STRATEGY, TECHNOLOGY AND PUBLIC POLICY

ECONOMISTS OF THE TWENTIETH CENTURY

General Editors: David Colander, *Christian A. Johnson Distinguished Professor of Economics, Middlebury College, Vermont, USA* and Mark Blaug, *Professor Emeritus, University of London, Professor Emeritus, University of Buckingham and Visiting Professor, University of Exeter*

This innovative series comprises specially invited collections of articles and papers by economists whose work has made an important contribution to economics in the late twentieth century.

The proliferation of new journals and the ever-increasing number of new articles make it difficult for even the most assiduous economist to keep track of all the important recent advances. By focusing on those economists whose work is generally recognized to be at the forefront of the discipline, the series will be an essential reference point for the different specialisms included.Wherever possible, the articles in these volumes have been reproduced as originally published using facsimile reproduction, inclusive of footnotes and pagination to facilitate ease of reference.

A list of published and future titles in this series is printed at the end of this volume.

Strategy, Technology and Public Policy

The Selected Papers of David J. Teece Volume Two

David J. Teece

Mitsubishi Bank Professor, Haas School of Business and Director, Institute of Management, Innovation and Organization, University of California, Berkeley, USA

ECONOMISTS OF THE TWENTIETH CENTURY

Edward Elgar
Cheltenham, UK • Northampton, MA, USA

Published by
Edward Elgar Publishing Limited
8 Lansdown Place
Cheltenham
Glos GL50 2HU
UK

Edward Elgar Publishing, Inc.
6 Market Street
Northampton
Massachusetts 01060
USA

A catalogue record for this book
is available from the British Library

Library of Congress Cataloguing in Publication Data

Teece, David J.
    Strategy, technology, and public policy / David J. Teece.
    (The selected papers of David J. Teece ; v. 2)
    Economists of the twentieth century
    A collection of articles previously published between 1977–1997.
    Includes bibliographical references and index.
    1. Economics. 2. Strategic planning. 3. Industrial policy.
4. International economic relations. 5. Technological innovations—
Economic aspects. 6. Teece, David J. 7. Economists—New Zealand—
Biography. I. Title. II. Series. III. Series: Teece, David J.
Selections. 1998 ; v. 2.
HB129.5.T44A25   1998b
338.9—dc21   96–21608
                                                                            CIP

ISBN 1 85898 336 3

Printed and bound in Great Britain by Bookcraft (Bath) Ltd.

Contents

Acknowledgements

The author and the publishers wish to thank the following who have kindly given permission for the use of copyright material.

American Bar Association for article: 'Information Sharing, Innovation, and Antitrust', *Antitrust Law Journal*, **62** (2), Winter 1994, 465–81.

American Economic Association and Thomas M. Jorde for article: 'Innovation and Cooperation: Implications for Competition and Antitrust', *Journal of Economic Perspectives*, **4** (3), Summer 1990, 75–96.

Blackwell Publishers for article: 'Technology Transfer by Multinational Firms: The Resource Cost of Transferring Technological Know-How', *Economic Journal*, **87**, June 1977, 242–61.

Elsevier Science Publishers B.V. for articles: 'Profiting from Technological Innovation: Implications for Integration, Collaboration, Licensing and Public Policy', *Research Policy*, **15** (6), December 1986, 285–305; 'Natural Resource Cartels', with David Sunding and Elaine Mosakowski, in *Handbook of Natural Resource and Energy Economics Volume III*, A.V. Kneese and J.L. Sweeney (eds), 1993, 1131–66; Elsevier Science B.V. and Gregory L. Rosston for excerpt: 'Competition and "Local" Communications: Innovation, Entry and Integration', in *Globalism and Localism in Telecommunications*, E.M. Noam and A.J. Wolfson (eds), 1997, 1–25.

Federal Legal Publications, Inc. for article: 'Systems Competition and Aftermarkets: An Economic Analysis of *Kodak*', with Carl Shapiro, *Antitrust Bulletin*, **XXXIX** (1), Spring 1994, 135–62.

Gordon and Breach Publishers for article: 'Product Emulation Strategies in the Presence of Reputation Effects and Network Externalities: Some Evidence from the Minicomputer Industry', with Raymond S. Hartman, *Economics of Innovation and New Technology*, **1**, 1990, 157–82.

Harper & Row for article: 'Contributions and Impediments of Economic Analysis to the Study of Strategic Management', in *Perspectives on Strategic Management*, James W. Fredrickson (ed.), 1990, 39–80.

Harvard Business School Press for excerpts: 'Fundamental Issues in Strategy', with Richard P. Rumelt and Dan E. Schendel, in *Fundamental Issues in Strategy: A Research Agenda*, Richard P. Rumelt, Dan E. Schendel and David J. Teece (eds),

1994, 9–47, references; 'Strategic Alliances and Industrial Research', with David E. Mowery, in *Engines of Innovation: U.S. Industrial Research at the End of an Era*, Richard S. Rosenbloom and William J. Spencer (eds), 1996, 111–29.

Institute for Operations Research and the Management Sciences for articles: 'Time–Cost Tradeoffs: Elasticity Estimates and Determinants for International Technology Transfer Projects', *Management Science*, **23** (8), April 1977, 830–37; 'Capturing Value from Technological Innovation: Integration, Strategic Partnering, and Licensing Decisions', *Interfaces*, **18** (3), May–June 1988, 46–61.

J.C.B. Mohr and Thomas M. Jorde for article: 'Antitrust Policy and Innovation: Taking Account of Performance Competition and Competitor Cooperation', *Journal of Institutional and Theoretical Economics*, **147** (1), March 1991, 118–44.

John Wiley and Sons Ltd for article: 'Strategic Management and Economics', with Richard P. Rumelt and Dan E. Schendel, *Strategic Management Journal*, **12**, 1991, 5–29; John Wiley and Sons Ltd and Gary Pisano for article: 'Dynamic Capabilities and Strategic Management', with Amy Shuen, *Strategic Management Journal*, **18** (7), 1997, 509–33; John Wiley and Sons Ltd for article: 'Inter-organizational Requirements of the Innovation Process', *Managerial and Decision Economics*, Special Issue, 1989, 35–42.

Journal of Business Administration for article: 'A Behavioural Analysis of OPEC: An Economic and Political Synthesis', **13**, 1982, 127–59.

Kluwer Academic Publishers, William F. Finan and Albert N. Link for article: 'Estimating the Benefits from Collaboration: The Case of SEMATECH', *Review of Industrial Organization*, **11**, 1996, 737–51.

Lawrence Erlbaum Associates, Inc., Robert G. Harris and Gregory L. Rosston for excerpt: 'Competition in Local Telecommunications: Implications of Unbundling for Antitrust Policy', in *Towards a Competitive Telecommunication Industry: Selected Papers from the 1994 Telecommunications Policy Research Conference*, Gerald W. Brock (ed.), 1995, 67–94.

OECD for excerpt: 'Technological Development and the Organisation of Industry', in *Technology and Productivity: The Challenge for Economic Policy*, 1991, 409–17, references.

Oxford University Press, Thomas M. Jorde and Will Mitchell for article: 'Assessing Market Power in Regimes of Rapid Technological Change', with Raymond Hartman, *Industrial and Corporate Change*, **2** (3), 1993, 317–50.

Praeger Publishers for article: 'The Uneasy Case for Mandatory Contract Carriage in the Natural Gas Industry', in *New Horizons in Natural Gas Deregulation*, Jerry Ellig and Joseph P. Kalt (eds), 1996, 43–73.

The Regents of the University of California for article: 'Economic Analysis and Strategic Management', *California Management Review*, **XXVI** (3), Spring 1984, 87–110; The Regents of the University of California and Thomas M. Jorde for article: 'Competition and Cooperation: Striking the Right Balance', *California Management Review*, **31** (3), Spring 1989, 25–37; The Regents of the University of California for article: 'Managing Intellectual Capital: Licensing and Cross-Licensing in Semiconductors and Electronics', with Peter C. Grindley, *California Management Review*, **39** (2), Winter 1997, 1–34; The Regents of the University of California and Michael V. Russo for excerpt: 'Natural Gas Distribution in California: Regulation, Strategy, and Market Structure', in *Regulatory Choices: A Perspective on Developments in Energy Policy*, R. Gilbert (ed.), 1991, 120–86; The Regents of the University of California for articles: 'Foreign Investment and Technological Development in Silicon Valley', *California Management Review*, **34** (2), Winter 1992, 88–106; 'Japan's Growing Capabilities in Industrial Technology: Implications for U.S. Managers and Policymakers', with David C. Mowery, *California Management Review*, **35** (2), Winter 1993, 9–34.

Sage Publications, Inc. for article: 'The Market for Know-How and the Efficient International Transfer of Technology', *Annals of the Academy of Political and Social Science*, **458**, November 1981, 81–96.

Every effort has been made to trace all the copyright holders but if any have been inadvertently overlooked the publishers will be pleased to make the necessary arrangements at the first opportunity.

Introduction

The publication of two volumes of one's selected publications is generally a time for stocktaking. When demanded by the publisher, it becomes a necessity. However, there is often benefit to oneself, if not to others (especially students), when one endeavours to explain one's research strategy, if there is one, and how his papers all fit together, if indeed they do.

In my case, I was grateful for the invitation and the opportunity because of the broader than usual range of topics I have addressed in my scholarly and professional writings. Given the evident trend towards specialization in economics, my situation is a little unusual. It also makes the assessment of scholarships more difficult, because one's reader is often interested in only a narrow slice of the work. In my case, I have not bothered as yet to pull my work together into an integrated monograph or series of monographs. Nor do these selections represent the totality of my publications. A full listing of my publications as of mid-1996 is contained in the Appendices to both Volume One and Volume Two. An orderly selection of pieces is however one step in the direction of making one's work a little more user friendly. It is in that spirit that I proceed.

Biographical sketch

I have studied economics since entering Canterbury University in Christchurch in 1967 at the age of 18. I had the good fortune to be born in New Zealand and to have access to good public schools. It's not that I studied economics in high school. Indeed, it was not available as a field. But I was taught to think for myself and to write. Not that we had a lot of grammar thrust upon us. But we were always writing essays, so it seemed.

I studied economics in my first year at the University of Canterbury. In New Zealand if you did not take a subject in your first (freshman) year, it was difficult to major in that field without delaying your graduation. However, while I was in high school at Waimea College, my brother had been studying economics at evening school, and he had fortunately left a copy of Bach's *Economics* (probably the 5th edition) lying around. I read several chapters and it was clear to me that if economics was a discipline, then this was the discipline for me. In those early years, being a bit naive I felt that politics was a noble profession, and the reason that society was getting bad government was that politicians and government officials did not understand economics. If they had only worked a little harder at their university studies, they would know more and deliver better policy. Notions of interest group politics were alien to me at the time. It was also my naive belief that there were clear answers to complex problems. Problems would always yield to thorough examination by knowledgeable individuals. I have since learned that this is only partially true.

This idealism fuelled my thirst for the study of economics at the university. And indeed economics was fun, and there were answers to many questions. I was mightily impressed by some of the results from international trade theory, such as the theory of comparative advantage and the Stolper–Samuelson theorem; and I was mightily impressed by the power of linear programming and other optimization techniques. Economics was heady stuff; one could make headway on big issues, so it seemed then and now. I finished my BA in 1969 (degree conferred in 1970) and launched into a masters programme.

A few extra courses beyond what was required for an MA would earn me a masters of commerce, similar to an MBA. Cheap diversification thereby obtained seem worthwhile, and I launched into a one year masters programme, majoring in economics, of course. So I studied more trade theory, economic development and economic history, in addition to the basic set of advanced courses in macro and micro theory.

But the competition was tough. The department chair (Bert Brownlie) set high standards, many of the faculty had advanced degrees from abroad, and the department chair had recently implemented a programme he called the 'knight's move', whereby graduates from mathematics and the sciences could enter *de novo* into the masters programme.

And some very bright folks did indeed do just that. Suddenly courses in micro theory were populated by mathematicians and physicists. I quickly worked out where my competitive advantages lay. I could always tussle with the fundamental economics, but my maths was too weak to enable me to formalize it all. My classmates could do that well, but I could also see that some of them did not understand much about what they modelled. Thus the tone was set for later.

Another wonderful gift associated with the University of Canterbury was the visits of distinguished faculty from abroad – mainly the United States. Once again, the department chair adopted a very international view of standards and wished to benchmark his faculty and his students among the best from anywhere. So during the northern summers, we had the great pleasure of hosting great economists at Canterbury, including Tjalling Koopmans from Yale, Charlie Kindleberger from MIT and Gerard Debreu from UC Berkeley. Indeed, struggling through Debreu's *Theory of Value* (New York, John Wiley, 1959) as a second year undergraduate student showed me the structure of economic theory. I respected its elegance, but had trouble appreciating its pratical significance. However, I did come to understand how it all fitted into the corpus of knowledge that we call economics. It was exhilarating to be exposed to all of this so early. I quickly figured out that I wanted to continue on and earn a doctorate in economics.

But there were two other essentials: one had to be accepted to a distinguished centre of learning, and one had to receive a scholarship. Brought up in the tradition of public education, it seemed unimaginable to me that one would shell out annually several years of savings for the privilege of studying abroad, especially because the alternatives in New Zealand seemed pretty good.

To meet the first prerequisite, I needed to get first honours. First honours were scarce currency, even at Canterbury, and those that got it were really very good. In some years none were awarded in economics, and usually at most one. Fortunately, my cohort was very good, and several were awarded. (Parenthetically,

I note that there is considerable support for the notion that it helps to be spurred by cooperative competition within one's cohort. Everyone helped each other until exam time, when each did one's personal best. I was a pretty good exam taker, which didn't hurt.)

With first honours in hand, I had a shot at good graduate schools abroad. The traditional trajectory for a top student from Canterbury was to head for Oxford or Cambridge or the London School of Economics. But my advisers, particularly the department chair Bert Brownlie (subsequently Vice Chancellor at the University of Canterbury) steered me towards North America. Brownlie argued that the torch in economic science had passed from Britain to America, and I believed then and now that he was substantially correct. I applied seriously to several Canadian schools (and was admitted to the University of British Columbia and the University of Toronto) and one US graduate programme. That programme was the Graduate Group in Economics at The Wharton School of Management at the University of Pennsylvania. Moreover, Penn offered a one year fellowship, and subsequently renewed support for my period of study (Autumn 1971 to Spring 1975).

Little did I know it, but I had stumbled on to an excellent programme that was to have a formative impact on my career and on my professional writings. My application to economics at Wharton indicates that I had visions of combining regional economics with trade theory. It was a poorly thought through vision, and in part was a pander to what I believed the Penn faculty was seeking. They took me anyway.

I had entered economics with a strong interest in the firm and in management. My father, Allan Teece, was a businessman. He had started a trucking company at the age of 18 and was, I believe, the first person to offer a regular scheduled overland freight service between the west coast of the Southern Island of New Zealand (Greymouth, Westport) and the northern part of the South Island (Nelson). When he left to go overseas in the New Zealand Expeditionary Force to assist the British in fighting against the Germans in North Africa, he participated in a buyout/merger and thereby became a founding shareholder in Transport Nelson Ltd, which by the 1960s had become, so local folks said, the largest freight hauler in the southern hemisphere. I am not sure there was any research to back this up, but certainly no local knew of a larger trucking enterprise.

Perhaps because of the department's existence at the time inside a great business school,[1] the study of the firm was reasonably well appreciated in the economics department at the University of Pennsylvania. More importantly, there was a marvellous trio of industrial organization faculty in Edwin Mansfield, Almarin Phillips and Oliver Williamson. But it would be a while before I could get to study with them. The first year in the programme was a breeze. It was familiar stuff and the competition was spotty. These poor American kids often had little prior training in economics, and I had had four years of it. But they caught up fast, and competition stiffened. I was pleased to do well in my theory classes. Steve Ross, now a very distinguished professor of finance at Yale, taught macro theory, and it didn't hurt that I outperformed my next classmates by ten points. Steve told others I was an excellent student, even though this wasn't quite true. It never hurts to have a champion or two.

But what was I to study for my field exams? Penn required two fields of specialization. International economics was to be one, but macro didn't appeal as the second. Given my background and interests, and with hindsight, I should have already selected industrial organization (IO). But I had not been exposed to the energetic and popular Oliver Williamson – for he was on leave in the United Kingdom, at Warwick I believe. Somehow I found my way into Almarin Phillips's class on IO and Edwin Mansfield's class on the economics of technological change. This was starting to feel better and I passed my field exams, well enough apparently to engender a call from Edwin Mansfield (who was always looking for graduate students) to invite me to work with him. Indeed, the Mansfield enterprise had money and energy, and was an alternative to the Larry Klein-inspired economic research unit, where one might be offered the chance to work on applied macro problems using econometrics and large data bases. Mansfield was the small sample advocate who insisted that one ought to understand precisely what the data were that one was working with. This philosophy was congruent with my own, and my confidence was reinforced.

Mansfield encouraged me to study international technology transfer. My background in the economics of technological change and international trade and finance seemed like good preparation. Eventually I did complete a decent thesis, and Chapters 9 and 10 in Volume Two are taken from the thesis. It was a daunting experience, however, to work in an area where there was basically no prior research and only a handful of loose conjectures. My treatment was entirely empirical, as Mansfield had developed a rather high degree of scepticism for economic theory. Had I to do it all over again, there is indeed a body of theory – barely emergent back then – on the nature of technology, that, had it been employed, would certainly have assisted. Still, my papers here stand alone. Nothing much before on the topic of transfer cost, and nothing much since. However, work in imitability, dynamic capabilities, and knowledge transfer is laying the foundation for further productive forays into the issues that were examined in my thesis.[2]

While I was waiting for my thesis to be read I had time on my hands. I volunteered my services free of charge to Oliver E. Williamson as a research assistant. He was now back from the UK and was working on a manuscript. His response to my offer was to provide me with an early draft of *Markets and Hierarchies* (New York, Free Press, 1975). I took it away, read it with undivided attention, and reported back that he had a truly significant contribution in the making. It was the first framework I had encountered in all of my studies that gave me a handle on the firm. And I was really interested in firms and managerial questions. My economics training in New Zealand had not exposed me in any way to the field of IO. Indeed, I had not known it existed. Nor was I aware of the literature on managerialism or firm structure, or of issues in competition policy. Perhaps that's not surprising. At the time New Zealand, like Denmark, had few large firms, and the government ran all the large projects.

My only awareness of IO issues had stemmed from my struggling efforts to understand direct foreign investment and the multinational firm. I had selected direct foreign investment as a term paper topic at Penn, and was thoroughly disillusioned by the contributions of international finance to the study of foreign direct investment and the multinational enterprise. But I got hold of the doctoral thesis of Stephen Hymer, who was, I believe, the first to cast direct foreign investment as a topic in IO and the theory of the firm. This provided direction, but the story was wrong.

Phillips's and Williamson's teachings were inspirational. It was *Markets and Hierarchies*, however, that fired my passions. It played into my strong belief that economics needed a theory of the firm and did not as yet have one. *Markets and Hierarchies* appeared to offer powerful new insights about the firm, and particularly about firm boundaries. I had no doubt that Williamson was on to something very important, and I was fortunate to have had early exposure.

With my degree almost in hand, I started thinking about employment. When entering the graduate programme, I believed I was on a career path for the World Bank's Young Professionals Programme. I had not dreamed that I might be qualified for an academic appointment.

I put myself on the market and was interviewed in the Spring of 1975. I applied to every advertised academic position placed in the job openings for economists. The leading opportunities turned out to be MIT (joint between the economics department and the Sloan School) and Stanford (in the Graduate School of Business with a courtesy appointment in economics). I momentarily accepted the former because my advisers at Penn argued that it was the superior opportunity. But I really wanted to go to the San Francisco Bay area. Positioned as it was on the Pacific, it felt more like home to a New Zealander. Lee Bach increased the offer by $750 and explained how I was really a business school guy (I was) and how 'inside the firm' and technology issues were just what Stanford needed and wanted. Within the hour I joyfully told MIT that I had changed my mind, accepted the Stanford job, and drove my 1971 Buick convertible across country with all my worldly possessions in the trunk and a few on the back seat. I had room to spare and offered a ride to another student to help keep costs down.

Post-doctoral research

Stanford
At Stanford, Lee Bach, a macro economist and keen mentor of young talent, was my chief colleague and main source of inspiration. He had been dean at Carnegie Mellon during its heyday in the 1960s when March, Simon, Mansfield, Nelson, Williamson, Winter and many other highly creative and imaginative minds opened the doors to the field of organizational economics. I was indeed fortunate to have the guidance and encouragement of the late Lee Bach. It was Bach who, with deans Ernie Arbuckle and Arjay Miller, mapped the road to Stanford's greatness as a business school. His encouragement was all I needed, and I launched into a series of studies that early on were basically empirical tests or applications of Williamson's ideas. James Griffin, now a distinguished professor at Texas A&M, was on the faculty at Penn when I was a student there, and had convinced me that the *Markets and Hierarchies* framework was not going to go anywhere until economists saw some empirical 'proof'. I believe I was the first to provide statistical 'proof'.[3]

As I was finishing my thesis, the oil crisis threw a spotlight on the oil industry.

Senators Kennedy and Hart and others began scapegoating the oil companies. Nothing was of course further from the truth – the companies had largely neutralized the effect of the embargo on the United States by spreading the shortfall around among embargoed and non-embargoed countries. They argued that the problem lay with the industry's vertical structure.

The oil companies were surprisingly slow to explain to the world why they were organized the way they were. Their tardiness provided an excellent opportunity to show that transaction cost economics could at least join the issues. Somehow I had to explain to applied IO economists what the framework was all about. There was no one more willing and able to do that than myself, now an assistant professor of business economics at Stanford. This resulted in a little monograph (now out of print) entitled *Vertical Integration and Vertical Divestiture in the U.S. Petroleum Industry*, which was published in 1976 by the now defunct Stanford University Institute for Energy Studies. This is excerpted in 'Vertical Integration in the U.S. Oil Industry' (Chapter 9 of Volume One). Many applied economists and organizational behaviour scholars found this a useful way to understand what the *Markets and Hierarchies* framework was about. Transaction costs helped to explain the industry's structure, but it left many questions unanswered. However, it was the most credible interpretation available.

I then took the framework and was, I believe, the first to apply it to the lateral integration/diversification question. 'Economies of Scope and the Scope of the Enterprise' and 'Towards an Economic Theory of the Multiproduct Firm' (Chapters 6 and 7 of Volume One) were efforts to understand a critical aspect of business organization about which we knew, and still know, very little. The first paper of this duo drew upon my background in innovation and in transaction cost economics. It was quite original and very problem driven. In the policy debate, some argued that the diversification of the oil companies into alternative fuels was driven by anti-competitive considerations. I argued otherwise and built a theory of diversification around the technology transfer problem. The second paper represented the first showing of another watershed in my growth as a scholar, as it displayed a self-conscious effort to inject evolutionary thinking. Both papers did much to resurrect Edith Penrose's early work on the theory of the firm. In addition, these papers propelled me somewhat unwittingly into the field of business strategy. Subsequent work on the resource-based theory of the firm took inspiration and encouragement from these papers.

But I am getting a little bit ahead of myself. The Williamson frameworks were begging for at least quasi rigorous empirical support, and I figured I had a good chance of delivering it.

I did so first with 'Organizational Structure and Economic Performance: A Test of the Multidivisional Hypothesis'. This showed a transitional m-form effect on profit. I believe this may well be the first study in economics or organization theory to show a statistically significant effect between organizational structure and performance. It was thus a watershed article for organization theory, if not for economics. Published soon thereafter a similar study by Cable and Steer using UK data found a far larger effect from the adoption of the m-form on accounting profits. The 'principal firm' study (Chapter 18 of Volume One) extended my findings beyond the petroleum industry. Together these articles showed the power of the Chandler–Williamson hypothesis, but left many questions unanswered with respect to just why the organizational change was adopted when it was, and so forth. Partial answers can be found in Chapter 19 of Volume One, which is an infrequently cited analysis on the diffusion history of the *m*-form structure.

On a parallel track I continued to work on the multinational firm. Stephen Hymer's work had convinced me that one had to look at firms, not capital markets, to understand the multinational enterprise. But Hymer had cast the multinational enterprise into the straitjacket of the old Mason–Bain view of the world, where market power was used to explain the multinational enterprise. It seemed to me that there was something much deeper at work – the role of the firm as a developer of technology and intangible assets. The multinational enterprise was an efficiency instrument well suited for transferring technology across national borders. Viewed this way, of course, public policy towards direct foreign investment ought to be friendly and not hostile as Hymer proposed. Several others seemed to be working on these issues more or less simultaneously. Buckley and Casson were chronologically out ahead. Each of us has stressed different aspects, but our work here flows in a common stream.

Berkeley
I moved to Berkeley in 1982.[4] UC Berkeley not only gave me tenure but advanced me immediately to full professor. A year later I inherited a moribund centre, the Center for Research in Management, with a mandate to revitalize it.

Since moving to Berkeley I have made several discoveries. One was that my work not only had relevance for the theory of the firm, but that it was being cited in the field of strategic management. This development led me to begin self-consciously paying attention to that field. Scholars in this area had a deep and enduring interest in the issues I was interested in but had little in the way of a conceptual apparatus for grappling with them. Michael Porter had rejuvenated the field by showing that the structuralist approach to IO could speak to certain strategy questions. However, while Porter could speak on issues about how to analyse markets and industries, there was little to help one analyse firms. It thus appeared that both IO and strategy needed a theory of the firm. Williamson had provided powerful insights in questions relating to the boundaries of the firm, but no one seemed to have much of a framework for explaining what firms were all about, that is, what were the differences (besides incentives) between organizing something inside a firm and across a market, and what were the con-ditions that led to organizational failure. I was convinced that the answers lay somewhere in the domain of organizational structure/capabilities.

However, my first self-conscious foray into strategy came with firm boundary/outsourcing issues in the context of innovation. In 'Profiting from Technological Innovation', (Chapter 2 of Volume Two), I set up a framework that could enable one systematically to address technology strategy issues such as when to license and when not to license. The framework also had predictive power in that the ability of a firm to profit from innovation (and hold off the imitators and emulators) was a function of both the firm's intellectual property position and its prior positioning in the relevant specialized or co-specialized assets. When first presented at the Stanford Asilomar Conference in 1984, this paper, then entitled 'Firm Boundaries, Technological Innovation and Strategy Management' (subsequently published in L.G. Thomas (ed.), *Economics of Strategic Planning* (1986)), engendered little interest. However, when presented in Venice a few months later at a conference on innovation organized by Giovanni Dosi, the reaction was quite different. My discussant, Richard Nelson, commented that 'I believe we have just heard an important paper'. The paper has now been republished at least half a dozen times in one form or another, and has been translated into Italian[5] and Japanese.[6] It was also selected by the editors of *Research Policy* as one of the ten best papers that the journal had published over the period 1971–91. I've been told it has over a thousand citations.

'Profiting from Technological Innovation' triggered two subsequent lines of research. One dealt with the role of strategic alliances and cooperation in the innovation process, and the second dealt with the topic of dynamic capabilities. As to the former, it became clear to me and many others that in the new global economy firms had to become more catholic with respect to the way they went about their business. In particular, global dispersion in the sources of knowledge meant that incumbent firms anywhere had to be cognizant of, and ideally have access to, relevant new technology everywhere. This was one type of motivation for strategic alliances. Second, innovators, particularly new companies, needed to quickly access complementary assets, if possible on very competitive terms. These two forces, coupled with much stronger competition, have been the main factors propelling the proliferation of alliances. 'Competition, Cooperation, and Innovation' (Chapter 23 of Volume One) encapsulated my analysis (much of it contained in Volume One, Part VI) of alliances as a new organizational form, outlining in particular how they can assist the innovation process. Alliances and cooperative arrangements among firms also brush up against antitrust issues. Indeed, to many antitrust lawyers and some economists, cooperation among competitors is the leitmotif of anti-competitive behaviour. However, in the new world order, it is increasingly common to find situations where firms are simultaneously buying/supplying their competitors. The papers in Part III of Volume Two urge policy makers and the courts to be open-minded about cooperation. Indeed, in this stream of research with my law school colleague and friend, Thomas Jorde, we observed that antitrust law in the United States treated cooperative relationships among unaffiliated firms more harshly than it would treat a merger among the entities. Congress eventually saw the inconsistency and in 1994 passed an amendment to the National Cooperative Research Act that softened the antitrust treatment of cooperative arrangements to commercialize new technology by eliminating the detrebbling aspects of antitrust enforcement for registered cooperative research/commercialization projects.

The second stream of research emanating from my work on innovation relates to corporate capabilities. As I explored the innovation process, and 'competitiveness' more generally, it became apparent that organizational processes underpinned what firms were about and their capacity to innovate and grow. The work of C.K. Prahalad and Gary Hamel in 'The Core Competencies of the Corporation' (*Harvard Business Review*, 1990) set the tone, but it did not promote much of the content. Clues as to content lay in the work by Richard Nelson and Sidney Winter on routines (Richard Nelson and Sidney Winter, *An Evolutionary Theory of Economic Change*, Cambridge, MA, Harvard University Press, 1982), and work by organization theorists on learning. It seemed then, and still now, that a theory of the firm may well reside in the rather jumbled set of ideas we call the competences/capabilities literature. Several of the articles in Volume One provided early foundations for the capabilities paradigm. This is particularly true of Chapters 1 and 7. As I note (with Gary Pisano) in Chapter 3, 'we offer dynamic capabilities as an emerging paradigm of the modern business firm'. This is still very much unfinished business.

A final note is probably warranted with respect to the section on public policy (Volume Two, Part III). In the main, my work on public policy has been part and parcel of my interest in deeper phenomena, for example the theory of the firm. Indeed, at the most abstract level, my fundamental interest is in building a unifying theory of the firm that will help us understand business behaviour and business organization. Accordingly, I have rarely explored a public policy issue for its own sake, and indeed practically all of my writings in public policy display strong linkages through to underlying issues in the theory of the firm. This is especially true of my work on cooperation and on cartels. Cartels are, of course, a form of economic organization. The other theme in my writings on antitrust policy is that antitrust ought to be more concerned with 'dynamic competition', by which I mean competition that is fuelled by innovation. The Chicago school performed an important function by injecting economics into antritrust analysis. However, in the main what was supplied was static (intermediate) price theory with its assumptions of un-changing technology and homogeneous goods. I developed a high level of frustration with the naive and often rather misleading orientation of the antitrust literature; several of my papers challenged some of the conventional wisdom, including Chapter 21 of Volume Two on 'Information Sharing, Innovation and Antitrust' and Chapter 17 on 'Assessing Market Power in Regimes of Rapid Technological Change'.

My work in technology policy (see Volume Two, Part III, Section C) likewise flows from my interest in innovation and dynamic competition. The papers in this section are a miscellany, but generally deal with business organization, particularly its international scope, or the role of intellectual property. The latter topic is an intriguing one. Indeed, I expect to do more work on intellectual property in the years ahead. It is increasingly salient in the global economy, yet the economics of intellectual property is still in its infancy.

The future

Two decades have passed since I received my doctorate. I am happy with the turf I have staked out for my research and scholarly activities. Economics is still quite a young field. It was first developed to help explain the wealth of nations, not the value of the business enterprise. Indeed, it is only in the last half century, beginning in my view with Coase's article on 'The Nature of the Firm' (*Economica*, **4**, 1937, pp. 386–405), that economists have tried to grapple with the economics of the business enterprise. Despite a few false starts, we are gradually beginning to develop an understanding of the firm. However, we have many decades of research ahead of us before we begin to have a theory of the firm that is anywhere near as sophisticated as our theory of markets.

I plan to keep pressing forward with the agenda that is already set. It's big enough to keep armies of scholars working for decades before there is any danger that the opportunities for discovery will be anywhere near exhausted. As we get near a viable theory of the firm, we will be able to predict firm behaviour and firm performance with some confidence. This will simplify the teaching of management and the diagnosis of organizational maladies. It will enable us to refine regulation and public policy. Clearly, significant private and public benefit can flow from this enterprise. Accordingly, it is one that I shall continue to pursue both inside and outside the university.

Notes

1. As a graduate student I did not know such institutions as business schools existed, for there were none I knew about at the time (1971) in New Zealand, Australia or the United Kingdom.
2. My doctoral thesis was published in its entirety by Ballinger as *The Multinational Corporation and the Resource Cost of International Technology Transfer* (1977).
3. See Armour and Teece, 'Organizational Structure and Economic Performance: A Test of the Multi-divisional Hypothesis', *Bell Journal of Economics* (Spring 1978), published here as Chapter 17 of Volume One; and Monteverde and Teece, 'Supplier Switching Costs and Vertical Integration in the Automobile Industry', *Bell Journal of Economics* (Spring 1982), published here as Chapter 10 of Volume One.
4. My years at Stanford were truly delightful. However, the business school was in the throes of trying to work out what to do with a business economics group. Stanford wavered in this in the late 1970s and early 1980s. I was hired by Bach, who saw the importance of looking 'inside the firm' and stressed organizational economics as the most fruitful path. After an unsuccessful attempt to hire Oliver Williamson, excellent faculty from the decision sciences group got the upper hand and saw game theory and agency theory as the more promising approach. This was obviously an environment less congenial to interests. After very rapid promotion to associate professor (without tenure), I asked for an early tenure review before the game theorists and agency theorists were firmly entrenched. They were entrenched enough to block early tenure, so I moved to Berkeley rather than waiting for a second try. With hindsight, the Graduate School of Business did me quite a favour, to which I remain indebted. I have only the most positive views of my Stanford experience and I remain in close contact with Stanford colleagues, though my contacts are ironically with colleagues in the economics department! Stanford has put the theorists in the business school, while the applied faculty flourish in the economics department. This is quite incongruous; it also diminishes what both groups can do. It's like putting the Jeep logo on a Cadillac. However, there is unquestionably great talent in both places. It is a pity, however, that the business school at Stanford has not as yet attained its full potential in the study of the business enterprise. Its excellence lies elsewhere.
5. *Ricerche Economiche*, **4** (Oct./Dec. 1986), and as 'Innovazione Technologica e Successo Imprenditoriale', *L'Industria*, **7**, 4 (Oct./Dec. 1986).
6. Chapter 9 in D.J. Teece (ed.), *The Competitive Challenge* (1987). Japanese edition.

PART I

STRATEGY

[1]

CALIFORNIA MANAGEMENT REVIEW
Vol. XXVI, No. 3, Spring 1984
Copyright © 1984, The Regents of the University of California

Economic Analysis and Strategic Management

David J. Teece

The basic idea behind strategic management is that a firm needs to match its capabilities to its ever-changing environment if it is to attain its best performance.[1] This will typically involve the formulation and execution of plans relating to the establishment and deployment of a firm's assets. It would seem on its face, therefore, that resource allocation issues are involved in strategic management, and that there ought to be a well-known set of economic principles to guide strategic management decisions. But this is not the case. Economic analysis employing standard economic theories of the textbook variety is virtually unknown in strategic management.

The purpose of this article is to explain why economic analysis has until recently yielded few insights into strategic management issues, to examine the intellectual roots of several recent contributions from industrial organization economists, and to develop in an illustrative fashion several strategic management principles regarding enterprise structure. This last endeavor will involve mining the emerging economic theory of internal organization for normative propositions of practical import to those concerned with organizational design and "efficient boundary" issues.

In outlining and assessing the contribution of economics and economists, the treatment is necessarily incomplete. Many important contributions have been omitted. The aim is to capture the essence of the economists' contribution, to trace its antecedents, to suggest the importance of heterodox approaches, and to urge the development and testing of theory-based principles which can supplant the ad hoc approach so prevalent even in contemporary strategic management research.

This article is forthcoming in Johannes M. Pennings, ed., *Strategy for Decision Making In Complex Organizations* (San Francisco, CA: Jossey-Bass, forthcoming 1984). Printed here by permission of the publisher.

DAVID J. TEECE

The Tension Between Orthodox Economic Theory And Strategic Management

The concept of strategy itself, at least as used in the field of strategic management, is somewhat alien to economic thinking. The term rarely appears in micro-economic texts, except in game-theoretic discussions of pricing, advertising policies, and the like. It is, therefore, in need of some translation before it can be examined in terms that most economists will find meaningful.

The notion that a firm can choose from a finite set of strategies (e.g., low cost high-volume strategies vs. high cost innovative-product strategies) implies that a firm's resources and capabilities are not completely fungible and generalizable, certainly in the short run, if not in the long run. Particular strategies imply particular investment decisions, organizational structures, and possibly particular organizational cultures. Put differently, the concept implies that certain factors of production are "semi-permanently tied to the firm by recontracting costs and, perhaps, market imperfections."[2] The assumption that resources are immobile and heterogeneous is implicitly if not explicitly embedded in the strategic manager's view of the world. However, this world view does not sit comfortably with the models and theories contained in most micro-economic texts, although the tension is not as great with the industrial organization literature. The problem is that the micro-economic theory of firms and markets was not developed with the education of business managers in mind. Indeed, in some contexts economists will point out that their characterizations of rationality do not pretend to describe how decisions are actually taken or ought to be taken. The discipline of economics in general, and formal economic theory in particular, is shaped by a concern with normative questions in public policy that are very different from the problems general managers must face. In addition, economics as an empirical science has long been determinedly oblivious to the problems of predicting behavior of the individual decision unit, and has focused its attention and developed its specialized tools for the statistical analysis of patterns of behavior of whole populations of economic actors. The fact that very different success criteria and information resources are associated with the normative study of the problems of the individual entity is often missed, and when noted is often underestimated in importance. Finally, and perhaps most importantly, the dominant mode of theorizing in contemporary microeconomics tends to distance the discipline from management problems, with the important exception of problems relating primarily to the functioning of organized auction markets operating under high information conditions (i.e. finance). The dominant mode combines unquestioning faith in the rational behavior paradigm as a framework, relative indifference to the delineation of the empirical phenomena that are thought to require theoretical explanation, and a delight in the construction of "parables of mechanism." Such parables provide a sharply defined view of an imaginary world in which the logic of a particular economic mechanism stands out with particular clarity. The insights generated by this method often seem valuable and compelling, but unfortunately there is often no attempt to bridge the vast gulf that separates the simple imaginary world with its isolated mechanism from the complex real world in which some analogous mechanism may, perhaps, operate.

Without doubting the legitimacy or importance of the concerns and objectives that have shaped mainstream economics, one can doubt very seriously that the discipline thus shaped makes a wholly constructive contribution to strategic management. The following section examines some areas where such doubt seems particularly well justified.

Treatment of Know-How—The production and utilization of technological and organizational knowledge is a central economic activity that is handled in a most cavalier way within economic theory. By far the most common theoretical approach is simply to take technology as given, ignoring entirely the fact that the options open to a manager almost always include an attempt at some degree of innovative improvement in existing ways of doing things. On the occasions when this pattern is broken by explicit attention to technological change, the treatment of states of knowledge and the changes therein is often simplistic and undifferentiated. It is common to assume that technology is uniformly available to all, or, if technology is proprietary, that it is embedded in a "book of blueprints." However, in reality, know-how is commonly not of this form. It is often tacit, in that those practicing a technique can do so with great facility, but they may not be able to transfer the skill to others without demonstration and involvement. [3] To assume otherwise often obscures issues relating to the generation and transfer of know-how.

In general, the fact that technological and organizational change is such an important and pervasive aspect of reality, and yet so peripheral in economic theory, may be the single most important consideration limiting the contribution of orthodox economics to issues in strategic management.

Focus on Static Analysis—Strategic management issues are centrally concerned with dynamics. Economic theory, on the other hand, deals almost exclusively with equilibrium analyses, which are very often static. In recent years, much greater attention has been given to theoretical formulations which are dynamic in nature, but formal modeling endeavors of this kind are often exceedingly difficult to perform. Accordingly, only very simple problems can be dealt with mathematically, and certainly not the kinds of problems of concern to managers. While comparative statics is one way to get at dynamic issues, it suffers from inattention to the path of equilibrium. These matters are usually exceedingly important. Managers are often as concerned with the journey as they are with the destination when industries and markets are being transformed.

Focus on Equilibrium—Economic analysis widely employs equilibrium analysis. (An equilibrium is where "the intended actions of rational economic agents are mutually consistent and can, therefore, be implemented."[4]) In fact, almost all of the central propositions of economics rely on the assumption that markets are in equilibrium. Clearly, equilibrium is a fictitious state. The justification for its use is the supposed tendency towards equilibrium, which is, however, an empirical rather than a theoretical proposition. Indeed, G. B. Richardson argues that "the general equilibrium of production and exchange . . . cannot properly be regarded as a configuration toward which a hypothetical perfectly competitive economy would gravitate or at which it would remain at rest."[5] His argument is the obvious one, that for equilibrium to be attained, firms need information about each other's investment plans. In the absence of collusion, however, this is not going to be fully and accurately revealed. Accordingly, "it is difficult to see what but an act of faith can enable us to believe that equilibrium would be reached."[6] Indeed, as Hahn has pointed out, the basic purpose of the famous Arrow-Debreu model of equilibrium is "to show why the economy cannot be in this state."[7] While equilibrium analysis yields valuable insights into certain public policy issues, it is of rather limited utility to managers of the strategic process. Indeed, it may obscure as well as clarify. It certainly distracts attention from process issues.

Inadequacy of the Theory of the Firm—With little exaggeration, we can assert that, until very recently, economics lacked a theory of the firm. To be sure, textbooks contain chapter headings labeled "the theory of the firm," but on closer examination one finds a theory of production masquerading as a theory of the firm. Firms are typically represented as production functions, or, in some formulations, production sets. These constructs relate a firm's inputs to its outputs. The firm is a "black box" which transforms the factors of production into usually just one output. Firms are thus single-product in their focus. If multiproduct firms exist, then they are flukes in that they have no distinct efficiency dimensions.[8]

The boundaries of the firm—the appropriate degree of vertical, lateral, or horizontal integration—thus lie outside the domain of traditional economic analysis. Moreover, the theory is completely silent with respect to the internal structure of the firm. In short, the firm is an entity which barely exists within received neoclassical theory. The only dimension of its activities which is given much play is the volume of its output and the price at which that output is sold.

Suppression of Entrepreneurship—Because equilibrium analysis plays such a dominant position within received theory, and because change is so often modeled as a movement from one equilibrium condition to another, the role of entrepreneurship tends to be downplayed, if not outright suppressed. In fact, "it may be said quite categorically that at present there is no established economic theory of the entrepreneur. The subject area has been surrendered by economists to sociologists, psychologists, and political scientists. Indeed, almost all the social sciences have a theory of the entrepreneur, except economics."[9] Casson goes on to identify two villains. One is "the very extreme assumptions about access to information which are implicit in orthodox economics . . . simple neoclassical models assume that everyone has free access to all the information they require for making decisions,"[10] an assumption which reduces decision-making to the mechanical application of mathematical rules for optimization. This trivializes decision-making, and makes it impossible to analyze the role of entrepreneurs. Moreover, the Austrian school, which does take the entrepreneur more seriously, is trapped by extreme subjectivism, rendering predictive theory-building impossible. A predictive theory of the entrepreneur is impossible with the Austrian school because "anyone who has the sort of information necessary to predict the behavior of entrepreneurs has a strong incentive to stop theorizing and become an entrepreneur himself."[11] The need for a theory of enterpreneurship—or at least a theory which does not suppress the process of entrepreneurship—is of considerable importance to strategic management.

Stylized Markets—In neoclassical theory, transactions are performed by faceless economic agents operating in impersonal markets. However, markets are not nearly so anonymous. Even traders on the New York Stock Exchange—supposedly the most "objective" of all markets—know a good deal about each other. Reputation effects, experience ratings, and the like are the very stuff which permits markets to operate efficiently. To strip such considerations out of the theory renders it impotent before many strategic management problems. Where managers know each other, trust relationships abound, and fly-by-night operators can generally be exposed.

Not only are markets characterized by a variety of information conditions, but they differ widely in the frequency with which transactions and the opportunities for and costs of disruption occur (compare the sale of nuclear power plants with the sale of a bushel of wheat). Intermediate markets and relational contracting[12] are virtually absent from the textbooks and most advanced theorizing. By neglecting the institutional foundations of market structure, the conventional tools of economic analysis are rendered impotent before many strategic management problems.

Assumptions with Respect to Decision-Maker Attributes— Economic analysis commonly assumes a form of behavior which has been referred to as superrational or hyperrational.[13] Decision makers are supersmart, don't have problems with memory loss or memory recall, and can instantly formulate and solve problems of great complexity. Even their expectations are rational. This is, of course, a caricature of real-world decision makers. The abstraction may be appropriate for framing certain problems, but it is generally an approach which managers find quite unhelpful. It is not a characterization of individual behavior and, even more so, of organizational behavior. Little can be learned from treating firms in this fashion.

Behavior of Cost—In micro-economic theory, and in practically all textbook treatments, costs in the short run are considered to rise with increasing output because of the law of diminishing returns. While the empirical evidence generally contradicts the assumption of increasing short run marginal cost, the rising marginal cost curve persists in the textbooks because it must, if much of the rest of the paraphernalia of neoclassical micro-economic theory and welfare economics is to survive. Without the rising marginal cost curve, it is often harder to derive industry equilibria and to arrive at normative conclusions. Hence, the reluctance to push it into the appendices, where it might well belong in many instances.

That's not to say that economists have not been involved in an important stream of research on alternative cost structures, particularly the progress function. In essence, the progress function implies that unit costs fall with cumulative volume, because of learning by doing efforts. T. P. Wright, working as chief engineer and general manager at Curtis Aeroplane in Long Island, played a catalytic role in developing, applying and diffusing the progress function concept.[14] After the war, industrial engineers and production managers pushed the construct empirically, while economists explored some of the theoretical implications.[15] In the 1960s the concept was applied (and sometimes misapplied) by the Boston Consulting Group and others to strategic management.

The progress function and various derivative concepts have proved quite valuable in linking cost behavior to strategic choices. But the literature on it within economics remains somewhat enigmatic and apart from mainstream treatments of cost. The concept has meanwhile become an important, though perhaps an overused concept in strategy management. In fact, Richard Pascale has invented the term "Honda Effect" to describe how consultants, academics, and executives have tended to squeeze reality into the strait-jacket of the experience curve and other parables, "to the neglect of the process through which organizations experiment, adapt, and learn."[16]

Assessment—Orthodox micro-economic theory, useful as it is for understanding many important economic and public policy issues, is of little value to the strategic manager. Indeed, it can be suggested that received theory, standing alone, tends to saddle the practitioner with perceptual blinders which block peripheral vision. However, economics is a very diverse discipline and within the field of industrial organization, broadly defined, greater realism is permitted to operate, although several of the central problems just surveyed are still pervasive. Since the field is developing very rapidly, the potential for positive contributions is considerable. Therefore, a brief journey through several of the streams of research in industrial organization which seem to be relevant to strategic management would appear to be warranted.

Industrial organization is that field of economics which has traditionally dealt with the structure of markets, the behavior of firms, and the social benefits and costs associated with various forms of market structure and firm behavior.[17] As the author of the leading text points out, "the name is a curious one . . . [as the field] has little or nothing to say about how one organizes and directs a particular industrial enterprise."[18] Rather, the focus of much of the industrial organization literature is on how particular forms of price and output behavior by firms affect consumer welfare.

There is now sufficient variety within the industrial organization literature that it is extremely difficult to characterize it as a whole. While research continues within the traditional structure-conduct-performance paradigm, interest is also being shown by economists within a variety of other traditions. These include transactions cost, game theory, and evolutionary theory. There are a number of other related fields as well such as information theory and agency theory, which are possibly relevant. I will discuss the contribution from several traditions, particularly those which are either already visible or offer considerable promise for future contributions.

The Structural Analysis of Industries

The Strucure-Conduct-Performance Paradigm—The first and most visible contribution from industrial organization to strategic management has come, not surprisingly, from employing the first and most visible paradigm in industrial organization, namely the structure-conduct-performance paradigm. The most notable early developers of the structuralist paradigm were Edward Mason at Harvard during the 1930s and Joe Bain at Berkeley during the 1950s. Within the paradigm, the performance (profitability, efficiency, etc.) of firms in particular industries or markets depends upon the conduct of buyers and sellers in matters such as pricing practices and policies, tacit and overt inter-firm coordination and cooperation, research and development commitments, advertising and product-line strategies, investment in production facilities and the like. Conduct in turn depends on the *structure* of the relevant market, as determined by features such as the number and size distribution of buyers and sellers, the degree of product differentiation, the existence of barriers blocking the entry of new firms into the industry, the degree of vertical integration, and the ratio of fixed to variable costs associated with the industry's technology. Market structure and conduct are also influenced by various fundamental or basic conditions. On the demand side these include the price elasticity of demand at various prices, the availablity of substitutes, buyers' practices, and the like. On the supply side, basic conditions include the nature of access to raw materials, characteristics of the industry's technology and production processes (fixed or flexible, continuous flow or batch, etc.), product durability, and shipping and inventory costs. Other basic conditions include aspects of the regulatory and community environment. The causation runs from structure to conduct to performance, although most treatments recognize feedback effects, and some stress circumstances under which causation may run the other way, that is from performance to structure. The basic theme, though, is that the market structure is the critical factor, and the paradigm focuses on exploring its many facets and tying those to conduct and performance.

The trick that has been used to apply this paradigm to strategic analysis is to treat the normative theory of industrial organization as a positive theory of strategic management. The principal focus becomes not one of how to select antitrust and regulatory policies to increase consumer welfare by enhancing competition but rather how to increase profits (and, if necessary, reduce consumer welfare) by containing or restricting competition. The principle weapon is the erection of various forms or entry barriers. As Michael Porter has explained, "public policymakers could use their knowledge of the sources of entry barriers to lower them, whereas business strategists could use theirs to raise barriers, within the rules of the game set by anti-trust policy."[19]

The essence of strategic management in the structuralist framework is thus to shield the firm, to the maximum extent legally possible, from competitive forces.[20] In Porter's words, "The goal of competitive strategy for a business unit in an industry is to find a position in the industry where the company can best defend itself against these competitive forces or can influence them in its favor. Since the collective strength of the forces may well be painfully apparent to all competitors, the key for developing strategy is to delve below the surface and analyze the sources of each. Knowledge of those underlying sources of competitive pressure highlights the critical strengths and weaknesses of the company, animates its positioning in its industry, clarifies the areas where strategic changes may yield the greatest payoff, and highlights the areas where industry trends promise to hold the greatest significance as either opportunities or threats."[21] This is simply a translation, redirection, and refinement of the Mason/Bain structure-conduct-performance paradigm of industrial organization, made visually apparent by comparing Porter's approach as presented in Figure 1A with the basic industrial organization (structuralist) paradigm as summarized by Scherer in Figure 1B.

Besides refashioning existing constructs, this tradition has also made considerable progress in refining the concept of entry barriers, which has led to the related concept of mobility barriers and strategic groups. Con-

The Structure – Conduct – Performance Paradigm
of Industrial Organization Applied to Competitive Strategy

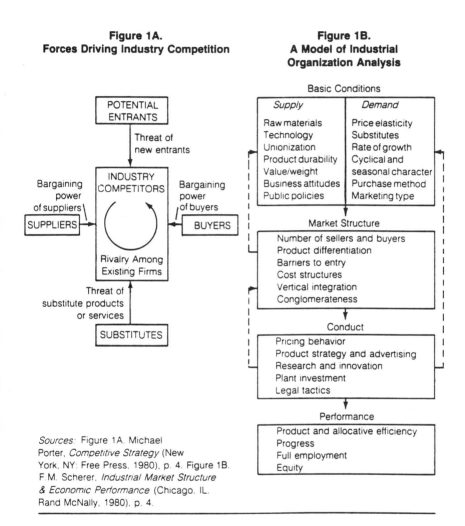

Figure 1A.
Forces Driving Industry Competition

Figure 1B.
A Model of Industrial
Organization Analysis

Basic Conditions

Supply	Demand
Raw materials	Price elasticity
Technology	Substitutes
Unionization	Rate of growth
Product durability	Cyclical and
Value/weight	seasonal character
Business attitudes	Purchase method
Public policies	Marketing type

Market Structure

Number of sellers and buyers
Product differentiation
Barriers to entry
Cost structures
Vertical integration
Conglomerateness

Conduct

Pricing behavior
Product strategy and advertising
Research and innovation
Plant investment
Legal tactics

Performance

Product and allocative efficiency
Progress
Full employment
Equity

Sources: Figure 1A. Michael
Porter, *Competitive Strategy* (New
York, NY: Free Press. 1980), p. 4. Figure 1B.
F.M. Scherer, *Industrial Market Structure
& Economic Performance* (Chicago. IL.
Rand McNally, 1980), p. 4.

sider entry deterrence through the erection of industry entry barriers.
Such barriers are exposed to free rider "abuses" and hence underprovision.
In order to overcome this problem, collusion amongst incumbents is
needed. Overt collusion is of course illegal in many industrial settings.
However, tacit collusion *is* legal, and possibly viable if firms' reactions to
each other's strategic moves are predictable. This is conceivable where
spatial elements in markets make some incumbents closer rivals than
others. Hence, behavior by certain groups of firms to deter rival incumbents

may be more viable and valuable than deterring potential entrants through the erection of entry barriers at the industry level. One can thus arrive at the concept of *strategic groups*.

Committed strategic choices and industry heterogeneity obviously underlie the strategic group concept. Fine-grain differences in market requirements, firm capabilities, and transactional relationships allow for differentiation amongst strategies. Firms occupying the same market niche are likely to be more aware of each other's behavioral reactions than of the behavioral reactions to be expected by others. Mobility barriers separate the various groups from each other. According to Caves, the concepts of strategic groups and mobility barriers "do not add up to a tight formal model. Rather they serve [as] . . . a dynamized add-on to the traditional structure-conduct-performance paradigm."[2]

With the redirection and refinement of structural analysis, a good start has been made towards the systematic understanding of the competitive environment of an industry. However, despite the useful work on strategic groups, this tradition does not provide much of a framework for assessing the capabilities and behavioral responses of individual firms, so that if the essence of formulating a competition strategy is relating a firm to its environment, the structuralist paradigm has dealt with only one half of the problem. As will be shown in the section below on transactions cost economics, recent work on the theory of the firm within a somewhat different industrial organization paradigm is helping to redress this deficiency. The complementary nature of these endeavors does not appear to have been fully recognized and exploited at this point in time.

Contestability, Sustainability, and Committed Competition—In the last few years, some old ideas have been repackaged and some new ones developed which, while often advanced by a group of scholars rather distinct from the structuralist school, nevertheless have a structuralist overtone. Some of these developments will be briefly surveyed and assessed with respect to their relevance to strategic management.

Consider, first, the concept of contestability.[23] A perfectly *contestable* market is one that is accessible to potential entrants and has the following two properties:

- The potential entrant can serve the same market and has access to the same technology on the same terms as incumbent firms. Thus, there are no entry barriers, if entry barriers are defined in the sense of potential entrants facing greater costs than those incurred by incumbent firms.
- The potential entrants evaluate the profitability of entry at the incumbent firms' pre-entry prices.

A *sustainable* industry configuration or structure involves prices and outputs such that supply equals demand and there are zero excess profits available to potential entrants if they take the prices of incumbent firms as given. Clearly, only sustainable industry configurations are consistent with contestability and equilibrium. Contestability of course requires that potential entrants have available to them the same technology as does the incumbent, and on the same terms and conditions.

It is clear that the classical case of a perfectly competitive market satisfies the condition of perfect contestability, but so might a natural monopolist if potential competitors have access to the same technology and costs as does the incumbent. Thus, markets may be natural monopolies and remain contestable, thereby earning zero economic rents for the incumbents.

One example may be small airline markets where demand is satisfied before economies of scale are exhausted. Consider two small towns where the demand for travel is only sufficient to support a single daily non-stop flight. It is a natural monopoly market and yet, because air transport equipment is highly mobile and can thus be redeployed ("flown") at low cost, entry into *and* exit from the market ought to be easy. If the incumbent prices so as to capture higher-than-competitive returns, an entrant need only deploy an aircraft to the market and undercut the incumbent's price. Should the incumbent lower prices to competitive levels, the new entrant can exit as effortlessly as he entered, so long as there are other hit-and-run opportunities, or so long as there is a well-developed aircraft leasing market, as is apparently the case. It ought to be clear that the reversibility of sunk costs[24] (or equivalently the non-existence of transaction-specific assets) and the absence of customer loyalties is essential for contestability. A contestable market is thus one subject to "hit-and-run" entry. Were it not for such exposure, some firms might want to lower their output and raise prices. However, the threat of hit-and-run entry prevents the exercise of market power.

The utility of the concept of contestability for short-to-medium term strategy formulation is limited by the widespread existence of some degree of investment irreversibility. The assumptions may be met in some transportation industries and in various other service industries, e.g. circuses. But whenever irreversible investments in physical and human capital must be made, a market is unlikely to be contestable. Thus, while contestable market theory is useful for sharpening one's appreciation of the role of costs, technology, and potential competition, it is of limited applicability as it suppresses the role of irreversibilities, strategic interactions, and demand variability. Nevertheless, it is a lens through which one can view certain types of service industries. Where entry barriers lack durability, it is a framework that has applicability for evaluating the long run as well as the short run.

A concept orthogonal to and more relevant than contestability is *committed competition*. Whereas contestability assumes that investments are reversible, committed competition assumes that they are not. As suggested earlier, the concept of entry barriers implicitly rests on irreversible commitments by industry incumbents. Entry barriers are therefore exit barriers as well.[25]

Recent research on entry deterrence has identified ways in which it may pay to expand the commitment of irreversible investments in order to make entry unfeasible. Expanding production capacity ahead of demand, advertising outlays, brand proliferation, and the like may sometimes be effective. Whether such strategies can be profitable is another matter.

Transactions Cost Economics

Within a somewhat different tradition of industrial organization, sometimes referred to as the transactions cost or markets and hierarchies literature, an important set of new ideas and theories has emerged with strong normative implications for several central strategic management issues, including: the degree to which a firm should integrate (backward, forward, lateral, multinational, and conglomerate) and the appropriate internal structure for the large enterprise. The first set of issues can be labeled efficient boundary issues, and the second, internal organization issues.

The transactions cost approach starts with Coase's observation that markets and hierarchies are alternative organizational mechanisms for supporting transactions, and that the choice of the one or the other ought to be made according to which is the more efficient way to support the transaction in question.[26] Thus, arms-length transactions in markets, such as when one firm purchases an input from another, and "in-house" production, as with vertical integration, can be thought of as alternatives. Table One identifies several market forms and their corporate equivalents. Note that the economic transactions conducted within the corporate form could conceivably take place in a market. One must, therefore, investigate why it may not always be desirable to push economic activity into the market, and vice versa. In order to do so, one must explore the nature of market processes in some detail. The development below owes much to Oliver Williamson, although many others have contributed as well, as indicated by the footnotes.[27]

One feature of markets is that they are informationally economical. If prices are left free to clear markets, they will often do so quickly. However, the adjustment features of markets are often illustrated in the textbooks with markets for highly standardized commodities, such as wheat or cloth. But in modern industrial socieities, some rather unique and nonstandardized products often need to be procured or traded, for instance, electronic switches in the telecommunications network, weapons, aircraft engines, low sulfur crude oil, experienced scientists and engineers. Unassisted spot markets, such as those used to trade wheat, do not always work well as

Table 1. Organizational Alternatives

Market Form	Corporate Form
Intermediate Product Markets	Vertical Integration
Capital Markets	Conglomerate
Markets for Know-how	
(a) Horizontal	Multinational Firms*
(b) Lateral	Lateral Diversification†

* David J. Teece, "Technological and Organizational Factors in the Theory of the Multinational Enterprise," in Mark Casson, ed., *The Growth of International Business* (London: George Allen & Unwin, 1983).

† David J. Teece, "Economies of Scope and the Scope of the Enterprise." *Journal of Economic Behavior and Organization. Vol. 1,* No. 3 (1980):223-247; David J. Teece, "Towards an Economic Theory of the Multiproduct Firm," *Journal of Economic Behavior and Organization,* 3 (1982):39-63.

---

some alternative arrangements. To see why this is so, one must zero in on the properties of transactions.

A transaction occurs when a good or service is transferred across a technologically separable interface, such as when a firm buys an input from an independent supplier. The attributes of transactions that are of special interest are: the frequency with which they recur, the uncertainty to which they are subject, and the degree to which the transfer of technological and managerial know-how is involved.[28] In most textbook descriptions of the functioning of markets, it is usually assumed that transactions are frequent, uncertainty is low or non-existent, transaction specific investment is not involved, and the commodities traded are tangible or at least can be packaged and clearly labeled as to their performance features. But in the real world, commodities are not always that standardized. Let's see how it matters.

Infrequent exchange prevents purchasers from building up an experience rating on particular suppliers, such as when a new company offers an (allegedly superior) microprocessor to board designers and manufacturers. Uncertainty means that writing, executing, and enforcing contracts that are anywhere near complete is extraordinarily difficult since many contingencies cannot be identified and responded to during the contract negotiation period. As a result, exchange is governed by incomplete contracts, and unexpected contingencies will surely arise—a potentially hazardous situation for all of the parties. Asset specificity can occur because of locational imperatives, (as with iron and steel production, residuum and petroleum manufacture, R&D and first commercialization of complex petrochemical processes), physical asset specificity (as when specialized tools and dies are needed to produce a component), or knowledge specificity (as when research and developed knowledge is generated which is specialized to a particular firm's requirement). The reason why asset specificity is critical is that once the investment has been made it is largely irreversible, so that buyers and sellers may be operating in a bilateral exchange relation for a considerable period thereafter. To the degree that the value of highly specific capital in other uses is, by definition, much smaller than the specialized use for which it has been designed, the buyer is "locked in" to the transaction to a significant degree. The buyer and seller must thus make special efforts to protect the relationship, since both can be injured if it breaks down.

The criterion for organizing commercial transactions is assumed to be cost minimization. For analytical purposes, this can be broken down into two parts: minimizing production costs and minimizing transactions costs.[29] The former are fairly well understood and will not receive much attention here. Rather, it is the relatively poorly understood transaction costs which will be emphasized.

It is convenient to assume that transactions will be organized by markets unless market exchange gives rise to contractual difficulties, and hence transactions costs. In other words, the presumption is that economic activity is best organized by markets as this seems to reduce various bureaucratic distortions to which internal exchange may be subject. Furthermore, there are obvious production cost advantages associated with using markets. For instance, scale economies can be more fully exhausted by buying rather than making if the firm's own needs are insufficient to exhaust scale economies. Furthermore, markets can aggregate uncorrelated demands, thereby achieving intertemporal efficiencies. Finally, contracting out may avoid diseconomies of scope when a particular firm's requirements are only one of several which can be produced using the same equipment. Accordingly, we should presume that firms will contract out unless contractual difficulties can be anticipated. There are a number of such regularities which can be used to derive several principles of organizational design.[30]

The Sunkcost Principle—If a firm, in order to minimize costs, must put in place specialized and hence dedicated assets in order to keep costs to the minimum, then it ought to protect itself against the possibility that the supporting transactions will be upset in an opportunistic way by suppliers, purchasers, or rivals. Thus, if an aluminum refinery is to some degree dedicated to a particular grade or type of bauxite, then the owner of the refinery ought to be sure that the ore will be available on competitive terms. Integration generally affords more control than relying on arms-length contracts with unaffiliated enterprises. Accordingly, the supply relationship should involve a progressive degree of vertical integration as the extent of the dedication increases.[31] Hence the following principle:

Principle 1: As asset dedication increases (so that once committed, invest-

ment decisions involve some degree of irreversibility) bring the supporting transactions under tighter control, vertically integrating if necessary to ensure the continued supply of raw materials and other inputs necessary to keep the specialized asset fully employed.[32]

Quality Assurance Principles—For many goods and services, the provision of product quality has economic value to the consumer enabling the quality product to support a higher price. In some cases, such as the camshaft of an engine, the buyer may not be able to establish the quality of the good by inspection of the final product, and may not even be able to screen for quality with trial use. If the potential damage caused by utilization of a substandard good is great, it is essential that quality be checked before the buyer takes delivery. This is a special case of the more general proposition that the seller of a product has a natural advantage over the buyer in screening for product quality because he is one step closer to the producer and may, in fact, be the producer himself. Information about product quality is generated naturally as a joint product of the production process and accrues in the first instance to the person supervising production. The costs of quality control may be reduced significantly by drawing upon this information instead of replicating its discovery at a subsequent stage.

For an intermediate product, there are three main strategies available for giving assemblers confidence in the supplier's quality control. The first is simply to build up confidence through successful experience through frequent trade between the same buyer and seller. The second strategy is for the seller to agree to the buyer supervising the production of the component/product in question, and the third is for the buyer to integrate backward into the manufacture of the component, i.e., to bring the production process in-house, where the buyer has maximum access to information and is able to take remedial measures without having to negotiate with an independent enterprise. The argument is also symmetric in the sense that a seller who feels that it will be slow or difficult to build up confidence among buyers may decide to integrate forward into the user's business. This suggests the following principle:

Principle 2 (a): Producers of high-quality products ought to be vertically integrated into component production when the costs of product failure are high, when limited opportunity exists to develop an experience rating on suppliers, and when effective in-plant monitoring of the supplier's production activities involves significant contracting costs.[33]

Quality-assurance issues also explain the incentive to forward integrate in situations where the activities of individual distributors affect one another (rather than the manufacturer as in the situation just considered), as when one retailer's poor service injures the product's reputation and limits the sales of other retailers. Independent forward integration, or possibly franchising, will thus tend to displace independent distributors as the most efficient mode of organization, leading to the following principle:

Principle 2 (b):   Franchising and forward integration become progressively desirable as spillover effects among retailers become more significant.[34]

The Systemic-Innovation Principle—As discussed earlier, uncertainty makes contractual relations especially complex, since it is impossible to write all contingencies into a contract. One of the activities in which a corporation may engage and which gives rise to uncertainty is innovation. Innovation by its very nature involves uncertainty. Costs and outcomes of the innovation process are never clear until commercialization and significant market penetration have occurred.

Technological innovations vary enormously in nature and characteristics. For present purposes, it is useful to distinguish between two types of innovation: autonomous (or "stand-alone") and systemic. An autonomous innovation is one which can be introduced without modifying other components or items of equipment. The component or device in that sense "stands alone." A systemic innovation, on the other hand, requires significant readjustment to other parts of the system. The major distinction relates to the amount of design coordination which development and commercialization are likely to require. An example of a systemic innovation would be electronic funds transfer, instant photography (it required redesign of the camera and the film), front wheel drive, and the jet airliner (it required new stress resistant airframes). An autonomous innovation does not require modification to other parts of a system for first commercialization, although modification may be necessary to capture all of the advantages of the innovation in question. The transistor, for example, originally replaced vacuum tubes and the early transistor radios were not much different from the old ones, although they were more reliable and used much less power. But one did not have to change radio transmission in order to commercialize transistor radios. Another example would be power steering—the automobile did not have to be redesigned to facilitate the introduction of this innovation, although it did permit designs which placed more weight over the front wheels. A faster microprocessor or a larger memory would be further examples. The third principle of efficient organizational design relates the firm's boundaries—the degree of vertical integration in particular—and the rate and direction of technological innovation.

When technological interdependencies are important, it is likely that the commercialization of an innovation will require complementary investments in several different parts of the industry. Thus, suppose that a cost saving (equipment) innovation has been generated which can enhance efficiency if successfully introduced into an industry, and suppose that introduction into one part requires that complementary investments be made in other parts. If the subparts are independently owned, cooperation will have to be obtained in order for the innovation to be commercialized.

There are two powerful reasons why common ownership of the parts will speed both the adoption and the subsequent diffusion of the innovation. Where there are significant interdependencies, introduction of an innovation will often result in differing benefits and cost to various parties. This effect makes it difficult if not impossible to coordinate the introduction of such an innovation. While a system of frictionless markets could overcome this problem—the firms obtaining the benefits could compensate those incurring the costs so that the introduction of the innovation would not depend on the degree of integration in the industry—it is commonly recognized that it may be extremely difficult to engineer a workable compensation agreement, in part because all relevant contingencies are not known when the contract would need to be drawn up.

For example, inasmuch as innovation involves uncertainty and difficulty in measuring costs and benefits, the *distribution* of costs and benefits cannot be evaluated as accurately as the net total effects, and it is this distribution among separate firms which would premise any agreement to introduce the innovation and the requisite adjustments in the production process. Thus, genuine differences can arise among the parties in their assessment of cost and benefits. Moreover, even if the costs and benefits are perceived similarly by the parties involved, differences in risk preferences may affect the manner in which the risks are priced. These problems will make it difficult to reach agreement with attendant delays in commercialization. Even if an arrangement for sharing costs and benefits is devised, initial terms and conditions can be circumvented, and unforeseen contingencies—of which there are likely to be many—can be interpreted opportunistically. By rendering distributional and contracting issues irrelevant, integration reduces contractual problems and facilitates the commercialization of innovation which affects several stages of production or several parts of an operating system.

Therefore, in the absence of integration, commercialization can be slowed or completely stalled. Considerable cost disparities can open up between old and new methods, yet the new method may not be implemented because the individual parties cannot agree upon the terms under which it will be introduced. There can be a reluctance on the part of both parties to make the necessary investments in specialized assets, and to exchange information about each other's needs and opportunities— even if cooperation would yield mutual gains, and certainly if the gains will go to one party at the expense of the other. Hence, in the absence of integration, there can be a reluctance on the part of one or more of the parties in an industry to develop or commercialize a systemic innovation requiring the participation of two or more firms.

To summarize, integration facilitates systemic innovations by facilitating information flows, and the coordination of investment plans. It also removes institutional barriers to innovation where the innovation in question requires allocating costs and benefits, or placing specializing investments into several parts of an industry. In the absence of integration, there will be a reluctance on the part of both parties to make the necessary investments in specialized assets, even if this would yield mutual gains. One reason is that both parties know that the exercise of opportunism might yield even greater benefits to one of the parties. Hence, in the absence of common ownership of the parts, there will be reluctance on the part of one or more of the parties to adopt a systemic innovation. This leads to the third principle of organizational design:

Principle 3: A structure which displays common ownership of the various organizational units which must participate in the adoption of an innovation is the structure which, ceteris paribus, *is the most likely to facilitate the innovation in question.*

> *Corollary I:*
>   Autonomous innovations do not require complex transactions amongst organizational units and will proceed efficiently in (small) unintegrated enterprises.
>
> *Corollary II:*
>   Systemic innovations require transactions amongst several organizational units, and will proceed most efficiently in (integrated) enterprises whose boundaries span the various participating organizations.

The Appropriability and Efficient Technology Transfer Principle—Successful firms possess one or more forms of intangible assets, such as technological or managerial know-how. Over time, these assets may expand beyond the point of profitable reinvestment in a firm's traditional market. Accordingly, the firm may consider deploying its intangible assets in different product or geographical markets, where the expected returns are higher, if efficient transfer modes exist.

The arms-length market for know-how and other intangible assets is, however, riddled with transactional difficulties and costs. There are both problems of recognition and disclosure—potential trading opportunities may go unrealized because it is difficult to fully publicize the availablity of certain forms of highly proprietary know-how, and when publicity is attempted, the buyer may thereby be able to obtain much of know-how without actualy paying for it. The buyer often needs to be fully informed about the technology before he is able to value it, but once he knows all the pertinent aspects of the technology needed to evaluate it, he no longer needs to purchase it! Accordingly, it is often risky for the seller to rely on licensing to nonaffiliated enterprises as a mechanism for appropriating the returns to its intangible assets. However, if the "buyer" is an affiliated enterprise, such as a foreign subsidiary, or another domestic division selling in a different market, the spillover effects mentioned above will wash out and will not effect the overall returns to stockholders unless divisional profits are taxed differently in different markets. This suggests the following principle:

Principle 4: When know-how licensing leads to significant transactions cost and substantial spillovers to nonaffiliated enterprises, the firm ought, ceteris paribus, to adjust its boundaries so as to internalize the transactions in question. This implies foreign direct investment when the markets in question are international, and lateral integration when the markets in question involve modification of the primary production process.

The Hierarchical Decomposition Principle—If a transaction is moved in-house, there is no necessary assurance that the activity will be effectively organized thereafter. Decision making must be factored into relatively independent subsystems, each of which can be designed with only minimal concern for its interactions with the others. The other operating parts must be grouped into separable entities, the interactions within which are strong and between which are weak. The strategic function, involving lower frequency interactions, needs also to be separated and associated with higher levels in the organizational hierarchy. The hierarchical decomposition principle has been stated by Alfred Chandler and Oliver Williamson approximately as follows:

Principle 5: The internal structure of an enterprise should be designed so as to effect quasi-independence between the parts. Operations management and strategic planning should be clearly distinguished and incentives should be aligned so as to promote global profitability rather than group or divisional goals.[35]

Other Contributions

The two streams of industrial organization research identified above are the most developed, although the second is more recent and is not frequently applied in current strategic management practice. As mentioned earlier, there are a number of additional streams that appear promising in terms of their potential contributions to economic science and to strategic management. Prominent among them is an evolutionary theory of economic change which has recently been outlined by Nelson and Winter.[36]

The Nelson & Winter framework is significant because it promises to address an important deficiency in the existing literature: a theory which can delineate the firm's distinctive capabilities. Existing theory is almost completely silent on this matter, and the field of strategic management often succumbs to an ad hoc approach. Yet the whole concept of strategy involves matching the firm's capabilities to its environment, so that in the absence of an adequate theory of the firm's capabilities, one is absent an adequate theory for addressing important issues in strategy formulation.

The firm in evolutionary theory is conceived as having a distinctive package of economic capabilities of relatively narrow scope. The information required for the functioning of the enterprise is stored in routines, in which much of the underlying knowledge is tacit, not consciously known or articulatable by anyone in particular. As Nelson & Winter point out: "Routines are the skills of an Organization."[37] Prevailing routines define a truce, and attempts to change routines often provoke a renewal of conflict which is destructive to the participants and to the organization in routine operation, but it is a flow that is continuously primed by external message sources.

For such a system to perform production activities, some highly specific conditions must be satisfied, and these will be different in particular cases. The specific features that account for the ability of a particular organization to accomplish particular things are reflected in the character of the collection of individual member's repertoires, and the possession of particular collections of specialized plant and equipment. Restaurants have chefs and kitchens, while universities have professors, research laboratories, libraries, and classrooms. Central to productive activity is coordination and central to coordination are individual skills and the existence of an information and control system which enables the right skills to be exercised at the right time.

What emerges is a conception of the firm with a limited range of capabilities based on its available routines and physical assets. There is no "shelf of technologies" external to the firm and available to all industry participants. A firm's capabilities are defined very much by where it has been in the past, and what it has done. History becomes important, as the firm's performance is a function of deeply engrained repertoires.

Nelson and Winter's concept of routines thus cuts across orthodox notions of capabilities (the techniques that a firm can use) and of choice, and treats these as similar features of a firm. To view firm behavior as governed by routines implies that what a firm is currently doing or has recently done defines its capabilities more appropriately than the set of abstract possibilities which an external observer might conceive to be available to the firm.[38] Thus a firm's flexibility is constrained not only by the irreversible investments which it may have made, but also by its limited range of available routines. Identifying these for a firm and its rivals thus becomes an important part of strategy formulation.

This view also suggests, however, that the strategy lever may not be as powerful as is commonly supposed. If a firm has only a limited range of repertoires, its range of strategic choices is correspondingly limited. However, if its distinctive skill—be it innovation, service, or quality—is not readily imitable, it can be an almost unassailable source of above-normal profits.

Evolutionary theory also directs one's attention to the process and mechanisms of imitation.[39] The interest in imitation arises because it often happens that a firm observes that some other firm is achieving the success that it would like for itself. The envious firm may then try to duplicate this imperfectly observed success. If the envious firm does not have open access to the target firm's internal operations, then the target firm's routines are not available as a template, so that when problems arise in the copy, it is not possible to resolve them by closer scrutiny of the original (the target). This implies that the copy may construct a substandard mutation of the original. At one extreme, the target routine may involve so much idiosyncratic and difficult-to-unravel tacit knowledge that even if the organization tried to replicate itself, success would be highly problematic, and imitation from a distance would be completely impossible. [40]

At the other extreme, the product in question may be a novel combination of highly standardized technological elements, so that engineering may suffice for successful imitation. Even vague rumors from good sources may provide enough clues to permit almost complete replication.

The theory of imitation, which may be lurking here, can be linked back to the structuralist concept of entry barriers, and its group level equivalent, mobility barriers. Individual firms as well as groups or industries may be insulated from competition by the high costs or impossibility of imitation. Richard Rumelt has used the term *isolating mechanism* to refer to phenomena which limit the *exposte* equilibration of rents among individual firms. Isolating mechanisms include patents, trade secrets, and tacit knowledge. The importance of isolating mechanisms in business strategy is that they are the phenomena which make competitive positions stable and defensible. They may appear as first mover advantages which can only be undone by changes in the environment which cause the value of the underlying inimitable assets to dissipate.

Conclusion

The economic theory of the firm and of markets is to the point where, if correctly applied, it can have a constructive impact on the field of strategic management. As a robust theory of the firm with strong normative implications develops, and as the structural analysis of markets improves so as to focus more attention on the fine-grained aspects of structure and conduct, and as theorists and practitioners find ways of blending together the theories and various findings of research and best business practice, the possibility arises that economics can make an increasingly positive contribution to certain aspects of strategic management, especially questions relating to the design of business strategies. However, it is most important that the analysis of strategic positioning, to which economic analysis has much to contribute , be balanced with concern for the building of distinctive competences, and with strategy implementation and execution. In fact, some argue—correctly in many instances—the execution is strategy.[41] One thing is clear. It is not enough to choose fundamental competitive strategies which *assume* the performance of the production system. In some instances one may be able to attain superior performance by reorganizing existing competences, or by positioning business units more advantageously. In general, however, it is critically important to focus on the building of distinctive competences. Thus in suggesting above that there are important contributions to management to be derived from economic analysis, particularly through employing a heterodox theoretical framework, I do not mean to suggest that this is a priority matter for the field of management. American management is more in need of sharpening basic skills in the stimulation and management of innovation and human resources in a global context.

I wish to thank Sidney Winter of Yale University for helpful discussion on many points in this paper. Part II ("The Tension Between Orthodox Economic Theory & Strategic Management") of this article is drawn from David J. Teece and Sidney Winter, "The Limits of Neoclassical Theory in Management Education," *American Economic Review* (May 1984). I have also benefited from useful discussion with Richard Rumelt of UCLA and Wes Cohen of Carnegie-Mellon University.

References

1. For an excellent recent statement and development of this, see the article by Raymond E. Miles and Charles C. Snow elsewhere in this issue.

2. Richard Caves, "Corporate Strategy and Structure," *Journal of Economic Literature*, Vol. 18 (1980): 65.

3. David J. Teece, "The Market for Knowhow and the Efficient International Transfer of Technology," *The Annals of the Academy of Political and Social Science* (November 1981).

4. F. H. Hahn. *On the Notion of Equilibrium in Economics* (Oxford: Oxford University Press, 1960), pp. 21.

5. G. B. Richardson, *Information and Investment* (Oxford: Oxford University Press, 1960), pp. 1-2.

6. Ibid., p. 11.

7. Hahn, op. cit., p. 4.

8. David J. Teece, "Economics of Scope and the Scope of the Enterprise," *Journal of Economic Behavior and Organization*, Vol. 1, No. 3 (1980): 223–247; David J. Teece, "Towards an Economic Theory of the Multiproduct Firm," *Journal of Economic Behavior and Organization* 3 (1982): 39–63.

9. Mark Casson, *The Entrepreneur: An Economic Theory* (Totawa, NJ: Barnes and Noble, 1982), p. 9.

10. Ibid.

11. Ibid.

12. Oliver E. Williamson, "Transactions Cost Economics: The Governance of Contractual Relations," *Journal of Law and Economics* 22 (1979): 223–261.

13. H. A. Simon, "Rationality as Process and Product of Thought," *American Economic Review*, Vol. 68, No. 2 (1978): 1–16.

14. John Dutton, Annie Thomas, and John E. Butler, "The History of Progress Functions as a Managerial Technology," unpublished manuscript, Graduate School of Business Administration, New York University, October 1983.

15. Armen Alchian, "Costs and Outputs," in Moses Abramovitz, ed., *The Allocation of Economic Resources: Essays in Honor of B. F. Haley* (Berkeley, CA: University of California

Press, 1959); Alchian's research was performed at RAND in the late 1940s, but the classified nature of sources prevented publication until much later. See also, Jack Hirschleifer, "The Firm's Cost Function: A Successful Reconstruction," *Journal of Business* (July 1962), pp. 235–253.

16. See the article by Richard T. Pascale elsewhere in this issue. Pascale juxtaposes the Boston Consulting Group's (BCG) parable of Honda's entry into the British and American motorcycle industry with the reality as seen by Honda's management team. The BCG paradigm imputes coherence and purposive rationality when, in Pascale's view, the opposite was closer to the truth.

17. As one text puts it, "the field of industrial organizations is about: (1) how enterprises function within a variety of market structures, and (2) how well the outcomes fit the public interest." William Shephard, *The Economics of Industrial Organization* (Englewood Cliffs, NJ: Prentice Hall, 1979), p. 4.

18. F. M. Scherer, *Industrial Market Structure & Economic Performance* (Chicago, IL: Rand-McNally, 1980).

19. Michael Porter, "The Contributions of Industrial Organizations to Strategic Management," *Academy of Management Review*, Vol. 6, No. 4 (1981): 612.

20. The structuralist approach is in marked contrast to the transactions-cost paradigm, outlined below, which focuses on economic efficiency as the mechanism to achieve advantage against one's rivals. It could be argued that some forms of strategic positioning which the structuralist paradigm helps identify involve contrived barriers to entry, and are contrary to the public interest, whether or not they violate the antitrust laws.

21. Michael Porter, *Competitive Strategy* (New York, NY: Free Press, 1980), p. 4.

22. Richard Caves, "Economic Analysis and the Quest for Competitive Advantage," *American Economic Review* (May 1984).

23. William Baumol, John Panzar, and Robert Willig, *Contestable Markets and the Theory of Industry Structure* (New York, NY: Harcourt Brace Jovanovich, 1982).

24. Sunk costs would include the cost of shutting down and opening up plants.

25. Richard Caves and Michael Porter, "From Entry Barriers to Mobility Barriers," *Quarterly Journal of Economics* 91 (1977): 241–262.

26. Ronald Coase, "The Nature of the Firm," *Economica* (1937), p. 386–405.

27. Oliver E. Williamson, *Markets and Hierarchies* (New York, NY: Free Press, 1975); Oliver E. Williamson, "The Modern Corporation: Origins, Evolution, Attributes," *Journal of Economic Literature* 19 (1981): 4; and Williamson, op. cit., 1979.

28. Williamson, op. cit., 1979, 1981; David J. Teece, "Technology Transfer by Multinational Firms: The Resource Cost of International Technology Transfer," *Economic Journal* (June 1977); Teece, op. cit., 1982; Kirk Monteverde and David J. Teece, "Supplier Switching Costs and Vertical Integration in the Automobile Industry," *Bell Journal of Economics*, Vol. 13, No. 1 (Spring 1982).

29. Williamson, op. cit., 1981.

30. Several of these are from Williamson (op. cit., 1981), some are derived from my earlier work, and some are presented here for the first time. Subsequent footnotes attempt to trace the antecedents.

31. Where the input in question is a specialized component, the buyer may be in a position to demand that the seller license out his know-how so that the component in question can be second-sourced. In some cases, this will overcome the need for vertical integration.

32. See Williamson, op. cit., 1981, p. 1548.

33. For an earlier treatment, see David J. Teece, *Vertical Integration and Vertical Divestiture in the U.S. Oil Industry* (Stanford, CA: Stanford University Institute for Energy Studies, 1976).

34. See Williamson, op. cit., 1981, p. 1549.

35. Ibid., p. 1550. Empirical support for this principle can be found in H. O. Armour and

110   DAVID J. TEECE

David J. Teece, "Organizational Structure and Economic Performance: A Test of the Multitudinal Hypothesis," *Bell Journal of Economics*, 9 (Spring 1978): 106-122.

36. R. R. Nelson and S. G. Winter, *An Evolutionary Theory of Economic Change* (Cambridge, MA: Harvard Univeristy Press, 1982).

37. Ibid., p. 124.

38. This is unlikely to be news to strategy practitioners but it does bear an uneasy tension with textbook treatments of the firm's technological choice set as contained in most micro theory texts.

39. Nelson & Winter, op. cit., pp. 123–124.

40. This may be at the heart of what Lippman and Rumelt (S. A. Lippman and R. P. Rumelt, "Uncertain Imitability: An Analysis of Interfirm Differences in Efficiency Under Competition," *Bell Journal of Economics*, Vol. 13, No. 2 (Autumn 1982): 418–438) refer to as "uncertain imitability." Uncertainty in their model arises from ambiguity as to the factors of production and how they interact. If the precise reasons for success and failure cannot be discerned, even *ex poste*, then replication is impossible. Given uncertain imitability, the average firm will earn positive economic profit and incumbents will be more efficient than new entrants. With uncertain imitability, new entry activity will be essentially a function of market growth rather than industry profitability. High levels of profitability in stable markets may well signal incumbents possessing difficult-to-imitate skills that deter entry.

41. See the article by Thomas J. Peters elsewhere in this issue.

[2]

Profiting from technological innovation: Implications for integration, collaboration, licensing and public policy

David J. TEECE *

School of Business Administration, University of California, Berkeley, CA 94720, U.S.A.

Final version received June 1986

This paper attempts to explain why innovating firms often fail to obtain significant economic returns from an innovation, while customers, imitators and other industry participants benefit. Business strategy – particularly as it relates to the firm's decision to integrate and collaborate – is shown to be an important factor. The paper demonstrates that when imitation is easy, markets don't work well, and the profits from innovation may accrue to the owners of certain complementary assets, rather than to the developers of the intellectual property. This speaks to the need, in certain cases, for the innovating firm to establish a prior position in these complementary assets. The paper also indicates that innovators with new products and processes which provide value to consumers may sometimes be so ill positioned in the market that they necessarily will fail. The analysis provides a theoretical foundation for the proposition that manufacturing often matters, particularly to innovating nations. Innovating firms without the requisite manufacturing and related capacities may die, even though they are the best at innovation. Implications for trade policy and domestic economic policy are examined.

* I thank Raphael Amit, Harvey Brooks, Chris Chapin, Therese Flaherty, Richard Gilbert, Heather Haveman, Mel Horwitch, David Hulbert, Carl Jacobsen, Michael Porter, Gary Pisano, Richard Rumelt, Raymond Vernon and Sidney Winter for helpful discussions relating to the subject matter of this paper. Three anonymous referees also provided valuable criticisms. I gratefully acknowledge the financial support of the National Science Foundation under grant no. SRS-8410556 to the Center for Research in Management, University of California Berkeley. Earlier versions of this paper were presented at a National Academy of Engineering Symposium titled "World Technologies and National Sovereignty," February 1986, and at a conference on innovation at the University of Venice, March 1986.

Research Policy 15 (1986) 285–305
North-Holland

1. Introduction

It is quite common for innovators – those firms which are first to commercialize a new product or process in the market – to lament the fact that competitors/imitators have profited more from the innovation than the firm first to commercialize it! Since it is often held that being first to market is a source of strategic advantage, the clear existence and persistence of this phenomenon may appear perplexing if not troubling. The aim of this article is to explain why a fast second or even a slow third might outperform the innovator. The message is particularly pertinent to those science and engineering driven companies that harbor the mistaken illusion that developing new products which meet customer needs will ensure fabulous success. It may possibly do so for the product, but not for the innovator.

In this paper, a framework is offered which identifies the factors which determine who wins from innovation: the firm which is first to market, follower firms, or firms that have related capabilities that the innovator needs. The follower firms may or may not be imitators in the narrow sense of the term, although they sometimes are. The framework appears to have utility for explaining the share of the profits from innovation accruing to the innovator compared to its followers and suppliers (see fig. 1), as well as for explaining a variety of interfirm activities such as joint ventures, coproduction agreements, cross distribution arrangements, and technology licensing. Implications for strategic management, public policy, and international trade and investment are then discussed.

What determines the share of profits captured by the innovator?

Fig. 1. Explaining the distribution of the profits from innovation.

2. The phenomenon

Figure 2 presents a simplified taxonomy of the possible outcomes from innovation. Quadrant 1 represents positive outcomes for the innovator. A first-to-market advantage is translated into a sustained competitive advantage which either creates a new earnings stream or enhances an existing one. Quadrant 4 and its corollary quadrant 2 are the ones which are the focus of this paper.

The EMI CAT scanner is a classic case of the phenomenon to be investigated. [1] By the early 1970s, the UK firm Electrical Musical Industries (EMI) Ltd. was in a variety of product lines including phonographic records, movies, and advanced electronics. EMI had developed high resolution TVs in the 1930s, pioneered airborne radar during World War II, and developed the UK's first all solid-state computers in 1952.

In the late 1960s Godfrey Houndsfield, an EMI senior research engineer engaged in pattern recognition research which resulted in his displaying a scan of a pig's brain. Subsequent clinical work established that computerized axial tomography (CAT) was viable for generating cross-sectional "views" of the human body, the greatest advance in radiology since the discovery of X rays in 1895. While EMI was initially successful with its CAT

[1] The EMI story is summarized in Michael Martin, *Managing Technological Innovation and Entrepreneurship*, (Reston Publishing Company, Reston, VA, 1984).

scanner, within 6 years of its introduction into the US in 1973 the company had lost market leadership, and by the eighth year had dropped out of the CT scanner business. Other companies successfully dominated the market, though they were late entrants, and are still profiting in the business today.

Other examples include RC Cola, a small beverage company that was the first to introduce cola in a can, and the first to introduce diet cola. Both Coca Cola and Pepsi followed almost immediately and deprived RC of any significant advantage from its innovation. Bowmar, which introduced the pocket calculator, was not able to withstand competition from Texas Instruments, Hewlett Packard and others, and went out of business. Xerox failed to succeed with its entry into the office computer business, even though Apple succeeded with the MacIntosh which contained many of Xerox's key product ideas, such as the mouse and icons. The de Havilland Comet saga has some of the same features. The Comet I jet was introduced into the commercial airline business 2 years or so before Boeing introduced the 707, but de Havilland failed to capitalize on its substantial early advantage. MITS introduced the first personal computer, the Altair, experienced a burst of sales, then slid quietly into oblivion.

If there are innovators who lose there must be followers/imitators who win. A classic example is IBM with its PC, a great success since the time it was introduced in 1981. Neither the architecture nor components embedded in the IBM PC were considered advanced when introduced; nor was the way the technology was packaged a significant departure from then-current practice. Yet the IBM PC was fabulously successful and established MS-DOS as the leading operating system for 16-bit PCs. By the end of 1984, IBM has shipped over 500 000 PCs, and many considered that it had irreversibly eclipsed Apple in the PC industry.

3. Profiting from innovation: Basic building blocks

In order to develop a coherent framework within which to explain the distribution of outcomes illustrated in fig. 2, three fundamental building blocks must first be put in place: the appropriability regime, complementary assets, and the dominant design paradigm.

D.J. Teece / Profiting from technological innovation 287

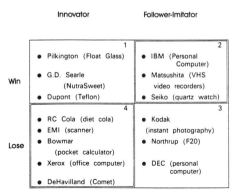

Fig. 2. Taxonomy of outcomes from the innovation process.

3.1. Regimes of appropriability

A regime of appropriability refers to the environmental factors, excluding firm and market structure, that govern an innovator's ability to capture the profits generated by an innovation. The most important dimensions of such a regime are the nature of the technology, and the efficacy of legal mechanisms of protection (fig. 3).

It has long been known that patents do not work in practice as they do in theory. Rarely, if ever, do patents confer perfect appropriability, although they do afford considerable protection on new chemical products and rather simple mechanical inventions. Many patents can be "invented around" at modest costs. They are especially ineffective at protecting process innovations. Often patents provide little protection because the legal requirements for upholding their validity or for proving their infringement are high.

In some industries, particularly where the innovation is embedded in processes, trade secrets are a viable alternative to patents. Trade secret protection is possible, however, only if a firm can put its product before the public and still keep the underlying technology secret. Usually only chemical formulas and industrial-commercial processes (e.g., cosmetics and recipes) can be protected as trade secrets after they're "out".

The degree to which knowledge is tacit or codified also affects ease of imitation. Codified knowledge is easier to transmit and receive, and is more exposed to industrial espionage and the like. Tacit knowledge by definition is difficult to articulate, and so transfer is hard unless those who possess the know how in question can demonstrate it to others (Teece [9]). Survey research indicates that methods of appropriability vary markedly across industries, and probably within industries as well (Levin et al. [5]).

The property rights environment within which a firm operates can thus be classified according to the nature of the technology and the efficacy of the legal system to assign and protect intellectual property. While a gross simplification, a dichotomy can be drawn between environments in which the appropriability regime is "tight" (technology is relatively easy to protect) and "weak" (technology is almost impossible to protect). Examples of the former include the formula for Coca Cola syrup; an example of the latter would be the Simplex algorithm in linear programming.

3.2. The dominant design paradigm

It is commonly recognized that there are two stages in the evolutionary development of a given branch of a science: the preparadigmatic stage when there is no single generally accepted conceptual treatment of the phenomenon in a field of study, and the paradigmatic stage which begins when a body of theory appears to have passed the canons of scientific acceptability. The emergence of a dominant paradigm signals scientific maturity and the acceptance of agreed upon "standards" by which what has been referred to as "normal" scientific research can proceed. These "standards" remain in force unless or until the paradigm is overturned. Revolutionary science is what overturns normal science, as when the Copernicus's theories of astronomy overturned Ptolemy's in the seventeenth century.

Abernathy and Utterback [1] and Dosi [3] have provided a treatment of the technological evolution of an industry which appears to parallel

- Legal instruments
  - Patents
  - Copyrights
  - Trade secrets
- Nature of technology
  - Product
  - Process
  - Tacit
  - Codified

Fig. 3. Appropriability regime: Key dimensions.

Kuhnian notions of scientific evolution. [2] In the early stages of industry development, product designs are fluid, manufacturing processes are loosely and adaptively organized, and generalized capital is used in production. Competition amongst firms manifests itself in competition amongst designs, which are markedly different from each other. This might be called the preparadigmatic stage of an industry.

At some point in time, and after considerable trial and error in the marketplace, one design or a narrow class of designs begins to emerge as the more promising. Such a design must be able to meet a whole set of user needs in a relatively complete fashion. The Model T Ford, the IBM 360, and the Douglas DC-3 are examples of dominant designs in the automobile, computer, and aircraft industry respectively.

Once a dominant design emerges, competition shifts to price and away from design. Competitive success then shifts to a whole new set of variables. Scale and learning become much more important, and specialized capital gets deployed as incumbent's seek to lower unit costs through exploiting economies of scale and learning. Reduced uncertainty over product design provides an opportunity to amortize specialized long-lived investments.

Innovation is not necessarily halted once the dominant design emerges; as Clarke [2] points out, it can occur lower down in the design hierarchy. For instance, a "v" cylinder configuration emerged in automobile engine blocks during the 1930s with the emergence of the Ford V-8 engine. Niches were quickly found for it. Moreover, once the product design stabilizes, there is likely to be a surge of process innovation as producers attempt to lower production costs for the new product (see fig. 4).

The Abernathy–Utterback framework does not characterize all industries. It seems more suited to mass markets where consumer tastes are relatively homogeneous. It would appear to be less characteristic of small niche markets where the absence of scale and learning economies attaches much less of a penalty to multiple designs. In these instances, generalized equipment will be employed in production.

---

[2] See Kuhn [4].

The existence of a dominant design watershed is of great significance to the distribution of profits between innovator and follower. The innovator may have been responsible for the fundamental scientific breakthroughs as well as the basic design of the new product. However, if imitation is relatively easy, imitators may enter the fray, modifying the product in important ways, yet relying on the fundamental designs pioneered by the innovator. When the game of musical chairs stops, and a dominant design emerges, the innovator might well end up positioned disadvantageously relative to a follower. Hence, when imitation is possible and occurs coupled with design modification before the emergence of a dominant design, followers have a good chance of having their modified product annointed as the industry standard, often to the great disadvantage of the innovator.

3.3. Complementary assets

Let the unit of analysis be an innovation. An innovation consists of certain technical knowledge about how to do things better than the existing state of the art. Assume that the know-how in question is partly codified and partly tacit. In order for such know-how to generate profits, it must be sold or utilized in some fashion in the market.

In almost all cases, the successful commercialization of an innovation requires that the know-how in question be utilized in conjunction with other capabilities or assets. Services such as marketing, competitive manufacturing, and after-sales support are almost always needed. These services are often obtained from complementary assets which are specialized. For example, the commercialization of a new drug is likely to require the dissemination of information over a specialized information channel. In some cases, as when the innovation is systemic, the complementary assets may be other parts of a system. For instance; computer hardware typically requires specialized software, both for the operating system, as well as for applications. Even when an innovation is autonomous, as with plug compatible components, certain complementary capabilities or assets will be needed for successful commercialization. Figure 5 summarizes this schematically.

Whether the assets required for least cost production and distribution are specialized to the

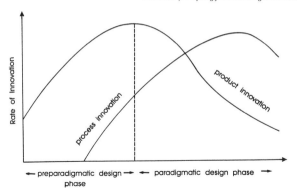

Fig. 4. Innovation over the product/industry life cycle.

innovation turns out to be important in the development presented below. Accordingly, the nature of complementary assets are explained in some detail. Figure 6 differentiates between complementary assets which are generic, specialized, and cospecialized.

Generic assets are general purpose assets which do not need to be tailored to the innovation in question. Specialized assets are those where there is unilateral dependence between the innovation and the complementary asset. Cospecialized assets are those for which there is a bilateral dependence. For instance, specialized repair facilities˙ were needed to support the introduction of the rotary engine by Mazda. These assets are cospecialized because of the mutual dependence of the innovation on the repair facility. Containerization similarly required the deployment of some cospecialized assets in ocean shipping and terminals. However, the dependence of trucking on containerized shipping was less than that of containerized shipping on trucking, as trucks can convert from containers to flat beds at low cost. An example of a generic asset would be the manufacturing facilities needed to make running shoes. Generalized

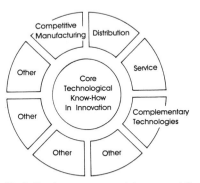

Fig. 5. Complementary assets needed to commercialize an innovation.

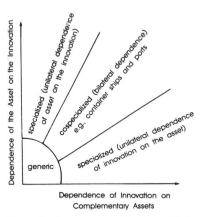

Fig. 6. Complementary assets: Generic, specialized, and cospecialized.

equipment can be employed in the main, exceptions being the molds for the soles.

4. Implications for profitability

These three concepts can now be related in a way which will shed light on the imitation process, and the distribution of profits between innovator and follower. We begin by examining tight appropriability regimes.

4.1. Tight appropriability regimes

In those few instances where the innovator has an iron clad patent or copyright protection, or where the nature of the product is such that trade secrets effectively deny imitators access to the relevant knowledge, the innovator is almost assured of translating its innovation into market value for some period of time. Even if the innovator does not possess the desirable endowment of complementary costs, iron clad protection of intellectual property will afford the innovator the time to access these assets. If these assets are generic, contractual relation may well suffice, and the innovator may simply license its technology. Specialized R & D firms are viable in such an environment. Universal Oil Products, an R & D firm developing refining processes for the petroleum industry was one such case in point. If, however, the complementary assets are specialized or cospecialized, contractual relationships are exposed to hazards, because one or both parties will have to commit capital to certain irreversible investments which will be valueless if the relationship between innovator and licensee breaks down. Accordingly, the innovator may find it prudent to expand its boundaries by integrating into specialized and cospecialized assets. Fortunately, the factors which make for difficult imitation will enable the innovator to build or acquire those complementary assets without competing with innovators for their control.

Competition from imitators is muted in this type of regime, which sometimes characterizes the petrochemical industry. In this industry, the protection offered by patents is fairly easily enforced. One factor assisting the licensee in this regard is that most petrochemical processes are designed around a specific variety of catalysts which can be

kept proprietory. An agreement not to analyze the catalyst can be extracted from licensees, affording extra protection. However, even if such requirements are violated by licensees, the innovator is still well positioned, as the most important properties of a catalyst are related to its physical structure, and the process for generating this structure cannot be deduced from structural analysis alone. Every reaction technology a company acquires is thus accompanied by an ongoing dependence on the innovating company for the catalyst appropriate to the plant design. Failure to comply with various elements of the licensing contract can thus result in a cutoff in the supply of the catalyst, and possibly facility closure.

Similarly, if the innovator comes to market in the preparadigmatic phase with a sound product concept but the wrong design, a tight appropriability regime will afford the innovator the time needed to perform the trials needed to get the design right. As discussed earlier, the best initial design concepts often turn out to be hopelessly wrong, but if the innovator possesses an impenetrable thicket of patents, or has technology which is simply difficult to copy, then the market may well afford the innovator the necessary time to ascertain the right design before being eclipsed by imitators.

4.2. Weak appropriability

Tight appropriability is the exception rather than the rule. Accordingly, innovators must turn to business strategy if they are to keep imitators/followers at bay. The nature of the competitive process will vary according to whether the industry is in the paradigmatic or preparadigmatic phase.

4.2.1. Preparadigmatic phase

In the preparadigmatic phase, the innovator must be careful to let the basic design "float" until sufficient evidence has accumulated that a design has been delivered which is likely to become the industry standard. In some industries there may be little opportunity for product modification. In microelectronics, for example, designs become locked in when the circuitry is chosen. Product modification is limited to "debugging" and software modification. An innovator must begin the design process anew if the product doesn't fit the market well. In some respects, however, selecting designs is dictated by the need to meet certain compatibility standards so that new hardware can interface with existing applications software. In one sense, therefore, the design issue for the microprocessor industry today is relatively straightforward: deliver greater power and speed while meeting the the computer industry standards of the existing software base. However, from time to time windows of opportunity emerge for the introduction of entirely new families of microprocessors which will define a new industry and software standard. In these instances, basic design parameters are less well defined, and can be permitted to "float" until market acceptance is apparent.

The early history of the automobile industry exemplifies exceedingly well the importance for subsequent success of selecting the right design in the preparadigmatic stages. None of the early producers of steam cars survived the early shakeout when the closed body internal combusion engine automobile emerged as the dominant design. The steam car, nevertheless, had numerous early virtues, such as reliability, which the internal combustion engine autos could not deliver.

The British fiasco with the Comet I is also instructive. De Havilland had picked an early design with both technical and commercial flaws. By moving into production, significant irreversibilities and loss of reputation hobbled de Havilland to such a degree that it was unable to convert to the Boeing design which subsequently emerged as dominant. It wasn't even able to occupy second place, which went instead to Douglas.

As a general principle, it appears that innovators in weak appropriability regimes need to be intimately coupled to the market so that user needs can fully impact designs. When multiple parallel and sequential prototyping is feasible, it has clear advantages. Generally such an approach is simply prohibitively costly. When development costs for a large commercial aircraft exceed one billion dollars, variations on a theme are all that is possible.

Hence, the probability that an innovator – defined here as a firm that is first to commercialize a new product design concept – will enter the paradigmatic phase possessing the dominant design is problematic. The probabilities will be higher the lower the relative cost of prototyping,

and the more tightly coupled the firm is to the market. The later is a function of organizational design, and can be influenced by managerial choices. The former is embedded in the technology, and cannot be influenced, except in minor ways, by managerial decisions. Hence, in industries with large developmental and prototyping costs – and hence significant irreversibilities – and where innovation of the product concept is easy, then one would expect that the probability that the innovator would emerge as the winner or amongst the winners at the end of the preparadigmatic stage is low.

4.2.2. Paradigmatic stage

In the preparadigmatic phase, complementary assets do not loom large. Rivalry is focused on trying to identify the design which will be dominant. Production volumes are low, and there is little to be gained in deploying specialized assets, as scale economies are unavailable, and price is not a principal competitive factor. However, as the leading design or designs begin to be revealed by the market, volumes increase and opportunities for economies of scale will induce firms to begin gearing up for mass production by acquiring specialized tooling and equipment, and possibly specialized distribution as well. Since these investments involve significant irreversibilities, producers are likely to proceed with caution. Islands of specialized capital will begin to appear in an industry, which otherwise features a sea of general purpose manufacturing equipment.

However, as the terms of competition begin to change, and prices become increasingly unimportant, access to complementary assets becomes absolutely critical. Since the core technology is easy to imitate, by assumption, commercial success swings upon the terms and conditions upon which the required complementary assets can be accessed.

It is at this point that specialized and cospecialized assets become critically important. Generalized equipment and skills, almost by definition, are always available in an industry, and even if they are not, they do not involve significant irreversibilities. Accordingly, firms have easy access to this type of capital, and even if there is insufficient capacity available in the relevant assets, it can easily be put in place as it involves few risks. Specialized assets, on the other hand, involve significant irreversibilities and cannot be easily accessed by contract, as the risks are significant for the party making the dedicated investment. The firms which control the cospecialized assets, such as distribution channels, specialized manufacturing capacity, etc. are clearly advantageously positioned relative to an innovator. Indeed, in rare instances where incumbent firms possess an airtight monopoly over specialized assets, and the innovator is in a regime of weak appropriability, all of the profits to the innovation could conceivably innure to the firms possessing the specialized assets who should be able to get the upper hand.

Even when the innovator is not confronted by situations where competitors or potential competitors control key assets, the innovator may still be disadvantaged. For instance, the technology embedded in cardiac pacemakers was easy to imitate, and so competitive outcomes quickly came to be determined by who had easiest access to the complementary assets, in this case specialized marketing. A similar situation has recently arisen in the United States with respect to personal computers. As an industry participant recently observed: "There are a huge numbers of computer manufacturers, companies that make peripherals (e.g. printers, hard disk drives, floppy disk drives), and software companies. They are all trying to get marketing distributors because they cannot afford to call on all of the US companies directly. They need to go through retail distribution channels, such as Businessland, in order to reach the marketplace. The problem today, however, is that many of these companies are not able to get shelf space and thus are having a very difficult time marketing their products. The point of distribution is where the profit and the power are in the marketplace today". (Norman [8, p.438])

5. Channel strategy issues

The above analysis indicates how access to complementary assets, such as manufacturing and distribution, on competitive teams is critical if the innovator is to avoid handling over the lion's share of the profits to imitators, and/or to the owners of the complementary assets that are specialized or cospecialized to the innovation. It is now necessary to delve deeper into the appropriate control structure that the innovator ideally ought to establish over these critical assets.

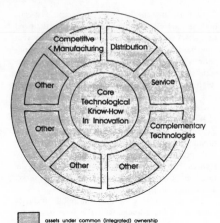

assets under common (integrated) ownership

Fig. 7. Complementary assets internalized for innovation: Hypothetical case #1 (innovator integrated into all complementary assets).

There are a myriad of possible channels which could be employed. At one extreme the innovator could integrate into all of the necessary comple-

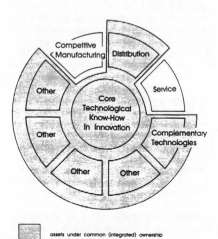

assets under common (integrated) ownership

Fig. 8. Complementary assets internalized for innovation: Hypothetical case #2 (innovator subcontracts for manufacturing and service).

mentary assets, as illustrated in fig. 7, or just a few of them, as illustrated in fig. 8. Complete integration (fig. 7) is likely to be unnecessary as well as prohibitively expensive. It is well to recognize that the variety of assets and competences which need to be accessed is likely to be quite large, even for only modestly complex technologies. To produce a personal computer, for instance, a company needs access to expertise in semiconductor technology, display technology, disk drive technology, networking technology, keyboard technology, and several others. No company can keep pace in all of these areas by itself.

At the other extreme, the innovator could attempt to access these assets through straightforward contractual relationships (e.g. component supply contracts, fabrication contracts, service contracts, etc.). In many instances such contracts may suffice, although it sometimes exposes the innovator to various hazards and dependencies that it may well wish to avoid. In between the fully integrated and full contractual extremes, there are a myriad of intermediate forms and channels available. An analysis of the properties of the two extreme forms is presented below. A brief synopsis of mixed modes then follows.

5.1. Contractual modes

The advantages of a contractual solution – whereby the innovator signs a contract, such as a license, with independent suppliers, manufacturers or distributors – are obvious. The innovator will not have to make the upfront capital expenditures needed to build or buy the assets in question. This reduces risks as well as cash requirements.

Contracting rather than integrating is likely to be the optimal strategy when the innovators appropriability regime is tight and the complementary assets are available in competitive supply (i.e. there is adequate capacity and a choice of sources).

Both conditions apply in petrochemicals for instance, so an innovator doesn't need to be integrated to be a successful. Consider, first, the appropriability regime. As discussed earlier, the protection offered by patents is fairly easily enforced, particularly for process technology, in the petrochemical industry. Given the advantageous feedstock prices available in hydrocarbon rich petrochemical exporters, and the appropriability regime characteristic of this industry, there is no

incentive or advantage in owning the complementary assets (production facilities) as they are not typically highly specialized to the innovation. Union Carbide appears to realize this, and has recently adjusted its strategy accordingly. Essentially, Carbide is placing its existing technology into a new subsidiary, Engineering and Hydrocarbons Service. The company is engaging in licensing and offers engineering, construction, and management services to customers who want to take their feedstocks and integrate them forward into petrochemicals. But Carbide itself appears to be backing away from an integration strategy.

Chemical and petrochemical product innovations are not quite so easy to protect, which should raise new challenges to innovating firms in the developed nations as they attempt to shift out of commodity petrochemicals. There are already numerous examples of new products that made it to the marketplace, filled a customer need, but never generated competitive returns to the innovator because of imitation. For example, in the 1960s Dow decided to start manufacturing rigid polyurethene foam. However, it was imitated very quickly by numerous small firms which had lower costs. [3] The absence of low cost manufacturing capability left Dow vulnerable.

Contractual relationships can bring added credibility to the innovator, especially if the innovator is relatively unknown when the contractual partner is established and viable. Indeed, arms-length contracting which embodies more than a simple buy-sell agreement is becoming so common, and is so multifaceted, that the term strategic partnering has been devised to describe it. Even large companies such as IBM are now engaging in it. For IBM, partnering buys access to new technologies enabling the company to "learn things we couldn't have learned without many years of trial and error." [4] IBM's arrangement with Microsoft to use the latter's MS-DOS operating system software on the IBM PC facilitated the timely introduction of IBM's personal computer into the market.

---

[3] Executive V.P. Union Carbide, Robert D. Kennedy, quoted in *Chemical Week*, Nov. 16, 1983, p. 48.

[4] Comment attributed to Peter Olson III, IBM's director of business development, as reported in The Strategy Behind IBM's Strategic Alliances, *Electronic Business*, October 1 (1985) 126.

Smaller less integrated companies are often eager to sign on with established companies because of the name recognition and reputation spillovers. For instance Cipher Data Products, Inc. contracted with IBM to develop a low-priced version of IBM's 3480 0.5 inch streaming cartridge drive, which is likely to become the industry standard. As Cipher management points out, "one of the biggest advantages to dealing with IBM is that, once you've created a product that meets the high quality standards necessary to sell into the IBM world, you can sell into any arena." [5] Similarly, IBM's contract with Microsoft "meant instant credibility" to Microsoft (McKenna, 1985, p. 94).

It is most important to recognize, however, that strategic (contractual) partnering, which is currently very fashionable, is exposed to certain hazards, particularly for the innovator, when the innovator is trying to use contracts to access specialized capabilities. First, it may be difficult to induce suppliers to make costly irreversible commitments which depend for their success on the success of the innovation. To expect suppliers, manufacturers, and distributors to do so is to invite them to take risks along with the innovator. The problem which this poses for the innovator is similar to the problems associated with attracting venture capital. The innovator must persuade its prospective partner that the risk is a good one. The situation is one open to opportunistic abuses on both sides. The innovator has incentives to overstate the value of the innovation, while the supplier has incentives to "run with the technology" should the innovation be a success.

Instances of both parties making irreversible capital commitments nevertheless exist. Apple's Laserwriter – a high resolution laser printer which allows PC users to produce near typeset quality text and art department graphics – is a case in point. Apple persuaded Canon to participate in the development of the Laserwriter by providing subsystems from its copiers – but only after Apple contracted to pay for a certain number of copier engines and cases. In short, Apple accepted a good deal of the financial risk in order to induce Canon to assist in the development and produc-

tion of the Laserwriter. The arrangement appears to have been prudent, yet there were clearly hazards for both sides. It is difficult to write, execute, and enforce complex development contracts, particularly when the design of the new product is still "floating." Apple was exposed to the risk that its co-innovator Canon would fail to deliver, and Canon was exposed to the risk that the Apple design and marketing effort would not succeed. Still, Apple's alternatives may have been rather limited, inasmuch as it didn't command the requisite technology to "go it alone."

In short, the current euphoria over "strategic partnering" may be partially misplaced. The advantages are being stressed (for example, McKenna [6]) without a balanced presentation of costs and risks. Briefly, there is the risk that the partner won't perform according to the innovator's perception of what the contract requires; there is the added danger that the partner may imitate the innovator's technology and attempt to compete with the innovator. This latter possibility is particularly acute if the provider of the complementary asset is uniquely situated with respect to the complementary asset in question and has the capacity to imitate the technology, which the innovator is unable to protect. The innovator will then find that it has created a competitor who is better positioned than the innovator to take advantage of the market opportunity at hand. *Business Week* has expressed concerns along these lines in its discussion of the "Hollow Corporation." [6]

It is important to bear in mind, however, that contractual or partnering strategies in certain cases are ideal. If the innovator's technology is well protected, and if what the partner has to provide is a "generic" capacity available from many potential partners, then the innovator will be able to maintain the upper hand while avoiding the costs of duplicating downstream capacity. Even if the partner fails to perform, adequate alternatives exist (by assumption, the partners' capacities are commonly available) so the innovator's efforts to successfully commercialize its technology ought to proceed profitably.

---

[5] Comment attributed to Norman Farquhar, Cipher's vice president for strategic development, as reported in *Electronic Business*, October 1 (1985) 128.

[6] See *Business Week*, March 3 (1986) 57–59. *Business Week* uses the term to describe a corporation which lacks in-house manufacturing capability.

5.2. Integration modes

Integration, which by definition involves ownership, is distinguished from pure contractual modes in that it typically facilitates incentive alignment and control. If an innovator owns rather than rents the complementary assets needed to commercialize, then it is in a position to capture spillover benefits stemming from increased demand for the complementary assets caused by the innovation.

Indeed, an innovator might be in the position, at least before its innovation is announced, to buy up capacity in the complementary assets, possibly to its great subsequent advantage. If futures markets exist, simply taking forward positions in the complementary assets may suffice to capture much of the spillovers.

Even after the innovation is announced, the innovator might still be able to build or buy complementary capacities at competitive prices if the innovation has iron clad legal protection (i.e. if the innovation is in a tight appropriability regime). However, if the innovation is not tightly protected and once "out" is easy to imitate, then securing control of complementary capacities is likely to be the key success factor, particularly if those capacities are in fixed supply – so called "bottlenecks." Distribution and specialized manufacturing competences often become bottlenecks.

As a practical matter, however, an innovator may not have the time to acquire or build the complementary assets that ideally it would like to control. This is particularly true when imitation is easy, so that timing becomes critical. Additionally, the innovator may simply not have the financial resources to proceed. The implications of timing and cash constraints are summarized in fig. 9.

Accordingly, in weak appropriability regimes innovators need to rank complementary assets as to their importance. If the complementary assets are critical, ownership is warranted, although if the firm is cash constrained a minority position may well represent a sensible tradeoff.

Needless to say, when imitation is easy, strategic moves to build or buy complementary assets which are specialized must occur with due reference to the moves of competitors. There is no point moving to build a specialized asset, for instance, if one's imitators can do it faster and cheaper.

It is hopefully self evident that if the innovator is already a large enterprise with many of the relevant complementary assets under its control, integration is not likely to be the issue that it might otherwise be, as the innovating firm will already control many of the relevant specialized and cospecialized assets. However, in industries experiencing rapid technological change, technologies advance so rapidly that it is unlikely that a single company has the full range of expertise needed to bring advanced products to market in a timely and cost effective fashion. Hence, the integration issue is not just a small firm issue.

**Time Required to Position
(Relative to Competitors)**

		Long	Short
Investment Required	**Minor**	OK If Timing Not Critical	Full Steam Ahead
	Major	Forget It	OK If Cost Position Tolerable

Optimum Investment for Business in Question

		Minor	Major
How Critical to Success?	**Critical**	Internalize (majority ownership)	Internalize (but if cash constrained, take minority position)
	Not Critical	Discretionary	Do Not Internalize (contract out)

Fig. 9. Specialized complementary assets and weak appropriability: Integration calculus.

5.3. Integration versus contract strategies: An analytic summary

Figure 10 summarizes some of the relevant considerations in the form of a decision flow chart. It indicates that a profit seeking innovator, confronted by weak intellectual property protection and the need to access specialized complementary assets and/or capabilities, is forced to expand its activities through integration if it is to prevail over imitators. Put differently, innovators who develop new products that possess poor intellectual property protection but which requires specialized complementary capacities are more likely to parlay their technology into a commercial advantage, rather than see it prevail in the hands of imitators.

Figure 10 makes it apparent that the difficult strategic decisions arise in situations where the appropriability regime is weak and where specialized assets are critical to profitable commercialization. These situations, which in reality are very common, require that a fine-grained competitor analysis be part of the innovator's strategic assessment of its opportunities and threats. This is carried a step further in fig. 11, which looks only at situations where commercialization requires certain specialized capabilities. It indicates the appropriate strategies for the innovators and predicts the outcomes to be expected for the various players.

Three classes of players are of interst: innovators, imitators, and the owners of cospecialized assets (e.g. distributors). All three can potentially benefit or lose from the innovation process. The latter can potentially benefit from the additional business which the innovation may direct in the asset owners direction. Should the asset turn out

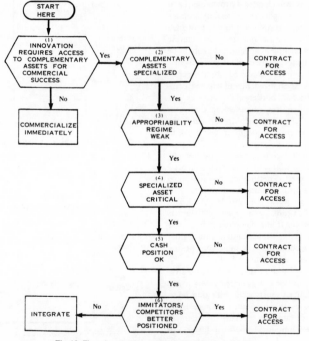

Fig. 10. Flow chart for integration versus contract decision.

to be a bottleneck with respect to commercializing the innovation, the owner of the bottleneck facilities is obviously in a position to extract profits from the innovator and/or imitators.

The vertical axis in fig. 11 measures how those who possess the technology (the innovator or possibly its imitators) are positioned vis à vis those firms that possess required specialized assets. The horizontal axis measures the "tightness" of the appropriability regime, tight regimes being evidence by iron clad legal protection coupled with technology that is simply difficult to copy; weak regimes offer little in the way of legal protection and the essence of the technology, once released, is transparent to the imitator. Weak regimes are further subdivided according to how the innovator and imitators are positioned vis à vis each other. This is likely to be a function of factors such as lead time and prior positioning in the requisite complementary assets.

Figure 11 makes it apparent that even when firms pursue the optimal strategy, other industry participants may take the jackpot. This possibility is unlikely when the intellectual property in question is tightly protected. The only serious threat to the innovator is where a specialized complementary asset is completely "locked up," a possibility recognized in cell 4. This can rarely be done without the cooperation of government. But it frequently occurs, as when a foreign government closes off access to a foreign market, forcing the innovators to license to foreign firms, but with the government effectively cartelizing the potential licensees. With weak intellectual property protection, however, it is quite clear that the innovator will often loose out to imitators and/or asset holders, even when the innovator is pursuing the appropriate strategy (cell 6). Clearly, incorrect strategies can compound problems. For instance, if innovators integrate when they should contract,

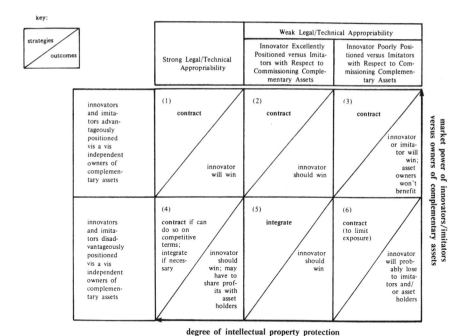

Fig. 11. Contract and integration strategies and outcomes for innovators: Specialized asset case.

a heavy commitment of resources will be incurred for little if any strategic benefit, thereby exposing the innovator to even greater losses than would otherwise be the case. On the other hand, if an innovator tries to contract for the supply of a critical capability when it should build the capability itself, it may well find it has nutured an imitator better able to serve the market than the innovator itself.

5.4. Mixed modes

The real world rarely provides extreme or pure cases. Decisions to integrate or·license involve tradeoffs, compromises, and mixed approaches. It is not surprising therefore that the real world is characterized by mixed modes of organization, involving judicious blends of integration and contracting. Sometimes mixed modes represent transitional phases. For instance, because of the convergence of computer and telecommunication technology, firms in each industry are discovering that they often lack the requisite technical capabilities in the other. Since the technological interdependence of the two requires collaboration amongst those who design different parts of the system, intense cross-boundary coordination and information flows are required. When separate enterprises are involved, agreement must be reached on complex protocol issues amongst parties who see their interests differently. Contractual difficulties can be anticipated since the selection of common technical protocols amongst the parties will often be followed by transaction-specific investments in hardware and software. There is little doubt that this was the motivation behind IBM's purchase of 15 percent of PBX manufacturer Rolm in 1983, a position that was expanded to 100 percent in 1984. IBM's stake in Intel, which began with a 12 percent purchase in 1982, is most probably not a transitional phase leading to 100 percent purchase, because both companies realized that the two corporate cultures are not very compatible, and IBM may not be as impressed with Intel's technology as it once was.

5.5. The CAT scanner, the IBM PC, and Nutra-Sweet: Insights from the framework

EMI's failure to reap significant returns from the CAT scanner can be explained in large mea-

sure by reference to the concepts developed above. The scanner which EMI developed was of a technical sophistication much higher than would normally be found in a hospital, requiring a high level of training, support, and servicing. EMI had none of these capabilities, could not easily contract for them, and was slow to realize their importance. It most probably could have formed a partnership with a company like Siemens to access the requisite capabilities. Its failure to do so was a strategic error compounded by the very limited intellectual property protection which the law afforded the scanner. Although subsequent court decisions have upheld some of EMI's patent claims, once the product was in the market it could be reverse engineered and its essential features copied. Two competitors, GE and Technicare, already possessed the complementary capabilities that the scanner required, and they were also technologically capable. In addition, both were experienced marketers of medical equipment, and had reputations for quality, reliability and service. GE and Technicare were thus able to commit their R&D resources to developing a competitive scanner, borrowing ideas from EMI's scanner, which they undoubtedly had access to through cooperative hospitals, and improving on it where they could while they rushed to market. GE began taking orders in 1976 and soon after made inroads on EMI. In 1977 concern for rising health care costs caused the Carter Administration to introduce "certificate of need' regulation, which required HEW's approval on expenditures on big ticket items like CAT scanners. This severely cut the size of the available market.

By 1978 EMI had lost market share leadership to Technicare, which was in turn quickly overtaken by GE. In October 1979, Godfrey Hounsfield of EMI shared the Nobel prize for invention of the CT scanner. Despite this honor, and the public recognition of its role in bringing this medical breakthrough to the world, the collapse of its scanner business forced EMI in the same year into the arms of a rescuer, Thorn Electrical Industries, Ltd. GE subsequently acquired what was EMI's scanner business from Thorn for what amounted to a pittance. [7] Though royalties continued to flow to EMI, the company had failed to capture the

---

[7]   See GE Gobbles a Rival in CT Scanners, *Business Week*, May 19, 1980, issue no. 2637.

lion's share of the profits generated by the innovation it had pioneered and successfully commercialized.

If EMI illustrates how a company with outstanding technology and an excellent product can fail to profit from innovation while the imitators succeeded, the story of the IBM PC indicates how a new product representing a very modest technological advance can yield remarkable returns to the developer.

The IBM PC, introduced in 1981, was a success despite the fact that the architecture was ordinary and the components standard. Philip Estridge's design team in Boca Raton, Florida, decided to use existing technology to produce a solid, reliable micro rather than state of the art. With a one-year mandate to develop a PC, Estridge's team could do little else.

However, the IBM PC did use what at the time was a new 16-bit microprocessor (the Intel 8088) and a new disk operating system (DOS) adapted for IBM by Microsoft. Other than the microprocessor and the operating system, the IBM PC incorporated existing micro "standards" and used off-the-shelf parts from outside vendors. IBM did write its own BIOS (Basic Input/Output System) which is embedded in ROM, but this was a relatively straightforward programming exercise.

The key to the PC's success was not the technology. It was the set of complementary assets which IBM either had or quickly assembled around the PC. In order to expand the market for PCs, there was a clear need for an expandable, flexible microcomputer system with extensive applications software. IBM could have based its PC system on its own patented hardware and copyrighted software. Such an approach would cause complementary products to be cospecialized, forcing IBM to develop peripherals and a comprehensive library of software in a very short time. Instead, IBM adopted what might be called an "induced contractual" approach. By adopting an open system architecture, as Apple had done, and by making the operating system information publicly available, a spectacular output of third part software was induced. IBM estimated that by mid-1983, at least 3000 hardware and software products were available for the PC. [8] Put differently, IBM pulled together the complementary assets, particularly software, which success required, without even using contracts, let alone integration. This was despite the fact that the software developers were creating assets that were in part cospecialized with the IBM PC, at least in the first instance.

A number of special factors made this seem a reasonable risk to the software writers. A critical one was IBM's name and commitment to the project. The reputation behind the letters I.B.M. is perhaps the greatest cospecialized asset the company possesses. The name implied that the product would be marketed and serviced in the IBM tradition. It guaranteed that PC-DOS would become an industry standard, so that the software business would not be solely dependent on IBM, because emulators were sure to enter. It guaranteed access to retail distribution outlets on competitive terms. The consequences was that IBM was able to take a product which represented at best a modest technological accomplishment, and turn into a fabulous commercial success. The case demonstrates the role that complementary assets play in determining outcomes.

The spectacular success and profitability of G.D. Searle's NutraSweet is an uncommon story which is also consistent with the above framework. In 1982, Searle reported combined sales of $74 million for NutraSweet and its table top version, Equal. In 1983, this surged to $336 million. In 1985, NutraSweet sales exceeded $700 million [9] and Equal had captured 50 percent of the U.S. sugar substitute market and was number one in five other countries.

NutraSweet, which is Searle's tradename for aspartame, has achieved rapid acceptance in each of its FDA approved categories because of its good taste and ability to substitute directly for sugar in many applications. However, Searle's earnings from NutraSweet and the absence of a strategic challenge can be traced in part to Searle's clever strategy.

It appears that Searle has managed to establish an exceptionally tight appropriability regime around NutraSweet – one that may well continue for some time after the patent has expired. No competitor appears to have successfully "invented around" the Searle patent and commercialized an alternative, no doubt in part because the FDA

[8] F. Gens and C. Christiansen, Could 1,000,000 IBM PC Users Be Wrong, *Byte*, November 1983, 88.

[9] See *Monsanto Annual Report, 1985.*

approval process would have to begin anew for an imitator who was not violating Searle's patents. A competitor who tried to replicate the aspartame molecule with minor modification to circumvent the patent would probably be forced to replicate the hundreds of tests and experiments which proved aspartame's safety. Without patent protection, FDA approval would provide no shield against imitators coming to market with an identical chemical and who could establish to the FDA that it is the same compound that had already been approved. Without FDA approval on the other hand, the patent protection would be worthless for the product would not be sold for human consumption.

Searle has aggressively pushed to strengthen its patent protection. The company was granted U.S. patent protection in 1970. It has also obtained patent protection in Japan, Canada, Australia, U.K., France, Germany, and a number of other countries. However, most of these patents carry a 17-year life. Since the product was only approved for human consumption in 1982, the 17-year patent life was effectively reduced to five. Recognizing the obvious importance of its patent, Searle pressed for and obtained special legislation in November 1984 extending the patent protection on aspartame for another 5 years. The U.K. provided a similar extension. In almost every other nation, however, 1987 will mark the expiration of the patent.

When the patent expires, however, Searle will still have several valuable assets to help keep imitators at bay. Searle has gone to great lengths to create and promulgate the use of its NutraSweet name and a distinctive "Swirl" logo on all goods licensed to use the ingredient. The company has also developed the "Equal" tradename for a table top version of the sweetener. Trademark law in the U.S. provides protection against "unfair" competition in branded products for as long as the owner of the mark continues to use it. Both the NutraSweet and Equal trademarks will become essential assets when the patents on aspartame expire. Searle may well have convinced consumers that the only real form of sweetener is Nutra-Sweet/Equal. Consumers know most other artificial sweeteners by their generic names – saccharin and cyclamates.

Clearly, Searle is trying to build a position in complementary assets to prepare for the competi-

tion which will surely arise. Searle's joint venture with Ajinomoto ensures them access to that company's many years of experience in the production of biochemical agents. Much of this knowledge is associated with techniques for distillation and synthesis of the delicate hydrocarbon compounds that are the ingredients of NutraSweet, and is therefore more tacit than codified. Searle has begun to put these techniques to use in its own $160 million Georgia production facility. It can be expected that Searle will use trade secrets to the maximum to keep this know-how proprietary.

By the time its patent expires, Searle's extensive research into production techniques for L-phenylalanine, and its 8 years of experience in the Georgia plant, should give it a significant cost advantage over potential aspartame competitors. Trade secret protection, unlike patents, has no fixed lifetime and may well sustain Searle's position for years to come.

Moreover, Searle has wisely avoided renewing contracts with suppliers when they have expired. [10] Had Searle subcontracted manufacturing for NutraSweet, it would have created a manufacturer who would then be in a position to enter the aspartame market itself, or to team up with a marketer of artificial sweeteners. But keeping manufacturing inhouse, and by developing a valuable tradename, Searle has a good chance of protecting its market position from dramatic inroads once patents expire. Clearly, Searle seems to be astutely aware of the importance of maintaining a "tight appropriability regime" and using cospecialized assets strategically.

6. Implications for R&D strategy, industry structure, and trade policy

6.1. Allocating R&D resources

The analysis so far assumes that the firm has developed an innovation for which a market exists. It indicates the strategies which the firm must

---

[10] Purification Engineering, which had spent $5 million to build a phenylalanine production facility, was told in January 1985 that their contract would not be renewed. In May, Genex, which claimed to have invested $25 million, was given the same message, A Bad Aftertaste, *Business Week*, July 15, 1985, issue 2903.

follow to maximize its share of industry profits relative to imitators and other competitors. There is no guarantee of success even if optimal strategies are followed.

The innovator can improve its total return to R&D, however, by adjusting its R&D investment portfolio to maximize the probability that technological discoveries will emerge that are either easy to protect with existing intellectual property law, or which require for commercialization cospecialized assets already within the firm's repertoire of capabilities. Put differently, if an innovating firm does not target its R&D resources towards new products and processes which it can commercialize advantageously relative to potential imitators and/or followers, then it is unlikely to profit from its investment in R&D. In this sense, a firm's history – and the assets it already has in place – ought to condition its R&D investment decisions. Clearly, an innovating firm with considerable assets already in place is free to strike out in new directions, so long as in doing so it is cognizant of the kinds of capabilities required to successfully commercialize the innovation. It is therefore rather clear that the R&D investment decision cannot be divorced from the strategic analysis of markets and industries, and the firm's position within them.

6.2. Small firm versus large firm comparisons

Business commentators often remark that many small entrepreneurial firms which generate new, commercially valuable technology fail while large multinational firms, often with a less meritorious record with respect to innovation, survive and prosper. One set of reasons for this phenomenon is now clear. Large firms are more likely to possess the relevant specialized and cospecialized assets within their boundaries at the time of new product introduction. They can therefore do a better job of milking their technology, however meager, to maximum advantage. Small domestic firms are less likely to have the relevant specialized and cospecialized assets within their boundaries and so will either have to incur the expense of trying to build them, or of trying to develop coalitions with competitors/owners of the specialized assets.

6.3. Regimes of appropriability and industry structure

In industries where legal methods of protection are effective, or where new products are just hard to copy, the strategic necessity for innovating firms to integrate into cospecialized assets would appear to be less compelling than in industries where legal protection is weak. In cases where legal protection is weak or nonexistent, the control of cospecialized assets will be needed for long-run survival.

In this regard, it is instructive to examine the U.S. drug industry (Temin [10]). Beginning in the 1940s, the U.S. Patent Office began, for the first time, to grant patents on certain natural substances that involved difficult extraction procedures. Thus, in 1948 Merck received a patent on streptomycin, which was a natural substance. However, it was not the extraction process but the drug itself which received the patent. Hence, patents were important to the drug industry in terms of what could be patented (drugs), but they did not prevent imitation [10, p.436]. Sometimes just changing one molecule will enable a company to come up with a different substance which does not violate the patent. Had patents been more all-inclusive – and I am not suggesting they should – licensing would have been an effective mechanism for Merck to extract profits from its innovation. As it turns out, the emergence of close substitutes, coupled with FDA regulation which had the de facto effect of reducing the elasticity of demand for drugs, placed high rewards on a product differentiation strategy. This required extensive marketing, including a sales force that could directly contact doctors, who were the purchasers of drugs through their ability to create prescriptions. [11] The result was exclusive production (i.e., the earlier industry practice of licensing was dropped) and forward integration into marketing (the relevant cospecialized asset).

Generally, if legal protection of the innovator's profits is secure, innovating firms can select their

---

[11] In the period before FDA regulation, all drugs other than narcotics were available over-the-counter. Since the end user could purchase drugs directly, sales were price sensitive. Once prescriptions were required, this price sensitivity collapsed; the doctors not only did not have to pay for the drugs, but in most cases they were unaware of the prices of the drugs they were prescribing.

boundaries based simply on their ability to identify user needs and respond to those through research and development. The weaker the legal methods of protection, the greater the incentive to integrate into the relevant cospecialized assets. Hence, as industries in which legal protection is weak begin to mature, integration into innovation-specific cospecialized assets will occur. Often this will take the form of backward, forward and lateral integration. (Conglomerate integration is not part of this phenomenon.) For example, IBM's purchase of Rolm can be seen as a response to the impact of technological change on the identity of the cospecialized assets relevant to IBM's future growth.

6.4. Industry maturity, new entry, and history

As technologically progressive industries mature, and a greater proportion of the relevant cospecialized assets are brought in under the corporate umbrellas of incumbents, new entry becomes more difficult. Moreover, when it does occur it is more likely to involve coalition formation very early on. Incumbents will for sure own the cospecialized assets, and new entrants will find it necessary to forge links with them. Here lies the explanation for the sudden surge in "strategic partnering" now occurring internationally, and particularly in the computer and telecommunications industry. Note that it should not be interpreted in anti-competitive terms. Given existing industry structure, coalitions ought to be seen not as attempts to stifle competition, but as mechanisms for lowering entry requirements for innovators.

In industries in which technological change of a particular kind has occurred, which required deployment of specialized and/or cospecialized assets at the time, a configuration of firm boundaries may well have arisen which no longer has compelling efficiencies. Considerations which once dictated integration may no longer hold, yet there may not be strong forces leading to divestiture. Hence existing firm boundaries may in some industries – especially those where the technological trajectory and attendant specialized asset requirements has changed – be rather fragile. In short, history matters in terms of understanding the structure of the modern business enterprise. Existing firm boundaries cannot always be assumed to have obvious rationales in terms of today's requirements.

6.5. The importance of manufacturing to international competitiveness

Practically all forms of technological know-how must be embedded in goods and services to yield value to the consumer. An important policy for the innovating nation is whether the identity of the firms and nations performing this function matter.

In a world of tight appropriability and zero transactions cost – the world of neoclassical trade theory – it is a matter of indifference whether an innovating firm has an in-house manufacturing capability, domestic or foreign. It can simply engage in arms-length contracting (patent licensing, know-how licensing, co-production, etc.) for the sale of the output of the activity in which it has a comparative advantage (in this case R & D) and will maximize returns by specializing in what it does best.

However, in a regime of weak appropriability, and especially where the requisite manufacturing assets are specialized to the innovation, which is often the case, participation in manufacturing may be necessary if an innovator is to appropriate the rents from its innovation. Hence, if an innovator's manufacturing costs are higher than those of its imitators, the innovator may well end up ceding the lion's share of profits to the imitator.

In a weak appropriability regime, low cost imitator-manufacturers may end up capturing all of the profits from innovation. In a weak appropriability regime where specialized manufacturing capabilities are required to produce new products, an innovator with a manufacturing disadvantage may find that its advantage at early stage research and development will have no commercial value. This will eventually cripple the innovator, unless it is assisted by governmental processes. For example, it appears that one of the reasons why U.S. color TV manufacturers did not capture the lion's share of the profits from the innovation, for which RCA was primarily responsible, was that RCA and its American licenses were not competitive at manufacturing. In this context, concerns that the decline of manufacturing threatens the entire economy appear to be well founded.

A related implication is that as the technology gap closes, the basis of competition in an industry will shift to the cospecialized assets. This appears to be what is happening in microprocessors. Intel is no longer out ahead technologically. As Gordon Moore, CEO of Intel points out, "Take the top 10 [semiconductor] companies in the world...and it is hard to tell at any time who is ahead of whom.... It is clear that we have to be pretty damn close to the Japanese from a manufacturing standpoint to compete." [12] It is not just that strength in one area is necessary to compensate for weakness in another. As technology becomes more public and less proprietary through easier imitation, then strength in manufacturing and other capabilities is necessary to derive advantage from whatever technological advantages an innovator may possess.

Put differently, the notion that the United States can adopt a "designer role" in international commerce, while letting independent firms in other countries such as Japan, Korea, Taiwan, or Mexico do the manufacturing, is unlikely to be viable as a long-run strategy. This is because profits will accrue primarily to the low cost manufacturers (by providing a larger sales base over which they can exploit their special skills). Where imitation is easy, and even where it is not, there are obvious problems in transacting in the market for know-how, problems which are described in more detail elsewhere [9]. In particular, there are difficulties in pricing an intangible asset whose true performance features are difficult to ascertain ex ante.

The trend in international business towards what Miles and Snow [7] call "dynamic networks" – characterized by vertical disintegration and contracting – ought thus be viewed with concern. (*Business Week*, March 3, 1986, has referred to the same phenomenon as the Hollow Corporation.) "Dynamic networks" may not so much reflect innovative organizational forms, but the disassembly of the modern corporation because of deterioration in national capacities, manufacturing in particular, which are complementary to technological innovation. Dynamic networks may therefore signal not so much the rejuvenation of American enterprise, but its piecemeal demise.

6.6. How trade and investment barriers can impact innovators' profits

In regimes of weak appropriability, governments can move to shift the distribution of the

gains from innovation away from foreign innovators and towards domestic firms by denying innovators ownership of specialized assets. The foreign firm, which by assumption is an innovator, will be left with the option of selling its intangible assets in the market for know how if both trade and investment are foreclosed by government policy. This option may appear better than the alternative (no renumeration at all from the market in question). Licensing may then appear profitable, but only because access to the complementary assets is blocked by government.

Thus when an innovating firm generating profits needs to access complementary assets abroad, host governments, by limiting access, can sometimes milk the innovators for a share of the profits, particularly that portion which originates from sales in the host country. However, the ability of host governments to do so depends importantly on the criticality of the host country's assets to the innovator. If the cost and infrastructure characteristics of the host country are such that it is the world's lowest cost manufacturing site, and if domestic industry is competitive, then by acting as a de facto monopsonist the host country government ought to be able to adjust the terms of access to the complementary assets so as to appropriate a greater share of the profits generated by the innovation. [13]

If, on the other hand, the host country offers no unique complementary assets, except access to its own market, restrictive practices by the government will only redistribute profits with respect to domestic rather than worldwide sales.

6.7. Implications for the international distribution of the benefits from innovation

The above analysis makes transparent that innovators who do not have access to the relevant specialized and cospecialized assets may end up ceding profits to imitators and other competitors, or simply to the owners of the specialized or cospecialized assets.

Even when the specialized assets are possessed by the innovating firm, they may be located abroad. Foreign factors of production are thus

---

[12] Institutionalizing the Revolution, *Forbes*, June 16, 1986, 35.

[13] If the host country market structure is monopolistic in the first instance, private actors might be able to achieve the same benefit. What government can do is to force collusion of domestic enterprises to their mutual benefit.

likely to benefit from research and development activities occurring across borders. There is little doubt, for instance, that the inability of many American multinationals to sustain competitive manufacturing in the U.S. is resulting in declining returns to U.S. labor. Stockholders and top management probably do as well if not better when a multinational accesses cospecialized assets in the firm's foreign subsidiaries; however, if there is unemployment in the factors of production supporting the specialized and cospecialized assets in question, then the foreign factors of production will benefit from innovation originating beyond national borders. This speaks to the importance to innovating nations of maintaining competence and competitiveness in the assets which complement technological innovation, manufacturing being a case in point. It also speaks to the importance to innovating nations of enhancing the protection afforded worldwide to intellectual property.

However, it must be recognized that there are inherent limits to the legal protection of intellectual property, and that business and national strategy are therefore likely to the critical factors in determining how the gains from innovation are shared worldwide. By making the correct strategic decision, innovating firms can move to protect the interests of stockholders; however, to ensure that domestic rather than foreign cospecialized assets capture the lion's share of the externalities spilling over to complementary assets, the supporting infrastructure for those complementary assets must not be allowed to decay. In short, if a nation has prowess at innovation, then in the absence of iron clad protection for intellectual property, it must maintain well-developed complementary assets if it is to capture the spillover benefits from innovation

7. Conclusion

The above analysis has attempted to synthesize from recent research in industrial organization and strategic management a framework within which to analyze the distribution of the profits from innovation. The framework indicates that the boundaries of the firm are an important strategic variable for innovating firms. The ownership of complementary assets, particularly when they are specialized and/or cospecialized, help establish who wins and who loses from innovation. Imitators can often outperform innovators if they are better positioned with respect to critical complementary assets. Hence, public policy aimed at promoting innovation must focus not only on R&D, but also on complementary assets, as well as the underlying infrastructure. If government decides to stimulate innovation, it would seem important to clear away barriers which impede the development of complementary assets which tend to be specialized or cospecialized to innovation. To fail to do so will cause an unnecessary large portion of the profits from innovation to flow to imitators and other competitors. If these firms lie beyond one's national borders, there are obvious implications for the internal distribution of income.

When applied to world markets, results similar to those obtained from the "new trade theory" are suggested by the framework. In particular, tariffs and other restrictions on trade can in some cases injure innovating firms while simultaneously benefiting protected firms when they are imitators. However, the propositions suggested by the framework are particularized to appropriability regimes, suggesting that economy-wide conclusions will be illusive. The policy conclusions derivable for commodity petrochemicals, for instance, are likely to be different than those that would be arrived at for semiconductors.

The approach also suggests that the product life cycle model of international trade will play itself out very differently in different industries and markets, in part according to appropriability regimes and the nature of the assets which need to be employed to convert a technological success into a commercial one. Whatever its limitations, the approach establishes that it is not so much the structure of markets but the structure of firms, particularly the scope of their boundaries, coupled with national policies with respect to the development of complementary assets, which determines the distribution of the profits amongst innovators and imitator/followers.

References

[1] W.J. Abernathy and J.M. Utterback, Patterns of Industrial Innovation, *Technology Review* 80(7) (January/July 1978) 40–47.

[2] Kim B. Clarke, The Interaction of Design Hierarchies and Market Concepts in Technological Evolution, *Research Policy* 14 (1985) 235–251.

[3] G. Dosi, Technological Paradigms and Technological Trajectories, *Research Policy* 11 (1982) 147–162.

[4] Thomas Kuhn, *The Structure of Scientifc Revolutions*, 2nd ed (University of Chicago Press, Chicago, 1970).

[5] R. Levin, A. Klevorick, N. Nelson, and S. Winter, Survey Research on R&D Appropriability and Technological Opportunity, unpublished manuscript, Yale University, 1984.

[6] Regis McKenna, Market Positioning in High Technology, *California Management Review*, XXVII (3) (spring 1985).

[7] R.E. Miles and C.C. Snow, Network Organizations: New Concepts for New Forms, *California Management Review* (spring 1986) 62–73.

[8] David A. Norman, Impact of Entrepreneurship and Innovations on the Distribution of Personal Computers, in: R. Landau and N. Rosenberg (eds.), *The Positive Sum Strategy* (National Academy Press, Washington, DC, 1986).

[9] D.J. Teece, The Market for Know how and the Efficient International Transfer of Technology, *Annals of the American Academy of Political and Social Science*, November 1981.

[10] P. Temin, Technology, Regulation, and Market Structure in the Modern Pharmaceutical Industry, *The Bell Journal of Economics* (autumn 1979) 429–446.

[3]

CALIFORNIA MANAGEMENT REVIEW Reprint Series
©1989 by The Regents of the University of California
CMR, Volume 31, Number 3, Spring 1989

Business & Public Policy

Competition and Cooperation: Striking the Right Balance

Thomas M. Jorde   **David J. Teece**

Two somewhat independent shifts are causing academics, businessmen, and policy makers to rethink fundamental ideas about competition and cooperation. The first is the increased level of international competition, particularly from Japan and other developmental states which have relentlessly been challenging American and European corporations in the global marketplace. These competitive pressures are leading, at least in some circles, to a re-evaluation of American institutions, policies, and ideology. The second and more subtle shift is occurring within business, government, and academia, and it concerns the role of interfirm agreements—one aspect of the corporation's new relationships. Whereas cooperation among firms was once a subject confined to antitrust case books, it is increasingly a topic for discussion in schools of management. Indeed, ways in which firms can cooperate to compete are receiving considerable attention, especially in courses on the management of technology and in corporate strategy. Yet firms wanting to experiment with new ways of organizing businesses contractually rather than by merger run the risk of getting snagged on out-of-date antitrust ideology. In this article, the need for cooperative agreement in the context of innovation are briefly surveyed, opportunities are assessed, and public policy problems confronted. A new balance between cooperation and competition is suggested, with strong implications for corporate strategy and public policy.

The authors wish to thank Michael Gerlach, Oliver Williamson, and Patrizia Zagnoli for helpful insights.

Traditional Views

The basic tenet of textbook orthodoxy is that competition drives resource allocation towards efficient outcomes, while market power distorts outcomes and
creates inefficiencies. The image of competition which informs this view is
that of neoclassical perfect competition. In the standard formulation, price is
considered to be the sharpest competitive weapon. Non-price competition,
through product and process innovation, "can have real effects but is less direct
and hard hitting."[1] Cooperation is generally analyzed *only* in terms of its negative impacts on economic welfare. Indeed, coordination of prices is often the
only form of cooperation recognized in economic textbooks. For instance,
Shepherd has an entire chapter devoted to the topic of "cooperation among
firms," yet this chapter only discusses cartels as if they were the only kind of
interfirm cooperation.[2] One must look in vain before 1980 for conclusions that
interfirm cooperation can be beneficial to the public. Economists fear cooperation between competing firms because it might preclude multiple paths to invention and dull the incentives to be creative. Furthermore, collaborative
habits might migrate from the laboratory to product development and marketing, with attendant antisocial consequences. The conventional conceptualization of competition thus leads to a hostility towards many forms of business
conduct, particularly if they involve agreements with competitors. The result
is a world in which the antitrust law inhibits certain interfirm activities such as
cooperation with respect to new product commercialization, while finding
nothing objectionable about conglomerate mergers, even if they are efficiency
destroying.[3]

Challenges to Orthodoxy

A reconceptualization of competition, and in particular a reassessment of horizontal cooperation, is urgently needed. The underpinnings of a new approach
begin with the observation that an essential aspect of economic organization is
the need to coordinate economic activity and, in particular, investments. It is a
characteristic of the private enterprise economy that although its individual
members are independent, their activivities are nevertheless interrelated. Any
single investment will, in general, only be profitable provided first, that the
volume of competitive investment does not exceed a limit set by demand, and
second, that the volume of complementary investment reaches the correct
level.[4]

However, orthodox thinking often fails to recognize that there is no special
machinery in a private enterprise, market economy to ensure that these two
conditions will be met. Price movements, by themselves, do not generally
form an adequate system of signalling. Indeed, Tjalling Koopmans has been
rather critical of what he calls "the overextended belief" of certain economists
in the efficiency of competitive markets as a means of allocating resources in

a world characterized by ubiquitous uncertainty.[5] The main source of this uncertainty is the ignorance which firms have with respect to their competitors' future actions, preferences, and states of technological information. In the absence of a complete set of forward markets in which anticipation and intentions could be tested and adjusted, there is no reason to believe that with uncertainty, competitive markets of the kind which American antitrust laws seek to foster can produce efficient outcomes.[6] The information-circulating function which economic theory attributes to competitive markets is quite simply not discharged by any existing arrangements with the detail and forward extension necessary to support efficient outcomes.[7]

Today, there is no arena in which uncertainty is higher and the need to coordinate investment decisions greater than in the development, and in some instances the commercialization, of certain new technologies. In many industries, the stupendous foreshortening of product life cycles and the tremendous escalation of development and commercialization costs have increased the technological, managerial, and financial resource requirements for marketplace success. Moreover, the sources of innovation have become geographically and organizationally more dispersed. At the same time, imitation and idea borrowing is becoming increasingly easy and common. Most scientific know-how and new product concepts are available to all firms willing and able to invest in the relevant information-collection activities. Low-cost travel and telecommunications means that the natural protection of distance and language has all but evaporated. While intellectual property law is moving in a direction which favors innovators, the instruments of the law (patents, copyrights, trademarks, etc.) are inherently weak and cannot provide much protection to the innovator, except in special instances. Appropriating the benefits from investment in new technology is thus inherently difficult.

Today, there is no arena in which uncertainty is higher and the need to coordinate investment decisions greater than in the development and commercialization of new technologies.

Nor surprisingly, some analysts are coming to realize that cooperative activity among firms which may be competitors in product markets is likely to improve economic welfare. Cooperative activity can assist firms to overcome appropriability (technology spillover) problems because research development and manufacturing costs can be shared.[8] The effect of greater appropriability is generally to stimulate greater investment in new technology. It is well understood that competitive markets tend to underinvest in new technology because innovators have limited capacity to extract "fees" from the imitators, who are thus able to get a free ride on their competitors' investments.

In addition, collaborative research can reduce, if not eliminate, what William Norris, CEO of Control Data Corporation, refers to as "shameful and needless duplication of effort."[9] Independent research activities often proceed down identical or near-identical technological paths. When there is uncertainty as to which technology will turn out to be the best, it is desirable to have a variety of approaches to a problem. But just because there are several firms working on a technology, there is no guarantee that there will not be a considerable duplication of efforts. This is wasteful and can be avoided if research plans are coordinated. Moreover, cooperation helps in the provision of information about complementary investment decisions. Indeed, complementary investments can be coordinated by cooperation so that both under capacity and over capacity are more likely to be avoided. Indeed, in order to capture value from innovation, it is often necessary for a number of firms to cooperate, with different firms being responsible for different activities.[10]

The manifold benefits from cooperative activity have been recognized abroad and, more recently, in the U.S. as well.[11] One assessment of the U.S. is that "up until now, however, we have taken it for granted as an article of faith that no cooperation should be permitted, that it is best that we keep companies apart from one another."[12] Japanese firms have engaged in deep cooperation for decades and have received de facto exemption from Japanese antitrust laws to do so. Japanese cooperative activity is primarily vertical (upstream and downstream) but from time to time is horizontal as well (that is, it involves competitors). For instance, by the end of 1971, the entire Japanese computer industry (six firms) was paired in order to compete with IBM and its system 370.[13] While the research was done in existing corporate labs, there was intense interaction and information sharing. Another celebrated example of Japanese collaboration was the VSLSI (Very Large Scale Integrated Circuit) Research Association which was an R&D joint venture formed in 1975 with the capital contributed by NEC, Toshiba, Hitachi, Mitsubishi, and Fujitsu.[14] At the successful conclusion of the project in 1979, the laboratory was dissoved and the scientists went back to their sponsoring companies. More recently, in January 1988 the Ministry of International Trade and Industry established the International Superconductivity Technology Center (ISTEC) to conduct basic research and development on high temperature superconductors and processing technology. Participation in this effort is open to foreign as well as Japanese companies for payment of an annual fee.[15] Many of the firms involved in the Center could be considered competitors.

Industrial Policy, Internal Organization, and Business Alliances

If this analysis is correct, we need to achieve greater coordination than the price system alone can effectuate. The need for coordination has led some economists to advocate a role for government planning of resource allocation. Indeed, the case for indicative planning and industrial policy is often made at least in part on the basis of the arguments just outlined.[16] But there are other mechanisms for enhancing cooperation among competing firms that do not require government planning.

It is important to recognize that industrial organization also has an impact on the functioning of markets. A company's internal organization, augmented by interfirm agreements, can serve to shore up some market imperfections and provide some of the necessary coordination. As Alfred Chandler has explained, the modern multidivisional business enterprise "took over from the market the coordination and intergration of the flow of goods and services from the production of raw materials through the several processes of production to the sale to the ultimate consumer . . . administrative coordination replaced market coordination in an increasingly large portion of the economy."[17]

Chandler's analysis did not, however, continue into the 1970s and 1980s, where much of what he observed earlier began to unravel. By drawing his analysis to a close in the early post-war period, Chandler did not have to contend with a relatively new phenomenon, the venture capital funded entrepreneurial firm. Companies like Sun Microsystems, Genentech, Compaq, Advanced Microdevices, and Apple Computer are archetypical examples. Whereas large integrated firms like IBM and Exxon have relied upon integration and administrative processes to effectuate coordination, the "Silicon Valley" startups have in the main eschewed integration and relied extensively on outsourcing. What has been created in many instances is thus a fragmented industrial structure, horizontally as well as vertically. This is particularly evident today in the micro-electronics industry. In short, in many industries, and in particular high-technology industries, contractual arrangements among firms effectuate coordination. Market processes have in some instances replaced administrative ones. This is particularly true where "hollow corporations"—those without significant in-house research, manufacturing, and distribution—have come to displace economic activity that in an earlier period took place inside vertical integrated enterprises. In some cases this has left industries with inadequate strategic coordination, particularly when they are competing against firms located in industrial structures that are less fragmented and which are supported by governments that engage in directed industrial policies.

However, many of the disabilities associated with fragmented industries can be overcome by interfirm agreements. Interfirm agreements can be classified as unilateral (where A sells X to B) or bilateral (whereby A agrees to buy Y from B as a condition for making the sale of X, and both parties understand that the transaction will be continued only if reciprocity is observed).[18] A strategic alliance can be defined as a bilateral relationship characterized by the commitment of two or more partner firms to reach a common goal,[19] and which entails the pooling of specialized assets and capabilities. Thus a strategic alliance might include one or more of

- technology swaps,
- joint R&D or co-development, and
- the sharing of complementary assets, e.g., one party does manufacturing, the other distribution, for a co-developed product.

Strategic allinances can be differentiated from exchange transactions, such as a simple licensing agreement with specified royalties, because in an exchange transaction the object of the transaction is supplied by the selling firm to the buying firm in exchange for cash. Exchange transactions are unilateral and not bilateral. A strategic alliance by definition can never have one side receiving cash alone. Nor do strategic alliances include mergers, because by definition alliances cannot involve acquisition of another firm's assets or controlling interest in another firm's stock. Alliances need not involve equity swaps or equity investments, though they often do. Strategic alliances without equity typically consist of contracts between or among partner firms that are nonaffiliated. Equity alliances can take many forms, including minority equity holdings, consortia, and joint ventures.

Strategic alliances have increased in frequency in recent years and are particularly characteristic of high-technology industries.[20] Joint R&D, know-how, manufacturing, and marketing agreements go well beyond exchange agreements because they can be used to access complementary technologies and complementary assets. The object of the transaction, such as the development of launch of a new product, usually does not exist at the time the contracts are inked.

Alternative governance structures are summarized in Table 1. Strategic alliances, including consortia and joint ventures, are often an effective and efficient way to organize for innovation, particularly when an industry is fragmented. Some of the objectives that national planning sets out to complete can thus be accomplished by private agreements. Whereas full-blown national planning entails the abolition of the market as an organizing mechanism— techniques of production and new technologies are no longer to be selected by competition but instead are to be consciously, deliberately decided upon, carefully inserted into a scientific plan, and then carried out by fiat—interfirm cooperation still preserves market selection but augments selection processes with limited, bilateral interfirm cooperation. Thus, the case for planning and industrial policy is pushed back if a degree of operational and strategic coordination can be attained through private agreements.

As compared to mergers, strategic alliances and other forms of interfirm agreements are of course far less restrictive and are conceptually different from cartels. First, interfirm agreements are usually temporary by design and are assembled and disassembled as circumstances warrant. Second, they are less comprehensive, as typically only a limited range of the firm's activities are enveloped in such agreements. Accordingly, it is ironic that, as explained below, U.S. antitrust laws treat cooperative agreements less permissively than they do mergers. This is an unfortunate circumstance which needs to be readdressed.

Table 1. Taxonomy of Interfirm Arrangements

	Nonequity	Equity
Exchange	short-medium term cash-based contracts	passive stock holdings portfolio diversification
Alliance	mid-long term bilateral contracts (non cash-based)	joint venture (operating or non-operating), consortium, minority equity holdings, and cross holdings
Merger	–0–	wholly-owned affiliate or subsidiary
Cartel	price fixing and/or output restricting agreements	price fixing and/or output restricting agreements

The National Cooperative Research Act of 1984

In order to relieve some of the antitrust uncertainties associated with certain interfirm agreements, Congress in 1984 unanimously passed the National Cooperative Research Act (NCRA). The act, the full import and scope of which has yet to be tested in the courts, covers only R&D activities up the prototype stage. In incorporates two significant developments.

First, the NCRA requires that "joint research and development venture(s) shall not be deemed illegal per se," and that such ventures instead shall be "judged on the basis of [their] reasonableness, taking into account all relevant factors affecting competition, including, but not limited to, effects on competition in properly defined, relevant research and development markets."[21] Thus, Congress made clear that any antitrust litigation concerning cooperative research efforts should be judged under the rule of reason. In doing so, Congress broke no new ground; rather, it codified existing laws.[22]

The NCRA establishes a registration procedure for joint research and development ventures[23] and limits the antitrust recovery by any plaintiff challenging a registered venture to single damages, interest, and the costs of suit, including a reasonable attorney's fee in limited circumstances.[24] Thus, Congress eliminated the threat of treble damages for litigation challenging cooperative innovation arrangements, provided that the parties to the arrangement first registered their venture.

The NCRA is a significant piece of legislation, as it demonstrates that Congress has recognized the importance of innovation to the American economy and to America's competitiveness in a world marketplace. Congress also grasped that traditional antitrust treatment of innovation and cooperative innovation arrangements was inhibiting desirable activities.

Examples of endeavors registered under the Act include consortia such as the Microelectronics and Computer Technology Corporation (MCC) with 19 firms that have chosen to fund and perform research in house on four major industry objectives; the Semiconductor Research Consortium with a longer term and more basic agenda which is pursued by contracting all research to universities; the 56-member Corporation for Open Systems which aims at assuming widespread customer acceptance of an open-system network architecture in world markets by both computer vendors and users; and the 13 members Sematech that plans to engage in R&D related to advanced semiconductor manufacturing techniques that can be used by Sematech's members in their own manufacturing process. Also registered under the Act are the two-party cooperative research arrangements, such as between Bellcore (itself registered under the Act) and NHK of Japan to collaborate in early stage research in the area of high-definition television, and between Bellcore and NEC to collaborate on research in high-speed and coherent optical devices.

Although the Act does take useful steps to assist innovation, the limited shelter it provides from antitrust covers only research and development activity. This is one reason why only 111 ventures had been registered under the Act from 1984 through June 1988. An effort to categorize filings over this period is found in Table 2. What is striking is the rather modest number of registrations (that is, not much economic activity has so far been affected by the Act) and the relatively larger number of endeavors aimed at solving environmental and health problems. The Motor Vehicle Manufacturers Association, for instance, has 15 endeavors dealing with research on diesel emissions, benzene emissions, acid rain, long-range transportation of air pollutants, vehicle side impact test procedures, etc. In short, there has not been a particularly significant surge of cooperative activity under the Act.

Untapped Opportunities

There are various reasons why American firms have been slow to take advantage of the opportunities provided by the 1984 statute. One reason is that there is little tradition and experience with cooperative activities. However, a more important reason is that the antitrust law remains a significant deterrent, particularly for cooperative activity that goes beyond prototyping and involves commercialization. At least two kinds of potentially beneficial opportunities for cooperation are discouraged by the antitrust laws. The first involves big technology endeavors like superconductors and HDTV; the second involves cases where smaller firms could benefit from shared facilities, such as with flexible computer-integrated manufacturing, or with next generation DRAMs.

The real challenges lie not just in developing new technologies, but in commercializing them. The best organizational approaches to commercialization usually involve competition, but will sometimes involve cooperation. Firms involved with these technologies are usually capable of working out the best

Table 2. Registration of Cooperative Endeavors Under the National Cooperative Research Act*

Categories†	Number	Percent of Total
Advanced Materials	4	3.6
Biotechnology	3	2.7
Energy	10	9.0
Environmental, Health and Medical	33	29.7
Information	33	29.7
Manufacturing	28	25.2
Totals	111	100

*As published in the *Federal Register,* January 1985-June 1988 inclusive. We have excluded notification of membership changes. The total number of registrations would otherwise be 80.

†Authors' categories. Classifications are based on limited data and may not be accurate.

approach. Because of the great diversity in the sources of innovation, U.S. firms acting collectively are rarely able to cartelize an industry and injure consumers. Consumers are more likely to be injured if these firms attempt to go it alone and fail as a result, or if they do nothing. Hence, it is unfortunate that antitrust still casts a shadow over cooperative efforts involving commercialization. The rationale advanced for restricting the activity falling under the NCRA to research and development up through prototyping is not that early-stage costs are especially high—commercialization is almost always far more expensive—but that the typical spillover problems associated with R&D come to an end once a prototype has been developed. Therefore, so the argument goes, firms engaged in cooperative research should begin competing once they have the prototype, lest the final product market become monopolized.

However, in practically all areas of modern technology, U.S. firms face competition from abroad, and unless entire global industries are organized into just one or two consortia—a highly unlikely circumstance—concerns that cooperative activity will monopolize final product markets are quite misplaced. Moreover, spillovers continue with commercialization, because process learning leaks out and final products can often be reverse engineered. The limited nature of the NCRA will leave Sematech—after spending $1 billion over the next four years to develop what is expected to be the world's most advanced flexible computer-integrated semiconductor manufacturing facility—unable to operate it without substantial risk of an antitrust violation, for which it and its members would be exposed to treble damages.[25] Even if antitrust enforcement agencies were not inclined to prosecute, private antitrust suits could be forth-coming. Until further legislation is passed, U.S. firms are likely to continue to muddle along with inadequate, uncoordinated, and unfocussed, separate initiatives while foreign competitors take the lead.

With respect to the second category (namely, where smaller firms could benefit from sharing new facilities) considerable opportunities also remain. One example is flexible computer-integrated manufacturing facilities (FCIM) which are too expensive for second and third tier suppliers, but which could easily be shared by several firms. These facilities can be programmed to make a variety of products. In a sense, they are a generic facility, but they are too expensive for small companies. Cooperative efforts to build and operate such facilities would, however, but clouded by significant antitrust uncertainties. A second example might be DRAMs. The cost of a next generation DRAM facility is likely to be $200 to $400 million. To the highly fragmented merchant semiconductor firm, these price tags are out of range. A cooperative effort among two or three firms, however, would raise interesting possibilities.

Easing Antitrust Restraints
By Changing Rule of Reason Analysis[26]

The current antitrust law, while today much more sympathetic toward cooperative activity involving competitors than it was a decade ago, still inhibits beneficial cooperation. While it is clear that such agreements are to be assessed by rule of reason analysis, and are thus not per se illegal, the parameters of the rule of reason analysis are ambiguous and unstructured, resulting in uncertainty and unpredictability. Ironically, full-blown horizontal mergers are treated with greater certainty. These substantive problems are compounded by antitrust procedures which in the U.S., but nowhere else in the world, permit private litigants to pursue treble damages against parties to cooperative innovation agreements. Thus, even while governmental enforcement agencies are unlikely to act as a roadblock, the ability of third parties to sue creates a powerful disincentive to cooperative agreements. In many instances, it will be prudent for defendants to settle out of court rather than "bet the company," and the prospect of capitulation by one defendant spurs lawsuits against others.

What is needed from the courts or from Congress is the clear articulation of rule of reason standards. At minimum, these should include:

- a market power based "safe harbor" that would completely exempt from antitrust liability cooperative arrangements or strategic alliances, whether for research and development or for downstream activities, if the firm involved jointly possessed less than 20 percent of the relevant market;
- an administrative procedure, involving both the Justice and Commerce departments, to evaluate and approve cooperative arrangements among firms with higher market shares, when efficiency gains are promising and competition is not threatened;

- specific rule of reason criteria that focus analysis on the pace and stage of technological change, the diversity of sources of new technology, the need for both operational and strategic coordination to achieve success with the new product or process in the marketplace, and the need for innovative to use business strategies to keep imitators at bay for a reasonable period of time, particularly when intellectual property protection is ineffective as a mechanism for limiting entry; and
- finally, and perhaps most importantly, private antitrust suits challenging cooperative efforts to develop and commercialize new product processes and services should be limited to injunctive relief only (i.e., there will be no payment of damages) and attorney's fees should be awarded to the prevailing party.

The courts could conceivably accomplish the first three, while the last one would require an act of Congress. However, given the tardiness of the legal process and the low probability that a non-specialist court system would get it right, there is a strong need for immediate congressional action on all these points.

Easing Antitrust Restraints By Legislation: "The National Cooperative Research and Commercialization Act"[27]

The time is ripe for legislation that would incorporate the substantive changes we discussed under Rule of Reason analysis and that will remove the threat of private damage actions. If such legislation were passed, it would at least put cooperative agreements on an equivalent antitrust footing with mergers. At present, effective safeharbors exist for mergers and acquisition; they are clearly articulated in the Department of Justice *Merger Guidelines*. Once an acquisition or merger is consummated, there are no antitrust constraints on the agreements that headquarters can make with divisions. Inside a company, it is of course possible to engage in all kinds of restrictive agreements, including interdivisional price fixing. Thus, under current policy, interfirm agreements are exposed to antitrust constraints, even though if two firms were able to consummate a legal merger they would be free from antitrust with respect to their "joint" activities!

If enacted, the proposed legislation would enable consortia and alliances to be formed not only to attain world leadership, as might be the case with super-conductors, but also to catch up in certain areas where the U.S. is now behind, such as HDTV and DRAMs. Indeed, those who are skeptical of the benefits of cooperative activity often argue that it is really only effective for "catch up." Both theory and evidence would suggest otherwise, but be that as it may, catch up is, unfortunately, the game that many U.S. high-technology industries must now play. In doing so, it is foolish to deny U.S. firms the widest possible organizational menu for achieving catch up, particularly when their competitors in Europe and Japan face no such constraints.

Conclusion

American firms are in the midst of striking new relationships with other firms, domestic and foreign. Interfirm agreements and other forms of cooperative activity are becoming increasingly common here; they have always been common abroad. Without some measure of cooperation and planning among firms, the complementary investments needed to develop and commercialize new technologies will not get made, or they will get made inefficiently. On the other hand, without a high degree of competition, it will be difficult to check monopolistic exploitation of consumers. In the last two decades, however, the level of competition facing firms in the U.S. economy has risen to a new height, heights driven in part by competition from East Asian and European multinationals. While the possibilities and opportunities to cartelize industries have dwindled and will stay low so long as the U.S. economy remains open, the need for cooperative arrangements seems to have increased, driven by the fragmentation of new industries like electronics coupled with steady escalation in the costs of innovation. These developments occasion the need for a re-examination of our antitrust laws, which have been slow to recognize the benefits of cooperative activity as compared to the possible risk of cartelization. The new global economy, and the declining significance of American firms within it, requires a less restrictive approach toward interfirm agreements, alliances, and consortia. While these organizational arrangements are no panacea to American's declining technological and economic position, they ought to be made available to American businesses. Farsighted managers will then be faced with the challenge of finding ways to make them work.

References

1. W.G. Shepherd, *The Economics of Industrial Organization* (Englewood Cliffs, NJ: Prentice-Hall, 1979), p.301
2. Ibid., Chapter 15.
3. By assumption they could not be because if they were, no manager would seek to merge. At least this is the reasoning advanced by many orthodox financial economists.
4. G.B. Richardson, *Information and Investment* (Oxford: Oxford University Press, 1960), p.31.
5. T. Koopmans, *Three Essays on the State of Economic Science* (New York, NY: McGraw-Hill, 1957), p.146.
6. Koopmans (Ibid., p.147) goes on to point out that because of this deficiency economic theorists are not able to speak with anything approaching scientific authority on matters relating to individual versus collective enterprise.
7. Ibid., p.163.
8. If the R&D is industry specific and all firms in the industry participate in funding, the appropriability problem will be substantially solved, particularly if a coordinated manufacturing program is also put in place.
9. D. Davis, "R&D Consortia," *High Technology* (October 1985), p. 42.
10. See D. J. Teece, "Profiting from Technological Innovation," *Research Policy* (December 1986).

11. According to William Norris, U.S. corporations were not willing to give collaborative research a try until "these companies had the hell scared out of them by the Japanese" (Davis, op. cit., p.42).

12. W. Ouchi, *M-Form Society* (New York, NY: Avon Books, 1984), p. 103.

13. Ibid., p.105.

14. A Japanese government laboratory was also involved.

15. Set at $2 million a year for the Center, and an additional $12 million a year for participation in the associated laboratory work. By mid-1988, 55 companies had joined the Center (including three American companies: IBM, Dupont, and Rockwell), while 45 companies had agreed to participate in the laboratory activities as well. These members are invited to send one or two qualified researchers to the laboratory.

16. See J.E. Meade, *The Theory of Indicative Planning* (Manchester: Manchester University Press, 1970); and Stephen Cohen, *Modern Capitalist Planning: The French Model* (Berkeley, CA: University of California Press, 1969).

17. A. Chandler, *The Visible Hand* (Cambridge, MA: Harvard University Press, 1977), Chapter 1. Note, however, that Chandler was by no means the first to make the observation that administrative allocation inside the firm constituted a form of planning. Karl Marx was quite willing to credit the market with having introduced rational, scientific planning on a partial basis. However chaotic Marx thought competitive coordination processes between functions were, within the factory productive activity was seen as deliberately coordinated according to a plan conceived by the capitalist. See Karl Marx, *Capital*, Vol. 1 (New York, NY: International [1867], 1967), p.356.

18. O.E. Williamson, *Economic Institutions of Capitalism* (New York, NY: Free Press, 1985).

19. If the common goal was price fixing, or naked market share decisions without any efficiency effects, such an agreement would constitute a cartel, and not an alliance.

20. For a review and compendium of industry studies, see David Mowery, ed., *International Collaborative Ventures in U.S. Manufacturing* (Cambridge, MA: Ballinger, 1988).

21. 15 U.S.C. 4302.

22. See Wright, "The National Cooperative Research Act of 1984: A New Antitrust Regime for Joint Research and Development Ventures," *High Technology Law Journal*, 1 (1986), p.178. "The NCRA has, to a large extent, merely codified existing antitrust doctrine. This codification by itself is unlikely to have a significant effect on the nation's R&D output, which has prompted some to criticize the Act as unnecessary . . . [I]t is questionable how much uncertainty has actually be removed by the Act."

23. U.S.C. 4305(a)-(b).

24. 15 U.S.C. 4303(a). The Act also allows prevailing defendants to recover attorney's fees, but only "if the claim, or the claimant's conduct during the litigation of the claim, was frivolous, unreasonable, without foundation, or in bad faith." 15 U.S.C. 4304(a)(2).

25. Comments of D. Bruce Marrifield, Assistant Secretary of Commerce for Productivity, Technology, and Innovation, January 1988.

26. This section and the next are based on T.M. Jorde and D.J. Teece, "Innovation, Cooperation, and Antitrust," Working Paper no. BPP-37, Center for Research in Management, University of California at Berkeley, October 1988 (forthcoming, *High Technology Law Journal*, 4/1, 1989).

27. T.M. Jorde and D.J. Teece have crafted such a proposal which, after some modifications, was introduced into Congress in February 1989 by Tom Campbell (R-CA) and Richard Boucher (D-VA) as the "National Cooperative Innovation and Commercialization Act of 1989," H.R. 1024.

[4]

Econ. Innov. New Techn., 1990, Vol. 1, pp. 157–182
Reprints available directly from the publisher
Photocopying permitted by license only

PRODUCT EMULATION STRATEGIES IN THE PRESENCE OF REPUTATION EFFECTS AND NETWORK EXTERNALITIES: SOME EVIDENCE FROM THE MINICOMPUTER INDUSTRY

RAYMOND S HARTMAN

Department of Economics, Boston University, Boston, MA 02215

and DAVID J TEECE

School of Business Administration, University of California, Berkeley, CA 94720

A model of firm performance in the minicomputer industry is developed and estimated. We use an hedonic price formulation to analyze product design and pricing issues and a market share model to assess the demand effects of price-performance characteristics, installed base advantages and manufacturer reputation. The results, which are based on 1976-1983 data, demonstrate the importance of network externalities, price-performance competition and reputation. We utilize the estimated models to quantify the implications of several emulation strategies and several defensive strategies of incumbent manufacturers.

KEY WORDS: minicomputer industry, hedonic price formulation, price–performance characteristics, network externalities, reputation

1. INTRODUCTION

In this paper, we explore the product emulation strategies available to a firm considering entry into an established market characterized by differentiated products, manufacturer reputation and network externalities. Concomitantly, we examine several recently advanced theoretical propositions regarding price and quality competition in network industries. Our empirical focus is the U.S. minicomputer industry over the period 1976 through 1983.

Product emulation strategies involve the introduction of technologically compatible products with superior price-performance characteristics. In the minicomputer industry, this usually means an emulator's computer system is able to execute the instruction set of an incumbent's system(s), without violating patents or copyrights. Generally, the emulator's products are more technologically advanced than the incumbents. This superiority usually stems from improved designs and/or components.

Emulation has obvious strategic advantages. It reduces the costs and market risk associated with establishing new technological standards and developing complementary products. However, emulation presents obvious risks. The incumbent may be well positioned with respect to distribution and sales, service and reputation, thereby making emulation difficult. Furthermore, the incumbent can defensively respond in a variety of strategic ways, including price reductions and especially surprise new

The authors gratefully acknowledge the assistance and/or comments of Ernst Berndt, Timothy Bresnahan, Harin DeSilva, Michael Doane, Zvi Griliches, Michael Katz, Marion Lieberman, Renee Rushnawitz, V. Kerry Smith, Jack Triplett and Paul Taylor.

product announcements targeted at the emulator. Depending upon the technological "closeness" of the emulation, the incumbent may be able to initiate or threaten to initiate legal actions based upon intellectual property infringement claims.

The advantages and hazards of emulation are intensified in markets with large network externalities. Such markets exhibit positive consumption externalities, which arise when the utility derived by a consumer of a given product or technology increases with the number of other individuals consuming identical or similar products. Network externalities can arise from a variety of sources. For instance, a technology or product which requires the provision of a complementary good or service will be subject to network externalities. In the computer industry, network externalities stem from the availability of compatible applications software induced by the existence of a large number of users. Any technology or product whose utility increases with the number of purchases will be subject to network externalities. Computer-based telecommunication networks fit into this category. Finally, a technology or product which requires specific training on the part of the user will be subject to network externalities. Again, the computer market is a good example; a firm's operating experience with hardware and specific applications programs will be more valuable the greater the diversity of computers compatible with the network. In all cases, there exist demand-side economies of scale. A given product or technology is more attractive the larger is the installed base of consumers using it.

The increased benefits and risks of emulation in network industries flow directly from the importance of an installed base of equipment. An emulator will do very well, if it can offer a product with a price-performance advantage which is *technologically compatible* with the installed network and which cannot *be excluded from the network*. In this case, the emulator (and its customers) will benefit from *both* the network effects *and* whatever price-performance advantage is offered. If, on the other hand, the incumbent is able to inhibit access to the network, entry will be more difficult. Consumers must now compare the emulator's price-performance advantage with the incumbent's installed-base advantage.

An incumbent's installed-base advantage will, in all likelihood, be accompanied by other incumbency effects, including reputation, all of which Teece (1987) characterizes as cospecialized assets.[1] Indeed, the interrelated effects of reputation and network size may prove insurmountable to an emulator, since technology/product choice depends crucially on market expectations. If consumers *expect* a given manufacturer with a growing network and established reputation to be dominant, they will be willing to pay more for that manufacturer's products and the expectations become self-fulfilling. For its technology to be adopted in this case, the emulator's price-performance advantage must be very substantial to outweigh the incumbent's network *and* reputation advantages. In some cases, there will be *no* price-performance advantage that will induce purchase, no matter how great.

To our knowledge, the theoretical literature has not formally addressed product emulation. Emulation has been indirectly examined in the context of product design or spatial location games [Eaton and Lipsey (1975), Economides (1986), Hausman and Wise (1978), Hay (1976), Michaels (1979), Prescott and Visscher (1977), Rosen (1974), Schmalensee (1978), Shaw (1982), Swann (1985)]; however, these treatments

---

[1]For example, two other confounding incumbency assets (positively correlated with installed base) are established sales/distribution networks and learning curve efficiencies [Lieberman (1984,1985)] in manufacture and use. We treat all such manufacturer-specific cospecialized assets as "reputation".

have been limited in their realism. For example, a common analytic structure is a duopoly game with differentiated products possessing only one or two attributes. The results of the analyses have been decidedly non-robust. More importantly, these analyses have ignored network effects and other important phenomena.

We approach the emulation decision as a game in prices and product attributes. We develop a strategic framework that explicitly recognizes the importance of price/performance competition, manufacturer reputation, and network effects in determining the market potential of an emulator's products and technologies. Our framework is distinctly empirical. We integrate hedonic price analysis into a demand model for differentiated products. Using the hedonic price model, we estimate the expected hedonic price of each "quality-differentiated" product (computer) – that is, how the market values, on average, the performance attributes of each product. We compare this hedonic price with the actual price. When the actual price is strategically set below (above) its hedonic price, the product offers a price-performance advantage (or disadvantage). We treat emulation strategy as the variation of the prices and attributes of the emulating products in order to offer significant price-performance advantages. We use the demand model to estimate how such price-performance advantages stimulate product demand, while accounting for the independent effects of network externalities and the reputation of the established incumbents.[2]

Having estimated these models, we explore and quantify how an emulator can strategically benefit by targeting the compatible products of strategically non-responsive incumbents with large market share when those products can be produced with a significant price-performance advantage. We also examine how several strategic responses by incumbents will affect the success of emulation.

Our model is presented in Section 2 below. In that Section, we also describe several network hypotheses that we plan to empirically examine. In Section 3, we estimate the models for the U.S. minicomputer industry, a market where products are highly differentiated by performance attributes; where product emulation has been successfully employed; and where reputation and network effects are purported to be significant. In Section 4, we describe how the estimated model can be used by an emulator to make product design, product pricing and market entry decisions. Section 5 summarizes the paper.

2.   THE MODEL

In this section, we assume (for notational simplicity) that all firms produce a single product and define the profit function for the emulating firm as

$$\Pi_e = q_e{}^*P_e - C_e(q_e,a_e) \qquad (1)$$

where q_e and P_e are the demand for and price of the emulating product and C_e is the emulator's hedonic cost function defined over production, q_e, and the attributes of the product, vector a_e. Demand for the emulator's differentiated product is assumed to be a function of total market demand for all products, Q; the price and performance

---

[2]We still abstract from the full reality of product emulation. For example, because of measurement difficulties, we do not incorporate the emulator's or incumbent's organizational assets, including the capabilities and entrepreneurial experience of the managerial, technical and financial personnel. We abstract from the prefunding characteristics of the emulator.

attributes of the product, P_e and a_e; and the prices and performance attributes of all incumbent differentiated products, P_i and a_i for $i = 1,. . .,I$. Therefore,

$$\Pi_e = q_e(Q,P_e,a_e; P_i,a_i \text{ all } i)^*P_e - C_e(q_e,a_e). \tag{1a}$$

An emulator will seek to maximize Π_e by varying price P_e and attributes a_{ej}, $j = 1,. . ., J$. Therefore, his $J+1$ first order conditions are

$$\partial\Pi_e/\partial P_e = q_e + P_e^*(\partial q_e/\partial P_e) - (\partial C_e/\partial q_e)(\partial q_e/\partial P_e) + \{[\Sigma_i[(\partial q_e/\partial P_i)(\partial P_i/\partial P_e)$$
$$+ \Sigma_k(\partial q_e/\partial a_{ik})(\partial a_{ik}/\partial P_e)]]^*(P_e - \partial C_e/\partial q_e)\}; \tag{2}$$

$$\partial\Pi_e/\partial a_{ej} = P_e^*\partial q_e/\partial a_{ej} - (\partial C_e/\partial a_{ej} + (\partial C_e/\partial q_e)(\partial q_e/\partial a_{ej})) + \{[\Sigma_i[(\partial q_e/\partial P_i)(\partial P_i/\partial a_{ej})$$
$$+ \Sigma_k(\partial q_e/\partial a_{ik})(\partial a_{ik}/\partial a_{ej})]]^*(P_e - \partial C_e/\partial q_e)\}, \text{ for all } j = 1, . . ., J.$$

The terms in brackets $\{\}$ summarize the profit effects of the emulator's conjectural variations regarding the I incumbents' price (P_i) and design $(a_{ik}, i = 1, . . ., I; k = 1, . . ., J)$ responses to the emulator's product.

We use the hedonic literature to give this profit criterion empirical content. Hedonic price analysis has been used extensively to measure how particular markets value the quality and performance attributes of differentiated products [Brown and Rosen (1982), Griliches (1971), Hartman (1987), Michaels (1979), Ohta (1975), Ohta and Griliches (1976)]. These models make the price of product i in period t (P_{it}) a function of its attributes (the J vector a_{it}) and a random error term ξ_{it}; or

$$P_{it} = f_1 (a_{it}, \xi_{it}). \tag{3}$$

f_1 is usually specified as semilog. However, a variety of functional forms can be utilized, and the one providing the best empirical results is frequently selected [Brown and Rosen (1982), Griliches (1971)].

It is well known that f_1 simultaneously summarizes supply and demand behavior in the market [Rosen (1974)]. Therefore, estimation of f_1 using single-equation estimation techniques will identify neither the supply nor demand curves for product attributes unless we impose restrictive assumptions on the underlying models of production and demand. For present purposes, we do not seek to recover demand preferences or the parameters of production. We are specifically interested in the "market" for product attributes and how the pricing of a specific product may strategically undercut the "market". $\hat{\varepsilon}_{it} = P_{it} - \hat{P}_{it}$ provides such a measure; it indicates how the actual product price differs from its expected "quality-corrected" price. $\hat{\varepsilon}_{it}$ measures the price-performance advantage (or disadvantage) of each product i in period t, relative to the market. If $\hat{\varepsilon}_{it}$ is large and negative (positive), the actual price of product i is well below (above) its expected market price, given its attributes, thereby offering a substantial price-performance advantage (disadvantage).

While most firms try to establish a price-performance advantage for their products as part of a broader set of strategies, the emulation strategy generally focuses solely on offering a price-performance advantage. An incumbent may have strategically offered a price performance advantage in the early stages of the life cycle of its technology by "penetration pricing" below cost to establish a reputation and/or a network [see Katz (1986), Katz and Shapiro (1985,1986), Shapiro (1983)]. However, an emulator specifically attempts to offer such an advantage while pricing above cost, by avoiding much of the original market development costs, by taking advantage of subsequent component innovations or by designing and producing a functionally equivalent or superior product more efficiently than the incumbent. The greater is the emulator's price-performance advantage, the greater will be the demand (and market share) for its product relative to the emulated incumbent and relative to the market at large, given existing networks and incumbent reputations.

We introduce the price-performance advantage, $\hat{\varepsilon}_{it}$, for *any* product i, into demand while including the effects of reputation and network externalities, as follows:

$$q_{it}{}^* = f_2 (Q_t, \hat{\varepsilon}_{it}, MR_{it}, Adv_{it}, NW_{it}; \hat{\varepsilon}_{kt}, \text{all } k \neq i; v_{it}), \qquad (4)$$

where $q_{it}{}^*$, the desired demand for product i in period t, is hypothesized to be determined by the total market demand Q_t; by the product's price-performance advantage ($\hat{\varepsilon}_{it}$) relative to the price-performance advantage of *all* competing products ($\hat{\varepsilon}_{kt}$); by the promotional efforts of the firm producing i in t (Adv_{it}, the advertising of product i in t); by the reputation (i.e., all cospecialized assets) of the manufacturer of product i (which will be measured with a manufacturer-specific dummy variable, MR_{it}); by the size of the existing network (NW_{it}) with which q_{it} is compatible; and a residual error (v_{it}).[3] In keeping with the literature on network externalities, NW_{it} will be a measure of the installed base of equipment with which product i is compatible. Notice that $\hat{\varepsilon}_{it}$ neatly summarizes the price P_{it} *and* design attributes of each product i.

Without specifying the underlying production or utility functions, we assume that f_2 is derived from either utility or profit maximization. As is done elsewhere, we assume that the elasticity of demand for product i ($q_{it}{}^*$) with respect to total market demand (Q_t) is unity. This implies that, *ceteris paribus*, if the total market demand doubles, the desired demand for each differentiated product doubles. The relative demand (market share) for each product will therefore be determined by the comparative attributes of each product. The *desired* market share of product i in t, $MS_{it}{}^* = q_{it}{}^*/Q_t$, is therefore

$$MS_{it}{}^* = f_3(\hat{\varepsilon}_{it}, MR_{it}, Adv_{it}, NW_{it}; \hat{\varepsilon}_{kt}, \text{all } k \neq i; v_{it}), \qquad (5)$$

Finally, we recognize that demand for durables in (4) and (5) will not respond immediately to changes in a product's price-performance characteristics, reputation and advertising. Rather, purchases of product i will occur with a lag, as consumers retire existing durables that are no longer economically desirable. This dynamic behavior is traditionally approximated with the following partial adjustment formulation:

$$MS_{it} - MS_{it-1} = \lambda (MS_{it}{}^* - MS_{it-1}); \qquad (6a)$$

$$MS_{it} = \lambda MS_{it}{}^* + (1 - \lambda) MS_{it-1}; \text{ and} \qquad (6b)$$

$$MS_{it} = f_4(\hat{\varepsilon}_{it}, MR_{it}, Adv_{it}, NW_{it}; \hat{\varepsilon}_{kt}, \text{all } k \neq i; (1 - \lambda) MS_{it-1}; v_{it}); \qquad (7)$$

where λ is a measure of the speed of demand adjustment.

---

[3] While Equations 3 and 4 may be thought of as simultaneous, they are somewhat recursive. The q_{it} underlying Equation 4 enter Equation 3 only indirectly – in estimation as the population weights for the different products in the sample. As we indicate in Section 2, experimentation with alternative estimation weights did not change our estimated results. Once Equation 3 is estimated, the residuals enter Equations 4-5 simultaneously. We explore this simultaneity with two stage techniques. The basic structure of equations (3) and (4) will be recognized as those used by Cowling and Cubbin(1971) and Cowling and Rayner. Our contribution involves the inclusion of network effects and reputation and our focus on emulation strategies.

Substituting Equation (7) into (1a) and dropping the time subscript for convenience, the profit criterion for *any* product ibecomes

$$\Pi_i = MS_i {}^* Q {}^* P_i - C_i(MS_i {}^* Q, a_i). \tag{8}$$

For an emulator, $i = e$ and we have an empirically implementable design and pricing criterion, the first-order conditions of which are derived as in Equation (2).

We shall primarily use our estimated model to examine alternative emulation strategies. However, its estimation allows us to throw some light on several theoretical propositions regarding pricing strategies, reputation and network effects. The specific hypotheses we examine are the following:

Hypothesis I:
  Firms investing in reputation or network development practice "penetration pricing" as a form of product or technology sponsoring. These firms price below cost during the early stages of a product's or technology's life cycle and above cost once the reputation or network has been established. [Katz(1986), Katz and Shapiro (1985,1986)]

Hypothesis II:
  Firms exploiting learning curve efficiencies will strategically lower product prices over time. The optimal price decline will be determined by demand, the number of competitors and the firm's discount rate. [Lieberman (1984,1985)]

To formally examine these hypotheses, we require cost information. Our model involves no direct information on production costs; however, these costs do enter into the determination of the hedonic price locus in Equation (3). Using the data available to us, we examine whether there is any evidence of penetration pricing by observing if there is any pattern in the price-performance characteristics of each product in our sample. If penetration pricing is pursued as a practical strategy, the measure of price-performance advantage of a given product ($\hat{\varepsilon}_{it}$) should be negative and large in the early stages of product life and positive and large in the later stages. On the other hand, if pricing reflects learning curve efficiencies, we would expect to find prices declining over a product's life cycle. We shall find in Section 3 that these hypotheses are not mutually exclusive.

Hypothesis III:
  In markets where optimizing firms establish reputations by providing high quality products, equilibrium implies constant product quality over time. [Shapiro(1983)]

We examine whether there is any evidence for such equilibrium constancy of product quality by examining the temporal pattern of expected hedonic prices ($\hat{P}_{it}$).

3.   MODEL ESTIMATION

Table 1 summarizes the 25 minicomputer manufacturers and their 103 products included in the empirical analysis. The specific products are computer systems. We selected a cross-section of manufacturers that accounted for most of the worldwide minicomputer sales during the years 1976 through 1983. The cross-section includes

Table 1. Manufacturers and Computer Systems Included in the Empirical Analysis

Manufacturer	Manufacturer label	System
Basic Four	BASE4	All Models
BTI	BTI	4000;5000;8000 Series
Burroughs	BURR	1720;1800;1900 Series; B700;B800;B80/90;B900
Control Data Corp.	CDC	1700/SYSTEM 17/CYBER 18
Data General Corp.	DAG	Nova 1200 Series; Nova 2 Series; Nova 3D; Nova 3/12; Nova 3/4; Nova 800/820; Nova 830/850; Nova 4/C,S,X; Eclipse C/300, 330; Eclipse S/100, 130, 140, AP130; Eclipse M/600; Eclipse C/350; Eclipse C/150; Eclipse S/200,230; Eclipse S/250
Digital Computer Controls	DCC	D-116
Digital Equipment Corp.	DEC	PDP 11/03,23;LSI 11/03,23; PDP 11/ 04,05,10,15,20; PDP 11/34,35,40;PDP 11/44; PDP 11/45,50,55;PDP 11/60;PDP 11/70 PDP 15 XSVM;8/A,E,F,M VAX 11/730,11/750,11/780,11/ 782
Digital Scientific Corp.	DSC	All Models
Four Phase	4PHS	IV/40-IV/95
General Automation	GA	All Models
Harris	HAR	All Models
Honeywell	HONY	Level 6;Level 62
Hewlett-Packard	HP	1000 Series;2100 Series 250;300;3000I,II;3000/ 30,33,40,44,64
IBM	IBM	8100;Series 1; System 23,3,32,34,36,38
Jacquard	JACQ	J100:200,300,600,J500
Modular Computer	MODC	Classic II;Cls 7810-70; Modcomp I–IV
NCR	NCR	8200,30/31,50/51;8270; Century 151
Nixdorf	NIX	8870/1,3
Perkin Elmer	PERK	7/32;8/32;Series 16
Prime	PRIME	100;150II;200;250II;300;350;400/500;450;500/ 550II; 650;750
Point 4	PT4	Point 4
Quantel	QUAN	20;200 Series;800-970
Sperry-Univac	SPER	90/30;BC 7V 70,77 Series
Texas Instruments	TI	990 Series
Wang	WANG	2200 Series;VS

successful firms and products, in addition to unsuccessful firms and emulating entrants. For each of these minicomputers, we collected annual data summarizing sales, product prices, physical and performance attributes and aggregate market sales (i.e., installed base) since market introduction. The sample information is summarized in Table 2.

Table 3 summarizes the estimated hedonic price equations for the 1976–1983

Table 2. Sample Information

System Attributes	System Performance
Word Size, bits	Ease of System Operation
Number of Workstations	Reliability of Mainframe
Cycle Time, microseconds	Responsiveness of Maintainance
Access Time, microseconds	Operating System
Add Time, microseconds	Compilers and Assemblers
Year of Introduction	Applications Programs
Disk Pack/Cartridge Drive	Ease of Conversion
Storage, Megabytes	Overall Satisfaction
Drum/Fixed Head Disk Storage, Megabytes	
Minimum Memory, Kbytes	
Monthly Maintenance ($)	
Number of Processors	
Computer Size Class, IDC Classification*	

Data Sources:
* System Sales and Installed Base: *Monthly EDP Industry Report*, International Data Corporation (IDC), Newton, MA.
* Physical and Performance Attributes: *All About Minicomputers*, annual, Datapro Research Corporation, Delran, NJ.
* System Sales and Overall Market Size: *Mini-Micro Computer Market Report*, Mini-Micro Systems, Boston, MA. and DataQuest Corporation, Cupertino, CA.

period.[4] The reported regressions are log linear. The first regression makes minicomputer price a function of computer size (using the IDC SIZE classification), speed (in terms of ADD TIME), the size of the minimum memory in the basic system (MEMORY) and an "extended system price" dummy variable (PRICE DUMMY). This dummy variable indicates whether the product price includes only a basic system or a more extended system configuration.[5]

The estimated coefficients in Regression 1 of Table 3 have the correct signs, and all but one are statistically significant. They indicate that a 100% increase in the overall size of a computer system, *ceteris paribus*, will increase market price 158%. A doubling of the speed of the CPU will approximately halve the add time; this improved performance will raise the market valuation. However, the estimated effect is small and statistically insignificant. Increasing the minimum memory of the basic system by 100% increases the market value 60%. The coefficient of the extended system price dummy corrects for the nature of the price data (footnote 5).

While the other physical and performance attributes (from Table 2) were included in initial regressions, they were all statistically insignificant. The results for Regression 1 indicate overall system size, the size of minimum memory and system speed are the most important determinants of market valuation. These attributes *alone* explain 72% of the variation of observed prices.

---

[4]The estimated results were robust to the use of OLS and alternative sales-weighted (Weighted Least Squares) estimation techniques. We estimated separate regressions for the 1976–1979 and 1980–1983 periods. The estimated price effects of the *physical* attributes were not statistically different for the two periods; however, different manufacturer dummies were significant. The inclusion of time effects in Regression 1 did not change the estimated coefficients for the physical attributes; the two sets of results were not statistically different. Traditional semilog, translog and Box-Cox estimates of the price equation yielded coefficients of the same sign. The Box-Cox and log-log results were essentially the same.

[5]For most of the systems in our sample, our price variable is the price of a basic system configuration – the CPU, power supply, front panel and minimum memory. However, for some systems, the price reflects a more complete configuration including some peripherals, operating systems, etc. We were not able to gather data on the degree of these system extensions. Therefore, we captured the presence of their effect on price with this dummy variable.

Table 3. Estimated Results for the Hedonic Price Equation – 1976–1983

	Regression 1	*Regression 2*	*Regression 3*
Dependent Variable	Log Price	Log Price	Log Price
Independent Variables			
Intercept	6.045 (33.0)	6.957 (38.3)	6.909 (38.1)
log SIZE	1.584 (7.29)	1.442 (7.62)	1.378 (7.21)
log ADD TIME	−0.019 (−0.47)	−0.327 (−6.13)	−0.308 (−5.76)
log MEMORY	0.603 (19.68)	0.517 (17.58)	0.555 (16.80)
System PRICE DUMMY	0.306 (2.88)	0.308 (3.10)	0.278 (2.80)
Manufacturer Dummy Variables			
BTI		0.929 (4.66)	0.931 (4.70)
Data General – DAG		−0.773 (−7.62)	−0.719 (−6.97)
Digital Equipment – DEC		−0.377 (−3.99)	−0.380 (−4.05)
General Automation – GA		−0.835 (−4.53)	−0.812 (−4.42)
Hewlett Packard – HP		−0.391 (−3.02)	−0.360 (−2.79)
IBM		−0.666 (−3.36)	−0.608 (−3.06)
Modular Computer – MODC		−0.690 (−4.87)	−0.667 (−4.72)
National Cash Register – NCR		0.595 (2.36)	0.505 (2.00)
Perkin Elmer – PERK		−0.559 (−2.32)	−0.485 (−2.01)
Point 4 – PT4		−1.443 (−6.48)	−1.376 (−6.17)
Sperry Univac – SPER		−0.728 (−4.13)	−0.703 (−4.01)
Texas Instruments – TI		−0.648 (−3.64)	−0.626 (−3.53)
Period Dummies			
1980			−0.122 (−1.37)
1981			−0.227 (−2.42)
1982			−0.084 (−0.86)
1983			−0.194 (−1.67)
R^2	.72	.82	.82
Mean, Dependent Variable	9.633	9.633	9.633
F Value	162.24	66.36	54.16
Observations	257	257	257

Notes:

t statistics for H_0: parameter = 0 in parentheses.

SIZE (IDC computer size class); ADD TIME (speed); and MEMORY (minimum memory) are described in Table 2. The PRICE DUMMY is described in footnote 5.

The residuals from Regression 1 indicate the price-performance characteristics of each sample system over time. This information is summarized in Table 4. The price-performance characteristics are measured relative to the system's hedonic price ($\hat{P}_{it}$). For example, in 1977, BTI priced its series 4000 systems 81% above the hedonic price, implying a serious price-performance disadvantage. The PDP-11/03,23 and LSI-11/03,23 systems of Digital Equipment (DEC) were priced 54% below their hedonic prices, thereby offering a significant price-performance advantage.

The patterns in Table 4 are robust to the inclusion of period effects to estimate a "pure" hedonic price deflator; they are robust to the specification of the price equation as semilog, translog and Box-Cox. Furthermore, they are quite informative. Some firms almost uniformly offer systems with price-performance disadvantages – for example, BTI, CDC and NCR. Some firms predominantly offer systems with price-performance advantages – for example, TI, Sperry, ModComp, Point 4 and IBM. Some firms offer a mix of systems with price-performance advantages and disadvantages that vary over time – most notably, Data General, Digital Equipment, Hewlett Packard and Prime.

There seems to be little evidence in Table 4 supporting the hypothesis that minicom-

Table 4. Price Performance[1] Characteristics of Sample Systems (in percent)

Manufacturer	System	Range of List Prices ($000)	Year of Introduction	Relative Price/Performance							
				1976	1977	1978	1979	1980	1981	1982	1983
BTI	4000 Series	36	1976		81	81					
	5000	30–39	1970			197	50	50	104	50	50
	8000	87	1981						−4		
CDC	1700/SYSTEM 17/ CYBER 18	14–28	1966	103	65	51	51	104	104	104	
DAG	Nova 1200 Series	5	1971	6							
	Nova 2 Series	4	1973	0	0	0					
	Nova 3D	4–13	1976	−19	−19	−19	−19	29	29	29	29
	Nova 3/12	4–5	1976	−19	−19	−19	−19	−23	−23	−23	−23
	Nova 3/4	3–4	1976	−57	−57	−42	−42	−40	−40	−40	−40
	Nova 800/820	8	1971	15							
	Nova 830/850	15	1973	43							
	Nova 4/C,S,X	6–7	1979								
	Eclipse C/300,330	30–32	1975	2	2	1	−60	−60	−58	−53	−53
	Eclipse S100,130 .140,AP/130	9–17	1975	36			63	27			
	Eclipse M/600	80	1978			−14	36	−31	−29	−7	−7
	Eclipse C/350	50–54	1978			32	−14	−14	−14		
	Eclipse C/150	28–34	1978			20	32	−19	−19		
	Eclipse S200,230	15–17	1975	52	52	46	46	20	43	−21	−16
	Eclipse S250	32–35	1978			−24	−24	62	62	62	
DCC	D-116	3–9	1971	−9	225	225		6			
DEC	PDP-11/03,23; LSI-11/03,23	2–6	1975	−54	−54	−54	−54	−70	−69	−68	−68
	PDP-11/04,05,10,15,20	4–8	1970	−23	−60	−60	−60	−39			
	PDP-11/34,35,40	13–15	1973	43	24	25	25	25	−16	37	37
	PDP-11/44	24–32	1980					−33	−21	−11	−11
	PDP-11/45,50,55	42–43	1972	171	74	78	78	78			
	PDP-11/70	60–90	1975	64	72	72	72	72	0	61	61
	PDP-11/60	36–62	1977		134	134	134	134	29	29	
DSC	All Models	23–34	—			265	180	22	−18		

	Model	Range	Year	1	2	3	4	5	6	7
GA	All Models	2–16	—	0	22	−33	−56	−52	−58	−40
HONY	Level 6	6–24	—	−12	−30	32	41	−13	6	605
HP	2100 Series	10	—	129	129	129				
	3000 I,II	82–93	—	52	53					
	1000 Series	9–11	—							
	250	17	1978			−54	−36	−56	−40	−67
	300	35–40	1978			68	72	51	−43	−74
IBM	Series 1	4–5	1977		−31	−34	−34	−40	−49	−20
JACQ	J100,200,300,600	15–21	1975	11	57	11	11	−23	−49	−23
	J500	10	1979				−1	−1	−35	−2
MODC	Modcomp I–IV	5–18	—	−27	−16	−3	−13	−14	8	8
	Cls 7810–70	27–37	—		14	−20	−23	−23	−22	−23
	Classic II	36	1971							14
NCR	8200,30/31,50/51	16–29	1974	74	145	21	21	21		
PERK	Series 16	9–31	1979				−7	−7	−1	15
PRIME	100	5–6	1973	6	−17	−17	−17	−17		
	200	6–7	1972	28	2	2	2	2		
	300	13–18	1973	87	164	164	164	164		
	400/500	49–95	1976	105	214	214	214	214		
	450	65	1979					82	82	
	550	80	1979					−22	−22	−22
	650	105	1979					2	2	
	750	130	1979					24	24	24
PT4	Point 4	6–13	—	66	−32	−65	−65	−64	−31	−29
SPER	V-70&77 Series	6–43	—	−43	−14	−22	−42	−33	−41	−38
TI	990 Series	1–15	—	−48	−43	−50	−40	−31	−3	−1

Notes:
1 Price performance defined relative to the hedonic price: $(P_{i1} - \hat{P}_{i1})/\hat{P}_{i1}$. A positive value reflects a disadvantage; a negative value reflects an advantage.

puter firms practice penetration pricing *on a system basis*. If such penetration pricing were prevalent, we would expect to find firms offering systems with a large price-performance advantage when the systems are first introduced to the market, thereby establishing reputation and networks. We would expect that these price-performance advantages would decline with the life of the system (i.e., the negative percentages in Table 4 would decline to 0), ultimately becoming a price-performance disadvantage as the firms recouped their initial investment at the later stages of the product life cycle. While examples of such penetration pricing patterns do occur (ModComp's systems I-IV and DAG's Nova 4, 3D and 3/4), statistically significant evidence of such a pattern does not obtain.[6]

The results, however, offer evidence of more sophisticated penetration pricing *across systems*. Since Katz (1986) and Katz and Shapiro (1985,1986) have focussed their discussions on single product firms, their hypothesized penetration pricing occurs over the life cycle of a single product. In the minicomputer market, however, manufacturers offer a variety of systems; indeed, some offer a full array of micros through mainframes. A manufacturer offering an array of products can use penetration pricing with models initially purchased, thereby tying users into a network through loss leaders. Once the users commit themselves to *the network* of *a particular manufacturer*, they will naturally migrate upward through the network toward the manufacturer's more powerful powerful computers as their computer requirements expand. The major reason for the network commitment is network-compatible applications software, which is designed to operate on the introductory systems *and* larger follow-on systems. Evidence of penetration pricing *across* systems is visible in the systems offered by Data General (DAG) and Digital Equipment (DEC). Thus, for the most part, DAG's lower-end Nova systems (list prices below $7500) offer price-performance advantages while the higher-priced systems sell at a price performance disadvantage. A similar pattern occurs with the DEC systems.[7]

Our results also provide modest support for learning curve efficiencies on a system basis. Corroborating Lieberman (Hypothesis II), we find that computer list prices *and* hedonic prices decline with the number of systems produced (installed base) *and* with the product life cycle.[8]

---

[6]A regression of the price-performance percentages (PPP_{it}) in Table 4 against a variable measuring years from system introduction (YFI_{it}) produces the following positive but statistically insignificant result (standard errors in parentheses):

$$PPP_{it} = 17.9 + 0.73*YFI_{it}.$$
$$\quad\;\; (7.9)\quad (1.4)$$

[7]A regression of the price-performance percentages (PPP_{it}) against system list price (P_{it}) for all systems yields the following results (standard errors in parentheses):

$$PPP_{it} = -2.14 + 0.00074\, P_{it}$$
$$\quad\;\; (6.2)\qquad (0.00016)$$

[8]Lieberman [1984] finds prices (hence costs) of 37 chemical products decline with time and cumulative output. For our sample, we find

$$P_{it} = 40119 - 2753.60*YFI_{it} \text{ and } P_{it} = 29141 - 0.89*IB_{it}$$
$$\quad\;\;\; (3467)\quad\; (624) \qquad\qquad\qquad (1866)\quad (.21)$$

$$\hat{P}_{it} = 39685 - 2912.74*YFI_{it} \text{ and } \hat{P}_{it} = 27758 - 0.71*IB_{it}$$
$$\quad\;\;\; (4007)\quad\; (721) \qquad\qquad\qquad (2174)\quad (.25)$$

where P_{it} and $\hat{P}_{it}$ are defined in the text: YFI_{it} is defined in footnote 6; and IB_{it} is the installed base of system i in the beginning of year t. Standard errors are in parentheses.

While we could examine the implications of the information summarized in Table 4 in greater detail, we mention only a few more here. First, we find that the expected hedonic prices ($\hat{P}_{it}$) of many of the systems vary substantially over the product's life cycle. To the extent that these hedonic prices summarize product quality as expected by the market, Shapiro's hypothesized reputation equilibrium (Hypothesis III) is not supported by our results. Second, we observe that actual company-specific phenomena are captured. For example, DCC entered the minicomputer industry in 1971 as a well-regarded successful emulator of the Nova systems of Data General (DAG). As an emulator, DCC offered its systems at a considerable price-performance advantage relative to DAG. DAG, however, aggressively combatted DCC's entry, alleging trade secret violations. DAG finally acquired DCC in 1976. Under this new ownership, DCC priced itself out of existence. The price-performance patterns corroborate these events. Even in 1976, after 5 years of litigation with DAG, DCC equipment still provided a marginal price-performance advantage. Once it was acquired, however, the "quality" of the equipment declined (the expected hedonic price declined from $3300 to $2800) while the equipment list prices rose substantially (from $3000 to $9400). The price-performance advantage (-9%) thereby changed into a substantial disadvantage ($+225\%$) over 1976–1977. For a second example, when A.M. Jacquard offered several smaller minis in the mid 1970's, they pursued a strategy counter to penetration pricing. In 1976, this firm priced its J100-600 systems 11% above the expected hedonic price. In 1977, while offering the same product with the same attributes, it raised its list price approximately 50%, thereby increasing the system's price-performance disadvantage to 57%. By 1980, the firm apparently realized that its pricing strategy was not working; it, thereafter, lowered list prices below hedonic prices. However, the company did not survive. No Jacquard reputation or network had developed.

The price-performance patterns in Table 4 provide strategic information to an emulator, indicating how different manufacturers utilize pricing strategies of differing sophistication, relative to the market and to one another. The strategies apparently differ across systems and over time. To the extent that the strategic pricing behavior varies *across manufacturers*, we can improve the explanatory power of Regression 1 by including manufacturer dummy variables as Regression 2 in Table 3. It is a considerable improvement over Regression 1. We now explain 82% of the observed variation in market prices using performance attributes plus manufacturer dummies for BTI, Data General, Digital Equipment, General Automation, Hewlett Packard, IBM, Modular Computers, NCR, Perkin Elmer, Point 4, Sperry and Texas Instruments. All regression coefficients are now very statistically significant, including computer speed.

The estimated coefficients in Regression 2 indicate that the systems of Data General, DEC, General Automation, Hewlett Packard, IBM, Modular Computer, Perkin Elmer, Point 4, Sperry and TI are *in general* priced below market expectations, given their price/performance characteristics. An entering emulator can expect that a variety of the systems of these manufacturers would be sold at a price-performance advantage, relative to the market. These estimates are robust to the inclusion of period-specific dummies (Regression 3) and to the specification of the price equation as semilog, log-log and Box-Cox. By comparison, the BTI and NCR systems were consistently priced above what the market expected, given their performance attributes. Thus, the systems of these two manufacturers' offered a price-performance disadvantage over the sample period. For the most part, the remaining manufacturers in the sample priced "at the market" – they offered neither a price-performance advantage nor disadvantage that was consistently statistically significant over time. With these latter systems, the purchasers got, on average, the performance attributes for which they paid.

Of course, given the simultaneity underlying Equation 1, we cannot claim to have fully disentangled whether the observed measures of price-performance advantage (disadvantage) and manufacturer dummies reflect pricing strategies, production efficiencies (inefficiencies) and/or negative (positive) reputation effects for these manufacturers.[9] However, given the manufacturers and systems involved, we believe the results primarily summarize a combination of supply effects – production efficiencies and pricing strategies. We shall see a more reasonable reputation effect for the manufacturers in the market share model below.

We turn now to our market share. Table 5 presents two linear, OLS formulations of Equation (7). Log-linear estimates yielded similar results. Given the simultaneity of MS_{it} and ($\hat{\varepsilon}_{it}$, $\hat{\varepsilon}_{kt}$ for $k \neq i$) and the potential correlation of MS_{it-1} with the regression error if v_{it} is autocorrelated, 2SLS is necessary for consistency. 2SLS corroborated the reported results; however, given the difficulty of finding good instruments, the statistical significance of the 2SLS results was quite weak.[10]

Regression 4 indicates that the price/performance characteristics of a given system and its competition affect market share. The coefficient of $\hat{\varepsilon}_{it}$ is appropriately negative and significant statistically. The coefficient of the price-performance of competing systems is appropriately positive and significant statistically. This competition is measured by the weighted average of the price-performance characteristics of all competing systems. Because a given system will compete more vigorously with "closer" (in attribute space) systems, the weights (ψ_{kt}) should measure the technological "closeness" and effective competition of all other systems. In the absence of such information, we use a simple average ($\psi_{kt} = 1/$ number of competitors).

The network effects on market share i in t are important. In Table 5, we have *conservatively* defined the network to be the installed base of system i at the beginning of t. We tested other network definitions for system i of manufacturer m including: a) all sample systems less expensive than i produced by manufacturer m; b) all sample

---

[9] That is, whether the dummy variables and pattern of residuals summarize demand and/or supply factors.

Another issue that we do not try to disentangle here is the relationship of our estimated list prices to actual transactions prices. In our data, P_{it} is system list price. By imputation $\hat{\varepsilon}_{it}$ is the price-performance advantage in terms of list price. Our results must be interpreted in that vein. Data on transactions prices were unavailable. Anecdotal information suggested that discounts from list were fairly standard across most of the systems in our sample.

[10] For example, comparing OLS and 2SLS for Regression 4 on a consistent subsample for which first-stage regressors were available:

2SLS: $MS_{it} = .0056 - 4.51*10^{-8} X_1 + 2.87*10^{-6} X_2 + 3.75*10^{-6} X_3 + 0.023$ DEC $+ 0.055$ IBM; and
            (2.08)   (−0.153)   (3.6)   (10.9)   (3.77)   (4.53)

OLS: $MS_{it} = .0069 - 4.15*10^{-8} X_1 + 1.91*10^{-6} X_2 + 3.50*10^{-6} X_3 + 0.027$ DEC $+ 0.057$ IBM,
           (2.64)   (−2.60)   (3.10)   (10.81)   (4.62)   (4.73)

where $X_1 = \hat{\varepsilon}_{it}$; $X_2 = NW_{it}$; $X_3 = \Sigma_{k \neq i} \psi_{kt}*\hat{\varepsilon}_{kt}$. t statistics for $H_0: \beta_i = 0$ in parentheses. The signs and sizes of the OLS and 2SLS coefficient estimates for Regression 5 were also comparable; however, *all* 2SLS estimates except lagged market share were statistically insignificant.

systems, across all manufacturers, that are plug-compatible with i; and c) all sample systems capable of RJE terminal emulation, if system i were capable of such emulation. The first definition assumes upward-compatibility among the systems of a given manufacturer. The last definition includes all systems that can act as a terminal for IBM mainframes, implying IBM compatibility. Only the plug-compatible definition produced reasonable econometric results,[11] which were still inferior to those in Table 5.

Focusing on the conservative own-system network definition in Table 5, we find the network effect twice as large in the static version of the model as in the dynamic version (i.e., including MS_{it-1}). The reason is that in the static version, NW_{it} picks up some of the effect of aggregated past demand. In the dynamic version, the speed of demand adjustment is a reasonable 57% per year (1-.429). The Table indicates the relative importance of the independent variables by presenting market share elasticities with respect to own-system price-performance, competitors' price-performance and network effects. The elasticities are short-run. The first set of elasticities are estimated at the sample means, reflecting values of an "average incumbent". For the "average incumbent," the proportional effect on market share of own-system price-performance is small (−.008) and about one half the effect of competitors' price-performance. The network effect is comparatively much greater (.205). However, these sample means are not the appropriate values for *an emulator*, who will design a product with price-performance characteristics *better than the mean* and aim it at a *relatively large network*. We incorporate these more realistic assumptions into the second column of "entrant" elasticities. Using these elasticities, we find that a one percent increase in price-performance advantage increases the emulator's (small) market share 41 times. The effect of the competitors' price-performance characteristics is about 22.5. The proportional effect of the compatible network remains comparatively large (125).

Finally, we *cautiously* proxy manufacturer reputation in Table 5 using manufacturer-specific dummy variables. We realize that such dummy variables will summarize *both* reputation *and* all other cospecialized assets such as learning curve efficiencies, established innovational creativity and established distribution networks. We believe, however, that learning curve efficiencies and innovational creativity will reveal themselves predominantly in the price and performance ($\hat{\varepsilon}_{it}$) of the manufacturer's systems. We believe the remaining fixed effect will summarize reputation, to a large extent.

With these cautions in mind, we find several manufacturers have market loyalty *across their systems*, in the form of market share independent of price-performance

---

[11]The network coefficient was quite insignificant statistically when we defined network as all upwardly compatible systems of a given manufacturer or as all systems capable of RJE terminal emulation. In both cases, the coefficient of the competitive systems' price-performance became insignificant and the wrong sign. The remaining regression coefficients were robust to these alternative network definitions. The estimated version of regression 5 using plug compatibility as the network definition is

$$MS_{it} = 0.0037 - 5.31*10^{-7}\,\hat{\varepsilon}_{it} + 1.11*10^{-7}\,NW_{it} + 4.74*10^{-7}\,X_3 + 0.62\ MS_{it-1} + 0.02\ DEC$$
$$\quad\ (1.32)\quad\ (-3.04)\qquad\ (1.2)\qquad\quad (0.79)\qquad\quad (11.0)\qquad\quad (2.6)$$

$$+\ 0.058\ IBM\ +\ 0.03\ TI;\ R2\ =\ .67;\ F\ =\ 57.3;$$
$$\quad\ (4.4)\qquad\quad (2.3)$$

where $X_3 = \Sigma_{k \neq i}\ \psi_{kt}*\hat{\varepsilon}_{kt}$. The inclusion of our sample systems into each of these network definitions was developed with the assistance of several computer engineers.

competition and network effects. In Regression 4, the dummies for DCC, DEC, IBM and TI are found to have statistically significant effects. Their inclusion adds about 20% to the explanatory power of the regression. In the dynamic Regression 5, DEC, IBM and TI exhibit "reputation" effects, relative to the remaining companies. We expected such large companies to exhibit positive market share effects, independent of network and price-performance competition. We believe that it is quite reasonable to attribute a residual reputation effect to these dummy variables. Furthermore, the fact that DCC has a positive dummy supports the reputation interpretation. As discussed with Table 4 above, DCC was a small yet highly-regarded emulator of Data General, whose sole incumbency effect was a good reputation. It was defensively acquired by Data General in 1977. Until acquisition, DCC produced more-powerful less-costly clones (i.e., with very favorable price-performance characteristics) of several Data General machines. The good reputation of these systems seems to have produced an independent demand effect.

We experimented with several specifications allowing the price/performance and network effects to vary over the technological life cycle of the computers. We find little evidence that price-performance characteristics or network effects diminish in importance over the life of a given system.

Table 5. Estimated Market Share Model – 1976–1983

	Regression 4 OLS	Regression 5 OLS	Short Run Elasticities Average Incumbent	Entrant
Dependent Variable				
Market Share$_{it}$ (MS$_{it}$)	MS$_{it}$	MS$_{it}$		
Independent Variables				
Intercept	0.0074(3.45)	0.0049(2.1)		
System Price-Performance ($\hat{\varepsilon}_{it}$)	$-3.82*10^{-7}(-2.96)$	$-4.6*10^{-7}(-2.75)$	$-.008$	-41
Network (NW$_{it}$)	$3.26*10^{-6}$ (11.8)	$1.55*10^{-6}$ (4.1)	.20	125
Competitors' Price-Performance ($\Sigma_{k \neq i}\, \psi_{kt}*\hat{\varepsilon}_{kt}$)	$1.56*10^{-6}$ (2.99)	$8.19*10^{-7}(1.50)$	.015	22.5
Lagged Market Share (MS$_{it-1}$)		0.429 (5.89)		
Manufacturer Dummy – Reputation Effect				
DCC	0.033 (1.96)	–		
DEC	0.029 (5.43)	0.022 (3.71)		
IBM	0.059 (4.97)	0.055 (4.31)		
TI	0.049 (4.56)	0.025 (2.01)		
R^2	.62	.70		
Mean, Dependent Variable	0.031	0.033		
Observations	256	202		
F Value	57.2	64.1		

Notes:
t statistics for H_0: parameter = 0 in parentheses.

$\hat{\varepsilon}_{it} = P_{it} - \hat{P}_{it}$ estimated from Regression 2, Table 3. The network, NW$_{it}$, is defined conservatively to be system-specific, that is the installed base of system i at the beginning of period t. The measure of competitors' price performance is calculated as a weighted average (weights ψ_{kt}) of the price-performance ($\hat{\varepsilon}_{kt}$) of all *other* competitive systems (k ≠ i) in the market in period t.

"Average Incumbent" elasticities calculated at the means of the independent variables. "Entrant" elasticities calculated at values of the independent variables most *relevant and favorable* to the emulator – i.e., own-system $\hat{\varepsilon}_{it}$ and MS$_{it}$ one standard deviation below the mean; competitors' $\hat{\varepsilon}_{kt}$ one standard deviation above the mean; emulator's compatible network, NW$_{it}$, one standard deviation above the mean.

4.   INTERPRETATION OF RESULTS – FORMULATING SUCCESSFUL PRODUCT EMULATION STRATEGIES

Our results have important implications. We discuss product development and pricing strategies, the role of reputation and international commercial implications in order. We conclude with a parametric simulation of several emulator and incumbent strategies.

A. Product Development Strategies

We believe that hedonic price analysis offers an important tool for the product development process. Product development is often confounded by the inability of management to identify the combination of new product features that consumers want and manufacturing can support. The hedonic equation can assist management in this identification. In our example, we demonstrate that minicomputer design should *begin* with a limited number of product features, specifically system size, speed and the size of memory. We indicate the relative importance of each of these features by measuring the extent to which they independently affect market valuation. Specialty options can later be added to these basic features, reflecting the insights and intuitions of engineering and market research.

B. Product Pricing Strategies Within Network Industries

Hedonic analysis can assist a firm in establishing prices and predicting the resulting outcomes. Comparison of prices contemplated for new products with the "market" will indicate the extent to which a price-performance advantage is being offered. Incorporation of that information, in addition to all other relevant factors, into a demand model will allow a firm to identify the independent effects of the pricing strategies. The firm will thereby be able to explore the revenue and profit effects with a higher degree of accuracy.

In our example, we find that system price and performance are   important in determining market success. However, for the incumbent, network and reputation effects are more important. The market share effects of own-system and competitive systems' price-performance characteristics are considerably greater for an emulating entrant, particularly since an emulator usually offers substantial price-performance advantage over incumbents. However, network effects will still be more important than pricing strategies in determining an emulator's success.

Several implications follow.

   (i)   One viable emulation strategy involves targeting incumbents with large networks who do not have significant advantages with respect to other cospecialized assets, including reputation. Timing is of the essence for this strategy.   The emulator must be able to wait in the wings and quickly introduce competitive and compatible products once a standard emerges and network economies have developed. In the minicomputer industry, this means that the operating system and applications software base must be present.

  (ii) Incumbents cannot expect much deterrence to flow from defensive price reductions. More effective strategies should aim at impeding network access and introducing new products which match or exceed the performance of the emulator's products.

(iii)   Because network effects appear so important, there is a large payoff to strategies that create networks and restrict entry. A firm that becomes dominant within a network will be able to exercise considerable market power, in the sense of pricing above cost. Since the network economies flow primarily from specialized investments made by customers (applications software in the minicomputer industry), market power within a network may be extremely profitable. Once the captive network is established, the incumbent will be in a position to establish prices that extract much of the quasi-rents produced with such   specialized investments. Minicomputer applications software investments typically involve billions of dollars of sunk costs.

(iv)   One standard intertemporal strategy for network sponsoring initially involves pricing below cost – penetration   pricing. We observe a richer set of network-sponsoring strategies which involve a variety of price-performance advantages and disadvantages across introductory and "follow-along" products. Accordingly, large price-performance advantages are offered on early products to attract customers to the network, while higher prices and consequential price-performance disadvantages characterize the subsequent upwardly-compatible products. In this way, customers become locked into the network and pay a "fee" once the lock-in has occurred.

   No doubt, antitrust scholars will query whether such behavior invites antitrust restraint. Classical notions of "predatory" pricing generally focus on pricing a *particular* product below cost to eliminate competition and subsequently pricing above cost once market power has been consolidated. We have found that minicomputer manufacturers price below cost to establish market power within a network and exploit that market power, in a potentially predatory fashion, on later network-compatible products. Such cross-subsidization may be necessary to provide the private incentives to create networks. However, given the social value arising from the networks, such pricing may decrease welfare. This matter obviously invites further research.

C. The Role Of Reputation

While we find no evidence for what Shapiro (1983) characterizes as a reputation equilibrium, we find what we believe to be strong reputation effects. Using manufacturer-specific dummy variables to summarize an array of cospecialized assets as "reputation," we explain about 20% of the variation in market share. Reputation effects are ascribed to DEC, IBM, TI and DCC which accords with our expectations and knowledge of the industry. DEC, IBM and TI are multi-market firms, with differential access to marketing channels and financial resources. They are consequentially viewed as able to effectively compete across many markets. DCC is the only small firm with a demonstrated reputation effect, due in part to the high market regard for its products and possibly due in part to its comparison with Data General. DCC emulated Data General during this time period and Data General was purported to have a negative reputation at the time as a result of tying sale of its hardware to its operating system (RDOS). Parenthetically, the tie was subsequently determined to be illegal.

The size of the specific effects is also of interest. IBM's reputation was worth between 5 and 6 percentage points of market share during the period of our study.

D. The Role Of Government Policy And National Endowments

While our results do not address complicated questions of *ex ante* network promotion, they indicate that the rights to manufacture and sell according to technical specifications insuring compatibility with an installed base of users is of great competitive significance. As a result, nations can engage in the erection of non-tariff barriers to trade in industries with large network effects, such as telecommunications and computers, by promoting domestic standards different from international standards. By fragmenting networks in this fashion, the returns to emulation, whether conducted by domestic or foreign firms, are likely to be attenuated. Nations with firms capable of building low-cost emulating products, such as Korea, Japan and Taiwan, will therefore promote uniform standards *outside* of their home markets. Network users similarly have the incentive to promote the entry of low cost producers.

The greater importance of network effects relative to price-performance characteristics, perhaps also explains why U.S. firms have dominated, and continue to dominate, the computer industry worldwide. Not only is the U.S. market large, thereby encouraging large network externalities, but U.S. firms have been traditionally better positioned to embark upon network promotion strategies, by virtue of their product development activities. The traditional advantage of the Japanese – low-cost manufacturing – does not have as much leverage in industries with network externalities because, as we have seen, a superior price performance advantage can be overridden by incumbents network, reputation and other incumbency factors. Still, the extent to which network economies are available to all entrants, a firm with low-cost manufacturing will find market entry more feasible.

E. A Parametric Simulation Of Emulator And Incumbent Strategies

Tables 6A and 6B quantify these insights through a parametric simulation of several emulation and incumbent strategies. Using Equation (8), the simulations focus on the revenue effects of the strategies; we assume that the cost effects are similar across the scenarios.

Table 6A identifies five of our sample computer systems as potential targets of emulation. The systems were offered by four manufacturers: the Nova 3/12 of Data General; the PDP/LSI 11/03, 23 and the PDP 11/70 of Digital Equipment; the Hewlett Packard 1000 Series; and the CDC System 17 (1700) and Cyber 18. For each system, Table 6A indicates the size of the relevant network using the two definitions in Section 3 – the system-specific installed base (Table 5) and the installed base of plug-compatible systems(footnote 11). We report the system list prices and the estimated price-performance advantages and disadvantages. For example, in 1976 DEC offered its PDP 11/03,23 at an average list price of $1995, $1807 *below* its hedonic value, implying a price-performance advantage of (– $1807). The PDP 11/70, on the other hand, was marketed at a list price of $60,000 in 1976, $9150 *above* it's market valuation (a price-performance disadvantage). The Data General (DAG) and HP systems were offered at price-performance advantages; the CDC system was sold at a price-performance disadvantage ($ + 8511 to $ + 1549) over the period.

An emulator contemplating entry against any of these systems would examine the size of the potential network, the price-performance advantage/disadvantages offered by the incumbents and the possible retaliatory strategies each incumbent might undertake. Clearly, Data General and Digital Equipment offered large own-system and plug-compatible networks; however, the Nova 3/12 and the DEC PDP 11/03,23

Table 6A. Assumed Emulation Strategies and Conjectural Variations

EMULATION TARGET		1976	1977	1978	1979	1980	1981	1982	1983
DATA GENERAL (NOVA 3/12)	network: Nova 3/12	–	225	4400	6420	8160	9400	10570	15570
	network: all plug compatables	13655	15505	21425	23905	26145	27725	29335	34415
	price performance	–731	–731	–731	–731	–1015	–1015	–1015	–1015
	list price	3600	3600	3600	3600	5180	5180	5180	5180
	STRATEGIC ASSUMPTIONS:								
	A1) emulator price performance	–731	–731	–731	–731	–1015	–1015	–1015	–1015
	A2) emulator price performance	–1462	–1462	–1462	–1462	–2030	–2030	–2030	–2030
	B) incumbent price performance	–1462	–1462	–1462	–1462	–2030	–2030	–2030	–2030
DIGITAL EQUIPMENT CORP (PDP & LSI 11/03,23)	network: PDP & LSI 11/03,23	350	1650	7450	15850	22050	31590	41080	52170
	network: all plug compatables	17560	26220	40770	57070	75470	93330	110550	132185
	price performance	–1807	–1807	–1807	–1807	–3443	–9152	–8145	–8145
	list price	1995	1995	1995	1995	1995	5950	5600	5600
	STRATEGIC ASSUMPTIONS:								
	A1) emulator price performance	–1807	–1807	–1807	–1807	–3443	–9152	–8145	–8145
	A2) emulator price performance	–3614	–3614	–3614	–3614	–6886	–18304	–16290	–16290
	B) incumbent price performance	–3614	–3614	–3614	–3614	–6886	–18304	–16290	–16290
DIGITAL EQUIPMENT CORP (PDP 11/70)	network: PDP 11/70	50	920	2050	3500	5200	6510	7480	8055
	network: all plug compatables	17560	26220	40770	57070	75470	93330	110550	132185
	price performance	9150	12150	12150	12150	12150	14000	16761	16761
	list price	60000	63000	63000	63000	63000	84500	89500	89500
	STRATEGIC ASSUMPTIONS:								
	A1) emulator price performance	9150	12150	12150	12150	12150	14000	16761	16761
	A2) emulator price performance	–12150	–12150	–12150	–12150	–12150	–12150	–12150	–12150
	B) incumbent price performance	–12150	–12150	–12150	–12150	–12150	–12150	–12150	–12150
HEWLETT PACKARD (1000 SEIES)	network: 1000 Series	–	–	7700	10150	13500	17551	22500	28380
	network: all plug compatables	–	–	17675	20125	23735	28157	33135	39365
	price performance	–	–	–13286	–7557	–12762	–6451	–21742	–28705
	list price	–	–	9605	12141	9323	9310	11175	11249
	STRATEGIC ASSUMPTIONS:								
	A1) emulator price performance	–	–	–13286	–7557	–12762	–6451	–21742	–28705
	A2) emulator price performance	–	–	–26572	–15114	–25524	–12902	–43484	–57410
	B) incumbent price performance	–	–	–26572	–15114	–25524	–12902	–43484	–57410
CONTROL DATA CORP (1700, SYS 17, CYBER 18)	network: 1700, Sys 17, CYBER 18	550	750	970	1430	1800	1920	2060	–
	network: all plug compatables	550	750	970	1430	1800	1920	2060	–

price performance	8511	2493	1093	1093	1549	1549	1549	—
list price	27840	16700	15300	15300	13700	13700	13700	—
STRATEGIC ASSUMPTIONS:								
A1) emulator price performance	8511	2493	1093	1093	1549	1549	1549	—
A2) emulator price performance	-8511	-2493	-1093	-1093	-1549	-1549	-1549	—
B) incumbent price performance	-8511	-2493	-1093	-1093	-1549	-1549	-1549	—
TOTAL MINICOMPUTER SALES	26013	33821	37926	48938	53408	52039	63900	44559

NOTES:
STRATEGIC ASSUMPTION A1) Assumed price performance advantage offered by emulator $(P_{it} - \hat{P}_{it})$.
STRATEGIC ASSUMPTION A2) Assumed price performance advantage offered by emulator $(P_{it} - \hat{P}_{it})$.
STRATEGIC ASSUMPTION B) Assumed price performance response offered by incumbent $(P_{kt} - \hat{P}_{kt})$.
STRATEGIC ASSUMPTION C) Assumed network available to emulator after legal action by incumbent $(NW_{it} = 0)$.

Table 6b. Revenue Implications of Alternative Emulation Scenarios ($)

EMULATION TARGET: FIRM (SYSTEM)		1976	1977	1978	1979	1980	1981	1982	1983
DAG (NOVA 3/12)	A1)	434,294	849,347	1,972,939	3,662,312	7,221,081	8,168,586	11,227,316	9,975,953
	A2)	465,783	907,853	2,046,995	3,762,548	7,417,776	8,376,663	11,491,472	10,162,744
	B)	409,718	803,688	1,915,143	3,584,085	7,067,574	8,006,194	11,021,159	9,830,175
	C)	409,718	761,225	963,556	1,304,187	2,032,572	1,974,027	2,420,563	1,686,901
DEC (PDP 11/03,23) LSI 11/03,23)	A1)	248,778	598,169	1,483,135	3,634,623	5,733,644	22,808,861	34,800,647	31,081,642
	A2)	291,915	678,314	1,584,582	3,771,934	5,966,681	24,402,909	36,931,684	32,654,061
	B)	215,112	535,621	1,403,961	3,527,461	5,551,774	21,564,811	33,137,512	29,854,471
	C)	186,959	347,356	439,682	595,115	537,317	152,423	(263,701)	(315,469)
DEC (PDP 11/70)	A1)	12,895,711	30,325,298	44,310,390	69,809,498	90,966,650	139,019,417	206,308,602	155,047,305
	A2)	28,188,233	63,098,677	86,784,685	127,784,490	155,720,326	228,218,989	332,135,520	245,725,733
	B)	960,894	4,747,813	11,161,972	24,563,798	40,430,629	69,404,969	108,108,897	84,278,706
	C)	839,934	1,638,561	2,074,084	2,807,302	3,125,052	4,118,482	5,375,615	3,754,284
HP (1000)	A1)	—	—	5,489,406	14,488,046	15,786,283	21,021,371	36,120,879	30,217,145
	A2)	—	—	7,715,721	18,111,258	20,011,952	24,222,937	45,287,015	39,595,949
	B)	—	—	3,751,913	11,660,365	12,488,423	18,522,757	28,967,308	22,897,600
	C)	—	—	(595,759)	(729,346)	(2,384,914)	(865,583)	(8,195,676)	(10,342,630)
CDC (1700, SYS 17 CYBER 18)	A1)	6,378,734	6,063,863	6,616,024	9,284,671	9,925,939	10,160,604	12,924,076	—
	A2)	12,049,322	9,256,558	8,606,667	11,139,530	11,746,258	11,937,492	15,107,663	—
	B)	1,953,210	3,572,172	5,062,456	7,837,074	8,505,299	8,773,859	11,219,929	—
	C)	1,335,827	2,709,016	3,809,595	5,483,930	5,477,390	5,386,490	6,640,283	—

STRATEGIC ASSUMPTION A1) Assumed price performance advantage offered by emulator $(P_{it} - P_{it})$.
STRATEGIC ASSUMPTION A2) Assumed price performance advantage offered by emulator $(P_{it} - P_{it})$.
STRATEGIC ASSUMPTION B) Assumed price performance response offered by incumbent $(P_{kt} - P_{kt})$.
STRATEGIC ASSUMPTION C) Assumed network not available to emulator after legal action by incumbent $(NW_{it} = 0)$.
NETWORK DEFINED AS COMPUTER−SPECIFIC (Using regression 5, Table 5 in Equation 8)

were being sold with price-performance advantages. TheDEC PDP 11/70 offers an inviting target, since it was part of a large network *and* was being sold at a price-performance disadvantage. The price-performance disadvantage of the CDC system makes it a target; however, it has a small network by both network definitions.

For each of these potential emulation targets, we quantify the effects of four strategic scenarios. Scenario A1 assumes that the emulator offers its system with price-performance characteristics *equal* to those of the incumbent system. Scenario A2 is more realistic, assuming that the emulator offers its system at a substantial price-performance advantage *relative* to the incumbent. For example, under scenario A1, the emulator is assumed to offer a product functionally equivalent to the PDP 11/70 with the same price-performance *disadvantage* ($9150 to $16761) as the DEC system. Under Scenario A2, the emulator offers the same product with a significant price-performance *advantage* (− $12,150). Under Scenario B, we assume that the incumbent strategically meets the price-performance competition of the emulator assumed in scenario A2. In Scenario C, we assume that the incumbent meets the price-performance competition (as in B) *and simultaneously* defends his network by initiating a patent or copyright infringement suit to restrict the emulator's access to the incumbent's network. Continuing with the DEC 11/70 example, under Scenario B we assume that DEC reconfigures the PDP 11/70 to offer a price-performance advantage of − $12150 throughout the period. Under Scenario C, we assume even more aggressive action; DEC competes on price-performance *and* excludes the emulator from the network.

The revenue implications of these four scenarios for each incumbent target are presented in Table 6B using the system-specific network definition.[12] Several conclusions are evident. First, we observe the importance of network. Emulation of the DAG and particularly DEC equipment offers much greater revenue potential then emulation of CDC. However, the importance of the network is a two-edged sword; exclusion of the emulator from the network is the incumbent's most powerful strategic weapon. Thus, the emulator's potential revenue falls precipitously given network exclusion. Second, we find that price-performance competition matters; it just doesn't matter as much. For example, we find that if the emulator offers a system functionally equivalent to the Nova 3/12 with the *same* price-performance characteristics, revenues are $434,294 in 1976, rising to $9.97 million in 1983. If the emulator offers the same product with *twice* the price-performance advantage (scenario A2), revenues rise only modestly. Likewise, when DAG matches the emulator's enhanced price-performance (in Scenario B), revenues drop only modestly. When DAG excludes the emulator from the network, however, revenues drop precipitously. For some systems, revenues become negative under Scenario C. Similar *patterns* are found for all incumbents and price-performance scenarios.

Of course, if the change in price-performance is large enough, then the revenue effects of price-performance will matter more. For example, if the emulator merely matches DEC's price-performance (a disadvantage of $9,150 to $16,761) on the PDP 11/70, its revenues range from $12.9 to $155 million. However, if the emulator offers a *substantial* price-performance advantage relative to DEC (-$12,150), its revenue

---

[12]The market shares are estimated as in Regression 5. *Total* market sales are presented in Table 6A; they are the total annual computer sales for our sample systems. We assume that all emulator systems are offered at the same list price as the targeted incumbent. Revenue and market share results were similar using the plug-compatible network definition (footnote 11).

rises to $28.2 to $245.7 million. Furthermore, *both* price-performance competition and network exclusion are powerful strategic responses for DEC in this case.

5.   SUMMARY AND CONCLUSIONS

Using data on the U.S. minicomputer industry over 1976-1983, this paper attempts to empirically test propositions from the burgeoning theoretical literature on industrial organization, innovation and business strategy. To date there is little empirical evidence available, other than anecdotal. While we focus specifically on product emulation strategies, our analysis sheds light on aspects of competition in markets characterized by differentiated products, network externalities and reputation. We find that competition in such markets revolve around issues of price-performance, compatibility standards and prior positioning in the relevant cospecialized assets including reputation. Our evidence separates these effects.

We specifically examine the determinants of market share obtained by producers of minicomputers. Our methodological approach involves embedding hedonic price analysis into a reduced form demand model for differentiated products. An hedonic price is estimated indicating the market valuation of each computer's performance attributes. Comparison of the hedonic and actual price provides an estimate of the price-performance advantage or disadvantage offered by each system. We estimate the market effect of such a price-performance advantage, in addition to network and reputation, in our demand model.

Using the model, we treat emulation strategies as the variation of price and performance attributes in order to offer significant price-performance advantages, while taking advantage of technical compatibility with complementary assets, such as operating systems and application software.

Our statistical results are significant and quite robust. Our hedonic price analysis is robust to the standard specifications, including semilog, log-log and Box-Cox. Our final estimated equation explains 72% of computer price variability through variables measuring speed, size and memory of the systems. We observe differences among firms with regard to the price-performance characteristics of their products. Some firms consistently offer price-performance advantages (e.g., IBM and TI); some consistently offer price-performance disadvantages (e.g., CDC and NCR); some offer a mix (e.g., DAG and HP). While we interpret these patterns to reflect differential pricing strategies, we make such claims modestly since we have not formally untangled the simultaneous factors underlying the price equation. With that caveat in mind, we find no evidence of penetration pricing on a system basis. We do, however, observe a pattern of penetration pricing across systems, where some manufacturers (e.g., DAG and DEC) offer smaller introductory systems at a price-performance advantage and larger follow-on systems at a price-performance disadvantage. We also observe modest learning curve efficiencies.

Our market share model incorporates the residuals from the hedonic price equation as an independent variable. The estimated results are robust with respect to the specification of the hedonic price equation and with respect to the use of OLS and 2SLS. Our reported results explain 60-70% of the variation in market share; all of our independent variables are statistically significant and the expected sign. We demonstrate the extent to which market share of a given minicomputer is driven by the size of the relevant network, its price-performance characteristics and those of competing systems, and the "reputation" of the manufacturer.

We conclude, and simulate, that emulation strategies are indeed viable particularly when compatibility with a given network is feasible (i.e., does not involve infringement of patents and/or copyrights). Our model provides a potential emulator with methods for the following analyses: evaluation of the market acceptance of proposed product designs and pricing strategies; quantification of the revenue and profit effects of alternative emulation strategies; estimation of the profit and revenue effects of alternative incumbent strategies. We believe that the literatures in industrial organization, innovation and business strategy can benefit from these empirical methods.

References

Bresnahan, T.F. (1981), "Duopoly Models with Consistent Conjectures', *American Economic Review*, 71(5).

Brown, J.N. and H.S. Rosen (1982), "On the Estimation of Structural Hedonic Price Models", *Econometrica*, 50(3).

Cowling, K. and J. Cubbin (1971), "Price, Quality and Advertising Competition: An Econometric Investigation of the United Kingdom Car Market", *Economica*, November.

Cowling, K. and A.J. Rayner (1970), "Price, Quality and Market Share", *Journal of Political Economy*.

Eaton, B.and R. Lipsey (1975), "The Principle of Minimum Differentiation Reconsidered: Some New Developments in the Theory of Spatial Competition", *Review of Economic Studies*, 42.

Economides, N. (1986), "Nash Equilibrium in Duopoly with Products Defined by Two Characteristics", *The Rand Journal of Economics*, 17(2).

Farrell, J. and G. Saloner (1986), "Installed Base and Compatibility: Innovation, Product Preannouncements and Predation", *The American Economic Review*, 76(5).

Griliches, Z., ed. (1971), *Price Indexes and Quality Changes*, Cambridge, Mass: Harvard University Press.

Hartman, R.S. (1987), "Product Quality and Market Efficiency: The Effect of Product Recalls on Resale Prices and Firm Valuation", *Review of Economics and Statistics*, 69(2).

Hartman, R.S. (1982), "A Note on the Use of Aggregate Data in Individual Choice Models: Discrete Consumer Choice Among Alternative Fuels for Residential Appliances", *Journal of Econometrics*, 18.

Hausman, J.and D. Wise (1978), "A Conditional Probit Model for Qualitative Choice: Discrete Decisions Recognizing Interdependence and Heterogeneous Preferences", *Econometrica*, 46(2).

Hay, D.A. (1976), "Sequential Entry and Entry-Deterring Strategies in Spatial Competition', *Oxford Economic Papers*, 28(2).

Hotelling, H. (1929), "Stability in Competition", *Economic Journal*, 39.

Katz, M. (1986), "The Economics of Standardization in Networks Industries", paper presented at the Fourteenth Annual Telecommunications Policy Research Conference, April.

Katz, M. and C. Shapiro (1985), "Network Externalities, Competition, and Compatibility", *American Economic Review*, 75, June.

Katz, M. and C. Shapiro (1986), "Technology Adoption in the Presence of Network Externalities", *Journal of Political Economy*, 94(4).

Lieberman, M. B. (1984), "The Learning Curve and Pricing in the Chemical Processing Industries", *The Rand Journal of Economics*, 15(2).

Lieberman, M. B. (1985), "The Learning Curve, Diffusion and Competitive Strategy", Research Paper 766a, Strategic Management Program, Stanford Business School.

Michaels, R. (1979), "Hedonic Prices and the Structure of the Digital Computer Industry", *The Journal of Industrial Economics*, 27(3).

Ohta, M. (1975), "Production Technologies of the U.S.Boiler and Turbogenerator Industries and Price Indices for their Products: A Cost Function Approach", *Journal of Political Economy*, 83(1).

Ohta, M. and Z. Griliches (1976), "Automobile Prices Revisited: Extensions of the Hedonic Hypothesis", in N.E. Terleckyj (ed.), *Household Production and Consumption, Conference on Research in Income and Wealth: Studies in Income and Wealth*, Vol. 40, New York: National Bureau of Economic Research.

Prescott, E. and M. Visscher (1977), "Sequential Location Among Firms with Foresight", *The Bell Journal of Economics*, 8(2).

Rogerson, W. (1983), "Reputation and Product Quality", *Bell Journal of Economics*, 14(2).

Rosen, S. (1982), "Hedonic Prices and Implicit Markets: Product Differentiation in Pure Competition", *Journal of Political Economy*, 82.

Schmalensee, R. (1978), "Entry Deterrence in the Ready-to-Eat Breakfast Cereal Industry", *The Bell Journal of Economics*, 9(2).

Shapiro, C. (1983), "Premiums for High Quality Products as Returns to Reputations", *The Quarterly Journal of Economics*, 97.

Shaw, R. (1982), "Product Proliferation in Characteristics Space: The UK Fertilizer Industry", *The Journal of Industrial Economics*, 31(2).

Swann, G.H.P. (1985), "Product Competition in Microprocessors", *The Journal of Industrial Economics*, 34(1).

Teece, D. (1987), "Market Entry Strategies for Innovations: Avoiding Pyrrhic Victories", *Journal of Strategic Management*.

[5]

CONTRIBUTIONS AND IMPEDIMENTS OF ECONOMIC ANALYSIS TO THE STUDY OF STRATEGIC MANAGEMENT

David J. Teece

INTRODUCTION

This chapter attempts to identify, relate, and balance concepts from economic analysis that might assist in the development of the nascent field of strategic management. In particular, five streams of economic analysis are reviewed for their potential importance to strategic management: (1) neoclassical price and production theory, (2) the structuralist approach to industrial economics, (3) the transactions cost approach to industrial economics, (4) the organizational economics approach to industrial economics, and (5) evolutionary economics. An effort is then made to provide an integrative paradigm that shows where different types of economic analysis can be helpful, and how other disciplines and subject matters relate to each other and to the field of strategic management. Relatedly, the chapter contends that especially useful contributions to strategic management from economists are at present originating from recent work in organizational-institutional economics. Indeed, the standard neoclassical textbook approach to economic analysis often obscures more than it reveals; it is, moreover, not especially accommodating

This chapter builds on Teece and Winter (1984) and Teece (1984). I am very grateful to Robert G. Harris for his trenchant comments and helpful suggestions. I am also indebted to Richard Rumelt for his provocative comments and deep insights into what strategic management is all about.

and sometimes even hostile to the intellectual approaches that must be assembled if one is to come to grips with key issues in strategic management.

STRATEGIC MANAGEMENT AND ITS INTELLECTUAL ANTECEDENTS

Strategic management can be defined as the formulation, implementation, and evaluation of managerial actions that enhance the value of a business enterprise.[1] *Strategy formulation* includes identifying an organization's competitive strengths and weaknesses, determining the firm's external opportunities and threats, establishing operational goals aligned with value creation, developing and analyzing alternative strategic paths, and selecting among them. One must acknowledge, however, as Mintzberg (1987) and Weick (1987) emphasize, that strategies are formed as well as formulated. While strategy "formulation" might appear to imply deliberate planning and action, it can also emerge (or be inferred) from a pattern of actions not deliberately conceived as a "strategy." *Strategy implementation* requires the enterprise to devise policies, common values, and incentives to motivate employees appropriately and to allocate organizational, technical, and financial resources in a manner that will allow identified strategies to be pursued successfully.

The strategic management process can be described as an objective, systematic approach for making major decisions in a business enterprise. Hence, it is the hallmark of professional management today. It is more art than science.

The field of strategic management is an area of inquiry developed in most business schools in the United States, Europe, and Japan, as well as in some corporations. It is my view that the field seeks to provide an intellectual foundation to inform an established arena of practice in the modern business enterprise. In recent years, the field has both informed and been informed by practice. The field has a quality journal—*The Strategic Management Journal*—and an active society. Yet it is still searching for its intellectual roots.

While strategic management appears to be primarily concerned with normative questions of interest to top management, there are a number of key issues that scholars who do research in the area of strategic management seem to think of as fundamental. It is their focus on these issues that separates, or ought to separate, the study of strategic management from related fields.[2] However, discussions of these questions is rarely explicit. As a corollary, the assumptions used by theorists and practitioners are also often obscure and may require much probing before they are revealed, if they ever are. While not everyone would agree, key issues appear to include the following:[3]

1. What is the source of economic rents and differential performance for individual firms? How can the source of these rents be protected from competitors? (This issue is not typically addressed by other fields. Economists explore rent creation and protection at the industry level, but not at the firm level.) Why are intraindustry differences in profitability so large?

2. Are there limits to how large an organization can become and still remain innovative and efficient? How must organizations be structured and managed to be efficient and innovative? To what degree are efficiency and innovativeness in conflict?

3. What are the significant differences between contracting arrangements and internal organizations? How do the boundaries of the firm—lateral and vertical—affect performance? When is cooperation—upstream, downstream, later, or horizontal—with other enterprises superior to integration? How does institutional context (for example, United States vs. Japan) matter?

4. How does the degree of corporate "coherence" (that is, relatedness among product lines) affect performance? When do firms that show tight coherence outperform conglomerates, and why?

5. What constitutes corporate capabilities? What configuration of assets constitutes a capability? How, if at all, are capabilities transferred? Is it possible to identify a "core business"?[4]

6. Can a firm's knowledge assets be managed strategically? If so, how can knowledge assets be characterized?

7. What is a business? Is it a meaningful concept? How can a business be identified? How do boundaries of markets differ from those of businesses?

8. Do firms and industries evolve in predictable ways?

9. Are there distinctive models of decision making that are strategic? Are strategic decisions separated from others just by domain (as in Chandler's distinction between operating and strategic decisions), or is the mode of decision making different too?

How large is the opportunity for strategically directing or re-
directing a business enterprise?

10. What is needed to implement clever strategies, and how much
difference does good strategic management really make?

These questions are by no means exhaustive, but they are certainly challenging. No other field or discipline accepts them as mainstream issues. No field tackles them effectively, although progress is
being made through interdisciplinary efforts.

The field of strategic management is defined not by methodology,
discipline-based theories, or paradigms, but by a set of questions,
the answers to which have tremendous implications for management
practice. The field is interdisciplinary at present; the scholars are
intrigued by the questions the field raises, and are well aware of the
limited answers afforded by more established disciplines.

Because the fundamental issues in strategic management are big
and important, and our understanding of them so very limited, the
field is simultaneously much less satisfactory and more intellectually
challenging than established disciplines like economics, or other
fields of business inquiry such as accounting, finance, and marketing.
To practice the art of strategic management well requires an understanding of all the key business functions and their integration, as
well as of the global business environment, and human resource and
technological management. To research the field likewise requires
a broad-based interdisciplinary framework. It is perhaps because
strategic management problems cannot be conquered by breaking
them down into their most microcosmic parts (doing so eliminates
the field's inherent integrative perspective), that the field has yet to
be tamed by the mainstream theoretical techniques of the basic
social science disciplines.

Relatedly, while numerous "single variable" theories of strategy
("market share," "focus," "culture") are always being propounded,
particularly by management consultants, strategic management is
far too complicated to be understood in these terms. To improve
understanding, the next section provides a cursory sketch of the
history of the field. It can be usefully divided into what might be
called the preanalytic and the analytic periods. Mel Horwitch (1988)
has provided the most insightful treatment to date, and what follows
has benefited from his insights and capabilities.

Preanalytic Era (up to 1970)

The study of what is now called "strategic management" (formerly called "business policy") began at the Harvard Business School with a case study approach that emphasized the role of the general manager, the importance of leadership, and a top-down view.[5] The case study approach was useful not only as a pedagogic mechanism but also because it immediately made it apparent to the professor, if not to the student, that firms engaged in the same activity and using the same technology, in stark contrast to predictions from models of perfect competition, often performed differently. Firms in the same industry could also be shown to have different product approaches, different approaches to distribution, and different organizational structures (Chandler 1962). These differences in approach in similar market environments came to be called "strategies." In this first era of strategic management—the "preanalytic era"—there was little if any role for economic analysis and for strategic planning techniques. The focus was on the CEO and how he or she could and should direct the enterprise.

During this era, most large companies were organized along functional lines. Most of the study and teaching of management was, accordingly, functionally oriented. Strategic management, or business policy as it was then still called, was concerned principally with *general* management, that is, with decisions, actions, structures, and systems that integrated functional activities or, at a minimum, were conducted at levels *above* functional management. The emergence of multidivisional and diversified forms of corporate organization based on disparate lines of business heightened awareness of the explicit need for *strategic*, as opposed to *operational*, management. It also made apparent the differences between business strategy and corporate strategy.

Analytic Era (late 1960s to 1980)

A second era, which began in the late 1960s, is what Horwitch (1988) has called the "golden age" of strategic planning. This epoch saw the development and utilization of tools—particularly product-portfolio analysis and the experience curve—and the rise of a staff-oriented strategic planning function in the business enterprise. Management consulting firms selling sets of techniques that had limited empirical or theoretical foundations blossomed at about the same time.

It was in this second era that economic analysis came to play a more significant role in strategic management. Empirical studies in industrial organization led to the identification of significant intra-industry differences in profitability. This in turn induced Caves and Porter (1977) to develop the concept of mobility barriers as an intra-industry analogue to Bain's (1956) concept of entry barriers at the interindustry level. Armed with these concepts and others from industrial organization, Michael Porter (1980) articulated an extensive compendium of concepts for analyzing industries and competitors. These concepts were presented in clear, forceful language and have subsequently become widely adopted by practitioners in the United States and abroad. They revolutionized the field.

New Questions (the 1980s)

The 1980s have seen a reaction to some of the overselling of analytic techniques during the 1960s and 1970s. Probably the most oversold technique was that of the learning curve. The Boston Consulting Group (BCG) in particular advanced learning economies at certain times to explain just about everything. This led to the recommendation that firms should obtain market dominance, almost no matter what the cost.

The field of strategic management and the practice of management consulting are still growth industries, but rigid and stupefying adherence to particular analytical tools is on the decline. Nevertheless, it is my view that the field remains, unfortunately, theoretically unsatisfactory. It purports to be normative, but the foundations for particular policies or strategies are rarely articulated in ways that are likely to satisfy the inquiring minds of either academics or executives. There is a tendency to overuse contingency tables, which implicitly contain special theories with unspecified assumptions. The field still employs many anecdotes and war stories; only a small body of careful empirical and theoretical work has emerged. As discussed earlier, there is also no generally accepted paradigm to pull together the many valid components of strategic management work.

When theoretical propositions are put forward, it is often without attention to underlying theoretical constructs. For example, concepts as basic as mobility barriers and entry barriers imply certain investment irreversibilities that are not spelled out. Why cannot firms instantaneously change strategic direction? What are the underlying organizational processes that render change difficult? When and under what circumstances is strategic change possible? Correct answers to such questions probably depend on issues in organizational and institutional economics that have themselves received scant theoretical attention. Until an empirically valid theory emerges, the field of strategic management will remain confused and contentious and will present normative principles of dubious value.

In order to prepare the subject matter of strategic management for theoretical development, it is useful to specify a fundamental problem or question. Namely, what is the big question that strategic management scholars are trying to answer? What outcome does one want to attain through the creation of a body of theory and the derivation of normative principles of strategic management? Fundamental as it may appear to be, this question is rarely addressed in the literature. The approach offered here is to view the fundamental problem of strategic management as the derivation and implementation of strategies to enhance the value of the enterprise. This is not the only possible approach, but it is one that is likely to yield insightful answers.

STRATEGIC MANAGEMENT AS RENT-SEEKING HEURISTICS FOR TOP MANAGEMENT

Many scholars of strategic management might agree—though they often do not say so—that a key, if not *the* key, issue is one of how to position and manage the firm so as to generate, augment, and protect "economic rents." Economic rents are the returns above those necessary to keep the underlying assets available to the firm in the long run.[6] Rent-seeking is not just the search for static efficiencies, because even the most efficient internal activities supporting the wrong products or markets will generate losses. Nor is it just market share acquisition, as sales or market shares do not automatically translate into profits. It is—or can and should be—what economists refer to as the "study of rent-seeking by the enterprise." (This leaves to one side just how corporate profits are distributed among stockholders, managers, workers, and other stakeholders.) My contention is that a rent-seeking orientation is useful in the field of strategic management because there is a chance that a viable paradigm can be crafted with such a focus.

As an alternative, however, the goals of strategic management could be defined in process terms. For instance, a recent textbook defines the ultimate objective of strategic management as "the development of corporate values, managerial capabilities, organizational responsibilities, and administrative systems that link strategic and operational decision making at all hierarchical levels, across all businesses, and across functional lines of authority in a firm" (Hax and Majhuf 1984: 71). The approach I am advocating, by contrast, looks at how strategic management enhances the difference between the market value of the firm and the capital its owners have invested.[7] It is important to recognize at the outset that rents are fundamentally derived from some unique or idiosyncratic asset owned or controlled by the firm. For if the supply of the asset—whether human, physical, locational, organizational, or legal capital—that is the source of the rent stream could be expanded by competitors, the returns to market participants would be brought down to competitive levels.

Needless to say, the art of identifying and creating new rent streams constitutes what might be thought of as entrepreneurship. Enhancing and protecting the rent stream from an existing product or process is not, of course, just a function of strategic management: it is what management, organization, and planning are all about. But certain key decision variables are usually the responsibility of the top management team. It is that subset of decisions that can be thought of as strategic decisions.

CONTRIBUTIONS (AND IMPEDIMENTS) MADE BY ECONOMIC ANALYSIS TO THE STUDY OF STRATEGIC MANAGEMENT

In recent years, economic analysis has made and continues to make contributions to the emerging field of strategic management. The contention advanced in this chapter is that some branches of economic analysis have illuminated while other branches have obfuscated the

Figure 3-1. Taxonomy of Economic Theories Pertinent
to Strategic Management.

Focal Concern:	Production	Exchange	Production and Exchange
Hyper	[1] Neoclassical economics (textbook orthodoxy)	[2] Neoclassical economics (working paper orthodoxy)	[3] 0
Bounded	[4] Evolutionary economics	[5] Industrial economics (structural and transactions cost perspectives)	[6] Organizational economics

Rationality Assumptions

Source: Based in part on Winter (1988).

study of strategic management. Noneconomists may see economics as a monolithic body of theory and all economists as believing in the same creed and adopting the same deductive method; that is not the case. Economics is becoming increasingly heterodox, although this is more the case in Europe and Japan than in the United States. Indeed, in the language of Kuhn (1962), the "protective belt" around the basic mainstream paradigm has been drawn rather tight in the United States. Interestingly, the belt is beginning to loosen as it becomes increasingly clear that received theory has been unable to comprehend economic reality in many areas. Figure 3-1 illustrates some of the variety that exists in the economic approaches that are pertinent to strategic management.

As noted in the figure, these approaches differ not only in their focal concerns (production, exchange, or both), but also in the rationality assumptions employed (bounded or hyper). Production theory addresses how goods are produced, while exchange theory addresses how goods are traded and priced. Under the assumption of bounded rationality, individuals are assumed to have limited cognitive capacities to store, retrieve, and compute information. Under the assumption of hyper rationality, no such constraints are assumed. Thus, economic models that assume hyper rationality impute godlike characteristics to economic agents.

In the discussion that follows, all the cells (except 3) will be covered approximately in the order in which they have developed historically. Cell 3 is, for practical purposes, an empty set. Neoclassical economists have very little to say about the boundaries of the firm and how they relate to changing technologies. What does exist comes out of monopoly and conspiracy theory and has not been satisfactorily verified.

Neoclassical Price and Production Theory

Modern post-Marshallian microeconomics is nicely laid out in all the standard microeconomic texts. This body of learning provides the intellectual foundations for most academic economists and is useful for understanding price determination in simplified auction markets (for example, stocks, bonds, wheat, corn, crude oil, cotton). Indeed, most examples in the texts are from such simplified markets. These texts also provide clear expositions of the theory of perfect competition and the pure theory of monopoly. The concepts of competition and monopoly are valuable constructs that should be understood—and typically they are, by managers, academics, and consultants interested in strategic management. However, the underlying model of markets, and especially of the firm, is severely limited and sometimes obscures more than it reveals.

In neoclassical analysis, economic systems are conceived in terms of firms (producers) facing households (consumers) and exchanging commodities and factor services in markets that express the forces of supply and demand. Markets are always predisposed to "clear" since prices will *equilibriate* at precisely that point at which there is no excess supply or demand. (When markets are characterized by neither excess demand nor excess supply, they are often said to have cleared.) Moreover, it is assumed that prices provide all the information necessary to allow all entities to behave optimally. Markets are assumed to be complete and to clear instantly with zero transaction costs, and future states of nature have probabilities of occurrence assigned to them. There is no role for organizations or institutions (other than markets and governments), nor is there typically an endogenous treatment of technological change or changing consumer tastes.

Neoclassical analysis is extremely limited in its usefulness to the manager—not because it involves abstraction, but because the abstraction so often caricatures economic reality. Without doubting the legitimacy, concerns, and objectives that have shaped mainstream economics, one can doubt very seriously that a discipline thus shaped makes a wholly constructive contribution to strategic management. The following paragraphs examine some areas where such doubt seems particularly well justified.[8]

Treatment of Know-how.   The production and utilization of technological and organizational knowledge is a central economic activity. Yet it is handled in a most cavalier way in neoclassical economic theory. By far the most common theoretical approach is simply to take technology as given, ignoring the fact that the options open to a manager almost always include some degree of innovative improvement in existing ways of doing things. On the occasions when this pattern is broken by explicit attention to technology change, the treatment of states of knowledge and the changes therein is often simplistic and undifferentiated. For example, it is common to assume that technology is uniformly available to all. Or, if technology is proprietary, then it is information that can be embedded in a "book of blueprints." In reality, however, know-how is commonly not of this form. Know-how is often tacit, in that those practicing a technique can do so with great facility but they may not be able to transfer the skill to others without demonstration and involvement (Teece 1981). To assume otherwise obscures issues relating to the generation and transfer of know-how. In general, the fact that technological and organizational change is such an important and pervasive aspect of reality, and yet so peripheral in economic theory, may be the single most important factor that limits the contribution of orthodox economics to strategic management.

Focus on Static Analysis.   Strategic management issues are centrally concerned with dynamics. Economic theory, on the other hand, deals almost exclusively with equilibrium analyses, which are very often static. In recent years, much greater attention has been given to theoretical formulations that are dynamic in nature, but formal modeling endeavors of this kind are often exceedingly difficult to perform. Accordingly, only very simple problems can be dealt with mathematically, and these are certainly not the kinds of problems that concern top-level managers. While comparative statics is one way to get at dynamic issues, it suffers from inattention to the path of equilibrium. Yet these matters are usually exceedingly important. When industries and markets are being transformed, top management must be as concerned with the journey as with the destination.

Focus on Equilibrium.   Economic analysis makes wide use of equilibrium analysis. An equilibrium is a state where the intended actions of rational economic agents are mutually consistent and can therefore be implemented. In fact, almost all of the central propositions of economics rely on the assumption that markets are in equilibrium. But equilibrium is clearly a fictitious state. The justification for its use is the supposed tendency toward equilibrium, which is, however, an empirical rather than a theoretical proposition. Indeed, G. B. Richardson (1960: 1-2) argues that "the general equilibrium of production and exchange . . . cannot properly be regarded as a configuration toward which a hypothetical, perfectly competitive economy would gravitate or at which it would remain at rest." His argument is the obvious one: that for equilibrium to be attained, firms need information about each other's investment plans. In the absence of collusion or a complete set of forward markets, however, such plans are not going to be fully and accurately revealed. Accordingly, "it is difficult to see what but an act of faith can enable us to believe that equilibrium would be reached" (Richardson 1960: 11). Indeed, as Hahn (1973: 4) has pointed out, the basic purpose of the famous Arrow-Debreu model of equilibrium is "to show why the economy cannot be in this state." While equilibrium analysis yields valuable insights into certain public policy issues, it is of limited use to managers of the strategic process. Indeed, it obscures more than it clarifies. It certainly distracts attention from process issues.

Inadequacy of the Theory of the Firm.   With little exaggeration, one can assert that until very recently, economics lacked a theory of the firm. To be sure, textbooks often contain the chapter heading for "The Theory of the Firm." But on closer examination, one finds a theory of production masquerading as a theory of the firm. Firms are typically represented as production functions or, in some formulations, as production sets. These constructs relate a firm's inputs to its outputs. The firm is a "black box" that transforms the factors of production into usually just one output. Therefore, firms are single-product in their focus. If multiproduct firms exist, then they are flukes in that they have no distinct efficiency dimensions (Teece 1982). The boundaries of the firm—the appropriate degree of vertical, lateral, or horizontal integration—thus cannot be explained by traditional economic analysis. Moreover, the theory is completely silent with respect to the internal structure of the firm. In short, the firm is an entity that barely exists in the received neoclassical theory. The only dimensions of its activities that are given much play are the volume of its output and the price at which that output is sold. Yet this limited scope is clearly inadequate for the problems of strategic management.

Suppression of Entrepreneurship. Because equilibrium analysis has such a dominant position in received economic theory, and because change is so often modeled as a movement from one equilibrium condition to another, the role of entrepreneurship (used here to mean the process of effectuating change) tends to be downplayed, if not outrightly suppressed. In fact, "it may be said quite categorically that at present there is no established economic theory of the entrepreneur. The subject area has been surrendered by economists to sociologists, psychologists, and political scientists. Indeed, almost all the social sciences have a theory of the entrepreneur, except economics" (Casson 1982: 9).

Casson goes on to identify two villains. One is "the very extreme assumptions about access to information which are implicit in orthodox economics. . . . Simple neoclassical models assume that everyone has free access to all the information they require for making decisions" (p. 9). Such an assumption reduces decision making to the mechanical application of mathematical rules for optimization. This trivializes decision making and makes it impossible to analyze the role of entrepreneurs. Moreover, even the Austrian school (for example, Hayek or Mises), which does take the entrepreneur more seriously, is often trapped by subjectivism, rendering predictive theory-building difficult. A predictive theory of the entrepreneur is impossible for the Austrian school because "anyone who has the sort of information necessary to predict the behavior of entrepreneurs has a strong incentive to stop theorizing and become an entrepreneur himself" (p. 9). The need for a theory of entrepreneurship—or at least a theory that does not suppress the process of entrepreneurship—is of considerable importance to strategic management. And it is not likely to be provided by neoclassical economics.

Stylized Markets.   In neoclassical theory, transactions are performed by faceless economic agents operating in impersonal markets. However, markets are not nearly so anonymous. Even traders on the New York Stock Exchange—supposedly the most "objective" of all markets—know a good deal about each other. Reputation, experience ratings, and the like are the very stuff that permits markets to operate. To strip such considerations from the theory—or to try and add them just one at a time—renders economic theory impotent before many strategic management problems. Where managers know each other, trust relationships abound, and fly-by-night operators can generally be exposed.

Real-world markets are characterized not only by a variety of information conditions; they also differ widely in the frequency with which transactions and the opportunities for, and costs of, disruption occur. (For instance, compare the sale of a nuclear power plant with the sale of a bushel of wheat.) Yet the analysis of intermediate markets and relational contracting (Williamson 1979) is virtually absent from the neoclassical textbooks and most advanced theorizing. By neglecting the institutional foundations of market structure, therefore, the conventional tools of economic analysis are rendered of little use in most strategic management problems.

Assumptions about Decision Makers.   Economic analysis commonly assumes a form of behavior that has been referred to as "superrational," or "hyperrational" (Simon 1978). Decision makers are supersmart, do not have problems with memory loss or memory recall, and can instantly formulate and solve problems of great complexity. Even their expectations are assumed to be rational. This is not an abstraction but a caricature of the business decision maker. It is clear that hyperrationality is simply not an adequate characterization of individual behavior, much less of organizational behavior. It is equally clear that strategic management can learn little from abstractions of this kind.

Behavior of Cost.   In microeconomic theory, and in practically all textbook treatments, short-run costs are considered to rise with increasing output because of the law of diminishing returns. While the empirical evidence generally contradicts the assumption of increasing short-run marginal cost, the rising marginal-cost curve persists in the textbooks. This is because it must, if much of the rest of the paraphernalia of neoclassical microeconomic theory and welfare economics is to survive. Without the rising marginal-cost curve, it is often harder to derive industry equilibriums and to arrive at normative conclusions—hence the reluctance to push it into the appendixes, where it might well belong.

The above point is not meant to suggest that economists have not been involved in an important stream of research on alternative cost structures, such as the progress function (Alchian 1959). In the 1960s, the concept was applied (and sometimes misapplied) to strategic management by BCG and others. Indeed, the progress function and various derivative concepts have proved quite valuable in linking cost behavior to strategic choices. But the economics literature on it remains somewhat enigmatic, as well as detached from mainstream treatments of cost.

Yet the concept has become an important, possibly overused, concept in strategy management. In fact, Richard Pascale has invented the term "Honda effect" to describe how consultants, academics, and executives have tended to squeeze reality into the straightjacket of the experience curve and other parables, "to the neglect of the process through which organizations experience, adapt, and learn" (Pascale 1984: 3). Pascale juxtaposes BCG's parable of Honda's entry into the British and American motorcycle industry with reality as seen by Honda's management team. The BCG paradigm imputes coherence and purposive rationality when, in Pascale's view, the opposite was closer to the truth.

The previous discussion suggests that orthodox microeconomic theory, useful as it is for understanding many important economic and public policy issues, is of little value to the strategic manager. In fact, received theory tends to saddle the practitioner with perceptual blinders that block peripheral vision. Oddly enough, it appears that the strong bias in neoclassical thinking toward equilibrium and reductionism may be due to economists imitating the discipline of physics. (Unfortunately, this imitation does not extend to the principle of empirical verification. In physics, theories must undergo and survive empirical verification before being accepted as scientific knowledge. This does not appear to be the case in many branches of economics, where theories that are at odds with the empirical evidence often seem to have a life of their own.) But while physics began to change course during the nineteenth century—toward a more organic, indeterminate perspective on natural events—neoclassical economics has tended to reinforce its addiction to the style of Newtonian physics. Neoclassical economics remains strongly mechanistic, not adaptive. Technological change, so critical to the understanding of today's global economy, remains exogenous in practically all neoclassical economic models, if it is included in them at all. Accordingly, it is difficult to see how neoclassical economics could provide the starting point for serious forays into the intellectual problems staked out by scholars and practitioners in the field of strategic management.

Needless to say, the neoclassical textbook approach (cell 1 in figure 3–1) is being rapidly supplemented by numerous working papers and journal articles—what is referred to as "working paper orthodoxy" (cell 2 in figure 3–1)—which attempt to shore up the neoclassical deficiencies, but typically only one at a time! This means that on just about every issue and proposition in economics, theorists—and in particular, game theorists—almost always have at least one special theory to offer. However, this burgeoning class of special theories is decidedly unrobust and is rarely exposed to the chill of empirical verification. Consequently, it is not reviewed here, as it has almost nothing to offer at this time to key issues in strategic management. By explaining everything, it explains nothing. I challenge proponents of game theory to demonstrate otherwise. Unfortunately, this last wave in the 1980s was itself preceded by an earlier wave in the 1960s which turned out to be almost equally as barren. Given the significant intellectual investment in these activities, the outcomes are quite pathetic—at least in terms of their utility to students of the field of strategic management.

Industrial Economics: The Structuralist Perspective

As mentioned earlier, Michael Porter (1980) revolutionized the study of strategy by demonstrating the utility of industrial economics to the formulation of business strategy. Inasmuch as his work draws heavily on the received industrial organization literature circa 1970, it is instructive to review the basic approach underlying Porter's "five forces" model (see figure 3–2) and its usefulness to strategic

Figure 3-2. Forces Driving Industry Competition.

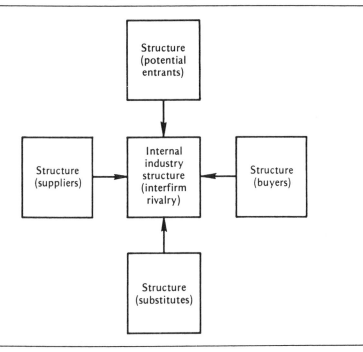

Source: Adapted from Porter (1980: 4).

management. The basic idea is that each set of forces conditions the level of rents. This approach has its roots in the structure-conduct-performance paradigm. Indeed, the four "parameter" forces (substitutes, suppliers, buyers, and potential entrants) are all elements of market structure, while the fifth (intraindustry competition) captures the concept of "conduct." As Porter (1980: 3) notes, competition in an industry is rooted in its underlying economic structure.

The structure-conduct-performance paradigm was developed by Ed Mason at Harvard in the 1930s and Joe Bain at Berkeley in the 1940s. A highly stylized version is represented in figure 3-3. According to this model, the conduct (C) of firms is somehow determined out of market structure (S). Conduct refers to the degree of collusiveness, R&D behavior, price-output policies, advertising, and so forth. Market performance (P) ultimately depends on structure alone, since conduct is seen as uniquely related to structure. Cournot (1938) was perhaps the first to employ this paradigm, and Stigler's (1963) theory of oligopoly also relied on it; structure determines the

Figure 3-3.   Structure-Conduct-Performance Paradigm.

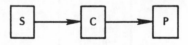

extent to which firms collude, and hence the performance of firms in the market.

Porter's model, while rooted in this paradigm, is considerably richer than the industrial economics textbook approach. He recognizes strategic groups within an industry, market signaling, commitment, and the dynamics of structural evolution. Moreover, he observes that industry structures are segregated and strategy is formulated according to whether industries are fragmented, emerging, mature, or declining. In fragmented industries, for instance, various ways of coping with fragmentation are outlined, such as specialization by customer type, order type, or geographical area. Strategic traps, such as attempting to seek dominance in an inherently fragmented structure, are also flagged by Porter. In emerging industries, various strategic decisions are outlined (such as timing). As with the other structural types, a contour map is drawn and obstacles are flagged, but no clear pathway towards higher profits is identified. However, useful lists of what to look for and what to avoid are provided.

What Porter encounters in *Competitive Strategy* is the limits of the structure-conduct-performance paradigm that he so successfully employed. The utility of this framework is to be found in formulating business unit strategy, not corporate strategy. There is no theory of the enterprise embedded in his analysis, nor is there a theory of organizational economics or organizational behavior. The reason for this is obvious. What Porter has to work with in the structure-conduct-performance paradigm is a theory of market structure and industry performance, not a theory of organization, of institutions, or of firm-level performance. While Porter does make efforts to focus on individual firm performance issues, there is no intellectual framework available for him to employ. Porter's second book, *Competitive Advantage* (1985), contends with these same deficiencies.

Figure 3-4. Corporate-Level Strategies.

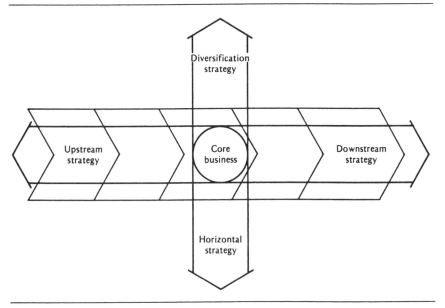

Source: Adapted from a slide presentation by Torger Reve at the meeting of the Strategic Management Society, Singapore, October 1986.

Industrial Economics: The Transaction Cost Approach

Until recently, strategic management lacked a plausible paradigm for thinking about corporate-level strategy as compared to business unit strategy. Corporate-level strategy engages such critical issues as diversification and vertical and horizontal integration. These issues are mapped in figure 3-4.

The fundamental question here is whether rents can be generated by combining businesses (vertically, horizontally, laterally, and so forth), using hierarchical methods (integration), market methods (contracts), or hybrid forms (for example, joint ventures). Such rents are to be expected if integration economies exist, and if these economies have not already been fully captured. The strategic question is not just whether a firm should move into related businesses (lateral, backward, forward, horizontal), but *how* it should do so. There are a number of organizational choices, including contracts, franchises, joint ventures, "alliances," and integration.

58   PERSPECTIVES ON STRATEGIC MANAGEMENT

To ascertain whether institutional/organizational or contractual methods should be used to mediate these transactions, transaction cost analysis can be profitably employed. The basic approach is as follows: Suppose amalgamation economies exist through the establishment of organizational linkages. The choice of governance structure ought to evolve around the relative efficiency properties of the alternatives. To start the analysis, the a priori assumption can be that arm's-length contractual relationships are the most efficient, since they require the least organizational overhead. However, the presumption can be easily overturned if, in order to obtain the amalgamation economies in question, one or both parties must dedicate specialized (irreversible) investments to the relationship. Then, in the absence of safeguards, one or both parties are likely to prefer common ownership of the amalgamated activities. Otherwise, they will be exposed to "recontracting" hazards (that is, one party may take advantage of contractual ambiguities). In the absence of adequate safeguards, such exposure can cripple incentives to cooperate, or at least change the terms upon which cooperation proceeds. In short, *transaction costs* of one kind or another will arise when *specialized assets* (equipment, know-how, and so on) need to be deployed. Depending on the nature of the specialized assets, *integration* can turn out to be the most efficient strategy for the economic units in question. These matters have now been afforded extensive treatment in the literature (Williamson 1975, 1979, 1981, 1985; Teece 1982, 1986; Monteverde and Teece 1982a, 1982b), and so they are not delved into further here. But they are ripe for further incorporation into the strategic management literature.

Transaction cost economics also provides certain insights into the internal structures needed to support specific strategies. Oliver Williamson, the leading contributor, has developed theories, and others have provided evidence to support some of the following conclusions:

1. There are basically only two fundamental internal forms: the unitary and the multidivisional.
2. The unitary form works adequately for small organizations, but with radial expansion it is exposed to control problems and a confounding of operating and strategic decisions.
3. The multidivisional form is ideal for multiproduct activity.[9]

But beyond such conclusions, economists of practically all persuasions have little to say about internal organization, or about related issues such as corporate culture.

In order to fully develop its capabilities, transaction cost economics must be joined with a theory of knowledge and production. This is because the corporation is not just an instrument for organizing transactions; it is also an instrument for learning. Important characteristics of this learning are: (1) it involves organizational as well as individual skill, (2) it is cumulative activity (as discussed below), (3) it is path dependent, and (4) the knowledge generated lies somewhere in organizational methods or routines. As transaction cost economics begins to incorporate such notions into its core, it will provide powerful insights into an additional set of strategic management issues.[10]

Evolutionary Economics and Related Approaches

For want of a better label, I refer to an emerging branch of analysis, one that has technological change as its core, as "evolutionary economics." Sidney Winter (1988: 173) points out that evolutionary economics

> emphasizes the inevitability of mistaken decisions in an uncertain world, and the active, observable role of the economic environment in defining "mistakes" and suppressing the mistakes it defines. Relatedly, the sort of explanation it offers for states of affairs is an evolutionary explanation—some antecedent condition existed, and the state of affairs now observable reflects the cumulative effect of the laws of change operating on that antecedent condition. In other words, the focus of explanatory effort is on dynamics. Like transaction cost economics, evolutionary economics tends to direct attention to observed economic behavior rather than hypothetical sets of alternatives. Like evolutionary biology, it is much concerned with how patterns are reproduced through time in the face of continuing turnover in the population of individuals displaying the pattern. Finally, it regards understanding of the ongoing, interrelated processes of change in technology and organization as the central intellectual problem to be confronted by a theory of the firm.

There has been a recent burst of writings in evolutionary economics and related approaches, and a remarkable convergence of thinking on many important issues. Yet there has been practically no carry-over to strategic management. The opportunities, however, exist. Admittedly, strong ecological positions that see firms as being unable to engage in significant change and as not having any choices available other than possibly their birth dates, obviously do not provide foundations for thinking about strategy; they only serve to suggest that strategy cannot matter, or that it is "all in the timing."[11]

The utility of less extreme evolutionary approaches to strategic management stems from the focus of evolutionary theories on three concerns. First, they are concerned with technological change and its implications for economic processes, and they focus attention on key issues of interest to management in industries experiencing, or exposed to, rapid technological change. Second, evolutionary approaches take into account production processes, learning, and innovation. These issues are of great significance to both strategy formulation and implementation. And third, these approaches examine dynamics and change processes, which are, of course, the very stuff that strategic management is all about.

Certain elements of evolutionary economics were developed by Schumpeter (1934) decades ago. In doing so, Schumpeter questioned the static underpinnings of neoclassical economics and at the same time suggested an alternative approach. He adopted an evolutionary model in which technological change and the efficacy of the entrepreneur as an innovative agent played the most significant roles; processes of industrial mutation increasingly revolutionize the economic structure from within. Schumpeter saw this "creative destruction" as the essential fact of capitalism.

But the evolutionary economics described here is much more. Schumpeter attempted to place technical change at the heart of his system and also addressed problems of social, institutional, and political change. He consistently emphasized innovation as the main source of dynamism and competition in capitalist development. Schumpeter sometimes emphasized the role of the small firm as the driver of innovation and change, but at other times described large firms with market power as the principal contributors. Schumpeter had almost nothing to say, however, about issues of strategy and public policy, as these were not his concerns. His purpose was to explain capitalism, not to suggest how it could be invigorated or what corporate and business strategies had the best chance of being profitable in a world where the leitmotiv was creative destruction.

Nevertheless, those economists who have taken their cue from Schumpeter have, half a century later, created a field of innovation studies that can inform the field of strategic management. Key concepts that can be associated with the evolutionary school and appear to have relevance to strategic management include the six discussed below.

Technological Regimes. Whereas research on innovation a decade ago tended to focus on particular innovations, innovations are now commonly viewed as connected, and attention has been shifted from the individual innovation to the connecting structure. The basic idea is that innovation must be understood as an evolutionary process, punctuated by periods of rapid change. Nelson and Winter (1977, 1982) have used the term "technological regimes," and Rosenberg (1976) has referred to "technological trajectories," to describe the underlying technical and learning structures guiding technical change at any time.

The application of the paradigm concept has affected thinking about technology policy, both public and private. This concept causes the focus to shift from particular innovations to classes of innovations, where a cumulative effect can be felt. DNA and monoclonal antibodies in biotechnology are examples of technology paradigms, as is solid-state, silicon-based memories in microelectronics.

The notion of a paradigm or trajectory for technology undercuts the view that industry structure is a key to the process. The notion of trajectory suggests a certain technological determinacy and the need for firms to adjust to it, and propel it, if possible. Paradigm shifts have obvious implications for entry barriers and entry timing, key issues in strategic management.

Path Dependencies. Closely related to the paradigm concept are path dependencies. Technology sometimes evolves with significant irreversibilities, as well as forward constraints. That is, the path along which the technology can evolve in the future is often highly constrained—as well as cumulative, with one improvement building on the next in serial fashion. The development of dynamic random-access memories (DRAMS), from 64 through 256 to one megabyte and beyond, is a case in point. A firm that did not participate in the development and production of one vintage had a slim chance of participating in the next. Technological paradigms may afford one or more paths, each of which is characterized by path dependency. This can create a kind of dynamic "lock-in" phenomenon with powerful implications for industry and firm development.

Selection.   The level of competition, the frequency of technological discontinuities, and the nature of government policy (for example, antitrust or trade policy) govern the strength of a *firm's* selection environment. The selection environment for a *business* may be more or less demanding, depending upon the policies and practices of the enterprise within which the business is embedded. In weak selection environments—that is, where lackluster performers are not quickly weeded out—inefficiency can live on in some business units for decades, particularly if the firm's selection environment is also weak, as may be the case in some regulated industries.

Technological Opportunities.   An important characterization of an industry is the technological opportunity available to it. Technological opportunities are determined in part by discoveries in basic science and the degree to which they open up fruitful avenues for new applications. In biotechnology, for instance, scientific discoveries that enabled the genetic structure of microorganisms to be modified (for example, Watson and Cricks' 1956 discovery of the double helix structure of DNA), augmented by the discovery of techniques such as recombinant DNA (a technique for removing specific genes from one organism and implanting them into the DNA structure of another), have provided enormous commercial opportunities for both incumbent firms and new entrants in many industries. These include pharmaceuticals, agricultural chemicals, materials, and electronics. The number and diversity of technological opportunities that exist in an industry are important characteristics likely to have a marked impact on industry dynamics. Therefore, they should be part of the analytic apparatus employed by strategic management.

Appropriability Regime.   The availability, or lack thereof, and scope of enforceable intellectual property rights are important features of industrial dynamics. If an industry is one in which intellectual property protection (patents, trade secrets, and so on) is effective, as in pharmaceuticals and organic and inorganic chemicals, then the manner in which competition will play itself out is markedly different from competition in other industries, such as financial services or semiconductors. The intellectual property protection afforded in these last two industries is intrinsically weak. Indeed, one writer recently noted that "in a world where there are no secrets, where innovations are quickly imitated or become obsolete, the theory of competitive advantage may have had its day. . . . Nowhere are the limits of the big play better demonstrated than in financial service industries" (Bhide 1986: 59). My contention here is that these statements reflect a failure of the strategic management literature to partition industry environments according to the nature of the intellectual property regime. This is a critical factor in all industries.

A second characteristic of the intellectual property regime, which is analytically separate from the first, is the distance that exists between the proprietary and the public knowledge bases. If the public knowledge base is on a par with the proprietary, as when university research opens up a new technological paradigm, or if elements of the public research enterprise outpace private efforts, then entry costs are drastically lowered. The asymmetry between new entrants and incumbents is of critical importance to the way in which competition plays itself out.

The above and other related issues can be developed much more fully; at present, they are not discussed in either the industrial organization literature or the strategic management literature. The implicit assumptions in neoclassical economics are that all industries have the same intellectual property protection and that new technology can be protected through the mechanism of intellectual property law. This is rarely the case, and both innovation strategy and business strategy must be adjusted accordingly.

Dominant Designs and Lock-in by Small Events. Abernathy and Utterback (1978) have postulated a life cycle model of industry development. That model is instructive because it highlights the impact that the emergence of a dominant design can have on industry structure and firm profitability. A related literature on competing technologies highlights the phenomenon of market "lock-in" and the implications for firm performance. Each will be briefly reviewed.

According to the Abernathy-Utterback model, the evolution of an industry is often characterized by early focus on product innovation and a neglect of process innovation. The latter occurs because in the early stages of a product life cycle, competition is on the basis of product performance, design changes are still occurring, and there is little incentive or need to manufacture in volume at low cost. Production processes remain unspecialized, and general purpose equipment and job shop production methods characterize production. Once a dominant design emerges from this competition among alternative designs, the terms of competition switch, and price becomes critical.

The implicit assumption in the above argument is that the industry in question is in a regime of weak appropriability, so that rivals can copy the designs that users appear to favor. With product imitation, competition thus switches to cost; access to, or possession of, a low-cost product delivery capacity becomes critical. Process technology is usually the key to achieving such low cost: competitors usually have similar factor costs because they are free to locate facilities wherever costs are lowest. Process technology also becomes critical because it is much harder to copy than product technology and it does not have to be released in order to yield benefits to its owners. Moreover, process technology can be protected by trade secret law, a form of intellectual property protection that is often stronger than patent protection.

The concept of the dominant design reinforces the importance to industry dynamics and individual firm performance of timing and the possession by innovators and imitators of relevant cospecialized assets. Thus, early success in pioneering a new product concept is often for naught if a firm exits before the dominant design has emerged. Witness AMPEX's inability to profitably participate in the home videocassette recorder (VCR) market. Product pioneering is also for naught if the innovating firm fails to assemble the relevant cospecialized assets (Teece 1986). Indeed, Flaherty's (1983) methodologically appealing empirical study of market share determination in the U.S. semiconductor industry confirms the importance of technological leadership; but it also highlights the importance of applications engineering, as well as sales and service support. Likewise, Hartman and Teece (1988) establish the performance impact of manufacturer reputation and the size of the installed base on firm performance in the minicomputer business.

It should be recognized that the design that dominates is not always that which is intrinsically, or ultimately would be, the best. In an insightful treatment of competing technologies, Brian Arthur (1988) explains how technologies become more attractive the more they are adopted, so much so that competition among technologies usually becomes a competition between bandwagons. Increasing returns to adoption can arise from several sources, including learning by using, network externalities, production scale economies, informational increasing returns, and technological interrelatedness. Arthur points out that in a world in which consumers are ignorant about future paths of technological activity, inferior designs that provide initial appeal can sometimes get selected over long-term superior designs. This lock-in can be triggered by small, chance events. For example, the selection by electric utilities of light-water reactors over what would have been (given equal development efforts) superior, gas-cooled designs is probably due to the U.S. Navy's selection (in the early 1950s) of light-water reactors to power submarines. The gains in learning and construction experience locked the market into this technology by the mid-1960s.

It should be apparent that evolutionary and ecological views provide fewer opportunities for adaptive behavior than do other approaches. Pure ecological perspectives reject the feasibility of adaptation and rely instead on selection. But more balanced views recognize that although organizations are characterized by strong inertial forces that severely limit change, they do not make it impossible. "Genetic engineering" is possible with organizations, but as with biological systems, it is not easy. In spite of such limitations, the evolutionary perspective is likely to make the strategy manager more keenly aware of aspects of the enterprise that cannot be changed, thereby directing attention to feasible "organizational engineering." Organizational engineering is likely to be "frame-breaking" in its impact, as when the whole top management team is replaced, or where poor performance leads to a crisis and the imposition of severe constraints by the company bank. It is also likely to cause management to focus on the buying and selling of organizational units as the only way to quickly reconfigure an enterprise—although what is changing might be simply what lies inside the firm's boundaries, rather than the subunits themselves. In short, an evolutionary perspective is likely to cause a keener awareness of: (1) constraints in implementing strategy, (2) the influence of timing, (3) the importance and the ramifications of setting strategic direction early in the life of the enterprise, and (4) the need to engage in mergers and acquisitions to effectuate strategy. Just how all of this plays out has yet to be addressed in ways likely to assist managers, but the possibilities are apparent. The next section elaborates.

Organizational Economics

The term "organizational economics" was coined by Barney and Ouchi (1986). For them, it denotes the study of organizations and organizational phenomena using concepts taken from contemporary organization theory, organization behavior, and microeconomics. Moreover, a small but growing body of work in the strategy area is being built through a melding of transaction cost economics and evolutionary economics. The organizational economics approach contends that firms need to be understood, and their boundaries explained, in terms of learning, path dependencies, selection, and transaction costs. (This contention has not been previously articulated in the literature, but appears to follow from a joining of the various concepts introduced earlier.) The organizational economics approach embeds a theory of production and enterprise development inside the transaction cost paradigm. It purports to provide a framework to explain corporate coherence and corporate diversification by developing the concept of a firm's "core business," which in turn is the set of competencies that define a firm's distinctive advantage.

A firm's core business, according to the organizational economics approach, stems from the underlying, natural trajectory embedded in the firm's knowledge base. Thus, new product development usually proceeds along the lines of previous successes. A wave of improvements, often dramatic in their significance, may follow the introduction of a major new technology. Of course, the desirability of seeking further improvement depends upon the commercial promise that market entry may have yielded, or at least signaled. The history of prior commercialization efforts may indicate the most promising technological neighborhoods to explore for market acceptance. However, sometimes there may be a kind of inevitability to the direction of search, driven by what was referred to earlier as "technological imperatives." A change in technological regime—where regime is defined by the convergence of engineering beliefs about what is feasible, or at least worth attempting—or the simultaneous coexistence of several related technological regimes (as with both [CMOS] and [NMOS] technologies in semiconductors) may soften technological imperatives, making them less path-dependent. Of course, technological discontinuities may blow path dependencies asunder.

There are important implications in the above concept for economic theory, for strategic management, and for the organization of economic activity more generally. First, because promising areas of research inquiry lie close to the firm's existing knowledge base, and because a set of production/manufacturing activities are typically implied by a particular research focus, a firm's core business (or possibly core businesses) can be expected to display a certain stability and coherence. Path dependencies inherent in technological progress and business development can be expected, at least partially, to drive the definition of a firm's capabilities, and therefore the business in which it has a comparative advantage.

Path dependency is reinforced as a limiting factor by a set of organizational routines that develop once a particular research endeavor bears fruit. Whereas the creative part of research is at least partly ad hoc, routines characterize efficient postdevelopment behavior in production, marketing, distribution, and sales. A routine is defined by repeatedly putting a skill, or set of skills, to use in a particular or distinctive environment. As mentioned earlier, path dependencies define the neighborhoods/environments in which skills can be most productively applied. Hence, a firm's initial point of entry in a technological regime, and the trajectories/paths that it initially selects, will define in large measure the kinds of competencies that the firm will generate, as well as the products it will develop and commercialize. After first commercialization, a set of routines will develop that will lead to stronger competencies in certain areas.

The skillful performance of organizational routines provides the underpinnings for what is commonly thought of as the firm's distinctive competency. The competencies, coupled with a modicum of strategic vision, will in turn help define a firm's core business. A firm's core business is necessarily bounded by particularized competencies in production, marketing, and R&D. Employees will tend to form natural teams that do not regroup or absorb new members easily.

Since routines cannot be codified, they must be constantly practiced to achieve high performance. This in turn suggests that the firm must remain in certain activities even though short-run considerations would suggest abandonment. Put differently, core business skills need to be constantly exercised to maintain corporate fitness.

A firm's learning domain is defined in part by where it has been, and by the technological imperatives and opportunities thus encountered. Therefore, it is readily apparent that a firm has a limited, but by no means nonexistent, ability to change its business. The products it can produce and the technologies it employs are highly path-dependent, at least at the level of the individual business unit. More can be done at the level of the corporation, but this typically involves entering the corporate control market (that is, buying and selling businesses), not the market for factors of production. This is where transaction cost analysis is relevant.

The implications for strategy management should be obvious. Specifically, profit-seeking firms have limited abilities to change products and technologies, except by entering the market for corporate control. In addition, economies of scope appear to be constrained by the limited ability to apply routines across different product and technological environments/neighborhoods. "Related" diversification would appear to be feasible so long as it is consistent with the underlying path dependencies and/or imperatives, a matter which is to be discussed in more detail later.

The analysis has so far assumed relative stability with respect to technological regimes. Suppose, however, that the firm experiences a discontinuity in its technological environment that makes its skills obsolete and possibly renders its downstream assets valueless. In these circumstances, established firms will lack many of the research competencies needed in the new business environment. However, downstream competencies, particularly in sales and distribution, may remain relevant to the new technological regime. When the technology necessary for survival is well out of the neighborhood of the firm's traditional research inquiry, it may be extremely difficult to utilize existing in-house research competencies within the new paradigm. This is because of the path dependencies noted earlier. Accordingly, the relevant competencies may have to be purchased en masse, or collaborative technology transfer programs may have to be employed to educate existing personnel in the assumptions and logic of the new technology. Here, in-licensing and collaboration with the organizations responsible for pioneering the new paradigm (typically universities or new business firms) may be necessary. Organizational economics helps to establish when such collaboration is necessary, and the forms it should take.

Incumbent firms can thus be expected to change their boundaries when technological regimes shift, unless, of course, incumbents have been responsible for the shifts. However, if the know-how in question is not protected by intellectual property law, then the collaboration at issue is likely to be more in the form of imitation than of in-licensing. If the technology has a large tacit component, know-how licensing may still be necessary.

Technological change is often driven by certain imperatives in a trajectory that help define the firm's core business. However, the diversity of applications for a given technology is often quite broad, and there is the possibility of applying the firm's capabilities to different market opportunities, especially after growth opportunities in existing markets are exhausted. Suppose application areas outside of the core business do in fact open up. The question arises as to whether the potential scope economies are best captured through diversification or licensing. According to the organizational economics approach, whether the firm ought to integrate is likely to depend on four sets of factors: (1) whether the technology can be transferred to an unaffiliated entity at higher or lower resource cost than it can be transferred to an affiliated entity; (2) the degree of intellectual property protection afforded to the technology in question; (3) whether a contract can be crafted that will regulate the sale of technology with greater or lesser efficiency and effectiveness than department-to-department or division-to-division sales can be regulated by internal administrative procedures; and (4) whether the set of complementary competencies possessed by the potential licensee can be accessed by the licensor at a competitive price. If the licensee's competencies can be made available cheaper than the licensee's other alternatives, the available returns from the market will be higher, and the opportunity for a satisfactory royalty or profit-sharing arrangement will be correspondingly greater.

The above issues are explored in more detail elsewhere (Teece 1981, 1982, 1986). Suffice it to say that contractual mechanisms are often less satisfactory than the alternative. Proprietary considerations are more often than not served by integration, and technology transfer is difficult, both to unaffiliated and affiliated partners. The result is that integration (or multiproduct diversification) is the more attractive alternative, except where incumbents are already competitively established in downstream activities and are in a position to make de novo entry by the technology-based firms unattractive. Hence, multiproduct firms can be expected to appear as efficient responses to contractual, proprietary, and technology transfer problems in some circumstances. Mixed modes, such as joint ventures and complex forms of profit-sharing collaboration, will also be common, according to how the set of transactions in question stacks up against the criteria identified above.

To summarize, a firm's core business is usually tightly circum-scribed by evolutionary considerations (learning, path dependencies, selection, and the like). However, at the corporate level there is con-siderable opportunity to adjust the firm's boundaries to either in-clude or exclude certain businesses. The choice open to management depends very much on the selection environment, as well as on the specificity of the assets involved, issues discussed more fully else-where (Dosi, Teece, and Winter 1987). But even with the admittedly general discussion provided above, it seems that organizational eco-nomics does provide considerable promise for informing the field of strategic management.

TOWARD A SYNTHESIS

The above four economic literatures—neoclassical economics, in-dustrial economics (structural and transaction cost), evolutionary economics, and organizational economics—provide varying, comple-mentary, but sometimes contradictory, normative insights into strat-egy formulation and implementation. Table 3–1 illustrates and sum-marizes how these different literatures might inform various elements of strategic management. From these literatures, one can find help in understanding rent-generating opportunities and mechanisms for the isolation and capture of rents. Yet they do not help in matters of implementation. Economists know little about implementing change and must rely on other disciplines for insights into such matters.

Admittedly, to disaggregate the strategic process—whether in the-ory or in practice—into sensing, formulation, and implementation may be hazardous, especially for the practitioner. Recent compari-sons of Japanese and Western models of management have shown two significant facts: (1) the strategic process tends to work more effectively in Japanese enterprises, and (2) the process used by the Japanese is not serial, but parallel. This is particularly so with respect to new product identification and development. (An appropriate metaphor, discussed by Takeuchi and Nonaka [1986], is relay versus rugby.) Elements of sensing, deciding, and executing are present throughout the strategic process, but in Japan there seems to be a

Table 3-1. Illustrative Concepts from Different Paradigms.

Elements of Strategy	Neoclassical Price and Production Economics	Industrial Economics		Evolutionary Economics	Organizational Economics
		Structural	Transactions Costs		
Size, market share	Economies of scale	Learning economies	Power structure of incentives, limits to control	Path dependency, learning, selection	Path dependency, learning, selection, organizational limits
Scope: vertical, lateral, conglomerate	Variable proportions theory	Foreclosure theory, leverage theories, economies of scope	Contractual theory, specialized assets	Path dependency, routines, cumulative learning	Cospecialized assets, core business, contractual theory
Product, price, and performance	Game theory	Cartel theory, oligopoly theory	Safeguards, hostages	Path-dependent learning, appropriability "lock in"	Cospecialized assets, path-dependent learning, appropriability regime
Internal organization	0	0	Multidivisional hypothesis	0	Multidivisional hypothesis
Financial structure	Modigliani-Miller irrelevance theory	0	Governance theory	0	Governance theory

greater recognition of constraints on change and of the importance of learning. As several eminent observers note, "U.S. companies actively develop and organize resources after relatively elaborate analysis and recognition of environmental opportunities and risks, while Japanese companies place more importance upon continuous in-house resource accumulation and development with a view towards survival under any type of environmental change" (Kagono, et al. 1985: 57).

In spite of the potential hazards, it seems appropriate to attempt to relate and synthesize the various aspects of strategic management, including the ones discussed above, to indicate where economic concepts may be useful. Such a synthesis is attempted in figure 3-5, which is highly stylized. It portrays a simultaneous system in which science, technology, and entrepreneurship shape revenues, costs, and ultimately, profits. Profits in turn shape entry, exit, asset accumulation, and next-period performance. The model assumes that the fundamental drivers of the business system are the rents available for distribution among what economists call the "factors of production"; others typically call them "stakeholders."

The logic of figure 3-5 can be best explained by example, Assume a change in (exogenous) science due, for instance, to breakthroughs in university research (point A in the figure). If these changes can provide the foundations for new products, opportunities for profit arise. Depending on the innovators' capabilities, skills, and assets, these opportunities can be sensed (point B), identified (point C), and converted into rent-yielding assets (point D). The point here is that not all opportunities are perceived correctly and acted upon; such activity is necessary before the possibility of capturing rents arises. Whether these rents are captured by the innovator or by imitators will depend on a variety of factors. On the revenue side, the key question is whether the rent stream can be shielded from the inroads of entrants, either incumbents or new entrants (points E_1, E_2, and E_3). The generation of rents will also depend on the availability of close substitutes. Needless to say, if incumbents and potential entrants can be effectively cartelized, an additional element of rent protection can be obtained and profits should be enhanced accordingly. So far, this is not too different from the structure-conduct-performance approach.

However, we also recognize the "lower loop" in figure 3-5, as well as feedback effects. The lower loop summarizes a set of factors typically dropped out of the picture in economic treatments of strategic management. We refer to internal operations, internal governance (such as appropriate organizational structure), and external governance (that is, the various structures the firm uses to couple with suppliers, customers, financial institutions, and the like). The lower loop corresponds more or less with efficiency concerns, while the upper loop corresponds with market control stemming from exclusionary behavior of one kind or another. Moreover, the lower loop is where transaction cost economics connects with corporate strategy; the upper loop is the domain of Porter's *Competitive Strategy* and its sequel. Feedback loops signal that there are steps in this process that must occur simultaneously, not sequentially, and that market structure and internal processes are as much a consequence of performance as they are a cause of it.

While the synthesis provided in figure 3-5 might seem appealing, it is at odds with much current practice, and with academic research and teaching. With respect to the latter, American business schools typically adopt one of two models for doing research and teaching in strategic management. First, because it has been a field with a weak paradigm, strategic management is not considered legitimate in some schools. Accordingly, these schools simply emphasize basic functions (for example, finance, accounting, marketing) and fail to give any attention to strategic or general management. Another approach is to separate the study of strategic management and treat it as a stand-alone field. Those taking this approach hope that the individuals assigned to teach and research in the area will grapple with the tough issues on the table and make some intellectual headway. However, both approaches are flawed, though the second less so.

As is apparent from figure 3-5, the subject matter and literature relevant to strategic management is extremely broad. Therefore, strategic management cannot be a specialist function, though it can be assisted by the specialist. As a result, it might make sense to organize strategic management in business schools not as a department but as an interdisciplinary program, with a focus on key issues such as those identified above. Once a central paradigm emerges and stands up to rigorous testing, the field of strategic management can more readily attain departmental status. Until then, an interdisciplinary program approach will prevent the gangplank from being drawn up too soon.

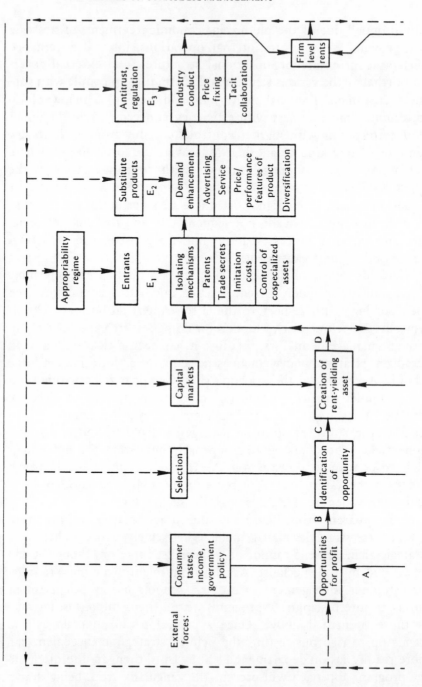

Figure 3–5.   Forces and Mechanisms Impacting Firm-Level Profits: Simplified View.

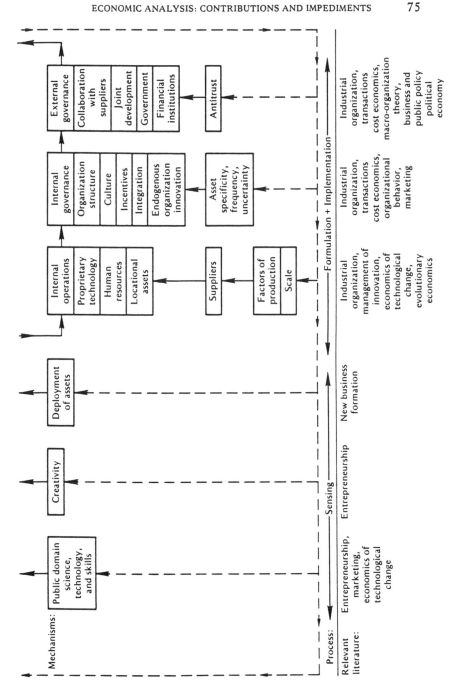

CONCLUSION

The field of strategic management is a new one with shallow intellectual roots. Yet the issues the field addresses are of central concern to both top management and students of the business enterprise. They are extremely challenging issues. Moreover, to admit weakness in the field of strategic management is to admit a more basic weakness in our understanding of the corporation, of competition, and of organizational growth and change.

In the last decade or so, the net contribution of economics to the study of strategic management has turned positive. While neoclassical economics provides both intellectual clutter and blinders, recent developments in industrial economics, in transaction cost economics, and in evolutionary and organizational economics have begun to provide the platform from which a powerful intellectual contribution can be made. Some of these concepts have been referenced here. Much more needs to be done in developing these concepts, testing them, and deriving their normative import. An organizing framework must also be developed to integrate these various contributions, as well as contributions from other fields, such as marketing and organizational behavior. One possible approach was sketched in the last section of this paper.

If strategic management can productively organize itself around such an approach, powerful linkages to other disciplines will be easier to forge. For instance, capital budgeting techniques for choosing among investments exist in corporate finance. However, these techniques cannot be intelligently employed as decision aids without a sense of the nature of the rent streams being evaluated. As a leading textbook in corporate finance (Brealy and Myers 1984: 786) laments, "Why do some companies earn economic rents while others in the same industry do not? Are the rents mere windfall gains, or can they be anticipated and planned for? What is their source and how long do they persist before competition destroys them? Very little is known about any of these important questions." A related question that Brealy and Myers seek answers to is, "Why are some real assets risky and others relatively safe?" (p. 786). Strategic management addresses just such questions. Once answers emerge, our understanding of basic issues in economics, finance, industrial development, and management will have advanced considerably. Only then can business school faculties feel confident that they are imparting to students an adequate understanding of the corporation and competition.

NOTES

1. Mintzberg (1987) suggests that strategic management cannot afford to rely on a single definition of strategy, and that multiple definitions can help practitioners and researchers alike. This position may well be valid. However, it is necessary to define terms in order for debate to proceed. The definition offered here is not the only one that could be offered, but it is one that helps frame the discussion that follows.

2. Carroll and Vogel (1987: 1) note that "for research to be legitimately labelled as being in the strategy area, it appears that only one of several sufficient criteria need be satisfied. These are:

    a concern with *performance* as the outcome variable of major interest;
    a *normative* orientation to research problems leading to discussion (if not investigation) of implications for managers; and
    an emphasis on the issues of interest to *top management*, including especially the decisions they face."

    As is apparent from what follows, the argument here is that it is the focus, explicitly or implicitly, on certain fundamental questions which is the key discriminating factor.

3. This treatment has benefited from many discussions with Richard Rumelt of UCLA who has helped shape my views on strategic management.

4. See Teece (1988) for a discussion of the concept of core business.

5. This history is documented by Mel Horwitch (1988).

6. Economic rents can be proxied at any point in time by Tobin's Q ratio, which is the firm's market value divided by the replacement cost of its invested capital.

7. This is consistent with Thomas (1986: 1).

8. This section is based partially on Teece and Winter (1984).

9. An excellent survey of empirical findings is contained in Thompson and Wright (1988: ch. 2).

10. For tentative steps in this direction, see Dosi, Teece, and Winter (1987).

11. For a clear statement of this position, see Hannan and Freeman (1984).

REFERENCES

Abernathy, W. J., and J. M. Utterback. 1978. "Patterns of Industrial Innovation." *Technology Review* 80, no. 7 (January/July): 40–47.

Alchian, A. 1959. "Costs and Outputs." In *The Allocation of Economic Resources: Essays in Honor of B. F. Haley*, edited by M. Abramovitz. Berkeley, Calif.: University of California Press.

Arthur, W. B. 1988. "Competing Technologies: An Overview." In *Technical Change and Economic Theory*, edited by G. Dosi, C. Freeman, R. Nelson, G. Silverberg, and L. Soete, ch. 26, pp. 590–607. London: Pinter.

Bain, J. S. 1956. *Barriers to New Competition*. Cambridge, Mass.: Harvard University Press.

Barney, J., and W. Ouchi. 1986. *Organizational Economics*. San Francisco: Jossey-Bass.

Bhide, A. 1986. "Hustle as Strategy." *Harvard Business Review* (September-October): 59–65.

Brealey, R., and S. Myers. 1984. *Principles of Corporate Finance*. New York: McGraw-Hill.

Carroll, G. 1988. *Ecological Models of Organizations*. Cambridge, Mass.: Ballinger.

Carroll, G., and D. Vogel. 1987. *Organizational Approaches to Strategy*. Cambridge, Mass.: Ballinger.

Casson, M. 1982. *The Entrepreneur: An Economic Theory*. Totowa, N. J.: Barnes and Noble.

Caves, R. E., and M. E. Porter. 1977. "From Entry Barriers to Mobility Barriers." *Quarterly Journal of Economics* 91 (May): 241–262.

Chandler, A. 1962. *Strategy and Structure*. Cambridge, Mass.: MIT Press.

Cournot, A. 1960. *Researches into the Mathematical Principles of the Theory of Wealth*. Translated by Nathaniel T. Bacon. Homewood, Ill.: Irwin Publishing. Originally published as *Recherches sur la Principes Mathematiques de la Theorie de Richesses* (Paris: L. Hachette, 1839).

Dosi, G., D. J. Teece, and S. G. Winter. 1987. "Towards a Theory of Corporate Coherence." Unpublished working paper (October).

Flaherty, M. T. 1983. "Market Share, Technology Leadership, and Competition in International Semiconductor Markets." In *Research on Technological Innovation, Management and Policy*, Vol. 1, edited by R. Rosenbloom, pp. 69–102. Greenwich, Conn.: JAI Press.

Hahn, F. H. 1973. *On the Notion of Equilibrium in Economics*. Cambridge, Eng.: Cambridge University Press.

Hannan, M., and J. Freeman. 1984. "Structural Inertia and Organizational Change." *American Sociological Review* 49 (April): 149–164.

Hartman, R., and D. J. Teece. 1988. "Product Emulation Strategies in the Presence of Reputation and Network Externalities." Working Paper EAP-27, Center for Research in Management, University of California at Berkeley (February). Forthcoming, *Economics of Innovation and New Technologies*.

Hax, A. C., and N. S. Majuf. 1984. *Strategic Management*. Englewood Cliffs, N. J.: Prentice-Hall.

Horwitch, M. 1988. "Post Modern Management." Unpublished book manuscript.

Kagono, T., K. Nonaka, K. Sakakibara, and A. Okumura. 1985. *Strategic Versus Evolutionary Management: A U.S.-Japan Comparison of Strategy and Organization.* Amsterdam: North Holland.

Kuhn, T.S. 1962. *The Structure of Scientific Revolution.* Chicago: University of Chicago Press.

Mintzberg, H. 1987. "The Strategy Concept: Five P's for Strategy." *California Management Review* 30, no. 1 (Fall): 25–32.

Monteverde, K., and D.J. Teece. 1982a. "Supplier Switching Costs and Vertical Integration in the U.S. Automobile Industry." *Bell Journal of Economics* 13, no. 1 (Spring): 206–213.

———. 1982b. "Appropriable Rents and Quasi-Vertical Integration." *Journal of Law and Economics* (October): 321–328.

Nelson, R., and S. Winter. 1977. "In Search of a Useful Theory of Innovations." *Research Policy* 6, no. 1 (January): 36–77.

———. 1982. *An Evolutionary Theory of Economic Change.* Cambridge, Mass.: Harvard University Press.

Pascale, R.T. 1984. "Perspectives on Strategy: The Real Story Behind Honda's Success." *California Management Review* 26, no. 3 (Spring): 47–72.

Phillips, A. 1971. *Technology and Market Structure.* Lexington, Mass.: Heath.

Porter, M.E. 1980. *Competitive Strategy: Techniques for Analyzing Industries and Competitors.* New York: Free Press.

———. 1985. *Competitive Advantage.* New York: Free Press.

Richardson, G.B. 1960. *Information and Investment.* Oxford: Oxford University Press.

Rosenberg, N. 1976. *Perspectives on Technology.* Cambridge, Mass.: Harvard University Press.

Schumpeter, J.A. 1934. *The Theory of Economic Development.* Cambridge, Mass.: Harvard University Press.

Simon, H. 1978. "Rationality as Process and as Product of Thought." *American Economic Review* 68 (May): 1–16.

Stigler, G. 1964. "A Theory of Oligopoly." *Journal of Political Economy* 72 (February): 44–61.

Takeuchi, H., and I. Nonaka. 1986. "The New Product Development Game." *Harvard Business Review* (January–February): 137–146.

Teece, D.J. 1981. "The Market for Know-how and the Efficient International Transfer of Technology." *Annals of the Academy of Political and Social Science* 26 (November): 81–96.

———. 1982. "Towards an Economic Theory of the Multiproduct Firm." *Journal of Economic Behavior and Organization* 3, no. 1 (March): 39–63.

———. 1984. "Economic Analysis and Strategic Management." *California Management Review* 26, no. 3 (Spring): 87–110.

_____. 1986. "Profiting from Technological Innovation." *Research Policy* 15, no. 6 (December): 286–305.

_____. 1988. "Technological Change and the Nature of the Firm." In *Technical Change and Economic Theory*, edited by G. Dosi, C. Freeman, R. Nelson, G. Silverberg, and L. Soete. London: Pinter.

Teece, D. J., and S. G. Winter. 1984. "The Limits of Neoclassical Theory in Management Education." *American Economic Review* 74, no. 2 (May): 116–126.

Thompson, S., and M. Wright, eds. 1988. *Internal Organization, Efficiency and Profit.* Oxford: Philip Alan.

Weick, K. E. 1987. "Substitutes for Corporate Strategy." In *The Competitive Challenge: Strategies for Industrial Innovation and Renewal*, edited by D. J. Teece, ch. 10, pp. 221–233. Cambridge, Mass.: Ballinger.

Williamson, O. E. 1975. *Markets and Hierarchies: Analysis and Antitrust Implications.* New York: Free Press.

_____. 1979. "Transaction-Cost Economics: The Governance of Contractual Relations." *Journal of Law and Economics* 22 (October): 3–61.

_____. 1981. "The Modern Corporation: Origins, Evolution, Attributes." *Journal of Economic Literature* 19, no. 4 (December): 1537–1568.

_____. 1985. *The Economic Institutions of Capitalism.* New York: Free Press.

Winter, S. G. 1988. "On Coase, Competence, and the Corporation." *Journal of Law, Economics, and Organizations* 4, no. 1 (Spring): 163–180.

[6]

Strategic Management Journal, Vol. 12, 5–29 (1991)

STRATEGIC MANAGEMENT AND ECONOMICS

RICHARD P. RUMELT
Anderson Graduate School of Management, University of California, Los Angeles, California, U.S.A.

DAN SCHENDEL
Krannert Graduate School of Management, Purdue University, West Lafayette, Indiana, U.S.A.

DAVID J. TEECE
Haas School of Business, University of California, Berkeley, California, U.S.A.

This essay examines the relationship between strategic management and economics. It introduces the special issue on this same topic by providing a guide to the eight papers contained in the special issue, and it offers the guest editors viewpoints on the contributions of each discipline to the other. The essay notes the major contribution from economics has been primarily from the industrial organization literature, with promises of important gains to be made from the 'new' economics as it breaks away from the neoclassical theory of the firm. Contributions from strategic management to economics are noted. Areas for further research utilizing the relationship between strategic management and economics are also indicated.

INTRODUCTION

The last decade has witnessed a minor revolution in strategic management research and writing. As never before, academics have adopted the language and logic of economics. This change is owed to the increased use of economics by strategy scholars and to the increased ability of economists, armed with new tools and richer theories, to attack problems of central interest to strategic management. Thus, during this past decade we have seen strategy scholars reaching out to use or reformulate economic theory, as in Porter's (1980) influential treatment of industry structure. In the other direction, we have seen some economists positioning their work as

relevant to general managers, as in Jensen's (1989) views on corporate control and Williamson's (1975, 1985) analysis of the efficiency properties of the institutions of capitalism.

Although there can be little doubt that economic thinking is reshaping strategic management, opinion is divided as to the usefulness of this trend. Within strategic management, there is a growing group who cross over between the fields, but maintain an understanding of their distinct strengths and weaknesses. However, there are also some who see economics as the 'solution' to the strategy problem (or, perhaps, to the 'tenure' problem), rejecting the field's traditional preoccupation with situational complexity and managerial processes. Finally, there are some who strongly oppose the confluence, seeing economics as 'imperialistic,' as taking undue credit for formalizing that which was already known by others, and as insensitive to

Key words: Editor's comment, strategic management, economics, research issues

0143–2095/91/100005–25$12.50

6   *R. P. Rumelt, D. Schendel and D. J. Teece*

aspects of the human situation other than the rational pursuit of gain. Within economics, the situation is simpler: there are those who follow and appreciate the contributions of strategic management research, but there is a much larger group who are unaware of traditions outside of economics and apprehend business management only through their own constructs (and an occasional reading of the *Wall Street Journal*).

Our purpose for this special issue of the *Strategic Management Journal* is to examine the state of the current connection between strategic management and economics. This examination will be done in two ways. The first way will be in presenting papers from a larger collection of commissioned papers and commentaries that appear elsewhere[1] and which provide particularly salient examples of the intersection of the two fields. The second way is through this editorial essay which, in addition to providing our interpretations of the papers selected for this special issue, is extended to provide our own views about the connection between strategy and economics. These views are intended to challenge both economists and strategists to recognize each others' contributions, limitations, and the opportunities each faces in connecting theory and application. Along the way we hope that new directions and priorities for research will be surfaced for our readers, whether their primary interest is strategy or economics. Some comment will also be provided on the issue: What (and who) should guide the intellectual development of the strategic management field: strategic thinking and strategists, or economic theory and economists?

Our essay is organized in this way: the next section briefly reviews the evolution of the connection between economics and strategic management. The third section addresses important forces that have induced this connection. The fourth section examines the future of strategic management and economics, high-lighting salient research issues. The fifth section provides a guide to the papers in this issue. Our summary comments close the essay.

A BRIEF HISTORY OF ECONOMICS WITHIN STRATEGIC MANAGEMENT

Strategic management, often called 'policy' or nowadays simply 'strategy,' is about the direction of organizations, and most often, business firms.[2] It includes those subjects which are of primary concern to senior management, or to anyone seeking reasons for the success and failure among organizations. Firms, if not all organizations, are in competition, competition for factor inputs, competition for customers, and ultimately, competition for revenues that cover the costs of their chosen manner of surviving. Firms have choices to make if they are to survive. Those which are *strategic* include: the selection of goals, the choice of products and services to offer; the design and configuration of policies determining how the firm positions itself to compete in product-markets (e.g. competitive strategy); the choice of an appropriate level of scope and diversity; and the design of organization structure, administrative systems and policies used to define and coordinate work. It is a basic proposition of the strategy field that these choices have critical influence on the success or failure of the enterprise, and, that they must be integrated. It is the integration (or reinforcing pattern) among these choices that makes the set a strategy.

Strategic management as a field of inquiry is firmly grounded in practice and exists because of the importance of its subject. The strategic direction of business organizations is at the heart of wealth creation in modern industrial society. The field has not, like political science, grown from ancient roots in philosophy, nor does it, like parts of economics, attract scholars because of the elegance of its theoretical underpinnings. Rather, like medicine or engineering, it exists

[1] The larger collection of papers appears in *Fundamental Issues in Strategy*, Richard P. Rumelt, Dan Schendel, and David J. Teece, (Eds.), Harvard Business School Press, 1992. This book contains the papers in this special issue, in some cases in extended form. This companion volume extends the discussion of strategic management and economics presented in this special issue, broadens the scope to include other social science disciplines, and provides a wider discussion of research issues facing the field.

[2] We will use a variety of terms interchangeably and assume throughout the reader will interchange them easily as well. Such alternatives as firm/organization/enterprise; product/service; policy/strategy/strategic management; administrative structure/organization structure/management process are examples of terms and concepts we use more or less interchangeably for sake of variety and convenience, and we trust, with no loss of generality.

because it is worthwhile to codify, teach, and expand what is known about the skilled performance of roles and tasks that are a necessary part of our civilization. While its origins lie in practice and codification, its advancement as a field increasingly depends upon building theory that helps explain and predict organizational success and failure. In the sense of expansion, codification, and teaching, theory is necessary, tested theory capable of prediction desirable, and the search and creation of both to better practice, absolutely at the heart of the field. Society is served by efficient, well-adapted organizations and strategic management is concerned with delivering them through the study of their creation, success, and survival, as well as with understanding their failure, its costs, and its lessons.

Strategic management has a rich tradition and long history as a teaching area in business schools, a history virtually as long as that of business schools themselves. Prior to the 1960s, the underlying metaphor of the (teaching) field was that of functional integration. Under this metaphor, the value-added by what was then called 'business policy' came from integration of specialized knowledge within broader perspectives. The perspectives were dual: that of the firm as a whole, including its performance, and that of the role of the general manager. Together with an intellectual style that stresses pragmatic realism over abstraction, these perspectives remain at the center of the field and distinguish it from other fields with different perspectives, but with similar interests in the same core issues.

A new metaphor was introduced in the 1960s, that of 'strategy.' Strategy was seen as more than just coordination or integration of functions—it embodied the joint selection of the product-market arenas in which the firm would compete, and the key policies defining how it would compete. Strategy was not necessarily a single decision or a primal action, but was a collection of related, reinforcing, resource-allocating decisions and implementing actions. Depending upon whether one read Selznick's *Leadership in Administration* (1957), Chandler's *Strategy and Structure* (1962), Andrew's material in *Business Policy: Text and Cases* (1965), or Ansoff's *Corporate Strategy* (1965), a company's mission or strategy built upon 'distinctive competence,' constituted the firm's method of expansion, involved a

balanced consideration of the firm's 'strengths and weakness,' and defined its use of 'synergy and competitive advantage' to develop new markets and new products. Ever since the sixties, the strategy metaphor has survived as a central construct of the field, even without the careful definition necessary for research purposes.

Where the sixties gave rise to basic concepts, the decade of the 1970s brought their development and application to practice, and in turn gave rise to research in the field as we now know it. The seventies were marked by the rapid expansion[3] of consulting firms specializing in strategy, the establishment of professional societies, and the advent of journals publishing material on strategy.[4] Three forces helped strategy flourish in the 1970s. First, the hostility and instability of the environment of the seventies led to a disenchantment with 'planning' and the search for methods of adapting to and taking advantage of the unexpected. The strategy doctrines of the seventies offered an alternative: building and protecting specialized strengths that weather change and expressing those strengths in new products and services as markets shift. The second important force was the continued expansion and further development of strategy consulting practices based on analytical tools and concepts. The Boston Consulting Group pioneered in this regard, creating the 'experience curve' and deriving the 'growth-share matrix.' The third key force at work was the maturation and predominance of the diversified firm. Top management began to see their corporations as portfolios of business units and their primary responsibility as capital allocation among business units. The new systems that evolved, dubbed 'strategic management,' forced business managers to define their plans and goals in competitive terms and generated a brisk demand for strategic tools and strategy analysis.

---

[3] It should be noted that The Boston Consulting Group, the first of the firms specializing in strategy, and the firm that spun off many similar firms, was started by Bruce Henderson in the early sixties.

[4] Technically, journals specializing in strategy such as this one, began publication in the eighties. However, the agreement to launch the SMJ was made in 1978. The Strategic Management Society started in 1981, but other groups such as the North American Society of Corporate Planners, Division of Business Policy and Planning of the Academy of Management, The Planning College of TIMS, and others can be traced to the seventies.

8   *R. P. Rumelt, D. Schendel and D. J. Teece*

Until the seventies, academic strategy research consisted chiefly of clinical case studies of actual situations, with generalizations sought through induction. Although this style of research continues to play an important role, the seventies saw the rise of a new research style, one based in deductive methods, the falsification philosophy of Popper, and the multivariate statistical methods characteristic of econometrics. Almost simultaneously, three different streams of work were changing the face of the field. Two of these streams were conducted at Harvard, the third at Purdue University. At the Harvard Business School, students of Bruce Scott built on Chandler's (1962) pioneering work and inaugurated a stream of research on diversification and firm performance. At the Harvard Department of Economics, Richard Caves' students began to modify traditional Mason/Bain studies of structure and performance to include differing positions of firms within industries, inaugurating the study of 'strategic groups' within industries. Meanwhile, at Purdue University, Dan Schendel, together with his and Arnold Cooper's students, began the so-called 'brewing' studies which explored the empirical links between organizational resource choices, interpreted as 'strategy,' and firm performance.[5] This work demonstrated for the first time the existence of structural heterogeneity within industries, and led to the first hard empirical evidence of the 'strategic groups' under discussion and development at Harvard. More important than the content of the Purdue and Harvard studies, however, was the different empirical nature of the work. In addition to cases used for induction, this new work used difficult data collection, and the rapidly growing power of the computer and multivariate statistical methods capable of handling large data bases, to test hypotheses in a deductive style of research.

This shift in research style ultimately led to questions that case research and simple hypothesis testing could not illuminate. Results were difficult to interpret, lacking any theory in which to embed them. Cumulation of questions occurred, but not of results that led to advice for practitioners, or to tests of theory useful for practice. Hence, the work of the seventies was instrumental in motivating the work of the

eighties and its search for linkages to theory. As importantly, this work and style led to a new generation of researchers better equipped to handle the new style of research and its intellectual demands.

During the 1980s, owing to the changes noted, the pace of change accelerated; economic thinking moved closer to center stage in strategic management as disciplines were examined for theoretical motivation for the empirical work then building. The most influential contribution of the decade from economics was undoubtedly Porter's *Competitive Strategy* (1980). In a remarkably short time, Porter's applications of mobility barriers, industry analysis, and generic strategies became broadly accepted and used in teaching, consultation, and many research projects.

Whereas Porter's approach to strategy built on the structure-conduct-performance tradition, which studied market power, there was another tradition, associated with the University of Chicago, which saw industry structure as reflecting efficiency outcomes rather than market power. In this tradition differences in performance tend to signal differences in resource endowments. In addition, another new stream of thought began to emphasize the importance of unique, difficult-to-imitate resources in sustaining performance. Within strategic management, these approaches have flowed together and have been dubbed the *resource-based view* of the firm.[6]

In addition to these broad perspectives developed within the field, during the 1980s strategy scholars dramatically increased their use of economic theory and their sophistication in doing so as the examples that follow indicate. The event-study methods of financial economics were used to investigate strategic and organizational change as well as the strategic fit of acquisitions. New security-market performance measures were applied to old questions of diversification and performance, market share and performance, as well as new areas of inquiry. Transaction-cost viewpoints on scope and integration were adopted and new theories of the efficiency of social bonding advanced. Studies

---

[5] See Hatten and Schendel (1977), Hatten, Schendel, and Cooper (1978), and Schendel and Patton (1978).

[6] This view was named and defined by Wernerfelt (1984a). Additional contributions were made by Teece (1982), Lippman and Rumelt (1982), Rumelt (1984, 1987), Barney (1986), and Teece, Pisano, and Shuen (1990). Grant (1991) reviews the subject and Conner (1991) provides a comprehensive evaluation.

of innovation began to use the language and logic of rents and appropriability, and research in venture capital responded to the agency and adverse selection problems characteristic of that activity. Agency theory perspectives have been used in the study of firm size, diversification, top-management compensation, and growth. The new game-theoretic approach to industrial organization has informed studies of producer reputations, entry and exit, technological change, and the adoption of standards.

In looking backward over these three decades, what comes into focus is the search for theoretical explanations of very complex phenomena. A linking occurred for the first time between basic disciplines of the social sciences,[7] especially economics, and practical issues involved in managing the firm. What had begun in the sixties as rather simple concepts that gave insight into phenomena described in cases, ended in the eighties motivating a search for theory with causal and predictive power able to be used in practice.

WHY ECONOMICS IN STRATEGIC MANAGEMENT?

Why has the 'content' side of strategic management come to draw so heavily on economics? The trend cannot have been driven by practice; very few, if any, of the unregulated firms in the U.S. employ microeconomists to analyze strategies or help chart strategic direction. It cannot have been driven by teaching; most strategic management courses continue to rely on cases that are more integrative than analytic. We contend that the infusion of economic thinking has been driven by five forces or events, all connected with the research program of strategic management. They are: (1) the need to interpret performance data, (2) the experience curve, (3) the problem of persistent profit, (4) the changing nature of economics, and (5) the changing climate within business schools. Each of the forces or events has shaped the connection

between economics and strategic management and each continues to pose practical and intellectual challenges that will shape future developments.

The need to interpret performance data

In the early 1970s strategy researchers began to look systematically at corporate performance data, particularly return on investment, in attempts to link results to managerial action. Fruhan's (1972) study of the airline industry, Rumelt's (1974) study of diversification strategy, Hatten, Schendel and Cooper's (1978) brewing industry study, Biggadike's (1979) study of entry and diversification, and the PIMS studies were the early examples of this new style of research. The problem implicit in each of these studies was that of interpreting the observed performance differentials. What meaning should be ascribed to performance differences between groups, or to variables that correlate with performance? The need to find an adequate answer to these questions was one of the forces engendering economic thinking among strategy researchers.

The story of the market-share effect provides a good illustration of this dynamic. The empirical association between market share and profitability was first discerned in IO economics research[8] where the relationship was intepreted as evidence of 'market power.' Why? Because using the structure-conduct-performance paradigm as the driver, market share represented 'structure' ('conduct' was implicit) and supernormal returns were interpreted as poor social 'performance.' Within the strategic management community, the market-share issue was raised by the Boston Consulting Group (BCG) and sharpened by the PIMS studies, carried out on the first business-level data base available for economic research. The leading role both BCG and PIMS gave to market share helped shape thought about strategic management in the late 1970s. The viewpoint they espoused saw market-share as an asset that could be 'bought' and 'sold' for strategic

---

[7] It should be understood that this special issue of the SMJ focuses on economics and strategy, but theoretical contributions were also forthcoming from other basic disciplines such as psychology, sociology, political science, and anthropology. Indeed, the theoretical linkage search was conducted on a broad scale and was by no means limited to economics alone.

[8] Imel and Helmberger (1971), Shepherd (1972), and Gale (1972) all address this phenomena. In the marketing literature there were also models proposed and studied that linked market share to profitability, but without much attention paid to the underlying theoretical issues involved.

10   *R. P. Rumelt, D. Schendel and D. J. Teece*

purposes.[9] BCG advised its clients to 'invest' in share in growing industries (where competitive reaction was either absent or dulled) and 'harvest' share in declining industries. PIMS researchers and consultants went further and told managers they could increase share, and thus profit, by redefining their markets (i.e. redefine their competitors and presumably their share position).

In 1979, Rumelt and Wensley (1981) began an empirical study using PIMS data that was designed to estimate the 'cost' of gaining market share. Their motivation was discomfort with the consultants' advice to gain share in growing markets (or new industries, etc.). The advice seemed to be too much of a 'free lunch.' Were there really simple rules of strategy that could always be expected to pay off? Expecting to find the cost of share-gains to be at least their worth in each context, they were quite surprised to find no cost to share-gains. Changes in share and changes in profitability were positively related in every context examined. *It was not possible to interpret this result without extensive forays into economic theory and advanced econometrics.* In the end, they adopted the assumption that share changes were properly 'priced' and interpreted their results as implying that the share-profit association was causally spurious. Instead, an unobserved stochastic process (i.e. luck, good management) was jointly driving both share and profitability. Subsequent empirical research has generally supported their view.[10] The market share issue also stimulated efforts to model competitive equilibria in which share and profitability are associated. Note that most of this work has been carried out within strategic management rather than by economists.[11]

The market share story exemplifies an argument over data analysis and equilibrium which continues in new forms today. Simply stated, equilibrium means that all actors have exploited the opportunities they face. Thus, competitive equilibrium rules out, (by assumption), the possibility that differences in firm wealth can be attributed to differences in freely variable strategy choices, or easily reversible decisions. Instead, observed differences in wealth must be attributed to phenomena that are uncontrollable or unpredictable, for example order of entry, nonimitable differences in quality or efficiency, and of course, luck. By making the assumption, the widely-used study of performance vs. some parameter or other loses much of its value. For example, if the world is in equilibrium, the fact that growing industries are more profitable does not mean that one should invest in growing industries. Instead, the assumption of equilibrium leads the researcher to presume that the observed profitability is balanced by the expectation of future losses, risk, or is sustained by impediments to entry, or is a reputation-based premium, or is otherwise balanced by unseen scarcity and cost.

Equilibrium assumptions are the cornerstone of most economic thinking and are the most straightforward way of modeling competition. Researchers who eschew equilibrium assumptions risk gross errors in the causal interpretation of data. On the other hand, the risk in adopting an equilibrium assumption is that it may be unwarranted. Observed differences in performance may actually reflect widespread ignorance about the phenomena being studied. Which risk is being undertaken is not just a matter of preference, but more likely one of conditions, especially in the presence of innovation and change. The general approach to making this judgement is to rule in favor of equilibrium when the underlying assets or positions are frequently traded or contested, when the level of aggregation and the type of data is familiar to actors in the industry, when the data is widely available and frequently reviewed, and when the connections between the data and profits are widely understood.

While equilibrium assumptions often drive out consideration of innovation, change, and heterogeneity, this does not need to be the case. In the neoclassical world, equilibrium meant that profits were everywhere zero, or more generally, that all opportunities had been exploited. But

---

[9] Their views were also echoed by some economists. Shepherd [1979: 185] claimed that 'present market share. . .will yield a given profit rate. . .The firm can maintain that profit rate. Or it can raise it now, while yielding up some of its market share to other firms. Or it can 'invest' present profits in building up a higher future market share.'

[10] See Jacobson (1990). For an intermediate view, see Boulding and Staelin (1990). Schendel and Patton (1978) as part of the Purdue brewing studies provided a simultaneous view of the search for market share, profitability, and growth.

[11] Lippman and Rumelt's (1982) theory of uncertain imitability generates this sort of equilibrium as does the differentiated oligopoly modeled by Karnani (1985). Elegant models in which market share 'matters' have been developed by Wernerfelt (1984b, 1991).

more sophisticated views now permit more sophisticated equilibria. The basic idea of Nash equilibrium, wherein each actor does the best he or she can with what they individually know and control, especially when coupled with uncertainty, asymmetric information and unequal resource endowments, permits a broad range of intriguing outcomes. For example, one could model the gradual imitation of an innovation as a process in which competitors observe its operation and market results, and then gradually learn what the leader already knows. In such a model large profits would be earned, firms might enter and then exit, and competition would gradually increase. Although the product market would not be in neoclassical equilibrium, the behavior described is still equilibrium behavior in that no one has passed up any opportunities for profit that are *known to them*. Thus, it is possible to describe many aspects of innovation and the profit-creating transient responses they induce with 'equilibrium' models, although a plethora of nonneoclassical assumptions will be required.

An example of an equilibrium assumption of use in strategic management is that of 'no rule for riches'—that there can be no *general* rules for generating wealth. There is no substitute for judgement in deciding whether or not this exclusion should be applied to a particular context (that is, deciding how general is 'general'). Interestingly, this equilibrium assumption rationalizes traditional case-based situational analysis that has been the hallmark of strategic management instruction. If there are no general rules for riches, then a strategy based on generally available information and unspecialized resources should be rejected. Opportunities worth undertaking must be rooted in the particulars of the situation. They must flow from special information possessed by the firm or its managers, from the special resources, skills, and market positions that the firm possesses. Viewed in this light, traditional case analysis is a legitimate search for opportunity. What is worth recognizing is that the acceptance of this level of economic equilibrium does not nullify strategic management, nor does it imply that one should teach economic theorems rather than management. What it does imply is that professional educators are right in their focus on developing skills in the analysis of the particular rather than the general. In addition, it suggests a framework for

where to look for opportunities and, once identified, a basis for judging their relative merits. Theory alone is insufficient absent intimate, unique knowledge of technical conditions and the ability to position assets and skills to create favorable competitive positions.

The experience curve

During the 1970s the experience curve doctrine, developed by the Boston Consulting Group,[12] was a powerful force within strategic management. Although the idea that some costs followed a learning-by-doing pattern had been around since the 1920s, it was largely ignored by economists because it was a theoretical nuisance; it destroyed the ability of standard models to reach equilibrium. BCG added four critical ingredients: (1) they argued that the pattern applied not just to direct labor, but to all deflated cost elements of value added; this expanded version of the learning curve was called the experience curve; (2) they provided convincing data showing experience effects in a broad variety of industries; (3) they argued that experience-based cost reduction was not restricted to the early stages of production, but continued indefinitely;[13] and (4) they explored the competitive implications of the experience effect. An example of the latter is BCG's suggestion that '. . .there is no naturally stable relationship with competitors on any product until some one competitor has a commanding market share of the normal market for that product and until the product's growth slows. Furthermore, under stable conditions, the profitability of each competitor should be a function of his accumulated experience with that product.' (1970: 29)

The idea that cumulative production experience, not scale, could be a primary driver of unit costs implied a value in doing business apart from the immediate profits earned. In the second-half of the seventies, virtually every article, book,

---

[12] See, *Perspectives on Experience*, The Boston Consulting Group, 1970.
[13] This was a critical issue. Scherer's [1970: 74] contemporaneous· industrial organization text dismissed the importance of learning-by-doing in mass production industries because 'the rate of cost reduction evidently declines as cumulative output rises beyond several thousand units.' Interestingly, the second revised edition, published in 1980, abandoned the disclaimer and treated learning-by-doing as an important phenomena, citing BCG, among others.

and presentation on strategy referred in some way to the experience curve. The idea's power was that it provided an explanation for the sustained dominance of leaders, and for heterogeneity, despite competition. There was also the simple fact that it supported many managers' tastes for pursuing dominance and growth at the expense of current profit.

The impact of the experience curve on the strategic management community extended beyond the overt content or correctness of the doctrine. The experience curve was the first wedge driven in the split that widened between the study of management process and the study of competitive action and market outcomes. In a field which had traditionally seen the firm as embedded within an 'environment,' the experience curve focused attention on the actions of alert rivals. Most importantly, the logic of the experience curve engendered a taste for a microeconomic style of explanation: For the first time there was a simple, parsimonious account of what competitive advantage was, how it was gained, and where it should be sought. Adding piquancy was the fact that the logic of experience-based competition was not imported from economics, but was instead developed within strategic management and then exported to economics. Finally, among those who sought more precision, there was the need to clarify assumptions about competitive behavior, to more exactly characterize the resulting equilibria,[14] and to empirically estimate the relative importance of scale, industry-experience, and firm-experience effects.[15] Thus, the very act of developing and grappling with the logic of experience-based competition encouraged economic thinking within strategic management.

The problem of persistent profit

One of the key empirical observations made by traditional strategy case research was that firms within the same industry differ from one another, and that there seems to be an inertia associated

[14] Experience-based equilibria are analytically intractable. Spence's [1974] work remains the best analysis, accomplished by ignoring discounting.
[15] Lieberman [1984], studying 37 chemical products, found learning effects much larger than scale economies and showed that they were associated with cumulative output rather than calendar time.

with these differences. Some firms simply do better than others, and they do so consistently. Indeed, it is the fact of these differences that was the origin of the strategy concept. In standard neoclassical economics, competition should erode the extra profits earned by successful firms, leaving each firm just enough to pay factor costs. Yet empirical studies show that if you do well today, you tend to do well tomorrow; good results persist.

One of the factors in the 1970s that drove strategy researchers to search for theoretical explanations for persistent performance differences was the enormous success and legitimacy of the capital asset pricing model (CAPM). Developed by financial economists, the CAPM not only had practical usefulness, it gave great strength to the idea that markets were *efficient*. Consequently, an intellectual climate developed in the academy which tended to presume efficiency in all markets, even product-markets, and aggressively challenged assertions to the contrary. The experience curve doctrine provided a partial response to this challenge, but it clearly was not the whole story.

In searching for explanations for enduring success it was natural to reach for relevant economic theory. The most obvious theory was that of industrial organization economics and its various explanations for abnormal returns. Traditional entry-barrier theory yielded the concepts of scale economies and sunk costs; mobility barrier theory stressed the importance of learning and first-mover advantages in making specialized investments in positions within industries. The 'Chicago' tradition supported the notion that high profits were returns to specialized, high-quality resources. Game theory provided models of firms which use preemption, brand crowding, dynamic limit-pricing, signaling, and reputations for toughness to strategically protect market positions. The economics of innovation brought a focus on Schumpeterian competition, intellectual property, and the costs of technology transfer. And evolutionary economics yielded the idea that skills, embedded in organizational routines, resisted imitation and had to be developed anew by each firm.

Within strategic management there has been a great deal of work aimed at synthesizing these ideas into coherent frameworks. The most prominent effort is Porter's (1980, 1985). Taking the basic ideas of the Mason/Bain structure-conduct-performance paradigm, Porter changed the perspective from that of the industry to that of the firm, and formulated what had been learned from this perspective into a theory of competitive strategy. Porter catalogued, described, and discussed a wide range of phenomena which interfered with free competition, thus allowing abnormal returns, and suggested how their interaction and relative importance varied across contexts. Porter's (1985) later approach, delineated in *Competitive Advantage*, extended the earlier analysis of competitive strategy to encompass positioning within an industry (or strategic group) so as to achieve sustained competitive advantage. Positing two basic types of firm-specific advantage (cost-based or differentiation-based), Porter argued that advantage could be sustained from a product-market position and a configuration of internal activities that were mutually reinforcing (i.e. strong complementarities amongst activities and the conditions of demand).[16]

A second effort at synthesis is the resource-based view of strategy. This view shifts attention away from product-market barriers to competition, and towards factor-market impediments to resource flows. Identifying abnormal returns as rents to unique resource combinations, rather than market power, this perspective emphasizes the importance of specialized, difficult-to-imitate resources. The creation of such resources is seen as entrepreneurship: strategic management consists of properly identifying the existence and quality of resources, and in building product-market positions and contractual arrangements that most effectively utilize, maintain, and extend these resources. This perspective finds its greatest use in examining heterogeneity within industries, and in the discussion of 'relatedness' among diversified businesses. Nelson (this issue) discusses a recent version of this viewpoint, incorporating learning, that is called the 'dynamic capabilities' approach. Prahalad and Hamel's [1990] recent discussion of core competences is an expression of the resource-based view.

Ghemawat [1991] provides a new attempt at synthesis around the idea of *commitment*. His

view is that the persistence of strategies and of performance both stem from mechanisms which link and bind actions over time. He identifies lock-in, lock-out, lags, and inertia as the key irreversibilities at work and reinterprets a great deal of strategic doctrine in terms of the selection and management of commitments.

In summary, the single most significant impact of economics in strategic management has been to radically alter explanations of success. Where the traditional frameworks had success follow leadership, clarity of purpose, and a general notion of 'fit' between the enterprise and its environment, the new framework focused on the impediments to the elimination of abnormal returns. Depending upon the framework employed, success is now seen as sustained by mobility barriers, entry barriers, market preemption, asset specificity, learning, ambiguity, tacit knowledge, nonimitable resources and skills, the sharing of core competences, and commitment. That 'fit' was correlated with success can be argued, that it is causal cannot be. The fit argument lies in the long line of work that Porter (this issue) describes as a continuing search for causal explanation. Teaching frameworks that suggest the importance of fit are correct so far as they go, but it is the new economic frameworks which establish the causal linkages. That has been learned from the pressure of asking questions from an economics perspective.

The changing nature of economics

The economist's neoclassical model of the firm, enshrined in textbooks, was a smoothly running machine in a world without secrets, without frictions or uncertainty, and without a temporal dimension. That such a theory, so obviously divorced from the most elementary conditions of real firms, should continue to be taught in most business schools as the 'theory of the firm' is a truly amazing victory of doctrine over reality. This era may, however, finally be coming to an end as the cumulative impact of new insights take their toll. During the past 30 years, and especially during the last 20 years, at least five substantial monkey wrenches have been thrown into what was a smoothly running machine. They are called *uncertainty, information asymmetry, bounded rationality, opportunism,* and *asset specificity*. Each of these phenomena, taken alone,

---

[16] This argument can be couched in strict equilibrium terms by introducing strategy-specific assets or other sources of first-mover advantage.

violate crucial axioms in the neoclassical model. In various combinations they are the essential ingredients of new subfields within economics. Transaction cost economics rests primarily on the conjunction of bounded rationality, asset specificity, and opportunism. Agency theory rests on the combination of opportunism and information asymmetry. The new game-theoretic industrial organization derives much of its punch from asymmetries in information and/or in the timing of irreversible expenditures (asset specificity). The evolutionary theory of the firm and of technological change rests chiefly on uncertainty and bounded rationality. Each of these new subfields has generated insights and research themes that are important to strategic management. Each is briefly treated in turn.

Transaction cost economics

Of all the new subfields of economics, the transactions cost branch of organizational economics has the greatest affinity with strategic management. The links derive, in part, from common interests in organizational form, including a shared concern with the Chandler–Williamson M-form hypothesis. They also derive from a common intellectual style which legitimizes inquiry into the reasons for specific institutional details. The clinical studies conducted by strategy researchers and business historians are grist for the transaction cost mill. A theory which seeks to explain why one particular clause appears in a contract is clearly of great interest to strategic management scholars, who have a definite taste for disaggregation.[17]

For many economists, the assumption of unlimitedly rational actors is the defining characteristic of their field. Consequently, transaction cost economics, which follows Simon in positing bounded rationality, has had a difficult uphill struggle for recognition and acceptance. The subfield got its start in the mid-1970s as some economists, building on Coase's (1937) seminal work, began to systematically probe questions of firm boundaries and internal organization. Williamson (1975) was the chief architect of a framework that explored the limits or boundaries of both markets and business firms as arrange-

ments for conducting economic activity. His basic point was that transactions should take place in that regime which best economizes on the costs imposed by bounded rationality and opportunism. This framework was explicitly comparative (the relative efficiencies of markets and hierarchies were exposed) and enabled economists for the first time to say something about the *efficiency* properties of different organizational forms. (Previously economists had commonly sought and found monopoly explanations for complex forms of business organization; efficiency explanations were ignored or denigrated.) In addition to comparing markets and hierarchies, transaction cost researchers also began to look at questions of internal structure and the manner in which specific decisions and actions were taken. In particular, the Chandler–Williamson M-form hypothesis raised important issues relating to corporate control. These ideas began to achieve wider acceptance after being supported in a number of empirical studies.[18]

Within strategic management, transaction cost economics is the ground where economic thinking, strategy, and organizational theory meet. Because of its focus on institutional detail, rather than mathematical display, it has a broader audience among noneconomists than other branches of organizational economics. During the 1980s, a considerable amount of work was done in applying the transaction cost framework to issues in organizational structure. In particular, research has been carried out on vertical supply arrangements in a number of industries,[19] the structure of multinational firms (Buckley and Casson, 1976; Teece, 1981; Kogut, 1988), sales force organization (Anderson and Schmittlein, 1984), joint ventures (Hennart, 1988; Pisano, 1990), and franchising (Klein, 1980). Williamson [this issue] provides a useful review of additional applications of interest to strategic management.

---

[17] See, for example, Joskow's [1988] treatment of price-adjustment clauses in long-term coal contracts.

[18] Armour and Teece [1978] demonstrated returns to the adoption of the M-form as well as showing eventual dissipation of excess returns through imitation; Monteverde and Teece [1982] established that specific assets affected the vertical structure of organizations.
[19] Early contributions were Monteverde and Teece's [1982] study of auto components and Masten's [1988] study of aerospace.

Agency theory

Agency theory concerns the design of incentive agreements and the allocation of decision rights among individuals with conflicting preferences or interests. Although it deals with the employment transaction, agency theory is not compatible with transaction cost theory. Whereas transaction cost economics begins with the assertion that one cannot write enforceable contracts that cover all contingencies, agency theorists make no such presumption, and instead seek the optimal form of such a contract.

Agency theory has developed in two branches. The *principal-agent* literature is chiefly concerned with the design of optimal incentive contracts between principals and their employees or agents. Principal-agent economics is largely mathematical in form and relatively inaccessible to those who have not made investments in its special technology. The standard problem has the agent shirking unless rewards can be properly conditioned on informative signals about effort. The interesting aspect of the problem is that both parties suffer if good measures are not available. A version of the problem that links with strategic management concerns project selection and the design of incentives so that agents will not distort the capital budgeting process.

The second *corporate control* branch of the agency literature is less technical and is concerned with the design of the financial claims and overall governance structure of the firm. It is this branch which is most significant to strategic management. The corporate control hypothesis most familiar to strategic management is Jensen's (1986) 'free cash flow' theory of leverage and takeovers. According to Jensen, in many firms, managers have inappropriately directed free cash flow towards wasteful investments or uses. Two cures to this problem have been proposed: use of high levels of debt to commit managements to payouts and hostile takeovers, which put new management teams in place. What should strike strategic management scholars is that BCG offered precisely this diagnosis for many diversified firms in the early 1970s. According to BCG, most firms mismanaged their portfolios, misusing the funds generated by mature cash-rich businesses ('cows'), usually by continuing to reinvest long after growth opportunities had evaporated.

The corporate control perspective provides a valuable framework for strategic management research. By recognizing the existence of 'bad' management, identifying remedial instruments, and emphasizing the importance of proper incentive arrangements, it takes a more normative stand than most other subfields of economics. However, scholars working in this area also have the tendency to see all managerial problems as due to incorrect incentives—a tautology for a perspective which assumes away any other sources of dysfunction (e.g. capital markets problems like those discussed by Shleifer and Vishny in this issue, managerial beliefs about cause and effect, management skills in coordination, and the presence or lack of character and self-control).

Game-theory and the new IO

Three of the papers in this special issue deal with implications of game theory for strategic management, so our remarks here will be brief. Mathematical game theory was invented by von Neumann and Morgenstern (1944) and Nash (1950). However, little progress was made in developing economic applications until the late 1970s. It was probably Spence's (1974) work on market signalling that sparked the modern interest of economists and it was Stanford's 'gang of four,' Kreps, Milgrom, Roberts and Wilson, (1982), who codified the treatment of sequential games with imperfect information.[20]

Modern game theory raises deep questions about the nature of rational behavior. The idea that a rational individual is one who maximizes utility in the face of available information is simply not sufficient to generate 'sensible' equilibria in many noncooperative games with asymmetric information. To obtain 'sensible' equilibria, actors must be assigned beliefs about what others' beliefs will be in the event of irrational acts. Research into the technical and philosophical foundations of game theory has, at present, little to do directly with strategic management, but much to do with the future of economics as the science of 'rational' behavior.

Game theory as applied to industrial organization has two basic themes of most interest to strategic management: commitment strategies

---

[20] Much of the technical foundation they used had been laid by Selten [1965] and Harsanyi [1967].

and reputations. Commitment, as Ghemawat (1991) emphasizes, can be seen as central to strategy. Among the commitment games that have been analyzed are those involving investment in specific assets and excess capacity, research and development with and without spillovers, horizontal merger, and financial structure. Reputations arise in games where a firm or actor can have various 'types' and others must form beliefs about which type is the true one. Thus, for example, a customer's belief (probability) that a seller is of the 'honest' type constitutes the seller's reputation and that reputation can be lost if the seller behaves so as to change the customer's beliefs. Reputations can also describe relationships within the firm, and the collection of employee beliefs and reputations can be called its 'culture.' Given the competitive importance of external reputations, the efficiency properties of internal reputations, and the relative silence of game theorists about how various equilibria are actually achieved, there is clearly much room for contributions, including those from strategic management research.

Evolutionary economics

There has been a long-standing analogy drawn between biological competition (and resulting evolution) and economic competition, with both fields often pointing towards the other to ground ideas. Making the analogy concrete, however, has largely been the work of Nelson and Winter (1982), who married the concepts of tacit knowledge and routines to the dynamics of Schumpeterian competition. In their framework, firms compete primarily through a struggle to improve or innovate. In this struggle, firms grope towards better methods with only a partial understanding of the causal structure of their own capabilities and of the technological opportunity set. Key to their view is the idea that organizational capacities are based on routines which are not explicitly comprehended, but which are developed and bettered with repetition and practice. This micro-link to learning-by-doing means that the current capability of the firm is a function of history, making it impossible to simply copy best practice even when it is observed.

Because evolutionary economics posits a firm which cannot change its strategy or its structure

easily or quickly, the field has a very close affinity to population ecology views in organization theory. Researchers interested in the evolution of populations tend to work in the sociology tradition, while those more interested in the evolution of firm capabilities and technical progress tend to work in the economics tradition. Both frameworks challenge the naive view that firms can change strategies easily, or that such changes will even matter when attempted and made.

The changing climate within business schools

Business schools have transformed themselves profoundly over the past 30 years. Business schools and their faculty have moved from collecting and transmitting best current practice to developing and communicating theoretical understandings of phenomena connected with management, principally, the management of complex business firms. This transformation, which occurred for larger reasons, has influenced the strategy field and its connection to economics in important ways. There are several reasons why that transformation has occurred: the impetus of the Ford Foundation and Carnegie Foundation; university hiring and promotion practices, the rise of consulting firms as repositories of best practice, and the relative proximity of economics departments. Without these changes collectively, the field as we know it would be different, and economics involvement in strategy would have been less.

In the late fifties, the so-called Gordon and Howell (1959), and the Pierson (1959) reports were published, both critiquing the business schools of their day. The criticisms were many and the changes they prompted were extensive, but one of the most far-reaching recommendations was that business schools needed to be infused with rigor, methods, and content of basic disciplines: mathematics, economics, sociology, and psychology. This recommendation was avidly followed, with the result that a good many economists, psychologists, and others trained soley in the basic social science disciplines found employment in business schools alongside traditional, professionally-oriented faculty members. The traditional faculty found its scholarship in studying business firms, identifying the best practice they could find, and transmitting what they learned in the classroom, typically through a case, and the occasional published article. Along the way such faculties were frequently cast in the role of consultants to practicing business managers and many found greater financial reward in such work than they did from their scholarship alone. The new, discipline-based faculty on the other hand found their scholarship inside the academy, in the writings of others similarly placed, and in advancing the theory of their field, often without resort to practice and application of what they learned. Their minds and rewards were concentrated on what they produced inside the academy. Set in motion was a process that retired practice-based scholars in favor of discipline-based ones.

In time, probably longer than anticipated, the discipline based preference in hiring and promotion led to a stronger and stronger presence of discipline based scholars, including economists. Indeed, some newer business schools and some older ones as well, were organized with the economics departments as part of their faculty. As business schools became more discipline based, their standards for hiring and promotion came into alignment with the social sciences. The primary measure of excellence became publication in discipline-based journals and acceptance by the community of discipline-based scholars, rather than relevance to practice or contributions to professional education. Discipline-based scholars not only earned internal rewards more easily, they also typically lacked the cushion of consultation that would otherwise allow a greater adaptation to the special circumstances of professional schools. This self reinforcing cycle is still present today.

Throughout most of this period very high growth rates characterized business schools, as they moved from granting about 12,000 to over 70,000 MBA degrees per year, and to many more schools offering the MBA. Well-trained faculties in specialty areas such as marketing, finance, accounting, and other functions were in short supply, especially in the earlier years of greatest growth. To fuel expansion it was a short step to hire disciplined based faculties directly, and worry about their adaptation to applications in business firms later. Some made the transition, some did not, but many who did retained an allegiance to their base disciplines that included seeking publication reputations, not in the field in which they were to profess, but in the

basic discipline in which the faculty member had been trained.

In the world of business, more and more large firms began to create their own management development programs, aimed at filling the gap between the increasingly theoretical MBA education and the needs of practice. In addition, consulting firms grew in scope and sophistication. In many functional areas, including management and strategy, specialist consulting firms replaced business schools as repositories of best practice.

These factors led to an increased proportion of business school faculties either trained in economics directly, or importantly influenced by the standards common to discipline based scholars. Unforeseen by Gordon, Howell, and Pierson was the changing character of economics, and other social sciences. Less and less concerned with empiricism, economics became increasingly concerned with working out the internal logic of its theoretical structure and less and less concerned with describing real institutions. This trend continues today, with 'advanced' departments of economics offering Ph. D. programs in which price-theory is considered applied and not even covered during the first year of study.

These changes in business schools forced those interested in strategic management to 'take sides,' and adopt a discipline. Early on, the typical faculty member in strategic management (then called business policy) was recruited from those with experience and high rank in a functional area (e.g. marketing). The switch required was to that of the total enterprise and its general management function. The increased discipline base of business schools made this switch more difficult, and many schools began to hire young faculties and expect them to move up through the ranks on the merit of work done in strategy. To move through the system in this 'new' field was especially difficult, as it tended to lack the infrastructure peculiar to promotion needs: patrons, senior faculties who had been through the system; journals, venues for exchange of views. Additionally, it had a case-based tradition of research increasingly shunned by the academy. Consequently, groups interested in general management and strategy began to take either organization theory or economics as their base discipline.

Throughout the 1970s it appeared that organization theory was the discipline of choice for strategy groups. However, this balance was reversed in the 1980s, largely due to the success of Porter's approach to strategy. While some schools and their strategy faculty retained an essentially behaviorally focused group, many others moved to economics based views. Like economics itself, economic-based strategy groups now also differentiate themselves on their commitment to mathematical modeling vs. verbal reasoning and their interest in theory vs. empiricism. Within the behavioral groups, the split is chiefly between those following organization theory and those taking a managerial process view of strategic management.

Which group has the better idea? Who will dominate? That remains to be seen, but if what the top research-oriented (i.e. Stanford, Northwestern, Chicago, Berkeley, etc.) schools are doing now is any guide you have to bet on those emphasizing contribution of economics, if not total reliance on economists. If, on the other hand, the top European schools or practice is your guide, if what managers listen to makes a difference, those who combine a modicum of economics with a focus on managerial process are clear winners. No matter what you believe will be the outcome of this contest, economics has clearly infused and informed strategic management, not only by the power of its theory to yield insights, but by the transformation of the business school host, and the evolution of strategic management as a field.

However, from the viewpoint of strategic management we see a danger in these trends. We advocate a balanced view of the field, perhaps tipped slightly in favor of tests of theoretical constructs by practice and application. If the balance, as it has at some schools, goes too far toward theory or toward a single discipline base such as economics, there is no counterweight from practice and application likely in either research or teaching. Likewise, if the balance tips too far toward managerial process or even best practice, as it has at other schools, there are no theoretical constructions to accumulate and build for the good of the field. Either unbalanced outcome is bad. In our view, balance requires both theory and application, in their fullest and finest representations, in our research, in our teaching, and in our faculty. That such balanced views represented by portfolios of scholars, some at the discipline end, others at

the practice end, do not exist, especially at our best schools, is a sad comment on the lack of administrative leadership and faculty understanding that exists about strategic management, its content, and its challenges. Simon's (1967) description of the problem of running a professional school has special relevance to strategic management:

> Organizing a professional school. . .is very much like mixing oil with water. . .Left to themselves, oil and water will separate again [p. 16]. . .A professional school administration—the dean and senior faculty—have an unceasing task of fighting the natural increase of entropy, of preventing the system from moving toward the equilibrium it would otherwise seek. When the school is no longer able, by continual activity, to maintain the gradients that differentiate it from the environment, it reaches that equilibrium with the world which is death. In the professional school, 'death' means mediocrity and inability to fulfill its special functions [p. 12].

Unfortunately, strategic management is too often inhabited (inhibited?) by those who see no need for (fear?) the balance we advocate.

THE FUTURE OF THE CONNECTION BETWEEN ECONOMICS AND STRATEGIC MANAGEMENT

We believe that strategic management has clearly profited from the infusion of economic thinking. There is no question that the presumption of equilibrium and the specification of alert rivals, rather than an amorphous 'environment,' has generated valuable new frameworks, new insights, and greatly sharpened thinking among strategy scholars. Nevertheless, it is vital also to recognize that this infusion has come only after the weakening of orthodoxy within economics. For decades economics impeded research into strategy by committing its intellectual capital and influence to static analysis, an almost exclusive focus on price competition, the suppression of entrepreneurship, a too stylized treatment of markets, hyper-rationality assumptions, and the cavalier treatment of know-how. Had orthodoxy weakened sooner, strategy would have had the benefits from useful economic thinking earlier. That orthodoxy weakened was perhaps partially a result of research in strategic management.

Economics has been chiefly concerned with the performance of markets in the allocation and coordination of resources. By contrast, strategic management is about coordination and resource allocation *inside the firm*. This distinction is crucial and explains why so much of economics is not readily applicable to the study of strategy, and why strategy can inform economics as much as economics can inform strategy. Twenty-five years ago economists, asked how a firm should be managed, would have (and did) argue that subunits should be measured on profit, they should transfer products, services, and capital to one another at marginal cost, and the more internal competition the better. Today, we know that this advice, to run a firm as if it were a set of markets, is ill-founded. Firms replace markets when *nonmarket* means of coordination and commitment are superior. Splendid progress has been made in defining the efficient boundaries of firms—where markets fail and hierarchies are superior—but there are limits to building a theory of management and strategy around market failures. It is up to strategy scholars to flesh out the inverse approach, supplying a coherent theory of effective internal coordination and resource allocation, of entrepreneurship and technical progress, so that markets can be identified as beginning where organizations fail.

The most interesting issue regards the future of the competitive strategy portion of strategic management. It is this subfield which has turned most wholeheartedly towards the use of economic reasoning and models. If the trend continues, does the competitive strategy subject matter have an independent future, or will it become just a branch of applied economics? There are two reasons for concern about this. The first is parochial: The field's most elementary wisdom suggests that competing head on with economics departments in their own domain is a losing strategy. The second has to do with the internal integrity of the field. To split off part of a problem for separate inquiry is to presume its independence from other elements of the problem. Yet, the sources of success and failure in firms, and therefore the proper concerns of general management, remain an issue of debate (see, for example, Williamson's argument in this issue). It would be a great loss if the study of competitive strategy became divorced from the other elements of strategic management.

We believe that competitive strategy will remain an integral part of strategic management and that its connection with economics will evolve and take on new forms in the future. We believe that fears of 'absorption' will not be realized for these reasons: (1) strategy is not 'applied' economics; (2) economists will not learn about business; (3) microeconomics is a collage and apparently cannot provide a coherent integrated theory of the firm or of management; (4) that which is strategically critical changes over time; and (5) organizational capability, not market exchange, may increasingly assume center stage in strategic management research.

Strategy is not applied microeconomics

We assert this because it is patently clear that skilled practitioners do not develop or implement business or corporate strategies by 'applying' economics or any other discipline. There are economists who argue that this only proves that practitioners are not very skilled after all, but such a response is neither social science, which studies natural order, nor good professionalism, which seeks to solve, rather than ignore, the expressed problems of practitioners. We do not deny that economic analysis may be useful to a strategist, but so may demography, law, social psychology, and an understanding of political trends, as well as an appreciation for product design, process technology, and the physical sciences underlying the business. Part of any competitive strategy can be tested against known economic theory and models of competitive reaction; but most business strategies also contain implicit hypotheses concerning organizational behavior, political behavior, technological relationships and trends, and rely on judgements about the perceptions, feelings, and beliefs of customers, suppliers, employees, and competitors. Competitive strategy is integrative—not just because it integrates business functions and helps create patterns of consistent, reinforcing decisions, but also because creating and evaluating business strategies requires insights and judgements based on a broad variety of knowledge bases.

Economists will not learn about business

Economics has a strong doctrinal component that resists displacement. Strategic management, by its nature and audience, is pragmatic. If certain approaches do not shed light on business practices, or if practitioners deny their validity, the proclivity of the strategy field will be, and should be, to reject them. In addition, we believe that economics will not delve very deeply into business practices to generate new theory. This belief is based on judgements about long-term trends in academia. As Simon (1969: 56) commented on academic tastes, 'why would anyone in a university stoop to teach or learn about designing machines or planning market strategies when he could concern himself with solid-state physics? The answer has been clear: he usually wouldn't.' Having become as mathematical as physics, and more axiomatic, mainstream economics will not learn enough about business and management to challenge strategic management in its domain. Thus, for example, as industrial organization increasingly becomes infatuated with formal modeling (it didn't until the mid-1970s), it may lose the rich empirical base that made it possible for the Mason/Bain tradition to undergird Porter's work. Put differently, industrial organization may have already made its important contributions to strategy.

An example may help illustrate the very real gap between theory, economic or otherwise, and the need to internalize a vast amount of information pertaining to business practice. A case instructor used to ask 'What are this company's strengths?' Economic reasoning has now helped us understand that what we may mean to ask is 'What firm-specific, nonimitable resources or sustainable market positions are presently under-utilized?' The restatement helps: it is more precise, it provides a definition of 'strength,' and it defends against critics who insist on a discipline base behind university education. But are economists better equipped to answer the question? We suspect not. It is probably much easier to teach these economic concepts to a generalist than it is to teach economists about business.

Microeconomics is a collage

The upshot of all the ferment in economics is that with regard to issues of most concern to strategic management, the neoclassical theory of the firm is no longer a contender. However, there is no new 'theory of the firm' to replace it. Instead, there are areas of inquiry characterized by the assumptions that are acceptable in building models and by the phenomena to be explained. There is excitement and vitality in the new economics because the range of phenomena that can be explained has been dramatically enlarged. However, there is also confusion over the loss of the old determinism. With the old theory of the firm, everyone knew how to price—you just set marginal revenue equal to marginal cost. But now price can signal quality to customers and price may tell a potential entrant something about the profits to be made. With the old theory of the firm, a topic like 'corporate culture' was outside the realm of consideration, and classified with faith healing and voodoo. But now it is clear that there can be many types of social equilibria among the actors within a firm, with the equilibria depending upon sets of beliefs and history, and that these equilibria have radically different efficiency properties. More generally, it used to be that given a technology, the neoclassical theory delivered a prediction about the allocation of resources. But now one has to specify the technology, the information sets of the actors, including their beliefs, and the order of play and one still usually obtains many possible equilibria. The descriptive power of the new economics has been paid for by the loss of determinism.

The limitation of the new microeconomics is that it *explains* rather than *predicts*. That is, it tends to consist of a series of models, each of which has been purposefully engineered to capture and illustrate a particular phenomena. Models have been constructed to examine markets with consumer loyalty, experience effects, producer reputations, complex signaling games, the strategic use of debt, multimarket deterrence, and causal ambiguity. In addition, models have been used to explore joint ventures, venture capital, vertical integration, the appropriability of intellectual capital, governance structures, and many other phenomena. All of this has been informative and provides strategic management with a panoply of useful insights. However, these phenomena have not been *deduced* from these models or from some general theory. Rather, each of these many models has been carefully engineered to deliver the phenomena being studied. The contribution of a good modeler is in finding the least aggressive assumptions that enable the phenomena in question. Consequently, the new microeconomics is essentially a formal language for expressing knowledge elsewhere obtained. Camerer (this issue) calls this the 'collage problem.'

The 'collage problem' is simply that formal theorizing has collapsed to examples. Consequently, part of the intellectual structure of the new microeconomics is evolving to look more like strategic management. Any scholar working in strategic management must be aware of the traditional economist's normal reaction to most of the work in our field: 'The subject is interesting, but there is no tight theory—it looks like a bunch of lists.' But the new economics, taken as a whole, is a 'bunch of lists.' More precisely, it delivers a large number of tightly reasoned submodels, but no strong guidance as to which will be important in a particular situation.

The new microeconomics is still a developing field and in the future we will see further elaboration of existing frameworks. But we can also confidently expect to hear the clangs of new monkey wrenches being thrown. One already in the air is the strong evidence for persistent biases in human judgement and decision-making. Another which can be anticipated is the fact that managers not only have different information sets, they also differ in their beliefs[21] and in their understandings of the causal mechanisms they face. A third, emphasized by Nelson (this issue), is that firms do not apprehend complete sets of alternatives, but grope forward with but limited understanding of their own capabilities and the opportunities they face.

The implications of this research style for strategic management are several. First, it should be clear that knowledge about what phenomena need be studied is outside its scope. Hence, there remains a central and important role for scholars who identify phenomena worth studying. For example, it is up to strategy and management scholars to convince financial economists that most firms really do budget as if they were equity constrained—only then will useful models of this phenomena appear. Similarly, it is up to strategy researchers to reveal the patterns of global

interdependence and competition—economic modeling will come after the fact. Second, the economist's approach to these phenomena is to show their existence; yet this is rarely sufficient to help in practical strategy work. Yes, it is useful to know that reputational equilibria are enabled when product quality cannot be determined by inspection and warranties are unavailable, but this is of little help to a firm that wants to know whether or not its reputation in the U.S. for workshirts will help it in Eastern Europe. It is up to strategy (or marketing, or other functional fields) to develop the measures, tools, and methods to help in specific situations. Third, each of the economist's models tends to be minimal and independent of the others—they do not integrate into any cohesive theory of the firm. For example, game theorists can model entry deterrence as based on reputations for toughness, as flowing from asset specificity, as responsive to uncertainty about post entry performance, and find that entry is encouraged by opportunities for learning, by the presence of technology options, and by economics of scope involving related products. However, these separate models provide little or no information about which of these phenomena, if any, will predominate in a specific situation, nor do they help much in determining even the rough magnitudes of the wealth impacts each of these phenomena can induce. This lack of specificity not only hinders empirical testing, it renders the professional utility of these concepts dramatically smaller than model builders imagine.

What is strategic changes over time

What is strategic changes as time and discovery alter the basis of competition. These changes arise, in part, because of technological, legal, social, and political changes. They also arise because education and research disseminate knowledge, reducing the degree to which a particular issue can be a source of advantage. The rise of Japanese competition, for example, has substantially altered the research agenda for strategy scholars. By contrast, little or no accommodation to such changes is seen in microeconomics. Business school deans like to argue that their research programs, though abstract, constitute the practices of tomorrow. The opposite is closer to the truth. Yesterday's

---

[21] A belief is a prior probability assignment to an unobservable variable. Interesting beliefs are those which affect decisions yet which are not significantly updated by events.

business strategies are the subject of today's research in strategic management (e.g. takeovers and LBOs, Kaizen), and economics is just beginning to theorize about phenomena that developed half a century ago (e.g. separation of ownership and control, the diversified firm, national advantages). Today's strategic issues (e.g. the growth of new 'network' empires in Europe and Asia, time-based competition) are only dimly perceived by anyone within the academy.

Advantage may be internal

Both theoretical and empirical research into the sources of advantage has begun to point to organizational capabilities, rather than product-market positions or tactics, as the enduring sources of advantage. If this is so, our investigations will increasingly take us into domains where economics is presently at its weakest— inside the firm. There are bids by transaction cost economics and agency theory to become 'organization science,' and we can expect new and important insights from these fields. However, their comparative advantage is the analysis of individual responses to incentives. If behavior turns on interacting expectations, beliefs and routines, and if diagnosis, problem solving, and the coordination of knowledge rather than effort are central, then economic views of organization will continue to be useful, but also will be only one part of the story.

For this set of reasons we believe the boundaries between strategic management and economics will remain distinct, but proximate and somtimes fuzzy. But the applied nature of strategic management and its extensive scope will require intersection with theory from other social science disciplines as well.

A GUIDE TO THE PAPERS

The eight papers in this special issue each raise or address issues which lie in the terrain between economics and strategic management. The authors are leaders in their fields: Colin Camerer in competitive strategy and the experimental economics of games, Alfred Chandler in business history as well as corporate strategy and structure,

Richard Nelson in the economics of technological change, Michael Porter in competitive strategy, Garth Saloner in game-theoretic industrial organization economics, Andrei Shleifer and Robert Vishny in financial economics and corporate control, and Oliver Williamson in organizational economics. The commentator on Camerer's and Saloner's papers, Steven Postrel, is a contributor to both game-theory and competitive strategy.

It is worth emphasizing that each author was assigned the topic for his paper by the editors. The topics were selected to reveal the state-of-the-art in the connection between economics and strategic management. The happy consequence of having this uniquely talented group respond to our requests is that we obtain an unobstructed view of our subject. Because each author has been involved in the development of the concepts and theories they use and describe, there are no problems of misinterpretation, lack of comprehension, or misinformation.

The very heartening aspect of these papers, especially those written by discipline-based economists, is that no one questions the importance of the issues that are raised in strategic management. Twenty five years ago there would have been no such agreement. Furthermore, there is general agreement that neoclassical microeconomics is woefully inadequate to deal with important issues of strategy. The fracture lines begin to appear over which of the newer economic subfields supply the greatest insights into strategic advantage. Not surprisingly, game theorists tend to bet on game theory. . .and so on.

The alert reader will discern three basic frameworks in these papers (some papers use more than one). The first stresses the centrality of avoiding direct competition and has no great problem with fairly strong rationality and equilibrium assumptions (e.g. Saloner and Camerer, as well as Porter's treatment of the structure of advantage). The second framework stresses the importance of governance and of getting the match right between the technologies to be managed and the system of ownership, administration, planning, and control. The writers using this framework (Chandler, Shleifer and Vishny, and Williamson) mix a static model of efficient arrangement with the willingness to see real firms as making mistakes and learning from them. The third framework stresses the centrality of innovation, learning, and discovery in shaping advantage (e.g. Nelson, as well as Porter's treatment of the origin of advantage).

The papers

The development and proper scope and structure of the diversified firm is one of the central issues in our field. Alfred Chandler's original study of this subject was a key stimulus for the development of a scholarly research tradition in strategic management. In this paper he revisits the question, using the events of the last 25 years to inform a new view of the administrative limits of corporate headquarters units. In particular, he examines how continued growth forced the standard M-form organizations of the immediate post-WWII era to a three-tiered structure, and how prosperity (and hubris) led to diversification strategies that overtaxed these structures.

The basic conceptual scheme Chandler brings to this paper is that developed in *Scale and Scope*, (Chandler, 1990). Heavy and technologically complex industries are characterized by inexhaustible technical economies of scale and scope, but the ability of firms to exploit these economies is limited by their entrepreneurial skill in guiding complementary investments and their administrative skill in coordination of the resultant operations. Thus, it is the managerial capabilities of the corporate office that ultimately determines the size, scope, and success of the enterprise. In this paper, Chandler uses Goold and Campbell's [1987] topology of headquarters styles, identifying those using purely financial controls as essentially administrative and those using strategic planning or strategic control methods as performing some entrepreneurial functions. He analyzes the recent histories of British and U.S. firms and concludes that multibusiness companies employing financial controls have been successful only when they have restricted their ownership to firms in services and in simply mature industries. Where industries are mature, but complex and require substantial investments, headquarters units must engage in strategic control. And where complexity is combined with technological advance, headquarters offices must supply entrepreneurially oriented strategic planning.

As in Chandler's other works, many of his conclusions fit easily within an 'economizing' institutional economics framework. Thus, for example, the fact that advancing technology increases the need for headquarters strategic planning can be seen as induced by the costs of haggling and hold-up that would be borne were the divisions to plan on a decentralized basis. However, Chandler's essential contributions go far beyond this static picture. In reaching his conclusions, Chandler uses the methods he has perfected: the historical analysis of challenge and managerial response. In this paper we do not see firms 'applying' concepts or somehow driven to the efficient response by selection pressure. Instead, we see management getting it wrong, suffering consequences, struggling to understand the nature of their dilemmas, and then, perhaps, creating new structures, policies, and methods to cope with, and perhaps transcend, the problem. Chandler's real message is not that one must get the headquarters design just right, but that those firms which dominate their industries are those which have shown the most resilience and insight in responding to the challenges that their own growth and expansion have generated.

Andrei Shleifer and Robert Vishny investigate some of the same terrain as Chandler—the wave of unrelated diversification followed by a wave of restructuring and retrenchment. Shleifer and Vishny review the available evidence and conclude that unrelated diversification did not improve economic efficiency. Unrelated diversification was carried too far in the 1960s, they argue, because of antitrust enforcement as well as agency problems connected with multidivisional structures: 'The M-form begot the monster of the conglomerate.'

What makes Shleifer and Vishny's paper especially interesting is their treatment of the efficient market hypothesis. Since the stock market responded to conglomerate acquisitions in the 1960s, many researchers have concluded that they created value. This paper argues that the stock market was merely reflecting the *mistaken* beliefs of a majority of investors. Drawing on their research on arbitrage and market fads, Shleifer and Vishny contend that fads persist because it is too costly for the best-informed investors to bet against them.

The boom and bust of conglomerates is a convenient vehicle for this argument, but its implications extend well beyond the issue of conglomeration. Event studies, using stock market residuals, have become a standard way of investigating the 'value' of various policies and strategies. If these studies do not really measure value, but only what investors think is value, then this whole methodology may be significantly weakened.

Richard Nelson's paper addresses the question of how and why firms differ, an extremely deep question in strategic management. If different firms display different levels of performance or competitive advantage, despite competition, then the reasons for these persistent differences reveal the basis of competitive advantage. In this paper Nelson tackles the especially difficult version of this question: how *discretionary* considerations—such as the strategies and structures adopted by management—help underpin such differences. Although the existence of discretionary differences is comfortable for many students of strategy, it is at odds with neoclassical microeconomic theory, which Nelson sees as 'badly limited' and hence unhelpful to the field of strategy. It is badly limited because it is often too abstract and rarely deals with economic aggregates smaller than the industry, and because economists see the economic problem as basically about getting private incentives right, not about identifying the best things to do, and how to do them. In this regard, Nelson and Williamson see eye-to-eye. Neither has much time (nor do the editors of this special issue) for the long, but gradually eroding tradition in economics which treats firms as black boxes.

Nelson stresses that if economics is to inform fundamental questions in strategy, economists must break away from the assumption of clear and obvious choice sets and correct understanding of consequences of making various choices. He offers a Schumpeterian perspective, one which stresses the importance of fundamental uncertainty, perceptions about feasible paths, and trial and error learning, as a better way to come to grips with firms and firm behavior. More particularly, he argues that it is the differences among firms in their abilities to generate and profit from innovation, not differences in command over particular technologies, that are the basis of durable, difficult-to-imitate differences in firm performance. It is the issue of firms' *capabilities to innovate* which the strategy and competitiveness literature ought to be more forthright in tackling.

Oliver Williamson's paper is a call to arms. The war is against the idea that strategizing is a source of competitive advantage, and in favor of stressing the importance of economizing. It argues that whereas the field of strategy should be concerned with first-order economizing ('rectangles'), it has imported doctrines from industrial organization economics which are focused on second-order economizing ('triangles'). Williamson contends that if strategic management is to unlock the sources of long-run competitive advantage, and if it is going to rely on economic thinking to assist it, then it ought not to rely so uncritically on economic perspectives which appeal to market power (strategies that restrict product competition) as the source of advantage. Rather, the field should develop more of an efficiency perspective—that being good at what you do and avoiding waste is more important than exploiting switching costs or playing oligopoly games.

Note that Williamson's *economizing* firm is miles away from Porter's *low-cost producer*; the economizer is not necessarily efficient at production, but in the broad range of business functions. For example, the economizer may be very efficient at managing the transition from design to production, or at tailoring products to local tastes. Williamson's position on this issue is at variance with the traditional (economic) assumption that firms are 'on their cost curves.' If firms are assumed to be technically efficient, the problem is simply to determine the level of output. Williamson, by contrast, sees the fundamental challenge as organizing and governing activities so as to eliminate waste.

Because transaction cost economics, which Williamson pioneered, is concerned with first-order economizing, he suggests that it has much to offer the field of strategy. (Of course, there are other approaches which focus on economizing too.) His paper goes on to identify several important insights from transaction cost theory which are relevant to strategy. Transaction costs are the costs of organizing the economic system. Internal structures, managerial control systems, and the positioning of the boundaries of the firm all impact transaction costs. Williamson outlines a framework which helps explain why these costs differ across organization forms and then shows how the framework applies to several issues in strategic management.

Michael Porter has played the key role in shaping the currently dominant perspective on competitive strategy. That perspective attempts to explain how a particular configuration of activities, resources, and industry characteristics combine to shield a firm's profits from rapid competitive erosion. In this paper Porter makes the point that the dominant perspective explains competitive success at a given point in time, solving what he labels the *cross-sectional problem*, but that the dynamic process by which firms perceive or attain superior market position, what he labels the time series or *longitudinal problem*, is much less developed. His paper attempts to suggest what we know and what we need to know to develop a theory of firm performance linked to managerial choice, initial conditions, and environmental circumstance.

Porter begins with what he labels the chain of causality (Figure 2 in his paper). In his cross-sectional explanation, success flows from advantage inherent in industry structure and relative position. Advantage, in turn, is due to the configuration of activities. The activities provide support to the configuration, in turn, because of drivers (i.e. activity-level sources of advantage). Backing up longitudinally, activity configurations and drivers arise from 'initial conditions' and managerial choices. In the paper he then moves even further back, noting that initial conditions are the result of past managerial choices, luck, and the nature and quality of the local (business) environment. One can, of course, then step back again, seeing the character of the local environment as due to the policy choices made by a variety of institutional leaders and natural physical endowments. This chain of causality map not only helps unify Porter's own theorizing on competitive strategy, it also clarifies the different levels at which explanation can be attempted or equilibrium assumptions applied.

Why do some managements make the right choices in selecting products, industries, and activity configurations? Porter reviews the degree to which game theory, commitment views (Ghemawat, 1991), and the resource-based theory of strategy can provide answers. Not surprisingly, none does the job, but we obtain insights about each approach along the way. Where, then, to turn? Porter's (1990) own current answer is luck and local environment. Drawing on his research in *The Competitive Advantage of Nations*, he argues that managerial insight does not spring up randomly, but is concentrated, in each industry, in certain locales. In those locations, clusters of competing and supporting firms have grown up which collectively embody a great deal of specialized know-how. One of the most intriguing ideas advanced here, one drawn from *The Competitive Advantage of Nations*, is that strength is frequently the fruit of adversity.

What seems to keep us from making better progress on understanding managerial choice? Porter suggests that a key missing element is a theory of action that is not rooted in choice, but which deals with creating new options and discovering new approaches. In this sense, he joins forces with Nelson who also calls for a model of search and discovery to help inform the discussion of innovation and change.

Three papers in this special issue address the connections between modern game theory and strategic management. Garth Saloner provides a viewpoint on the usefulness of game theoretic modeling in strategic management. His basically positive view is conditioned by two major cautions: there is no evidence of any real-world use of game theory by companies, and game theoretic approaches are 'too hard' to be applied to anything but very simple 'boiled down' models of reality. The second issue may, of course, be the reason for the first and it is interesting to speculate on what consequences would flow from the invention of a game theory 'engine' that quickly and clearly yielded the equilibria of very complex models.

Saloner's enthusiasm for game theoretic models survives these two considerations and is based on their necessity, the 'audit trail' they provide, their metaphorical value, and their growing importance in empirical research. Once you begin to consider the reactions of rivals to one another's moves, he argues, you are doing game analysis, and the current theory is simply the distilled wisdom about the most sensible way to do it. The great value of explicit modeling is the clear record of assumptions and logic—the audit trail—that permits others to verify and modify one's analysis. Saloner dismisses the use of game theory to calculate actual behavior, stressing instead the value of understanding why certain results obtain in certain situations and the possibility of novel insights. As work progresses, he argues, research will build up a mosaic of models, each providing insights about a particular aspect of strategic interaction. Game theory's contribution to strategic management will be the sum total of the insights this mosaic provides.

One of the most challenging questions Saloner tackles is the reasonableness of the rationality imputed to players in game theory. He points out that in many games, such as Cournot competition, the rationality required is not very great. However, in many modern game models, equilibria are based on quite complex considerations, straining the credulity of the rationality assumption. There is no escape, he suggests, from using judgement on this matter and notes that your own play in a game might be affected by whether your opponent was David Kreps, a fourth grader, an average undergraduate, or the CEO of a typical U.S. firm.

Colin Camerer also addresses the utility of game theory to strategic management. Like Saloner, Camerer is concerned with the sparseness of modern analysis, termed 'no fat' modeling, and with the fact that game analysis is hard. If neoclassical analysis is like eating with a fork, he analogizes, game theory is like using chopsticks. Game theory is not only hard, Camerer stresses, it is also too easy. That is, it is too easy to generate explanations for all sorts of behavior. This happens because behavior is not just determined by preferences, but also by the presence of hidden information.

The heart of Camerer's essay addresses the rationality assumption—is it too demanding to be reasonable? His own laboratory work on games shows that people do not arrive at strategies using the cognitive methods of the theorist. Consequently, theoretical equilibria are usually approached only after repeated play. Nonetheless, through processes of adaptation and/or evolution, theoretical equilibria are approached. Camerer also points out that the strict rationality assumptions of the theorist are sometimes only an analytical convenience; the same equilibria can often be justified with weaker assumptions, though the analysis is more difficult.

Despite these and other difficulties in living with game theory, Camerer favors welcoming it into the strategic management family. Like Saloner, he feels that it is the best way to look at interactions among alert rivals. In addition, Camerer sees opportunities to inform areas of interest to strategic management, such as the properties of collective resources (reputations and capabilities). Finally, he argues that the

problem of too many explanations and too many equilibria provides opportunities for good empirical work to point the way.

Steven Postrel's paper is a comment on Saloner's and Camerer's discussions of game theory and strategy, especially the 'Pandora's Box' problem that the theory has too few constraints on generating explanations of behavior. Using a humorous setting, Postrel shows how a game-theorist could build a model to rationalize unreasonable behavior. His point is that game theory is not really a theory of strategy but is only a methodology for analyzing games. Other than rationality, the substantive theory present in a model is in the assumptions, not in the mechanics.

These then are the papers offered in the special issue. All offer informed and interesting views, and we hope will in their own right inform the reader on boundary conditions, future challenges, and research opportunities that lie in considering economic reasoning on strategic management issues.

SUMMARY AND CONCLUSIONS

We have tried to show the relationship between economics and strategic management in this essay. It is more than some admit, and less than some would hope. We have tried to show that economics and strategic management are not the same thing, in research or in practice. We have tried to indicate that it is the new economics that offers the most promise, but it is old economics in the form of industrial organization that, thus far, has made the greatest contribution. There can be little question that the development of the strategic management field has benefited from the influence of economics, but the influence is not unidirectional either.

Where do we go from here? One trend that has recently emerged and deserves mention is the new attention to internal organization. Strategic management is increasingly concerned with understanding the administrative processes that select and coordinate the firm's activities. The capabilities of the firm, and the asset structures that accumulate, appear central to advantage and success. The assets that matter do not appear purely physical or separable. The conjunction of physical and intangible assets results from innovative managerial choice and action not easily duplicated. About such matters the new economics cited and discussed here, both in the papers, and this essay, are just beginning to have something to say. However, in this new and complex realm, economics will be only one of the logical systems in use. Where organizational relationships turn on exchange and on individual incentives, various economic approaches will have much to say. Where the coordination and accumulation of knowledge is key, and where patterns of belief and attitude are important, other disciplines will have more to say.

Along with the internal turn taken by research, comes increasing concern over dynamic explanation. Game-theory brings a fanatical attention to sequences of action and reaction, history provides stories of challenge and response, innovation is inherently dynamic, and so are the processes whereby skillful managers make sense of and respond to an evolving environment. In the more practice-oriented side of the field there is great interest in time-based competition and in the interplay between product-market strategy and the development of organizational capabilities.

More important than these trends in subject matter is the gradual enlargement of strategic management to include discipline-based scholars who share our interest in understanding the direction of enterprises. Caution in this regard is only reasonable. Strategic management scholars are small in number and struggle to maintain integration amongst frameworks and between theory and practice; most disciplines are populous and tend to compete, rather than cooperate, with other disciplines. Nonetheless, intellectual and social mechanisms must be found to make the very best of the discipline-based scholars welcome in strategic management. Their participation and *variety* are key to the long-run survival of our field.

REFERENCES

Anderson, E. and D. C. Schmittlein. 'Integration of the sales force: An empirical examination', *Rand Journal of Economics*, 15, 1984, pp. 385–395.

Ansoff, H. I. *Corporate Strategy*, McGraw-Hill, New York, 1965.

Armour, H. O. and D. J. Teece. 'Organizational structure and economic performance: A test of the multidivisional hypothesis', *Bell Journal of Economics*, 9, Spring 1978, pp. 106–122.

Barney J. B. 'Strategic factor markets: Expectations, luck, and business strategy', *Management Science*, 32, October 1986, pp. 1231–1241.

Biggadike, R. E. *Corporate Diversification: Entry, Strategy, and Performance*, Division of Research, Harvard Business School, 1979.

Boston Consulting Group. *Perspectives on Experience*, Boston Consulting Group, Boston, MA, 1968, 1970.

Boulding, W. and R. Staelin. 'Environment, market share, and market power', *Management Science*, 10, 1990, pp. 1160–1177.

Buckley, P. J. and M. Casson. *The Future of the Multinational Enterprise*, Macmillan, New York, 1976.

Caves, R. E. and M. E. Porter. 'From entry barriers to mobility barriers: Conjectural decisions and contrived deterrence to new competition', *Quarterly Journal of Economics*, 91, May 1977, pp. 241–261.

Chandler, A. D., Jr. *Strategy and Structure*, The MIT Press, Cambridge, MA, 1962.

Chandler, A. D., Jr. *Scale and Scope: The Dynamics of Industrial Capitalism*, Harvard University Press, Cambridge, MA, 1990.

Coase, R. H. 'The nature of the firm', *Economica*, 4, 1937, pp. 386–406.

Conner, K. R. 'A historical comparison of resource-based theory and five schools of thought within industrial organization economics: Do we have a new theory of the firm?' *Journal of Management*, 17, 1991, pp. 121–154.

Demsetz, H. 'Industry structure, market rivalry, and public policy', *Journal of Law and Economics*, 16, April 1973, pp. 1–9.

Fruhan, W. E., Jr. *The Fight for Competitive Advantage*, Division of Research, Harvard Business School, 1972.

Gale, B. T. 'Market share and rate of return', *Review of Economics and Statistics*, 54, (4), November 1972, pp. 412–423.

Ghemawat, P. *Commitment: The Dynamic of Strategy*, The Free Press, New York, 1991.

Goold, M. and A. Campbell. *Strategies and Styles: The Role of the Center in Diversified Corporations*, Basil Blackwell, Oxford, 1987.

Gordon, R. and J. Howell. *Higher Education for Business*, Columbia University Press, New York, 1959.

Grant, R. M. 'The resource-based theory of competitive advantage', *California Management Review*, 33, 1991, pp. 114–135.

Hansen, G. S. and B. Wernerfelt. 'Determinants of firm performance: The relative importance of economic and organizational factors', *Strategic Management Journal*, 10, September–October 1989, pp. 399–411.

Hatten, K. J. and D. E. Schendel. 'Heterogeneity within an industry', *Journal of Industrial Economics*, 26, December 1977, pp. 97–113.

Hatten, K. J., D. E. Schendel and A. C. Cooper. 'A strategic model of the U.S. brewing industry:

1952–1971', *American Management Journal*, **21**, 1978, pp. 592–610.

Harsanyi, J. 'Games with incomplete information played by 'Bayesian' Players. I: The basic model'. *Management Science*, **14**, 1967, pp. 159–182.

Hennart, J.-F. 'A transactions cost theory of equity joint ventures', *Strategic Management Journal*, **9**, 1988, pp. 361–374.

Imel, B. and P. Helmberger, 'Estimation of structure–profit relationships with application to the food processing sector'. *American Economic Review*, **62**, 1971, pp. 614–627.

Jacobson, R. 'What *really* determines business performance? Unobservable effects—The key to profitability'. *Management Science*, **9**, 1990, pp. 74–85.

Jensen, M. 'Agency costs of free cash flow, corporate finance, and takeovers'. *American Economic Review*, **76**, 1986, pp. 323–329.

Jensen, M. 'The eclipse of the public corporation'. *Harvard Business Review*, **67**, 1989, pp. 61–74.

Joskow, P. L. 'Price adjustment in long-term contracts: The case of coal'. *Journal of Law and Economics*, **31**, 1988, pp. 47–83.

Karnani, A. 'Generic competitive strategies', *Strategic Management Journal*, **5**, 1985, pp. 367–380.

Klein, B. 'Transaction cost determinants of 'unfair' contractual arrangements'. *American Economic Review*, **70**, 1980, pp. 356–362.

Kogut, B. 'Joint ventures: Theoretical and empirical perspectives', *Strategic Management Journal*, **9**, 1988, pp. 319–332.

Kreps, D., P. Milgrom, J. Roberts and R. Wilson. 'Rational cooperation in the finitely repeated prisoners' dilemma'. *Journal of Economic Theory*, **27**, 1982, pp. 245–252.

Learned, E. P., C. R. Christensen, K. R. Andrews and W. D. Guth. *Business Policy: Text and Cases*. Richard D. Irwin, Homewood, IL, 1965.

Lieberman, M. 'The learning curve and pricing in the chemical processing industries'. *Rand Journal of Economics*, **15**, 1984, pp. 213–228.

Lippman, S. A. and R. P. Rumelt. 'Uncertain imitability: An analysis of interfirm differences in efficiency under competition'. *Bell Journal of Economics*, **13**, 1982, pp. 418–438.

McGee, J. and H. Thomas. 'Strategic groups: Theory, research and taxonomy', *Strategic Management Journal*, 7, March–April 1986, pp. 141–160.

Masten, S. E. 'The organization of production: Evidence from the aerospace industry'. *Journal of Law, Economics, and Organization*, **4**, 1988, pp. 403–418.

Monteverde, K. and D. J. Teece. 'Supplier switching costs and vertical integration. *Bell Journal of Economics*, **13**, 1982, pp. 206–213.

Nash, J. 'The bargaining problem'. *Econometrica*, **18**, 1950, pp. 155–162.

Nelson, R. R. and S. G. Winter. *An Evolutionary Theory of Economic Change*, Harvard University Press, Cambridge, MA, 1982.

Pierson, F. *The Education of American Businessmen: A Study of University-College Programs in Business Administration*, McGraw-Hill, New York, 1959.

Pisano, G. 'The R&D boundaries of the firm'. *Administrative Science Quarterly*, **34**, 1990, pp. 153–176.

Porter, M. E. *Competitive Strategy: Techniques for Analyzing Industries and Competitors*, The Free Press, New York, 1980.

Porter, M. E. *Competitive Advantage*. The Free Press, New York, 1985.

Porter, M. E. *The Competitive Advantage of Nations*, The Free Press, New York, 1990.

Prahalad, C. K. and G. Hamel. 'The core competence of the corporation', *Harvard Business Review*, May–June 1990, pp. 79–91.

Rumelt, R. P. *Strategy, Structure, and Economic Performance*. Division of Research, Harvard Business School, 1974.

Rumelt, R. P. 'Towards a strategic theory of the firm'. In R. B. Lamb (ed.), *Competitive Strategic Management*. Prentice-Hall, Englewood Cliffs, NJ, 1984, pp. 556–570.

Rumelt, R. P. 'Theory, strategy, and entrepreneurship'. In D. J. Teece (ed.) *The Competitive Challenge: Strategies for Industrial Innovation and Renewal*, Ballinger, Cambridge, MA, 1987, pp. 137–158.

Rumelt, R. P., D. Schendel and D. J. Teece. (eds) *Fundamental Issues in Strategy*, Boston, MA, Harvard Business School Press, forthcoming (1992).

Rumelt, R. P. and R. Wensley. 'In search of the market share effect', *Proceedings of the Academy of Management*, August 1981, pp. 1–5.

Schendel, D. and R. Patton. 'A simultaneous equation model of corporate strategy', *Management Science*, **24**, 1978, pp. 1611–1621.

Scherer, F. M. *Industrial Market Structure and Economic Performance*, Rand McNally, Boston, MA, 1970, (2nd edn), 1980.

Selten, R. 'Spieltheoretische behandlung eines oligopolmodells mit nachfrägetragheit', *Zeitschrift für die gesamte Staatswissenschaft*, **12**, 1965, pp. 301–324.

Selznick, P. *Leadership in Administration*, Harper & Row, New York, 1957.

Shepherd, W. G. 'The elements of market structure', *Review of Economics and Statistics*, **54**, 1972, pp. 25–37.

Shepherd, W. G. *The Economics of Industrial Organization*, Prentice-Hall, Englewood Cliffs, NJ, 1979.

Simon, H. A. 'The business school: A problem in organizational design', *Journal of Management Studies*, **4**, 1967, pp. 1–16.

Simon, H. A. *The Sciences of the Artificial*, The MIT Press, Cambridge, MA, 1969.

Spence, M. *Market Signaling*, Harvard University Press, Cambridge, MA, 1974.

Spence, A. M. 'Investment strategy and growth in a new market', *Bell Journal of Economics*, **10**, 1979, pp. 1–19.

Teece, D. J. 'The market for know-how and the efficient transfer of technology'. *The Annals of the Academy of Political and Social Science*, 1981, pp. 81–96.

Teece, D. J. 'Towards an economic theory of the

multiproduct firm'. *Journal of Economic Behavior and Organization*, **3**, 1982, pp. 39–63.

Teece, D. J., G. Pisano and A. Shuen. 'Firm capabilities, resources, and the concept of strategy', Working Paper, University of California, Berkeley, 1990.

von Neumann, J. and O. Morgenstern. *The Theory of Games and Economic Behavior*, John Wiley and Sons, New York, 1944.

Wernerfelt, B. 'A resource-based view of the firm', *Strategic Management Journal*, **5**, 1984a, pp. 171–180.

Wernerfelt, B. 'Consumers with differing reaction speeds, scale advantages, and industry structure'.

European Economic Review, **24**, 1984b, pp. 257–270.

Wernerfelt, B. 'Brand loyalty and market equilibrium'. *Marketing Science*, **10**, 1991, pp. 229–246.

Wernerfelt, B. and C. A. Montgomery, 'Tobin's q and the importance of focus in firm performance', *American Economic Review*, **78**, March 1988, pp. 246–251.

Williamson, O. E. *Markets and Hierarchies: Analysis and Antitrust Implications*, The Free Press, New York, 1975.

Williamson, O. E. *The Economic Institutions of Capitalism: Firms, Markets, Relational Contracting*, The Free Press, New York, 1985.

[7]

Fundamental Issues in Strategy

Richard P. Rumelt, Dan E. Schendel and David J. Teece

History of Strategic Management

Strategic management, often called "policy" or nowadays simply "strategy," is about the direction of organizations, and most often, business firms. It includes those subjects of primary concern to senior management, or to anyone seeking reasons for success and failure among organizations. Firms, if not all organizations, are in competition—competition for factor inputs, competition for customers, and ultimately, competition for revenues that cover the costs of their chosen manner of surviving. Because of competition, firms have choices to make if they are to survive. Those that are *strategic* include: the selection of goals; the choice of products and services to offer; the design and configuration of policies determining how the firm positions itself to compete in product markets (e.g., competitive strategy); the choice of an appropriate level of scope and diversity; and the design of organization structure, administrative systems, and policies used to define and coordinate work. It is a basic proposition of the strategy field that these choices have critical influence on the success or failure of the enterprise, and that they must be integrated. It is the integration (or reinforcing pattern) among these choices that makes the set a strategy.

Strategic management as a field of inquiry is firmly grounded in practice and exists because of the importance of its subject. The strategic direction of business organizations is at the heart of wealth creation in modern industrial society. The field has not, like political science, grown from ancient roots in philosophy, nor does it, like parts of economics, attract scholars because of the elegance of its theoretical underpinnings. Rather, like medicine or engineering, it exists because it is worthwhile to codify, teach, and expand what is known about the skilled performance of roles and tasks that are a necessary part of our civilization. While its origins lie in practice and codification, its advancement as a field increasingly depends upon building theory that helps explain and predict organizational success and failure.

Strategic management as an academic field is much younger than its actual practice. While its date of conception (not to mention parentage) is somewhat uncertain, the academic field of strategic management is certainly a child of the 1960s. As such, it is now entering upon its "thirty-something" decade, a time of self-examination and of coming into its own. The premise of this book, and of the conference which preceded it, is that academic strategic management is indeed ready to come into its own, through the identification and clarification of the fundamental issues of scientific interest that distinguish it as a field of scholarly inquiry.

As an introduction to those fundamental issues, we briefly review the history of the academic field. If the child is indeed father to the man, a look back will help put the fundamental issues we identify into perspective, provide context, and clarify terms.

The Business Policy Course and Faculty

Strategic management, as a field of study, originated as a teaching area in business schools. The first business school, The Wharton School, was established at the University of Pennsylvania over 100 years ago. Harvard established its school some years later, but soon assumed a leadership role in business education. As far as can be determined, it was at Harvard that the first business policy course was taught.

The Harvard curriculum was built out of so-called functional courses, corresponding to business functions like accounting, marketing, and manufacturing. The policy course "integrated" what the student had learned in the functional courses, serving as a capstone to the core curriculum. True to Harvard tradition, the case method was employed. The course was not burdened with teaching substantive mechanisms of achieving integration—it simply presented administrative problems faced by senior executives that naturally required a multifunctional perspective.

Harvard served as an important model for other business and management schools, leading many to imitate its design. Business policy as a capstone course became a standard part of the curriculum across the United States. Indeed, today, the Association of American Collegiate Schools of Business (AACSB) includes instruction in business policy among its guideline requirements for accreditation. Tellingly, though, the AACSB has left "business policy" open to very broad interpretation.

As an integrative capstone course, business policy may have had some measure of prestige, but it had no prescribed content. No received theory grounded in the professional norms of a business function, or in the basic disciplines of the social sciences, needed to be taught. Historically, the course was often staffed by full professors, experienced teachers thought to have developed a broad view of business, or by adjunct professors, often former general managers with the wisdom of experience to transmit. With no theory to teach, any discipline or experience base seemed satisfactory, and indeed, eclecticism and a holistic view were valued.

Relegation of strategic management to a capstone course in business policy had serious structural consequences for the development of strategic management as a scholarly field of inquiry, however, and probably stifled its emergence for many years. A single, capstone course permitted no development of follow-on courses, and in turn limited the scope for expanding consideration of the subject. Since the teachers used to staff the course were either already full professors or were adjunct teachers without hope of tenure or interest in full rank, there was no evolutionary career path from assistant to full professor. The career paths to tenure and advanced rank remained in functional areas of business (e.g., marketing, finance) or in the traditional social science disciplines (e.g., economics, organization theory).

Faculty for the business policy course made their intellectual homes elsewhere. If serious research was done, it was done for the basic disciplines in which faculty members were trained. Moreover, the acceptability of using senior faculty members from a variety of disciplines often meant, as a practical matter, that the business policy course became something of a burying ground for academic white elephants long in the tusk but short on remaining research potential.

Some work had to be done, of course, to support course development. This scholarship tended to result in cases and notes of value to teaching, not articles and books of interest to other researchers, and it generated little theory or academic debate. One of the positive legacies of this practice, however, was extensive institutional knowledge and rich general descriptions of practice as observed from case writing and consulting.

In important respects, the field of strategic management only began to develop in terms of research accumulation in the early 1970s. It was then that the first faculty were hired as "policy" teachers, as pioneers expected to find their way up the promotion system to gain tenure in their own field, that of strategic management, by developing research records. Then the questioning of constructs and attention to tools and techniques of scientific research began in earnest. Then, too, professional associations and journals began to be needed.

Journals and Professional Societies

Any field develops around an infrastructure of journals and professional meetings, through which results are argued and disseminated. Initially, strategic management took advantage of the infrastructure built in the 1950s and 1960s to accommodate the increased interest in business and administrative organization. Before 1970, there were no distinct professional societies or publications devoted to the field.

The early history of strategic management showed remarkable interest in "planning," and although it proved short-lived, enthusiasm for planning dominated strategic management in the late 1960s and early 1970s. Consequently, some of the earliest efforts to organize societies and publications centered on planning per se. The Institute of Management Sciences developed a College on Planning, which attracted a small band of workers interested in formal models of the firm useful for planning long-range operation of organizations. The college did not flourish and was ultimately abandoned. The Planning Executives Institute (PEI) devoted its energy to budgeting and short-term financial planning, and was not truly interested in strategy concepts. PEI later was to combine with a practitioner group, the North American Society of Corporate Planners, to form The Planning Forum, which continues to operate throughout North America. Planning societies devoted to improving the state of practice for professional planners formed in various countries in Europe and elsewhere. Some, such as the Strategic Planning Society of the United Kingdom, are quite large.

Publications like *Long Range Planning* and *The Planning Review* were among the early outlets for work in strategy. Early work in strategy also found its way into general management journals such as the *Harvard Business Review, Sloan Management Review, Journal of Business, Business Horizons,* and *California Management Review.* Academic journals devoted to management topics, such as *Administrative Science Quarterly, Academy of Management Journal,* and *Management Science,* also provided important opportunities to publish scholarly research.

About 1969, the Academy of Management elected to form professional divisions to better reflect the specialized interests of its members. One of the first divisions formed, in 1971, was the Business Policy and Planning Division, since renamed the Business Policy and Strategy Division to reflect the ascendance of strategy concepts and the decline of planning. The division became an important base of support for the establishment of tenure-track strategy faculty.

Although interest in planning per se fell off, the number of practitioners and academics interested in topics of strategic management grew steadily through the 1970s. The growth of interest and support was reflected in the 1980s in the formation of societies and publications specialized to strategic management. In 1980, two journals devoted exclusively to strategy commenced publication: the *Strategic Management Journal (SMJ)* and the *Journal of Business Strategy,* the former oriented to academic research and the latter to practice. Both flourished, and *SMJ* rapidly became the leading research journal in the field, as reported in the Social Science Citation Index.

Also in the early 1980s, the Strategic Management Society was formed as an organization of practitioners, consultants, and academics interested in developing the field. Unlike predecessor organizations, it held international meetings and tried to attract members from all over the world. With members from about 50 countries, it sponsors meetings around the world and a publication (*SMJ*) devoted to advancing scholarship in the field.

The Development of Strategy Theory and Research

Precursors. The prehistory of strategic management as an academic field lies in studies of economic organization and bureaucracy. The vigorous interaction with economics and the study of organization, which characterizes the field today, reflects its origins in these disciplines. Work in a wide variety of areas contributed to a single task vital to the emergence of strategic management: preparing the ground for concepts of strategy.

Mainstream economic theory—price theory—has traditionally ignored the role of managers and left little scope for strategic choice in economic affairs. From the time of Adam Smith down to the present day, economists have sought to show that a completely decentralized economic system, coordinated only through market prices, could and would be efficient. Little attention has been given to why private firms might make use of managerial hierarchies to plan and coordinate. Institutional settings and arrangements have been largely abstracted away. The varied character and capabilities of actual business organizations have not been considered. The firm of economic theory observes market prices and then makes an efficient choice of output quantities; all firms are essentially alike, having the same access to information and technology, and the decisions they make are essentially rational and predictable, virtually compelled by cost and demand conditions.

While conventional economic theory did not recognize most of the choices open to managers of firms, work in a wide variety of areas—more than can be cited here—served to establish a basis for studying the role of management and the possibilities for strategic choices, before strategic management began to emerge as a field of study.

In the mid-twentieth century Taylor (1947) initiated a "science of work" in an organizational setting, beginning the effort to understand what economists might call "technical efficiency" or "x-efficiency." Taylor's enduring contribution was the conviction, and demonstration, that "natural" practices could be improved through careful observation and analysis.

Barnard (1938) elevated the analysis of organizational work from Taylor's shop floor to the executive ranks in his classic work, *Functions of the Executive*. He stressed the difference between managerial work directed at making the organization efficient, and work that made the organization effective, a distinction critical to the concept of strategy. Simon (1947) extended Barnard's ideas in his attempt to build a framework for analyzing administration. Selznick (1957) explored the roles of institutional commitment and introduced the idea of an organization's "distinctive competence."

The difficult economic conditions of the 1930s raised many questions about capitalism and the real efficiency of business. During this period, theories of imperfect competition were developed by Robinson ([1933] 1959) and Chamberlin (1933). Schumpeter's (1934) innovative entrepreneur and agent of creative destruction provided an alternative to the static concept of competitive efficiency favored by most economists. Later, Frank Knight's (1965) work on the risk-bearing function of entrepreneurs laid an early foundation for much of what we now call organizational economics.

Despite the increasing interest in business organization from the turn of the century on, there was no sustained debate about business strategy and its role in the success of firms. The founder of McKinsey & Co. evidently wrote about strategy in the 1930s. Newman (1951) used the concept of strategy to differentiate certain important work of the manager from the day-to-day work of running an organization. However, it was not until the 1960s that a field of interest could be seen forming.

1960s: Birth. The birth of strategic management in the 1960s took place against a background of tremendous ferment in organization theory. Universalistic principles and maxims of administration were being overthrown in favor of concepts of contingent design. March and Simon (1958) had developed the cybernetic or information-processing metaphor for management structure. Cyert and March (1963) had laid out a behavioral theory of the firm. Open systems theories and approaches, which tended to suggest that organizations were somewhat akin to organisms in a natural environment, had a major influence. Burns and Stalker (1961) contrasted organic and mechanistic types of management organization. Woodward (1965) showed how production process technology influenced organizational structure. Thompson (1967), in a bold, propositional inventory, and Lawrence and Lorsch (1967), in a more empirical work, proposed that managerial organization was contingent on "environmental uncertainty." The 1960s were a propitious time to introduce concepts of strategic adaptation by organizations.

The birth of the field of strategic management can be traced to three works of the 1960s: Alfred Chandler's *Strategy and Structure* (1962); Igor Ansoff's *Corporate Strategy* (1965); and the Harvard textbook, *Business Policy: Text and Cases* (Learned et al., 1965), the declarative text of which is attributed to Kenneth Andrews.

The foundation of strategic management as a field may very well be traced to the 1962 publication of Chandler's *Strategy and Structure*. Chandler's seminal book, subtitled "Chapters in the History of the Industrial Enterprise," was about the growth of large businesses and explored how their administrative structures had been adapted to accommodate that growth. In the process of telling the story of growth and administrative change at General Motors, Sears, Standard Oil of New Jersey (Exxon), and DuPont, Chandler showed how executives at these companies discovered and developed roles for themselves in making long-term decisions about the direction of their enterprises and then made investments and modified organizational structure to make those strategies work. A compelling and fascinating story of economic innovation, organizational behavior, and managerial achievement, it naturally attracted much interest and attention. Most important for the field, Chandler showed executives doing strategic management work and achieving remarkable performance outcomes. Moreover, he showed a process of administrative change within organizations that involved shifts in strategic direction, rather than adjustments for simple efficiency.

In formulating a thesis to summarize his findings, Chandler found it convenient to define two terms, strategy and structure:

> The thesis that different organization forms result from different types of growth can be stated more precisely if the planning and carrying out of such growth is considered a strategy, and the organization devised to administer these enlarged activities and resources, a structure. Strategy can be defined as the determination of the basic long-term goals and objectives of an enterprise, and the adoption of courses of action and the allocation of resources necessary for carrying out these goals. (pp. 15–16)

The concept of strategy used by Chandler was a handy way of characterizing the relationship among a set of managerial purposes and choices, and was explicitly distinct from a structure.

Andrews, in his text for Business Policy, accepted the strategy idea from Chandler, but added Selznick's "distinctive competence" and the notion of an uncertain environment to which management and the firm had to adapt. In Andrews's view, the environment, through constant change, gave rise to opportunities and threats, and the organization's strengths and weaknesses were adapted to avoid the threats and take advantage of the opportunities. An internal appraisal of strengths and weaknesses led to identification of distinctive competencies; an external appraisal of environmental threats and opportunities led to identification of potential success factors. These twin appraisals were the foundation for strategy formulation, a process analytically (if not practically) distinct from strategy implementation. Andrews conceived of strategy as akin to identity, defining it as "the pattern of objectives, purposes, or goals and major policies and plans for achieving these goals, stated in such a way as to define what business the company is in or is to be in and the kind of company it is or is to be" (p. 15). Andrews considered it a "matter of indifference" whether to include selection of goals as well as the deployment of resources in pursuit of goals as part of strategy. He regarded strategy formulation as "analytically objective," while implementation was "primarily administrative."

H. Igor Ansoff was general manager of the Lockheed Electronics Company (New Jersey) and developed his strategy concepts out of frustration with planning as the naive extrapolation of past trends. Ansoff was more explicitly interested in understanding what was meant by "strategy" and took some care to develop his ideas. He accepted that the objective for the firm ought to be to maximize economic return, which he distinguished from accounting return. For Ansoff, strategy provided a "common thread" for five component choices: (1) product-market scope; (2) growth vector (the direction in which scope was changing, e.g., the emphasis on old versus new products or markets); (3) competitive advantage (unique opportunities in terms of product or market attributes); (4) synergy internally generated by a combination of capabilities or competencies; and (5) the make or buy decision. In tracing this common thread of strategy through its components, Ansoff emphasized the potential for success arising from mutual reinforcement among the components.

In retrospect, it seems that Ansoff was more interested in what we would today call *corporate* strategy, while Andrews was more focused on *business* strategy. Ansoff's more elaborate analysis of the *concept* of strategy was also reflected in a more elaborate view of the *process* of creating strategy, a difference in emphasis that promoted the cause of strategic planning. Both Ansoff and Andrews, however, had gone beyond the traditional Business Policy course metaphor of functional integration.

These three authors—Chandler, Andrews, and Ansoff—gave first form to the basic concepts of strategic management. Nearly all of the ideas and issues that concern us today can be found in at least embryonic form in these key writings of the 1960s. It should be acknowledged, though, that their audience was primarily students and professors. None of these three authors directly and immediately influenced practice. Many of the changes in practice that occurred by the late 1960s can instead be traced to the influence of consulting firms. Leadership in this arena was provided by the exemplar of strategy consulting firms, The Boston Consulting Group.

Founded by Bruce Henderson in the mid-1960s, The Boston Consulting Group (BCG) had a major impact on the strategy field. Although a great deal of BCG's practice consisted of "segmentation studies" which simply reanalyzed cost and profit data using economic concepts rather than accounting measures, BCG became best known for its two related conceptual inventions: the experience curve, and the growth-share matrix. In brief, experience curve theory maintained that whoever captured market share early, whoever gained the most experience in production would end up with the lowest cost (assuming efficient operational management practice), and whoever had the lowest cost would have the highest margin. With the highest margin came cash flow and an ability to withstand competition and whatever actions it required. Within a few years, such reasoning led to the growth-share matrix, whose terminology of cash cows, dogs, stars, and question marks became famous and widely used.

The rapid expansion of the firm, successful spin-offs like Bain, and imitation by old-line rivals like McKinsey, attests to the influence that BCG had on practice. In contrast to many other consultants to top management, who emphasized long-term planning without much attention to strategy, BCG made strategic conception central. The experience curve and growth-share matrix drew a sharp, clear line between operational decision making and corporate strategy, highlighting the latter. The corporate strategist was encouraged to assume that efficient operations management would achieve the cost reductions projected along the experience curve and to make corporate investment decisions and plans accordingly. Moreover, the dynamic aspect of competition implied by the experience curve clearly called for strategic behavior: preemption of rivals with commitment today was necessary for success tomorrow.

Together with the work of Chandler, Andrews, and Ansoff, the developments at The Boston Consulting Group gave a powerful new thrust to managerial work and responsibility during the 1960s. The entrepreneurial responsibility of management was recognized—not just an act performed at birth—but as a continuing, pervasive responsibility to consider the long-run, dynamic direction of the firm, even while maintaining routine and efficient operations.

1970s: Transition toward a research orientation. While the work of Andrews and Ansoff, and of others who aimed to provide material for the policy course, expanded consideration of strategy concepts, there was no early reflection on the normative character of the statements made. Experiential, case-based evidence lay behind the writing, but there was little analysis, and no evidence was offered to satisfy a critical reader. Chandler's work, supported by historical methods, was much less aggressively normative and prescriptive, of course, but was still essentially inductive in character. At best, these first works offered a set of constructs and propositions about how strategies formed and how they affected the performance of business enterprises. Systematic observation, deductive analysis and modeling, and careful empirical testing had to wait for the 1970s.

As strategic management began to advance in the direction of positive science in the 1970s, a dichotomy developed between those pursuing essentially descriptive studies of how strategies were formed and implemented (process) and those seeking to understand the relationship between strategic choice and performance (content). It is not clear that the work of Chandler, Andrews, or Ansoff fits easily into either category. The work of all three appears to have implications for both content and process. The seeds of division between process and content may have been sown by distinctions made for rhetorical or expository reasons. Andrews, for example, wrote: "Corporate strategy has two equally important aspects, interrelated in life but separated to the extent practicable in our study of the concept. The first of these is formulation; the second is implementation" (p. 17).

The convenience of analytically isolating strategic choice remains difficult to reconcile with the reality of organizational, strategy-making processes. However, today we are seeing signs of a reconciliation that promises new gains. The developments yielded by recent research efforts suggest that processes to formulate strategy themselves have asset-generating capability.

Late in the 1960s and early in the 1970s, concepts of strategic and long-term planning played important roles in the field. This movement owed much to the diffusion of war-based planning experience in the corporate world. For example, George Steiner had learned planning by working on materials allocation in Washington during World War II, by serving as director of policy in the Office of Defense Mobilization during the Korean War, and then as chief economist at Lockheed (1953–1954). Later, as an academic, he wrote extensively on formal long-range planning processes. Much of this literature was descriptive of selected industry practices and was strongly prescriptive, never attempting to be analytical or empirical.

The prominence of long-range planning, and then strategic planning, failed to survive the economic turmoil that began with the oil embargo of 1973 and continued with the advent of floating exchange rates, high inflation, and increasing international competition; organizations learned from practical experience that simple extrapolations of history and cadres of professional planners failed to lead to innovation, adaptation to change, or even survival. Planning processes too easily degenerated into goal-setting exercises, failing to embody any real understanding of competitive advantage. Moreover, when more sophisticated planning process designs were advanced, problems of execution or implementation increased. An organizational process to both create and execute strategy proved to be poor at conception and not influential enough to make a substantial difference in implementation.

Careful observation of actual organizational decision making gave rise to more subtle conceptions of process, in which strategies were arrived at indirectly and, to some degree, unintentionally. Uncertainty ex ante led to tentativeness, search and serial trial, and some learning—a somewhat chaotic process—which, with a certain amount of luck, might accumulate to a strategy, which could be named and described as coherent only ex post. Lindblom's (1959) "muddling through," Quinn's (1980) "logical incrementalism," and Mintzberg and Waters's (1978) "emergent strategy" all attempted to gain insight into organizational processes which produced strategy as a somewhat unintended outcome.

Attempts to understand and test the connection between strategy and performance also began in the 1970s. In this work, three streams ought to be highlighted. One, centered at Harvard and following on Chandler, generated and tested propositions about corporate growth and diversification strategies. A second, focusing on business strategies, began with the so-called brewing studies at Purdue. The third, also at Harvard, used an industrial organization economics perspective to study business strategy, and culminated in Michael Porter's work on analyzing competitive strategy and competitive advantage.

The brewing studies done in the early 1970s at Purdue examined the strategies and performance of major U.S. brewers over time. Their goal was to explore the proposition that performance was a function of strategy and environment. The brewers were chosen because they represented a group of mostly undiversified firms, and because, due to product taxation and heavy regulation, good data were available for representing the constructs (i.e., strategy and environment) and functional form of the relationship.

The brewing study results (Hatten and Schendel, 1977; Hatten, Schendel, and Cooper, 1978), were generally consistent with the notion that strategy, in addition to "environment," mattered, so that a "better" strategy, relative to competitors, was associated with better performance. The studies also revealed the considerable heterogeneity in strategy and performance that can exist within a single industry; the differences were far greater than was generally presumed in industrial organization economics and, indeed, in most management and strategy thinking. These differences led to very interesting research on strategic groups and to further explanations of performance differences based on concepts of competitive advantage.

The brewing studies demonstrated that the strategy construct could be represented by measurable variables, and that empirical evidence supported the usefulness of the strategy construct itself. What had been derived on the basis of experiential, inductive methods had been supported by more objective, deductive methods of research. This represented a new departure in research philosophy for the field, and changed the direction of research in the field in ways that were more significant than the findings themselves.

At about the same time as the brewing studies, enthusiasm for Chandler's historical work had inspired further interest in empirically demonstrating a relationship between growth strategy, organization form, and the expected performance of the enterprise. This work led ultimately to important findings concerning the forms of diversification that improved performance and those that did not. Wrigley (1970), working under Bruce Scott, did the first work in trying to classify diversification strategies. Other dissertation work followed, conducted in a variety of national economies: Channon (1973) studied the United Kingdom; Pavan (1972) studied Italy; Thanheiser (1972) studied Germany; and Pooley-Dias (1972) studied France. Rumelt (1974) pushed this stream of work even further, contributing more discriminating measures of diversification and testing the impact of diversification strategy and organizational structure on performance. Like the brewing studies, this work was at least as significant for introducing new methodological approaches to the field as for its findings.

In a third major departure for studies of the relationship of performance and strategy, Porter (1980) imported into the strategy field the concepts developed over the years in industrial organization (IO) economics. Using a large number of case studies as a factual base, Porter employed IO concepts concerning market power and profitability to build a general, cross-sectional framework for explaining individual firm performance. Until Porter, firms in strategic management had been seen as adapting to general, even rather vague environments.

Porter's "Five Forces" framework substituted a structured, competitive economic environment, in which the ability to bargain effectively in the face of an "extended rivalry" of competing firms, customers, and suppliers determined profit performance. By making managerial choice in an explicitly economic environment the focal point of analysis, Porter succeeded in turning IO economics on its head. Its traditional role was to identify socially wasteful sources of "monopoly" profits, but Porter instead used the framework to define and explain the strategies available to firms in their quest for survival and profit. Drawing on his extensive case study research, he catalogued, described, and discussed a wide range of phenomena that interfered with free competition and thus allowed abnormal returns, and he suggested how their interaction and relative importance varied across contexts.

Porter's work opened an important bridge to IO economics across which traveled more than the Structure-Conduct-Performance paradigm he employed himself. The "Chicago" critique of traditional entry barrier theory, which supported the alternative view that high profits were returns to specialized, high-quality resources or capabilities, became an important inspiration for the resource-based theory of the firm. Game theory modeling in industrial organization found applications in strategic management, too.

In addition to these broad perspectives developed *within* the field during the 1980s, strategy scholars dramatically increased their use of economic theory and their sophistication in doing so, as the examples that follow indicate. The event-study methods of financial economics were used to investigate strategic and organizational change as well as the strategic fit of acquisitions. New security-market performance measures were applied to old questions of diversification and performance, market share and performance, as well as other new areas of inquiry. Transaction cost viewpoints on scope and integration were adopted and new theories of the efficiency of social bonding were advanced. Studies of innovation began to use the language and logic of economic rents and appropriability, and research in venture capital responded to the agency and adverse selection problems characteristic of that activity. Agency theory perspectives have been used in the study of firm size, diversification, top management compensation, and growth. The new game-theoretic approach to industrial organization has informed studies of producer reputations, entry and exit, technological change, and the adoption of standards.

At the same time, research on the strategy process continued apace. Interestingly, the most vital new ideas were generated by those studying global firms. In the 1980s, the increasing globalization of the world's economy was leading students of general management to look ever more carefully at how large multinational corporations directed and coordinated their myriad resources and activities. An important early work was Stopford and Wells (1972). The new framework is first seen in the dissertations of the key authors: Prahalad (1975), Doz (1976), Bartlett (1979), and Ghoshal (1986). Their insights began to challenge the received wisdom about structure and process. In particular, the need to consider functional, product, and geographical bases for specialization forced thinking beyond the increasingly stale product-function dichotomy. The emerging framework represents management as needing to maintain "differentiation" in some activities to achieve gains from specialization or administrative isolation, and tight integration in other areas to achieve economies of scale and focus.[1] In addition, management is seen as actively managing a complex system of linkages among activities, which enables critical coordination and facilitates organizational learning.

In looking back over these three decades, what comes into focus is the search, sometimes in vain, for theoretical explanations of very complex phenomena. The purpose has been to understand real-world phenomena and establish a base for making useful prescriptions. For the first time, basic disciplines of the social sciences, especially economics, have been linked with practical issues involved in managing the firm. What began in the 1960s as rather simple concepts of strategy intended to give insight into the phenomena described in cases has evolved into a serious search for intellectual foundations with explanatory and predictive power.

Developments and Trends in Allied Disciplines

During the past decade strategic management research has increasingly relied on the theories and methods of economics

---

[1]   See Chapter 17 of this volume.

and organizational sociology, as well as (but to a lesser extent) on political science and psychology. As a consequence, the boundaries that mark the strategy field have been blurred. Not so long ago there was no doubt about what "policy" or "strategy" research was, and certainly there was no difficulty in separating it from work in economics or other disciplines. Now those distinctions are less clear.

Given these trends, it is important to understand the fundamental questions being asked in the allied disciplines and to be aware of the changes sweeping these fields. This understanding will serve two purposes. First, it will help us to place strategic management's fundamental questions in context, and to see how strategic management is related to, yet differentiated from, its allied disciplines. Second, the blurring of boundaries makes it important to examine the interrelationships between strategy and its allied disciplines. As the strategy field begins to adopt the language and tools of agency theory, population ecology, behavioral decision theory, political science, and so on, and as scholars in those fields realize that the strategy field addresses truly important and significant questions and issues, how should the relationship between strategy and its allied disciplines be viewed, and in particular, what does it mean for a research agenda for strategy? Indeed, does strategy have an independent research future, or should it merely wait for research developments to occur and then give attention to their application? Even more pointedly, does strategy have a future as a field at top research universities, or will its subject matter be taught and researched by economists, sociologists, political scientists, and psychologists?

Economics

In the beginning, economics was centrally concerned with understanding what governed the efficient generation of goods and services and what determined the distribution of wealth in society. However, in this century classical economics, now called microeconomics, has been driven more by its internal logic than by external phenomena in need of explanation. The overriding fundamental question has been, What phenomena can be explained by models that assume that human action is rational? And even in cases where no human agent has made a coherent choice, economists ask, Which institutions can be explained by assuming they were designed and stuctured by a rational actor? This program of research, begun by the Enlightenment thinkers of the eighteenth century, has reached its full flower in the economics departments of U.S. universities during the last 30 years. Indeed, Gary Becker's recent Nobel Prize was awarded for his work on extending economic reasoning to the family and beyond—his boldest work asserts that drug addiction can be explained as a rational choice.

Although the central quest of economics, the explication of phenomena as the products of rational action, is unchanged, the context within which action is envisioned has undergone a dramatic evolution. During the first half of this century the great task before economics was the mathematization of Marshall's theories to produce the "neoclassical" theory of the firm. The economist's neoclassical model of the firm, still enshrined in textbooks, is a smoothly running machine in a world without secrets, without frictions or uncertainty, and without a temporal dimension. That such a theory, so obviously divorced from the most elementary conditions of real firms, should continue to be taught in most business schools as the "theory of the firm" is a truly amazing victory of doctrine over reality. This era may, however, finally be coming to an end as the cumulative impact of new insights takes its toll.

During the past 30 years, and especially during the last 20, at least five conceptual monkey wrenches have been thrown into what was once a smoothly running machine. These five are: *uncertainty, information asymmetry, bounded rationality, opportunism,* and *asset specificity.* Each of these phenomena, taken alone, violates crucial axioms in the neoclassical model. In various combinations they are the essential ingredients of new subfields within economics. For example, transaction cost economics rests primarily on the conjunction of bounded rationality, asset specificity, and opportunism. Agency theory rests on the combination of opportunism and information asymmetry. The new game-theoretic industrial organization derives much of its punch from asymmetries in information and/or in the timing of irreversible expenditures (asset specificity). The evolutionary theory of the firm and of technological change rests chiefly on uncertainty and bounded rationality. Each of these new subfields has generated insights and research themes that are important to strategic management. Here each is briefly treated in turn.

Transaction cost economics.   Of all the new subfields of economics, the transaction cost branch of organizational economics has the greatest affinity with strategic management. The links derive, in part, from common interests in organizational form, including a shared concern with the Chandler-Williamson M-form hypothesis. They also derive from a common intellectual style, which legitimizes inquiry into the reasons for specific institutional details. The clinical studies conducted by strategy researchers and business historians are grist for the transaction cost mill. A theory that seeks to explain why one particular clause appears in a contract is clearly of great interest to strategic management scholars, who have a definite taste for disaggregation. For an example of such detail, see Joskow's (1988) study of price-adjustment clauses in long-term coal contracts.

For many economists, the assumption of unlimitedly rational actors is the defining characteristic of their field. Consequently, transaction cost economics, which follows Simon in positing bounded rationality, has had an uphill struggle for recognition and acceptance. The subfield got its start in the mid-1970s as some economists, building on Coase's (1937) seminal work, began to systematically probe questions of firm boundaries and internal organization. Williamson (1975) was the chief architect of a framework that explored the limits or boundaries of both markets and business firms as arrangements for conducting economic activity. His basic point was that transactions should take place in the regime which best economizes on the costs imposed by bounded rationality and opportunism. This framework was explicitly comparative (the relative efficiencies of markets and hierarchies were exposed) and enabled economists for the first time to say something about the *efficiency* properties of different organizational forms. (Previously economists had commonly sought and found monopoly explanations for complex forms of business organization; efficiency explanations were ignored or denigrated.) In addition to comparing markets and hierarchies, transaction cost researchers also began to look at questions of internal structure and the manner in which specific decisions and actions were taken. In particular, the Chandler-Williamson M-form hypothesis raised important issues relating to corporate control. These ideas began to achieve wider acceptance after being supported in a number of empirical studies (Armour and Teece, 1978; Monteverde and Teece, 1982).

Within strategic management, transaction cost economics is

the ground where economic thinking, strategy, and organizational theory meet. Because of its focus on institutional detail rather than mathematical display, it has a broader audience among noneconomists than other branches of organizational economics. During the 1980s, a considerable amount of work was done in applying the transaction cost framework to issues in organizational structure. In particular, research has been carried out on vertical supply arrangements in a number of industries,[2] the structure of multinational firms (Buckley and Casson, 1976; Teece, 1985; Kogut, 1988), sales force organization (Anderson and Schmittlein, 1984), joint ventures (Hennart, 1988; Pisano, 1990), and franchising. Williamson (Chapter 13, this volume) provides a useful review of additional applications of interest to strategic management.

Agency theory. Agency theory concerns the design of incentive agreements and the allocation of decision rights among individuals with conflicting preferences or interests. Although it deals with the employment transaction, agency theory is not compatible with transaction cost theory. Whereas transaction cost economics begins with the assertion that one cannot write enforceable contracts that cover all contingencies, agency theorists make no such presumption, and instead seek the optimal form of such a contract.

Agency theory has developed in two branches. The *principal-agent* literature is chiefly concerned with the design of optimal incentive contracts between principals and their employees or agents. Principal-agent economics is largely mathematical in form and is relatively inaccessible to those who have not made investments in its special technology. The standard problem has the agent shirking unless rewards can be properly conditioned on informative signals about effort. The interesting aspect of the problem is that both parties suffer if good measures are not available. A version of the problem that links with strategic management concerns project selection and the design of incentives so that agents will not distort the capital budgeting process.

The second, *corporate control* branch of the agency literature is less technical and is concerned with the design of the financial

---

[2] Early contributions were Monteverde and Teece's (1982) study of auto components and Masten's (1988) study of aerospace.

claims and overall governance structure of the firm. It is this branch which is most significant to strategic management. The corporate control hypothesis most familiar to strategic management is Jensen's (1986) "free cash flow" theory of leverage and takeovers. According to Jensen, in many firms, managers have inappropriately directed free cash flow toward wasteful investments or uses. Two cures for this problem have been proposed: use of high levels of debt to commit managements to payouts, and hostile takeovers, which put new management teams in place. What should strike strategic management scholars is that BCG offered precisely this diagnosis for many diversified firms in the early 1970s. According to BCG, most firms mismanaged their portfolios, misusing the funds generated by mature cash-rich businesses ("cows"), usually by continuing to reinvest long after growth opportunities had evaporated.

The corporate control perspective provides a valuable framework for strategic management research. By recognizing the existence of "bad" management, identifying remedial instruments, and emphasizing the importance of proper incentive arrangements, it takes a more normative stand than most other subfields of economics. However, scholars working in this area of agency theory also have the tendency to see all managerial problems as due to incorrect incentives—a tautology for a perspective that assumes away any other sources of dysfunction (e.g., capital markets problems like those discussed by Shleifer and Vishny later in this book, managerial beliefs about cause and effect, management skills in coordination, and the presence or lack of character and self-control).

Game theory and the new IO.   Three of the papers in this book deal with implications of game theory for strategic management, so our remarks here will be brief. Mathematical game theory was invented by von Neumann and Morgenstern (1944) and Nash (1950). However, little progress was made in developing economic applications until the late 1970s. It was probably Spence's (1974) work on market signaling that sparked the modern interest of economists, and it was Stanford's "gang of four," Kreps, Milgrom, Roberts, and Wilson (1982), who codified the treatment of sequential games with imperfect information.[3]

---

[3]   Much of the technical foundation they used had been laid by Selten (1965) and Harsanyi (1967).

Modern game theory raises deep questions about the nature of rational behavior. The idea that a rational individual is one who maximizes utility in the face of available information is simply not sufficient to generate "sensible" equilibria in many noncooperative games with asymmetric information. To obtain "sensible" equilibria, actors must be assigned beliefs about what others' beliefs will be in the event of irrational acts. Research into the technical and philosophical foundations of game theory has, at present, little to do directly with strategic management, but much to do with the future of economics as the science of "rational" behavior.

Game theory as applied to industrial organization has two basic themes of particular interest to strategic management: commitment strategies and reputations. Commitment, as Ghemawat (1991) emphasizes, can be seen as central to strategy. Among the commitment games that have been analyzed are those involving investment in specific assets and excess capacity, research and development with and without spillovers, horizontal mergers, and financial structure.

Reputations arise in games where firms or actors may belong to various "types" and others must form beliefs about which type is the true one. Thus, for example, a customer's belief (probability) that a seller is of the "honest" type constitutes the seller's reputation, and that reputation can be lost if the seller behaves in a way that changes the customer's beliefs. Reputations can also describe relationships within the firm, and the collection of employee beliefs and reputations can be called its "culture." Given the competitive importance of external reputations, the efficiency properties of internal reputations, and the relative silence of game theorists about how various equilibria are actually achieved, there is clearly much room for contributions, including those from strategic management research.

Evolutionary economics. There has been a long-standing analogy drawn between biological competition (and resulting evolution) and economic competition, and students of both phenomena often ground ideas by pointing to the parallel. Making the analogy concrete, however, has largely been the work of Nelson and Winter (1982), who married the concepts of tacit knowledge and routines to the dynamics of Schumpeterian competition. In their framework, firms compete primarily through a struggle to improve or innovate. In this struggle, firms grope toward better methods with only a partial understanding of the causal structure of their own capabilities and of the technological opportunity set. Key to their view is the idea that organizational capacities are based on routines which are not explicitly comprehended, but which are developed and bettered with repetition and practice. This micro-link to learning-by-doing means that the current capability of the firm is a function of history, and implies that it is impossible to simply copy best practice even when it is observed.

Because evolutionary economics posits a firm that cannot change its strategy or its structure easily or quickly, the field has a very close affinity to population ecology views in organization theory. Researchers interested in the evolution of populations tend to work in the sociology tradition, while those more interested in the evolution of firm capabilities and technical progress tend to work in the economics tradition. Both frameworks challenge the naive view that firms can change strategies easily, or that such changes will even matter when attempted and made.

Organizational Sociology

The fundamental issue addressed by sociology is the structure and subjective meaning of social interaction. The center of the puzzle was and continues to be the stability of social structures and the amazingly strong controlling forces they exert on their members' actions. Although economists are also interested in patterns of exchange, two concerns distinguish the sociologists' approach: an interest in authority and a real concern with the subjective experience of social interaction. Whereas economists almost always study voluntary exchange, sociologists normally begin with the presumption that authority is a key source of social order. Equally distinctive and crucial is the sociologist's concern with the subjective. To an economist, exchange is a means to an end. When an employee exchanges labor for pay, for example, the economist sees two gains: the employee values the pay more than the discomfort of work, and the employer values the labor received at least as greatly as the cost of employment. To a sociologist, the exchange itself, and the system of exchanges within which it is embedded, generate value and meaning apart from their instrumental worth.

Organizational sociology grew from two important traditions. The "main line" flows from the work of Durkheim ([1893] 1984) and Weber (1947) through Parsons (1937), Merton (1940), and Homans (1950), to Selznick (1949, 1957) and Blau and Scott (1962). In general, this tradition has been concerned with the processes whereby authority is legitimized (accepted), with the general problem of social structure in society, and with the limits and dysfunctions of bureaucracy. The second tradition is more normative and practice-oriented, and springs from the early management theorists and from the "human relations" movement inaugurated by industrial psychologists.

From the mid-1960s through the 1970s, the contingency theory synthesis emerged and was widely disseminated. Contingency theory built on a variety of earlier insights: Woodward (1965) and Burns and Stalker (1961) showed that high-performing organizations did not have the same structure, but matched structure to the technological demands of production; the Aston studies established that there is no single factor with which organizational characteristics covary; Emery and Trist (1965) stressed the importance of the environment in determining structure; and Lawrence and Lorsch (1967) drew from their empirical work the picture of an organization with subunits adapted to differing local environments and with integrative mechanisms that assert the interests of the whole. Contingency theory hypothesized that organizations which contain subsystems "matched" to their environments perform better than those with a less perfect fit. Under competition, this implies that structure follows environment and must be able to cope with uncertainty, the most important variable in the environment. If strategy is taken to include the choice of environment, this hypothesis is consistent with Chandler's (and now strategic management's) dictum that structure follows strategy.

But contingency theory's apparent success at solving the puzzle of formal structure did not ensure its longevity. Carroll (1988: 1) gives a vivid explanation of what happened in the mid-1970s:

> Although its adherents continue working at a feverish pace, the once hegemonic contingency theory of organization has been deposed by a paradigmatic revolution. The beginnings of the revolution can be dated sometime around 1975, a period marked by the appearance of four new seminal theoretical statements about organizations: (1) the book on transaction

cost economics by Oliver Williamson (1975), *Markets and Hierarchies;*
(2) the article on the population ecology of organizations by Michael T.
Hannan and John Freeman (1977); (3) the article on institutionalized
organizations by John Meyer and Brian Rowen (1977); and (4) the book
on resource dependence theory by Jeffrey Pfeffer and Gerald Salancik
(1978), *The External Control of Organizations.*

Each of these subfields of organizational sociology is relevant
to strategic management (we have already viewed transaction
cost economics in the previous section).

Resource dependence.   Who or what determines what organizations do? The resource dependence model argues that much
of what organizations do is determined by outsiders—by those
parties who control the flow of critical resources upon which the
organization depends. The strategic activities of management,
according to this perspective, are those of accommodating or
finding ways to insulate the organization from the demands of
those who control critical resources. Resource dependence explains mergers, joint ventures, diversification, and board mem-
berships in this way, and scholars working in this tradition have
provided empirical support for these claims. Note that there is
an affinity between resource dependence theory and transaction
cost theory. Both are concerned with the governance of critical
transactions, and both are concerned with the power of one party
to damage the other.

Resource dependence theory also speaks to the distribution of
power within organizations. Power, it is argued, is possessed by
those who can influence the flow of critical resources from external sources and by those who have influence over the flow of
discretionary resources. Thus, power in a consulting firm resides
in those who can generate new business or influence clients,
and great power in universities can be wielded by those who
control relatively small discretionary funds.

Organization ecology.   Economics and, to a large extent, strategic management view the firm as actively adapting to changed
conditions. Organization ecology makes the opposite presumption—that firms do not adapt. Instead of the adaptive firm, organization ecology sees a population of firms that changes in composition over time as some flourish, others perish, and new
organizations are born. The metaphor of biology has been frequently used by economists and strategy researchers, but Hannan and Freeman (1977) were the first to complete the metaphor, placing firms in the position of individuals with fixed

genetic endowments and advocating the study of a population of firms (i.e., a species) over time, rather than the idiosyncratic features of individuals.

Although it assumes that firms do not adapt, organization ecology is much more receptive to the concept that firms have strategies than traditional organization theory. The critical difference is that organization ecology sees the strategy of a firm as fixed at its inception and as unchanging over time.[4] Once it is fixed, of course no further room is left for the strategic manager. This view is obviously at odds with much of the literature in strategic management, especially that which emphasizes strategic change, organization renewal and transformation, and flexibility. Nevertheless, it may be that strategic management scholars need to reexamine their assumptions—strategic change may well be the exception rather than the rule. Given the large number of case studies that feature companies unable to perceive or cope with a changing environment, it may be that the ecologist's assumption of strategic inertia is more realistic than the economist's assumption of rapid, rational response to change.

Much of the research in organization ecology has been directed at measuring the birth and death rates of organizations and, therefore, the rate of expansion or decline of the population under study. More recently, interest has focused on *density dependence:* the degree to which birth and/or death rates vary with the size of the population. In addition, interest attaches to niching, niche-overlap, and measures of competition across subpopulations. By keeping the economist's notion that the environment changes and selects the most efficient organizations, but abandoning rational adaptation, organization ecologists are able to measure "niche-width," competition, and similar concepts using straightforward data. This is in marked contrast to the difficulty in developing proper empirical measures of economic concepts, such as cross-elasticity of demand, or strategic management concepts such as "mobility barriers."

Of course, the fact that some organizations do adapt creates a natural tension within organization ecology. A natural response is to shift the locus of selection from the firm as a whole

---

[4]   More precisely, organization ecologists assume strategic change is infrequent and independent of immediate environmental demands.

to some part of the firm, say its policies or its organizational subunits, and to see these subunits as unchanging but also subject to birth, proliferation, and extinction (Burgelman, 1990). It remains to be seen whether an empirical demography of policies or subunit forms can be created.

New institutionalism. The basic tenet of economics, much of strategic management, and a great deal of sociology and organization theory is rationality or functionalism—that the structures, concepts, and social arrangements which evolve are the "rational" or "efficient" solutions to the problems of production, coordination, and change. These functional structures are either designed, selected, or otherwise evolve. It is this view that motivates case studies of successful firms and that lies behind the economic analysis of institutions.

The new institutionalism[5] provides a contrary view. It claims that whereas some organizations survive through technical efficiency, there are others that survive through legitimacy—by acting in socially expected ways. Put differently, whereas an economist might see a joint venture as an arrangement for efficiently dealing with certain forms of co-specialized assets in a context of opportunism, the (new) institutionalist would see it as a currently accepted (or rationalized) activity. Joint ventures are undertaken, it might be argued, because other firms have done them and because academics have rationalized them. Hence, more firms undertake them. From this point of view, joint ventures may be something like a virus, multiplying in the social, cognitive, and economic context of modern corporate life. They proliferate not because they are efficient, but because they have become *institutionalized* (and are not obviously dysfunctional). As DiMaggio and Powell (1988: 3) put it, "The distinguishing contribution of institutional theory rests in the identification of causal mechanisms leading to organizational change and stability on the basis of preconscious understandings that organizational actors share, independent of their interests."

The new institutionalism is an intellectual descendant of the old, which was best represented by Selznick (1957). But Selznick used the word to denote the way value and meaning attached to a specific organization and its mission. To the new writers,

---

[5]   The best survey is Powell and DiMaggio (1991), especially their introductory essay.

society at large is the source of concepts, professional roles, rules, standards, expectations, policies, strategies, and standard organizational arrangements. Organizations institutionalize (adopt) these things and thereby gain legitimacy. Thus, business schools teach business policy because it is "the thing to do" rather than because it is technically necessary. This form of nonrational behavior draws on new work in cognitive psychology that identifies behavior derived from unconscious scripts, rules, and routines. It is also akin to that studied by Elster (1988), who distinguishes between consequentialist and nonconsequentialist behavior: the first is action impelled by a consideration of consequences or payoffs; the second is action chosen according to a rule or according to its "appropriateness" in the context. Finally, and perhaps most simply, it should be recognizable as the logic of the legal system—procedural rationality.

Institutional theory is at its strongest in explaining those aspects of organizational life that are taken for granted. For example, the fact that superiors judge the performance of subordinates but not vice versa, the annual planning cycle, and the general use of financial measures of subunit performance are "institutions" which are accepted virtually without question. This viewpoint has obvious bite with regard to the diffusion of many new management concepts and fads (e.g., quality circles, value-based strategy, and TQM).

Another developing stream of thought that intersects organizational sociology in many areas is concerned with organization culture.[6] The study of organization culture derives from functional anthropology, semiotics, and phenomenology. It tends to reject reductionism, seeing culture as something that must be comprehended as a whole, and perhaps only by direct participation. It is a nonrational view to the extent that social behavior cannot be expressed as the outcome of individual rational optimizing behavior. Some scholars, however, do view the culture as a whole as the functional solution to problems of communication, cooperation, and intertemporal opportunism. Culture is sometimes seen as the impediment to change and at other times as the source of unusual excellence; in either case, the technology of changing, protecting, or creating culture is at a very primitive state of development.

---

[6]   See Ouchi and Wilkins (1985) for an insightful review.

Political Science

The systematic investigation of political structures and processes has a tradition extending back to the Greek philosophers. And most political science has been within the classical form: the discussion of ideal states, the histories of particular political conflicts or events, descriptions of political structures and the rules governing their operation, and framers' expectations as to the value and functioning of various political structures. Like strategic management, political science lacks a central, generally accepted paradigm, and its many streams are not tied together in any coherent way.

However, two dramatic shifts in paradigm have occurred in American political science in the last 50 years. The first was the "behavioral revolution" that commenced in the 1950s. Just as the Carnegie School's views on behavioral, rather than "rational," models of human behavior influenced research and thinking in management schools, they also had an impact on political science. The new mode saw researchers looking at what political actors actually did rather than at descriptions of rules and structure or at a framer's expectations. For example, see Kaufman (1960) for a fascinating account of the Forest Service.

The second paradigm shift was political science's own "new institutionalism." Among its antecedents were the many empirical studies of voting that had been carried out over the years. These studies examined the effects of blocs, splinter groups, rules, and so forth, on voting behavior and outcomes. New institutionalism in political science also included abstract and rigorous analysis of how individual preferences combine through voting to produce political outcomes. This avenue of study had its origins in Arrow's (1951) Impossibility Theorem, which showed that literally centuries of talk about "the public interest" was vacuous—that one cannot aggregate preferences and treat a collection like an individual. The early attempts to model democratic processes took their structure from economics; voters were likened to consumers, policy makers to producers, and politics and voting to market competition. Of the many important contributions to this literature, two that stand out are Black's (1958) analysis of bloc voting and Buchanan and Tullock's (1962) analysis of when collective democratic action is individually preferred.

One might expect an economic metaphor applied to politics to produce the same conclusion—that competitive markets maximize welfare—but political scientists discovered substantial difficulties. When preferences were modeled as differing in only one dimension, everything worked well, with the policy outcome being the preferences of the median voter. But with two or more dimensions to preferences, outcomes were indeterminate. McKelvey (1976) is credited with the first "chaos theorem," proving that if there is no clearly dominating policy, any policy can be made the outcome through some adjustment of the agenda. That is, given majority-rule voting, a sufficiently clever chairperson can obtain any result he or she desires.

Although analysis showed chaos, real political institutions demonstrated substantial stability and predictability. Thus, the actual outcome of democratic processes, or at least their stability, it was argued, must be at least as greatly determined by the structure of institutions as by the preferences of voters. This insight generated a renewed interest in the structure of institutions, and a great deal of research has been done on the committee structures of the U.S. Congress and on its voting rules (Shepsle, 1979; Weingast, 1989).

A final stream of political science research of interest to strategic management is the study of bureaucratic biases or failures. The studies in this stream most familiar to strategic management are Selznick's (1949) study of the TVA and Allison's (1971) analysis of the Cuban missile crisis. Other important works in this genre are Downs's (1967) study of bureaucracy and Wilson's (1989) analysis of the properties and behavior of government agencies.

Summary

Each of the allied disciplines speaks to a unique metaphor. Economics is concerned with public welfare and wealth distribution in society. Sociology is concerned with groups of individuals and their activities as groups. Political science is concerned with choices made by groups where the objective function is diffuse and specified by the group itself. Psychology is concerned with individuals, the mind, and individual behavior. That all of these have something to do with individuals in combination with group choices and welfare is evident. But what of strategic management? What is its metaphor, and what is its domain? And how does it relate to these basic disciplines?

Strategic management has to do with groups, their birth and their continuing success. It does not assume that the group's purpose is beneficial, but simply that the group forms and tries to exist because it has purpose. Moreover, the group exists within a context, and the context governs conditions of success. It is management's responsibility to see that the group adapts to its context, and survival in the end is an objective definition of success. So the perspective is that of the management team assigned the responsibility of ensuring success, with success defined as either the entrepreneurial act of starting an organization, or those acts that condition survival.

The fundamental issues addressed by strategic management then are different from those addressed by the allied disciplines themselves. Related they are to be sure, but different perspectives separate their domains of inquiry, and one must expect different fundamental questions to be addressed by each discipline.

We turn now to an examination of what we see as fundamental questions of interest to strategic management. In so doing, we define the field as we see it today, and further, we separate the field from the allied disciplines with which it overlaps and with which it has common interests. Perhaps most important, by posing fundamental questions, we outline what we believe to be the boundaries of the field and its current and ongoing agenda for research.

The Fundamental Questions in Strategy

The Value of Fundamental Questions

A fundamental question acts to define a field of inquiry and to orient the efforts of researchers who work in that domain. Ronald Coase, for example, defined the field of institutional economics by asking, Why are there firms? Despite its apparent simplicity, this question has great power. When it was posed, the neoclassical theory of the firm was well advanced, but that theory sought to characterize the behavior of the firm, taking its existence as a given. Thus, Coase's question was a subtle critique of the state of microeconomics, and it proved to be an extremely fruitful impetus to new thinking. The value of the question is undiminished by the fact that it has not yet been answered entirely satisfactorily.

Fundamental questions are not necessarily the most often stated or the most fashionable; nevertheless, they serve to highlight the issues and presumptions that differentiate a field of inquiry, making its axioms, its methods, and the phenomena it studies different from those of other related fields. Thus, one of the fundamental questions for the strategy field is, Why are firms different?—a question that echoes Coase's but that directs attention away from common properties of all firms and focuses instead on the phenomena which produce and sustain continuing heterogeneity among firms.

For a fundamental question to energize research it must not only address a critical issue, it must also offer at least one clear path to follow in seeking answers. Thus, the power of Coase's question derives not only from its focus on the basics, but also from its association with a method for seeking its answer—comparative institutional analysis. Adam Smith invented economics by coupling the question, What determines the wealth of nations? with a new method of analyzing the collective results of individual self-seeking behavior. Durkheim virtually invented sociology by asking, What binds individuals into societies? and advocating the statistical comparison of behavior and social structure in various settings.

There are many questions addressing important issues that cannot motivate useful research. Some are too general; others lack connection to any usable theoretical structure or research methodology. For example, the question, What is good management? is too general, given our current knowledge, to be fundamental. We know that managerial work depends sharply on the task, the role, and the organization. In business research there is also the problem of asking questions that are too close to the entrepreneurial heart of the matter. In a competitive world, there can be no general answer to the query, How can a firm increase its market share? because if it were really general, it would also apply to the firm's competitors.

What questions energize research around a critical issue in the strategy field? And which of these provide a clear path to follow in seeking answers? Clearly, we need to understand how firms and organizations in general make assumptions and decisions about context. In other words, we need to learn more about just how organizations reach conclusions about action, and whether they can in fact be more rational than the individuals that comprise them. Certainly none of the basic and allied disciplines we have examined tells us how firms behave. All seem either to be passively descriptive or to postulate behavior from the outset.

We can also wonder how competition among organizations influences their nature. Among competitive business firms, we see a variety of successful firms with very different natures. Yet theory would suggest this should not be true. No good explanations exist for the difference.

There are concerns about the role of senior management that span several strategically distinctive business firms. Why are they needed and what do they do? All theory available suggests they add costs without corresponding value. Yet they persist, and though we know much about their activities, which are typically strategic in character, we don't know enough about the value they create.

As the world shrinks, competition intensifies, environments grow more complex, and it becomes increasingly difficult to survive. We know too little about these complex processes on an international scale, and we know too little about competitiveness. Nothing in theory much helps to explain this dynamic process of birth, survival, and death.

These kinds of concerns lead us to four fundamental questions that we believe characterize major concerns of the strategic management field. We now turn to their specific development.

The four questions addressed in this volume represent some of the most crucial puzzles in the strategy field, and emphasize the links between strategy and its allied disciplines. While other questions can be posed, almost all relate in one way or another to the four developed here. To satisfy the curious, we include a brief summary of some of the "also-ran" questions in the Afterword.

How Do Firms Behave?

Or, do firms really behave like rational actors, and, if not, what models of their behavior should be used by researchers and policy makers?

Strategy is about the choice of direction for the firm.[7] But what assumptions should the strategist entertain about the choices made by competitive firms, choices that inevitably are interdependent? Is it even reasonable to think of the behavior of a firm as reflecting "choices," or should a much less rational model be used? Thus, the question of how firms behave has two components: (1) the empirical issue of the actual patterns of behavior observed among firms, and (2) the more abstract question of what modeling assumptions are most fruitful in explaining observed patterns or guiding competitive strategy.

The dominant assumption used by economists is that the firm behaves like a rational individual. Therefore, the question, How do firms behave? directs attention toward situations in which the dominant assumption is unwise. Since there is good empirical evidence that individual behavior does not meet strict norms of rationality, even when it is intendedly rational, and since most firm behavior reflects organizational outcomes rather than individual action, it is a reasonable conjecture that the standard rational model of firm behavior is rarely accurate.

The subquestions that appear appropriate to this fundamental question are these:

- What are the foundation assumptions that differentiate among various models of firm behavior (e.g., resource dependence, "garbage can" models, Nelson and Winter's routines, and population ecology models)?
- According to behavioral decision scientists, there are predictable biases in human decision making. Are there predictable biases in firm or organizational behavior? What do we know about the relationships between organizational size (or other stable characteristics) and behavior?
- "Rational" models of competitive interaction posit players who engage in very subtle and complex reasoning. Yet our common experience is that decision makers are far less analytic and perform far less comprehensive analyses than these models posit. If one is a player, is it really "rational" to posit such complex behavior in others?
- Can game theorists deal with biased behavior or with the

---

[7]   Clearly, the organization does not have to be a business firm. Any type of organization could be substituted in the remarks made here and those that follow.

nonrational aspects of firm behavior? Can analytic models of nonrational or extrarational behavior move beyond their present ad hoc status?

Why Are Firms Different?

Or, what sustains the heterogeneity in resources and performance among close competitors despite competition and imitative attempts?

One of the key empirical observations made by strategy researchers, an observation as well as a perspective that sets the strategy field apart from industrial organization economics, is that firms within the same industry differ from one another, often dramatically. In a recent study, Rumelt (1991:179) found that among businesses in the FTC Line of Business sample, the variance in return on capital could be apportioned as follows: 0.8% due to corporate effects, 8.3% due to stable industry effects, and 46.4% due to stable business-unit effects. Thus, the differences among business units within the same industry were eight times as great as the differences among industries. The source of this heterogeneity lies at the root of competitive advantage, and understanding *why* it arises and translating that into *how* it can be achieved is of central concern to the field.

For those who do not accept the idea of equilibrium, there is, of course, no puzzle in heterogeneity—people differ and so must firms. But competition, it is normally thought, should eliminate differences among competitors; good practices and successful techniques will be imitated, and firms that cannot or will not adopt good practices will be driven from the field. Therefore, the challenge is to retain the power of equilibrium thinking and still correctly explain the observed differences among competitors.

Differences among firms may arise from intention, or stochastically, and they may be created and sustained through property rights, active prevention of imitation, or through natural impediments of limitation and resource flows. In addition, these differences may also arise and be sustained through differing conceptual views, theories, or causal maps, differing organizational processes within firms, different levels of organizational learning and team skills, and/or through the action of ambiguity.

There are many different theories that can be used to deal with this question. The following subsidiary questions suggest the range of these theories and the underlying disciplines that may have something to offer:

- To what extent are the differences among firms the results of purposeful differentiation rather than unavoidable heterogeneity in resources and their combinations? That is, should strategy be thought of as the exploitation of existing asymmetry, or the search for and creation of unique resources or market positions?
- Are the most important impediments to equilibration rooted in market phenomena (e.g., first-mover advantages), or are they chiefly rooted in internal organizational phenomena (e.g., cultural differences or learning)?
- Is the search for rents based on resource heterogeneity contrary to public welfare, or does it act in the public's welfare?

What Is the Function of or Value Added by the Headquarters Unit in a Diversified Firm?

Or, what limits the scope of the firm?

The diversified corporation is the dominant form of business firm in the industrialized world. The creation and management of these enterprises has been heavily researched by strategy scholars. Nevertheless, the relative strengths and weaknesses of this organizational form remain poorly understood. In particular, the question of what is, or should be, the value added by the headquarters unit of such firms is of central concern to the strategy field.

There appear to be two general points of view with regard to the role of the headquarters unit in multibusiness firms: the first emphasizes value creation, and the second emphasizes loss prevention. According to the first viewpoint, the headquarters unit formulates the overall strategy for the corporation, including its degree of diversification and organizational form. Also, it manages the process of resource allocation among constituent businesses, apparently better than would the unaided capital markets. Finally, the headquarters unit maintains the existence of key shared resources and manages the processes by which business units share these resources.

By contrast, the loss prevention school of thought sees management as reviewing the strategies of the business units (strategic management), apparently to make sure that egregious logical errors are not made. Second, the headquarters unit monitors the operations of the subunits, providing surer supervision of the agents operating the businesses than would independent boards of directors or the competitive marketplace. Finally, the headquarters unit can extract free cash flow from a mature business unit at much lower cost than can the unaided capital markets or the market for corporate control.

There are, of course, perspectives beyond these two. Financial economics suggests gains from corporate diversification if bankruptcy is costly, and transaction cost economics suggests gains from internalizing businesses sharing co-specialized assets. Finally, there is a skeptical perspective that sees these complex firms as the result of agency problems—as long as managers prefer to invest excess cash rather than pay it back to stockholders, and as long as they can do so, maturing profitable businesses will spawn diversified firms.

The persistence of multibusiness firms cannot be ignored. However, it is no trivial task to isolate the forces that generate and sustain these firms. The subsidiary questions that may aid inquiry into these considerations include:

- Which is primary, strategy or structure? That is, is the multidivisional form (M-form) the administrative solution to the problems created by product-market diversification and/or the need to internalize transactions, or is it itself the innovation that permits efficiencies from the assembly of various business units in a common hierarchy?
- Which is primary, the entrepreneurial (value-creating) role of the headquarters unit, or the administrative (loss-preventing) role? Can a headquarters unit simultaneously perform both roles?
- What, if any, are the limits to the amalgamation of business units in multibusiness firms? Relatedly, how can the value now being created by the breakup of diversified firms be reconciled with the value created by their formation in the past?
- Strategic management is normally taken to mean the explicit oversight and review of the strategy formulation pro-

cess together with systems for allocating resources among businesses. Do firms that impose "strategic management" on portfolios of businesses add value, and if so, what is the mechanism?

- Are there corollaries to headquarters units in nonbusiness organizations and, if so, what are the comparative lessons to be learned?

What Determines Success or Failure in International Competition?

Or, what are the origins of success and what are their particular manifestations in international settings or global competition?

This question has two parts of interest. One part is the more fundamental issue of why some firms enjoy more success than others. What is the dynamic competitive process that leads to the relative success of some firms, and what causes some to decline and some to fail (or, more commonly, to be sold to other firms that more efficiently employ their assets)? This issue is at the heart of competitive dynamics and the workings of capitalism and needs to be understood better in its own right.

Another part of the question deals with international competition and the competitiveness of firms, and indeed, of nations and cultures. At stake is not just firm survival or success, but the quality of life in economies and their respective cultures.

There are a number of disciplines that can shed light on these fundamental issues, including international trade theory, political science, and organizational theory. Subsidiary questions that need to be addressed include these:

- To what extent do firms from different countries (cultures) possess inherent competitive advantages in certain arenas? The issue at stake is not simply the economists' comparative advantage, which would not operate when a domestic firm invests abroad, but a subtler set of management skills, technologies, and norms of work.
- Are there "strategic" industries and, if so, what makes them strategic? That is, are there significant positive externalities associated with the presence of a particular industry within a nation? Note that the often postulated efficacy of

Japan's MITI or an "industrial policy" in the United States
rests on the presumption that there are strategic industries.
• Are there rules for global competition that are not simply
the extension of rules for competition within a large nation-
state or continent?

Summary

These four questions help define the field of strategic management. In our view they are fundamental to understanding the
matter of managing groups, their formation or birth, their relative success, and ultimately their adaptation and survival.
These questions relate to allied disciplines, but they are not
central to them, and their perspectives differ.

The next four sections of the book present the papers that
deal with each of the four questions, and the papers in turn
present the perspectives of authors whose disciplines are not
necessarily those of strategic management. Collectively, the
perspectives offered raise research questions and practice issues
we believe can help set important research and practice agendas
within the strategic management field.

References

Allison, G. (1971). *Essence of Decision*. Boston: Little, Brown.

Anderson, E., and D. C. Schmittlein (1984). "Integration of the Sales Force: An Empirical Examination." *Rand Journal of Economics* 15, pp. 385–395.

Ansoff, H. I. (1965). *Corporate Strategy: An Analytical Approach to Business Policy for Growth and Expansion*. New York: McGraw-Hill.

Armour, H. O., and D. J. Teece (1978). "Organizational Structure and Economic Performance: A Test of the Multidivisional Hypothesis." *Bell Journal of Economics* 9, pp. 106–122.

Arrow, K. J. (1951). *Social Choice and Individual Values*. New York: John Wiley.

Barnard, C. (1938). *The Functions of the Executive*, fifteenth printing, 1962. Cambridge, Mass.: Harvard University Press.

Bartlett, C. A. (1979). "Multinational Structural Evolution: The Changing Decision Environment in International Divisions." Unpublished dissertation, Harvard Business School.

Black, D. (1958). *The Theory of Committees and Elections*. Cambridge: Cambridge University Press.

Blau, P. M., and W. R. Scott (1962). *Formal Organizations*. San Francisco: Chandler.

Buchanan, J. M., and G. Tullock (1962). *The Calculus of Consent*. Ann Arbor: University of Michigan Press.

Buckley, P. J., and M. C. Casson (1976). *The Future of the Multinational Enterprise*. New York: Macmillan.

Burgelman, R. A. (1990). "Strategy-Making and Organizational Ecology: A Conceptual Integration." In J. V. Singh (ed.), *Organizational Evolution: New Directions*. Newbury Park, Cal.: Sage, pp. 164–181.

Burns, T., and E. Stalker (1961). *The Management of Innovation*. London: Tavistock.

Carroll, G. R. (1988). *Ecological Models of Organizations*. Cambridge, Mass.: Ballinger.

Chamberlin, E. H. (1933). *The Theory of Monopolistic Competition*. Cambridge, Mass.: Harvard University Press.

Chandler, A. D., Jr. (1962). *Strategy and Structure: Chapters in the History of the Industrial Enterprise,* Cambridge, Mass.: MIT Press.

Channon, D. F. (1973). *The Strategy and Structure of British Enterprise*. London: Macmillan.

Coase, R. H. (1937). "The Nature of the Firm." *Economica* 4, pp. 386–405.

Cyert, R., and J. March (1963). *A Behavioral Theory of the Firm*. Englewood Cliffs, N. J.: Prentice-Hall.

DiMaggio, J., and W. Powell (1988). "Interest and Agency in Institutional Theory." In L. G. Zucker (ed.), *Industrial Patterns and Organization*. Cambridge, Mass.: Ballinger, pp. 3–22.

Downs, A. (1967). *Inside Bureaucracy*. Boston: Little, Brown.

Doz, Y. (1976). "National Policies and Multinational Management." Unpublished doctoral dissertation, Harvard Business School.

Durkheim, E. (1984, originally published in 1893). *The Division of Labor in Society*. New York: Free Press.

Elster, J. (1989). *The Cement of Society*. Cambridge: Cambridge University Press.

Emery, F. E., and E. L. Trist (1965). "The Causal Texture of Organizational Environments." *Human Relations* 18, pp. 21–32.

Ghemawat, P. (1991). *Commitment: The Dynamic of Strategy*. New York: Free Press.

Ghoshal, S.(1986). "The Innovative Multinational: A Differentiated Network of Organizational Roles and Management Processes." Unpublished doctoral dissertation, Harvard Business School.

Hannan, M. T., and J. Freeman (1977). "The Population Ecology of Organizations." *American Journal of Sociology* 82, pp. 929–964.

Harsanyi, J. (1967). "Games with Incomplete Information Played by 'Bayesian' Players. I: The Basic Model." *Management Science* 14, pp. 159–182.

Hatten, K. J., and D. E. Schendel (1977). "Heterogeneity Within an Industry: Firm Conduct in the U.S. Brewing Industry, 1952–1971." *Journal of Industrial Economics* 26, pp. 97–113.

Hatten, K. J., D. E. Schendel, and Arnold C. Cooper (1978). "A Strategic Model of the U.S. Brewing Industry: 1952–1971." *Academy of Management Journal* 21(4), pp. 592–610.

Hennart, J. F. (1988). "A Transactions Cost Theory of Equity Joint Ventures." *Strategic Management Journal* 9, pp. 361–374.

Homans, G. C. (1950). *The Human Group*. New York: Harcourt.

Jensen, M. C. (1986). "Agency Cost of Free Cash Flow, Corporate Finance, and Takeovers." *American Economic Review Papers and Proceedings* 76, pp. 323–329.

Joskow, P. L. (1988). "Price Adjustment in Long-Term Contracts: The Case of Coal." *Journal of Law and Economics* 31, pp. 47–83.

Kaufman, H. (1960). *The Forest Ranger: A Study in Administrative Behavior*. Baltimore: Johns Hopkins Press.

Knight, F. H. (1965). *Risk, Uncertainty, and Profit*. New York: Harper & Row.

Kogut, B. (1988). "Joint Ventures: Theoretical and Empirical Predictions." *Strategic Management Journal* 9, pp. 319–332.

Kreps, D., P. Milgrom, J. Roberts, and R. Wilson (1982). "Rational Cooperation in the Finitely Repeated Prisoner's Dilemma." *Journal of Economic Theory* 27, pp. 245–252.

Lawrence, P. R., and J. W. Lorsch (1967). *Organization and Environment: Managing Differentiation and Integration*. Boston: Division of Research, Harvard Business School.

Learned, E. P., C. R. Christensen, K. R. Andrews, and W. D. Guth (1965). *Business Policy: Text and Cases*. Homewood, Ill.: Richard D. Irwin.

Lindblom, C. E. (1959). "The Science of 'Muddling Through'." *Public Administration Review* 19, pp. 79–88.

McKelvey, R. (1976). "Intransitivities in Multidimensional Voting Models and Some Implications for Agenda Control." *Journal of Economic Theory* 16, pp. 472–482.

March, J. G., and H. A. Simon (1958). *Organizations.* New York: John Wiley.

Masten, S. (1988). "The Organization of Production: Evidence from the Aerospace Industry." *Journal of Law, Economics, and Organization* 4, pp. 403–418.

Merton, R. K. (1940). "Bureaucratic Structure and Personality." *Social Forces* 18, pp. 16–19.

Meyer, J. W., and B. Rowan (1977). "Institutionalized Organizations: Formal Structure as Myth and Ceremony." *American Journal of Sociology* 83, pp. 340–363.

Mintzberg, H., and J. A. Waters (1978). "Patterns in Strategy Formation." *Management Science* 24, pp. 934–948.

Monteverde, K., and D. J. Teece (1982). "Supplier Switching Costs and Vertical Integration in the Automobile Industry." *Bell Journal of Economics* 13, pp. 206–213.

Nash, J. (1950). "The Bargaining Problem." *Econometrica* 18, pp. 155–162.

Nelson, R., and S. Winter (1982). *An Evolutionary Theory of Economic Change.* Cambridge, Mass.: Harvard University Press.

Newman, W. H. (1951). *Administrative Action: The Techniques of Organization and Management.* Englewood Cliffs, N.J.: Prentice-Hall.

Ouchi, W. G., and A. L. Wilkins (1985). "Organizational Culture." *Annual Review of Sociology* 11, pp. 457–483.

Parsons, T. (1937). *The Structure of Social Action.* New York: McGraw-Hill.

Pavan, R. J. (1972). *Strategy and Structure of Italian Enterprise.* Unpublished doctoral dissertation, Harvard Business School.

Pfeffer, J., and G. R. Salancik (1978). *The External Control of Organizations: A Resource Dependence Perspective.* New York: Harper & Row.

Pisano, G. (1990). "The R&D Boundaries of the Firm." *Administrative Science Quarterly* 34, pp. 153–176.

Pooley-Dias, G. (1972). *Strategy and Structure of French Enterprise.* Doctoral dissertation, Harvard University.

Porter, M. E. (1980). *Competitive Strategy: Techniques for Analyzing Industries and Competitors.* New York: Free Press.

Powell, W. W., and P. J. DiMaggio (1991). *The New Institutionalism in Organizational Analysis.* Chicago: University of Chicago Press.

Prahalad, C. K. (1975). *The Strategic Process in a Multinational Corporation.* Unpublished doctoral dissertation, Harvard Business School.

Quinn, J. B. (1980). *Strategies for Change: Logical Incrementalism.* Homewood, Ill.: Dow Jones-Irwin.

Robinson, J. (1959). *The Economics of Imperfect Competition.* New York: St. Martin's Press. Originally published in 1933.

Rumelt, R. P. (1974). *Strategy, Structure and Economic Performance.* Boston: Division of Research, Harvard Business School.

Rumelt, R. P. (1991). "How Much Does Industry Matter?" *Strategic Management Journal* 12(3), pp. 167–185.

Schumpter, J. A. (1911/1934). *The Theory of Economic Development.* Cambridge, Mass.: Harvard University Press.

Selten, R. (1965). "Spieltheoretische Behandlung eines Oligopolmodells mit Nachfragetragheit." *Zeitschrift für die gesamte Staatswissenschaft* 12, pp. 301–324.

Selznick, P. (1949). *TVA and the Grass Roots.* Berkeley: University of California Press.

Selznick, P. (1957). *Leadership in Administration: A Sociological Interpretation.* New York: Harper & Row.

Shepsle, K. A. (1979). "Institutional Arrangements and Equilibrium in Multidimensional Voting Models." *American Journal of Political Science* 23, pp. 27–59.

Simon, H. A. (1947). *Administrative Behavior.* New York: Macmillan.

Spence, A. M. (1974). *Market Signaling.* Cambridge: Mass.: Harvard University Press.

Stopford, J., and L. T. Wells, Jr. (1972). *Managing the Multinational Enterprise.* New York: Basic Books.

Taylor, F. W. (1947). *Scientific Management.* New York: Harper.

Teece, D. J. (1985). "Multinational Enterprise, Internal Governance and Economic Organization." *American Economic Review* 75, pp. 233–238.

Thanheiser, H. (1972). *Strategy and Structure of German Enterprise.* Unpublished doctoral dissertation, Harvard Business School.

Thompson, J. D. (1967). *Organizations in Action.* New York: McGraw-Hill.

von Neumann, J., and O. Morgenstern (1944). *The Theory of Games and Economic Behavior.* New York: John Wiley.

Weber, M. (1947). "The Theory of Social and Economic Organization." In A. H. Henderson and T. Parsons (trans.), Glencoe, Ill.: Free Press (originally published in 1924).

Weingast, B. R. (1989). "Floor Behavior in the U.S. Congress: Committee Power under the Open Rule." *American Political Science Review* 83, September, pp. 795–815.

Williamson, O. E. (1975). *Markets and Hierarchies: Analysis and Antitrust Implications.* New York: Free Press.

Wilson, J. Q. (1989). *Bureaucracy.* New York: Basic Books.

Woodward, J. (1965). *Industrial Organization: Theory and Practice.* New York: Oxford University Press.

Wrigley, L. (1970). *Divisional Autonomy and Diversification.* Unpublished doctoral dissertation, Harvard Business School.

[8]

Strategic Management Journal, Vol. 18:7, 509–533 (1997)

DYNAMIC CAPABILITIES AND STRATEGIC MANAGEMENT

DAVID J. TEECE[1]*, GARY PISANO[2] and AMY SHUEN[3]
[1]*Haas School of Business, University of California, Berkeley, California, U.S.A.*
[2]*Graduate School of Business Administration, Harvard University, Boston, Massachusetts, U.S.A.*
[3]*School of Business, San Jose State University, San Jose, California, U.S.A.*

The dynamic capabilities framework analyzes the sources and methods of wealth creation and capture by private enterprise firms operating in environments of rapid technological change. The competitive advantage of firms is seen as resting on distinctive processes (ways of coordinating and combining), shaped by the firm's (specific) asset positions (such as the firm's portfolio of difficult-to-trade knowledge assets and complementary assets), and the evolution path(s) it has adopted or inherited. The importance of path dependencies is amplified where conditions of increasing returns exist. Whether and how a firm's competitive advantage is eroded depends on the stability of market demand, and the ease of replicability (expanding internally) and imitatability (replication by competitors). If correct, the framework suggests that private wealth creation in regimes of rapid technological change depends in large measure on honing internal technological, organizational, and managerial processes inside the firm. In short, identifying new opportunities and organizing effectively and efficiently to embrace them are generally more fundamental to private wealth creation than is strategizing, if by strategizing one means engaging in business conduct that keeps competitors off balance, raises rival's costs, and excludes new entrants. © 1997 by John Wiley & Sons, Ltd.

INTRODUCTION

The fundamental question in the field of strategic management is how firms achieve and sustain competitive advantage.[1] We confront this question here by developing the dynamic capabilities approach, which endeavors to analyze the sources of wealth creation and capture by firms. The development of this framework flows from a recognition by the authors that strategic theory is replete with analyses of firm-level strategies for sustaining and safeguarding extant competitive advantage, but has performed less well with

Key words: competences; capabilities; innovation; strategy; path dependency; knowledge assets

*Correspondence to: David J. Teece, Institute of Management, Innovation and Organization, Haas School of Business, University of California, Berkeley, CA 94720–1930, U.S.A.
[1] For a review of the fundamental questions in the field of strategy, see Rumelt, Schendel, and Teece (1994).

CCC 0143–2095/97/070509–25$17.50
© 1997 by John Wiley & Sons, Ltd.

respect to assisting in the understanding of how and why certain firms build competitive advantage in regimes of rapid change. Our approach is especially relevant in a Schumpeterian world of innovation-based competition, price/performance rivalry, increasing returns, and the 'creative destruction' of existing competences. The approach endeavors to explain firm-level success and failure. We are interested in both building a better theory of firm performance, as well as informing managerial practice.

In order to position our analysis in a manner that displays similarities and differences with existing approaches, we begin by briefly reviewing accepted frameworks for strategic management. We endeavor to expose implicit assumptions, and identify competitive circumstances where each paradigm might display some relative advantage as both a useful descriptive and normative theory of competitive strategy. While numerous theories have been advanced over the past

Received 17 April 1991
Final revision received 4 March 1997

two decades about the sources of competitive advantage, many cluster around just a few loosely structured frameworks or paradigms. In this paper we attempt to identify three existing paradigms and describe aspects of an emerging new paradigm that we label dynamic capabilities.

The dominant paradigm in the field during the 1980s was the competitive forces approach developed by Porter (1980). This approach, rooted in the structure–conduct–performance paradigm of industrial organization (Mason, 1949; Bain, 1959), emphasizes the actions a firm can take to create defensible positions against competitive forces. A second approach, referred to as a strategic conflict approach (e.g., Shapiro, 1989), is closely related to the first in its focus on product market imperfections, entry deterrence, and strategic interaction. The strategic conflict approach uses the tools of game theory and thus implicitly views competitive outcomes as a function of the effectiveness with which firms keep their rivals off balance through strategic investments, pricing strategies, signaling, and the control of information. Both the competitive forces and the strategic conflict approaches appear to share the view that rents flow from privileged product market positions.

Another distinct class of approaches emphasizes building competitive advantage through capturing entrepreneurial rents stemming from fundamental firm-level efficiency advantages. These approaches have their roots in a much older discussion of corporate strengths and weaknesses; they have taken on new life as evidence suggests that firms build enduring advantages only through efficiency and effectiveness, and as developments in organizational economics and the study of technological and organizational change become applied to strategy questions. One strand of this literature, often referred to as the 'resource-based perspective,' emphasizes firm-specific capabilities and assets and the existence of isolating mechanisms as the fundamental determinants of firm performance (Penrose, 1959; Rumelt, 1984; Teece, 1984; Wernerfelt, 1984).[2] This perspective

recognizes but does not attempt to explain the nature of the isolating mechanisms that enable entrepreneurial rents and competitive advantage to be sustained.

Another component of the efficiency-based approach is developed in this paper. Rudimentary efforts are made to identify the dimensions of firm-specific capabilities that can be sources of advantage, and to explain how combinations of competences and resources can be developed, deployed, and protected. We refer to this as the 'dynamic capabilities' approach in order to stress exploiting existing internal and external firm-specific competences to address changing environments. Elements of the approach can be found in Schumpeter (1942), Penrose (1959), Nelson and Winter (1982), Prahalad and Hamel (1990), Teece (1976, 1986a, 1986b, 1988) and in Hayes, Wheelwright, and Clark (1988): Because this approach emphasizes the development of management capabilities, and difficult-to-imitate combinations of organizational, functional and technological skills, it integrates and draws upon research in such areas as the management of R&D, product and process development, technology transfer, intellectual property, manufacturing, human resources, and organizational learning. Because these fields are often viewed as outside the traditional boundaries of strategy, much of this research has not been incorporated into existing economic approaches to strategy issues. As a result, dynamic capabilities can be seen as an emerging and potentially integrative approach to understanding the newer sources of competitive advantage.

We suggest that the dynamic capabilities approach is promising both in terms of future research potential and as an aid to management endeavoring to gain competitive advantage in increasingly demanding environments. To illustrate the essential elements of the dynamic capabilities approach, the sections that follow compare and contrast this approach to other models of strategy. Each section highlights the strategic

---

[2] Of these authors, Rumelt may have been the first to self-consciously apply a resource perspective to the field of strategy. Rumelt (1984: 561) notes that the strategic firm 'is characterized by a bundle of linked and idiosyncratic resources and resource conversion activities.' Similarly, Teece (1984: 95) notes: 'Successful firms possess one or more forms of intangible assets, such as technological or managerial know-

how. Over time, these assets may expand beyond the point of profitable reinvestment in a firm's traditional market. Accordingly, the firm may consider deploying its intangible assets in different product or geographical markets, where the expected returns are higher, if efficient transfer modes exist.' Wernerfelt (1984) was early to recognize that this approach was at odds with product market approaches and might constitute a distinct paradigm of strategy.

insights provided by each approach as well as the different competitive circumstances in which it might be most appropriate. Needless to say, these approaches are in many ways complementary and a full understanding of firm-level, competitive advantage requires an appreciation of all four approaches and more.

MODELS OF STRATEGY EMPHASIZING THE EXPLOITATION OF MARKET POWER

Competitive forces

The dominant paradigm in strategy at least during the 1980s was the competitive forces approach. Pioneered by Porter (1980), the competitive forces approach views the essence of competitive strategy formulation as 'relating a company to its environment ... [T]he key aspect of the firm's environment is the industry or industries in which it competes.' Industry structure strongly influences the competitive rules of the game as well as the strategies potentially available to firms.

In the competitive forces model, five industry-level forces—entry barriers, threat of substitution, bargaining power of buyers, bargaining power of suppliers, and rivalry among industry incumbents—determine the inherent profit potential of an industry or subsegment of an industry. The approach can be used to help the firm find a position in an industry from which it can best defend itself against competitive forces or influence them in its favor (Porter, 1980: 4).

This 'five-forces' framework provides a systematic way of thinking about how competitive forces work at the industry level and how these forces determine the profitability of different industries and industry segments. The competitive forces framework also contains a number of underlying assumptions about the sources of competition and the nature of the strategy process. To facilitate comparisons with other approaches, we highlight several distinctive characteristics of the framework.

Economic rents in the competitive forces framework are monopoly rents (Teece, 1984). Firms in an industry earn rents when they are somehow able to impede the competitive forces (in either factor markets or product markets) which tend to drive economic returns to zero. Available strategies are described in Porter (1980). Competitive strategies are often aimed at altering the firm's position in the industry *vis-à-vis* competitors and suppliers. Industry structure plays a central role in determining and limiting strategic action.

Some industries or subsectors of industries become more 'attractive' because they have structural impediments to competitive forces (e.g., entry barriers) that allow firms better opportunities for creating sustainable competitive advantages. Rents are created largely at the industry or subsector level rather than at the firm level. While there is some recognition given to firm-specific assets, differences among firms relate primarily to scale. This approach to strategy reflects its incubation inside the field of industrial organization and in particular the industrial structure school of Mason and Bain[3] (Teece, 1984).

Strategic conflict

The publication of Carl Shapiro's 1989 article, confidently titled 'The Theory of Business Strategy,' announced the emergence of a new approach to business strategy, if not strategic management. This approach utilizes the tools of game theory to analyze the nature of competitive interaction between rival firms. The main thrust of work in this tradition is to reveal how a firm can influence the behavior and actions of rival firms and thus the market environment.[4] Examples of such moves are investment in capacity (Dixit, 1980), R&D (Gilbert and Newberry, 1982), and advertising (Schmalensee, 1983). To be effective, these strategic moves require irreversible commitments.[5] The moves in question will have no effect if they can be costlessly undone. A key idea is that by manipulating the market environment, a firm may be able to increase its profits.

---

[3] In competitive environments characterized by sustainable and stable mobility and structural barriers, these forces may become the determinants of industry-level profitability. However, competitive advantage is more complex to ascertain in environments of rapid technological change where specific assets owned by heterogeneous firms can be expected to play a larger role in explaining rents.

[4] The market environment is all factors that influence market outcomes (prices, quantities, profits) including the beliefs of customers and of rivals, the number of potential technologies employed, and the costs or speed with which a rival can enter the industry.

[5] For an excellent discussion of committed competition in multiple contexts, see Ghemawat (1991).

512   *D. J. Teece, G. Pisano and A. Shuen*

This literature, together with the contestability literature (Baumol, Panzar, and Willig, 1982), has led to a greater appreciation of the role of sunk costs, as opposed to fixed costs, in determining competitive outcomes. Strategic moves can also be designed to influence rivals' behavior through signaling. Strategic signaling has been examined in a number of contexts, including predatory pricing (Kreps and Wilson, 1982a, 1982b) and limit pricing (Milgrom and Roberts, 1982a, 1982b). More recent treatments have emphasized the role of commitment and reputation (e.g., Ghemawat, 1991) and the benefits of firms simultaneously pursuing competition and cooperation[6] (Brandenburger and Nalebuff, 1995, 1996).

In many instances, game theory formalizes long-standing intuitive arguments about various types of business behavior (e.g., predatory pricing, patent races), though in some instances it has induced a substantial change in the conventional wisdom. But by rationalizing observed behavior by reference to suitably designed games, in explaining everything these models also explain nothing, as they do not generate testable predictions (Sutton, 1992). Many specific game-theoretic models admit multiple equilibrium, and a wide range of choice exists as to the design of the appropriate game form to be used. Unfortunately, the results often depend on the precise specification chosen. The equilibrium in models of strategic behavior crucially depends on what one rival believes another rival will do in a particular situation. Thus the qualitative features of the results may depend on the way price competition is modeled (e.g., Bertrand or Cournot) or on the presence or absence of strategic asymmetries such as first-mover advantages. The analysis of strategic moves using game theory can be thought of as 'dynamic' in the sense that multiperiod analyses can be pursued both intuitively and formally. However, we use the term 'dynamic' in this paper in a different sense, referring to situations where there is rapid change in technology and market forces, and 'feedback' effects on firms.[7]

We have a particular view of the contexts in which the strategic conflict literature is relevant to strategic management. Firms that have a tremendous cost or other competitive advantage *vis-à-vis* their rivals ought not be transfixed by the moves and countermoves of their rivals. Their competitive fortunes will swing more on total demand conditions, not on how competitors deploy and redeploy their competitive assets. Put differently, when there are gross asymmetries in competitive advantage between firms, the results of game-theoretic analysis are likely to be obvious and uninteresting. The stronger competitor will generally advance, even if disadvantaged by certain information asymmetries. To be sure, incumbent firms can be undone by new entrants with a dramatic cost advantage, but no 'gaming' will overturn that outcome. On the other hand, if firms' competitive positions are more delicately balanced, as with Coke and Pepsi, and United Airlines and American Airlines, then strategic conflict is of interest to competitive outcomes. Needless to say, there are many such circumstances, but they are rare in industries where there is rapid technological change and fast-shifting market circumstances.

In short, where competitors do not have deep-seated competitive advantages, the moves and countermoves of competitors can often be usefully formulated in game-theoretic terms. However, we doubt that game theory can comprehensively illuminate how Chrysler should compete against Toyota and Honda, or how United Airlines can best respond to Southwest Airlines since Southwest's advantage is built on organizational attributes which United cannot readily replicate.[8] Indeed, the entrepreneurial side of strategy—how significant new rent streams are created and protected—is largely ignored by the game-theoretic approach.[9] Accordingly, we find that the approach, while important, is most relevant

---

[6] Competition and cooperation have also been analyzed ouside of this tradition. See, for example, Teece (1992) and Link, Teece and Finan (1996).

[7] Accordingly, both approaches are dynamic, but in very different senses.

---

[8] Thus even in the air transport industry game-theoretic formulations by no means capture all the relevant dimensions of competitive rivalry. United Airlines' and United Express's difficulties in competing with Southwest Airlines because of United's inability to fully replicate Southwest's operation capabilities is documented in Gittel (1995).

[9] Important exceptions can be found in Brandenburger and Nalebuff (1996) such as their emphasis on the role of complements. However, these insights do not flow uniquely from game theory and can be found in the organizational economics literature (e.g., Teece, 1986a, 1986b; de Figueiredo and Teece, 1996).

when competitors are closely matched[10] and the population of relevant competitors and the identity of their strategic alternatives can be readily ascertained. Nevertheless, coupled with other approaches it can sometimes yield powerful insights.

However, this research has an orientation that we are concerned about in terms of the implicit framing of strategic issues. Rents, from a game-theoretic perspective, are ultimately a result of managers' intellectual ability to 'play the game.' The adage of the strategist steeped in this approach is 'do unto others before they do unto you.' We worry that fascination with strategic moves and Machiavellian tricks will distract managers from seeking to build more enduring sources of competitive advantage. The approach unfortunately ignores competition as a process involving the development, accumulation, combination, and protection of unique skills and capabilities. Since strategic interactions are what receive focal attention, the impression one might receive from this literature is that success in the marketplace is the result of sophisticated plays and counterplays, when this is generally not the case at all.[11]

In what follows, we suggest that building a dynamic view of the business enterprise—something missing from the two approaches we have so far identified—enhances the probability of establishing an acceptable descriptive theory of strategy that can assist practitioners in the building of long-run advantage and competitive flexibility. Below, we discuss first the resource-based perspective and then an extension we call the dynamic capabilities approach.

MODELS OF STRATEGY EMPHASIZING EFFICIENCY

Resource-based perspective

The resource-based approach sees firms with superior systems and structures being profitable not because they engage in strategic investments that may deter entry and raise prices above long-run costs, but because they have markedly lower costs, or offer markedly higher quality or product performance. This approach focuses on the rents accruing to the owners of scarce firm-specific resources rather than the economic profits from product market positioning.[12] Competitive advantage lies 'upstream' of product markets and rests on the firm's idiosyncratic and difficult-to-imitate resources.[13]

One can find the resources approach suggested by the earlier preanalytic strategy literature. A leading text of the 1960s (Learned *et al.*, 1969) noted that 'the capability of an organization is its demonstrated and potential ability to accomplish against the opposition of circumstance or competition, whatever it sets out to do. Every organization has actual and potential strengths and weaknesses; it is important to try to determine what they are and to distinguish one from the other.' Thus what a firm can do is not just a function of the opportunities it confronts; it also depends on what resources the organization can muster.

Learned *et al.* proposed that the real key to a company's success or even to its future development lies in its ability to find or create 'a competence that is truly distinctive.'[14] This literature also recognized the constraints on firm behavior and, in particular, noted that one should not assume that management 'can rise to any occasion.' These insights do appear to keenly anticipate the resource-based approach that has since emerged, but they did not provide a theory or systematic framework for analyzing business strategies. Indeed, Andrews (1987: 46) noted that 'much of what is intuitive in this process is yet to be identified.' Unfortunately, the academic literature on capabilities stalled for a couple of decades.

New impetus has been given to the resource-based approach by recent theoretical developments in organizational economics and in the theory of strategy, as well as by a growing

---

[10] When closely matched in an aggregate sense, they may nevertheless display asymmetries which game theorists can analyze.
[11] The strategic conflict literature also tends to focus practitioners on product market positioning rather than on developing the unique assets which make possible superior product market positions (Dierickx and Cool, 1989).

[12] In the language of economics, rents flow from unique firm-specific assets that cannot readily be replicated, rather than from tactics which deter entry and keep competitors off balance. In short, rents are Ricardian.
[13] Teece (1982: 46) saw the firm as having 'a variety of end products which it can produce with its organizational technology.'
[14] Elsewhere Andrews (1987: 47) defined a distinctive competence as what an organization can do particularly well.

body of anecdotal and empirical literature[15] that highlights the importance of firm-specific factors in explaining firm performance. Cool and Schendel (1988) have shown that there are systematic and significant performance differences among firms which belong to the same strategic group within the U.S. pharmaceutical industry. Rumelt (1991) has shown that intraindustry differences in profits are greater than interindustry differences in profits, strongly suggesting the importance of firm-specific factors and the relative unimportance of industry effects.[16] Jacobsen (1988) and Hansen and Wernerfelt (1989) made similar findings.

A comparison of the resource-based approach and the competitive forces approach (discussed earlier in the paper) in terms of their implications for the strategy process is revealing. From the first perspective, an entry decision looks roughly as follows: (1) pick an industry (based on its 'structural attractiveness'); (2) choose an entry strategy based on conjectures about competitors' rational strategies; (3) if not already possessed, acquire or otherwise obtain the requisite assets to compete in the market. From this perspective, the process of identifying and developing the requisite assets is not particularly problematic. The process involves nothing more than choosing rationally among a well-defined set of investment alternatives. If assets are not already owned, they can be bought. The resource-based perspective is strongly at odds with this conceptualization.

From the resource-based perspective, firms are heterogeneous with respect to their resources/ capabilities/endowments. Further, resource endowments are 'sticky:' at least in the short run, firms are to some degree stuck with what they have and may have to live with what they lack.[17] This stickiness arises for three reasons. First, business development is viewed as an extremely complex

process.[18] Quite simply, firms lack the organizational capacity to develop new competences quickly (Dierickx and Cool, 1989). Secondly, some assets are simply not readily tradeable, for example, tacit know-how (Teece, 1976, 1980) and reputation (Dierickx and Cool, 1989). Thus, resource endowments cannot equilibrate through factor input markets. Finally, even when an asset can be purchased, firms may stand to gain little by doing so. As Barney (1986) points out, unless a firm is lucky, possesses superior information, or both, the price it pays in a competitive factor market will fully capitalize the rents from the asset.

Given that in the resources perspective firms possess heterogeneous and sticky resource bundles, the entry decision process suggested by this approach is as follows: (1) identify your firm's unique resources; (2) decide in which markets those resources can earn the highest rents; and (3) decide whether the rents from those assets are most effectively utilized by (a) integrating into related market(s), (b) selling the relevant intermediate output to related firms, or (c) selling the assets themselves to a firm in related businesses (Teece, 1980, 1982).

The resource-based perspective puts both vertical integration and diversification into a new strategic light. Both can be viewed as ways of capturing rents on scarce, firm-specific assets whose services are difficult to sell in intermediate markets (Penrose, 1959; Williamson, 1975; Teece, 1980, 1982, 1986a, 1986b; Wernerfelt, 1984). Empirical work on the relationship between performance and diversification by Wernerfelt and Montgomery (1988) provides evidence for this proposition. It is evident that the resource-based perspective focuses on strategies for exploiting existing firm-specific assets.

However, the resource-based perspective also invites consideration of managerial strategies for developing new capabilities (Wernerfelt, 1984). Indeed, if control over scarce resources is the source of economic profits, then it follows that such issues as skill acquisition, the management of knowledge and know-how (Shuen, 1994), and learning become fundamental strategic issues. It is in this second dimension, encompassing skill acquisition, learning, and accumulation of organizational and intangible or 'invisible' assets (Itami

---

[15] Studies of the automobile and other industries displayed differences in organization which often underlay differences amongst firms. See, for example, Womack, Jones, and Roos, 1991; Hayes and Clark, 1985; Barney, Spender and Reve, 1994; Clark and Fujimoto, 1991; Henderson and Cockburn, 1994; Nelson, 1991; Levinthal and Myatt, 1994.

[16] Using FTC line of business data, Rumelt showed that stable industry effects account for only 8 percent of the variance in business unit returns. Furthermore, only about 40 percent of the dispersion in industry returns is due to stable industry effects.

[17] In this regard, this approach has much in common with recent work on organizational ecology (e.g., Freeman and Boeker, 1984) and also on commitment (Ghemawat, 1991: 17–25).

---

[18] Capability development, however, is not really analyzed.

and Roehl, 1987), that we believe lies the greatest potential for contributions to strategy.

The dynamic capabilities approach: Overview

The global competitive battles in high-technology industries such as semiconductors, information services, and software have demonstrated the need for an expanded paradigm to understand how competitive advantage is achieved. Well-known companies like IBM, Texas Instruments, Philips, and others appear to have followed a 'resource-based strategy' of accumulating valuable technology assets, often guarded by an aggressive intellectual property stance. However, this strategy is often not enough to support a significant competitive advantage. Winners in the global marketplace have been firms that can demonstrate timely responsiveness and rapid and flexible product innovation, coupled with the management capability to effectively coordinate and redeploy internal and external competences. Not surprisingly, industry observers have remarked that companies can accumulate a large stock of valuable technology assets and still not have many useful capabilities.

We refer to this ability to achieve new forms of competitive advantage as 'dynamic capabilities' to emphasize two key aspects that were not the main focus of attention in previous strategy perspectives. The term 'dynamic' refers to the capacity to renew competences so as to achieve congruence with the changing business environment; certain innovative responses are required when time-to-market and timing are critical, the rate of technological change is rapid, and the nature of future competition and markets difficult to determine. The term 'capabilities' emphasizes the key role of strategic management in appropriately adapting, integrating, and reconfiguring internal and external organizational skills, resources, and functional competences to match the requirements of a changing environment.

One aspect of the strategic problem facing an innovating firm in a world of Schumpeterian competition is to identify difficult-to-imitate internal and external competences most likely to support valuable products and services. Thus, as argued by Dierickx and Cool (1989), choices about how much to spend (invest) on different possible areas are central to the firm's strategy. However, choices about domains of competence are influenced by past choices. At any given point in time, firms must follow a certain trajectory or path of competence development. This path not only defines what choices are open to the firm today, but it also puts bounds around what its internal repertoire is likely to be in the future. Thus, firms, at various points in time, make long-term, quasi-irreversible commitments to certain domains of competence.[19]

The notion that competitive advantage requires both the exploitation of existing internal and external firm-specific capabilities, and developing new ones is partially developed in Penrose (1959), Teece (1982), and Wernerfelt (1984). However, only recently have researchers begun to focus on the specifics of how some organizations first develop firm-specific capabilities and how they renew competences to respond to shifts in the business environment.[20] These issues are intimately tied to the firm's business processes, market positions, and expansion paths. Several writers have recently offered insights and evidence on how firms can develop their capability to adapt and even capitalize on rapidly changing environments.[21] The dynamic capabilities approach seeks to provide a coherent framework which can both integrate existing conceptual and empirical knowledge, and facilitate prescription. In doing so, it builds upon the theoretical foundations provided by Schumpeter (1934), Penrose (1959), Williamson (1975, 1985), Barney (1986), Nelson and Winter (1982), Teece (1988), and Teece *et al.* (1994).

TOWARD A DYNAMIC CAPABILITIES FRAMEWORK

Terminology

In order to facilitate theory development and intellectual dialogue, some acceptable definitions are desirable. We propose the following.

---

[19] Deciding, under significant uncertainty about future states of the world, which long-term paths to commit to and when to change paths is the central strategic problem confronting the firm. In this regard, the work of Ghemawat (1991) is highly germane to the dynamic capabilities approach to strategy.
[20] See, for example, Iansiti and Clark (1994) and Henderson (1994).
[21] See Hayes *et al.* (1988), Prahalad and Hamel (1990), Dierickx and Cool (1989), Chandler (1990), and Teece (1993).

516   *D. J. Teece, G. Pisano and A. Shuen*

Factors of production

These are 'undifferentiated' inputs available in disaggregate form in factor markets. By undifferentiated we mean that they lack a firm-specific component. Land, unskilled labor, and capital are typical examples. Some factors may be available for the taking, such as public knowledge. In the language of Arrow, such resources must be 'non-fugitive.'[22] Property rights are usually well defined for factors of production.

Resources[23]

Resources are firm-specific assets that are difficult if not impossible to imitate. Trade secrets and certain specialized production facilities and engineering experience are examples. Such assets are difficult to transfer among firms because of transactions costs and transfer costs, and because the assets may contain tacit knowledge.

Organizational routines/competences

When firm-specific assets are assembled in integrated clusters spanning individuals and groups so that they enable distinctive activities to be performed, these activities constitute organizational routines and processes. Examples include quality, miniaturization, and systems integration. Such competences are typically viable across multiple product lines, and may extend outside the firm to embrace alliance partners.

Core competences

We define those competences that define a firm's fundamental business as core. Core competences must accordingly be derived by looking across the range of a firm's (and its competitors') products and services.[24] The value of core competences can be enhanced by combination with the appropriate complementary assets. The degree

to which a core competence is distinctive depends on how well endowed the firm is relative to its competitors, and on how difficult it is for competitors to replicate its competences.

Dynamic capabilities

We define dynamic capabilities as the firm's ability to integrate, build, and reconfigure internal and external competences to address rapidly changing environments. Dynamic capabilities thus reflect an organization's ability to achieve new and innovative forms of competitive advantage given path dependencies and market positions (Leonard-Barton, 1992).

Products

End products are the final goods and services produced by the firm based on utilizing the competences that it possesses. The performance (price, quality, etc.) of a firm's products relative to its competitors at any point in time will depend upon its competences (which over time depend on its capabilities).

Markets and strategic capabilities

Different approaches to strategy view sources of wealth creation and the essence of the strategic problem faced by firms differently. The competitive forces framework sees the strategic problem in terms of industry structure, entry deterrence, and positioning; game-theoretic models view the strategic problem as one of interaction between rivals with certain expectations about how each other will behave;[25] resource-based perspectives have focused on the exploitation of firm-specific assets. Each approach asks different, often complementary questions. A key step in building a conceptual framework related to dynamic capabilities is to identify the foundations upon which distinctive and difficult-to-replicate advantages can be built, maintained, and enhanced.

A useful way to vector in on the strategic elements of the business enterprise is first to identify what is not strategic. To be strategic, a

---

[22] Arrow (1996) defines fugitive resources as ones that can move cheaply amongst individuals and firms.
[23] We do not like the term 'resource' and believe it is misleading. We prefer to use the term firm-specific asset. We use it here to try and maintain links to the literature on the resource-based approach which we believe is important.
[24] Thus Eastman Kodak's core competence might be considered imaging, IBM's might be considered integrated data processing and service, and Motorola's untethered communications.

[25] In sequential move games, each player looks ahead and anticipates his rival's future responses in order to reason back and decide action, i.e., look forward, reason backward.

capability must be honed to a user need[26] (so there is a source of revenues), unique (so that the products/services produced can be priced without too much regard to competition) and difficult to replicate (so profits will not be competed away). Accordingly, any assets or entity which are homogeneous and can be bought and sold at an established price cannot be all that strategic (Barney, 1986). What is it, then, about firms which undergirds competitive advantage?

To answer this, one must first make some fundamental distinctions between markets and internal organization (firms). The essence of the firm, as Coase (1937) pointed out, is that it displaces market organization. It does so in the main because inside the firms one can organize certain types of economic activity in ways one cannot using markets. This is not only because of transaction costs, as Williamson (1975, 1985) emphasized, but also because there are many types of arrangements where injecting high-powered (market like) incentives might well be quite destructive of cooperative activity and learning.[27] Inside an organization, exchange cannot take place in the same manner that it can outside an organization, not just because it might be destructive to provide high-powered individual incentives, but because it is difficult if not impossible to tightly calibrate individual contribution to a joint effort. Hence, contrary to Arrow's (1969) view of firms as quasi markets, and the task of management to inject markets into firms, we recognize the inherent limits and possible counterproductive results of attempting to fashion firms into simply clusters of internal markets. In particular, learning and internal technology transfer may well be jeopardized.

Indeed, what is distinctive about firms is that they are domains for organizing activity in a nonmarket-like fashion. Accordingly, as we discuss what is distinctive about firms, we stress competences/capabilities which are ways of organizing and getting things done which cannot be accomplished merely by using the price system

to coordinate activity.[28] The very essence of most capabilities/competences is that they cannot be readily assembled through markets (Teece, 1982, 1986a; Zander and Kogut, 1995). If the ability to assemble competences using markets is what is meant by the firm as a nexus of contracts (Fama, 1980), then we unequivocally state that the firm about which we theorize cannot be usefully modeled as a nexus of contracts. By 'contract' we are referring to a transaction undergirded by a legal agreement, or some other arrangement which clearly spells out rights, rewards, and responsibilities. Moreover, the firm as a nexus of contracts suggests a series of bilateral contracts orchestrated by a coordinator. Our view of the firm is that the organization takes place in a more multilateral fashion, with patterns of behavior and learning being orchestrated in a much more decentralized fashion, but with a viable headquarters operation.

The key point, however, is that the properties of internal organization cannot be replicated by a portfolio of business units amalgamated just through formal contracts as many distinctive elements of internal organization simply cannot be replicated in the market.[29] That is, entrepreneurial activity cannot lead to the immediate replication of unique organizational skills through simply entering a market and piecing the parts together overnight. Replication takes time, and the replication of best practice may be illusive. Indeed, firm capabilities need to be understood not in terms of balance sheet items, but mainly in terms of the organizational structures and managerial processes which support productive activity. By construction, the firm's balance sheet contains items that can be valued, at least at original market prices (cost). It is necessarily the case, therefore, that the balance sheet is a poor shadow of a firm's distinctive competences.[30]

---

[26] Needless to say, users need not be the current customers of the enterprise. Thus a capability can be the basis for diversification into new product markets.

[27] Indeed, the essence of internal organization is that it is a domain of unleveraged or low-powered incentives. By unleveraged we mean that rewards are determined at the group or organization level, not primarily at the individual level, in an effort to encourage team behavior, not individual behavior.

[28] We see the problem of market contracting as a matter of coordination as much as we see it a problem of opportunism in the fact of contractual hazards. In this sense, we are consonant with both Richardson (1960) and Williamson (1975, 1985).

[29] As we note in Teece *et al.* (1994), the conglomerate offers few if any efficiencies because there is little provided by the conglomerate form that shareholders cannot obtain for themselves simply by holding a diversified portfolio of stocks.

[30] Owners' equity may reflect, in part, certain historic capabilities. Recently, some scholars have begun to attempt to measure organizational capability using financial statement data. See Baldwin and Clark (1991) and Lev and Sougiannis (1992).

518   *D. J. Teece, G. Pisano and A. Shuen*

That which is distinctive cannot be bought and sold short of buying the firm itself, or one or more of its subunits.

There are many dimensions of the business firm that must be understood if one is to grasp firm-level distinctive competences/capabilities. In this paper we merely identify several classes of factors that will help determine a firm's distinctive competence and dynamic capabilities. We organize these in three categories: processes, positions, and paths. The essence of competences and capabilities is embedded in organizational processes of one kind or another. But the content of these processes and the opportunities they afford for developing competitive advantage at any point in time are shaped significantly by the assets the firm possesses (internal and market) and by the evolutionary path it has adopted/inherited. Hence organizational processes, shaped by the firm's asset positions and molded by its evolutionary and co-evolutionary paths, explain the essence of the firm's dynamic capabilities and its competitive advantage.

Processes, positions, and paths

We thus advance the argument that the competitive advantage of firms lies with its managerial and organizational processes, shaped by its (specific) asset position, and the paths available to it.[31] By managerial and organizational processes, we refer to the way things are done in the firm, or what might be referred to as its routines, or patterns of current practice and learning. By position we refer to its current specific endowments of technology, intellectual property, complementary assets, customer base, and its external relations with suppliers and complementors. By paths we refer to the strategic alternatives available to the firm, and the presence or absence of increasing returns and attendant path dependencies.

Our focus throughout is on asset structures for which no ready market exists, as these are the only assets of strategic interest. A final section

focuses on replication and imitation, as it is these phenomena which determine how readily a competence or capability can be cloned by competitors, and therefore distinctiveness of its competences and the durability of its advantage.

The firm's processes and positions collectively encompass its competences and capabilities. A hierarchy of competences/capabilities ought to be recognized, as some competences may be on the factory floor, some in the R&D labs, some in the executive suites, and some in the way everything is integrated. A difficult-to-replicate or difficult-to-imitate competence was defined earlier as a distinctive competence. As indicated, the key feature of distinctive competence is that there is not a market for it, except possibly through the market for business units. Hence competences and capabilities are intriguing assets as they typically must be built because they cannot be bought.

Organizational and managerial processes

Organizational processes have three roles: coordination/integration (a static concept); learning (a dynamic concept); and reconfiguration (a transformational concept). We discuss each in turn.

Coordination/integration. While the price system supposedly coordinates the economy,[32] managers coordinate or integrate activity inside the firm. How efficiently and effectively internal coordination or integration is achieved is very important (Aoki, 1990).[33] Likewise for external coordination.[34] Increasingly, strategic advantage requires the integration of external activities and technologies. The growing literature on strategic

---

[31] We are implicitly saying that fixed assets, like plant and equipment which can be purchased off-the-shelf by all industry participants, cannot be the source of a firm's competitive advantage. In asmuch as financial balance sheets typically reflect such assets, we point out that the assets that matter for competitive advantage are rarely reflected in the balance sheet, while those that do not are.

[32] The coordinative properties of markets depend on prices being "sufficient" upon which to base resource allocation decisions.
[33] Indeed, Ronald Coase, author of the pathbreaking 1937 article 'The nature of the firm,' which focused on the costs of organizational coordination inside the firm as compared to across the market, half a century later has identified as critical the understanding of 'why the costs of organizing particular activities differs among firms' (Coase, 1988: 47). We argue that a firm's distinctive ability needs to be understood as a reflection of distinctive organizational or coordinative capabilities. This form of integration (i.e., inside business units) is different from the integration between business units; they could be viable on a stand-alone basis (external integration). For a useful taxonomy, see Iansiti and Clark (1994).
[34] Shuen (1994) examines the gains and hazards of the technology make-vs.-buy decision and supplier codevelopment.

alliances, the virtual corporation, and buyer–supplier relations and technology collaboration evidences the importance of external integration and sourcing.

There is some field-based empirical research that provides support for the notion that the way production is organized by management inside the firm is the source of differences in firms' competence in various domains. For example, Garvin's (1988) study of 18 room air-conditioning plants reveals that quality performance was not related to either capital investment or the degree of automation of the facilities. Instead, quality performance was driven by special organizational routines. These included routines for gathering and processing information, for linking customer experiences with engineering design choices, and for coordinating factories and component suppliers.[35] The work of Clark and Fujimoto (1991) on project development in the automobile industry also illustrates the role played by coordinative routines. Their study reveals a significant degree of variation in how different firms coordinate the various activities required to bring a new model from concept to market. These differences in coordinative routines and capabilities seem to have a significant impact on such performance variables as development cost, development lead times, and quality. Furthermore, Clark and Fujimoto tended to find significant firm-level differences in coordination routines and these differences seemed to have persisted for a long time. This suggests that routines related to coordination are firm-specific in nature.

Also, the notion that competence/capability is embedded in distinct ways of coordinating and combining helps to explain how and why seemingly minor technological changes can have devastating impacts on incumbent firms' abilities to compete in a market. Henderson and Clark (1990), for example, have shown that incumbments in the photolithographic equipment industry were sequentially devasted by seemingly minor innovations that, nevertheless, had major impacts on how systems had to be configured. They attribute these difficulties to the fact that systems-level or 'architectural' innovations often require new routines to integrate and coordinate engineering tasks. These findings and others suggest that productive systems display high interdependency, and that it may not be possible to change one level without changing others. This appears to be true with respect to the 'lean production' model (Womack *et al.*, 1991) which has now transformed the Taylor or Ford model of manufacturing organization in the automobile industry.[36] Lean production requires distinctive shop floor practices and processes as well as distinctive higher-order managerial processes. Put differently, organizational processes often display high levels of coherence, and when they do, replication may be difficult because it requires systemic changes throughout the organization and also among interorganizational linkages, which might be very hard to effectuate. Put differently, partial imitation or replication of a successful model may yield zero benefits.[37]

---

[35] Garvin (1994) provides a typology of organizational processes.

[36] Fujimoto (1994: 18–20) describes key elements as they existed in the Japanese auto industry as follows: 'The typical volume production system of effective Japanese makers of the 1980s (e.g., Toyota) consists of various intertwined elements that might lead to competitive advantages. Just-in-Time (JIT), Jidoka (automatic defect detection and machine stop), Total Quality Control (TQC), and continuous improvement (Kaizen) are often pointed out as its core subsystems. The elements of such a system include inventory reduction mechanisms by Kanban system; levelization of production volume and product mix (heijunka); reduction of 'muda' (non-value adding activities), 'mura' (uneven pace of production) and muri (excessive workload); production plans based on dealers' order volume (genyo seisan); reduction of die set-up time and lot size in stamping operation; mixed model assembly; piece-by-piece transfer of parts between machines (ikko-nagashi); flexible task assignment for volume changes and productivity improvement (shojinka); multi-task job assignment along the process flow (takotei-mochi); U-shape machine layout that facilitates flexible and multiple task assignment, on-the-spot inspection by direct workers (tsukurikomi); fool-proof prevention of defects (poka-yoke); real-time feedback of production troubles (andon); assembly line stop cord; emphasis on cleanliness, order and discipline on the shop floor (5-S); frequent revision of standard operating procedures by supervisors; quality control circles; standardized tools for quality improvement (e.g., 7 tools for QC, QC story); worker involvement in preventive maintenance (Total Productive Maintenance); low cost automation or semi-automation with just-enough functions); reduction of process steps for saving of tools and dies, and so on. The human-resource management factors that back up the above elements include stable employment of core workers (with temporary workers in the periphery); long-term training of multi-skilled (multi-task) workers; wage system based in part on skill accumulation; internal promotion to shop floor supervisors; cooperative relationships with labor unions; inclusion of production supervisors in union members; generally egalitarian policies for corporate welfare, communication and worker motivation. Parts procurement policies are also pointed out often as a source of the competitive advantage.

[37] For a theoretical argument along these lines, see Milgrom and Roberts (1990).

The notion that there is a certain rationality or coherence to processes and systems is not quite the same concept as corporate culture, as we understand the latter. Corporate culture refers to the values and beliefs that employees hold; culture can be a *de facto* governance system as it mediates the behavior of individuals and economizes on more formal administrative methods. Rationality or coherence notions are more akin to the Nelson and Winter (1982) notion of organizational routines. However, the routines concept is a little too amorphous to properly capture the congruence amongst processes and between processes and incentives that we have in mind. Consider a professional service organization like an accounting firm. If it is to have relatively high-powered incentives that reward individual performance, then it must build organizational processes that channel individual behavior; if it has weak or low-powered incentives, it must find symbolic ways to recognize the high performers, and it must use alternative methods to build effort and enthusiasm. What one may think of as styles of organization in fact contain necessary, not discretionary, elements to achieve performance.

Recognizing the congruences and complementarities among processes, and between processes and incentives, is critical to the understanding of organizational capabilities. In particular, they can help us explain why architectural and radical innovations are so often introduced into an industry by new entrants. The incumbents develop distinctive organizational processes that cannot support the new technology, despite certain overt similarities between the old and the new. The frequent failure of incumbents to introduce new technologies can thus be seen as a consequence of the mismatch that so often exists between the set of organizational processes needed to support the conventional product/service and the requirements of the new. Radical organizational re-engineering will usually be required to support the new product, which may well do better embedded in a separate subsidiary where a new set of coherent organizatonal processes can be fashioned.[38]

Learning. Perhaps even more important than integration is learning. Learning is a process by which repetition and experimentation enable tasks to be performed better and quicker. It also enables new production opportunities to be identified.[39] In the context of the firm, if not more generally, learning has several key characteristics. First, learning involves organizational as well as individual skills.[40] While individual skills are of relevance, their value depends upon their employment, in particular organizational settings. Learning processes are intrinsically social and collective and occur not only through the imitation and emulation of individuals, as with teacher–student or master–apprentice, but also because of joint contributions to the understanding of complex problems.[41] Learning requires common codes of communication and coordinated search procedures. Second, the organizational knowledge generated by such activity resides in new patterns of activity, in 'routines,' or a new logic of organization. As indicated earlier, routines are patterns of interactions that represent successful solutions to particular problems. These patterns of interaction are resident in group behavior, though certain subroutines may be resident in individual behavior. The concept of dynamic capabilities as a coordinative management process opens the door to the potential for interorganizational learning. Researchers (Doz and Shuen, 1990; Mody, 1993) have pointed out that collaborations and partnerships can be a vehicle for new organizational learning, helping firms to recognize dysfunctional routines, and preventing strategic blindspots.

Reconfiguration and transformation.   In rapidly changing environments, there is obviously value in the ability to sense the need to reconfigure the firm's asset structure, and to accomplish the necessary internal and external transformation (Amit and Schoemaker, 1993; Langlois, 1994). This requires constant surveillance of markets and technologies and the willingness to adopt best practice. In this regard, benchmarking is of con-

---

[38] See Abernathy and Clark (1985).

[39] For a useful review and contribution, see Levitt and March (1988).
[40] Levinthal and March, 1993. Mahoney (1992) and Mahoney and Pandian (1995) suggest that both resources and mental models are intertwined in firm-level learning.
[41] There is a large literature on learning, although only a small fraction of it deals with organizational learning. Relevant contributors include Levitt and March (1988), Argyris and Schon (1978), Levinthal and March (1981), Nelson and Winter (1982), and Leonard-Barton (1995).

siderable value as an organized process for accomplishing such ends (Camp, 1989). In dynamic environments, narcissistic organizations are likely to be impaired. The capacity to reconfigure and transform is itself a learned organizational skill. The more frequently practiced, the easier accomplished.

Change is costly and so firms must develop processes to minimize low pay-off change. The ability to calibrate the requirements for change and to effectuate the necessary adjustments would appear to depend on the ability to scan the environment, to evaluate markets and competitors, and to quickly accomplish reconfiguration and transformation ahead of competition. Decentralization and local autonomy assist these processes. Firms that have honed these capabilities are sometimes referred to as 'high-flex'.

Positions

The strategic posture of a firm is determined not only by its learning processes and by the coherence of its internal and external processes and incentives, but also by its specific assets. By specific assets we mean for example its specialized plant and equipment. These include its difficult-to-trade knowledge assets and assets complementary to them, as well as its reputational and relational assets. Such assets determine its competitive advantage at any point in time. We identify several illustrative classes.

Technological assets. While there is an emerging market for know-how (Teece, 1981), much technology does not enter it. This is either because the firm is unwilling to sell it[42] or because of difficulties in transacting in the market for know-how (Teece, 1980). A firm's technological assets may or may not be protected by the standard instruments of intellectual property law. Either way, the ownership protection and utilization of technological assets are clearly key differentiators among firms. Likewise for complementary assets.

Complementary assets. Technological innovations require the use of certain related assets to produce and deliver new products and services.

---

[42] Managers often evoke the 'crown jewels' metaphor. That is, if the technology is released, the kingdom will be lost.

Prior commercialization activities require and enable firms to build such complementarities (Teece, 1986b). Such capabilities and assets, while necessary for the firm's established activities, may have other uses as well. These assets typically lie downstream. New products and processes either can enhance or destroy the value of such assets (Tushman, Newman, and Romanelli, 1986). Thus the development of computers enhanced the value of IBM's direct sales force in office products, while disk brakes rendered useless much of the auto industry's investment in drum brakes.

Financial assets. In the short run, a firm's cash position and degree of leverage may have strategic implications. While there is nothing more fungible than cash, it cannot always be raised from external markets without the dissemination of considerable information to potential investors. Accordingly, what a firm can do in short order is often a function of its balance sheet. In the longer run, that ought not to be so, as cash flow ought be more determinative.

Reputational assets. Firms, like individuals, have reputations. Reputations often summarize a good deal of information about firms and shape the responses of customers, suppliers, and competitors. It is sometimes difficult to disentangle reputation from the firm's current asset and market position. However, in our view, reputational assets are best viewed as an intangible asset that enables firms to achieve various goals in the market. Its main value is external, since what is critical about reputation is that it is a kind of summary statistic about the firm's current assets and position, and its likely future behavior. Because there is generally a strong asymmetry between what is known inside the firm and what is known externally, reputations may sometimes be more salient than the true state of affairs, in the sense that external actors must respond to what they know rather than what is knowable.

Structural assets. The formal and informal structure of organizations and their external linkages have an important bearing on the rate and direction of innovation, and how competences and capabilities co-evolve (Argyres, 1995; Teece, 1996). The degree of hierarchy and the level of vertical and lateral integration are elements of firm-specific structure. Distinctive governance modes can be recognized (e.g., multiproduct, integrated firms; high 'flex' firms; virtual corporations; conglomerates), and these modes support different types of innovation to a greater or lesser degree. For instance, virtual structures work well when innovation is autonomous; integrated structures work better for systemic innovations.

Institutional assets. Environments cannot be defined in terms of markets alone. While public policies are usually recognized as important in constraining what firms can do, there is a tendency, particularly by economists, to see these as acting through markets or through incentives. However, institutions themselves are a critical element of the business environment. Regulatory systems, as well as intellectual property regimes, tort laws, and antitrust laws, are also part of the environment. So is the system of higher education and national culture. There are significant national differences here, which is just one of the reasons geographic location matters (Nelson, 1994). Such assets may not be entirely firm specific; firms of different national and regional origin may have quite different institutional assets to call upon because their institutional/policy settings are so different.

Market (structure) assets. Product market position matters, but it is often not at all determinative of the fundamental position of the enterprise in its external environment. Part of the problem lies in defining the market in which a firm competes in a way that gives economic meaning. More importantly, market position in regimes of rapid technological change is often extremely fragile. This is in part because time moves on a different clock in such environments.[43] Moreover, the link between market share and innovation has long been broken, if it ever existed (Teece, 1996). All of this is to suggest that product market position, while important, is too often overplayed. Strategy should be formulated with regard to the more fundamental aspects of firm performance, which we believe are rooted in competences and capabilities and shaped by positions and paths.

Organizational boundaries. An important dimension of 'position' is the location of a firm's boundaries. Put differently, the degree of integration (vertical, lateral, and horizontal) is of quite some significance. Boundaries are not only significant with respect to the technological and complementary assets contained within, but also with respect to the nature of the coordination that can be achieved internally as compared to through markets. When specific assets or poorly protected intellectual capital are at issue, pure market arrangements expose the parties to recontracting hazards or appropriability hazards. In such circumstances, hierarchical control structures may work better than pure arms-length contracts.[44]

Paths

Path dependencies. Where a firm can go is a function of its current position and the paths ahead. Its current position is often shaped by the path it has traveled. In standard economics textbooks, firms have an infinite range of technologies from which they can choose and markets they can occupy. Changes in product or factor prices will be responded to instantaneously, with technologies moving in and out according to value maximization criteria. Only in the short run are irreversibilities recognized. Fixed costs—such as equipment and overheads—cause firms to price below fully amortized costs but never constrain future investment choices. 'Bygones are bygones.' Path dependencies are simply not recognized. This is a major limitation of microeconomic theory.

The notion of path dependencies recognizes that 'history matters.' Bygones are rarely bygones, despite the predictions of rational actor theory. Thus a firm's previous investments and

---

[43] For instance, an Internet year might well be thought of as equivalent to 10 years on many industry clocks, because as much change occurs in the Internet business in a year that occurs in say the auto industry in a decade.

[44] Williamson (1996: 102–103) has observed, failures of coordination may arise because 'parties that bear a long term bilateral dependency relationship to one another must recognize that incomplete contracts require gap filling and sometimes get out of alignment. Although it is always in the collective interest of autonomous parties to fill gaps, correct errors, and affect efficient realignments, it is also the case that the distribution of the resulting gains is indeterminate. Self-interested bargaining predictably obtains. Such bargaining is itself costly. The main costs, however, are that transactions are maladapted to the environment during the bargaining interval. Also, the prospect of ex post bargaining invites ex ante prepositioning of an inefficient kind.'

its repertoire of routines (its 'history') constrain its future behavior.[45] This follows because learning tends to be local. That is, opportunities for learning will be 'close in' to previous activities and thus will be transaction and production specific (Teece, 1988). This is because learning is often a process of trial, feedback, and evaluation. If too many parameters are changed simultaneously, the ability of firms to conduct meaningful natural quasi experiments is attenuated. If many aspects of a firm's learning environment change simultaneously, the ability to ascertain cause–effect relationships is confounded because cognitive structures will not be formed and rates of learning diminish as a result. One implication is that many investments are much longer term than is commonly thought.

The importance of path dependencies is amplified where conditions of increasing returns to adoption exist. This is a demand-side phenomenon, and it tends to make technologies and products embodying those technologies more attractive the more they are adopted. Attractiveness flows from the greater adoption of the product amongst users, which in turn enables them to become more developed and hence more useful. Increasing returns to adoption has many sources including network externalities (Katz and Shapiro, 1985), the presence of complementary assets (Teece, 1986b) and supporting infrastructure (Nelson, 1996), learning by using (Rosenberg, 1982), and scale economies in production and distribution. Competition between and amongst technologies is shaped by increasing returns. Early leads won by good luck or special circumstances (Arthur, 1983) can become amplified by increasing returns. This is not to suggest that first movers necessarily win. Because increasing returns have multiple sources, the prior positioning of firms can affect their capacity to exploit increasing returns. Thus, in Mitchell's (1989) study of medical diagnostic imaging, firms already controlling the relevant complementary assets could in theory start last and finish first.

In the presence of increasing returns, firms can compete passively, or they may compete strategically through technology-sponsoring activities.[46] The first type of competition is not unlike biological competition amongst species, although it can be sharpened by managerial activities that enhance the performance of products and processes. The reality is that companies with the best products will not always win, as chance events may cause 'lock-in' on inferior technologies (Arthur, 1983) and may even in special cases generate switching costs for consumers. However, while switching costs may favor the incumbent, in regimes of rapid technological change switching costs can become quickly swamped by switching benefits. Put differently, new products employing different standards often appear with alacrity in market environments experiencing rapid technological change, and incumbents can be readily challenged by superior products and services that yield switching benefits. Thus the degree to which switching costs cause 'lock-in' is a function of factors such as user learning, rapidity of technological change, and the amount of ferment in the competitive environment.

Technological opportunities. The concept of path dependencies is given forward meaning through the consideration of an industry's technological opportunities. It is well recognized that how far and how fast a particular area of industrial activity can proceed is in part due to the technological opportunities that lie before it. Such opportunities are usually a lagged function of foment and diversity in basic science, and the rapidity with which new scientific breakthroughs are being made.

However, technological opportunities may not be completely exogenous to industry, not only because some firms have the capacity to engage in or at least support basic research, but also because technological opportunities are often fed by innovative activity itself. Moreover, the recognition of such opportunities is affected by the

---

[45] For further development, see Bercovitz, de Figueiredo, and Teece, 1996.

[46] Because of huge uncertainties, it may be extremely difficult to determine viable strategies early on. Since the rules of the game and the identity of the players will be revealed only after the market has begun to evolve, the pay-off is likely to lie with building and maintaining organizational capabilities that support flexibility. For example, Microsoft's recent about-face and vigorous pursuit of Internet business once the Net-Scape phenomenon became apparent is impressive, not so much because it perceived the need to change strategy, but because of its organizational capacity to effectuate a strategic shift.

organizational structures that link the institutions engaging in basic research (primarily the university) to the business enterprise. Hence, the existence of technological opportunities can be quite firm specific.

Important for our purposes is the rate and direction in which relevant scientific frontiers are being rolled back. Firms engaging in R&D may find the path dead ahead closed off, though breakthroughs in related areas may be sufficiently close to be attractive. Likewise, if the path dead ahead is extremely attractive, there may be no incentive for firms to shift the allocation of resources away from traditional pursuits. The depth and width of technological opportunities in the neighborhood of a firm's prior research activities thus are likely to impact a firm's options with respect to both the amount and level of R&D activity that it can justify. In addition, a firm's past experience conditions the alternatives management is able to perceive. Thus, not only do firms in the same industry face 'menus' with different costs associated with particular technological choices, they also are looking at menus containing different choices.[47]

Assessment

The essence of a firm's competence and dynamic capabilities is presented here as being resident in the firm's organizational processes, that are in turn shaped by the firm's assets (positions) and its evolutionary path. Its evolutionary path, despite managerial hubris that might suggest otherwise, is often rather narrow.[48] What the firm can do and where it can go are thus rather constrained by its positions and paths. Its competitors are likewise constrained. Rents (profits) thus tend to flow not just from the asset structure of the firm and, as we shall see, the degree of its imitability, but also by the firm's ability to reconfigure and transform.

The parameters we have identified for determining performance are quite different from those in the standard textbook theory of the firm, and in the competitive forces and strategic conflict

approaches to the firm and to strategy.[49] Moreover, the agency theoretic view of the firm as a nexus of contracts would put no weight on processes, positions, and paths. While agency approaches to the firm may recognize that opportunism and shirking may limit what a firm can do, they do not recognize the opportunities and constraints imposed by processes, positions, and paths.

Moreover, the firm in our conceptualization is much more than the sum of its parts—or a team tied together by contracts.[50] Indeed, to some extent individuals can be moved in and out of organizations and, so long as the internal processes and structures remain in place, performance will not necessarily be impaired. A shift in the environment is a far more serious threat to the firm than is the loss of key individuals, as individuals can be replaced more readily than organizations can be transformed. Furthermore, the dynamic capabilities view of the firm would suggest that the behavior and performance of particular firms may be quite hard to replicate, even if its coherence and rationality are observable. This matter and related issues involving replication and imitation are taken up in the section that follows.

Replicability and imitatability of organizational processes and positions

Thus far, we have argued that the competences and capabilities (and hence competitive advantage) of a firm rest fundamentally on processes, shaped by positions and paths. However, competences can provide competitive advantage and generate rents only if they are based on a collection of routines, skills, and complementary assets that are difficult to imitate.[51] A particular set of routines can lose their value if they support a competence which no longer matters in the marketplace, or if they can be readily replicated or emulated by competitors. Imitation occurs when firms discover and simply copy a firm's organizational routines and procedures. Emulation occurs when firms

---

[47] This is a critical element in Nelson and Winter's (1982) view of firms and technical change.

[48] We also recognize that the processes, positions, and paths of customers also matter. See our discussion above on increasing returns, including customer learning and network externalities.

[49] In both the firm is still largely a black box. Certainly, little or no attention is given to processes, positions, and paths.

[50] See Alchian and Demsetz (1972).

[51] We call such competences distinctive. See also Dierickx and Cool (1989) for a discussion of the characteristics of assets which make them a source of rents.

discover alternative ways of achieving the same functionality.[52]

Replication

To understand imitation, one must first understand replication. Replication involves transferring or redeploying competences from one concrete economic setting to another. Since productive knowledge is embodied, this cannot be accomplished by simply transmitting information. Only in those instances where all relevant knowledge is fully codified and understood can replication be collapsed into a simple problem of information transfer. Too often, the contextual dependence of original performance is poorly appreciated, so unless firms have replicated their systems of productive knowledge on many prior occasions, the act of replication is likely to be difficult (Teece, 1976). Indeed, replication and transfer are often impossible absent the transfer of people, though this can be minimized if investments are made to convert tacit knowledge to codified knowledge. Often, however, this is simply not possible.

In short, competences and capabilities, and the routines upon which they rest, are normally rather difficult to replicate.[53] Even understanding what all the relevant routines are that support a particular competence may not be transparent. Indeed, Lippman and Rumelt (1992) have argued that some sources of competitive advantage are so complex that the firm itself, let alone its competitors, does not understand them.[54] As Nelson and Winter (1982) and Teece (1982) have explained, many organizational routines are quite tacit in nature. Imitation can also be hindered by the fact few routines are 'stand-alone;' coherence may require that a change in one set of routines in one part of the firm (e.g., production) requires changes in some other part (e.g., R&D).

Some routines and competences seem to be attributable to local or regional forces that shape firms' capabilities at early stages in their lives. Porter (1990), for example, shows that differences in local product markets, local factor markets, and institutions play an important role in shaping competitive capabilities. Differences also exist within populations of firms from the same country. Various studies of the automobile industry, for example, show that not all Japanese automobile companies are top performers in terms of quality, productivity, or product development (see, for example, Clark and Fujimoto, 1991). The role of firm-specific history has been highlighted as a critical factor explaining such firm-level (as opposed to regional or national-level) differences (Nelson and Winter, 1982). Replication in a different context may thus be rather difficult.

At least two types of strategic value flow from replication. One is the ability to support geographic and product line expansion. To the extent that the capabilities in question are relevant to customer needs elsewhere, replication can confer value.[55] Another is that the ability to replicate also indicates that the firm has the foundations in place for learning and improvement. Considerable empirical evidence supports the notion that the understanding of processes, both in production and in management, is the key to process improvement. In short, an organization cannot improve that which it does not understand. Deep process understanding is often required to accomplish codification. Indeed, if knowledge is highly tacit, it indicates that underlying structures are not well understood, which limits learning because scientific and engineering principles cannot be as systematically applied.[56] Instead, learning is confined to proceeding through trial and error, and the

---

[52] There is ample evidence that a given type of competence (e.g., quality) can be supported by different routines and combinations of skills. For example, the Garvin (1988) and Clark and Fujimoto (1991) studies both indicate that there was no one 'formula' for achieving either high quality or high product development performance.

[53] See Szulanski's (1995) discussion of the intrafirm transfer of best practice. He quotes a senior vice president of Xerox as saying 'you can see a high performance factory or office, but it just doesn't spread. I don't know why.' Szulanski also discusses the role of benchmarking in facilitating the transfer of best practice.

[54] If so, it is our belief that the firm's advantage is likely to fade, as luck does run out.

[55] Needless to say, there are many examples of firms replicating their capabilities inappropriately by applying extant routines to circumstances where they may not be applicable, e.g., Nestle's transfer of developed-country marketing methods for infant formula to the Third World (Hartley, 1989). A key strategic need is for firms to screen capabilities for their applicability to new environments.

[56] Different approaches to learning are required depending on the depth of knowledge. Where knowledge is less articulated and structured, trial and error and learning-by-doing are necessary, whereas in mature environments where the underlying engineering science is better understood, organizations can undertake more deductive approaches or what Pisano (1994) refers to as 'learning-before-doing.'

leverage that might otherwise come from the application of scientific theory is denied.

Imitation

Imitation is simply replication performed by a competitor. If self-replication is difficult, imitation is likely to be harder. In competitive markets, it is the ease of imitation that determines the sustainability of competitive advantage. Easy imitation implies the rapid dissipation of rents.

Factors that make replication difficult also make imitation difficult. Thus, the more tacit the firm's productive knowledge, the harder it is to replicate by the firm itself or its competitors. When the tacit component is high, imitation may well be impossible, absent the hiring away of key individuals and the transfers of key organization processes.

However, another set of barriers impedes imitation of certain capabilities in advanced industrial countries. This is the system of intellectual property rights, such as patents, trade secrets, and trademarks, and even trade dress.[57] Intellectual property protection is of increasing importance in the United States, as since 1982 the legal system has adopted a more pro-patent posture. Similar trends are evident outside the United States. Besides the patent system, several other factors cause there to be a difference between replication costs and imitation costs. The observability of the technology or the organization is one such important factor. Whereas vistas into product technology can be obtained through strategies such as reverse engineering, this is not the case for process technology, as a firm need not expose its process technology to the outside in order to benefit from it.[58] Firms with product technology, on the other hand, confront the unfortunate circumstances that they must expose what they have got in order to profit from the technology. Secrets

are thus more protectable if there is no need to expose them in contexts where competitors can learn about them.

One should not, however, overestimate the overall importance of intellectual property protection; yet it presents a formidable imitation barrier in certain particular contexts. Intellectual property protection is not uniform across products, processes, and technologies, and is best thought of as islands in a sea of open competition. If one is not able to place the fruits of one's investment, ingenuity, or creativity on one or more of the islands, then one indeed is at sea.

We use the term appropriability regimes to describe the ease of imitation. Appropriability is a function both of the ease of replication and the efficacy of intellectual property rights as a barrier to imitation. Appropriability is strong when a technology is both inherently difficult to replicate and the intellectual property system provides legal barriers to imitation. When it is inherently easy to replicate and intellectual property protection is either unavailable or ineffectual, then appropriability is weak. Intermediate conditions also exist.

CONCLUSION

The four paradigms discussed above are quite different, though the first two have much in common with each other (strategizing) as do the last two (economizing). But are these paradigms complementary or competitive? According to some authors, 'the resource perspective complements the industry analysis framework' (Amit and Schoemaker, 1993: 35). While this is undoubtedly true, we think that in several important respects the perspectives are also competitive. While this should be recognized, it is not to suggest that there is only one framework that has value. Indeed, complex problems are likely to benefit from insights obtained from all of the paradigms we have identified plus more. The trick is to work out which frameworks are appropriate for the problem at hand. Slavish adherence to one class to the neglect of all others is likely to generate strategic blindspots. The tools themselves then generate strategic vulnerability. We now explore these issues further. Table 1 summarizes some similarities and differences.

---

[57] Trade dress refers to the 'look and feel' of a retail establishment, e.g., the distinctive marketing and presentation style of The Nature Company.

[58] An interesting but important exception to this can be found in second sourcing. In the microprocessor business, until the introduction of the 386 chip, Intel and most other merchant semi producers were encouraged by large customers like IBM to provide second sources, i.e., to license and share their proprietary process technology with competitors like AMD and NEC. The microprocessor developers did so to assure customers that they had sufficient manufacturing capability to meet demand at all times.

Table 1. Paradigms of strategy: Salient characteristics

Paradigm	Intellectual roots	Representative authors addressing strategic management questions	Nature of rents	Rationality assumptions of managers	Fundamental units of analysis	Short-run capacity for strategic reorientation	Role of industrial structure	Focal concern
(1) Attenuating competitive forces	Mason, Bain	Porter (1980)	Chamberlinean	Rational	Industries, firms, products	High	Exogenous	Structural conditions and competitor positioning
(2) Strategic conflict	Machiavelli, Schelling, Cournot, Nash, Harsanyi, Shapiro	Ghemawat (1986) Shapiro (1989) Brandenburger and Nalebuff (1995)	Chamberlinean	Hyper-rational	Firms, products	Often infinite	Endogenous	Strategic interactions
(3) Resource-based perspectives	Penrose, Selznick, Christensen, Andrews	Rumelt (1984) Chandler (1966) Wernerfelt (1984) Teece (1980, 1982)	Ricardian	Rational	Resources	Low	Endogenous	Asset fungibility
(4) Dynamic capabilities perspective	Schumpeter, Nelson, Winter, Teece	Dosi, Teece, and Winter (1989) Prahalad and Hamel (1990) Hayes and Wheelwright (1984) Dierickx and Cool (1989) Porter (1990)	Schumpeterian	Rational	Processes, positions, paths	Low	Endogenous	Asset accumulation, replicability and inimitability

528   *D. J. Teece, G. Pisano and A. Shuen*

Efficiency vs. market power

The competitive forces and strategic conflict approaches generally see profits as stemming from strategizing—that is, from limitations on competition which firms achieve through raising rivals' costs and exclusionary behavior (Teece, 1984). The competitive forces approach in particular leads one to see concentrated industries as being attractive—market positions can be shielded behind entry barriers, and rivals costs can be raised. It also suggests that the sources of competitive advantage lie at the level of the industry, or possibly groups within an industry. In text book presentations, there is almost no attention at all devoted to discovering, creating, and commercializing new sources of value.

The dynamic capabilities and resources approaches clearly have a different orientation. They see competitive advantage stemming from high-performance routines operating 'inside the firm,' shaped by processes and positions. Path dependencies (including increasing returns) and technological opportunities mark the road ahead. Because of imperfect factor markets, or more precisely the nontradability of 'soft' assets like values, culture, and organizational experience, distinctive competences and capabilities generally cannot be acquired; they must be built. This sometimes takes years—possibly decades. In some cases, as when the competence is protected by patents, replication by a competitor is ineffectual as a means to access the technology. The capabilities approach accordingly sees definite limits on strategic options, at least in the short run. Competitive success occurs in part because of policies pursued and experience and efficiency obtained in earlier periods.

Competitive success can undoubtedly flow from both strategizing and economizing,[59] but along with Williamson (1991) we believe that 'economizing is more fundamental than strategizing .... or put differently, that economy is the best strategy.'[60] Indeed, we suggest that, except

in special circumstances, too much 'strategizing' can lead firms to underinvest in core competences and neglect dynamic capabilities, and thus harm long-term competitiveness.

Normative implications

The field of strategic management is avowedly normative. It seeks to guide those aspects of general management that have material effects on the survival and success of the business enterprise. Unless these various approaches differ in terms of the framework and heuristics they offer management, then the discourse we have gone through is of limited immediate value. In this paper, we have already alluded to the fact that the capabilities approach tends to steer managers toward creating distinctive and difficult-to-imitate advantages and avoiding games with customers and competitors. We now survey possible differences, recognizing that the paradigms are still in their infancy and cannot confidently support strong normative conclusions.

Unit of analysis and analytic focus

Because in the capabilities and the resources framework business opportunities flow from a firm's unique processes, strategy analysis must be situational.[61] This is also true with the strategic conflict approach. There is no algorithm for creating wealth for the entire industry. Prescriptions they apply to industries or groups of firms at best suggest overall direction, and may indicate errors to be avoided. In contrast, the competitive forces approach is not particularly firm specific; it is industry and group specific.

Strategic change

The competitive forces and the strategic conflict approach, since they pay little attention to skills, know-how, and path dependency, tend to see

---

[59] Phillips (1971) and Demsetz (1974) also made the case that market concentration resulted from the competitive success of more efficient firms, and not from entry barriers and restrictive practices.
[60] We concur with Williamson that economizing and strategizing are not mutually exclusive. Strategic ploys can be used to disguise inefficiencies and to promote economizing outcomes, as with pricing with reference to learning curve costs. Our view of economizing is perhaps more expansive than

Williamson's as it embraces more than efficient contract design and the minimization of transactions costs. We also address production and organizational economies, and the distinctive ways that things are accomplished inside the business enterprise.
[61] On this point, the strategic conflict and the resources and capabilities are congruent. However, the aspects of 'situation' that matter are dramatically different, as described earlier in this paper.

strategic choice occurring with relative facility. The capabiliies approach sees value augmenting strategic change as being difficult and costly. Moreover, it can generally only occur incrementally. Capabilities cannot easily be bought; they must be built. From the capabilities perspective, strategy involves choosing among and committing to long-term paths or trajectories of competence development.

In this regard, we speculate that the dominance of competitive forces and the strategic conflict approaches in the United States may have something to do with observed differences in strategic approaches adopted by some U.S. and some foreign firms. Hayes (1985) has noted that American companies tend to favor 'strategic leaps' while, in contrast, Japanese and German companies tend to favor incremental, but rapid, improvements.

Entry strategies

Here the resources and the capabilities approaches suggest that entry decisions must be made with reference to the competences and capabilities which new entrants have, relative to the competition. Whereas the other approaches tell you little about where to look to find likely entrants, the capabilities approach identifies likely entrants. Relatedly, whereas the entry deterrence approach suggests an unconstrained search for new business opportunities, the capabilities approach suggests that such opportunities lie close in to one's existing business. As Richard Rumelt has explained it in conversation, 'the capabilities approach suggests that if a firm looks inside itself, and at its market environment, sooner or later it will find a business opportunity.'

Entry timing

Whereas the strategic conflict approach tells little abut where to look to find likely entrants, the resources and the capabilities approach identifies likely entrants and their timing of entry. Brittain and Freeman (1980) using population ecology methodologies argued that an organization is quick to expand when there is a significant overlap between its core capabilities and those needed to survive in a new market. Recent research (Mitchell, 1989) showed that the more industry-specialized assets or capabilities a firm possesses, the more likely it is to enter an emerging technical subfield in its industry, following a technological discontinuity. Additionally, the interaction between specialized assets such as firm-specific capabilities and rivalry had the greatest influence on entry timing.

Diversification

Related diversification—that is, diversification that builds upon or extends existing capabilities—is about the only form of diversification that a resources/capabilities framework is likely to view as meritorious (Rumelt, 1974; Teece, 1980, 1982; Teece *et al.*, 1994). Such diversification will be justifiable when the firms' traditional markets decline.[62] The strategic conflict approach is likely to be a little more permissive; acquisitions that raise rivals' costs or enable firms to effectuate exclusive arrangements are likely to be seen as efficacious in certain circumstances.

Focus and specialization

Focus needs to be defined in terms of distinctive competences or capability, not products. Products are the manifestation of competences, as competences can be molded into a variety of products. Product market specialization and decentalization configured around product markets may cause firms to neglect the development of core competences and dynamic capabilities, to the extent to which competences require accessing assets across divisions.

The capabilities approach places emphasis on the internal processes that a firm utilizes, as well as how they are deployed and how they will evolve. The approach has the benefit of indicating that competitive advantage is not just a function of how one plays the game; it is also a function of the 'assets' one has to play with, and how these assets can be deployed and redeployed in a changing market.

---

[62] Cantwell shows that the technological competence of firms persists over time, gradually evolving through firm-specific learning. He shows that technological diversification has been greater for chemicals and pharmaceuticals than for electrical and electronic-related fields., and he offers as an explanation the greater straight-ahead opportunities in electrical and electronic fields than in chemicals and pharmaceuticals. See Cantwell (1993).

530   *D. J. Teece, G. Pisano and A. Shuen*

Future directions

We have merely sketched an outline for a dynamic capabilities approach. Further theoretical work is needed to tighten the framework, and empirical research is critical to helping us understand how firms get to be good, how they sometimes stay that way, why and how they improve, and why they sometimes decline.[63] Researchers in the field of strategy need to join forces with researchers in the fields of innovation, manufacturing, and organizational behavior and business history if they are to unlock the riddles that lie behind corporate as well as national competitive advantage. There could hardly be a more ambitious research agenda in the social sciences today.

ACKNOWLEDGEMENTS

Research for this paper was aided by support from the Alfred P. Sloan Foundation through the Consortium on Competitiveness and Cooperation at the University of California, Berkeley. The authors are grateful for helpful comments from two anonymous referees, as well as from Raffi Amit, Jay Barney, Joseph Bower, Henry Chesbrough, Giovanni Dosi, Sumantra Goshal, Pankaj Ghemawat, Connie Helfat, Rebecca Henderson, Dan Levinthal, Richard Nelson, Margie Peteraf, Richard Rosenbloom, Richard Rumelt, Carl Shapiro, Oliver Williamson, and Sidney Winter. Useful feedback was obtained from workshops at the Haas School of Business, the Wharton School, the Kellogg School (Northwestern), the Harvard Business School, and the International Institute of Applied Systems Analysis (IIASA) in Vienna, the London School of Economics, and the London Business School.

REFERENCES

Abernathy, W. J. and K. Clark (1985). 'Innovation: Mapping the winds of creative destruction', *Research Policy*, 14, pp. 3–22.

---

[63] For a gallant start, see Miyazaki (1995) and McGrath *et al.* (1996). Chandler's (1990) work on scale and scope, summarized in Teece (1993), provides some historical support for the capabilities approach. Other relevant studies can be found in a special issue of *Industrial and Corporate Change* 3(3), 1994, that was devoted to dynamic capabilities.

Alchian, A. A. and H. Demsetz (1972). 'Production, information costs, and economic organization', *American Economic Review*, 62, pp. 777–795.

Amit, R. and P. Schoemaker (1993). 'Strategic assets and organizational rent', *Strategic Management Journal* 14(1), pp. 33–46.

Andrews, K. (1987). *The Concept of Corporate Strategy* (3rd ed.). Dow Jones-Irwin, Homewood, IL.

Aoki, M. (1990). 'The participatory generation of information rents and the theory of the firm'. In M. Aoki, B. Gustafsson and O. E. Williamson (eds.), *The Firm as a Nexus of Treaties*. Sage, London, pp. 26–52.

Argyres, N. (1995). 'Technology strategy, governance structure and interdivisional coordination', *Journal of Economic Behavior and Organization*, 28, pp. 337–358.

Argyris, C. and D. Schon (1978). *Organizational Learning*. Addison-Wesley, Reading, MA.

Arrow, K. (1969). 'The organization of economic activity: Issues pertinent to the choice of market vs. nonmarket allocation'. In *The Analysis and Evaluation of Public Expenditures: The PPB System*, 1. U.S. Joint Economic Committee, 91st Session. U.S. Government Printing Office, Washington, DC, pp. 59–73.

Arrow, K. (1996) 'Technical information and industrial structure', *Industrial and Corporate Change*, 5(2), pp. 645–652.

Arthur, W. B. (1983). 'Competing technologies and lock-in by historical events: The dynamics of allocation under increasing returns', working paper WP-83-90, International Institute for Applied Systems Analysis, Laxenburg, Austria.

Bain, J. S. (1959). *Industrial Organization*. Wiley, New York.

Baldwin, C. and K. Clark (1991). 'Capabilities and capital investment: New perspectives on capital budgeting', Harvard Business School working paper #92–004.

Barney, J. B. (1986). 'Strategic factor markets: Expectations, luck, and business strategy', *Management Science* 32(10), pp. 1231–1241.

Barney, J. B., J.-C. Spender and T. Reve (1994). *Craoford Lectures*, Vol. 6. Chartwell-Bratt, Bromley, U.K. and Lund University Press, Lund, Sweden.

Baumol, W., J. Panzar and R. Willig (1982). *Contestable Markets and the Theory of Industry Structure*. Harcourt Brace Jovanovich, New York.

Bercovitz, J. E. L., J. M. de Figueiredo and D. J. Teece (1996). 'Firm capabilities and managerial decision-making: A theory of innovation biases'. In R. Garud, P. Nayyar and Z. Shapira (eds), *Innovation: Oversights and Foresights*. Cambridge University Press, Cambridge, U.K. pp. 233–259.

Brandenburger, A. M. and B. J. Nalebuff (1996). *Co-opetition*. Doubleday, New York.

Brandenburger, A. M. and B. J. Nalebuff (1995). 'The right game: Use game theory to shape strategy', *Harvard Business Review*, 73(4), pp. 57–71.

Brittain, J. and J. Freeman (1980). 'Organizational proliferation and density-dependent selection'. In J. R. Kimberly and R. Miles (eds.), *The Organizational*

Life Cycle. Jossey-Bass, San Francisco, CA, pp. 291–338.

Camp, R. (1989). *Benchmarking: The Search for Industry Best practices that Lead to Superior Performance.* Quality Press, Milwaukee, WI.

Cantwell, J. (1993). 'Corporate technological specialization in international industries'. In M. Casson and J. Creedy (eds.), *Industrial Concentration and Economic Inequality.* Edward Elgar, Aldershot, pp. 216–232.

Chandler, A.D., Jr. (1966). *Strategy and Structure.* Doubleday, Anchor Books Edition, New York.

Chandler, A. D., Jr. (1990). *Scale and Scope: The Dynamics of Industrial Competition.* Harvard University Press, Cambridge, MA.

Clark, K. and T. Fujimoto (1991). *Product Development Performance: Strategy, Organization and Management in the World Auto Industries.* Harvard Buiness School Press, Cambridge, MA.

Coase, R. (1937). 'The nature of the firm', *Economica*, **4**, pp. 386–405.

Coase, R. (1988). 'Lecture on the Nature of the Firm, III', *Journal of Law, Economics and Organization*, **4**, pp. 33–47.

Cool, K. and D. Schendel (1988). 'Performance differences among strategic group members', *Strategic Management Journal*, **9**(3), pp. 207–223.

de Figueiredo, J. M. and D. J. Teece (1996). 'Mitigating procurement hazards in the context of innovation', *Industrial and Corporate Change*, **5**(2), pp. 537–559.

Demsetz, H. (1974). 'Two systems of belief about monopoly'. In H. Goldschmid, M. Mann and J. F. Weston (eds.), *Industrial Concentration: The New Learning.* Little, Brown, Boston, MA, pp. 161–184.

Dierickx. I. and K. Cool (1989). 'Asset stock accumulation and sustainability of competitive advantage', *Management Science*, **35**(12), pp. 1504–1511.

Dixit, A. (1980). 'The role of investment in entry deterrence', *Economic Journal*, **90**, pp. 95–106.

Dosi, G., D. J. Teece and S. Winter (1989). 'Toward a theory of corporate coherence: Preliminary remarks', unpublished paper, Center for Research in Management, University of California at Berkeley.

Doz, Y. and A. Shuen (1990). 'From intent to outcome: A process framework for partnerships', INSEAD working paper.

Fama, E. F. (1980). 'Agency problems and the theory of the firm', *Journal of Political Economy*, **88**, pp. 288–307.

Freeman, J. and W. Boeker (1984). 'The ecological analysis of business strategy'. In G. Carroll and D. Vogel (eds.), *Strategy and Organization.* Pitman, Boston, MA, pp. 64–77.

Fujimoto. T. (1994). 'Reinterpreting the resource-capability view of the firm: A case of the development-production systems of the Japanese automakers', draft working paper, Faculty of Economics, University of Tokyo.

Garvin, D. (1988). *Managing Quality.* Free Press, New York.

Garvin, D. (1994). 'The processes of organization and management', Harvard Business School working paper #94–084.

Ghemawat, P. (1986). 'Sustainable advantage', *Harvard Business Review*, **64**(5), pp. 53–58.

Ghemawat, P. (1991). *Commitment: The Dynamics of Strategy.* Free Press, New York.

Gilbert, R. J. and D. M. G. Newberry (1982). 'Preemptive patenting and the persistence of monopoly', *American Economic Review*, **72**, pp. 514–526.

Gittell, J. H. (1995). 'Cross functional coordination, control and human resource systems: Evidence from the airline industry', unpublished Ph.D. thesis, Massachusetts Institute of Technology.

Hansen, G. S. and B. Wernerfelt (1989). 'Determinants of firm performance: The relative importance of economic and organizational factors', *Strategic Management Journal*, **10**(5), pp. 399–411.

Hartley, R. F. (1989). *Marketing Mistakes.* Wiley, New York.

Hayes, R. (1985). 'Strategic planning: Forward in reverse', *Harvard Business Review*, **63**(6), pp. 111–119.

Hayes, R. and K. Clark (1985). 'Exploring the sources of productivity differences at the factory level'. In K. Clark, R. H. Hayes and C. Lorenz (eds.), *The Uneasy Alliance: Managing the Productivity–Technology Dilemma.* Harvard Business School Press, Boston, MA, pp. 151–188.

Hayes, R. and S. Wheelwright (1984). *Restoring our Competitive Edge: Competing Through Manufacturing.* Wiley, New York.

Hayes, R., S. Wheelwright and K. Clark (1988). *Dynamic Manufacturing: Creating the Learning Organization.* Free Press, New York.

Henderson, R. M. (1994). 'The evolution of integrative capability: Innovation in cardiovascular drug discovery', *Industrial and Corporate Change*, **3**(3), pp. 607–630.

Henderson, R. M. and K. B. Clark (1990). 'Architectural innovation: The reconfiguration of existing product technologies and the failure of established firms', *Administrative Science Quarterly*, **35**, pp. 9–30.

Henderson, R. M. and I. Cockburn (1994). 'Measuring competence? Exploring firm effects in pharmaceutical research, *Strategic Management Journal*, Summer Special Issue, **15**, pp. 63–84.

Iansiti, M. and K. B. Clark (1994). 'Integration and dynamic capability: Evidence from product development in automobiles and mainframe computers', *Industrial and Corporate Change*, **3**(3), pp. 557–661.

Itami, H. and T. W. Roehl (1987). *Mobilizing Invisible Assets.* Harvard University Press, Cambridge, MA.

Jacobsen, R. (1988). 'The persistence of abnormal returns', *Strategic Management Journal*, **9**(5), pp. 415–430.

Katz, M. and C. Shapiro (1985). 'Network externalities, competition and compatibility', *American Economic Review*, **75**, pp. 424–440.

Kreps, D. M. and R. Wilson (1982a). 'Sequential equilibria', *Econometrica*, **50**, pp. 863–894.

Kreps, D. M. and R. Wilson (1982b). 'Reputation and imperfect information', *Journal of Economic Theory*, **27**, pp. 253–279.

Langlois, R. (1994). 'Cognition and capabilities:

Opportunities seized and missed in the history of the computer industry', working paper, University of Connecticut. Presented at the conference on Technological Oversights and Foresights, Stern School of Business, New York University, 11–12 March 1994.

Learned, E., C. Christensen, K. Andrews and W. Guth (1969). *Business Policy: Text and Cases.* Irwin, Homewood, IL.

Leonard-Barton, D. (1992). 'Core capabilities and core rigidities: A paradox in managing new product development', *Strategic Management Journal*, Summer Special Issue, **13**, pp. 111–125.

Leonard-Barton, D. (1995). *Wellsprings of Knowledge.* Harvard Business School Press, Boston, MA.

Lev, B. and T. Sougiannis (1992). 'The capitalization, amortization and value-relevance of R&D', unpublished manuscript, University of California, Berkeley, and University of Illinois, Urbana–Champaign.

Levinthal, D. and J. March (1981). 'A model of adaptive organizational search', *Journal of Economic Behavior and Organization*, **2**, pp. 307–333.

Levinthal, D. A. and J. G. March (1993). 'The myopia of learning', *Strategic Management Journal*, Winter Special Issue, **14**, pp. 95–112.

Levinthal, D. and J. Myatt (1994). 'Co-evolution of capabilities and industry: The evolution of mutual fund processing', *Strategic Management Journal*, Winter Special Issue, **15**, pp. 45–62.

Levitt, B. and J. March (1988). 'Organizational learning', *Annual Review of Sociology*, **14**, pp. 319–340.

Link, A. N., D. J. Teece and W. F. Finan (October 1996). 'Estimating the benefits from collaboration: The Case of SEMATECH', *Review of Industrial Organization*, **11**, pp. 737–751.

Lippman, S. A. and R. P. Rumelt (1992) 'Demand uncertainty and investment in industry-specific capital', *Industrial and Corporate Change*, **1**(1), pp. 235–262.

Mahoney, J. (1995). 'The management of resources and the resources of management', *Journal of Business Research*, **33**(2), pp. 91–101.

Mahoney, J. T. and J. R. Pandian (1992). 'The resource-based view within the conversation of strategic management', *Strategic Management Journal*, **13**(5), pp. 363–380.

Mason, E. (1949). 'The current state of the monopoly problem in the U.S.', *Harvard Law Review*, **62**, pp. 1265–1285.

McGrath, R. G., M-H. Tsai, S. Venkataraman and I. C. MacMillan (1996). 'Innovation, competitive advantage and rent: A model and test', *Management Science*, **42**(3), pp. 389–403.

Milgrom, P. and J. Roberts (1982a). 'Limit pricing and entry under incomplete information: An equilibrium analysis', *Econometrica*, **50**, pp. 443–459.

Milgrom, P. and J. Roberts (1982b). 'Predation, reputation and entry deterrence', *Journal of Economic Theory*, **27**, pp. 280–312.

Milgrom, P. and J. Roberts (1990). 'The economics of modern manufacturing: Technology, strategy, and organization', *American Economic Review*, **80**(3), pp. 511–528.

Mitchell, W. (1989). 'Whether and when? Probability and timing of incumbents' entry into emerging industrial subfields', *Administrative Science Quarterly*, **34**, pp. 208–230.

Miyazaki, K. (1995). *Building Competences in the Firm: Lessons from Japanese and European Optoelectronics.* St. Martins Press, New York.

Mody, A. (1993). 'Learning through alliances', *Journal of Economic Behavior and Organization*, **20**(2), pp. 151–170.

Nelson, R. R. (1991). 'Why do firms differ, and how does it matter?' *Strategic Management Journal*, Winter Special Issue, **12**, pp. 61–74.

Nelson, R. R. (1994). 'The co-evolution of technology, industrial structure, and supporting institutions', *Industrial and Corporate Change*, **3**(1), pp. 47–63.

Nelson, R. (1996). 'The evolution of competitive or comparative advantage: A preliminary report on a study', WP-96-21, International Institute for Applied Systems Analysis, Laxemberg, Austria.

Nelson, R. and S. Winter (1982). *An Evolutionary Theory of Economic change.* Harvard University Press, Cambridge, MA.

Penrose, E. (1959). *The Theory of the Growth of the Firm.* Basil Blackwell, London.

Phillips, A. C. (1971). *Technology and Market Structure.* Lexington Books, Toronto.

Pisano, G. (1994). 'Knowledge integration and the locus of learning: An empirical analysis of process development', *Strategic Management Journal*, Winter Special Issue, **15**, pp. 85–100.

Porter, M. E. (1980). *Competitive Strategy.* Free Press, New York.

Porter, M. E. (1990). *The Competitive Advantage of Nations.* Free Press, New York.

Prahalad, C. K. and G. Hamel (1990). 'The core competence of the corporation', *Harvard Business Review*, **68**(3), pp. 79–91.

Richardson, G. B. H. (1960, 1990). *Information and Investment.* Oxford University Press, New York.

Rosenberg, N. (1982). *Inside the Black Box: Technology and Economics.* Cambridge University Press, Cambridge, MA

Rumelt, R. P. (1974). *Strategy, Structure, and Economic Performance.* Harvard University Press, Cambridge, MA.

Rumelt, R. P. (1984). 'Towards a strategic theory of the firm'. In R. B. Lamb (ed.), *Competitive Strategic Management.* Prentice-Hall, Englewood Cliffs, NJ, pp. 556–570.

Rumelt, R. P. (1991). 'How much does industry matter?', *Strategic Management Journal*, **12**(3), pp. 167–185.

Rumelt, R. P., D. Schendel and D. Teece (1994). *Fundamental Issues in Strategy.* Harvard Business School Press, Cambridge, MA.

Schmalensee, R. (1983). 'Advertising and entry deterrence: An exploratory model', *Journal of Political Economy*, **91**(4), pp. 636–653.

Schumpeter, J. A. (1934). *Theory of Economic Development.* Harvard University Press, Cambridge, MA.

Schumpeter, J. A. (1942). *Capitalism, Socialism, and Democracy.* Harper, New York.

Shapiro, C. (1989). 'The theory of business strategy', *RAND Journal of Economics*, 20(1), pp. 125–137.

Shuen, A. (1994). 'Technology sourcing and learning strategies in the semiconductor industry', unpublished Ph.D. dissertation, University of California, Berkeley.

Sutton, J. (1992). 'Implementing game theoretical models in industrial economies', In A. Del Monte (ed.), *Recent Developments in the Theory of Industrial Organization*. University of Michigan Press, Ann Arbor, MI, pp. 19–33.

Szulanski, G. (1995). 'Unpacking stickiness: An empirical investigation of the barriers to transfer best practice inside the firm', *Academy of Management Journal*, Best Papers Proceedings, pp. 437–441.

Teece, D. J. (1976). *The Multinational Corporation and the Resource Cost of International Technology Transfer*. Ballinger, Cambridge, MA.

Teece, D. J. (1980). 'Economics of scope and the scope of the enterprise', *Journal of Economic Behavior and Organization*, 1, pp. 223–247.

Teece, D. J. (1981). 'The market for know-how and the efficient international transfer of technology', *Annals of the Academy of Political and Social Science*, 458, pp. 81–96.

Teece, D. J. (1982). 'Towards an economic theory of the multiproduct firm', *Journal of Economic Behavior and Organization*, 3, pp. 39–63.

Teece, D. J. (1984). 'Economic analysis and strategic management', *California Management Review*, 26(3), pp. 87–110.

Teece, D. J. (1986a). 'Transactions cost economics and the multinational enterprise', *Journal of Economic Behavior and Organization*, 7, pp. 21–45.

Teece, D. J. (1986b). 'Profiting from technological innovation', *Research Policy*, 15(6), pp. 285–305.

Teece, D. J. 1988. 'Technological change and the nature of the firm'. In G. Dosi, C. Freeman, R. Nelson, G. Silverberg and L. Soete (eds.), *Technical Change and Economic Theory*. Pinter Publishers, New York, pp. 256–281.

Teece, D. J. (1992). 'Competition, cooperation, and innovation: Organizational arrangements for regimes of rapid technological progress', *Journal of Economic Behavior and Organization*, 18(1), pp. 1–25.

Teece, D. J. (1993). 'The dynamics of industrial capitalism: Perspectives on Alfred Chandler's *Scale and Scope* (1990)', *Journal of Economic Literature*, 31(1), pp. 199–225.

Teece, D. J. (1996) 'Firm organization, industrial structure, and technological innovation', *Journal of Economic Behavior and Organization*, 31, pp. 193–224.

Teece, D. J. and G. Pisano (1994). 'The dynamic capabilities of firms: An introduction', *Industrial and Corporate Change*, 3(3), pp. 537–556.

Teece, D. J., R. Rumelt, G. Dosi and S. Winter (1994). 'Understanding corporate coherence: Theory and evidence', *Journal of Economic Behavior and Organization*, 23, pp. 1–30.

Tushman, M. L., W. H. Newman and E. Romanelli (1986). 'Convergence and upheaval: Managing the unsteady pace of organizational evolution', *California Management Review*, 29(1), pp. 29–44.

Wernerfelt, B. (1984). 'A resource-based view of the firm', *Strategic Management Journal*, 5(2), pp. 171–180.

Wernerfelt, B. and C. Montgomery (1988). 'Tobin's Q and the importance of focus in firm performance', *American Economic Review*, 78(1), pp. 246–250.

Williamson, O. E. (1975). *Markets and Hierarchies*. Free Press, New York.

Williamson, O. E. (1985). *The Economic Institutions of Capitalism*. Free Press, New York.

Williamson, O. E. (1991). 'Strategizing, economizing, and economic organization', *Strategic Management Journal*, Winter Special Issue, 12, pp. 75–94.

Williamson, O. E. (1996) *The Mechanisms of Governance*. Oxford University Press, New York.

Womack, J., D. Jones and D. Roos (1991). *The Machine that Changed the World*. Harper-Perennial, New York.

Zander, U. and B. Kogut (1995). 'Knowledge and the speed of the transfer and imitation of organizational capabilities: An empirical test', *Organization Science*, 6(1), pp. 76–92.

PART II

TECHNOLOGY TRANSFER
AND LICENSING

[9]

The Economic Journal, **87** *(June 1977)*, 242–261
Printed in Great Britain

TECHNOLOGY TRANSFER BY MULTINATIONAL FIRMS: THE RESOURCE COST OF TRANSFERRING TECHNOLOGICAL KNOW-HOW*

I. INTRODUCTION

The essence of modern economic growth is the increase in the stock of useful knowledge and the extension of its application. Since the origins of technical and social innovations have never been confined to the borders of any one nation, the economic growth of all countries depends to some degree on the successful application of a transnational stock of knowledge (Kuznets, 1966). In other words, the economic growth of every nation is inextricably linked to the successful international transfer of technology. Nevertheless, economists have been remarkably slow in addressing themselves to the economics of international technology transfer. The result is that "at both the analytic and factual level very little is known about the international transfer of knowhow" (Reynolds, 1966).

This paper addresses itself to this need. The starting-point is Arrow's suggestion that the cost of communication, or information transfer, is a fundamental factor influencing the world-wide diffusion of technology (Arrow, 1969).[1] The purpose of the paper is to examine the level and determinants of the costs involved in transferring technology. The value of the resources which have to be utilised to accomplish the successful transfer of a given manufacturing technology is used as a measure of the cost of transfer. The resource cost concept is therefore designed to reflect the ease or difficulty of transferring technological know-how from manufacturing plants in one country to manufacturing plants in another.

II. TECHNOLOGY TRANSFER AND THE PRODUCTION OF KNOWLEDGE

The literature on technological change recognises that it takes substantial resources to make a new process or product feasible (Mansfield, 1968). However, it is common to assume that the cost of transferring the innovation to other firms is very much less, so that the marginal costs of successive application is trivial compared to the average cost of research, development, and application. This paradigm is sometimes extended to international as well as domestic technology transfer (Rodriguez, 1975).[2] Buttressing this view is a common belief that

* The findings described in this paper resulted from research undertaken for my Ph.D. dissertation, "The Multinational Corporation and the Resource Cost of International Technology Transfer" (Cambridge, Mass.: Ballinger, 1976). The trenchant comments of Professor Edwin Mansfield were much appreciated during all phases of the study. My particular gratitude goes to the participating firms, without whose co-operation this paper would not have been possible. I should also like to acknowledge the financial support provided for this study by the National Science Foundation, under a grant to Professor Edwin Mansfield of the University of Pennsylvania.

[1] Arrow asks: "If one nation or class has the knowledge which enables it to achieve high productivity, why is not the other acquiring that information?...The problem turns on the differential between costs of communication within and between classes" (or nations). P. 33.

[2] "Transmission of technology between countries is assumed costless. Thus, it is possible for the

technology is nothing but a set of blueprints that is usable at nominal cost tò all. Nevertheless, it has been pointed out that generally "only the broad outlines of technical knowledge are codified by non-personal means of intellectual communication, or communication by teaching outside the production process itself" (Berrill, 1964). The cost of transfer, which can be defined to include both transmission and absorption costs, may therefore be considerable when the technology is complex and the recipient firm does not have the capabilities to absorb the technology. The available evidence is unfortunately very sketchy. From the case studies of Mueller and Peck, Arrow inferred that transfer costs must be high (Arrow, 1962). From the Hall and Johnson study of the transfer of aerospace technology from the United States to Japan, it is not clear that this is true (Hall and Johnson, 1970). Robinson believes that economists' views on transfer costs are exaggerated (Robinson, 1973) while Mansfield and Freeman take the opposite view (Freeman, 1965; Mansfield, 1973). The lack of compelling evidence is apparent, and the appeals for further research (Mansfield, 1974; UNCTAD, 1970) seem to be well founded.

III. THE SAMPLE

The domain of this study is the transfer of the capability to manufacture a product or process from firms in one country to firms in another. Consequently the transfers can be considered as horizontal,[1] and in the design phase.[2] Data on 26 fairly recent international technology transfer projects were obtained. The proprietary nature of much of the data meant that sampling costs were high, which in turn severely limited the size of the sample that could be collected. All 26 transfers were conducted by firms which were multinational in the scope of their manufacturing activity, although they varied considerably in sales value (10–20 billion U.S. dollars) and R & D expenditures (1·2–12·5% of sales value). All had headquarters in the United States. The transferees were on the average much smaller and less research-intensive. In 12 instances they were wholly owned subsidiaries of the transferor, in 8 instances the transferor and transferee were joint ventures partners, in 4 instances transfers were to wholly independent private enterprises, and the remaining 3 were to government enterprises. Table 1 shows that 17 of the projects fall into a broad category which will be labelled "chemicals and petroleum refining." The remaining 9 projects fall into a category which will be labelled "machinery".[3] Table 1 also indicates the wide geographical dispersion of the transferees.

---

country which owns the technology to operate a plant in a foreign country without any transfer of factors." P. 122.

   [1] Horizontal transfer refers to the transfer of technical information from one project to another. It can be distinguished from vertical transfer, which refers to the transfer of technical information within the various stages of a particular innovation process, e.g. from the basic research stage to the applied research stage.

   [2] For the distinctions between materials transfer, design transfer, and capacity transfer, see Hayami and Ruttan (1971).

   [3] Chemicals and petroleum refining thus embrace ISIC categories (United Nations, 1968), 351, 353, and 356, while "machinery" embraces categories 381, 382, and 383.

Table I

Twenty-six Technology Transfer Projects: 3 Digit ISIC Category and Transferee Location

Location	"Chemicals and Petroleum Refining"			"Machinery"			Total
	351: industrial chemicals	353: petroleum refineries	356: plastic products	381: fabricated metal products machinery and equipment	382: machinery except electrical	383: electrical machinery, appliances, and supplies	
Canada	1	1	0	1	0	0	3
Northern and Western Europe	3	1	0	0	4	1	9
Australia	0	0	1	0	0	0	1
Japan	3	0	0	0	1	0	4
Eastern Europe	2	0	0	0	0	0	2
Latin America	3	0	0	0	0	1	4
Asia (excluding Japan)	0	1	0	0	0	1	2
Africa	1	0	0	0	0	0	1
Total	13	3	1	1	5	3	26

IV. DEFINITION OF TECHNOLOGY TRANSFER COSTS

An economic definition of transfer cost is developed below. The emphasis is on the resources which must be utilised to transfer technological know-how. Of course royalty costs or rents must be incurred merely to secure access to the technology, but these costs are not the focus of attention of this paper.[1] In order to appreciate the import of the definition that will be presented, a distinction must first be made between two basic forms in which technology can be transferred. The first form embraces physical items such as tooling, equipment, and blue prints. Technology can be embodied in these objects. The second form of technology is the information that must be acquired if the physical equipment or "hardware" is to be utilised effectively. This information relates to methods of organisation and operation, quality control, and various other manufacturing procedures. The effective conveyance of such "peripheral" support constitutes the crux of the process of technology transfer, and it typically generates the associated information flows. It is towards discovery of the cost of transfer of this "unembodied"[2] knowledge that the attention is directed.

Technology transfer costs are therefore defined as the costs of transmitting and absorbing all of the relevant unembodied knowledge. The costs of performing the various activities which have to be conducted to ensure the transfer of the necessary technological know-how will represent the cost of technology transfer.[3] Clearly, a great many skills from other industries (e.g. design engineering) will be needed for plant design, plant construction, and equipment installation. However, not all of these skills will have to be transferred to ensure the success of the project. As defined, the costs of transfer clearly do not include all of the costs of establishing a plant abroad and bringing it on stream.

The definition of transfer costs presented at the conceptual level can be translated into operational measures by considering the nature of a given project activity. At the operational level the subset of project costs identified as transfer costs fall into four groups. The first group is the cost of pre-engineering technological exchanges. During these exchanges the basic characteristics of the technology are revealed to the transferee, and the necessary theoretical insights are conveyed. The second group of costs included are the engineering costs associated with transferring the process design and the associated process engineering[4] in the case of process innovations, or the product design and production engineering[5] in the case of product innovations. If the technology has already

---

[1] Many observers equate the cost of technology with royalty fees (Mason, 1973; Gillette, 1973). Royalty costs are considered in the dissertation from which this paper was taken.

[2] Unembodied knowledge is the term used here to denote knowledge not embodied in capital goods, blueprints, and technical specifications, etc.

[3] All of the relevant costs are included, irrespective of which entity initially or eventually incurs them.

[4] Process engineering for continuous flow technology involves the compilation of flow diagrams, heat balances, control instrumentation, etc. It can be distinguished from detailed engineering which involves the translation and elaboration of the process engineering into a manufacturing facility.

[5] Production engineering for a specified item can be divided into two phases: production design and process planning. Production design is the modification of the functional design in order to reduce manufacturing costs. (Functional product design is the design of a product to fulfil certain specifications and requirements.) Given the design, process planning for manufacture must be carried out to specify,

been commercialised,[1] transmission may simply involve transferring existing drawings and specifications with the minimum of modification. However, the process of absorption may be more difficult, requiring the utilisation of considerable consulting or advisory resources. "Engineering" costs not falling into the specified categories[2] are excluded from transfer costs. The excluded engineering costs are essentially the plant or detailed engineering costs, net of advisory or consulting costs. This residual is assumed to correspond with routine drafting costs. Routine drafting is generally performed by technicians under the supervision of engineers. Drafting skills do not have to be transferred for the viability of the project to be assured. Accordingly, drafting is not considered to represent a transfer activity.[3]

The third group of costs are those of R & D personnel (salaries and expenses) during all phases of the transfer project. These are not the R & D costs associated with developing the underlying process or product innovations. Rather, they are the R & D costs associated with solving unexpected problems and adapting or modifying the technology. For instance, research scientists may be utilised during the transfer if new and unusual technical problems are encountered[4] with the production inputs. These R & D costs are generally small or non-existent for international transfers falling into the "design transfer" category.

The fourth group of costs are the pre-start-up training costs and the "excess manufacturing costs". The latter represent the learning and debugging costs incurred during the start-up phase, and before the plant achieves the design performance specifications. It is quite possible that no marketable output will be produced during the initial phases of the start-up. Nevertheless, normal labour, materials, utilities, and depreciation costs will be incurred, together with the costs of the extra supervisory personnel that will inevitably be required to

---

in careful detail, the processes required and their sequence. The production design first sets the minimum possible costs that can be achieved through the specification of materials, tolerances, basic configurations, methods of joining parts, etc. Process planning then attempts to achieve that minimum through the specification of processes and their sequence to meet the exacting requirements of the design specifications. The accepted end-point for production design is manifested by the drawing release. Process planning takes over from this point and develops the broad plan of manufacture of the part or product. A distinction can also be drawn between process planning and the layout of the physical facilities. Some process planning will take place during the layout phases of the design of a production system, Process plans can be regarded as inputs to the development of a layout. (*McGraw-Hill Encyclopedia.* 1960.)

[1] An innovation is said to have been commercialised if it has already been applied in a facility of economic size which is essentially non-experimental in nature. Thus pilot plant or prototype application is not considered to represent commercialisation.

[2] These categories are (a) process or design engineering costs and related consultation for process innovations or (b) production engineering expenses for product innovations; and (c) costs of engineering supervision and consultation (salaries plus travel and living) for the plant engineering.

[3] Drafting costs can be considered an implementation cost rather than a transfer cost, the implication being that if the host country does not have these skills, the viability and cost of the project is unlikely to be affected. The advisory and consulting costs, on the other hand, represent transfer costs since these activities are necessary if the technology is to be adjusted to the local circumstance and requirements. Clearly, if an existing plant was to be duplicated in its own environment, consulting costs could be expected to go to zero, whereas routine drafting would still have to be performed.

[4] Referring to process technologies, it is possible that differences in feedstocks amongst various locations may create problems that only research scientists can effectively handle. Similarly, changes in atmospheric conditions or water supply could have unexpected consequences for some highly complex processes.

assist in the start-up. The operating losses incurred during initial production are very often a close approximation to excess manufacturing costs.[1]

V. TRANSFER COSTS: DATA AND HYPOTHESES

1. *The Level of Transfer Costs*

The above definition was used to calculate the transfer costs for 26 projects. The results are presented in Table 2. The costs are given in absolute dollars, and then normalised by total project costs.[2] For the sample as a whole, transfer costs average 19 % of total project costs. Clearly, the data do not support the notion that technology is a stock of blueprints usable at nominal cost to all. Nevertheless, there is considerable variation in the sample data, with transfer costs ranging from 2 % to 59 % of total project costs. The number of factors influencing transfer costs is undoubtedly very great,[3] but some factors are likely to have a more pervasive influence than others. The discussion to follow is restricted to hypotheses for which statistical testing is feasible, given the available data. Two groupings of testable hypotheses can be identified: characteristics of the technology/transferor, and characteristics of the transferee/host country.

2. *Technology/Transferor Characteristics*

A critical factor in the transfer of technology is the extent to which the technology is completely understood by the transferor. The number of manufacturing start-ups[4] or applications which the transferor has already conducted with a specific technology can be used as an index of this knowledge.[5] An increase in the number of applications is likely to lower transfer costs since with each start-up additional knowledge about the technology is acquired. Since no two manufacturing start-ups are identical, each start-up provides the firm with the opportunity to observe the effects of different operating parameters and differences in equipment design. Each application can be regarded as a new experiment which

---

[1] An important consideration is the extent to which excess manufacturing costs correctly reflect technology transfer costs rather than the costs of discovering and overcoming the idiosyncrasies of a new plant. One way to confront this issue is to consider the level of excess manufacturing costs when an absolutely identical plant is constructed in a location adjacent to an existing plant. Further, assume the second plant embodies the same technology as the first plant, and the labour force from the first is transferred to the second for the purpose of performing the manufacturing start-up. The assumption is that under these circumstances excess manufacturing costs in the second plant will be zero, or very nearly so. The correctness of this assumption was corroborated by a subsample of project managers subsequently questioned about this matter. The postulated circumstance would be identical to shutting down the first plant and then starting it up again. Some excess manufacturing costs might be incurred during the initial hours of operation if the plant embodies flow process technology. (For the projects in the sample the average duration of the manufacturing start-up was 8·2 months.) However, these costs are unlikely to be of sufficient magnitude to challenge the validity of classifying excess manufacturing costs as a component of technology transfer costs.

[2] Total project costs are measured according to the inside boundary limits definition commonly employed by project accountants. Installations outside the plant perimeter are thereby excluded.

[3] For a broader view of the spectrum of hypotheses, see the author's Ph.D. dissertation.

[4] Manufacturing start-ups are synonymous with the number of applications of the technology. If a new plant is built for each application, it would also by synonymous with the number of plants that are built which utilise the technology.

[5] Corporations engaged in technology transfer ventures not grounded on their own technology are known to have encountered massive transfer problems and costs.

yields new information and new experience.[1] Transfer will be facilitated the more fully the technology is understood. Besides these engineering economies, additional applications provide expanded opportunities for the pre-start-up, training of the labour force. Clearly, if identical or similar plants exist elsewhere,

Table 2

Sample Data on the Resource Costs of Technology Transfer: 26 International Projects

Chemicals and Petroleum Refining		Machinery	
Transfer costs: dollar amount (thousands)	Transfer costs: dollar amount total project cost	Transfer costs: dollar amount (thousands)	Transfer costs: dollar amount total project cost
49	18	198	26
185	8	360	32
683	11	1,006	38
137	17	5,850	45
449	8	555	10
362	7	1,530	42
643	6	33	59
75	10	968	24
780	13	270	45
2,142	6		
161	2		
586	7		
877	7		
66	4		
2,850	19		
7,425	22		
3,341	4		

then experienced operators from these plants can be used to assist the start-up in the new plant. In addition, untrained operators can be brought into existing plants for pre-start-up training.

The second variable to be considered is the age of the technology. The age of the technology is defined as the number of years since the beginning of the first commercial application of the technology[2] anywhere in the world, and the end[3] of the technology transfer programme. The age of an innovation will determine the stability of the engineering designs and the transferor's knowledge of the manufacturing procedures. The older the technology, *ceteris paribus*, then the greater have been the opportunities for interaction between the development groups and the manufacturing and operating groups within the firm. Problems

[1] The first application represents first commercialisation of the technology. This will result in the creation of a set of basic engineering drawings and specifications. Duplication and alteration of these for subsequent start-ups will involve a modest cost compared to the initial cost of constructing them.

[2] If there is more than one key innovation embodied in the technology, then the date of commercial application of the most recent key innovation is the reference date.

[3] Age is defined up to the end of the transfer programme since any knowledge about the technology acquired up to this point is potentially useful for the transfer. For the very first start-up, age will be the length of the transfer minus the development overlap.

stand a better chance of already being ironed out, and the drawings are likely to be more secure. Further, since technology is not embodied in drawings alone, there is a great deal of uncodified information – the relevant "art". This kind of knowledge is carried by the supervisors, engineers, and operators. As the age of the technology increases, more individuals in the firm have the opportunity to acquire this non-codified information, and hence are potentially available to assist in the transfer. There will, however, be some point after which greater age will begin to increase the cost of transfer. When the length of stay of corporate personnel begins to be outstripped by the age of technology, then the non-codified dimensions of design knowledge may be lost to the firm.[1]

It is necessary to distinguish the cost reductions resulting from additional start-ups from the cost reductions resulting from greater age of the technology. For continuous flow technologies, additional applications of an innovation in entirely new plants will allow experimentation with scale and with the basic parameters of the design. This will generate a greater understanding of the technology. On the other hand, greater age, given the number of applications or start-ups, generally permits experimentation only with operating parameters, the design of the plant remaining fixed throughout.

The third technology variable to be considered is the number of firms utilising the technology, or one that is "similar and competitive". This is taken to represent the degree to which the innovation and the associated manufacturing technology is already diffused throughout the industry. The greater the number of firms with the same or similar and competitive technology, then the greater the likelihood that technology is more generally available, and can therefore be acquired at lower cost.[2]

These technology variables and the attendant hypotheses begin to take on some extra significance when viewed together. Taken singly they define the technology to only a limited degree. Together, they hypothesise, *ceteris paribus*, that the most difficult and hence costly technology to transfer is characterised by very few previous applications, a short elapsed time since development, and limited diffusion. Technology displaying such characteristics can be termed "leading-edge" technology. "Leading-edge" technology is likely to be in a state of flux; the engineering drawings will be constantly altering, thus frustrating the transfer. In comparison, state-of-the-art technology is hypothesised, *ceteris paribus*, to involve lower transfer costs since the engineering drawings are more likely to be finalised and the fundamentals of the technology stand a better chance of being more fully understood.

---

[1] In the limit, the firm could terminate its utilisation of a particular technology, and the non-codified information associated with it could be gradually lost for ever as the technology becomes historic. Further, the drawings associated with technology that is very old may suffer from so many small alterations that the very essence of even the codified technology may become quite obscure. Since none of the technology transfer projects in the sample were historic in the above sense, the relevant range of the hypothesised age–transfer cost function involves an inverse relationship between the age of the technology and the cost of transfer.

[2] An identification problem may exist here because more firms may have applied the technology because the transfer cost is low.

3. *Transferee and Host Country Characteristics*

The technical and managerial competence of the transferee will be presented. as an important determinant of the ease with which technology can be absorbed. The years of manufacturing experience of the transferee in a given 4-digit ISIC industry (United Nations, 1968) is used as an index of the extent to which managers, engineers, and operators have command over the general manufacturing skills of an industry. A firm skilled in the manufacture of a group of products is likely to have less difficulty absorbing a new innovation in that industry group than is the firm which has had no previous experience manufacturing products in a particular industry group (Rawski, 1975). Older enterprises, with their skilled manufacturing personnel, seem more likely to be able to understand and apply codified knowledge to the manufacture of a new product, or the utilisation of a new process.[1]

Another variable to be considered is the size of the transferee. Although less compelling, the reasoning behind the hypothesis that transfer costs decline with firm size is that larger firms generally have a wider spectrum of technical and managerial talent which can be called on for assistance during the transfer. A small firm may be technically and managerially quite competent yet unable to absorb new technology easily because of the extra demands placed on its scarce managerial and technical manpower. Consultants may have to be engaged by the smaller firms to perform tasks that are typically handled internally in larger firms.

A third variable considered is the R & D activity of the transferee. When unusual technical problems are unexpectedly encountered, an in-house R & D capability is likely to be of value. Oshima has argued that the R & D capability of Japanese firms facilitated the low-cost importation of foreign technology by Japanese firms (Oshima, 1973). The R & D to sales ratio of the transferee is taken as an index of its R & D capability, and an inverse relationship between this and transfer cost is postulated.

The final variable considered is designed to reflect the level of development of the host country infrastructure, which is hypothesised to be a determinant of the cost of transfer. For example, the level of skill formation in the host country will influence the amount and type of training that the labour force will require. Similarly, if the new venture is to acquire its inputs domestically, the quality of the inputs available will undoubtedly influence the level of start-up costs. There are many other considerations of similar kind which could be discussed. However, the high degree of cross-sectional collinearity between indices of development (Kuznets, 1966) makes the identification of separate effects statistically difficult. However, GNP *per capita*, a measure of productive capacity, can

---

[1] According to Rawski, recent experience of the People's Republic of China shows that during at least some phases of industrialisation, production experience may be a key determinant of the level and fungibility of industrial skills. Rawski notes that "with their skilled veteran workers and experienced technical persons, old industrial bases and old enterprises find it easier to tackle complicated technical problems than new enterprises and new industrial bases. With these advantages, it is the established centers which are best able to copy foreign equipment samples, to extract useful information from foreign technological publications, and to apply it to current domestic problem areas." (Rawski (1975), p. 386.)

be expected to capture some of the above considerations, and it will be used in this study as an index of economic development. A negative relationship between transfer cost and GNP/*per capita* is postulated.[1]

VI. DETERMINANTS OF THE COST OF INTERNATIONAL TECHNOLOGY TRANSFER: TESTS AND RESULTS

1. *The Model*

The basic model to be tested is

$$C_i = f(U_i, G_i, E_i, R_i, S_i, N_i, P_i, Z_i), \tag{1}$$

where C_i is the transfer cost divided by the total project cost for the ith transfer; U_i is the number of previous applications or start-ups that the technology of the ith transfer has undergone by the transferor;[2] G_i is the age of the technology in years; E_i is the number of years of manufacturing experience that the recipient of the ith transfer has accumulated; R_i is the ratio of research and development to sales for the recipient of the ith transfer, calculated for the year the transfer commenced; S_i is the volume of sales, measured in millions of dollars, of the recipient of the ith transfer; N_i is the number of firms identified by the transferor as having a technology that is identical or "technically similar and economically competitive" to the technology underlying the ith transfer; P_i is the level of GNP *per capita* of the host country (International Bank, 1973); Z_i is the random error term for the ith transfer. The expected derivatives are:

$$\frac{\partial C_i}{\partial U_i} < 0, \quad \frac{\partial C_i}{\partial G_i} < 0, \quad \frac{\partial C_i}{\partial E_i} < 0, \quad \frac{\partial C_i}{\partial R_i} < 0, \quad \frac{\partial C_i}{\partial S_i} < 0, \quad \frac{\partial C_i}{\partial N_i} < 0, \quad \frac{\partial C_i}{\partial P_i} < 0.$$

Since one of the best tests of any hypothesis is to look for the convergence of independent lines of evidence, the testing of this model will proceed in two phases. First, cross-section data on 26 completed projects is utilised in a linear version of the model estimated by ordinary least-squares procedures. Secondly, cost estimates provided by project managers for comparable projects are pooled to test a more specific non-linear version of the model.

2. *Statistical Tests: Phase I*

The model to be tested is

$$C_i = \alpha_0 + \alpha_1 \bar{U}_i + \alpha_2 G_i + \alpha_3 E_i + \alpha_4 R_i + \alpha_5 S_i + \alpha_6 N_i + \alpha_7 P_i + Z_i, \tag{2}$$

where $\bar{U}_i$ is a dummy variable taking the value 1 if the transfer represents the first manufacturing start-up, and zero otherwise. $\bar{U}_i$ is used rather than U_i for empirical reasons, since the first start-up is often of critical importance. The sample was dichotomised because of the large differences between continuous flow process technology, and product technology. One category includes chemicals and petroleum refining and the other includes machinery (see Table 1).

---

[1] The sample did not include countries where high GNP statistics were grossly dependent on oil revenues.

[2] The number of previous manufacturing start-ups was significant in Phase I only when it was included as a dummy variable taking the value 1 if there had been no previous manufacturing start-ups of this technology by the transferring firm, and zero otherwise.

The results in Table 3 indicate that in chemicals and petroleum refining $\bar{U}_i$, N_i, and E_i are significant at the 0·05 level and carry the expected signs. In the machinery category the variables N_i, G_i, and E_i all carry the expected signs and are significant at the 0·05 level. N_i and E_i are thus significant in both industry

Table 3

*Regression of Coefficients and t Statistics in Regression
Equations to Explain C (The Cost of Transfer)*

Independent variable	Chemicals and petroleum refining		Machinery	
	Equation (1)*	Equation (2)*	Equation (1)*	Equation (2)*
Constant	12·79	13·42	16·67	65·98
	(6·82)	(6·98)	(8·27)	(6·60)
Novelty dummy variable $\bar{U}$†	6·73	6·11	—	1·62
	(1·92)	(1·75)		(0·15)
Number of firms variable	−0·37	−0·39	−1·29	−1·26
	(−2·06)	(−2·22)	(−2·28)	(−1·95)
Age of technology variable (years)	—	—	−2·43	−2·35
			(−3·53)	(−2·51)
Experience of transference variable (years in 4-digit ISIC)	−0·09	−0·08	−0·84	−0·85
	(−1·66)	(−1·42)	(−3·37)	(−2·95)
Size of transferee variable (thousands of dollars of sales)	—	−0·0009	—	—
		(−1·18)		
Number of observations	17	17	9	9
R^2	0·56	0·61	0·78	0·78
F	5·66	4·73	6·00	3·22
Significance level of F	0·01	0·02	0·04	0·12

* Omitted coefficient indicates variable dropped from the regression equation.
† Note 2, p. 251.

groupings, strongly supporting the hypothesis that transfer costs decline as the number of firms with identical or "similar and competitive" technology increases, and as the experience of the transferee increases. However, R_i and P_i were not significant in any of the equations, and although S_i carries the expected sign and approaches significance in one of the regressions it is not possible to be more than 85 % sure that the sign is correct or that the coefficient is different from zero.[1]

[1] Multicollinearity does not appear to be a serious problem in any of the equations. Correlations amongst pairs of the independent variables were never significant at the 0·05 level. The stability of the regression coefficients further suggests that multicollinearity is not a serious problem. Dummy variables were introduced to test for the effects of the organisational relationship between transferor and transferee (affiliate/non affiliate, public enterprise/private enterprise), but they were not found to be statistically significant determinant of transfer costs. Application of a forward step by step procedure did not reveal a preferred subset of variables. However, it is possible that the correct model is the simultaneous equation model $Ci = f(N_i, ...)$, $N_i = f(C_i, ...)$. To eliminate simultaneous equation bias it would be desirable to use a two-stage procedure. A predictor of N could first be obtained by regressing N_i on arguments other than C_i. This could then be used as an argument in the transfer cost regression. It was not possible to obtain a good predictor of N using the available cross-section data, so this procedure was not employed. Consistency was sacrificed for efficiency. It is therefore possible that simultaneous equation bias remains in the model. Therefore, the estimates of the parameters may not be consistent.

The results therefore generally support the hypotheses advanced earlier, but there are differences in the size of coefficients as well as in the specification of the equations between the industry groups. In particular, the novelty variable $\bar{U}_i$ is significant in chemicals and petroleum refining, but insignificant in machinery. The converse is true for the age variable G_i. The reason may be that there exists relatively less latitude for production experimentation with continuous flow process technology than with product technology. Once the plant is constructed, the extent to which the design parameters can be changed is rather minimal because of the degree of interdependence in the production system. In comparison, many product technologies allow greater design flexibility. Innumerable small changes to the technology are very often possible without massive reconstruction of the plant. It is also of interest that the coefficient of the experience variable E_i is considerably larger in machinery than in chemicals and petroleum refining. This is consistent with other findings that reveal important learning economies in fabrication and assembling (Tilton, 1971).

3. *Statistical Tests: Phase II*

The above analysis is handicapped by the small sample size and the very high costs of adding additional observations. Limited variation in exogenous variables coupled with the problem of omitted variables can imply difficulties with bias and identification. For the projects in the sample, a procedure was therefore devised to hold the missing variables constant while generating large variation in the exogenous variables. The respondent firms were asked to estimate how the total transfer costs would vary for each project if one particular exogenous variable happened to take a different value, assuming all other variables remain constant. The responses were taken into account only if the exercise generated circumstances within the bounds of an executive's experience. Given these limitations, the change specified was quite large in order to provide a robust sample. Generally the actual value of a selected variable was hypothesised first to halve and then to double. The estimated impact on transfer costs was noted. The exercise was performed for the following independent variables: the number of applications or start-ups that the technology has undergone; the age of the technology; the number of years of previous manufacturing experience possessed by the transferee in a given four-digit industry; the research and development expenditures to sales ratio for the transferee; the size (measured by sales value) of the transferee. For each variable this exercise generated at most three observations (including the actual) or transfer costs for each project. Pooling across projects produces enough observations for ordinary least-squares regression analysis.

The estimation procedure is commenced by assuming that the shape of the cost function can be represented by the following relatively simple but quite specific equation

$$C_j = V e^{\phi/X_j}. \tag{3}$$

C is the estimated transfer cost as a percentage of total project cost, X represents the value of various independent variables, j refers to the jth observation.

With this specification, the transfer cost for a project asymptotically approaches a minimum non-zero value as the value of each X increases. That is, as X goes to infinity, C goes to V. Therefore V is the minimum transfer cost with respect to the X variable. However, there is no maximum cost asymptote for the range of the data. The expression for the elasticity of transfer cost with respect to X is given by

$$\frac{-X}{C}\frac{dC}{dX} = \frac{\phi}{X}. \tag{4}$$

Thus for a specified value of X, the elasticity of transfer cost with respect to X is determined by ϕ. Hence the elasticity depends only on ϕ and X. In order to estimate the function, the log of the arguments in (3) are taken:

$$\log C_j = \log V + \frac{\phi}{X_j}. \tag{5}$$

Dummy variables are used to pool the observations across projects. Inclusion of dummy variables allows the minimum cost asymptote to vary from project to project. It is assumed that ϕ is constant across projects. These assumptions provide a pooled sample with intercepts which vary across projects.

Ordinary least-squares regressions of $\log C_j$ on the dummy variables and $1/X_j$ then proceeded for five different X variables, and for five data sets. These were: total transfers; transfers within the chemical and petroleum refining category; transfers in the machinery category; transfers of chemicals and petroleum refining technology to developed countries; and transfers of chemical and petroleum refining technology to less developed countries.[1] The Chow test (Chow, 1960) of equality between sets of coefficients in two linear regressions revealed that the separation of the sample along industry lines was valid, except for the research and development variable. However, there was no statistically valid reason for disaggregating the chemical and petroleum refining subsample according to differences in GNP *per capita* in the host countries.

The results of the estimation are contained in Table 4. The high R^2 values are partly because the large across-project variation in costs is being captured by the project dummies. The intercept term was always highly significant and the coefficients on all the dummies were significantly different from each other. All of the coefficients are significantly greater than zero at the 0·20 level and the age of the technology, the number of manufacturing start-ups, transferee size and experience achieve at least the 0·05 significance level in one or other of the subsamples. In several cases the coefficients are highly significant, providing strong statistical support for the hypotheses that have been advanced. The number of previous applications once again has a sizeable impact. Diffusion and manufacturing experience are particularly important in the machinery category.

The calculation of elasticities allows interpretation and comparisons of estimated effects. Average or point elasticities for some typical sample values of X are presented in Table 5. These estimates suggest that in the chemicals and petroleum-refining category, the second start-up could lower transfer costs by

---

[1] A purely arbitrary classification was used where less developed countries were defined as those with GNP/*per capita* less than $1,000.

34 % over the first start-up, other variables held constant. The corresponding change for conducting a third start-up is 19 %. The other elasticities can be interpreted similarly.

Table 4

Estimated values of ϕ (obtained from regressing $\log C_j$ on $\log V + \phi/X_j$) together with corresponding t-statistics, sample size, degrees of freedom, and coefficient of determination R^2

Variable	ϕ	t-statistic	Sample size	Degrees of freedom	R^2
Start-ups					
Chemicals and petroleum refining	0·46	4·23	45	25	0·92
Machinery	0·19	1·76	20	10	0·91
Age					
Chemicals and petroleum refining	0·04	1·29	47	30	0·89
Machinery	0·41	2·19	21	13	0·94
Experience					
Chemicals and petroleum refining	0·007	0·85	52	33	0·78
Machinery	0·57	6·08	23	14	0·91
Size					
Chemicals and petroleum refining	0·008	1·17	54	35	0·88
Machinery	0·081	5·18	17	10	0·99
R & D sales					
Total sample	0·06	1·58	59	30	0·90

VII. DIFFERENCES BETWEEN INTERNATIONAL AND DOMESTIC TECHNOLOGY TRANSFER

Although this is primarily a study of international technology transfer, it is apparent that many of the characteristics of international technology transfer are also characteristic of the technology transfer that occurs within national borders, but there are differences. For instance, distance and communication costs very often differentiate international from domestic transfers. Although the communications revolution of the twentieth century has enormously reduced the barriers imposed by distance,[1] the costs of international communication are often significant.[2] Language differences can also add to communication costs, especially if the translation of engineering drawings is required. The experience of Polyspinners Ltd at Mogilev in the Soviet Union (Jones, 1973) is ample testimony to the extra costs that can be encountered.[3] International differences in units of measurements and engineering standards can compound the problems encountered (Meursinge, 1971). Additional sources of difficulty are rooted in

[1] Facsimile equipment exists which can be used to transmit messages and drawings across the Atlantic instantaneously.

[2] One of the participating companies indicated that travel, telegraph, freight, and insurance added about 10 % to the total cost of a project established in New Zealand.

[3] The project manager estimated that documentation alone cost £500,000, and the translation a similar amount.

the cultural and attitudinal differences between nations, as well as differences in
the level of economic development and the attendant socioeconomic structure.

It is of interest to know the magnitude and determinants of the "international
component" of the transfer cost. Unfortunately, foreign and domestic transfers

Table 5

*Arc or Point Elasticity of Transfer Costs With Respect to Number of Start-ups,
Age of Technology, Experience, Size and R & D/Sales of Transferee*

Independent variable	Chemicals and petroleum refining	Machinery
	Arc elasticity	
Number of start-ups		
1–2	0·34	0·14
2–3	0·19	0·08
3–4	0·13	0·05
9–10	0·05	0·02
14–15	0·03	0·01
Age of technology (years)	Point elasticity	
1	0·04	0·41
2	0·02	0·20
3	0·01	0·14
10	0·00	0·04
20	0·00	0·02
Experience of transferee (years)	Point elasticity	
1	0·007	0·57
2	0·003	0·28
3	0·002	0·19
10	0·001	0·06
20	0·000	0·03
Size of transferee (millions of sales dollars)	Point elasticity	
1·0	0·008	0·081
10	0·001	0·008
20	0·000	0·004
100	0·000	0·001
1000	0·000	0·000
R & D/Sales of transferee (%)	Total sample point elasticity	
1	0·06	
2	0·03	
3	0·02	
4	0·01	
5	0·01	
6	0·01	

are rarely identical in scope or in timing, and so it is not possible to gather
comparative data on implemented projects at home and abroad. It was therefore found necessary to rely on estimates provided by the firms involved in international transfers. For the projects in the sample, project managers were asked
to estimate the dollar amount by which transfer costs would be different if the

international transfers in the sample had occurred domestically, holding firm and technology characteristics constant. The procedure was designed to highlight the effects of country characteristics such as differences in language, differences in engineering and measurement standards, differences in economic infrastructure and business environment, and geographical distance from the transferor. The international component of the transfer cost for the projects in the sample could be obtained by subtracting the estimated transfer cost from the

Table 6

International Component* of Transfer Cost

Chemicals and petroleum refining		Machinery	
Dollar amount (thousands)	As % of actual transfer cost	Dollar amount (thousands)	As % of actual transfer cost
3·03	6·07	35·55	17·88
0·00	0·00	− 399·37	− 110·93
− 12·81	− 1·87	50·06	4·93
43·90	31·00	830·70	14·20
0·00	0·00	− 4·59	− 0·02
5·17	1·42	226·80	14·82
132·75	20·63	0·67	1·99
0·00	0·00	− 134·40	13·87
342·00	43·84	34·98	12·95
0·00	—		
0·00	—		
0·00	0·00		
− 10·77	− 6·66		
− 50·16	− 8·52		
0·00	—		
637·32	72·60		
− 1·33	− 1·99		
1,723·81	60·48		
1,370·25	18·45		
524·25	15·69		

* Amount of actual transfer costs attributable to the fact that transfer was international rather than domestic. (Accordingly negative values indicate that firms estimated that transfer costs would be higher had the transfer been domestic.) In general, these numbers were derived from taking the weighted average of estimated changes in the various identifiable components of transfer costs.

actual transfer cost. The data, contained in Table 6, reveal that the difference in cost is not always positive. This indicates that in at least some of the cases, the international transfer of an innovation was estimated to cost less than a comparable domestic transfer. This may seem paradoxical at first, given that international technology transfer generally augments the transfer activities that have to be performed.[1] An analysis of the determinants of the international component of transfer costs may yield an explanation.

Several hypotheses are presented and tested. The first is that the difference is

---

[1] The source of the apparent paradox may be differences in labour costs. Nevertheless, the identification of the transfer for which international transfer costs less than domestic transfer is an issue of importance.

large and positive when the technology has not been previously commercialised. National boundaries are often surrogates for cultural and language barriers, differences in methods and standards of measurement, and distance from the home country. During first commercialisation of a product or process, there are generally enormous information flows across the development-manufacturing interface. The hypothesis is that placing a national boundary at this interface can complicate matters considerably, and escalate the costs enormously. The second hypothesis is that transfers to government enterprises in centrally planned economies will involve higher transfer costs. Transferors can expect numerous delays and large documentation requirements (Jones, 1973). The third hypothesis is that the less the diffusion of the technology, measured as before by the number of firms utilising the innovation, the greater the positive differential associated with international technology transfer. The fourth hypothesis is that whereas, in general, low levels of economic development are likely to add to transfer costs because of inadequacies in the economic infrastructure, this may be more than offset, in some circumstances, by low labour costs. Labour costs can have a substantial impact on excess manufacturing costs, especially in relatively labour intensive industries. Since machinery manufacture is relatively labour intensive, the hypothesis is that the GNP *per capita* in the host country is positively related to the transfer cost differential in this classification, but is negatively associated with the differential in the chemicals and petroleum refining category.

To test these hypotheses it is assumed that

$$D_i = \alpha_0 + \alpha_1 d_i + \alpha_2 \bar{U}_i + \alpha_3 N_i + \alpha_4 P_i + Z_i,$$

where D_i is the "international component" as a percentage of actual transfer cost for the ith transfer. d_i is a dummy variable which takes the value 1 if the recipient of the ith transfer is a government enterprise in a centrally planned economy, and zero otherwise. The other variables carry the same definitions as previously. The expected derivations are:

$$\frac{\partial D_i}{\partial d_i} > 0, \quad \frac{\partial D_i}{\partial \bar{U}_i} > 0, \quad \frac{\partial D_i}{\partial N_i} < 0;$$

$\partial D_i / \partial P_i \gtrless 0$ according to the industry category (the partial is postulated positive for the machinery category, and negative otherwise). Least-squares estimates of the α's were obtained, the results being:

Chemicals and petroleum:

$$D_i = 0.285 + 3.84 d_i + 4.46 \bar{U}_i \quad (n = 17, r^2 = 0.71).$$
$$\quad\;\; (0.91) \quad (5.01) \quad (4.89)$$

Machinery:[1]

$$D_i = -8.59 \quad - 1.39 N_i + 0.005 P_i \quad (n = 9, r^2 = 0.94).$$
$$\quad\;\; (-1.96) \; (-5.98) \quad (3.90)$$

---

[1] O_i was omitted from the machinery regression since none of the actual transfers in this category were to government enterprises in centrally planned economies.

The hypotheses are to some extent borne out by the data, but the small sample size must counsel caution in the interpretation of these results.[1] In chemicals and petroleum, the results indicate that transfers to government enterprises, and transfers before first commercialisation, involve substantial extra costs. Furthermore, both N_i and P_i are significant in the machinery category, despite the small number of observations, yet they are insignificant in chemicals and petroleum refining, where there are more than twice as many degrees of freedom. Apparently, the level of host country development and the degree of diffusion of an innovation have no bearing on the international–domestic transfer cost differential in the chemicals and petroleum grouping. This calls for an explanation. The diffusion variable N_i is taken to indicate the degree to which the requisite skills are generally available. The statistical results suggest that the relevant skills for highly capital intensive industries, such as chemicals and petroleum refining, are more easily transferred internationally than are the requisite skills in the machinery category.[2] Furthermore, P_i was not significant in chemicals and petroleum refining, suggesting that costs of transfer are independent of the level of economic development in this category. This is consistent with speculation that international transfer is no more difficult than domestic transfer when the underlying technology is highly capital intensive. The perceived reluctance of multinational firms to adapt technology to suit the capital–labour endowments of less developed countries could well be rooted in the desire to avoid escalating transfer costs to unacceptable levels.

VIII. CONCLUSION

The resources required to transfer technology internationally are considerable. Accordingly, it is quite inappropriate to regard existing technology as something that can be made available to all at zero social cost. Furthermore, transfer costs vary considerably, especially according to the number of previous applications of the innovation, and how well the innovation is understood by the parties involved. It is equally inappropriate, therefore, to make sweeping generalisations about the process of technology transfer and the costs involved. For instance, technology transfer in chemicals and petroleum refining displayed relatively low transfer costs, presumably because it is possible to embody sophisticated process technology in capital equipment, which in turn facilitates the transfer process.

The analysis of the determinants of technology transfer costs provided some interesting findings with development implications. The success of the more experienced enterprises, indicated by lower transfer costs, points towards economic models which emphasise the accumulation of skills, rather than fixed

---

[1] If the second observation on D_i in the machinery category is excluded, and the regression results recomputed, the estimates of the coefficients exhibit considerable instability and the "goodness of fit" deteriorates. The estimated equation is

$$D_i = -4 \cdot 96 \quad -0 \cdot 66 N_i + 0 \cdot 003 P_i \quad (n = 8, r^2 = 0 \cdot 45).$$
$$ (1 \cdot 14) \quad (2 \cdot 40) \quad (1 \cdot 94)$$

These estimates are nevertheless significant at the $0 \cdot 05$ level for a one-tail test.

[2] This is consonant with the views expressed by several project managers in the chemical industry. It was asserted that technology could be transferred with equal facility to almost anywhere in the world, including less developed countries, assuming host government interference is held constant.

assets or capital, in facilitating the technology transfer process. This seems consonant with the findings of several economic historians (Rosenberg, 1970; Rawski, 1975).

The results also provide some managerial implications for the multinational firm. Consider the costs associated with separating production from development (Arditti, 1968). The results indicate that the international transfer of technology is most likely to be viable when production runs are long enough to allow second sourcing. The especially high cost of transfer before first application favours the development location, at least for production of initial units. However, transfer costs will be lowered once the first production run has been commenced, and international transfer then becomes more likely, a finding consistent with the product cycle model (Vernon, 1966). However, inter-industry differences are important, and the costs involved in separating first production from development did not prove to be an insurmountable transfer barrier for an important subset of the sample projects.

A second implication is that since transfer costs decline with each application of a given innovation, technology transfer is a decreasing cost activity. This can be advanced as an explanation for the specialisation often exhibited by engineering firms in the design and installation of particular turnkey plants,[1] a characteristic particularly noteworthy of the petrochemical industry.

A third set of managerial implications relate to the criteria which might be used for the selection of a joint venture or licensing partner to utilise the innovating firms' technology abroad. While the manufacturing experience, size, and R & D to sales ratio of the transferee were identified as statistically significant determinants of transfer costs for the sample, there was also evidence to suggest that, *ceteris paribus*, any firm moderately matured in these dimensions is a good candidate to absorb the technology at the minimum possible transfer cost. It is not clear, therefore, that super giant firms have any advantage in this respect over moderately sized firms. Nor is it clear that highly research intensive firms have more than a slight cost advantage in absorbing technology over firms with a minimal commitment to research and development activity. However, manufacturing experience is important, especially for transferring machinery technology. In addition, there is evidence that transfers to governments in centrally planned economies involve substantial extra costs, perhaps because of high documentation requirements, or differences in language and managerial procedures.

Technology transfer by multinational firms is clearly a complex matter. Collection and analysis of proprietary data has provided some helpful insights. Few issues have been settled although many have been raised. Further analytic research and more extensive data collection is required if our understanding of international technology transfer is to be improved.

D. J. TEECE

Stanford University, California

Date of receipt of final typescript: November 1976

[1] Turnkey plants generally embody state-of-the-art technology.

REFERENCES

Arrow, K. (1969). "Classificatory Notes on the Production and Transmission of Technological Knowledge." *Amercian Economic Review; Papers and Proceedings*, vol. 52 (May), pp. 29–35.
—— (1962). Comment in Universities-National Bureau Committee for Economic Research. *The Rate and Direction of Inventive Activity*. Princeton: Princeton University Press.
Arditti, F. (1968). "On the Separation of Production from the Developer." *Journal of Business*, vol. 41 (July), pp. 317–28.
Baranson, J. (1967): *Manufacturing Problems in India: The Cummings Diesel Experience*. Syracuse, N.Y.: Syracuse University Press.
Berrill, K. (ed.) (1964). *Economic Development with Special Reference to East Asia*. New York: St Martins Press.
Chow, G. C. (1960). "Tests of Equality between Sets of Coefficients in Two Linear Regressions." *Econometrica*, vol. 28 (July), pp. 591–605.
Freeman, C. (1965). "Research and Development in Electronic Capital Goods." *National Institute Economic Review*, no. 34, vol. 34 (November), pp. 1–70.
Gillette, R. (1973). "Latin America: Is Imported Technology Too Expensive?" *Science*, vol. 191 (6 July), pp. 4–44.
Hall, G. R. and Johnson, R. E. (1970). "Transfers of United States Aerospace Technology to Japan." In *The Technology Factor in International Trade* (ed. R. Vernon). N.Y.: National Bureau of Economic Research.
Hayami, Y. and Ruttan, V. (1971). *Agricultural Development and International Perspective*. Baltimore: Johns Hopkins.
International Bank for Reconstruction and Development (1973). *World Bank Atlas*. Washington, D.C.: I.B.R.D.
Jones, D. (1973). "The 'Extra Costs' in Europe's Biggest Synthetic Fiber Complex at Mogilev, U.S.S.R." *Worldwide Projects and Installations*, vol. 7 (May/June), pp. 30–5.
Kuznets, S. (1966). *Modern Economic Growth: Rate, Structure, Spread*. New Haven: Yale University Press.
Mansfield, E. (1974). "Technology and Technical Change." In *Economic Analysis and the Multinational Enterprise* (ed. J. Dunning). London: Allen and Unwin.
—— (1968) *The Economics of Technological Change*. New York: Norton.
—— (1973). "Discussion of the Paper by Professor Griliches." In *Science and Technology in Economic Growth* (ed. B. R. Williams). New York: John Wiley.
Mansfield, E., Rapoport, J., Schnee, J., Wagner, S. and Hamburger, M. (1971). *Research and Innovation In the Modern Corporation*. New York: W. W. Norton.
Mason, R. Hal (1973). "The Multinational Firm and the Cost of Technology to Developing Countries." *California Management Review*, vol. 15 (Summer), pp. 5–13.
Meursinge, J. (1971). "Practical Experience in the Transfer of Technology." *Technology and Culture*, vol. 12 (July), pp. 469–70.
McGraw-Hill Encyclopedia of Science and Technology (1960). Vols. 4, 10, pp. 639–44. New York: McGraw-Hill.
Oshima, K. (1973). "Research and Development and Economic Growth in Japan." In *Science and Technology in Economic Growth* (ed. B. R. Williams). New York: John Wiley.
Rawski, T. (1975). "Problems of Technology and Absorption in Chinese Industry." *American Economic Review*, vol. 65 (May), pp. 363–88.
Reynolds, L. (1966). Discussion. *American Economic Review*, vol. 56 (May), pp. 112–14.
Robinson, E. A. G. (1973). "Discussion of the Paper by Professor Hsia." In *Science and Technology in Economic Growth* (ed. B. R. Williams). New York: John Wiley.
Rodriguez, C. A. (1975). "Trade in Technical Knowledge and the National Advantage." *Journal of Political Economy*, vol. 93 (February), pp. 121–35.
Rosenberg, N. (1970). "Economic Development and the Transfer of Technology: Some Historical Perspectives." *Technology and Culture*, vol. 11 (October), pp. 550–75.
Teece, D. (1976). *The Multinational Corporation and the Resource Cost of International Technology Transfer*. Cambridge: Ballinger.
—— (1977). "Time–Cost Tradeoffs: Elasticity Estimates and Determinants for International Technology Transfer Projects." *Management Science*, vol. 23 (April).
Tilton, J. (1971). *International Diffusion of Technology: The Case of Semiconductors*. Washington, D.C.: Brookings Institution.
United Nations (1968). *International Standard Industrial Classification of all Economic Activities*. United Nations Statistical Papers, Series M., Number 4. New York: United Nations.
UNCTAD (1970). "The Transfer of Technology." *Journal of World Trade Law*, vol. 4 (September/October), pp. 692–718.
Vernon, R. (1966). "International Investment and International Trade in the Product Cycle. *Quarterly Journal of Economics*, vol. 80 (May), pp. 190–207.

[10]

MANAGEMENT SCIENCE
Vol. 23, No. 8, April, 1977
Printed in U.S.A.

TIME-COST TRADEOFFS: ELASTICITY ESTIMATES AND DETERMINANTS FOR INTERNATIONAL TECHNOLOGY TRANSFER PROJECTS*

DAVID TEECE†

This paper postulates and tests for a time-cost tradeoff during the establishment of manufacturing plants abroad based on U.S. technology. Data on twenty international projects are used to estimate negatively sloped tradeoff functions for which time-cost elasticities are subsequently calculated. The determinants of these elasticities are then analyzed and shown to bear some similarities with the determinants of time-cost tradeoffs in technological innovation. The elasticity measurements were higher for projects where the technology had not been previously commercialized, for large-scale projects, and for projects carried out by the larger firms.

1. Introduction

This paper shows that a time-cost tradeoff confronts the multinational firm in the scheduling of the design, construction, and startup of a manufacturing project abroad based on U.S. technology. In other words, the total cost of a project is revealed to increase if the time span between project commencement and project completion is reduced. Furthermore, the elasticity of this tradeoff can be explained by reference to characteristics of the technology being transferred and to characteristics of the participating firms.

Although the establishment of foreign plants is by no means an everyday activity for most multinational firms, foreign direct investment and international technology transfer is of some consequence for many U.S. and foreign firms. Therefore, the time-cost tradeoff identified is of practical importance.[1] The concept also has analytic interest, since the identification of the tradeoff under a number of different guises strengthens the generality of the principle that "buying" time in various kinds of investment decisions will require additional resources. Furthermore, an understanding of the concept is enhanced if comparisons can be made of the various kinds of time-cost tradeoff.

In the following sections reasons will be advanced for the existence of a time-cost tradeoff during the establishment of a manufacturing plant abroad. Using data from a sample of twenty such projects, the parameters of a tradeoff function will then be estimated. Finally, hypotheses will be advanced and tested to explain variation in the elasticity of the tradeoff function for these same twenty projects.

2. Foundations of the Time-Cost Tradeoff

While the existence of a time-cost tradeoff for research and development has been recognized [5] and demonstrated [3], the applicability of this discovery to nonresearch activity has at the same time been questioned [5].[2] Foreign direct investment, not obviously a research related activity, nevertheless seems to be rooted in the exploita-

---

* Accepted by Burton V. Dean; received December 8, 1975. This paper has been with the author 1 month, for 1 revision.

† Stanford University.

[1] The importance of the concept has been recognized in a number of different applications, and critical path analysis has been used to operationalize the time-cost tradeoff for the purpose of assisting in the efficient scheduling of complex development and construction projects. See, for example, [4, Chapter 7] and [2].

[2] Scherer contends that the time-cost tradeoff in research and development has "few close parallels in nonresearch activities."

tion of technological know-how [1]. Furthermore, the application of U.S. technology abroad is often replete with technological uncertainty, just as is the development of new technology itself [6]. The utilization of a technological innovation in a new context is likely to require, among other things, adjustment of some of the basic design parameters. For example, differences in the market size between home and abroad will induce scale adaptations to the plant; and differences in materials inputs, operator skills and engineering standards will frequently necessitate design changes in the process and/or the product. The implementation of design changes will produce uncertain responses in the quality and cost of the final product. Although the uncertainties generated are undoubtedly modest compared to those encountered during the original product or process development, they are still important. When uncertainty precludes immediate identification of the best design, it may be desirable to "hedge" by supporting several different designs [5]. By incurring higher project costs, hedging can reduce the project time relative to a procedure which explores different designs sequentially.

Besides "hedging" activities there are a number of other procedures which can be used to reduce project time, but they can all be expected to increase project costs. As additional engineers are brought on to the project to speed the design, diminishing returns can generally be expected. The concomitant increases in job segmentation will eventually augment coordination costs. Attempts to reduce project time by speeding equipment procurement can also be expected to increase project costs. Lead-times on major items of equipment can be reduced in a number of ways. For instance, the multinational firm can by-pass the equipment bidding procedure and the attendant delays by negotiating cost plus contracts with equipment suppliers. The disabilities and costs associated with this kind of contracting have been set out adequately elsewhere [7]. An alternative procedure is to solicit bids before the plant and equipment designs have been finalized. This may save several weeks, but firms generally run the risk of incurring penalty fees if the design specifications are subsequently modified. A number of procedures are also available to reduce manufacturing startup time, which commonly accounts for about 20% of total project time. For instance, the number and duration of pre-startup training programs can be increased. A more radical and costly procedure to facilitate a quick and smooth startup would involve the importation of large numbers of trained operators from established plants to assist during the startup period. Of course, if the new plant is the first of its kind, there may be little advantage to be gained from such costly procedures.

All of these various considerations provide the foundation for postulating a time-cost tradeoff that within some range has a negative slope and is convex to the origin. If the existence of some fixed costs is also postulated, then increasing project time need not always lower expected costs. The postulated tradeoff function is therefore

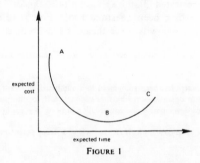

FIGURE 1

DAVID TEECE

U-shaped (see Figure 1). Clearly the firm will not wish to operate to the right of B under any sort of sensible conditions, and so the range of the tradeoff function that is of greatest interest is AB.

3. Estimation of the Time-Cost Tradeoff

The relevant tradeoff function is hypothesized to be negatively sloped and convex to the origin. $\partial C/\partial T < 0$, $\partial^2 C/\partial T^2 > 0$, where C is the expected project cost, and T is the expected project time. In order to test this hypothesis, data were obtained for a sample of twenty international projects. All of the projects embodied U.S. technology, and fifteen of the twenty were in chemicals or petroleum refining. The remainder were in the machinery industry. The projects varied considerably in size and in geographical dispersion.[3]

Project managers were asked to estimate the percentage change in the actual cost of the project that would result from expected changes in the actual time.[4] The actual project cost and time were used as reference points. The project managers were also asked to estimate the minimum possible time in which the project could be completed. Five observations on time and cost were obtained for each project, including the actual time and cost.[5]

In order to estimate the function, the assumption is made that the downward sloping section of the time-cost tradeoff can be represented by:

$$C = V \exp\{\phi/((t/\alpha) - 1)\} \tag{1}$$

where C is the expected cost of the projects, t is the expected time, and V, α, and ϕ are parameters that vary from project to project. Figure 2 shows the nature of this function. It is convex and has time and cost asymptotes.

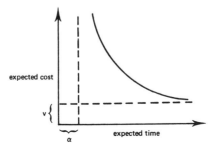

FIGURE 2. Graphical Representation of (1).

---

[3] For a detailed description of the sample see [6].

[4] Managers were asked to estimate the change in cost that would result for different time spans, such as half the actual time, twice the actual time, actual time ± 10% and so forth. Generally, five points on the negatively sloped portion of the tradeoff were obtained including the actual cost-time configuration. Since this was an experiment conducted by a disinterested party, and since the confidentiality of the data was guaranteed, the respondents had no incentive to deliberately distort the data. Furthermore, the time-cost tradeoff by itself implies very little about the optimal scheduling of the project. To discover this, a revenue function must also be estimated. The optimal project time occurs when the marginal revenue from time shaving equals the marginal cost from time shaving. Accordingly, the data supplied could not possibly be used to make inferences about the performance records of the respondent managers. These factors attenuate whatever opportunistic proclivities managers might possibly entertain.

[5] Although it was decided to estimate only the negatively sloped portion of the time-cost tradeoff, it is of interest to note that for 13 of the projects in the sample, costs would have increased if the expected time were doubled. Several respondents pointed out that inept management could quite easily create situations where it might be realized ex post that a project had proceeded on the positively sloped portion of the tradeoff.

Since C approaches V as t becomes larger, V can be considered the minimum expected cost of the project. Since t approaches α as C becomes larger, α can be considered the minimum expected time to complete the innovation. The elasticity of cost with respect to time, $(-dC/dt) \cdot (t/C)$, is equal to $\phi(t/\alpha)/[(t/\alpha) - 1]^2$. Thus, for a given value of t/α, the elasticity of cost with respect to time is determined by ϕ. A logarithmic transformation of (1) together with the addition of an error term yields:

$$\ln C_i = \ln V_i + \phi[(t_i/\alpha) - 1]^{-1} + Z_i. \tag{2}$$

Since for each project direct estimates of α have been obtained from the respondents, estimates of V_i and ϕ could be obtained by regressing $\ln C_i$ on $1/[(t_i/\alpha) - 1]$. The error term Z_i is assumed to be distributed with mean zero and constant variance. The results are summarized in Table 1. In general, it can be said that the goodness of fit is acceptable, although in each case the number of observations is very small.

Using the estimated value of ϕ, the elasticity of cost with respect to time was calculated for a given value of t_i/α. (t_i was set at its actual value.) The results, given in Table 2, show that in fifteen out of twenty cases, strategies aimed at shaving the

TABLE 1
Estimates of V, α, and ϕ: 20 International Projects

Project	V (Thousands of Dollars)	α (Months)	ϕ	r^2
1	260	9	0.024	0.61
2	1,998	20	0.068	0.69
3	3,964	14	0.065	0.99
4	796	11	0.146	0.99
5	578	32	0.174	0.90
6	1,808	28	0.070	0.98
7	9,228	24	0.089	0.55
8	3,197	15	0.030	0.95
9	111	3	0.279	0.96
10	459	10	0.072	0.94
11	1,615	21	0.007	0.82
12	11,395	30	0.119	0.96
13	29,971	61	0.028	0.98
14	2,470	20	0.115	0.95
15	654	12	0.053	0.94
16	3,901	22	0.122	0.91
17	12,100	27	0.560	0.79
18	4,745	36	0.185	0.78
19	10,872	36	0.021	0.97
20	620	17	0.041	0.97

TABLE 2
Estimates of Elasticity of Cost with Respect to Time:
20 International Projects

Point Elasticity	Realized t/α				Total
	1.00–1.25	1.26–1.50	1.51–1.75	1.76–2.00	
0–0.50	1	0	1	0	2
0.51–1.00	2	1	0	0	3
1.01–1.50	1	1	0	1	3
1.51–2.00	4	0	0	0	3
2.01–2.50	3	1	0	0	3
2.51–3.00	1	1	0	0	2
3.01–3.50	2	1	0	0	3
Over 3.50	1	0	0	0	1
Total	13	5	1	1	20

actual time by one percent would raise costs by more than one percent. By comparison, Mansfield [3] discovered that for innovation, a one percent shaving in project time could be obtained for a cost increase of less than one percent for almost three quarters of the innovation projects examined. Mansfield's results are contained in Table 3. The time cost tradeoff function for international transfer of manufacturing technology is apparently much more elastic than the time cost tradeoff for innovation.

TABLE 3

Number of Innovations with Indicated Values of
Elasticity of Cost with Respect to Time,
at Actually Realized Values of t/α,
for 29 Innovations

Value of Elasticity*	Actually Realized Value of t/α			
	1.00–1.50	1.51–2.00	Over 2.00	Total
	(Numbers of Innovations)			
0	0	0	1	1
0.01–0.49	1	2	7	10
0.50–0.99	2	3	0	5
1.00–2.00	1	3	2	6
Over 2.00	5	1	1	7
Total	9	9	11	29

* Arc elasticities were computed between the point at the actually realized value of t and the point at the next lower value of t given by the respondent. The difference in t/α is often quite large.

Source: Mansfield [3, p. 140].

4. Determinants of the Elasticity of Cost with Respect to Time

If seems likely that the elasticity is related in some way to the structure of the network of tasks involved in the technology transfer project. Ideally, resources should be provisionally allocated in a project so that all tasks on the critical path are at the same marginal cost level [4]. In order to reduce total project time, resources are allocated to the critical path tasks. If in this process the critical path shifts widely, the elasticity of the time-cost tradeoff is apt to be high. If, on the other hand, the critical path involves much the same tasks throughout the process, the elasticity of the time-cost tradeoff is apt to be lower. The elasticity is also likely to be higher the higher the proportion of critical path task expenditures are to total project expenditures.

Unfortunately, data on these underlying considerations are not readily available, and it is therefore difficult to test the above hypotheses directly. In the analysis of the determinants of the time-cost elasticity which follows, attention is confined to variables for which data are readily available. Nevertheless, it is recognized that some of the variables selected may simply be surrogates for more fundamental considerations such as the ones outlined above.

The first hypothesis to be advanced is that the elasticity will be lower the longer the duration of the preliminary planning stage, hereafter stage A,[6] relative to the other stages. Stage A usually can be telescoped, if the need arises, since it utilizes resources entirely at the firm's own command. The converse of this hypothesis is that the engineering, construction, installation, and startup can be telescoped, but only at a relatively greater expense. This is because these activities generally involve contractual relations with other firms in which the authority of the transferor is diminished.

The second hypothesis is that the elasticity will be lower if the technology to be embodied in the new facility has been applied previously. If there has been at least

[6] For a detailed elaboration of the sequence of activities in transferring technology. see [6].

one previous application, then attention can be directed away from problems of the technology per se to problems of the transfer; that is, because of the uncertainty involved, a strategy to speed up the project by maximizing overlap will present colossal problems if the technology has not been applied previously.

The third hypothesis is that the elasticity will also be determined by the size of the primary transfer agent. The primary transfer agent is defined as the enterprise with the controlling equity in the new venture. Thus, the transferor will be the primary agent if the transfer is to a subsidiary, but the transferee will be the primary agent if the transfer is to an independent enterprise. The primary agent is generally the entity which will hire the engineering contractors and authorize the bidding on key pieces of equipment. It will have the responsibility for expediting the project. It seems reasonable to hypothesize that insofar as speeding up a project requires a certain flexibility of approach, a larger organization may be handicapped by inertia and a more complex decision making procedure. Even reaching agreement on how to proceed will take longer if more people and a longer chain of command are involved.

The fourth hypothesis is that the elasticity may be influenced by total project costs. On a priori grounds it seems reasonable to hypothesize that because large projects require more coordination and integration of different tasks, they may be more costly to speed up than smaller projects.

Finally, it is hypothesized that the actually realized value of the elasticity is also a function of whether or not the foreign market can be satisfactorily supplied by exports in the interim. If trade barriers are not prohibitive, and if exporting has traditionally been used to supply a particular foreign market, then the marginal profits from bringing the new plant on stream more quickly are not likely to be enormous. If, on the other hand, prohibitive tariffs or import controls prohibit sourcing from abroad, then the returns from time shaving are likely to be enhanced and the elasticity measure higher since the project will be pushed a little faster.[7]

To test these hypotheses it was assumed that

$$\epsilon_i = \alpha_0 + \alpha_1 A_i + \alpha_2 U_i + \alpha_3 S_i + \alpha_4 C_i + \alpha_5 X_i + Z_i,$$

where ϵ_i is the estimated elasticity of cost with respect to time for the ith project calculated at the actual time taken for the transfer; A_i is the percentage of total time allocated to stage A of the ith project; U_i is a dummy variable that takes the value 1 if the ith project represents the first application of the technology, and 0 otherwise; S_i is the sales volume (in millions of dollars) of the primary transfer agent for the ith project; C_i is the total cost of the ith project (measured in thousands of dollars); X_i is a dummy variable which takes the value 1 if the foreign market which the new plant will supply was previously supplied by export by the transferor. (If it was not supplied in this manner $X_i = 0$.) Z_i is a random error term with mean zero and constant variance. The expected derivatives are

$$\partial\epsilon/\partial A_i < 0, \quad \partial\epsilon/\partial U_i > 0, \quad \partial\epsilon/\partial S_i < 0, \quad \partial\epsilon/\partial C_i > 0, \quad \partial\epsilon/\partial X_i < 0.$$

Ordinary least square estimates of the α's yielded:

$$\epsilon_i = \underset{(10.11)}{2.20} - \underset{(2.02)}{1.82 A_i} + \underset{(2.81)}{1.20 U_i} + \underset{(2.15)}{0.00014 S_i} + \underset{(1.48)}{0.00011 C_i} - \underset{(2.39)}{0.83 X_i}$$

$$r^2 = 0.71, \quad n = 20.$$

[7] A profit maximizing firm will choose a location on the tradeoff function such that the marginal benefit and the marginal cost of time shaving are equalized. The actually realized elasticity measure will therefore be sensitive to both the parameters of the time-cost tradeoff, as well as the parameters of the benefit function. The four previous hypotheses represent parameters entering the cost function, whereas the existence of a viable export option will be a parameter entering the benefit function.

All of the variables are significant and take the expected signs. Most interestingly, U_i is highly significant and has a sizable impact. If the technology has not been previously commercialized, the elasticity measure is increased by 1.20. Technological uncertainty is clearly an important determinant of the elasticity estimates. X_i is also highly significant, suggesting that the incentive to shave time is reduced if the market can be simultaneously supplied from the parent plant or from foreign subsidiaries. The coefficient on S_i indicates that a hundred million dollar increase in the size of the primary transfer agent increases the elasticity by 0.14. A million dollar increase in project size increases the elasticity by a similar amount. The large coefficient on A_i indicates considerable potential for shaving time when the preliminary planning stage has been protracted. By juxtaposing these results against those derived from analysis of the time-cost tradeoff in technological innovation [3], it becomes apparent that variables indicating how well a technology is understood[8] are particularly significant determinants of the time-cost elasticity. Measures of project size and firm size are likewise significant in both studies.

5. Conclusion

The examination and estimation of time-cost tradeoff for the establishment of foreign manufacturing facilities have been instructive for several reasons. First, the existence of a negatively sloped function has once more been demonstrated. This is of some importance since the existence of time-cost tradeoffs has at times been treated with considerable skepticism.[9] Second, the elasticity estimates were generally greater than one, indicating that time shaving would involve rather high incremental costs. Third, it was observed that the elasticity estimates were highest for projects where the technology had not been previously commercialized, for projects that were large, and for projects carried out by the larger firms.

Several important implications follow from the analysis. First, when the transferred technology involves a change in the state of the art, the extra costs of speeding a project would seem to be considerable. In fact, the sensitivity of cost with respect to time indicates the extreme importance of scheduling the project precisely. Alternatively, if accurate scheduling is difficult to achieve, the necessity of commercializing the technology at home before its transfer abroad is suggested. Secondly, smaller firms implementing smaller projects seem to possess more versatility than the larger firms implementing the larger projects. Both of these implications rest comfortably with a view of technological change which recognizes the deficiencies as well as the strengths of the larger firm as agents of technological change, and which also recognizes the high cost of innovation and technology transfer when an alteration of the state of the art is involved.[10]

[8] The variables referred to are the extent of the "state of the art" advance in the study of innovation [3], and secondly, a dummy variable used to indicate whether or not the technology has been previously applied.

[9] The reference is to military men who have argued that although hastening a project will undoubtedly increase costs per time period, the reduction in total project time will offset the higher rates of expenditure (see [5]).

[10] This paper is based on the author's Ph.D. dissertation, "The Multinational Corporation and the Resource Cost of International Technology Transfer," University of Pennsylvania, 1975. The research was supported by a grant from the National Science Foundation to Professor Edwin Mansfield of the University of Pennsylvania, whose trenchant comments were much appreciated during all phases of the study. The author's particular gratitude goes to the participating firms, without whose cooperation this paper would not have been possible.

References

1. CAVES, R., "International Corporations: The Industrial Economics of Foreign Investment," *Economica*, Vol. 38 (Feb. 1971), pp. 1–27.
2. MALCOLM, D., "Integrated Research and Development Management Systems," in *Operations Research in Research and Development*, Burton Dean, ed., John Wiley, New York, 1963.
3. MANSFIELD, E., RAPOPORT, J., SCHNEE, WAGNER, S. AND HAMBURGER, M., *Research and Innovation in the Modern Corporation*, W. W. Norton, New York, 1971.
4. MODER, J. AND PHILLIPS, C., *Project Management with CPM and PERT*, Reinhold, New York, 1964.
5. SCHERER, F. M., "Government Research and Development Programs," in *Measuring Benefits of Government Expenditures*, R. Dorfman, ed., The Brookings Institution, Washington, D. C., 1965.
6. TEECE, DAVID, *The Multinational Corporation and the Resource Cost of International Technology Transfer*, Ballinger, Cambridge, 1977.
7. WILLIAMSON, O. E., *Markets and Hierarchies: Analysis and Antitrust Implications*, Free Press, New York, 1975.

[11]

The market for know-how and the efficient international transfer of technology

Economic prosperity rests upon knowledge and its useful application. International, inter-regional, and interpersonal differences in levels of living can be explained, at least in part, by differences in the production techniques employed. Throughout history, advances in knowledge have not been uniformly distributed across nations and peoples, but have been concentrated in particular nations at particular times. According to Kuznets,

> ... the increase in the stock of useful knowledge and the extension of its application are of the essence of modern economic growth. ... No matter where these technological and social innovations emerge ... the economic growth of any given nation depends on their adoption. In that sense, whatever the national affiliation of resources used, any single nation's economic growth has its base somewhere outside its boundaries – with the single exception of the pioneering nations.[1]

The rate at which technology is diffused worldwide depends heavily on the resource costs of transfer – both transmittal and absorption costs – and on the magnitude of the economic rents obtained by the seller. The resource costs of transfer depend on the characteristics of the transmitter, the receiver, the technology being transferred, and the institutional mode chosen for transfer.[2] These are matters explored in the following section. The rents obtained are a function of the working of the market for know-how, a matter explored in a subsequent section. The last two sections explore regulatory issues with respect to this market from the perspective first of less-developed country (LDC) importers and from the perspective of the United States as a net exporter of know-how. What emerges is an understanding of the technology transfer process, the role of the multinationals, and the difficulties and occasional contradictions associated with regulation. In no sense can the market for know-how and the transfer process be said to operate in an ideal fashion. However, internalization of the process appears to offer considerable efficiencies, and 'codes of conduct' are likely to confound the very objectives of importers, while export controls can be expected to yield only limited benefits, and then only under special conditions.

Codification and transfer costs
The fact that different individuals, organizations, or nations possess different types of knowledge and experience creates opportunities for communication and mutually profitable transfer. Yet, paradoxically, such transfer as does take place among individuals and organizations can only do so on the basis of similarities in the knowledge and experience each possess. A shared context appears necessary

for the formulation of meaningful messages. Transmittal and receiving costs are lower the greater the similarities in the experience of the transmitting unit and the receiving unit; for the greater these similarities, the easier it is to transfer technology in codified form, such as [82] blueprints, formulas, or computer languages.

Furthermore, there appears to be a simple but powerful relationship between codification[3] of knowledge and the costs of its transfer. Simply stated, the more a given item of knowledge or experience has been codified, the more economically it can be transferred. This is a purely technical property that depends on the ready availability of channels of communication suitable for the transmission of well-codified information – for example, printing, radio, telegraph, and data networks. Whether information so transferred will be considered meaningful by those who receive it will depend on whether they are familiar with the code selected as well as the different contexts in which it is used.[4]

Uncodified or tacit knowledge, on the other hand, is slow and costly to transmit. Ambiguities abound and can be overcome only when communications take place in face-to-face situations. Errors of interpretation can be corrected by a prompt use of personal feedback. Consider the apprenticeship system as an example. First, a master craftsman can cope with only a limited number of pupils at a time; second, his teaching has to be dispensed mostly through examples rather than by precept – he cannot easily put the intangible elements of his skill into words; third, the examples he offers will be initially confusing and ambiguous for his pupils so that learning has to take place through extensive and time-consuming repetition, and mastery will occur gradually on the basis of 'feel'; finally, the pupil's eventual mastery of a craft or skill will remain idiosyncratic and will never be a carbon copy of his master's. It is the scope provided for the development of a personal style that defines a craft as something that goes beyond the routine and hence programmable application of a skill.

The transmission of codified knowledge, on the other hand, does not necessarily require face-to-face contact and can often be carried out largely by impersonal means, such as when one computer 'talks' to another, or when a technical manual is passed from one individual to another. Messages are better structured and less ambiguous if they can be transferred in codified form. Take for example Paul Samuelson's introductory textbook for students of economics. Year after year, thousands of students all over the globe are introduced to Samuelson's economic thinking without being introduced to Samuelson himself. The knowledge acquired will be elementary and standardized, an idiosyncratic approach at this level being considered by many as a symptom of error rather than of style. Moreover [83] the student can pick up the sage's book or put it down according to caprice; he can scan it, refer to it, reflect upon it, or forget it. This freedom to allocate one's attention or not to the message source is much more restricted where learning requires interpersonal contact.

With respect to the international transfer of technology, the costs of transfer are very much a function of the degree to which know-how can be codified and under-stood in that form by the recipient. Typically, only the broad outline of technical knowledge can be codified by non-personal means of intellectual communication or communication by teaching outside the production process itself. Accordingly, the transfer of technology generally requires the transfer of skilled personnel, even when the cultural and infrastructural differences are not great. History has illustrated this time and time again. For instance, the transfer of technological skills between the United States and Britain at the end of the nineteenth century was dependent upon the transfer of skilled personnel. One also observes that the diffusion of crafts from one country to another depends on the migration of groups of craftsmen, such as when the Huguenots were driven from France by the repeal of the Edict of Nantes under Louis XIV.

The costs of transfer so far examined are simply the resource costs of transfer – the costs of the labor and capital that must be employed to effect transfer. An empirical investigation of these issues based upon a sample of 26 international transfers indicated that the resource cost of international transfer is non-trivial.[5] Transfer costs ranged from 2.25 percent to 59 percent of total project costs with a mean of 19.16 percent. They declined with each subsequent application of the technology and were typically lower the greater the amount of related manufacturing experience possessed by the transferee. Experience with transfer and experience with the technology appear to be key considerations with respect to the ease with which technology can be transferred abroad. In order to understand these costs, as well as other aspects of the transfer process, it will be necessary to examine the market for know-how. In so doing, the focus is on private transactions between firms of different national origins.

Characteristics of the market for know-how
The differential distribution of know-how and expertise among the world's enterprises means that mutually advantageous opportunities for the trading of know-how commonly exist. However, these opportunities will be realized only if the institutional framework exists to provide the appropriate linkage mechanisms and governance structures to identify trading opportunities and to surround and protect the associated know-how transfers. Unfortunately, unassisted markets are seriously faulted as institutional devices for facilitating trading in many kinds of technological and managerial know-how.

The imperfections in the market for know-how for the most part can be traced to the nature of the commodity in question. Know-how has some of the characteristics of a public good, since it can often be used in another enterprise without its value being substantially impaired. Furthermore the marginal cost of [84] employing know-how abroad is likely to be much less than its average cost of production and transfer. Accordingly the international transfer of proprietary know-how is likely to be profitable if organizational modes can be discovered to conduct and protect the transfer at low cost.

An examination of the properties of markets for know-how readily leads to the identification of several transactional difficulties. These difficulties can be summarized in terms of recognition, disclosure, and team organization. Consider a team that has accumulated know-how that can potentially find application in foreign markets. If there are firms abroad that can apply this know-how with profit, then according to traditional microeconomic theory, trading will ensue until the gains from trade are exhausted. Or, as Calabresi has put it, 'if one assumes rationality, no transactions costs, and no legal impediments to bargaining, all misallocations of resources would be fully cured in the market by bargains.'[6] However, one generally cannot expect this happy result in the market for proprietary know-how. Not only are there high costs associated with obtaining the requisite information, but there are also organizational and strategic impediments associated with using the market to effect transfer.

Consider the information requirements associated with using markets. In order to carry out a market transaction, it is necessary to discover potential trading partners and acceptable terms of trade. It is also necessary to conduct negotiations leading up to the bargain, to draw up the contract, to undertake the inspection needed to make sure that the terms of the contract are being observed, and so on. As Kirzner has explained,

> for an exchange transaction to be completed it is not sufficient merely that the conditions for exchange which prospectively will be mutually beneficial be present; it is necessary also that each participant be aware of his opportunity to gain through the exchange. . . . It is usually assumed . . . that where such scope is present, exchange will in fact occur. . . . In fact, of course, exchange may fail to occur because knowledge is imperfect, in spite of the presence of the conditions for mutually profitable exchange.[7]

The transactional difficulties identified by Kirzner are especially compelling when the commodity in question is proprietary information. One reason is that protecting the ownership of technological know-how often requires the suppression of information on exchange possibilities. By its very nature, industrial R&D (research and development) requires that the activities and outcomes of the R&D establishment be disguised or concealed.

Even where the possessor of the technology recognizes the opportunity and has the capability to absorb know-how, markets may break down. This is because of the problems of disclosing value to buyers in a way that is convincing and that does not destroy the basis for exchange. Due to informational asymmetries, the less informed party must be wary of opportunistic representations by the seller. Moreover, if there is sufficient disclosure to assure the buyer that the information possesses great value, the 'fundamental paradox' of information arises: 'its value for the purchaser is not known until he has the [85] information, but then he has in effect acquired it without cost.' [8]

Appropriability issues emerge not only at the negotiating stage but also at all subsequent stages of the transfer. Indeed, as discussed elsewhere in this issue, Magee has built a theory of multinational enterprise around the issue of appropriability, hypothesizing that

> multinational corporations are specialists in the production of information that is less efficient to transmit through markets than within firms.[9]

However, the transactional difficulties in the market for know-how that provide an incentive for firms to internalize technology transfer go beyond issues of recognition and appropriability. Thus suppose that recognition is no problem, that buyers concede value and are prepared to pay for information in the seller's possession, and that enforceable use restrictions soften subsequent appropriability problems. Even if these assumptions are satisfied, there is still the problem of actually transferring the technology.

In some cases the transfer of a formula or a chemical compound, the blueprints for a special device, or a special mathematical algorithm may be all that is needed to effect the transfer. However, more is frequently needed. As mentioned earlier, know-how cannot always be codified, since it often has an important tacit dimension. Individuals may know more than they are able to articulate.[10] When knowledge has a high tacit component, it is extremely difficult to transfer without intimate personal contact, demonstration, and involvement. Indeed, in the absence of intimate human contact, technology transfer is sometimes impossible. In a slightly different context Polanyi has observed, 'It is pathetic to watch the endless efforts – equipped with microscopy and chemistry, with mathematics and electronics to reproduce a single violin of the kind the half literate Stradivarius turned out as a matter of routine more than 200 years ago.'[11]

In short, the transfer of knowledge may be impossible in the absence of the transfer of people. Furthermore, it will often not suffice just to transfer individuals. While a single individual may sometimes hold the key to much organizational knowledge, team support is often needed, since the organization's total capabilities must be brought to bear upon the transfer problem. In some instances the transfer can be effected through a one-time contract providing for a consulting team to assist in the start-up. Such contracts may be highly incomplete and may give rise to dissatisfaction during execution. This dissatisfaction may be an unavoidable – which is to say, an irremediable – result. Plainly, foreign investment would be a costly response to the need for a one-time international exchange. In the absence of a superior organizational alternative, one-time, incomplete contracting for a consulting team is likely to prevail.

Reliance on repeated contracting is less clearly warranted, however, where a succession of transfers is contemplated, or when two-way communication is needed to promote the recognition and disclosure of opportunities for information [86] transfer as well as the actual transfer itself. In these circumstances a more cooperative arrangement for joining the parties would enjoy a greater comparative institutional advantage. Specifically, intrafirm transfer to a foreign subsidiary, which avoids the need for repeated negotiations and attenuates the hazards of opportunism, has advantages over autonomous trading. Better disclosure, easier agreement, better governance, and more effective team organization and reconfiguration all result. Here lies the incentive for internalizing technology transfer within the multinational firm.

The preceding discussion has emphasized that an important attribute of the multinational firm is that it is an organizational mode capable of internally trans-ferring know-how among its various business units in a relatively efficient and effective fashion. Given the opportunities that apparently exist for international trade in know-how and given the transactional difficulties associated with relying on markets, one should expect to find multinational enterprises (MNEs) frequently selecting internal channels for technology transfer. However, when problems of recognition, disclosure, and team transfer are not severe, one should expect that market processes will be utilized, in which case the licensing of know-how among non-affiliated enterprises will be observed.

Recognition, disclosure, and team transfer problems will be modest, it would seem, when the following exist: (1) the know-how at issue is not recent in origin so that knowledge of its existence has diffused widely; (2) the know-how at issue has been commercialized several times so that its important parameters and performance in different situations are well understood, thereby reducing the need for start-up assistance; and (3) the receiving enterprise has a high level of technological sophistication. Some evidence supportive of these propositions has recently been presented. Mansfield, employing a sample of 23 multinationals, discovered that foreign subsidiaries were the principal channel of transfer during the first five years after commercialization.[12] For the second five-year period after commercialization, licensing turned out to be more important. Larger firms also tended to rely more on internal transfer than did smaller firms, although this might not reflect relative efficiency considerations but rather the sunk costs larger firms have already made in foreign subsidiaries.

One implication for a potential technology purchaser is that it will have to look among the smaller firms in the industry, and at firms in different industries, to find willing technology suppliers. This does not result in an easy search process. It is made more difficult by the fact that few firms actively market their know-how. Thus the apparent size and nature of the market is likely to be a function of the search costs buyers are willing to incur.

Another implication is that because the marginal cost of successive applications of a technology is less than the average cost of production and transfer, and because know-how is often unique – implying that trading relations are [87] characterized by small numbers – there is often a high degree of indeterminacy with respect to price. Killing's field research confirmed that 'neither buyer nor seller of tech-nology seems to have a clear idea of the value of the commodity in which they are trading,' fueling speculation that 'royalty rates may simply be a function of negotiating skills of the parties involved.' [13] This is because the market for know-how commonly displays aspects of bilateral monopoly, at least at the level of the individual transaction. So in many important cases there is likely to be a wide range of indeterminacy.

The existence of elements of bilateral monopoly has led some countries to advocate regulation of the market for know-how. Indeed, some Third World countries, as well as the antitrust authorities in some developed countries, have already imposed various regulatory regimes.

> By 1974, over 20 countries had enacted specific legislation to control and direct foreign capital and technology. Their actions and regulations focused on lowering the royalties paid for foreign technology, forcing local participation in management and ownership, and in increasing the government capability to screen and direct foreign activities – the major focus of the governments was initially to limit the kind of restrictive clauses allowed in contracts for technology transfer with foreign firms.[14]

Governmental and intergovernmental intervention in the market for know-how appears to be growing in significance. In the following sections, several dimensions of this phenomenon are explored in more detail.

Codes of conduct and the regulation of technology imports
Since the United Nations Conference on Trade and Development (UNCTAD) IV decided to set up an intergovernmental group of experts to prepare a draft of an international code of conduct on the transfer of technology, discussion has intensified on matters associated with the transfer and development of technology, particularly on topics of concern to developing countries.[15] A number of draft codes have emerged in which representatives from less-developed countries have argued that technology is part of the universal heritage of mankind and that all countries have right of access to technology in order to improve the standards of living of their peoples. Such contentions obviously involve fundamental challenges to the world's industrial property system. They also fail to recognize the constitutional restraints in countries such as the United States that prevent [88] the government from confiscating private property.

The stated objective of the UNCTAD code is 'to encourage the transfer of technology transactions, particularly those involving developing countries, under conditions where bargaining positions of the parties to the transaction are balanced in such a way so to avoid abuses of a stronger position and thereby to achieve mutually satisfactory agreement.' One of the principal mechanisms by which this is to be achieved is through the elimination of 'restrictive business practices.'[16] A long litany of these is typically advanced, including tying or packaging, use restrictions, exclusive dealing, and territorial restrictions. An examination of recent legislation on the transfer of technology, particularly in Latin America and Yugoslavia, shows that many of these ideas have been uncritically accepted into national law.[17]

It is not possible to attempt a comprehensive review of restrictive business practices in this article. However, I submit that insufficient analysis has been given to the efficiency-enhancing attributes of many practices surrounding the generation and transfer of technology. Many restrictive clauses in licensing and know-how agreements are designed to protect the transaction and the underlying know-how; in their absence less technology might be transferred, to the mutual detriment of all, or technology might be transferred less efficiently. In the space that follows, two 'restrictive business practices' – use restrictions and tying – are analyzed in order to illustrate that 'restrictive business practices' can be in fact procompetitive and may serve to promote economic efficiency.

Use restrictions
The interesting question associated with use restrictions is whether they are anticompetitive. designed merely to extract monopoly rents, or whether they are efficiency instruments, the removal of which might leave both parties worse off. Since know-how is the principal resource upon which the value of many private enterprise firms is based, firms facing market competition are not going to sell it *carte blanche* to a firm that might use it to compete with their own products, for to do so would reduce the value of the firm. Thus reasonable limitations on use are commonly necessary to provide adequate incentives for transfers to occur and

for those transfers to operate efficiently. This is especially true when the transferor and the transferee are competitors or potential competitors.

When know-how is transferred by a market transaction (contract) the buyer does not acquire the asset to the exclusion of use by the seller in the same sense as occurs when a physical item is bought and sold. The seller of know-how retains the knowledge even after it has been transferred to a buyer. Furthermore, technology is constantly evolving. Indeed, static technology is generally obsolete technology. Accordingly, a buyer of intangible know-how typically needs ongoing, future cooperation from the seller to obtain the full benefit of the know-how purchased, since all of the [89] learning and experience of the developer of the know-how cannot be captured in the codified descriptions, drawings, and data that are amenable to physical transfer.

Limitations on the use of technological know-how are often needed to provide adequate incentives for the buyer and the seller to effect a continuous transfer of the knowledge in question. If the seller is limited in his use of the know-how, the buyer can rely more confidently on the seller's full disclosure and cooperation in the buyer's use of the know-how. Where the seller contemplates some use of the know-how himself, limitations on the buyer's use of the know-how in competition with the seller are necessary to provide the seller with the incentive to transfer this know-how and to share fully in his mental perceptions, understandings, working experience, and expertise.

A partial analogue to these principles is when business enterprises are sold. These transactions have traditionally included ancillary limitations on the economic activities of the seller after the business is sold. Such limitations bring about economically efficient transfers of ongoing businesses by ensuring that the buyer acquires exclusively the enterprise – or part of the enterprise – he is contracting to purchase, including its intangible goodwill. Similarly, in the sale of a business the seller is often retained as a consultant for the purpose of ensuring that the intangible knowledge that comes from the seller's experiences in conducting the business is fully transferred in the transaction. Without contractual or other limitations on the seller's use of the assets being transferred, and without the seller's continued cooperation, a buyer would not pay the full economic value of those assets. As a result, the efficient transfer of the assets would be inhibited.

Use limitations are particularly beneficial when two or more uses exist for the products that can be derived from know-how and when some of the uses are for some reason foreclosed to the developer of the know-how. In this instance, transfer of the know-how to a buyer having access to one or more of these otherwise fore-closed uses may be beneficial to both parties, since economies of scope will be generated. The seller of the know-how requires adequate incentives to transfer his knowledge, however. The seller will not transfer the know-how to a buyer for the otherwise foreclosed uses if, in doing so, he is likely to lose more in the uses that are available to him with no transfer than he gains through the expanded uses made possible by transfers. The availability of limitations on the buyer's use of the know-how provides possible means to prevent such losses.

Use limitations are also beneficial in providing incentives for the contracting parties to share complementary know-how in order to reach a new market that neither acting independently could efficiently serve. If each of the parties has one or more of the technology elements critical for a particular new use, if neither of the parties has all of the critical technology elements for that use, and if through sharing of the complementary technologies for the new use one or both of the parties could enter markets that neither party could serve without sharing, then use limitations are necessary to effect the bilateral technology transfers. Without use limitations, one or both of the parties may lack the incentive to share, since the losses that might occur in an existing [90] market through sharing could exceed the gains derived from reaching the new market.

Tying and packaging
In a tying arrangement, the seller requires the buyer to purchase a second product as a condition of sale of the first, such as when a petrochemical firm licenses its process technology to another firm on the condition that it purchases certain inputs on a continuous basis, or when an automobile company agrees to build a facility abroad so long as it is able to select equipment and designs for the whole facility and not just for part of it.

In the context of the international transfer of technology, there are often very genuine managerial and technical reasons for tying the sale of products. For instance, coordinated design and construction might allow important systems engineering functions to be carried out more efficiently. Furthermore. processing facilities may require raw materials and components that meet certain narrow technological standards, and tying may be necessary to ensure that the requisite amount of quality control is exercised. These problems are likely to be especially severe when the technological distance between the transferor and transferee is great.

It is only under rather special circumstances that tying will enable a monopolist to expand the amount of monopoly profit that would be obtained in the absence of tying. One such circumstance is if tying can be used as a method of price discrimination.

Accordingly, blanket prohibitions against tying and packaging are likely to be costly to the country imposing the prohibitions. Technology suppliers may have good reasons for wanting to supply know-how and other products and services in a package. Certainly some striking examples exist of problems that have arisen when adequate packaging and systems design have not been performed. Consider the Soviet Union's experience in constructing and starting up its Kama River truck plant, as related by Lee Iacocca, then with Ford Motor Company:

> Well, one example of acquiring technology in its unbundled state is the Kama River truck plant in Russia. After first attempting to get a foreign company to build the plant (we were approached but decided against it) the Russians decided to do it themselves and to parcel out contracts to foreign firms for various parts of the project. That was in 1971. As of December 1976, the project was almost two years behind schedule. By year's end, only about 5,000 trucks were expected to roll off the line, instead of the 150,000 vehicles and 100,000 diesel engines and transmissions originally scheduled for annual production. According to published reports, only four of nine projected furnaces in the iron foundry were operating and those only at half capacity. What's more, 35 percent of the castings were being rejected as unserviceable. There were bottlenecks on the assembly line, and because the components and designs were bought from different suppliers all over the world, replacement parts were not interchangeable

Now compare that with Ford's recent investment in Spain. It took us just three years to the day to build a complex that includes an assembly plant, a stamping and body plant and an engine plant on a manufacturing site $2\frac{1}{2}$ miles long and half a mile wide, with 55 acres under roof. The first Fiesta, our new minicar, was driven off the assembly line last August, well ahead of schedule. To get from farmland to an annual capacity of 250,000 cars and 400,000 engines in [91] three years, we drew on the experience of our personnel and our technological resources from all over the world – experience and resources that couldn't be bought and that we probably wouldn't even know how to sell.[18]

Regulation of technology exports

Pressures for restricting trade in technological know-how have also come from technology exporters. The reasons advanced for controls are almost the complete opposite of those advanced by the LDCs. In the United States concern is often expressed in industry and government that the United States is either selling its technology for far less than its economic value, or allowing it to be stolen through industrial espionage, principally to other developed countries, or simply transferring it abroad too soon. According to J. Fred Bucy, the president of Texas Instruments:

Today our toughest competition is coming from foreign companies whose ability to compete with us rests in part on their acquisitions of U.S. technology . . . The time has come to stop selling our latest technologies, which are the most valuable things we've got.[19]

Labor groups in the United States go further and argue that not only is the know-how underpriced, but that one consequence of the export of technology is the export of jobs.[20] According to one labor leader:

I recognize that technology will flow across national lines no matter what we do. But certainly we do not have to cut our own throats with aid, trade, tax and tariff policies that actively encourage and promote the export of American jobs and technology, without regard for the impact on either those who give or those who receive.[21]

Before proceeding further, it will be helpful to outline the available evidence with respect to these considerations. Unfortunately, only very sketchy data are available. Conclusive evidence on the net impacts of foreign investment and technology transfer on US jobs and welfare does not exist. The available evidence suggests that the impact is likely to vary from one instance to another. Baranson has presented case studies that suggest that US-based firms, driven by competitive necessity, are transferring their newest technology abroad more frequently than in the past.[22] To investigate this issue further, Mansfield and Romeo obtained information concerning the age of the technology transferred abroad in a sample of 65 transfers taken from 31 US-based [92] multinationals.[23] As shown in Table 11.1, they found that the mean age of the technologies transferred to overseas subsidiaries in developed countries was about six years, which was significantly less than the mean age of technologies transferred to overseas subsidiaries in developing countries – about 10 years. Table 11.1 also suggests that the mean age of the technologies transferred through licenses, joint ventures, and channels other than subsidiaries is commonly higher than the mean age of the technologies

Table 11.1   *Mean and standard deviation of number of years between technology's transfer overseas and its initial introduction in the United States, for 65 technologies*

Channel of technology transfer	Mean (years)	Standard deviation (years)	Number of cases
Overseas subsidiary in developed country	5·8	5·5	27
Overseas subsidiary in developing country	9·8	8·4	12
Licensing or joint venture	13·1	13·4	26

Source Edwin Mansfield and Anthony Romeo, 'Technology Transfer to Overseas Subsidiaries by US-based Firms,' Research Paper, University of Pennsylvania, 1979.

technology overseas through wholly owned subsidiaries rather than via licenses or joint venture, but the latter channels become more important as the technology becomes older.

Another concern of countries that generate new technology is that the transfer of technology to overseas subsidiaries will hasten the time when foreign producers have access to this technology. Some evidence has recently become available on the speed with which technology 'leaks out' and the extent to which international transfer actually hastens its 'leaking out'. The evidence, which is based on a sample of 26 technologies transferred abroad, indicated that the mean lag between the transfer and the time when foreign firms had access to the technology was about four years.[24] In over half the cases, the technology transfer was estimated to have had no effect at all on how quickly foreign competitors had access to the technology. On the other hand, in about one-fourth of the cases, it was estimated to have hastened their access to the technology by at least three years.

Technology transfer hastened the spread of process technologies to a greater degree than it did the spread of product technologies. According to the study, the most frequent channel by which the technology 'leaked out' was reverse engineering.[25] That is, foreign competitors [93] took apart and analyzed the new or modified product to gain insights into the relevant technology. Clearly, this evidence gives only a very sketchy impression of the level and nature of the returns from international technology transfer, and the role that technology exports are having on the US competition position. However, there is little evidence that the technological lead of the United States in various industries is about to disappear as a result of the technology transfer activities of US firms. Indeed, there is some evidence, admittedly of a conjectural nature, that the international transfer of technology stimulated R&D activities by multinational firms.[26]

From a public policy perspective the interesting question is whether the United States could increase its economic welfare through restrictions on technology exports. It is a well-known theorem of international trade that if a country has monopoly (monopsony) power in world markets, then imposing a tax (tariff) on exports (imports) will serve to improve welfare in the absence of retaliation.

This, of course, assumes that such a policy can be effectively administered.

The economic intuition behind this theorem is fairly apparent. By transferring technology abroad, American firms increase the likelihood of foreign competition in the future. While firms face incentives to consider this when setting prices at which technology is transferred, each firm will evaluate the future effects on themselves, not on the rest of the economy. The company that exports the technology is not usually the one that loses out. It receives payment of some kind. The victim is likely to be another US company, one that prior to the technology transfer enjoyed a competitive advantage over the foreign company. Fujitsu, for example, has used the technology it got from Amdahl to compete with IBM. Therefore, in strictly nationalist terms, private firms will have a tendency to set the price of technology too low and to transfer too much technology abroad. Where several US firms have similar technology that does not exist abroad, their competition will tend to lower the price of technology transfers. The United States could prevent this by reducing competition and by establishing monopoly prices through control of such transfers. For instance, an export tax would serve to restrict exports, thereby driving up the price and enabling the US economy to capture monopoly rents from the export of know-how. A similar result could be obtained by enabling [94] domestic industry to cartelize foreign markets.[27]

There is, in fact, a long history of government attempts to limit the export of technology and trade secrets. A prime example is England during the Industrial Revolution. There are serious disadvantages in limiting technology transfers, however. One problem is that while levels of restriction that are optimal on nationalist grounds can be determined in theoretical models, there is little reason to be confident that government policies will approach such optima in practice. Domestic firms seem able to circumvent restrictions on the export of know-how,[28] while foreign firms can engage in 'reverse engineering of products and designs' to circumvent many controls.

An alternative approach to technology controls might involve placing more emphasis on technical data and critical manufacturing equipment and less on commodities.[29] However, it is enormously difficult to control the export of technical data. Since it can move in many informal ways that are often difficult to detect.[30] Clearly the transfer of highly visible turnkey plants is more readily controlled than are surreptitious, casual conversations. Furthermore, the effectiveness of controls depends on the degree of monopoly power poossessed by the United States. In most instances where controls are applicable, the United States does not have a clear superiority *vis-à-vis* other Western countries. The effectiveness of controls therefore depends upon cooperation with other suppliers and potential suppliers.[31]

Conclusion

In the foregoing discussion, the arm's-length market for know-how has been shown to be exposed to a number of hazards and inefficiencies, many of which can be overcome by internalizing the process within the multinational firm. Despite the shortcomings identified, it was not apparent that regulation by either technology importers or exporters could substantially improve the efficiency with which this market operates; indeed, for the instances examined it appeared that the impairment of efficiency through regulation was the more likely outcome. Yet the strongest argument against controls on the transfer of [95] technology is the same as the argument for liberal trade policies in general. Many kinds of economic restrictions can be used to bring gains to some at the expense of others. But almost everyone is likely to end up worse off if they all succeed. This holds just as true for nations within the world economy as for individuals and groups within a national economy. The basic case for liberal policies is not that they always maximize short-run gains, but that they serve enlightened and longer-run interests in avoiding a world riddled with restrictions. [96]

Notes

The financial support of the National Science Foundation is gratefully acknowledged, together with the valuable comments from Max Boisot, Almarin Phillips, and Oliver Williamson.

1. S. Kuznets, *Modern Economic Growth: Rate, Structure, Spread* (New Haven: Yale University Press, 1966).
2. The concept and measurement of the resource cost of transfer can be found in David Teece, *The Multinational Corporation and the Resource Cost of International Technology Transfer* (Cambridge: Ballinger, 1976), and in 'Technology Transfer by Multinational Firms The Resource Cost of International Technology Transfer,' *Economic Journal* (June 1977).
3. Codification – the transformation of experience and information into symbolic form – is an exercise in abstraction that often economizes on bounded rationality. Instead of having to respond to a hopelessly extensive and varied range of phenomena, the mind can respond instead to a much more restricted set of information. At least two obstacles stand in the way of effective codification. First, abstracting from experience can be accomplished in an almost infinite number of ways. Ask a group of painters to depict a given object and each will select different facets or features for emphasis. Furthermore, the choice of what to codify and how to codify it is often personal. Second, to structure and codify experience one way can make it difficult, subsequently, to do so in an alternative way. The conceptual channels through which experience is made to flow appear to run deep and resist rerouteing.
4. These ideas are developed further in C.E. Shannon and W. Weaver, The Mathematical Theory of Communication (Chicago: University of Illinois Press, 1949). I am grateful to Max Boisot for drawing them to my attention.
5. See David Teece, 'Technology Transfer by Multinational Firms: The Resource Cost of International Technology Transfer,' *Economic Journal* (June 1977).
6. G. Calabresi, 'Transactions Costs, Resource Allocation, and Liability Rules: A Comment,' *Journal of Law and Economics* (April 1968).
7. I.Kirzner, *Competition and Entrepreneurship* (Chicago: University of Chicago Press, 1962), p. 215.
8. K.J. Arrow, *Essays in the Theory of Risk Bearing* (Chicago: Chicago University Press, 1971).
9. See Stephen Magee, 'Information and Multinational Corporation: An Appropriability Theory of Direct Foreign Investment,' in *The New International Economic Order*, ed. Jagdish Bhagwati (Cambridge, MA: MIT Press, 1977), p. 318.
10. See Michael Polanyi, *Personal Knowledge: Towards a Post Critical Philosophy* (Chicago: University of Chicago Press, 1958).
11. Polanyi.
12. See Edwin Mansfield, 'Statement to the Senate Commerce Committee Conc erning International Technology Transfer and Overseas Research and Development,' Hearings before the Subcommittee on International Finance of the Committee on Banking, Housing, and Urban Affairs of the Committee on Commerce, Science, and Transportation, United States Senate, Ninety-fifth Congress, Second Session, Part 7: Oversight on US High Technology E.xports (Washington, DC: Government Printing Office, May 1978).
13. Peter Killing, Technology Acquisition: License Agreement or Joint Venture,' *Columbia Journal of World Business* (Fall 1980)
14. See Harvey Wallender, 'Developing Country Orientations Towards Foreign Technology in the Eighties: Implications for New Negotiation Approaches,' *Columbia Journal of World Business* (Summer 1980), pp 21–22.

15. The movement toward an international code on the transfer of technology is but a reflection of larger, exceedingly complex political problems that have been engendered by an international society undergoing profound changes. Demands for a new international economic order, international regulation of transnational enterprises, and the like form the backdrop of UNCTAD's activities in the technology transfer area. These broader demands raise the possibility that the work now being carried on by UNCTAD in moving toward a code of conduct for the transfer of technology will be subsumed by the development of a more comprehensive code of conduct for transnational enterprises by the UN Commission on Transnational Corporations.

16. See UNCTAD, 'Draft International Code of Conduct on the Transfer of Technology,' TD/CODE/TOT/20.

17. See UNCTAD, 'Selected Legislation, Policies and Practices on the Transfer of Technology, TD/B/C.6/48.

18. See Lee Iacocca, 'Multinational Investment and Global Purpose,' speech delivered before the Swiss-American Chamber of Commerce,' Zurich, 17 June 1977. Reprinted in *Vital Speeches*, 15 Sept. 1977.

19. See 'Those Worrisome Technology Exports,' *Fortune*, 22 May 1978, p. 106.

20. An example commonly cited is that of Piper aircraft. Until a few years ago, Brazil was the leading purchaser of light aircraft manufactured in the United States. However, the Brazilian government levied prohibitive taxes on the import of US-produced light aircraft and it invited a US manufacturer, Piper, to bring in US technology and produce with Brazilian workers. As a result, hundreds of US citizens who were directly employed in light aircraft production became unemployed, some permanently. Now Brazil is selling light aircraft to other Latin American countries and is also planning to export planes to the United States in competition with US producers.

21. William Winpisinger, 'The Case Against Exporting US Technology,' *Research Management* (March 1978): 21.

22. Jack Baranson, 'Technology Exports Can Hurt,' *Foreign Policy*, 25 (Winter 1976–77).

23. See Edwin Mansfield and Anthony Romeo, 'Technology Transfer to Overseas Subsidiaries by US-based Firms,' Research Paper, University of Pennsylvania, 1979.

24. Ibid.

25. Reverse engineering is very common in the semiconductor industry. It involves stripping down a competitor's chip to recreate an outright copy, to figure out how a chip works in order to design a functionally equivalent emulator chip, or merely to determine whether a new chip contains any new ideas that might be adaptable to other products. Creating a copy is surprisingly simple: the necessary tools include a microscope, acid to etch away the circuits layer by layer, and a camera to record the successive steps; $50,000 of equipment will suffice. Reverse engineering enables a rival to obtain the same advantages as could be obtained by pirating the masks – the negatives that are used to lay down the circuit elements on silicon wafers – used in manufacturing the product. Intel Corporation of California has accused the Soviet Union of copying one of its 4K memory chips and Japan's Toshiba Corporation of making a 'dead ringer' of another. See *Business Week*, 21 April 1980, p. 182.

26. See Edwin Mansfield, Anthony Romeo, and Samuel Wagner, 'Foreign Trade and US Research and Development,' *Review of Economics and Statistics*, 1979.

27. One difference is that with a cartel as compared with a tax, the industry would capture a larger portion of the economic rents, as there would be no revenues accruing to the government.

28. In 1980, allegations of export control violations in the United States numbered 350, up from 200 in 1979. *Business Week*, 27 April 1981, p. 131.

29. On the other hand, some authorities suggest that Soviet spies might do better acquiring consumer products in large department stores. Buying consumer and industrial products such as toys, appliances, and industrial tools in many cases may be more useful than technical data because of the delays in Defense Department procurement of new chips and the rapidity with which new chips become incorporated into consumer products.

30. According to one source, the KGB has 30 agents in California's Silicon Valley, plus others in Phoenix and Dallas, charged with obtaining data on microelectronics technology. *Business Week*, 27 April 1980, p. 128.

31. The Coordinating Committee on Export Controls (COCOM), an organization consisting of all NATO members plus Iceland and Japan, is the forum usually chosen to attempt the necessary coordination. However, the members have no legal obligation to participate in COCOM or to abide by its recommendations.

[12]

Capturing Value from Technological Innovation: Integration, Strategic Partnering, and Licensing Decisions

DAVID J. TEECE

School of Business Administration
University of California
Berkeley, California 94720

The competitive potential embedded in new technology is not always captured by the innovator. Follower firms, customers, and suppliers are often the principal beneficiaries. When innovating firms lose to followers or imitators, the reason is often the failure of the innovator to build or access competitive capacity in activities, such as manufacturing, which are complementary to the innovation. This paper analyzes the make-or-buy decision with respect to these capacities in different competitive environments, including that of rapid technological change and easy imitation. Often it is pointless for firms to invest in R&D unless they are also willing to invest in the development of certain complementary capacities, at home or abroad.

It is commonly recognized that firms responsible for technological breakthroughs and for technological enhancement of existing products and processes are often unable to commercialize the product so that the product concept ultimately fails. Myriads of would-be innovators have discovered that technical success is necessary but not sufficient for establishing economic utility and commercial acceptance. A less commonly recognized but equally important phenomenon is the firm that is first to commercialize a new product concept but fails to extract economic value from the innovation, even though it is of great value to consumers

MARKETING — NEW PRODUCTS
PLANNING — CORPORATE

INTERFACES 18: 3 May-June 1988 (pp. 46-61)

INNOVATION

and is the source of economic rents (profits) to competitors. The phenomenon unquestionably exists and has obvious significance for the dynamic efficiency of the economy as well as for the distribution of income, domestically and internationally. In the international context, it has important ramifications for economic relations, for commercial policy, and for corporate strategy.

I offer a framework that may shed light on the factors that determine who wins from innovation: the firm that is first to market or those that follow. The follower firms may or may not be imitators. The framework seems useful for explaining the share of the profits from innovation accruing to the innovator compared to the followers (Figure 1), and for explaining a variety of interfirm activities such as joint ventures, coproduction agreements, cross

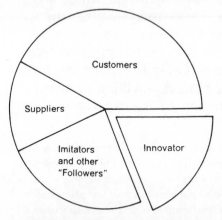

Figure 1: The benefits from innovation, sometimes referred to as economic rents, are divided among innovator, imitators, suppliers, and customers. A normative framework developed in this paper can guide innovating firms to capture a large portion of the rents in environments where imitation is easy.

distribution arrangements, and technological licensing.

The Phenomenon

The EMI Scanner is a classic case of a losing innovation [Martin 1984]. By the early '70s, the UK firm, Electrical Musical Industries (EMI) Ltd., was producing a variety of products including phonographic records, movies, and advanced electronics. EMI had developed high resolution TVs in the '30s, pioneered airborne radar during World War II, and developed the UK's first all solid-state computers in 1952.

In the late '60s Godfrey Houndsfield, an EMI senior research engineer, engaged in research on pattern recognition, which resulted in his displaying a scan of a pig's brain. Subsequent clinical work established that computerized axial tomography (CAT) was viable for generating cross-sectional "views" of the human body; this was the greatest advance in radiology since the discovery of X-rays in 1895.

The US was the major market for the product. However, EMI was UK based and lacked a marketing capability or presence in medical electronics in the United States. Because the scanner was a complex product, it required an organization that had service and training capacity as well as marketing ability. EMI's competitors, such as Siemens and GE, had these assets.

A market for CAT scanners rapidly emerged after EMI displayed advanced prototypes in Chicago in November 1972. By 1975, EMI had an order backlog of £55 million. Expectations of £100 million a year in scanner sales by EMI were

TEECE

projected by investors, and stock analysts began to think of EMI as shaping up for a success of the magnitude of Xerox's in the previous decade.

By the mid-'70s imitators had emerged, most notably GE with faster scanners tailored more closely to the needs of the medical profession and supported in the field by experienced marketing and service personnel. Simultaneously, health care regulations in the United States imposed a requirement that hospitals obtain certificates of need before purchasing high priced items like scanners. EMI was forced to sell its scanner business and in April of 1980 announced a sale to GE. At that time EMI indicated that it had lost £26 million on the business. Meanwhile, GE's operations were believed to be quite profitable. Subsequently, GE and Johnson & Johnson each paid EMI $100 million in damages for patent infringement.

Other examples of losing innovators are RC Cola, Bowmar, Xerox, and de Havilland. RC Cola, a small beverage company, was the first to introduce cola in a can and the first to introduce diet cola. Both Coca Cola and Pepsi followed almost immediately, depriving RC of any significant advantage from its innovation. Bowmar, which introduced the pocket calculator, was not able to withstand competition from Texas Instruments, Hewlett Packard, and others and went out of business. Xerox failed to succeed with its entry into the office computer business, even though Apple succeeded with the MacIntosh, which contained many of Xerox's key product ideas, such as the mouse and icons. The de Havilland Comet saga has some of the same features. The Comet I

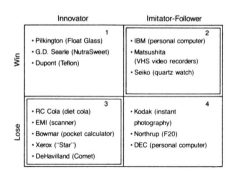

Figure 2: There is lore, but little analytics, to explain when and why innovators lose out to imitators and followers. Xerox, for instance, has been first to commercialize key computer technologies developed in its Parc facility; however, in several instances it has failed to recover its investment, while competitors, such as Apple, have done fabulously well with derivative technology.

jet was introduced into the commercial airline business two years or so before Boeing introduced the 707, but through an unfortunate series of events, de Havilland failed to capitalize on its substantial early advantage.

Capturing the Rent Stream from Innovation: Basic Building Blocks

In order to develop a coherent framework within which to explain the distribution of outcomes illustrated in Figure 2, three fundamental building blocks must first be described: the appropriability regime, complementary assets, and the dominant design paradigm.

Regimes of Appropriability

The term *regime of appropriability* refers to aspects of the commercial environment, excluding firm and market structure, that govern an innovator's ability to capture the rents associated with innovation. The most important dimensions of such a regime are the nature of the

INNOVATION

technology and the efficacy of legal mechanisms of protection such as patents, copyrights, and trade secrets.

It has long been known that patents do not work in practice as they do in theory. Rarely, if ever, do patents confer perfect appropriability, although they do afford considerable protection on new chemical products and on some mechanical inventions. Many patents can be "invented around" at modest costs. They are especially ineffective at protecting process innovations. Often patents provide little protection because the legal requirements for upholding their validity or for proving their infringement are high.

In some industries, particularly where the innovation is embedded in processes, trade secrets are a viable alternative to patents. Trade secret protection is possible, however, only if a firm can put its product before the public and still keep the underlying technology secret. Usually only chemical formulas and industrial-commercial processes (for example, cosmetics and recipes) can be protected as trade secrets after the products are "out."

The degree to which knowledge is tacit or codified also affects the ease with which it can be imitated. Codified knowledge is easy to transmit and receive and is more exposed to industrial espionage and the like. Tacit knowledge by definition is difficult to articulate, and so its transfer is difficult unless those with the know-how can demonstrate it to others [Teece 1981].

Empirical research by Levin, Klevorick, Nelson, and Winter [1984] demonstrates that patents and trade secrets often do not afford significant protection. Their results show considerable collinearity among certain mechanisms of appropriability. They conclude that "at the expense of some oversimplification, the data suggest that the mechanism of appropriation may reduce to two dimensions: one associated with the use of patents, the other with lead time and learning-curve advantages. For process innovations, secrecy is closely connected with exploiting lead time and learning advantages. For product innovation, sales and service efforts

Who wins from innovation?

are part of the package" [p. 18]. These findings are tentative and must be interpreted with care. They do, however, indicate that methods of appropriability vary markedly across industries and probably within industries as well.

The property rights environment within which a firm operates can thus be classified according to the nature of the technology and the efficacy of the legal system to assign and protect intellectual property. While a gross simplification, a dichotomy can be drawn between products for which the appropriability regime is "tight" (technology is relatively easy to protect) and those for which it is "weak" (technology is almost impossible to protect). An example of the former is the formula for Coca Cola syrup; an example of the latter is the Simplex algorithm in linear programming.

The Dominant Design Paradigm

Thomas Kuhn's seminal work [1970] describes the history and social psychology of science on the basis of the notion of a paradigm. The concept of a paradigm

TEECE

as applied to scientific development is broader than that of a theory. In fact, a paradigm is a Gestalt that embodies a set of scientific assumptions and beliefs about certain classes of phenomenon. Kuhn suggests that there are two stages in the evolutionary development of a given branch of a science: the preparadigmatic stage, when there is no single generally accepted conceptual treatment of the phenomenon in a field of study, and the paradigmatic stage, which begins when a body of theory appears to have passed the canons of scientific acceptability. The emergence of a dominant paradigm signals scientific maturity, and the acceptance of agreed upon standards by which what Kuhn calls "normal" scientific research can proceed. These standards remain in force unless or until the paradigm is overturned. Revolutionary science is what overturns normal science, as when the Copernicus theories of astronomy overturned Ptolemy's in the 17th century.

Abernathy and Utterback [1978] and Dosi [1982] have provided a treatment of the technological evolution of an industry which appears to parallel Kuhnian notions of scientific evolution. In the early stages of industry development, product designs are fluid, manufacturing processes are loosely and adaptively organized, and generalized capital is used in production. Competition among firms manifests itself in competition among designs, which are markedly different from each other. This might be called the preparadigmatic stage of an industry.

At some point after considerable trial and error in the marketplace, one design

or a narrow class of designs begins to emerge as the more promising. Such a design must be able to meet a whole set of user needs in a relatively complete fashion. The Model T Ford, the IBM 360, and the Douglas DC-3 are examples of dominant designs in the automobile, computer, and aircraft industries.

Once a dominant design emerges, competition shifts to price and away from design. Competitive success then shifts to a

---

Expectations of £100 million a year in scanner sales by EMI were projected.

---

whole new set of variables. Scale and learning become much more important, and specialized capital is deployed as competing firms seek to lower unit costs by exploiting economies of scale and learning. Reduced uncertainty over product design provides an opportunity to amortize specialized long-lived investments.

Innovation is not necessarily halted once the dominant design emerges; as Clarke [1985] points out, it can occur lower down in the design hierarchy. For instance, a "V" cylinder configuration emerged in automobile engine blocks during the 1930s with the emergence of the Ford V-8 engine. Niches were quickly found for it. Moreover, once the product design stabilizes, there is likely to be a surge of process innovation as producers attempt to lower production costs for the new product (Figure 3).

The Abernathy-Utterback framework does not characterize all industries. It

INNOVATION

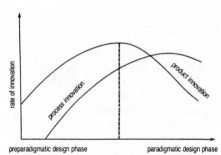

preparadigmatic design phase   paradigmatic design phase

Figure 3: When new technologies are commercialized, process innovation often follows product innovation. As the rate of product innovation slows, designs in the marketplace tend to become more standardized, providing the opportunity for large-scale production and the deployment of specialized assets. The nature of competition and the requirements for marketplace success shift dramatically as the market evolves from its early preparadigmatic phase (with competition based on features and product performance) to its post paradigmatic phase (with competition based more on price).

seems more suited to mass markets where consumer tastes are relatively homogeneous. It appears less characteristic of small niche markets where the absence of scale and learning economies attaches much less of a penalty to multiple designs. In these instances, generalized equipment will be employed in production.

The existence of a dominant design watershed is of great significance to the distribution of rents between innovator and follower. The innovator may have been responsible for the fundamental scientific breakthroughs as well as the basic design of the new product. However, if imitation is relatively easy, imitators may enter the fray, modifying the product in important ways, yet relying on the fundamental designs pioneered by the innovator. When the game of musical chairs

stops, and a dominant design emerges, the innovator might well end up at a disadvantage. Hence, when imitation is possible, and when it occurs coupled with design modification before a dominant design emerges, a follower's modified product has a good chance of being anointed as the industry standard.

Complementary Assets

Let the unit of analysis be innovation. An innovation consists of certain technical knowledge about how to do things better. Assume that the know-how in question is partly codified and partly tacit. In order for such know-how to generate a rent stream, it must be sold or used in the market.

In almost all cases, the successful commercialization of an innovation requires that the know-how in question be utilized in conjunction with such services as marketing, competitive manufacturing, and after-sales support. These services are often obtained from complementary assets that are specialized. For example, the commercialization of a new drug is likely to require the dissemination of information over a specialized information channel. In some cases, as when the innovation is systemic, the complementary assets may be other parts of a system. For instance, computer hardware typically requires the development of specialized software, both for the operating system and for applications. Even when an innovation is autonomous, the services of certain complementary assets will be needed for successful commercialization (Figure 4).

Whether the assets required for least cost production and distribution are specialized to the innovation turns out to be

TEECE

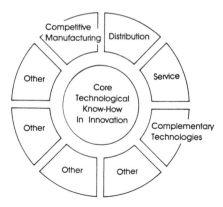

Figure 4: In order to innovate, firms need complementary assets and technologies to support the commercialization of some core technology. These assets typically include manufacturing, distribution, and sales and service. They may already reside in-house. If not, they are conceivably available through merger, acquisition, or contract. The key consideration is the terms upon which they are available to the innovator.

important in the development presented below. Complementary assets can be generic, specialized, or cospecialized.

Generic assets are general purpose assets that do not need to be tailored to the innovation. Specialized assets are those on which the innovation depends, tailored to that innovation. Cospecialized assets are those for which there is a bilateral dependence. For instance, specialized repair facilities are needed to support Mazda's rotary engine. These assets are cospecialized because of the mutual dependence of the innovation and the repair facility. Container shipping required a similar deployment of cospecialized assets in specially designed ships and terminals. However, the dependence of trucking on containerized shipping was less than that of containerized shipping on trucking:

trucks can convert from containers to flat beds at low cost. An example of a generic asset would be the manufacturing facilities needed to make running shoes. Generalized equipment can be used except for the mold for the sole.

Implications for Profitability

These three concepts can now be related in a way that will shed light on the imitation process and the distribution of rents between innovator and follower. In those few instances where the innovator has ironclad patent or copyright protection, or where trade secrets effectively deny imitators access to the product, the innovator is almost assured of capturing the lion's share of available profits for some period of time. Even if the innovator does not have the desirable complementary assets, ironclad protection of intellectual property will afford it time to obtain them. If these assets are generic, a contractual relationship may suffice; the innovator may simply license its technology. Specialized R&D firms are viable in such an environment. Universal Oil Products, an R&D firm developing refining processes for the petroleum industry, was such an innovator. If, however, the needed complementary assets are specialized or cospecialized, contractual relationships are exposed to hazards, because one or both parties will have to commit capital to certain irreversible investments, which will be valueless if the relationship between innovator and licensee breaks down. Accordingly, the innovator may want to integrate by owning the specialized and cospecialized assets. Fortunately, the factors which make for difficult imitation will enable the

INNOVATION

innovator to build or acquire those complementary assets without competing with innovators for their control.

Competition from imitators is thus muted in tight appropriability regimes, which sometimes characterizes the petrochemical industry. In this industry, the protection offered by patents is fairly easily enforced. A factor that helps the licensor is that most petrochemical processes

---

RC Cola was the first to introduce cola in a can and the first to introduce diet cola.

---

are designed around a specific variety of catalysts that can be kept proprietary. An agreement not to analyze the catalyst can be extracted from licensees, affording extra protection. Even if such requirements are violated by licensees, the innovator is still well positioned: the most important properties of a catalyst are related to its physical structure, and the process for generating this structure cannot be deduced from structural analysis alone. Every reaction technology a company acquires is thus accompanied by an ongoing dependence on the innovating company for the catalyst appropriate to the plant design. Failure to comply with the licensing contract can result in a cutoff in the supply of the catalyst and possibly in facility closure.

Similarly, if an innovator comes to market in the preparadigmatic phase with a sound product concept but the wrong design, a tight appropriability regime will afford it the time needed to get the

design right. The best initial design concepts often turn out to be hopelessly wrong, but if the innovator possesses an impenetrable thicket of patents, or simply has technology that is difficult to copy, then the market may well afford the innovator the time necessary to find the right design.

However, tight appropriability is the exception rather than the rule. Most innovators must formulate and implement complex business strategies to keep imitators at bay. The nature of the strategic challenge will vary according to whether the industry is in the paradigmatic or preparadigmatic phase.

In the preparadigmatic phase, the innovator, with little or no intellectual property protection available for its technology, must be careful to let the basic design float until the design seems likely to become the industry standard. In some industries this may be difficult as little opportunity exists for product modification. In microelectronics, for example, designs become locked in when the circuitry is chosen. Product modification is limited to debugging and software changes. An innovator must begin the design process anew if the product does not fit the market well. To some extent, new designs are dictated by the need to meet certain compatibility standards so that the new hardware can interface with existing applications software. In one sense, therefore, design for the microprocessor industry today is relatively straightforward: deliver greater power and speed while meeting the industry standards of the existing software base. However, from time to time windows of opportunity

TEECE

allow the introduction of entirely new families of microprocessors that will define a new industry and software standard. Then basic design parameters are less defined and can float until market acceptance is apparent.

The early history of the automobile industry — an industry characterized by a weak appropriability regime — exemplifies the importance of selecting the right design in the preparadigmatic stages. None of the early steam cars survived when the closed-body, internal combustion engine automobile emerged as the dominant design. The steam car, nevertheless, had virtues, such as reliability, that the internal combustion engine autos of that time did not.

The British fiasco with the Comet I is also instructive. De Havilland had picked an early design with significant flaws. By racing on to production, the innovator suffered an irreversible loss of reputation that seemed to prevent it from converting to what subsequently became the dominant design.

In general, innovators in weak appropriability regimes need to be intimately connected with the market so that designs are based on user needs. When multiple parallel and sequential prototyping is feasible, it has clear advantages. Usually, it is too costly. Development costs for a large commercial aircraft can exceed one billion dollars; variations on one theme are all that is possible.

Hence, the probability that the first firm to commercialize a new product design will enter the paradigmatic phase with the dominant design is problematic. The probabilities will be higher the lower the cost of prototyping and the more tightly coupled the firm is to the market. The firm's relationship to the market is a function of organizational design and can be influenced by managerial choices. The cost of prototyping is embedded in the technology and cannot be greatly influenced by managerial decisions. Hence, in industries with large developmental and prototyping costs — where choices are irreversible and where innovation of the product concept is easy — the innovator would be unlikely to emerge as a winner at the end of the preparadigmatic stage if the appropriability regime is weak.

In the preparadigmatic phase, complementary assets do not loom large. Rivalry is focused on trying to identify the design that will dominate the industry. Production volumes are low, and little can be gained from deploying specialized assets since scale economies are unavailable and price is not a principle competitive factor. However, as the leading design or designs are revealed by the market, volumes increase and firms gear up for mass production by acquiring specialized tooling and equipment, and possibly specialized distribution as well. Since these investments are irreversible, they are likely to proceed with caution. Islands of asset specificity will thus begin to form in a sea of generalized assets.

However, as the terms of competition begin to change and prices become increasingly unimportant, complementary assets become critical. Since the core technology is easy to imitate, commercial success depends on the terms under which the required complementary assets can be accessed.

INNOVATION

At this point, specialized and cospecialized assets become critically important. Generalized assets, almost by definition, are always available in an industry, and even if they are not, they do not involve significant irreversibilities. Even if there is insufficient capacity, additional capacity can be put in place with little risk. Specialized assets, on the other hand, involve significant irreversibilities and cannot be easily accessed by contract. Recontracting hazards abound when dedicated assets that do not have alternative uses are supported entirely by contractual arrangement [Williamson 1975, 1981, 1985, Teece 1980, 1982, 1985]. Owners of cospecialized assets, such as distribution channels or specialized manufacturing capacity, are clearly advantageously positioned relative to an innovator. Indeed, when they hold an airtight monopoly over specialized assets, and the innovator is in a regime of weak appropriability, they could command all of the rents to the innovation. Even without a monopoly, specialized assets are often not as easy to replicate as the technology. For instance, the technology in cardiac pacemakers was easy to imitate; competitive success was determined by who controlled the specialized marketing. A similar situation exists in the US for personal computers:

There are a huge number of computer manufacturers, companies that make peripherals (e.g., printers, hard disk drives, floppy disk drives), and software companies. They are all trying to get marketing distributors because they cannot afford to call on all of the US companies directly. They need to go through retail distribution channels, such as Businessland, in order to reach the marketplace. The problem today, however, is that many of these companies are not able to get shelf space and thus are having a very difficult time marketing

their products. The point of distribution is where the profit and the power are in the marketplace today [Norman 1986, p. 438].

Channel Selection Issues

Access to complementary assets is critical if the innovator is to avoid handing over the lion's share of the profits to imitators or to the owners of specialized and cospecialized complementary assets. What controls should the imitator establish over these critical assets?

Many channels can be employed. At one extreme, the innovator could integrate into all of the necessary complementary assets, an option that is probably

---

Patents do not work in practice as they do in theory.

---

unnecessary and prohibitively expensive. The assets and competencies needed may be numerous, even for quite simple technologies. To produce a personal computer, for instance, a company needs expertise in semiconductor technology, display technology, disk-drive technology, networking technology, keyboard technology, and several others. No company, not even IBM, has kept pace in all of these areas by itself.

At the other extreme, from handling all technologies internally the innovator could attempt to access these assets through contractual relationships (for example, component supply contracts, fabrication contracts, and distribution contracts). In many instances, contracts may suffice, although they expose the innovator to various hazards and dependencies that it may want to avoid. In between

TEECE

these two extremes are a myriad of intermediate forms and channels. I will analyze the properties of two extremes and also describe a mixture.

Contractual Modes

The advantages of a contractual solution — whereby the innovator contracts with independent suppliers, manufacturers or distributors — are obvious. The innovator will not have to make the capital expenditures needed to build or buy the assets. This reduces risks as well as cash requirements. Also, contractual relationships can bring added credibility to the innovator, especially if the innovator is unknown and the contractual partner is established and viable. Indeed, armslength contracting which embodies more than a simple buy-sell agreement is becoming so common and is so multifaceted that the term strategic partnering has been devised to describe it. Even large companies such as IBM are now engaging in it. For IBM, partnering buys access to new technologies enabling the company to learn things they couldn't have learned without many years of trial and error. IBM's arrangement to use Microsoft's MS-DOS operating system software on the IBM PC facilitated the timely introduction of IBM's personal computer into the market. Had IBM developed its own operating system, it would probably have missed the market window.

Smaller, less integrated companies are often eager to sign on with established companies because of the name recognition and reputation spillovers. For instance, Cipher Data Products contracted with IBM to develop a low-priced version of IBM's 3480 0.5 inch streaming cartridge drive, which is likely to become the industry standard. Cipher management recognizes that one of the biggest advantages to dealing with IBM is that, once you've created a product that meets the high quality standards necessary to sell into the IBM world, you can sell into any arena. Similarly, IBM's contract with Microsoft meant instant credibility to Microsoft [McKenna 1985, p. 94].

It is important to recognize that strategic partnering, which is currently very fashionable, exposes the innovator to certain hazards, particularly when the innovator is trying to use contracts to access special capabilities. First, it may be difficult to induce suppliers to make costly irreversible commitments which depend for their success on the success of the innovation. To expect suppliers, manufacturers, and distributors to do so is to expect them to take risks along with the innovator. For the innovator, this poses problems similar to those associated with attracting venture capital. The innovator must persuade its prospective partner that the risk is a good one. The situation is open to opportunistic abuses on both sides. The innovator has incentives to overstate the value of the innovation, while the supplier has incentives to "run with the technology" should the innovation be a success.

Instances of both parties making irreversible capital commitments nevertheless exist. Apple's Laserwriter — a high resolution laser printer which produces near typeset quality text graphics — is a case in point. Apple persuaded Canon to participate in the development of the Laserwriter; Canon provided subsystems from

INNOVATION

its copiers, but only after Apple contracted to pay for a certain number of copier engines and cases. In short, Apple accepted a good deal of the financial risk in order to induce Canon to assist in the development and production of the Laserwriter. The arrangement appears to have been prudent, yet there were clearly hazards for both sides. It is difficult to write, execute, and enforce complex development contracts, particularly when the design of the new product is still floating, which it often is, even after commercialization. Apple was exposed to the risk that its co-innovator Canon would fail to deliver, and Canon was exposed to the risk that the Apple design and marketing effort would not succeed. Still, Apple's alternatives may have been rather limited, in that it did not have the technology to go it alone.

The current euphoria over strategic partnering may be partially misplaced. Its advantages are being stressed (for example, by McKenna [1985]) without a balanced presentation of costs and risks. These have been described by Williamson [1975, 1985]. Briefly, there is the risk that the partner will not perform according to the innovator's perception of what the contract requires; there is the added danger that the partner may imitate the innovator's technology and attempt to compete with the innovator. The danger is particularly acute if the provider of the complementary asset is uniquely situated with respect to that asset and also can absorb and imitate the technology. Contractual or partnering strategies are unambiguously preferred, however, where the complementary assets are generic and in competitive supply. Because alternatives exist, failure of the partner to perform according to the contract is not particularly damaging on the innovator.

Integration Modes

An alternative organizational arrangement is for the firm to provide the necessary complementary assets internally. This in-house approach facilitates greater control, but it is costly in terms of managerial and financial resources.

There are clear advantages to integration when assets are in fixed supply over the relevant time period. To avoid a speculative price run-up, the assets in question must be acquired by the innovator before their connection with the innovation is public knowledge. If the value of the complementary asset to the innovator leaks out, the owner of a critical complementarity could extract a portion of the rent stream that the innovation was expected to generate. Such bottleneck situations are not uncommon, particularly in distribution.

However, an innovator may not have the time or the money to acquire or build the complementary assets it would like to control. Particularly when imitation is easy, timing becomes critical. Innovators, therefore, need to rank complementary assets as to their importance. If the complementary assets are critical, ownership is warranted, although if the firm is cash constrained, a minority equity position may well be a sensible trade-off. If the complementary asset in question is technology, this calculus needs to be revised in terms of the desired equity position. This is because ownership of complementary enterprises appears to be fraught

TEECE

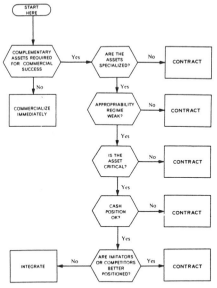

Figure 5: **When making R&D and commercialization decisions, managers must identify, preferably ahead of time, the complementary assets the innovation will need for successful commercialization. Contractual alternatives will make strategic sense if the complementary assets are not specialized, or if the innovators' position regarding its intellectual property is ironclad, or for assets which are not critical, or for assets in which the innovator does not have or cannot obtain the necessary financial resources, or for assets in which imitators are in any case already irrevocably better positioned. Otherwise, the integration (in-house) alternative ought to be preferred.**

with hazards, as integration tends to destroy incentives and cultures, particularly when a deep hierarchy is involved.

When imitation is easy, building or buying specialized complementary assets must be considered in light of the moves of competitors. Building loses its point if one's imitators can do it faster. Figure 5 summarizes the factors to be considered in deciding between contracting and

building or buying (mixed modes and intermediate solutions are ignored in order to simplify the analysis.)

If the innovator is a large enterprise that controls many of the relevant complementary assets, integration is not likely to be the issue it might be for a smaller company. However, in industries experiencing rapid technological change, no single company is likely to have the full range of expertise needed to bring advanced products to market in a timely and cost-effective fashion. In such industries, integration is an issue for large as well as small firms.

Mixed Modes

Organizational reality rarely affords the possibility of choice among pure forms of economic organization. Integration and contract are, accordingly, rarely seen without some accommodation to each other. The reality of business is that mixed modes — involving the blending of elements of integration and contract — are rather common. Still, in examining such intermediate forms, it is instructive to bear in mind the simple economics of pure forms.

Sometimes mixed modes represent transitional phases. For instance, because computer and telecommunication technologies are converging, firms in each industry are discovering that they need the technical capabilities of the other. This interdependence requires the collaboration of those who design different parts of the system; intense cross-boundary coordination and information flows must be supported. When separate companies collaborate, the parties must often agree on complex protocol issues. Contractual

INNOVATION

difficulties can be anticipated since the selection of common technical protocols among the parties will often be followed by investments in specialized hardware and software. There is little doubt that this was a key part of IBM's motivation in purchasing 15 percent of PBX manufacturer Rolm in 1983 and expanding that position to 100 percent in 1984. IBM's stake in Intel, which began with a 12 percent purchase in 1982, is most probably not a transitional phase leading to 100 percent purchase, because both companies realized that the two corporate cultures are not very compatible.

An example of how profoundly changing technology can affect the boundaries of the firm — and the identity of the firm at the nexus of contracts needed to develop and manufacture complex products — can be found in the jet fighter business. Avionics now constitutes about one third of the cost of a fighter, up from about 15 percent a decade ago (Figure 6). Avionics is expected to be even more important in the future, both in terms of cost and in terms of performance. Given

the fairly widespread diffusion of airframe and propulsion technology, the superiority of fighters today and in the future will depend primarily upon the sophistication and capability of the aircraft's electronics. Indeed, in the future, computer manufacturers like AT&T and IBM may become prime contractors for advanced weapons systems, including fighters. In a related way, VHSIC technology is regarded as a key factor in reestablishing what the US sees as a necessary degree of operational supremacy for its forces against the numerical superiority of the Soviet Union and the Warsaw Pact. It will be an essential ingredient of new aircraft programs such as the USAF's ATF advanced tactical fighter, the US Navy's VFMX air superiority fighter, and the US Army's LHX light battlefield helicopter, not to mention extensive upgrading of current equipment such as the F-15 and F-16 fighters and AH-64 helicopter [*Jane's All the World's Aircraft* 1983-84, p. 24].

Of particular relevance here is the USAF's advanced tactical fighter (ATF). While it is still too early to discuss

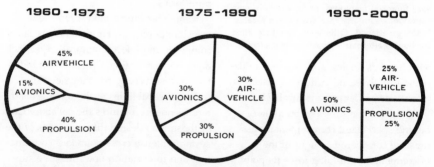

Figure 6: The trend in fighter plane subsystem costs has been away from air vehicle and propulsion and toward avionics, and this trend is likely to continue. An implication is that companies in the electronics industry, like IBM and AT&T, may be prime contractors for future generations of aircraft.

TEECE

electronics definitively, according to *Jane's* [1983-84, p. 26], a number of technological areas can be identified that will be required in the ATF, including the integration of flight and propulsion control systems, fly-by-wire, and integration of cockpit displays, probably with a voice command system to enhance the HOTAS (hands on throttle and stick). Advanced heads-up display and VHSIC technology will also be critical.

In order to compete in the advanced fighter market in the future, prime contractors will have to be on the leading edge with respect to avionics technology. A manufacturer that fails to develop or acquire such technology must expect to be shut out of a growing portion of the market.

Airframe companies without considerable in-house electronics capability will probably not be able to contract with electronics companies for the requisite subsystems. Because avionics is becoming the core technology that dictates other elements of design, it will not be enough for airframe companies to contract with both avionics and propulsion companies. Indeed, the leading fighter manufacturers — such as General Dynamics and McDonnell Douglas — have developed in-house avionics capabilities. Were these companies to fail to build a substantial in-house capability, it might be impossible, in the future, for them to design competitive fighter planes using avionics subcontractors.

The reason is that complex trade-offs often exist between avionics and air-vehicle design — trade-offs that are much more complex and dynamic than between

air vehicle and propulsion. Moreover, much of the avionics of a fighter plane is specific to that aircraft. In the absence of in-house avionics capabilities, jet fighter manufacturers would be unable, without extremely close collaboration with avionics' subcontractors, to formulate and implement new fighter plane concepts. Moreover, the kind of collaboration required would require deep dependence of a kind very likely to lead to contractual vulnerabilities.

Conclusion

Clearly, the boundaries of an innovating firm are an important strategic variable, particularly when intellectual property protection is weak, as with microelectronics. The control of complementary assets, particularly when they are specialized or cospecialized, helps establish who wins and who loses from innovation. Imitators can do better than innovators if they are better positioned on cost and quality with respect to critical complementary assets, such as manufacturing.

There are important implications for corporate strategy. Except in unusual circumstances, innovating firms must emphasize the development of cost-competitive capabilities in the activities downstream from R&D if they are to profit from investment in R&D. Being first to market is no longer a guarantee of commercial success, particularly if to achieve early market entry the innovating firm engages in risky contracts with manufacturers, distributors, and developers of complementary technologies.

For public policy, a related set of implications follow. Government policy which equates policies to assist innovation with

INNOVATION

policies to assist R&D is increasingly wide of the mark. Except in special circumstances, national prowess in research and development is neither necessary nor sufficient to ensure that the innovator (rather than followers) captures the greater share of the profits available from innovation. Public policy towards science and technology must recognize how important the technological infrastructure (particularly education at all levels and manufacturing) is to the ability of domestically-based firms to build the requisite competitive capacities needed to capture value from innovation.

Acknowledgments

I thank Raphael Amit, Harvey Brooks, Therese Flaherty, Richard Gilbert, Heather Haveman, Mel Horwitch, Gary Pisano, Richard Rumelt, Raymond Vernon, and Sidney Winter for helpful discussions relating to the subject matter of this paper. A related treatment of the issues in this paper was published in *Research Policy* 1986, Vol. 15, No. 6.

References

Abernathy, W. J. and Utterback, J. M. 1978, "Patterns of industrial innovation," *Technology Review*, Vol. 80, No. 7 (January/July), pp. 40–47.

Clarke, Kim B. 1985, "The interaction of design hierarchies and market concepts in technological evolution," *Research Policy*, Vol. 14, No. 5 (October), pp. 235–251.

Dosi, G. 1982, "Technological paradigms and technological trajectories," *Research Policy*, Vol. 11, No. 3 (June), pp. 147–162.

Jane's All the World's Aircraft 1983-84, McGraw-Hill, New York.

Kuhn, T. 1970. *The Structure of Scientific Revolutions*, University of Chicago Press, Chicago, Illinois.

Levin, R.; Klevorick, A.; Nelson, N.; and Winter, S. 1984, "Survey research on R&D appropriability and technological opportunity,"

unpublished manuscript, Yale University.

Martin, Michael 1984, *Managing Technological Innovation and Enterpreneurship*, Reston Publishing Company, Reston, Virginia.

McKenna, R. 1985, "Market positioning in high technology," *California Management Review*, Vol. 27, No. 3 (Spring), pp. 82–108.

Norman, D. A. 1986, "Impact of entrepreneurship and innovations on the distribution of personal computers," in *The Positive Sum Strategy*, eds. R. Landau and N. Rosenberg, National Academy Press, Washington, DC, pp. 437–439.

Teece, D. J. 1980, "Economics of scope and the scope of the enterprise," *Journal of Economic Behavior and Organization*, Vol. 1, No. 3, pp. 223–247.

Teece, D. J. 1981, "The market for know-how and the efficient international transfer of technology," *Annals of the American Academy of Political and Social Science*, Vol. 458 (November), pp. 81–96.

Teece, D. J. 1982, "Towards an economic theory of the multiproduct firm," *Journal of Economic Behavior and Organization*, Vol. 3, No. 1, pp. 39–63.

Teece, D. J. 1985, "Multinational enterprise, internal governance, and industrial organization," *American Economic Review*, Vol. 75, No. 2 (May), pp. 233–238.

Williamson, O. E. 1975, *Markets and Hierarchies*, The Free Press, New York.

Williamson, O. E. 1981, "The modern corporation: Origins, evolution, attributes," *Journal of Economic Literature*, Vol. 19, No. 4 (December), pp. 1537–1568.

Williamson, O. E. 1985, *The Economic Institutions of Capitalism*, The Free Press, New York.

[13]

Inter-organizational Requirements of the Innovation Process

INTRODUCTION

At the heart of the innovation process in the United States is the modern corporate R&D facility, found in giant corporations and in small start-up enterprises. However, the institutional structure of innovation in capitalist economies is extremely variegated and involves a complex network of backward, forward, horizontal, lateral relationships and linkages within, among and between firms and other organizations such as universities.

Studies designed to explain innovation and to understand the success of particular firms have been somewhat remiss in not analyzing these linkages, which, we propose, have a significant impact on the productivity and profitability of R&D. In this paper attention will be given to inter-firm and inter-organizational relationships and linkages. An attempt will be made to assess their importance to the development and profitable commercialization of new technology. In addition, an effort will be made to identify appropriate organizational designs for managing them. Before doing so, it will be useful to specify key transactions among the various groups and individuals typically involved in the innovation process.

MODELS OF THE INNOVATION PROCESS

Because of the complexity of the innovation process it is important to build some kind of conceptual model of what is involved in the activity that we commonly refer to as innovation. The dominant model, having its origins in the description and analysis of 'big technology' projects, is described below. Its inadequacies are then addressed in the light of the more 'simultaneous' nature of the process, particularly in certain industries experiencing high rates of technological change.

The 'Serial' Model

In the traditional description of the innovation process it is not uncommon to break the process down into a number of stages which proceed sequentially, albeit with significant overlaps if the project is on a fast track. The innovation process thus proceeds from research to development, to design, to production and finally to marketing, sales and service (see Fig. 1). In simple versions of this model there is no feedback or overlap between and among stages. This view of the process may represent an appropriate summary, in some very limited instances, such as where a very modest product improvement is at issue.

The serial or assembly line model of product development with feedback and overlaps has been a reasonable approximation of what went on in many large US corporations at home and abroad for many years. The approach worked well in many areas, including aircraft, automobiles and telecommunications (especially central office switches). Examples of products developed in this fashion include the 7×7 series of Boeing aircraft, the Mercury and Apollo programs, many large DoD programs, the IBM 360 and the Xerox 9000 family of high-speed copiers. This method of management had its advantages whenever large idiosyncratic fixed investments were required for successful commercialization. It is a method of organizaiton in which many large companies are comfortable, as it includes clear reponsibility for each part of a complex delivery system.

However, this assembly line or pipeline representation of a new product delivery system is increasingly a caricature of what actually takes place, or what needs to take place. At the center of the innovation process is design, not science. Research is often stimulated by the problems associated with trying to get the design right. Contrary to the view inherent in the serial model, technology is not merely applied science. Any technological development draws on an array of science, not

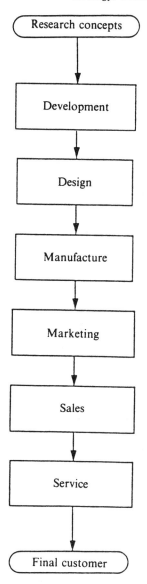

Figure 1. Simplified serial product-delivery process.

only that which is embedded in one or two recent findings.

Moreover, important technological breakthroughs can often proceed even when the underlying science is not understood well (for example, the IUD for birth control). Products can often be made to work without much knowledge of why. Airframe design in the aircraft industry, for instance, has a large empirical component. Certain designs are known, from experimentation, to have certain performance features. However, the underlying scientific understanding of [35] airframe design is rudimentary. Accordingly, wind tunnel testing is still an essential part of the development process.

The serial model also underemphasizes the importance of process innovation. Indeed, if the scheme fits innovation at all it is perhaps only for product innovations. Process innovations often do not require marketing, and may not even require new tooling. Nor does the serial model highlight the many small but cumulatively important incremental innovations which are often at the heart of technological change. The serial model has a macro project orientation; but as we know, this is not the way in which most innovation proceeds.

Serial Model with Links and Feedback

In reality, with uncertainty, learning and short product lifecycles, innovation requires rapid feedback, midcourse corrections to designs, and redesign. Feedbacks and trials are essential, whether it is incremental or radical innovation which is at issue. The demands of innovation often lead to scientific developments just as often as innovation draws on science.

Kline and Rosenberg (1986) have proposed what they call a chain-linked model as an alternative (Fig. 2). This model recognizes aspects of the linear one—such as a flow of activity through design to development production and marketing—but also recognizes constant feedback between and among 'stages'. Moreover, 'the linkage from science to innovation is not solely or even preponderantly at the beginning of typical innovations, but rather extends all through the process . . . science can be visualized as lying alongside development processes, to be used when needed' (Kline and Rosenberg, 1986, pp. 290–91).

The identification of needs is critical to the profitable expenditure of R&D dollars. R&D personnel must thus be closely conntected to the market and to marketing personnel. Scientists must have one foot in the laboratory and one in the marketplace. Knowing *what* to develop and design, rather than just how to do

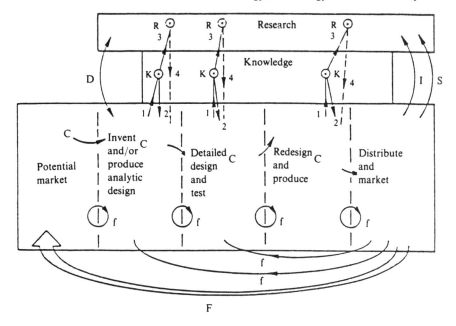

Figure 2. Model showing flow paths of information and co-operation (Kline and Rosenberg, 1986, p. 290.)

Symbols used on arrows:

C: Central chain of innovation
f: Feedback loops
F: Particularly important feedback

K–R: Links through knowledge to research and return paths. If problem solved at node K, link 3 to R not activated. Return from research (link 4) is problematic—therefore dashed line.
  D: Direct link to and from research from problems in invention and design.
  I: Support of scientific research by instruments, machines, tools and procedures of technology.
  S: Support of research in sciences underlying product area to gain information directly and by monitoring outside work. The information obtained may apply anywhere along the chain.

it, is absolutely essential for commercial success. Developing this understanding involves a complex interplay between science and engineering, manufacturing and marketing in order to specify product functions and features. It is not just a matter of identifying user needs and assessing engineering feasibility. One must also separate those user needs which are being met by competition and those which are not. This may not become clear until the product is introduced, in which case the ability to redesign quickly and efficiently may be of the utmost importance.

This model recognizes the existence and exercise of tight linkages and feedback mechanisms which must operate quickly and efficiently. These linkages must exist within, among and between firms and other organizations, such as universities. Of course, the positioning of the firm's boundaries (for example, its level of vertical integration) determines in part whether the required interactions are intrafirm or interfirm.

Parallel (Simultaneous) Model

Both versions of the serial model have embedded within them elements of a sequential process. In some circumstances, however, the sequential nature of activity can and should be compressed to such a degree that a parallel model is in fact required. (Fig. 3).

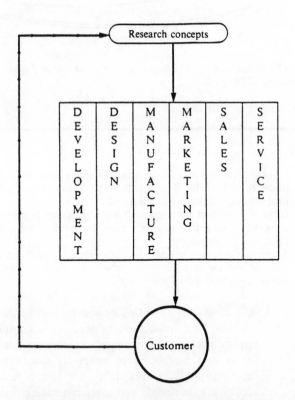

Figure 3. Parallel product-delivery process.

The 'parallel' model, it should be recognized, has been facilitated by a lowering of the cost of changes in digital electronic circuits. While in some domains such as aircraft engines the costs of development have increased, in others (for example, computers) the costs of development per unit of performance have fallen considerably. As a result of this and the great amount of innovation which has occurred and is still continuing in components, major new computer companies such as Apple, Sun, Apollo, Commodore and others have been born and have grown extremely fast. Generally, the hallmark of these new companies is the ability to develop new products quickly. In these companies the linear model has been collapsed and [36] some of the work in product development is done in parallel, a process which requires an entirely new approach to management. New information systems and collaboration with outside vendors and partners is often essential.

Clearly, a parallel approach to development requires intense communication, because various downstream activities may be in progress before product features and specifications are finally determined. Hence the amount of information which must be communicated among the various activities is necessarily large, as it is often changing. Workstations and modern communications facilitate the necessary timely technology transfer. Moreover, the simulation of manufacturing facilities can lead to early feedback with respect to the cost ramifications alternative product designs.

LINKAGES TO EXTERNAL INSTITUTIONS

Whether innovation proceeds according to either the serial or the parallel model, it is likely to require access to capabilities which lie beyond the innovating entity. These may be found in universities, other parts of the [37] enterprise or in other unaffiliated enterprises. The roles of some of these key organizational units are now explored.

University–industry Interaction

The US university has made an important contribution to the innovation process since the late nineteenth century, and university science and engineering and science-based industries grew up together in the United States. Universities have provided industry with technical people, and with ideas about product and process innovation (Nelson, 1988).

University research finds its way to industry through a variety of channels, including graduate students, publications, research contracts, technical conferences, industry affiliate programs, personnel exchanges (for example, adjunct professors), consultants, as well as in some cases through directed mechanisms such as research consortia and university industrial liaison offices and licensing offices which market proprietary university technology at universities like Stanford and MIT. Most universities, however, are relatively passive with respect to directed efforts to market university technology, patented or unpatented, to industry. UC Berkeley and UCLA, which have great technological resources, are cases in point.

Two somewhat contradictory threads have been observed in the business perspectives on the commercial applicability and value of university technology. On the one hand, there is a body of evidence that US industry on the whole does not consider universities a viable source of new products. Peters and Fusfeld (1982) examined 464 examples of university–industry research collaboration, but could rarely identify instances where a commercially marketable product or process was an immediate and direct outcome of research interactions or processes. On the other hand, industrial enterprises are often eager to develop good relationships with universities, most probably to get access to the best graduate students, to attract away faculty as partners in new business ventures, and to encourage faculty and students to become familiar with their equipment (as in computers). Even if there are few new products and processes which can be attributed directly to the university, the university connection enables firms to preserve an open window on science and technology and to be alert to changing opportunities and threats.

That university–industry connections rarely result in new patentable products and processes is evident from the minuscule (in relationship to university research budgets) royalties which universities earn (there are some examples where universities have taken equity in exchange for technology and have had a payoff in terms of capital gains or dividends). Table 1 shows annual royalty income for nine US universities and demonstrates, for instance, that the entire university of California (nine campuses) earned only $4 million in gross royalty income in 1986/7.

It would appear that the intensity and necessity for

Table 1. Estimates of Royalty Income at Certain Universities, 1984.

Institution	Annual royalty income ($000)
Johns Hopkins	90
MIT	1500
Stanford University	2500[a]
University of Washington	120
University of California	1700[b]
Harvard University	50
Columbia University	Minimal
University of Wisconsin	6000[c]
Cornell University	1300

[a] $6.5 million gross in 1986/7. (Source: W. Mitchell.)
[b] $4.0 million gross in 1986/7. (Source: W. Mitchell.)
[c] Investment income is a substantial portion. Comparable number for 1986/7 was $10 million. (Source: OTA, 1984, p. 412.)

---

industry–university interaction varies by field and over time. As Nelson (1988) notes, there is evidence that academic research in chemistry and electrical engineering has, over the years, diminished as a source of important new knowledge for industry. Academic researchers were very important to technological developments in the early days of the semiconductor industry, but, as time went by, R&D in industry increasingly separated itself from what academics were doing. In the late 1980s certain areas of academic biology and computer science and metallurgy are very important sources of new ideas and techniques for industry. The industries in which these sciences are important must look to universities for new knowledge and techniques, as well as training. In recent years a number of new models have been developed to facilitate these linkages at some campuses. However, few tight linkages exist, even today. Nevertheless, close links to the university are critical requirements for success in certain industries at certain times.

Vertical Linkages

In a series of important publications Von Hippel (1977, 1988) has presented evidence that, in some industries, industrial products judged by users to offer them a significant performance improvement are usually conceived and prototyped by users, not by the manufacturers. The manufacturers' role in the innovation process in these industries is somehow to become aware of the user innovation and its value and then to manufacture a commercial version of the device for sale to user firms. This pattern of innovation by product users is contrary to the usual assumption that product manufacturers are responsible for the innovation process from finding to filling the need. Figure 4

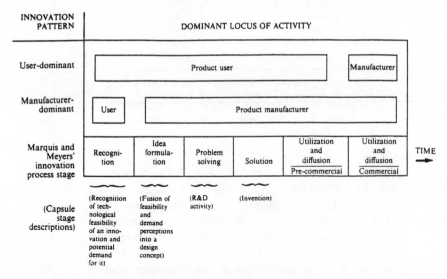

Figure 4. User and manufacturer roles in the innovation process charted against Marquis and Meyers' (1969) innovation process stages (Von Hippel, 1977).

from Von Hippel (1977, p. 61) contrasts such user-dominated involvement with the more typical manufacturer-dominant innovation. The transfer from user to manufacturer may be initiated by the user, or by the manufacturer, who may have already hired individuals with experience from the user firms.   [38]

Von Hippel found that user-dominated innovation accounted for more than two-thirds of first-to-market innovations in scientific instruments and in process machinery used in semiconductor and electronic sub-assembly manufacture. Successful management of the process requires that product engineering (rather than R&D) skills be resident in the manufacturer, and that manufacturers search to identify user solutions rather than user needs.[1] A further implication is that there may be a symbiotic relationship between users and equipment manufacturers which depends upon social and geographical proximity. If user industries migrate offshore, then the manufactures of equipment will disappear from the domestic scene as well. Hence, the decline of the US semiconductor industry can be expected to threaten the US semiconductor equipment industry unless close ties can be developed between foreign users (domestic and offshore) and domestic manufacturers.

Balancing the role that users play in stimulating innovation upstream is the role that suppliers play in stimulating downstream innovation. Much of the innovation in the automobile industry, including fuel injection, alternators and power steering, has its origins in upstream component suppliers.[2] The challenge then becomes how to 'design in' the new components and avoid sole source dependency on the part of the automotive companies. As discussed below, deep and enduring relationships need to be established between component developer–manufacturer and supplier to ensure adoption and diffusion of the technology.

A related set of vertical relationships involving innovation has been commented upon by Rosenberg (1972) in his treatise on technology and US economic growth. The machine tool industry in the nineteenth century played a unique role both in the initial solution of technical problems in user industries, such as textiles, and as the disseminator of these techniques to other industries, such as railroad locomotive manufacture. Rosenberg's description seems to suggest that the users played some role in the development of new equipment. He notes that before 1820 in the United States one could not identify a distinct set of firms who were specialists in the design and manufacture of machinery. Machines were either produced by users or by firms engaged in the production of metal or wooden products (pp. 98–9). Machinery-producing firms were thus first observed as adjuncts to textile factories. However, once established, these firms played an important role as the transmission center in the diffusion of new technology (Rosenberg, 1972, p. 102).

Horizontal Linkages

Successful innovation often requires horizontal as well as vertical co-operation. Horizontal linkages can help reduce spillover externalities and unnecessary duplication of research efforts and can also assist in the definition of technical standards for systemic innovation.

Horizontal linkages can help firms to overcome the appropriability (spillover) problems because the set of firms receiving the benefits is likely to include a greater portion of firms which have incurred R&D costs. The effect of greater appropriability is, of course, to encourage greater investment in new technology. It is well understood that competitive markets tend to under-invest in new technology because those firms which support R&D have limited capacity to extract 'fees' from the imitators (free riders).

In addition, collaborative reduces, if not eliminates, what William Norris, CEO of Control Data Corporation, refers to as 'shameful and needless duplication of effort' (Davis, 1985, p. 42). Independent [39] research activities often proceed down identical or near-identical technological paths. This is often wasteful and can be minimized if research plans are co-ordinated.[3]

This is not to imply that research activity in the United States has not traditionally displayed important co-operative elements. Von Hippel (1988, Ch. 6) has observed informal knowhow trading between engineers from different companies[4] who have common professional interests, and he describes the process as follows:

> In general such trading networks appear to be formed and refined as engineers get to know each other at professional conferences and elsewhere. In the course of such contracts, an engineer builds his personal informal list of possibly useful expert con-

tacts by making private judgments as to the areas of expertise and abilities of those he meets. Later, when engineer A encounters a difficult product or process development problem, A activates his network by calling Engineer B—an appropriately knowledgeable contact who works at a competing (or non-competing) firm—for advice.

The manifold benefits from broad-scale collaboration activity have been recognized abroad, and more recently in the United States as well.[5] One assessment of the United States is that 'up until now, however, we have taken it for granted as an article of faith that no co-operation should be permitted, that it is best that we keep companies apart from one another' (Ouchi, 1984, p. 103). Meanwhile, other countries have adopted different models. For instance, Japanese co-operative activity is ubiquitous and is not only in the form of R&D joint ventures but also R&D collaboration. By the end of 1971 the entire Japanese computer industry (six firms) was paired in order to compete with IBM and its System 370 (Ouchi, 1984, p. 105). While the research was done in existing co-operative laboratories there was intense interaction and information sharing. Another celebrated example of Japanese collaboration was the VLSI (Very Large Scale Integrated Circuit) Research Association, which was an R&D joint venture formed in 1975 with the capital contributed by NEC, Toshiba, Hitachi, Mitsubishi and Fujitsu. At the successful conclusion of the project in 1979 the laboratory was dissolved and the scientists went back to their sponsoring companies.

Since the National Co-operative Research Act of 1984, which limits but does not eliminate antitrust risks, interest has been shown in R&D joint ventures in the United States. Well-known ventures include the Microelectronics and Computer Technology Corp. (MCC) in Austin, Texas; the Semiconductor Research Corporation (SRC) in Research Triangle Park, North Carolina; and Bell Communication Research (Bellcore). Collaboration under the Act is restricted at some undefined point as the product approaches commercialization. MCC's objective is to engage in advanced long-term research and development in computer architecture, semiconductor packaging and interconnect, software technology, VLSI and CAD. Its members include AMD, Boeing, Control Data, Harris, Motorola, Sperry and others. (IBM is conspicuously absent, as are Japanese and European-based firms).

The only form of co-operative research which receives special antitrust treatment (but not exemption) in the United States is the R&D joint venture. Other forms of collaborative R&D activity, such as the pooling of R&D projects and the sharing of development data, are subject to ordinary antitrust scrutiny. Co-operation using existing facilities is thus perceived to be exposed to serious antitrust risk, particularly if participating firms have significant market shares.

However, the successful commercialization of technology often requires collaboration among horizontal competitors that have different capabilities. For instance, the relevant manufacturing capacities need not be resident within the firm responsible for the other activities in the innovation process. In order to capture value from the innovation it may therefore be necessary for a number of firms to collaborate, with different firms being responsible for different activities (Teece, 1986). In some cases these firms may be horizontal competitors and antitrust may block desirable collaboration.

A further area in which horizontal linkages may be critical is where network technologies exist, as is currently the case with teletext and videotext. A careful reconsideration of US antitrust policy is clearly warranted. Subscribers will tend to wait in the hope that others will achieve the cost of achieving compatibility with them. Collaboration among horizontal competitors can then assist in the derivation and implementation of a network standard which would speed adoption of the network technologies.

ORGANIZATIONAL IMPLICATIONS: CO-OPERATION VERSUS INTEGRATION

The need for several kinds of linkages among different organizational units and groups raises basic questions about the organizational structures which should govern these linkages if they are to be developed and maintained in the most (dynamically) efficient way. All kinds of market failures can exist if these interactions are left to unassisted markets fettered by antitrust policies uninformed by the requirements of dynamic competition. (Teece, 1981, 1988). Vertical integration between R&D and production can help overcome a whole set of contracting problems which can be predicted to emerge in pure market transactions. Indeed, in a capitalist economy characterized by weak intellectual property protection and perfect competition, neoclassical markets and specialized (non-integrated) firms, product innovation could not be supported.[6] Indeed, at a highly abstract level a socialist economy should be expected to overcome many of the critical information and exchange problems implicit in the above analysis of interaction and linkages.   [40]

However, in real-world situations markets are characterized by a variety of supporting relationships and non-market exchanges. Trust relationships can develop, supported by norms of reciprocity. Generally, the smaller the amount of committed capital which is at stake, the looser the governance structure required. Equity ties can be expected in environments characterized by fewer potential partners and transaction-specific investments in physical and human capital.

Hence technological change itself, as well as changing competition, suggests that different organizational models may be appropriate for different innovation projects. Unfortunately, space constraints do not afford the opportunity for anything but a superficial treatment of the issue. As mentioned earlier, the lowering of the costs of digital electronics by complex silicon-integrated circuits has opened up new possibilities. Many new products, such as the Sun workstations, can be developed using off-the-shelf components and technologies. 'Ferraris' can be made out of spare parts, according to Sun's CEO, Scott McNealey. This reduces the sunk costs in certain development activities and suggests not only a parallel type development process but also one that need not involve high levels of organizational integration. Hence a high range of less hierarchical structures can be used to commercialize new technologies in certain industries at certain times. Collaboration with component suppliers, can thus substitute for integration in many important circumstances. When feasible, it can also lead to a reduction in development costs, by drawing on established competences.

In some instances equity linkages may not be feasible or desirable, as with linkages to the university. However, enduring relationships can and must be built using mechanisms which support stable and close relationships. De facto integration must be attained.

CONCLUSIONS

Innovation requires complex interactions and de facto integration among a multiplicity of organizational units. These interactions are vertical, horizontal and lateral and require special infrastructure to proceed smoothly and efficiently.

Capitalist economies have, over time, developed much of the organizational and incentive apparatus that is required, so that it is not surprising that innovation proceeds most efficiently in capitalist economies. However, advanced capitalist economies are not all identical, and a variety of models within and across economies exist by which to organize innovative activity.

The linkages discussed in this paper facilitate the process of coupling user needs to technological opportunities, and of commercializing new products and processes in a timely fashion. These linkages can either be intra-organizational (within firms) or inter-organizational (between and among firms). If attainable with non-hierarchical decentralized modes of organization, the former is generally preferred, as it increases the probability that innovators rather than follower-imitators will capture value from new technology. Nevertheless, collaboration among unaffiliated enterprises will often suffice, and is imperative in instances where firms conducting R&D must catch up, as where hierarchical internal structures would otherwise suffocate the innovation process.

Acknowledgements

The author is especially grateful to William Spencer of Xerox Corp. for valuable insights and comments. The intellectual debt to Richard Nelson, Nathan Rosenberg and Oliver Williamson will be readily apparent to the reader. Will Mitchell provided helpful assistance and comments.

NOTES

1. Note that user innovation requires two kinds of technology transfer: first from user to manufacturer, and then from manufacturer to the developer–user and other users.
2. Bendix and Bosch developed fuel injection and Motorola the alternator.
3. Needless to say, uncertainty often requires that multiple (but not identical) technological paths be pursued simultaneously. See, for example, Nelson (1984, Ch. 2).
4. The companies he observed were in the US steel minimill industry.
5. According to William Norris, US corporations were not willing to give collaborative research a try until 'these companies had the hell scared out of them by the Japanese' (Davis, 1985, p. 42).
6. With vertical integration, product innovations would be converted to process innovations and would not have to be revealed to others in order to be profitably commercialised.

REFERENCES

D. Davis (1985). R&D consortia. *High Technology* October.

S. J. Kline and N. Rosenberg (1986). An overview of innovation. In N. Rosenberg and R. Landau (eds), *The Positive Sum Strategy*, Washington, DC: National Academy Press.

D. Marquis and S. Meyers (1969) *Successful Industrial Innovations*, National Science Foundation, May.

R. R. Nelson (1984). *High Technology Policies*, Washington, DC: American Enterprise Institute.

R. R. Nelson (1988). The roles of firms in technical advance: a perspective from evolutionary theory. Unpublished manuscript, Columbia University, January.

OTA (1984). *Commercial Biotechnology: An International Analysis*, Washington, DC: Office of Technology Assessment, January.

L. Peters and H. Fusfeld (1982). Current U.S. university/industry research connections. *University/Industry Research Relationship*, National Science Foundation.

N. Rosenberg (1972). *Technology and American Economic Growth*, New York: Harper & Row.

D. Teece (1981). The market for know-how and the efficient international transfer of technology. *Annals of the American Academy of Political and Social Science* November, 81–96. [41]

D. Teece (1986). Profiting from technological innovation: implications for integration, collaboration, licensing, and public policy. *Research Policy* **15**(6) December, 285–305.

D. Teece (1988). Technological change and the nature of the firm. In G. Dosi, C. Freeman, R. Nelson, G. Silverberg and L. Soete (eds), *Technical Change and Economic Theory*, (London: Pinter publishers).

E. Von Hippel (1977). The dominant role of the user in semiconductor and electronic subassembly process innovation *IEEE Transactions on Engineering Management* **EM-24**, 2, May.

E. Von Hippel (1988). *The Sources of Innovation*, New York: Oxford University Press. [42]

[14]

Managing Intellectual Capital:

LICENSING AND CROSS-LICENSING IN SEMICONDUCTORS AND ELECTRONICS

Peter C. Grindley
David J. Teece

O ne of the most significant emerging business developments in the last decade has been the proactive management of intellectual capital by innovating firms. While firms have for decades actively managed their physical and financial assets, until quite recently intellectual property (IP) management was a backwater. Top management paid little attention and legal counsel did not participate in major managerial decisions. This is changing. High-technology firms now often have "IP" managers as well as "IT" managers.[1] In some firms considerations of intellectual capital management have expanded from the mere licensing of residual technology to become a central element in technology strategy. This development is spurred by the increasing protection afforded IP worldwide and by the greater importance of technological know-how to competitive advantage. These developments herald a new era for management.

Patents and trade secrets have become a key element of competition in high-technology industries. In electronics and semiconductors, firms continually make large investments in R&D in their attempts to stay at the frontier and to utilize technological developments external to the firm. Fierce competition has put a premium on innovation and on defending IP from unlicensed imitators. As IP owners have taken a more active stance regarding their patent portfolios, industry participants increasingly find it necessary to engage in licensing and cross-licensing.[2] Moreover, and relatedly, royalty rates have risen. The effect has been positive for firms with strong portfolios, who are now able to capture considerable benefit from their patent estates. Firms that are high net users of others' patents have a choice. They must increasingly pay royalties, or they must develop their own portfolios so as to bring something to the table in cross-licensing negotiations.

CALIFORNIA MANAGEMENT REVIEW   VOL 39, NO. 2   WINTER 1997

The new environment affords new challenges. If a firm is to compete with advanced products and processes, it is likely to utilize not only its own technology, but also the patents of others. In many advanced products, the range of technology is too great for a single firm to develop its entire needs internally. In cumulative technology fields such as electronics and semiconductors, one innovation builds on another. There are inevitably overlapping developments and mutually blocking patents. It is likely that firms will need to cross-license patents from others to ensure that they have freedom to manufacture without infringement. Thus in many industries today, firms can generate value from their innovation not only by embedding it in new products and processes, but also through engaging in licensing and cross-licensing.

In electronics and semiconductors, cross-licensing is generally more complex than the exchange of individual patent rights. The size of the patent portfolios of some firms is often too great for it to be feasible to identify individual infringements. Companies may own thousands of patents, used in literally tens of thousands of products, and may add hundreds more each year. With this degree of overlap of technology, companies protect themselves against mutual infringement by cross-licensing portfolios of all current and future patents in a field-of-use, without making specific reference to individual patents. It is simply too cumbersome and costly to license only the specific patents you need for specific products. The portfolio approach reduces transactions costs and allows licensees freedom to design and manufacture without infringement.[3]

An important dimension of field-of-use cross-licensing is the calculation of balancing royalty payments, according to the relative value of the patent portfolios of each party. This calculation is made prospectively, based on a sample of each firm's leading patents. Weight is given to the quality and market coverage of the patents. Desirable portfolios have excellent patents covering technology widely used in the industry. A quality portfolio is a powerful lever in negotiating access to required technology and may lead to significant royalty earnings or, at a minimum, to reduced payments to others. Obviously, a firm which is a large net user of other firms' patents, without contributing comparable IP in exchange, is likely to have to pay significant royalties.

Many managers now understand the use of licensing and cross-licensing as part of business strategy as well as the importance of a valuable patent portfolio. The key to successful cross-licensing is a portfolio of quality patents that covers large areas of the partner's product markets. Significantly, for the balancing process, the firm should not necessarily emulate the portfolio of its cross-licensing partner. Rather it should concentrate R&D in those areas in which it does best and has the most comparative advantage to develop patents that its partners need. This will give maximum leverage in negotiating access and balancing royalties. This might be in product design, software, or manufacturing processes, wherever the firm's R&D is most effective and its IP most widely used. In this sense, cross-licensing has a double positive effect on innovation. It allows firms greater means of earning a return on innovation (to help fund further

R&D), while allowing firms to concentrate their innovation and patenting activities according to their comparative advantage. In this way, firms can develop complementary rather than duplicative technology, thereby benefiting the public interest.

The unprecedented rates of technological development in the electronics industries have been made possible by a combination of the ability to capture value from innovation and the freedom to design and manufacture. Cross-licensing has been crucial. A key lesson for managers is to be aware of the value of developing a strong, high-quality IP portfolio and the effect this can have on licensing and cross-licensing strategies. This protects the firm's innovations and may significantly reduce royalty payments and fund further R&D.

The Licensing Legacy

Background—The Formation of RCA

Cross-licensing is not a new phenomenon in electronics; it goes back almost to the beginning of the industry. Cross-licensing is typical of industries involved in "cumulative systems technologies," where one innovation builds on another and products may draw on several related technologies. Multiple firms develop patented innovations in the same technological fields, and the "state of the art" of the technology tends to be covered by a large number of different patents held by different firms. Because of the potential for mutually blocking patents, firms typically cross-license all patents in a field-of-use to ensure adequate access to technology. The strongest examples of cumulative systems technologies are in electronics, including computers and semiconductors, where extensive cross-licensing ensures "design freedom" or "freedom-to-manufacture."[4] Note that this is a different situation than in some other industries not characterized by cumulative systems technologies, such as chemicals and pharmaceuticals, where cross-licensing, or, rather, reciprocal licensing, is typically aimed at exchanging technology rather than avoiding patent interference.[5]

An important instance of field-of-use cross-licensing is the development of radio in the first quarter of this century.[6] It epitomizes the complexities surrounding intellectual property arrangements that may be encountered with cumulative systems technologies. Also, many of the cross-licensing ideas used later by the electronics industry were pioneered during the early days of radio.

The commercialization of radio required a number of basic inventions. The scientific basis for wireless was developed by university scientists such as Maxwell, Hertz, and Lodge in the 19th century. Their discoveries were first applied to practical communication with the development of wireless telegraphy by Marconi in Britain in 1896. The first speech transmissions were made in the U.S. by Fessenden in 1900, using a high-frequency alternator. Further basic innovations were made over the next two decades.[7]

Many of these inventions were initially developed by individuals working independently of each other. Indeed, many carry the name of the inventor, such as the Poulsen arc, the Fleming valve, and the de Forest triode.[8] As the potential for radio became apparent, and the need for large-scale R&D and investment grew, large corporations entered the field. The pace of development accelerated and the number of patents multiplied. The companies involved included Marconi, General Electric (GE), Westinghouse, AT&T, Telefunken, and others. In addition to their considerable R&D effort, these corporations also acquired key patents where appropriate.[9] There was considerable competition, and with research teams in different companies working in parallel, patent interferences were common.[10] By 1918, it was apparent that several technologies were needed to manufacture radio systems, and each of these technologies itself involved multiple patents from different firms. In the words of Armstrong, one of the pioneers of radio, "It was absolutely impossible to manufacture any kind of workable apparatus without using practically all of the inventions which were then known."[11]

The result was deadlock. A number of firms had important patent positions and could block each other's access to key components. They refused to cross-license each other. It was a "Mexican standoff," with each firm holding up the development of the industry.[12] The situation arose in large part as a result of the way radio had developed. Key patent portfolios had been developed by different individuals and corporations, who were often adamant about refusing to cross-license competitors. Also, in a new industry in which large scale interference was a novel problem, there was no well developed means of coordinating cross-licensing agreements between these groups.

The situation was resolved in the U.S. only when, under prompting by the U.S. Navy, the various pioneers formed the Radio Corporation of America (RCA) in 1919.[13] This broke a key source of the deadlock. RCA acquired the U.S. rights to the Marconi patents, and cross-licensed the U.S. rights for other major patent portfolios.[14] The major U.S. patent holders became shareholders in RCA. In this way, RCA acquired the U.S. rights to all the constituent radio patents under one roof—amounting to over 2,000 patents.[15] It established RCA as the technical leader in radio, but also enabled the other cross-licensees to continue their own development of the technology for use in other fields or as suppliers to RCA. The RCA cross-licensing agreements became a model for the future.[16]

The case shows that because of the reluctance of the parties to cross-license, technological progress and the further commercialization of radio was halted. In this case, the debacle was resolved only by the formation of RCA, a rather radical organizational solution. However, it became clear from the experience that the same ends—namely design freedom—may be achieved more simply, without such fundamental reorganization, by cross-licensing alone. This helped set the stage for further development of cross-licensing in electronics.

AT&T's Cross-Licensing Practices

The need to achieve design freedom was soon experienced in other fields of electronics and resulted in patent cross-licensing agreements. One of the most influential firms in shaping the industry practices was AT&T, whose licensing and cross-licensing policy, especially from the 1940s until its breakup in 1984, has been crucial to the development of similar practices in U.S. electronics and semiconductor industries.

Over its long history, AT&T's licensing policy has had three phases, reflecting changes in its overall business strategy. First, from AT&T's establishment in 1885 until its first antitrust-related commitment in 1913, it used its IP rights in a forthright fashion to establish itself in the service market.[17] In the second phase, from 1914 until 1984, AT&T became a regulated monopoly. Its policy (as a matter of law under the 1956 antitrust consent decree) was to openly license its IP to everyone for minimal fees. Reasons of technology access similar to those in radio led to patent cross-license agreements between the major producers of telephone equipment, starting in the 1920s. This developed into a more widespread policy. It was during this period that the transistor was invented at Bell Labs. This and other breakthroughs laid the foundation for the semiconductor industry and shaped the development of the telecommunications, computer, and electronics industries. In the current phase, dating from divestiture in 1984, AT&T is no longer bound by the consent decree, and its IP licensing can be aligned with its proprietary needs.[18]

The 1956 antitrust consent decree required AT&T to openly license all patents controlled by the Bell System to any applicant at "reasonable royalties," provided that the licensee also grant licenses at reasonable royalties in return. AT&T was also required to provide technical information with the licenses on payment of reasonable fees; licensees had the right to sublicense the technology to their associates.[19] The impact of AT&T's liberal licensing on the industry was considerable, especially when considered in parallel with that at IBM.[20]

To a large extent, the licensing terms in AT&T's 1956 decree simply codified what was already AT&T policy. As an enterprise under rate-of-return regulation, it had little reason to maximize royalty income from its IP. Instead, it used its technology and IP to promote new services and reduce costs. It procured a tremendous amount of equipment and materials on the open market and apparently figured that its service customers would be better off if its technologies were widely diffused amongst its actual and potential suppliers, as this would lower prices and increase the performance of procured components.[21] It was the first company we are aware of to have "design freedom" as a core component of its patent strategy. It did not see licensing income as a source of funds for R&D, as Bell Labs research was largely funded by the "license contract fee," assessed on the annual revenues of the Bell operating companies. This very stable source of research funding supported a constant stream of basic innovations.[22] Using its own portfolio as leverage, AT&T was able to obtain the (reciprocal) rights it needed to continue to innovate, unimpeded by the IP of others. It successfully accomplished this limited objective.

An interesting aspect of AT&T's IP strategy was that technologies (though not R&D programs) were often selected for patent protection based on their potential interest to other firms generating technology of interest to AT&T. Since the legal requirement for open licensing specifically did not extinguish all of AT&T's intellectual property rights, the company was able to gain access to the external technology that it needed, while contributing enormously to innovation in telecommunications, computers, and electronics worldwide.[23]

The terms of AT&T's licenses set a pattern that is still commonplace in the electronics industries. The "capture model" was defined in the consent decree.[24] Under this arrangement, the licensee is granted the right to use existing patents and any obtained for inventions made during a fixed capture period of no more than five years, followed by a survivorship period until the expiration of these patents and with subsequent agreement renewals. The open licensing regimes this led to were persistent, since with the long survivorship period on many of the basic patents, there was limited scope to introduce more stringent conditions for new patents.

AT&T's licensing policy had the effect of making its tremendously large IP portfolio available to the industry worldwide for next to nothing. This portfolio included fundamental patents such as the transistor, basic semiconductor technology, and the laser, and included many other basic patents in telecommunications, computing, optoelectronics, and superconductivity. Shaped under antitrust policy reflecting the needs and beliefs of an era in which U.S. firms did not have to worry much about foreign competition, such a liberal policy appears quite anachronistic today. However, there is no doubt that it provided a tremendous contribution to world welfare. It remains as one of the most unheralded contributions to economic development—possibly far exceeding the Marshall Plan in terms of the wealth generation capability it established abroad and in the United States.

The traditional cross-licensing policy of AT&T was greatly extended following the invention of the transistor. Widespread "field-of-use" licenses in the semiconductor industry is a legacy, as the industry was founded on the basic semiconductor technology developed by AT&T. In the early days of semiconductor technology, AT&T controlled most of the key patents in the field. It soon realized that, given the importance of semiconductor technology, other electronics companies were developing their own technologies and could eventually invent around the AT&T patents. Cross-licensing ensured that AT&T would have reciprocal access to this technology and be able to develop its own technology without risking patent interference.[25]

AT&T's liberal licensing allowed the semiconductor industry to grow rapidly, and members of the industry did not care much about individual patents. The culture of the industry still reflects this, with a tradition of spin-outs and new ventures, open communications and frequent job changes.[26] The continued speed of technological progress in the industry and the difficulty of monitoring technological use are reasons why there is still a need for the transactional simplicity associated with "lump-sum" or bundled licensing.[27] With individual product life cycles short compared with the long patent lives, any new innovation is likely to infringe several existing patents. Licensing thus typically involves clusters of patents.

Not surprisingly, AT&T now uses its IP more strategically. No longer bound by the consent decree, and with R&D funding no longer guaranteed by the telephone subscribers, its IP policy is necessarily linked more closely to individual business opportunities. This is especially true of trade secret licensing, which is often a key component of international joint ventures, involving omnibus IP agreements combining patents, trademarks, and know-how.

Cross-Licensing in the Computer Industry—IBM

A second major influence on licensing practice across the electronics industry has been IBM. It has long been heavily involved in licensing and cross-licensing its technology, both as a means of accessing external technology and to earn revenues. In many ways, it has been in a similar position to AT&T in that it has been a wellspring of new technology but was also subject to a consent decree in 1956 that had certain compulsory licensing terms. Under the IBM consent decree, IBM was required to grant non-exclusive, non-transferable, worldwide licenses for any or all of its patents at reasonable royalties (royalty free for existing tabulating card/machinery patents) to any applicant—provided the applicant also offered to cross-license its patents to IBM on similar terms. The provision covered all existing patents at the time of the decree (i.e., as of 1956) plus any that were filed during the next five years. The rights lasted for the full term of the patents.[28]

IBM's cross-licensing activity continues today. IBM states that it is "exploiting our technology in the industry through agreements with companies like Hitachi, Toshiba, Canon, and Cyrix." Patent and technology licensing agreements earned $640 million in cash for IBM in 1994.[29] IBM is one of the world's leading innovators, with more U.S. patents granted in each of the three years from 1993 to 1995 than any other company (see Table 1).

The central importance IBM attaches to its patent portfolio in providing an arsenal of patents for use in cross-licensing and negotiating access to outside technology has been borne out in public statements by the company.[30] For IBM, the main object of its licensing policy has been "design freedom," to ensure "the right to manufacture and market products." To be able to manufacture products, IBM needs rights to technology owned by others:

> Market driven quality demands that we shorten our cycle times. This means we have to speed up the process of innovation. And that means there is less time to invent everything we need. We can't do everything ourselves. IBM needs to have access to the inventions of others.[31]

TABLE 1. Top Ten U.S. Patent Recipients (1990-1995)

Company	US Patents Received					
	1990	**1991**	**1992**	**1993**	**1994**	**1995**
IBM	608	684	851	1,088	1,305	1,383
Canon	868	831	1,115	1,039	1,100	1,088
Motorola	396	614	662	731	839	1,012
NEC	448	441	462	602	901	1,005
Mitsubishi	862	964	977	944	998	971
Toshiba	891	1,031	1,036	1,064	985	970
Hitachi	902	962	973	949	1,002	909
Matsushita	351	467	616	722	782	852
Eastman Kodak	720	863	778	1008	890	772
General Electric	785	818	943	942	973	757

Source: IFI/Plenum Data Corp., USPTO

It acquires these rights "primarily by trading access to its own patents, a process called 'cross-licensing'."[32] IBM has often had the reputation of being a "fast follower" in some areas of technology, and it has used the power of its patent portfolio to negotiate the access needed. The company notes that:

> You get value from patents in two ways: through fees, and through licensing negotiations that give IBM access to other patents. Access is far more valuable to IBM than the fees it receives from its 9,000 active [U.S.] patents. There is no direct calculation of this value, but it is many times larger than the fee income, perhaps an order of magnitude larger.[33]

The effect of the consent decree for IBM, as for AT&T, was in large part to formalize policies that were already partly in effect. While IBM already used cross-licensing for design freedom where appropriate, the consent decree expanded the scope and in a sense prodded IBM into treating licensing and cross-licensing as a central aspect of its business.

Impact of Consent Decrees on Industry Development

The combined cross-licensing of basic technology by the technologically leading firms—AT&T, IBM, and others—had a profound influence on the development of the post-war electronics industry. The effect of the 1956 AT&T and IBM consent decrees was to make a huge range of basic semiconductor and telecommunications technology widely available for next to nothing to domestic and foreign firms. Even so, for AT&T and its existing cross-licensing partners, the AT&T 1956 consent decree merely formalized what was already established corporate policy. This was exchanged for rights to related technology where this was available; otherwise it was offered at low royalty payments. The availability

of the basic technology formed the basis for the rapid growth of the semiconductor industry. Given the common technological base, firms relied on the rapid
development and introduction of new products to succeed.

Yet the very prevalence of AT&T, IBM, and others in licensing at low
royalties also created a mind set in the industry that became accustomed to
artificially low royalties. This contributed to some initial agitation, if not outrage,
in some quarters when in the 1980s some intellectual property owners such as
Texas Instruments began to seek market returns on their IP.[34]

Licensing Practice at a Semiconductor Company— Texas Instruments[35]

Licensing Objectives

In the semiconductor industry, IP licensing is an integral and essential
element of competition, and a corollary of innovation. As noted above, the
industry was launched with the invention of the transistor by Bell Laboratories
in 1947. First commercial transistor production took place in 1952. By 1995,
worldwide sales of the industry were over $150 billion. Like other parts of the
electronics industry, the semiconductor industry is characterized by wide use
of cross-licensing. The main purpose of cross-licensing is to ensure "freedom-to-
operate" or "design freedom" in an industry where there are likely to be large
numbers of overlapping patents. Given rapid technological development and
many industry participants, the probability is high that any new product or
process will overlap technology developed by other firms pursuing parallel
paths. Also, the technology often overlaps that developed in related industries,
such as computers and telecommunications.

The licensing procedures and royalty rate determination process at Texas
Instruments (TI) illustrates the ways in which cross-licensing agreements are.
used in practice. TI has two main licensing objectives. The first and primary
objective is to ensure freedom to operate in broad areas of technology supporting given product markets, without running the risk of patent infringement litigation by other firms with similar technology. Agreements cover groups of
patents within designated "fields-of-use," including existing and new patents
developed within the fixed term of the agreement. The second objective is to
obtain value from the firm's IP, in the form of its patent portfolio, by generating
royalty income. The purpose and result of royalty payments received under
cross-licensing agreements is "competitive re-balancing," which equalizes the
net cost and profit advantage for imitators who otherwise might free-ride on
technology TI developed.

Buying "freedom-to-operate" is vital in the semiconductor industry, with
its rapid innovation, short product life cycles, and ubiquity of patents. In a typical technological field, there may be as many as a half dozen other firms with
patents that an innovator could potentially infringe while implementing its

independent research strategy. In semiconductor devices and manufacture, there are huge numbers of patents to consider, with many more generated each year, as seen in Table 2. Bear in mind that a particular product can utilize technology from several other technology fields, such as computers, software, materials, communications, and general systems, each with large patent establishments.

At the start of an R&D program, possible infringements cannot be easily predicted, as firms are quite ignorant of the R&D and product development plans of competitors. Yet a firm investing in R&D and product development needs to be confident that patents developed through independent R&D efforts by others will not hinder commercialization of its technology. Consider that a wafer production facility now costs $1 billion.[36] The facility may have a five-year life or longer, and it is not known in advance what products will be developed for manufacture during that time. R&D is similarly becoming more expensive. Companies need to be able to develop new products to fill the wafer fabrication facilities without being concerned that startup may be blocked by patents owned by competitors and other companies inside and outside the industry.

TABLE 2. U.S. Patents Granted in Semiconductor Devices and Manufacture (1969-1994)

Company*	Patents granted (1969-94)	Patents granted (1994)
IBM	3,435	220
Toshiba	2,492	245
Texas Instruments	2,366	231
AT&T	2,342	110
Hitachi	2,218	170
Motorola	1,882	210
Mitsubishi	1,691	275
RCA	1,601	0
Siemens	1,518	46
U.S. Philips	1,482	61
General Electric	1,446	48
NEC	1,360	261
Fujitsu	1,335	125

* Companies with over 1,000 semiconductor patents granted (1969-94).
Source: USPTO, 1995

One approach for a developer to deal with the IP rights of others would be simply to identify all infringements as they arise, and negotiate separate licenses for each. However, the transactions costs of such an approach would be inordinate.[37] Moreover, it would expose the potential licensee to large risks.

A typical cross-license includes all patents that licensees may own in a given field-of-use, giving each firm the freedom to infringe the other's existing and future patents for a given period, typically five years. Such licenses are typically non-exclusive and rarely include any trade-secret or know-how transfer or sublicensing rights.[38]

In a cross-license, technology is not usually transferred, as the parties each are capable of using the technology in question without assistance. Firms will usually gain access to the relevant technology either by developing it themselves, or by other means such as reverse engineering, hiring consultants, other technical agreements, or technical publications.[39] In either case, the cross-license primarily confers the right to use the patented technology without being sued for infringement. This avoids monitoring costs and adjusts royalty payments to reflect overall contributions to the stock of IP currently in use.[40]

In the semiconductor industry, licensing agreements sometimes go further, and may include transfer of trade secrets and know-how. However, trade secret licenses are quite different, typically involve technology transfer, and often accompany a joint venture or strategic alliance. Technology transfer involves significant costs and managerial effort, and often "creates competitors', as it frequently transfers to the licensee important technological capabilities otherwise inaccessible.[41]

Types of Cross-Licenses

There are two main models for cross-licensing agreements in the semiconductor industry: "capture" and "fixed period." In the "capture" model the licensee has rights to use, in a given field-of-use, all patents within a technological field which exist or are applied for during the license period, usually five years, and, importantly, retains "survivorship" rights to use the patents until they expire, up to 20 years later. The agreement does not generally list individual patents, but some patents of particular strategic importance to the licensor may be excluded. In the "fixed period" model the licensee has similar rights to use patents existing or applied for during the license period, but with no survivorship rights once the license period has expired. This requires full renegotiation of the cross-license for succeeding periods.

TI has been a leader in the use of fixed period licensing, which is becoming more widely used. The capture model became widespread through the industry following its use by AT&T and IBM. It gives broad rights to patents for a long period. The fixed period model allows more flexible commercialization of patent portfolios, since licensing terms can be periodically adjusted to account for changes in competitive conditions and the value of the technology. This increases strategic flexibility and allows the parties more freedom to negotiate royalty terms so that they more closely mirror the value of the patents. It is a logical evolution of licensing practices reflecting the difficulties and changes in the market for know-how.

"Proud List" Royalty Valuation Process

Balancing payments are negotiated as part of the agreement, to account for the relative value of the IP contributed by two firms. Each firm's contribution is evaluated by estimating the value of a firm's patent portfolio to its licensing partner, with the net royalty payment to the one with the greater contribution. Where both firms contribute similar portfolio values, the net payment will be small or zero. Where one firm has developed little technology and the other a great deal, the payments may be significant. Occasionally, cross-licenses are royalty-free because contributions are either very close or difficult to assess. However, even in royalty-free agreements it should not be assumed that a detailed patent balancing process has not taken place. Also, the cross-license may be included as part of a larger joint venture.

Royalty balancing is performed according to a "proud list" procedure. In this procedure, each firm identifies a sample list of its most valuable patents and this is used as a representative proxy group for estimating the value of the entire portfolio. There is a great deal of preparation before the negotiations. Having identified a potential cross-licensing candidate, TI first performs extensive reverse engineering of the other's products to assess the extent of any infringement—called "reading" the patents on the infringer's products—and identifies product market sizes involved. This may take a year of effort.[42] As part of this effort, it generates the proud list of about 50 of its major patents which it believes are being infringed, and which apply over a large product base of the other firm. The other firm also prepares a proud list of its own strongest patents.

In the negotiations, each of the sample patents is evaluated by both sides according to its quality and coverage. Quality measures include: the legal validity and enforceability of the patent; the technological significance of this feature to the product compared with other (non-infringing) ways of achieving the same end; and the similarity between the infringing features and the patent. These determine quality weighting factors for each patent so that a legally strong patent, which is hard to invent-around and is close to the infringing feature, has a high relative weight. The coverage is the size of the infringer's product market using the patent. Each patent is assigned a nominal royalty rate, which is then multiplied by its quality weighting factor and the annual sales of the affected product base to arrive at a dollar amount. Certain patents of particular strategic significance to the technology are assigned a flat rate as a group and do not go through the weighting process.

The dollar amounts are summed for all the listed patents and expressed as a royalty rate percentage of the licensee's total sales. Typically, the values of each side's estimated royalty payments are netted out to give a single royalty rate paid by the firm with the less valuable portfolio.[43] This royalty rate applies to the licensee's sales for the term of the license. When the license expires the same procedure will be used to reevaluate the relative portfolio values for the next five years.[44]

Strategic Considerations

TI's procedures provide a formal mechanism for determining royalty rates based on best estimates of the economic and technological contribution of the patent portfolios of the two firms. These procedures have been applied to a wide variety of relative IP contributions, both where these are roughly in balance and where not. Even so, there are often other considerations to include in final negotiations of a licensing agreement. Much depends on the individual needs of the parties, their negotiating strength, and the broader strategic considerations of each firm. Individual rates and the overall rates also tend to recognize overall competitive effects of the royalty payments, as well as "what the market will bear."[45]

There is obviously an upper limit on royalties, since royalties that are too high will cripple the competitive capacities of the licensee, causing royalty payments to decline. If a potential problem in this respect exists, it is usually not with an individual agreement, which is likely to be set at reasonable royalty rates. Rather, problems may arise when a licensee is subject to claims from several licensors and the cumulative royalty payments become onerous. This can create serious problems in negotiating agreements with would-be licensees. There does not seem to be an easy solution to this problem, given that agreements are negotiated individually.[46]

Royalty rates may also be affected by longer-term strategic considerations. For one thing, both parties are likely to need to renew the agreement in future, and an aggressive royalty rate now may make negotiations more difficult later, when the balance of IP may have shifted in a different direction. The firms may have, or expect to have, overlapping interests in other market areas, which will also condition negotiations. Licenses often may also be part of a cooperative venture of some kind. Patents can often be traded for know-how, or used as an entry ticket to a joint development arrangement. For example, rather than seek royalties, TI has had technology development agreements with Hitachi. It also has several manufacturing joint ventures around the world.

Strategic considerations may also affect the usual licensing process where the technology is intended to become part of an industry standard. Industry standards bodies sometimes require that patent holders agree to license their patents with low or zero royalty fees, often on a non-discriminatory basis. Similarly, when trying to establish a *de facto* market standard, a firm may charge low royalty rates.[47] The aim is to ensure the wide adoption of the technology as an industry-wide standard. Value from the technology may then be earned through product sales in an expanded market. The "reasonable rate" royalty involved is likely to be low, though need not be zero.[48]

Impact of TI's Licensing Strategy

TI has led industry moves to take a more active stance on licensing and cross-licensing. The impact of its licensing strategy on its capability to compete and innovate is of particular interest. TI instituted its current licensing strategy in 1985. Cumulative royalty earnings of over $1.8 billion had been achieved during the period from 1986 to 1993. Among other effects, this enabled TI to maintain a high level of R&D spending during 1989-91, when the semiconductor market was in a downturn, as shown in Figure 1. However, moving to a more active licensing strategy and the aggressive assertion of its IP rights was a major step for the company—and the industry—and involved considerable risk.[49] TI's strategy was enhanced by the stronger U.S. treatment of IP after 1982.

Managing Intellectual Capital

FIGURE I.   Texas Instruments: Royalty Earnings, Net Income and R&D

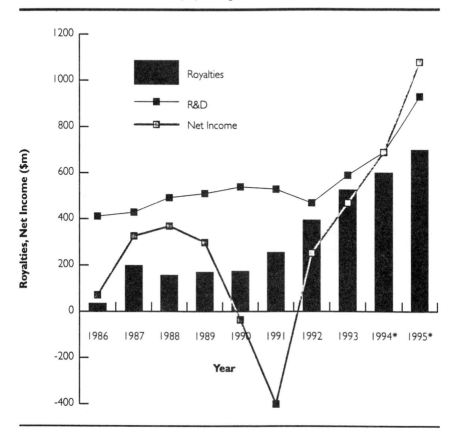

*Royalties for 1994 and 1995 estimated
Source: Annual Reports

TI's IP portfolio has been valuable in negotiating R&D cooperation. For example, TI has had a series of ventures with Hitachi for the joint technological development of DRAM memory chips. TI's ability to supply technology, supported by its IP rights, was a crucial component in making these agreements.[50] TI's changed IP strategy has allowed it to implement new product market strategies to expand its manufacturing capacity by means of joint ventures, based partly on the negotiating value of its IP portfolio, and expanding its development of high value added components. It has been a partner in a number of international manufacturing joint ventures to set up production facilities for memory

Managing Intellectual Capital

TABLE 3. Top 10 Merchant Semiconductor Firms: 1980-1995

	1980			1990			1995		
	Company	$m	%	Company	$m	%	Company	$m	%
1	Texas Inst.	1,580	12.2	NEC	4,952	8.6	Intel	13,830	8.9
2	Motorola	1,110	8.5	Toshiba	4,905	8.5	NEC	11,360	7.3
3	Philips	935	7.2	Hitachi	3,927	6.8	Toshiba	10,190	6.6
4	NEC	787	6.1	Intel	3,135	5.5	Hitachi	9,420	6.1
5	National	747	5.7	Fujitsu	3,019	5.3	Motorola	9,170	5.9
6	Toshiba	629	4.8	Motorola	3,692	6.4	Samsung	8,340	5.4
7	Hitachi	622	4.8	Texas Inst.	2,574	4.5	Texas Inst.	8,000	5.2
8	Intel	575	4.4	Mitsubishi	2,476	4.3	Fujitsu	5,510	3.6
9	Fairchild	566	4.4	Matsushita	1,945	3.4	Mitsubishi	5,150	3.3
10	Siemens	413	3.2	Philips	1,932	3.4	Philips	4,040	2.6
	Others	5036	38.7	Others	24,943	43.4	Others	69,990	45.2
	Total	**13,000**	**100.0**	**Total**	**57,500**	**100.0**	**Total**	**155,000**	**100.0**

Source: Dataquest

chip production.[51] TI and Hitachi also entered a joint venture in 1996 to manu-facture DRAMs in Texas.

These changes have had a major impact on TI's performance, helping the company to grow and to increase its world market share since the mid 1980s. This helped reverse a relative decline in its position beginning in the mid-1970s due to inroads made in world markets by foreign producers, as seen in Table 3.

IP Management and Cross-Licensing in an Electronics Company—Hewlett-Packard[52]

Innovation Strategy

Many aspects of licensing elsewhere in electronics are similar to those described for semiconductors. The electronics industry shares many of the basic features of the semiconductor industry: rapid technological innovation, short product life cycles, and significant patenting. The computer, telecommunica-tions, electronics, and semiconductor industries also use many of the same tech-nologies and have been influenced by the practices of AT&T and other major corporations. Field-of-use cross-licensing is used widely.

However, a difference between many electronics firms outside of semiconductors is the breadth of technologies that are practiced. In addition to semiconductor technology, product development may involve integrating many aspects of computing, telecommunications, software, systems design, mechanical engineering, ergonomics and so forth. There are also likely to be complex manufacturing and marketing requirements. Thus, IP strategies in such firms are likely to involve broader considerations.

Hewlett-Packard (HP) produces many different types of products, from laser printers and computers to hand-held calculators and electronic instruments. HP is currently organized into Computer Products, Systems, Measurement Systems, and Test and Measurement organizations.

To maintain its high rate of innovation, a high priority for HP in its IP strategy is maintaining "design freedom." It has two principal objectives: ensuring that its own technology is not blocked by competitors' patents; and ensuring that it has access to outside technology. HP's products include complex systems that typically involve several different technologies, some of which may be developed by other firms and other industries. HP alone can not develop the complete range of technologies used in its products. To obtain access to needed technologies, Hewlett-Packard needs patents to trade in cross-licensing agreements. The company has a huge portfolio of patents and know-how in leading-edge technologies, developed as part of its extensive R&D programs. This IP portfolio is the basis for protecting HP's own products; it is also invaluable as leverage to ensure access to outside technology.

Licensing Objectives

One type of HP cross-licensing takes place as "program licensing," which is aimed at acquiring access to specific technologies. The company identifies firms with technologies of interest. There may be several different technologies at a given firm so the strategic overlaps must be considered in assessing each licensing opportunity.

HP's licensing activities are not focused primarily on cash income. With a wide range of products, the company's interests in one area are likely to overlap with those in other areas. It may encounter licensing partners in several different markets in a variety of circumstances—a competitor in one field may be a supplier or customer in another. HP does not want negotiations in one product group to interfere with those in another. This leads to a long-term bias towards meaningful cross-licensing agreements and a soft approach to royalties. HP recognizes that it is likely to deal with the same partners repeatedly and therefore normally does not require high royalty rates that could be used as a precedent against it in the future.

There are some exceptions in that some strategic patents are only licensed at high royalty rates, or more likely are not licensed at all. In products where HP has a strong leadership position (e.g. printers), it is unlikely to license out its core IP rights. HP's IP policy in this area is aimed, as it must be, at the aggressive protection of a key source of competitive advantage. The company would normally consider licensing such IP rights only as part of a specific strategic alliance and would normally exclude such technology from cross-licensing agreements.

The form of the cross-license agreements is quite standard, with a limited capture period, usually with survivorship rights. The objective is to estimate the relative value of the infringements that are likely to take place over a five-year period. Other inputs to the licensing decision include the expected R&D spending in the field by each firm, the number of patents held by each party in the particular field, and determination of the value to the infringer of a limited number of pertinent patents. Each side to the agreement may select a limited number of patents which it has determined are being infringed by the other party's products. This may be as few as six to twelve patents each. The imputed royalty fee for these patents over the next five years becomes one of the inputs to the negotiation. In general, this balancing process is not unlike that which exists in the semiconductor industry.

Royalties are often paid as a lump sum. Agreements almost never include sublicensing rights, since the company could lose control of its own technology if sublicensing were permitted. Exclusive licensing is also rare, partly because of potential antitrust concerns, but also because the historical practice of non-exclusive cross-licensing leaves fewer innovations that could be treated as exclusive.

Even after a patent cross-license agreement is concluded, HP policy is not to over-use the technology of the other party to the agreement. This is again related to a long-term view of licensing. The agreement will probably need to be renewed in the future and the more of the other party's technology HP uses, the greater the leverage the other party would have the next time around. Also, patents are lagging indicators of research, so that to be at the forefront of technology each party will need to have developed its own application of the technology well before the patents are issued. One purpose of the agreement is to be able to use the technology in the development of new products without worrying about "accidental infringement."

Licensing is only secondarily seen as a source of royalty earnings. Royalty earnings are significant but not material, given the overall size of HP's operations. However, there are some cases where licensing for revenue is pursued. One is where the company has world-class technology and is approached by others seeking a license. If the technology is not of strategic importance to HP, the company may license it out for profit. Another is the "rifle shot" license, where a single patent may be licensed, if it has specific value to a licensee. Licensing terms in either case are usually very simple, amounting to an agreement to allow use of the innovation for a royalty payment or lump sum without being subject to an infringement claim.

IP Management

Given the importance of IP to Hewlett-Packard, a formal IP strategy has been developed for managing its large and diverse IP portfolio. Since products combine many technologies, IP may need to be even more closely integrated with business strategy than at a single product corporation. HP has a series of

FIGURE 2. Intellectual Property and Patenting Decision Process at HP

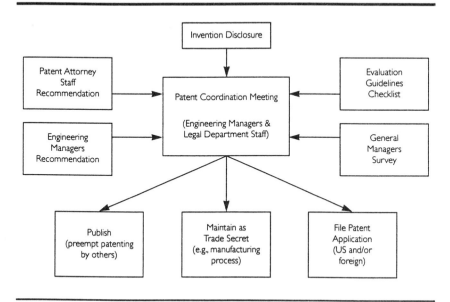

procedures for identifying technological areas to stress for patent protection and for making individual decisions about the best method of protecting innovations. Obtaining and maintaining patent protection is costly, and hence only selected innovations are patented. This process starts with "templates" to guide what IP should be protected. The templates are updated each year to protect technologies that will be strategically important to the company in the future. These templates are developed by a process that rates and prioritizes products and technologies and reviews patent needs throughout the world. This does not go as far as targeting R&D programs at innovations that will be useful in negotiating cross-licenses; rather it aims to make maximum use of innovations by creating patent portfolios that will be strategically valuable. This supports rather than directs corporate strategy.

The IP protection decision process for individual innovations is shown in Figure 2. When a product or process innovation is developed, a determination is made whether to patent it, to keep it as a trade secret, or, if not believed worthwhile to patent, to publish it. The inputs to this decision take place in an internal committee process, with inputs from engineering management and the legal (IP) department. Innovations that are likely to be of strategic value are either patented immediately or, if they are not yet completed or proven, are reviewed again at a later time. If the innovation is valuable but its use by an imitator would be undetectable (such as for some process innovations), then the innovation may be kept as a trade secret. Marginal ideas are published immediately to preempt patenting by a competitor who might later block their use by HP. "Vanity publishers" for publicly disclosing the results of research exist for this purpose.[53]

Managing Intellectual Capital in the Electronics Industry

Contrasting IP Management Objectives

The case studies indicate several similarities in the way firms in the electronics industry use licensing and cross-licensing to ensure design freedom as well as some level of licensing earnings. They also illustrate how differences in management objectives are reflected in cross-licensing strategies.

RCA represents a rather complex organizational response to the problem of design freedom, in which a single company acquired exclusive cross-licensed rights to all the patents needed for radio manufacture. It then licensed out these rights to other manufacturers. Partly as a result, RCA was able to dominate the radio market for many years.

AT&T, as a regulated monopoly before 1984, was primarily interested in the dissemination of technology to as many producers as possible, to develop technologies that would be useful in its telecommunications services—as purchased components or in its own systems development. It was barred from competing in product markets, so it cross-licensed on liberal terms with the aim of stimulating development and obtaining access to new technology.

A primary concern of IBM in cross-licensing has been design freedom. As one of the world's leading innovators it has been very active in using its IP for competitive advantage, both in products and to obtain the widest possible access to other technology. IBM's interests have spanned a wide range of computer related markets and it has needed broad access to many different technologies. It also obtains significant income from its licenses.

TI's interests have generally been more specific to the semiconductor industry, although it also has interests in other areas of electronics. Its concerns have been to obtain freedom-to-operate given the dense patent concentration in semiconductors, and to obtain cash from cross-licensing its IP, to help fund R&D and to equalize any advantage it would otherwise be allowing competitors using its IP.

Finally, HP is in a somewhat similar position to IBM in having a broad range of interests in different markets and being especially interested in design freedom for products spanning many technologies. HP's breadth of interests—in which a competitor in one field may be a customer, supplier, or venture partner in another—moderates its approach to seeking high royalties. IP is central to its business, needed to support its rapid product innovation and to trade for technology access. It has well developed procedures for developing and protecting IP across its diverse fields.

Changing IP Modes in the Semiconductor Industry

The strengthening of IP rights and increased licensing and cross-licensing have extended the ability of the innovator to earn a reward from R&D. In addition to providing better IP protection for new products, there are greater opportunities for earning value via access to technology, joint ventures, technology exchanges, and R&D collaboration. Royalty earnings have become more significant. Much of this is a recent development and there are many questions as to how much strategic emphasis firms should place on licensing and cross-licensing compared with manufacturing, and on the importance of licensing revenue earning compared with freedom-to-operate.

It may help put these questions in context by reviewing the changing modes of competition in semiconductors, where firms have gradually needed to place increased stress on innovation, IP protection, and licensing and cross-licensing as a basis for product competition. There have been major changes in the way firms have obtained value from innovation as the industry has developed. The weak IP regime in effect during the first two or three decades of the industry was not a barrier to R&D and investment, and the liberal licensing practices used by AT&T and others accelerated the initial diffusion of the technology. This nurtured the early growth of a new industry. However, firms could not operate successfully in today's technological and competitive environment with the strategies and policies in place in the 1950s and 1960s. Competition to stay at the forefront of innovation is sharper and R&D and investment take place on a much bigger scale. AT&T no longer has a franchise monopoly, the market power of other industry participants is at best a phantom, and the industry is global.

Initial Growth Phase

From 1950 until the late 1970s, semiconductor and electronics firms used technology to open up new markets. Semiconductor technology was new and developing rapidly, and was too big and too important to be developed and commercialized adequately within one organization. There were benefits from having multiple sources of innovation. This was epitomized by AT&T's policy. As a major consumer of semiconductors, it wished to spread the use of the technology as widely as possible. Elements of this reasoning applied to other firms, who benefited from the rapid expansion of technology and markets. And, given the weak protection of IP afforded by the courts at this time, patents were not seen as a major factor in building competitive advantage.[54]

At that time, firms relied primarily on time-to-market advantages to keep ahead. The basic semiconductor patents were already widely licensed, so any individual patent had limited power.[55] Product life cycles were short and often firms would simply not bother to patent inventions, believing that there was no point in patenting products and processes that would soon be obsolete. The fragmented structure of the new "merchant" semiconductor industry (which had grown up around spin-offs from Bell Labs and others), the rapidity of innovation, and the high level of competition reflected the fact that not much attention was paid to protecting IP.[56] The predominant strategy for capturing value from technology involved "riding the experience curve"—reducing prices rapidly as unit costs fell with the hope of earning enough to fund the next round of development.[57]

Second sourcing, licensed or not, was often required by many of the large customers to ensure continuous and competitive supplies. There was significant cross-licensing (often associated with second sourcing), but it rarely involved significant royalty payments.[58] Customers like the Department of Defense (DOD) had sufficient clout to force small suppliers like Intel to second source. During this period, licenses were mainly used to get some residual value from an innovation when it could not be recovered via the product market because of investment restrictions or trade restrictions. An example is the difficulty U.S. firms had selling products in Japan. Faced with effective trade protection, most U.S. firms' only recourse was to license technology to Japanese firms.[59]

At this time, TI was one of the first firms to make strategic use of its IP. It established a production plant in Japan in 1968, one of the very few foreign firms to do so. It achieved these rights from MITI by using the power of its patent portfolio.[60] This heralded a new role for IP in global commerce and firm competitiveness.

Increased Global Competition

The competitive environment began to change during the 1970s. The complexity of the technology and the scale of investment in R&D and capacity were rising, increasing the business risk of each new development. Moreover, as requirements for specialized investment increased, the business risk associated with a patent holder's ability to obtain an injunction (in the case of inadvertent or intentional infringement) increased.

Managers were at first distracted by the increasing size of the total market when new mass markets opened up in the 1970s for consumer electronics (including calculators, watches, and later personal computers) and computer memories. By the early 1980s, new competitors from Japan (and later Korea) had entered the world markets and were challenging the U.S. firms, using technology largely developed in the United States. Changes were most dramatic in the manufacture of "commodity" DRAM memory chips, in which U.S. manufacturers' share of the world market fell from 75% in 1980 to 17% in 1986, while over the same period Japanese memory share rose from 25% to 79%.[61] U.S. firms could no longer rely on success in the product market alone to obtain returns from innovation.

The new entrants to the industry depended on access to existing technology and often sought to cross-license it. Yet nominal or royalty-free cross-licenses, which had been common in the industry prior to the 1980s, came to be seen as unfair when the entrants from outside the industry offered to pay the nominal cross-license fees, but with no balancing portfolios of patents to offer. Royalty fees also reflect payment for access to technology accumulated in prior years, often at great expense. TI and others realized that more detailed evaluation of relative contributions to cross-licenses were required.

Innovation Leadership

The situation today is that, with numerous qualified competitors, competitive advantage requires more emphasis on strong IP rights. Stronger IP protection calls for dual strategies for capturing value from technology—the simultaneous use of product manufacturing using the IP in question together with IP licensing. Market developments have put more emphasis on chip design, developed close to the customer, and on being able to protect this and leading-edge process technology from imitation by fully able competitors. The increase in cooperative R&D and manufacturing joint ventures, often underpinned by IP rights, represent a market response to increased costs and the risks of development.

A regime shift occurred when many of the once small semiconductor firms such as Intel could no longer be forced into second sourcing their products. The demise of contractually required second sourcing suddenly made the value of IP more significant. The successful blunting of buyers' demand for second sourcing made IP more important—so much so that many companies, such as Intel, now have designated IP managers.

Many in the semiconductor industry have been opposed to stronger assertion of IP rights, having grown accustomed to a relatively open exchange of ideas and personnel. Not surprisingly, advocates of this view include start-ups, who claim that if they pay the full price of technology, it would limit their ability to compete. This may be true, but it is also trite. We observe that supporters of open ideas often become more protective once they have invested heavily in R&D. Most significantly, there has been a change in the global competitive reality. What may have been a useful model in the early days of the industry (in which it may be argued that all firms in a local market benefit from mutual exchange of ideas), becomes a different equation when firms are global.[62]

Lessons for Innovation Management

To an extent, management today has little choice but to adopt a more active IP and licensing stance. IP rights have been strengthened and, not surprisingly, firms have become more strategic about commercializing IP. Cross-licensing enables firms to protect their IP while at the same time obtaining freedom to manufacture. The new IP and licensing circumstances have increased incentives to build IP portfolios and to innovate. In these new circumstances, there are some key lessons for innovation management.

Using IP to Support Core Business

Despite, or because of, the growing importance of licensing and cross-licensing, IP strategy should still be designed primarily to support technological developments and strategies surrounding the firm's core business. The global marketplace still rewards firms primarily for developing and commercializing products and processes as such, not for developing IP. Accordingly, few firms target technologies primarily for their value in earning royalties or for trading IP rights in future cross-licensing agreements.

Furthermore, for long-term success, firms typically need to be closely involved with the markets in which they operate and to develop core capabilities (in manufacture and design) closely linked to the products and processes. Maintaining a stream of valuable innovations requires extensive, up-to-date information about market demand and technological possibilities, especially in industries where technology is changing rapidly. Although this depends on the nature of the product, it usually also calls for close functional links between design, production, and marketing. These needs are typically best served by active participation in the product market.[63]

The alternative—becoming a pure "licensing company" not directly involved in the product market and increasingly remote from the manufacture and design of the product itself—can be a risky strategy. Such a strategy, on its own, not only risks the erosion of the dynamic capabilities of the firm to continue innovating, it also is likely to be less financially rewarding than developing and commercializing products.[64]

Importance of Developing a Valuable Patent Portfolio

Developing a valuable patent portfolio is an increasingly important part of strategy. In the electronics industry, patents are valuable because they provide protection from imitation for new proprietary products and services; they provide bargaining chips in negotiating access to other firms' technology (to avoid patent blocking and ensure freedom-to-operate); and patents may be an additional source of earnings or of reduced royalty fees the firm might otherwise have to pay.

The value of a portfolio is greatest when it has a high proportion of high-quality patents that cover significant product markets. These patents affect each of the reasons for holding a portfolio, but are seen most directly in the effect on cross-licensing. Patents have greatest cross-licensing value when they give the firm maximum leverage to obtain a favorable cross-license. This means that the patents should be legally and technically strong and should cover key aspects of the licensee's product base.

Concentrate R&D Where the Firm Is Strongest

In developing its patent portfolio, the firm can concentrate its R&D in those areas where it has the greatest competitive advantage in developing valuable innovations, provided these are also areas needed by other firms. It need not focus on those technological areas where its cross-licensee is strongest in an attempt to duplicate or avoid the licensee's patents—a hopeless task with complex cumulative technology, such as electronics, where infringement is almost inevitable.[65] This might be in the same fields that it wishes to cross-license from its partners, or it might be in a more specialized area. For cross-licensing with a multidivisional corporation with interests in several markets, it might be in a different business area or field-of-use than the one from which it wishes to access technology. As argued above, a firm is most likely to create valuable IP where it is actively involved in the market, i.e., its core business. Provided this is also a commercially important field to cross-licensing partners, the firm can concentrate on developing and protecting IP in this field, rather than seeking another.

Licensing and cross-licensing enable firms to capture value from technology so long as they contribute to the common pool of industry knowledge. Innovators who are contributors have every incentive to avoid duplicative R&D investments, since a contribution to an industry's useful stock of proprietary knowledge is recognized no matter what the precise domain of applicability. Firms are advised to focus on innovating where they can best make a contribution to the development of quality patents they and other firms are likely to need. Cross-licensing thus enables firms to play to their technological strengths.

Although the number of patents a firm holds is important, of even greater importance is their quality. A single key patent is often worth more than a portfolio of questionable ones when it comes to assessing the ability of a patent owner to stop an infringer. The most effective way to acquire a portfolio of valuable patents is likely to be through in-house R&D. Occasionally, firms can purchase a portfolio of patents with which to establish cross-licensing relationships; but quality patents often are not available in this fashion.

In summary, the reality of the global marketplace today indicates that firms should proactively develop IP portfolios with an eye towards value in the market for know-how. A corollary is that to create a valuable patent portfolio for cross-licensing, it matters little where R&D is aimed, so long as it creates quality patents in a field that one's competitors need to license.

Policy Issues

Intellectual property is more critical than ever to competitive advantage and, as a result, is being given increasing attention by strategists and policy makers. IP protection has been strengthened and firms are more actively defending and exploiting their IP. Coincident with the increased importance of patents is the increased importance of licensing and cross-licensing. Cross-licensing has become a significant dimension of competition. Absent the ability to offer an equivalent IP portfolio, licensees must incur considerable costs. This in and of itself is a spur to innovation.

Cross-licensing outcomes do not, however, tilt towards the large firm at the expense of the small. Rather, they favor firms with significant IP regardless of size. In a particular market niche where patents from two firms overlap, a small firm may have as many patents as a large firm, and as much bargaining power as the large firm. It may have sufficient IP leverage to block a larger competitor by pursuing a claim in court (or credibly threatening to do so). Indeed, in the evaluation process, a small innovator with a strong patent may be the net gainer, if the patent applies to a high-volume product of a large corporation.[66] Some competitors may possess "equal patents but unequal products." Nor need the licensing process disadvantage a new entrant firm. If a new entrant has significant relevant technology, it can in principle be a beneficiary of the cross-licensing regime.

Those investing in R&D need to ensure that they earn an adequate return, and royalties from licensing are an increasingly significant part. A company that develops technology will be at a competitive disadvantage in the market if its competitors are free to use its technology without incurring any expenses. Licensing fees on patented technology help ensure that the innovator earns an adequate return, which helps support future R&D. Cross-licensing helps balance the costs for developers and imitators. Thus, products manufactured by imitators who have not performed R&D do not have a competitive advantage merely by virtue of engaging in "copycat" imitation. If both parties to a licensing agreement have contributed similarly to a product field-of-use—in terms of the number, quality, product base coverage, and commercial significance of the patents included in the agreement—then the net royalty payments will be small, or possibly zero. In short, royalty payments help level the playing field, thereby ensuring competition on the merits.

The result is that IP now often has great value, both as a lever to obtain design freedom and as a vehicle to assist innovators in capturing value from innovation. This is of considerable consequence to firms without much IP—they must expect to pay—and also for firms with significant IP portfolios. IP and other knowledge assets are the core assets of many high-technology companies.

However, and perhaps because IP rights have become more valuable, infringers do not always step forward and offer to pay royalties. Accordingly, patent owners must often be proactive in obtaining royalty payments. Litigation or the threat of it may sometimes be necessary to enforce one's rights. Unfortunately, at least in the U.S., litigation is often slow and costly, and antitrust and patent misuse defenses are often raised, sometimes frivolously. The archaic state of the law on patent misuse may further handicap the chances of efficient and socially desirable outcomes.[67] Moreover, antitrust attorneys are often ready to argue that a package license is a tying arrangement with anticompetitive effects, and/or that cross-licensing is a front for collusion. However, the truth of the matter is that such arguments are out of step with the new competitive order.

Such arrangements are pro-innovation and pro-competitive. There would appear to be a significant knowledge gap in some circles with respect to the nature, purposes, and effects of cross-licensing. For instance, the field-of-use cross-licensing of patents in widespread use today is quite different from the traditional practice of licensing and cross-licensing involving individual patents. In the electronics industries, it is simply too cumbersome and transactionally costly to license specific patents for specific products, and so licensing commonly proceeds on a portfolio basis. Yet patent misuse and patent antitrust arguments often assume a world where infringement is easy to detect and costless to enforce. This is rarely the case in the electronics industry today.

At the most elementary level, licensing and cross-licensing involve merely the sale or exchange of property rights. Indeed, it often involves precisely that and no more. However, such arrangements ensure that firms have freedom-to-operate in developing and using innovations, without risking infringement claims from holders of patents in the same field of technology. In industries experiencing rapid technological innovation, patents, even when developed independently, will inevitably overlap technological domains worked by other firms. Cross-licensing agreements provide firms active in R&D with protection against inadvertent infringement and the rights to use the licensee's patents. Cross-licensing arrangements provide a mechanism for recognizing contributions through the establishment of balancing royalty payments. Royalty flows thus recognize the relative contributions to the product technology of the parties, thereby providing a mechanism for net takers to compensate net contributors. The arrangements thereby provide some limited protection against "free riders" who wish to use an industry's stock of proprietary knowledge without contributing. Balancing royalty payments are part of most cross-licenses, even when the main purpose is freedom-to-operate. "Pure" royalty free cross-licenses are rare for some companies and nowadays tend only to apply where the patent portfolios of both firms are large and the overall technological balance is both hard to assess and roughly equal.

Conclusion

Licensing is no longer a marginal activity in semiconductors and electronics. Whereas the management of patents and other forms of IP have always been of great importance in some industries like chemicals and pharmaceuticals, the ascendancy of IP in electronics is relatively recent. This is not just because the industry is new, but because regulatory and judicial distortions which impaired the value of IP have now been substantially rectified. The U.S. Department of Justice (DOJ) and the Courts forced AT&T, and to a lesser extent IBM, to license their technologies way below market value.[68] Not surprisingly, the electronics industry worldwide grew up with a distorted view of the value of intellectual property. This was reinforced by second sourcing requirements imposed by the DOD and other large buyers of integrated circuits that could, and did, insist on licensing for second sourcing purposes at low or zero royalties. Moreover, AT&T itself, being a significant purchaser of telecommunications and electronic equipment, and with protected service markets, had private incentives to diffuse technology rather than use it to build competitive advantage.

This confluence of very special factors has ended. The AT&T consent decree is gone, and AT&T must now be far more proprietary with its technology. The IBM patent provisions ended in 1961. Intel, TI, and other integrated circuit producers are no longer forced to second source. Moreover, the courts are more inclined to enforce IP rights than ever before. In these respects, hopefully the DOJ/FTC 1995 Antitrust Guidelines for the Licensing of IP, which include statements regarding the potential efficiency benefits of licensing and cross-licensing, are an important step in the right direction and reflect more modern thinking about IP.[69] However, these guidelines are non-binding in litigation, though one would of course hope that the courts would take them into account.

The old regime—whereby the antitrust authorities pressed major IP owners to give up whatever rights they held, where the courts were reluctant to enforce IP rights and were eager to see IP as a barrier to competition rather than as an instrument of it—has faded away. Meanwhile, the ability of the buyers of electronic componentry to bargain for and achieve second source arrangements (which indirectly lowered the value of IP by causing owners to create their own competition) has declined. As a result of these developments, a new order has emerged in which IP rights are valuable. Firms must either invest in R&D and develop patentable technology, or pay to license the patent portfolios of others. The free ride appears to be coming to an end, and IP management is now critical to the success of new entrants and incumbents alike.

Notes

1. By "IT," we refer of course to information technology.
2. In cross-licensing, two or more firms license their IP to each other.
3. Cross-licensing is not the same as a patent pool, in which member firms contribute patents to a common pool and each member accesses them on the same conditions. In cross-licensing, firms agree one-on-one to license their IP to each other and retain control over their proprietary technology, which is used for competitive advantage via product manufacturing and further licensing.
4. Other examples of "cumulative systems" include aircraft and automobiles. In aircraft, problems of blocking patents, stemming from different approaches by pioneers such as the Wright Brothers and Curtiss, were only resolved during World War II when automatic cross-licensing was introduced. In automobiles, the Association of Licensed Automobile Manufacturers (although formed to exploit the Selden patent) developed means for automatic cross-licensing of patents early this century. In both cases, the lack of cross-licensing probably held up industry development. R. Merges and R. Nelson, "On the Complex Economics of Patent Scope," *Columbia Law Review*, 90 (1990): 839-916.
5. In chemicals and pharmaceuticals, although patenting is extensive, individual technology development paths are less likely to overlap, and cross-licensing may be used to ensure broad product lines. For licensing strategy in the chemicals industry, see P. Grindley and J. Nickerson, "Licensing and Business Strategy in the

Chemicals Industry," in R. Parr and P. Sullivan, eds., *Technology Licensing Strategies* (New York, NY, NY: Wiley, 1996), pp. 97-120.

6. The early history of radio is described in: G. Archer, *History of Radio to 1926* (New York, NY: American Historical Society, 1938); W. Maclaurin, *Invention and Innovation in the Radio Industry* (New York, NY: Macmillan, 1949); J. Jewkes, D. Sawers, and R. Stillerman, *The Sources of Innovation* (New York, NY: Norton, 1969), pp. 286-288; G. Douglas, *The Early Days of Radio Broadcasting* (Jefferson, NC: McFarland, 1987); Merges and Nelson, op. cit., pp. 891-896.

7. These included the high-frequency alternator, high-frequency transmission arc, magnetic amplifier, selective tuning, crystal detector, heterodyne signal detection, diode valve, triode valve, high vacuum tube, and directional aerials.

8. Not all early inventors were independent. Alexanderson—who improved the Fessenden alternator, invented a magnetic amplifier, electronic amplifier, and multiple tuned antenna, and co-invented the "Alexanderson-Beverage static eliminator"—was a General Electric employee.

9. AT&T acquired the de Forest triode and feedback patents in 1913-1914 for $90,000, and his remaining feedback patents in 1917 for $250,000; Westinghouse cross-licensed the Fessenden heterodyne interests in 1920, and acquired the Armstrong super heterodyne patents in 1920 for $335,000. Archer, op. cit., p. 135; Maclaurin, op. cit., p. 106.

10. The fact that GE and AT&T alone were each devoting major research attention to the vacuum tube led to no less than twenty important patent interferences in this area. Maclaurin, op. cit., p. 97.

11. Federal Trade Commission, *The Radio Industry* (Washington DC: FTC, 1923); Maclaurin, op. cit., p. 99.

12. To cite one important example, Marconi and de Forest both had critical valve patents. Marconi's diode patent was held to dominate de Forest's triode patent. Both technologies were vital to radio, yet the interests refused to cross-license. [Archer, op. cit., pp. 113-114; Douglas, op. cit., p. 12.] The application of the triode (audion) to feedback amplification was also the subject of a long-running patent priority dispute between de Forest and Armstrong (finally resolved in de Forest's favor by the Supreme Court in 1934). Its use in transmission oscillation was the subject of four-way patent interference between Langmuir, Meissner, Armstrong, and de Forest. [Maclaurin, op. cit., p. 77.] These problems held up the use of the triode—a crucial component of signal transmission, detection, and amplification, which has been called "the heart and soul of radio" [Douglas, op. cit., p. 8], and "so outstanding in its consequences it almost ranks with the greatest inventions of all time" [Nobel Prize physicist Rabi, quoted in Maclaurin, op. cit., p. 70].

13. A main concern of the U.S. Navy was that international wireless communications were dominated by the British firm Marconi, and the patent impasse helped perpetuate this. It favored the establishment of an "All American" company in international communications. RCA was formed by GE in 1919, and simultaneously acquired the American Marconi Corp. Major shareholders included GE, AT&T (1920) and Westinghouse (1921). Archer, op. cit., pp. 176-189; Maclaurin, op. cit., p. 105.

14. As part of its role in the formation of RCA, the U.S. Navy also initiated cross-licensing to resolve the patent situation in radio manufacture. It wished to have clear rights to use the radio equipment it purchased, without risking litigation due to the complex patent ownership—noting in 1919 that "there was not a single company among those making radio sets for the Navy which possessed basic patents sufficient to enable them to supply, without infringement, . . . a complete transmitter or receiver." A formal letter suggesting "some agreement between the

Managing Intellectual Capital

several holders of permanent patents whereby the market can be freely supplied
with [vacuum] tubes," sent from the Navy to GE and AT&T in January 1920, may
be seen as an initiating point for cross-licensing in the industry. Archer, op. cit.,
pp. 180-186; Maclaurin, op. cit., pp. 99-110.

15. RCA concluded cross-license agreements with firms including GE, Westinghouse,
AT&T, United Fruit Company, Wireless Specialty Apparatus Company, Marconi
(Britain), CCTF (France), and Telefunken (Germany). Archer, op. cit., p. 195;
Maclaurin, op. cit., p. 107.

16. A distinction was that the RCA cross-licenses typically granted (reciprocal) exclusive rights to use the patents in given territories or markets, compared with the
non-exclusive cross-licenses that became the norm later. The cross-license with
GE (and later Westinghouse) included provisions for the supply of components to
RCA. The RCA cross-licenses were for very long terms—many for 25 years, from
1919 to 1945. They covered current and future patents. Other radio manufacturers took licenses with RCA, starting in the late 1920s. Some of RCA's cross-licensing policies were later questioned on antitrust grounds, and modified following a
consent decree in 1932. Archer, op. cit., pp. 381-387; Maclaurin, op. cit., pp. 107-
109, 132-152.

17. Historical perspective on competition in the telecommunications industry is given
in: M. Irwin, "The Telephone Industry," in W. Adams, ed., *The Structure of American
Industry*, 5th ed. (New York, NY: Macmillan, 1977), pp. 312-333; G. Brock, *The
Telecommunications Industry: The Dynamics of Market Structure* (Cambridge, MA: Har-
vard University Press, 1981); Office of Technology Assessment, *Information Tech-
nology Research and Development: Critical Trends and Issues* (New York, NY: Pergamon
Press, 1985); R. Noll and B. Owen, "The Anticompetitive Uses of Regulation:
United States *v.* AT&T," in J. Kwoka and L. White, eds., *The Antitrust Revolution*
(New York, NY: Macmillan, 1989); G. Rosston and D. Teece, "Competition and
"Local" Communications: Innovation, Entry, and Integration," *Industrial and
Corporate Change*, 4/4 (1995).

18. OTA, op. cit.; M. Noll, "Bell System R&D Activities: The Impact of Divestiture,"
Telecommunications Policy, 11 (1987): 161-178; R. Harris, "Divestiture and Regulatory Policies," *Telecommunications Policy*, 14 (1990): 105-124.

19. The two substantive provisions of the 1956 consent decree were that (a) it confined AT&T to providing regulated telecommunications services, and its manufacturing subsidiary Western Electric to making equipment for those services
(effectively prohibiting it from selling semiconductors in the commercial market),
and (b) all patents controlled by the Bell System should be licensed to others on
request. Licenses for the 8,600 patents included in existing cross-licensing agreements were royalty free to new applicants, and licenses to all other existing or
future patents were to be issued at a non-discriminatory "reasonable royalty"
(determined by the court if necessary). AT&T was also to provide technical information along with the patent licenses for reasonable fees. Licenses were unre-
stricted, other than being non-transferable. [*USA v. Western Electric Co. Inc. and
AT&T*, Civil Action, 17-49, Final Judgment, January 24, 1956; Brock, op. cit., pp.
166, 191-194; R. Levin, "The Semiconductor Industry," in R. Nelson, ed., *Government and Technical Progress* (New York, NY: Pergamon, 1982), pp. 9-101.] In fact,
AT&T went beyond the Consent Decree in its efforts to diffuse transistor technology, including symposia and direct efforts to spread know-how. [Levin, op. cit.,
pp. 76-77.]

20. See section later in this article on "Lessons for Innovation Management."

21. "We realized that if [the transistor] was as big as we thought, we couldn't keep
it to ourselves and we couldn't make all the technical contributions. It was to our
interest to spread it around." AT&T executive, quoted in Levin, op. cit., p. 77, after

J. Tilton, *International Diffusion of Technology: The Case of Semiconductors* (Washington, D.C.: The Brookings Institution, 1971).

22. By 1983, Bell Labs had received 20,000 patents. This may be compared to about 10,000 currently at IBM and 6,000 at Texas Instruments.

23. W. Kefauver, "Intellectual Property Rights and Competitive Strategy: An International Telecommunications Firm," in M. Wallerstein, M. E. Mogee, and R. Schoen, eds., *Global Dimensions of Intellectual Property Rights in Science and Technology* (Washington, D.C.: National Academy Press, 1993), pp. 236-240.

24. For the capture model, see section below on "Policy Issues." The survivorship period could be as much as 17 years from the grant date (possibly several years after filing), under U.S. patent rules prior to 1995, or 20 years from the filing date, after 1995.

25. In the U.S., during 1953-1968, 5,128 semiconductor patents were awarded. Bell Laboratories was granted 16% of these; the next five firms were RCA, General Electric, Westinghouse, IBM, and Texas Instruments. Tilton, op. cit.

26. E. von Hippel, "Cooperation Between Rivals: Informal Know-How Trading," *Research Policy*, 16 (1987): 416-424; A. Saxenian, "Regional Networks and the Resurgence of Silicon Valley," *California Management Review*, 33/1 (Fall 1990): 89-112.

27. There are also transactions costs reasons for using bundled licensing, as noted previously.

28. If the parties could not agree on a reasonable royalty rate, the court could impose one. Patent rights could be very long lived, since, at that time, patent life was 17 years from the grant date, which might be some years after the filing date. The patent licensing provisions ended in 1961. The decree also included other provisions related to the sale of IBM products and services. USA v. International Business Machines Corporation, CCH 1956 Trade Cases para. 68, 245, SDNY 1956.

29. This increased from $345 million in 1993 [IBM Annual Report, 1994]. IBM initiated a more active approach to licensing in 1988, when it increased the royalty rates sought on its patents from 1% of sales revenue on products using IBM patents to a range of 1% to 5%. Computerworld, April 11, 1988, p. 105.

30. R. Smith, "Management of a Corporate Intellectual Property Law Department," *AIPLA Bulletin* (April/June 1989), pp. 817-823; C. Boyer, "The Power of the Patent Portfolio," *Think*, 5 (1990): 10-11.

31. Gary Markovits, IBM patent process manager, in Boyer, op. cit., p. 10.

32. Jim McGrody, IBM VP and director of research, in Boyer, op. cit.

33. Roger Smith, IBM assistant general counsel, in Boyer op. cit. In all, IBM has about 11,000 active inventions, with about 35,000 active patents around the world. Smith, op. cit.

34. Many firms in the U.S. semiconductor industry were reported to be "dismayed" and "outraged" over the higher royalties and more active IP strategies of TI and others. [S. Weber, "The Chip Industry is Up in Arms Over TI's Pursuit of Intellectual Property Rights at the ITC," *Electronics* (February 1991), p. 51.] For example, T. J. Rodgers, CEO of Cypress Semiconductor described the practice of increased litigation over patent rights as a "venture capital investment." [*Upside* (December 1990).] Others have questioned whether the strengthening of patent rights might be hindering innovation, by enabling IP holders to demand "crippling royalties from young companies." Several small Silicon Valley semiconductor firms, including Cypress Semiconductor, LSI Logic, and VLSI Technology, formed a consortium to defend themselves against patent suits. [B. Glass, "Patently Unfair: The System Created to Protect the Individual Inventor May be Hindering Innovation," *InfoWorld*, October 29, 1990, p. 56.] Although some Japanese manufacturers reportedly described royalty demands as "possibly exorbitant," the Japanese

Managing Intellectual Capital

response has generally been to increase their own patenting effort. [*Computergram*, September 14, 1990; Weber, op. cit.] Similar objections to increased patent strength and licensing activity have also been evident in resistance to the growing use of patents for computer software, which it has been claimed may restrict innovation by small enterprises. [B. Kahin, "The Software Patent Crisis," *Technology Review* (April 1990), pp. 53-58.] However, here too, many software firms who at first resisted the trend have now accepted the need to build their own patent portfolios. [M. Walsh, "Bowing to Reality, Software Maker Begins Building a Patent Portfolio," *The Recorder*, August 17, 1995, p. 1.]

35. This section is based in part on discussions with Texas Instruments executives. However, the views expressed here are those of the authors and should not be seen as necessarily reflecting those of Texas Instruments.

36. The costs of manufacturing facilities have risen dramatically. A new wafer fabrication plant cost $10-20 million in 1975 (4-kilobit DRAM), $300-400 million in 1990 (16-megabit DRAM) and over $1 billion in 1991 (256-megabit DRAM). SEMATECH, *Annual Report, 1991*; "Foreign Alliances Which Make Sense," *Electronic Business*, September 3, 1990, p. 68.

37. Without field-of-use cross-licenses, a typical semiconductor firm might need to reverse engineer an average of two or three competitors' products a day, as each is introduced over the course of a five-year license, to ascertain whether these are infringing its patents. It must do the same for its own products. This would be prohibitively expensive. Tracking sales by each of hundreds of affected products, on a patent by patent basis, to ascertain royalties, would be virtually impossible.

38. In some cases, where there are only a few very specific overlaps between two firms' technology needs, firms may choose to license single patents. Although an option, it is rarely convenient compared with field-of-use cross-licensing when there are substantial technology overlaps.

39. R. Levin, A. Klevorick, R. Nelson, and S. Winter, "Appropriating the Returns to Industrial R&D," *Brookings Papers on Economic Activity*, 3 (1987): 783-820. Of course, even reading the patent is a helpful guide to someone knowledgeable in the field.

40. The most powerful threat to enforce a patent is an injunction to close down the infringer's production line. This could be ruinous for a manufacturing corporation, especially in fast developing markets such as electronics and semiconductors. The threat of damages may also be important, but as these are often based on projected royalties (and hence may be little worse than freely negotiated licensing terms) they are less potent, unless multiplied by the court.

41. For the economics of technology transfer see D. Teece, "The Market for Know-How and the Efficient International Transfer of Technology," *Annals of the American Academy of Political and Social Science*, 458 (1981): 81-96.

42. Reverse engineering a semiconductor product is not a simple matter, involving as it does decapping and microscopic examination at the submicron level. Although the process is by now largely automated, it can take 400-500 man-hours per device.

43. For cross-licenses with firms outside the semiconductor industry, such as the personal computer industry, the process used is simpler. In this case, there may be few patents to balance against the proffered patents. Licensing follows precedents long established in the computer industry, primarily under the leadership of IBM, as the holder of many of the patents used in the industry. The negotiations are similar, but the weighting process is not involved. Royalty rates are influenced by industry norms.

44. In some cases licensees may only wish to license a few selected patents, rather than all patents in a field-of-use. For this reason licenses are generally also offered

for individual or specific patents, as well as for all patents in a given field. However, there are significant transactions savings to both sides from a field-of-use license, and the cost per patent is likely to be higher when only a few patents are licensed.

45. For general considerations affecting royalty rates, see M. Lee, "Determining Reasonable Royalty," *Les Nouvelles*, 27 (1992): 124-128; R. Parr, *Intellectual Property Infringement Damages: A Litigation Support Handbook* (New York, NY: Wiley, 1993).

46. To an extent this may be a transitional problem. As licensing becomes more widespread, individual licenses are more likely to be negotiated in the knowledge that other licenses, potential or actual, must be taken into account.

47. For strategies to establish standards see R. Hartman and D. Teece, "Product Emulation Strategies in the Presence of Reputation Effects and Network Externalities," *Economics of Innovation and New Technology*, 1 (1990): 157-182; L. Gabel, *Competitive Strategies and Product Standards* (London: McGraw-Hill, 1991); P. Grindley, *Standards, Strategy, and Policy: Cases and Stories* (Oxford: Oxford University Press, 1995).

48. However liberal the licensing terms, the patent holder should not inadvertently assign away IP rights beyond those specifically needed to operate the standard, and may need to condition rights over its IP to uses related to the standard. The innovator might otherwise be deterred from participating in standards setting. There is a balance to be drawn between committing to an open standard and limiting that commitment to what is needed for the standard and to keep access open in future.

49. Risks include the likelihood that the validity of the patents would be challenged in court, that firms—and nations—would retaliate, and that the corporate image with customers would suffer. Patent assertion against customers and partners is an especially sensitive area.

50. R&D agreements with Hitachi have ranged from a 4-megabit DRAM know-how exchange in 1988 to a 256-megabit DRAM co-development agreement in 1994. According to Yasutsugu Takeda of Hitachi, "You can't create [a successful cooperative venture] just because you sign up a lot of companies that are barely committed and don't have anything to bring." The Hitachi-TI collaboration on 256-megabit memory chips has been successful because it is a "meeting of equals" [*Business Week*, June 27, 1994, p. 79]. Complementary capabilities are generally considered important factors in selecting international collaborative venture partners. D. Mowery, "International Collaborative Ventures and the Commercialization of New Technologies," in N. Rosenberg, R. Landau, and D. Mowery, *Technology and the Wealth of Nations* (Stanford, CA: Stanford University Press, 1992), pp. 345-380.

51. TI entered joint ventures during 1989-1990 to build manufacturing plants with total investments over $1 billion: with the Italian government; Acer (Taiwan); Kobe Steel (Japan); and the Singapore government, HP, and Canon (Singapore).

52. This section is based in part on discussions with Hewlett-Packard executives. However, the views expressed here are those of the authors, and should not be seen as necessarily reflecting those of Hewlett-Packard.

53. Examples include *Research Disclosure* and other publications. Such journals charge fees to authors, yet often have large circulations for reference libraries and research laboratories.

54. Surveys of executives in a range of industries taken in the early 1980s typically rated methods such as lead time and superior sales and service effort as the most effective means of protecting innovations, rather than patent protection, which was considered relatively ineffective. Levin et al., op. cit.

55. The original transistor process patents were held by AT&T, so that all transistor manufacturers needed to cross-license their own patents at least with AT&T.

Managing Intellectual Capital

Similarly, the key patents for the integrated circuit (IC) technology were held by two firms, TI and Fairchild, ensuring that these too were widely licensed. With the critical patents widely available, the cumulative nature of innovation guaranteed broad cross-licensing. Levin, op. cit., pp. 79-82.

56. The first commercial producers of transistors in the 1950s, using AT&T licenses, included Shockley Labs, Fairchild, Motorola and TI. These gave rise to a wave of spin-off companies in the 1960s, such as National Semiconductor, Intel, AMD, Signetics and AMI, which in turn gave rise to subsequent waves of new companies, such as, Cypress Semiconductor, Cyrix, LSI Logic, Chips and Technologies, Brooktree Semiconductor, and others.

57. At TI this approach was formalized in the Objectives, Strategies, and Tactics (OST) product development management process, including "design to cost" methods formalizing experience curve pricing procedures. *Business Week*, September 18, 1978; B. Uttal, "TI Regroups," *Fortune*, August 9, 1982, p. 40; M. Martin, *Managing Technological Innovation and Entrepreneurship* (Reston, VA: Reston, 1984).; R. Burgelman and M. Maidique, *Strategic Management of Technology and Innovation* (Homewood, IL: Irwin, 1988).

58. Tilton, op. cit.; M. Borrus, J. Millstein, and J. Zysman, *International Competition in Advanced Industrial Sectors: Trade and Development in the Semiconductor Industry* (Washington, D.C.: U.S. Department of Commerce, 1982).

59. Borrus et al., op. cit.

60. The same is broadly true of IBM's entry into Japan.

61. Dataquest figures, quoted in United Nations Organization (UNO), *The Competitive Status of the U.S. Electronics Sector* (New York, NY: United Nations Organization, 1990). For comments on the U.S. recovery since the late 1980s, see W. Spencer and P. Grindley, "SEMATECH After Five Years: High-Technology Consortia and U.S. Competitiveness," *California Management Review*, 35/4 (Summer 1993): 9-32; P. Grindley, D. Mowery, and B. Silverman, "SEMATECH and Collaborative Research: Lessons in the Design of High-Technology Consortia," *Journal of Policy Analysis and Management*, 13 (1994): 723-758.

62. For contrasting views on the responses of Silicon Valley to international competition, see R. Florida and M. Kenney, "Why Silicon Valley and Route 128 Can't Save Us," *California Management Review*, 33/1 (Fall 1990): 66-88; Saxenian, op. cit.

63. Hazards for innovation when a firm is remote from business transactions, and hence from the technological frontier, are outlined in J. de Figueiredo and D. Teece, "Strategic Hazards and Safeguards in Competitor Supply," *Industrial and Corporate Change*, vol. 5.2 (1996). The similar vulnerability of the "virtual corporation," which contracts out development and manufacturing, is discussed in H. Chesbrough and D. Teece, "When Is Virtual Virtuous: Organizing for Innovation," *Harvard Business Review* (January/February 1996), pp. 65-73.

64. For the nature of dynamic capabilities of firms and their relationship to innovation, see D. Teece and G. Pisano, "The Dynamic Capabilities of Firms: An Introduction," *Industrial and Corporate Change*, 3.3 (1994): 537-556; D. Teece, G. Pisano, and A. Shuen, "Dynamic Capabilities and Strategic Management," *Strategic Management Journal* (forthcoming in 1997). For the role of complementary assets in commercializing innovation, see D. Teece, "Profiting from Technological Innovation," *Research Policy*, 15 (1986): 285-305.

65. Indeed, in some cases the firm might conceivably do better if it has strengths in an area where the licensee is relatively weak, since it will have greatest difficulty avoiding their patents in those areas, whereas where it is strongest it may have more ability to invent around the patents.

66. An example is Brooktree Corporation, a small semiconductor design company in San Diego, which concluded a favorable cross-licensing agreement with TI in 1993.
67. See E. Sherry and D. Teece, "The Patent Misuse Doctrine: An Economic Reassessment," in *Antitrust Fundamentals*, ABA Section of Antitrust Law, Chicago (forthcoming).
68. IP rights to the transistor were given away to U.S. and foreign firms for very small amounts. Levin, op. cit.
69. DOJ/FTC, *Antitrust Guidelines for the Licensing of IP,* April 6, 1995 (Washington, DC: U.S. Department of Justice and the Federal Trade Commission, 1995).

PART III

PUBLIC POLICY

A

Antitrust: Innovation and Antitrust

15

Journal of Economic Perspectives—Volume 4, Number 3—Summer 1990—Pages 75–96

Innovation and Cooperation: Implications for Competition and Antitrust

Thomas M. Jorde and David J. Teece

Nobel Laureate Robert Solow and his colleagues on MIT's Industrial Productivity Commission recently noted (Dertouzos, Lester, and Solow, 1989, p. 7): "Undeveloped cooperative relationships between individuals and between organizations stand out in our industry studies as obstacles to technological innovation and the improvement of industrial performance" and later (p. 105) that "interfirm cooperation in the U.S. has often, though not always, been inhibited by government antitrust regulation." These striking conclusions warrant further exploration.

Unfortunately, industrial organization textbooks still discuss horizontal cooperation and competition almost exclusively in terms of standard cartel theory. (On the other hand, vertical cooperation/contracting is viewed differently, and some textbooks provide treatments of supplier-buyer relationships in which cooperation is viewed as enhancing efficiency.) Both in the textbooks and in policy discussion among economists, cooperation among competitors is highly suspect, being perhaps the last bastion of what was once referred to as the "inhospitality tradition" in antitrust. As a result, very little literature addresses how cooperation among competitors can promote competition, notwithstanding that cooperation among competitors may sometimes be essential if innovating firms are to compete in today's increasingly global markets (Imai and Baba, 1989). Such cooperation is already important in Japan and in Europe.[1]

---

[1]For instance, cooperative R&D and related activities have been important to the success of the Western German machine tool industry. The industry formed a strong association that has a research and teaching institute at Aachen. The West German industry has been described as

■ *Thomas M. Jorde is Professor of Law, University of California, Berkeley, California. David J. Teece is Mitsubishi Bank Professor, Walter A. Haas School of Business, University of California, Berkeley, California.*

This paper begins by describing the nature of the innovation process. We then explore socially beneficial forms of cooperation that can assist the development and commercialization of new technology, and suggest modifications to current U.S. antitrust law that would remove unnecessary impediments to organizational arrangements that support innovation and stimulate competition in the United States. The modifications we propose would create "safe harbors" for various forms of cooperative activities among competitors in unconcentrated markets, and they would permit cooperation in concentrated markets if commercialization and appropriability were thereby facilitated. These modifications would bring U.S. antitrust laws closer to what is already in place in Europe and Japan and would promote competition more assuredly than would existing law.[2]

We have no illusion that our proposed changes, standing alone, would dramatically improve the performance of U.S. industry, though specific industries might be transformed. However, the changes we propose in antitrust have the attraction that they do not require the expenditure of public funds. In short, we see existing law as a self-imposed impediment to U.S. economic performance.[3]

The Nature of Innovation

Innovation is the search for, and the discovery, development, improvement, adoption and commercialization of new processes, new products, and new organizational structures and procedures.[4] It involves uncertainty, risk taking, probing and reprobing, experimenting, and testing. It is an activity in which "dry holes" and "blind alleys" are the rule, not the exception. Many of these aspects are well-known and have been frequently analyzed in the economics literature.

"groups of clubs" (Collis, 1988, p. 95) because of the nature of the cooperation displayed. The Italian machine tool industry around Modena is similarly organized, as is the Italian textile industry and the Danish furniture industry. A review of examples of cooperative activity abroad is part of the authors' ongoing research.

[2] There is no necessary conflict between promoting cooperation and competition, if the cooperation improves efficiency or advances innovation. As Schumpeter (1942, p. 85) pointed out, when compared to competition among firms with similar products and technologies, the competition that counts "comes from the new commodity, the new technology, the new source of supply.... This kind of competition is as much more effective than the other as bombardment is in comparison with forcing a door, and so much more important that it becomes a matter of comparative indifference whether competition in the ordinary sense functions more or less promptly."

[3] As this *Journal of Economic Perspectives* issue goes to press, the House Judiciary Committee approved the "National Cooperative Production Amendments of 1990" (H.R. 4611), a bill that incorporates many of the changes we suggest in this article and which we have been advocating since 1988. We discuss the provisions of H.R. 4611 and additional antitrust changes that we believe would advance innovation and U.S. competitiveness later in this article.

[4] Dosi (1988) provides an excellent review of the innovation literature.

However, other aspects of innovation, particularly its organizational requirements, have not been sufficiently explored. The traditional serial model that has served as the basis for current antitrust policy is described below. Its inadequacies are then addressed in light of the "simultaneous" nature of the process, which is particularly relevant in certain industries, like microelectronics, experiencing high rates of technological change.[5]

The Traditional Serial Model

Traditional descriptions of the innovation process commonly break it down into a number of stages which proceed sequentially and theoretical treatments of R&D in industrial organization reflect this model. According to this view, the innovation process proceeds in a linear and predictable fashion from research to development, design, production, and then finally to marketing, sales, and service (Grossman and Shapiro, 1986, p. 319; Tirole, 1988, p. 389). In simple models, there is not even any feedback or overlap between and among stages.

If the serial model adequately characterizes innovation today, then it is mainly the innovation which occurs in some scale-intensive industries. The initial development of nylon at Dupont perhaps fits this model. The Manhattan Project during World War II is also illustrative. The serial model does not address the many small but cumulatively important incremental innovations that are at the heart of technological change in many industries, especially well-established industries like semiconductors, computers, and automobiles. The serial model of innovation is an analytic convenience which no longer adequately characterizes the innovation process, except in special circumstances.

The serial model has enabled economists to model innovation as a vertical process. Inasmuch as antitrust policy toward vertical restraints is very permissive, many economists and legal scholars do not understand how U.S. antitrust laws could stand in the way of the various kinds of standard and non-standard contracting often needed to support the commercialization of innovation. But as we shall see, matters are not so simple.

The Simultaneous Model

The simultaneous model of innovation recognizes the existence of tight linkages and feedback mechanisms which must operate quickly and efficiently, including links between firms, within firms, and sometimes between firms and other organizations like universities. From this perspective, innovation does not necessarily begin with research; nor is the process serial. But it does require rapid feedback, mid-course corrections to designs, and redesign.[6] This concep-

---

[5] This argument is presented at greater length in D. Teece (1989a).

[6] This process has also been termed "cyclic" (Gomory, 1987, p. 72). The popular press has even begun to recognize and discuss the simultaneous nature of innovation and effective commercialization. See "A Smarter Way to Manufacture," *Business Week*, April 30, 1990, 110–117 (discussing "concurrent engineering").

tualization recognizes aspects of the serial model—such as the flow of activity, in certain cases through design to development, production and marketing—but also recognizes the constant feedback between and among activities, and the involvement of a wide variety of economic actors and organizations that need not have a simple upstream-downstream relationship to each other.[7] It suggests that R&D personnel must be closely connected to the manufacturing and to marketing personnel and to external sources of supply of new components and complementary technologies, so that supplier, manufacturer and customer reactions can be fed back into the design process rapidly. In this way new technology, whether internal or external, becomes embedded into designs which meet customer needs quickly and efficiently.

The simultaneous model visualizes innovation as an incremental and cumulative activity that involves building on what went before, whether it is inside the organization or outside the organization, and whether the knowledge is proprietary or in the public domain. The simultaneous model also stresses the importance of the speed of the design cycle, and flexibility. IBM followed this model in developing its first PC, employing alliances with Microsoft and others to launch a successful personal computer system. Sun Microsystems and NeXT Computer launched themselves in this way and have remained in this mode for subsequent new product development. Microprocessor development at Intel often follows this logic too.

When innovation has this character, the company which is quickest in product design and development will appear to be the pioneer, even if its own contribution to science and technology is minimal, because it can be first to "design in" science and technology already in the public domain. Both small and large organizations operate by this model, reaching out upstream and downstream, horizontally and laterally to develop and assemble leading edge systems.

In short, much innovation today is likely to require lateral and horizontal linkages as well as vertical ones. As we discuss below, and particularly for small firms, innovation may require accessing complementary assets which lie outside the organization. If innovating firms do not have the necessary capabilities in-house, they may need to engage in various forms of restrictive contracts with providers of inputs and complementary assets. The possibility that antitrust laws could be invoked, particularly by excluded competitors, thus arises. Lying in the weeds to create mischief for unsuspecting firms engaged in socially desirable but poorly understood business practices are plaintiffs' attorneys and their expert economists entreating the courts to view reality through the lens of monopoly theory and modern variants such as raising rivals. These theories

---

[7]Moreover, the linkage from science to innovation is not solely or even preponderantly at the beginning of typical innovations, but rather extends all through the process. "Science can be visualized as lying alongside development processes, to be used when needed" (Kline and Rosenberg, 1986). Design is often at the center of the innovation process. Research is often spawned by the problems associated with trying to get the design right. Indeed, important technological breakthroughs can often proceed even when the underlying science is not understood.

have been honed in the context of a hypothetical world of unchanging technology. If new technology does arrive it often falls like manna from heaven; behavior which is anticompetitive in the static context may be procompetitive in a dynamic one. Because the study of innovation is largely outside the mainstream of economic research and antitrust jurisprudence, the possibility of expensive and distracting litigation followed by judicial error is significant.

Paradoxically, the giant integrated enterprises are not most heavily at risk. Instead, most at risk are mid-sized enterprises that have developed and commercialized important innovations, because such firms are likely to have some market power (under orthodox definitions) and have the need to engage in complex forms of interfirm cooperation. Because of these risks, managers may choose to forego socially desirable arrangements and investments, and innovation and the competition it engenders will be attenuated.

Organizational Requirements of Innovation

Whether innovation is serial or simultaneous, it requires the coordination of various activities. The serial model suggests a rather simple organizational problem; the simultaneous model a more complex one, often employing various forms of non-standard contracting. To the extent that economists employ just the serial model, they greatly oversimplify the organizational challenges which innovation provides and underestimate potential antitrust problems. Also, they probably exaggerate the importance of research and downplay the importance of other factors. As discussed below, except in special cases, a firm's R&D capability is for naught if it cannot organize the rest of the innovation process efficiently and effectively, particularly if that innovation is taking place in an already-established industry.

For innovations to be commercialized, the economic system must somehow assemble all the relevant complementary assets and create an interactive and dynamically efficient system of learning and information exchange. The necessary complementary assets can conceivably be assembled by administrative processes, or by market processes, as when the innovator simply licenses the technology to firms that already own the relevant assets, or are willing to create them. These organizational choices have received scant attention in the context of innovation. Indeed, the serial model relies on an implicit belief that arms-length contracts between unaffiliated firms in the vertical chain from research to customer will suffice to commercialize technology. In particular, there has been little consideration of how complex contractual arrangements among firms can assist commercialization—that is, translating R&D capability into profitable new products and processes. The one partial exception is a tiny literature on joint R&D activity (Grossman and Shapiro, 1986; Ordover and Willig, 1985); but this literature addresses the organization of R&D and not the organization of innovation.[8]

---

[8] For a more complete statement of our own views on this, see Teece (1977, 1989b).

If innovation takes place in a regime of tight appropriability—that is, if the technological leader can secure legal protection, perhaps by obtaining an ironclad patent (Teece, 1986)—and if technology can be transferred at zero cost as is commonly assumed in theoretical models, the organizational challenge that is created by innovation is relatively simple. In these instances, the market for intellectual property is likely to support transactions enabling the developer of the technology to simply sell its intellectual property for cash, or at least license it to downstream firms who can then engage in whatever value-added activities are necessary to extract value from the technology. With a well-functioning market for know-how, markets can provide the structure for the requisite organization to be accomplished.

But in reality, the market for know-how is riddled with imperfections (Arrow, 1962). Simple unilateral contracts, where technology is sold for cash, are unlikely to be efficient (Teece, 1980, 1982). Complex bilateral and multilateral contracts, internal organization, or various hybrid structures are often required to shore up obvious market failures (Williamson, 1985; Teece, 1986). This section will examine various market failures and the institutional arrangements which can ameliorate them.

Technology Transfer Efficiency

The transfer of technology among the various activities that constitute innovation is not costless. This is especially true if the know-how to be transferred cannot be easily bundled and shipped out in one lot—which is clearly the case when the development activity must proceed simultaneously and when the knowledge has a high tacit component.[9] In these instances, the required transfer of technology cannot be separated from the transfer of personnel, which is typically difficult if the contractual relationship is arms-length and non-exclusive.

Besides the problems of getting technology-driven concepts to market, there is the converse problem of getting user-driven innovations to developers. In some industries, users other than the manufacturers conceive of and design innovative prototypes. The manufacturers' role in the innovation process is somehow to become aware of the user innovation and its value, and then to manufacture a commercial version of the device for sale to other users. User-dominated innovation accounts for more than two-thirds of first-to-market innovations in scientific instruments and in process machinery used in semiconductor and electronic subassembly manufacture (von Hippel, 1988). Clearly, user innovation requires two kinds of technology transfer: first from user to manufacturer, and then from the manufacturer to the developer-user and other users.

Mirroring the role that users play in stimulating innovation upstream is the role that suppliers play in stimulating downstream innovation. For example, a good deal of the innovation in the automobile industry, including fuel injection,

---

[9] For a review of the characteristics of know-how, see Winter (1987) and Teece (1989b).

alternators and power steering, has its origins in upstream component suppliers. Bendix and Bosch developed fuel injection and Motorola the alternator. The challenge to the manufacturer then becomes how to "design in" the new components and how to avoid sole source dependency. As discussed below, deep and enduring relationships need to be established between component developer-manufacturers and suppliers to ensure adoption and diffusion of the technology.[10] These relationships, while functionally vertical, could well turn out to be viewed as horizontal by a court. Unless the courts have an adequate model of innovation and competition presented to them, beneficial contractual arrangements with attendant restraints could well be viewed negatively.

Scale, Scope, and Duplication Issues

Successful new product and process development innovation often requires horizontal and lateral as well as vertical cooperation. It is well understood that horizontal linkages can help overcome scale barriers in research; they can also assist in defining technical standards. But it is common to assert that if firms need to engage in joint research to achieve these economies, the maintenance of competition requires that firms participating in joint research work go their own way with respect to related activities such as manufacturing. However, a requirement that firms participating in a joint research arrangement commercialize the technology independently can impose an unnecessary technology transfer burden. As discussed above, the imposition of a market interface between "research" and "commercialization" activities will most assuredly create a technology transfer challenge, a loss of effectiveness and timeliness, and higher costs.

Collaborative research also reduces what William Norris, CEO of Control Data Corporation, refers to as "shameful and needless duplication of effort" (David, 1985). Independent research activities often proceed down identical or near-identical technological paths. This is sometimes wasteful and can be minimized if research plans are coordinated. The danger of horizontal cooperation, on the other hand, is that it may reduce diversity. This concern is legitimate and is commonly stressed by economists.[11] Unquestionably, a system

---

[10]A related set of vertical relationships involving innovation has been remarked upon by Rosenberg (1972, pp. 98–102) in his treatise on technology and American economic growth. The machine tool industry in the 19th century played a unique role both in the initial solution of technical problems in user industries, such as textiles, and as the disseminator of these techniques to other industries, such as railroad locomotive manufacture. Rosenberg's description suggests that the users played a role in the development of new equipment. He notes that before 1820 in the United States, one could not identify a distinct set of firms that were specialists in the design and manufacture of machinery. Machines were either produced by users or by firms engaged in the production of metal or wooden products. Machinery-producing firms were thus first observed as adjuncts to textile factories. However, once established, these firms played an important role as the transmission center in the diffusion of new technology.

[11]Nalebuff and Stiglitz (1983) argue that the gains from competition may more than offset the losses from duplication. Also, Sah and Stiglitz (1989) show that in a model with ex post Bertrand competition where there is knowledge of which research projects others are undertaking, the number and range of research projects undertaken will be a constrained Pareto optimum.

of innovation that converges on just one view of the technological possibilities is likely to close off productive avenues of inquiry.

However, a private enterprise economy without horizontal coordination and communication offers no guarantee that the desired level of diversity is achieved at the lowest cost. In addition, cooperation need not be the enemy of diversity. If firms can coordinate their research programs to some degree, duplication can be minimized without the industry converging on a single technological approach. Indeed, Bell Labs has been noted for the very considerable internal diversity it has been able to achieve, at least in the pre-divestiture period.

Rent Dissipation Issues

Innovation has well-known free rider and public good characteristics. Know-how leakage and other spillovers impair incentives to innovate by redistributing benefits to others, particularly competitors and users. To maintain adequate incentives to invest in innovative activity, without providing government subsidies, free riding must be curtailed. This is how economists justify patents, copyrights, trade secrets, and other aspects of intellectual property law.

The organizational form in which innovation takes place, interacting with the protection provided by intellectual property law (Teece, 1986), will affect the degree of rent dissipation which the innovator experiences. If the innovation has value and intellectual property protection is effective, an innovator specializing just in early stage activity is in a good position to capture a portion of the returns from innovation.

But surveys show that intellectual property law has a limited ability to provide protection from imitation,[12] even though there have been recent efforts by the courts to tighten enforcement. For a sample of 48 patented product innovations in the chemical, drug, electronics and machinery industry, one group of researchers found that within four years of their introduction, 60 percent of the patented successful innovations in the sample were imitated (Mansfield et al, 1982). Not surprisingly, the social returns to innovation are greater than the private returns. Underinvestment in innovative activities is to be expected.

A "research joint venture" may not do enough to overcome appropriability problems, unless many potential competitors are in the joint venture. Thus, a

---

[12]See Levin, Klevorick, Nelson, and Winter (1987). These researchers surveyed R&D managers in various industries. The survey shows that, on a seven-point scale (1 = not at all effective, 7 = very effective) for 18 industry categories with 10 or more respondents, managers in only chemicals (specifically drugs, plastic materials, inorganic chemicals, and organic chemicals) and petroleum refining rated process patents effectiveness higher than 4 on the scale, and only these same chemical industries and steel mills rated product patents higher than 5. These findings make very clear that managers have little confidence that patents suffice as mechanisms to protect intellectual property from free riders. The results also show that other methods of appropriation such as first mover advantages (lead time and learning curve advantages), secrecy, and investment in sales or service support were more effective.

single firm or even a consortium with good intellectual property protection will often need to bolster its market position and its stream of rents by other strategies and mechanisms. These mechanisms include building, acquiring, or renting (on an exclusive basis) complementary assets and exploiting first-mover advantages. We use the term *complementary assets* to refer to those assets and capabilities that need to be employed to package new technology so that it is valuable to the end user.[13] Broad categories of complementary assets include complementary technologies, manufacturing, marketing, distribution, sales, and service.

It is essential to distinguish further between generic and specific complementary assets. Generic assets include general purpose facilities and equipment and nonspecific skills; they tend to be disembodied and codified and hence easy to transfer. Specific assets, on the other hand, include highly differentiated system and firm-specific assets and skills. Specific assets and capabilities are typically embedded in the organization; or even if not embedded in the organization (like a specialized machine) are of reduced value in a different organizational context. In a sense, specific assets represent the firm's particular assemblage of physical assets and prior learning. Accordingly, they are difficult for competitors to replicate.

Thus, when imitation of aspects of a firm's technology is easy, it is essential for firms to be world-class—or to be linked to partners who are world-class—in the less imitable complementary activities. Accordingly, the best defense against product imitators may well be the development of a less easily imitatable superior manufacturing process to make the product, or it may be the firm's superior service capability. In short, because a firm's comparative advantage in research does not necessarily coincide with an advantage in the relevant complementary assets, the expert performance of the innovator's contractual partners in certain key activities complementary to the easily imitatable activities is often essential if the innovator is to capture a portion of the profits that the innovation generates. The antitrust laws must be shaped so that they do not impair such beneficial linkages.

In this regard, many British and American firms responsible for important product innovations have captured very little value from innovations for which they have been responsible because of their weaknesses in manufacturing. Often competitors can quickly reverse engineer new products. Once the new product design is apparent to competitors, success in the marketplace is determined by manufacturing costs and quality. In these circumstances, firms that are excellent at manufacturing—and this excellence is often harder to replicate than a new product is to reverse engineer—can garner practically all of the profits associated with the new product designs. Hence it is critical that

---

[13] There has been almost no treatment in the economic literature of the concept of complementary assets. It does not map easily into the familiar concept of indivisibilities, which is perhaps the closest analogue. For a more complete treatment, see Teece (1986).

innovating firms protect themselves from such outcomes by developing or somehow uniquely accessing the requisite complementary assets. The next section explains why cooperation may be necessary for firms to perform this function.

Governance Alternatives

The previous section has argued that innovation often requires firms to enter complex contracts and relationships with other firms to bring technology to the market, and to hold imitators at bay. This section considers in more detail the range of organizational alternatives available to the innovator to generate, coordinate and control such complementary assets.

Consider first the price mechanism. Theoretical treatments generally assume that the requisite coordination and control can be achieved by the invisible hand. Efficient levels of investment in complementary assets are brought forward at the right time and place by price signals. Entrepreneurship is automatic and costless. This is the view implicit in textbook presentations; in turn, the textbook view seems implicit in U.S. antitrust law.

However, many economists seem to have what Tjalling Koopmans calls an "overextended belief" regarding the efficiency of competitive markets as a means of allocating resources in a world characterized by ubiquitous uncertainty. Market failures are likely to arise because of the ignorance which firms have with respect to their competitors' future actions, preferences, and states of technological information (Koopmans, 1957, part II). In reality, nothing guarantees that investment programs are made known to all concerned at the time of their inception. This uncertainty is especially high for the development and commercialization of new technology. Accordingly, innovating firms need to achieve greater coordination than the price system alone appears to be able to bring about.

A second mechanism for effectuating coordination is the administrative processes within the firm. A company's internal organization can serve to shore up some market imperfections and provide some of the necessary coordination. As Alfred Chandler (1977) has explained, the modern multidivisional business enterprise "took over from the market the coordination and integration of the flow of goods and services from the production of raw materials through the several processes of production to the sale to the ultimate consumer ... administrative coordination replaced market coordination in an increasingly large portion of the economy." Oliver Williamson (1985) has developed an elegant and powerful framework to explain the relative efficiencies of markets and administrative processes. However, one property of large integrated structures is that they have the potential to become excessively hierarchical and less responsive to market needs (Teece, 1989c). Accordingly, at least for some aspects of innovative activity, smaller organizations are often superior.

In between pure market and full administrative solutions are many intermediate and hybrid possibilities, including interfirm agreements. Interfirm agreements can be classified as unilateral (where *A* sells *X* to *B*) or bilateral (whereby *A* agrees to buy *Y* from *B* as a condition for making the sale of *X*, and both parties understand that the transaction will be continued only if reciprocity is observed). Such arrangements can also be multilateral.

An especially interesting interfirm agreement is the strategic alliance, which can be defined as a bilateral or multilateral relationship characterized by the commitment of two or more partner firms to a common goal. A strategic alliance might include (1) technology swaps, (2) joint R&D or co-development, and/or (3) the sharing of complementary assets, such as where one party does manufacturing and the other distribution for a co-developed product. If the common goal was simply price-fixing or market-sharing, such an agreement might constitute a cartel, especially if the agreement included substantially all members of an industry.

By definition, a strategic alliance can never have one side receiving cash alone; it is not a unilateral exchange transaction. Nor do strategic alliances include mergers, because alliances by definition cannot involve acquisition of another firm's assets or controlling interest in another firm's stock. Alliances need not involve equity swaps or equity investments, though they often do. Strategic alliances without equity typically consist of contracts between or among partner firms that are nonaffiliated. Equity alliances can take many forms, including minority equity holdings, consortia, and joint ventures. Such interfirm agreements are usually temporary, and are assembled and disassembled as circumstances warrant. Typically, only a limited range of the firm's activities are enveloped in such agreements, and many competitors are excluded.

Strategic alliances, including consortia and joint ventures, are often an effective and efficient way to organize for innovation, particularly when an industry is fragmented. Interfirm cooperation preserves market selection and responsiveness; in a sense, it is the pure private enterprise solution. The case for planning and industrial policy recedes if a degree of operational and strategic coordination can be attained through private agreements. The benefits associated with less hierarchical structures can be obtained without incurring the disadvantages of insufficient scale and scope.

Antitrust Treatment of Interfirm Agreements

Current U.S. antitrust law needlessly inhibits interfirm agreements designed to develop and commercialize new technology. The problem is that the legal standards for interfirm agreements are ambiguous. While "rule of reason" analysis will generally be applied to contractual arrangements designed to advance innovation, the elements of rule of reason analysis are quite muddled.

In addition, although current law seems to recognize a "safe harbor" for mergers and acquisitions between firms that will have less than 20 percent market share, it does not recognize a similar safe harbor for horizontal contractual arrangements among firms.

The Clayton Act also permits private parties to sue for treble damages for alleged antitrust injuries, and allows state attorney generals to recover treble damages on behalf of persons residing in the state. Successful plaintiffs can also recover attorneys' fees. These remedies are available only in the United States. They provide a powerful incentive for plaintiffs to litigate, and given the current state of the law, a powerful disincentive for businesses to form cooperative innovation arrangements and strategic alliances. While measuring the missed opportunities for cooperative innovation caused by the threat of treble damage litigation is difficult, we believe the loss is substantial. Moreover, these disincentives work to the particular detriment of small and medium-sized innovative firms in industries where the innovative process is simultaneous.

Congress has recognized that these provisions may inhibit technological innovation, and the National Cooperative Research Act (NCRA) of 1984 took two significant steps to remove legal disincentives to cooperative research. First, the NCRA provides that "joint research and development ventures" must not be held illegal per se, and that such ventures instead should be "judged on the basis of [their] reasonableness, taking into account all relevant factors affecting competition, including, but not limited to, effects on competition in properly defined, relevant research and development markets." Second, the NCRA establishes a registration procedure for joint research and development ventures, limiting antitrust recoveries against registered ventures to single damages, interest, and costs, including attorney's fees. Thus, Congress eliminated the threat of treble damages for litigation challenging cooperative R&D arrangements, provided that the parties to the arrangement first register their venture. But R&D is only a small piece of the innovation puzzle.

In our view, the NCRA is not sufficiently permissive. The substantive protections provided by the NCRA—guaranteed rule of reason treatment and reduction of damages—extend only to research, and downstream commercial activity "reasonably required" for research and narrowly confined to marketing intellectual property developed through a joint R&D program. Treatment of other agreements designed to facilitate innovation is thus left uncertain, to be determined only by interpretation of the "reasonably required" standard. The NCRA unwisely precludes joint manufacturing and production of innovative products and processes, which is often necessary to provide the cooperating ventures with significant feedback information to aid in further innovation and product development, and to make the joint activity profitable. The NCRA implicitly accepts the serial and not the simultaneous model of innovation.

In addition, the NCRA gives little guidance concerning the substantive content of its rule of reason approach. While the Act did require that markets be defined in the context of research and not the products that might result from it, the NCRA fails to specify factors to be considered within rule of reason analysis. It simply requires consideration of "all relevant factors affecting competition," paying no special attention to the special characteristics of the innovation process in a quickly changing industry.

Finally, while the NCRA's elimination of treble damages for registered ventures is an important step forward, cooperating firms are still not protected from antitrust litigation. Even after the NCRA, antitrust law still permits private plaintiffs to engage in treble damage litigation against cooperative arrangements facilitating commercialization. Moreover, single damages are still available even against those registered under NCRA. The cost of defending antitrust suits is not materially reduced by the exceedingly narrow circumstances in which the Act permits an award of attorneys' fees to prevailing defendants. Moreover, the threat of litigation, with attendant managerial distraction, can be extremely damaging to the competitive performance of a fast-paced industry.

Businesses seem to have recognized the limited nature of the steps taken by the NCRA. Not surprisingly, only 111 separate cooperative ventures registered under the NCRA between 1984 and June 1988. Our review of these filings indicates that they are very modest endeavors that are aimed at solving industry problems and are not of great competitive moment. We believe that if an approval procedure existed under which procompetitive arrangements could obtain exemptions from further antitrust exposure to private damage actions, then many more competitively beneficial ventures would utilize the NCRA.

In contrast to this picture of U.S. antitrust law, the antitrust and business environment in Japan and Europe is more hospitable to strategic alliances and cooperative arrangements for innovation. The basic Japanese attitude is that joint R&D activities are procompetitive and thus should not be touched by the Antimonopoly Act. Significantly, the literal Japanese translation of "R&D" —*kenkyu kaihatsu*—implicitly includes commercialization; there is no semantic distinction between the concepts of R&D and commercialization.

In Japan, the Fair Trade Commission is responsible for executing and enforcing the Antimonopoly Act of 1947, which (like the Sherman Act) broadly prohibits unreasonable restraints of trade. While the Act provides no specific legislative exemption for joint innovation arrangements, Japan's FTC has been able to exempt cooperative innovation efforts from the scope of the law by virtue of its power as the primary enforcer of the Act.[14] FTC policy also states

---

[14]The basic adminstrative policy outlining the standards by which such joint innovation efforts are to be scrutinized is contained in a report of Japan's Fair Trade Commission (1984, 37-39). The report states that the evaluation of the anticompetitive effect of joint R&D at the product market stage will depend significantly "on the competition and market shares among the participants and the market structure of the industry to which the participants belong.... In cases where the market shares of the participants are small ... the effects will be small." Although "small" is not defined in the report, Japan's Merger Guidelines state that the FTC is not likely to closely examine cases in which the combined market share of the merging parties is less than 25 percent. See H. Iyori and A. Yesugi (1983, pp. 86–88). Our discussions with MITI and FTC officials confirm that the horizontal merger safe harbors would be equally applicable to cooperative contractual arrangements.

that if anticompetitive effects are alleged, the procompetitiveness benefits of innovation must be balanced, too. Balancing will take place not only within a particular market but also across markets (FTC, 1984), because "there is a possibility of the emergence of competition at the intersection of industrial sectors as a result of joint R&D between firms in different sectors."

In considering anticompetitive effects of cooperative innovation arrangements, Japan's FTC analyzes market shares and market structure. The FTC specifically recognizes the needs of innovators and articulates procompetitive justifications that include: (1) the difficulty of single-firm innovation; (2) the faster innovation created by cooperation and specialization between joint participants; (3) the pursuit of innovation in new fields by utilizing shared technology and know-how; and (4) enhancement of the technological level of each participant through the interchange of technology.

When MITI seeks to promote cooperative R&D activities (for example, as authorized by the Act for Facilitation of Research in Key Technology, or the Research Association for Mining and Manufacturing Technology Act), the FTC is consulted in advance. Once the FTC clears an activity, it is extraordinarily unlikely to pursue antitrust remedies at a future time. Significantly, treble damages are not available to private parties seeking to enforce Japanese antitrust laws, and private suits for single damages are very rare and usually unsuccessful. Thus, Japanese firms cooperating on innovation and commercialization of innovation have little to fear from Japanese antitrust laws.

Under this type of antitrust environment, it is not surprising that collaboration for innovation is frequent. Although regular statistics are not kept in Japan, because there is no reporting requirement for collaborative research and commercialization activities, a Fair Trade Commission report issued in 1984 contains statistics suggestive of the quantity and variety of joint innovation activities in Japan. The survey results indicate that joint R&D projects among corporations in the same industrial sector, which might be classified as horizontal collaboration, represent 19.1 percent of total projects.[15]

The antitrust environment shaping cooperation in the European Community is also markedly different from the United States. In 1968, the European Commission issued a "Notice of Cooperation between Enterprises" which indicates that horizontal collaboration for purposes of R&D is normally outside the scope of antitrust concerns as defined in Articles 85 and 86 of the EEC Treaty. The Commission has consistently taken a favorable position on R&D

---

[15]Questionnaires were sent to 484 manufacturing corporations in the fields of electronics, telecommunications, automobiles, chemicals, ceramics, steel and nonferrous metals, whose stocks were listed in Tokyo and Osaka Stock Exchanges. Data was provided by 242 corporations, representing 1.9 percent of the total manufacturing industry that engage in R&D activities in terms of the number of corporations and 16.7 percent in terms of sales. As to the nature of the joint R&D projects, 54.3 percent of the total cases were developmental research. Basic and applied research were 13.6 and 32.1 percent respectively. In the case of large corporations with capital of more than 10 billion yen, the total basic and application research amounted to 52.1 percent.

agreements unless the large entities involved imply serious anticompetitive consequences.

In 1984, the European Commission adopted Regulation No. 418/85 (hereafter Reg. 418) expanding the favorable antitrust treatment of R&D. For firms whose total market share does not exceed 20 percent, it provides blanket exceptions for horizontal R&D arrangements, including commercialization— which the Commission views as "the natural consequence of joint R&D"—up to the point of distribution and sales.[16] In addition, under Article 85(3), the Commission is authorized to grant exemptions for cooperative efforts that do not fall within the automatic safe harbor. Such exemptions may be granted when a horizontal agreement contributes to economic or technological progress in the research, production, or distribution of goods, and when procompetitive features outweigh anticompetitive aspects.

Proposed Modifications to U.S. Antitrust Law

To insure that antitrust law is responsive to the needs of innovating firms and does not inhibit U.S. firms from competing effectively in global markets experiencing rapid technological change, we believe the following changes are in order:

First, the rule of reason should be clarified to take specific account of the appropriability regime, the pace of technological change, the diversity of sources of new technology, the need to access complementary assets and technologies, and the need to have cheek-by-jowl cooperation to manage the innovation process simultaneously rather than serially.

Second, a safe harbor defined according to market power should be expressly adopted that would shield from antitrust liability interfirm agreements that involve less than 20 to 25 percent of the relevant market.

Third, market definition should be tailored to the context of innovation and should focus primarily on the market for know-how; specific product markets become relevant only when commercialization is included within the scope of the cooperative agreement. Even then, the extent of appropriability should be factored in when analyzing product market issues. The geographic market should be presumed to be worldwide, with the burden upon the challenger to demonstrate otherwise.

[16]Regulation No. 418/85 of 19 December 1984 on the application of Art. 85(3) of the Treaty to categories of research and development agreements, *O. J. Eur. Comm.* (No. L 53) 5 (1985), entered into force March 1, 1985, and applicable until December 31, 1997. The statutory framework of Reg. 418 is complex. It applies to three categories of agreements involving R&D: (1) joint research and development of products or processes and joint exploitation of the results of the R&D; (2) joint exploitation of the results of R&D product or processes pursuant to a prior agreements between the same parties; and (3) joint research and development of products without joint exploitation should the agreement fall within the purview of Art. 85(1). Under Reg. 418, joint exploitation is interpreted to mean joint manufacturing and licensing to third parties. Joint distribution and sales, however, are not covered and required individual exemptions pursuant to Art. 85(3).

Fourth, antitrust law should not bias the selection of interfirm organizational forms; at a minimum, integration by contract or alliance should be treated no less favorably than full mergers.

Fifth, the NCRA should be amended to include joint commercialization efforts to exploit innovation.

Sixth, an administrative procedure should be created, involving both the Justice and Commerce Departments, to allow evaluation and possible certification of cooperative arrangements among firms with higher market shares, when dynamic efficiency gains are likely and rivalry robust. We favor providing the opportunity for firms to either simply register and receive relief from treble damages as with the NCRA, or to apply for a certificate of exemption from the Justice and Commerce Departments that would provide even more protection. However, the quid pro quo would be greater disclosure and scrutiny of business plans. The firms themselves would choose which path to take.

Seventh, private antitrust suits challenging cooperative innovation arrangements should be limited to equitable relief, and attorneys' fees should be awarded to the prevailing party.

The first four of these proposals could be accomplished by courts interpreting the rule of reason and the National Cooperative Research Act. We hope courts will not hesitate to employ the tools of evolutionary, common law interpretation and development to achieve these changes. However, to achieve the complete package of substantive and procedural changes most quickly, and thus assure certainty and predictability, legislation is the best overall solution. At a U.C. Berkeley Conference on "Antitrust, Innovation and Competitiveness" in October 1988, we distributed a draft of legislation that combined a "registration" and "certification" approach for cooperative commercialization ventures. Shortly thereafter, Congressmen Edwards (H.R. 1025) and Congressman Fish (H.R. 2264) advanced a "registration" approach to cooperative commercialization efforts and Congressmen Boucher and Campbell (H.R. 1024) proposed a "certification" approach. After three hearings on these bills, Chairman Jack Brooks of the House Judiciary Committee introduced and the Judiciary Committee passed the National Cooperative Production Amendments of 1990 (H.R. 4611). H.R. 4611 would amend the National Cooperative Research Act to extend its registration approach to joint production ventures.[17] At the same time, Attorney General Richard Thornburgh and Commerce Secretary Robert

---

[17]Professor Jorde testified on July 26, 1989, in favor of both a registration and certification approach. See "Legislative Proposals to Modify the U.S. Antitrust Laws to Facilitate Cooperative Arrangements to Commercialize Innovation" (with David Teece), in *Hearings Before the Subcommittee on Economics and Commercial Law*, Committee on the Judiciary, U.S. House of Representatives (July 26, 1989). Legislation advancing a registration approach for production joint ventures has also been introduced in the Senate by Senators Patrick Leahy (D-VT) and Strom Thurmond (R-SC) (S.1006). Three aspects of H.R. 4611 bear noting. First, relevant market definition under rule of reason analysis would specifically consider the worldwide capacity of suppliers. Second, foreign participation in a production joint venture would be limited to 30 percent of the voting securities or equity interests, and all production facilities would have to be located in the United States or its

Mosbacher announced the Bush Administration's support of a registration approach for production joint ventures.[18]

As mentioned above, we support *both* a registration and certification approach. We do not see them as alternatives. Rather, we believe they should be combined into a single, two-track approach. Firms could choose the level and then form of protection most appropriate for their joint activity. Greater disclosure could buy greater protection.

The case for these changes rests on three fundamental pillars. The first is that the innovation process is terribly important to economic growth and development, because it yields social returns in excess of private returns, and because innovation is a powerful spur to competition. Hence, if antitrust policy is going to err, it ought to do so by facilitating innovation, rather than inhibiting it. This principle is well-understood in Europe and Japan.

Second, economic theory tells us that if certain organizational arrangements are exposed to governmentally-imposed costs while others are not, firms will substitute away from the burdened forms (in this context, interfirm agreements) and in favor of the unburdened forms (in this context, hierarchy), even when the former are potentially economically superior. According to Aoki (1989), the slowdown in total factor productivity in the United States can be attributed in large part to a mismatch between organizational form and the requirements of new technology; in particular, he is concerned that hierarchical solutions are overused, at least in the United States. As we have explained at some length above, we are concerned that present laws do not give full recognition to the interorganizational requirements of the innovation process; failure to do so is damaging when innovation must proceed according to the simultaneous model.

Third, cartelization of industries experiencing rapid technological change, and which are open to international trade and investment, is very difficult. So long as these industries remain open and innovative, antitrust policy should err on the side of permitting rather than restricting interfirm contracts.

Beneficial cooperation will eventually expand if antitrust laws are revised along the lines we propose. The response may not be immediate, particularly with respect to consortia, because the experience base in U.S. industry in this area is thin, because of our antitrust history, and because U.S. firms, at least in the postwar period, have been large relative to their foreign competitors. Accordingly, the need to cooperate has not been as powerful in the past as it is now. However, once organizational learning accumulates, we expect consortia to begin to flourish even in the absence of government funding. We also expect

---

territories. Third, apparently production joint ventures would not be limited to efforts designed to commercialize joint R&D, nor need they be related to innovation.

[18]See Department of Justice release, "Thornburgh Mosbacher Send Revision Legislation to Congress" (May 7, 1990) (supporting and detailing "legislation designed to facilitate joint production ventures"), reported at *Antitrust and Trade Regulation Report*, p. 701 (Vol. 58, No. 1465) (May 10, 1990).

the reinforcement of bilateral alliances already common in U.S. industry. We briefly discuss the kinds of activities that might take place.

Cooperative Manufacturing and Commercialization

In a number of circumstances, cooperative activity beyond early stages will benefit innovating firms. As discussed, sometimes this is true because of scale, risk, and appropriability considerations. Sometimes it is true because prohibition of cooperative commercialization imposes a significant technology transfer problem, for instance from the research joint venture (if there is one) back to the funding companies. In most cases, firms will not wish to cooperate all the way from research through to commercialization. But in some instances they will, or they will wish to cooperate simply on a downstream production venture. When cartelization of the industry is not a threat, we see no reason for antitrust restraints.

The now defunct U.S. Memories, Inc. consortium wanted to invest $500 million to $1 billion to develop and manufacture for its members and for the market advanced dynamic random access memories (DRAMs). With fabrication facilities costing hundreds of millions, acting alone is beyond the financial resources of many companies in this industry who might otherwise wish to have some control over their DRAM supply. This proposed consortium had to contend with a number of difficulties, including threats of third party litigation (Jorde and Teece, 1989b). While antitrust was not the main reason for the failure of this enterprise, the antitrust environment did nothing to help it succeed. A certification procedure would have provided important certainty to this venture, and others like it. A registration procedure would provide less certainty, but still would be a significant advance over current antitrust law.

Similarly, in the area of superconductors, it is likely that the real challenges will come not in developing superconductors, but in their commercialization. Applying superconductors in systems like railroads, computers, and electricity distribution will require great amounts of time, resources, and capital— probably greater than any single business can muster internally. Accordingly, a public policy stance that treats only early stage activity as potentially requiring cooperation is misguided and will thwart both early and later stage activities. Most firms will not have much incentive to engage in early stage, joint development if later stage, stand-alone commercialization appears too expensive to accomplish profitably.

Cooperative Innovation Designed to Achieve Catch-Up

Cooperative activities in Japan and Europe have frequently been motivated by a desire to catch up with the world's technological frontier, which in the postwar years was usually the technology of U.S. firms. However, U.S. firms are increasingly slipping behind the frontier. For instance, U.S. firms are now behind in areas like ceramics and robotics, and in products like VCRs, facsimiles, and HDTV. Just as foreign firms have found cooperative ventures useful for catch-up in the past, U.S. firms could utilize cooperation for this purpose. For example, U.S.-based firms, acting together and with foreign firms, may still have a slender chance of competing in the market for high definition televisions (HDTV) and related products expected to evolve in the 1990s. In the absence of cooperative interfirm agreements, we doubt that development of HDTV systems is possible in the United States. If America's potential "reentrants" to the consumer electronics business combine to attempt reentry, they cannot be sure of avoiding serious antitrust problems involving treble damages, particularly if they are successful.

At minimum, the legislative changes proposed would facilitate unfettered information exchange and strategic coordination with respect to reentry strategies. If such efforts facilitated profitable reentry into high technology businesses when reentering would otherwise not occur, or would occur in a more limited and unprofitable way, we do not see why antitrust concerns ought to interfere.

Cooperation in Response to Foreign Industrial and Technology Policy

In high technology industries, both European and East Asian nations have active industrial and technology policies that significantly impact market outcomes, both in their own countries and abroad. Airbus is a case in point. The dominant U.S. attitude is one of laissez-faire, and many economists are of the view that the United States should send a letter of thanks to foreign governments who subsidize exports to the United States. Such a view is insensitive to the dynamics of technological change, to the importance of cumulative learning, and to reentry costs.

Some U.S. policy makers, however, favor retaliation against foreign countries which have active industrial policies. We support a modification of U.S. antitrust laws which in some circumstances would permit a competitive response by U.S. industry acting collectively. The proposals we advance to encourage greater cooperation among U.S. firms do not require government expenditures nor do they involve the government "picking winners." But they would soften the tensions emerging in the United States between technology, antitrust and trade policies.

Conclusion

The past two decades have wrought significant changes in the business environment. Markets have become globalized, sources of new technology are increasingly pluralistic, and "simultaneous" systems of innovation have substituted for linear, hierarchical ones. Moreover, the ability of foreign firms to utilize technology developed in the United States has increased markedly. Imitation is easier, not harder, in spite of recent court decisions which have strengthened patents.

Accordingly, innovative firms confront significant challenges in capturing value from new technology. Success in research and development does not automatically translate into a financial success, even if the technology developed meets a significant market need. To succeed financially, innovative firms must quickly position themselves advantageously in the appropriate complementary assets and technologies. If they are not already integrated, the best solution often involves bilateral and multilateral cooperative agreements.[19]

U.S. antitrust policy, like so much of our economic policy, has been preoccupied with static rather than intertemporal concerns. Despite important recent developments, it is informed by naive theories of the innovation process, and in particular is insensitive to the organizational needs of innovation. U.S. antitrust scholars still harbor suspicion of cooperative agreements among competitors, and do not appreciate the benefits. This suspicion fuels uncertainty about how the courts would view interfirm arrangements to promote technological progress and competition.

The policy changes we advance are certainly no panacea for the severe problems U.S. high technology industry is currently experiencing. But in bringing American policy closer to Europe and Japan, we will at least purge dogma that no longer deserves a place in U.S. industrial policy. In time, reduced antitrust exposure will help clear the way for beneficial cooperation, thereby reducing incentives for mergers and acquisitions.

The 1990 centennial of the Sherman Act would be a good occasion to set things right. The economics profession, which in the past has had a significant impact on the law of vertical restraints, can provide the intellectual leadership necessary to propel adjustments in the horizontal area, thereby helping to align U.S. policies with the technological and competitive realities of today's global economy.

■ *This paper is based in part on Jorde and Teece (1989a) and Teece (1986). We are extremely grateful for financial support from the Alfred P. Sloan Foundation, the Smith-Richardson Foundation, The Pew Foundation, and the Sasakawa Peace Foundation. We wish to thank Joseph Stiglitz, Carl Shapiro, and Timothy Taylor for valuable substantive and editorial comments. Bill Baxter, Oliver Williamson, and Dick Nelson made helpful comments on earlier drafts and oral presentations. We implicate none of the above in our conclusions.*

---

[19]As Richard Nelson (1990) notes, a wide variety of new kinds of organizational arrangements is emerging to support innovation. He predicts, and we concur, that some will succeed, and some will not. Our concern is that because the requirements of innovation are not well understood in mainstream economics and in contemporary antitrust analysis, there is significant danger that the performance of U.S. firms will be impaired by outdated antitrust law.

References

Aoki, M., "Global Competition, Firm Organization, and Total Factor Productivity: A Comparative Micro Perspective." Paper presented at the International Seminar on Science, Technology, and Economic Growth, OECD, Paris, June 1989.

Arrow, Kenneth J., "Economic Welfare and the Allocation of Resources for Invention." In National Bureau of Economic Research, ed., *The Rate and Direction of Inventive Activity.* Princeton: Princeton University Press, 1962, pp. 609–625.

Chandler, Alfred D. Jr., *The Visible Hand: The Managerial Revolution in American Business.* Cambridge: Harvard University Press, 1977.

Collis, David, "The Machine Tool Industry and Industrial Policy, 1955-1982." In Spence, A. Michael, and Heather A. Hazard, eds., *International Competitiveness.* Cambridge: Ballinger, 1988, pp.

David, D., "R&D Consortia," *High Technology,* October 1985, p. 42.

Dertouzos, Michael L., Richard K. Lester, and Robert M. Solow, *Made in America: Regaining the Productive Edge.* Cambridge: MIT Press, 1989.

Dosi, Giovanni, "Sources, Procedures, and Microeconomic Effects of Innovation," *Journal of Economic Literature,* September 1988, *26,* 1120–1171.

Fair Trade Commission (Japan), *Research and Development Activities in Private Enterprises and Problems They Pose in the Competition Policy* (*Minkan kigyo ni okeru kenkyu kaihatsu katsudo no jttai to kyoso seidaku jo no kaidai*), 1984.

Gomory, R., "Dominant Science Does Not Mean Dominant Product," *Research and Development,* November 1987, p. 72.

Grossman, Gene M., and Carl Shapiro, "Research Joint Ventures: An Antitrust Analysis," *Journal of Law and Economics,* Fall 1986, *2,* pp. 315–337.

von Hippel, Eric, *The Sources of Innovation.* Cambridge: MIT Press, 1988.

Imai, Ken-ichi, and Yasunori Baba, "Systemic Innovation and Cross Border Networks." Paper presented at Seminar on the Contributions of Science and Technology to Economic Growth, OECD, Paris, June 1989.

Iyori, H., and A. Yesugi, *The Antimonopoly Laws of Japan,* New York: Federal Legal Publications, 2nd edition, 1983.

Jorde, Thomas M., and David J. Teece, "Innovation, Cooperation, and Antitrust: Balancing Competition and Cooperation," *High Technology Law Journal,* Spring 1989a, *4,* pp. 1–113.

Jorde, Thomas M., and David J. Teece, "To Keep U.S. in the Chips, Modify the Antitrust Laws," *Los Angeles Times,* July 24, 1989b, Part II, p. 5.

Kline, S. J., and Nathan Rosenberg, "An Overview of Innovation." In Rosenberg, Nathan, and R. Landau, eds., *The Positive Sum Strategy.* Washington, DC: National Academy Press, 1986, pp. 275–305.

Koopmans, Tjalling, *Three Essays in the State of Economic Science.* New York: McGraw Hill, 1957.

Levin, Richard, A. Klevorick, R. Nelson, and S. Winter, "Appropriating the Returns from Industrial Research and Development," *Brookings Papers on Economic Activity,* Winter 1987, *3,* 783–820.

Mansfield, E., A. Romeo, M. Schwartz, D. Teece, S. Wagner and P. Brach, *Technology Transfer, Productivity, and Economic Policy.* New York: W. W. Norton, 1982.

Nalebuff, Barry, and Joseph Stiglitz, "Information, Competition and Markets," *American Economic Review,* May 1983, *72,* 278–284.

Nelson, Richard, "Capitalism as an Enigma of Progress," *Research Policy,* 1990, *19,* 193–214.

Ordover, Janusz, and Robert Willig, "Antitrust for High Technology Industries: Assessing Research Joint Ventures and Mergers," *Journal of Law and Economics,* May 1985, *28,* 311–33.

Rosenberg, Nathan, *Technology and American Economic Growth.* Armonk: M. E. Sharpe, 1972.

Sah, Raaj, and Joseph Stiglitz, "Technological Learning, Social Learning and Technological Change." In Chakravarty, S., ed., *The Balance between Industry and Agriculture in Economic Development.* New York: St. Martin's/International Economic Association, 1989, pp. 285–298.

Schumpeter, J. A., *Capitalism, Socialism and Democracy.* New York: Harper Brothers, 1942.

Teece, David J., "Technology Transfer by Multinational Firms: The Resource Costs of Transferring Technological Know-how," *The Economic Journal,* June 1977, *87,* 242–261.

Teece, David J., "Economies of Scope and the Scope of the Enterprise," *Journal of Economic Behavior and Organization,* 1980, *1,* 223–247.

Teece, David J., "Towards an Economic Theory of the Multiproduct Firm," *Journal of Economic Behavior and Organization*, 1982, *3*, 39–63.

Teece, David J., "Profiting from Technological Innovation," *Research Policy*, December 1986, 285–305.

Teece, David J., "Inter-organizational Requirements of the Innovation Process," *Managerial and Decision Economics*, 1989a, *10*, 35–42.

Teece, David J., "Innovation and the Organization of Industry." Unpublished working paper, Center for Research in Management, University of California at Berkeley, 1989b.

Teece, David J., "Market Entry Strategies for Innovators: Avoiding Pyrrhic Victories," *Strategic Management Journal*, 1991.

Tirole, Jean, *The Theory of Industrial Organization*. Cambridge: MIT Press, 1988.

Williamson, Oliver E., *The Economic Institutions of Capitalism: Firms, Markets, Relational Contracting*. New York: Free Press, 1985.

Winter, Sidney J., "Knowledge and Competence as Strategic Assets." In Teece, David J., ed., *The Competitive Challenge*. Cambridge: Ballinger, 1987.

16

Journal of Institutional and Theoretical Economics (JITE) 147 (1991), 118–144
Zeitschrift für die gesamte Staatswissenschaft

Antitrust Policy and Innovation: Taking Account of Performance Competition and Competitor Cooperation*

by

THOMAS M. JORDE and DAVID J. TEECE

1. Overview

The beginning of a new decade is a good time for stock taking – to reflect upon past accomplishments and to survey future challenges. In the field of antitrust, 1990 has special significance because this year marks the centennial of the Sherman Act. Our own reflections on antitrust policy, particularly as practiced in the United States, cause us to express certain concerns about the relevance of today's antitrust policy for the future and for the global economic environment. Though we certainly do not advocate its abolition, we suggest that antitrust may be anachronistic in certain contexts, and indeed, may actually inhibit effective competition.

Antitrust law has undergone significant changes since the passage of the Sherman Act in 1890. But the U.S. and world economies have undergone even greater changes. We do not intend in this paper to recount the major developments in antitrust over the past century. Nor do we intend to survey comprehensively the many changes that have occurred in our economic system and in the global economy. Rather, we will describe in general terms ways in which antitrust law and policy can be "out of touch" with other important goals. In particular, we suggest that if society wishes to promote competition, the best way to do so is to promote innovation. That in turn may require dismantling portions of our antitrust laws. To be sure, other policies affecting innovation are also important, such as savings rates, investment in education and technological skills, and appropriate financial and tax incentives. Our focus, however, is upon antitrust and its impact on innovation and competitiveness.

In our view, antitrust is being rendered increasingly superfluous by dispersion in the sources of innovation and the associated growth in international

* This paper is based in part on JORDE and TEECE [1989a], [1990a], [1990b] and TEECE [1986]. We are extremely grateful for financial support from the Alfred P. Sloan Foundation, the Smith-Richardson Foundation, The Pew Foundation, and the Sasakawa Peace Foundation. Bill Baxter, Oliver Williamson, and Dick Nelson made helpful comments on earlier drafts and oral presentations. We implicate none of the above in our conclusions.

competition. So long as U.S. markets remain open to global competition, antitrust may soon become an expensive ornament that more often than not gets in the way of competition, though it need not in an ideal world with an efficient system of adjudication and enforcement. The basis of our argument is that technological innovation drives competition, that the sources of innovation are remarkably diverse, and the antitrust laws which we have inherited are informed by static theories of market performance and therefore are as likely to throttle innovation as to stimulate it. In short, we believe (1) that stimulating rivalry ought to be an important policy goal, (2) that the form of competition the antitrust laws should embrace is Schumpeterian dynamic competition, (3) that current antitrust is not designed to achieve this, (4) that the best guarantor of dynamic competition is a system that is open to international trade and has policies which facilitate innovation, and (5) that internal organization and intercorporate links, and not government intervention, is important for successful innovation and commercialization. Accordingly, we are uncomfortable with an approach to antitrust which measures market power from a static perspective and is inhospitable to a great deal of cooperative behavior among competitors. If economic welfare is the goal of antitrust, then the promotion of innovation may henceforth need to take precedence over standard antitrust concerns. At minimum, we offer certain modest changes in the antitrust laws which would alter the way that market power is measured and cooperation among competitors assessed, when credible claims of innovation and its commercialization are present.

The organization of this paper is as follows. In the next section we discuss the nature of competition and its importance to a properly functioning market economy. We distinguish between two types of competition. The first we call "price competition." This kind of competition occurs among firms in mature industries and stems from differences in scale economies and the like. The second kind of competition we simply label "performance competition." This competition originates from innovations which fuel the introduction of new products, or old products at drastically lower prices. Performance competition stimulates rivalry and promotes economic welfare far more effectively than does price competition. Yet it is not what U.S. antitrust laws seem to emphasize. We discuss the implications of this for market definition and market power analysis in section 3, and for the antitrust treatment of agreements among competitors in section 4. Our conclusion in section 5 discusses the benefits we believe would flow from an antitrust jurisprudence that was more Schumpeterian.

2. The Nature and Importance of Competition and the Goals of Antitrust

Americans have a long-standing and well-founded belief in competition. This tradition is rooted in part in political beliefs. Competitive systems that are open to newcomers provide important checks and balances on monopoly power; monopoly power sometimes impairs resource allocations and is often seen as being correlated with political influence. Promoting competition can thus be seen as a corollary of democracy. Indeed, it was concern about the political power of the trusts that helped motivate the passage of the Sherman Act in the first place.

But while political concerns helped motivate passage of the Sherman Act, the economics profession has, particularly in the post-war period, spilled a great deal of economic content into the various antitrust vessels which Congress created. Antitrust law and policy have generally benefitted. The economic theory that has been supplied falls into two broad classes: neoclassical (textbook) microeconomics, and to a much more limited but growing extent, transaction cost economics. Neoclassical microeconomics is a very powerful lens for analyzing the behavior of certain types of markets. It is particularly useful for explaining commodity-type markets characterized either by perfect competition or pure monopoly. Textbook microeconomic analysis often rests on the following assumptions: (1) markets are characterized by perfect information; (2) economic agents are hyper-rational; (3) markets are always in equilibrium; and (4) technology is uniformly available to all firms (and therefore costlessly transferrable among them).

This results in a view of competition that is highly stylized: firms compete primarily by offering lower prices; competition is characterized by the zero profit condition; adjustments from equilibrium occur instantaneously; new entry is always good; technology is uniformly available to all firms; communication among competitors is probably for the purpose and will have the effect of cartelizing. Unfortunately, this view of economics, which informs antitrust analysis today, overlooks important aspects of the competitive process, and distorts others. Indeed, as Schumpeter suggested half a century ago, the kind of competition embedded in standard microeconomic analysis may not be the kind of competition that really matters if enhancing economic welfare is the goal of antitrust. Rather, it is dynamic competition that really counts.[1]

Dynamic competition is the competition that comes from the new product or the new process. There are at least two types of innovative regimes which stimulate rivalry. First, there is incremental innovation. In this type of innovative system new products are introduced in rapid succession, each one such an improvement on the prior product that the new drives out the old. In regimes characterized by incremental innovation, the population of firms in an industry is likely to be relatively stable. However, established firms will fall into relative decline if they do not keep up with changing technology. Good examples of industrial regimes characterized by incremental innovation today are the aircraft, chemical, and VCR industries.

---

[1] See Joseph SCHUMPETER [1942].

The other regime is one where radical innovation is predominant. Few industries are characterized by this for long periods of time. However, when the transistor arrived it clearly did more to invigorate competition and provide economic benefits than did any level of rivalrous behavior among the manufacturers of vacuum tubes. Likewise, the invention of the video disc and compact disc engendered competition into the recording business of a kind that firms competing with the standard vinyl records could not supply. And the arrival of the steamship sharpened competition on ocean freight in ways that intense competition among sail ships could never engender.

Recognizing these forms of dynamic competition would not cause any tension with existing antitrust laws if the world of competition envisaged in the textbook was the ideal structure from which innovation and its successful commercialization would emerge. However, there is no evidence that the world of perfect competition to which antitrust doctrine often aspires is in fact ideal for promoting innovation. The weight of the evidence appears to suggest that the structure of markets – whether competitive or monopolized – is relatively unimportant in impacting innovation.[2] The evidence does suggest that current monopoly is usually transitory and is rarely a barrier; most truly radical innovations emerge from outside an established industry, and access to the infrastructure provided by incumbent firms is rarely critical for ultimate success. Incremental innovation is not much impacted by market structure either.

What, then, does innovation require? The evidence is sketchy. However, we can identify several classes of factors that are important: availability of a labor force with the requisite technical skills; economic structures which permit considerable autonomy and entrepreneurship; economic systems which permit and encourage a variety of approaches to technological and market opportunities; access to "venture" capital, either from a firm's existing cash flow or from an external venture capital community; good connections between the scientific community, especially the universities, and the technological community, and between users and developers of technology; strong protection of intellectual property; the availability of strategies and structures to enable innovating firms to capture a return from their investment; in fragmented industries, the ability to quickly build or access cospecialized assets inside or outside the industry.

Few of these considerations are impacted positively by antitrust policy. However, we contend that antitrust negatively affects the ability of innovating firms to cooperate in the development and commercialization of innovation, or engage in business strategies or interfirm agreements to keep "me too"-type imitators at bay.[3] In our view, dynamic, not static, competition is what the antitrust laws should be seeking to promote if enhancing economic welfare over time is the goal. We believe that the implicit acceptance of current antitrust law,

---

[2] See BALDWIN and SCOTT [1987], and TEECE [1990].
[3] See generally, JORDE and TEECE [1989 a] for a detailed assessment of antitrust law and enforcement.

and infatuation with the inherently short run model of perfect competition, may be counterproductive long run. There is no good theoretical reason nor any evidence to support the contention that present antitrust policy advances dynamic competition and economic growth. In sections III and IV, we explore areas in which we believe antitrust is likely to stand in the way.

We take it as axiomatic that innovation and its rapid and profitable commercialization is the key factor driving productivity improvement in the economy.[4] Accordingly, the focus of antitrust on consumer welfare is possibly misplaced. Consumer welfare is enhanced long term only if productivity increases; and that requires technological innovation. Hence, an economic welfare calculus which includes future benefits, appropriately discounted of course, requires the promotion of innovation. Modern efforts to promote consumer welfare as the goal of antitrust fall wide of the mark whenever the focus is on present consumer welfare.[5a] This is unfortunately exactly what the standard static analysis accomplishes. Accordingly, if consumer welfare is to be the goal of antitrust, it needs to be couched in a forward-looking, innovation-centered context.[5b] Otherwise, antitrust policy may unwittingly diminish a nation's economic welfare.

Alternatively, one might consider the abandonment of a consumer welfare orientation, and the substitution of innovation and its rapid diffusion as the goal of antitrust policy. At minimum, we would propose that when the promotion of static consumer welfare and innovation are in conflict, the courts and administrative agencies should favor innovation. Adopting dynamic competition and innovation as the goal of antitrust would, in our view, serve consumer welfare over time more assuredly than would the current focus on short-run consumer welfare. We will return to this topic in our discussion of industrial policy in section 5. We next turn to two areas of antitrust law that are insufficiently sensitive to dynamic competition and its benefits: market power assessment and competitor agreements.

3. Innovation and Market Power Assessment [6]

There is no area where antitrust policy so clearly displays its focus on static competition than in the treatment of market definition. Market definition is the key pillar to antitrust theory and enforcement policy. In the absence of market power, practically every form of business behavior, other than price fixing and

---

[4] For a brief review of this literature, see JORDE and TEECE [1989].

[5a] BORK [1978] has been a strong advocate of the consumer welfare approach.

[5b] Interestingly, in the economic analysis of international trade policy, both producer and consumer welfare are advanced, along with tariff revenues, as legitimate components of domestic economic welfare.

[6] This section is based on JORDE and TEECE [1988] and HARTMAN, TEECE, MITCHELL and JORDE [1990].

its economic equivalents, is legal. Once market power is proven, business practices will be closely scrutinized to determine whether they are reasonable.

Standard approaches to competition can assign market power incorrectly to an innovating firm. Even though the market power associated with innovation is often quite transitory, standard entry barrier analysis – with its one to two year fuse for entry[7] – will often not undo a finding of market dominance and associated market power for an innovator. Accordingly, innovators may need to constrain severely their business conduct in order to avoid violating the antitrust laws or the threat of private treble damage actions. Ironically, in today's global economy, with low or nonexistent tariffs, one of the few ways to build market share in the United States is through innovative success.

With a Schumpeterian concept of competition in mind, one finds the current methodology for defining product markets troublesome. This is because, in the Schumpeterian conception of things, market power can be ephemeral in industries characterized by rapid technological change. Schumpeterian competition is not readily incorporated into the standard analytical frameworks used to define relevant antitrust markets.

For example, consider how the U.S. Department of Justice (DOJ) approaches market definition.[8] As explained in the *Merger Guidelines* [1984], the DOJ will include in the product market a group of products such that "a hypothetical firm that was the only present and future seller of these products ('the monopolist') could profitably impose a small but significant and nontransitory increase in price – generally five percent lasting one year." Our focus here is not so much on the 5 percent threshold, but on the fact that the implicit assumption adopted is that products in a market are homogeneous and competitors compete on price. Such is often not the case. As a result, application of the 5 percent test in an industry where competition is Schumpeterian rather than neoclassical is likely to create a downward bias in the definition of the size of the relevant product market, and a corresponding upward bias in the assessment of market power.

Consider the minicomputer industry. In the minicomputer industry, a variety of systems compete on price and performance while exhibiting price differences of several 100 percent.[9] Too literal an application of the DOJ's 5 percent test would suggest that each manufacturer is in a different market, because otherwise product substitution would occur which would stimulate pressures for price equalization.

Such an interpretation, however, would ignore the realities of competition in the computer industry. A variety of systems with quite different price-performance attributes successfully occupy the same market at a given point in time.

---

[7] See *U.S. Department of Justice Merger Guidelines*, June 14, 1984.

[8] While frequently criticized, this approach is widely accepted by scholars and the courts. For a critique, see HARRIS and JORDE [1983].

[9] See HARTMAN and TEECE [1990].

As new systems are introduced and the prices of existing systems change, it takes some time for resulting price-performance implications to be digested and understood by the market. One reason is simply that it takes time for users to experience and test the products. Moreover, to the extent that the product is durable and a replacement for existing equipment, purchase decisions are complicated by the need to retire existing equipment. In addition, new computer systems usually require new supporting systems to be developed and acquired, so that even computer systems that are consensually superior on price and performance dimensions will take time to diffuse and be adapted. In such situations, 5 percent or even 25 percent price increases may be met with no substitution until the performance of the products can be assessed and existing equipment can be economically replaced. Even a 25 percent price increase may seem insignificant if accompanied by a performance enhancement. In such circumstances, where competition is performance based, the DOJ's 5%-one-year rule is not likely to identify markets that are in any way meaningful.[10] We outline our approach to this problem, which is more fully developed in HART-MAN, TEECE, MITCHELL and JORDE [1990].

When competition proceeds primarily on the basis of features and performance, the pertinent question to ask is whether a change in the performance attributes of one commodity would induce substitution to or from another. If the answer is affirmative, then the differentiated products, even if based on alternative technologies, should be included in the relevant product market. Furthermore, when assessing such performance-induced substitutability, a one-year or two-year period is simply too short, because enhancement of performance attributes involves a longer time to accomplish than price changes. While it is difficult to state precisely (and generally) what the length of time should be, it is clear that the time frame should be determined by technological concerns. As a result, it may be necessary to apply different time frames to different products/technologies.

When assessing performance-based competition among existing producers, the product changes to be included as a metric should involve re-engineering of existing products using technologies currently known to existing competitors. Product changes which depend on anticipated technologies, that are not currently commercial, should be excluded. Thus if firm A, by modifying its product X using its existing proprietary product and process technology and public

---

[10] In Section 3.411, the *U.S. Department of Justice Merger Guidelines* state that with heterogeneous products "the problems facing a cartel become more complex. Instead of a single price, it may be necessary to establish and enforce a complex schedule of prices corresponding to gradations in actual or perceived quality attributes among competing products. ...Product variation is arguably relevant in all cases, but *practical consider-ations dictate a more limited use of the factor.*" As a rule of thumb, if the product is completely homogeneous (very heterogeneous), "the Department of Justice is more (less) likely to challenge the merger."

knowledge, could draw sales away from product Y of firm B, such that B would need to improve its products to avoid losing market share to A, then X and Y are in the same relevant market. If such changes are likely to occur yet would take longer than one year, the one-year rule should be modified.

When assessing potential competition and entry barriers, the two-year-5% rule must also be modified to include variations in performance attributes in existing and new technologies. In high-technology innovative industries, it is this competition that is often most threatening, often the most important from a welfare standpoint,[11] takes the longest time to play out, and is the most difficult to fully anticipate. A more realistic time frame must be determined over which the new products/technologies may be allowed to enter. The precise length of time allowed for the entry of potential competitors must also reflect technological realities. Hence, it too may vary by product and technology.

The need to assess performance competition argues for the use of "hedonic methods." A growing hedonic literature has addressed the importance of product attributes in economic behavior. This literature has been both theoretical and empirical. It has focused upon product demand and production cost. The demand literature has addressed the importance of product attributes in determining prices[12] and market share.[13] The cost literature demonstrates and measures the impact of product attributes on production costs.[14]

Thus assume that several firms offer various products with different attributes. Assume that one producer improves the performance of a certain attribute, holding price and other attributes constant. If the demand of a similar product decreases, there exists a performance cross-elasticity between the two products. If this cross elasticity is high enough, the products are in the same market. However, if the producer were to improve the performance of a certain attribute, but simultaneously raises the product's price such that no substitution occurs, this does not necessarily mean that the products are in different markets.

---

[11] As noted earlier, SCHUMPETER [1942] stressed that potential competition from new products and processes is the most powerful form of competition. stating "in capitalist reality, as distinguished from its textbook picture, it is not that kind [price] of competition that counts but the competition that comes from the new commodity, the new technology. the new source of supply... This kind of competition is as much more effective than the other as bombardment is in comparison with forcing a door, and so much more important that it becomes a matter of comparative indifference whether competition in the ordinary sense functions more or less promptly."

[12] See BROWN and MENDELSOHN [1984]; BROWN and ROSEN [1982]; EPPLE [1987]; HARTMAN [1987]; HARTMAN and DOANE [1987]; HARTMAN and TEECE [1990]; OHTA and GRILICHES [1976]; and ROSEN [1974].

[13] See ATKINSON and HALVORSEN [1984]; HARTMAN [1982]; HAUSMAN [1979]; and MANNERING and WINSTON [1984].

[14] See EPPLE [1987]; FRIEDLAENDER et al. [1983]; FUSS [1984]; FUSS and WAVERMAN [1981]; and SPADY and FRIEDLAENDER [1978].

This framework allows one to anaylze and quantify both price and performance (attribute) competition. Using it, one can retain the 5 percent price rule while extending the DOJ approach to incorporate performance competition. For example, analogous to the 5 percent price rule, one could assess the effects of percentage changes in performance. However, such an extension is far from straightforward. One needs to carefully specify rules of thumb regarding the threshold size of performance competition and the time period over which such competition is allowed to unfold.

In general, performance changes are more difficult to quantify than price changes because performance is multi-dimensional. As a result, quantification requires measuring both the change in an individual attribute and the relative importance of that attribute. Unlike price changes which involve altering the value of a common base unit (dollars), performance changes often involve changing the units by which performance is measured. Nonetheless, rough quantification is possible, based on the pooled judgments of competent observers, particularly product users.

In terms of threshold effects, we tentatively suggest introducing a 25 percent rule for a change in any key performance attribute. This threshold implies the following. Assume that an existing manufacturer lowers the quality of a key performance attribute of an existing product up to 25 percent, *ceteris paribus*. If no substitution to other products occurs, then the original product constitutes a distinct antitrust market. If substitution to other products does occur, then those other products share the market with the original product. Conversely, assume that a new product is introduced that is identical to an existing product in all ways except that it offers up to a 25 percent improvement in a key performance attribute. If there is no substitution to the new product, then the products represent distinct markets. If there is substitution from the existing product to the new product, then the two products share the same antitrust market.

The criterion of 25 percent performance improvement for a single key performance attribute is conservative. Not only is a 25 percent improvement small compared to those that commonly occur in industries experiencing rapid technological change, but a 25 percent improvement in a single attribute is likely to imply an overall performance improvement of considerably less than 25 percent. This performance threshold must furthermore be judged in terms of feasibility. While it is always possible to raise prices, it is not always possible to increase performance. This problem is most severe in the case of quantum changes, such as the introduction of a specific application for a device. Following introduction, however, most product changes take place along a relatively continuous trajectory of technological improvement. Many product users are familiar with the key development programs of their suppliers and are able to assess the likelihood that a particular product change will emerge in the near future.

An effective measurement procedure, therefore, would be to rely on the informed judgments of users of existing products. This procedure would involve identifying market experts, asking them to list key performance attributes, and then asking them to assess the substitutive effects of changes in the attributes. The sample of product users could be supplemented by a corresponding sample of commercial participants, although care would be required to avoid introducing competitive bias into the judgments.[15] A sample of such participants could be asked whether a 25 percent change in the performance of any one attribute would lead to product substitution.

In addition to threshold rules regarding performance changes, market definition requires an identification of a time frame for the competitive product changes – that is, the definition of the "near future." We argued above that the DOJ one-year and two-year rules are too short for almost any case of serious technical advance. Indeed, because there is significant variation among products, no single number will be appropriate for all cases. Nonetheless, we suggest that a four-year period be established as a default time frame, with the option of adjusting the period if strong evidence suggests that would be appropriate in an individual case. Like the DOJ's one-year rule, or the patent law's 17-year grant, a fixed four-year rule will not be optimal in all cases. It could provide too broad a market definition in some cases and too narrow a definition for others; however, its unambiguous nature has the advantage of being easily understood and not requiring negotiation or litigation to determine an appropriate frame.

Finally, one needs to address the question of the appropriate HHI thresholds. The Merger Guidelines selects critical HHIs at 1000 and 1800. It is difficult to hypothesize and propose alternative HHIs for technologically dynamic markets. However, the inclusion of performance competition and the extension of the time frame of competitive response may mean that it is not necessary to change these critical HHIs. Furthermore, we believe that with technologically dynamic markets, the dynamics of market structure in the past should provide some guidance to assessing market definition and predicting likely changes in market concentration. Key factors are the change in concentration and the trend in the number of competitors.

Failure to recognize that competition is often on the basis of performance attributes and not price will lead courts and the Department of Justice to underestimate the breadth of product markets in industries characterized by rapid technological change. This process, in turn, will lead courts and the DOJ to exaggerate antitrust dangers.[16]

---

[15] If an employee of a competitor of a firm for which market power was being determined were included in the sample, for instance, that person would have incentives to overestimate the difficulty of performance improvement. The need to inform these economic decisions with technological reality would argue for a closer working relationship between the Antitrust Division of the Justice Department and the National Science Foundation and/or the Office of Technology Assessment.

[16] One example was the Justice Department's challenge to the sale of EMI's U.S. operations to General Electric.

4. Innovation and Cooperative Agreements Among Competitors

A second area in which traditional antitrust analysis may impede innovation is in the analysis of cooperative agreements among competitors. The problem arises because of a naïve view of innovation, embedded in current antitrust economics and jurisprudence, that fails to recognize that innovating firms may need to cooperate to promote innovation. We next briefly explain two different models of the innovation process and explore implications for antitrust policy.

4.1 The (Traditional) Serial Model

Traditional descriptions of the innovation process commonly break it down into a number of stages which proceed sequentially. This view is reflected in theoretical treatments of R&D in industrial organization. According to this view, the innovation process proceeds in a linear and predictable fashion from research to development, design, production, and then finally to marketing, sales, and service.[17] In simple models, there is not even any feedback or overlap between and among stages.

The serial model of innovation is an analytic convenience which no longer adequately characterizes the innovation process, except in special circumstances, such as in some scale-intensive industries. The initial development of nylon at Dupont perhaps fits this model. The Manhattan project during World War II is also illustrative. The serial model does not address the many small but cumulatively important incremental innovations that are at the heart of technological change in many industries, especially well-established industries like semiconductors, computers, and automobiles.

The serial model has enabled economists to model innovation as a vertical process. Inasmuch as antitrust policy toward vertical restraints is very permissive, many economists and legal scholars do not understand how U.S. antitrust laws could stand in the way of the various kinds of standard and non-standard contracting often needed to support the commercialization of innovation. But matters are not so simple.

4.2 The Simultaneous Model

The simultaneous model of innovation recognizes the existence of tight linkages and feedback mechanisms which must operate quickly and efficiently, including links between firms, within firms, and sometimes between firms and other organizations like universities. From this perspective, innovation does not necessarily begin with research; nor is the process serial. But it does require

---

[17] See GROSSMAN and SHAPIRO [1986].

rapid feedback, mid-course corrections to designs, and redesign.[18] This conceptualization recognizes aspects of the serial model – such as the flow of activity,
in certain cases through design to development, production and marketing –
but also recognizes the constant feedback between and among activities, and
the involvement of a wide variety of economic actors and organizations that
need not have a simple upstream-downstream relationship to each other.[19] It
suggests that R & D personnel must be closely connected to manufacturing and
marketing personnel and to external sources of supply of new components and
complementary technologies, so that supplier, manufacturer and customer reactions can be fed back into the design process rapidly. In this way new
technology, whether internal or external, becomes embedded into designs
which meet customer needs quickly and efficiently.

The simultaneous model visualizes innovation as an incremental and cumulative activity that involves building on what went before, whether it is inside
the organization or outside the organization, and whether the knowledge is
proprietary or in the public domain. The simultaneous model also stresses the
importance of the speed of the design cycle, and flexibility. IBM followed this
model in developing its first PC, employing alliances with Microsoft and others
to launch a successful personal computer system. Sun Microsystems and NeXT
Computer launched themselves in this way and have remained in this mode for
subsequent new product development. Microprocessor development at Intel
often follows this logic too.

When innovation has this character, the company which is quickest in product design and development will appear to be the pioneer, even if its own
contribution to science and technology is minimal, because it can be first to
"design in" science and technology already in the public domain. Both small
and large organizations operate by this model, reaching out upstream and
downstream, horizontally and laterally to develop and assemble leading edge
systems.

In short, much innovation today is likely to require lateral and horizontal
linkages as well as vertical ones. As we discuss below, and particularly for small
firms, innovation may require accessing complementary assets which lie outside
the organization. If innovating firms do not have the necessary capabilities
in-house, they will need to engage in various forms of restrictive contracts with
providers of inputs and complementary assets. The possibility that antitrust
laws could be invoked, particularly by excluded competitors, thus arises. Lying

---

[18]   This process has also been termed "cyclic." See GOMORY [1987].

[19]   Moreover, the linkage from science to innovation is not solely or even preponderantly at the beginning of typical innovations, but rather extends all through the process.
"Science can be visualized as lying alongside development processes, to be used when
needed." (KLINE and ROSENBERG [1986]) Design is often at the center of the innovation
process. Research is often spawned by the problems associated with trying to get the
design right. Indeed, important technological breakthroughs can often proceed even
when the underlying science is not understood.

ready to snare these firms are plaintiffs' attorneys appealing to cartel and "raising rivals' costs" theories. With the required forms of contracting necessarily complex, and an understanding of the requirements of the innovation process largely absent from antitrust doctrine, the possibility of judicial error is significant. Paradoxically, it is not the giant integrated enterprise which is most exposed to these risks. Most at risk are mid-sized enterprises that have developed and commercialized important innovations, because such firms are likely to have market power (under orthodox definitions) and have the need to engage in complex forms of interfirm cooperation.

4.3 Organizational Requirements of Innovation

Whether innovation is serial or simultaneous, it requires the coordination of various activities. The serial model suggests a rather simple organizational problem; the simultaneous model a more complex one, often employing various forms of non-standard contracting. To the extent that economists employ just the serial model, they greatly oversimplify the organizational challenges which innovation provides and underestimate potential antitrust problems. Also, they probably exaggerate the importance of research and downplay the importance of other factors. Except in special cases, a firm's R&D capability is for naught if it cannot organize the rest of the innovation process efficiently and effectively, particularly if that innovation is taking place in an already-established industry.

For innovations to be commercialized, the economic system must somehow assemble all the relevant complementary assets and create a dynamically-efficient interactive system of learning and information exchange. The necessary complementary assets can conceivably be assembled by administrative processes, or by market processes, as when the innovator simply licenses the technology to firms that already own the relevant assets, or are willing to create them. These organizational choices have received scant attention in the context of innovation. Indeed, the serial model relies on an implicit belief that arms-length contracts between unaffiliated firms in the vertical chain from research to customer will suffice to commercialize technology. In particular, there has been little consideration of how complex contractual arrangements among firms can assist commercialization – that is, translating R&D capability into profitable new products and processes. The one partial exception is a tiny literature on joint R&D activity;[20] but this literature addresses the organization of R&D and not the organization of innovation.

If innovation takes place in a regime of tight appropriability – that is, if the technological leader can secure legal protection (as when it obtains an ironclad patent[21]) – and if technology can be transferred at zero cost as is commonly

---

[20] See GROSSMAN and SHAPIRO [1986], and ORDOVER and WILLIG [1985].

[21] See TEECE [1986].

assumed in theoretical models, the organizational challenge that is created by innovation is relatively simple. In these instances, the market for intellectual property is likely to support transactions enabling the developer of the technology simply to sell its intellectual property for cash, or at least license it to downstream firms who can then engage in whatever value-added activities are necessary to extract value from the technology. With a well-functioning market for know-how, markets can provide the structure for the requisite organization to be accomplished.

But in reality, the market for know-how is riddled with imperfections.[22] Simple unilateral contracts – where technology is sold for cash – are unlikely to be efficient.[23] Complex bilateral and multilateral contracts, internal organization, or various hybrid structures are often required to shore up obvious market failures.[24]

4.4 Governance Alternatives for Innovation

The previous section has argued that innovation often requires firms to entrepreneur complex contracts and relationships with other firms in order to bring technology to the market, and to hold "me too" imitators at bay. This section considers in more detail the range of organizational alternatives available to the innovator to generate, coordinate and control such complementary assets.

4.4.1 The Price Mechanism

Consider first the price mechanism. Theoretical treatments generally assume that the requisite coordination and control can be achieved by the invisible hand. Efficient levels of investment in complementary assets are brought forward at the right time and place by price signals. Entrepreneurship is automatic and costless. This is the view implicit in textbook presentations; in turn, the textbook view often influences U.S. antitrust law.

However, many scholars have been rather critical of what Tjalling Koopmans calls the "overextended belief" of many economists regarding the efficiency of competitive markets as a means of allocating resources in a world characterized by ubiquitous uncertainty. Market failures are likely to arise because of the ignorance which firms have with respect to their competitors' future actions, preferences, and states of technological information.[25] In reality, there is no special means to ensure that investment programs are made known to all concerned at the time of their inception. This uncertainty is especially high for

---

[22] See ARROW [1962].
[23] See TEECE [1980], [1982].
[24] See WILLIAMSON [1985] and TEECE [1986].
[25] See KOOPMANS [1957, part II].

the development and commercialization of new technology. Acordingly, innovating firms need to achieve greater coordination than the price system alone appears to be able to effectuate.

4.4.2 Internal Organization

A second mechanism for effectuating coordination is the administrative processes within the firm. A company's internal organization can serve to shore up some market imperfections and provide some of the necessary coordination. As Alfred CHANDLER [1977] has explained, the modern multidivisional business enterprise "took over from the market the coordination and integration of the flow of goods and services from the production of raw materials through the several processes of production to the sale to the ultimate consumer ... administrative coordination replaced market coordination in an increasingly large portion of the economy." Oliver WILLIAMSON [1985] has developed a framework, both elegant and powerful, to explain the relative efficiencies of markets and administrative processes. One property of large integrated structures is that they have the potential to become excessively hierarchical and less responsive to market needs.[26] Accordingly, at least for some aspects of innovative activity, smaller organizations are often superior. Unfortunately, as we discuss below, antitrust law appears to favor merger over interfirm agreements and thus burdens innovation by attaching disincentives to otherwise appropriate organizational forms.

4.4.3 Strategic Alliances

Lying in between pure market and full administrative solutions are many intermediate and hybrid possibilities, including interfirm agreements. Interfirm agreements can be classified as unilateral (where A sells X to B) or bilateral (whereby A agrees to buy Y from B as a condition for making the sale of X, and both parties understand that the transaction will be continued only if reciprocity is observed). Such arrangements can also be multilateral if they involve more than two parties.

An especially interesting interfirm agreement is the strategic alliance, which can be defined as a bilateral or multilateral relationship characterized by the commitment of two or more partner firms to a common goal. A strategic alliance might include (1) technology swaps, (2) joint R & D or co-development, and/or (3) the sharing of complementary assets, such as where one party does manufacturing and the other distribution for a co-developed product. Of course, if the common goals were simply price-fixing or market-sharing, then such an agreement would constitute a cartel, especially if the agreement included substantially all members of an industry.

---

[26] See TEECE [1989].

By definition, a strategic alliance can never have one side receiving cash alone; it is not a unilateral exchange transaction. Nor do strategic alliances include mergers, because alliances by definition cannot involve acquisition of another firm's assets or controlling interest in another firm's stock. Alliances need not involve equity swaps or equity investments, though they often do. Strategic alliances without equity typically consist of contracts between or among partner firms that are nonaffiliated. Equity alliances can take many forms, including minority equity holdings, consortia, and joint ventures. Such interfirm agreements are usually temporary, and are assembled and disassembled as circumstances warrant. Typically, only a limited range of the firm's activities are enveloped in such agreements, and many competitors are excluded.

Strategic alliances, including consortia and joint ventures, are often an effective and efficient way to organize for innovation, particularly when an industry is fragmented. Whereas full-blown national planning entails the abolition of the market as an organizing mechanism, and large hierarchies are exposed to bureaucratic limits, interfirm cooperation preserves market selection and responsiveness. In a sense, interfirm cooperation is the pure private enterprise solution. The case for planning and industrial policy recedes if a degree of operational and strategic coordination can be attained through private agreements. The benefits associated with less hierarchical structures can be obtained without incurring the disadvantages of insufficient scale and scope.

4.5 *Antitrust Treatment of Agreements Among Competitors*[27]

Current U.S. antitrust law needlessly inhibits agreements among competition designed to develop and commercialize new technology. The problem is that the legal standards for interfirm agreements are ambiguous. While it is generally true that "rule of reason" anaylsis – rather than per se rules – will be applied to contractual arrangements designed to advance innovation, the elements of rule of reason analysis are muddled. In addition, although current law, as a practical matter, recognizes a "safe harbor" for mergers between firms that will have less than 20 percent market share, it does not recognize a similar safe harbor for horizontal contractual arrangements among firms.

The Clayton Act also permits private parties to sue for treble damages for alleged antitrust injuries, and allows state attorney generals to recover treble damages on behalf of persons residing in the state. Successful plaintiffs can also recover attorneys' fees. These remedies are available only in the United States. They provide a powerful incentive for plaintiffs to litigate, and given the current state of the law, a powerful disincentive for businesses to form cooperative

---

[27] See generally, JORDE and TEECE [1989a] for a detailed assessment of antitrust law and enforcement.

innovation arrangements and strategic alliances. While it is difficult to measure the missed opportunities for cooperative innovation caused by the threat of treble damage litigation, we believe it is substantial. Moreover, it works to the particular detriment of small and medium-sized innovative firms in industries where the innovative process is simultaneous.

Congress has recognized that these provisions may inhibit technological innovation, and the National Cooperative Research Act (NCRA) of 1984 took two significant steps to remove legal disincentives to cooperative research. First, the NCRA provides that "joint research and development ventures" must not be held illegal per se, and that such ventures instead should be "judged on the basis of [their] reasonableness, taking into account all relevant factors affecting competition, including, but not limited to, effects on competition in properly defined, relevant research and development markets." Second, the NCRA establishes a registration procedure for joint research and development ventures, limiting antitrust recoveries against registered ventures to single damages, interest, and costs, including attorneys' fees. Thus, Congress eliminated the threat of treble damages for litigation challenging cooperative R&D arrangements, provided that the parties to the arrangement first register their venture. But R&D is only a small piece of the innovation puzzle.

In our view, the NCRA is not sufficiently permissive. The substantive protection provided by the NCRA – guaranteed rule of reason treatment and reduction of damages – extend only to research, and downstream commercial activity "reasonably required" for research and narrowly confined to marketing intellectual property developed through a joint R&D program. Treatment of other agreements designed to facilitate innovation is thus left uncertain, to be determined only by interpretation of the "reasonably required" standard. The NCRA unwisely precludes joint manufacturing and production of innovative products and processes, which is often necessary to provide the cooperating ventures with significant feedback information to aid in further innovation and product development, and to make the joint activity profitable. The NCRA implicitly accepts the serial and not the simultaneous model of innovation.

In addition, the NCRA gives little guidance concerning the substantive content of its rule of reason approach. While the Act did require that markets be defined in the context of research and not the products that might result from it, the NCRA fails to specify factors to be considered within rule of reason analysis. It simply requires consideration of "all relevant factors affecting competition," paying no special attention to the special characteristics of the innovation process in a quickly changing industry.

Finally, while the NCRA's elimination of treble damages for registered ventures is an important step forward, cooperating firms are still not protected from antitrust litigation. Even after the NCRA, antitrust laws still permit private plaintiffs to engage in treble damage litigation against cooperative arrangements facilitating commercialization. Moreover, single damages are still available even against those registered under NCRA. The cost of defending antitrust suits is not materially reduced by the exceedingly narrow circumstances in which the Act permits an award of attorneys' fees to prevailing defendants. The threat of litigation, with attendant managerial distraction, can be extremely damaging to the competitive performance of a fast-paced industry.

Businesses seem to have recognized the limited nature of the steps taken by the NCRA. Not surprisingly, only 111 separate cooperative ventures registered under the NCRA between 1984 and June 1988. Our review of these filings indicates that they are very modest endeavors that are aimed at solving industry problems and are not of great competitive moment. We believe that if an approval procedure existed under which procompetitive arrangements could obtain exemptions from further antitrust exposure to private damage actions, then many more competitively beneficial ventures would utilize the NCRA.

In contrast to this picture of U.S. antitrust law, the antitrust and business environments in Japan and Europe are more hospitable to strategic alliances and cooperative arrangements for innovation. The basic Japanese attitude is that joint R & D activities are procompetitive and thus should not be touched by the Antimonopoly Act. Significantly, the literal Japanese translation of "R & D" – *kenkyu kaihatsu* – implicitly includes commercialization; there is no semantic distinction between the concepts of R & D and commercialization.

In Japan, the Fair Trade Commission is responsible for executing and enforcing the Antimonopoly Act of 1947, which (like the Sherman Act) broadly prohibits unreasonable restraints of trade. While there is no specific legislative exemption for joint innovation arrangements under the Act, Japan's FTC has been able to exempt cooperative innovation efforts from the scope of the law by virtue of its power as the primary enforcer of the Act.[28] FTC policy also states that if anticompetitive effects are alleged, the procompetitiveness benefits of innovation must be balanced, too. Balancing will take place not only within a particular market but also across markets,[29] because "there is a possibility of the emergence of competition at the intersection of industrial sectors as a result of joint R & D between firms in different sectors."

---

[28] The basic administrative policy outlining the standards by which such joint innovation efforts are to be scrutinized is contained in a Report of Japan's FAIR TRADE COMMISSION [1984, 37–39]. The Report states that the evaluation of the anticompetitive effect of joint R & D at the product market stage will depend significantly "on the competition and market shares among the participants and the market structure of the industry to which the participants belong... In cases where the market shares of the participants are small... the effects will be small." Although "small" is not defined in the Report, Japan's Merger Guidelines state that the FTC is not likely to closely examine cases in which the combined market share of the merging parties is less than 25 percent. See IYORI and YESUGI [1983, 86–88]. Our discussions with MITI and FTC officials confirm that the horizontal merger safe harbors would be equally applicable to cooperative contractual arrangements.

[29] *Fair Trade Commission* (Japan) [1984].

In considering anticompetitive effects of cooperative innovation arrangements, Japan's FTC analyzes market shares and market structure. The FTC specifically recognizes the needs of innovators and articulates procompetitive justifications that include: (1) the difficulty of single-firm innovation; (2) the faster innovation created by cooperation and specialization between joint participants; (3) the pursuit of innovation in new fields by utilizing shared technology and know-how; and (4) enhancement of the technological level of each participant through the interchange of technology.

When MITI seeks to promote cooperative R & D activities (for example, as authorized by the Act for Facilitation of Research in Key Technology, or the Research Association for Mining and Manufacturing Technology Act), the FTC is consulted in advance. Once the activities are cleared by the FTC, it is extraordinarily unlikely that the FTC would pursue antitrust remedies at a future time. Significantly, treble damages are not available to private parties seeking to enforce Japanese antitrust laws, and private suits for single damages are very rare and usually unsuccessful. Thus, Japanese firms cooperating on innovation and commercialization of innovation have little to fear from Japanese antitrust laws.

Under this type of antitrust environment, it is not surprising that there is frequent collaboration for innovation. Although regular statistics are not kept in Japan, because there is no reporting requirement for collaborative research and commercialization activities, a Fair Trade Commission report issued in 1984 contains statistics suggestive of the quantity and variety of joint innovation activities in Japan. The survey results indicate that joint R & D projects among corporations in the same industrial sector, which might be classified as horizontal collaboration, represent 19.1 percent of total projects.[30] The antitrust environment shaping cooperation in the European Community is also markedly different from the United States. In 1968, the European Commission issued a "Notice of Cooperation between Enterprises" which indicates that horizontal collaboration for purposes of R & D is normally outside the scope of antitrust concerns as defined in Articles 85 and 86 of the EEC Treaty. The Commission has consistently taken a favorable position on R & D agreements unless the large entities involved imply serious anticompetitive consequences.

In 1984, the European Commission adopted Regulation No. 418/85 (hereafter Reg. 418) expanding the favorable antitrust treatment of R & D. For firms

---

[30] Questionnaires were sent to 484 manufacturing corporations in the fields of electronics, telecommunications, automobiles, chemicals, ceramics, steel and nonferrous metals, whose stocks were listed in Tokyo and Osaka Stock Exchanges. Data was provided by 242 corporations, representing 1.9 percent of the total manufacturing industry that engage in R & D activities in terms of the number of corporations and 16.7 percent in terms of sales. As to the nature of the joint R & D projects, 54.3 percent of the total cases were developmental research. Basic and applied research were 13.6 and 32.1 percent respectively. In the case of large corporations with capital of more than 10 billion yen, the total basic and application research amounted to 52.1 percent.

whose total market share does not exceed 20 percent, it provides blanket exceptions for horizontal R & D arrangements, including commercialization – which the Commission views as "the natural consequence of joint R & D" – up to the point of distribution and sales.[31] In addition, the Commission is authorized to grant exemptions for cooperative efforts that do not fall within the automatic safe harbor.

4.6 Proposed Modifications to U.S. Antitrust Law Affecting Cooperative Agreements Among Competitors

To insure that antitrust law is responsive to the needs of innovating firms and does not inhibit U.S. firms from competing effectively in global markets experiencing rapid technological change, we believe the following changes are in order:

First, as discussed in section III, market definition should be tailored to the context of innovation and should focus primarily on the market for know-how. Specific product markets become relevant only when commercialization is included within the scope of the cooperative agreement.

Second, the rule of reason should be clarified to take specific account of the appropriability regime, the pace of technological change, the diversity of sources of new technology, the need to access complementary assets and technologies, and the need to have cheek-by-jowl cooperation to manage the innovation process simultaneously rather than serially.

Third, a safe harbor defined according to market power should be expressly adopted that would shield from antitrust liability interfirm agreements among competitors that involve less than 20 to 25 percent of the relevant market.

Fourth, antitrust law should not bias the selection of interfirm organizational forms; at a minimum, integration by contract or alliance should be treated no less favorably than full mergers.[32]

Fifth, the NCRA should be amended to include joint production and commercialization efforts to exploit innovation.

---

[31] Regulation No. 418/85 of 19 December 1984 on the application of Art. 85(3) of the Treaty to categories of research and development agreement, *O. J. Eur. Comm.* (No. L 53) 5 [1985], entered into force March 1, 1985, and applicable until December 31, 1997. The statutory framework of Reg. 418 is complex. It applies to three categories of agreements involving R & D: (1) joint research and development of products or processes and joint exploitation of the results of the R & D; (2) joint exploitation of the results of R & D product or processes pursuant to a prior agreement between the same parties; and (3) joint research and development of products without joint exploitation should the agreement fall within the purview of Art. 85(1). Under Reg. 418, joint exploitation is interpreted to mean joint manufacturing and licensing to third parties. Joint distribution and sales, however, are not covered and require individual exemptions pursuant to Art. 85(3).

[32] At present, the *U.S. Department of Justice Merger Guidelines* provide a degree of certainty for cooperation achieved by merger, which is absent for cooperation achieved contractually.

Sixth, an administrative procedure should be created, involving both the Justice and Commerce Departments, to allow evaluation and possible certification of cooperative arrangements among firms with market shares higher than 20 to 25 percent, when dynamic efficiency gains are likely and rivalry robust.

Seventh, private antitrust suits challenging cooperative innovation arrangements should be limited to equitable relief, and attorneys' fees should be awarded to the prevailing party.

The first four of these proposals could be accomplished by courts interpreting the rule of reason and the National Cooperative Research Act. We hope courts will not hesitate to employ the tools of evolutionary, common law interpretation and development to achieve these changes. However, to achieve the complete package of substantive and procedural changes most quickly, and thus assure certainty and predictability, legislation is the best overall solution. At a U.C. Berkeley Conference on "Antitrust, Innovation and Competitiveness" in October 1988, we distributed a draft of legislation that combined a "registration" and "certification" approach for cooperative commercialization ventures. Shortly thereafter, Congressman Edwards (H.R. 1025) and Congressman Fish (H.R. 2264) advanced a "registration" approach to cooperative commercialization efforts and Congressman Boucher and Campbell (H.R. 1024) proposed a "certification" approach. After three hearings on these bills, Chairman Jack Brooks of the House Judiciary Committee introduced and the Judiciary Committee passed the National Cooperative Production Amendments of 1990 (H.R. 4611). H.R. 4611 would amend the National Cooperative Research Act to extend its registration approach to joint production ventures.[33] At the same time, Attorney General Richard Thornburgh and Commerce Secretary Robert Mosbacher announced the Bush Administration's support of a registration approach for production joint ventures.[34]

5. Conclusion

The case for changes in the way antitrust law analyzes and assesses market power and agreements among competitors rests on three fundamental pillars.

---

[33] Professor Jorde testified on July 26, 1989, in favor of both a registration and certification approach. See JORDE and TEECE [1989c]. Legislation advancing a registration approach for production joint ventures has also been introduced in the Senate by Senators Patrick Leahy (D-VT) and Strom Thurmond (R-SC) (S. 1006). Three aspects of H.R. 4611 bear noting. First, relevant market definition under rule of reason analysis would specifically consider the worldwide capacity of suppliers. Second, foreign participation in a production joint venture would be limited to 30 percent of the voting securities or equity interests, and all production facilities would have to be located in the United States or its territories. Third, apparently production joint ventures would not be limited to efforts designed to commercialize joint R & D, nor need they be related to innovation.

[34] See *Department of Justice* release, May 10, 1990, p. 701.

The first is that the innovation process is terribly important to economic growth and development, because it yields social returns in excess of private returns, and because innovation is a powerful spur to competition. Hence, if antitrust policy is going to err, it ought to do so by being on the facilitating rather than on the inhibiting side of innovation. This principle is well-understood in Europe and Japan. Second, economic theory tells us that if certain organizational arrangements are exposed to governmentally-imposed costs while others are not, firms will substitute away from the burdened forms (in this context, inter-firm agreements) and in favor of the unburdened forms (in this context, hierarchy), even when the former are potentially economically superior. According to Aoki,[35] the slowdown in total factor productivity in the United States can be attributed in large part to a mismatch between organizational form and the requirements of new technology; in particular, he is concerned that hierarchical solutions are overused, at least in the United States. We are concerned that present law does not give full recognition to the interorganizational require-ments of the innovation process; failure to do so is damaging when innovation must proceed according to the simultaneous model. Third, cartelization of industries experiencing rapid technological change, and which are open to international trade and investment, is very difficult. So long as these industries remain open and innovative, antitrust policy should err on the side of permit-ting rather than restricting interfirm contracts.

There are several classes of circumstances where beneficial cooperation will eventually expand if antitrust laws are revised along the lines we propose. The response may not be immediate, particularly with respect to consortia, because the experience base in U.S. industry in this area is thin, because of our antitrust history, and because U.S. firms, at least in the post-war period, have been large relative to their foreign competitors. Accordingly, the need to cooperate has not been as powerful in the past as it is now. However, once organizational learning accumulates, we expect consortia to begin to flourish even in the absence of government funding. We also expect the reinforcement of bilateral alliances already common in U.S. industry. We briefly discuss the kinds of activities that might take place.

(1) *Cooperative Manufacturing and Commercialization.* There are a number of circumstances where cooperative activity beyond early stage activity is ben-eficial to innovating firms. As discussed, sometimes this is true because of scale, risk, and appropriability considerations. Sometimes it is true because prohibi-tion of cooperative commercialization imposes a significant technology transfer problem, for instance from the research joint venture (if there is one) back to the funding companies. In most cases firms will not wish to cooperate all the way from research through to commercialization. But in some instances they will, or they will wish to cooperate simply on a downstream production venture.

---

[35] See AOKI [1989].

When cartelization of the industry is not a threat, we see no reasons for antitrust restraints. The now defunct U.S. Memories, Inc. consortium wanted to invest $500 million to $1 billion to develop and manufacture for its members and for the market advanced dynamic random access memories (DRAMs). With fabrication facilities costing hundreds of millions, acting alone is beyond the financial resources of many companies in this industry who might otherwise wish to have some control over their DRAM supply. This proposed consortium had to contend with a number of difficulties, including threats of third party litigation.[36] While antitrust was probably not the main reason for the failure of this enterprise, the antitrust environment did nothing to help. A certification procedure would have provided important certainty to this venture, and others like it. A registration procedure would provide less certainty, but still would be a significant advance over current antitrust law.

Similarly, in the area of superconductors, it is likely that the real challenges will come not in developing superconductors, but in their commercialization. Applying superconductors in systems like railroads, computers, and electricity distribution will require great amounts of time, resources, and capital – probably greater than any single business can muster internally. Accordingly, a public policy stance that treats only early stage activity as potentially requiring cooperation is misguided and will thwart both early and later stage activities. Most firms will not have much incentive to engage in early stage, joint development if later stage, stand-alone commercialization appears too expensive to accomplish profitably.

(2) *Cooperative Innovation Designed to Achieve Catch-up.* Cooperative activities in Japan and Europe have frequently been motivated by a desire to catch-up with the world's technological frontier, which in the postwar years was usually the technology of U.S. firms. However, U.S. firms are increasingly slipping behind the frontier. For instance, U.S. firms are now behind in areas like ceramics and robotics, and in products like VCRs, facsimiles, and HDTV. Just as foreign firms have found cooperative ventures useful for catch-up in the past, U.S. firms could utilize cooperation for this purpose. For example, U.S.-based firms, acting together and with foreign firms, may still have a slender chance of competing in the market for high definition televisions (HDTV) and related products expected to evolve in the 1990s. In the absence of cooperative interfirm agreements, we doubt that development of HDTV systems is possible in the United States. If America's potential "re-entrants" to the consumer electronics business combine to attempt re-entry, they cannot be sure of avoiding serious antitrust problems involving treble damages, particularly if they are successful.

At minimum, the legislative changes proposed would facilitate unfettered information exchange and strategic coordination with respect to re-entry strate-

---

[36] See JORDE and TEECE [1989b].

gies. If such efforts facilitated profitable re-entry into high technology business-es when re-entering would otherwise not occur, or would occur in a more limited and unprofitable way, we do not see why antitrust concerns ought to interfere.

(3) *Cooperation in Response to Foreign Industrial and Technology Policy.* In high technology industries, both European and East Asian nations have active industrial and technology policies that significantly impact market outcomes, both in their own countries and abroad. Airbus is a case in point. The dominant U.S. attitude is one of laissez-faire, and many economists are of the view that the United States should send a letter of thanks to foreign governments who subsidize exports to the United States. Such a view is insensitive to the dynam-ics of technological change, to the importance of cumulative learning, and to re-entry costs.

Some U.S. policy makers, however, favor retaliation against foreign coun-tries which have active industrial policies. We support a modification of U.S. antitrust laws which in some circumstances would permit a competitive re-sponse by U.S. industry acting collectively. The proposals we advance to en-courage greater cooperation among U.S. firms do not require government expenditures nor do they involve the government "picking winners." But they would soften the tensions emerging in the United States between technology, antitrust and trade policies.

U.S. antitrust policy, like so much of our economic policy, has been preoccu-pied with static rather than intertemporal concerns. Despite important recent developments, it is informed by naïve theories of the innovation process, and in particular is insensitive to the organizational needs of innovation. U.S. antitrust scholars still harbor suspicion of cooperative agreements among com-petitors, and do not appreciate the benefits. This suspicion helps fuel uncertain-ty about how the courts would view interfirm arrangements to promote techno-logical progress and competition.

The modest policy changes we advance are certainly no panacea for the severe problems U.S. high-technology industry is currently experiencing. But in bringing our policy closer to Europe and Japan in the way we propose, we will at least purge dogma that no longer deserves a place in our industrial policy. In time, reduced antitrust exposure will help clear the way for beneficial coop-eration, thereby reducing incentives for mergers and acquisitions.

The 1990 centennial of the Sherman Act provides a good occasion to begin to set things right. The economics profession, which in the past has had a signi-ficant impact on the law of vertical restraints, can provide the intellectual leader-ship necessary to propel adjustments in the manner in which market power and horizontal agreements are assessed, thereby helping to align U.S. policies with the technological and competitive realities of today's global economy.

But scholarship should not rest once such modest goals are accomplished. Antitrust policy, like much of our economic policy, needs more serious overhaul. We challenge scholars and ourselves to tease out more fully the implications of Schumpeterian competition for antitrust policy.

Summary

Technological innovation drives the competitive process. It yields new products and processes, and sharpens the performance attributes of existing products and processes. Yet economic analysis, infatuated with price competition, too often ignores the role of innovation in the competitive process. The static bias is manifested in antitrust policy, at least in the United States. Accordingly, markets may be defined too narrowly in high technology industries, because price competition is the only form of competition that is recognized. Moreover, antitrust law is hostile to cooperation to effectuate innovation, unless it is strictly vertical, because of the spectre of cartels. This paper suggests how in context of innovation market definition techniques need to be modified to avoid error, and how the law affecting cooperation among competitors needs to be adjusted to ensure that antitrust policy assists rather than impedes competition.

Zusammenfassung

Technologische Innovation ist der wesentliche Motor des Wettbewerbsprozesses. Durch Innovation entstehen neue Produkte und Verfahren und die Qualität existierender Produkte und Verfahren wird erhöht. Dennoch hat sich die ökonomische Analyse überwiegend mit Preiswettbewerb beschäftigt und dabei die Rolle von Innovationen im Wettbewerbsprozeß häufig ignoriert. Die einseitig statische Sichtweise hat sich zumindest in der Wettbewerbspolitik der Vereinigten Staaten niedergeschlagen. Im Bereich der Hochtechnologie können Märkte zu eng definiert sein, wenn Preiswettbewerb die einzige Wettbewerbsform ist, der Beachtung geschenkt wird. Darüber hinaus steht die Wettbewerbsgesetzgebung wegen des Schreckgespenstes der Kartellbildung eine Kooperation zur Durchführung von Innovationen zumindest dann ablehnend gegenüber, wenn sie nicht rein vertikaler Natur ist. In diesem Beitrag wird ein Vorschlag unterbreitet, wie bei Berücksichtigung des Innovationsaspektes bestehende Praktiken der Marktdefinition modifiziert werden müssen, um Fehler zu vermeiden. Ferner wird aufgezeigt, wie Gesetze, die Kooperation unter Wettbewerbern betreffen, zu verändern sind, damit die Wettbewerbspolitik den Wettbewerb fördert und nicht behindert.

References

AOKI, M. [1989], "Global Competition, Firm Organization, and Total Factor Productivity: A Comparative Micro Perspective," Paper presented at the International Seminar on Science, Technology, and Economic Growth, OECD, Paris (June).

ARROW, K. J. [1962], "Economic Welfare and the Allocation of Resources for Invention," pp. 609–625 in: National Bureau of Economic Research, *The Rate and Direction of Inventive Activity*, Princeton: Princeton University Press.

ATKINSON, S. E. and R. HALVORSEN [1984], "A New Hedonic Technique for Estimating Attribute Demand: An Application to the Demand for Automobile Fuel Efficiency," *Review of Economics and Statistics*, 66(3), 417–426.

BALDWIN, W. and J. T. SCOTT [1987], *Market Structure and Technological Change*, Chur, Switzerland: Harwood Publishers.

BORK, R. [1978], *The Antitrust Paradox: A Policy at War with Itself*, New York: Basic Books.

BROWN, G. Jr. and R. MENDELSOHN [1984], "The Hedonic Travel Cost Method," *Review of Economics and Statistics*, 66(3), 427–433.

BROWN, J. N. and H. S. ROSEN [1982], "On the Estimation of Structural Hedonic Price Models," *Econometrica*, 50(3), 765–768.

CHANDLER, A. D. Jr. [1977], *The Visible Hand: The Managerial Revolution in American Business*, Cambridge, Harvard University Press.

EPPLE, D. [1987], "Hedonic Prices and Implicit Markets: Estimating Demand and Supply Functions for Differentiated Products," *Journal of Political Economy*, 95(1), 59–80.

FAIR TRADE COMMISSION (Japan) [1984], *Research and Development Activities in Private Enterprises and Problems They Pose in the Competition Policy (Minkan kigyo ni okeru kenkyu kaihatsu katsudo no jttai to kyoso seidaku jo no kaidai)*.

FRIEDLAENDER, A. F., C. WINSTON and K. WANG [1983] "Costs, Technology and Productivity on the U.S. Automobile Industry," *Bell Journal of Economics*, 14(1), 1–20.

FUSS, M. A. [1984], "Cost Allocation: How Can the Costs of Postal Services Be Determined?" pp. 30–52 in: Roger Sherman (ed.), *Perspectives on Postal Service Issues*, Washington, D.C.: American Enterprises Institute.

— — and L. WAVERMAN [1981], "Regulation and the Multiproduct Firm: The Case of Telecommunications in Canada," in: G. Fromme (ed.), *Studies in Public Utility Regulation*, Cambridge, MA: MIT Press.

GOMORY, R. [1987], "Dominant Science Does Not Mean Dominant Product," *Research and Development*, 29 (11), 72–74.

GROSSMAN, G. M. and C. SHAPIRO [1986], "Research Joint Ventures: An Antitrust Analysis," *Journal of Law and Economics*, 2(2), 315–337.

HARRIS, G. and T. J. JORDE [1983], "Market Definition in the Merger Guidelines: Implications for Antitrust Enforcement," *California Law Review*, 71(2), 464–496.

HARTMAN, R. S. [1982], "A Note on the Use of Aggregate Data in Individuals Choice Models: Discrete Consumer Choice Among Alternative Fuels for Residential Appliances," *Journal of Econometrics*, 18(3), 313–336.

— — [1987], "Product Quality and Market Efficiency: The Effect of Product Recalls on Resale Prices and Firm Valuation," *Review of Economics and Statistics*, 39(2), 367–371.

— — and J. DOANE [1987], "The Use of Hedonic Analysis for Certification and Damage Calculations in Class Action Complaints," *The Journal of Law, Economics and Organization*, 32(2), 351–372.

— — and D. J. TEECE [1990], "Product Emulation Strategies in the Presence of Reputation Effects and Network Externalities: Some Evidence from the Minicomputer Industry," *Economics of Innovation and New Technology*, 1, 157–182.

— — and — — W. MITCHELL and T. JORDE [1990], "Product Market Definition in the Context of Innovation," unpublished working paper, September.

HAUSMAN, A. [1979], "Individual Discount Rates and the Purchase and Utilization of Energy-Using Durables," *Bell Journal of Economics*, 10(1), 33–54.

IYORI, H. and A. YESUGI [1983], *The Antimonopoly Laws of Japan*.

JORDE, T. M. and D. J. TEECE [1988], "Product Market Definition in the Context of Innovation," Working Paper No. BPP-29, Center for Research in Management, University of California at Berkeley (February).

-- and -- [1989a], "Innovation, Cooperation, and Antitrust," *High Technology Law Review*, 4(1), 1–113.

-- and -- [1989b], "To Keep U.S. in the Chips, Modify the Antitrust Laws," *Los Angeles Times*, July 24.

-- and -- [1989c], "Legislative Proposals to Modify the U.S. Antitrust Laws to Facilitate Cooperative Arrangements to Commercialize Innovation," In: Hearings Before the Subcommittee on Economics and Commercial Law, Committee on the Judiciary, U.S. House of Representatives (July 26).

JORDE, T. M. and D. J. TEECE [1990a], "Innovation and Cooperation: Implications for Competition and Antitrust," *Journal of Economic Perspectives*, 4(3), 75–96.

-- and -- [1990b], "Innovation, Dynamic Competition, and Antitrust Policy," *Regulation*, 13(3), 35–44.

KLINE, S. J. and N. ROSENBERG [1986], "An Overview of Innovation," pp. 275–305 in: N. Rosenberg and R. Landau (ed.), *The Positive Sum Strategy*, Washington, D.C.: National Academy Press.

KOOPMANS, T. [1957], *Three Essays on the State of Economic Science*, part II. New York: McGraw Hill.

MANNERING, F. and C. WINSTON [1984], "Consumer Demand for Automobile Safety," *American Economic Review*, 74(2), 316–318.

OHTA, M. and Z. GRILICHES [1976], "Automobile Prices Revisited: Extensions of the Hedonic Hypothesis," pp. 325–390 in: Nester E. Terleckyi (ed.), *Household Production and Consumption*, Washington, D.C.: National Bureau of Economic Research Conference on Research in Income and Wealth, Studies in Income and Wealth.

ORDOVER, J. and R. WILLIG [1985], "Antitrust for High Technology Industries: Assessing Research Joint Ventures and Mergers," *Journal of Law and Economics*, 28, 311–333.

SCHUMPETER, J. A. [1942] *Capitalism, Socialism and Democracy*, New York: Harper & Row.

SPADY, R. H. and A. F. FRIEDLAENDER [1978], "Hedonic Cost Functions for the Regulated Trucking Industry," *Bell Journal of Economics*, 9(1), 159–179.

TEECE, D. J. [1980], "Economies of Scope and the Scope of the Enterprise," *Journal of Economic Behavior and Organization*, 1(3), 223–247.

-- [1982], "Towards an Economic Theory of the Multiproduct Firm," *Journal of Economic Behavior and Organization*, 3, 39–63.

-- [1986], "Profiting from Technological Innovation," *Research Policy*, 15(6), 285–305.

-- [1990], "Innovation and the Organization of Industry," CCC Working Paper No. 90-6, Center of Research in Management, University of California at Berkeley.

-- [forthcoming], "Competition, Cooperation, and Innovation: Organizational Arrangements for Regimes of Rapid Technological Progress," *Journal of Economic Behavior and Organization*.

U.S. DEPARTMENT OF JUSTICE, ANTITRUST DIVISION [1984], *U.S. Department of Justice Merger Guidelines*, June 14.

WILLIAMSON, O. E. [1985], *The Economic Institutions of Capitalism: Firms, Markets, Relational Contracting*, New York: Free Press.

Professor Thomas M. Jorde
School of Law
University of California at Berkeley
Berkeley, CA 94720-2499
U.S.A.

Professor David J. Teece
Haas School of Business
University of California at Berkeley
Berkeley, CA 94720
U.S.A.

B

Antitrust: Market Definition

[17]

Assessing Market Power in Regimes of Rapid Technological Change*

RAYMOND HARTMAN§, DAVID TEECE†, WILL
MITCHELL‡, THOMAS JORDE§

(University of California at Berkeley,§ Law and Economics Consulting Group and
‡University of Michigan)

1. Introduction and Overview

For quite some time now it has been apparent that the most distinctive hallmark of a private enterprise system of economic organization is its capacity to support innovation and change. Moreover, the capacity of the system to develop, adapt, and introduce new products and methods of production provides the foundation for economic prosperity. Indeed this is such an obvious feature of well-functioning market economies that it seems almost too trite to mention. Driving new product and process development is technological innovation. Technological innovation not only is the basis of wealth creation, it is also the process most responsible for keeping the positions of competitors in flux. Of course, at any point in time some industries may be experiencing more rapid change than others. Moreover, change can be either gradual or discontinuous, propelled by incumbents or new entrants. It can completely and irreversibly overturn the existing competitive order in an industry.

Success in one round of innovation does not guarantee success in the next—it merely gives incumbents the opportunity to compete again. Positions lost are often impossible to regain. No amount of improvement in the horse-drawn carriage would have resulted in a transport system competitive

* This is a revised version of 'Product Market Definition in the Context of Innovation', Business and Public Policy Working Paper number BPP-47, Center for Research in Management, University of California at Berkeley, August 1990, and 'Product Market Definition in the Context of Innovation: An Exploration' working paper number BPP-29 by Thomas Jorde and David Teece.

†David Teece and Thomas Jorde are on the faculty at the University of California at Berkeley. Raymond Hartman is principal in the Law and Economics Consulting Group, as are Thomas Jorde and David Teece. Will Mitchell is on the faculty at the University of Michigan. Please address all correspondence to Professor David J. Teece, Center for Research in Management, Haas School of Business, University of California, Berkeley, CA 94720, USA.

Industrial and Corporate Change Volume 2 Number 3 1993

with the railroad. Western Union is unlikely to ever regain its once significant position in communications, nor Singer its lead in light machinery, nor Unisys its position in electronic operating.

The proper assessment of competition and competitive dynamics is important in many contexts. Firms obviously need to take account of changing technologies in their product planning and competitor analyses. Investors need to factor it into their assessment of risk. Governments also need to take it into account in many contexts including the design of regulation and the formulation and implementation of industrial and antitrust policies. It is the last context that concerns us in this paper. In particular, we are interested in the question of how should the formulation and implementation of competition/antitrust policy take into account different competitive regimes, particularly for purposes of determining whether a single firm has market power.

This purpose is of some significance in the United States, the EC, Canada, Australia, and New Zealand, where business behavior that is permissible for firms without market power suddenly becomes illegal if they are found to possess it.[1] Getting technology into antitrust analysis is, in our view, of some moment as the dominant conceptual approaches ignore it or recognizes only a subsidiary role. Indeed, it is remarkable the proclivity some policy analysts exhibit toward assessing competition in purely static terms. Thus, sometimes only four firm concentration ratios (and possibly Herfindahls) are still relied upon exclusively to assess the terms of competition. If there is any consideration of dynamics, it tends to be backward looking (historical) rather than forward looking. Too often 'the problem that is usually being visualized is how capitalism administers existing structures, whereas the relevant problem is how it creates and destroys them. As long as this is not recognized, the investigator does a meaningless job. As soon as it is recognized, his outlook on capitalist practice and its social results changes considerably (Schumpeter, 1942, p. 85).

2. *Conceptions of the Firm and Competitive Regimes*

In our view, one of the reasons why many economists are so wooden in this approach to competition is that they frequently adopt a highly stylized caricature of the business enterprise. In standard textbook treatments, it is common to assume that all technology is public and that firms produce homogeneous products. Firms are either price takers (perfect competition) or price makers (monopoly); and so competition is not particularly interesting.

---

[1] For instance, in the United States tying appears in violation of antitrust laws if the producer of the tying good has market power and there is no compelling efficiency reason for the tie. Absent market power, it raises no concerns.

—— *Assessing Market Power in Regimes of Rapid Technological Change* ——

Firms increase output when profitable and decrease it (or go out of business) when unprofitable. Firms cannot afford significant price cuts or they will fail. Price competition, and especially discounting, is often considered the leitmotif of competition.

In an alternative (neo-Schumpeterian) conceptualization of industry, one which we favor in many contexts, firms are investing in R&D and technology acquisition and adaptation, discovering new ways of designing and manufacturing products, and experimenting with new methods of organization. Firms are highly individualized repositories of productive knowledge, much of which is tacit and therefore difficult to describe and convey to others (Teece, 1980, 1981). The competition which is manifested in industries containing such firms must admit additional dimensions to the competitive process other than price competition, even though output decisions will still be guided by current or expected prices. In such industries firms compete not just by lowering price or increasing output but by developing or otherwise acquiring technologies that can dramatically enhance product and process performance.

Indeed, it is generally the industries in which firms do not compete primarily on price that have the highest productivity growth and which yield the most dramatic benefits for consumers. In those industries where the firm's competitive repertoire includes costly efforts to innovate, to improve, to adapt, and to build complementary assets with the objective of capturing value from innovation through the competitive advantage it supports, the winners will be those that strike a favorable balance between the rents captured from successive rounds of innovation and the costs of investing in innovation, including R&D, complementary assets, and intellectual property protection (Teece, 1986). The absence of at least some temporary period of monopoly power—in which prices are above recurring costs—causes innovation to be non-viable. As the work of Nelson and Winter (1982) has shown, sufficiently high costs of innovation and low costs of imitation will cause firms that continue to attempt innovation to die.

In high technology industries, the competitive positions of firms are never secure; incumbents, even those that appear dominant, can be unseated with alacrity by new technologies developed by others. Market positions built on a technological base which is changing rapidly are vulnerable to being overturned by new entrants from outside the industry as well as by competitors from within. Texas Instruments' early lead in memory devices came to be challenged not by IBM but by NEC and Toshiba, which had hitherto hardly been significant in the global semiconductor industry. Sun Microsystems, a new entrant, in less than a half decade completely overturned the position of IBM, DEC, and Hewlett Packard in workstations. Moreover, competitive

—— *Assessing Market Power in Regimes of Rapid Technological Change* ——

effects often take place long before there is any outward manifestation of new entry. The ever present threat of new technologies can cause firms to moderate price increases, to invest in R&D, and engage in technology acquisition strategies and cost-cutting activities long before the tangible presence of the competitor is evident in the market. As Schumpeter noted:

> It is hardly necessary to point out that competition of the kind we now have in mind acts not only when in being but also when it is merely an ever-present threat. It disciplines before it attacks. The businessman feels himself to be in a competitive situation even if he is alone in his field or if, although not alone, he holds a position such that investigating government experts fail to see any effective competition between him and any other firms in the same or a neighboring field and in consequence conclude that his talk, under examination, about his competitive sorrows is all make-believe. (Schumpeter, 1942, p. 85)

The reason why a firm might feel competitive pressures when 'alone in its field' is because new technologies can radically alter cost structures and the price performance attributes of products. Therefore, at least until others catch on, significant competitive advantage can be attained, often at the expense of incumbents who are exposed to the decline in value of the specialized investments and intangible assets. For publicly traded companies, this can lead to dramatic drops in share prices, with attendant implications for the cost of capital.

The rapidity with which incumbents can be unseated in high technology industries is remarkable, and more dramatic than is commonly observed in industries that are less R&D intensive. The example of Sun Microsystems was mentioned earlier. Dell Computer grew from nothing to a significant position in the personal computer industry in half a decade; in less than two decades Microsoft came to have a market value approaching that of IBM, which was widely considered to be the industry leader at the time. Osborn Computer was the pioneer in portables, grew rapidly, but was then quickly displaced by Compaq Computer. Telephony is currently on the threshold of experiencing similar turmoil, with wireline being challenged by wireless technologies, generating a new competition arena in which companies like Motorola will come to challenge the regional telephone companies. It is performance competition brought by such companies, underpinned by rapid technological or organizational innovation, that typically offers the most powerful challenge to the existing order and is the more likely to overturn incumbents. Rapid technological change and the possession of market-wide 'monopoly power' (which is in any case economically meaningful) are basically incompatible, except in rare instances.[2] This property of competition needs to be factored into the formal analysis of market power.

The proper assessment of monopoly power always requires identifying a relevant market. In markets where there is rapid technological change, identifying the right competitive arenas within which to assess competition is often complex. Unfortunately, standard approaches to the problem are designed for assessing market power in static contexts, and are often biased downward in that they adopt definitions of (relevant) markets that are too narrow, and they use the wrong metrics to gauge competition within the market. At an intuitive level many professionals inside the enforcement agencies are aware of these problems and sometimes informally adjust their analyses accordingly. However, in our view, it is better to formally recognize the shortcomings in existing frameworks and press forward to address conceptual and analytical weaknesses. In particular, we suggest that the Department of Justice and Federal Trade Commission's *Horizontal Merger Guidelines* (1992) would be improved if they were to specifically address the concerns raised in this paper. Later in this paper we suggest how this might be achieved.

3. *Defining (Antitrust) Markets and Identifying Competitors*

There are several ways that one could attempt to assess market power. Tobins Q (the ratio of the market value of the firm's equity divided by the replacement cost of its assets) is one basis for inferring market power, but the approach presents the problem of properly calibrating a firm's tangible and intangible assets so as to correctly measure the denominator. Earnings-based measures of market power, such as the Lerner Index, attempt to infer monopoly power from accounting data, but they are subject to their own difficulties and often prove to be inconclusive.[3] In an attempt to resolve attendant uncertainty and to legitimize an approach that is not quite so data hungry, the antitrust agencies in the United States advance guidelines suggest the following criterion for defining a market:[4]

---

[2] Obviously patents can exclude competitors; rarely, however, does a single patent, or even a cluster of patents, confer monopoly power over a relevant market, even though they can exclude competitors from a particular technological domain.

[3] Liebowitz (1987) identifies problems arising with the use of such earnings-based measures as profit/sales ratios, profit/equity ratios, and the Lerner Index. Cowling and Waterson (1976) demonstrate that the Lerner Index is determined by levels of concentration, the elasticity of demand *and* the conjectural variation of the other firms in the market. As a result, two industries with the same level of concentration may reveal widely different price-cost margins. Likewise, two industries with the same price-cost margins can exhibit widely different levels of concentration.

[4] US Department of Justice and Federal Trade Commission, *Horizontal Merger Guidelines*, April 2, 1992.

——— *Assessing Market Power in Regimes of Rapid Technological Change* ———

> A market is defined as a product or group of products and a geographical
> area in which it is produced or sold such that a hypothetical profit-
> maximizing firm, not subject to price regulation that was the only present
> and future producer or seller of those products in that area would impose a
> 'small but significant and nontransitory' increase in price, assuming the
> terms of sale of all other products are held constant. A relevant market is a
> group of products and a geographic area that is no bigger than necessary to
> satisfy this test.

In most applications the Justice Department takes 'a small but significant'
increase to be 5%. It has taken 'nontransitory' to be the foreseeable future,
usually one year.

The *Guidelines* approach to market definition has been widely accepted by
the courts in the United States, and the methodology advanced has helped
eliminate judicial uncertainty in many areas of antitrust. To the DOJ and
many economists the central question in market definition is the degree of
demand side substitution possible among products in the relevant market,
and the threshold is clear. Will a price rise of 5% generate sufficient
switching to alternative products by customers to include those alternative
products in the market?

While a valuable conceptual tool, the *Guidelines* approach to market
definition is incomplete. Most importantly, it addresses only price competition, as if that were the only kind of competition that mattered. As a result,
it biases market definition downward (i.e. markets become defined too
narrowly) in industries experiencing rapid technological change, where competition often takes place on performance attributes and not price. Moreover,
in terms of identifying competitors (firms that participate in the market for
purposes of determining concentration and the market power of various
incumbents) the *Guidelines* approach is likewise incomplete. While the
Agency will identify other firms not currently producing or selling the
relevant product as participating in the relevant market if their inclusion
would more accurately reflect probable supply responses, 'these supply responses must be likely to occur within one year and without the expenditure
of significant sunk costs of entry and exit in response to a small but
significant and non-transitory' price increase. If a firm has the technological
capability to achieve such an uncommitted supply response, but likely would
not (e.g. because difficulties in achieving product acceptance, distribution,
or production would render such response unprofitable), that firm will not be
considered a market participant.[5]

Such an approach to entry analysis puts little weight on Schumpeterian
factors, i.e. the technological capacity of the new entrant, the disciplinary

---

[5] *Guidelines*, 1992, pp. 20–21.

─── *Assessing Market Power in Regimes of Rapid Technological Change* ───

effects of the R&D programs of competitors even if new products are not yet in the market, and the magnitude of the creative destruction that a new entrant can impose on incumbents. Put differently, the calibration of competition in terms of the responses of consumers and producers to small price increases caricatures competition in many high technology industries where price is almost a subsidiary competitive variable. As noted earlier, Schumpeter was quite clear about how potential entrants could in fact have competitive impacts before they entered, even if entry would involve irreversible investments. He was also clear that the kind of competition that comes from 'the firms with new technology,' as compared to 'the textbook picture' of price competition among firms possessing no proprietary technology, 'is much more effective than the other as a bombardment is in comparison with forcing a door' (Schumpeter, 1942, p. 84).

A price-based approach to assessing markets and identifying competitors is more appropriate in markets characterized by complete information, simple technologies and/or homogeneous products. In such markets, supply and demand responses are fairly well understood, and competition often does in fact take place primarily on the basis of price. If, on the other hand, markets are characterized by incomplete information, price *and* performance competition, and substantial uncertainty regarding both product performance and the technological possibilities for substitution in supply and demand, the 5%-1-yr-price threshold seems too limiting. The approach evokes an economy of small shopkeepers in Adam Smith's 18th century Scotland and does not register the kind of rivalry characteristic of California's Silicon Valley in the closing decade of the 20th century.

One can illustrate the weaknesses of the *Guidelines* approach by considering the minicomputer industry in the 1970s. During that decade a variety of systems competed on price and performance while exhibiting price differences of several hundred percent.[6] Strict interpretation of the *Merger Guidelines* might suggest that such price differences imply that the products are in different markets and that a Hewlett Packard minicomputer did not compete with a DEC machine. Such an interpretation, however, would ignore the realities of competition in the computer industry, or in any industry experiencing rapid process and product innovation. A variety of systems with quite different price–performance attributes successfully occupy the same market and compete with each other at a given point in time. As new systems are introduced and the prices of existing systems change, it takes some time for resulting price–performance implications to be digested and

---

[6] See Hartman and Teece (1990).

[7] If we were discussing a component market, it would take time to arrange 'design ins' of such components into new products.

understood by the market. One reason is simply that it takes time for users to experience and test the products.[7] Moreover, to the extent that the product is durable and a replacement for existing equipment, purchase decisions are complicated by the need to retire existing equipment. In addition, new computers usually require new support systems to be developed and acquired so that even computer systems that are consensually superior on price and performance dimensions will take time to diffuse and be adapted. In such situations, 5% or even 25% price increases may be met with no substitution *until* the performance of the products can be assessed and existing equipment can be economically replaced. Call this switching costs if you wish. In such circumstances, where competition is performance based, the 5%-1-yr rule used by the antitrust enforcement agencies in the United States is not likely to identify markets that are economically meaningful,[8] for different mini-computer systems surely competed with each other during the 1970s. Products will be put in separate markets when in fact they belong together in the same market because the producers of each are engaged in a life and death struggle to survive and prosper.

To summarize, the static, short-run notions informing key components of competition policy are inadequate to assess the longer-run behavioral issues and the welfare implications of innovative activities. The static price-driven approach will often lead to the conclusion that an innovating firm has market power when it really does not in any economically meaningful way. The more innovative the new product or process, the greater the conventional market power will appear, because price changes will in the short run have little or no influence on demand for a truly innovative product. Complex innovative activities and their resulting products take time to unfold and develop. Moreover, in the early stages of the life cycle of a new product or process, incomplete information is available regarding performance attributes. Few of the possible uses, hence few of the markets in which the product will compete, are fully anticipated. Biotechnological products and processes, for example, may find uses in medicine, agriculture, brewing, chemistry and other sectors of the economy. To the extent that the new product and/or process is technologically complex, these uncertainties are aggravated. The heterogeneous markets in which the new product will compete are revealed slowly. Hence, attempts to use standard price-elasticity-of-demand based methods to define markets for such products and

[8] The 1984 *Merger Guidelines*, Section 3.411, state that with heterogeneous products 'the problems facing a cartel become more complex. Instead of a single price, it may be necessary to establish and enforce a complex schedule of prices corresponding to gradations in actual or perceived quality attributes among competing products . . . Product variation is arguable relevant in all cases, but *practical considerations dictate a more limited use of the factor.*' As a rule of thumb, if the product is completely homogeneous (very heterogeneous), 'the Department of Justice is more (less) likely to challenge the merger.' See Brunner *et al.*, 1985.

processes will grossly understate the size of the markets, possibly resulting in antitrust interference when it is not at all warranted. What is required is a method that takes account of both the price and the performance competition that will unfold over a realistic time frame. Before discussing such a method, we first describe in more specific terms the issues involved by examining the evolution of a particular set of products.

4. The Medical Diagnostic Device Industry as an Exemplar

Overview

The transient nature of market power or 'dominance' in industries experiencing rapid innovation—suggesting the absence of economically meaningful market power—can be illustrated by an examination of diagnostic imaging devices. These are used by physicians and other health care professionals to view inside the human body without intervention. Examples of such devices (and their underlying technologies) include traditional X-ray instrumentation, nuclear imaging, ultrasonic devices (ultrasound), computer tomography (CT scanners), magnetic resonance imaging (MRI) and digital radiography.

For most of these imaging modalities,[9] there has been a period during which one or a few firms were 'dominant.' If one were to consider each new device as a distinct product market, then each market experienced a period in which concentration was very high and a 'monopoly' situation existed if one simply took a snapshot of the market. Such a definition of the market flows naturally from the 5% test embedded in *Merger Guidelines*, given that the demand cross-price elasticities were perceived to be quite low across modalities, particularly during the early introduction stages for each device.

However, as described below, entry by competing firms occurred quickly and concentration fell rapidly as a result of price–performance competition over time within and among modalities. Table 1 and Figure 1 (based on Table A in the Appendix) illustrate these events by summarizing information on sales and the number of producers for each modality. The Tables also summarize total sales and producers across all modalities. Table B in the Appendix presents estimates of the Hirschman-Herfindahl Indices (HHIs) for the modalities, assuming each represents an antitrust market. Figure 2 charts this data. Note that several modalities display brief periods of 'monopoly' or very high concentration, as evidenced by HHI values near 10 000. Hence, the *Guidelines* approach might well suggest that the innovators possessed significant market power, at least initially. While the *Guidelines* do

---

[9] The term modality, which means 'way of doing,' is commonly used in the imaging industry to distinguish between different types of devices.

———— *Assessing Market Power in Regimes of Rapid Technological Change* ————

TABLE 1. Annual Sales of Diagnostic Imaging Modalities in the United States
($ million) (Deflated by the Producer Price Index)

Year	X-ray	Nuclear imaging	Diagnostic ultrasound	CT scan	Magnetic resonance	Digital radiography	All modalities
1954	45	<1	—	—	—	—	45
1955	43	<1	—	—	—	—	43
1956	42	<1	—	—	—	—	42
1957	41	<1	<1	—	—	—	41
1958	42	<1	<1	—	—	—	42
1959	42	<1	<1	—	—	—	42
1960	42	1	<1	—	—	—	43
1961	48	1	<1	—	—	—	49
1962	53	2	<1	—	—	—	55
1963	69	4	<1	—	—	—	73
1964	77	6	<1	—	—	—	83
1965	84	9	1	—	—	—	94
1966	85	10	1	—	—	—	96
1967	171	14	1	—	—	—	186
1968	180	17	1	—	—	—	198
1969	172	19	2	—	—	—	193
1970	173	24	3	—	—	—	200
1971	190	31	4	—	—	—	225
1972	206	39	7	—	—	—	252
1973	273	40	10	5	—	—	328
1974	281	42	15	13	—	—	351
1975	257	43	23	46	—	—	369
1976	230	46	41	87	—	—	404
1977	232	59	49	185	—	—	525
1978	239	69	60	115	—	—	483
1979	242	70	64	85	—	—	461
1980	238	69	77	97	<1	—	481
1981	242	68	80	133	<1	17	540
1982	262	63	77	175	5	55	637
1983	252	50	78	248	28	56	712
1984	257	47	90	185	39	81	699
1985	250	48	110	161	109	81	759
1986	247	51	127	153	143	82	803
1987	242	50	145	168	160	81	846

Source: Mitchell, 1988.

permit one to count potential entrants as being in the market if they can
enter without making irreversible investments, entry requirements were
generally not of that kind in the medical diagnostic device industry. However, a forward looking view of the market for any modality would have
undoubtedly recognized multiple sources of performance competition, which
would imply that the innovators never had market power that was economically
meaningful. Indeed, subsequent history has revealed the highly transient
nature of any monopoly—so transient that it suggests that market power
never really existed. The next two subsections make this apparent by examining both intramodal and intermodal competition.

—— *Assessing Market Power in Regimes of Rapid Technological Change* ——

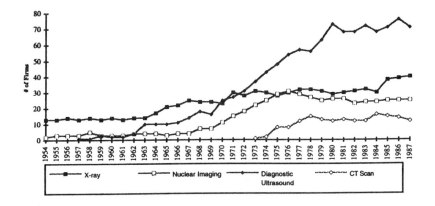

FIGURE 1. Number of Participants in Diagnostic Imaging Modalities in the United States. Source: Mitchell (1988).

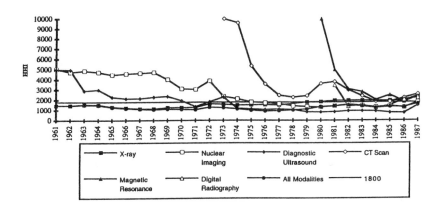

FIGURE 2. Implied Hirschman-Herfindahl Indices (HHI), 1961–1987. Source: based on Table A in the Appendix.

Intra-Modal (Within Modality) Competition in the Medical Diagnostic Device Industry

Consider a specific modality—computer tomographic scanners (CT scans). Godfrey Hounsfield was employed by the British firm EMI when he developed the first practical CT instrument, a head scanner.[10] EMI was the first firm to market CT instrumentation,[11] selling the first unit in London in 1972. In

---

[10] Hounsfield subsequently received a Nobel Prize for his contribution to humanity.

[11] EMI, to whom Hounsfield had assigned his patent, and UCLA's Oldendorf, who had a previous patent on CT technology, engaged in legal contention over the priority of their parents. The issue was resolved when Oldendorf transferred his rights to EMI.

—— *Assessing Market Power in Regimes of Rapid Technological Change* ——

1973 the Mayo Clinic received the first American unit. While the CT scanner market in the United States appears concentrated over the subsequent 2–3 yr period, entry was vigorous. During 1974, a Californian company marketed a competing head scanner. During 1975 several more companies began to sell head scanners, and two whole-body scanners were introduced. By 1977, 12 companies were manufacturing CT scanners for the American market (see Appendix, Table A). Indeed, the longer-term competition proved to be too much for EMI, the company that 6 yrs earlier some might have been (incorrectly) considered a 'monopolist' as it stood alone as the only producer in its modality. Because of severe financial pressure in 1979, EMI's scanner business was acquired by Thorn PLC. Thorn, in turn, divested the EMI CT business in 1980, selling the international operations to General Electric Company (GE). GE, a major competitor in the diagnostic imaging industry, had originally planned to purchase EMI's US operations also, but was deterred by a Justice Department investigation. As a result, the US operations were sold to Omnimedical Inc., a minor producer of CT instruments, which survived only into the early 1980s. [12] Other early participants were no more successful. Most had exited by the early 1980s while new entrants dominated the market.

Thus, we see that despite the existence of patents and early 'monopoly' positions within a given imaging modality, competition was rapid and severe. In fact, the innovator in this field, EMI, was unable to exclude imitators and emulators in spite of its patents. Ironically, its tremendous contribution to the industry and society was rewarded by financial losses. [13] In the process, industry concentration quickly declined. Changes in the HHI reflect the entry of competing CT firms. From a 1972 level of 10 000, the HHI declined below 2500 by 1977 (see Figure 2). Following a brief rise, as several companies left the market, it fell again during the 1980s, as several Japanese and European firms began to market CT systems.

[12] As part of the sale of EMI's international operations to General Electric, EMI and GE settled a patent infringement suit that the British company had initiated during the 1970s.

[13] From the point of view of providing the proper incentives for innovative effort, one might argue that despite its 'monopoly' position, EMI still did not possess sufficient market power to deter entry enough to make the innovation profitable. Entry was 'too' easy from the point of view of the innovator, EMI, and arguably from society's perspective as well. Nevertheless, entry did have some positive effects. The public benefitted from the availability of a broad selection of high-quality CT instruments, most far better than those introduced by EMI. Arguably EMI would have taken much longer to introduce a whole-body instrument, for instance were it not for the pressure of Pfizer and Technicare. However, the core issue here is not that EMI failed and lost money, but that its early monopoly and near-monopoly positions were transient and needed no attention. Moreover, the Justice Department's challenge to the sale of EMI's US operations to GE, which scuttled the deal and caused the American operations to be sold to a minor competitor (Omnimedical), was unnecessary and costly. It was unnecessary because there were many serious competitors to GE and costly because Omnimedical was not capable of managing the assets which it acquired.

———— *Assessing Market Power in Regimes of Rapid Technological Change* ————

Inter-Modal (Between Modality) Competition

When one recognizes price–performance competition between modalities, the degree of concentration and the market power implied by a structuralist approach is attenuated even further. As argued earlier, innovative products compete in terms of price and performance and usually exhibit very different performance attributes. At the center of the competitive innovative process is a period, often long, during which users test the performance attributes of new products under different conditions. For the diagnostic imaging modalities, Table 2 summarizes the relevant performance attributes by which the modalities compete and the range of values of the price–performance attributes over which they compete.

The principal performance attributes recognized in this industry are the following: the variety of tissue applications in which diagnostic information can be obtained, the degree of invasiveness involved with the device, the clarity of the image, and the degree to which a specific tissue can be targeted. These are summarized in the Appendix. In general, there is a rough trade-off between price and performance. However, the trade-off is far from stable, given the coincident evolution of price and performance attributes. Table 3 summarizes the introductory dates for each of the modalities. The specific performance characteristics of the devices/modalities, summarized in Table C in the Appendix, were highly uncertain when the devices were first introduced. Many of the applications have emerged as standard clinical practices only after years of experience and the development of supporting products. Nuclear imaging, for instance, began as a tool for obtaining information about thyroid glands. It evolved in general neurological practice when appropriate radiopharmaceuticals were developed which could

TABLE 2. Summary of Price and Performance Characteristics

Modality	Applications	Relative invasiveness	Relative clarity	Relative tissue-specificity	Relative cost
X-ray	Many	High	Low	Low	Low–medium
Nuclear	Brain/heart	Low–medium	Low	Highest	Low–medium (except PET)
Ultrasound	Heart/fetus eyes/other	Low	Low–high	Medium	Low (except digital)[a]
CT	Brain (heart)	Medium	High	High	Medium–high
MRI	Brain (heart)	Low	High	High	Medium–high
Digital X-ray	Heart (other)	Medium	Medium	High	Medium

Applications in parenthesis are primarily potential applications.
[a] PET and digital technologies are described in the Appendix.

—— *Assessing Market Power in Regimes of Rapid Technological Change* ——

TABLE 3. Research Start, Commercial Entry, Commercial Success

Modality	First research prototype	Commercial introduction		Commercial success assured
		US	Non-US	
Conventional X-ray	1895	1896	1986	c. 1905
Nuclear imaging	c. 1941	1950	c. 1952	c. 1961
Ultrasound	c. 1942	1957	c. 1954	c. 1963
Computed tomography	c. 1961	1973	1972	c. 1975
Magnetic resonance	c. 1974	1980	1978	c. 1984
Digital radiography	c. 1974	1981	1981	c. 1984

target specific lesions in the brain. It found further use in cardiac imaging following additional radiopharmaceutical development and advances in computer enhancement techniques. Invasiveness, which is the degree to which the patient suffers trauma as a result of the imaging procedure, sometimes becomes apparent only after decades of use. Ionizing radiation (of which X-rays are one type), for instance, was routinely used in obtaining fetal images until the 1940s, when the carcinogenic effect of such radiation was finally recognized. Clarity and tissue-specificity, meanwhile, are evolving attributes. Early nuclear imaging devices, for instance, could distinguish only between tissues that were centimeters apart while newer equipment has spatial resolution of a few millimeters.

Prices have also changed as the modalities have evolved. Some products have been introduced at low prices, which were then raised as the products became refined technologically. Other equipment has been introduced at high prices, which then decreased. For instance, nuclear imaging scanners of the late 1950s were priced at about $10,000 (see the Appendix). The nuclear imaging devices of the 1990s cost several hundred thousand dollars for the basic system and up to $5,000,000 for esoteric positron emission tomography systems. Magnetic resonance imaging (MRI) devices, on the other hand, were introduced at prices in the hundreds of thousands of dollars. Prices moved quickly to the range of $1–2 million and, for some MRI scanners, have recently moved back to the hundreds of thousands of dollars as competition and advances in less-expensive magnet technology have emerged.[14]

Closer scrutiny of the details of price–performance competition among the equipment and producers of nuclear medical, computed tomographic and magnetic resonance imaging devices is also very informative regarding the

---

[14] Although MRI systems based on superconducting magnets are still priced at more than $1 million, high-quality permanent magnet systems are available for less than $500 000.

evolution of price and performance attributes. Nuclear medicine was introduced to therapeutic clinical research during the 1930s and diagnostic research during the 1940s. Commercial prototypes of hand-held nuclear probes for obtaining images of thyroid glands were introduced by about 1950, but received little use because the images were unclear and prohibitive amounts of radioactive material were required. Mechanical scanners, introduced commercially about 1954, produced somewhat clearer images, but did not achieve significant clinical success until the early 1960s, when the development of better electronics, the design of complementary glass phantoms for fine-tuning and the accumulation of clinical experience led to their acceptance.

As the nuclear scanners evolved technically, competition evolved commercially. By the time the devices had been accepted generally, the first dozen manufacturers had left the market because their products, although innovative, were commercially inadequate. Brief periods of dominance gave them no protection from technical and commercial competition. Only with the entry of an established manufacturer of radiographic imaging equipment, the Picker X-Ray Corporation, did a stable manufacturer emerge. Picker coupled nuclear scanner technical advances with its established commercial distribution system and reputation to become the dominant nuclear imaging firm during the 1960s. However, Picker's position did not last long. The company quickly faced challenges from two quarters. Some competitors introduced scanners that would obtain images of the entire body, rather than just the head, while other competitors introduced devices that took a stationary snapshot, rather than moved across the body. The stationary cameras, introduced by the Nuclear Chicago Corporation were the major competitive challenge. They were faster, produced fewer imperfections and were better-suited to use with newly-developed radiopharmaceuticals that could be targeted to more organs. The newer devices were more expensive—$25,000 compared to $10,000, which was a significant difference during the 1960s. But the devices offered much greater performance—greater functionality of applications, clarity, tissue specificity and speed. As a result, the price differential was acceptable in the market, and by 1970 the cameras had supplanted the scanner as the dominant instrument. Picker attempted to react, developing two new scanner designs and two different camera designs; however, it was forced into a secondary position. Nuclear Chicago, after being acquired by the GD Searle pharmaceutical company in 1966, became the most successful manufacturer within this modality.[15] However, even this

---

[15] Searle acquired Nuclear Chicago after Abbott Laboratories was deterred from doing so by a Justice Department investigation. The department was concerned that if Abbott acquired Nuclear Chicago, it would control the radiopharmaceutical side of the nuclear market (in which Abbott was then the dominant player) and also become a major instrument player.

—— *Assessing Market Power in Regimes of Rapid Technological Change* ——

dominant position was transitory; Searle/Nuclear Chicago was significantly challenged by competitors who introduced incremental improvements to the camera.[16]

However, the market 'dominance' of nuclear imaging devices was short-lived. In 1973, X-ray computed tomographic (CT) instruments were introduced, which obtained radiographic images of single slices of the body. CT received its first accepted use in neurological imaging, the primary application of nuclear imaging devices during the early 1970s. CT, although more expensive by a factor of 4–5, produced much clearer images. As a result, nuclear imaging equipment manufacturers were facing major sales reductions.

The leading nuclear device producers responded to the new CT devices by introducing other CT instruments to compete with those offered by the early innovator, EMI. At the same time, they worked with nuclear clinicians to expand the number of applications of nuclear devices and improve their brain-imaging applications. The expanded applications took two forms. The first involved emerging cardiac applications, which could not be achieved with CT equipment. Drawing on computing advances, the new cardiac applications stimulated a market for nuclear imaging devices in the late 1970s, although at a significantly higher price than earlier brain applications. The second application advance was the development of several types of tomographic nuclear devices, to compete with X-ray CT in obtaining images of the brain and other organs. Several such general-purpose devices had been accepted by the late 1980s, although X-ray CT continued to receive far greater use.

CT, however, was itself partially supplanted during the early 1980s by the emergence of magnetic resonance imaging (MRI) equipment. MRI, although even more expensive than CT, produced clearer images with less invasiveness, and the device was commercially successful, in spite of its higher price. The early entrants, however, were not successful. The first three firms into the MRI business had either exited or were facing financial trouble by the late 1980s. Instead, later entrants introduced technically superior products and offered better commercial support.

This concern was ungrounded. There was enough competition from established radiography firms such as Picker and General Electric, enough product-specific potential competition from innovative entrants such as Ohio Nuclear (which was later acquired by Technicare), and enough intermodal competition from X-ray CT several years later. Abbott would have had little chance to exploit a combined position in radiopharmaceuticals and instruments to achieve market power. Indeed, even in radiopharmaceuticals, Abbott's position has slipped drastically.

[16] Nuclear Chicago reacted to competitive introduction of gamma cameras by filing patent infringement suits against the competing firms. Most of the suits were settled out of court, with the competitors signing royalty agreements with Nuclear Chicago. Similarly, one defendant (Nuclear Data) which took the matter to trial was forced to sign a royalty agreement.

——— *Assessing Market Power in Regimes of Rapid Technological Change* ———

To summarize, although each 'market' defined by modality has exhibited extremely high HHIs, dynamic competition flourished and drove down concentration over periods of 5–10 yrs. As a result, the within-modality HHIs, while conforming with the static price-based competitive notions of the *Merger Guidelines*, clearly overstate market power. Indeed, the 'monopolists' were usually displaced by competitors producing devices in the same or different modalities. Moreover, the fragility of their positions was apparent at the time, suggesting that the usual static structuralists' approach to assessing market power is highly misleading in the context of industries experiencing rapid technological change. A more realistic approach to assessing competition should make explicit the price *and* performance competition across all devices in the six modalities. If we measure HHIs, including all modalities in a unified market, on the assumption that performance substitution existed across the six technical subfields even if price competition was negligible, the resulting measures of concentration are found to be low, with the HHIs generally below 1500 (see Table B in the Appendix). These lower measures of market power more realistically summarize the competitive dynamism observed in this industry. Indeed, the industry was viewed as highly competitive by analysts at the time, despite the absence of price discounting.

A Formal Method for Identifying Competitors in Markets Experiencing Rapid Technological Change

Overview. The history of the medical diagnostics industry indicates that price and performance competition amongst equipment producers within and across imaging modalities was ever present, though it evolved over time. In light of the understanding provided by the case study, we now ask what is the analytic framework most likely to capture the realities of competition situation. The correct methodology will 'recognize competition where, in fact, competition exists'[17] by identifying all competitive products and the firms producing them.

In assessing where competition indeed exists, the *Merger Guidelines* has distinguished between firms currently producing the market's products, and any potential entrant that could do so quickly in response to a 5% price increase without making irreversible investments. The 5% rule highlights customer and producer switching induced by price changes, and only by price changes. However, for reasons discussed above, price is only one of

---

[17] *Transamerican Computer Co. v International Business Machines Corp.*, 481 F. Supp. 965, 978 (N.D. Cal. 1979) (quoting *Brown Shoe Co. v United States*) 370 US 294, 326 (1962), aff'd, 698 F. 2d 1377 (9th Cir) cert. denied, 464 US 955 (1983).

—— *Assessing Market Power in Regimes of Rapid Technological Change* ——

many product dimensions by which innovative high technology firms compete. Indeed, in high technology industries, customer switching is often more powerfully induced by performance competition involving changes in quality, features, service and other non-price factors.

The evolution of the diagnostic imaging industry was found to be replete with successful challenges from more expensive but better performing new products, delivered by 'committed' entrants as well as by incumbents. Thus, the prices of CT instruments were found to exceed those of nuclear imaging and conventional X-ray devices by several orders of magnitude. However, substitution in favor of CT instruments occurred anyway, given its better performance attributes, in particular, its greater image clarity. The competitive challenge delivered by the new technology to the old had little to do with price. If the price of existing nuclear imaging devices had been lowered by 5% in 1973, we doubt there would have been any effect whatsoever on the sales of CT instruments. Conversely, an increase or decrease of 5% in the price of CT instruments would have had no effect on sales of nuclear imaging equipment. Indeed, CT instrument prices escalated rapidly after introduction, moving from about $200,000 to $1 million and more, without leading to renewed reliance on nuclear or X-ray devices. But this is insensitivity of competition to price does not imply that the two modalities nevertheless competed. Indeed, competition was vigorous, but it was simply not price dependent. Rather it was performance-related. The competitive challenge came from new technology, as did the competitive response, as manufacturers of nuclear devices responded with performance enhancements. They developed and introduced equipment that would approach the image clarity offered by CT instruments, while offering greater tissue specificity. Similarly, the response of the manufacturers of conventional X-ray equipment was to develop expensive digital radiographic devices, thereby competing through performance enhancements, rather than by discounting the price. To ask what incremental competition to CT instrumentation a hypothetical monopolist would confront from an assumed 5% price increase thus frames the market definition question incorrectly, and produces the wrong answer.

When competition proceeds primarily on the basis of features and performance, the pertinent question to ask is whether a change in the performance attributes of one commodity would induce substitution to or from another. If the answer is affirmative, then the differentiated products, even if based on alternative technologies, ought to be included in the relevant product market. Furthermore, when assessing such performance-induced substitutability, a 1-yr or 2-yr period is simply too short because enhancement of performance attributes takes time, yet can be devastating in competitive impact. For example, in each of the six imaging modalities, the cycle from

R&D to commercial success exceeded 10 yrs (see Table 3). Even the period between commercial introduction and assured commercial success has never been less than 3 yrs. Furthermore, once success of a given device/modality had been achieved, the major competitive technical responses and counter-responses have generally played out over a period of years. For instance, the commercial assessment regarding whether tomographic nuclear imaging devices dedicated to brain scanning will be an effective substitute for X-ray CT devices was still underway in 1990, despite the fact that the first devices were introduced in 1976. While it is difficult to state precisely (and generally) what the length of time should be, it is clear that the time frame is determined by technological concerns. As a result, it may be necessary to apply different time frames to different products/technologies.

When assessing performance-based competition among existing producers, the product changes to be included should involve re-engineering of existing products using technologies currently known to existing competitors. Product changes which depend on anticipated technologies, that are not currently commercial in any market, should be excluded. Thus if firm A, by modifying its product X using its existing proprietary product and process technology, and public knowledge, could draw sales away from product Y or firm B, such that B would need to improve its products to avoid losing market share to A, then X and Y are in the same relevant market. If such changes are likely to occur yet would take longer than 1 yr, the 1-yr rule should be modified.

When assessing potential competition and entry barriers, the 2-yr-5% rule must also be extended to include variations in performance attributes in existing and potentially new technologies.[18] In high technology innovative industries, it is this potential competition that is often most threatening,[19] takes the longest time to play out, and is the most difficult to fully anticipate. The reason is that potential competition from new technologies can destroy the value not only of a firm's market position in a particular product, but also

---

[18] Recall that the *Guidelines* suggest that the agencies will include in the market firms with existing assets that likely would be shifted or extended into production of the relevant product within a year, without incurring significant entry and exit loss. The agencies also recognize that even a concentrated market is exposed to competition if entry is timely, likely, and sufficient. The agencies consider timely only those committed entry alternatives that can be achieved within 2 yrs from initial planning to significant market impact (p. 51).

[19] Schumpeter (1942) stressed that potential competition from new products and processes is the most powerful form of competition, stating 'in capitalist reality, as distinguished from its textbook picture, it is not that kind [price] of competition that counts but the competition that comes from the new commodity, the new technology, the new source of supply . . . This kind of competition is as much more effective than the other as bombardment is in comparison with forcing a door, and so much more important that it becomes a matter of comparative indifference whether competition in the ordinary sense functions more or less promptly.'

—— *Assessing Market Power in Regimes of Rapid Technological Change* ——

the value of its underlying technological, physical, and human assets. Price competition, on the other hand, can only erode profit margins. A more realistic time frame must therefore be established over which the new products/technologies may be allowed to enter. The precise length of time allowed for the entry of potential competitors must also reflect technological realities. Hence, it too may vary by product and technology.

Our Proposed Methodology. We focus here on the analytic techniques which aid the assessment of price and performance competition. The need to assess performance based competition argues for the use of 'hedonic methods' which address the importance of product attributes in economic behavior. The 'hedonic' literature has been both theoretical and empirical. It focuses on product demand and production costs, with the demand literature addressing the importance of product attributes in determining prices[20] and market share,[21] the cost literature demonstrating and measuring the impact of product attributes on production costs.[22] Finally, Hartman (1989a, 1989b) integrates hedonic demand and cost analysis into corporate stragegy models focusing on product pricing and design.

In order to demonstrate the contribution of hedonic methods, we begin with a discussion of the more traditional methods underlying application of the *Merger Guidelines*. To that end, assume we are assessing whether each of the six product lines of medical diagnostic imaging modalities in Table 1 represents a distinct product market. In the process, we must assess whether the equipment of manufacturers within a product line really compete. According to the *Merger Guidelines*, producers O and m are assumed to be in the same market if sales of manufacturer O (q_o) are found to compete (within a year) with the sales of manufacturer m (q_m), given a 5% rise in the price of manufacturer m(p_m) and given that the price of manufacturer O (p_o) and all other exogenous factors are held constant. This sensitivity of q_o to p_m can be summarized by the following inverse supply and inverse demand functions:

$$q_0 = S(p_m, p_0, Z_s) \text{ and}$$
$$q_0 = D(p_m, p_0, Z_d), \qquad (1)$$

where Z_s and Z_d summarize all exogenous factors affecting supply and demand. Notice further that if producers O and m are in the same market and

---

[20] See Brown and Mendelsohn (1984), Brown and Rosen (1982), Epple (1987), Hartman (1987), Hartman and Doane (1987), Hartman and Teece (1990), Ohta and Griliches (1976), and Rosen (1974).
[21] See Atkinson and Halvorsen (1984), Hartman (1982), Hausman (1979), and Mannering and Winston (1984).
[22] See Epple (1987), Friedlaender *et al.* (1983), Fuss (1984), Fuss and Waverman (1981), and Spady and Friedlaender (1978).

—— *Assessing Market Power in Regimes of Rapid Technological Change* ——

produce homogeneous products, $p_m = p_o = p$ for all O and m, $q = q_o + q_m$ and equations (1) reduce to standard supply and demand specifications for the market, or

$$q = S(p, Z_s) \text{ and}$$
$$q = D(p, Z_d). \tag{1a}$$

The price test underlying equations (1) can analogously be extended to assess whether price competition exists across product lines in Table 1. To do so, let p_m be the price of the equipment of producer(s) m in one product line and assume that this price is raised by 5%. Let p_o be the price of equipment of producer(s) O in the other product line; let q_o be the sales of the equipment of producer(s) O to customers of producer(s) m; and let Z_d and Z_s be exogenous factors. If we find sensitivity of q_o to price p_m across product lines, then the product lines are part of the same market. In this case, if we allow p_o and q_o to represent the price and quantity of equipment in one product line and p_m and q_m to represent the price and quantity of equipment sold in the second product line, equations (1) become traditional demand and supply curves for all products/producers O with a cross-price elasticity with respect to products/producers m. If that cross elasticity is high enough, products/producers m and O belong in the same market.

As indicated earlier, however, such price competition within and across product lines is considerably less important than performance competition in innovative, high technology industries. Excluding performance competition from the calculation will grossly mis-state observed and apparent price sensitivity, and hence the boundaries of the market. We can introduce such competition into equations (1) by formally including vectors of performance attributes, a_m and a_o for the products produced by manufacturers m and O. For example, a_m would include the performance attributes of the imaging modalities presented in Table 1.[23] Using these extended demand and supply formulations, given as equations (2), we can formally assess sensitivity to price and performance both within and across product lines as

$$q_0 = S(p_m, p_0; a_m, a_0; Z_s) \text{ and}$$
$$q_0 = D(p_m, p_0; a_m, a_0; Z_d). \tag{2}$$

For example, suppose a manufacturer, m, reduces one (or several) of the performance attributes of its product, say a_{mi}, holding price and other attributes constant. If an increase in demand for the product of producer O

---

[23] Any number of attributes can be included. Table 2 identifies five attributes. Hartman includes nine attributes to describe alternative hotel rooms (1989a) and microcomputers (1989b).

results, there exists a performance cross-elasticity between products m and O. If this cross-elasticity is high enough, the products are in the same market. Furthermore, if producer m raises his price 5% and simultaneously increases some of the performance attributes of his product, a_{mi}, 5% or more, there may be no increase in the demand for product O.[24] However, that does not mean that the products are in different markets. In this example, producer m has lowered its price–performance attributes. Using our more explicit formulation in equations (2), we can see that we would not expect demand for product/producer O to increase in this case, because we have accounted for both price and performance changes. Indeed, equations (2) indicate that the improved performance accompanying the hypothetical price rise should generate substitution away from product O.

The inclusion of performance attributes not only allows for formally assessing price and performance competition in the shorter run, it also allows for assessing (qualitatively and quantitatively) the dynamic effects of such competition upon total demand in the longer run. In particular, anecdotal and formal theoretical developments indicate that in rapidly expanding innovation industries, the existence of price–performance competition among several producers is important in dynamically inducing increases in total demand. This importance is characterized in equation (3) where the demand for any product O is determined by both the market share (MS_o) attained by product O [based upon price–performance competition (p_o, a_o) with other producers (producer $m(p_m, a_m)$ and all other producers $j \neq O$ or $m(p_j, a_j)$] and the total market demand for the class of products (Q). Notice that in equation (3) the market share function incorporates all of the price–performance competition discussed with equation (2). Additionally, it incorporates the dynamically-induced demand effects of all price–performance competition upon total market acceptance (Q). An example would be that total market demand for all diagnostic imaging devices increased considerably with the introduction of newer modalities that competed with traditional X-ray devices and led to the broader use of imaging devices generally.

The relevance of this dynamically induced competition is the following. It is possible that two product lines, say O and m, compete but not vigorously. In particular, they may represent fairly distinct price–performance bands, for which it is possible to argue that the two bands represent fairly distinct markets. However, the presence of the two (or more) innovators across the price–performance spectrum can induce greater total market demand over

---

[24] Indeed, there may be an increase in the demand for product m, as in the CT instrument example above.

———— *Assessing Market Power in Regimes of Rapid Technological Change* ————

time, given the resulting information effects and the perceived existence of several suppliers. In this case, variation of price and performance of producer *m* relative to producer O may have little immediate effect upon market share. This fact may persuade analysts to conclude that the markets are separate. However, to the extent that the price and performance variation in (p_m, a_m) stimulates greater total market demand (Q) while market shares remain the same, the price–performance variation (p_m, a_m) will still increase q_0 in equation (3) over time.

$$q_0 = MS_0(p_m, a_m; p_0, a_0; p_j, aj \neq i; Z) *$$
$$Q(P_m, a_m; p_0, a_0; p_j, a_j, j \neq i; Z). \tag{3}$$

To the extent that an increase in q_0 is thereby induced, products O and *m* should be thought of as belonging to the same market.[25]

Methodological Implementation.   The framework presented above explicitly allows us to analyze and quantify both price and performance competition. Using it, we can retain the 5% price rule while extending the *Merger Guidelines* to address performance competition. For example, analogous to the 5% price rule, we could assess the effects of 5% performance changes. However, such an extension is far from straightforward. We need to carefully identify rules of thumb regarding the threshold size of performance competition and the time period over which such competition is allowed to unfold. Using out case study of the diagnostic imaging industry, let us see what can be said about such an extension.

In general, performance changes are more difficult to quantify than price changes because performance is multi-dimensional. As a result, quantification requires measuring both the change in an individual attribute and the relative importance of that attribute. Unlike price changes that involve altering the value of a common base unit (dollars), performance changes often involve changing the units by which performance is measured.[26] Nonetheless, rough quantification is possible, based on the pooled judgments of competent observers, particularly product users.

In terms of threshold effects, we tentatively suggest introducing a 25% rule for a change in any key performance attribute. Such a rule implies that if

---

[25] An example of such non-vigorous competition is ultrasound versus CT, which have only slight overlap of applications. Nonetheless, there are some spill-overs of competence and reputation, so that a firm's performance in the CT modality will increase its success in the ultrasound modality. As advances in one modality improve the performance of another, overall market demand (Q) can increase. Computer techniques successfully applied to CT devices during the 1970s, for instance, underlay the explosion in demand for ultrasound instruments during the 1980s.

[26] Image clarity, for example, once involved only spatial resolution (distance between points). It now also includes temporal resolution (time between images).

an existing manufacturer lowers the quality of a key performance attribute of an existing product up to 25%, *ceteris paribus*, and no substitution to other products occurs, then the original product constitutes a distinct antitrust market. If substitution to other products does occur, then those other products share the market with the original product. Conversely, assume that a new product is introduced which is identical to an existing product in all ways except that it offers up to a 25% improvement in a key performance attribute. If there is no substitution to the new product, then the products represent distinct markets. If there is substitution from the existing product to the new product, then the two products share the same antitrust market. In proposing this threshold, we have attempted to be conservative. The 25% criterion for a single key performance attribute appears to us conservative because a 25% improvement is small compared to those that actually occurred in the diagnostic imaging and minicomputer industries. Moreover, a 25% improvement in a single attribute is likely to imply an overall performance improvement of considerably less than 25%.

A performance threshold must also be judged in terms of feasibility. While it is always possible to raise prices, it is not always possible to increase performance. Nevertheless, it is often the case that following introduction, most product changes take place along a relatively continuous trajectory of technological improvement. Many product users are familiar with the key development programs of their suppliers and are able to assess the likelihood that a particular product change will emerge in the near future. This predictability will be greatest in the science-based industries, where regular product development interaction takes place between product commercializers and users. However, it will also be possible in other settings. In markets with long distribution chains, for instance, large wholesalers will be familiar with the development efforts of their suppliers, even if the eventual end-users are not.

An effective measurement procedure, therefore, would be to rely on the informed judgments of users of existing products or of industry experts. This procedure would involve identifying market experts, asking them to list key performance attributes, and then asking them to assess the substitutive effects of changes in the attributes. The sample of product users could be supplemented by a corresponding sample of commercial participants, although care would be required to avoid introducing competitive bias into the judgments.[27] A sample of such participants could be asked whether a

---

[27] Independent industry experts are well qualified to make these judgments. In some cases government agencies may house individuals with the requisite skills. The general approach advanced here would argue for a closer working relationship between the Antitrust Division of the Justice Department, the Office of Technology Assessment, and the national academies of science and engineering.

25 % change in the performance of any one attribute would lead to product substitution. In the diagnostic imaging equipment market, for instance, radiologists, hospital administrators, marketing personnel, and engineering staff could assess the performance change in computed tomography instrumentation that would likely lead to decreased purchases of magnetic resonance imaging equipment. If improved CT image clarity of 25 % would lead to significant substitution of CT for MRI devices, and if the panel or the industry expert judged that such changes were technically feasible in the 'near future', then the conclusion would be that the two devices were part of the same market. If greater changes in performance were needed to induce substitution, or if no technically feasible changes in performance would induce substitution, then the products might be judged to be in different markets.

If market and industry experts were unable or unwilling to assign percentage values to performance attributes, an alternative would be to simply rely on their estimation of the technical feasibility of near-term product changes. For example, if changes to CT equipment expected in the near-term would influence the buying decisions for magnetic resonance imaging equipment, the two types of products would be judged to be in the same market. If the experts did not expect near-term changes in CT performance to influence their MRI purchase decisions, then the products would be judged to be in different markets.

In addition to threshold rules regarding performance changes, market definition requires an identification of time frame for the competitive product changes—that is, the definition of the 'near future.' We argued above that the DOJ 1-yr and 2-yr rules are too short for almost any case of serious technical advance. However, because there is significant variation among products, no single number will be appropriate for all cases. Nonetheless, we suggest that a 4-yr period be established as a default time frame, with the option of adjusting the period if it seems appropriate in any individual case. Based upon our diagnostic imaging case study, we believe that 4 yrs is conservative. Our rationale for not selecting a longer period rests somewhat on predictive feasibility. Even partially-accurate predictions of feasible technical change often simply fall apart if industry and market experts are asked to project much beyond 4 yrs. A 1981 survey of medical sector experts conducted by the Food and Drug Administration (FDA), for instance, was close to the mark for product changes that occurred during the first half of the 1980s, but was far from accurate for changes predicted to take place during the second half of the decade. The general tendency was to underestimate the time and difficulty that would be required to introduce new and reconfigured products that were in early developmental

―――― *Assessing Market Power in Regimes of Rapid Technological Change* ――――

and commercial stages at the time of the survey.[28]

Like the DOJ's 1-yr rule or the patent law's 17-yr grant, a fixed 4-yr rule is somewhat arbitrary. In some cases, however, industry and market experts will be able to forecast beyond the 4-yr limit. In those cases the option of changing the default 4-yr period should exist. Such cases are likely to occur when a competitive improvement will (i) combine existing physical and knowledge-based resources, and (ii) be used by existing users in existing markets. Experts in the diagnostic imaging market in 1990 were likely to be aware, for instance, that two or three established imaging equipment manufacturers were designing fourth-generation CT devices to compete with the established third-generation product, and that the new device may also perform some of the imaging procedures now most effectively carried out by MRI. Likewise, the history of the diagnostic imaging industry indicates that the success or failure of new devices is unlikely to be apparent until at least 4 or 5 yrs in the future. In such cases, if the experts believe the new devices are likely to influence purchase decisions, the time frame should be widened beyond the 4-yr time frame to reflect this better information.

Finally, we need to assess the appropriate HHI thresholds. The merger guidelines define critical HHIs to be 1000 and 1800 for purposes of assessing mergers.[29] It is difficult to hypothesize and propose alternative HHIs for technologically dynamic markets. However, the inclusion of performance competition, and the inclusion as competitors of firms engaged in relevant R&D, and the extension of the time frame of competition may render increases in these critical HHIs less important.

Furthermore, we believe that with technologically dynamic markets, the pattern of past changes and expected future changes in the HHIs merit as much weight as their current level. The dynamics of market structure in the past provide some guidance to assessing market definition and predicting likely changes in market concentration. For instance if one looks at the 1976 HHI for the CT modality in Table B (Appendix) we find that it is a relatively high 3570. However, the HHI had declined from 10 000 in 1973, indicating a significant trend toward deconcentration. If we find that concentration is declining in this fashion, market power is unlikely to be an issue. Only when the market is defined correctly and when concentration is both high and stable and there is nothing on the horizon to upset the status quo

---

[28] For example, the 1981 FDA report predicted that by 1990 transmission and storage systems would provide central access to all of a patients' health care records, so that information from primary care facilities, clinical specialists, hospitals, pharmacies, dentists and insurance companies would be available simultaneously. By 1990, however, information systems did not yet span all departments within an individual hospital, let alone reach into external facilities such as pharmacies and insurance companies. See US Department of Health and Human Services, *Forecast of Emerging Technologies*, 1981.

[29] See *Merger Guidelines*, 1992.

will current HHIs provide a good indicator of long-term market power.

In addition to the change in concentration, the trend in the number of competitors will provide guidance to the estimation of future market power. Note that the computed tomography HHI grew to 3805 in 1981, after falling to 2268 in 1977 (Appendix, Table B). At the same time, the number of competitors rose from 12 to 13. The expanded pool of actual competitors provided the basis for the decline in concentration which took place after 1981. Thus, if the number of competitors is growing, market power is likely to be transient, even if concentration is stable.

Further refinement can be carried out by examining the capabilities of the current members of the industry. Consider again the 3805 computed tomography HHI in 1981, which was the result of market success of General Electric. When we observe that GE's 12 competitors included well-established imaging industry manufacturers, such as Siemens AG, NV Philips, Picker International, and the Toshiba Corporation, we should not be surprised at the subsequent decline in concentration. Thus, if the pool of current competitors includes several well-established participants in related industrial and market sectors, the 'market power' suggested by simple structured tests is likely to be transient.

One will, of course, also need to examine the capabilities of firms which are not yet competing in the US, but are selling similar products in foreign markets. In 1981, for instance, the Hitachi Corporation was successfully manufacturing CT instruments for sale in Japan, but was just introducing computed tomography devices to the United States. Part of the decline in US concentration that took place after 1981 occurred because of the success of Hitachi's product.

In summary, suggesting extremely high concentration is likely to indicate market power in technologically dynamic industries only if four conditions are met: (i) measures of concentration are stable; (ii) the incumbent controls all the relevant technology; (iii) the number of actual competitors is small and declining; (iv) the pool of potential competitors does not include well-established firms in related sectors or in other geographic areas. When these conditions do not hold, very little can be inferred about the presence of market power from high concentration because transient monopoly is not monopoly at all. In short, even when the market is defined correctly, there is much to be learned from examining the incumbents' competitive position in detail as well as looking at entry conditions.

5. *Summary and Conclusion*

The static economic theory which has traditionally been embraced by many

────── *Assessing Market Power in Regimes of Rapid Technological Change* ──────

economists and many courts does not adequately reflect the role of innovation as the driving force of competition.[30] This has led courts and the antitrust enforcement agencies in the United States to underestimate the breadth of product markets in industries characterized by rapid technological change. In the process, we believe that the courts and the DOJ have, at times, exaggerated antitrust dangers and may consequently have retarded technological development by penalizing innovators.[31] One example was the Justice Department's challenge to the sale of EMI's US operations to General Electric.

In this paper we have suggested in a tentative way how the static approach to product market definition should be modified if the antitrust laws are to fully embrace the kind of competition that really counts—competition driven by product and process innovators. We have argued that competition is seldom based on price alone, as appears presumed by the *Merger Guidelines*. Competition on product attributes is as important as competition on price in most markets; in technologically dynamic markets, product attributes and performance competition are typically more important than price competition. Furthermore, performance competition requires a longer time period to unfold than does price competition.

Taking these insights as a point of departure, we have proposed a 'hedonic' framework through which the courts and the enforcement agencies can explicitly formulate, quantify and analyze both price and performance competition. We have tentatively suggested a 25% threshold and a 4-yr period for delineating market boundaries. We view these thresholds as conservative and propose them as supplements to the existing 5%-1-yr and 5%-2-yr rules of the *Merger Guidelines*. We believe these steps are warranted because we agree with William Baxter (1985, pp. 80–81), that 'the contribution of technological advances to our economic well being is very substantial when compared to the damage that could be caused by restrictive behavior the antitrust laws seek to halt. If our antitrust laws were to impede technological development to any substantial degree, the net effect of those laws on our well being would surely be negative.'

References

Atkinson, S. E. and R. Halvorsen (1984), 'A New Hedonic Technique for Estimating Attribute Demand: An Application to the Demand for Automobile Fuel Efficiency,' *Review of Economics and Statistics*, 66, 417–426.

Armentano, D. T. (1982), *Antitrust and Monopoly: Anatomy of a Policy Failure*, Wiley and Sons: New York.

[30] It is not the courts as much as the economists that are at fault. Mainstream economic theory has been slow to incorporate the dynamics of technological change into its corpus, as is apparent from inspecting practically all introductory, intermediate, and advanced microeconomic textbooks.

[31] This will be dealt with more extensively in subsequent papers planned by the authors.

—— *Assessing Market Power in Regimes of Rapid Technological Change* ——

Baxter, W. F. (1985), 'Antitrust Law and Technological Innovation,' *Issues in Science and Technology*, Winter, 80–81.

Brown, G. Jr. and R. Mendelsohn (1984), 'The Hedonic Travel Cost Method,' *Review of Economics and Statistics*, 66, 427–433.

Brown, J. N. and H. S. Rosen (1982), 'On the Estimation of Structural Hedonic Price Models,' *Econometrica*, 50, 765–768.

Brunner, T. W., T. G. Krattenmaker, R. A. Skitol and A. A. Webster (1985), *Mergers in the New Antitrust Era*, The Bureau of National Affairs, Inc.: Washington.

Cowling, K. and M. Waterson (1976), 'Price-Cost Margins and Market Structure,' *Economica*, 43, 267–274.

Epple, D. (1987), 'Hedonic Prices and Implicit Markets: Estimating Demand and Supply Functions for Differentiated Products,' *Journal of Political Economy*, 95, 59–80.

Freeman, C. (1982), *The Economics of Industrial Innovation*, MIT Press: Cambridge, Mass.

Friedlaender, A. F., C. Winston and K. Wang (1983), 'Costs, Technology and Productivity on the US Automobile Industry,' *Bell Journal of Economics*, 14, 1–20.

Fuss, M. A. (1984), 'Cost Allocation: How Can the Cost of Postal Services be Determined?', in R. Sherman, (ed.), *Perspectives on Postal Service Issues*, American Enterprises Institute, pp. 30–52.

Fuss, M. A. and L. Waverman (1981), 'Regulation and the Multiproduct Firm: The Case of Telecom-munications in Canada,' in G. Fromme (ed.), *Studies in Public Utility Regulation*, MIT Press: Cambridge, MA.

Hartman, R. S. (1982), 'A Note on the Use of Aggregate Data in Individual Choice Models: Discrete Consumer Choice Among Alternative Fuels for Residential Appliance,' *Journal of Econometrics*, 18, 313–336.

Hartman, R. S. (1987), 'Product Quality and Market Efficiency: The Effect of Product Recalls on Resale Prices and Firm Valuation,' *Review of Economics and Statistics*, 69(2).

Hartman, R. S. (1989a), 'Hedonic Methods for Evaluating Product Design and Pricing Strategies,' *Journal of Economics and Business*, 41, 197–212.

Hartman, R. S. (1989b), 'An Empirical Model for Evaluating Product Design and Pricing Strategy,' *International Journal of Industrial Organization*, 7, 419–436.

Hartman, R. S. and M. J. Doane, (1987), 'The Use of Hedonic Analysis for Certification and Damage Calculations in Class Action Complaints,' *The Journal of Law, Economics and Organization*, 3, 351–372.

Hartman, R. S. and D. Teece (1990), 'Product Emulation Strategies in the Presence of Reputation Effects and Network Externalities: Some Evidence from the Minicomputer Industry,' *Economics of Innovation and New Technology*, 1, 157–182.

Hausman, J. A. (1979), 'Individual Discount Rates and the Purchase and Utilization of Energy-Using Durables,' *Bell Journal of Economics*, 10.

Liebowitz, S. J. (1987), 'The Measurement and Mismeasurement of Monopoly Power,' *International Review of Law and Economics*, 7, 89–99.

Mannering, F. and C. Winston (1984), 'Consumer Demand for Automobile Safety,' *American Economic Review*, 74, 316–318.

Mitchell, W. (1988), 'Dynamic Commercialization: Innovation in the Medical Diagnostic Imaging Industry,' unpublished Doctoral Dissertation, School of Business, University of California, Berkeley.

Mitchell, W. (1989), 'Whether and When? Probability and Timing of Incumbents' Entry into Emerging Industrial Subfields,' *Administrative Science Quarterly*, 34, 208–230.

Nelson, R. R. (1984), *High Technology Policies*, American Enterprise Institute: Washington, DC.

Nelson, R. R. and S. G. Winter (1982), 'The Schumpeterian Trade-Off Revisited,' *American Economic Review*, 72, 114–132.

Ohta, M. and Z. Griliches (1976) 'Automobile Prices Revisited: Extensions of the Hedonic Hypothesis,' in N. E. Terleckyj, (ed.), *Household Production and Consumption*, National Bureau of Economic Research Conference on Research in Income and Wealth: Studies in Income and Wealth, 40, 325–390.

Rosen, S. (1974), 'Hedonic Prices and Implicit Markets: Product Differentiation in Pure Competition,' *Journal of Political Economy*, 82, 34–55.

—— *Assessing Market Power in Regimes of Rapid Technological Change* ——

Schumpeter, J. A. (1942), *Capitalism, Socialism and Democracy*, Harper & Row: NY.

Spady, R. H. and A. F. Friedlaender (1978), 'Hedonic Cost Functions for the Regulated Trucking Industry,' *Bell Journal of Economics*, 9, 159–179.

Teece, D. J. (1980), 'Economics of Scope and the Scope of an Enterprise,' *Journal of Economic Behavior and Organization*, 1, 223–247. Reprinted in 'La Diversificazione Strategica: Condizione de Efficienza in Organizzazione e Mercato,' in R. C. D. Nacamulli and A. Rugiadini (eds), *Organizzazione e Mercato:*, Mulino: Bologna, Italy, pp. 447–476.

Teece, D. J. (1981), 'The Market for Know-How and the Efficient International Transfer of Technology,' *The Annals of the Academy of Political and Social Science*, 81–96.

Teece, D. J. (1983), 'Towards an Economic Theory of the Multipoint Firm,' *Journal of Economic Behavior and Organization*, 3, 39–63. Reprinted in L. Putterman (ed.), *The Economic Nature of the Firm: A Reader*, Cambridge University Press: Cambridge, MA, 1986.

Teece, D. J. (1986), 'Profiting from Technological Innovation,' *Research Policy*, 15(6). Reprinted in Industria Ricerche Economiche, 4 (October/December 1986 and 1987).

Teece, D. J. (ed.) (1987), *The Competitive Challenge: Strategy and Organization for Industrial Innovation and Renewal*, Ballinger: Cambridge, MA.

US Department of Justice and Federal Trade Commission, *Horizontal Merger Guidelines*, April 2, 1992.

Appendix

TABLE A. Number of Participants in Diagnostic Imaging Modalities in the United States

Year	X-ray	Nuclear imaging	Diagnostic ultrasound	CT scan	Magnetic resonance	Digital radiography	All modalities
1954	13	2	—	—	—	—	15
1955	13	3	—	—	—	—	16
1956	14	3	—	—	—	—	17
1957	13	3	1	—	—	—	17
1958	14	5	1	—	—	—	20
1959	13	3	3	—	—	—	18
1960	14	3	2	—	—	—	18
1961	13	3	2	—	—	—	17
1962	14	4	4	—	—	—	21
1963	14	4	10	—	—	—	27
1964	17	4	10	—	—	—	30
1965	21	3	10	—	—	—	32
1966	22	4	11	—	—	—	35
1967	25	4	14	—	—	—	40
1968	24	7	18	—	—	—	46
1969	24	7	16	—	—	—	44
1970	23	11	25	—	—	—	51
1971	30	15	27	—	—	—	63
1972	28	18	31	—	—	—	67
1973	31	22	37	1	—	—	78
1974	30	25	43	2	—	—	86
1975	28	29	48	8	—	—	91
1976	30	31	54	8	—	—	96
1977	32	29	57	12	—	—	99
1978	32	27	56	15	—	—	94
1979	31	25	63	13	—	—	96

———— *Assessing Market Power in Regimes of Rapid Technological Change* ————

TABLE A. (continued)

Year	X-ray	Nuclear imaging	Diagnostic ultrasound	CT scan	Magnetic resonance	Digital radiography	All modalities
1980	29	26	73	12	1	—	106
1981	30	26	68	13	3	3	103
1982	31	23	68	12	6	17	108
1983	32	24	72	12	9	23	111
1984	30	24	68	16	12	21	111
1985	38	25	71	15	13	20	124
1986	39	25	76	14	18	17	134
1987	40	25	71	12	16	18	129

Source: Mitchell, 1988.

TABLE B. Implied Hirschman-Herfindahl indices (HHI) 1961–1987

Year	X-ray	Nuclear imaging	Diagnostic ultrasound	CT scan	Magnetic resonance	Digital radiography	All modalities
1961	1469	5048	5000	—	—	—	1464
1962	1467	4718	4950	—	—	—	1461
1963	1548	4859	2904	—	—	—	1533
1964	1529	4719	3004	—	—	—	1494
1965	1326	4472	2293	—	—	—	1281
1966	1239	4582	2143	—	—	—	1173
1967	1158	4638	2152	—	—	—	1102
1968	1158	4715	2292	—	—	—	1060
1969	1268	4019	2363	—	—	—	1122
1970	1273	3089	1944	—	—	—	1089
1971	1284	3054	1353	—	—	—	1060
1972	1631	3894	1836	—	—	—	1297
1973	1578	2353	2293	10000	—	—	1253
1974	1507	2130	1190	9608	—	—	1133
1975	1527	1807	1141	5335	—	—	1005
1976	1556	1733	1073	3570	—	—	928
1977	1508	1648	1117	2468	—	—	961
1978	1675	1438	1072	2268	—	—	1033
1979	1813	1354	830	2428	—	—	1122
1980	1842	1319	822	3620	10000	—	1361
1981	1965	1424	860	3805	5000	3464	1418
1982	1965	1578	945	2992	3082	1404	1519
1983	1957	1450	942	2385	2794	1511	1408
1984	1948	1317	915	1848	2024	1220	1240
1985	1949	1426	772	1826	2489	1491	1341
1986	1949	1285	743	2212	1843	2043	1328
1987	2414	1794	1475	2576	2374	2222	1637

——— *Assessing Market Power in Regimes of Rapid Technological Change* ———

TABLE C. Comparison of Six Diagnostic Imaging Methods (Modalities)

1. Relevant Science Base

Conventional X-ray. Images based on differences in tissue density observed by passing X-ray through body. Produces image on film.

Nuclear medicine. Images and other diagnostic information based on analysis of gamma-ray emitting radioactive materials placed into body. Most images produced on film; may be stored and reproduced on monitor.

Ultrasound. Images and other diagnostic information obtained from sonic pulse echoes or shift in frequency (Doppler effect). Images produced on film or monitor; film images may be stored and reproduced on monitor.

Computed tomography (CT). X-ray based technique which uses sequence of scans and computer image processing to produce image of slice. Images produced on film; may be stored and reproduced on monitor.

Magnetic resonance (MRI, NMR). Magnetic fields used to stimulate cell nuclei which produce radio frequency signals. Images produced on film; may be stored and reproduced on monitor.

Digital radiography (computed radiography). X-ray enhanced by computer image processing and contrast agents. Uses several X-ray detection methods, including phosphor plate. Images produced on film; may be stored and reproduced on monitor.

2. Common Applications

Conventional X-ray. Used throughout body. Accounts for about 70% of current imaging procedures (not including electrodiagnostic procedures such as electrocardiograms and electroencephalograms). Mainly static images (snapshot of current state).

Nuclear medicine. First success was with brain imaging, but was largely supplanted by CT. Found new life in dynamic studies of cardiac function and detection of abnormalities in bones. New role in brain imaging emerging with single photon emission computed tomography (SPECT) and positron emission tomography (PET). Has emerging applications, through PET, that combine images with information about biochemical changes in brain and other tissues. Dependent on development of radioactive materials that have appropriate half-life and will concentrate in specific tissues. Both static and dynamic analysis (heart valve function, for instance).

Ultrasound. Found first wide-scale use outside radiology, in specialties such as neurology, cardiology, obstetrics, ophthalmology, urology, and office-based practice. Some functions, such as neurology, supplanted by other imaging advances. Growing applications in radiology for solid organ imaging. Cardiac applications also growing with integration of pulse-based images, Doppler-based flow analysis, and color options. Cannot image bone. Sound waves distorted when air is present, such as in embolisms. Static and dynamic analysis (heart rhythm, for instance).

Computed tomography (CT). Widely used for brain, stem, and spinal column, which are largely unapproachable with conventional X-ray. Effectively supplanted nuclear medicine for neurological work. Has presently limited cardiac applications.

Magnetic resonance imaging. Competes with CT, and is widely used for brain, stem, and spine imaging. Has limited cardiac applications. Cannot image bone. Depends on availability of powerful magnets; most powerful superconducting magnets are both large and expensive; resistive magnets are lighter and less expensive, but less powerful; permanent magnets are less expensive and sometimes lighter, but less powerful. Has potential, through high-magnetic-field spectroscopy, to combine images with information about biochemical changes in tissues.

——— *Assessing Market Power in Regimes of Rapid Technological Change* ———

TABLE C. (*continued*)

Digital radiography. Image subtraction capabilities used for imaging blood vessels and measuring arterial circulation. This involves injecting contrast media into an artery and measuring over time the changing concentration of contrast medium passing through the artery; using a computer, the images before the contrast injection are subtracted from those after the injection, leaving only the path of the contrast medium. Experienced initial rapid diffusion of systems that were designed to be added-on to existing conventional X-ray systems, but add-ons turned out to be technically flawed. Reasonable success with stand-along systems that replace/augment conventional X-ray angiography systems. Phosphor-plate systems may offer wider applications.

3. Invasiveness

	Exposure to ionizing radiation	*Requires catheter incision*
Conventional X-ray	Yes	Angiography
Nuclear medicine	Little, but radioactive materials present storage and supply problem	No
Ultrasound	No	No
CT	Yes, less than X-ray	No, except some contrast media applications
MRI	No, but magnetic field might turn out to have side effects	No, except some contrast media applications
Digital radiography	Yes, less than X-ray	Angiography

4. Image Clarity*

Conventional X-ray. Relatively poor. Can distinguish among only 5–20 scales of gray, with basic distinctions being between air (black), fat (dark gray), soft tissue (lighter grey), bone (moderately white), and metal (white). Superimposes three-dimensional structures into single two-dimensional image. Cannot observe tissue obstructed by higher-density tissue, such as an organ obstructed by bone.

Nuclear medicine. Traditionally, relatively poor. Recent advances in single photon emission computed tomography (SPECT) and positron emission tomography (PET) have improved clarity, but still lags CT and MRI.

Ultrasound. Traditionally, relatively poor. Until early 1980s interpreting images accurately required several years of experience on part of technician. Digital advances in last 8–10 years have led to much clearer images. Fetuses now look like proto-babies, not fuzzy insects.

Computed tomography. Relatively high. Produces images in slices of single planes. Can detect up to 2000 shades of gray; not only can fat be distinguished from other soft tissues, but gradations of density within soft tissue can be recognized; for example, tumor from surrounding normal tissue. Suffers from motion artifacts (patient moved during scan). But still has some difficulty differentiating early-stage tumors.

Magnetic resonance. High clarity. Produces images in slices of single planes. But clinical data on imaging protocols required to establish comparability of images still being developed. Suffers from motion artifacts (patient moved during scan).

*Image clarity defined as the ability to distinguish between adjacent parts of the body.

—— *Assessing Market Power in Regimes of Rapid Technological Change* ——

TABLE C. (*continued*)

Digital radiography. Potentially high, but early subtraction techniques left as much distortion as image. Newer digital angiography systems provided better images than conventional X-ray angiography.

5. Tissue Specificity*

Conventional X-ray	Low
Nuclear medicine	Highest and most flexible, with constraints of radioactive material and carrying agent.
Ultrasound	Reasonable
CT	High
Magnetic resonance	High
Digital radiography	High, when coupled with contrast media injection.

*Note: Tissue specificity defined a the ability to target specific organ or other tissues.

6. Cost Estimate*

	Introduction (current US $)	Present (US $, 1990)
Conventional X-ray	5000	100 000–1 million
Nuclear medicine	10 000	100 000–5 million
Ultrasound	1000	10 000–1 million
Computed tomography	250 000	250 000–3 million
Magnetic resonance	1000 000	500 000–3 million
Digital radiography	500 000	500 000–2 million

*Note: Includes site preparation; excludes service and parts.

7a. Relative Importance of Several Factors to US Research-Oriented Hospitals

Primary	Image quality (clarity, specificity, invasiveness)
	Availability of upgrades from manufacturer
	After-sales service and maintenance
Secondary	Applications (breadth within main application), Price
Tertiary	Financing
	Availability
	Ability to generate referrals

7b. Relative Importance of Several Factors to US Community Hospitals

Primary	Image quality (clarity, specificity, invasiveness)
	Availability of upgrades from manufacturer
	Applications: breadth within main application
Secondary	Price
	Financing
	After-sales service and maintenance
Tertiary	Availability
	Ability to generate referrals

Systems competition and aftermarkets: an economic analysis of *Kodak*

BY CARL SHAPIRO* and DAVID J. TEECE**

I. Introduction

The Supreme Court's recent (1992) *Kodak* decision[1] has put the spotlight on important economic as well as legal issues. The economic issues relate to the relationship between what the Supreme Court calls "equipment markets," and "aftermarkets." In *Kodak*, the equipment markets were for photocopiers and micrographic

* Professor of Business and Economics, Haas School of Business and the Department of Economics, University of California at Berkeley.

** Mitsubishi Bank Professor and Director of the Center for Research in Management, Haas School of Business, University of California at Berkeley.

AUTHORS' NOTE: *We thank Severin Borenstein, Joseph Farrell, Richard Gilbert, Thomas Jorde, Michael Katz, and Paul Klemperer for stimulating discussions on the issues addressed in this article. Shapiro also thanks the National Science Foundation for financial support. Teece thanks the Alfred P. Sloan Foundation.*

[1] Eastman Kodak Company v. Image Technical Services, Inc. et al., 112 S. Ct. 2072 (1992).

136 : *The antitrust bulletin*

equipment, and the aftermarkets involved the parts and service needed to keep these machines in good running condition.[2] The *Kodak* decision has raised many questions, among both economists and lawyers, regarding aftermarkets, and especially about the circumstances under which behavior by equipment man-ufacturers can have anticompetitive effects in aftermarkets. The Court's ruling in *Kodak* also has focused attention on the role of economic theory and economic analysis in antitrust cases.

We view *Kodak* as the Court's most recent foray into the law and economics of *systems*, i.e., groupings of products that work together. Kodak's "copier system" includes a Kodak copier, spare parts that fit that copier, and service for that copier.[3] In *Kodak* the Court rejected the notion that competition between rival systems (interbrand competition) inevitably precludes any finding of monopoly power in derivative aftermarkets. The Court also pro-vided guidance as to some of the factors that might enable market power to be exercised in aftermarkets, although the factors dis-cussed by the Court by no means represent a comprehensive or particularly lucid treatment of the economics of aftermarkets. Nevertheless, the Court has raised important issues, issues that have been explored in the economics literature under the rubrics of *lock-in* and *switching costs*.[4]

---

[2]   As we discuss below, the concept of aftermarkets is not restricted to the sale of equipment, parts and service as in *Kodak*.

[3]   For a more complete discussion of systems competition, see Michael Katz & Carl Shapiro, *Systems Competition and Network Effects*, 8 J. Econ. Persp. (forthcoming Spring 1994).

[4]   *See, for example*, the theories developed by Joseph Farrell & Carl Shapiro, *Optimal Contracts with Lock-in*, 79 Am. Econ. Rev. 51 (1989) [hereinafter *Optimal Contracts*]; *Dynamic Competition With Switching Costs*, 19 Rand J. Econ. 123 (1988); and Alan Beggs & Paul Klemperer, *Multi-Period Competition With Switching Costs*, 651 Econometrica 60 (1992). See also the general discussion of lock-in and opportunism in Oliver Williamson, The Economic Institutions of Capitalism (1985). For an empirical assessment of switching costs and the organizational implications that flow from them, see Kirk Monteverde & David J. Teece, *Supplier Switching Cost and Vertical Integration in the U.S. Auto-mobile Industry*, 13 Bell J. Econ. 206 (1982).

Since the *Kodak* decision makes it very clear that plaintiffs are entitled to a full opportunity to conduct discovery necessary to withstand defendants' summary judgment motions, lower courts and antitrust practitioners can expect future antitrust cases involving aftermarkets to involve more discovery and more analysis than has hitherto been the case. In this article we sketch out the key economic questions and analytical steps that will arise in *Kodak*-style cases. Specifically, we discuss: (1) the economic concept of an aftermarket; (2) how to assess market power in aftermarkets; (3) tying claims involving aftermarket products and services; (4) the role of intellectual property rights in aftermarkets; and (5) class certification and damages in *Kodak*-style cases.

We devote much of our article to assessing market power in aftermarkets. Based on the analytical steps we have identified, we suspect that market power in aftermarkets usually goes hand-in-hand with market power in equipment markets. But we recognize that this is ultimately an empirical matter that will be highly fact-dependent. Our goal is to lay out the questions an economist must explore to determine whether a firm facing equipment competition nonetheless has genuine market power in an aftermarket. For this to happen requires the confluence of several circumstances. We predict, therefore, that plaintiffs' economic arguments will prove weak in most *Kodak*-style cases where market power is absent in the original equipment market.

II. Background

In *Kodak*, independent service organizations (ISOs) brought an antitrust action against Kodak to recover for policies Kodak introduced that limited the availability to ISOs of replacement parts for copying and micrographic equipment manufactured and sold by Kodak. The ISOs alleged that Kodak had unlawfully tied the sale of service for its machines to the sale of parts, in violation of section 1 of the Sherman Act, and had unlawfully monopolized and attempted to monopolize the sale of service and parts in violation of section 2 of the Sherman Act. The district court granted summary judgment.

The Court of Appeals for the Ninth Circuit reversed and remanded, and certiorari was granted. The Supreme Court found that the ISOs had presented sufficient evidence to raise genuine issues concerning Kodak's market power in the service and parts markets, and rejected Kodak's contention that lack of market power in service and parts must be assumed when such power is absent in the equipment market. The ISOs successfully argued that aftermarkets might not be competitive, despite the presence of equipment (or interbrand) competition, because significant information and switching costs could confound competition in the aftermarket. Customer lock-in, high information costs, and price discrimination against locked-in customers could plausibly enable a manufacturer to elevate service prices above competitive levels. Proper market definition and the measurement of market power could not, the Supreme Court reasoned, be determined as a matter of law, but required factual inquiry.

In this article, we argue that, as a matter of economic logic, one cannot positively infer the absence of market power in aftermarkets from competitive equipment markets. The Supreme Court was therefore on firm theoretical ground in denying summary judgment, even given the high thresholds of *Matsushita*,[5] if indeed the limited factual record presented to the Court did not render the plaintiffs' claim inherently implausible or illogical.[6] Quoting the court of appeals approvingly, the Supreme Court concluded that the plaintiffs' claims cannot be rejected a priori because "market imperfections can keep economic theories about how consumers will react from mirroring reality."[7]

---

[5] Matsushita Electric Industrial Co. v. Zenith Radio Corp., 475 U.S. 574 (1986).

[6] We are far from fully informed about the factual record in *Kodak* on at least two important issues. In particular, Kodak's attorneys clearly feel that the record included evidence that Kodak's customers were sophisticated and well informed, and evidence that Kodak's policies were imposed only prospectively on new customers, not retroactively on old customers. *See* Daniel M. Wall, Kodak: *A Personal Perspective*, ANTITRUST, Fall/Winter 1992, at 5.

[7] 112 S. Ct. 2078, quoting 903 F.2d 617.

The *Kodak* decision has triggered a vigorous debate among economists about the costs and benefits of denying summary judgment to firms that face strong competition in "primary" markets.[8] Even though such firms may have some transitory market power in their own proprietary aftermarkets, the costs of identifying and limiting that power may be substantial, and the benefits will be low if such market power is rare or typically short lived. This debate is likely to continue—economists never tire of comparing costs and benefits—but it is largely academic at this point. *The key practical question now is how to assess market power in aftermarkets and how to analyze the effects of firms' aftermarket policies on competition.* That is the primary focus of this article.

III. The concept of an aftermarket

Kodak may be the first occasion in which the Supreme Court has explicitly used the term "aftermarket." While not explicitly defined, the Court seems to have in mind the sale of parts and service, transactions that often take place at a point in time after the purchase of equipment. We define an "aftermarket transaction" to be any transaction with two characteristics: (1) the aftermarket product or service is *used together with a primary product*, and (2) the aftermarket product or service is *purchased after the primary product*.

Aftermarkets are not restricted to the equipment-parts-service pattern present in *Kodak*. The primary product may be a computer operating system such as Microsoft's MS-DOS or Windows, with aftermarkets consisting of applications software (e.g., word processing, spreadsheet, and database software) designed to run on that operating system. Or the primary product may be a brand of word processing software such as WordPerfect, with aftermarkets

---

[8] A public-policy analysis of the *Kodak* decision involves trading off extra litigation and compliance costs (including any chilling of procompetitive behavior) vs. the deterrence of anticompetitive behavior. We suspect that the costs imposed by the *Kodak* decision will ultimately outweigh the benefits; time will tell. *See* Severin Borenstein, Jeffrey Mackie-Mason, and Janet Netz, Exercising Market Power in Proprietary Aftermarkets (Oct. 1992) (unpublished manuscript) for a contrary view.

for upgrades or enhancements to WordPerfect. Following the Court, however, we will refer to the primary market as the "equipment" market and the aftermarket products as "parts" and "service."[9]

The industrial market structures for the primary product and its aftermarkets can follow several patterns. Certainly, equipment and service markets can both be competitive (telephones, fax machines); or both can be monopolized, either by the same firm or by separate firms. It is also possible for the primary market to be competitive and the aftermarket monopolized: if a single firm were to develop a proprietary technology to service refrigerators in compliance with new environmental restrictions, that firm could conceivably monopolize the refrigerator service business, even if sales of refrigerators is competitive. The fourth logical possibility, a monopolized equipment market and a competitive aftermarket, arises if an equipment manufacturer has monopoly power and many firms service its equipment.

Aftermarkets need not be brand-specific, i.e., *proprietary*, as they were in *Kodak*. For standardized parts, one cannot talk of markets for Kodak parts, for Xerox parts, etc., but rather of markets for parts that fit all brands of machines. Likewise, if service skills are transferable from one brand of machine to another, there cannot be brand-specific service aftermarkets. Of course, market power by equipment manufacturers in aftermarkets is more likely to arise if aftermarkets are proprietary. The remainder of our discussion is restricted to proprietary aftermarkets.

Some important insights into aftermarkets can be gleaned from the recognition that the parts and service are complements to equipment in the economic sense: lowering the price of equipment raises the demand for parts and service, and vice versa. As a general rule, there are economic benefits from coordinating the sale of complementary goods, very possibly within the same firm.[10]

---

[9]   The primary market may in fact be for the entire system of equipment, parts, and service, but we shall refer to the "equipment" market for ease of exposition.

[10]   There is a large economics literature exploring the benefits of coordinating the sale of complementary goods, including the literature on

The basic economics of complementary goods tells us that an equipment vendor should welcome the emergence of high-quality, low-cost repair services for its machines, as this will make the machines more attractive, just as a lower price of gasoline stimulates the demand for automobiles and the availability of cheap compact disks stimulates the demand for CD players.

The temporal relationship between equipment markets and their associated aftermarkets goes beyond mere complementarity, however. Customers rarely arrange for all of their parts and service needs when they purchase a machine, and years can go by between a buyer's original-equipment purchase and aftermarket transactions by that same buyer. Most important for our purposes, a customer who owns one brand of machine may face high switching costs in adopting another brand, e.g., because the buyer has made investments in brand-specific skills or complementary assets.

With high switching costs, the number of users at any point in time who are using a particular brand of equipment, i.e., the installed base of equipment of that brand, is significant.[11] However, the mere fact that some consumers face high switching costs does not in and of itself imply that a firm with a large market share in an aftermarket has genuine market power.

---

vertical integration, the so-called double marginalization problem, and the literature on vertical contracting. *See, for example,* David J. Teece, *Toward an Economic Theory of the Multiproduct Firm,* 3 J. ECON. BEHAVIOR & ORGANIZATION 39 and D. Teece et al., *Understanding Corporate Coherence: Theory & Evidence,* J. ECON. BEHAVIOR & ORGANIZATION (1993).

[11] For economic analyses of competition with installed bases, see Michael Katz & Carl Shapiro, *Technology Adoption in the Presence of Network Externalities,* 94 J. POL. ECON. 822 (1986), and *Product Introduction With Network Externalities,* 40 J. INDUS. ECON. 55 (1992); and Joseph Farrell & Garth Saloner, *Installed Base and Compatibility: Innovation, Product Preannouncements, and Predation,* 76 AM. ECON. REV. 940 (1986); and Raymond Hartman & David Teece, *Product Emulation Strategies in the Presence of Reputation Effects and Network Externalities: Some Evidence from the Microcomputer Industry,* 1 ECON. INNOVATION & NEW TECHNOLOGY 157 (1990).

142 : *The antitrust bulletin*

IV. Assessing market power in aftermarkets

The Supreme Court attempted to identify circumstances where market power is possible in aftermarkets even though the equipment market is competitive. That is our focus as well; the analysis below is confined to aftermarkets associated with competitive equipment markets.

In principle, assessing market power in aftermarkets is no different from assessing market power in any other context.[12] We ask whether a single entity controlling the aftermarket could profitably raise price above competitive levels.[13] This question can be posed as a market-definition question—Is the aftermarket a proper antitrust market?—or as a market-power question—Does a manufacturer have market power in its proprietary aftermarkets?[14]

The new twist in looking at an aftermarket is its close connection to the equipment market that spawned it. Specifically, a manufacturer that attempts to exploit its position in aftermarkets may suffer adverse consequences in equipment markets. This implies that one cannot properly analyze aftermarkets in isolation. An aftermarket can exist as a distinct relevant antitrust market only if such *ex post* exploitation is profitable for a manufacturer controlling its own aftermarket. A primary reason such exploitation may not be profitable is that a manufacturer engaging in opportunism faces the risk of alienating its customers and damaging its reputa-

---

[12]   In *Kodak*, the Court defined market power as the power to force a purchaser to do something that he would not do in a competitive market, and as the ability of a single seller to raise price and restrict output. 112 S. Ct. 2080–81.

[13]   If the equipment market is competitive, the prices prevailing based on equipment, or systems competition naturally serve as a competitive benchmark.

[14]   As the Court stated in *Kodak*: "Whether considered in the conceptual category of 'market definition' or 'market power,' the ultimate inquiry is the same—whether competition in the equipment market will significantly restrain power in the service and parts markets." (112 S. Ct. 2072 n.15.)

tion and credibility. More specifically, current aftermarket prices have a direct impact on current and future equipment sales.[15]

The Court identified switching costs and information costs as important factors in aftermarkets for complex equipment.[16] Large switching costs make existing equipment owners more vulnerable to price increases for parts and service, and high information costs can attenuate the link between today's aftermarket and tomorrow's new equipment sales if customers are poorly informed.

A. Switching costs

The first economic question in looking at an aftermarket is to determine whether there exists a significant group of customers who purchase in the aftermarket and face high costs of switching to other brands of equipment and thus are potentially vulnerable. If consumers' brand-switching costs are uniformly low, there can be no monopoly power in aftermarkets.

How are brand-switching costs measured? A consumer's brand-switching cost is the extra cost that would be incurred by that consumer in replacing its current equipment with equipment made by another manufacturer. These costs could include the cost of training personnel to use the new equipment, the cost of rewriting computer programming to work on a new brand of machine or a new operating system, etc.

Customers with high brand-switching costs face a genuine obstacle to selecting a new brand of equipment. As a general proposition, the maximum dollar amount by which a "locked-in" customer can be "exploited" in a proprietary aftermarket for parts and service, i.e., the maximum premium such a customer would

---

[15]   The Court noted that if consumers assess the total systems price and engage in "accurate life cycle pricing," then service market prices will affect equipment demand and a separate market for parts and/or service is unlikely.

[16]   112 S. Ct. 2085.

pay over prevailing systems prices, in present-value, is exactly equal to that customer's brand-switching cost.[17]

One should not think of customer lock-in as an absolute concept; even an equipment vendor with 100% of its aftermarket cannot set aftermarket prices with impunity. Since customers differ in their switching costs, and since customers can choose how carefully to maintain their machines and when to replace them, an equipment manufacturer, even one whose customers face switching costs, will sell fewer parts and less service, the higher price is charged for parts and service. Any attempt to charge a premium for aftermarket service will induce those customers with low switching costs to replace their equipment.[18]

Customers most likely to switch brands in response to super-competitive aftermarket prices are those who have made the least brand-specific investments such as training, computer programming, etc.; those who already use multiple brands and can simply shift their mix of equipment; and those with older equipment in need of replacement in any event. Other things equal, brand-switching costs are lower in markets with rapid technological progress. If rival equipment has superior performance to installed machines, these performance advantages must be offset against any costs of switching. Effectively, there is a "switching benefit" in the form of the superior equipment.

A given customer's switching costs will typically change over time. As already noted, a customer with a machine in need of replacement may have low switching costs. However, in some cases brand-specific investments will last longer than a single machine, as when buyers write software to a brand-specific standard that is carried from one generation of hardware to another.

If the bulk of a firm's customers face low brand-switching costs, aftermarket power will be minimal. More generally, one

---

[17]   *See* Farrell & Shapiro, *supra* note 4, *Optimal Contracts,* for a formal analysis of lock-in and market power.

[18]   *See id.* for an analysis of pricing when customers differ in their switching costs.

must look to see if there is any significant group of customers who have high switching costs and can be discriminated against. If no such group exists, the inquiry into aftermarket power ends.

Switching costs certainly can be significant, both for low- and high-technology products. With large switching costs, the possibility of aftermarket power exists. Yet for this very reason, customers often protect themselves from exposure to *ex post* exploitation, and these protections can nullify aftermarket power.

B. *Contractual protections for locked-in buyers*

Buyers choosing a system can directly protect themselves from any *ex post* exploitation by obtaining contractual protections at the time they purchase equipment. These protections can take the form of extended warranty coverage, long-term service contracts, guaranteed multiple-sourcing of parts or service, or price-protection clauses for parts and service. Some protection, but less, is offered by a long-term service contract in which the manufacturer promises to charge the "generally prevailing" price for service and parts. In this case, the manufacturer is contractually prevented from discriminating against locked-in customers on service and parts prices.[19]

When customers purchase parts and service along with their equipment, they are shifting transactions from the aftermarket, where they might otherwise be in a poor bargaining position, to the primary systems market. If customers sign long-term service contracts when they purchase equipment, or if they lease equipment rather than buy it, market power in aftermarkets will be sharply limited for the simple reason that few parts and service are actually sold in the aftermarket.[20] However, a long-term con-

---

[19]   This protection is incomplete since the manufacturer might raise all parts and/or service prices and offer discounts on new equipment to attract new customers, or the manufacturer might raise the price of parts or service on models of machines no longer being sold new.

[20]   Here, "long-term" should include any warranty period and should be evaluated in comparison with the life of the equipment. If a piece of equipment is usually kept for 7 years, and the buyer purchases a 5-year

146 : *The antitrust bulletin*

tract can actually reduce the protection enjoyed by buyers, unless such a contract protects the buyer on all significant dimensions.[21] In any event, buyers rarely contract for all of their aftermarket requirements when they purchase equipment.

C. *Information costs and life-cycle costing*

If brand-switching costs are significant and customers are not directly protected by long-term contracts, the primary reason for a manufacturer controlling its proprietary aftermarkets not to engage in installed-base opportunism is the prospect that such behavior will lead to a loss of future equipment sales. Evaluating the strength of the linkage between a firm's aftermarket terms and conditions and its future equipment sales requires an understanding of the factors that buyers consider in choosing a brand of equipment. Specifically, a key question is whether or not buyers engage in an integrated assessment of the life-cycle costs of rival brands of equipment.

Life-cycle costing requires some delineation. We define life-cycle costing as decision making in which buyers of durable goods take into account not only the original purchase price of the equipment, but also expected maintenance costs including supplies, parts, and service.[22] It is well known that many buyers rou-

---

service contract beginning after the 1-year warranty period expires, we would certainly consider the service contract "long-term." The key point is that any lock-in remaining in the seventh year will be small, since the equipment is about to be replaced, unless the buyer has made significant brand-specific investments that are transferable only to replacement equipment made by the same manufacturer.

[21] This is the "Principle of Negative Protection" developed in Farrell & Shapiro, *supra* note 4, *Optimal Contracts.*

[22] In its purest form, life-cycle costing boils down to a single output-oriented measure: for copiers, this measure would be the cost per copy over the lifetime of the equipment, including equipment, parts, service, suppliers, and the cost of operator time. For a medical device, the measure might be the cost per patient-treatment, again taken over the lifetime of the equipment and including all costs.

tinely engage in such calculus, albeit with varying degrees of sophistication. Buyers of automobiles consider fuel costs, service costs, and parts costs, although their information about parts and service costs may be poor. Volume buyers in particular—such as fleet operators (e.g., rental cars, taxis)—have explicit and highly refined estimates of expected costs. Even households buying white goods take operating, service, and repair costs into account. As a consequence, producers will often make these features an explicit part of their marketing strategy (e.g., Japanese auto companies stress fuel economy; Maytag often stresses the minimal repairs owners of their product can expect). The accuracy of such information obviously varies from circumstance to circumstance, and is greater for large buyers and for big-ticket items where information costs are small relative to overall expenditures, but it is a safe generalization that in mature, established, durable-goods industries such information is readily available from equipment producers and distributors, third parties, and buyers themselves.

The Court was skeptical of the linkages between today's parts and service markets and tomorrow's equipment sales, stating that "life-cycle pricing of complex, durable equipment is difficult and costly." As an empirical matter, we do not agree. To the contrary, at least in mature markets, and often in emerging ones as well, implicit and often explicit life-cycle cost comparisons are frequently made.[23] Indeed, we are familiar with cases in which buyers use computer models to compare the life-cycle costs of different machines. And surely in many markets sales typically occur to repeat customers who have excellent information about and experience with the life-cycle costs of equipment.

There are strong economic forces helping buyers to become well informed: buyers have much to save by avoiding brands with expensive aftermarket costs, and an equipment vendor with inexpensive parts and service has very strong incentives to communicate its competitive advantage to customers. Information costs are

---

[23]   One of the ironies of the *Kodak* case is that the markets Kodak competes in involve expensive equipment and what appear to be sophisticated, well-informed customers, precisely the conditions under which the Court agreed aftermarket market power is likely to be sharply limited.

lowered when customers buy multiple machines; when consultants and other third parties help buyers compare equipment brands; when vendors provide information to customers comparing the cost of different machines; and when buyers have life-cycle experience with similar equipment. In some cases, banks or other financing entities even *require* an analysis of life-cycle costs before issuing a loan for the equipment, or government entities may be required to use life-cycle costing. For all of these reasons, we expect in most cases involving expensive equipment or sophisticated customers that a detailed analysis will reveal customers to be employing life-cycle costing.

Even if customers are not capable of evaluating life-cycle costs, competition in the equipment market may still protect them. Suppose that buyers naively pick the machine with the cheapest equipment price. Ignoring reputation effects in other product lines, all manufacturers will charge monopolistic parts and service prices (assuming they can control their proprietary aftermarkets). Anticipating these monopoly margins in the aftermarket, manufacturers will discount equipment to generate those aftermarket margins. This is, of course, the classic strategy of giving away the razor to sell blades at big markups, or of selling the video game hardware at or below cost in order to sell video game cartridges at large markups. So long as sellers anticipate aftermarket revenues and costs, consumers will ultimately pay a competitive price for systems, even if they are not sophisticated or well informed.

To summarize, aftermarket power is most likely to be significant if switching costs are high and long lived, if customers lack the protection of long-term contracts, and if information costs prevent most customers from engaging in life-cycle costing. Based on our experience in business strategy and antitrust, we suspect that this confluence of circumstances is relatively rare; detailed factual inquiry in post-*Kodak* cases will reveal whether we are correct in this assessment.

D. The economics of installed-base opportunism

We now turn to the fact pattern that we believe is common: customers have genuine switching costs, and are well informed, but do not actually sign long-term service contracts when buying equipment. Suppose, for example, buyers choose equipment based on estimates of aftermarket costs provided by sellers or based on historical experience. This circumstance is common for sophisticated, expensive machinery purchased by businesses. In this case, an equipment manufacturer controlling its own proprietary aftermarkets may have the ability to engage in *ex post* exploitation of its installed base, by unexpectedly raising its parts or service prices or by degrading quality.

The key practical economic problem in this situation is to measure the cost to the manufacturer of engaging in such installed-base opportunism. How are such costs properly measured?

1. ANTITRUST OR CONTRACT CASE? Before answering this question, we pause to make an important related point that we believe has received insufficient attention in the discussion following *Kodak*. Specifically, there should be little or no concern about policy changes that are announced in advance of equipment sales and anticipated by buyers. Suppose an equipment vendor in a competitive market announces to its prospective customers: We retain exclusive rights to service our equipment, and we will charge you dearly for parts and service, according to the attached pricing schedule. Well-informed customers will pay no more than the competitive price for this vendor's system, so long as competition exists in the primary equipment market. Likewise, a policy restricting the sale of parts to ISOs prospectively for new machines does not constitute installed-base opportunism.[24] In our

---

[24] It could be argued that ISOs might have difficulty surviving if they could only service older-model machines, due to a restrictive parts policy for newer models, and the decline in ISOs might ultimately lead to higher service prices on older machines, even if parts for those machines were readily available. While possibly true in some cases, we believe that equipment manufacturers must be given some flexibility to adjust their aftermarket policies to compete in the primary market. Otherwise, ineffi-

view, the discussion of market power in aftermarkets is properly restricted to policy changes that are imposed unexpectedly on a captive installed base.[25]

The majority opinion does not appear to make much of the fact that Kodak's policies were largely, or entirely, imposed prospectively. However, it appears clear to us that any harm to end users that might have been caused by Kodak's policy must flow from the policy change being a "surprise." To the extent that buyers made product-specific investments around their equipment purchases, then a change in behavior by Kodak might indeed enable Kodak to extract rents from its customers' non-redeployable assets.[26]

As we discuss immediately below, such behavior could be extremely short-sighted as the customer might well switch in the future, even though switching at present is too costly. Such behavior might better be viewed as a contractual violation. If Kodak's customers had a constructive contract with Kodak, then opportunistic behavior by Kodak could well represent a breech. For this reason, many economists regard *Kodak* as an attempt by the Court to apply antitrust law to a problem that would better be served by

---

cient aftermarket policies may be perpetuated (hardly a desirable goal of antitrust law) and firms may refuse ever to sell parts to ISOs for fear of having to do so forever once they start (again, this lack of flexibility would ultimately injure customers, contrary to the goals of antitrust law). If antitrust really is to protect competition, not competitors, the possibility of some indirect injury to ISOs should not stand in the way of interbrand competition. ISOs have no more guarantee of survival than other firms in a competitive marketplace.

[25]　As pointed out in the minority opinion in *Kodak* (112 S. Ct. 2095), "the restrictive parts policy, with respect to micrographics equipment at least, was not even alleged to be anything but prospective."

[26]　Note that a firm controlling the supply of parts for its own machines may well be able to exploit its installed base simply by charging more for those parts. A consistent theory of installed-base opportunism based on monopolization of a service aftermarket must explain why the firm could extract more from its customers by controlling service than simply by controlling parts. If parts and service are used in fixed proportions, this will not be the case.

contract law, either by encouraging buyers to obtain additional contractual protections before making specific investments, or by holding sellers accountable for representations they make about aftermarket terms and conditions when selling their equipment.

2. IS *EX POST* EXPLOITATION PROFITABLE? By definition, customers with high switching costs are potentially vulnerable to some *ex post* exploitation, or opportunism, on the part of the equipment manufacturer.[27] A key economic issue in many cases will be to ascertain whether the equipment manufacturer controlling aftermarkets can profitably engage in installed-base opportunism, e.g., by raising parts or service prices above competitive levels. Ultimately, this comes down to a comparison of any extra profits earned on the locked-in buyers with any profits lost in selling to new customers.

Measuring incremental profits on locked-in customers from higher parts or service prices is a relatively straightforward pricing question. It hinges on the elasticity of demand for parts and service and the markups for parts and service. We must point out, however, that the mere presence of switching costs does not imply that the manufacturer has an incentive to raise parts or service prices. To the contrary: if parts and service prices are at their "monopoly" levels, i.e., the profit-maximizing levels facing locked-in customers, as part of the overall systems pricing, further increases in parts and service prices will lower, not raise, the manufacturer's profits.

Measuring the profits lost on new equipment sales by a firm engaging in installed-based opportunism is empirically a much more difficult matter. In principle, the calculation is straightforward: how many new system sales are lost, and what is the life-cycle profit margin on those systems? In practice, this is not an easy matter, since the answers to these questions are not tied tightly to historical data. Nonetheless, we can sketch out the major analytical steps here.

---

[27]   As we noted above, if switching costs are low, even the installed base will not tolerate supercompetitive service or parts pricing, and any attempt to set aftermarket prices above competitive levels would fail.

First, *ex post* exploitation is not a trick that the manufacturer can play over and over, unless customers are extraordinarily inept. Thus, the proper comparison is between the one-time extra profits gained from opportunistic behavior and the present value of the stream of profits earned indefinitely from refraining from opportunism. This is a general principle in the economics of reputation, as developed by Carl Shapiro.[28]

Second, we agree with other commentators that the penalty for opportunistic behavior is smaller, *ceteris paribus*, the less equipment the firm expects to sell in the future. In the extreme case where no new equipment is being sold, these costs could be zero. Thus, a firm is more likely, *ceteris paribus*, to have the incentive to engage in opportunistic behavior if that firm is exiting the market; if that firm anticipates a relatively small share of new equipment sales relative to its share of the installed base of equipment; or if that firm is selling in a sharply declining market. The ratio of expected future sales to the size of the installed base is thus an important economic variable in this analysis.

Third, the profits lost through opportunistic behavior depend upon the life-cycle margin on sales of new systems, not merely on the equipment margins, and not merely on the unit sales of equipment.

Fourth, we must stress that there is nothing confining the firm's damaged reputation and lost equipment sales to a single relevant antitrust market. A firm engaging in installed-base opportunism may well lose sales in other markets, if buyers participate in several equipment markets, or if information about the firm's behavior leaks out to buyers in other markets.

Fifth, it may be very difficult for a manufacturer to overcome a reputation for taking advantage of its locked-in customers. Some commentators have suggested that the manufacturer can neutralize a reputation for *ex post* exploitation by pricing its equipment below cost. This is likely to be very expensive, simply

---

[28]   Carl Shapiro, *Premium for High Quality Products as Rents to Reputation*, 98 Q.J. Econ. 659 (1983).

because of the distortions caused by the peculiar combination of pricing one component of the system (equipment) below cost and other components (parts and service) at monopoly levels.[29] Furthermore, a firm that has violated the trust of its customers by raising aftermarket prices will probably be suspected of engaging in other tactics, such as withdrawing support for aging models of equipment.

To summarize, the fly-by-night strategy of exploiting loyal customers is more likely to be attractive (a) in a declining market, so future sales are less important relative to the size of the installed base; (b) for a firm that is having trouble competing in the market, so it discounts the importance of future sales; (c) for products that are marginally profitable or unprofitable on a life-cycle basis, so that future sales are not likely to generate significant profits, even when viewed on a life-cycle basis; (d) for a firm with few other products whose goodwill will be hurt; or (e) for a firm in financial distress, or one with a very high cost of capital, which places unusual weight on current profits relative to future profits.

E. Competition in aftermarkets

Even customers for whom it is expensive to switch brands of equipment may have options that will limit the market power of the equipment manufacturer. In other words, even if proprietary aftermarkets are relevant antitrust markets, it does not automatically follow that the equipment manufacturer has market power in those markets.

Alternative sources of supply may exist, even for brand-specific parts. Several sources of parts are possible: (a) third-party manufacturers of parts may offer actual or potential competition; (b) parts may be salvaged from used machines or from equipment

---

[29]   Because of the inefficiencies (deadweight loss) associated with monopoly pricing in aftermarkets, a firm employing a strategy of charging monopolistic prices for parts and service and discounting its equipment to attract customers will be at a competitive disadvantage relative to firms that can credibly commit to competitive aftermarket prices.

154 : *The antitrust bulletin*

that has already been junked (indeed, there may be an active salvage market); (c) there may exist a gray market, whereby parts are transshipped from other parts of the world; or (d) parts from other equipment manufacturers may be substitutable at little or no cost. Clearly, any of these factors may sharply limit the ability of a parts provider to exercise monopoly profits. In addition, arbitrage may prevent the manufacturer from selling parts to end users but not to ISOs: some end users may purchase extra parts and sell them "on the street."

Likewise, the equipment manufacturer may face competition in the service aftermarket. Of course, this is precisely the competition ISOs hope to offer. In some cases, the barriers to entry into such service may be low, especially if service skills are general, and not machine- or brand-specific. On the other hand, there may be quite insurmountable barriers to entry, as when copyrighted service manuals or access to copyrighted software is required to perform service.

V. Tying claims in aftermarkets

Suppose now that a manufacturer does indeed have market power in a proprietary aftermarket. In this case, antitrust law treats the tying of service to parts rather harshly, even though economic analysis shows that the economic effects of tying are ambiguous.[30] It is well to keep in mind that a firm with a monopoly in parts can simply price the parts noncompetitively and then sell them to ISOs. Indeed, if ISOs provide superior service or have lower costs than the original equipment manufacturer, this strategy will typically be more profitable than the tie. It usually will not be rational for a manufacturer to attempt to provide service itself if the ISOs can do it better or more cheaply. The

---

[30] If parts and service are used together in fixed proportions, the manufacturer controlling the supply of parts gains no extra ability to price discriminate by controlling service prices as well. And, even if tying does allow the manufacturer to price discriminate more effectively, this could well lead to an increase in output and greater consumer benefits.

Supreme Court did not seem particularly adept at analyzing this issue, yet it remains an important one in the economic theory of tying.

In addition, of course, there are business justifications for tying. These include control of free riding, quality control, inventory management, distribution economies, and so forth. We suspect that when *Kodak*-type cases go to trial, such factors will often turn out to be very important.

We question, however, whether the central economic issues in post-*Kodak* cases will revolve around tying claims. We understand that other companies have used policies that would be hard to describe as a tie. For example, Xerox sells its repair parts to end users, who are free to use ISOs to service their machines with these parts, but does not knowingly sell parts to ISOs (except in their role as end users). Unless the courts take a very broad definition of what constitutes a tie, a refusal to deal is simply not the same as a tie, whether or not the manufacturer has market power.

VI. Intellectual property rights in aftermarkets

Consider now an aspect of aftermarkets not mentioned by the Supreme Court in *Kodak*. In the copier industry, as well as for many other durable products, aftermarket products and services have embedded within them intellectual property of some significance. It is common for manufacturers of machines to obtain patents on those machines, and these patents typically extend to the specific replacement parts and subassemblies in those machines. In addition, the installation of the parts often will involve propriety techniques, techniques that may be protected by trade secrets and/or copyrights. Copyrighted service manuals may be indispensable to service technicians. In addition, as more and more machines contain sophisticated electronics, repair services will increasingly involve the use of diagnostic software embedded in the machine. This software too is likely to have copyright or patent protection.

Viewing the *Kodak* case in this light, we see that imposing a duty on a manufacturer to sell its parts to ISOs, or to let ISOs use its copyrighted diagnostic software, is likely to diminish the value of the manufacturer's intellectual property. If parts must be sold, at what price? If the courts require sale of parts on "reasonable terms," the manufacturer's right to do as it pleases with its intellectual property has been undermined. Likewise, if the manufacturer is required to let independent service technicians use the diagnostic software built into the machine, will the licensing terms for the use of that software be regulated by the courts? The courts may find themselves enmeshed in the well-known dangers of compulsory licensing.

Ultimately, imposing a duty to deal on manufacturers who possess intellectual property can only diminish the returns to innovation and work at odds with the patent and copyright systems. As one of us has argued elsewhere, the legitimate exercise of the monopoly right afforded by intellectual property ought to be presumed efficiency enhancing.[31] We expect that defendants like Kodak will be able to demonstrate substantial investment in their systems. Likewise, it should not be difficult to demonstrate that innovation has been the most important form of competition, in terms of customer benefits, in many equipment markets. Together, these demonstrations should alert judges and juries to the very real dangers to competition of undermining the intellectual property rights awarded to successful innovators.

VII. Damages and class certification

The special relationship between equipment markets and proprietary aftermarkets discussed above has some strong and important implications for damages in *Kodak*-style cases.

---

[31]   *See* David J. Teece, *Profiting From Technological Innovation*, 6 RESEARCH POLICY (1986), and THOMAS JORDE & DAVID J. TEECE, ANTITRUST, INNOVATION, AND COMPETITIVENESS (1992).

A. *Damages with competitive equipment markets*

Suppose that it has been determined that a manufacturer indeed has market power in its aftermarkets, despite a competitive primary equipment market, and that the manufacturer has monopolized its service aftermarket, e.g., by refusing to sell parts to ISOs. Who is injured and by how much?

If the policies were implemented prospectively, as was true in *Kodak* at least for micrographics equipment, it is hard to see how end users can claim any damages from service overcharges. As argued above, equipment competition forces a manufacturer with supercompetitive aftermarket prices to discount its equipment in order to make its offerings attractive relative to other brands.[32] Ultimately, removing the restrictive parts policies would shift the manufacturer's revenues to the equipment side of its business from the service side, but would have no significant effect on buyers' total cost of ownership. Hence there would be little or no damages to end users. This conclusion follows inevitably from interbrand competition.

If the policies were implemented retrospectively, the argument just given would still apply to all customers buying equipment after the policies were implemented. Only customers who already owned machines when the policy was changed would have a claim for service overcharges. Even their claims will be substantially tempered by considerations of competitive response given below. In particular, there is every reason to believe that the manufacturer would charge end users (and ISOs) more for parts if it were forced to make parts available to ISOs.[33] An economically accurate assessment of end-user damage claims should include

---

[32] This is certainly true if customers are well informed. Even if they are not, however, as noted above, manufacturers will compete with equipment discounts, knowing that these uninformed customers can be later charged monopoly aftermarket prices.

[33] The manufacturer may well be able to raise its parts prices without altering the total price it charges its service customers for parts and service. It is harder for the manufacturer to immunize self-service customers from any widespread increase in the price of parts, however.

upward adjustments in parts prices as an offset to any reductions in the price of service.

Finally, there is the question of which end users could legitimately make service overcharge claims. There is no reason to believe that the manufacturer would lower its service prices across the board, even facing additional ISO competition. ISOs may have only a limited ability to expand, even in the absence of any restrictive parts policies, because of a shortage of qualified personnel, limited access to copyrighted service manuals, etc. Certain customers may strongly prefer brand-name service, or even be required to obtain brand-name service. And ISOs may not be qualified to service certain machines, such as new-model machines for which they have not received training, or for which they lack access to copyrighted diagnostic software.

For all of these reasons, broad classes of end users in post-*Kodak* cases will face significant obstacles to certification.

ISOs' claims of lost profits also will face significant hurdles. If the but-for world involves ISOs freely buying parts from the manufacturer, the damage analysis must recognize that the manufacturer has a strong incentive to raise the price of those parts. The analysis must also consider the other obstacles ISOs would have faced, such as limited access to diagnostic software or training, and any legitimate competitive responses of the manufacturer to any additional actual or potential competition by ISOs.

B. *Competitive response*

A manufacturer seeking to retain the business of servicing its own machines has many alternatives to a parts policy of the type used by Kodak. A proper damages analysis should account for a reasonable competitive response in the absence of the challenged parts policies.

Whether one adopts an economics or a business-strategy perspective, it is apparent that there are a host of alternative strategies available to manufacturers, many of which may be quite effective in certain markets. We list a few here.

1. A manufacturer could extend the length of its warranty coverage, raising the price of its equipment to maintain competitive parity in the primary equipment market. A longer warranty period would reduce the amount of service business available to ISOs. In the limit, the manufacturer could include lifetime service and parts with its machine.[34]

2. A manufacturer could shift from selling machines to leasing or renting machines. Parts and service could either be included with the lease, or brand-name service and parts could be required for leasing customers in order to assure that the manufacturer's machine is well maintained. This shift from selling to leasing could be accomplished by raising the price at which machines are sold but not changing the terms on which machines are leased.

3. A manufacturer could simply raise the price of parts, whether sold to ISOs, end users, or anyone. No change need be implemented for service contracts. So long as the incremental price of service (comparing a service contract including parts with the price of parts alone) is at least as large as the cost of providing that service, so there could be no legitimate claim of predatory pricing of service.

4. A manufacturer could act to retain its service employees who are the source of technical expertise for ISOs. These responses include higher salaries for service technicians, limited noncompete clauses in employment contracts, or a provision that technicians pay the manufacturer back for their training if they leave before a reasonable recoupment period has elapsed.

5. A manufacturer could enforce its intellectual property rights. ISOs might well be unable to compete without infringing on the manufacturer's intellectual property, such as the copyrighted service manuals or diagnostic software noted above.

It appears to us that many manufacturers have quite a few entirely legitimate competitive weapons in their arsenal. For firms with secure control over their proprietary parts, therefore, we find it hard to believe that ISOs could play a major role in the servic-

---

[34] As Justice Scalia pointed out in the minority opinion (112 S. Ct. 2095), this would in fact be a tie between equipment, parts, and service, but "it would be immune from per se scrutiny under the antitrust laws because the tying product would be equipment, a market in which (we assume) Kodak has no power to influence price or quantity."

160 : *The antitrust bulletin*

ing aftermarket, even without Kodak-style parts polices, unless their presence is welcomed by the brand-name manufacturer.[35]

VIII. Competitive strategy in a post-*Kodak* world

One of the recent themes in the literature on competitive strategy is that U.S. firms, to compete effectively in international markets, must understand their customers' needs and offer the quality their customers want. Successful companies are those that learned to coordinate the chain of production from customer service to R&D effectively, very possibly through vertical integration.[36]

It would be unfortunate if the *Kodak* decision hampered the ability of American firms to vertically integrate into service when necessary to remain close to their customers, and generally to flexibly choose their distribution strategy in competitive markets. Fortunately, we do not believe that *Kodak* will have any such impact. Instead, firms should, with careful antitrust advice, be able to flexibly craft their strategies in competitive markets despite *Kodak*. Indeed, the competitive response strategies listed above indicate the many ways in which firms can achieve their quality-control aims, their aims to remain close to customers, and their goal of recouping R&D investments with aftermarket revenues.

Further discovery in *Kodak* and in many other durable-goods industries will undoubtedly yield a plethora of different contractual arrangements with respect to parts and service quality. Arranged from more to less restrictive approaches, one can identify the following generic policies:

1. Full integration with a parts and service contract for the life of the product bundled with equipment purchase and service performed by the manufacturer.

---

[35] Remember, in many cases manufacturers *will* welcome ISOs, so long as ISOs can efficiently offer good quality service.

[36] *See* David J. Teece, *Interorganizational Requirements of the Innovation Process*, 10 MANAGERIAL & DECISION ECON. 135 (1989), and David J. Teece, *Technological Change and the Nature of the Firm*, in TECHNOLOGICAL CHANGE AND ECONOMIC THEORY (G. Dosi, et al., eds., 1988).

2. Same as (1) with service contracted out to a single independent dealer network.

3. Parts sold to equipment owners (not to ISOs); service provision made available but an exclusive service contract is not required by purchaser.

4. Parts sold to both ISOs and own service network.

5. No parts or service provided; design rights to parts supplied to all upon request; any intellectual property in parts supplied free of charge under automatic license arrangement.

While antitrust presumptions would have it that (5) is preferable to (1) from the point of view of competition, such a finding is by no means assured. If vertical integration economies are important, the competitive process is more confidently assisted if firms are free to choose their own organizational arrangements.[37]

IX. Significance of the decision

Kodak is obviously an important case. Some have argued that it is the most important antitrust case of the decade; in particular, some suggest that it indicates that antitrust analysis has moved into a new "post-Chicago" era and that *Kodak* represents some kind of a legal climacteric.

We shall not attempt to assess the legal significance of the decision, as this article is primarily economic in its orientation. However, in essence it appears that the Supreme Court has merely reaffirmed the basic standards for summary judgment in antitrust cases—the plaintiff's theory must be inconsistent with rational behavior by the defendant on the stipulated facts. The Court has reaffirmed that findings requiring factual determination cannot be opined simply as a matter of law.

But is the economics advanced here all that new? The Court explicitly addressed such concepts as information costs, switching costs, and lock-in. Steven Salop for one has stated that this indi-

---

[37]   *See* OLIVER WILLIAMSON, *supra* note 4.

162 : *The antitrust bulletin*

cates a new "post-Chicago" era for antitrust analysis.[38] However, many economists at Chicago would no doubt be surprised to learn that information costs, switching costs, etc., are alien ideas to Chicagoans. Indeed, the late George Stigler of Chicago is favorably cited, as he ought to be, for his insights into the role of consumer information on market outcomes. Indeed, one of the key articles cited by the Nobel Prize Committee in awarding the prize to Stigler was his study of consumer information costs.[39]

The Court was simply not willing to simply assume well-informed buyers, or the absence of switching costs.[40] The Court correctly identified these as matters for a trier of fact to ascertain. However, it does not seem that this is a break with prior law, and it is certainly *not* a break with contemporary economic analysis.[41] True, some members of the Chicago school were frequently guilty of adopting the fiction of frictionless markets; but the founders of the school, such as Stigler, are not at all culpable. Accordingly, if *Kodak* is post-Chicago, it is also pre-Chicago and Chicago.

---

[38]   Steven Salop, *Exclusionary Vertical Restraints Law—Has Economics Mattered?*, 83 AM. ECON. REV. 168 (1993).

[39]   George Stigler, *The Economics of Information*, 72 J. POL. ECON. 213 (1964).

[40]   Let us stress again that we are not sufficiently familiar with the factual record that was available to the Court in *Kodak* to know whether, in fact, Kodak established, on the basis of the limited discovery that was permitted, key facts about switching costs, information costs, or the timing of Kodak's policy changes.

[41]   *See, for example,* Carl Shapiro, *The Theory of Business Strategy*, 20 RAND J. ECON. 125 (1989), for a discussion of competition in the presence of switching costs, information costs, installed bases, etc.

C

Antitrust: Information Sharing and Cartels

A Behavioural
Analysis of OPEC:
An Economic and
Political Synthesis

by
David J. Teece

Introduction

In recent years, economists and policy analysts have exhibited considerable puzzlement over the role that the Organization of Petroleum Exporting Countries (OPEC) as an organization plays in determining the world price of crude oil. Most Western economists refer to OPEC as a cartel, while OPEC representatives and Arab scholars commonly argue that OPEC is not a cartel and that the current world price is competitive (Griffin and Teece, 1982, Chap. 1). Given that the community of professional analysts has had such a disappointing track record with respect to predicting OPEC behaviour and the world price of oil,[1] it seems appropriate to question the conceptual lens through which OPEC behaviour is commonly evaluated.

This paper indicates that wealth-maximizing classical cartel models relying on co-ordinated behaviour and comprehensive collusion provide an inappropriate model for analysing OPEC behaviour. Rather, an alternative view is offered that can be summarized as follows. Several important OPEC producers set oil production with reference to budgetary "requirements"[2] and internal and external political constraints. If export receipts plus other capital inflows are such as to satisfy expenditure "requirements," oil production policies will be determined by "conservation" considerations, where "conservation" involves shutting in production for future generations, even if this is not consistent with maximizing the present value of oil reserves. Conversely, if export receipts plus capital inflows are such that expenditure requirements are not being met, production and capacity will be expanded, so long as technical conditions permit. Expenditure "requirements" are determined by applying some percentage growth factor to last year's expenditure levels, where the growth factor is always positive, or very nearly so.

In economic parlance, it appears that at least for an important subset of OPEC producers, the relationship between current price and current output is best represented by a backward-bending supply curve[3] for the short run. One implication is that once a producer is on the backward-bending portion of this curve, there is no proclivity to "cheat" on other OPEC members. Conversely, if a producer is not on the backward-bending portion of the (short run) supply curve, it will display proclivities to expand output in an attempt to increase current revenues. This hypothesis has remarkable implications for OPEC behaviour. First, it indicates that the monopoly price level is not exposed to the hazards of cheating, just so long as oil revenues plus capital inflows meet budgetary "needs." But once "needs" catch up with revenues, pressures to expand production will be evident. Secondly, it indicates that the stability of OPEC over the period 1974–1980 need not have been the consequence of collusion. The backward-bending supply curve construct implies that monopolization is possible without collusion, at least in the short run. By implication, OPEC has yet to prove that it is capable of supporting the world price through co-ordinated action.

This view relegates wealth-maximizing considerations to a secondary role in explaining OPEC behaviour. In particular, if optimizing criteria were to indicate that significantly higher current exports would maximize wealth, the revenues from which would then be converted into foreign assets because they cannot be productively employed domestically in the current period, then these dictates will be ignored in large measure. The reason is that foreign assets are not always viewed as desirable investments, except for liquidity purposes. Not only are there considered to be internal and external political risks[4] associated with foreign investments, but they are perceived to yield returns less than can be obtained from keeping oil in the ground. Furthermore, the objectives of most OPEC states are not consistent with creating a nation of *rentiers* dependent on "coupon clipping" for their economic survival, even if this were the wealth-maximizing strategy. The *rentier* concept is simply perceived to be inconsistent with national aspirations for economic development and political independence. As Turner and Bedore (1979, p. 75) have noted, "producer governments would have political difficulties in remaining mere exporters of crude oil."

This view of OPEC explains why the price level did not collapse under the weight of cheating in the decade of the 1970s.[5] It also indicates that OPEC behaviour in a tight market and in a prolonged soft market will be markedly different. With a continued soft market through to the mid-1980s, coupled with the absence of a political upheaval large enough to take another 5 million barrels per day (MMBPD) or more off the market, there is a good chance that the OPEC producers with the technical capacity to do so will expand production in order to generate higher revenues to meet internal budgetary requirements.[6] The result could well be that the price of crude will remain in the $30 per barrel range (in 1980$) through to the end of this century. However, a major disruption in supplies could once again lift the real price, at least for several years. In short, uncertainty with respect to prices is not just simply on the upside; there is downside uncertainty as well. The theoretical and empirical underpinnings of this view are developed in more detail below.

Production Policies in OPEC

There is growing evidence that a number of important OPEC producers adjust output, at least in the short run, in a manner that appears to be at odds with the view that OPEC is a wealth-maximizing cartel. If discount rates, oil reserves, demand elasticities, and expectations about future prices are held constant, exhaustible resource theory indicates that current production will increase if current prices increase (Griffin and Teece, 1982, Chap. 1). Furthermore, at prices significantly above competitive levels, there are enormous incentives to increase output to obtain higher current revenues. However, OPEC production policies appear to march to a different drummer, with some producers reducing output, holding it constant, or abolishing expansion plans when prices rise. Furthermore, "cheating" in the form of output expansion was almost completely absent in the 1970s. OPEC output fell from 31.8 MMBPD in 1973 to 26.9 MMBPD in 1980.

This apparently anomalous behaviour has a ready explanation if production decisions are made in some states with the principal objective of generating sufficient income to meet the budgetary requirements of the nations in question. Accordingly, price escalation in a given period can lead to decreased production if the additional revenues resulting from higher prices are greater than the desired expansion in government expenditures for the same period. Clearly, this explanation assumes that in some sense there are steeply diminishing returns to current revenues for some producing states. This is quite at odds with neoclausical investment and consumption theory. However, the economic and political realities of certain less developed economies render standard analysis of limited value.

Thus, consider an oil-producing nation like Kuwait where oil revenues are a very large component of export receipts and government revenues. Such a nation-state can allocate revenues to domestic consumption, domestic investment, or foreign investment. Each of these opportunities is now examined in turn.

Opportunities for increasing domestic expenditures are severely constrained in the short to medium run by the lack of a supporting infrastructure in areas such as transportation and distribution, and by the inability of the labour force to rapidly acquire the skills needed for economic development. The concept of absorptive capacity has been developed to give content to this notion. According to Rosenstein-Rodan (1961, p. 108), "absorptive capacity relates to the ability to use capital productively. .... There are ... narrow limits to the pace and extent at which a country's absorptive capacity can be expanded." Absorptive capacity can be defined as the amount of investment that can be made at some acceptable threshold rate of return, with the supply of complementary factors considered as given. What is involved is a decline in the marginal productivity of capital resulting from the inability to augment the human factors of production as fast as the capital stock. The result is "a kind of inevitable decreasing returns to the scale of investment" (Eckaus, 1972, p. 80) and a backward-bending supply curve for crude oil. This is more formally portrayed in the Appendix.

Buttressing these economic factors are important political constraints in several OPEC countries where fundamentalist Islamic groups are vying for political power. Rapid economic development involves the transformation of social, cultural, and religious values. If these are cherished and provide the foundation for the existing political order, expenditure growth will be constrained on this account.

For a different set of economic and political considerations, the desirability of increased foreign investment is also at issue for several OPEC producers. While some amount of investment in foreign securities and short-term obligations is considered desirable for liquidity and diversification reasons, there appears to be a perception by certain OPEC states that these investments are risky and subject to expropriation by foreign governments or by inflation. The American freeze on Iranian assets has fuelled this belief, while inflation-corrected returns were very modest through the 1970s, averaging less than the rate of inflation by some estimates.[7] While myopic, these beliefs were common through the 1970s, leading certain key OPEC countries to conclude that oil in the ground constituted a wiser investment than did the acquisition of various foreign financial assets.[8]

These views are powerfully bolstered by the following consideration. Most OPEC producers are loath to consider the possibility that their wealth-maximizing strategy may well be to become *rentiers* — mere "coupon clippers" — dependent on investments in the West for their succour. Powerful evidence that this alternative has been rejected can be seen in the billions of dollars sunk into domestic projects that offer no prospect of ever becoming economic by objective efficiency standards.

Of course, there are noticeable differences among the OPEC producers with respect to their attitudes and policies towards foreign investment. The Kuwaitis, for instance, have made sizeable investments in the West, including equity participation. As Table 1 indicates, their investments abroad are much larger, relative to annual revenues, than those of any other OPEC state. Nevertheless, Kuwait has held considerable excess capacity, apparently preferring oil in the ground to money in the bank.

Table 1
ESTIMATED FOREIGN ASSETS, SELECTED OPEC MEMBERS
(US $ million)

	End of 1972	End of 1978	End of 1979
Iraq	720	8 619	17 500
Iran	884	11 977	15 900
Kuwait	2 418	28 000	40 000
Libya	2 694	4 105	6 344
Qatar	414	2 967	4 267
Saudi Arabia	2 303	64 000	75 000
United Arab Emirates	300	9 307	12 707
Total	9 733	128 975	171 718

INVESTMENT INCOME, SELECTED OPEC MEMBERS
(US $ million)

	1972	1973	1974	1975	1976	1977	1978	1979
Iraq	28.4	65.7	275	191	146	288	755	1 750
Iran	18	54	424	745	784	739	1 078	1 590
Kuwait	410	559	767	1 361	1 821	2 111	2 500	4 000
Libya	152	123.7	312	228	202	266	370	634
Qatar	28	24.8	75.5	128	138	157	267	426
Saudi Arabia	125	221.7	1 305.7	1 961.8	3 226.6	4 447	5 750	7 600
United Arab Emirates	20	49.6	143.8	268	470	731	838	1 270
Total	781.4	1 098.5	3 303	4 882.8	6 787.6	8 739	11 558	17 270

Source: Middle East Economic Survey (28 April 1980).

So long as the above perceptions remain firm, OPEC producers cannot be expected to expand production for the principal purpose of acquiring foreign assets, even if by doing so they would enhance the present value of their oil reserves. Furthermore, if the domestic economy is already burdened with all the investment that can be supported prudently, then there are no internal reasons for a producer to expand production. If this is an appropriate representation of reality for a significant portion of OPEC capacity, then supply responses will be quite perverse in that large increases in the world price in one period need not occasion any increase in output in the same period. In fact the opposite is possible.[9] Conversely, falling world prices will sooner or later lead to production expansion, at least in certain countries.[10]

The strength of the above considerations depends, in part, on the extent to which economic development is constrained by the economic and political considerations mentioned earlier. Absorptive capacity constraints rooted in political considerations appear to be especially important in Islamic countries; absorptive capacity constraints rooted in economic considerations will be more powerful the lower the level of economic development and the smaller the population in relation to revenues from oil. Table 2 categorizes the OPEC states according to this last criterion. Countries classified as group I (low absorptive capacity) had average revenues per inhabitant of $5799 in 1978, while the corresponding figures for group II (moderate absorptive capacity) and group III (high absorptive capacity) were $602 and $72 respectively. These classifications are at best highly approximate as absorptive capacity is determined in part by political factors as well as other economic considerations not captured in Table 2. Additional information is therefore needed if the classifications are to be refined.

What makes these categories significant in terms of cartel theory is that, as of 1980−81, the data indicate that countries with low absorptive capacity have considerably more short-run excess capacity than do producers with higher absorptive capacity (Table 3). Group I countries have about 3 millon barrels per day or about two-thirds of OPEC's excess short-run capacity. Furthermore, these countries have higher reserve-to-production ratios than do countries in other categories. At 1978 levels of production, remaining reserves for group I, group II, and group III countries were 54, 26, and 22 years respectively (Table 2). This indicates the existence of greater capacity expansion possibilities for group I countries. In short, those producers with low absorptive capacities are also the countries possessing the greatest amount of short- to medium-run excess capacity. As such, their production behaviour will be of very great importance to the world oil market, at least over the next decade. Their existing excess capacity and their ability to add to this capacity are the priccipalisupply-side threat to the monopoly prices that producers have attained.

There is mounting evidence that group I producers behave according to the considerations specified above. The clearest evidence is the absence of widespread cheating, by which is meant the tendency to offer price discounts in order to sell more oil. While this might be explained in terms of OPEC solidarity, it is argued below that OPEC solidarity, in the sense of individual countries adjusting their production decisions in order to meet group goals, is of minor importance. Of greater significance are various natural characteristics of OPEC economies coupled with internal and external political factors that explain why group I producers have not, as of 1981, engaged in competitive output expansion.

Besides the absence of cheating, there are .numerous public statements by key OPEC ministers indicating that production decisions are made in reference to internal budgetary targets. Also consistent with such behaviour are various endeavours to cut production or restrain output increases when prices rise. Clearly, if OPEC producers are shooting at some target level of production, they will tend to cut production if prices rise, and increase production if prices fall. (In economic language, target revenue producers will have a backward-bending supply curve). For instance, the Algerian Energy and Petro Chemicals Minister has stated that, "If the terms of trade improve, Algerian exports will drop."[11] Similarly, Kuwait's Minister of Oil has stated that, "The big increase in oil prices has given us the opportunity to review production,"[12] adding that the Kuwait Council of Ministers was discussing the question of lowering production. Libya, Abu Dhabi, Qatar, and occasionally Saudi Arabia can be expected to display similar proclivities. OPEC members and other producers with modest production in relation to absorptive capacity, such as Nigeria, Ecuador, and Mexico, are less able to adjust production in this fashion, although they sometimes exhibit similar tendencies.

The increasing reluctance of OPEC countries to produce today in order to build financial assets abroad is also supportive of the view that production decisions are made with reference to domestic budgetary targets. Perhaps the one exception is Saudi Arabia. As is pointed out below, there are complex political reasons why Saudi Arabia behaves differently, producing, if necessary, beyond its domestic budgetary needs and investing the surpluses in financial assets. Yet even in the case of Saudi Arabia, there is increasing reluctance to do so. An objective assessment based on economic analysis might indicate an incentive to build financial assets, but this is of little importance for predicting OPEC behaviour if production decisions are made on a different set of criteria.

An important implication of this analysis is that in a tight crude market, collusion among producers is not necessary for the price to remain at levels generating large monopoly rents.[13] This explains why the price during the 1970s did not collapse under the pressures of competitive output expansion. It also indicates that OPEC, as an organization, has been essentially irrelevant to price determination in the 1970s. With only modest exaggeration, OPEC can be considered a price-stamping organization, attempting to ratify market-place prices resulting from the actions of individual producers. In short, OPEC

Table 2
OPEC COUNTRIES[a]: 1978 POPULATION, RESERVES, AND REVENUES PER CAPITA

	Population (million)	Proven Reserve (millions of barrels)	Output (thousands barrels per day)	Reserves Years (at 1978 output rate)	Revenue from Oil Exports (millions $US)	Revenues per Inhabitant ($US)
Group I (Low Absorptive Capacity)						
Saudi Arabia	6.89	153 100	8 059	52.05	38 736	5 622.06
Libya	2.73	25 000	1 982	34.58	9 490	3 476.19
Kuwait	1.18	70 100	1 865	102.98	9 575	8 114.41
Qatar	0.23	5 600	485	31.63	2 315	10 065.22
United Arab Emirates	0.83	32 425	1 832	40.49	8 658	10 431.33
Subtotal	11.86	286 225	14 223	54	68 774	—
Share of Total	3.7%	65.70%	48.96%	—	51.5%	—
Average revenues per inhabitant[b]	—	—	—	—	—	$5 799

Group II (Moderate Absorptive Capacity)

Irac	36.64	62 000	5 264	32.27	21 766	594.05
Venezuela	13.1	18 200	2 163	23.05	9 187	701.30
Iraq	12.65	34 500	2 629	35.95	11 008	870.20
Algeria	17.25	6 000	1 225	13.42	6 015	348.70
Subtotal	79.64	120 700	11 281	26	47 976	—
Share of Total	24.6%	27.71%	38.83%	—	35.9%	—
Average revenues per inhabitant[b]	—	—	—	—	—	$ 602

Group III (High Absorptive Capacity)

Nigeria	91.17	18 700	1 910	26.82	9 318	102.20
Indonesia	141.28	10 000	1 637	16.74	7 439	52.65
Subtotal	232.45	28 700	3 547	22	16 757	—
Share of Total	71.7%	6.59%	12.21%	—	12.6%	—
Average revenues per inhabitant[b]	—	—	—	—	—	$ 72
TOTAL	323.95	435 625	29 051	—	133 507	

Sources: 1. *World Energy Industry* I (Second Quarter, 1978).
         2. *Background Notes*, U.S. Department of State, various dates.

Notes: a   Excludes Ecuador and Gabon.
       b   Subtotal revenue divided by subtotal population.

Table 3
OPEC COUNTRIES[a]: 1981 PRODUCTION AND SHORT-RUN EXCESS CAPACITY (1000 b/d)

	Capacity			Production		Short-Run Excess Capacity[f]
	Installed[b]	Maximum Sustainable[c]	Available[d]	Latest Post Embargo Peak	Current[e] (JFMA 81)	
Group I (Low Absorptive Capacity)						
Saudi Arabia[1]	12 500	9 500	9 500	10 200 (Jan. 81)	10 209	0
Libya	2 500	2 100	1 750	2 210 (Mar. 77)	1 612	598
Kuwait[1]	2 900	2 500	1 500	2 990 (Dec. 76)	1 471	1 519
Qatar	650	600	600	610 (Dec. 75)	501	109
United Arab Emirates	2 570	2 415	1 630	2 260[g]	1 601	659
Subtotal	21 120	17 115	14 980	18 270	15,394	2 885
Share of Total	52.5%	51.1%	51.6%	49.5%	62.9%	63.4%
Group II (Moderate Absorptive Capacity)						
Iran	7 000	5 500[h]	3 500[l]	6 680 (Nov. 76)	1 650	—
Venezuela	2 600	2 400	2 200	2 950 (June 74)	2 214	736
Iraq	4 000	3 500	3 500	3 500 (June 79)	825	—
Algeria	1 200	1 100	1 000	1 160 (Dec. 78)	938	222
Subtotal	14 800	12 500	10 200	14 290	5 627	958
Share of Total	36.8%	37.4%	35.1%	39.1%	23.0%	21.0%

Group III (High Absorptive Capacity)

Nigeria	2 500	2 200	2 200	2 440 (Jan. 79)	1 840	600
Indonesia	1 800	1 650	1 650	1 740 (Mar. 77)	1 629	111
Subtotal	4 300	3 850	3 850	4 180	3 469	711
Share of Total	10.7%	11.5%	13.3%	11.4%	14.1%	15.6%
TOTAL	40 220	33 465	29 030	36 740	24 490	4 554

Sources: *International Energy Statistical Review*, CIA (28 April 1981) and *Monthly Energy Review*, DOE (Auguut 1981).

Notes:
a Excluding Ecuador and Gabon.
b Installed capacity, also called nameplate or design capacity, includes all aspects of crude oil production, processing, transportation, and storage. Installed capacity is generally the highest capacity estimate.
c Maximum sustainable or operational capacity is the maximum production rate that can be sustained for several months; it considers the experience of operating the total system and is generally some 90–95 per cent of installed capacity. This capacity concept does not necessarily reflect the maximum production rate sustainable without damage to the fields.
d Available or allowable capacity reflects production ceilings applied by Abu Dhabi, Kuwait, Iran, and Saudi Arabia. These ceilings usually represent a constraict only on annual average output, and thus production may exceed the ceilings in a given month. These ceilings are frequently altered and not always enforced.
e Production estimates are the average for January, February, March, and April 1981 as reported in *Monthly Energy Review*, U.S. Department of Energy, Energy Information Administration, August 1981.
f Except in the case of Iran and Iraq, this is calculated by subtracting current production from the latest post-embargo peak. In the case of Iran and Iraq, it is assumed that there is no excess capacity because of the dysfunctional effects of revolution and war.
g This figure is constructed from the following: Abu Dhabi 1930 (July 1975), Dubai 370 (July 1979), Sharjah 60 (December 1974).
h The precise loss in sustainable capacity remains uncertain.
i This figure represents the upper end of the range of available capacity, according to government statements.

does not appear to be a cartel. The trappings of a cartel are absent, other than the frequent price conferences, which are of little consequence. There are no prorationing and policing mechanisms in place; nor is there agreement about how this should be accomplished if it were needed.

This view of OPEC has important implications for the behaviour one can expect in the future. It means that OPEC has yet to demonstrate that it has the ability to obtain the co-ordination necessary to support the monopoly price should pressures arise that would threaten to unravel the benefits acquired in the 1970s. Accordingly, there are conditions under which expanded production, or the failure to curtail production in the face of falling demand, is to be expected.

This possibility becomes apparent when OPEC behaviour is considered under conditions in which crude prices fail to rise for a prolonged period. If production and prices are constant, export revenues are constant. However, as explained earlier, revenue "requirements" in the next period depend on a mark-up over the previous period's "requirements" in order to accommodate rising expectations and increased absorptive capacity. Depending on the rapidity with which expenditures expand, it might take only a few years for expenditures to catch up with receipts. At this point, pressures arise to draw down liquid foreign assets, take on indebtedness, and then to increase revenues via increased crude oil production. If OPEC is unable to construct and police a prorationing agreement — and there is as yet no tangible evidence that it can do so over a prolonged period — competitive output expansion would commence, creating downward pressures on prices. As discussed below, there are reasons to believe that this scenario might arrive during the 1980s, provided there is no major disruption that takes a significant amount of production off the market.

In the sections that follow, OPEC behaviour since 1970 is reviewed against this conceptual background. There appears to be evidence in support of the model presented. The final section evaluates implications for the future.

OPEC Behaviour, 1970–1974

At a minimum, a theory of OPEC behaviour must be able to explain why the price quadrupled in 1973–74. This is a particularly challenging task for those who assert that the world oil market is competitive. Proponents of the competitive view (Johany, 1978; Mead 1979) argue that this turbulent period witnessed a fundamental reassignment of ownership rights and control of production policy from the multinational oil companies to the producer states. As the rapacious policies of the multinationals were abandoned in favour of policies that paid proper attention to conservation goals and the welfare of future generations, then the constriction of output that followed led to the restoration of the price to a much higher but, nevertheless, competitive level.[14] If this argument is correct, then one need not search further for an explanation of OPEC stability, since there are no monopoly profits to be competed away. However, this explanation must confront many economic studies that indicate that the world price since 1973−74 contains a large element of monopoly profit.[15]

The alternative explanation offered here recognizes that in the early 1970s there occurred a transfer of control from the companies to the countries. The attendant modification to property rights can explain part of the price increase. But of far greater importance is the fact that in the period 1970−74, a series of events unravelled in an unplanned, uncoordinated fashion, which elevated the price considerably above competitive levels. Once established, this price yielded such an enormous increment to revenues in relation to the ability of the producers to absorb them domestically that the proclivities of individual producers to capture a greater share of the monopoly rents through output expansion were severely attenuated in several important cases. This explains why the price level did not collapse to previous levels.

Indeed, what is remarkable about the 1970−74 transformation is that few of the key changes were achieved by OPEC countries acting together. Generally, one or a few governments drove the bargains and OPEC subsequently ratified the results. Of enormous significance was Libya's successful attempt to negotiate higher prices with the companies. Libyan pressures were severe and included threats of nationalization and enforced reduction in output.[16] Ghaddafi received some encouragement but no tangible help from Algeria and Iraq, but because of the peculiar market conditions prevailing at the time, Ghaddafi prevailed. His success can be attributed to a combination of factors. First of all, the 1967 Arab-Israeli war caused the closure of the Suez Canal and the interruption of the "Tapline" (the oil pipeline that carries oil from Saudi Arabia to the Mediterranean). Both events served to raise freight rates from the Gulf substantially. Secondly, the Biafra war stopped oil production in Nigeria. Thirdly, new environmental regulations in Europe made the low sulphur Libyan crudes especially desirable. As a result of these factors, there was a strong demand for the short-haul low sulphur Mediterranean oil. Fourthly, a large quantity of Libyan oil was produced by "independents" who had no alternative sources of supply to honour their previous contracts and to keep their refineries in operation. Competition among the majors and independents prevented the companies from presenting a unified front.

The terms negotiated by Libya were generalized to other OPEC countries in the Tehran and Tripoli agreements of 1971. These agreements were designed to raise the revenues per barrel and also to stabilize them in real terms. However, the devaluation of the U.S. dollar reduced the real price of oil to the producers, thereby challenging the sanctity of the agreements, since posted price escalators had been specified in U.S. dollars. An additional threat to the agreement came from enhanced market demand, especially in the United States, as domestic consumption began to outstrip production at a quickening rate. In addition, the integrated multinationals became increasingly concerned about the extent to which the participation of host governments in their major concessions would affect the availability of crude for their downstream operations. As a consequence, they began reducing their outside sales of crude oil, which increased the competitive pressures on less integrated refiners.

Spurred by these considerations, Iraq led a move at the OPEC Vienna Conference in June 1973 to scrap the Tehran and Tripoli agreements, but the effort failed. By September 1973, all OPEC countries were prepared formally to request a revision of the price agreements, and new negotiations with the companies to revise the Tehran agreement opened on 8 October in Vienna. On 6 October, Egypt and Israel had gone to war. On 16 October the ministerial committee representing the six Gulf States of OPEC, including Iran, decided to negotiate no further. The governments henceforth posted their own prices, thus completing the transfer of control over pricing policy, taxes, and production to the producer states. New posted prices were announced that embodied a 70 per cent increase for Gulf crudes (from $3.01 to $5.12 for 34° API Arabian Light).

The output and destination restrictions imposed by the Arabs on 27 October 1973 further tightened the market for oil and, in particular, for oil free of destination restrictions. Spot prices soared, which led some OPEC members, especially Iran, to demand that the posted price match the spot price. The Saudis resisted the increase, on the grounds that the high prices reflected the embargo situation. A compromise was reached on a posted price of $11.65 a barrel for 34° API Arabian Light. Thus, the posted price was quadrupled from where it existed before the outbreak of the Arab-Israeli war.

The transfer of oil policy from the companies to the countries can explain at least a portion of this price increase since some concessionaires had been producing as if there was no tomorrow; but while this conflicted with underlying conservation aspirations of several producer states, it was encouraged by others such as Iran, which had ambitious development plans. In short, fear of nationalization may have led some companies to produce at higher rates in the 1960s, thereby contributing to the downward drift of prices in that period. Accordingly, the ownership changes brought about in 1970−74 may account for some part of the price increase. More important, however, is the fact that with demand very insensitive to price changes in the short run, the embargo sent prices rocketing. Once flooded with additional revenues, it became both possible and convenient for the producers to cut back production, or attenuate scheduled increases, while sanctimoniously proclaiming conservation objectives. There was no proclivity to cheat because internal budgetary needs were being satisfied.[17] In short, the nature of the market and the goals of the key producers were such that a quadrupling of the world oil price could be engineered and sustained with the minimum of collusion. More explicit treatment of this phenomenon as well as competing views are offered for the post-embargo period below.

OPEC Behaviour, 1974–1980

The classical cartel of the economics textbooks raises price by restricting output. The restriction of output is a result of a concerted and co-ordinated action on the part of cartel members. Price generally does not act as the rationing mechanism to allocate sales among the cartel members. Rather, sales are allocated among cartel members on the basis of a quota or prorationing system that is agreed upon by cartel members. The quota system may be specified in terms of percentage market share, physical units of output, assignment of particular customers or regional markets, or some combination of all of these arrangements. The basis for the quota system is typically historical market share or the producing capacity of the individual cartel members. In the classical cartel, there is a strong incentive for the members to cheat on the cartel price. Cheating by one of the cartel members initially increases the cartel members' market share at the expense of the other members of the cartel. The cheating may take the form of secret price concessions, enhancement of product quality, special credit terms, and so on. But as cheating, particularly price cheating, is detected, other cartel members attempt to first attenuate such behaviour, but the lack of effective policing and disciplinary measures typically leads producers to retaliate in kind to protect their monopoly profits. The result is a violation of the quota system, a scramble for market shares, and the collapse of the cartel. In the classical formulation, this is supposed to be the fate of all successful cartels. Why has it not happened to OPEC?

A satisfactory theory of OPEC behaviour must be able to explain why cheating has not driven the price down to competitive levels in the post-embargo period. One explanation is that the monopoly profits are just so huge that every member recognizes the importance of solidarity and tacitly refrains from cheating. But the opposing argument seems just as plausible. If monopoly profits are huge, the incremental profits, and therefore the incentives to cheat, are also huge for an individual producer. Another explanation is that the multinational oil companies prorate output for the OPEC states, thereby minimizing the amount of co-ordination needed at the national level. Others have postulated that by agreeing to agree on just one price — the price of the marker crude — the process of collusion is greatly simplified and cartel stability is thereby secured. A close examination of OPEC, however, would seem to indicate that it has few if any of the hallmarks of a classical cartel. It has displayed unstable market shares and chaotic prices. Furthermore, OPEC had no prorationing agreement, and even if it were to devise one, its success would be very problematic.

Consider pricing. OPEC has attempted to administer prices rather than output, at least through the 1970s. As discussed below, it does not control the market share of the member-states, although in the early 1980s it will be forced to try. Attempts at price administration are focused on a single type of crude, the marker crude, which is currently Saudi Arabian Light, 34° API. Efforts to administer the entire price structure to take account of crude oil quality and location differentials have never been successful. Rather, the OPEC meetings attempt to determine the price of just *one* particular kind of crude, the marker. Each producer is then free to set differentials for their own crudes at whatever level seems appropriate. In the absence of production ceilings, this means that each and every producer — OPEC member or otherwise — has complete liberty over its pricing decisions, subject, of course, to market acceptance. There is no mechanism to solicit and police agreements over "appropriate" differentials — a near impossibility to determine objectively.

Not surprisingly, OPEC's pricing structure has, at various times, been rather chaotic. Whatever pricing uniformity existed in earlier years has evaporated. By February 1980, four distinct tiers of prices could be recognized (Table 4). The chasm between Saudi Arabia and the rest of OPEC had widened in 1980 to the point where some Middle East crudes were $7 more per barrel than the bench-mark Arabian Light, and African crudes were $10 more a barrel.[18] The dividing line between the various pricing policies pursued by individual producer nations cuts across any geographical or commercial considerations, and appears to reflect political decisions.

One of the most intriguing aspects of the pricing regime that emerged was that Saudi Arabia consistently attempted to moderate increase in the world price of oil and has under-priced its oil on the market. Saudi Arabia stated that it will cut back output if and when the "radicals" exercise pricing restraint. Furthermore, on several occasions the Saudi's increased crude oil production in order to moderate increases in the world price. A very important question in terms of understanding the behaviour of OPEC is the motivation for this action. One interpretation — and the one favoured by most economists — is that the Saudis, being net wealth maximizers,

Table 4
OPEC CRUDE OIL PRICE SPLIT IN 1979−1980

	Selling Prices ($/barrel)		
	Feb. 1980	Dec. 1978	Total Rise
The 'Bench-mark'			
Arabian Light-34	26.00	12.70	13.30
The 'Moderates'			
Venezuela Medium-24	25.93	12.39	13.54
Venezuela Light-31	28.90	13.54	15.36
Kuwait-31	27.50	12.22	15.28
Iraq Basrah Light-35	27.96	12.66	15.30
The 'Intermediates'			
Indonesia Sumatran-34	29.50	13.55	15.95
Abu Dhabi Murban-39	29.56	13.17	16.29
Qatar Marine-36	29.23	13.00	16.23
The 'Radicals'			
Iranian Light-24	32.87	12.81	20.06
Nigerian Bonny-37	34.20	14.12	20.08
Libyan Zueitina-41	34.72	13.90	20.82
Algerian Saharan-44	37.21	14.10	23.11

recognize that higher prices today will provide incentives for conservation and the development of substitutes in consuming nations, all of which will serve to shrink the market for crude, especially in the long run. Saudi Arabia having the largest reserves and the highest reserves-to-production ratio, has the most to lose from such a policy.

This explanation is only partially correct. An additional consideration is that the Saudis do not have a very accurate estimate of the price at which substitutes will become a threat because the large-scale development of substitutes depends on political decisions to be made in the importing countries, and especially in the United States. Furthermore, whatever threat from substitutes exists lies in the distant future, given the long gestation period for the development of most synthetic fuels. In any case, so long as their oil can fetch the cost of production for substitutes, the economic welfare of the Saudi people is guaranteed for the foreseeable future.[19] Rather, the more immediate concern of the Saudis is that higher oil prices will create greater instability in the West and especially in the Gulf, since the additional revenues occasioned by higher prices can be used to fuel the military machines of various "radical" producers. Furthermore, by appearing as the moderating element in the market, the Saudis are able to cement their alliance with the West and particularly the United

States, an alliance that the Saudis consider essential for their survival. With the Gulf exposed to external and internal threats, this view posits that the oil policy of the conservative Saudis is driven as much by political as by economic considerations.

Now consider output. Does OPEC orchestrate production restraints? At least until 1982, OPEC had not attempted production prorationing since the abortive attempts of the 1960s. Indeed, having failed to observe OPEC exercising any form of prorationing mechanism, some observers have imputed the function to the multinational oil companies. Adelman's view is that:

> The oil cartel nations do not face the difficult, divisive, and probably impossible task of setting production shares. They need not meet together to quarrel over the gain of one being the loss of another. The governments need only agree that they will sell the bulk of their output through the oil companies, whose margins are too narrow to allow any but trifling price cuts. . . . So long as nearly every government refrains from independent offers, the total offered in the market by the companies adds up to the total demanded by consumers at the going price (Adelman, 1977, pp. 7–8).

This statement seems to suggest that formal prorationing is being conducted for OPEC by the companies. Blair (1976, p. 375) is more explicit on this point, claiming that "if . . . the OPEC members have neither agreed on standards of allocation nor set up the necessary allocating machinery, the responsibility for the curtailments necessarily rests with the companies." In particular:

> . . . the initiative for the 1975 production cutbacks came from the oil companies. Had it not been for the cutbacks, the market would have been flooded with "distressed" oil, OPEC would indeed have broken down, and oil prices would have fallen sharply. That none of this occurred stems from the nature of the relationship between the companies and the countries (Blair, 1976, p. 293).

Although OPEC has, on occasion, tried to devise formal prorationing agreements, including one in 1982, there is little evidence that these agreements have been honoured or enforced. In any case, the analysis here indicates that once a producer has attained its target revenue goals, prorationing is unnecessary to sustain the world price, since the proclivities to cheat by the key producers are attenuated by limited absorptive capacity and aversion to foreign investment. But the proclivities change dramatically if the target is missed on the low side.

A form of voluntary "prorationing" does, however, occur. For instance, in the first half of 1980, supply cuts of 200 000 BPD, 350 000 BPD, and 500 000 BPD, were announced by Venezuela, Libya, and Kuwait respectively. Algeria announced a 15 per cent reduction in contract volumes in March 1980 citing "conservation" as the reason. Of course, there is a delicate line between output restriction based on "conservation" considerations and output restrictions based on the desire to contrive a scarcity and drive up the world price. The difference is that whereas output restrictions for monopoly purposes will require explicit or tacit collusion, output restrictions for conservation reasons need not. Conservation amongst OPEC producers appears to be motivated by political and absorptive capacity considerations. Further, oil production policy is considered a matter of national sovereignty, and not a matter that can be determined by OPEC.

The nation with the largest oil reserves and the largest export volume is Saudi Arabia. One interpretation of OPEC stability in the 1974–1980 period is that Saudi Arabia is the dominant producer adjusting world supply so as to maintain the cartel price. This "dominant producer" monopoly model bears some similarities to reality, but there are very important differences. In particular, Saudi Arabia has in no sense fine-tuned the world market to the degree that, say, the Texas Railroad Commission fine-tuned the American domestic market before the removal of import controls. Indeed, Sheikh Yamani has announced on several occasions that Saudi Arabia will bear no more than its fair share of production cuts should prorationing appear necessary. Furthermore, Saudi Arabia is severely constrained in its ability to administer the world price; it could not sustain the OPEC price on the face of large-scale discounting by other members, and it cannot restrain price increases once it is producing at full capacity, as it was through much of the 1980–81 period. While Saudi Arabia undoubtedly has more influence on the pricing structure than any other producer, it does not appear to have used this influence with the sole objective of maximizing the net present value of its oil reserves. It has given considerable weight to important political objectives, and the pricing policy prevailing at any point very much reflects the political and economic context of the time.[20] Thus to the extent that it is able to restrain the excess of the radicals, Saudi Arabia is able to capture political benefits from the oil-importing nations. By helping to moderate price increases, it not only denies revenues to other oil producers, but receives credit for the savings across the total volume of OPEC exports, not just those exports emanating from Saudi Arabia. Clearly, Saudi Arabia has enough leverage over price to make other producers share the costs of the political favours it wins abroad.

In this regard, consider some of the reasons advanced by Saudi Arabia for pursuing a policy of moderate price increases. Sheikh Yamani has stated that Saudi Arabia's reasons for advocating a moderate price posture during the two-tier pricing episode following the Doha meeting were related to Saudi fears of renewed economic recession in the West, Communist gains in Italy and France, and concern over the shaky situations in Britain, Spain, and Portugal. "The Kingdom is very anxious to prevent any deterioration of the world economy because that would hurt us financially in view of the large investments we have in the western countries. To increase oil prices now would also expose us to certain political repercussions because we are bound to the West by clearly defined political interests."[21] Yamani has also expressed fears about Soviet designs on Mideast oil, making it clear that he considered the economic prosperity and goodwill of the West, and particularly the United States, important to countering Soviet ambitions. These worries have been sharpened by the invasion of Afghanistan, and help explain why the Saudis and several other Gulf producers have, from time to time, adopted policies that involve economic costs in the form of forgone profits. For instance, following the Iranian revolution, Saudi Arabia, Kuwait, and the United Arab Emirates increased their production by 3 MMBPD to compensate for the Iranian shortfall "earning in the process unwanted revenues." The Saudis took this initiative "in order to avoid disaster in the West." With the outbreak of hostilities and loss of production as a result of the Iran-Iraq war, the Saudis again increased output in order to relieve pressure on the price. Such behaviour is not consistent with the pursuit of economic self-interest narrowly defined.

In short, the limited absorptive capacity-cum-target revenue view of OPEC provides a viable explanation of the underlying production policies of OPEC. However, additional political factors intervene as well, at least in the case of Saudi Arabia. The Saudis have a large enough market position that their production policies are under close scrutiny from the West. Given the precarious military and security conditions that prevail in the Gulf, Saudi production decisions are exposed to an additional set of political influences stemming from its delicate relation with the United States and the rest of the Arab world. These pressures will remain as long as tensions in the Gulf are high, which appears to be the case for the foreseeable future.

OPEC Behaviour, 1981–2000

OPEC behaviour in the future will depend on economic and political considerations, as it has in the past. The analysis to follow focuses principally on the economic factors, especially OPEC production decisions, since these are the central focus of the target revenue model.

One distinct possibility is that the conventional wisdom — that OPEC production will remain about where it is today — will prevail. According to one leading expert, there is "growing recognition that the Saudis and other Persian Gulf producers will not expand their production to meet the demand growth that would be generated at today's energy prices" (Manne, 1979, p. 2). There is, in fact, a possibility that because of political disruption or because of rapidly increasing demand, prices might tend upwards rapidly, moderated only by the possibility of Saudi attempts to restrain them.

However, the above is by no means a foregone conclusion. As the demand for crude oil, and especially OPEC oil, begins to moderate in the early 1980s, a window of opportunity for consumers will open should demand for OPEC oil remain stationary for several years — or at least long enough to enable OPEC expenditure growth to encounter a revenue constraint. There are several powerful reasons suggesting that this may occur. One is the fast clip with which OPEC expenditures have grown in the past; another is the perception that financial assets invested abroad now yield attractive real returns; a third is the impact on consumption of the previous crude price increases. Each will be examined briefly.

Table 5 summarizes rates of growth of oil income and government expenditures within OPEC. It is quite apparent that expenditures have grown almost as fast as oil revenues, a situation also reflected in Table 6, which shows that the foreign assets of selected OPEC members are modest relative to annual oil revenues.

Clearly, if oil revenues stay constant for several years, past rates of expansion of government revenues cannot be sustained. The data in Table 6 indicate that foreign assets, relative to annual expenditures, are not enormous, amounting at the end of 1979 to about two years for Saudi Arabia, four years for Kuwait, two years for Qatar, eighteen months for Iran and Iraq, and less than a year for Libya. By 1981, Iraq and Iran had largely exhausted their liquid assets. To the extent that some foreign assets are illiquid, as with Kuwait, the period would be shorter. Conversely, a producer's ability to obtain and service foreign debt would delay adjustment. This is not to imply that the OPEC producers would necessarily deplete their liquid assets and credit lines before adjusting production upwards. The point is merely that the foreign assets of the OPEC producers are not enormous relative to the levels of government expenditure and their annual increments.

Confronted with zero increase in oil revenues, OPEC governments could undoubtedly slow the rate of increase of government expenditure, without creating economic hardship. However, it is generally easier to win friends and placate enemies at home and abroad when prosperity is increasing rather than decreasing. Obviously, the degree to which this is true will vary according to society's value structure and the desire for consumption of imported commodities. Islamic fundamentalists might be heartened by a slacking of economic development, but professional and commercial groups are likely to see it otherwise. In short, if the world price of crude were to stay constant for several years, pressures for increased revenues, and hence

Table 5
RATES OF GROWTH OF OIL INCOME, GOVERNMENT EXPENDITURES
(annual averages, percentage)

Country	Oil Income[a]	Government Expenditure[b]	Time Period
Kuwait	31.2	38.2	1972−79
Libya	29.8	20.0	1972−78
Qatar	116.0	50.0	1972−77
Saudi Arabia	46.5	42.7	1972−79
United Arab Emirates	43.7	39.0	1972−79
Algeria	41.5	22.3	1972−79
Ecuador	49.6	20.0	1972−79
Indonesia	57.7	38.9	1972−78
Iran	43.1	40.5	1972−78
Iraq	65.0	35.7	1972−79
Nigeria	36.9	33.6	1972−78
Venezuela	20.0	24.3	1972−78
Simple Average	48.41	33.76	1972−79

Notes: [a] *OPEC Bulletin* (January 1981).
  [b] *OPEC Statistical Bulletin* (1979).

Table 6
SELECTED OPEC PRODUCERS
Foreign Assets, Oil Revenues, and Total Foreign
Assets as a Percentage of Annual Revenues, 1979
($U.S. millions)

	Foreign Assets[a]	Revenues from Oil 1979	Foreign Assets Divided by Annual Revenues 1979
Iraq	17 500	11 008	1.589
Iran	15 900	21 766	.730
Kuwait	40 000	9 575	4.177
Libya	6 344	9 490	.668
Qatar	4 267	2 315	1.843
Saudi Arabia	75 000	38 736	1.936
United Arab Emirates	12 707	8 658	1.467
TOTAL	171 718	101 548	1.691

Note: [a] *Middle East Economic Survey* (18 April 1980).

production, would mount in various OPEC countries, especially once debt capacity was exhausted. This could be fuelled by changing expectations with respect to the attractiveness of foreign investments. As mentioned earlier, foreign investment has never been embraced enthusiastically by any OPEC producer because the notion of a *rentier* nation is not compatible with national pride. However, the apparent failures and inefficiencies of many domestic development programs may eventually serve to ameliorate the stigma attached to "coupon clipping." Couple this with the generous real returns on financial assets experienced during the early 1980s, and widely held perceptions that oil in the ground is better than money in the bank will start to crumble. This is especially likely if the price of crude oil stays flat into the mid-1980s.

There are demand-side reasons to expect such an outcome. Griffin and Teece (1982, Chap. 6) indicate that the long-run elasticity for total energy is around −.73. Furthermore, the reduction in oil consumption evident by 1981 can be explained by the original price jump of 1973−74, the point being that the effects of the first price increases have been only about half-way felt, and the 1979 impact is only just beginning to register. If economic growth at the abnormally slow rate of 2.5 per cent per year experienced since 1973 is coupled with the continued decline of energy and oil demand per unit output, total energy consumption will grow only very slowly. This means that oil consumption throughout the period will be flat and may drift downward very slightly. If similar trends are experienced elsewhere in the world, oil will no longer be a growth industry.[22] Meanwhile, the supply of non-OPEC oil is inching upward, which means that OPEC exports must decline, or the price must fall. In 1980 they were about 26 MMBPD, below the 1973 peak of 31 MMBPD. If OPEC exports fall to around 20 MMBPD annually for several years, the pressures for output expansion will be considerable. Considering that OPEC has yet to demonstrate that it has the wherewithal to delimit competitive output expansion, two decades of constant real prices is a strong possibility — absent a supply disruption of significance. This is all the more likely if Iran and Iraq restore production to pre-1978 levels.

Conclusion

This paper has advanced the somewhat novel position that the world oil price was elevated above competitive levels by good luck and special circumstances. Individual OPEC nations forged gains that might not have been obtained had collective action been necessary. Furthermore, competitive output expansion has been absent not out of recognition of mutual interdependence among producers, but simply because internal economic and political circumstances have so far displaced desires for higher current revenues. A backward-bending supply curve for OPEC oil is thereby postulated, at least for the short run. This indicates that the world price is subject to considerable instability, with modest increases (decreases) in demand translating into sizeable price increases (decreases) in the absence of Saudi ability and willingness to stabilize the market.

Whereas the possibility of upward instability is commonly recognized, the possibility that OPEC production may expand significantly, or fail to contract in the face of falling demand, is commonly dismissed by most OPEC analysts. The conceptual view advanced here indicates that competitive output expansion is possible if real prices can remain constant long enough to permit expenditures to press up against revenue constraints in countries that have excess capacity or the ability to add to it at low cost. Modest output expansion by OPEC will suffice to keep real prices constant through the 1980s and perhaps to the year 2000, absent a serious oil supply disruption.

A number of policy implications for the industrialized oil importers follow from these observations. The most conspicuous is the need for policies to further reduce demand for imported oil. Sustained demand reduction can be expected to foster competitive output expansion by producers, and hence lower prices. Since OPEC constitutes the world's residual supply for energy, energy conservation and production enhancement anywhere in the world are likely to reduce the demand for OPEC oil.

The need to reduce imports is all the more apparent whenever the market is tight, such as in periods of disruption or rapid economic growth. Because of the inelastic and perhaps even backward-bending nature of the aggregate supply curve when exporters are attaining their expenditure targets, demand reduction policies are essential to curb price hikes and the associated wealth transfers from consumers to producers. A tariff on imported oil ought to be implemented in all consuming nations to reduce oil consumption and to switch demand towards domestic crudes and alternate fuels (Teece and Griffin, 1982). The tariff should be permanent and ought not be reviewed until the world price is closer to competitive levels. Supplementary tariffs coupled with redistributive mechanisms (such as reduced withholding taxes in the United States) ought to be imposed immediately in the event of a supply disruption.

Another implication is that sovereign states should avoid the temptation to restrict investments abroad by OPEC states since factors that encourage the false notion that oil in the ground is a good investment tends to discourage production expansion in producing countries. It might even be worthwhile to provide instruments designed to meet OPEC objectives for a guaranteed return. However, as discussed earlier, the principal reasons why certain Arab states are cautious about investing abroad are political, and these concerns cannot be relieved by the verbal guarantees of host countries. Nevertheless, foreign investment policies should be liberalized world wide to facilitate diversified long-term investment by oil-exporting nations. European and Japanese capital markets need to be receptive to investments of all nationalities.[23] The implementation of policies along these lines should hasten the dissipation of OPEC's monopoly profits, and the restoration of a more equitable international economic order.

Epilogue (February 1983)

This article was written in 1980 and revised in 1981. The author received the page proofs in February 1983, just as OPEC ministers were meeting in London to try to thrash out a new pricing and prorationing agreement. The editor kindly permitted this short epilogue to be added in February 1983.

It appears that the low-price scenario advanced in the paper is gradually unfolding in a fashion consistent with the basic theory outlined. OPEC production in February 1983 is down to about 15 MMBPD and the pressures for expansion within OPEC are intense. If the above model is correct, it seems doubtful that OPEC will be able to hold the line on production and, hence, prices. Competitive output expansion will occur as budgetary requirements gradually force an expansion in production. Only a very rapid recovery in oil demand can save OPEC's pricing structure. This seems unlikely, so that oil prices in the range of $20 a barrel or less seem quite likely. This could become a certainty if the major importing nations were to impose a tariff on imported oil. Such a device would keep domestic prices high and sustain incentives for conservation. It will be all the more necessary if prices fall of their own volition.

It is rather striking that the "new orthodoxy" on prices, strongly critiqued by Griffin and Teece (1982), is turning out to be erroneous. The mainstream modellers have had a rough time of it. Part of the problem was their inability to estimate long-run price elasticities, a problem shared with many others in the profession. Another part was their inability to model OPEC behaviour correctly, and to perceive that OPEC was really not a cartel, or at least not a cartel with significant powers of decision making and enforcement. Slavish adherence to conventional theorizing has certainly paid pathetic dividends in the area of OPEC analysis and price forecasting. Hopefully this can be remedied in future studies of industrial organization, especially where nation-states are important actors in economic decision making.

Appendix

A Backward-Bending Supply Curve for OPEC Oil

The backward-bending supply curve is more than a theoretical curiosity; it has found useful application in labour economics. It may also have applicability to the export of exhaustible natural resources by developing countries where the natural resource in question is the dominant export industry. With respect to oil, there is some evidence that a number of important OPEC producers first determine their domestic investment requirements and then set production goals that will reach this target. This notion can be formulated in terms of investment theory as follows. A marginal efficiency of investment schedule exists that displays the investment opportunities open to an economy. There are a few projects that yield high returns, but as the rate-of-return requirement is lowered, more and more projects become viable. If planners pick a threshold rate-of-return level $\bar{r}$ below which investment projects will be rejected, then the level of desired domestic investment requirements I can be readily determined (see Figure 1). Once investment needs are determined, an isorevenue curve showing different combinations of prices and quantities for the natural resource can be constructed. This is drawn to show export earnings equal to I^* (it is assumed that the natural resource in question is the only export commodity and that export earnings constitute the only source of investment funds). In Figure 2 this is represented by the hyperbola $P = I/Q$. The isorevenue curve also represents the individual producer's supply curve for production levels involving less than full capacity production.

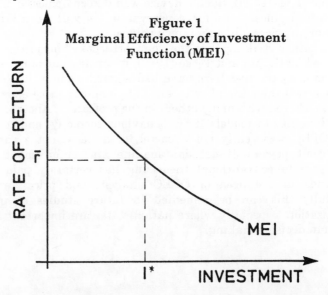

Figure 1
Marginal Efficiency of Investment
Function (MEI)

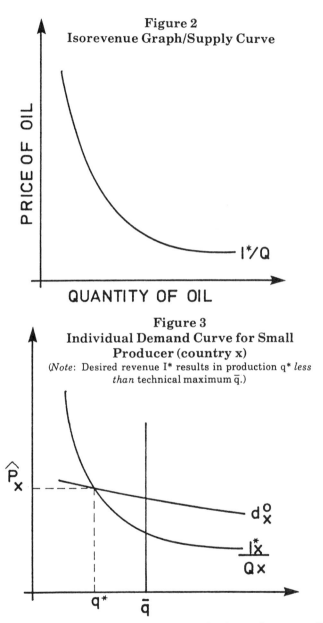

Figure 2
Isorevenue Graph/Supply Curve

Figure 3
Individual Demand Curve for Small
Producer (country x)
(*Note*: Desired revenue I* results in production q* *less*
than technical maximum q̄.)

If the demand curve facing the individual producer is d_x^o, the
country's desired production is q^* (Figure 3). The curve d_x^o has
some slope because of quality and location differences among producers of the natural resource. However, because this producer is
small relative to the market, d_x^o is shown to be highly elastic.

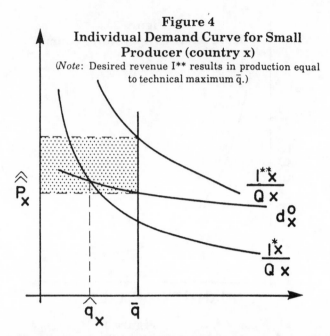

Figure 4
Individual Demand Curve for Small
Producer (country x)
(*Note*: Desired revenue I** results in production equal
to technical maximum q̄.)

If the producer has a very high target income, as represented by I^{**} (Figure 4), then production is adjusted to the technical maximum $\bar{q}$, but revenues fall short of the target in the amount of the cross-hatched area. If revenues always fall short of the target, then production will remain at capacity $\bar{q}$, irrespective of the price. The supply curve will be vertical at $\bar{q}$, at least in the short run. The producer's only hope of reaching its revenue target is if world supply and demand intersect in a fashion that raises the world price, and hence d_x^o.

It is of some importance to observe that the target revenue approach implies a backward-bending supply curve for prices above those needed to support the target revenue. If the world price increases, and the isorevenue curve is stationary (Figure 5a), then production falls. Output can increase in the absence of a price decline if the marginal efficiency of investment, and hence the isorevenue curve, moves to the right (Figure 5b). If there are a sufficient number of countries with backward-bending supply curves, then the market supply curve will take the same shape. This is represented in Figures 6a and 6b. If world demand is inelastic (as in Figure 6b), then the price is unstable in the range over which the supply curve is backward bending. An initial price at P_a will collapse to the lower equilibrium P_b or may spiral up above P_a. The more realistic case, where demand is elastic (as in Figure 6a), results in a stable equilibrium. However, the near parallelism of the supply and demand curve means that an increase in demand will generate a large price increase. Conversely, a decrease in demand will generate a large price decrease.[24]

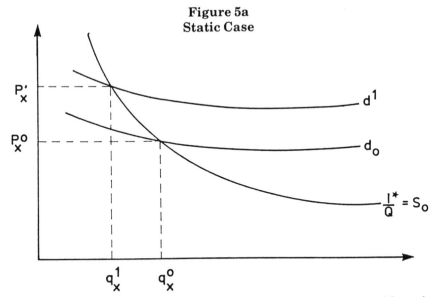

Figure 5a
Static Case

(*Note*: Backward-bending supply curve for country x showing implications of demand
shift (d^0 to d^1) with unchanged absorptive capacity. Demand shift leads to higher price
and output reduction. Supply curve is S_0.)

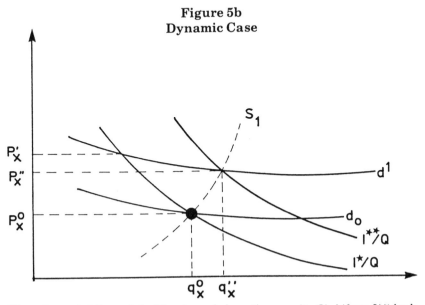

Figure 5b
Dynamic Case

(*Note*: Demand shift coupled with enhanced absorptive capacity (I* shifts to I**) leads
to output expansion and smaller price increase. Supply-price path is S_1.)

Figure 6a
World Supply and Demand
(Elastic Demand)

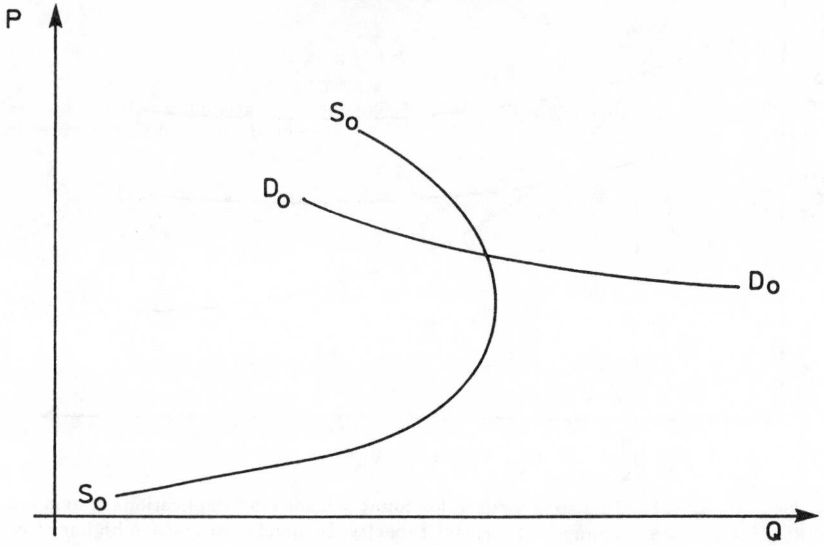

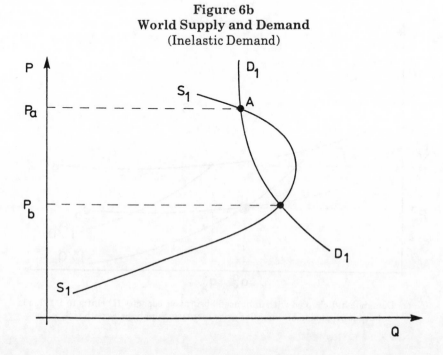

Figure 6b
World Supply and Demand
(Inelastic Demand)

Notes

[1] Nobel Laureat Milton Friedman reflected the views of many in the economics profession when in 1974 he predicted the imminent collapse of OPEC world crude prices.

[2] Further definition of what is meant by "needs," "requirements," and cheating is provided below.

[3] A backward-bending supply curve implies a negative relationship between current price and current production. This construct is developed more fully in the second section and the Appendix.

[4] The political risks are not just the expropriation risk but the internal political risk stemming from the negative reaction of Islamic fundamentalists to a perception that conservation is being abandoned in favour of profligate policies that serve the interests of the oil-consuming nations.

[5] Quite simply, export receipts at existing levels of production have been more than adequate to meet current budgetary requirements. The loss of Iranian production in 1978–79 is partly responsible for this outcome.

[6] As explained below, this will be assisted by the new investment environment of the 1980s, which promises to yield real returns to producing-country investments.

[7] As one Kuwaiti observed, "Kuwait was losing a large amount of money in its portfolio investments as a result of rising inflation and currency depreciation. Oil in the ground is better than continuously depreciating cash" (Al-Sabah, 1980, p. 35).

[8] It is not uncommon for OPEC ministers to appeal for lower production on grounds that (1) development is a slow process, and (2) that the real price of oil will "increase." Sheikh Ali of Kuwait, for instance, has advocated that OPEC countries adopt a 100:1 reserve-to-production ratio, arguing as follows:

> The attitude of the OPEC countries, amongst them Kuwait, on production should be to adopt a reserves to production ratio of 100:1, for two important economic reasons. The first is that economic development is a very long process. It is not a five or ten-year plan, but takes hundreds of years. Change does not come overnight or from one year to another. It is a question of social development and of changing certain concepts. The second reason is that we will always be in need of oil supplies, and the real price of oil will increase over the next 20 years and, for that matter, in the first part of the next century (*Middle East Economic Survey*, 29 October 1979, p. 4).

[9] As discussed below, placating foreign consumers and political allies in the West may provide a reason.

[10] As discussed below, oil-producing nations with small oil revenues (as a percentage of GNP) or large economies, such as Mexico and Nigeria, are unlikely to have a backward-bending supply curve in the relevant range of prices; the opposite can be expected for several OPEC nations including Libya, Kuwait, Abu Dhabi, and Qatar, which have low or moderate absorptive capacities. In the Saudi case, these proclivities are attenuated by political considerations (see the text).

[11] *Petroleum Intelligence Weekly* (12 May 1980), p. 4.

[12] *Middle East Economic Survey* (29 October 1979).

[13] This might appear to be a contradiction in that monopoly rents are attached to a market structure that is "competitive" in the sense that each producer is independently pursuing its own "best" interests. However, the result is the same as would be obtained under monopoly — namely, the existence of substantial economic rents, where per barrel rents are the difference between price and the sum of marginal costs and user costs determined on reasonable discount rate, elasticity, and reserve assumptions.

[14] See Griffin and Teece (1982, Chap. 1) for a discussion of the property rights perspective.

[15] See Griffin and Teece (1982, Chap. 1) for a discussion of monopoly profits in a Hotelling framework.

[16] Ghaddafi ordered a cut-back in output for the companies operating in Libya. Occidental Petroleum was forced to cut back by more than 50 per cent at which point Oxy capitulated by agreeing to pay $0.30 more per barrel by raising posted prices from $2.23 to $2.55 per barrel for 40° API Arabian Light.

[17] This is not withstanding that if wealth maximizing were the goal, each producer would have powerful incentives to cheat.

[18] The chasm had narrowed by October 1981 as OPEC appeared somewhat closer to an agreement on a unified price of $34 a barrel.

[19] Unless, of course, synthetics turn out to be a decreasing cost industry, which appears highly unlikely.

[20] This view is quite at odds with Professor Adelman, who has argued as follows:

> Nor shall we be distracted by the alleged political objectives of the oil producing nations, which are served perfectly by economic gain. There is no sacrifice or trade off of one or the other. The more money one has, the better position one is to make friends and put down enemies (Adelman, 1977, p. 28).

[21] *Middle East Economic Survey* (19 June 1978).

[22] See Adelman (1982).

[23] Consuming countries should also recognize that the removal of developmental bottle-necks (such as skills and transportation facilities) in key OPEC states will also serve to increase production to the extent to which it enhances domestic absorptive capacity.

[24] Consider the effect of a shift in the demand curve. Let $p(\lambda)$ be a solution of $k\,D(p) = S(p)$. We have $\hat{p} = \hat{p}(1)$. The elasticity of $\hat{p}$ with respect to λ, for $\lambda = 1$, is equal to $\dfrac{1}{E_s - E_d}$ where E_s and E_d are the elasticities of supply and demand. On the backward-bending part of the supply curve, $E_s > 1$; on the downward part, $E_s < 1$. Hence, assuming a constant elasticity of demand, the elasticity of p with respect to λ is higher in the downward-sloping part of the supply curve.

References

Adelman, M.A. (1977) "The Changing Structure of Big International Oil." In *Oil, Divestiture and National Security*, edited by Frank N. Trager, pp. 1–10. New York: Crane, Russak.

Adelman, Morris. (1982) "OPEC as a Cartel." In *OPEC Behavior & World Oil Prices*, edited by J.M. Griffin and D.J. Teece, pp. 37–63. London: Allen and Unwin.

Al-Sabah, Y.S.F. (1980) *The Oil Economy of Kuwait*. London: Kegan Paul.

Blair, John M. (1976) *The Control of Oil*. New York: Pantheon.

Eckaus, R.S. (1972) "Absorptive Capacity as a Constraint Due to Maturation Processes." In *Development and Planning: Essays in Honour of Paul Rosenstein-Rodan*, edited by Jagdish Bhagwati and Richard S. Eckaus, pp. 79–108. London: Allen and Unwin.

Griffin, J.M. and Teece, D.J., eds. (1982) *OPEC Behavior & World Oil Prices*. London: Allen and Unwin.

Johany, Ali D. (1978) "OPEC Is Not a Cartel: A Property Rights Explanation of the Rise in Crude Oil Prices." Ph.D. dissertation, University of California, Santa Barbara.

Manne, Alan. (1979) "International Energy Supplies and Demands: A Long Term Perspective." Stanford, Calif.: Stanford University International Energy Program.

Mead, Walter J. (1979) "The Performance of Government in Energy Regulations." *American Economic Review* 69 (May): 352–56.

Rosenstein-Rodan, P.N. (1961) "International Aid for Underdeveloped Countries." *The Review of Economics and Statistics* 43 (May): 107–38.

Teece, David J. and Griffin, James. (1982) "A Tariff on Imported Oil." *Journal of Contemporary Studies* (Winter): 89–92.

Turner, Louis and Bedore, James M. (1979) *Middle East Industrialisation: A Study of Saudi and Iranian Downstream Investments.* Westmead: Saxon House for Royal Institute of International Affairs.

[20]

Chapter 24

NATURAL RESOURCE CARTELS*

DAVID J. TEECE

Haas School of Business, University of California, 554 Barrows Hall, Berkeley, CA 94720, USA

DAVID SUNDING

Law and Economics Consulting Group (LECG), Parker Plaza, 2560 9th Street, Suite 212, Berkeley, CA 94710, USA

ELAINE MOSAKOWSKI

Graduate School of Management, University of California at Los Angeles (UCLA), 6359 Anderson, 405 Hilgard Avenue, Los Angeles, CA 90024-1482, USA

1. Introduction

The defining characteristic of cartels is that they involve explicit communication and agreement among competitors to control output and price. Various synonyms are commonly used to describe these arrangements, including combine, conference, and syndicate. The loosest form of cartel is a 'gentleman's agreement' to fix prices and/or control output. A tighter form would involve separately owned, independent or public enterprises unified under a formal charter or agreement to engage in restrictive practices. The cartel concept as defined does not include collusion which is merely tacit and which does not involve an agreement, although it is recognized that the market outcomes associated with tacit collusion may sometimes be quite similar to those obtained from cartelization.

A cartel, if it is to be successful, must confront and surmount several organizational and market challenges. The external challenge is to discourage and, if possible, prevent production by non-members. The internal challenges are more numerous, although arguably not so severe: to calculate the optimal level of production and prices for the commodity being cartelized; to allocate that production, or the returns from it, among the members of the cartel; and to detect and punish cheating.

---

* We thank Robert Pindyck and James Griffin for helpful criticism. This paper was drafted in 1984 and revised in 1992.

Handbook of Natural Resource and Energy Economics, vol. III, edited by A.V. Kneese and J.L. Sweeney

Conventional textbook theory teaches that cartels are inherently unstable because of the difficulties associated with sharing, detecting and punishing. Unless the cartel members have identical cost functions, discount rates, and a host of other common attributes, profit-maximizing members will disagree about the appropriate level of cartel output and the division of that output among the cartel members. When government entities are involved, with discount rates set by political whim rather than by objective market consideration, this later problem will be particularly serious, as many observers, including Osborne (1976) and Griffin and Teece (1982, ch. 1) have indicated. Those members that judge the production agreement as unfair will cheat on that account alone, while all members will have an incentive to cheat if they believe that deterrence is weak. In the standard formulation, cheating dominates over observing the agreement; so the cartel collapses, assuming it were ever to become established in the first place.

The traditional cartel theory based on maximizing behavior of cartel members tends to be somewhat strained. Both the creation and maintenance of cartels is difficult, though not impossible, to explain. Game theory addresses some of these deficiencies. The most important results in this recent effort stem from 'Folk Theorems' for repeated games such as that described by Fudenberg and Maskin (1986) and reputation models of the type formalized by Kreps et al. (1982). These theorems show the types of cooperative behavior that are attainable with repeated contact when cartel members employ sophisticated monitoring and punishment strategies. Their results indicate that in theory cartels can achieve a high degree of cooperation, thus laying a foundation for the treatment of cartels as cooperative institutions.

In Section 2 we consider the major classes of theories of cartel objectives and behavior. Whether cartels can solve their problems in principle is not as interesting as the question of whether they can solve their problems in practice. Some clearly have, at least for certain periods. Successful cartels include a number of exhaustible resource cartels.

Section 3 presents a number of theoretical and empirical results on the durability of cartels. In Section 4 we consider some propositions concerning the welfare implications of cartels. The typical argument treats cartels as monopolists, and concludes that cartels subtract from social welfare by choosing suboptimal extraction paths. While we largely agree with this treatment of the problem, we also consider conditions under which such cooperation is socially beneficial. Finally, in Section 5 we discuss in detail some natural resource cartels and use this evidence to assess the cartel theories presented in Section 2. We consider the international oil, mercury, uranium, and diamond cartels.

2. The cartel problem

There are three major classes of theories concerning the nature of exhaustible resource cartels: (1) The behavior of resource cartels can be described by a simple welfare diminishing monopoly model or by treating a subset of producers (or countries) as a dominant firm, with the remaining producers behaving as a competitive fringe. (2) Cartel behavior can be described by non-traditional objectives, particularly satisfaction of target revenue requirements. (3) Cartel behavior can in some circumstances generate positive welfare gains. We consider (1) and (2) below. In Section 3 we briefly touch upon (3).

2.1. Monopoly

The behavior of a cartel can be considered to approximate a single-firm monopoly. This is a rather extreme characterization of cartel behavior, but is nevertheless a useful starting point. Thus consider a natural resource cartel in which the decision to produce today does not influence future production costs.

Even in this simple world it is important to recognize that the decision to produce today precludes the possibility of producing at some time in the future. In effect, there is an opportunity cost, or user cost, associated with the decision to produce. Harold Hotelling (1931) first articulated the intertemporal conditions for profit maximization in extractive industries. Hotelling chose to make the simplifying assumption that marginal production costs are zero. His now-standard arbitrage rule holds that prices will rise at the rate of interest under competitive market conditions, or

$$P_0 = \frac{P_1}{1 + r} = \frac{P_2}{(1 + r)^2} = \cdots = \frac{P_T}{(1 + r)^T}, \tag{1}$$

where P_t is the market price in period t, and r is the (common) rate of discount.

For the monopolist (or the cartel), marginal revenues, which are less than price as in the static case, will rise over time at the rate of interest, or

$$\mathrm{MR}_0 = \frac{\mathrm{MR}_1}{1 + r} = \frac{\mathrm{MR}_2}{(1 + r)^2} = \cdots = \frac{\mathrm{MR}_T}{(1 + r)^T}. \tag{2}$$

We should note that eq. (2) is both a flow and a stock equilibrium condition, as discussed by Solow (1974) and Dasgupta and Heal (1979).

Monopoly prices determined by eq. (2) obviously rise over time with marginal revenue, but the rate of increase depends on the characteristics of the market demand curve. It is natural to investigate the competitive and monopoly price paths

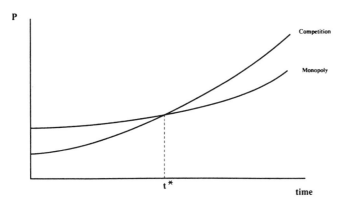

Fig. 1. Alternative price paths for an exhaustible resource.

governed by eqs. (1) and (2), respectively, by making alternative assumptions about how the elasticity of demand varies along the demand curve.

In the case of a constant elasticity of demand, the depletion policy undertaken by a cartel is identical to that undertaken under perfect competition. The intuition is simple: the price resulting from an intertemporal competitive equilibrium rises at the rate of interest, while under monopoly marginal revenue rises at this rate. Marginal revenue is proportional to price when the demand function has constant elasticity, so eqs. (1) and (2) imply the same extraction paths.

A more plausible situation is one in which the elasticity of demand increases with the price of the resource. This may arise, for example, when there exist actual or potential substitute technologies for the resource in question that are viable at high prices or, somewhat more mechanically, when the cartel faces a linear demand curve. In this case, the monopoly price path is always flatter than the competitive price path, and must cross the competitive price path once from above. Figure 1 contrasts the price paths. This argument illustrates the adage that "The monopolist is the conservationist's best friend". The monopoly extraction agreement distorts the socially optimal pattern of resource depletion by encouraging too much conservation initially, that is before t^* in Figure 1.

Hotelling's arbitrage principle provides the most fundamental characterization of the behavior of resource cartels as monopolies. It is not, however, sufficient to describe the behavior of even a simple monopolist in several significant and realistic cases. Perhaps most important is a situation in which there exists a 'backstop technology'. In this case, it is common to assume that there is some price above which the resource cannot be sold. The optimal monopoly price trajectory may

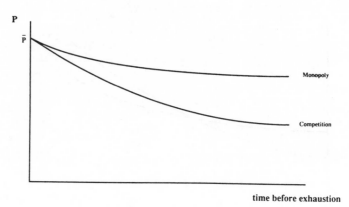

Fig. 2. Alternative price paths with backstop.

then be derived by working backwards from the backstop price with the arbitrage condition.

To determine the date of exhaustion under these conditions, it is analytically convenient to move backwards through time from the date at which price equals its maximum and note that the price falls for reasons just discussed. Price determines consumption at each date, and also cumulative consumption. The time to exhaustion is simply determined by stopping the clock when cumulative consumption equals the total stock. Figure 2 gives price and depletion paths for a monopoly cartel and a competitive industry in the presence of a backstop technology for the case of a linear demand curve.

This analysis highlights the fact that resource cartels are even more difficult to form and maintain than are collusive institutions in the more familiar static case. Members must agree on the size of the total stock, future demand conditions, substitute goods, and discount rates; otherwise they will disagree as to the optimal price path. In some cases, however, the problems faced by resource cartels may not be so different from those faced by static cartels since Hotelling rents are small for many commodities in relation to costs. In this event, agreement on depletion rates will not be an empirically decisive factor in determining cartel behavior or success.

A closely related class of models of cartel behavior envisions the cartel as consisting of a core number of firms or countries acting cooperatively in the presence of a competitive fringe. These models typically treat the cartel as a Stackelberg leader that announces a time-path of prices. The fringe reacts to this announcement by choosing a profit-maximizing extraction path. Papers in this genre include Salant (1976), Gilbert (1978), Lewis and Schmalensee (1978, 1982), Ulph and Folie (1980), and Ulph (1982). The analysis in this case is considerably

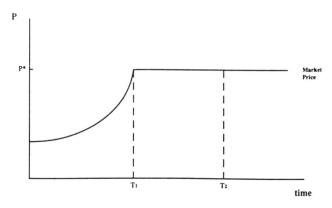

Fig. 3. Limit pricing.

more complicated than in the case of either perfect competition or monopoly. The previous section indicated that the extraction behavior of a monopoly cartel could be described by the Hotelling rule and, where necessary, by consideration of the constraints imposed by a backstop technology. In the case of a dominant firm facing a competitive fringe, the relationship between price and marginal revenue becomes more complex. We illustrate some of the complexities here by considering one important, although admittedly special, case: limit pricing.

Suppose that a cartel must decide on an extraction plan in the presence of a fringe that supplies elastically above a certain price, say p. The cartel's marginal revenue schedule then has a kink at p since it cannot feasibly set a higher price and faces no competition at lower prices. Suppose further that the demand function is iso-elastic and has greater than unitary elasticity below p^*. There is a familiar equilibrium in this case shown in Figure 3. Initially the cartel prices below p^* and prices rise at the rate of interest. Between T_1 and T_2 the cartel sells its remaining stock at p^*. Finally, the fringe produces at p^* until its stock is exhausted. Gilbert (1978) and Dasgupta and Heal (1979) consider the more complex cases of unitary and inelastic demand at p^*.

This core–fringe market structure highlights another important problem faced by a resource cartel in addition to those faced by static cartels: the possibility of the dynamic inconsistency of extraction plans derived via the maximum principle. Our analysis to this point has assumed that all members of the cartel, and indeed all fringe firms, commit to extraction paths and do not deviate from these plans. Modelling cartel behavior with commitment is equivalent to assuming the existence of well-functioning futures markets wherein producers can contract with consumers for current and future delivery of the resource at prespecified prices. In the

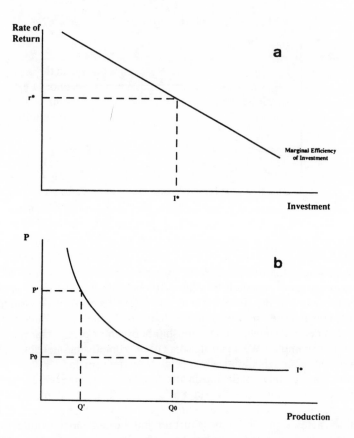

Fig. 4. Target revenue model: (a) investment determination; (b) output determination.

absence of futures markets, commitments to price paths are typically not credible. Newbery (1981) and Ulph (1982) were among the first to show that there is an incentive to deviate from these plans derived from the maximum principle in a number of realistic cases. In particular, they show that the problem of dynamic inconsistency is especially important in the case of a cartel facing a competitive fringe. Computation of dynamically consistent plans, defined as extraction plans and implied price paths that maximize discounted profit for each firm at each date, imposes a significant burden on industry participants. To the extent that these plans differ from desired behavior at any instant in time, dynamic inconsistency is a basis for conflict.

2.2. *Target revenue models*

Target revenue models depict resource cartels as a collection of firms whose production decisions are made with reference to budgetary requirements. As described in Teece (1982), these budgetary requirements are, in the case of nation-states, determined by absorptive capacity and other macroeconomic concerns.

More formally, cartel revenues can be considered as the source of funding for potential investment projects, which can be arrayed along a representative marginal efficiency of investment schedule (see Figure 4a). If a country is unwilling to invest for return less than r^* then investment needs are limited by I^*. In Figure 4b, if production decisions are made in order to meet the investment objective represented by I^*, then increases in the world price (from P_0 to P') in the current period will tend to result in reduced production (Q_0 to Q') in the current period, and conversely. The supply schedule thereby generated will have the 'wrong' slope; that is, it will be backward bending, at least over the relevant range. This property also exists in Cremer and Salehi-Isfahani's (1980) consideration of OPEC and in Griffin and Steele (1980) [1].

An intertemporal dimension can be readily added: economic development can be viewed as expanding investment opportunities and thereby raising the revenue target. Consequently, any specific backward-bending supply curve is dependent on a given level of infrastructure. Given adjustment time, the target revenue can rise substantially; so the target revenue model might be thought of as a more adequate description of cartel behavior in the short run than in the long run, and more for economies highly dependent on oil revenues than for economies that are diversified. However, it can be argued that the target revenue model has long-run predictive implications for countries with more limited potential for expanding domestic investments. Earnings from current investment activity may generate sufficient returns to partially finance future investment plans, enabling a lower dependency on revenues for domestic investment programs.

3. The durability of cartels

The cartel problem involves surmounting both external challenges (production by nonmembers) and internal problems (calculating the optimal cartel production, allocating production, detecting cheating, and deterring cheating). In this section we examine factors which seem to influence the ability of producers to meet these challenges. In short, we examine conditions that favor cartel formation and factors which contribute to cartel durability.

---

[1] The target revenue model and the backward sloped supply schedule were first put forward by industry economists in the 1970s.

We begin by noting that the answers to these questions are complex and not well understood in any systematic way. Nevertheless, received theory does provide some valuable insights. In a strictly rational world where cartel agreements were enforceable a cartel would be undertaken if and only if the present value of the cartel's joint profits from monopoly pricing exceeded the present value of the expected cost of operation and enforcement. In such a world, the formation of potentially profitable cartels is blocked only by its lack of inventiveness with respect to mechanisms for detection and deterrence.

In reality, the existence of net gains from cartelization will generally not suffice to enable a cartel to be formed. Cartel formation is often hampered by the inability of the potential cartel members to strike a deal, and to manage a deal once it is struck. For an efficient cartel, it is not enough to divide markets or agree on a common price. In order to minimize the aggregate cost of producing the joint profit-maximizing output, it will ordinarily be necessary to devise some revenue-sharing scheme involving side payments. Without side payments, the feasible locus of efficient profit outcomes will contain points inconsistent with joint profit maximization. Thus, an important potential limit on the ability of producers to reach an agreement is posed by contractual difficulties and uncertainty. Differences in sellers' objectives (assuming they are not strict profit maximizers) and their forecasts of market demand contribute to these costs. Where a depletable natural resource is involved in which user costs are substantial, then differences in discount rates and forecasts of future reserve additions compound the problem. Oligopoly theory in the Fellner (1965) and Williamson (1975, ch. 12) tradition recognizes how such inconsistencies prevent cartels from ever simulating pure monopoly outcomes.

In an interesting paper, Cramton and Palfrey (1990) highlight the difficulties posed by asymmetric information about cost and demand for cartel members bargaining about production and revenue-sharing rules. They show that, for at least some common environments attaining in the absence of collusion, the excess payments necessary to induce truth-telling in the revelation mechanism with incomplete cost information are larger than the gains from collusion when the number of industry participants is sufficiently large. The opposite result holds for the common value situation of asymmetric demand information.

Even though theory indicates that cartels fall short of complete joint profit maximization, they can extract monopoly rents of nontrivial magnitudes, and the industrial organization literature has endeavored to identify the structural conditions and sellers' strategies capable of sustaining a noncooperative market bargain. It emphasizes the importance of market structure and the fewness and similarity of producers. Few sellers are a necessary but not sufficient condition for collusion; many sellers are a sufficient though not necessary condition for competition. It also emphasizes the importance of inelastic demand, not so much because it implies that the monopoly price premium is larger the more inelastic the demand, but because it suggests the absence of competition from outside the industry that might tend to upset and undo the collusive deal worked out among the industry participants.

Economic theory emphasizes the fragility of cartels in the face of the temptation which every member has to cheat by surreptitiously providing the market with a little extra production. The size of the temptation swings on at least three classes of factors, which we now examine.

The first is the behavior of short-run marginal cost in the neighborhood of the individual firms post cartel level of output. If the gap between marginal cost and price is large and if marginal cost continues to fall for the individual producer, the per unit profit is likely to be substantial and the incentive to cheat enormous.

The second factor is the elasticity of the individual producer's demand curve. This determines the responsiveness of sales to whatever discounts the cheater offers to move his output. Obviously, the more elastic the demand, the less the discount that must be offered and the greater the incremental profit. The less the product differentiation, the higher the elasticity. The ability of the cheater to price discriminate also affects the profitability of this behavior. If clandestine price cuts can be offered to lure new buyers while preserving the price structure in place to existing buyers, then cheating is especially seductive to the producer.

A third influence on the incentive to cheat is the probability of detection and the costliness of the punishment which the other cartel members are able to impose. Orr and MacAvoy (1965) have developed a model in which the price information is transmitted only with a lag so that the price cutter enjoys some increased profits before discovery, although reduced profits afterward. If enforcement takes the form of matching the cheater's price cuts, the potential cheater can calculate the optimal price cut. The present value of the profits expected from cheating will exceed those of remaining loyal if the lag before detection is long enough. Besides the lag, the price cutter's expected return depends on the likelihood of detection, which depends upon the form in which information passes through the market. The 'trigger price' literature [most notably Stigler (1964), Green and Porter (1984) and Abreu, Pearce and Stacchetti (1985)] reinforces the difficulty of collusion when prices are imperfectly known.

A system of open price quotas often confounds cheating as the same price will generally have to be offered to all buyers and will become known to all sellers simultaneously. If price quotations are made on a customer-by-customer basis, several outcomes appear possible. The buyer with the special deal may wish to cooperate in keeping it secret, fearing that if other buyers hear of it they will demand equally favorable terms. This is likely if the cartel commodity is an intermediate product, the acquisition price of which affects the buyers' competitive position in downstream markets. It is possible, however, that the buyer may judge the best course of action to be playing one cartel member off against another in the hope of getting a better price. This runs the risk, however, of providing other cartel members with the information they need to share in order to discipline the cheater.

Obviously, the most likely outcome is difficult to predict except upon various assumptions about the internal structure and operating mechanisms of the cartel.

The fundamental tension in cartel arrangements is that there are incentives for firms both to form and to undermine cooperative institutions. There has been a great deal of attention paid in the last few years to models that exploit these incentives to predict when in the business cycle cartels are most likely to occur. Stigler (1964) and Green and Porter (1984) note that when prices are not directly observable and demand is subject to random fluctuations, undercutting an agreement on prices is observationally equivalent to an inward shift of the demand curve. When cartel members see market price falling below a certain level (the trigger price), they rationally respond by expanding their own outputs for a finite period of time, even if there has been no cheating and members *know* there has been no cheating! Despite the eventual occurrence of this unwarranted punishment, a trigger price scheme is attractive to the cartel since a sufficiently long reversion phase will deter cheating. The empirical implication of the trigger price mechanism is that cartel agreements are more likely to break down when demand is falling, as during business cycle downturns.

Recently, Rotemberg and Saloner (1986) have argued that they expect exactly the opposite result: cartels are more likely to fail when demand is rising since this increases the benefit from cheating. Thus, while theory has identified economic fluctuation as an important determinant of cartel durability, it is unable to predict the direction of incentives in this case; we must rely on empirical evidence to sort things out.

In an important test of these competing theories and other predictions about cartel behavior, Suslow (1992) examined the durability of international cartels in 45 industries between 1920 and 1939. During this period cartels were often overt, with European firms taking the lead due to relatively lax antitrust laws. Most of the cartels considered were governed by formal contracts between members, with United States participants being an occasional exception.

Suslow finds that the average non-censored cartel episode lasted 2.8 years, and the longest episode was more than 13 years. Censoring in this case means that the cartel agreement was cut short by an exogenous factor. Table 1 lists the reasons, endogenous and exogenous, for the demise of cartels studied by Suslow.

The number of firms comprising the cartel appears to influence durability. Information on firm membership was available for 41 episodes; of these 64% had five or fewer members, and 83% had 10 or fewer members. Further, "formal cooperation, rather than tacit coordination, is chosen in markets with relatively few firms." [Suslow (1992) p. 12]

Another significant finding of Suslow's study is that longer-lived cartels tended to employ more complex and specialized governance structures. In particular, there seems to be a requirement that successful cartels put production quotas and punishments into the contract.

Table 1
Reasons for termination of cartel contract[a]

Cause of termination	Frequency
Cheating on agreement	11
Defection of important cartel member	5
Fringe production undermines agreement	11
Tariff	2
Direct government intervention	1
Antitrust indictment	13
World War II	27
	——— +
Total	71

[a] From Suslow (1992), p. 42.

Finally, economic activity appears to be an important factor governing cartel durability. Using indices of industrial production for the United States, the United Kingdom, and France, Suslow concludes that economic volatility, or positive *and* negative 'surprises', contributes to the collapse of cartels. Her results also indicate that sub-trend economic activity tends to decrease cartel survival. Suslow's investigation thus lends empirical support to Green and Porter's characterization of cartel behavior.

4. Welfare implications of cartels

In standard treatments, the welfare implications of cartels are usually presented in a fairly straightforward and unambiguous fashion: cartels, to the extent to which they are successful, promote adoption of suboptimal extraction plans. In short, cartels are typically folded into the standard treatment of market power with the associated deadweight losses. However, the literature does contain threads of arguments indicating that the negative welfare implications of cartels rest upon the assumption that in their absence competition would reign and moreover would yield a superior allocation of the economy's resources. We outline these arguments below and use them to argue that the received doctrine is probably correct, but that under certain conditions cartels may in fact augment, rather than subtract from, economic efficiency in a laissez-faire economy.

4.1. The coordination of complementary and competitive investments

The ideal state to which cartels are usually compared is that of the perfectly competitive economy in equilibrium. Serious scholars have questioned the ability of an economy to reach this state. The justification for use of the concept is the supposed tendency toward equilibrium, which is, however, an empirical rather than a theoretical proposition. Indeed, G.B. Richardson (1960, pp. 1–2) argues that "the general equilibrium of production and exchange ... cannot properly be regarded as a configuration toward which a hypothetical perfectly competitive economy would gravitate or at which it would remain at rest." His argument is the obvious one, that for equilibrium to be attained, firms need information about each other's investment plans. In the absence of the sharing of investment plans, however, this is not going to be fully and accurately revealed. Accordingly, "it is difficult to see what but an act of faith can enable us to believe that equilibrium would be reached" [Richardson (1960) p. 11]. Indeed, as Hahn (1973) has pointed out, the basic purpose of the Arrow–Debreu model of equilibrium is to show why the economy cannot be in this state.

As explained by Richardson (1960, p. 36), the problem with the model of perfect competition is that it contains no special machinery to ensure that investment programs are made known to all concerned at the time of their conception. "Price movements, by themselves, do not form an adequate system of signalling" (p. 37). Koopmans (1958, pp. 146–147) recognizes the same deficiency in competitive theory noting that "To my knowledge no formal model of resource allocation through competitive markets has been developed, which recognizes ignorance about decision makers' future actions, preferences or states of technological information as the main source of uncertainty confronting each individual decision maker and which at the same time acknowledges the fact that forward markets on which anticipations and intentions could be tested and adjusted do not exist in sufficient variety and with a sufficient span of foresight to make presently developed theory regarding the efficiency of competitive markets applicable."

It may be that certain kinds of cartel arrangements, particularly those that involve the disclosure of information on investment plans, and perhaps even the coordination of them, may contribute to rather than subtract from economic welfare. Demesetz (1982, p. 50) has suggested that a similar quandary exists with respect to the role of trade associations which distribute price information among their members.

Recent economic theory lends some credence to this assertion, particularly regarding the welfare-enhancing effects of information exchange. While the literature has pointed out that the type of competition (Bertrand vs. Cournot) and uncertainty (private values vs. common values) have pivoted importance in explaining the incentives for information exchange, Vives (1990) has shown that exclusionary disclosure is much easier to motivate than nonexclusionary disclosure. That is, if information can be limited to a subset of firms, then exchanges (via institutions such as cartels or trade associations) is easy to explain. Vives also points out that, at least under Cournot competition, exclusionary disclosure increases total surplus.

The notion that cartels may perform a socially beneficial function in this regard is closely akin to arguments commonly advanced in favor of indicative planning [Meade (1970)]. Indicative planning has been used in France and other countries in an attempt to improve the information available to decision makers, supposedly reducing uncertainty [Cohen (1969)]. The questionable success of the process may not be so much the result of a flawed concept as of flawed implementation. For instance, if the important competitive factors are international, an indicative planning exercise which is domestic in scope is doomed to failure. However, it does seem possible, theoretically at least, that a cartel could inspire efficiency relative to alternatives if it could select and trace an expansion or contraction path for industry capacity that was more closely matched to long-run demand than a laissez-faire competitive economy without cooperation could generate. Our position in this regard is very tentative and is best viewed as a hypothesis. The literature on the issue is extremely sketchy, although earlier treatment of cartels did distinguish between 'cartels of conditions' and those that regulate output, sales, and prices. 'Cartels of conditions' [Plummer (1951) p. 18] include agreements relating to information exchange, product standardization, patent exchanging and pooling, and the like. According to Plummer, "Standardization, cooperative research, and similar arrangements help to increase efficiency and economy; and therefore little or no objection can be raised to 'cartels of conditions,' unless patents are deliberately acquired and put into 'cold storage' to keep them from producers not in the cartel, or similar policies, advantageous to the private interests concerned but against the public interest, are pursued. But we must not overlook the fact that cartels of the first type can pave the way to those of the second type, so that 'closer cooperation' may ultimately evolve out of an apparently harmless 'cartel of conditions'." If advantages do exist from cartelization, the welfare analysis is not simple. Our point is that the case against *all* forms of industry coordination and cooperation among competitors is rather weak and is based on the assumption that the available adjustment processes enable equilibrium conditions to be selected and implemented in a frictionless fashion – or at least more efficiently than an alternative process based upon cooperation and coordination [Jorde and Teece (1992)].

4.2. Price stabilization cartels

A discussion of cartels would not be complete without mention of international commodity agreements, which often have many cartel-like features. They are often directed at stabilizing export prices, if not export receipts, for countries whose exports are specialized in the traded commodity in question. Economists generally view such arrangements with great suspicion because the implicit agenda is often to raise as well as stabilize prices. To the extent that the objective is to raise prices, the analysis of cartels presented above seems to be applicable.

The more intriguing questions relate to whether price stabilization can augment economic welfare. Once again the answer swings importantly on the alternatives. If it is the model of perfect competition with fully developed futures markets and mechanisms to attain instant equilibrium, then the welfare implications would appear to be negative. On the other hand, if futures markets are nonexistent or highly incomplete and price information is the only investment signal available to producers, the results may be quite different. As Behrman (1978) suggests, the issues are empirical rather than theoretical. Given that the empirical base which affords commentary is rather thin, we simply note this is a relatively unexplored area and an important direction for future research.

5. A synopsis of some natural resource cartels

5.1. Cartel issues raised with respect to world oil in the immediate post-embargo period

Two decades after the first oil shock of 1973–1974 there remains disagreement about the reasons for the price increase and the role that classical cartelization had to play. Aside from political explanations of what went on, there are three main classes of economic explanation that have been advanced. They are labelled here as the cartel explanation, the competitive explanation, and the target revenue explanation. Each is briefly surveyed below. More complete surveys can be found in Griffin and Teece (1982) and Teece (1983).

5.1.1. The cartel explanation

The view most widely accepted by economists is that OPEC effectively cartelized the world oil market, fixing prices above competitive levels and restricting output to support the common price. There are many early statements of this view, but the representation by Pindyck (1978) of OPEC as a monopolist is perhaps the starkest and most precise. In other versions, the dominant producer, Saudi Arabia, sets the price, allows the other OPEC producers to sell all they want, and supplies the remaining demand. Saudi Arabia is thus the 'balance wheel' or 'swing producer', absorbing demand and supply fluctuations in order to maintain the monopoly price. Such an arrangement creates no cartel problems. However, it does run the risk of inducing sufficient new production outside of Saudi Arabia to make the strategy nonviable for the Saudis. The stability of OPEC turns on whether world supply and demand at the monopoly price results in sufficient demand for Saudi oil to satisfy Saudi objectives. Put another way, the world price does not necessarily depend upon the strengths and weaknesses of cartel cohesion. In the simplest version of this model, the dominant producer chooses the best price from its own viewpoint, taking into account both present and future demand and supply of the competitive fringe at whatever price the dominant producer may choose. The problem facing Saudi Arabia is to choose a price path which maximizes its wealth over time. If the price set by the dominant producer is high enough to let fringe producers earn monopoly rents, they will have an incentive to expand their capacity. Also, new entrants will be attracted into the fringe. This causes a reduction in the residual demand confronting the dominant producer. If Saudi Arabia adopts a high discount rate, implicitly setting a low value on future profits, the dominant producer selects a higher initial price and makes room for an expanded competitive fringe, earning higher profits initially than later on. Its high prices and profits in the current period set into motion a chain of repercussions reducing the dominant producer's market share in future years.

In many instances, there is only one way for the dominant producer to avoid this outcome: it must adopt a lower discount rate, reducing its current price to a level at which new entry and the expansion of fringe members are discouraged. An overly simple but useful first approximation is to view the dominant producer's decision problems as dichotomous: either it sets high prices and accepts declining future market shares and profits, or it sets low current prices to deter all entry and expansion by fringe competitors. The latter strategy is commonly referred to as limit pricing, in that a price is selected which limits entry to zero. In reality, depending on the rate of discount, intermediate outcomes between these two extremes may well be chosen. Limit pricing is particularly germane with reference to synthetic oil production from shales, tar sands, and coal liquefaction. Since these fuel sources can be likened to a backstop fuel, available in elastic supply, a wealth-maximizing dominant producer with huge reserves would probably choose a price path below the price at which large quantities of synthetic fuels would be produced.

To introduce collusive elements into the model, a number of variants of the dominant-producer model have emerged, with a group of OPEC producers acting essentially as the single dominant producer. One popular view is that there is a 'cartel core' (e.g., Saudi Arabia, the United Arab Emirates, Kuwait, Qatar, and Libya) which behaves like a dominant firm. Analytically, this model is basically the same as what we have just described. The only significant difference is that the 'cartel core' version depends on cooperative behavior within the core; the dominant-producer version does not depend on collusion, explicit or tacit, for the generation of rents. This difference is important for assessing the stability of the cartel arrangement.

Models of this genre are the conventional wisdom among most economists. Adelman (1982), an influential disciple of this traditional view, has set forth the factual argument in support of this genre of models. Milton Friedman appears to adhere to it, as he predicted that OPEC will quickly go the way of other cartels and collapse, and along with it the price of crude oil. (Having been awarded a booby prize for his prediction by the Society for the Promotion of Humor in International Affairs, Friedman has confessed to a predictive error in timing, but not direction. The cartel will collapse 'sooner or later' according to his March 21, 1980 *Newsweek* column.)

5.1.2. Competitive views

An alternate view, advanced in one form by MacAvoy (1982) and in another by Johany (1978) and Mead (1979), is that the price increases merely reflect a shift in underlying supply and demand conditions. MacAvoy argues that a tight market with minimal excess capacity in 1973 and spot prices above contract prices was pushed over the brink by demand growth coupled with the embargo. MacAvoy (1982, p. 57) concludes that because of politically induced supply interruptions (the 1973–1974 embargo and the turmoil in Iran and Iraq during 1979–1980) "prices would have risen to four-fifths or more of present prices under open market conditions. This would have required a tripling of constant dollar crude prices. The operations of an open market would have been subject to fundamental constraints in accumulation of reserves and to income determined increases of year-to-year demand. **The conditions, and not OPEC caused most of the crude oil price increases in the 1970's**" (emphasis added). The argument is buttressed by an econometric model of the world petroleum market using parameter values derived where possible from the pre-1972 era. The model is then used to predict demand, supply, and price in the post-1973 era. The difference between simulated prices based on 'market fundamentals" and prices simulated with actual OPEC production is then attributed to cartel behavior.

While MacAvoy's concept of market fundamentals is never fully explained, it turns out to be critical to the interpretation and evaluation of his study. He hints that it is a market 'without cartels', one characterized by an 'open market'[2]. If this is the case, then a price path generated by market fundamentals need not be a Hotelling-type competitive price path calculated on the basis of known reserves, reasonable discount rates, and expectations as to future oil demand and reserve conditions. It is simply one generated in the absence of collusion and coordinated behavior. Such a price path might be well above or well below the (Hotelling) competitive path, especially if the production decisions of some producers are made with reference to revenue targets, as emphasized below. It seems important to know not only whether OPEC is a cartel, but also whether the price is above or below the Hotelling price path as this path is likely to be close to what would be observed were producers to behave according to the classical competitive model. MacAvoy does

---

[2] Further confusing the issue is mention that OPEC could conceivable "have been a factor in determining the fundamentals" [MacAvoy (1982) p. 3].

not distinguish between the two concepts, and this carelessness is likely to mean that too few readers will realize that the market fundamentals concept may refer to a set of conditions quite different from the usual conception of a competitive market. The MacAvoy argument can be labeled as a competitive interpretation of the world crude market.

In another version, henceforth labeled the property-rights view, Johany (1978) and Mead (1979) argue that the price regimes prevailing before and after 1973–1974 are best explained by appealing to the change in ownership patterns that transpired in the early 1970s. Until that time, the concessions granted by the producing countries to the oil companies permitted the companies to make unilateral production decisions. Accordingly, since production policies were essentially the prerogative of the companies, discount rate assumptions were made on the basis of the companies' perceptions of the future. Since expropriation risk was nontrivial in many countries in the 1960s, the wealth-maximizing strategy for the companies involved a high discount rate and rapid depletion. This was fueled by forever escalating royalty and tax demands by producer countries, which further served to reinforce expectations that profits would decline in the future. The result, according to Johany, was that the companies produced as if there were no tomorrow, depressing world crude oil prices in the process.

According to the property rights view, the events of 1973–74 marked a watershed in the world oil market, principally because of the transfer of control over production policies that occurred at that time. As Johany (1978, p. 107) explains it, "the oil producers decided to determine the price of their oil unilaterally rather than through negotiations with the oil companies as had been done in the past. Once the host countries became the ones who decided the rate of oil output and its price, the role of the companies had been essentially reduced to that of contractors. That amounted to a *de facto* nationalization of the crude oil deposits."

This reassignment of property rights was significant because the companies and the host countries had different discount rates and that implied different rates of output [Johany (1978) p. 107]. These differences would be traced to intrinsic differences in the discount rate, as well as to differences in risk evaluation. With lower discount rates, current production would fall, thereby driving up the world price. At the time of the transition, production would drop sharply, causing a switch to the higher price path. According to this line of reasoning, 1973–1974 represented such a transition period and switching to a higher price path.

The property-rights interpretation of the transformation of the world oil market is consistent with the observation that the world price during the 1970s did not appear to be threatened by cheating – such as the granting of secret price concessions by some members of OPEC in order to capture market shares from the others. Furthermore, there is evidence that the companies considered the expropriation risk in the 1960s to be real. In fact, significant episodes took place in Algeria, Iraq, Egypt, Iran, Libya, and Peru. These episodes illustrated the latent power of governments over the companies and the reality of the political risks inherent in the industry. The nationalization of foreign oil companies was an appealing way for governments to develop government-owned enterprises and to win popular support. Implicit threats of expropriation stood behind many less extreme forms of regulation.

It is instructive to set forth the major inadequacies of this theory. The most obvious inadequacy is that most oil-producing countries in the 1950s and 1960s were demanding that the companies expand production. The Shah of Iran pushed hard on the companies to expand production. This is completely at odds with the property-rights model. However, Iran might be considered an exception as the Shah's lust for current revenues was legend. Unfortunately, one is never likely to be entirely sure as to the relations between the companies and the countries as 'behind the doors' manipulation is likely to have been of some importance. Still another objection is that while this theory could presumably explain a portion of the 1973–1974 price increase, it offers no obvious interpretation to the doubling of prices in 1978–1979. As the transfer of ownership had long since occurred, further reductions in the discount rate are not apparent. Similarly, the rationale for changed expectations in other factors that could allow competitive prices to double is not apparent. It is not obvious that producers altered their long-run expectations in 1978–1979 regarding future reserves, future demand growth, the price of the backstop fuel, and so forth. Rather, following the rationale of a competitive model, one would expect that following the 1978–1979 price rise due to short-run supply constraints, the price would return to the initial price path, with an easing of these constraints.

5.1.3. The target revenue model

In its pure form the target revenue model explanation depicts OPEC, or at least its principal members, as a collection of nation states whose oil production decisions are made with reference to the requirements of the national budget. Budgetary needs are in turn a function of absorptive capacity which is limited where the economy is small in relation to oil revenues or where the infrastructure is inadequate to support rapid escalation in consumption and investment levels.

A challenge can be mounted to the target-revenue approach on grounds that it is unrealistic to assume that foreign investment is not a viable alternative to domestic investment, for this is the assumption implicit in the analysis. One reply is that for various periods of history OPEC producers have perceived foreign investment to be unattractive, not only from perceived low returns (generally when the dollar was depreciating in relation to other key currencies and producers held dollar-denominated assets) but also because of political risks. These risks are of several kinds. One is the risk that the nation in which the funds were deposited might confiscate, freeze, or otherwise manipulate financial assets for political reasons.

The other is that the existence of huge external liquid assets might facilitate the survival of revolutionary regimes, which if successful in displacing existing governments would have command over liquid assets that could be used to placate friends and buy off enemies. While admittedly such risks exist, it seems highly implausible that wealth-maximizing agents in selecting a portfolio of assets would limit those portfolios to oil in the ground and domestic investments. As the Iranian experience proves, the latter are not devoid of their risks. A portfolio including foreign debt and equity securities would presumably both increase the expected return and reduce the overall risk of the portfolio. In view of these considerations, our interpretation of the target revenue model is that it eschews wealth-maximizing behavior.

An important implication for OPEC, as explained in Teece (1982), is that prices can rise above the Hotelling competitive price path even in the absence of coordinated action by OPEC members. If an event such as the embargo brings current oil revenues into the target revenue range, there is no desire for individual producers to cheat by expanding production. Conversely, if demand reduction or rapid expansion in absorptive capacity creates a situation in which revenue needs are not met, then the producer in question will expand production until revenue objectives are satisfied. With these characteristics of instability, the model allows for behavior by a number of producers which could lead to a collapse of the cartel price.

5.1.4. Evidence

It is perhaps amazing that such a variety of models can exist contemporaneously, and sometimes contemptuously, without much in the way of serious empirical efforts to select among them. As Gately (1984) points out, initially there was much optimism that the wealth-maximizing approach would help us understand OPEC behavior. But disillusionment has set in. It seems that from a theoretical point of view, models of OPEC oil pricing have reached practical limits as tools of analysis [Pindyck (1982) p. 109]. The normative sensibility of such models has been questioned by many, including Teece (1982) and Gately (1984).

In addition to the formulation of more robust models of the world oil market, the predictive power of existing models needs to be tested. This task has been much neglected to date, the standard practice being to validate the choice of model by arbitrarily pointing to selected events which are consistent with the model and then ignoring anomalies. Such an approach is obviously unscientific.

Part of the difficulty is in specifying a valid test. Considerable progress in this direction has recently been made by Griffin (1985). To test competing models, he focuses on each individual country's production decision. The determinants of each OPEC country's oil production (Q) are formalized based on various competing models of OPEC behavior. These determinants are then systematically

Table 2
Hypothesized coefficient signs of various models. [Source: Griffin (1985).]

Model[a]	Sign β_i	Sign γ_i	Sign δ_i	Sign ϕ_i
I. Cartel model: $\ln Q_{i,t} = \alpha_i + \beta_i \ln Q_{i,t}^{00} + \gamma_i \ln P_i$				
1. Strict market sharing	$\beta_i = 1$	$\gamma_i = 0$		
2. Market sharing	$\beta_i = 1$	$\gamma_i \gtreqqless 0$		
3. Partial market sharing	$\beta_i > 1$	$\gamma_i \gtreqqless 0$		
II. Competitive model				
1. Standard model: $\ln Q_{i,t} = \alpha_i + \gamma_i \ln P_t$		$\gamma_i > 0$		
2. Property rights model: $\ln Q_{i,t} = \alpha_i + \phi_i G_{i,t}$				$\phi_i < 0$
III. Target revenue model: $\ln Q_{i,t} = \alpha_i + \delta_i \ln I_{i,t}^* + \gamma_i \ln P_t$				
1. Strict version		$\gamma_i = -1$	$\delta_i = 1$	
2. Partial version		$\gamma_i < 0$	$\delta_i > 0$	

[a] Symbols:
Q: production in barrels per day;
Q^{00}: production of OPEC oil less that of the ith producer;
P: price of Saudi Light 34° API;
G: government production divided by total production;
I: gross fixed capital formation.

assessed with respect to their conformity with resulting hypotheses. The advantage of focusing on the individual country's production behavior, as Griffin points out, is that "each model yields quite disparate hypotheses about the determinants of production. The emphasis here is on testing the simplest version of the model, necessarily omitting nuances which would improve the explanation power of the model" [Griffin (1985) p. 2]. Table 2 summarizes Griffin's formulations and the signs of the hypothesized coefficients.

The simplified models were then tested with quarterly data for the period 1971:I through 1983:III [3] for the 13 OPEC countries with the exception, for data availability reasons, of Ecuador and Gabon. For Iran and Iraq, respectively, the sample is truncated to delete the period following the revolution in Iran (78:III) and the beginning of the Iran/Iraq war (80:III).

Griffin's results (summarized in Table 3) are suggestive, if not instructive. Cartel-like behavior was rejected for Iraq only, classical competitive behavior was rejected for six of the 11 countries, the property rights model rejected for eight of the 11 countries, and the target revenue approach was rejected for all but Algeria. However, if the sample is restricted to the period 74:I to 81:IV, the target revenue hypothesis cannot be rejected for four of the 10 countries. Clearly, this model seems to work best when prices are rising. However, Griffin concludes that "the results

---

[3] The exception was the property-rights model.

Table 3
Results of tests: four models of OPEC behavior[a]

Country	Partial market sharing cartel	Classical competitive	Property rights (competitive)	Target revenue
Saudi Arabia	NR	NR	R	R
Kuwait	NR	R	NR	R
Qatar	NR	R	R	R
UAE	NR	NR	R	R
Iraq	R	NR	R	R
Libya	NR	R	NR	R
Algeria	NR	R	R	NR
Iran	NR	NR	R	R
Nigeria	NR	R	R	R
Indonesia	NR	NR	R	R
Venezuela	NR	R	NR	R

[a] Adapted from Griffin (1985), Tables 2–5.
Codes: R, hypothesis rejected; NR, hypothesis not rejected.

give considerable support to the cartel model. Not only does this model apply to a greater number of countries modelled, but the overall level of explanation dominates other models" [Griffin (1985) p. 24].

The principal weakness of the above approach is that the results are somewhat dependent upon the particular test devised for each model. The burden, Griffin claims, rests upon the advocates of particular models to specify precisely the criteria by which these models should be accepted or rejected. Another weakness of the approach is that certain models are empirically more demanding that others so that the comparative nature of the tests must be viewed cautiously. For instance, the target revenue model is empirically the most explicit and demanding. At the other extreme is the classical competitive model which needs only a positive price coefficient coupled with a positive investment coefficient, as is required for the target-revenue approach. The analysis has thus not entirely laid matters to rest. This is especially so as OPEC's behavior may well be changing over time. This simply reflects the complexity of the problem and the necessity for approaching modeling exercises with temerity.

5.2. Cartel experience in the world mercury market [4]

The international mercury market displays a long history of cartel activity. A recent study [MacKie-Mason and Pindyck (1987)] identifies a long period of successful

---

[4] This section draws heavily on the excellent treatment in MacKie-Mason and Pindyck (1987).

Table 4
World price and production of mercury (1972$/flask of 76 lbs, and 1000 flasks)[a]

Year	Price	Spain	Italy	USSR	Mex.	USA	China[b]	Yug.	Alg.	Total
1941		86.5	94.2	NA	23.1	44.9	6.6	b	0.0	275.0
1942		72.3	75.9	NA	32.4	50.8	4.7	b	0.0	260.0
1943		47.8	58.0	NA	28.3	51.9	3.1	b	0.0	236.0
1944		34.4	28.7	NA	26.1	37.7	3.5	b	0.0	163.0
1945		40.7	25.4	NA	16.4	30.8	1.8	b	0.0	131.0
1946		41.8	50.8	NA	11.7	25.3	1.2	8.9	0.0	154.0
1947	168.49	55.6	54.0	NA	9.7	23.2	0.3	9.5	0.0	168.0
1948	143.97	22.7	38.2	NA	4.8	14.4	0.3	10.9	0.0	107.0
1949	151.09	32.3	44.5	NA	5.3	9.9	0.3	12.8	0.0	121.0
1950	151.49	51.8	53.3	11.6	3.8	4.5	1.5	14.4	0.0	143.3
1951	368.07	44.5	53.8	11.6	8.1	7.3	4.0	14.6	0.0	146.7
1952	343.75	39.1	55.9	11.6	8.7	12.5	4.0	14.6	0.0	150.5
1953	328.17	43.5	51.7	12.3	11.6	14.3	5.0	14.3	0.0	159.7
1954	443.98	43.1	54.5	12.3	14.8	18.5	10.0	14.4	0.0	179.3
1955	477.24	36.2	53.5	12.3	29.9	19.0	11.5	14.6	0.0	185.1
1956	413.95	55.4	62.3	22.0	19.5	24.2	17.0	13.2	0.0	228.1
1957	380.38	51.7	62.2	25.0	21.1	34.6	17.0	12.3	0.0	243.3
1958	333.22	56.0[c]	58.7	25.0	22.6	38.1	17.0	12.3	0.0	251.9
1959	336.51	51.7	45.8	25.0	16.4	31.3	23.0	13.3	0.0	223.3
1960	306.78	53.4	55.5	25.0	20.1	33.2	23.0	14.0	0.0	241.7
1961	285.03	51.2	55.4	25.0	1.1	31.7	26.0	16.0	0.0	239.7
1962	270.80	52.8	54.5	35.0	18.9	26.3	26.0	16.3	0.0	244.6
1963	264.34	57.0	54.4	35.0	17.2	19.1	26.0	15.8	0.0	239.7
1964	432.58	7.3	57.0	35.0	12.6	14.1	26.0	17.3	0.0	255.0
1965	767.55	74.7	57.3	40.0	19.2	19.6	26.0	16.4	0.0	267.7
1966	575.46	70.1	53.5	40.0	22.1	22.0	26.0	15.9	0.0	265.0
1967	618.97	49.2	48.0	45.0	23.9	23.9	20.0	15.9	0.0	241.3
1968	651.43	56.9	53.2	45.0	17.2	28.9	20.0	14.8	0.0	259.7
1969	587.51	65.0	48.7	47.0	22.5	29.6	20.0	14.3	0.0	290.0
1970	457.23	45.4	44.6	48.0	30.3	27.3	20.0	15.5	0.0	284.0
1971	315.54	50.8	42.6	50.0	35.4	17.9	26.0	16.6	7.1	298.6
1972	226.76	54.0	41.8	50.0	22.5	7.3	26.0	16.4	13.4	279.0
1973	275.59	60.1	32.7	52.0	2.0	2.2	26.0	15.6	13.3	262.3
1974	253.70	54.4	26.0	54.0	NA	2.2	26.0	NA	14.0	257.5
1975	132.86	44.0	31.7	55.0	NA	7.4	26.0	NA	28.0	252.4
1976	94.05	42.7	22.3	56.0	NA	23.1	26.0	NA	30.9	234.6
1977	99.91	26.9	0.4	58.0	NA	28.2	20.0	NA	30.4	190.7
1978	102.34	29.6	0.1	60.0	NA	24.2	20.0	NA	30.6	181.4
1979	177.54	33.3	0.0	61.0	NA	29.5	20.0	NA	30.0	190.0
1980	223.57	33.0	0.0	62.0	NA	30.7	20.0	NA	30.0	191.1
1981[c]	176.82	33.0	0.0	62.0	NA	28.0	20.0	NA	30.0	190.4

[a] 1951–1980 prices taken from *1981 Commodity Yearbook* (Commodity Research Bureau, 1981); 1981 prices from *Minerals Commodity Summaries 1982* (US Bureau of Mines, 1982).
Abbreviations: Mex., Mexico; Yug., Yugoslavia; Alg., Algeria.
[b] Data for China are estimates for 1949–1967. Output of India mine (Yugoslavia) included with Italy through 1945.
[c] Estimates.

two-country cartelizations by Spain and Italy (1928–1972) followed by years of unsuccessful many-country attempts at price fixing. Spain and Italy were the dominant producers, at least up until 1960, because of their low production costs. The potential for industry cartelization was enhanced by the small number of firms in each producing country and by the willingness of governments in the producing nations to exercise control. There were just a few mines in each country (Spain, Italy, Yugoslavia, Algeria, and the Soviet Union) that were wholly or partially state owned. Production and price data are contained in Table 4.

The formation of *Mercurio Europeo* by Spain and Italy in 1928 marked the emergence of the cartel. These two nations accounted for more than 80% of world production at that time. Buttressed by an understanding with Mexico, the cartel was apparently very successful until 1950 [Hexnes (1945)].

A market-sharing arrangement, by which Spain supplied the USA and Italy supplied Europe, was part of the cartel agreement. The agreement was formally terminated by Spain in January 1950 after Monte Amiata, the largest Italian mine, sold 80 000 flasks of mercury to the US government stockpile in 1949. Spain replied with a price cut, but cartel pricing, albeit informal, was soon restored. Prices rose sharply in 1950, and a formal cartel was secretly re-established in 1954.

Prices peaked in 1965 as the US government began to stockpile. The cartel's market share peaked in 1950 and fell to 32% in 1970, by which time, according to MacKie-Mason and Pindyck (1987, p. 11), its effectiveness had largely ended. Subsequently, several producing nations, including Spain, Italy, Algeria, Yugoslavia, Peru, and Turkey, have attempted to recartelize the industry, but without apparent success. In any case, MacKie-Mason and Pindyck (1987, p. 12) argue that in the past war period the external market conditions "explain mercury price movements in the last three decades, price movements which cannot be explained by (and in fact often run counter to) changes in internal cartel organization." In support of a general thesis that once minimal conditions of market concentration have been met, the controlling factors in cartel success or failure are not the internal problems of organization, but the external constraints imposed by the market, the Italian 'cheating' incident of late 1949 is cited:

> Italy's sale to the U.S. Government stockpile was two-thirds as large as the entire world output of mercury in 1949. The Mercurio Europeo agreement was terminated, and for about ten months Spain tried to retaliate by undercutting Italy's price. Spain offered mercury to the market at $120 (1972 dollars), approximately equal to Italy's cost of production. One might think that this apparent collapse of the cartel would lead to depressed, competitive pricing. In fact prices began to rise during the summer of 1950. Spain stopped undercutting and increased price to $385 in January 1951. Prices and profits reached historical highs just one year after the cartel's 'demise'. The average price for 1951 was $368, and it stayed near that level through 1953. The high prices of the early 1950s were the result of the extremely low short-run elasticities of supply and demand. When Spain tried to undercut Italy in 1950, its production

capacity, combined with that of fringe suppliers, was too constrained in the short run to fulfill demand at the low ($120) price. Italy was able to sell at higher prices in the disequilibrium of the market; demand held strong as Italy gradually raised price. As long as the market was unresponsive, it was in Spain's interest to raise its price, which it did, and Italy followed suit. Thus any internal problems the cartel faced were irrelevant to its success in exploiting market power to obtain excess profits. None of the internal problems were overcome: Spain and Italy did not reach a new agreement until 1954, cheating was not deterred, and retaliation was unsuccessful. If anything, these events made the cartel more aware of its strength.

MacKie-Mason and Pindyck (1987, pp. 17–18)

This outcome is very similar to that which was obtained in the world oil market after the Doha meeting in 1978, where a two-tier price structure prevailed as Saudi Arabia tried to keep prices down for various economic and political reasons. The Saudis could not prevail because they had insufficient spare capacity to impact the entire price structure through increased production. However, neither incident supports the inference that the internal mechanisms of cartelization are unimportant and that external market factors are deterministic.

Clearly the market is a tremendous force to be reckoned with, and attempts to tamper with it through complex forms of collusion are often fragile, though not totally ineffective. Inelastic demand and inelastic supply from non-cartel fringe producers are almost always necessary conditions for effective cartelization, but they are not sufficient. Some form of internal organization is also needed unless producers are satisficing, as is postulated in the case of the target revenue model of OPEC outlined earlier.

5.3. Cartel experience in the world uranium markets

From 1972 to 1976, the price of uranium ore rose from $6/pound to over $40/pound. Following this price increase, the existence of a secret international uranium cartel was revealed and a cross-fire of investigations and legal battles began. Although all the effects of the uranium cartel are unclear at best, its existence has significantly affected energy markets and the future of the nuclear industry.

This case is an interesting illustration of the interaction between privately held firms, host governments, and public interest concerns involved with a natural-resource cartel. It also illustrates many of the mechanisms necessary for the formation and maintenance of a cartel. The active participation of host governments, the cartel's secret and illegal status, and the use of national security reasons as a disguising mechanism all contribute interesting complexities to the case.

The attempt to cartelize the uranium industry in the early 1970s seems to have been triggered by an overabundance of mining and milling capacity in relation to

Table 5
US reserves and potential resource estimates (January 1, 1977)[a]

Cost per pound U_3O_8 cost category	Tons of U_3O_8 potential resources			
	Reserves	Probable	Possible	Speculative
$10	250 000	275 000	115 000	100 000
$10 to $15 increment	160 000	310 000	375 000	90 000
$15	410 000	585 000	490 000	190 000
$15 to 30 increment	270 000	505 000	630 000	290 000
$30	680 000	1 090 000	1 120 000	480 000
$30 to $50 increment	160 000	280 000	300 000	60 000
$50	840 000	1 370 000	1 420 000	540 000

[a] From US Department of Energy.

demand. Price competition, led by the French, was forcing producers to sell at prices covering only their marginal costs, around $5/pound in 1972.

The USA has the largest known uranium deposits in the world. Over 25% of 'reasonably assured' world reserves reside in the USA [Taylor and Yokell (1979)]. US resources can be categorized by their estimated costs of production, which are known as 'forward costs'. Forward costs are essentially marginal costs and do not include fixed costs (such as exploration and mine development if these costs have already been sunk) or the user costs discussed in Section 2. DOE estimates of US uranium reserves categorized by their forward costs are shown in Table 5. It can be seen that the forward costs were and still are significantly above the prices quoted in 1972. If forward costs are expanded to include user costs, the depressed situation of the industry in 1972 is readily apparent.

Estimates of potential reserves have been subject of much debate in the industry. Resource estimates have grown each year as new exploration and drilling have uncovered new deposits. In addition to holding the largest known reserves, the USA is also the world's largest producer of uranium ore. However, while US uranium reserves are large, they are and have been significantly more costly to produce than Australian, Canadian, or South African uranium. The USA has the strictest safety requirements and high labor costs. In addition, US deposits are not so rich as those of other producers and thus they are more costly to extract.

The international uranium cartel commenced with meetings in 1972 among uranium producers from France, England, Canada, Australia, and South Africa. It continued with meeting of a 'policy committee' and an 'operating committee' and with the support of a 'secretariat' to compile and circulate data. Some or all of these operations were taken over in 1975 by 'The Uranium Institute', headquartered in London, after its formation by the cartel participants.

A stated purpose of the series of producer meetings begun in Paris in February 1972 was "to discuss ways and means of assuring an adequate price of uranium in order to attract sufficient investment into the industry."[5] With the existing price at "about U.S. $4.5 per pound", an initial proposal was to set the price at "$6.25 per pound U_3O_8 in 1975" and that the 'Club' thereafter "agree upon a price for uranium from time to time ..."[6].

An elaborate cartel agreement was in fact arrived at during meetings in Johannesburg, South Africa, in June 1972. A written summary of the agreement worked out at the Johannesburg meetings was approved at the Paris meeting on July 6, 1972[7]. Among the constituent agreements were those relating to:

(1) "Market quotas" as follows:

Country	1972–1977	1978–1980
Canada	33.50%	23.22%
South Africa	23.75%	19.26%
France	21.75%	19.26%
Australia	17.00%	24.44%
RTZ (Rio Tinto Zinc)	4.00%	13.82%

(2) Sales to be allocated among members on the basis of "contracted tonnages" and "each group's quota to be filled at a uniform rate", with 'the Secretary' to report quarterly "on markets, contracts, deliveries and positions vis-a-vis quotas", and to "distribute price and quantity information to members on a routine basis".

(3) "Minimum prices" for all future bids as follows (with prices for customers in Japan, Taiwan, and Korea to be $0.20 per pound higher)[8]

1972	1973	1974	1975	1976	1977	1978
$5.40	5.75	6.10	6.45	6.80	7.15	7.50

(4) Quotations beyond 1978 to be no lower than the minimum prices or based on "world market price", with the "maximum validity period for any quotations" to be 90 days.

---

[5] *Report of the Discussions in Paris on the Uranium Industry,* Feb. 1–4, 1972.

[6] See previous footnote.

[7] The *Report of the Discussions in Paris on the Uranium Industry,* Feb. 1–4, 1972 and *Notes of the Johannesburg Meeting of the Uranium Producers Club* were released publicly by California officials on August 29, 1976. The documents were obtained from the files of an Australian uranium producer, Mary Kathleen Mines. They constitute some of the minutes and detailed reports of the 'Club'. The following points are extrapolated from the 'Notes'.

[8] The rationale for price discrimination appeared to be that these countries were pursuing large, well-publicized nuclear expansion programs and had few domestic sources as substitutes. Their demand could therefore be inferred to be more inelastic, thereby supporting a higher than competitive price.

(5) No uranium sales contract to contain a "consequential damage clause" and no producer to "waive a force majeure condition for any period in order to guarantee delivery".

(6) A leader and a runner-up to be selected by the Secretary for each bid after consultation with the (Operating) Committee, with the leader having the right to quote the appropriate minimum price; the runner-up having the right to quote only the minimum price plus 8¢/lb, and with all others having the right to quote the minimum price plus 15¢/lb. [9]

(7) "If a supplier not associated with the organization should quote under the minimum price, the leader will not match that quotation and the Operating Committee will review the situation and decide on a course of action as soon as possible".

Further meetings in Johannesburg on January 28 through February 1, 1974, led to additional increases in the agreed schedule of minimum prices previously increased three months earlier. The ninth session of the uranium producers 'Operating Committee', held at Las Palmas (Canary Islands) on November 23, 1973, adjusted upward the quota for the Australian group of producers for the period 1978–1980 because the political situation in Australia made it impossible for the Australian producers to sell their assigned quota for the period 1972–1977. The evidence and information publicly available amply demonstrate the existence and operation of the cartel, but they do not constitute a complete set of the minutes of the many meetings held over a five-year period or a complete record of the cartel's activities.

In connection with the impact of the cartel on the US market, it is clear that parties recognized early on that in the colluding formation of their cartel coordination with US uranium producers was necessary to ensure their overall objectives of raising prices and dividing the market. Beginning with contacts by Louis Mazel of Rio Tinto Zinc at least as early as the fall of 1972 [10], foreign producers increased the tempo of their coordination efforts with US producers to demonstrate the higher prices foreign producers were charging and to assure the US producers that foreign uranium would not be sold in the USA at prices below the US prices.

---

[9] The leader runner-up system was an attempt to make the bids look competitive when in fact they had been rigged.

[10] Louis Mazel of Rio Tinto Zinc in London addressed a meeting of US uranium producers in Washington, DC, in late 1972 on 'supply and demand'. On November 29, 1972, following the meeting, he wrote the secretary of the trade association which sponsored the meeting: "I would like to thank you for the pleasant and interesting breakfast at the Shoreham Hotel and I hope that my remarks on the foreign U_3O_8 supply and demand were not too shocking for some of the Mining and Milling Committee members.

Nevertheless, we sincerely believe that an exchange of information, and consequently an understanding of one another's position, will be helpful in solving problems which exist both in the USA and non-USA U_3O_8 market."

The cartel also refused to deal with so-called 'middlemen', like Westinghouse Electric. Apparently the foreign uranium producers were annoyed at the sale of uranium by Westinghouse at prices that were considered too low. Westinghouse was selling uranium forward in order to sweeten the sale of nuclear reactors to electric utilities. However, the producers were upset because in their view the effect of Westinghouse activities was to withhold demand from the market just at a time when the producers were hurting the most. Producers therefore agreed to deal with end-users only.

The ownership structure of the industry outside the USA seemed to favor cartelization. The number of parties was limited by the small number of commercial deposits and the cooperation that various governments were prepared to offer to help the cartel become effective. In addition, the demand facing uranium producers was very inelastic in the short run due to the high switching costs and long lead times associated with nuclear- and power-plant production. Finally, the USA had placed an embargo on the enrichment of foreign uranium, and this effectively protected the international market for US competition.

At the very inception, the cartel agreed that secrecy was a necessity. Violation of US antitrust laws was a danger, especially for those firms with US subsidiaries. Also, the US government might retaliate by withholding enrichment services to international producers. In addition, antitrust action was possible in other countries where the uranium was sold.

Governments actively participated in the cartel alongside the companies. The Canadian government was especially enthusiastic. The Canadian uranium industry suffered after the USA stopped purchasing foreign uranium in 1957, and the government had to step in with over $100 million to avert the collapse of the industry. However, because of this strong government participation in the cartel, the domestic markets of the four producing nations were initially excluded from the cartel-set price.

The cartel was not insensitive to monitoring and enforcement needs. Stringent disclosure requirements and selective punishments were established. All contracts, letters of intent, inquiries, quotations, and delivery invoices had to be turned over. If any were not, the offending producer was to be called before the Operating Committee which met bimonthly. Such checks were designed to eliminate overt cheating.

To prevent more covert actions, the cartel used the governments as an enforcement mechanism. In France and South Africa, marketing was controlled through a single corporation with government participation. In Canada and Australia, the government used the technique of withholding export licenses to ensure that no company exceeded its quota. This was possible because uranium was declared a commodity with national security implications. Price (the cartel-set price) was then incorporated as one of the criteria for government approval.

Infractions did occur. They were penalized by selectively levying a "fine" on the offending party that took the form of a reduced quota.

As mentioned earlier, one potential problem arose when Australian producers discovered new, low-cost sources of uranium. These new deposits threatened to undercut the existing cartel mechanism unless some entry was allowed on relatively good terms. The Australians threatened to stay outside, undersell the cartel, and capture an even larger market share unless accommodated. The cartel's response was twofold. First, Australia's entry was accommodated slowly by using a dual quota system. Australia was given a lower (ranging from 7% to 17%) market share for 1972–1977 and a larger one (from 24% to 28%) for 1978–1980. Second, existing producers forced the government to "institute some control to prevent new producers from coming into production too early" and exceeding the quotas set in the dual system. The result was that the government denied several export licenses.

An interesting but difficult question to answer about the cartel is whether it affected the price of uranium. Prices did rise in the 1972–1976 period, but it is not clear what if any part of this escalation was due to the cartel. During the period 1972 through 1976, production costs were increasing, supply uncertainties were exacerbated, and demand for international uranium was rising because of increased restrictions in US government enrichment policies. Whether the cartel had much impact in relation to these other factors is yet to be firmly established.

5.4. The diamond cartel

The monopolistic and cartelistic features of the diamond industry are more sensational than they are typical, but underlying and buttressing observed behavior is one fundamental fact: there is no close substitute for diamonds, especially for ornamental (gem) uses, but to a lesser degree for industrial uses as well.

Nevertheless, the internal organization of the cartel appears intriguing. The formal organization of the cartel was established in 1934 under the rubric of a trade association, the Diamond Producers' Association of London. The members of this trade association included representatives from the governments of the Union of South Africa and the Administration of Southwest Africa. The most significant member of this association was De Beers Consolidated Mines, Ltd[11], which was the controlling shareholder of the Diamond Corporation. De Beers was, and still is, the most important producer of diamonds. In fact, of all the world's major commodity markets, the market in diamonds comes nearest to being a monopoly. The world diamond industry might arguably be better read as a study in monopoly

---

[11] In the nineteenth century, Cecil Rhodes amalgamated the Kimberly diamond fields into de Beers Consolidated.

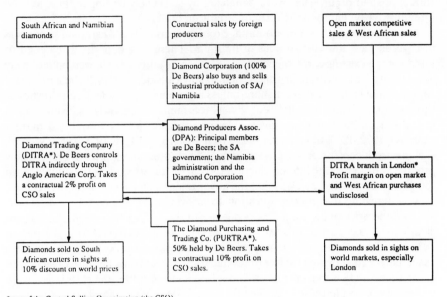

*part of the Central Selling Organization (the CSO)

Fig. 5. The De Beers supply and marketing system. (From *The Economist*, February 23, 1980, p. 102.)

than as a study in cartels [12]. Still, there are enough aspects of coordination amongst governments and independent private entities to warrant categorizing the industry as one organized as a cartel with a dominant player – De Beers.

Since the 1930s, De Beers has operated an elaborate apparatus of stockpiling and distribution under the Central Selling Organization (CSO). The CSO is an inextricably complex group of London-based companies, the major elements of which are controlled either directly by De Beers itself or by Anglo-American (Anglo-American and De Beers are both chaired by Harry Oppenheimer, whose shareholdings interlock in a group called E. Oppenheimer & Sons).

Figure 5 sketches the companies involved in the distribution system. The CSO, backed by De Beers, attempts to regulate prices to the benefit of De Beers, its dealers, and probably the producers as well. This involves adjusting stocks of diamonds to meet demand at smoothly rising prices and tightly managing the distribution system so as to exert maximum control over the way diamonds are distributed and priced. An important part of the apparatus in this regard is the

---

[12] Indeed, de Beers Chairman Harry Oppenheimer would seem to agree, stating: "We are a monopoly of the most unusual kind – you can say we handle at least 80% of the diamonds of the world." *Forbes*, May 28, 1979, p. 45.

fashion in which De Beers conducts sales, or 'sights' as they are called in the trade. These sales are by invitation only, and denial of access means that a dealer must buy from other dealers at prices considerably above De Beers' prices. De Beers thus uses access to their supply to 'bribe' dealers into 'responsible' behavior. The threat of black-balling can be serious. The dealers who are provided access are expected to avoid hoarding for speculative reasons and to accept consignments almost sight unseen. Price chiseling with De Beers is also unacceptable. In fact, Epstein (1982, ch. 6) identifies six 'rules of the game' that have been established by De Beers.

Rule one: No one may question the authority of the diamond trading company to decide who gets which diamonds (a block consignment rule). The De Beers director of operations is the sole arbiter of both the number and quality of the diamonds offered to each dealer. This enables Oppenheimer to largely control both the volume and profitability of the dealer's business.

Rule two: There shall be no haggling over price. De Beers is the sole arbiter of price, and it is able to do so since the price it charges averages about 20–25% below the wholesale price. Refusal to pay the price may foreclose future purchase opportunities. This effectively prevents price competition and helps De Beers stabilize the market so the profit margin provided to the dealers seems to vary with the business cycle.

Rule three: Take the entire offered arrangement, or none of it. This appears to be a form of price discrimination akin to the economics of block booking in the movie business.

Rule four: No client may resell the diamonds in his consignment in their uncut form without a special dispensation from the director of operations. To manage its international monopoly over the supply of diamonds and to maintain control over prices, De Beers needs to control the world stockpile of uncut diamonds. If it permitted its clients to resell their boxes, some outside party could amass its own stockpile of uncut diamonds.

Rule five: Clients will supply De Beers with whatever information it needs to assess the diamond market. Before attending a 'sight', a client must provide detailed information on the number of uncut diamonds in inventory, the number in the process of being cut, the number previously sold, forecasted sales, and the relevant details of his business. In fact, clients must also be open to a De Beers audit at any time. This information is obviously quite critical to maintaining control over supply and hence prices.

Rule six: Diamonds must never be sold into 'weak hands'. Since the marketing strategy of De Beers involves portraying diamonds as steadily appreciating in value, it is important to avoid 'fire sales' and the like. For this and other reasons, De Beers clients are prohibited from selling their diamonds to any wholesale or retail jewelers who undercut retail prices. De Beers clients are thus "forced to be silent partners with De Beers in maintaining an orderly retail market" [Epstein (1982) p. 64].

The penalty for violating the rules is either refusal to deal at all or refusal to deal in terms quite as favorable. Typically, the quality of the consignment is degraded for minor offenses, and refusals to deal are reserved to punish more severe departures from expected behavior. These rules could not be imposed but for De Beers's considerable control over production, which seems to have been maintained through nationalization and changing governments in the producing nations. Even production not under De Beers's ownership seems to have been controlled by the company. According to Epstein (pp. 97–98), Oppenheimer negotiated a series of secret arrangements to block the availability of diamonds from the sources that his company did not directly own or control. In South Africa and the Belgian Congo, he pressed the governments into passing laws that forced independent prospectors and diggers to sell their diamonds only to government-licensed diamond buyers, who in turn contracted to sell their diamonds to De Beers's subsidiary, the Diamond Trading Company. In British colonies, such as the Gold Coast (now Ghana) or Sierra Leone, he contracted to buy whatever diamonds were unearthed from British mining companies, such as the Selection Trust, which held the mining concessions there. In South America, where the alluvial diamond fields are scattered over vast areas, he arranged his deal with local buying agents. In all cases, Oppenheimer required that the total production of diamonds be turned over to De Beers or its subsidiaries at an agreed-upon price.

In recent years, De Beers's production has been increasing much faster outside South Africa than within it, at a time when political alignments are changing fast. A large and growing proportion of De Beers's production comes from Namibia and Botswana. In fact, Namibia is now the most important single source of gemstones.

Yet De Beers seems to have moved successfully against potential competitors. Marine Diamond Corporation, a new entrant which obtained a concession in Namibia, was unable to market its production profitably when De Beers unloaded from its stocks sufficient diamonds of similar size and grade to depress the market segment upon which Marine Diamond depended. By 1965, this had deprived the fledgling enterprise of cash and made it an easy buy-out for De Beers [Epstein (1982) pp. 212–213]. Attempts by others to obtain concessions in Angola and elsewhere similarly ran up against the economic and political ability of De Beers to foreclose them. The Soviet Union, on the other hand, was not driven out but accommodated when it began to sell its polished diamonds in the 1960s. According to Epstein, the Soviets became partners in the cartel (p. 255) and have relied upon the De Beers distribution system. As De Beers's upstream position has now eroded through the entry of the Soviet Union and the shifting political winds of Africa, De Beers has attempted to integrate downstream into cutting, distributing, and wholesaling. One reason was to monitor market conditions more closely, but another may have been to obtain market power in various downstream positions, an inherently difficult objective to attain.

6. Conclusion

The markets examined here – oil, mercury, uranium, and diamonds – are characterized to a greater or lesser degree by external market environments in which demand elasticities, as well as supply elasticities of non-members are relatively low. Still, success for the cartel seems to depend on a viable internal 'structure' – such as the CSO in the case of diamonds, and a 'club' in the case of uranium – bolstered by governments in all cases. The cartels selected seem to indicate that the external market environment molds the outcomes associated with attempts at cartelization, but that internal structure also matters. However, the need for tight internal governance is softened if the producers are satisfiers, as may be the case with certain OPEC producers.

The welfare implications of the four cartels examined were addressed only superficially. Effects on price are often difficult to ascertain, particularly in the case of natural resource cartels, where the calculation of monopoly rents requires measurement of user costs. Further, to the extent that cartels lower the adjustment costs associated with competitive markets, deadweight-loss calculations from monopolization fail to capture the totality of normative considerations. Economists, however, seem reluctant to address disequilibrium phenomena, and so our understanding of the causes and consequences of cartels is likely to be incomplete for quite some time.

References

Abreu, D., et al., 1985, "Optimal Cartel Equilibria with Imperfect Monitoring", *Journal of Economic Theory* 39, 251–269.

Adelman, M.A., 1982, "OPEC as a Cartel", in: J.M. Griffin and D.J. Teece (eds.), *OPEC Behavior and World Oil Prices* (Allen & Unwin, London).

Behrman, J.R., 1978, "Simple Theoretical Analysis of International Commodity Agreements", in: *Development, the International Economic Order and Commodity Agreements* (Addison-Wesley, Reading, MA).

Cohen, S.S., 1969, *Modern Capitalist Planning: The French Model* (University of California Press, Berkeley, CA).

Cremer, J., and I. Salehi-Isfahani, 1980, "Competitive Pricing in the Oil Market: How Important is OPEC?", CARESS Working Paper 80-4 (University of Pennsylvania, Philadelphia, PA).

Dasgupta, P., and G.M. Heal, 1979, *Economic Theory and Exhaustible Resources* (Cambridge University Press, Cambridge).

Epstein, E.J., 1982, *The Rise and Fall of Diamonds* (Simon & Schuster, New York).

Fellner, W., 1965, *Competition Among the Few* (Augustus Kelley, New York).

Fudenberg, D., and E. Maskin, 1986, "The Folk Theorem in Repeated Games with Discounting and Incomplete Information", *Econometrica* 54 (May) 533–554.

Gately, D., 1984, "A Ten-Year Retrospective on OPEC and the World Oil Market", *Journal of Economic Literature* 22 no. 3, 1100–1114.

Gilbert, R., 1978, "Dominant Firm Pricing in a Market for an Exhaustible Resource", *Bell Journal of Economics* 9, 385–395.

Green, E., and R. Porter, 1984, "Non-Cooperative Collusion under Imperfect Price Information", *Econometrica* 52, 82–100.

Griffin, J., 1985, "OPEC Behavior: A Test of Alternative Hypotheses", *American Economic Review* 75, 954–963.

Griffin, J.M., and D.J. Teece, eds, 1982, *OPEC Behavior and World Oil Prices* (Allen & Unwin, London).

Hahn, F., 1973, *On the Notion of Equilibrium in Economics* (Cambridge University Press, Cambridge).

Hexner, E., 1945, *International Cartels* (University of North Carolina Press, Chapel Hill, NC).

Hotelling, H., 1931, "The Economics of Exhaustible Resources", *Journal of Political Economy* (April).

Johany, A.D., 1978, "OPEC Is Not a Cartel: A Property Rights Explanation of the Rise in Crude Oil Prices", unpublished doctoral dissertation (University of California, Santa Barbara, CA).

Jorde, T.M., and D.J. Teece, 1992, *Antitrust, Innovation, and Competitiveness* (Oxford University Press, New York).

Koopmans, T.C., 1957, *Three Essays on the State of Economic Science* (McGraw-Hill, New York).

Kreps, D. et al., 1982, "Rational Cooperation in the Finitely Repeated Prisoner's Dilemma", *Journal of Economic Theory* 27, 245–252.

Lewis, T., and R. Schmalensee, 1978, "Cartel and Oligopoly Pricing of Nonreplenishable Natural Resources", in: P. Liu (ed.), *Dynamic Optimization and Application to Economics* (Plenum Press, New York).

Lewis, T.R., and R. Schmalensee, 1982, "Cartel Deception in Non-renewable Resource Markets", *Bell Journal of Economics* 13 no. 1, 263–271.

MacAvoy, P., 1982, *Crude Oil Prices as Determined by OPEC and Market Fundamentals* (Ballinger, Cambridge, MA).

MacKie-Mason, J., and R. Pindyck, 1987, "Cartel Theory and Cartel Experience in International Minerals Markets", in: R. Gordon et al. (eds.), *Energy: Markets and Regulation* (MIT Press, Cambridge, MA).

Mead, W.J., 1979, "The Performance of Government in Energy Regulations", *American Economic Review* 69 (Papers and Proceedings, May) 352–356.

Meade, J.E., 1970, *The Theory of Indicative Planning: Lectures Given in the University of Manchester* (Manchester University Press, Manchester, England).

Milgrom, P., and J. Roberts, 1982, "Predation, Reputation, and Entry Deterrence", *Journal of Economic Theory* 27, 280–312.

Newbery, D., 1981, "Oil Prices, Cartels, and the Problem of Dynamic Inconsistency", *Economic Journal* 91, 617–646.

Orr, D., and P. MacAvoy, 1965, "Price Strategies to Promote Cartel Stability", *Economica* 32, 186–197.

Osborne, D.K., 1976, "Cartel Problems", *American Economic Review* 66, 835–844.

Pindyck, R.S., 1978, "Gains to Producers from the Cartelization of Exhaustible Resources", *American Economic Review* 60 (May) 238–251.

Pindyck, R.S., 1982, "OPEC Oil Pricing and the Implications for Consumers and Producers", in: J.M. Griffin and D.J. Teece (eds.), *OPEC Behavior and World Oil Prices* (Allen & Unwin, London).

Plummer, A., 1951, *International Combines in Modern Industry* (Pitman, London).

Richardson, G.B., 1960, *Information and Investment* (Oxford University Press, London).

Rotemberg, J., and G. Saloner, 1986, "A Supergame-Theoretic Model of Price Wars During Booms", *American Economic Review* 76, 390–407.

Salant, S., 1976, "Exhaustible Resources and Industrial Structure: A Nash–Cournot Approach to the World Oil Market", *Journal of Political Economy* 84, 1079–1093.

Solow, R., 1974, "The Economics of Resources or the Resources of Economics", *American Economic Review* 64, 1–14.

Suslow, V.Y., 1992, "Cartel Contract Duration: Empirical Evidence from International Cartels", submitted.

Taylor, J., and M. Yorkel, 1979, *Yellowcake: The International Uranium Cartel* (Pergamon Press, New York).

Teece, D.J., 1982, "OPEC Behavior: An Alternative View", in: J.M. Griffin and D.J. Teece (eds.), *OPEC Behavior and World Prices* (Allen & Unwin, London).

Teece, D.J., 1983, "Assessing OPEC's Pricing Policies", *California Management Review* 26 (Fall) 69–87.

Ulph, A., 1982, "Modeling Partially Cartelized Markets for Exhaustible Resources", *Economic Theory of Natural Resources* (Physica-Verlag, Vienna).

Ulph, A., and G.M. Folie, 1980, "Exhaustible Resources and Cartels: An Intertemporal Nash–Cournot Model", *Canadian Journal of Economics* 13, 645–658.

US Bureau of Mines, 1960 and 1965 editions, *Mineral Facts and Problems* (US Government Printing Office, Washington, DC).

US Bureau of Mines, Various years, *Minerals Yearbook* (US Government Printing Office, Washington, DC).

US Bureau of Mines, Various years, *Commodity Data Summaries* (US Government Printing Office, Washington, DC).

US Congress, 1939, *Hearings Before the Temporary National Economic Committee,* 76th Congress, 1st Session, Part 5.

Vives, X., 1990, "Trade Association Disclosure Rules, Incentives to Share Information, and Welfare", *RAND Journal of Economics* 21 no. 3, 409–430.

Williamson, O.E., 1975, *Markets and Hierarchies* (Free Press, New York).

[21]

Information Sharing, Innovation, and Antitrust

David J. Teece*

1. Introduction

Antitrust analysis of vertical and horizontal agreements has evolved considerably in recent years. In the horizontal restraints area, this evolution is reflected in the Supreme Court's move away from the automatic application of the per se rule and toward a greater willingness to consider the context in which conduct occurs, employing rule of reason analysis to assess the reasonableness of behavior.[1] Both the Federal Trade Commission and the Department of Justice have developed tests that reflect in one way or another the evolution of the Supreme Court's analysis.[2] The passing of the traditional per se rule against horizontal restraints is widely recognized by economists as a desirable development.[3]

However, the implementation of rule of reason analysis requires that cooperative activity among firms be understood in a more fundamental way than is currently the case.[4] Of course there is nothing redeeming about some types of horizontal activity, such as price-fixing restraints, no matter how they are disguised, and it is not the purpose of this article to attempt to justify them. Price

---

* Reprinted from *Antitrust Law Journal*, Vol. 62 (Winter 1994), No. 2, David J. Teece, "Information Sharing, Innovation, and Antitrust", with kind permission from American Bar Association, Antitrust Law Section, 750 N. Lake Shore Dr., Chicago, IL 60611, USA.

The author thanks James Clifton, Ronald Davis, Thomas Jorde, and Robert Lande for helpful comments.

1 See, e.g., Northwest Wholesale Stationers, Inc. v. Pacific Stationery & Printing Co., 472 U.S. 284, 294 (1985); NCAA v. Board of Regents, 468 U.S. 85, 103-04 (1984); Jefferson Parish Hospital Dist. No. 2 v. Hyde, 466 U.S. 2 (1984).

2 For an excellent survey, see Winterscheid, J. H. and Thompson, J. E.: "Development in the Rule of Reason Analysis of Horizontal Restraints: The FTC, DOJ and Supreme Court Approaches". In: Fox, E. M. and Halverson, J. T. (eds.) (1992): *Collaborations among Competitors – Antitrust Policy and Economics.*

3 See, e.g., Schmalensee, R.: "Agreements Between Competitors". In: Jorde, T. M. and Teece, D. J. (eds.) (1992): *Antitrust, Innovation and Competitiveness.* New York, 98.

4 According to one economist, the acquisition and dissemination of information among competitors imposes "ticklish problems" for antitrust analysis. See Greer, D. F. (1980): *Industrial Organization and Public Policy.* New York.

fixing and output prorationing agreements ought to be and are illegal. Rather, this article will focus on certain forms of cooperation that relate to innovation and have received scant treatment in the literature. Such practices may superficially appear to restrict competition, when in a more fundamental way they in fact enhance it.

The context in which I have particular interest in examining cooperation and, in particular, information collection, dissemination, and exchange among "competitors"[5] is that of dynamic environments where markets are experiencing rapid change, often induced by technological innovation. This article presents examples of certain types of beneficial information exchange that have received limited review in the antitrust literature. Needless to say, that which promotes innovation also promotes competition, as innovation remains the primary driver of competition and economic welfare in all advanced economies.[6] Also analyzed are certain circumstances in which cooperation and information exchange among U.S.-based competitors at home may help strengthen their competitive posture vis à vis foreign firms at home and abroad.[7]

Certain kinds of efficient collaboration, if recognized and disseminated to the public, make antitrust exemptions unneeded. As Anne Bingaman, Assistant Attorney General for Antitrust, recently stated:

"I am not aware of any situation where existing law is not sufficiently flexible to allow desirable economic cooperation. To be sure, I have heard the argument that even if the antitrust laws are flexible, efficient collaboration nevertheless is deterred by legal uncertainty or unwarranted fear of antitrust liability or litigation. To the extent that is true, the preferable approach is to provide the public with accurate information rather than to create antitrust exemptions."[8]

---

5   I define competitors as firms operating in the same relevant market. However, not all exchanges among competitors are strictly horizontal, as when a firm's downstream unit cooperates with an upstream unit of another firm in the same market. Thus while much of what is said about information exchange in this article may involve vertical flows, the flows may nevertheless involve competitors.

6   See Jorde, T. M. and Teece, D. J.: "Innovation, Cooperation, and Antitrust". In: *Antitrust, Innovation and Competitiveness.* New York, 47, supra note 3.

7   Eleanor Fox is of the view that *"if, by its nature, the restraint goes to the process of rivalry, it requires weighty justification."* Fox, E.: "Competitors Collaboration: A Methodology for Analysis". In: Fox, E. M. and Halverson, J. T. (eds.) (1992): *Collaborations among Competitors – Antitrust Policy and Economics.* 829, supra note 2.

8   See Anne K. Bingaman, Assistant Attorney General, Antitrust Division, Remarks to the Antitrust Section of the American Bar Association Annual Meeting, New York, NY (Aug. 10, 1993).

2.   Prices as "Sufficient" Statistics[9]

The reason why cooperation and information exchange are regarded suspiciously in many commercial contexts seems to have its origins in two suppositions, one correct and one false. The first is the obvious one that cartel activity requires coordinated activity and the sharing of information to construct, monitor, and police agreements. Needless to say, information exchange for such purposes is anticompetitive and ought to be condemned. The second supposition commonly accepted is that information exchange among competitors is not necessary to achieve efficient outcomes; after all, prices are "sufficient" statistics and are all that firms need to know to make good decisions. If firms know market prices and adjust their output accordingly, the market will ensure that resources will be allocated efficiently. Cooperation is not needed. This proposition is false, or at best a gross caricature of economic organization, particularly in the context of innovation.

To understand why economists often have intellectual blinders when it comes to recognizing the affirmative characteristics of information transfer and exchange, one must appreciate the limitations of the economic theory of market adjustment that is still accepted wisdom in many elementary textbooks. In elementary treatments of market processes, knowledge of market prices is considered necessary but also sufficient for the efficient operation of markets, but if the "invisible" hand is going to properly guide resource allocation, then economic agents must know not only today's supply and demand but supply and demand for all future periods. That is because efficiency requires that the future as well as the present be taken into account in resource allocation decisions. In reality, competitors need a good deal of knowledge about each other's prices and plans and intentions for the economic system to be efficient.[10] Judge Richard Posner notes:

"[T]he producer's need to have information about his competitors ... including the prices they charge, their output, the quality and reliability of their services, their investment plans, their costs ... is not obviously less important from the standpoint of efficiency than the consumer's interest in knowing what the market has to offer."[11]

---

9   For a more complete development, see Teece, D. J. (1992): "Competition, Cooperation, and Innovation: Organizational Arrangements for Regimes of Rapid Technological Progress". In: *Journal of Economic Behavior and Organization*, 18, 1.

10   See Richardson, G. B. (2d ed. 1990): *Information and Investment*.

11   Posner, R. A. (1979): "Information and Antitrust: Reflections on the Gypsum and Engineers Decisions". In: *Geo. L. J.*, 67, 1187, 1194.

In short, producers must be well informed about competitors' prices and plans if resources are to be allocated efficiently. Ignorance is rarely a virtue. This is not to deny that prices summarize a remarkable amount of information. They signal changes in demand and supply in ways that enable consumers and producers to respond independently and quickly. Prices unquestionably work extremely well as signals of resource scarcity, at least compared to the clumsy apparatus of central planning.[12] However, while prices are useful summary statistics, and facilitate high levels of decentralization, the price system alone is not sufficient to guide efficient resource allocation in real world economics. One obvious reason is the absence of a complete set of markets (and hence a complete set of prices), future and current, for many commodities, particularly contingent commodities.[13] There are many reasons for the failure of the theoretically desirable contingent markets and their associated prices to exist. They include complexity (there are just too many relevant contingencies) and asymmetric information (which leads to moral hazard problems).[14] It follows that the information channels that supplement prices are important. As Nobel Laureate Kenneth Arrow notes:

"The possibility of using the price system to allocate uncertainty, to insure against risks, is limited by the structure of the information channels in existence. Put the other way, the value of nonmarket decision-making, the desirability of creating organizations of a scope more limited than the markets as a whole, is partially determined by the characteristics of the network of information flows."[15]

Put differently, there is an incentive for firms to engage in information collection and dissemination activities if by so doing superior information about relevant economic fundamentals can be generated.

The requirements of producers and consumers for information beyond that contained in available prices, always considerable, depend significantly on the rapidity of change that the economy is experiencing and the importance of the decisions that are being made. With an extremely stable industry (with, let us say, zero demand growth and no innovation) and for industries which do not need much specific investment, the informational requirements – and therefore the need

---

12 Hayek, F. A. (1945): "The Use of Knowledge in Society". In: *The American Economic Review*, 35, 519.

13 An example of a contingent commodity would be a sightseeing helicopter flight with the fare refundable if visibility turns out to be poor.

14 Moral hazard problems occur when economic agents refuse to self-reveal relevant aspects of their motivation and personal attributes.

15 See Arrow, K. J. (1974): *The Limits of Organization*. New York, 37. Note that Arrow uses the term 'organization' very broadly to include formal organizations (firms, labor unions, universities) and informal organizations (ethical codes, etc.). Id. at 33.

for information collection – will be less severe than for an industry experiencing turbulence and requiring specialized, risky investments. Once gathered, information will not decline in its value over time if the industry is static. Accordingly, the need for information transfer is limited. On the other hand, uncertainty and the turbulence it creates simultaneously increases the value of timely information while increasing the cost of information collection.

There is no arena in which uncertainty is higher and the need to gather information greater than in the development and commercialization of new technology. Adam Smith's warning – *"[p]eople of the same trade seldom meet together, even for merriment and diversion, but the conversation ends in a conspiracy against the public, or in some contrivance to raise prices"*[16] – is a bit anachronistic in such contexts. Moreover, the oft-quoted statement fails to recognize that in global industries experiencing rapid change, the difficulty of assembling all the relevant parties to effectuate an international conspiracy is an almost insurmountable challenge absent governmental assistance.

3.   Information Exchange and Systems of Innovation

3.1 National Systems of Innovation

One's appreciation for the need for information networks that go beyond observing prices is deepened if one recognizes the importance of innovation to competition and economic development, and if one also recognizes that innovation is often associated with multifaceted networks in which information exchange is frequent. Even the casual observer of global enterprise will notice that innovating firms are not distributed uniformly across nation states. The firms and industrial sectors introducing successful innovation and profiting from them are located in a small number of countries (United States, Britain, Germany, France, and Japan). Each innovating country has some sectors of greater competitive advantage, e.g., software, semiconductors, and biotechnology in the United States; machine tools and chemicals in Germany; automobiles and photographic equipment in Japan. Moreover, the configuration of successful innovators in the world economic system tends to show a considerable stability.

Put differently, there is a strikingly localized and asymmetric distribution of innovative performance in the world economic system. This specificity cannot be explained by factor endowments (land, labor, and capital) but arises from specific

---

16   Smith, A.: *The Wealth of Nations*, Edwin Cannan (ed.) (1976), 144.

institutional configurations, the character of the knowledge that the institution possesses, and by the patterns of interaction and information sharing among firms and supporting institutions. It is the collective and interactive aspects of organizations (including firms) that causes them to be effective innovators. Firms and other institutions contributing to the generation of innovations in particular countries do not act independently but are linked into networks of various kinds; firms and their supporting institutions constitute a system that might be called a National System of Innovation.[17] French writers have advanced an industry-level analogue called "filieres."[18]

The implication is that interactions among firms and institutions are important to the innovation process and that these interactions are much easier within a short geographical distance, and especially within the same social and cultural context. Information sharing lies at the very foundation of these systems (networks). Consider Silicon Valley where, one observer notes, *"information-exchange is a dominant, distinguishing characteristic."*[19] Information exchange and cooperative relationships of various kinds lie at the heart of this tremendously innovative assemblage of physical and human assets. Needless to say, rapid advances in communications and transportation technologies are undermining some of the geographical basis of national and regional systems. The institutional and cultural aspects of systems of innovation, however, are likely to remain even as geographical boundaries become permeable.

The concept of national (and regional) systems implies differential barriers to the flow of information between systems as compared to across systems. The information flows in question may be of many kinds: knowledge about customer needs, knowledge about new components and other technological opportunities, and knowledge about market developments, including the actions of competitors. The information flows supporting systems of innovation are by no means unilateral and are not always vertical. In Silicon Valley, for instance, Rogers and Larsen note that *"[i]nformation must he given in order for it to be obtained. The nature of the technical information-exchange process in the microelectronics industry demands a high degree of reciprocity among the participants."*[20] Such information exchange is often mutually beneficial (perhaps more beneficial than

---

17 Nelson, R. R. and Rosenberg, N.: "Technical Innovation and National Systems". In: Nelson, R. R. (ed.) (1993): *National Innovation Systems: A Comparative Analysis.* New York: Oxford University Press, 4-5.

18 Dosi, G. et al. (1990): *The Economics of Technical Change and International Trade.* New York: Harvester Whaetsheaf. Silicon Valley might well contain one or more filieres.

19 Rogers, E. M. and Larsen, J. K. (1984): *Silicon Valley Fever: Growth of High-Technology Culture,* 80.

20 Id. at 81.

unilateral transfers) as it supports incremental improvement with technological developments in one firm building on those of competitors reciprocally, with a general and rapid advance in technological capability resulting.

None of this is to say that anticompetitive purposes cannot be served by the exchange of information, particularly if the information is on prices and output. Rather, the purpose here is to indicate that information sharing is essential to economic organization, and that the frequency with which transfer will be required and the complexity of information exchanged are likely to increase with the rate and complexity of technological innovation. Accordingly, unless one is simply looking at the naked exchange of information on prices and output, information. sharing should be viewed neutrally, if not favorably: it lies at the heart of highly dynamic and competitive economic systems.

3.2 Industrial Clusters

The role of cooperation and information sharing among industrial and technical communities has recently been highlighted by research on global competitiveness, including the influential work of Michael Porter in *The Competitive Advantage of Nations.*[21] "Industry clusters" are central. to Porter's analysis. These are *"industries related by links of various kinds"*,[22] both vertical and horizontal, connecting users and suppliers, and enterprises that have common customers, employ related technologies, and use the same channels of communication. In Porter's framework, "groups of domestic rivals" are integral to the operation of industry clusters.

Cooperation, not competition, is implied by the interchange that needs to take place within industry clusters to build national advantage. According to Porter *"[m]echanisms that facilitate interchange within clusters are conditions that help information to flow more easily, or which unblock information as well as facilitate coordination by creating trust and mitigating perceived differences in economic interest between vertically and horizontally linked firms."*[23] Porter

---

21   Michael Porter seems reluctant to draw this conclusion from his work, stressing instead the need for domestic rivalry rather than cooperation. Porter, M. E. (1990): *The Competitive Advantage of Nations*, 143-44. However, in my view, the only legitimate interpretation of his anecdotes is that competition and cooperation are both important for competitive advantage. I share this view with William Lazonick whose writings on this point are compelling and are summarized here. See Lazonick, W. (1993): "Industry Clusters Versus Global Webs: Organizational Capabilities in the American Economy". In: *Industrial and Corporate Change*, 2, 1, 1-10 (1993).

22   Porter, supra note 21, at 131.

23   Id. at 152-53.

goes on to list a number of *"facilitators of information flow"* in which he includes: *"[p]ersonal relationships due to schooling, military service"*; *"[t]ies through the scientific community or professional associations"*; *"[c]ommunity ties due to geographic proximity"*; *"[t]rade associations encompassing clusters"*; and *"[n]orms of behavior such as belief in community and long-term relationships."*[24] He also lists a number of *"sources of goal congruence or compatibility within dusters"* that include family ties, common ownership, interlocking directors, and national patriotism, and that facilitate information exchange.[25] Porter states, *"Mechanisms that facilitate interchange within clusters are generally strongest in Japan, Sweden, and Italy, and are generally weakest in the United Kingdom and the United States ..."*[26]

In the United States, the best-functioning clusters appear to be in health care and computing, sectors that contain some of America's premier global competitors. *"Here,"* Porter observes, *"scientific ties often overcome the natural reticence of American managers toward interchange."*[27] Porter argues, and I agree, that such cooperation should not go so far as to blunt competition in any particular industry within the cluster. Rather, cooperation and competition must coexist. In Porter's words, when *"the exchange and flow of information about the needs, techniques and technology among buyer, suppliers and related industries ... occurs* at the same time that active rivalry is maintained in each separate industry, *the conditions for competitive advantage are most fertile."*[28]

Porter provides an instructive example of how cooperation among domestic competitors centered around the town of Sassuolo has constributed to the global competitive advantage attained by the Italian ceramic tile industry over the past four decades. Indeed, as Lazonick[29] points out, Porter's analysis of "Sassuolo Rivalry" reveals the importance of intra-industry cooperation to the industry's ability to develop and utilize productive resources.

"Competition among Italian tile producers was intensely personal. All of the producers were located close together ....

Assopiastrelle, the ceramic tile industry association, with membership concentrated in the Sassuolo area, gradually began offering services of common interest including bulk purchasing, foreign market research, and consulting on fiscal and legal matters. The association also took the lead in government and

---

24   Id. at 153.
25   Id.
26   Id. at 154.
27   Id.
28   Id. at 152.
29   Lazonick, supra note 21, at 6-7.

union-relations. The growing Italian tile cluster stimulated wider mechanisms for factor creation."[30]

Given this dynamic interaction of organization and technology, the rapid interfirm diffusion of product and process innovations that Porter identifies in Sassuolo are attributable to the existence of cohesive industrial and technological communities, rooted in cooperation. Indeed, Porter's analysis as well as research by others suggest that cooperation, not competition, is the root cause of Sassuolo success.[31] For example, Brusco likewise reports that *"in the [Sassuolo] ceramic tile industry, the machines which move the tiles uninterruptedly along the glazing lines, or which detect breakages through the. use of sonic waves, were not the product of formal research, but were rather developed through the collaboration of the tile firms with a number of small engineering firms."*[32]

The role of cooperation is again highlighted when Porter summarizes the Italian ceramic tile case. Foreign firms must compete not with a single firm, or even a group of firms, but with an entire subculture. The organic nature of this system is the hardest to duplicate and therefore the most sustainable advantage of Sassuolo firms.[33]

The ceramic tile case study is recounted here not to argue that domestic rivalry was absent, or that it did not create pressures on individual enterprises to respond to the innovations of their competitors. Rather, it is that rivalry in and of itself cannot explain the ability of an enterprise to respond innovatively to competitive challenges. Thus Porter's own case studies suggest that the basic problem many industries face in the United States is not insufficient rivalry but insufficient cooperation and information sharing.

---

30   Id. (quoting Porter, supra note 21, at 216).
31   Best, M. H. (1990): *The New Competition: Institutions of Industrial Restructuring.* Cambridge (Mass.): Harvard University Press.
32   Brusco, S. (1982): "The Emilian Model: Productive Decentralization and Social Integration". In: *Cambridge Journal of Economics*, 6, 167, 179.
33   Porter, supra note 21, at 225.

4. Some Additional Circumstances in which Information Sharing Can Support Innovation and/or Competition

4.1 Establishing Dominant Standards Through Information Sharing and Coordination[34]

Compatibility standards are essential if products and their complements are to be used in a system. Computers need software, compact disc players need compact discs, televisions need programs, and bolts need nuts. Compatibility standards define the format for the interface between the core and complementary goods, so that, for example, compact disc players from any manufacturer may use compact discs from any music company.

The advantage of a standard is that the greater the installed base of the core product, the more complementary goods are likely to be produced by independent vendors, in turn increasing demand for the core good. In the compact disc example, the more households that have disc players, the more titles record companies are likely to publish on compact disc. The same mechanism applies when the complement is a service, such as a maintenance network for aircraft, or when the complement is other users of the same product, as with a telephone network.

Standards apply not only to many products that use digital electronics but also to such mundane articles as ski bindings, flashlight batteries, bank cards, stapling guns, and petroleum products, and more generally to knowledge of how to use a product, such as prescribing a pharmaceutical or operating a computer. In each case the demand for the core product increases the larger the base of products using the same standard. The standard increases the total market for the product because it enables network externalities to be enjoyed.[35] Although the standard may only define the interface between core and complementary goods, this has a deep influence on the internal design of products so that common standards may require that compatible products employ similar technology.

---

34 The discussion of standards here is largely confined to compatibility standards. For an excellent survey, see Greenstein, S. (1993): "Invisible Hands Versus Invisible Advisors: Coordination Mechanism in Economic Networks". Department of Economics, University of Illinois, Champaign-Urbana, Working Paper No. 93-0111. This section draws heavily on Greenstein. See also Grindley, P. (1992): *Standards, Business Strategy and Policy: A Casebook*, for some useful case studies.

35 Grindley, P.: "Managing Technology: Organizing for Competitive Advantage". In: Swann, P. (ed.) (1993): *New Technologies and the Firm.*

The dynamics of a new standard are that once the installed base achieves critical mass, both core and complement producers join the bandwagon, often driving the rapid adoption of a new design, as happened recently with compact discs displacing the old vinyl records. The result is that a successful standard will usually dominate the whole market, leaving few if any niches for nonstandard products. An open standard, which is licensed cheaply to other manufacturers, is more likely to dominate the market than a protected standard, where the owner of the design must provide more of both core and complementary goods itself or sponsor others to do so.

To establish common standards, meetings and exchanges of technical information are often necessary.[36] Such meetings can cause antitrust suspicion. However, so long as prices are not the subject of discussion, and so long as an agreement on standards does not disguise coordinated efforts to reduce output, there is little that should warrant antitrust concern.[37] The advantages to society associated with the widespread adoption of common standards can be very large, as network externalities are often considerable. It is, therefore, critical that antitrust law and litigation do not stand in the way of such activities.

Trade associations, consortia, and professional societies often sponsor standards. Consortia also often have the capacity to stimulate nonaffiliated firms to produce complementary components, as the consortia's existence and mandate can help ensure that the standards' integrity will be met. Sometimes downstream (upstream) groups can help sponsor standards for suppliers (distributors). For instance, trade associations from the grocery business helped encourage manufacturers to support bar coding their packaging.[38] Consortia may also help overcome regional separations, as was necessary, for instance, to establish national automatic teller networks.[39]

Professional organizations have had a long history assisting in the formation and adoption of standards. The International Telegraph and Telephone Consultative Committee (CCITT), Institute of Electrical and Electronic Engineers (IEEE), American Society for Testing and Materials (ASTM), American National Standards Institute (ANSI), and other groups have had especially visible

---

36   Standards can be set by noncooperative means as well, by a dominant firm, or from a battle for a standard in an oligopoly.

37   It is usually very difficult to mask a cartel with a standard-setting ruse. Cartels require the involvement of senior management and require agreement on variables not normally part of the standard-setting activity.

38   Keen, S. A. (1988): "Adoption and Interfirm Diffusion of Innovation". Department of Economics, Stanford University, Working Paper.

39   Salop, S. C. (1990): "Deregulating Self-Regulated ATM Networks". In: *Economics of Innovation and New Technology*, 1, 85.

involvement in the development of technical standards.[40] These associations serve as forums for standards, development, and dissemination of information about standards.[41] Sometimes such groups merely ratify standards. determined by market processes. Usually they are more active, often even anticipating technical change in network industries and helping to guide design.[42]

One feature of these organizations is that many are voluntary.[43] Therefore, designers of new products must have some incentive for embedding a technical standard in their products since use is optional. Knowledge that the standard will become dominant is often sufficient motivation. Though most firms belong to the relevant associations and societies, their desire to participate in the development of standards can vary for a variety of technical and strategic reasons. This can lead to "free riding" on the involvement of others in the standard-setting function. It can sometimes also lead to the opposite.

Voluntary standards organizations play many useful roles in solving network coordination problems, especially those related to lack of communication. They can serve as a forum for providers or for users to educate each other about the

---

40 Cropper, W. V. (1980): "The Voluntary Development of Concensus Standards in ASTM". In: *ASTM Standardization News*, 8, 14. Hemenway, D. (1975): *Industrywide Voluntary Product Standards*; Cargill, C. F. (1983): *Information Technology Standardization: Theory, Process, and Organization*; Spring, M. B.: "Information Technology Standards", 26. In: Williams, M. (ed.) (1991): *Annual Review of Information Science and Technology*.

41 Weiss, M. B. H. and Sirbu, M. A. (1990): "Technological Choice in Voluntary Standards Setting Committees: An Empirical Analysis". In: *Economics of Innovation and New Technology*, 1, 111.

42 Witten, I. H. (1983): "Welcome to the Standard Jungle: An in Depth Look at the Confusing World of Computer Connections". In: *Byte*, 8, 146-78; C. F. Cargill, supra note 40; David, P. A. and Greenstein, S. (1989): "Compatibility Standards and Information Technology – Business Strategy, Market Development and Public Policies: A Synopsis of Panelists' Statements and the Discussion at the CEPR Compatibility Standards Workshop", Stanford University, Center for Economic Policy Research Publication, No. 159; Besen, S. M. (1990): "The European Telecommunications Standards Institute: A Preliminary Analysis". *Telecommuniations Pol'y*, 14, 521; OECD Committee for Information, Computers and Communication Policy (1991): *Information Technology Standards: The Economic Dimension*, 9.

43 The major exception in the United States is when standards written by voluntary standards groups are required by law or administrative fiat, as with building codes. Rosenberg, E. S. (1976): "Standards and Industry Self-Regulation". *Cal. Mgt. Rev.*, 19, 79. When governments get involved, it is often for the purpose of writing or choosing a standard directly. On occasion government bodies will also rely on those standards determined by an industry umbrella group.

nature of the problems to be solved.[44] They may also serve as a forum to discuss and plan the development of a system of compatible components.[45] They may also serve to document and disseminate agreements about technical specifications of standards.[46] Standards developed by such groups can serve as a focal point for designers who must choose among many technical solutions when embedding a standard in a component design. Such groups are most likely to succeed when market participants desire interoperability, need to establish a mechanism for communication, and lack an alternative means to develop or choose one of many technical alternatives.[47]

However, when technology is changing rapidly, standard-setting activities may get bypassed because cooperative efforts may simply be too slow.[48] When events become too technically complex and fluid, a focal point is easily lost. This problem is already arising in telecommunications as private networks proliferate. Reaching agreement on an Integrated Services Digital Network (ISDN), for instance, is complicated if once ISDN standards are written, the nature of technology has changed so that the standard is no longer ideal from a technical standpoint. Standards do not serve as a guide to component designers if the standards organization is overwhelmed by technical changes and must frequently amend its standards.

In sum, voluntary standard setting can improve outcomes for participants and society, particularly when markets are fragmented. Standard-setting organizations are one more avenue through which a system may develop. They are an important forum in which competitors may communicate. Since the societal benefits associated with capturing the network externalities made possible by common standards are considerable, antitrust analysts must be especially careful not to construe beneficial information sharing as collusion, which warrants legal interference.

---

44 Sirbu , M. A. and Hughes, K. (1986): "Standardization of Local Area Networks". Unpublished manuscript, Department of Engineering and Public Policy, Carnegie Mellon University.

45 Weiss and Sirbu, supra note 41.

46 Sirbu, M. A. and Zwimpfer, L. E. (1985): "Standards Setting for Computer Communication: The Case of X.25". In: *IEEE Communications*, 23, 35.

47 Besen, S. M. and Johnson, L. L. (1986): *Compatibility Standards, Competition, and Innovation in the Broadcasting Industry*. Santa Monica (Calif.): Rand.

48 Lehr, W. (1989): *ISDN: An Economist's Primer for a New Telecommunications Technology*, unpublished manuscript.

4.2 Benchmarking[49]

Another reason firms competing with each other may seek linkages and communication is to capture the stimulative benefits of benchmarking. Benchmarking is the process by which firms discover the degree to which they are not world-class in their various functional activities and institute programs to emulate best practices. Typically, benchmarking involves collecting information from excellent companies inside as well as outside the industry, either directly or through third parties.

While some aspects of benchmarking are little more than competitive intelligence gathering, what makes benchmarking distinctive is the focus on sharing information. As Robert Camp, an early champion of benchmarking, points out, *"We're beginning to recognize that sharing benchmarking data benefits everyone,"* and *"getting companies to share information readily is a significant directional change in the corporate culture of this country."*[50] It involves a recognition that cooperation in the sharing of information and experiences, even with one's competitors, is generally a stimulus to improvement.

Benchmarking, by bringing in external information to the firm, has a salutary effect in galvanizing companies to compete once they recognize how far behind they are and what they can do to improve. Benchmarking at the pace and scale now ongoing in the United States is a relatively new phenomenon. To some, benchmarking activities may appear contrary to sound antitrust policy because they often involve information sharing with competitors.[51] However, there is no evidence to support the notion, common in antitrust thinking, that ignorance of one's competitors' costs and/or internal quality programs is procompetitive. To the contrary, knowledge that one's competitors are ahead can be and has been a tremendous stimulus to action.[52] Moreover, knowledge of how competitors

---

49   This section is based in part on Jorde, T. M. and Teece, D. J. (1993): "Rule of Reason Analysis of Horizontal Arrangements: Agreements Designed to Advance Innovation and Commercialize Technology". In: *Antitrust Law Journal*, 61, 579.

50   See Camp, R. C, (1989): *Benchmarking: The Search for Industry Best Practices that Lead to Superior Performance*, 3.

51   Practitioners have recognized the potential for antitrust problems. As one practical guide notes, "Some types of data sharing (e.g., with out-of-industry companies) are clearly legal. Other types of data sharing go on all the time, with some corporations considering them proper and legal, and other corporations thinking overwise. Your own company rules and advice of your corporate attorney should be your guideline." Kaiser Associates, Inc., (1988): *Beating the Competition: A Practical Guide to Benchmarking*, 41.

52   These types of behavioral considerations, while obvious to most, are not part of the apparatus of neoclassical price theory. Accordingly, they tend to be unnecessarily denigrated.

achieved success can help guide a company committed to renovating its structures and systems, lowering costs, and achieving maximum efficiency.

By sharing benchmarking information with one or a small number of competitors, a firm might better position itself against other competitors. Sharing information of one's own successes may lead to the receipt of information from other firms concerning their successes. Overall, the exchanging firms are likely to he better off. Firms that are better at benchmarking will display superior financial performance.

As the number and market shares of the firms in an industry exchanging information increase, antitrust concerns may arise that will require careful assessment and balancing. Rule of reason analysis is the appropriate vehicle. Yet, in almost all circumstances there will be no anticompetitive harm. Indeed, were agencies and third parties to litigate over information exchange in bona fide benchmarking programs, it would have its own long run anticompetitive effects, throttling down one of the major forces of organizational renewal currently at work in America.

4.3 Information Exchanges on "Common Values"

There are often benefits when firms exchange or otherwise share information on "common values." Common values are industry or market aggregates. In the petroleum industry, an example would be industry (national or international) oil and gas reserves; in the hotel industry, it might be upcoming conferences and conventions in a particular city; in the auto industry, it might be changes in demand or in external technological developments; in the semiconductor industry, it might be the identity of future technologies and the limits of the present. Sharing such information improves forecasts of future supply and demand, and enables operations and investments to be scheduled more confidently and efficiently.

This phenomenon can be explained statistically. Suppose a firm has the task of estimating some parameter of great importance, such as future demand, the weather, or possibly even the price of a key input. The statistic of interest is quite uncertain. Each firm in the industry has some separate foundation for estimating its value. By sharing such imperfect knowledge, firms in an industry are likely to increase the accuracy of their judgments because their modal observations are likely to be better predictors than any one firm's observation. With better estimates of uncertain common values, operations and investments can be scheduled more confidently and efficiently, thereby lowering longterm costs. Basically, cost savings are generated because overinvestment and underinvestment are minimized, and operations are better tuned to supply and demand than might otherwise be the case.

Information sharing of this kind may tend to homogenize beliefs about key industry parameters. One consequence is that the quality of investment decisions is improved. Another may well be the reduction of price dispersion in an industry because firms will tend to make pricing errors less often. The level of prices is also likely to be reduced in the long term because of the efficiency consequences noted above, which competition will force to be passed on to consumers. These types of information exchanges do not constitute price-fixing agreements, and the benefits obtained by the firm in question do not come at the expense of the consumer. Similar observations regarding the effects of information exchange on prices have been advanced by Judge Richard Posner, who notes that the purpose of legitimate exchange of information is *"to narrow the dispersion of prices – that is, to eliminate, as far as possible, those prices in the tails of the price distribution that reflect the ignorance of buyers or sellers concerning the conditions of supply and demand. There is no reason to expect the price level – the average price in the market – to change."*[53]

4.4 Industry Visions

Ministry of International Trade and Industry (MITI) vision statements, an attempt by industry and government to identify emerging industries, are a recognized component of Japanese industrial policy. In the U.S. semiconductor industry, vision statements have now become a reality, along with plans for their implementation. A new form of industrial policy initiated not by government but by the private sector has thus now arrived in the United States. Its creation and implementation requires considerable information exchange.

The need for an industry vision in the U.S. semiconductor industry can be understood in terms of the common values discussion above; but it goes one step further. It takes into account Japanese competition and how to respond to it collectively. Cooperation is sought not only between industry, government, and academia but implicitly within industry as well, albeit for "precompetitive" activities where the definition of precompetitive is stretched to embrace certain basic manufacturing processes.

Currently, the U.S. semiconductor industry could claim to be the first U.S. electronics industry to have recaptured leadership from the Japanese in the postwar period. Cooperation within the industry and between the industry and government, including the use of an industrial consortium, Semiconductor

53   Posner, supra note 11, at 1197.

Manufacturing Technology Consortium (SEMA-TECH), appears to deserve some part of the credit. In 1993, the industry, through the Semiconductor Industry Association, published a fifteenyear "shared vision" for technological development, which was advanced as a "technological roadmap." Following the roadmap would require "a new infrastructure" to a new period of cooperation. This cooperation requires a common vision that spans the entire semiconductor industry (including its suppliers and customers) and extends as well to academia, government, and electronics users. The pervasive importance of semiconductor-based electronics, coupled with the high cost, complexity, and sophistication of integrated circuit technology of the late 1990s, compel the creation of this new shared vision. Success requires expanded teamwork and cooperation throughout the private and public domestic semiconductor infrastructure.

The essence of a common vision is strategic coordination, or at least strategic alignment. As Gordon Moore, Chairman of Intel, puts it, *"We must create a common national plan from these separate approaches so that the industry is all singing from the same sheet of music."*[54] He might also have added that effective coordination of government policy and private strategies is also critical. To my knowledge, the semiconductor industry's roadmaps, which include technological characteristics and cost targets, are the first time in recent history that a U.S. industry has engaged in a process to identify common objectives and has sought to align public and private investment behind it.

Old school antitrust analysts might view such activities inhospitably. Yet, such behavior should not be objectionable under current conditions. The most important reason that such activities should be supported is the existence of significant foreign competition, particularly from Japan. The existence of multiple centers of competition in an industry clearly softens any concerns that cooperation of this kind is the harbinger of cartelization. Antitrust theory and jurisprudence must accommodate rather than resist the new reality.

5. Conclusion

Concerted action among otherwise independent actors – contracts, combinations, and conspiracies – is judged sternly under Section I of the Sherman Act. Though the per se rule of horizontal restraints is almost dead, and rule of reason reigns, there are few guidelines with respect to what are legitimate rule of reason defenses and what are not. This vacuum exists because economic theory provides too few hints as to the efficiency properties (or lack thereof) of various forms of

---

54   Robinson, J. (1992): "Moore: Unity Tech Strategy". In: *Electronic News*, July 27, 1992, at 1, 23.

cooperation. The reason is that in economic theory the price system performs miracles. Extraordinary coordinating functions are imputed that it generally cannot attain, at least in the context of innovation, without being augmented by networks, information flows, and associated cooperation. Hence, economic arguments based on neoclassical theory often come up short in explaining the rationale for various forms of cooperation that either are or ought to be ubiquitous. Industrial clusters, benchmarking, and the formation of technology visions are striking examples of phenomena that seem quite anomalous if the only lens through which one is looking is neoclassical price theory.

If, however, one looks to organizational economics and puts innovation and change center stage, it can be seen that many forms of industrial cooperation and information sharing – just a few of which have been examined here – are very understandable and, in fact, desirable. One should not assume that one is looking at the innards of a cartel just because some economists with a limited understanding of business institutions and the role of cooperation may be stumped in explicating the rationale for complex organizational arrangements and forms of business behavior.

D

Regulation and Deregulation

[22]

Natural Gas Distribution in California

Regulation, Strategy, and Market Structure

Michael V. Russo and David J. Teece

I. INTRODUCTION

Though stability has nearly returned to America's natural gas industry, the tumultuous events of the late 1970s and early 1980s will not soon be forgotten. The period's disruptive effects, manifested in swings in prices and supply, profoundly affected California's natural gas market. Among the reasons why a study of policy making during this unsettled time is instructive are the unique structure of the state's supply system, the political and social forces that historically have characterized statewide regulation, and the potential for this experience to lead to major change in future years.

This chapter focuses on the distribution segment of the industry in the years 1972–1986, a period marked at its beginning by the highest level of natural gas sales nationally and at its end by a new approach to regulating the state's gas market. The analysis spotlights California's two major gas distribution companies, Pacific Gas and Electric Company (PG&E) and Southern California Gas Company (SCG). Together, their retail sales accounted for roughly 95% of statewide sales in 1982.[1]

No study would be complete without an examination of the regulatory structure in which these companies operate. The principal agencies involved are the Federal Energy Regulatory Commission (FERC) and the California Public Utilities Commission (CPUC). This chapter will de-

The authors are grateful to the American Gas Association, the California Public Utilities Commission, the Interstate Natural Gas Association, Pacific Gas and Electric Company, and Southern California Gas Company for cooperation and assistance in compiling data for this chapter.

1. The remainder was sold by several small private utilities and municipal services.

scribe the elements of regulation as used in practice by these agencies, particularly the CPUC. Textbook models of regulation that assume continuity and instantaneous adjustment will be shown to be particularly unhelpful in trying to understand the realities of natural gas regulation in California. We will demonstrate how the gas market responded to the pursuit of sociopolitical goals established by regulators and to sudden and unpredicted economic change, and how the policies of utilities and regulators have greatly affected the California market. We will show how the regulatory process is characterized by strategic behavior by both utilities and regulators, and we will attempt to capture the ultimate effect of this contentiousness on economic welfare in California. We will also analyze the costs of gas distribution to gain insight into economic efficiency and cost minimization under regulation.

Special attention is directed to the industrial sector, which is one of four retail classes commonly identified in California. The others are residential, commercial, and electricity generation. Although the cost of serving industrial customers is undoubtedly less than most of the other classes, until recent years customers in this class paid substantially higher rates than the residential, electricity generation, and commercial classes. Because during the initial years of the study industrial users paid less than the average, at prices presumably closer to actual costs, the transition to higher relative prices was both rapid and painful.[2]

The overall goals of this study are to develop a deeper understanding of the California natural gas market and to provide the foundation for policies that will facilitate the transition to a competitive future. We will use a strong historical perspective to gain a depth of awareness with respect to current problems and opportunities. Section II will describe the federal regulation of natural gas prices and sales. The natural gas market in the state of California is the focus of Section III. Section IV will discuss California gas ratemaking during the study period, considering the issue of imbedded cost of service estimates developed by the CPUC and one firm it regulates. Section V will investigate that portion of the burner-tip price associated with transporting the gas from the utility's border (generally referred to as the city-gate) to its ultimate end use (generally referred to as the burner tip). A description of the response of industrial users to the present conditions then follows. Finally, we conclude with recommendations as to policies that can assist in the further transition to an economically sustainable California gas market.

2. An illustration comes from SCG. While average delivered (burner-tip) prices to residential customers have risen about fivefold from 1972 to 1984, the increase was more than twelvefold for industrial users.

II. THE NATIONAL MARKET

Historical Background

Gas was first put to commercial use for lighting city streets. It was not natural gas but coal gas. Although electricity had replaced gas as the prime source of municipal lighting by the late 19th century, a new market for gas was to emerge, as the early 20th century saw the invention of appliances that used gas for household purposes, first for cooking, then for water and space heating. By the late 1920s, pipeline technologies had been developed that allowed low-cost long-distance transportation of natural gas from the newly discovered fields in the south-central states to urban markets to the east, north, and west (Tussig and Barlow, 1984). A rapidly expanding natural gas industry resulted.

Before its recognition and use as a valuable resource, natural gas production was influenced by regulations put in place by states in regard to oil drilling. Oil and gas ownership has long been governed by the rule of capture, which effectively means that oil or gas belongs to the owner from whose well it emerges. Because petroleum deposits do not respect property lines, the discovery of oil on a parcel of land usually meant that nearby land owners had to begin production immediately or lose their right to claim a share of the deposit. States, fearful of the waste associated with these practices, controlled the extraction procedures a producer could employ, such as a limit on spacing of wells. These conservation laws made it easier for the states to inhibit the waste of gas, originally seen as an unwanted by-product of oil extraction. They also set a precedent for state regulation of local gas industries.

Although states had the power to regulate local rates charged by gas distribution companies, interstate transactions were free from regulation until 1938. The absence of interstate regulation meant that the downstream control exercised by state commissions could not significantly affect the price paid by utilities at the city gates, where ownership passed from the pipeline to the distribution utility. Not surprisingly, many interstate pipeline companies were highly profitable during this period.

The Natural Gas Act of 1938 resulted from a comprehensive Federal Trade Commission study and lively congressional debate. The act subjected interstate transmission of gas to Federal Power Commission (FPC) control. Transportation rates were to be "just and reasonable." In addition, no company could extend an interstate pipeline into a market already served by an existing pipeline without the prior consent of the FPC. Although the FPC could regulate field sales by a gas producer to a pipeline if the two companies were affiliated, the FPC took the position that it had no purview over a transaction between separate companies. This interpretational issue was the subject of a number of congressional bills intended to explicitly exempt nonaffiliated sales from federal regulation, but for different reasons each was met with a presidential veto.[3] The courts were thus left with the responsibility of interpreting the act, and the Supreme Court got its opportunity with the Phillips Petroleum case in 1954.[4]

In 1954 Phillips Petroleum Company, the largest independent natural gas producer, raised its wholesale rates to pipelines. These pipelines passed along the higher costs, but the ultimate consumers, which in this case were states and cities to the north, complained bitterly. The Federal Trade Commission declined to review the case, and it was taken to court. The Supreme Court ruled in favor of the plaintiffs, assigning the FPC dominion over wellhead gas pricing.[5]

The case-by-case approach to rate setting initially employed by the FPC became onerous, so in 1960 it divided the country into several rate areas, setting ceiling prices for gas in each.[6] The only distinction within the areas was between "old" and "new" gas, where new gas was that discovered after 1960. Dissatisfaction with the operation of the gas industry under these controls led to further disaggregation of gas price categories. The cumbersome nature of ratemaking for the 23 geographic areas defined by the FPC led to the setting of a nationwide price in 1974 for gas discovered after 1973. This basic structure, which retained many of the various subcategories for gas discovered before 1973, remained in effect until the passage of the Natural Gas Policy Act of 1978.

The Natural Gas Policy Act of 1978

Passed amid widespread fear of gas shortages at prevailing, regulated prices, the NGPA was intended to stimulate the development of new sources by deregulating new and high-cost supplies. Old gas supplies dedicated to interstate commerce before the introduction of the NGPA in Congress were to remain regulated indefinitely. New gas, generally that developed after this introduction, remained regulated until January 1985 or July 1987, depending on the depth of the well. High-cost gas supplies produced from deep wells and other expensive sources after the enactment date were deregulated soon after the act's passage.

The act also gave the FERC, the successor agency to FPC, some power to control wellhead prices at sources destined for intrastate sales. A complicated set of rules controlled how interstate pipelines were to pass

3. An account of the politics behind these decisions is contained in Tussig and Barlow (1984).
4. See *Phillips Petroleum Company vs. Wisconsin et al.*, 342 US 672 (1954).
5. Ibid.
6. For a brief overview of the sequence of FERC pricing regimes, see Braeutigam (1981).

along costs of new gas to industrial users and power plants.[7] The intent of this provision was to equalize the Btu cost of distillate oil and natural gas used for boiler fuel.

Under the NGPA, the prospect for higher natural gas prices triggered exploration for new gas, but incentives to produce more old gas were weakened. Furthermore, the pipelines rolled in old gas with new and high-cost gas, so that prices to customers reflected the average cost rather than the marginal cost of gas. The NGPA thus inevitably caused distortions and inefficiencies (Braeutigam, 1981). However, because of the excess gas supply on hand on January 1, 1985, one anticipated effect of the NGPA never took place. That date passed without the sudden increase in price predicted by observers as late as 1982,[8] although price controls on vast amounts of new gas were lifted.

Recent Federal Regulatory Issues

The statutes of the NGPA were designed in anticipation of continued escalation in energy prices. For the first several years, this expectation proved accurate. As just mentioned, some of these distortions and inefficiencies were predicted. However, the effect that the NGPA would have on the ensuing soft natural gas market was not widely foreseen.

A combination of several factors, notably increased competition from distillate oil, the effect of conservation efforts, and warmer-than-expected winters caused an ebb in the demand for gas, starting in late 1982. Gas pipelines found themselves without markets for their gas supplies, but bound by take-or-pay contracts to continue accepting or paying for gas.[9] Estimates of the gas surplus vary, but the Department of Energy released figures in 1986 (Energy Information Administration, 1986) showing the surplus rising from 660 to 2036 billion cubic feet and staying at that high level through early 1986. During the post-1982 years, it became apparent that the NGPA offered little guidance when prices were in decline.

Previously, due to rolled-in pricing and the perception that gas prices would continue to climb, purchase prices for new and high-priced gas rose to record levels during the 1978–1982 period, topping out at over $11/thousand cubic feet.[10] The tendency to pay well above the prevailing

7. Braeutigam (1981) provides further depth on these policies.

8. Willis B. Wood, president of Pacific Lighting Gas Supply Company, testimony before the U.S. House of Representatives Subcommittee on Fossil Fuels, August 6, 1982 (in California Energy Commission, 1983, p. 32).

9. Take or pay provisions force a pipeline to pay for gas whether it is taken or not. Even if accepted later, the pipeline incurs major carrying costs through such delays.

10. Because gas greater than 15,000 feet below the surface was statutorily deregulated by NGPA, these reserves were the subject of great recovery efforts in the "deep-gas boom of 1978–1982," as Tussing and Barlow (1984) refer to it. There was a corresponding crash in these efforts in the soft gas market in subsequent years.

market price for new gas supplies may have been affected by a given pipeline's endowment of old gas; the more old gas it had to "cushion" the cost of the new and high-priced gas it purchased and rolled in, the more it could afford to pay for this gas and still remain competitive.[11] This strategy stemmed from the pipelines' expectation that a ready market for any gas existed, assuring the viability of rolled-in pricing. When the market softened, however, pressure on pipelines to curtail pipeline purchases of high-cost gas increased. The result has been the take-or-pay crisis, an important problem in the natural gas industry that will be addressed below.

In resolving take-or-pay liabilities and a host of other issues, the FERC has felt it necessary to balance equity and efficiency on several fronts. Consider the pressure exerted by end users and utilities to purchase gas directly from producers and pay pipelines only for transportation. Such contract carriage represents a more efficient option for end users and utilities because it reduces their costs. Unfortunately for the pipelines, gas purchased at levels too high to sell without rolling it in with lower-cost gas may remain unsold if the use of contract carriage broadens. Most of the commitments by pipelines to purchase high-cost gas reserves were made under a regulatory regime that assumed that parties at either end of the pipeline would never recontract. Therefore the issue of fairness to the pipelines became a salient one at the FERC. But the equity/efficiency trade-off also persists at the up- and downstream ends of the pipelines. Gas producers, who had installed facilities to extract higher-priced gas based on very favorable contracts with pipelines, and captive customers who have only one pipeline from which to purchase both complained bitterly (Stalon, 1986).

The FERC's early responses to these protests reflected the intent to phase in direct sales by producers to consumers. The FERC's Order 436 (Federal Energy Regulatory Commission, 1985) represented an attempt to respond to the needs of consumers by giving incentives to pipelines to offer contract carriage on a nondiscriminatory basis.[12] Although there were allegations that pipelines did, in fact, discriminate, the program appears to have gained acceptance among pipelines (Wall Street Journal, 1986). A second proposal is the so-called block-billing system. Under this program, gas would be separated into two blocks, essentially based on whether it was old gas (block 1) or new and high-cost gas (block

11. This tendency is not as straightforward as is sometimes asserted. For a statistical analysis of contracting practices by pipelines, see Energy Information Administration (1982b).

12. The most important of these incentives was that the pipelines could flow through into rates reasonable take-or-pay settlements if they joined the 436 program. Downstream, customers of participating pipelines would be allowed to reduce their minimum commitments for pipeline gas by 25%/year for four years (later extended to 20% for five years, beginning after an interim period).

2). Block 1 gas would be allocated to each pipeline customer based on historical usage; needs beyond that level could be met in a variety of ways. These FERC initiatives represent efforts to bring prices in line with marginal costs in the industry, while respecting equity considerations by preventing discriminatory pricing to the extent possible under existing regulatory conditions.

It will be helpful to review the prospects for deregulation of wellhead pricing and pipeline transportation. Given the FERC's public statements concerning the remission of regulation in the natural gas industry,[13] such an exercise is no longer academic.

Wellhead Deregulation

Under the NGPA, there is provision for deregulation of a majority of gas after 1985. By early 1985, gas purchased from price-controlled wells represented only about 36% of the total (Williams, 1985). One can expect that over the long run there will be some movement toward market-driven pricing in the industry, as supplies of indefinitely controlled old gas are depleted.[14] Although proponents of decontrol can take some comfort in this prospect, the depletion argument understates the magnitude of remaining distortions because the NGPA stipulates that the price of additions to reserves of old gas be controlled. Thus one lingering inefficiency will remain: if additions to old gas reservoirs cost more to recover than their controlled price, they will remain in situ, even though their value on the spot market or in contracts may be well in excess of the cost of recovery. A study by the Office of Technology Assessment (1984) estimated the incremental effect of decontrolling old gas reserves, the sum of additions due to delayed abandonment, infill drilling, and well stimulation, at 19–38 trillion cubic feet. This number represents a 9.5 to 19.0% increase in the nation's gas reserves, as measured on January 1, 1984. Insofar as these incremental supplies are instead replaced by higher-cost supplies, wasteful expenditures are made.

As described above, the historical reason generally advanced for the institution of wellhead price regulation under the *Phillips* decision was the perceived market power wielded by upstream producers. Regardless of whether producers did, in fact, have market power at that time, our opinion, as well as that of most observers, is that this is not the case today. This view is corroborated by a 1983 Department of Energy study (Energy Information Administration, 1983), which investigated seller concentration in major natural gas producing areas, each smaller than relevant markets. In no area of the country, except Alaska, did the own-

---

13. Stalon (1986) discusses FERC's visions of future regulatory reform.

14. According to Broadman (1987), "virtually all gas will be decontrolled" by the late 1990s.

ership percentage of the 16 largest producers exceed 61.3%. Furthermore, aside from Alaska, no Herfindahl-Hirschman Index for any of the nine major areas[15] was above 0.062, which, using the Department of Justice's criteria, makes each area "unconcentrated."

Thus on strictly economic efficiency terms, the argument for continued regulation of any gas reserves is weak. The preservation of this regulation can best be seen as politically motivated. As such, one can understand that the essential struggle is over the perceived benefits from regulation flowing to the various segments of the country's population. Evidence of the enormous importance attached by regional interests to the wellhead price deregulation issue is shown in a study by the National Regulatory Research Institute (1983). The study focused on 47 bills concerning the gas industry introduced into the House of Representatives in the first six months of 1983. Seventeen of these bills dealt with price controls.[16] What one clearly sees in this analysis is that major differences among states, generally based on whether they produce or consume gas, drive the activity of their representatives in these matters. Producing states want deregulation; consuming states favor continued regulation.[17] Given the different, and often conflicting, goals of politics and economics, this is not surprising, but it indicates the importance of leadership from the federal agencies, such as the FERC.

The impact of deregulation of wellhead prices depends in part, however, on the behavior of interstate pipelines and on the regulatory posture of the state regulatory commissions. The existence of any market power could impede the relay of marginal-cost pricing signals to final consumers.

Pipeline Deregulation Issues

To determine the feasibility of deregulation, a model to assess market power is needed. Analysis of oil pipelines (Teece, 1985) indicates that if workable competition exists in the relevant product markets, pipeline regulation is not needed. Some information on the relevance of this principle to interstate gas pipelines exists (German and Roland, 1985). Table 5.1 displays data on the number of pipelines serving producing

15. The other eight areas are Appalachian-Illinois, Other South, Southern Louisiana, Texas Gulf Coast, Permian Basin, Hugoton-Anadarko, Rocky Mountain, and California.

16. Other natural gas issues for which bills were initiated dealt with purchase contract provisions, pipeline carrier status, and other issues.

17. More recent evidence suggests that the issue of regional winners and losers is not as clear as it may appear. Kalt and Leone (1986) analyze decontrol, including important secondary effects. Among their findings are: (1) because ownership of reserves is not geographically limited, benefits of decontrol accrue to stockholders in all states, and (2) to the extent that consuming states can pass along increased gas costs in the form of higher product prices, their "trade surplus" with producing states will reduce the net income transfer.

areas. These data indicate that the larger fields, representing 95% of total production, are, on average, served by a large number of pipelines. The table, however, aggregates data in a way that may distort the apparent competition, because not all gas in a given area can be obtained by any pipeline operating there.

When one considers the downstream end of interstate pipelines, the issue becomes more complex. Table 5.2 describes aspects of the resale market. This information is based on a sample of 26 companies developed by the American Gas Association (AGA). Although German and Roland conclude that 84% (58% + 26%) of sales are to distribution companies with alternative suppliers, the data do not accurately reflect the degree of competition, because the presence of just one alternative supplier need not always generate adequate gas-to-gas competition. In addition, of course, one would also like to be able to account for interfuel competition.

Further insight is provided by a separate AGA publication (American Gas Association, 1985), which disaggregates the first category. After deleting pipelines that provide less than 5% of a distribution company's need, the 58% figure shrinks to 53%, distributed as shown in Table 5.3. But these data are based on volumes, not points of transactions. According to Mead (1981, cited in Broadman, 1986), about 70% of all distributors are served by a single pipeline. For the remaining 30%, Broadman (pp. 18–19) points out that:

> Even where distributors are served by more than one pipeline there is some question as to the technical feasibility of switching among suppliers. Some distribution companies have non-integrated supply systems which, in effect, segment the distribution network into two or more independent systems. More important, a pipeline's capacity at delivery points generally is tailored to meet a specific level of demand. In the short run, shifting the balance among pipeline-suppliers may well be constrained by limits on the physical capacity of one (or more) of the pipelines.

Unfortunately, simply counting interconnect possibilities is not a particularly good way to measure the state of competition that gas pipelines face, and further analysis is needed. This analysis should include the effect of competition in end markets, such as that from fuel oil and local gas producers.

Take-or-Pay Issues

One additional feature of the national gas market that should be mentioned involves the contracting practices of pipelines and producers. Along with the physical structure of the industry, regulation engendered unusual provisions in these contracts. Although once useful, the changing market for natural gas has undermined the viability of a number of these provisions and brought into question the enforceability of contractual commitments to purchase gas at the wellhead.

A number of provisions typically found in natural gas wellhead purchase agreements are peculiar and rather idiosyncratic to the natural gas industry. Virtually all contracts contain obligations for the purchaser to take a minimum amount of gas at the stipulated price. A number of methods for redressing the failure to draw such "minimum takes" have been used. The most popular is the so-called take-or-pay provision, wherein the pipeline agrees either to take a minimum amount of gas or pay for it as if it had. Pipelines generally can take delivery of the gas at later dates, but payment must be made in the specified period.

Masten and Crocker (1985) portray the take-or-pay stipulation as an efficiency mechanism that induces pipelines to refuse deliveries only at the point where an alternative purchaser would be willing to buy that gas. The level of gas the pipeline must take from the producer as a percentage of its total receivability varies with factors relating to the market structure of the gas field and the extent to which the price ceiling on that particular type of gas is binding. Masten and Crocker find that the take level varies directly with the number of sellers in a field and the free market value of the gas and inversely with the number of pipelines serving a field and their concentration.

Even though take-or-pay provisions may be rooted in the pursuit of economic efficiency, the extent to which pipelines exposed themselves to risk through these commitments indicates an industrywide bet that the gas market would not soften as it did. In fact, high demand for gas and continued shortages in the mid-1970s made the possibility of a gas surplus appear so remote to pipelines that they were willing, on average, to commit to take more than 80% of gas under contract to them.[18] Conditions changed somewhat from 1979 through 1982, but even in 1982, no NGPA category of gas had an average take below 75.8 percent (Energy Information Administration 1982b).

However, when the nationwide surplus of gas developed, a number of major pipelines began incurring enormous liabilities. In 1983, six had accrued potential liabilities in excess of $100 million (Energy Information Administration, 1986). In 1984, although over $3.6 billion of liabilities

18. It should be noted, however, that minimum bill provisions at the downstream end of the pipelines essentially passed along the commitments. As such, this system could have been viewed as an effective substitute for vertical integration. When the FERC eliminated the gas portion of minimum bill provisions with Order 380, it created a major assymmetry in incentives at the up- and downstream ends of the pipelines. This ruling placed the burden of gas surpluses solely on the pipeline companies. It also created a strong incentive for pipelines to integrate further downstream, which may take place in future years.

had been settled, another $3.4 billion remained outstanding. That figure rose to $5.6 billion in 1985.[19]

These consequences have sent gas pipeline legal staffs searching for ways to justify their unilateral cancellation of major contracts. A number of legal doctrines theoretically could be drawn upon to legitimize these actions. One is claiming umbrage under *force majeure* clauses, the same provisions that protect companies against uncontrollable natural events, as well as labor strikes and well blowouts on occasion. Another possible route is using the doctrine of commercial impracticability, which has generally been used when an unforeseen event makes contractual performance economically unviable.[20] Neither of these escape hatches, however, will necessarily lead to release of take-or-pay obligations for pipelines. The issue appears headed for the courts.

The Future Federal Role in Natural Gas Regulation

A bold policy initiative would be to deregulate the entire natural gas industry upstream from the city gate immediately. Advocates of a more measured approach advance three reasons why caution should be exercised.

First, gas that is controlled in price is held so far below its market value that a sudden increase in its price would have major short-term ramifications. New, high gas prices, which have been inflated by rolled-in pricing, could collapse. The ensuing adjustment period could be quite severe.

Second, and related to the first, is the issue of long-term contracts. In the event of decontrol of old gas, pressure for abbrogation of contracts for new, high-cost gas will mount. As described above, most of the contracts for these supplies executed in the post-NGPA period do contain provisions to protect the producer if decontrolled new prices result in higher prices but do not correspondingly protect pipelines if decontrol of old gas suppresses new gas supplies. Thus there are asymmetries in the response of old and new gas prices under decontrol, indicating that prices could rise in the short run.[21] Policymakers also have to consider this effect of deregulation before finalizing new rules in the gas industry.

Finally, although the data are not as conclusive as one could hope for, some analysts point to strong circumstantial evidence indicating that in-

19. The years actually relate to the fiscal years of the companies, which may not correspond exactly to calendar years.

20. For an overview of the legal issues, see Gentry (1984).

21. The effect of contract escalation clauses not tied to the market is crucial here. According to Interstate Natural Gas Association of America (1986a), in mid-1986, amidst a still-sizable gas glut, almost as much gas under contract was increasing in price as was decreasing.

terstate pipelines do possess some market power. To ensure that decontrol works properly, concurrent attention will have to be focused on pipelines to study the extent of this power. If market power has been present, we believe that Order 436 sufficiently addresses the situation. As more pipelines become "open" under 436, pipeline market power will be eliminated.

Thus the evidence surveyed in this section indicates that workable competition exists in wellhead markets, and it appears that decontrol of old gas prices would assist efficiency goals. For political reasons, contract carriage will probably need to accompany gas price decontrol to ensure that the benefits wellhead deregulation brings to consumers are not captured by upstream pipelines. If persistent evidence exists that nondiscriminatory voluntary carriage is being resisted by pipelines, the FERC might consider mandatory carriage as a solution. A more drastic policy would be to make pipelines common carriers.

We now turn our attention to positioning California in the national setting, with special emphasis on how the state would fare in a deregulated gas price regime.

California in the National Setting

The California natural gas market is large by national standards, accounting for 9.6% of the country's consumption in 1983 (American Gas Association, 1984). In addition, the prospect of an enormous new market for gas in Kern County ensures that California's role will be great in the foreseeable future. California is also a major market for Canadian gas, receiving 23% of that country's gas exports in the United States in 1982 (American Gas Association, 1984).

California is endowed with major in-state gas reserves. In 1982, it produced 385 billion cubic feet of gas, equal to about 13% of its consumption. California is one of only two states in which no in-state production enters interstate markets (Michigan is the other). Rather, whatever gas is not used by the owner is generally sold to the local distribution utilities. Because Canadian imports represent an additional 20% of the state's consumption,[22] in 1982, gas not regulated by the federal government comprised about 33% of California's usage.

For in-state production, a classic monopsony situation applies, with the local utility acting as the sole available purchaser of gas. This situation, along with the low cost of transportation to the utility system, has kept in-state reserves relatively inexpensive. For PG&E, California gas was priced an average of 17.3% below PG&E's average for the years 1981 through 1985. On the other hand, the Canadian gas that PG&E

22. All of this gas is purchased by PG&E.

purchases has cost as much as 51% more than the system average price.[23]
This situation may be the result of the relative bargaining position at the
time of the execution of the contract with Canada. In any case, the importance of long-term contracts is still very high; PG&E's minimum
takes of gas from its suppliers represent about half of all of its purchased
volumes.

It is difficult to assess the effect of gas price deregulation on California markets. Presumably, if a single (transportation-adjusted) price for
gas then prevailed, old gas prices would rise, while new gas prices would
fall. Complete decontrol of old gas, assuming that the market clearing
price were stable, would thus result in an income transfer to states currently consuming large quantitites of new gas. Although the data do not
permit one to trace from wellhead to burner tip exactly how much of a
given state's gas purchases is old gas, an examination of the gas purchases of two of the pipelines accounting for a majority of the 56% of
the gas coming to California from other states is instructive.

Table 5.4 gives information on gas purchases by the 25 largest interstate pipelines, as submitted to the FERC. These figures are based on
the purchased gas adjustment (PGA) filings, made on a staggered basis
from September 1984 through April 1985, representing purchases in
the previous six months.

Even for the two California suppliers, the endowments of old gas differ considerably. For the sample as a whole, the range of percentage of
reserves comprised by old gas runs from 3.7 to 64.7%. The weighted average cost of gas purchased by California's suppliers was more consistent, averaging $2.71 per thousand cubic feet, close to the national
average.[24] For the nationwide sample, this number ranged from $2.06
to $3.73, a considerable range.

These numbers seem to indicate that not just rolled-in pricing has
varied the purchasing behavior by the pipelines. If this were so, one
would expect a narrower range in weighted average purchase costs, regardless of the differing endowments of old and new gas. The range of
purchased costs may also provide a reason why pipelines may be resist-
ing the more competitive environment that contract carriage would engender; given these figures, high-cost pipelines would have difficulty
marketing their own supplies.

Because California appears to be near the median in terms of both
old gas endowment and average costs, decontrol would probably not
cause severe adjustment problems, assuming prices for higher-priced

23. These figures were developed using PG&E's Report 10-K for the year 1985.

24. California's receipts may not correspond exactly to the pipelines' purchases. The
implicit assumption here is that these receipts are similar in constitution to the makeup
of gas purchased by the pipelines.

gas are free to decline so that a market clearing price is sustained.[25] Also, because California receives large quantities from in-state and Canadian sources, the impact of any sudden increase in interstate costs would be softened somewhat.[26] We should point out that the lack of crucial data, such as the exact nature of contract provisions and of the makeup of gas reaching California from interstate pipelines, makes this analysis necessarily speculative.

As stated above, without pipeline contract carriage requirements being linked to further (or full) wellhead decontrol, the effect of price decontrol at the wellhead is uncertain. In the absence of contract carriage there is some chance that gas pipelines would be among the beneficiaries due to the concentration of interstate pipelines serving California.[27] Whether California consumers would lose from wellhead deregulation in the short run will depend on whether market and environmental conditions permit competition from fuel oil. In the long run, we expect that welfare gains from gas field decontrol will outweigh any short-run losses.

III. NATURAL GAS IN THE STATE OF CALIFORNIA

The purpose of this section is to provide background on the nature of the market for natural gas in California. We will examine gas distribution companies, the state regulatory agency, and retail gas customers, particularly those in the industrial sector.

California's Major Gas Distributors

Figure 5.1 shows the system of gas pipelines operating in and around California. Several large mains that originate in the Texas gas fields enter the state. The major lines are operated by the El Paso Company and Transwestern Pipeline Company. The former is a subsidiary of Burlington Northern, Inc., the latter of Houston Natural Gas Corporation. To the north, a large pipeline operated by Pacific Gas Transmission

25. A model developed by the National Regulatory Research Institute (1983) used the difference in percentage increases in city-gate prices to investigate the impact of decontrol. It estimated effects by the region of the country, finding a 10–14% increase for the average customer, depending on the region and the assumptions used in that scenario. No single scenario produced a difference of greater than 2% between any two regions.

26. As long as contract provisions for non-interstate supplies do not contain provisions tying the price of that gas to interstate gas.

27. According to the American Gas Association (personal communication, 1985), of forty-six states for which data were available, the four-firm concentration ratios serving those states exceeded 90% in twenty-one cases. Though not a fully satisfactory measure of markets or market power, this evidence indicates that some potential for anti-competitive practices exists.

Company, a subsidiary of PG&E, brings gas from the western provinces of Canada to California. The network of smaller lines in northern California represents the Sacramento Valley gas fields; the southern network represents those of the San Joaquin valley. Figure 5.2 shows service areas of the two main gas distribution companies in the state.

Table 5.5 shows how the supplier profiles of PG&E and SCG have changed by contrasting their gas sources for 1982 and 1986. Although Canadian supplies have remained its largest source, PG&E has reduced its purchase of higher-cost El Paso gas by over one-half, substituting it with spot purchases. After making its first spot purchase in 1985, PG&E has strikingly expanded the role of these spot markets. California and Rocky Mountain purchases remained steady. PG&E serves most of northern California. Of its total load, approximately 71% is sold to residential, commercial, and industrial customers; the rest is used for electricity generation (Table 5.6). These electricity generation requirements account for a large portion of the gas company's revenues, reflecting the resource mix of the PG&E electric utility, which depends heavily on fossil fuels.

SCG serves most of southern California. Like PG&E, it has reduced purchases from southwestern pipelines by about one-half and sharply increased its use of spot markets (Table 5.5). It has also increased its use of Canadian and California onshore producers and greatly expanded its purchases from offshore sources and PG&E (mainly the former source). Unlike PG&E, it is not integrated into power production, so it sells a large quantity of gas to electric utilities for power generation. It also provides the City of Long Beach and San Diego Gas & Electric Company with their natural gas needs. The latter transactions are termed sales for resale or wholesale sales and comprise approximately 14.5% of the gas sold annually. The majority of gas is sold to customer classes as shown in Table 5.6.

Sales to customers are made according to several different price schedules, which correspond to priorities set by the CPUC, as well as according to whether or not the supply is delivered on an interruptible basis. There is a lifeline allowance for residential users, which differs by location within the system, home heating equipment (gas or electric), and time of year. In this chapter, we will often use a classwide average to describe customer rates for simplicity.[28]

28. Sales for resale operations have not been included in most analyses. These transactions are similar to those typically made by interstate pipelines, rather than distribution utilities, so their inclusion would not further our understanding of the California distribution system. Their elimination from the SCG system would not have resulted in substantially different prices being paid by remaining customers.

Figure 5.3 shows the delivery profile for PG&E in 1984; SCG's is similar. Because gas can be stored for future use (usually underground in natural reservoirs), the utility has the ability to "bank" gas for later use. Fortunately, California's gas demand exhibits seasonal complementarities. Residential gas demand peaks during the winter, while utility gas demand peaks during the summer (generally the late summer, when hydroelectric resources are depleted). By using storage, the utilities are able to keep their gas demand at a nearly constant level, though it still peaks in the winter. Because their suppliers base part of the gas charge on the peak level of gas delivered to utilities, storage helps to moderate overall gas costs.

In contrast to most other states, no interstate pipelines pierce the state's borders, giving California gas utilities complete control over out-of-state gas sales in California. The gas line that brings Canadian gas to California terminates one foot from the border, where ownership is transferred from Pacific Gas Transmission Company to PG&E. Thus the FERC, which regulates gas destined for interstate sales, has no purview whatever within California.[29] Instead, the CPUC has almost complete control over rates, a powerful position that has been well exercised.

The California Public Utilities Commission

The CPUC exerts authority over a number of state industries, from telecommunications to commuter railroads. It has achieved a national reputation for technical expertise, regulatory zeal, and the willingness to experiment with new programs and technologies. Working with utilities, it has developed a number of progressive approaches to conservation. It also has been involved in soliciting private electricity generation in California. The CPUC has always championed low prices for consumers, and in 1976 it acted on a legislative mandate to set a lifeline allowance for residential customers.[30] After 1977, when appointees of Governor Jerry Brown achieved a majority on the commission, it increasingly pursued social goals, a thrust that more often than not translated into cross-subsidization of residential consumers by commercial and industrial classes. It also adopted several policies that have allowed certain price signals to reach the consumer sooner than otherwise. For instance, it instituted an adjustment mechanism in 1973 that allows utilities to raise or lower rates automatically every three months to account for

29. A minor exception is gas from federal offshore wells, those three miles or more from the coast.

30. The original 1975 lifeline bill (AB 167) set rates at 75% of the residential average rate. That rate was increased effectively to 85% in 1985 (AB 2443), under rates now known as baseline allowances.

changes in fuel costs. Current policies, described below, allow larger customers to recontract periodically for utility gas, in direct competition with other suppliers.

Ratemaking with respect to general rates takes place on a three-year cycle in California.[31] The rate base is generally set in accordance with the principles of original cost. Until 1987 rate design had ostensibly been based on value-of-service pricing, although this terminology had never been precisely defined by the commission. As practiced, value-of-service pricing is distinct from Ramsey pricing, with which it is often confused. Under Ramsey pricing, the ratio of the markups over marginal costs for two customer classes is set equal to the inverse of the ratio of their elasticities. Thus, the higher a class's elasticity, the lower its relative price.[32]

Under value-of-service pricing, prices are set in proportion to willingness to pay for a particular good or service. The important point is that willingness to pay is not necessarily equal to the inverse of a customer's elasticity. The assumptions employed by the Commission in choosing prices were that industrial and commercial customers had a higher willingness to pay than residential customers. In the case of industrial customers, the use of a willingness-to-pay criterion rather than the use of elasticity measures meant that their prices exceeded those of the residential sector. Under a Ramsey pricing regime, the industrial market would have received gas at the lowest prices because it is the most elastic.

Gas Utility Customer Classes
Residential customers form the largest component of demand for natural gas in California. Collectively, they purchase more cubic feet of gas than the industrial and commercial classes combined. It is residential customers who historically have been the recipient of cross-subsidies authorized by the CPUC. In part, this may have been due to their captive position. Unlike an industrial or electricity generation customer who can exercise some interfuel substitution if the price is right, residential customers have only conservation as a ready alternative.

Commercial classes fared the worst under value-of-service pricing. They experienced frequent rate increases, under the presumption that their willingness to pay was high. They have been squeezed even tighter in recent years, as pressure from the industrial sector has resulted in re-

31. Until 1984, a two-year cycle was used, but the administrative burden on both utility and regulator became excessive.

32. For information on Ramsey pricing and other nonuniform pricing structures for public utilities, see Brown and Sibley (1986).

lief for that class. In some cases, it was cost-effective for commercial customers to burn propane rather than natural gas. The main problem may be that, unlike other users, the commercial users have not yet developed any effective means for regulatory plea bargaining.[33]

Industrial customers have been in a very different situation from commercial customers. Historically, they have switched from natural gas to fuel oil based on economic conditions. Table 5.7, which displays California data, shows that industrial consumers do exhibit sensitivity to the relative price of gas and oil. Since 1982, regulations have prohibited the combustion of Nos. 5 and 6 fuel oil in industrial boilers, the reason later years are omitted. The figures indicate that a large number of users either cannot purchase fuel or have transportation costs that make oil use cost-ineffective, even given the average numbers above. The figures show that industrial customers do respond to changes in the relative prices of competing fuels, the correlation coefficient between the price ratio and gas sales being −0.658.[34]

Given the cleaner-burning characteristics of gas, state regulatory authorities have been reluctant to implement policies that would facilitate switching away from gas. This policy preference has, at times, clashed with federal regulation, notably in the case of the Power Plant and Industrial Fuel Use Act of 1978 (PIFUA). The act was passed to encourage the use of coal and synthetic fuels by large users, with the expectation that both sources would expand rapidly in coming years. Although this aim was understandable in the face of the expectations of dwindling natural gas supplies at the time of passage, the result in markets in which the primary choice is between oil and gas was to promote oil combustion implicitly.

The demand for gas for electricity generation by utilities forms a most interesting market segment. It is in this sector that the two major distributors differ. For PG&E and SCG, gas sales for utility electricity generation constitute internal and external transactions, respectively. Later sections will show that sales to gas-fired power plants, a major competitive nexus between electric and gas services in California, have been used strategically by both the utilities and the CPUC.

33. This development fits neatly both with Olson's (1965) theory of collective action in the case of industrial (but not commercial) customers organizing and with vote-maximizing models such as Peltzman's (1976) in the case of residential customers being respresented by grass roots groups.

34. This number does not include data from 1979. Were that year's data included, the coefficient would be −0.240. There are a number of reasons why the correlation is not unity, the most important being the gas-curtailments experience in the late 1970s. Others include conservation effects, cyclical business conditions, and customer-specific circumstances.

IV. THE VALUE-OF-SERVICE EXPERIENCE

This portion of the chapter evaluates the value-of-service structure employed by the CPUC until 1987. Our aim is to show how this pricing was used to pursue a number of social goals, how the CPUC grasped the opportunity, and how the distortions it created ultimately resulted in its abandonment. We discuss the historical background of value-of-service pricing, consider an interesting case concerning the problems with determining actual costs of service, and conclude with a description of the new direction of gas regulation in California.

Historical Background

We will investigate the setting and designing of gas rates by the CPUC in this section, drawing extensively on statistical information for PG&E and SCG. Figure 5.4 shows the historical trend of delivered gas prices for the retail classes for PG&E; the trends are very similar for SCG. With a few exceptions, the trend is monotonically upward. Although this course reflects the general rise in natural gas prices, a closer inspection reveals that the four retail classes—residential, commercial, industrial, and electricity generation—have fared differently from 1972 to 1985.

Before 1974, ratemaking was based on the principles of cost of service, so that residential and commercial customers paid rates in excess of the average retail rate, reflecting the fact that the provision of service to them was more costly. Beginning in 1975, rates began to move toward equality across the various classes, although ostensibly no change in ratemaking policy occurred. This movement may have been induced by consumer pressures, caused by the onset of higher energy prices in 1974. In 1977, however, the ascendancy of the Brown administration appointees to a majority in the CPUC, the prospect of severe gas shortages, and the legislative directing to establish baseline rates led to the formal adoption of value-of-service rates.

This method of designing rates can be used to keep total utility revenues at acceptable levels, given steady or declining sales. Prices are set based on willingness to pay, and for ratemaking purposes the CPUC placed industrial and commercial classes higher on this scale. In California this meant raising industrial and commercial rates substantially more than residential rates. Industrial rates (until 1984) and commercial rates have risen markedly with respect to average rates, while residential rates have declined. Electricity generation prices under value-of-service also rose. This growing cross-subsidy, which would be even more pronounced if actual cost-of-service figures were used rather than average retail rates, prompted increasing resistance from commercial and industrial customers. The cost-price distortion, as will be shown, had major structural ramifications in the industrial sector.

But these cost-price gaps were necessary to comply with the directives of the state legislature to suppress residential rates. In 1975, after several years of rapid gas cost escalation, legislation was passed calling for the CPUC to reconstitute gas rates so that the first portion of residential therms were priced under the residential class average. These new rates, now known as baseline rates, call for this allowance to be priced at 85% of the class average.[35] This policy forced the CPUC to make up these revenues elsewhere, a major factor contributing to its adoption of value-of-service pricing.

Even if the assumptions regarding the willingness of the various customer classes to pay were accurate, value-of-service rate design policies have drawbacks. Because gas faces interfuel competition, tariffs so determined for industrial users were no longer sustainable. As we shall see, this practice induced severe market distortions, such as "cream-skimming" entry in customer segments that provide high-margin contributions. In deciding to return to a rate design based on cost of service, other serious consequences may develop.

Abandoning value-of-service pricing involved several problems for the CPUC. There are a number of political and strategic reasons why the commission found that pricing structure attractive. Perhaps the most important is that it guaranteed the agency broad discretion in setting rates, because the key allocational tool, the relative willingness of the various classes to pay, could not be objectively and definitively determined. The CPUC, therefore, was free to adjust rates as it saw fit, as long as the total revenue received by a utility is held constant. In several cases, this discretion led to the reconfiguration of rates within various classes, to prevent oil combustion or to pursue political goals.

In the case of pricing natural gas to industrial customers capable of switching from natural gas to oil, the CPUC priced gas to these users in a way that precluded the combustion of residual oil. The policy involved calculating a proxy value for delivered oil and then setting the gas rate just below this value. To arrive at this value, the commission started with the price of Indonesian low-sulfur waxy residual oil, then added a factor for taxes and transportation to the ultimate consumers. This constituted a form of limit pricing, characterized by the posting of a price designed to deter entry by a competitor.

Not surprisingly, the combination of lags in rate setting during periods of falling oil prices and regional differences in actual oil transportation charges among industrial customers has meant that some oil, nonetheless, is burned for industrial purposes. In a more subtle vein, the difference in rates between industrial customers with and without boilers

35.   The original plan, in effect until 1985, set lifeline rates at 75% of the residential class average and froze that rate until the company's average gas supply cost rose 25%.

fitted for dual fuel combustion widened considerably during the early 1980s. Those customers without the capability to switch fuels were charged much higher rates (28% in the PG&E service area in 1984). The artificiality of this gap from a cost-of-service perspective is underscored by the fact that there is little basis to claim a difference in that cost between these two customer groups.

One fascinating example of the political factor in ratemaking as formerly practiced by the CPUC centers on the pricing of gas destined for use in electricity generating plants across California. These sales are made in a clearly identifiable transaction by SCG to Southern California Edison Company (SCE); for PG&E they represent an internal sale from the gas side to the electric side of the same company. Sales for electricity generation by both SCG and PG&E's gas side have presumably been held well above costs of service because of the CPUC value-of-service policies.[36]

Another reason why electricity generation rates have been held high is the set of social goals that the CPUC emphasized. Among these goals is the support for private electric power generation. According to the statutes of the Public Utility Regulatory Policies Act of 1978 (PURPA), electric utilities are required to purchase electricity generated at privately financed facilities, provided that this electricity is produced at qualifying facilities, defined as those using renewable or cogeneration technologies. The price paid by utilities per kilowatthour is to be its full avoided cost, that is, the savings to the utility for not having to produce that same kilowatthour of electricity itself. The typical California electric utility would have produced a kilowatthour on the margin during a large portion of the summer months by burning natural gas.[37] For this reason, the higher the purchase price of gas to the utility during this period, the higher the price paid to private power producers.

Because of the CPUC's strong support for the concept of small power production, it kept the gas price to electric utilities at levels that meant

36. If one considers the average annual price paid by electric utilities for gas and the average annual cost of gas supplies to gas utilities, the price-cost gap under value-of-service pricing for the electricity generation class was similar to commercial and industrial classes. In the case of electricity generation, the effect of this gap varied over the course of the year. The majority of gas used for electricity generation is burned during the peaking season, the summer months. During this period, natural gas supplies are plentiful, so that the actual marginal gas cost is well below the annual average gas cost. Therefore, comparing electricity generation gas rates to annual average city-gate prices considerably understates the actual price-cost gap.

37. The marginal source of electricity varies diurnally and seasonally. During winter evenings, for example, very cheap energy supplies are curtailed, as demand is at its lowest level. During most summer peak periods and many summer "shoulder" and winter peak hours, however, natural gas is the marginal fuel source.

a major incentive for qualifying-facility development in California. The policy has also had the effect of generating revenue to help keep the increase in residential gas rates relatively low as gas sales for electricity generation provided a source of cross-subsidies to gas recipient classes. However, in 1984 the CPUC began to recognize this pricing distortion, stating that in PG&E's case, the "[electricity generation] rate is out of touch with today's fuel markets" (California Public Utilities Commission, 1984, p. 76). In its 1986 decision discussed below, the CPUC decided to treat electricity generation loads as identical to large industrial loads and price accordingly.

The responses of the electric utilities to this policy shed light on the complex intertwining nature of ratemaking. In California, as elsewhere, new power plants are subject to a prudency review before being allowed into a utility's rate base. A crucial part of this review is the comparison of the fuel savings to the company to the cost of the new plant. Thus the higher the current and projected marginal-cost savings to the utility, the better a new plant looks economically. Because both PG&E and SCE have newly completed nuclear units, both targets of accusations of managerial bungling, they are anxious to have the specific question of economic need for the plants resolved. The ex post facto nature of this review certainly is open to criticism, but such examinations have become the rule for regulatory commissions. Because the marginal costs saved by its new nuclear plant (and projections for future savings) are strongly influenced by the price its electric side "pays" its gas side for gas supplies, until recently PG&E did not protest this price with much vigor.

Another possible reason for PG&E's acquiescence to the policy of maintaining a high electricity-to-gas transfer price was that it gave the company the opportunity to offer lower rates to industrial customers, including those able to switch from the SCG system to PG&E's. SCG could not respond directly to this challenge for two reasons. First, its electricity generation sales represent a real, external transaction. Second, SCE protested to the CPUC about the high price it was being charged by SCG for this gas. SCE, perhaps less concerned about the economics of its nuclear unit, threatened to begin widespread use of oil in its thermal plants as oil converged in price with gas. The CPUC responded by adopting an electricity generation gas rate schedule, which reduced SCE's gas rate, but only when air quality conditions allowed the burning of fuel oil. A much higher price is charged during episode days, when oil could not be used. The net result was a price decrease in SCE's gas bills.

Contemplating the Costs of Service

Our criticisms of value-of-service pricing should not be construed as implying that true costs of service can be determined unambiguously and uncontroversially. A clear example of how differently the CPUC and a company can compute the relative cost of serving various customer classes is illustrated in 1985 studies by the CPUC and SCG (California Public Utilities Commission, 1985a; Southern California Gas Company, 1985b). Table 5.8 shows the average imbedded costs of service for four retail classes and combined wholesale classes for SCG. Although these numbers represent imbedded costs, they are based on historical costs and so do not necessarily correspond to economic costs.[38]

The actual numbers represent rates in effect at the time of the studies, adjusted slightly for comparability.[39] SCG and CPUC calculations cover the 12 months beginning May 1, 1985, and are based on the same revenue requirement as the actual rates. The CPUC costs were developed using work papers supporting the analysis of the Public Staff Division (PSD). It should be pointed out that these figures do not necessarily represent the opinion of the CPUC as a whole. As such, they will be referred to as the PSD figures.[40] To keep the fine-class breakdown, assumptions regarding the rate structure below were made.[41] Also, the estimates were adjusted so that each corresponds to a purchased gas cost of $3.755/thousand cubic feet. Finally, each estimate would result in SCG meeting its nongas revenue requirement. The figures do not include the effect of regulatory balancing accounts. The differences between SCG and the PSD are illustrated in Figure 5.5. This figure summarizes very detailed and complicated allocation procedures used by both entities. These procedures are necessary to apportion costs other than that of gas, such as labor, new construction, and depreciation of existing infrastructure. The simplest allocation method is to add up all the

38. We focus on SCG in this section because PG&E did not perform a cost analysis that could be compared as readily as the SCG analysis.

39. To place each rate structure on equal terms, each was adjusted for a common purchased gas cost, sales volume level, and nongas margin level. In this way, the revenue requirement of SCG was met under each set of adjusted prices. In no case was a major adjustment of rates for revenue requirement purposes necessary. Details appear in Appendix A.

40. To cast the figures in comparable terms, we retraced some of the steps leading to the PSD costs; generally we placed the fixed (transmission and production) portion of gas costs back into the cost of gas purchased, so the cost categories were comparable to the SCG costs.

41. Because priority of supply in addition to customer class status determines ultimate rates, they are not set as commercial or industrial rates per se. For this reason, the decision was made to use the GN-1 rate as the proxy for commercial rates. It covers smaller nonresidential customers but is applied to some small industrial customers. Conversely, the GN-2 rate, which is typically applied to industrial customers, is applied to some large commercial customers. GN-3, GN-4, and GN-6 rates were allocated to the industrial class. Because all three estimates (actual, PSD, and SCG) were made in terms of the GN classes and not the retail designations, consistency was maintained in using this categorization.

nongas charges and spread them equally across all cubic feet of gas sold. This "commoditizing" process is the most straightforward way to allocate truly common costs.

The major proximate difference between the two approaches is that of the total nongas charges; each assumes its own estimate of how much of these nongas charges are common costs. The PSD figures allocate roughly 67% as common costs, whereas for SCG this share is 8%. Other costs are allocated according to formulas using peak and average demand, cold and average year sales, or direct cost-based allocations. Ostensibly, the PSD assumed that SCG's allocation procedures for apportioning common costs to customer classes were based on specific formulas. The PSD contended that commoditizing a major portion of the nongas margin constituted a more accurate and fair approach in the absence of more precise knowledge.

In some instances, the PSD approach is appropriate. In other instances, such as when part of the SCG distribution system operation and maintenance costs are allocated to wholesale customers, it is flawed. Although it is difficult to endorse either approach, there is no doubt that the PSD figures buttressed the CPUC's value-of-service rate structure. By placing so many nongas costs into the jointly allocated category, the PSD study flattens cost-of-service estimates across the various classes compared with the SCG figures. For this reason, cross-subsidy estimates based on the PSD cost estimates are lower than SCG figures. The SCG estimates supported that company's claim that there were major pricing distortions under value of service.

For the purposes of this study, an analysis comparing 1985 rates charged SCG customers to PSD and SCG cost estimates was conducted. Figure 5.6 displays the total cross-subsidies received or contributed by class and represents the cost per thousand cubic feet multiplied by total sales to that class.

Looking at Figure 5.6, the difference in conclusions concerning residential customers is startling. That class received a small subsidy according to PSD cost estimates, but for SCG, this subsidy swells to $337.0 million annually. If sales by PG&E and smaller utilities were supported by the same amount per cubic foot as SCG residential sales, a statewide estimate of the total subsidy to residential customers in 1985 would be in the neighborhood of $600 to $700 million per year. Both PSD and SCG agree that commercial customers supplied major revenues, $171.6 million and $137.5 million, respectively. For industrial customers, both estimates show that this class also provided net revenues, but the two figures vary, placed at $55.5 million by PSD and $126.5 million by SCG. Interestingly, the conclusion concerning the electricity generation class differs, depending on whose estimates are used. For PSD, the class receives a $133.9 million subsidy; for SCG, the class provides a $85.1 million contribution. Finally, although SCG cost figures set wholesale rates nearly at their cost, PSD cost figures show that wholesale customers receive $80.2 million annually from the SCG system.

The public policy implications of analyses based on the two estimates of cost are completely different. If one believes the PSD, residential customers have paid their way under value of service. The major subsidy ran from commercial users to the electricity generation and wholesale classes. If marginal rates were used, most of the subsidy to the electricity generation class would probably dissolve. However, the result that wholesale customers receive a major subsidy appears to be the result of the commoditizing of nongas costs, which perhaps should have been spread across the four retail classes, not all five classes. In any case, cross-subsidy figures based on PSD costs show that the value-of-service pricing system was much closer to one founded on costs than the SCG costs.

The SCG cross-subsidies show that residential customers were the recipients of huge benefits under this system, receiving about $100 to $130 million from each of the commercial, industrial, and electricity generation segments. This scenario appears to fit more closely with the outcome one would expect from a value-of-service format that assumes that residential customers are the least willing to pay for gas. The electricity generation subsidy, following the same logic as above, probably is much larger than the figures suggest. Most important, one can more easily see the impetus for entry into the industrial market. Entry by third parties was invited if they could price between current rates and imbedded costs.[42] As we discuss below, the threat of entry by dedicated pipelines has become a central issue in the California regulatory arena.

Above all, what this analysis demonstrates is that there is a tremendous degree of gamesmanship involved in the California regulatory process. The analysis confirms the observations of Owen and Braeutigam (1978) in regard to the strategic use of the administrative process and suggests that regulators are not strangers to the use of gaming apparatus. Furthermore, an assertion that rates should be based on the costs of service, implying that these costs are precisely determinate, carries an unsupportable assumption. Indeed, considerable factual reinforcement exists for each cost structure studied here. The supporting documents for both sets of figures (as if to discourage validation efforts) present the dispassionate analyst with a considerable tangle of details. At this point, given the new move to prices based closer to costs, a common costing methodology is compulsory.

42. It is highly unlikely at this time that gas transmission facilities could be constructed at capital costs below that of existing ones. This is in contrast to the case of telecommunications, where rapid technological change has resulted in the cost-effectiveness of retiring partially depreciated capital facilities.

It appears that the need for good estimates for the actual costs of service is a concern in most of the industries regulated as public utilities; the CPUC itself has made the determination of these costs a major priority in a study of the telecommunications industry (California Public Utilities Commission, 1985b). Given the threat of entry in California industrial gas markets, precise knowledge about the costs of service would be an invaluable policy tool for the gas industry as well.

The New Direction of California Natural Gas Regulation

Responding to an industrywide clamor for regulatory reform, the CPUC initiated an effort to restructure gas rates in 1985. At that time, although it adopted methods to make contract carriage easier for large users, the CPUC recognized that a more fundamental and broader reconfiguration was necessary. After a year of extensive study and numerous hearings, it issued new guidelines which became effective on January 1, 1987 (California Public Utilities Commission, 1986a, b).

At the heart of the plan is the explicit acknowledgment of the dual nature of California's gas market. The main division is between those customers who can and cannot switch between fuels, although it is defined in terms of service priorities. The two basic consumer sectors are referred to as core and noncore, where the latter class includes fuel switchers.[43] Within each sector are separate charges categorized as transportation and gas costs. Transportation tariffs are based on a formula that allocates each of the nongas charges between the core and noncore sectors using allocational techniques determined by the CPUC. These techniques recognize that both sectors should pay for existing infrastructure and demand charges, not just those customers who are captives of the utility. However, core customers do bear a larger portion of the cost burden, reflecting their higher service priority.

For the noncore sector, burner-tip gas rates will be determined individually because the CPUC has now allowed the utilities to individually negotiate transportation tariffs. The lowest tariff, based on short-run marginal cost estimates, is about 10¢/thousand cubic feet. The highest, based on a proxy for long-run costs, is about $1/thousand cubic feet. This provision allows noncore customers to negotiate for a level of transmission security commensurate with their needs. It also allows utilities to conduct auctions for scarce capacity. Under additional provisions of the new rate structure, customers switching completely away from gas will still have to pay stand-by charges to the utility, corresponding to the cost of having that ready alternative.

Gas procurement for the two sectors also varies. Procurement of gas for the core sector will be made with high supply security in mind. As

---

43. One exception to this typography is large commercial users who could burn propane instead of natural gas. They have been designated core customers.

such, it is expected to be more expensive and consist predominantly of long-term supplies, although the CPUC ordered the utilities to include some short-term and spot supplies in the core portfolio. For noncore customers, gas procurement will be made on a best-efforts basis, and supplies will be of a more short-term quality, so that prices will track national averages more closely. The obligation of the utility to serve noncore customers has been attenuated. In the case of gas procured by the utility for both noncore and core customers, the price will be the weighted average of the sector's portfolio. Thus even though transportation tariffs for noncore customers can be individually negotiated, gas commodity prices cannot. The adjustment mechanism by which fuel costs are included in rates will also be phased out for noncore customers.

The rules invite the noncore customers to seek out and contract for gas from other sources, paying the utility only for transportation. Large commercial customers in the core sector also have this option, although they must pay fixed transportation charges. Noncore customers can elect to receive gas from the core portfolio, although they can only switch back to noncore status when the noncore gas cost exceeds the core gas cost. However, these elected-core customers are subject to minimum billing, to ensure that they do not use core status to guarantee gas availability for large purchases made at infrequent intervals. This practice would have imposed the cost of insuring suppliability on other core customers.

On balance, the new guidelines are a giant step in the right direction. As we have argued, the natural gas distribution industry in California consists of not one but several markets, divided according to the nature of substitutability for gas. As now regulated, the particular needs of each market are better addressed. Except for residential and other small customers, transportation and gas services have been unbundled. Utilities are put under pressure to reduce their purchased gas costs, so as to retain the maximum number of customers for transmission plus gas. Industrial customers are free to cut their own deals if they are dissatisfied with utility gas; they are also free to suffer the consequences of poor decisions they may make. And costs are more properly borne by core customers for whom security of supply is a major priority.

There are possible problems that may have to be addressed. Utilities may view the ability to negotiate transmission tariffs as a license to price discriminate. Although discriminatory pricing has a long regulatory history, the ability to discriminate customer by customer is new to gas distribution. There will likely be complaints from customers who feel they have received unfair treatment, and the CPUC will have to decide how to deal with that issue. However, the competition to serve customers in the noncore sector is best addressed by allowing flexibility, not limiting it. The new rules may also have the effect of directing the lowest cost supplies to the largest customers, which has angered consumer groups. Large customers may get the cheapest supplies now, but the situation could reverse if increased demand causes marginal rates to rise. But the retention of these customers on the utility rolls is important; they make positive contributions to the recovery of the utility's fixed costs.

Twenty-two parties, ranging from the interstate pipelines serving California to industrial user groups, filed comments and participated in the proceedings leading to the formation and adoption of the CPUC's guidelines. Under these contentious conditions, it is a positive sign that progressive results were obtained. The regulatory approach taken appears well suited to the need and the responsibility of the large industry players to control their own destiny. As the system is fine-tuned, we hope it will further enhance the efficiency of gas distribution in the state.

V. ARE DISTRIBUTION COSTS EXCESSIVE?

Background

In the preceding discussion of the divergence of cost and price in the California natural gas market, we pointed out that this growing separation led to markedly increased prices over time for some classes. Another historical cost trend in California has received less attention. It is a tendency that has taken place within the utilities themselves, and its effect has been to raise rates for all users. The issue is organizational efficiency.

X-Efficiency is a term coined by Leibenstein (1966) to describe the sources of efficiency that are not captured in neoclassical economic theory, such as motivational and institutional factors. X-Inefficiency refers to firm behavior that is non–cost minimizing, often attributed to a lack of competition. The idea that monopolies, either regulated or unregulated, could display X-Inefficiency has many supporters.

If X-Inefficiency exists in the natural gas distribution industry, one would expect that the market would result in distribution margins larger than competitive levels. One would expect a system displaying greater X-Ineffiency over time to display higher employment and salary growth than that of comparable competitive firms. This section will explore these issues by studying the employee component of distribution (or gross) margins. The gross margin includes depreciation and return on plant, operating, and maintenance expenses; administrative costs; and other constituent costs. Labor comprises the major portion of most of these items.

An unfortunate fact is that the data necessary to prove relationships convincingly are not publicly available, due to a number of factors.

Isolating the direct effect of being sheltered from competition on employee growth is difficult. The nature of work differs across utilities, but more important, growth rates during the period under study have varied widely between different geographic sections of the country. One should not expect employment growth within California utilities to equal that of utilities located in the Northeast or even the country as a whole. The spatial organization of service territories varies also. Population densities vary widely.

For these reasons, the analysis of employee growth will be conducted in a less rigorous manner than the analysis of salary growth, although the study of the latter variable is troublesome as well. The main difficulty associated with the study of salary structure here is that only company-wide average salary data are available. Previous studies of several other utility industries (Hendricks, 1975; Weiss, 1966) have isolated salary by job classification, possible with the use of census data. This allowed direct comparison of wages in regulated industries to wages in unregulated manufacturing industries. Unfortunately, because census data by job classification is available for industries only up to three-digit Standard Industrial Classification code level, only certain regulated industries, such as electric power production, can be analyzed in this way. Because the relevant data for gas distribution companies and transmission companies is aggregated, there is no simple way to obtain salary information by job classification for gas distribution companies. However, a study looking at the effect of differing competitive environments on average company salaries is interesting and will be developed below. A somewhat circumstantial but nonetheless arguable case that inefficiencies exist will be constructed. We will begin our study of distribution margins at the California state level.

Historical Trends

Focusing on the California utilities, the social and political objectives pursued by the CPUC in the past clearly affected how the total gross margin has been allocated among the consumer classes. The gross margins for the utilities in the years 1972 through 1985, calculated as the difference between the ultimate sales price for the customer class less the average utility gas cost (city-gate cost), rose for all classes. However, for customer classes that have suffered the greatest price increases, such as the commercial class, the margin has risen at a more rapid rate. For residential customers, the margin increase has been moderated. To get an idea of whether this increase in margins is unusual, a comparison of California rates to national averages from 1972 to 1984 was made to national averages. The results appear in Table 5.9.

The greater increase in city-gate (CG) prices experienced by the California utilities is likely the result of their commitments to purchase gas at later dates than the typical gas utility. Many of these commitments call for gas to be purchased at new gas prices, higher than average gas prices.

Table 5.9 shows that distribution margins (M) increased enormously compared with national figures. Considering average annual percentage changes, this difference in overall increases appears to be rooted in the years from 1976 to 1980. During this period, while the national average margin grew at 4.02%, the corresponding figures for SCG and PG&E were 13.42% and 18.82%, respectively. This phenomenon appears to be the result mainly of growth in customers and employees, both of which outpaced the national growth rate. The period from 1976 to 1980 brought major construction inflation, and the inclusion of considerable new capital expenses into the rate base by both utilities no doubt contributed to the higher distribution margin for each. The difference between the SCG and PG&E margin growth figures may be the direct effect of the difference in sales between the two companies. For SCG, major sales gains allowed it to spread its fixed costs across more sales units than PG&E, which experienced a sales loss.

In the 12 years from 1972 through 1984, PG&E's sales per customer declined by 47%; SCG's corresponding decline was very close to the national figure of 33%. This change probably reflects the migration of industrial users from the system, customers who shouldered a large portion of the total gross margin. The much greater loss of sales by PG&E certainly resulted in proportionately more fixed costs being added to each sales unit in later years than SCG.

Although employee increases at SCG far outstripped the national figures, this may be the result of construction operations. The PG&E employment figures are puzzling. Their apparent decline may be the result of the company's use of a central construction department for both gas and electric operations.[44] For both SCG and PG&E, responding to CPUC mandates to pursue conservation and other demand-side approaches to controlling gas loads also influenced employee growth. In sum, it is difficult to make a conclusive case from these numbers either that employee growth has been excessive or that it has been appropriate. In the case of gas distribution salaries, a cross-sectional analysis can support more confident conclusions.

44. Separation of construction workers into the gas and electric sides of the company was given only for three of the listed years, and although the ratio of gas construction workers to total construction workers was nearly constant for those three observations, applying that ratio to years without specific breakdowns entails some uncertainty.

Wage Rates

Of the distribution margin, the share represented by labor costs, including overheads, is approximately 39%.[45] Thus the relative salary structure is a major determinant of the level of that margin. This section will test the hypothesis that the varying competitive conditions experienced by gas companies affect their salary structure.

Whether labor unions are able to extract premium wages from regulated utilities is an important issue, with a long history of economic inquiry. A recent installment in the ongoing debate on the subject of market power, unions, and wage rates has been provided by M. A. Salinger (1984). Employing a careful statistical analysis, Salinger finds that "the combination of concentration and entry barriers allows firms to raise price above cost and that the primary beneficiaries of the monopoly power are unionized workers" (p. 167). Extending this result to regulated utilities is not as simple as it may appear. Depending on the nature of regulation, the firm may be prevented from expanding wage rates. Furthermore, comparing salaries in regulated and unregulated firms is fraught with difficulty. For example, Weiss (1966) hypothesizes that regulated firms may obtain higher-quality labor.

Hendricks (1977) conducted an extensive investigation of wage rates in regulated utilities. In his analysis, salaries for similar jobs in regulated and manufacturing industries are compared. Because wages are not significantly higher for workers in regulated industries, he concludes that there is little evidence that economic rents are captured by the workers in regulated firms. This is especially true in industries with rate and entry regulation. The explanation is that maximum rate regulation puts pressure on managements to contain costs, pressure not felt by industries under minimum rate regulation, such as trucking.

As a measure of competition in each industry, Hendricks controlled the effect of the concentration ratio for both manufacturing and regulated industries. Whether this approach is appropriate for regional franchised monopolies, such as gas and electric services, is debatable.[46]

---

45. The 39% figure is based on the following 1984 estimates for SCG (the PG&E percentage would be similar):

		($ in thousands)
A. Nongas margin (see Appendix A)		$1,200,000
B. Direct employee salaries	334,000	
C. Indirect and overhead expenses, estimated at 40%	133,600	
D. Total employee expenses (B + C)		467,600
E. Ratio of total salary expense to nongas margin (D/A)		39.0%

46. This may be the reason for Hendrick's (1977) finding that variables measuring the concentration ratio and the product of unionization and concentration were not significant in the setting of wage levels.

Gas distribution utilities face competition not from other distribution companies but from interstate pipelines transversing service territories. These pipelines are able to make direct sales to industrial and electricity-generating stations, generally in competition with the local firm. Because rates for these sales are in general freely negotiated, one would expect that gas distribution companies facing competition would bargain more aggressively with their workers for salaries, so as to minimize their delivered costs and retain customers.

To test the hypothesis that competitive conditions affect the salary structure in gas utilities, a number of assumptions had to be made. An implicit assumption in using companywide salary data is that the relative task structure within companies is constant across companies. We use the state as the unit of analysis, because it allows us to use readily available data.

Also, a proxy for the competitiveness in a given state had to be constructed. It is misleading to use concentration ratios to measure the competitiveness faced by a utility. Because distribution companies have exclusive service territories, they do not compete with each other directly. For this reason, the relative concentration in a given state is a poor indicator of competition. However, although gas distribution companies do not compete directly with each other, many do compete with interstate pipelines. Adjacent large users have the technical ability to buy gas directly from these pipelines, bypassing the local distribution company. We use the ratio of direct sales to industrial customers by interstate pipelines to sales to industrial customers by gas utilities as a proxy for the level of competition prevailing in a given state. The ratio excludes the effect of sales made for electricity generation (SIC 49), because many of these plants lie well outside populated areas and generally purchase gas through long-term contracts. The industrial sales ratio is not strictly covariant with the amount of gas produced in a given state; a number of states that produce large amounts of gas have little or no direct sales by pipelines. Conversely, in some states where no gas is produced, direct sales are made by pipelines passing through that state. To formally control for states with major gas production, a variable to capture this effect was included in the analysis. Finally, because information on unionization of utilities by state is not available, a unionization measure using all nonagricultural workers by state was used.

Appendix B reports the results of this econometric analysis, testing whether utility wage rates are affected by competitive pressures. In summary, when a number of important variables, such as manufacturing wages, unionization rates, a southern location, and the presence or absence of gas production in the state are used to control for those influences, the presence of competition from pipelines has a small but significant negative effect on wage rates. Thus competition seems to induce cost-reducing activities by utilities.

We do not use this analysis to advise lacing the state of California with interstate pipelines but, rather, to inject, where sensible, some competition into the utility environment. The present national gas market structure offers the opportunity for some competition through the use of contract carriage, which may prod utilities in the direction of more efficient operation. Although the main result of this effort would be to reduce utility gas purchase prices, gross margins might be trimmed as well. The CPUC may have had this idea in mind when it designed the new gas rate structure.

VI. COPING WITH THE PRESSURE FOR CHANGE IN INDUSTRIAL MARKETS

We have described how in comparison to average system costs, historical rates charged to industrial customers have risen in overall terms, in real terms, and in relative terms. There are two main reasons for this escalation. Along with other classes, industrial users have had to pay a share of a nongas margin that has broadened considerably since 1972. In addition, due in large measure to value-of-service pricing and the growing cross-subsidies that it was used to provide, industrial rates have escalated until recent years.

Because most industrial users can switch from burning gas in their boilers to burning oil, unlike most other users they have the ability to substitute another fuel if the gas price exceeds that of oil. The price of these fuels can be compared using a heat-content-per-unit-cost scale. Although oil has historically been priced at levels that precluded major interfuel substitution, recent years witnessed the closing of this gap. This situation caused California utilities consternation for two related reasons. First, because they do not sell oil, they stood to lose part of their customer base. Second, any permanent loss would saddle other classes with a higher proportion of fixed costs per unit purchased.

The utilities, the CPUC, and industrial users responded to the situation. Utilities are busy trying to renegotiate the long-term contracts under which they purchase most of their gas. Many of these contracts were signed when prices were high and rising, and have turned out to favor producers as the prices contractually agreed upon are now well above prevailing spot rates. The renegotiation process has resulted in some concessions, but gas sold to the California utilities remains expensive. The CPUC has restructured gas rates to allow pricing flexibility, which should increase the pressure for lower prices. The new plan allows for a utility to act as a transporter only of gas, if a large user so requests. Interstate pipelines, which would bypass the state utilities completely, have been proposed as a means for serving a rapidly growing load associated with oil extraction in the San Joaquin Valley. These two strategies for reducing delivered costs to industrial users are the subject of this section.

The Rising Importance of Contract Carriage

Table 5.10 lists the wellhead prices through 1986, weighted by quantities delivered at the various sources nationwide, along with industrial rates by service area. Of course, these figures cannot be compared directly because the wellhead numbers are exclusive of transportation charges. But it is safe to say that if transportation could be arranged on competitive terms, industrial users (or any other customer class or the distribution company itself) would benefit from directly purchasing gas and contracting for its transportation to the state border.[47] This is the concept of contract carriage. The basic economics of contract carriage gave industrial users a strong incentive to push for permission to buy gas themselves.

The emergence of contract carriage as an issue in the mid-1980s is attributable to a number of factors. A major factor is that until the early 1980s, with prices constrained by federal ceilings, ready demand existed for any available gas. Little marketing effort on the part of producers was necessary. With prices partially decontrolled and demand below prior expectations, producers have embarked on major marketing initiatives.

However, the use of long-term supply contracts by utilities to ensure themselves of adequate gas supplies has prevented contract prices from tracking spot market rates. When a gas surplus developed, this price stickiness hurt the utilities and their customers. In a 1984 complaint filed with the CPUC, Owens-Illinois, Inc., (O-I) claimed that it could have gas transported to the PG&E city gate for $3.43–$3.75/thousand cubic feet, approximately 10 to 15% below PG&E's system average gas cost.[48]

Another reason for the pressure for contract carriage is interfuel competition, resulting from both policy and market forces, which drove the prices of gas and oil toward parity. Table 5.11 shows this convergence, using national figures. Since 1983 the gas/oil price ratio has exceeded 1.00 in many parts of the country.

---

47. One estimate places the transportation cost from the Colorado gas fields to the California border at 60¢ to 70¢ per therm (Rohan, 1984). [1 therm equals 100,000 Btu and is approximately equal to 100 cubic feet of gas.]

48. See *Owens-Illionis v. PG&E and SCG*, complaint filed February 10, 1984, to the CPUC (no docket number).

These figures understate the competitive effect on gas due to regional differences in fuel prices. For example, in 1982 the AGA estimated that the spread that caused industrial users to cease using gas ranged from a 4 to 41% cost savings for using residual oil (*Oil and Gas Journal*, 1983). Combined with the 1970s mandate to install facilities designed to burn both gas and oil, interfuel price competition accentuated industrial users' awareness of fuel substitution opportunities. Although it is difficult to separate the effect of price-induced conservation from fuel switching, it is safe to say that California utilities have felt the onset of gas-to-oil competition acutely. PG&E and SCG each lost more than 30% of their industrial loads in the two years from 1981 to 1983. In one interesting case, the Dow Chemical Company bypassed the PG&E system altogether by building its own dedicated pipeline to purchase gas directly from a California producer. The episode eventually led to accusations of franchise infringement and a settlement against Dow.[49]

The pressure for direct purchase of gas from out-of-state sources has been growing. Given the evidence presented above, it is easy to understand why industrial customers wanted contract carriage options. The collective anxiety of the utilities appears to have been grounded in concern over the long-term consequences of their actions. However, the new CPUC pricing guidelines invited large users to look at nonutility suppliers, so the utilities have moved to meet this competition.

There are a number of reasons why contract carriage makes sense. Gas-to-gas competition itself, although injurious to the utility sole franchise, is almost certainly a benefit to many parties. It would facilitate the transmission of price signals from producers to customers in California. This situation would surely motivate PG&E and SCG to intensify renegotiations with out-of-state producers. Also, now that residual oil prices are at a level that allows competition with current gas prices, companies are converting to oil combustion rather than continuing to purchase from utilities. Because gas could presumably be found outside the state for substantially less per Btu than fuel oil, a potential economic aberration can be avoided through contract carriage. Contract carriage, however, may have its own long-term hazards.

The gas/oil price disparity that had persisted in California caused O-I to file its 1984 complaint against both PG&E and SCG with the CPUC. O-I maintained that the utilities refused to exercise diligence in pursuing their chartered responsibility to provide energy at the lowest practi-

---

49. Dow Chemical constructed its own pipeline from a California producer to its plant in northern California. PG&E, with reserves in adjoining fields, reportedly began to extract gas from these fields at a rapid rate. Due to the law of capture, Dow was forced to pump more gas from its field than it could use. It sold the excess supplies to nearby industrial customers, violating the PG&E franchise.

cable cost. Their collective refusal caused O-I to begin preparing for combustion of fuel oil at a price below retail rates but above the cost of gas that it could contract to purchase from an out-of-state producer, even if the distributors' gross margin for industrial customers were added to the gas price. As stated previously, this potential deadweight loss does not include the greater societal cost caused by the additional pollutants discharged with oil combustion.

In the mid-1980s federal and state regulators began responding to market tensions by removing barriers to carriage. On the federal level, under Order 436, FERC directed pipeline companies that if they carry third-party gas for one customer, they must offer transportation services to all customers, without discrimination. Formerly, the pipelines refused carriage for their captive customers, forcing them to continue to purchase the pipeline-owned gas, which was often priced well in excess of spot-priced gas. This difference was largely due to contract provisions that the producers were able to impose on the pipelines when supplies were depleted. In addition, to bridge the gap separating contract and spot gas, FERC gave gas customers the ability to phase out their commitments to purchase pipeline-owned contract gas. Although the net result of this ruling may have been to encourage contract abrogations by pipelines (which are still bound to their purchase agreements with producers), it also hastened the conveyance of cheaper gas to consumers.

California regulators did not approve contract carriage to California customers until late 1985. This response was slow, given the national picture, which featured a large and growing carriage segment. Voluntary contract carriage is now a major component of interstate pipeline volume, accounting for over a third of the volume (Interstate Natural Gas Association of America, 1985, p. 2). The recipients of this gas, end users and distribution companies, both benefitted to a great degree. Table 5.12 provides information on contract carriage. These figures include both voluntary carriage and transportation offered under FERC programs designed to speed up carriage implementation, such as Order 436. The rise in total volumes over time indicates that on a nationwide basis, contract carriage became a major form of gas transport.[50]

Whether contract carriage will be the dominant method of serving industrial gas needs is an interesting question. As we stated, by unbundling gas procurement charges and nongas charges (mostly transmission), the CPUC invited large industrial customers to find and contract for their own supplies. Whether the greater national conditions will allow gas to be released at prices competitive with fuel oil remains to be

50. According to Interstate Natural Gas Association of America (INGAA) (personal communication), for 1987 more than *half* of total deliveries employed contract carriage.

seen. But a system for ensuring the ability of larger users to take advantage of this opportunity is now in place.

Interstate Pipeline Proposals

In the early 1960s, as the service territories of PG&E and SCG solidified, a mutually convenient agreement resulted in the current service territory boundaries shown in Figure 5.2. A portion of this boundary was drawn at the Kern County line. Because farming was then the dominant land use, little thought was given to the competitive pressures that would arise there two decades later. Yet, this area now appears to represent the largest undeveloped gas market in the United States. The demand for gas in Kern County has been promulgated by two interrelated factors. The first is the need for steam to inject into the wells to recover the heavy oil residing in the oil fields. The second factor is the air quality in the area, which is frequently in danger of violating state and federal standards. For this reason, oil producers prefer to use cleaner-burning natural gas as a steam source. Both utilities are eager to serve the Kern load. After the two could not agree on a definitive boundary between their two service territories there, the CPUC intervened and explicitly drew that line in early 1986. However, this boundary apparently has been perceived differently by SCG and PG&E, who claimed 80% and 37% of the same enhanced oil recovery (EOR) market, respectively.[51]

It is easy to understand the intense interest of these companies in serving Kern County when one considers the potential size of the new market for gas there. Usage in 1985 is about 150 million cubic feet/day. According to SCG, the total potential market for gas for EOR and associated cogeneration facilities in Kern is between 900 and 1,200 million cubic feet/day (Southern California Gas, 1985a). Because some of this demand will be met by locally produced gas and crude oil, the ultimate demand is roughly 700–900 million cubic feet. If so, the market represents an increase of perhaps 20% to the state's gas usage. Cogeneration facilities are able to sell electricity to the state's electric utilities under prices prescribed by PURPA. As described earlier in this chapter, the price inducements developed by the CPUC to support PURPA qualifying facility development have greatly improved the economics of oil- or gas-fired steam injection, one key reason that the market grew so quickly. These incentives mean that the electricity co-produced with gas-fired steam for injection into oil wells brings an attractive price, enhancing total project economics. Paradoxically, as explained later, this CPUC policy toward qualifying facilities may result in a major challenge to its own dominion in California.

51. See 1986 Report 10-Ks for the companies.

Several proposals for interstate pipelines to serve Kern County were submitted to FERC. Table 5.13 summarizes them. The Mojave pipeline was proposed by a consortium composed of a gas producer, a pipeline, and Pacific Lighting Company, parent company of SCG. That utility claimed that it could serve the area with existing facilities, but the oil producers were partial to an interstate pipeline (Southern California Gas, 1985b). On August 1, 1986, Pacific Lighting withdrew from the venture, arguing that depressed oil prices had reduced the development potential in Kern County, eliminating the need for a separate pipeline. PG&E, which has declined to participate in any interstate proposal, contends that such options represent wasteful duplication of existing facilities.

The oil companies in Kern County advanced the following reasons for preference for interstate service.

- Oil companies could make use of their own out-of-state gas supplies.

- Gas pricing would not fall under the jurisdiction of the CPUC, because it would be shipper-owned.

- The current CPUC-regulated service entails a substantial supply risk.

- Long-run costs of supplying operations with natural gas are cheaper with dedicated interstate pipelines.

Let us consider these points in order. The first point involves reasoning that has long confounded economists. Given the concept of opportunity costing, one would expect that the companies would be indifferent about the choice between sales at the wellhead and bringing the gas to California. The gas market in the central states is a competitive one, so that the company should be indifferent about the choice between using its wellhead supply and purchasing other companies' output at the wellhead. Because natural gas is a quintessential commodity, it is difficult to understand why an oil company would strongly favor use of its own gas supplies.[52]

The next two points bring into focus the strong secondary reasons for the pressure for interstate pipelines. Although pricing is certainly central to this pressure, industrial customers have long been at odds with

52. There is one interesting set of circumstances under which this conveyance would make sense. If an EOR company owned reserves consisting of price-controlled "old" gas, by bringing them to California, burning them, and selling the associated electricity to the local utility at a rate based on "new" gas, that company could actually extract a new gas price for its old gas. An earlier attempt at such "regulatory evasion" took place in the 1960s, when a pipeline from Texas to California through Mexico was proposed. See Palmer (1982).

the CPUC over its policies of prioritization of customers and cross-subsidization. As stated earlier, in 1983 California was one of only two states in which average industrial rates exceeded average residential rates. Supply risk also played an important role in the proponents' desire for a dedicated pipeline. Under the former priority structure, EOR customers had a low priority, meaning that their service could be curtailed in times of severe shortage. Remembering the supply curtailments of the late 1970s, they were concerned about the potential for future service disruptions.

The final point has been addressed sequentially by the CPUC. In its late 1985 order (California Public Utilities Commission, 1985c) it considered how best to meet the oil producers' pricing worries, while simultaneously keeping in mind the principle of "maximum possible ratepayer indifference" to new transportation rates. Wary of the threat of interstate pipelines, it used a new form of limit pricing. Using estimates from FERC filings of proposed interstate pipelines, it developed an estimate for a contract carriage transportation charge, 3.5¢/therm, which was slightly below what the new pipelines would charge under FERC regulations. The pipeline charge would be based on cost of service, including depreciation, using typical FERC pipeline accounting. The hope of the CPUC was to stop the interstate pipelines while extracting the maximum possible margin from EOR customers. This order also allowed utilities to enter into long-term contracts guaranteeing the EOR customers supplies for extended periods.

Those guidelines, which were still somewhat artificial, were superseded by newer regulations taking effect in 1987. Under these rules, EOR customers are treated as noncore customers and so can negotiate transportation prices, depending on the level of supply security necessary. The commission encouraged the utilities and the EOR producers to sign long-term transportation contracts, although it would review all agreements with terms longer than five years. The CPUC waived its general right to change contract provisions except "in circumstances in which those provisions unequivocally thwart the public interest" (California Public Utilities Commission 1986a, p. 70). In time, we will know whether the total package that utilities can offer the EOR producers is attractive enough to prevent the construction of interstate pipelines.

Taking a step back, the interstate pipeline case provides many insights into the impact that regulation can have on market structure. Service to the EOR market can be seen as analogous to service to long-distance telecommunications users. Industrial users were assumed to have the most inelastic demand for the service. This assumption was used as the justification for long-standing and growing cross-subsidization. Over time, to moderate increases in residential service, that sector saw rates increase at a disproportionately high rate. Finally, it became possible for dedicated systems to serve their customers' needs at a lower cost. Curiously, the providers of this dedicated service have in both cases claimed that they are serving a new market and that their operation would not draw revenue away from utility services. In the case of telecommunications, a lively and still unresolved debate centers on whether or not long-distance telephone service is now a workably competitive industry. In that industry, technological breakthroughs for which there are no analogues in gas transmission are central to the issue of competitiveness. Thus in the case of dedicated interstate pipelines, one must wonder how, without the gross margins charged under value-of-service pricing, the pipeline proposals described above could be cost-effective.

The issue of the relative economics of serving the EOR market as an incremental load has not received the attention it deserves. Cast in these terms, the interstate pipeline proposals are extremely expensive.

Table 5.13 provides information on the capital costs associated with the various service proposals for the EOR market. The interstate proposals range in price from 53¢ per cubic foot of additional volume to 85¢ per cubic foot for the Kern River project. In sharp contrast, the two California utilities claim that they can serve this market with relatively minor incremental expenditures.[53] The advantage to the utilities in operation and maintenance costs would widen this gap further.

Some caution must be exercised in comparing these figures. The utilities' deliverability depends on growth in other customer segments not greatly exceeding current projections. However, both utility cost estimates were based on facilities sized such that curtailment would occur, on average one day every 35 years. The main drawback of the utility estimates is their short timeframe. Each covers service only through 1995, beyond which further supplemental facilities would be needed. However, there is no reason to believe that the cost of those future additional facilities would elevate the life-cycle cost of utility upgrades to a level above the interstate pipelines.

One other point deserves mention. As we have argued, the effect of competition on gas distribution utilities is to encourage greater efficiency. If one of the interstate pipelines is built, it would have the positive effect of motivating California's gas utilities to minimize their costs

53. These costs do not include expenditures by PG&E for an expansion of one of its backbone lines, which some observers consider to be strategic in nature. This expansion will cost $110 million, bringing the utility upgrade figures to $157 million and a ratio of 0.22, respectively.

of service. Although this efficiency-inducing gain of competition is swamped by the waste associated with building a new pipeline, it is one advantage foregone if the utilities continue their sole transporter role.

Thus new pipelines have been proposed that apparently cost several times the marginal capital cost of utility upgrades to accomplish the same goal. Because the potential market represents a new load for the provider of gas, it is not unreasonable to consider the marginal cost of service. That is, the question that should be asked is: What is the cheapest way to increase the capability of the transmission and distribution system to provide gas to Kern County? Put this way, it is clear that utility upgrades, combined with contract carriage of supplies purchased by the EOR customers, are by far the cheapest method of serving the new load. Yet this greater social question of the cheapest overall method of meeting this new demand has been pushed aside, because private interests are making service decisions.

Unfortunately, even if the projected long-run cost of transportation by dedicated pipelines is perceived as being slightly above the ultimate rate utilities are directed to charge, it is likely that these pipelines still will be given serious consideration. The major reason why interstate pipelines still may enter California is the CPUC's failure to perceive that policies designed to affect customer decisions regarding fuel choice in the short run cannot be applied readily to capital asset decisions with long-run consequences.

Most industrial customers have dual boiler capabilities and can easily switch between gas and oil, depending on their relative price. If the price of gas is set just below that of oil, it will be the fuel of choice in most cases. But in the case of the Kern County EOR projects, the choice that the CPUC is attempting to influence involves the construction of a major dedicated asset. The consequences of choosing one fuel over another for a short time are limited; a user can switch back to the original fuel with relative ease. However, if the opportunity to construct a dedicated pipeline is passed up, the EOR customers will again be subject to pricing according to the CPUC's regulatory mood, even if they sign long-term contracts. EOR gas customers are thus anxious to act on their opportunities now. Another reason for this urgency comes from the general economic climate. Because the alternative to building this pipeline is using existing facilities with minor upgrades, future economic changes, such as major construction inflation, may render an interstate pipeline financially infeasible. For the EOR market, the interstate pipeline options may be "now or never."

Even if the CPUC's reworking of gas rates may not be satisfactory to the EOR producers, they have no problem with one of the commission's policies, which is the commission's strong support of cogeneration as a

California electricity resource. As described earlier, electric utilities are directed to pay high prices for power purchased from private sources, and the utilities have been anxious to sign up cogenerators, because unlike many PURPA power sources, they can deliver firm capacity.[54] Further strengthening the Kern County producers' negotiating position is the fact that they are situated near the border separating PG&E and SCE, the utility providing electric service to most of that portion of the state. This commission-driven competition was put to good use by producers, who have extracted numerous contract concessions from the utility with which they ultimately signed.[55]

This seeming choice of regulatory exposure by the EOR producers brings up an interesting point. Looking at their practices in pursuing FERC regulation of delivered gas pricing and commission regulation of electricity sales, it becomes clear that the practice reflects a strategic motive—one of seeking "optimal regulatory purview." That is, it is a policy wherein the firm selectively places each of its operations under the jurisdiction of whichever regulatory body will serve its interests with respect to that operation. This "unbundling" of regulatory oversight certainly is a rational practice on the part of these firms. But greater equity considerations seem to indicate that such a practice be subjected to closer scrutiny. Fairness dictates that largeness alone should not allow EOR customers this liberty.

VII. CONCLUSIONS AND RECOMMENDATIONS

The 1980s witnessed great change at every level of the natural gas industry. Distortions created at first by a federal policy of price controls and then by frictions in the adjustment process after partial deregulation profoundly affected national markets. On the local level regulators perservered in their support of social goals while working within the framework of this national market. Whether the policies that were sustained by the CPUC in this regard have been injurious to the state's long-term welfare cannot be easily determined; we suspect they have.

One can wind a spring only to a certain point. Tightened further, it will burst at its weakest point. In many ways the development of the

54. This eagerness has been replaced with caution in more recent years. In fact, the potential for large-scale private power production has caused the CPUC and the CEC to conclude that the proper posture toward development is a tough but fair policy of contract administration (CPUC and CEC, 1988, p. i).

55. The state's two largest electric utilities, SCE and PG&E's electricity side, offered competing concessions to induce cogeneration projects to sell electricity to their systems. Among these concessions were system operation guarantees that transferred risk to the utility and transmission credits that recognized the location of the producers on the utility grid.

CPUC's natural gas pricing policies until 1987 was analogous to the winding of a spring. In subsidizing residential rates, the commission continually increased rates to commercial and industrial customers. In doing so, it gradually and cumulatively put great pressure on these customers to seek alternatives to traditional utility service. The pressure was especially great on customers using large quantities of gas. Their use of propane and fuel oil indicates that the relative cost of gas has met or exceeded the level at which fuel switching was economic. The magnitude of the price-cost gap that characterized industrial rates until recently is epitomized by the threat of interstate pipelines entering California. Fortunately the CPUC has addressed the question of rate relief, adopting a new gas rate structure that recognizes the need for different regulations for core and noncore sectors.

Although baseline allowances were not addressed specifically in this paper, they probably will come into question in the near future. Now that cross-subsidies from large users are greatly curtailed, baseline rates have to be supported by the residential segment itself. That is, the gap between the gas costs of the baseline tier and the second tier will widen. An approach similar to that adopted by the CPUC in telephone pricing may be in order.[56] By setting up an income-level qualifying test for lower rates, it can more efficiently target the state's neediest citizens for concentrated subsidies.[57] Although precise estimates require knowledge of California demography, it seems safe to assume that the residential sector could produce greater contributions to utility revenues while rates to the neediest segments of the population could simultaneously be decreased. One advantage that this approach holds over the telephone plan is that the choice among service options that complicates telephone low-income lifeline rates would be absent in the case of natural gas.

The efficiency with which utilities carry out their franchised responsibilities should be made an issue in regulatory proceedings. Given that city-gate gas rates should eventually, if asymptotically, reach competitive levels, the next stage in bringing costs into line should be the installation of incentive systems for utilities to contain costs. As detailed above, linking contract carriage rates to organizational efficiency is one method of driving nongas costs down.

If, as suggested in our analysis, gas-to-gas competition can have efficiency-enhancing properties, perhaps so would electricity-to-gas competition. This would indicate that policymakers might consider separating the state's gas and electric utilities. The efficiency gained from

56. This approach has recently received legislative attention. See California Public Utilities Commission (1987).

57. As structured at present, baseline has very little income redistribution effects (Southern California Gas, 1986).

competition may exceed whatever scope economies exist in combined service; California might therefore benefit from the separation of gas and electric distribution.[58] Unfortunately, this subject has received very little attention, so that policymakers lack the evidence necessary to take action. Rigorous analysis to explore net efficiency gains from policy changes in this area should be undertaken.

With respect to the industrial sector, what is to be done? Clearly, given the incremental-cost approach, it is far less expensive to upgrade existing facilities than to allow the construction of interstate pipelines. One would hope the new gas rate design will permit these users to attain the security, flexibility, and economy they have sought for their operations. If so, these interstate pipeline proposals could be delayed until additional supplies for California are truly necessary.

Finally, we cannot overstate the role of strategy and gamesmanship in California regulatory proceedings. An objective that one might consider reasonably attainable, such as determining the imbedded costs of service, is difficult to reach conclusively and uncontroversially. Other tactics employed by the various actors in ratemaking reveal that strategy cannot be overlooked as a rationale for regulatory behavior. The strategic use of the interconnectedness of the California energy industry is clearly put in focus when one considers the case of pricing of electricity generation gas supplies. Because the chain of causation that started with higher interutility gas prices ended with greater incentives to private electric power generation, the CPUC kept these rates well above costs. The result was support for a key commission goal, small power production, but a weakened case for the assault on the need for newly completed electricity-generating stations in California.

The strategic side of public utility regulation is here to stay, although it can be attenuated. One would hope that a new collective agreement among the parties to rate proceedings could be struck, affirming the commitment of all to the efficient production and distribution of the state's natural gas resources. There is a chance that such a system could address important social goals, without inducing the unexpected and sometimes perverse consequences that mark the history of gas distribution in California.

REFERENCES

American Gas Association (1981). *Gas Facts: 1980 Data.* Arlington, Va.
American Gas Association (1984). *Gas Facts: 1983 Data.* Arlington, Va.

58. Note that the obvious economy of joint billing could be retained through an agreement between separate gas and electric companies. For an examination of the conditions in which economies of scope call for single ownership, see Teece (1980).

American Gas Association (1985). "Issue Paper: Competition in the Natural Gas Industry—Update." Arlington, Va.

Braeutigam, Ronald R. (1981). "The Deregulation of Natural Gas." In Leonard Weiss and Michael W. Klass (eds.), *Case Studies in Regulation: Revolution and Reform*, pp. 142–187. Boston: Little, Brown.

Broadman, Harry G. (1986). "Elements of Market Power in the Natural Gas Pipeline Industry." *The Energy Journal*, January, pp. 119–138.

Broadman, Harry G. (1987). "Competition in Natural Gas Pipeline Wellhead Supply Purchases." *The Energy Journal*, July, pp. 113–134.

Brown, Stephen J., and David S. Sibley (1986). *The Theory of Public Utility Pricing*. Cambridge: Cambridge University Press.

California Energy Commission (1981). *Energy Tomorrow: Challenges and Opportunities for California: The 1981 Biennial Report*. Sacramento.

California Energy Commission (1983). *Securing California's Energy Future: The 1983 Biennial Report*. Sacramento.

California Public Utilities Commission (1984). Decision 84-12-067, December 28, 1984.

California Public Utilities Commission (1985a). "Gas Rate Design Alternatives." Report of the Public Staff Division, April.

California Public Utilities Commission (1985b). "Charting a Sustainable Regulatory Course in Telecommunications." Report to the Commission by the Policy and Planning Division, October.

California Public Utilities Commission (1985c). Decision 84-04-079, October 17, 1985.

California Public Utilities Commission (1986a). Decision 86-12-009, December 3, 1986.

California Public Utilities Commission (1986b). Decision 86-12-010, December 3, 1986.

California Public Utilities Commission (1987) "Report to the Legislature Per AB 2764." July.

California Public Utilities Commission and California Energy Commission (1988). Final Report to the Legislature on Joint CEC/CPUC hearings on Excess Electrical Generating Capacity. June.

Cambridge Energy Research Associates (1984). *Mandatory Carriage: Consequences for the Natural Gas Industry*. Cambridge, Mass.

Energy Information Administration (1982a). *An Analysis of Post-NGPA Interstate Pipeline Wellhead Purchases*. DOE/EIA-0357. Washington, D.C.: U.S. Department of Energy.

Energy Information Administration (1982b). *Natural Gas Producer/Purchaser Contracts and Their Potential Impacts on the Natural Gas Market*. DOE/EIA-0330, Washington, D.C.: U.S. Department of Energy.

Energy Information Administration (1983). *Producer Revenues, Prices, and Concentration in the Natural Gas Market*. DOE/EIA-0404. Washington, D.C.: U.S. Department of Energy.

Energy Information Administration (1986). *Natural Gas Monthly*, DOE/EIA-0130 (86/03). Washington, D.C.: U.S. Department of Energy.

Federal Energy Regulatory Commission (1985). Docket No. RM85–1–000 (Order 436), issued October 9, 1985.

Filer, John E., and Daniel R. Hollas (1983). "Empirical Tests for the Effect of Regulation on Firm and Interruptible Gas Service." *Southern Economic Journal,* July, pp. 195–205.

Gentry, Charles R. (1984). "The Changing World of Natural Gas Purchase Agreements." *Natural Gas,* August, pp. 8–12.

German, Michael I., and Anne V. Roland (1985). "The Case Against Mandatory Carriage." *Public Utilities Fortnightly,* September 5, pp. 37–42.

Hendricks, Wallace (1975). "The Effect of Regulation on Collective Bargaining in Electric Utilities." *Bell Journal of Economics,* Autumn, pp. 451–465.

Hendricks, Wallace (1977). "Regulation and Labor Earnings." *Bell Journal of Economics,* Autumn, pp. 483–496.

Interstate Natural Gas Association of America (1985). "Voluntary Carriage Through 1984." May.

Interstate Natural Gas Association of America (1986a). "The Trend in Producer/Pipeline Gas Prices." June.

Interstate Natural Gas Association of America (1986b). "Interstate Natural Gas Transportation: An Analysis of Past-Order 436 Activity." July.

Jensen, James T. (1984). "Natural Gas Deregulation and the Clash of Cultures." *Public Utilities Fortnightly,* October 25, pp. 29–35; and November 8, pp. 29–35.

Kalt, Joseph P., and Robert A. Leone (1986). "Regional Effects of Energy Price Decontrol: The Roles of Interregional Trade, Stockholding, and Microeconomic Incidence." *The Rand Journal of Economics,* Summer, pp. 201–213.

Leibenstein, Harvey (1966). "Allocative Efficiency vs. X-Efficiency." *The American Economic Review,* June 1966, pp. 392–410.

Masten, S. E., and K. J. Crocker (1985). "Efficient Adaptation in Long-Term Contracts: Take-or-Pay Provisions for Natural Gas." *The American Economic Review,* December, pp. 1083–1093.

Mead, David E. (1981). "Concentration in the Natural Gas Pipeline Industry." Unpublished paper. Washington, D.C.: Office of Regulatory Analysis, Federal Energy Regulatory Commission.

National Regulatory Research Institute (1983). *State Regulatory Options for Dealing with Natural Gas Wellhead Deregulation.* Columbus, Ohio.

Office of Technology Assessment, United States Congress (1984). "Staff Memorandum on the Effects of Decontrol on Old Gas Recovery." February. Washington, D.C.: U.S. Congress.

Olson, Mancur (1965). *The Logic of Collective Action: Public Goods and the Theory of Groups.* Cambridge, Mass.: Harvard University Press.

Oil and Gas Journal (1983). "AGA: It's Possible to Trim Gas Surplus." August 22, p. 66.

Owen, Bruce M., and Ronald Braeutigam (1978). *The Regulation Game: Strategic Use of the Administrative Process.* Cambridge, Mass.: Ballinger.

Palmer, David R. (1982). "American Politics and Policies in the Regulation of Mexican Gas Imports." Unpublished PhD dissertation. Berkeley: University of California.

Peltzman, Sam (1976). "Toward a More General Theory of Regulation." *Journal of Law and Economics,* August, pp. 211–240.

Rohan, Dennis M. (1984). "Natural Gas Contract Carriage." Report to the California Manufacturers Association, July 9.

Salinger, Michael A. (1984). "Tobin's q, Unionization, and the Concentration-Profits Relationship." *The Rand Journal of Economics,* Summer, pp. 159–170.

Southern California Gas Company (1985a). "Base Supply and Load Equation Cost Allocation Study." May.

Southern California Gas Company (1985b). "Position Paper on the Proposed Mojave Pipeline Project." April.

Southern California Gas Company (1986). "The Impact of Baseline on Southern California Gas Company Customers." November.

Stalon, Charles G. (1986). "The Diminishing Role of Regulation in the Natural Gas Industry." *The Energy Journal,* April, pp. 1–12.

Teece, David J. (1980). "Economies of Scope and the Scope of the Enterprise." *Journal of Economic Behavior and Organization,* pp. 223–247.

Teece, David J. (1985). "The Economic Regulation of Oil Pipelines: The Implications of Competition for Regulatory Policy." Business and Public Policy Working Paper BPP-9. Berkeley Center For Research in Management.

Tussig, Arlon R., and Connie C. Barlow (1984). *The Natural Gas Industry: Evolution, Structure and Economics.* Cambridge, Mass.: Balinger.

U.S. Department of Energy (1981). "Main Line Natural Gas Sales to Industrial Users, 1980."

Wall Street Journal (1986). "Antitrust Officials Are Probing Charges Pipelines Won't Ship Lower-Priced Gas," January 31, p. 5.

Weiss, Leonard W. (1966). "Regulation and Labor Earnings." *American Economic Review,* March, pp. 96–117.

Williams, Stephen F. (1985). *The Natural Gas Revolution of 1985.* Washington, D.C.: American Enterprise Institute.

Appendix A: Methodology for Cross-subsidy Analysis

The main problem confronting the comparative analysis was how to put each set of estimates on a comparable basis. Each was developed using different costs of purchased gas and a slightly different sales profile. Fortunately, each set of costs, when adjusted for a common gas purchase price, yielded total revenues very close to a common value. Outside of adjusting for gas costs, the costs developed using this methodology differ from those appearing in Table 5.8 by a maximum of roughly three percent. Estimates for gas purchase costs, total nongas margins, and total sales volume are rounded to put them close to each of the three sets of estimates. Rates do not include the effect of adjustment clauses and balancing accounts.

1. THE COST STRUCTURE ASSUMED $ in thousands

Nongas Margin		$1,200,000
Cost of Gas Purchased ($/thousand cubic feet) (includes commodity, transmission, and production costs)	3.755	
Total Annual Sales (million cubic feet)	930,000	
Total Annual Cost of Gas Purchased		$3,492,150
Total Revenue Requirement		$4,692,150

2. THE ADJUSTMENT PROCESS

Costs for the five customer classes were first adjusted on an equal per million-cubic-feet basis to account for the common gas purchase cost. Remaining differences between the nongas margin and $1,200 million (a maximum adjustment of 5%) were allocated on a per thousand-cubic-feet basis to the four retail classes.

The distribution below shows how total sales were distributed among the five classes. It follows the PSD percentage distribution, and yields a distribution very close to the other two allocations. Commercial sales include only those to customers on the GN-1 schedule (see note 41).

Class	Annual Sales (million cubic feet)
Residential	271,814
Commercial	94,178
Industrial	162,374
Electricity Generation	274,386
Wholesale	127,248
Total	930,000

167

Appendix B: Competition and Wage Rate Analysis

A linear regression model was developed to test the hypothesis that wages are influenced by the degree of competition seen by gas utilities in that state. Data were assembled for 1980, a convenient year, because it antedates the movement for contract carriage. The exclusion of the effect of contract carriage in analyzing data from later years would constitute a dangerous omission. Variables marked with an asterisk (*) were taken from data released to the authors by the American Gas Association, based on the AGA's ongoing data compilation. The number of observations is 37. The 48 continental states were used, less 6 states for which the sample contained very small numbers of aggregated observations and 5 states with missing data. The most general form of the equation to be specified is:

$$\text{UWAGE} = a_0 + a_1 \cdot \text{MWAGE} + a_2 \cdot \text{UNION} + a_3 \cdot \text{UMMULT} + a_4 \cdot \text{RATEIDR} + a_5 \cdot \text{SOUTH} + a_6 \cdot \text{GASPROD} + a_7 \cdot \text{SGMULT} + a_8 \text{C4} + a_9 \text{RATEEDR} + e$$

where:

UWAGE* = Average wage in gas utilities for that state. Included is data for distribution companies, companies having pipeline transportation operations within their state in addition to distribution operations, and the gas sides of combination gas and electric utilities[59]

MWAGE = Average wage for manufacturing workers

UNION = Unionization rates for nonagricultural workers

UMMULT = An interaction term that is the product of MWAGE and UNION

RATEIDR = Ratio of direct sales by interstate pipelines to industrial customers divided by utility sales to industrial customers

SOUTH = Dummy variable set equal to one for south Atlantic, east south central, and west south central states

GASPROD = Dummy variable set equal to one for states where the ratio of marketed production to total utility sales exceeds 5%

SGMULT = product of SOUTH and GASPROD

C4* = Four-firm concentration ratio, based on sales to end users by all types of suppliers[59]

RATEEDR = Ratio of direct sales for electricity generation

e = Random disturbance term

Table 5.14 shows the range of values for these variables. The dependent variable is UWAGE. The expected signs of MWAGE and UNION are positive, whereas the expected sign of RATEIDR is negative. UMMULT was added with-

59. This calculation was made using data from various issues of *Natural Gas Monthly.*

out expectation as to sign, to test the linearity of MWAGE and UNION in the relationship. If the argument presented above is accurate, C4 and RATEEDR will not be significant, regardless of sign. The variables for southern states and gas-producing states were added to control for the effect of those particular market environments. The expected sign of the SOUTH coefficient cannot be deduced from theory. It is added following Hendricks (1977). The GASPROD coefficient is expected to be negative, reflecting the greater pool of gas-associated workers in states where gas production is a part of the economy.

The results are shown in Table 5.15. Equation 1 shows the results for the wage and union variables. Equation 2 adds the competition proxy, RATEIDR. Its estimated coefficient has the expected sign and is significant (at the 0.05 level), thereby supporting the principal research hypothesis being explored in this section. The addition of the southern and gas-producing state variables in equation 3 improves the overall explanatory power of the model. The GASPROD coefficient is negative and significant. Equation 4 has the highest adjusted R2, approximately 72%. In this equation, SOUTH is replaced by SGMULT, which has the effect of introducing a dummy variable to represent southern gas-producing states. Both it and GASPROD are nearly significant and negative in sign. Finally, equations 5 and 6 show the effect of adding the concentration variable, C4, and the electricity generation sales ratio, RATEEDR, to the other eight variables. As expected, neither is significant.

There are a number of reasons why the model is not perfect. In addition to reasons already discussed, we should mention that the aggregation to statewide data, a concession given to include more variables, reduces variation in a number of the variables. This, in turn, reduces the probability of finding statistical significance if it exists. The MWAGE variable is also influenced by the differential effect of international competition on manufacturing jobs across states, an influence not felt in the natural gas industry. The varying stringency of regulation may also affect the efficiency of utilities. Those in states with greater regulatory vigilance may make cost containment a higher priority.

Distilling policy conclusions from this exercise is most difficult. The information necessary to measure variables and confidently establish what has been strongly suggested by the regression analysis is not available. Nonetheless, the results enable one to tentatively predict the effect of the infusion of competition in California on nongas distribution costs. Assuming that the regression coefficients on RATEIDR from the equation 4 are correct, an increase of direct sales by interstate pipeline companies to industrial customers as a percent of similar sales by utilities has the effect of reducing wages by 15.6¢/hour for every 10 percentage points of that ratio. Another way of stating this result is that in two states where the only difference in the set of variables described is that one state has a RATEIDR value of 10% and the other has a RATEIDR value of 0%, average utility wages in the first state will be 15.6¢/hour lower.

Table 5.16, which compares actual and hypothetical employment costs, was developed using California data. It lists the labor cost savings (including overheads, at 40%) under competitive conditions represented by various RATEIDR values. Employment is fixed at the 1980 level. These costs are minor if compared to the total nongas margins of the two companies, each of which runs well over a billion dollars annually. However, the effect on wages of a RATEIDR of 10% is about a 1.5% decrease, which, though small, is not trivial. If the rest of the charges, which together comprise the entire nongas margin, are similarly higher than necessary, the net effect could be substantial inefficiency and excessive costs of distribution.

Some evidence of inefficiency in other portions of gas utility operations costs is already available from other studies that use national data. Filer and Hollas (1983), for example, found evidence of an Averch-Johnson overcapitalization effect in the building of storage facilities. The ultimate cost of such inefficiencies is borne primarily by consumers. Recently available data suggests that utilities in more competitive environments have negotiated contracts with pipeline suppliers with more vigor. This can be tested by comparing the decline in city-gate prices to the competition proxy RATEIDR. The correlation coefficient between the percentage change in city-gate prices for the 24 months prior to February 1986 and RATEIDR is −0.513.[59] That is, the stronger the competitive pressure in a state, the greater the drop in city-gate prices. This is evidence that competition puts force behind the effort to bargain aggressively.

TABLE 5.1
Natural Gas Production From Gas Reserves
Dedicated to Interstate Pipelines[a]
(1980)

1980 Area Production (billion cubic feet)	Average Number of Pipelines in Area	% of Total Production
Less than 10	2.8	1
10–99	5.0	4
100–1,000	11.3	63
Greater than 1,000	18.0	33
Average	8.2	
Total		100

[a]SOURCE: American Gas Association (1985).

TABLE 5.2
Interstate Pipeline Sales for Resale
by Customer Type[a]
(1983)

	% of Sales for Resale
Sales to Privately Owned Distribution Companies with With Two or More Suppliers	58
Sales to Other Pipelines	26
Sales to Privately Owned Distribution Companies with One Supplier	10
Sales to Municipal Distribution Companies	4
Not Known	2
Total	100

[a]SOURCE: American Gas Association (1985).

TABLE 5.3
Interstate Pipeline Sales for Resale
Suppliers Providing 5% or Greater
of a Distribution Company's Needs[a]

	% of Sales
Sales to Privately Owned Distribution Companies With:	
Two Suppliers	19
Three Suppliers	28
Four Suppliers	5
Five or More Suppliers	1
Total	53

[a]SOURCE: American Gas Association (1985).

TABLE 5.4
Gas Purchase Statistics of Major Interstate Pipelines
1984–1985[a]

	Block 1			Block 2		
	Cost ($/thousand cubic feet)	Volume (billion cubic feet)	% of Total	Cost ($/thousand cubic feet)	Volume (billion cubic feet)	Weighted Average Cost
El Paso Natural Gas	1.29	370.9	38.4	3.54	591.1	2.68
Transwestern Pipeline	1.38	41.3	15.6	3.14	223.4	2.86
Other Companies (23)	1.48	3,749.7	36.4	3.62	6,552.4	2.84
Total	1.46	4,161.9	36.1	3.60	7,366.9	2.83
California Suppliers (2)	1.30	412.2	33.6	3.43	814.5	2.71

[a]NOTE: This table is adapted from one appearing in Williams (1985). For our purposes, we assumed that block 1 gas can be taken as a proxy for old gas and block 2 for new and high-cost gas.

TABLE 5.5
PG&E and SCG Sources of Gas[a]
Percent of Purchases

	PG&E		SCG	
Source	1982	1986	1982	1986
Canadian	40.0	41.3	6.2	10.3
El Paso	34.7	16.7	60.6	30.3
Transwestern			27.3	14.7
California Producers	23.1	24.0	5.0	8.3
Other California Sources			0.9	5.2
Rocky Mountains	2.2	2.4		
Spot Market	0.0	15.6	0.0	31.2
Total:	100.0	100.0	100.0	100.0

[a]SOURCE: Company reports.
[b]NOTE: Includes purchases from PG&E and offshore sources.

TABLE 5.6
PG&E and SCG Revenues and Sales by Customer Classes
(1986)[a]

	PG&E		SCG	
Class	Revenues ($ millions)	Sales (billion cubic feet)	Revenues ($ millions)	Sales (billion cubic feet)
Residential	899.0	189.1	1,256.3	233.2
Commercial	435.4	78.1	519.0	83.7
Industrial	437.7	128.9	526.3	120.8
Electricity Generation	511.3[b]	158.5[b]	609.5	219.5
Total	2,283.4	554.6	2,911.1	657.2

[a]SOURCE: Company reports, personal communication.
[b]NOTE: Sales are considered internal to the company.

TABLE 5.7
Relative Price and Sales of Gas in California,
Industrial Users with Nos. 5 and 6 Residual Oil Alternative[a]

Year	Delivered Price ($/1.03 million Btu[b]) Gas	Oil	Ratio Gas/Oil	Gas Sales to Class (billion cubic feet)
1976	1.72	1.83	0.94	166.2
1977	2.15	1.86	1.16	132.3
1978	2.34	1.56	1.50	115.4
1979	3.93	2.74	1.42	162.2[c]
1980	4.22	3.44	1.23	138.8
1981	4.43	4.47	0.99	152.0
1982	5.14	4.50	1.14	114.0

[a]SOURCES: Platt's Oilgram, with 8% added to terminal price for taxes and transportation; PG&E records.
[b]NOTES: 1.03 million Btu is the energy content of 1,000 cubic feet of natural gas or approximately of 7.7 gallons of residual oil.
[c]Probably due to oil supply disruptions.

TABLE 5.8
Actual Rates and Rates Based on Estimates of Imbedded Cost of Service,
Southern California Gas Company
Twelve Months Beginning May 1, 1985[a]
(¢/thousand cubic feet)

Class	Actual Rates	Rates Based on Estimated Imbedded Costs of Service PSD	SCG
Residential	566	571	690
Commercial	685	503	539
Industrial	510	476	432
Electricity Generation	426	475	395
Wholesale	400	463	409

[a]SOURCE: SCG (1985b), CPUC (1985a). Author's calculations based on CPUC work papers.

TABLE 5.9
Comparative Distribution Costs
National Averages and California Utilities[a,b]
($/thousand cubic feet)

Year	National			SCG			PG&E		
	CG	BT	M	CG	BT	M	CG	BT	M
1972	0.43	0.73	0.30	0.40	0.73	0.33	0.36	0.58	0.22
1973	0.46	0.79	0.33	0.43	0.84	0.41	0.40	0.65	0.25
1974	0.57	0.95	0.38	0.56	1.03	0.46	0.53	0.88	0.35
1975	0.80	1.29	0.49	0.72	1.28	0.56	0.92	1.35	0.43
1976	0.98	1.60	0.62	0.86	1.49	0.63	1.28	1.73	0.45
1977	1.31	1.97	0.67	1.16	1.85	0.69	1.53	2.12	0.59
1978	1.47	2.18	0.72	1.40	2.05	0.65	1.81	2.24	0.43
1979	1.81	2.52	0.71	1.92	2.57	0.65	2.16	2.54	0.38
1980	2.41	3.13	0.72	2.46	3.51	1.05	3.10	3.99	0.89
1981	2.89	3.65	0.77	2.77	3.79	1.02	3.29	4.31	1.02
1982	3.60	4.46	0.86	3.92	4.96	1.04	4.04	4.99	0.95
1983	4.05	5.12	1.07	4.17	5.81	1.64	4.07	5.36	1.29
1984	3.89	5.13	1.24	3.97	5.89	1.92	3.97	5.56	1.59
Total Overall Percentage Change 1972–1984 (%)									
	806	602	311	892	703	477	100	864	633
Average Annual Percentage Change (%/year)									
1972–1976	22.9	2.7	19.6	21.1	19.4	17.4	37.3	31.5	19.7
1976–1980	25.2	18.3	4.0	30.0	23.8	13.4	24.7	23.3	18.8
1980–1984	12.7	13	14.5	12.7	13.8	16.4	6.8	8.7	15.6

[a]Source: American Gas Association (1981), company reports.
[b]Key: CG = city gate cost; BT = burner tip price; M = distribution margin.

TABLE 5.10   Gas Costs: National Average Wellhead
Prices and California Industrial Rates[a]
($/thousand cubic feet)

| Year | Wellhead | Average Industrial Delivered Rate | |
		PG&E	SCG
1977	0.79	2.24	1.80
1978	0.91	2.45	2.12
1979	1.18	2.68	2.50
1980	1.59	4.40	3.55
1981	1.98	4.62	3.80
1982	2.46	5.35	5.03
1983	2.62	5.69	6.26
1984	2.63	5.34	6.27
1985	2.48	4.49	5.66
1986	1.94	3.40	4.36

[a]SOURCES: Energy Information Administration (1986), company reports.

TABLE 5.11
Comparison of Residual Oil
and Natural Gas Prices, National Averages[a]
($/million Btu)

Year	Average Retail Price of Residual Fuel Oil	Average Gas Price to Industry	Ratio of Gas Price to Fuel Oil Price
1976	1.82	1.31	0.77
1977	2.10	1.69	0.80
1978	1.99	1.90	0.95
1979	2.91	2.23	0.77
1980	4.05	2.79	0.69
1981	5.05	3.29	0.63
1982	4.51	3.97	0.88
1983	4.34	4.32	1.00

[a]SOURCE: Cambridge Energy Research Associates (1984).

TABLE 5.12

Contract Carriage for Distributors and End Users, Nationwide Totals[a]
(billion cubic feet)

Year	Carriage for Distributors	Carriage for End Users	Total Carriage	Carriage Share of Total Delivered to Market (%)
1982	269	101	370	3
1983	479	206	685	5
1984	618	513	1,131	9
1985	1,357	800	2,157	17
1986	2,996	1,180	4,176	37

[a]SOURCE: Interstate Natural Gas Association of America (1986b), personal communication.

TABLE 5.13
Capital Cost Comparison of EOR Service Proposals[a]

Project (State)[b]	Sponsors	Distance (miles)	Capacity (million cubic feet/day)	Cost ($ in millions)	Capital Cost Ratio ($/cubic ft/day)
Mojave (Arizona)	El Paso Natural Gas Co. Houston Natural Gas Co. Pacific Lighting	385	600	320	0.53
El Dorado (Arizona)	Lear Petroleum	383	520	285	0.55
Kern River (Wyoming)	Tenneco Corp. Williams Co.	762	700	825	0.85
PG&E and SCG upgrade			700	47	0.07

[a]SOURCES: FERC submittals, PG&E and SCG documents.
[b]NOTE: State of origin.

TABLE 5.14
Sample Statistics—Gas Utility Wage Study
(N = 37)[a]

Variable	Mean	Standard Deviation	Minimum	Maximum
UWAGE	9.20	1.44	5.30	11.81
MWAGE	7.25	1.10	5.37	9.52
UNION	23.19	7.53	9.60	38.70
UMMULT	173.05	74.08	51.55	356.05
RATEIDR	0.18	0.21	0	0.67
SOUTH	0.30	0.46	0	1
GASPROD	0.38	0.49	0	1
SGMULT	0.19	0.40	0	1
C4	85.67	14.55	53.90	100.00
RATEEDR	0.51	1.55	0	8.83

[a]SOURCES: U.S Department of Energy (1981), personal communication.

TABLE 5.15
Regression Equation to Explain Utility Wage Rates
(T-statistics in parentheses)

Variable	Eq. 1	Eq. 2	Eq. 3	Eq. 4	Eq. 5	Eq. 6
CONSTANT	−2.366	−2.330	−1.406	−1.786	−1.229	−1.990
	(−0.622)	(−0.715)	(−0.461)	(−0.639)	(−0.363)	(−0.621)
MWAGE	1.365	1.503	1.402	1.458	1.450	1.473
	(2.411)	(3.139)	(3.180)	(3.558)	(3.231)	(3.199)
UNION	0.359	0.400	0.354	0.382	0.385	0.394
	(2.349)	(3.100)	(2.982)	(3.432)	(3.120)	(3.154)
UMMULT	−0.038	−0.040	−0.041	−0.045	−0.045	0.046
	(−1.827)	(−2.634)	(−2.501)	(−2.094)	(−2.652)	(−2.699)
RATEIDR		−2.890	−1.786	−1.557	−1.732	−1.638
		(−3.800)	(−2.921)	(−2.094)	(−2.294)	(−1.881)
SOUTH			−0.209		0.386	0.331
			(0.566)	(0.819)	(0.688)	
GASPROD			−0.869	−0.513	−0.434	−0.385
			(−2.729)	(−1.419)	(−1.157)	(−1.041)
SGMULT				−0.909	−1.331	−1.220
				(−1.890)	(−1.991)	(−1.807)
C4						−0.007
						(−0.696)
RATEEDR						−0.030
						(−0.265)
$\overline{R}^2$	0.457	0.614	0.687	0.704	0.699	
F	11.093	15.318	14.183	16.242	11.689	11.468

TABLE 5.16
1980 Estimated Cost Savings from Greater Competition
($ in millions)

RATEIDR	SCG	PG&E	Both Companies
5%	$1.96	$2.37	$4.43
10%	3.93	4.74	8.67
20%	7.86	9.48	17.34

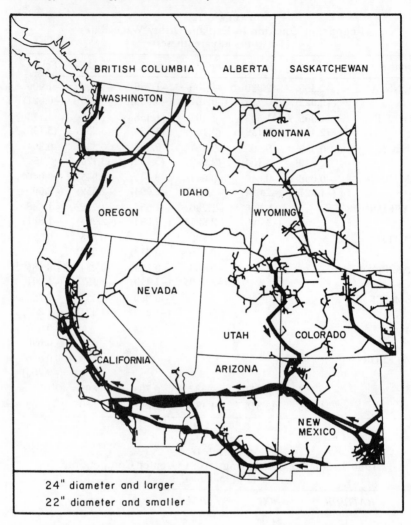

5.1. Natural gas pipelines—western states. Source: California Energy Commission (1981).

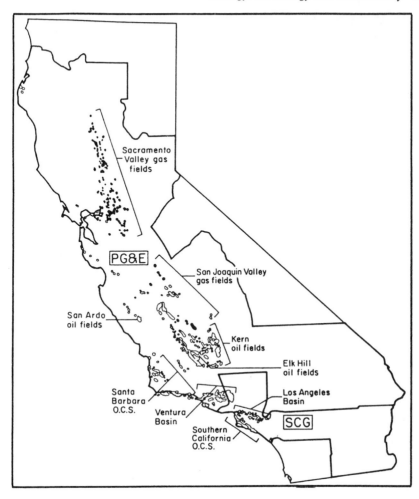

5.2. Gas utility service territories. Source: California Energy Commission (1981).

Billions of
cubic feet

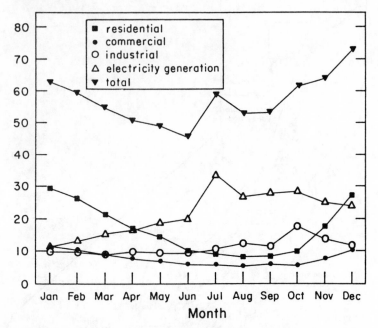

5.3. PG&E monthly gas deliveries profile, 1984.

¢/thousand cubic feet

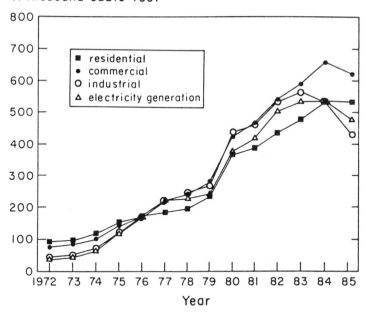

5.4. PG&E burner tip cost of natural gas by customer class.

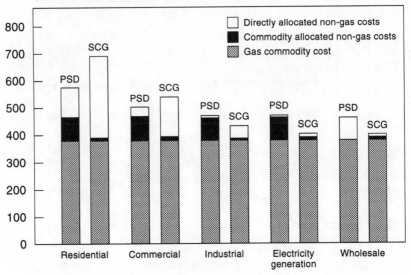

5.5. Imbedded cost of service estimates for SCG, 12 months beginning May 1, 1985.

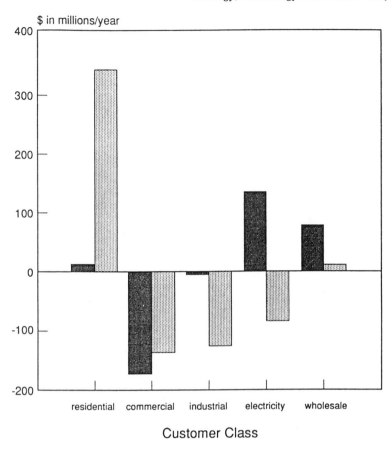

5.6. Estimates of total cross-subsidy for SCG. Positive value indicates recipient class.

[23]

The Uneasy Case for Mandatory Contract Carriage in the Natural Gas Industry

David J. Teece

The restructuring of the U.S. natural gas industry that has occurred in the 1980s and 1990s, involving as it does mandatory common carriage and the unbundling of pipeline services, is almost uniformly represented as a step in the direction of competition, which favors free enterprise and benefits the consumer. In this essay, I review the rationale for these policy moves and question the common assertion that mandatory carriage and unbundling unambiguously comprise a move that is to the ultimate benefit of the consumer. While these moves have supported the development of a spot gas market and enabled certain parties in the industry to dig out from prior regulatory distortions created by wellhead price regulation, these short-term benefits to consumers, some producers, and independent markets have required the construction by regulatory agencies of an industrial structure and system of competition that does not involve competition on the merits and that, therefore, involves unnecessary costs—albeit costs that are somewhat invisible. A more patient approach, less infected by the special interests of independent marketers and producers of spot gas, could have enabled the United States to completely deregulate the industry while maintaining the benefit of competition and integrated structures. Such a system has existed in Germany, and it has performed extremely well. Instead, however, the United States has stuck itself with a decidedly second-best system of organization, which is arguably better than the old regime but involves unnecessary costs.

This paper has not undergone significant revisions since its presentation in March 1993. Accordingly, it does not pretend to be current on all relevant regulatory developments.

ORGANIZATIONAL CHARACTERISTICS OF THE NATURAL GAS INDUSTRY

Technical Requirements and Organizational Consequences

Viewed functionally, the natural gas industry in the United States consists of a number of capital-intensive and technically demanding activities, including production, gathering, storage, pipeline transportation, distribution, and end-user consumption. Viewed organizationally, the industry worldwide displays certain common organizational characteristics. Consumers have traditionally purchased from a local distribution company (LDC), although the LDCs in some countries are "bypassed," as large end users buy directly from producers or pipelines.[1] In many countries, the entire structure is vertically integrated, from production through distribution to the end user.

Until very recently, pipelines everywhere (even when not vertically integrated) performed a "merchant" function, contracting for gas in the field and selling it at the city gate; performing the long-term scheduling, storing, and planning function for the industry; and generally serving as the balancer of supply and demand and the guarantor of supply to the customer. It is important to recognize that the natural gas industry is one that is capital-intensive throughout and, moreover, involves irreversible commitments of specialized plant and equipment for efficient production, distribution, and supply. There are also significant system interdependencies. Pressure control, load balancing, gas rerouting during line work, storage, and gas mix all require high levels of cooperation from one end of the system to the other.[2] Close coordination and cooperation allows customers to be alerted in a timely fashion to impending problems, and adjustments occur more smoothly and quickly.

Vertical Integration

Vertical integration refers to an organization of industry in which sequential stages of activity occur under common ownership. Thus, in vertically integrated industries, transactions between different stages are conducted internally (in-house) rather than via arm's-length relationships among unaffiliated firms. An alternative organizational form is the linkage of unaffiliated segments of the industry by long-term contracts. Vertical integration and long-term contracts are substitute organizational modes, but they tend to have different performance characteristics except when the business environment is stable and contract enforcement is not an issue. While more flexible, a series of end-to-end, short-term contracts are not a substitute for vertical integration since the incentives of the parties are different and contract terms can be renegotiated at the time of contract renewal. There is, therefore, no guarantee that contracting parties will be dealing with each other over the long term or that specialized irreversible investments can be efficiently and competitively utilized.

The vertical structure of a firm tells one almost nothing about the firm's market power, which is a horizontal, and not a vertical, concept. Economists generally recognize that, absent market power in one or more stages of an industry, vertically integrated firms cannot exercise any more market power than firms that are not vertically integrated. Put differently, vertically integrated structures and competitive markets can exist together, and they commonly do. There is no necessary connection between integration and market power.

Since the turn of the century, vertical integration has been a common feature of industry in advanced industrial nations. When specialized long-lived investments are needed for efficient, secure supply, long-term contracts and/or vertical integration emerge to ensure that the dedicated assets in question can be profitably amortized.[3] As modern industrial technology dictated increased requirements for specialized, nonredeployable investments, highly vertically integrated organizations emerged in many industries. Thus, by the turn of the century in the United States and elsewhere, considerable vertical integration characterized steel, chemicals, and many other industries. By the 1920s, vertical integration also came to characterize new industries like automobiles and oil, both in the United States and abroad.[4] While vertical integration in some form characterizes all industries, their level of integration varies. For example, steel, automobiles, and aluminum are more integrated than furniture and construction. Because these patterns are very often repeated (at least functionally) in different countries, one may infer that similar organizing principles and requirements are at work.

A reliance on contracts rather than vertical integration brings with it hazards, particularly when specialized assets have been committed in the expectation of contractual performance. In an industry organized by contracts rather than vertical integration, planning is necessarily incomplete (in the sense that adjustments to changed circumstances may require tampering with the contract), promises are not always honored (because of opportunism), and the efficacy of court ordering is problematic.[5] These considerations are of little import when investments are costlessly redeployable. When this is not so, vertical integration or its close equivalents are necessary to minimize industry costs and maximize supply security.

This can be demonstrated as follows.[6] Suppose a good or service can be supplied by either of two alternative technologies, one being general-purpose (with no commitment of dedicated assets), and the other, a special-purpose technology (that is, dedicated assets, as in natural gas). Thus, the special-purpose technology requires greater investment in dedicated special facilities and is more efficient if it can be kept in continuous use. However, in order to encourage investment in the efficient technology, investing firms need to be assured that their investments are protected, in the sense that they will be sufficiently utilized to ensure that the investment can be recouped. Unless safeguards to that effect are provided, the investments will not be made, or if they are, only if a higher return is made available to the provider to offset the higher risks that the assets might become stranded and economically valueless.

This is demonstrated in Figure 1. If the industry does not make the necessary specialized investments needed for efficient supply, it can provide consumers with product at the high price of P_3. If it does make the investment, it can price at either P_2 or P_1, with P_1 less than P_2. Whether the lowest price, P_1, is possible depends on whether organizational arrangements can be made to safeguard the economic value of the specialized investments. When suppliers do not have full confidence (safeguards) that their investments are protected because of regulatory or contractual uncertainties, the industry must establish the higher price, P_2. If safeguards can be worked out, as, for instance, with vertical integration, the industry's costs can be lowered and the goals of economic efficiency can be served.

Integration of Shipper and Merchant

A related, but different, form of integration is also relevant in the gas industry. A vertically fragmented industry, in which the gas producer, storage, and pipeline are under different ownership, may yet have a degree of integration in that while the producer and the pipelines are separate entities, the pipeline may nevertheless take on the core risk-bearing role, guaranteeing the customer certain service levels and contracting with producers to ensure it has sufficient deliverability to meet its obligations. In the United States, this function is typically referred to as the merchant function. Historically, the pipelines have generally provided both transportation services and the merchant function.

With open access and the emergence of a spot market, the system of long-term contracts, which previously tied the customer to the producer via the pipeline, has begun unraveling in the United States. Figure 2 summarizes various types of open access. There are powerful reasons for these changes, which will be described following identification of the inefficiencies that are potentially avoidable in the integration of the merchant and the shipper.

Informational Efficiencies

Because of unimpeded information flows and the absence of deep proprietary concerns, a merchant pipeline can learn about transportation bottlenecks, shut-in production, customer demand switches, and so on, far sooner than do pipelines that only provide the transportation function. This is a property of a well-managed, integrated system that can contribute to its superior efficiency vis-à-vis nonintegrated firms. Moreover, because such information is of a transitory nature, sharing it with other nonintegrated merchants on a timely basis is often impractical.

The Open Access Debate   47

Figure 1
Industry Supply Price Under Different Organizational Schemes

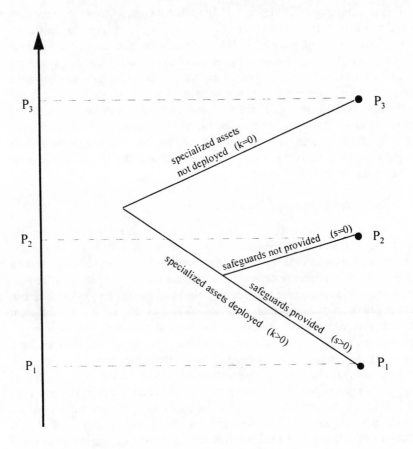

Source: Williamson, *Economic Institutions*, 33.

P ≡ breakeven price to final consumer, $P_3 > P_2 > P_1$

k ≡ level of specialized investments

s ≡ level of contractual "safeguards" available

Figure 2:
Forms of Open Access

TERMINOLOGY	ORGANIZATIONAL ARRANGEMENT
Private carriers	Transport own gas only
Contract carriers	Transport own gas, plus gas for others
Voluntary	On negotiated terms without regulatory interference
Mandated	On terms dictated by regulators
Common carriers	Mandatory transport of all gas on regulated and "nondiscriminatory terms and conditions"

Operating Efficiencies

Operational problems in the gas industry are often better handled by an integrated firm. Such problems include pressure control, balancing receipts and deliveries, and rerouting gas during line work. With gas entering or leaving a system at many points, a merchant pipeline, through close coordination, can aggregate demand and supply to meet particular requirements and respond to problems in an efficient and expeditious fashion. Customers are likewise alerted in a timely fashion to impending problems, and adjustments occur more quickly and smoothly.

Capital Utilization Efficiencies

It is critical that pipeline assets be efficiently utilized, as these are quite substantial. If a pipeline must leave the marketing of its excess capacity to others, and if it does not have long-term contracts both upstream and downstream, the risks associated with pipeline investments will increase for any particular pipeline and for the industry more generally.

Aggregation Economies/Transactional Efficiencies

It is rare that the needs of a particular customer match the supply of a particular producer. Generally, the needs of a large number of customers must be pooled and matched against the supply capabilities of several producers. Thus, a portfolio of contracts offers obvious transactional economies. There are economies associated with aggregating both supply and sales transactions, rather than brokering one at a time. Merchant pipelines are in a position to capture such economies, with concomitant benefits to customers.

Efficiencies Due to Credible Commitment and Supply

Local distribution companies must have assured supply to meet their obligations. The economic and political costs associated with failure to perform are tremendous. Integrated merchant pipelines are perceived to be backed by the substantial and irreversible assets of the pipeline and/or producer, while brokers are not. Moreover, merchant pipelines have incentives as well as the capacity to keep the pipeline full. The merchant pipeline, having much to lose by failing to perform, is a credible supply alternative. Therefore, it is likely to have a competitive advantage over pipelines that only provide transportation.

Summary

Basically, the integrated merchant pipeline can overcome several problems associated with relying exclusively on a fragmented system in which one party performs the merchant function and the other, the transportation function. Fundamentally, the efficiencies stem from the harmonizing of diverse expectations, plans, and interests.[7] Other organizational arrangements are often not as capable of coping with changes in customer requirements or of providing one-stop shopping. Furthermore, spot providers lack the same incentive as a pipeline to address long-term customer requirements. Accordingly, it is important to reiterate that there are considerable operational complexities in the gas industry, from wellhead to burner-tip. Moreover, there is a good deal of nonredeployable capacity, which needs to be utilized efficiently. Supply flexibility stems from storage, pipeline flow, and the ability to manage supply contracts. This means that production, transportation, distribution and storage must be coordinated and harmonized. Independent nonintegrated and nonaffiliated companies operating at arm's-length can perform all these functions if the relevant information moves rapidly and accurately and the objectives of all parties have been closely aligned. Often that is not the case, however. Integration, with its aligning of incentives and sharing of information, creates the potential for the industry to work better.[8] Integrated companies have emerged around the world to get the industry's business done, which is no accident, as there are real economies to be achieved through properly managed integrated structures.

Desirable Performance Characteristics

There are several desirable characteristics that most observers believe ought to characterize a properly functioning gas industry. First, the industry must be cost-competitive and be able to assure supply. Because the disruption costs to customers and the economy can be enormous if suppliers are cut off—there may not be adequate substitute supply in the short run—security of supply is paramount.[9]

Also paramount is "competitive" pricing. As a practical matter, the appropriate way to set a benchmark figure is by comparison with competing fuels. With a natural resource, competitive prices need not be the sum of production, transportation, and distribution costs. "User costs"—the opportunity costs of selling the product today rather than in the future—must also be taken into account.[10]

Relatedly, the industry ought to be in supply-demand balance without shortages or surpluses. If an industry is efficiently organized and competitive, shortages and gluts will rarely occur. Moreover, the industry ought to be able to adjust smoothly and efficiently to supply-and-demand shocks. It is against these criteria that the performance of the gas industry ought to be reviewed.

ORGANIZATIONAL STRUCTURE OF THE U.S. INDUSTRY: HISTORY AND RECENT DEVELOPMENTS

This American industry has been, and remains, highly regulated. Supply has been organized by a mixture of vertical integration and long-term contracts. The deployment of the specialized assets needed in this industry was facilitated because, at least historically, long-term durable relationships, supported by contracts and vertical integration, emerged and were supported by the courts. The pipelines, which traditionally combined the role of both merchant and shipper, bound themselves upstream to producers with long-term contracts and downstream to local distribution companies with balancing, long-term supply contracts. These customers reciprocated with "minimum-bill" contractual provisions, which guaranteed that they would purchase certain minimum volumes. This structure evolved over a long period, and historically, it has worked well. However, it has recently been undone by the regulators. Before discussing this process, a brief synopsis of the industry's organization will be given.

Early Development

The vertical integration of production and pipelines has been a feature of the natural gas industry since the early days, although upstream integration has never been particularly significant. Rather, long-term contracts induced by regulation provided many of the benefits commonly available from vertical integration. Some pipelines were joint ventures involving producing interests. During World War II, the government built two oil pipelines for the purpose of national defense from Texas to the New York–Philadelphia area. After the war, these lines were converted to gas transmission and then sold. Between 1950 and 1956, five gas pipelines, each over a thousand miles long, were built from the Gulf Coast to points north and east. These pipelines were not highly integrated.[11]

As these were expensive and long-lived capital intensive ventures with only one use—the transportation of gas—pipeline financing and viability often depended on guarantees of shipment by producers and guarantees of purchase by local distribution companies.[12] This could be obtained either by long-term contracts or via vertical integration, but mainly the former mechanism was used. Minimum-bill provisions of long-term contracts and their upstream counterparts, take-or-pay provisions with the producer, guaranteed the pipelines that their long-lived specialized asset would be in continuous use.[13] Hence, a pipeline company could confidently invest in new facilities if it could sign contracts with local distribution companies and producers guaranteeing both markets and supplies for decades into the future. Producers could likewise invest in production facilities, knowing that a guaranteed market was available and accessible. Moreover, once gas was dedicated to individual interstate pipelines, it could not be moved to other uses unless the gas contract was abandoned with Federal Power Commission approval.

In this environment, backward integration was useful to "anchor" a new field and provide the impetus for initial entry by a pipeline, but complete integration was neither a necessary nor a feasible means to ensure the effective utilization of the pipeline's assets. Long-term contracts plus the regulatory apparatus provided the instruments for effective organization of the industry and the recovery of investment in dedicated facilities.

It is important to bear in mind that organizational arrangements that provide safeguards to the owners of specialized assets ultimately benefit the users (i.e., customers) of the assets in question. If investors/owners of the specialized asset cannot be assured that the investment will be recovered, then the terms of finance will be adjusted against the firms making the investment in the assets in question. This ultimately will pull up the cost structure of the industry, to the detriment of the consumer.

During the 1950s and 1960s, pipelines began developing their own integrated production as a way to diversify into a less-regulated business. During the 1970s, interstate pipelines developed their own gas (supplied at the urging of the Federal Power Commission) to help solve the gas shortage problem.[14]

Though they had limited production, the pipelines engaged in a number of other activities besides transportation. Most notable was offering storage systems, to help balance supply and demand and meet contractual obligations with producers and customers, as well as gathering systems, designed to gather gas in the field for interstate and intrastate pipeline system supply. Although there are some stand-alone storage companies and gathering companies, these activities were generally an outgrowth of other pipeline operations.

Regulation and Integration

The vertical organization of the natural gas industry by contract was supported and encouraged by regulation. The NGA of 1938 assigned responsibility for pipeline regulation to the Federal Power Commission (FPC), which is now the Federal Energy Regulatory Commission (FERC). The essential feature of FPC pipeline regulation was the "certification" of facilities and a "tariff" governing rates and obligations to serve a system that is substantially intact today. The FPC set up procedures both for the certification of new pipeline facilities and the modification and abandonment of old ones. To gain a certificate of public convenience and necessity, pipelines had to enter into enough long-term purchase and sales contracts to demonstrate a 15- to 20-year supply of reserves and demand for gas. This meant not only that it was difficult to enter a market, but that an incumbent pipeline did not have to fear that competition would strand its enormous investment in pipe, an investment that had no alternative use.[15]

The pipeline tariffs governed the terms of the pipelines' jurisdictional sales. The rates in a tariff consisted of purchased gas costs and transportation costs. A pipeline's weighted average ("rolled-in") cost of buying gas was passed through to the LDC. Rates were regulated in public-utility fashion, providing an opportunity, but not the guarantee, of a specified regulated return.

The certificate also obligated a pipeline company to deliver to an LDC an obligation that extended beyond any given contract term. To offset this burden, customers were often obligated to make a minimum payment to the pipeline (the "minimum bill"). The minimum bill, and particularly the gas cost portion, provided the basis for the pipelines to write take-or-pay contracts with producers. The regulatory structure under the NGA thus eliminated incentives for forward integration. Regulation also reduced incentives for backward integration, at least by pipelines, though not necessarily by their integrated affiliates.[16] Moreover, the Public Utilities Holding Act of 1935 discouraged interstate gas pipelines in the United States from owning local distribution companies. The pipelines thus traditionally relied on the "minimum-bill" purchase provisions to ensure that contracted volumes would be moved. The minimum bill enabled pipelines to confidently amortize their pipeline investments while substantially meeting their take-or-pay obligations.[17] Hence, contractual instruments were developed by the industry that conferred functional integration, thereby reducing incentives for more formal vertical integration.[18]

Pipelines in the United States display modest but significant integration into gas production/reserve holdings. As a group, affiliates provided only 7.8 percent of domestic interstate pipeline supplies in 1983, while pipeline-owned production accounted for an additional 3.8 percent. This illustrates that the pipelines in the United States source predominantly from unaffiliated producers. Historically, the interstate pipelines bought gas on a "take-or-pay" basis. These contracts turned out to be burdensome during the gas bubble of the 1980s. The trend toward more flexible wellhead contracts evident in the early 1980s shifted some of this risk to the producer.

Thus, the vertical arrangements that emerged in the U.S. industry resulted from both economic requirements and federal regulations. The system that existed until about 1980 protected the pipelines' assets and appeared to offer supply reliability to LDCs, in return for minimum-bill commitments, and steady purchases from producers, with upstream take-or-pay provisions designed to roughly match downstream contracts to LDCs. There was a logic to the industrial structure that was rooted in the fundamental economics of the business. However, it was a system that was to come apart in the 1980s.

Wellhead Price Regulation and the First Gas Crisis

The Natural Gas Act and the Phillips *Decision*

Gas pipelines were unregulated in the United States until the passage of the Natural Gas Act (NGA) of 1938, which began regulating the type of service, entry, and rates charged by interstate pipelines. Wellhead price regulation came later. Federal regulation of wellhead prices began in 1954, after the Supreme Court's decision in the *Phillips* case.[19]   In that case, the court judged that producers were subject to the Federal Power Commission's (FPC) rate-setting authority under the NGA. Only gas entering the interstate market fell under federal jurisdiction; intrastate gas remained under state jurisdiction, and most states did not restrict wellhead prices. For the federal portion, the FPC attempted to set wellhead prices on a traditional public-utility cost basis.

None of the different rate-making techniques used by the FPC solved the problem of how to apply price regulation in a reasonably efficient manner. The FPC could not solve the wellhead pricing problem because of the incompatibility between the long-established NGA rate-setting principles and the economic conditions of the 1960s and 1970s. Under the NGA, the just-and-reasonable price had come to be associated with average cost. However, in the 1960s, and especially in the 1970s, the market value of natural gas exceeded, by a substantial margin, the average historical costs of production. The attempt to set cost-based prices meant that the FPC maintained the price of gas below its market-clearing price. This underpricing led to economically and socially pernicious results—namely, shortages—which continue to have ramifications even today. The basic problems inherent in trying to price gas on a cost basis, when the price of an equivalent amount per British thermal unit (Btu) in the form of oil far exceeded any cost-based prices for gas, were exacerbated by the existence of unregulated intrastate markets. When they could, producers naturally sold their gas in the intrastate markets, which resulted in many intrastate market gluts. The courts and the regulators created a fiasco par excellence, with shortages and curtailments in the interstate market existing side-by-side with oversupplies and dump sales in the intrastate markets. As time went on, the problem became worse. Clean air standards were tightened, thus increasing the advantage of gas as a fuel. Decreasing supplies of alternate low-cost fuels, particularly oil after the embargo of 1973, greatly increased the commodity value of gas relative to the cost of production from most wells.

The end result for much of the 1970s was that the interstate gas market would not "clear" at NGA just-and-reasonable prices. Consumers in the regulated market sought to purchase more than producers were willing to offer at the regulated prices, with the result that natural gas shortages arose in the interstate market and a curtailment system was imposed by the FPC.

As interstate pipelines found that they could not meet their contractual or certificate obligations, the FPC ordered jurisdictional pipelines facing natural gas shortages to file new rate schedules, under sections 4 and 5 of the NGA, that would provide "curtailment plans." Curtailment led industrial gas users, both those who had a low priority in the early 1970s and those who feared they might be curtailed at some future time, to develop dual fuel–using capabilities. Considerable doubt was generated on the part of industrial end users and electric utilities with respect to the reliability of the natural gas industry as a supplier of energy. Perhaps most important, many natural gas entities developed a shortage mentality, which greatly affected events in the 1970s and 1980s. By 1976, it was clear that the reform or elimination of natural gas regulation was imperative. A two-year legislative battle resulted in a complex and comprehensive compromise among the warring factions—the Natural Gas Policy Act (NGPA) of 1978.

The NGPA: Features

Title I of the NGPA changed wellhead price regulation in three fundamental ways. First, the interstate and intrastate natural gas markets were unified and placed under a common regulatory scheme. Second, incentive prices for all sales at the wellhead were set by Congress. Third, a phased deregulation program for some (but not all) natural gas was established.

The NGPA restricted the price of "old gas" and most categories of "new gas," but it provided strong price incentives for the development of new gas, particularly from sources that are expensive to exploit. Moreover, the deregulation section of the NGPA was based on the concept of deregulating new gas in the future but maintaining old gas under price regulation for the life of the well. "Vintage" regulation was maintained, but some (albeit not all) vintages were scheduled for deregulation. Figure 3 attempts to summarize the Byzantine complexity of the NGPA.

The NGPA and the Gas Glut

The NGPA had dramatic effects on natural gas prices. The increase in burner-tip prices engendered substantial conservation by all customer classes and fuel switching by consumers who were in a position to do so, as well as intense consumer and congressional discontent about the size and timing of natural gas price increases.

Meanwhile, on the production side, many interstate pipelines that had been hamstrung by the dual market, the low NGA prices, and the costs of demand curtailments responded with an aggressive campaign to acquire reserves. Many pipelines, and particularly those that had been in especially deep curtailment situations, were able to improve their reserve-to-production ratios significantly. However, this aggressive reserve-acquisition drive led some pipelines to contract for gas at very high prices, thus exacerbating the problem. The acquisition of high-cost reserves also aggravated gas marketing problems at both the city-gate and burner-tip levels.

The substantial production response to the NGPA, coupled with the conservation and fuel-switching response at the other end of the pipeline, led to

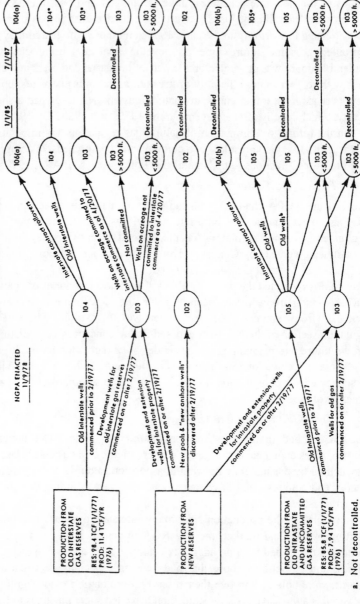

Figure 3

MAXIMUM CEILING PRICE CATEGORIES: NGPA TITLE I FOR ONSHORE
LOWER-48 NATURAL GAS ABOVE 15,000 FEET

a. Not decontrolled.
b. Price greater than $1.00 per million Btu under a definite escalator clause.

Note: Stripper wells and high cost gas omitted.

Source: U.S. Energy Information Administration, *Natural Gas Market* (1981), p. 16.

what was referred to in the late 1970s as the "gas bubble." For several years after passage of the NGPA, from .5 trillion cubic feet (Tcf) to up to 4 Tcf of gas were usually available for sale annually without takers. Thus, by 1982, the gas bubble had turned into what since then has been called a "gas glut." A severe economic recession, fuel switching by large industrial customers, the international competition difficulties of many "smokestack" industries such as steel and automotive, and conservation induced by high and increasing prices resulted in low levels of demand for gas. At the same time, the NGPA prices stimulated production. Since 1982, the gas surplus has probably been on the order of 10 to 15 percent of production.

Wellhead price deregulation under the NGPA thus came to result in a complete reversal of pricing relationships in the natural gas industry. The "add-on" system that had prevailed under total wellhead regulation was replaced by a system that more accurately could be described as "market-derived."

The emergence of a surplus was one factor that assisted in the development of a spot market for gas at the wellhead. The spot market settled in at prices that, not surprisingly, were lower than what pipelines had contracted for on a long-term basis during the gas shortage. These prices were reflected, in part if not in their entirety, in the prices that final customers paid for their gas supplies. The difference in price between what final customers were paying under long-term contract and the wellhead price created an economic incentive for end users to abandon prior commitments and seek the gas that was available in the spot market, where it could often be obtained at less than half the usual cost. The two major barriers to this strategy were (a) the "minimum-bill" feature of gas contracts, which required the gas purchaser to take negotiated amounts of gas from the pipelines, and (b) access to pipeline transportation.

The FERC released end users from the gas-cost portion of the minimum bill in Order 380 of June 1984 but did not simultaneously release the pipelines from their take-or-pay obligations with producers. This and other factors left the pipelines with commitments to take and without the guaranteed market that the pipeline customers had previously contracted to provide. This increased the political pressure still further for open-access or mandatory (that is, involuntary) carriage by gas pipelines. Open access began in earnest with FERC Order 436.[20]

Indirect Consequences of Wellhead Price Deregulation

The NGPA thus accomplished its primary goal of eliminating shortages and increasing supply, but it widened price differentials between the city gate and the wellhead. These price differences intensified political pressures on the pipelines and on the FERC because, prior to 1983, many interstate pipelines had contracted for more gas supplies than they were now able to market at the prices set forth in those contracts. The pipelines, of course, had no incentive to resume contracting for the less expensive new gas reserves until their existing, high-cost contracts were terminated or renegotiated to marketable levels. As the gas bubble turned into a glut and many wells of all vintages became shut in, it is not surprising that producers, particularly independent producers as well as certain end users, sought access to pipeline transportation. The merchant pipelines meanwhile sought new sales to fuel-switchable or pipeline-switchable customers, such as industrial-boiler fuel users or partial-requirement customers with multifuel (usually oil or coal) burning capacity.[21]   However, pipelines often stood to suffer huge losses if they were to transport gas that would displace a unit of gas they had contracted for at higher prices. The more gas they transported, the more money they would lose.[22]   An important consequence was that the average delivered prices of gas did not adjust downward toward the spot price, nor did average prices move with competing fuels.[23]   This is the background of FERC Order 436.

FERC ORDERS 436 AND 500 AND THE OPEN ACCESS ISSUE

Origins and Purpose

Bending to strong interest-group pressure from independent producers and end users, and desirous of patching up a regulatory disaster stemming from decades of wrongheaded policies, on May 30, 1985, the FERC issued a Notice of Proposed Rule Making (NOPR), seeking comments on a new program:

- to separate the pipelines' functions as transporters and sellers of gas;
- to offer choices to the buyers of gas. allowing LDCs to buy only what they wanted from pipelines;
- to relax entry and exit barriers:
- to allow pipelines to reduce their roles as buyers and sellers (i.e., the merchant function).

The FERC's attempts to deal with the quagmire that regulation had created culminated in Order 436, which was issued on October 9, 1985, to become effective November 1, 1985. The order incorporated most, but not all, of the NOPR's goals.

A pipeline volunteering for Order 436 was released from various regulatory requirements and had others imposed on it. The pipeline could receive a "blanket" certificate, allowing it to arrange contract carriage without the required contract-by-contract approval of the FERC. In return, the pipeline had to agree to offer both "firm" and "interruptible" service on a first-come, first-served basis, up to its capacity limits. Moreover, the pipeline had to set "firm" and "interruptible" rates for both peak and off-peak periods.

LDCs that purchased gas from a pipeline volunteering for Order 436 could lower their contract demand levels by up to 100 percent in five years. The pipeline was then able to abandon its service to the LDC, up to the level of the reduction in contract demand. Capacity was thereby made available on the pipeline so that it would offer contract carriage under Order 436.

Order 436 did not mandate open access, but it did try to achieve that objective without formally requiring it. In any event, in June 1987, a federal appeals court voided Order 436 because it did not provide sufficient take-or-pay relief to the pipelines. Subsequently, FERC Orders 500, 500B, and 500C granted modest take-or-pay relief while preserving the essence of Order 436. Over 90 percent of interstate gas was shipped under open access for the first half of 1989.

The implicit logic of Order 436 was that gas pipelines were an essential facility and that the owners of these assets ought, therefore, to be mandated to provide access to the facility to shippers on terms set by the regulators. It appears, however, that regulators simply assumed that these facilities were "essential." In truth, it is not at all clear that gas pipelines are essential facilities. The mere fact that a prospective competitor wishes access to a pipeline that is difficult or costly to duplicate is not enough to make the facility essential.[24] One suspects that the FERC, like other regulatory agencies, had, and possibly still has, a tendency to freely affix the label of "essential" or "bottleneck" to any network component or functionality that confers competitive advantage on its owner. This then enables the regulatory agency to feel justified in compelling access to the full extent that it is empowered to do so. This is unfortunate, as there are often harmful consequences from mandating access, and these are generally less visible than the benefits. Thus, regulators may believe they have promoted competition while, in fact, they have in some more fundamental sense, injured it.

As a general matter, forcing access to an incumbent's facilities may reduce incentives to engage in cost-reducing innovations. The incumbent incentives to undertake cost-reducing improvements will be dampened if it is known that the regulators will likely make the improvements available to competitors via open-access policies. Further, by guaranteeing access to an incumbent's facilities on favorable terms, regulation may dampen competitors' incentives to make their own facilities-based investments, which might, in the longer run, deliver more competition. There is a strong tendency for regulators to assume that technologies and costs are unchanging, when of course they are not—not even in the gas business.

The open-access provisions of Order 436 in essence forced the unbundling of the merchant and the transportation activities. It unraveled the integrated structures that had emerged based on historical market and regulatory forces. It is not by accident that nowhere in the world—Canada, the United States, Australia, or Europe—has the natural gas industry evolved by itself into a fragmented structure. Instead, integration efficiencies often dictate bundling. This view may be contrary to the new conventional wisdom, but it is consistent with historical evidence and recent developments in organizational economics.

Effects

The cumulative effect of Orders 380, 436, and 500 was that distribution obligations to purchase gas from pipeline suppliers according to the terms of long-term sales agreements were irrevocably altered. The consequence of the elimination of minimum bills and the advent of open-access transportation was the erosion of the mutual obligations between distributors and pipelines (see Figure 4). Because of political pressure by PUCs to lower short-term costs, without much regard for the implications for consumers beyond the period of the regulator's term, LDCs chose nonpipeline suppliers, causing a mismatch between the pipelines' service obligations and take-or-pay commitments to producers. These regulators' decisions, which in essence voided customers contractual obligations to take from the pipeline while leaving the pipeline with its obligations to buy from producers, were economically inexcusable and had disastrous consequences.

Short-Term Impact of Open Access

The total impact of Order 436, and its companion order, Order 500, will not be apparent for decades to come and cannot be assessed independent of subsequent regulatory developments.[25] Short-term ramifications included the following:

1. In many cases, 436/500 enabled end users to bypass their local distribution companies. This benefited the buyer, who thereby obtained cheaper gas, but it imposed a heavy burden on the local distribution company, whose costs are largely fixed. In many cases, these fixed costs had to be spread over the remaining customers on the system, leading to still higher gas prices and still greater incentives to bypass. This threatened a "death spiral," as steadily escalating rates caused still others to leave the system.[26]

2. Take-or-pay problems magnified. The FERC provided insufficient relief for the take-or-pay obligations of the pipelines. Hence, 436/500 increased the pipelines' take-or-pay exposure, causing many of them to teeter on the edge of bankruptcy. The combination of Orders 380 and 436 injured the financial health of the gas pipeline industry, as reflected in their declining bond ratings (see Figure 5). At least one pipeline, Columbia Gas Transmission, filed for Chapter 11 bankruptcy protection.

3. The transportation of customer-owned gas has emerged, not only as a means by which producers and end users bypass market distortions created by three decades of crippling wellhead price controls, but also as a means by which they can circumvent the embedded contractual obligations of pipelines and distributors. Both sources of the current movement for mandatory carriage are temporary, because high-priced long-term contracts will eventually expire.

Figure 4
Traditional and Post–380, 436, and 500 Pipeline/Distributor Functions and Responsibilities

Traditional Pipeline/Distributors Functions and Responsibilities

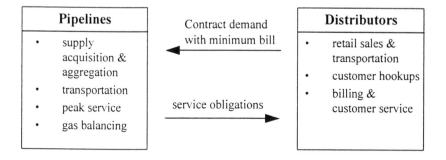

Post 380, 436 and 500 Pipeline/Distributor Functions and Responsibilities

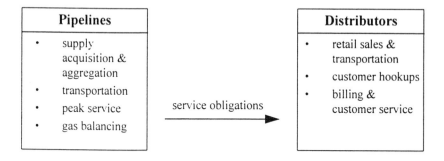

Customers and producers saw open access as a method to obtain cheap gas in a highly distorted market. Contract carriage, not surprisingly, increased from around 30 percent of deliveries in 1986 to over 70 percent by 1989 (Figure 6). Only 17 percent of the gas flowing the nation's interstate pipelines in 1991 was merchant sales.[27]

The pipelines did obtain some relief by simply welching on contracts. Massive load losses and the threat of bankruptcy forced interstate pipelines, such as Columbia, United, Panhandle, Tennessee, and Transco, to undertake drastic actions, including the refusal to honor their contractual obligations, thereby courting billions of dollars of fines in lawsuits for failing to perform on their contractual minimum bill or take-or-pay obligations.[28] These moves have been effective in reducing gas acquisition costs but not enough to placate affected interest groups, which have insisted on access to transportation.

Long-Term Impact of Open Access

The long-term implications of the FERC's action are yet to be felt. The FERC may have achieved the goal of bringing end-user prices and spot-wellhead prices closer together by facilitating entry into the merchant function, but it has left the pipelines with service obligations that they may be unable to meet when the gas glut disappears. Relatedly, the FERC has neglected to clarify the responsibility for acquiring new supplies in order to provide long-term security of supply. The pipelines are currently still left with an obligation to maintain supply for LDCs, but LDCs have no obligation to buy the gas. The FERC has not provided incentives for any party to shoulder all the risks of the merchant function in the long run. The pipeline service obligations remain in place, but customers are now often free to seek cheaper supplies from producers without fear of supply interruption. This amounts to courting another curtailment crisis in the future.

The situation raises long-run concerns. The pipelines' service obligations must be adjusted if the structure is to remain viable in the long run. Customers will then have to make their own efforts to ensure long-term supply. This was not a pressing issue during the glut, but it is becoming an issue as the glut disappears. Customers may be in for a tough time in the future unless they have fuel-switching capacity.

For example, Natural Gas Pipeline of America (NGPL) is taking steps to reduce its gas supply commitment to utilities. NGPL has asked the 49 utilities it supplies to take over responsibility for obtaining as much as 20 percent of the gas they can now elect to receive from the pipeline. Meanwhile, the pipeline customers are asking NGPL to stand ready to provide nearly as much gas in winter as they always have, but today many buy no system gas several days of the year. The pipeline has lost sales because 66 shippers are delivering gas into its market area via NGPL's own transportation facilities.

The NGPL situation is being repeated all over the country. Customers want, and think they have, cost-free supply insurance. However, regulatory changes have jeopardized the ability of many pipelines to maintain and acquire needed supplies. Under current FERC policy and case law, pipelines are forced to continue to provide traditional services as merchant suppliers, but they are generally permitted only to profit from the transportation function.

It is important to remind policy makers that "there is no such thing as a free lunch." Customers must either pay pipelines to guarantee supply or build inventories or fuel switching capacity themselves. In an open-access pipeline environment, the supply responsibility clearly falls on the pipeline customer. Currently, customers are attempting to have it both ways: to take advantage of supply security provided by the pipelines while simultaneously engaging in opportunistic buying strategies. These opportunities will come to an end with the gas glut, if not before, and some customers may find themselves caught short. Open access may have solved some short-run problems, but it may also have laid the foundations for another deliverability crisis in the future.

By 1989, the FERC had signaled that at some point it would have to put an end to this fool's paradise. Its mechanism for doing it may be the gas-inventory holding charge. This is a standby fee that is set to reflect actual costs. If widely adopted by pipelines, gas inventory charges will significantly affect the purchasing practices of pipeline sales customers, particularly those local distribution companies that purchase at a low-load factor. Although the gas-inventory charge is still in the early stages of its development, it appears that a key feature is that the charge would be based on nominated amounts of service that could be adjusted periodically. While the FERC maintains that deficiency-based, gas-inventory charges are not simply minimum commodity bills (previously eliminated by FERC Order 380) in slightly altered form, both charges are similar in that they require the customer either to purchase certain minimum quantities or pay a stated charge on each unit not purchased.

The integration of storage with the transportation and merchant function has obvious advantages. This is because the biggest problem with gas storage is not finding customers for the gas during peak-demand days; it is finding pipeline transportation to move the gas to them from the storage facility. Accordingly, the integration of the storage and transportation function has clear economies. Hence, new storage cannot be justified on a pure commodity-hedge basis. Long-term problems can be expected if the FERC expects storage to be provided on a stand-alone basis.

To summarize, FERC Orders 436 and 500 represented one more regulatory gyration as efforts were made to overcome past regulatory errors. Without wellhead price regulation and the sequence of shortages, and, subsequently, the tremendous glut that was created, and without FERC's cancellation of the gas portion of minimum bill, it is unlikely that the FERC would have been pressured to step forward and impose a form of mandatory carriage on the industry. If open access makes sense, it is only in the context of the U.S. industry's own regulatory history. Regulation begets regulation because one distortion always creates another. In this case, open access has been a response to previous regulatory errors, and it is not part of the natural evolution of the industry.

Open access in the United States has already resulted in predictable problems. In particular, arranging transportation in the U.S. interstate gas industry involves "chaotic monthly nominations to pipeline transport controllers."[29] As one observer noted:

The Open Access Debate   63

We have transportation and exchange people who stay up—24 hours a day for a couple of days during the week pipeline nominations are made. At the end of each month, you have one or two groups that end up spending a night here just to make sure all of the gas gets accounted. After you've been through this. it looks like the New York Stock Exchange at day's end, with paper all over the floor.[30]

This transactional complexity has translated through to higher costs and more manpower. Thus, whereas major pipelines before open access might have had 20 to 30 customers, with everyone else buying from the LDC, now a major pipeline might have over 1,000 customers, with perhaps 80 percent of this accounting for no more than 15 percent of the volume. Even brokers have standing to request transportation.[31]   The open-access environment has increased the cost of administering the system and accounting for and dispatching the gas on the order of 10 to 15 percent.

Figure 5
Interstate Pipeline Bond Ratings

Moody's/S&P Ratings

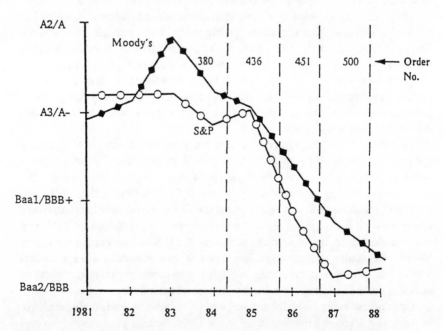

Source: Individual company bond ratings as reported by T.E. Desmond Co.
Note: S&P - Standard and Poor's

Natural Gas Deregulation

Figure 6
Carriage Share of Deliveries to Market
(Contract Share on Non-owner Shippers on a Percentage of Total Interstate Throughput)

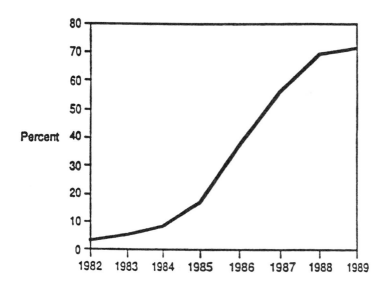

Source: Interstate Natural Gas Association of America (INGAA), *Interstate Pipeline Policy Issues*, February 1991, 47.

Moreover, many pipelines have huge imbalances on their systems. Hundreds of producers and purchasers are on the system, and it is an anomaly if they are matched. Many wells do not have an electronic read, so dispatchers sometimes cannot tell whether a particular well is delivering what was promised. Likewise, marketers will often go and sell more than their short-run capabilities at the well. With hundreds of producers (many with fractional interests in a well), hundreds of buyers, and the absence of real-time monitoring at each wellhead, the pipelines have horrendous problems figuring out where the gas came from and where it went. New computer and remote monitoring may eventually enable pipelines to reconcile gas balances on a daily basis—but only at a nontrivial cost. Even a 1 percent imbalance can involve significant dollar amounts.

None of this is to say that unbundling is not technically feasible; often, however, it is not economically efficient, nor need it support supply security.

Indeed, long-term contracts have now virtually disappeared from the industry. Most gas is now transported on 30-day contracts, and a 3-year contract is now considered long-term. Furthermore, these contracts typically contain low threshold triggering mechanisms to let either party out. In short, "take-or-pay" has vanished and been replaced by "take or release."[32]

UNBUNDLING AND ORDERS 636 AND 636-A

Order 636 ("Pipeline Service Obligations and Revisions to Regulations Governing Self-implementing Transportation") was intended by the FERC to complete the transition to a particular type of "competitive" natural gas industry, which was advanced by Orders 436 and 500. FERC believes that 636 will enable all natural gas suppliers, including merchant pipelines, to compete for gas purchases on an "equal footing." Specifically, 636 requires the unbundling of sales and transportation services at an upstream point near the production area; no notice transportation; and equality of service, whereby firm and interruptible services must be offered on a basis that is "equal" or "comparable" in quality for all gas supplies, whether purchased from the pipeline or not.[33] The idea is to permit third parties to provide a merchant function comparable to the pipelines' sales service. Order 636 also extends order 497 (the "Marketing Affiliates Rule") which prohibits a pipeline from preferring its marketing affiliate over unaffiliated shippers.[34] Order 636 also requires that storage be allocated on a nondiscriminatory basis among all shippers. Certain transaction costs massed by pipelines, as a result of implementing 636, can be recovered.[35] Order 636-A, which is almost 450 pages in length, also contained a plethora of open-access transportation rules. Moreover, these orders put pressure on the pipeline industry to develop interactive, user-friendly electronic bulletin boards so that a potential capacity buyer could respond to an offer and close the deal on the bulletin board without pipeline intervention.

Orders 636 and 636-A thus represent the culmination of a series of efforts by the FERC to decouple merchant and transportation services and to unbundle other services and resources that pipelines use in obtaining and delivering gas. The goal is to facilitate contracting between wellhead suppliers and end-use customers so that distinctions between merchant and nonmerchant gas evaporate and the end users have the maximum provider choice. The idea is that this will sharpen competition at the production end of the business, thereby resulting in lower prices to end users.

However, in attempting to engineer this outcome, the FERC appears to have taken for granted the continued provision of pipeline services to competitors and paid little attention to the operational and investment economics of the pipelines themselves. Thus, when customers are enabled to shop à la carte, there is no guarantee that the result will be efficient if the pricing rules do not reflect the relevant costs of operating and maintaining the system over the long term. Because pipeline segments do not have a fixed capacity at all times, proper pricing is likely to be extremely difficult.[36] To the extent that each service is based on its stand-alone cost, the aggregate revenues that the pipeline may be able to secure from each service may be insufficient to cover the costs of maintaining the system as a whole.

This is a likely outcome because the FERC seems implicitly to adopt a simple "straw" or "linear" model of a pipeline system, even though very few pipelines have such a simple configuration. It is extraordinarily common to have offtakes enroute, and possibly injections as well. Demands at intermediate points can readily reduce downstream supply, requiring the installation of compression facilities and/or careful attention to linepack to assure deliverability on a consistent basis. It is easy to see how a system of pricing based on the analysis of stand-alone costs could easily underestimate system costs. Moreover, uncoordinated demands on capacity could easily generate flow incompatibilities, causing problems for all. Pricing is also confounded by scale and scope economics, which imply that the equalization of unbundled and bundled service charges is impossible to reconcile with economic efficiency.

Furthermore, much more information is required to coordinate unbundled transactions than is needed to provide a bundled service. When customers have the ability and the right to schedule shipments on a competitor's pipeline, new operating and competitive constraints are imposed on pipeline managers.

SUBVERTING COMPETITION THROUGH OPEN ACCESS, UNBUNDLING, AND DISCLOSURE RULES

The FERC's proclivity to ignore integration economies, oversimplified model of pipeline economics, and readiness to tilt toward protecting competitors rather than advancing the process of competition has resulted in several unfortunate circumstances, which reveal the fundamental weaknesses in mandatory carriage as a solution to the industry's problem. In its effort to create a level playing field, the FERC, not unlike some other regulatory agencies, appears willing to eviscerate the competitive advantage of incumbents, even when they are efficiency-based. This amounts to equalizing the outcome, rather than the terms, of competition.

This is no more telling than in FERC's marketing affiliate rules. Order 497-D prevents pipelines from "favoring" marketing affiliates by disclosing to them proprietary information from the pipelines. However, one of the recognized efficiencies of vertically integrated systems lies with the information that can flow freely, both up- and downstream.[37] The FERC appears willing to squander these efficiencies in order to create a level playing field, which is, of course, completely contrary to the principles of economic efficiency and a perversion of competitive principles. It is tantamount to squandering an integrated pipeline's efficiency-based competitive advantage.[38]   Not surprisingly, gas distributors' stocks have outperformed gas pipeline stocks.[39]   Moreover, as shown in Figure 5, bond ratings plummeted from A minus in the early 1980s to an average of BBB in 1988 for 14 major interstate pipelines.[40]

A corollary has been the growth of independent marketers, organizations that are largely a regulatory artifact. Indeed, one of the largest, National Gas Clearinghouse, was cofounded by a law firm, Akin Gump Straus Elauer & Feld. The gas bubble, combined with Order 436, caused the rapid proliferation of independent marketers. By 1991, gas marketing was dominated by a mixture of competitors including pipeline affiliates, independents, and large producers (see Table 1).

It should be apparent that open access and unbundling are not, prima facie, a movement in the direction of competition. Rather, they replace one form of competition, which I will call system competition (whereby competition is between alternate fuels and gas, and in some cases is gas to gas), with another form of competition—let's call it fragmented competition—whereby pipelines are transformed into a nonproprietary input available to all at rental rates set by regulators. While in the short run this may sharpen competition in the spot market, it suffocates competition in transportation, and possibly also in the merchant function. Whether this is a movement toward or away from competition is thus difficult to determine in the short run; it certainly does not deserve to be trumpeted as being unequivocally procompetitive. Many other countries (for instance, Germany) have a completely unregulated natural gas industry. Instead, interfuel competition is relied upon to protect consumers. This method of organization has worked extremely well, and the industry has avoided the gyrations and crises that have characterized the United States. Ultimately, it ought to be the objective of public policy to establish a competitive system of this kind in the United States.

LESSONS FROM THE AMERICAN EXPERIENCE

Controls on natural gas in the United States were a misguided enterprise from the beginning. The gas industry and consumers abroad have faced far less trauma. For instance, the gas industry in Germany has been highly integrated and unregulated, yet it has performed extremely well for consumers.

During the middle and late 1960s in the United States, shortages began to develop, but they did not immediately manifest themselves. In the early 1970s, however, the latent shortage of natural gas became all too apparent. Beginning in 1968, total gas reserves in the lower 48 U.S. states declined each year until 1980. Warnings were issued. Two scholars, McAvoy and Pindyck, were among many who early on urged deregulation:

Table 1
Largest Natural Gas Marketers (1991)

Twelve Largest Natural Gas Marketers in 1991	
Chevron	3.0 Bcf/d
Texaco	2.9 Bcf/d
Natural Gas Clearinghouse	2.8 Bcf/d
Enron and affiliates	2.6 Bcf/d
Coastal and affiliates	2.5 Bcf/d
Amoco	2.4 Bcf/d
Transco and affiliates	2.1 Bcf/d
Exxon	2.0 Bcf/d
Mobil	1.7 Bcf/d
Tenneco and affiliates	1.7 Bcf/d
Arco	1.6 Bcf/d
Panhandle and affiliates	.5 Bcf/d
Ten Largest Independent Gas Marketers in 1991:	
Natural Gas Clearinghouse	2.8 Bcf/d
Aquila/Utilicorp	1.1 Bcf/d
Associated Natural Gas	1.0 Bcf/d
Tejas Gas	.9 Bcf/d
Hadson Gas	.7 Bcf/d
CanWest Gas Supply U.S.A.	.7 Bcf/d
Tejas Power	.6 Bcf/d
Vesta Energy	.5 Bcf/d
Entrade	.5 Bcf/d
Sunrise Energy	.4 Bcf/d

Source: Natural Gas Clearinghouse, as reported in *Natural Gas Intelligence* (April 13, 1992), 8.

The Federal Power Commission should consider relaxing, rather than tightening, its supervision of pipeline prices and profits. Our findings suggest that the pipelines face a certain amount of competition in many of their regulated markets. Such competition limits the extent to which they can raise prices above costs. That fact, together with the near impossibility of regulating prices in such a way as to eliminate monopoly profit, makes it most unlikely that regulation provides benefits worth its administrative cost. The commission should consider abandoning the cost-of-service price setting method and instead investigate the extent to which various pipeline markets are competitive. Where competition exists—where there are more than two gas pipelines and there are close substitutes of sources of energy—it could deregulate.[41]

However, rather than abandon the controls, the regulators and Congress stumbled around—modifying here, controlling there, and decontrolling elsewhere—until they had erected a patchwork of controls and regulations that begot more controls and regulations and continues to distort normal market forces even today. In particular, in order to relieve the pressure caused by the discrepancy between end-user prices and spot-wellhead prices, the FERC has moved the industry toward open access. By 1988, this was drawing to a close as the prices of system gas were below spot gas in some markets.[42]

In the short run, these recent FERC moves might appear like "deregulation" since they do let market forces express themselves to the end user in ways that were not possible under the inherited regulated structure. However, to do so, the regulators have regulated the construction of barriers between the merchant and the shipper. These barriers did not arise because of market forces. They were not erected because these functions no longer belonged together as a matter of economic efficiency. Moreover, the move will generate significant long-run costs, even though it may make some sense as a solution to a problem created by prior regulation.

The efficient future performance of the U.S. industry is thus in doubt, as the FERC has created a structure that attenuates incentives for acquiring new supplies and for making needed downstream commitments and investments. Moreover, merchants and shippers must now sleep in different beds, which has impaired communications and weakened incentives to shoulder the risks of the merchant function. Because of perceived pipeline service obligations, customers feel free to seek cheaper supplies from producers without fear of supply interruption (pipelines must "stand by," ready to supply in the event that customers' new supply arrangements should falter). Customers want, and think they have, cost-free supply insurance, but regulatory changes have jeopardized the ability of many pipelines to maintain needed supply. Under current FERC policy and case law, pipelines are forced to continue to provide a merchant function while permitted only to profit from the transportation function. Clearly, this is unsustainable.

Since the gas industry in America is well established, the dysfunction this will create may not be evident for quite some time, given that the existing asset structure is long-lived. However, problems can be anticipated at the point at which the gas bubble disappears and capital needs to be replaced.[43] They may be masked if customers in the meantime incur additional expense to insulate themselves from curtailment. However, the "insurance fee" they pay will be considerable, and will be another hidden cost imposed on the industry.

Indeed, when McAvoy and Pindyck looked at the U.S. situation in the early 1970s, their recommended solution—deregulation and price determination by interfuel and gas-to-gas competition—if adopted, would have brought the United States close to the German model. The gas shortages of the 1970s could have been avoided, along with the gas glut of the 1980s. Practically everyone would have been better off (except the regulators and the lawyers).

There is no doubt that regulation in the United States has provided work for an entire industry of consultants, experts, administrators, and lawyers. The impact of regulation is so significant that top management in the natural gas industry must devote as much time to regulation as to operations. Armies of lawyers and accountants are involved in the implementation and administration of regulations.

Perhaps even more significantly, investment decisions get delayed by lengthy hearings, slow rule making, and numerous court challenges. Often it is difficult to know exactly which regulations are valid, as the issuance of a regulation often does not make it valid unless or until it is affirmed by the courts. For instance, Order 436 was not fully clarified for several years after its issuance. The resulting operational and planning insecurity is simply stupendous.

CONCLUSIONS

The natural gas industry is a capital-intensive one and requires significant investment in irreversible plant and equipment for efficient operation and security of supply. In order to encourage these investments, stability is required in the business environment. Vertical integration can provide much of what is needed; so can long-term contracts, if the legal apparatus provides adequate enforcement. In addition, managers ought to be free to integrate the merchant and transportation functions, when needed, to obtain scheduling, information, and capital-utilization economies. This seems to have been the natural way in which the industry evolved in many different countries for similar economic reasons.

Fundamental economic imperatives cannot forever be denied, and so one might hope that regulators will eventually step away from the gas pipeline industry and completely deregulate it. The 1980s was a decade when actions were taken to ameliorate the problems that regulation had generated in prior decades. Perhaps the closing years of the twentieth century will see the beginning of an epoch in which the dysfunction of regulation will become even more widely recognized by the citizenry and in which competition will be more fully relied on to achieve desirable outcomes. Should that occur, the existing arrangement will change and integrated structures will reemerge and overpower the fragmented structures—many of them regulatory artifacts—that have been nurtured by FERC edicts.

The case for mandated carriage remains uneasy; regulatory intervention that forces incumbents to share their competitive advantage with new entrants is ultimately destructive of incentives to invest. There is an obvious tension when regulators commandeer one competitor's facilities and make them available to others. Such actions can only be justified in the most exceptional of circumstances, in which facilities are truly "essential." However, such circumstances are rare in the industry today.

NOTES

1.   Not all countries have LDCs. Both the United States and the Federal Republic of Germany have LDCs, but the British do not.

2.   In Germany, there are three different pipeline systems: one for high-calorie crude gas, another for low-calorie gas, and a third for cooking gas.

3.   See O. Williamson, *The Economic Institutions of Capitalism* (New York: Free Press, 1985), for the seminal treatment of these issues and the economics of organization more generally.

4.   See A. Chandler, *The Visible Hand* (Cambridge: Belknap Press, 1977); and D. Teece, *Vertical Integration and Vertical Divestiture in the U.S. Petroleum Industry* (Stanford, CA: Institute for Energy Studies, Stanford University, 1976).

5.   This treatment is based on Williamson, *Economic Institutions*, 32.

6.   Ibid., 32–35.

7.   For a more theoretical treatment of these issues, see G. B. Richardson, *Information and Investment* (London: Oxford University Press, 1960).

8.   See Williamson, *Economic Institutions*.

9.   If supply is insecure, users may have to invest heavily in their fuel-switching capacity. Of course, once such investments have been made, security of supply may become less important. However, if security of supply can be provided, it avoids expensive downstream investments in fuel-switching capacity. Needless to say, the real question is the price at which secure supply can be obtained. Historically, the biggest barrier to security of supply has been regulation.

10.   The importance of user costs is that there is no easy way to determine if prices are competitive by simply observing production costs. The most objective benchmark is thus the alternative fuels.

11.   See A. Tussing and C. Barlow, *The Natural Gas Industry: Evolution, Structure, and Economics* (Cambridge. MA: Ballinger Publishing Co., 1984).

12.   Similarly, oil pipelines typically require throughput guarantees from shippers before they can be financed. However, an important difference between oil pipelines and gas pipelines is that the former typically do not take title to the product shipped, whereas gas pipelines take on the merchant role as well.

13.   Take-or-pay provisions between producers and pipelines generally require pipelines to take certain prespecified volumes of gas or to pay anyway.

14.   Federal Trade Commission, Bureau of Economics, *The Economic Structure and Behavior in the Natural Gas Production Industry*, Staff Report (Washington, DC: U.S. Government Printing Office. 1979), 28–30.

15.   When considering whether to issue a certificate of public convenience and necessity, the FERC considers the existing capacity in the industry, thus offering some degree of protection for incumbents from new entries that would jeopardize dedicated facilities that were already in place.

16.   Under NGA, a pipeline's own production was subject to rate-of-return, cost-of-service regulation, while gas purchases from others were not.

17.   In this regard, note that only four pipelines did not have minimum bills from inception: Columbia, Consolidated, United, and Natural. Columbia and Consolidated are a part of firms that are vertically integrated downstream; Natural was part of such a firm in its early years (Insull Utility Investments, Inc.), and United was designed to serve primarily other pipelines (e.g., TETCO, Texas Gas, etc.) that had minimum bills with their customers.

18.   A key property of vertical integration is that it is an organization arrangement that ensures that long-lived, non-redeployable assets do not become stranded because of opportunism on the part of buyers or sellers. Long-term contracts could accomplish much the same objective, if they could be written to contain all relevant contingencies and be fully enforceable. This is not often the case. The use of long-term contracts as a way to organize industry encounters problems when contingencies arise that were not anticipated or contractual provisions once considered enforceable turn out to be unenforceable.

19.   *Phillips Petroleum Company v. State of Wisconsin.* 347 U.S. 672 (1954).

20.   Order 436 did not make contract carriage legally mandatory, but the FERC set out to make life difficult for those pipelines that did not go along with the FERC's ambitions.

21.   Because gas prices were no longer in tune with energy prices, some fuel-switchable customers were lost, and the merchant pipelines tried to replace these lost sales.

22.   For many years, the pipeline-regulated rate structures required the crediting to customers of all transportation revenues, so that even a pipeline with excess capacity and no take-or-pay obligations lacked an incentive to engage in contract carriage.

23.   It is interesting to compare these outcomes to what was happening abroad. Germany is a good example. Whereas in the United States, over the period 1978–1987, gas prices at the retail level rose to more than twice the 1978 levels, the rise in Germany was never more than 1.6 times the 1978 level. Moreover, whereas in Germany gas prices fell, so that by 1987 they were back to 1980 levels, in the United States, they remained almost 50 percent higher. Gas prices in Germany equilibrate against alternative fuels, while gas prices in the United States do not necessarily do so, despite open access.

24.   Customers may also appear before a regulatory agency and petition for open access. As in many regulatory circumstances, open-access rates for pipelines were set so as to take from the incumbent the competitive advantage that flows from its prior investments. Hence, the fact that customers may prefer unbundling once a pipeline has committed its capital is entirely consistent with the thesis advanced here.

25.   Order 500 requires producers to give pipelines take-or-pay relief in volumes equal to those that they want the lines to move under open-access transportation. *Oil and Gas Journal* 85(51) (December 21, 1987), 26.

26.   See J. S. Henderson. "Price Determination Limits in Relation to the Death Spiral." *Energy Journal* 7(3) (July 1986).

27.   Interstate Natural Gas Association of America, *Interstate Pipeline Policy Issues 1991* (February 1991), 47.

28.   Unfortunately, the sanctity of contracts may have been jeopardized by the pipelines' failure to perform on take-or-pay.

29.   "FERC's Open Access Rules Spawn Changes in Way Gas Transmission Lines." *Oil and Gas Journal* 87(16) (April 17, 1989), 14.

30.   Remarks attributable to Charles M. Ogelsby, executive vice president of Coastal Corporation's natural gas group. Ibid., 15.

31.   Transportation nominations are made once a month, though the nominator has the right to change nominations. Interrupted space is available to any customer on a first-come, first-served basis. Firm space is sold to historical customers.

32.   With such contracts, if the purchaser does not take the gas, the supplier will want it back.

33.   Notice transportation is defined as the ability of firm shippers to receive delivery of gas on demand up to their firm entitlements on a daily basis without incurring daily balancing and scheduling penalties. The idea is to enable pipeline customers to receive unnominated volumes in order to meet unexpected requirements caused by unexpected changes in temperature.

34.   Provisions of 497 include one stating that to the extent that information is provided to an affiliate, it must be disclosed contemporaneously to all potential shippers. In addition, if a pipeline offers a transportation discount to an affiliated marketer, it must make a "comparable and contemporaneous" discount available to all similarly situated, nonaffiliated shippers.

35.   Four types are recognized: (1) unrecovered gas costs remaining in the purchased gas adjustment account, (2) gas supply realignment costs, (3) standard costs, and (4) new facilities costs.

36.   FERC has mandated the use of the *straight/fixed-variable* (SFV) method of rate design for transportation rates under which all fixed costs are assigned to the reservation charge and all variable costs to the commodity charge.

37.   See Teece, *Vertical Integration.*

38.   FERC Commissioner Elizabeth Moler, in her dissent from 497-D, said as much when she wrote, "The order utterly fails to meet the burden of showing how this [potential information exchange] flows from the pipelines anticompetitive exercise of market power."

39.   March 1992 INGAA background report, as reported in *Washington Report,* March 20, 1992.

40.   Ibid.

41.   P. McAvoy and R. S. Pindyck, *Price Controls and the Natural Gas Shortage* (Washington, DC: American Enterprise Institute, 1975), 133.

42.   See *Oil and Gas Journal* (August 22, 1988).

43.   For a variety of reasons, in the summer of 1988 in California, certain classes of customers found themselves in curtailment.

[24]

Telecommunications in transition: unbundling, reintegration, and competition*

I. Introduction

The world economy is experiencing a technological revolution, fuelled by rapid advances in microelectronics, optics, and computer science, that in the 1990s and beyond will dramatically change the way people everywhere communicate, learn, and access information and entertainment. This technological revolution has been underway for about a decade. The emergence of a fully interactive communications network, sometimes referred to as the 'Information Superhighway', is now upon us. This highway, made possible by fibre optics and the convergence of several different technologies, is capable of delivering a plethora of new interactive entertainment, informational, and instructional services that are powerful and user-friendly. The transition from analogue to digital technologies, the expanding bandwidth of the enabling platform, and the shift from regulated to competitive environments have all served to make the 1990s the decade in which the Information Superhighway will be built and used. A true revolution in the delivery of enter-tainment, information, transactions, and telecommunications services is at hand.

This chapter outlines these technological changes and explores their implications for competition policy, industry structure and business organization. Part I introduces competition as an organizational model and discusses the existing structure of the telecommunications industry in the United States. Part II describes recent technological advances that change the conditions underlying the current regulatory structure of the telecommunications industry and challenges the effectiveness and validity of the current regulatory scheme. Part III discusses how innovation impacts what has been considered the natural monopoly of local exchange. Part IV advances five principles that should guide policy modification. Part V explores how eliminating the line-of-business restrictions created by the Modification of the Final Judgment[1] between the government and American Telephone and Telegraph Co. will accelerate competition and stimulate the development of the Information Superhighway. Ameritech's Customer First Plan is presented as a viable means to enhance competition, avoid redundant investment, and increase service innovations arid technological advances. Part VI discusses the impact of removing interLATA restrictions.

The organizational model most capable of delivering advanced services universally

*Presented at the University of Michigan Conference on Competition and the Information Superhighway, Ann Arbor, Michigan, 30 September 1994. The sources contained in this chapter include many difficult to obtain publications that are kept on file with the author. Sources have been updated since

and at low cost is one that relies on competition and cooperation.[2] Competition will ensure that incentives exist to provide new services at low cost. Cooperation, governed by antitrust laws, will ensure that the various networks based on copper wires, coaxial cables, fibre optic cables and airwaves are knit together into a 'network of networks'. In combination, competition and cooperation will ensure that vestigial elements of any remaining essential facilities in the local exchange business are accessible in a non-discriminatory fashion and that people can communicate anytime, anywhere, to anyone.

The United States has already moved quite some distance toward implementing this model. Since the late 1970s, the government has embraced competition as a matter of public policy for the telecommunications industry.[3] Moreover 'the genie of competition has been set loose from the bottle and is unlikely ever to be squeezed back in'.[4] Nor should it. In the United States, if not everywhere, competition is far and away the most promising route for efficiently bringing forward the advanced telecommunications services needed to enhance global competitiveness in the decades ahead. However the existing structure prevents realization of the benefits of integration. The predivestiture Bell companies, whatever their faults, did bring forward network innovation that kept the United States second to none in the efficient provision of telecommunications services for decades. The benefits of the former integrated system can be available today . Many of the problems of the existing system, such as declining investment, slow rates of new product innovation, and limited network innovation, can be addressed if the embargo under which the Regional Bell Operating Companies (RBOCs)[5] are operating is lifted. When coupled with unbundling of the local exchange, removal of the interLATA restriction[6] will create a framework that allows market forces to determine whether services are offered by an integrated or a non-integrated entity and how different services are priced. This will leave federal and state regulators more focused on monitoring safeguards and championing innovation rather than simply standing in innovation's way. Also inefficient investments that have sprung up purely as artefacts of regulation will fade away, as they should. Scarce investment dollars can then be steered where they need to go: not into the unnecessary duplication of facilities, but rather into the building of advanced digital intelligent networks.

This model based on competition is by no means a pipedream. It is the logical conclusion of the trend selected in the late 1970s and early 1980s to increasingly rely on competition rather than regulation to organize the market.[7] The model already finds full expression in New Zealand, where the Post and Telegraph Office (PTO) provider was privatized and the market was opened to competition.[8] The 'Kiwi share' set a price cap on residential rates that moves with the rate of inflation and New Zealand's antitrust laws safeguard the interconnection rights of new entrants. Tremendous productivity improvements followed privatization and deregulation bringing New Zealand to a leadership position in the modernization of telecommunications infrastructure.

II. Enabling techonlogies
The continued rapid evolution of a number of key technologies facilitates the development and deployment of advanced broadband telecommunications services

in the United States and abroad. These technologies enable voice, data, and images to be created, processed, stored, and delivered using a variety of wired and wireless technologies that were little known only a few years ago. Interactive multimedia, for instance, mixes and combines a variety of communication methods, sound, graphics, still photos, motion video, and the written and spoken word, in a computer-controlled environment. The familiar functions of the computer (manipulating databases) and the TV set (displaying pictures) now combine to give us an expanded concept of multimedia, drawing on advanced software developments and protocols and powerful microprocessor architectures.

Some key technologies that provide the enabling platform for these new telecommunications services are:

1. *Bandwidth explosion.* The conversion to digital systems permits expansion in the number of channels carried by a transmission media. Optical fibre also permits a dramatic increase in the bandwidth that can be transported from point to point.[9]
2. *Enhanced microprocessor power.* New RISC-based microprocessors and digital signal processors permit faster, more efficient, and thus lower cost switching, data access, and digital compression.[10]
3. R*eductions in memory cost.* In recent years, the unit cost of memory has fallen dramatically,[11] thus allowing cost-effective storage and retrieval of large libraries of digital context.
4. *Software breakthroughs.* Software developments are permitting quick, low-cost programming, access to large data bases, and interoperability, which facilitate the integration of different types of media into multimedia products. Stored program control has dramatically improved the versatility of tele-communications products. Software breakthroughs are also permitting seamless, user-friendly operation.
5. *Wireless modulation.* Techniques such as trunking[12] have been developed and are now being deployed that dramatically increase the capacity of the radio spectrum for voice data.

Many of these technological developments change the conditions that form the basis of the current regulatory structure of teleconuumunications, making many of those regulations obsolete. Recognizing this, regulators and courts have begun to promote competition as the underlying principle for the organization of the tele-communications industry. Some regulatory changes include additional spectrum allocations for new services such as Personal Communication Servers (PCS)[13] and Enhanced SMR,[14] Federal Communication Commission (FCC) co-location and open network architecture (ONA)[15] policies, the lifting of information-services content restrictions on the RBOCs in July 1991,[16] and a July 1992 FCC ruling permitting local exchange carrier deployment of video dial tone.[17] Without these and other regulatory changes, the Information Superhighway would be just a dream.

Indeed it is well to recognize that the United States no longer holds a commanding lead in telecommunications. As one observer has noted:

The rate of network improvement in other countries is more rapid than in the United States and we are in serious danger of falling behind. For example, both Europe and Japan have plans to have a universal broadband service available by the year 2015, with fiber connections to every subscriber.[18]

In addition cable telephony is offered in Great Britain.[19] Combinations of American telephone companies, including Nynex and Southwestern Bell, British cable companies, and American cable companies, including Cox, Comcast, and TeleCommunications Inc. (TCI), have begun to offer cable telephone services in competition with British Telecom.[20] The success of these ventures has resulted in lower prices for local and long-distance telephone services in Great Britain and an increase in the quality and variety of services offered.[21]

In order to capture the benefits associated with these technological developments and facilitate their deployment in the private sector, regulatory policies and competition policy must rapidly evolve. Because of the speed of technological change, radical changes in regulatory policy and industry structure are needed. Technological innovation makes increasing competition in telecommunications both possible and inevitable. For example, the application of microwave technology to telecommunications made possible the entry of MCI, Sprint, and others into the long-distance market. Today, dramatic breakthroughs in radio communications technologies are sharpening competition between wireless and wireline. Public policies are often slow to recognize the opportunities afforded by the new technologies, and regulatory and public policies often delay and distort competitive dynamics. In the United States, it is often the incumbent regulated firms that are most ensnared in policies that prevent new technologies from being rapidly embraced. This often impairs the ability of established firms to contribute to the investment needed to bring forth new services. The existing regulatory environment inhibits the most qualified providers of enhanced services to the obvious detriment of the nation.

III.   The impact of innovation on the local exchange 'natural monopoly'

John Maynard Keynes remarked over half a century ago 'in the field of economic and political philosophy there are not many who are influenced by new theories . . . so that the ideas which civil servants and politicians and even agitators apply . . . are not likely to be the newest'.[22] Civil servants, politicians, agitators and even some economists have been far too quick to see the local exchange as a natural monopoly. 'The defining characteristic of natural monopoly is the necessity to have production done by a single enterprise if costs are to be minimized'.[23] To the extent that the regulation of the local exchange has any grounding in economic theory, it is the theory of natural monopoly. According to this theory, society should accept the existence of a natural monopolist and regulate to prevent monopoly pricing in industries where cost conditions and market demand are such as to make it inefficient for all but one supplier (the natural monopolist) to install facilities of optimal scale. In such a situation, society theoretically is better off minimizing industrial costs.[24]

The traditional case for regulation assumed the existence of a natural monopoly:

a situation where economies of scale persist over all relevant ranges of demand so that a single firm can serve the market at lower cost than two or more firms. Textbook treatments then typically use electric power, gas distribution, local telephone service, rail transport between small and medium city pairs, and the long distance pipeline transport of petroleum and gasoline as examples of natural monopolies.[25] It was often assumed, because detailed analysis was rarely reported or even performed, that regulation was necessary in such instances to protect consumers from the monopoly pricing behaviour that was supposedly virtually inevitable when scale economies were achieved.

Recently, however, scholarly work has begun to recognize that natural monopolies are not only extremely rare, but also do not necessarily have to be regulated.[26] The theory of contestable markets demonstrates that the presence of a large number of actively producing firms is not necessary to produce efficient outcomes.[27] Where costless, reversible entry, sometimes referred to as 'hit-and-run' entry, is possible, firms that are characterized by economies of scale will still price at efficient levels. Put differently, the threat of potential competition can, under certain conditions, produce efficient outcomes even in markets where there is only one supplier or where a single supplier holds a substantial market share. However, the argument here is not that markets characterized by natural monopolies do not need to be regulated, although in some circumstances that is true, rather, the proposition is advanced that the local exchange is not a natural monopoly any more, if it ever was.

Almost since the beginning of the telephone business, local telephone service has been provided by a copper pair of wires strung to each house. Because the major cost of providing local phone service was the cost of the wire and the wire was sufficient to carry the calls of each customer, it was significantly cheaper to have a single provider of local services. The cost savings from a single provider led to the widespread belief that a natural monopoly existed.

For the past 20 years, technological change has transformed competitive conditions in the local exchange business. Technology is not only making the local exchange more susceptible to competition but also blurring the distinction between interexchange and intraexchange services.[28] The actual regulatory distinction between categories of service affects technical choice and network design and therefore may, itself, be an important factor in determining the direction of innovation and the nature of competition. For example, the introduction of fibre optics into the telephone networks has significantly reduced the cost of transport so that the cost of calls is very insensitive to distance.[29] As a result, depending on the amount of switching, the real resource cost of a 10-mile 'local' call may not be very different from the cost of a 100 or 1000 mile 'long-distance' call. However, because of regulation and imbedded subsidies, the prices charged for these calls remain different. In response to these price-cost discrepancies, many companies have been able to arbitrage the difference and route calls through the lowest priced jurisdiction even if it is not the least resource cost routeing. This results from the implicit subsidies as well as the decrease in the cost of call transport.

The implementation of fibre optic technology is not the only change that is affecting the economics of local communications. There are a variety of tech-exchange, which in turn threaten the natural monopoly and reduce the difference between long-distance and local telephone calls.[30]

New enabling technologies have led and will continue to lead to alternative and enhanced provision of telephone service. The advance of technology has come in many different arenas and from many different enterprises in response to several different regulatory regimes. Especially pertinent to the discussion of 'local' telephony are the impact of radio-based technology, the introduction of fibre optics, the significant advances in microelectronics and computing power, and the continued decrease in the cost of computers and microelectronics.

Radio-based technology

Radio-based technologies are rapidly increasing quality and capacity and decreasing costs of wireless telephone service. The combination of these three factors makes radio-based local loops a competitive threat to the traditional wireline-based local natural monopoly.

Radio has gone through a series of advances since it was first introduced. These advances are currently most evident in the explosion of cellular phone usage that has occurred over the last 10 years. More cellular phone 'lines' than new local exchange lines are activated each year.[31] Despite this growth and predictions that cellular might one day compete with landline service, cellular has not yet provided significant price competition with landline service. In some respects, this may be due to capacity limitations and the inability of providers to price discriminate between mobile and fixed services. The first problem, capacity constraints, is in the process of being rectified for the majority of the country with the conversion to digital signalling. Digital cellular transmission is expected to bring an immediate threefold increase capacity.[32] System capacity at that level will be sufficient to provide a competitive alternative to wireline service in all but the very largest areas of the country.

Although cellular is currently providing only modest competition to landline service, several factors are likely to reduce cellular prices in the near future and make it more of a competitive alternative to landline service. Cellular is likely to face price competition from two sides in the near future. Nextel recently began operation of its digital, cellular SMR service in Los Angeles.[33] It is expected that Nextel will be able to provide cellular quality service with advanced technology.[34] The addition of a third high-quality mobile service provider will expand capacity further and put downward pressure on prices. Other SMR operators also appear to have plans to introduce digital cellular technology to their networks.

In addition, future wireless competition will put pressure on both cellular and landline service. PCS is expected to provide mobile communications and to add significantly to wireless capacity. Because the higher PCS frequencies have limited effective ranges, the handsets will be smaller than comparable cellular phones. However, these systems will require significantly more cells which may limit mobility. This limited mobility will cause them to charge lower prices than cellular systems and serve as competitors to portable and wireline phones in addition to many portable cellular phones.

The additional capacity offered by the introduction of digital signalling and the increase in spectrum available for mobile communications will eliminate capacity constraints in most areas. At that time, service prices should be based on the cost of installing the infrastructure and maintaining the system. In many cases, these costs will be comparable to or lower than the costs faced by a traditional wireline company. Wireline costs diminish, the available spectrum widens, and cell-sitting becomes less expensive as you move further away from dense urban areas. As a result, the wireless technologies are much more competitive with wireline service in rural areas.

One additional future radio-based technology is the Iridium project proposed by Motorola. This project proposes a worldwide satellite network so that users can communicate anywhere throughout the world.[35] The signal will be directed to a satellite from the handset and then back to the other handset or local network. Although this is expected to be a relatively expensive service, it is another wireless technology that may some day turn 'local' communications into global communications.

Fibre optics

Fibre optics have dramatically changed the nature of competition in communications. Because fibre is so much more efficient than microwave technology, the cost of transmission of calls is much less sensitive to distance than it was at the time of the forced divestiture. Because of negligible cost differences, it is hard to determine why a 10-mile call should be 'local' and a 100-mile call should be 'long distance'. The decline in transmission costs will lead to the substitution of fibre for switching. It will become more cost effective to circuitously route calls over fibre networks in order to minimize switching costs if the cost of transmission decreases relative to the cost of switching.[36]

Fibre has not only affected the cost structure of the interLATA carriers but has also become an integral part of local exchange. Local telephone and cable companies are racing to introduce fibre into their networks. Just as Bell and the other telephone companies competed to wire networks, these two competitors are racing to be the first to have a high-capacity two-way network and to reap the benefits of early adoption. There are many issues to be resolved about the introduction of fibre: whether it will be fibre to the home, fibre to the curb, or fibre to the neighbourhood, for example. But it is clear that fibre and its carrying capacity have had, and will continue to have, a strong impact on the nature and cost structure of communications.

The development of fibre optic technology has led to the first competitive alternative to Local Exchange Carriers: Competitive Access Providers (CAPs). CAPs have deployed fibre optic networks through dense downtown areas. In addition to the arguments that they are able to avoid the subsidies embedded in LEC access rates, the CAPs claim that they are satisfying a need for high-capacity, high-quality, high-speed data transmission links. Without the transmission quality of fibre, CAPs would not be able to fill this need and therefore might not be able to exist and bring competitive pressure on LEC rates.

Cheap transmission has a significant impact on the economics of information services. Many information services rely on accessing databases. With cheap transmission it becomes economical to have a single version of a database and allow users from a wide area to access the single database. In this way, the provider does not have to duplicate the facilities to run the database, updates to the database are simplified, and all users accessing the database receive consistent information.

The preceding two sections show the complementary nature of the competitive effects of fibre and wireless technologies. Fibre is being introduced by CAPs and cable companies in dense urban areas to provide high-capacity service. In these areas the costs of wiring per telephone is relatively low since the density is high. Also, in these areas spectrum is relatively scarce and expensive. Construction and operation of a high-quality cellular-like system would be expensive because of the opportunity cost of the spectrum, the high price of the land rental for cell sites and the need for a large number of cell sites. On the other hand, in suburban and rural areas it is more expensive to string wires, spectrum is less intensely used, and there are more options for cell sites. As can be seen, technology is challenging the existence of the natural monopoly in areas of both high and low population density.

Equipmenl costs
The relentless advance in power and decrease in price of microelectronics and computing technology has had a large impact on the price and performance of Customer Premise Equipment (CPE)[37] as well as central office switching equipment. For example, the total cost of cellular service has decreased as handsets have become significantly cheaper and operators have paid lower prices for incremental switching capacity. Because switching and controller costs have decreased, the costs to provide alternative forms of local access have also decreased. Cable, CAPs, and radio-based carriers will benefit from these lower costs as they begin to compete with LECs.

The decline in microelectronics prices will make it easier for cable companies to compete with LECs. For example, if the cable version of a telecommunications provision is a 500-channel interactive broadband network, the cost of the CPE to link into that network will be significantly cheaper and more sophisticated than it would have been only a few years ago. As a result, even if the cable and telco networks are significantly different, the competition on a variety of features ensures that the reductions in cost for cable telephony will make them more competitive with LECs.[38]

The pace of electronics advance has blurred the distinction between transmission and switching as well as between central office equipment and CPE. For example, advancement in central office technology has allowed the offering of advanced voice messaging systems. Although these systems may offer more features than standard home answering machines, they none the less directly compete with home machines. PBXs[39] are another example of an advance outside the central office that has increased competition between central office services, Centrex,[40] and CPE. PBXs not only provide competition for central office services but also provide switching services, allowing users to reduce their use of loops and pay for fewer lines.

The next section analyses the effect of these technologies on the entry strategies of potential entrants into the local exchange.

Entry

Entry can be divided into two broad categories: entrants using existing local distribution technology and entrants using new technologies. This discussion will also consider entry in the context of an unbundled network[41] like the one proposed in Ameritech's Customer First Plan for Illinois.[42] This analysis seems to be applicable for other regions as well because the FCC has steadily been decreasing the size of the 'bottleneck' and allowing more competition. Recent switched and special access orders[43] and expanded interconnection have opened traffic on the local exchange network to competition just outside the local switch.

Entry using new technology

Cable company entry   Cable companies are positioning themselves to provide local exchange services. Cable companies have capacity to provide transport from LEC end offices to the points of presence (POP) of interexchange providers.[44] They are also interconnecting their headends, the originating points of cable TV signals, with fibre cable to offer advertisers the ability to reach region-wide audiences. One indirect, but non-trivial result of interconnection is the creation of capacity for the transport of telephone calls. Cable companies are also putting fibre further into their networks, giving them the ability to provide end-to-end voice and video service. In several instances, they are linking up with LECs to accelerate the introduction of new services. In one cable and RBOC joint effort, Time Warner and US West recently made a presentation disclosing that they intend to upgrade their physical plant to begin the provision of telephone service by the end of 1994.[45] Their proposed service seeks to target residences and both small and large businesses. Further, they can be expected to charge rates that will undercut LEC rates. The partners are both well-financed, experienced companies. Time Warner claimed in its presentation that it has been very successful competing against British Telecom in England.[46] Time Warner's success comes without the benefit of the unbundling and switch integration proposed in Ameritech's Plan. Thus, despite the assertion of opponents to Ameritech's CFP, the distinct possibility of exclusionary practices in England has not yet prevented competition.

Time Warner's Orlando, Florida trial is another example of cable competing for local service. Set to be completed next year, the system as envisioned will be based on a fibre optic backbone, copper to the home architecture, digital compression technology and digital storage and switching systems.[47] The network will give the cable company the ability to offer, among other things, voice and data transmission services and PCS.[48] Jones InterCable recently announced a test of telephone service over its cable system.[49] With the help of MCI and Scientific Atlanta, Jones InterCable will be able to allow users to bypass the LEC and receive faxes while using the phone and to have access to interactive games.

Comcast is also poised to begin telephone service.[50] The *New York Times* reported that Comcast had continuing talks with both AT&T and MCI, indicating their interest in telephone service.[51] Comcast also is one of the owners of Nextel, a specialized mobile radio company that recently received FCC approval to provide cellular-like service in a number of major cities.[52] Furthermore, Comcast offers cable and telephone service in Britain. In the United States, Brian Roberts, of Comcast says, 'Long term, the cable companies want to look like the phone companies with ubiquitous coverage. We've wired up nearly all the homes, but not the businesses. So that's why we're investing in Teleport'.[53]

Once these ventures and others begin offering services to consumers, a significant marketing advantage will emerge. A cable company can package its programming and phone service, offering the customer the convenience of one-stop shopping, and possibly adjust the prices of the individual services to convince the customer to subscribe. Such bundling has proven highly successful in the UK. As one example, Cable and Wireless, a British concern, is now signing-up close to 15 000 residential customers per month through the local cable companies.[54] There is no reason not to expect similar inroads here in the United States, especially with an interconnected network of networks.

Wireless entry   Wireless carriers provide both immediate and future competitive entry alternatives for local exchange service. AT&T's multi-billion dollar purchase of McCaw Cellular will position wireless technology as a direct competitor to the RBOCs' local telephone business. [55] The company's brand name, marketing prowess, and financial resources eliminate any doubt that an AT&T backed cellular venture could quickly become a nation-wide player in the local telecommunications services area. Furthermore, the merger places AT&T in the enviable position of being able to offer its subscribers a complete package of local, cellular, and long-distance calling.

'Non-wireline' cellular carriers provide nearly ubiquitous service throughout the country. While their 'loops' may not currently provide a complete, competitive alternative to LEC loops, they are positioned to do so easily. Cellular carriers have sophisticated switches and, in some cases, fully functional networks and office support in place that will allow them to use spectrum for 'fixed' loops and to provide competitive local service. Cellular carriers also possess a select list of customers with a high demand for telecommunications services. Cellular and other wireless carriers appear well-situated to provide future competition for the local loop, especially in relatively high-cost areas. Spectrum is used less intensively in rural areas than in major metropolitan areas. Therefore, providing competitive loops in these areas would not divert spectrum from a relatively more valuable use.

In the future, the combination of leased wireline access and wireless access may give the cellular carriers a unique advantage in marketing to customers. If they succeed in their drive to receive PCS licences, wireless carriers would provide customers with three options for 'loops'. Under one example, the cellular provider can position a cell site directly adjacent to a wireless PBX serving a large corporate complex. The cellular carrier could handle local mobile traffic and serve as the local carrier for all interLATA traffic originating and terminating at the PBX. Although the coverage for the cellular portion of the traffic would be more limited than for wireline traffic, the volume of traffic, combined with the absence of inter-connect charges for the cellular carrier, would offset at least some of the gap.[56]

With the imminent conversion to digital signalling for cellular, there are a number of cellular operators that will have significant excess capacity.[57] They can market this capacity for use as simple local service. in fact, products are being developed to allow cellular operators to sell service to wireline customers that is transparent to the user. Other implementations could include selling 'loops' to serve as connections for alarms that need only infrequent access.

Amalgamations and alliances   Given the infrastructure of cable companies, CAPs, and cellular carriers, and the emergence of alliances among them, possible future competitive alternatives would be a combination with CAPs providing loops for downtown areas, cable companies providing loops for suburban and residential customers, and cellular companies providing loops for rural areas. Combinations of the various technologies also lead to greater geographic coverage. An entry strategy using a combination of the assets of these companies would enable pervasive entry at multiple nodes.

Another group of potentially formidable competitors moving closer to actual entry with each passing month are the LECs from other regions. The RBOCs and GTE are all large, financially sound carriers with the requisite technical engineering, marketing, and billing capabilities to provide exchange services. As already noted, US West, with Time Warner, intends to enter other regions and will soon begin providing local exchange service.[59] Entry by the other LECs is just as likely. Both Sprint and GTE have local exchange operations[60] and it would be logical for them to expand their service areas through a combination of resale and facilities construction. Most RBOCs have cellular operations in areas outside their local exchange territories. The market presence of these companies provides a natural springboard for the extension of the scope of their services into the local exchange. Such a strategy could be accomplished via their own facilities or by a pooling of talents and resources with the other potential entrants other than the Interexchange Carriers (IXCs) who are restricted by the MFJ.

Entry using existing technology

Competitors using existing technology, depending on their specific capabilities, are poised to compete for either the entire market or for distinct subsets of customers. Because each potential competitor has different competitive advantages, the range of customers benefiting from new entry and expanded competition nearly spans the gamut of local exchange customers. In addition, the ability to enter with minimal investment and to act as a reseller in an unbundled local network gives an entrant complete market presence with little risk.

Interexchange carriers   The most likely source of immediate and influential entry into local service will be the ICXs, especially the large, nation-wide carriers like AT&T, MCI, and Sprint.[61] AT&T has itself advanced the case for seamless end-to-end integration through its Megacom service and private networks.[62] The McCaw acquisition is the epitome of a company positioning itself to provide end-to-end service. AT&T's purchase shows the obvious synergies existing between the two businesses in addition to the expected future possibilities. Indeed, AT&T's public statements suggest that the company's strategy is to provide their customers with end-to-end service.[63]

MCI, through its subsidiary Access Transmission Services, has filed for a permit to begin competitive access service provision in Indiana.[64] MCI also recently announced the planned test of cable telephony with Jones InterCable discussed above.[65] Sprint is already an active participant in local exchange telephony.[66] MCI and Sprint may have additional incentives to add end offices if prospective changes to switched and special access transport pricing make the IXCs more sensitive to the location of their switches. MCI and Sprint will then have incentives to provide their own links from high-volume end offices to their POPs. This will create excess capacity and position them to take advantage of the unbundling and switch integration plan.

All three companies have the ability to self-supply transport. Once the necessary construction and right-of-way expenses are incurred, the incremental cost to add traffic will be quite small.[67] Specifically, once the IXCs have successfully developed the transport segment of their network, they will be able to sign up additional subscribers at little added cost in an unbundled environment since they can rent loops from the LEC and transport traffic to their own switches. In addition, as a major manufacturer of switches, AT&T will be able to obtain switching at a lower cost than any of its competitors and could easily position switches for local service.[68]

Because IXCs enjoy their highest margins in the small and mid-size business segment, they are likely to pursue these customers first for their provision of end-to-end service. AT&T, as well as other large IXCs, could compete by installing switches (or using excess capacity on its existing switches) to supply dial tone and usage services and routeing the traffic to any of their many existing POPs. This could be economical even in an area with a small amount of traffic because the large IXCs could either share capacity on a nearby existing long-distance switch or economically use a somewhat distant switch to provide local dial tone until traffic justifies a truly local switch. Adding switch capacity is relatively simple with modern modular switches such as the 5ESS. Furthermore, because the IXCs have fibre facilities in place with excess capacity, the cost of transport to take advantage of a distant 'local' switch would be minimal.

Competitive access providers   Competitive access providers (CAPs) have entered many major cities by deploying fibre loops through dense downtown areas. They are already providing competition for local exchange carriers without the benefit of unbundled local networks, Competition for transport services will increase the traffic on CAP networks and decrease average unit costs, making CAPs more effective competitors for a larger portion of business.

The strategic intent of CAPs appears to involve providing expanded services.[69] MFS Communications, Inc. has recently announced that it will offer local and long-distance services in New York City.[70] To support this effort, it plans to install Ericsson switches in its network.[71] The service will be 'available immediately in Manhattan and will be extended to the rest of the New York metropolitan area over the next few months'.[72] MFS does not intend to stop with New York. According to its half-page advertisement for this new service, 'Service is available in New York now. National expansion is underway'.[73]

CAPs have invested in loops that give them access to a large number of customers with a relatively high demand for telephone service. CAPs may not he positioned to compete for customers throughout the local service areas, but they are well beyond the venture capital stage and now represent formidable competitors to the local exchange carriers. The largest CAP, Teleport, is owned by several large cable companies, including TCI, Comcast, and Cox and thus possesses the financial backing to ensure its ability to effectively compete.[74] This investment by the cable companies reveals their expectation that CAPs will provide telephony expertise and their belief that further synergies exist.

Investment advisers and the CAPs themselves believe CAPs have a significant role in the future of telecommunications. In discussing the acquisition of Teleport by TCI and Cox, Goldman Sachs says that the alternative access market is 'substantial' and represents a significant opportunity for cable companies.[75] TCI's CEO John Malone believes there is a potential market of $40 billion annually for alternative access carriers; he expects the alternative access market to generate revenues of at least $1 billion in three years and to potentially represent 25 per cent of the total access marketplace.[76] Such optimistic numbers, while obviously not precise, are indicative of the potential for CAPs to become significant access providers.

With switch integration, CAPs with switches can easily become the local phone service provider to those businesses their networks reach. In addition, the ability to rent loops in areas their networks do not reach will enable CAPs to provide service to businesses and residences with little incremental investment as long as those customers are served by end offices their networks do reach. CAPs can also expand their geographic coverage sequentially and determine the optimal path for their new fibre loops by leasing capacity in the short term while determining where to install plant expansions. Finally, the CAPs will be able to compete to serve multi-location businesses even when they do not have a physical presence near each of the satellite offices.

CAPs also will be able to increase their target customer base significantly with unbundling. CAPs are already reaching new customers. With unbundling, CAPs may deploy fibre in other areas and reach even more potential customers. CAPs can use unbundling to determine demand for their services and perform true market research by purchasing pieces of LECs' networks before determining where to construct their own facilities. Further, CAPs will be able greatly to reduce the risk of new construction by establishing an active customer base prior to completing their facilities.

Clearly local exchange services are exposed to forms of competition not imaginable even a decade ago. Local exchange is certainly not the monolithic essential facility once described in industrial organization textbooks. New technology and regulatory changes have brought fundamental transformation. Competition increases daily. Full-scale competition in access, exchange, and interexchange services is both inevitable and desirable. Competition in telecommunications has not advanced yet to the point where it alone will suffice to guarantee all the public policy objectives traditionally embraced in the United States.[77] The rapid expansion of competition in the local exchange permits and requires regulatory changes and the development of new policies to further the transition to a fully competitive tele-communications environment.

IV   The required policy framework[78]

In order to capture the benefits of innovation, policymakers must make aggressive moves to modify the regulatory institutional approaches in place in the United States today. The following principles should guide this process.

Replace regulation with competition. Enabling customers to choose among competitive service providers constitutes the most efficient form of 'regulation'. While competition will increase whether regulators want it to or not, good regulatory policy can ensure that competition proceeds more quickly and that all customers enjoy the benefits of competition. Also, good regulatory policy can promote the right kind of competition, that which responds to real market demands and reflects real economic efficiencies. Regulators should avoid policies that stimulate artificial competition wherein participants exploit regulatory distortions and arbitrage uneconomic pricing schemes.

Promote competitive neutrality. Because technology is proceeding at breath-taking speeds and advanced telecommunications are becoming absolutely crucial to competitive success in more and more industries, it is vital to adopt policies that promote continued development of healthy competition in telecommunications while ensuring that social policy objectives, such as universal service, are main-tained. Therefore, regulatory policies should be competitively neutral. Policies that treat competitors differently can bias customers' choices and distort entry and investment decisions. Policies should provide competitors with an opportunity to compete but should not attempt to guarantee their success. Policies should promote and protect competition, not protect competitors from competition.

Facilitate market responsiveness. Public policies should attempt to be responsive to current and expected market conditions in both the industry being regulated and related industries. Prices, as signals of cost and value, play a critical role in market exchange. Regulators should therefore allow prices to be set by market forces whenever possible, or, alternatively, emulate market forces when they do set prices or pricing parameters. Similarly regulators should allow, to the maximum extent possible, market forces to determine what variety of products and services will be offered. Regulators should recognize that market pressures have increased the rewards of good public policies (that is, those which stimulate investment, increase usage, and promote economic development in the states) and the costs of policies that are not consonant with market conditions (for example, uneconomic bypass, self-supply, and relocation of facilities).

Synchronize regulatory and competition policies. It is also important that rate regulation and competition policy are synchronized. As competition policies, whether by design or in effect, further open markets to competitive entry, regu-latory policies should be reformed to ensure that they are consistent with actual and expected conditions in the marketplace. For competition policy to work well, pricing should be market-driven with only limited, targeted exceptions. Com-petition policies should recognize when, and the degree to which, prices are not market-driven. In the best situation, prices are regulated only when competition customer discretion is inadequate to protect buyers from the exercise of market power.

Remove barriers to entry and competition. When technically feasible, and when balanced by appropriate changes in other regulations, regulations should be used to reduce or remove barriers to entry and competition. Probably the most important step in removing entry barriers in access and exchange services is unbundling the local network into its component parts. The most important step in removing entry barriers in interexchange competition is waiving or eliminating the MFJ line-of-business restriction that prevents the RBOCs from offering interLATA services.

V.   Unbundling and 'as if' contestability

One of the most exciting ways to accelerate competition in local exchange is unbundling. Both Ameritech and Rochester Telephone have advanced plans that would accomplish a dramatic restructuring of the industry by coupling unbundling with relief from the interLATA restructures in the MFJ.[79] If implemented, unbundling will reduce entry costs, increase competitive and entrepreneurial opportunities, and stimulate the development of the Information Superhighway. Unbundling, coupled with interLATA relief, would foster a competitive environ-ment where success is determined by market forces. rather than regulatory or judicially imposed asymmetries. Ameritech's unbundling plan, known as the Customer First Plan (CFP), offers the following:

1. *Loops.* Local loops on an unbundled basis at tariff rates established by state regulatory agencies. Ameritech will propose rates that are above long-run incremental costs but do not exceed fully distributed costs. Access to local loops would be at the main distribution frame or the digital cross-connect frame.
2. *Switching.* Interconnection to its local switching with loops provided by others. The switch integration of the Plan permits all providers to seamlessly connect to a 'network of networks'.
3. *Signalling.* Unbundling of SS7 80 call set-up capabilities and permitting competitors to access the SS7 signalling network without subscribing to Ameritech's transport or switching service.
4. *White pages listings, 911 service, deaf-relay services.* On an optional basis.
5. *Cooperative engineering.* Cooperative engineering, operation, maintenance, and administrative practices on an optional basis.
6. *Rights-of-way.* Where sufficient space permits, conduit and pole attachment space on a non-discriminatory basis to authorized interconnectors.
7. *Mutual compensation.* Mutual compensation arrangements at reciprocal rates for termination of traffic by state-certified alternate exchange providers.
8. *Numbering plans.* Complete NXX codes[81] to other qualified providers.
9. *Local telephone number portability.* Portability to the fullest extent permitted by current technology. The company is committed to supporting the develop-ment of more robust options through industry forums.
10. *Usage subscription.* Use of Ameritech's loops and local dial tone provision while they carry all outbound traffic on their networks. In essence, this might

be termed intraLATA presubscription. Thus, a new entrant can offer alternative service without requiring the customer to change telephone numbers.

The essence of the CFP is that it dramatically lowers entry barriers into the local exchange and quarantines residual sunk cost facilities, leaving the effectively contestable part of the local exchange under the control of market forces and the portion requiring substantial amounts of sunk capital (basically the local loop) subject to price cap regulation. The services of the sunk facility are provided to any industry participant, including Ameritech, on the same terms and conditions.

The key to guaranteeing competitive outcomes in any context is the existence of conditions enabling entry. Even the threat of entry disciplines prices. This well-accepted proposition, historically rooted in the analysis of eminent economists as diverse as Sylos-Labini[82] and Schumpeter,[83] and recently renovated and extended by the insightful work of Baumol, Panzar and Willig,[84] means that if one lowers artificial entry barriers and new entrants need not incur significant sunk costs then all the benefits of competition are available regardless of the market share of the incumbent. This is, in essence, the market discipline the CFP will create. Of course, the state of the current technology may not instantaneously enable all elements of the local exchange to be contestable. However, providing the elements on a non-discriminatory basis and at price levels no higher than their opportunity cost will ensure 'as if' contestability because the relevant businesses are effectively contestable. Professor Baumol is quite laudatory of Ameritech's efforts, noting that 'Ameritech should be commended for addressing itself to the principal preconditions for ultimate removal of the interexchange restriction, that is. the elimination of entry barriers into exchange operations and the encouragement of exchange competition'[85] Indeed, the CFP is the embodiment of principles developed and vigorously advanced in other contexts by Professor Baumol over the past decade. He also notes that 'unbundling, if it is carried out fully and effectively, can greatly facilitate the entry process'.[86] Baumol further points out that unbundling will not transform loops into contestable markets.[87] But that answers the wrong question. The relevant inquiry is whether the services of the loop will he provided to all on a non-discriminatory basis. Ameritech's recent tariff filings guarantee the answer to this question is affirmative.

One can measure the degree of contestability of a market by the 'share of the investment that is composed of capital that is sunk'.[88] Setting aside the loop, the CFP enables a new entrant to enter practically any segment of the local exchange with a truly minimal investment. In this manner, Ameritech's unbundling and switch integration will facilitate and assist entry. Through the CFP, Ameritech offers its competitors the right to access its network at non-disciminatory rates.[89] The CFP essentially confers on Ameritech's competitors whatever economies of scale and scope Ameritech possesses. Few, if any, irreversible investments will need to be deployed by new entrants in order to compete because new entrants can simply rent from Ameritech. As Baily and Baumol note, 'if an industry behaves as if if is contestable, most of the benefits of perfect competition can be attained without government intervention'.[90]

If implemented, Ameritech's unbundling plan will make the local exchange effectively contestable. A provider wanting to enter any segment could do so at relatively low cost. Entry barriers, in essence, would be eliminated. This flood of new entry will result in heightened competition, both in terms of price and service offerings. The latter is especially critical because service innovations and technological advances confer the greatest benefits upon telecommunications users. The competition to meet consumer needs and create new consumer demands will produce gains that dwarf the savings derived from intensified price competition.

VI.   Local exchange competition and interLATA relief

The consent decree and the MFJ entered into between the government and AT&T recognized that in the presence of monopoly power and rate of return regulation, the RBOCs might have the incentive and the ability to impede competition through integration into the interLATA business and, therefore, should be prevented from entering this business until such time as the ability or incentive to impede competition or circumvent regulation had disappeared.[91] This paper does not attempt to second guess the wisdom of these restrictions, but merely notes that accepted economic literature recognizes that the potential for adverse consequences from integration[92] occurs only when 'a non-trivial degree of monopoly exists'.[93] Absent the incentive or the ability to exercise market power, the rationale for the MFJ evaporates. Indeed, this has been explicitly recognized by the court:

> It is probable that, over time, the Operating Companies will lose the ability to leverage their monopoly power into the competitive markets from which they must now be barred. This change could occur as a result of technological developments which eliminate the Operating Companies' local exchange monopoly or from changes in the structures of the competitive markets. In either event, the need for the restrictions . . . will disappear, and the decree should therefore contain a mechanism by which they may be removed.[94]

The court further noted '[t]he restrictions imposed upon the separated BOCs by virtue of section II(D) [the line of business restrictions] shall be removed upon a showing by the petitioning BOC that there is no substantial possibility that it could use its monopoly power to impede competition in the market it seeks to enter'.[95]

Unbundling along the lines proposed by Ameritech, if faithfully implemented, would remove any residual concern that the RBOCs could upset the terms of competition in the interLATA business. Absent Congressional action, unbundling provides the best opportunity for breaking the regulatory and judicial gridlock that exists in the United States telecommunications industry by enabling the courts to do what is correct: eliminate prohibitions against RBOC entry into the long-distance business. Doing so will not only stimulate competition in the interLATA market but also yield some old-fashioned integration economies that will assist the development of the Information Superhighway.

It has long been recognized that economies of scope exist between the local and long-distance businesses. Indeed, Professor Baumol discusses 'efficiencies derived from coordinated operation of an integrated network'.[96] Network-wide planning decisions 'make production less costly when local and long-distance operations are contained within one firm'.[97] The RBOCs will recognize scope economies if waivers are granted since they will be able to use many of their embedded facilities to provide long-distance services. Excess capacity can thus be used to provide service that others might provide by making new investments. Savings in investment are thus recognized to the ultimate benefit of society. Likewise, with the CFP, IXCs and others will be able to recognize scope economies in providing local service.

Of perhaps greater quantitative significance are the economies that come from systems innovation which will be facilitated once interLATA waivers are granted. Innovation facilitates non-price competition in the form of new services in addition to price competition. Economists recognize that the MFJ restrictions 'ignore the foregone consumers' surplus [that would be available] from services that the RBOCs would and might offer but for the restrictions'.[98]

The restriction on the RBOCs from operating interLATA vitiates their capacity to deliver services customers want and in the manner customers prefer. LATAs are purely artificial constructs which make no geographical, technological, or organizational sense.[99] InterLATA restrictions are a primary reason for the slow adoption and diffusion of mobile data services, ISDN,[100] voice messaging and other network services.

The granting of interLATA waivers will increase the value to customers of many broadband services. Remote teaching via videoconference is such an opportunity. Because many businesses and educational institutions (for example, Ford, GM and the University of Illinois) have facilities which span several LATAs, the waivers will permit the local telephone company to provide these services on a company-wide or institution-wide basis. Moreover, because many network services have high fixed costs, the removal of interLATA restrictions will at minimum increase the size of the potential customer base and bring forward services which involve significant scale economies and network externalities.

Furthermore, the removal of the interLATA restriction would enhance the efficiency of RBOC services as they are currently configured, leading to lower prices and better services. Examples include Centrex, Caller ID, and enhanced facsimile services already offered by the RBOCs. Centrex is a service offering which competes with PBX equipment. Regional Centrex is a complete private network for a customer with locations in multiple LATAs connected via long-distance services. The interLATA restriction prevents the RBOCs from offering regional Centrex services.[101] If the RBOCs are able to offer the one-stop shopping for customers that regional Centrex entails, they could provide an important competitive alternative to the PBX-based private networks that have proliferated in the United States. Again, this increase in competition will reduce the costs of service and stimulate service innovation.

Removal of the interLATA restriction would also facilitate the commercialization of enhanced facsimile services. At present, a RBOC wishing to compete in such services has to install equipment in every LATA where service is desired. LATAs with a small amount of potential usage are not economic to serve under this arrangement but could be more efficiently served from another larger LATA with higher volumes. This innovative service is thus not available to customers who would have if but for the interLATA restriction.

The social cost imposed by the interLATA restrictions can be further illustrated by one of the RBOC's, in this case Ameritech's, abortive efforts to provide voice mail services through its acquisition of Tigon.[102] Ameritech was unable to achieve the benefits of integration that were necessary to profitably operate Tigon's voice mail service. MFJ restrictions have increased Ameritech's costs and lowered its revenues, thereby crimping the competitive operation of its business.[103]

Voice mail services such as Tigon are sold with two main components: mailboxes and an '800' telephone access. Because Ameritech could not resell or provide long-distance services and its competitors could, Ameritech could not factor in '800' service resale into its prices for voice mail services.[104] This meant that Ameritech could not take advantage of buying discounted '800' service and passing lower prices onto its customers. Ameritech could only sell the mailbox. This allowed Tigon's major competitors to heavily discount basic mailbox fees and earn healthy margins on 800 resale. Tigon, because of the interLATA restriction, did not have this pricing flexibility and as a result, had to either accept overall margins below those of its rivals or lose sales. More importantly, Tigon's customers were denied the price reductions others enjoyed through volume discounts.

Tigon was further disadvantaged by the confusion created among less sophisticated buyers. While Ameritech's Tigon customers were forced to purchase their own '800' services separate from the Tigon mailbox, a competitor's customers would find that feature bundled into its price for basic voice mail service. This created customer confusion, as competitors exploited the notion that with the Ameritech services the customer had to 'buy more'. Another disadvantage was Ameritech's inability to achieve scale and scope efficiencies. The MFJ prohibition and the attendant customer confusion forced Tigon to build a higher cost network than its competitors. In many instances, Ameritech erected a database in separate LATAs, even when engineering principles and marketing data would indicate the superiority of an alternative, central facilities strategy. As a consequence, it had to choose between not optimizing its network design or serving a more limited market area than its competitors. The Tigon example highlights the fact that artificial regulatory boundaries which cause duplicate investment are a subtle but costly tax on the economy. These real costs and foregone opportunities are no longer acceptable.

VII. Conclusion

The competitive model has been embraced, at least rhetorically, as the right way to organize the telecommunications industry in the United States in order to reflect new technological realities and opportunities. It is in fact the only model likely to facilitate the investment needed to put the Information Superhighway in place and provide the necessary off-ramps and on-ramps. The speed with which the model is being advanced in the United States, however, is alarmingly slow. Perhaps this would not matter very much if it did not involve high opportunity costs and if we did not face ubiquitous global competition in all aspects of our commercial life. However, falling behind has both economic and geopolitical consequences. Further, it denies the American people the fruits of technological innovation developed at home. Congress seems unable to grapple with the issues.[105] It is now, therefore, up to the regulators and the courts to embrace the policies needed to promote dynamic competition and the building of the Information Superhighway. Removing entry barriers everywhere, coupled with regulatory neutrality, is of critical importance. Once this is accomplished, incentives will exist to facilitate private investment in the provision of enhanced services on the Information Superhighway. If unbundling of the local exchange is necessary to unblock the political and judicial roadblocks to more substantial reforms (such as the interLATA and other entry barriers in the MFJ), then it should be universally embraced and rapidly implemented. The stakes are too high for dilatory behaviour in Congress and the courts to be tolerated any longer.

Afterword**

One noticeable feature of the telecommunications competitive landscape is the rapid pace at which events unfold. Since the presentation of this article in September 1994, Ameritech's Customer First Plan (CFP) has received the enthusiastic support of the Department of Justice (DOJ).[106] The DOJ has indicated that it will file a motion in support of the experimental implementation of CFP when Ameritech applies to United States District Judge Harold Greene for a waiver.[107] If the waiver is granted, we will see first hand whether the conclusions of this chapter are correct.

Under the terms of the proposed Order negotiated between the DOJ and Ameritech, Ameritech would be allowed to offer interLATA service on a provisional basis from the LATAs encompassing the Chicago, Illinois and Grand Rapids, Michigan areas. If the Order is approved by the court, Ameritech will not be allowed to enter into interLATA until the DOJ determines that 'actual' competitive conditions exist in local markets within the waiver area.[108] Once Ameritech begins operation as an independent carrier, the DOJ will continue to monitor the trial with a wide range of supervisory powers and will maintain the authority to terminate the experiment at any time.[109]

In the past six months, there have been a number of significant competitive developments in both Chicago and Grand Rapids. In Chicago, two competitive access providers, MFS Communications and Teleport, have been certified to offer local exchange service, and a third, MCI Metro, has applied to do the same.[110] City Signal, Inc., owned by Teledial America, already provides competitive local phone services in both Grand Rapids and Detroit.[111] Other alternative providers of local service are entering, including cable companies. Chicago is home of two separate tests of cable-based telephone service. MCI and Jones Lightwave intend to test linking a few residents in Chicago suburbs to MCI's long-distance service.[112] Motorola, Inc., TCI, and Teleport Communications Group are providing local phone service over cable lines on a test basis in Arlington Heights, Illinois.[113]

In addition to facing heightened competition in local exchange, Ameritech will he operating under additional guidelines that were not elements of the original CFP. Foremost, Ameritech is required to operate its interexchange business as a separate subsidiary.[114] Although I have never endorsed the idea that Ameritech has either the incentive or the ability to engage in cross-subsidization, this structural

**Written 10 April 1995

separation offers ironclad protection against such a possibility.

Developments over the last six months have confirmed many of the propositions advanced in this paper and elsewhere. The local exchange is not a natural monopoly and indeed stands on the brink of an explosion in the number of competitive alternatives. The proposed DOJ order safeguards any residual possibility of competitive harm by adopting the protections of the CFP, by calling for active monitoring of the local exchange market, and by requiring the structural separation of Ameritech's new long-distance business from its existing local business.

In sum, if the courts approve Ameritech's CFP in Illinois, we will shortly witness a major step in the structural reform of the United States telecommunications industry.

Notes

1. *United States v. Western Elec. Co.* (American Tele. & Tele. Co.), 552 F. Supp. 131, (D.D.C. 1982) *aff'd sub nom. Maryland v. United States*, 460 U.S. 1001(1983) [hereinafter *U.S. v. AT&T*]. Although the case is commonly referred to as the MFJ, the decision actually modified and approved the MFJ which is appended to the opinion at 552 F. Supp. at 226.
2. *Iacocca Institute, Lehigh University, 21st Century Manufacturing Enterprise Strategy*, at Foreword (1991) (concluding that an organzational model in which companies and industries learn to work together to build an infrastructure even while competing in products and services is the key component to America's future success in the global economy).
3. The model in the United States from 1913, when AT&T promulgated the 'Kingsbury Commitment to, inter alia, interconnect the independent telephone companies with AT&T, until the late 1970s was one that relied essentially on regulated monopoly. See Gerald W. Brock, *The Telecommunications Industry* 155–56 (1981); See generally *Heritage Foundation*, Issue Bulletin no. 191, *A Guide to Telecommunications Deregulation Legislation* (3 June 1993).
4. G. Noll, 'Telecommunications regulation in the 1990s', in *New Directions in Telecommunication Policy*, 11, 47 (P. Newberg ed., 1989).
5. The MFJ spawned seven regional Bell Operating Companies: Ameritech, Bell Atlantic, Bell South, Nynex, Pacific Telesis, SBC Communications (previously Southwestern Bell), and US West. See *United States v. Western Elec. Co.*, 990 F. 2d 283, 290 n.3 (*per curium*), *cert. denied*, 111 S. Ct. 283 (1990).
6. InterLATA restrictions prohibit the RBOCs from providing long-distance transmissions between Local Access Transport Areas. See *U.S. v. AT&T* supra note 1, at 141 n.39.
7. See, for example, Robert W. Crandall, *After the Breakup: U.S. Telecommunications in a More Competitive Era* (1991).
8. See generally L. Evans et al., 'Economy-wide reform: the case of New Zealand', *J. Econ. Literature* (forthcoming).
9. Fibre is generally considered to have nearly unlimited bandwidth potential. Larry Lannon, 'Is shorthaul microwave's future, well, short?', *Telephony*, Oct. 1993, at 67.
10. Reduced Instruction Set Chips (RISC) represent an advance in microprocessing. Conventional Instruction Set Chips (CISC) will have hundreds of instructions that are directly recognized. RISC microprocessors recognize only the 20–30 per cent of these instructions that are used most often. A smaller instruction set means the RISC microprocessors can do 'less' but much faster than CISC microprocessors. Mark Alpert, 'Why it's a RISC worth taking', *Fortune*, 10 Oct. 1988, at 112.
11. Robert L. Fike, 'Analog or digital the debate continues, transport facilities', *Telephony*, 17 Oct. 1994, at 35.
12. A trunked system is one in which a central computer assigns the first available channel to the user. See, for example, 'Motorola may finance California comms system', *News Byte News Network*, 14 Dec., 1995.
13. Personal Communications Servers are 'microcells' on microwave frequencies with low power, digital transmitters that provide mobile service over small areas, such as an office building or a neighbourhood. Michael K. Kellogg et al., *Federal Communications Law*, 860–61 (1992).
14. Enhanced SMR stands for Enhanced Specialized Mobile Radio which is digital radio service capable of providing mobile telephone service. Communications analysts believe enhanced SMR telephone service may be competitive with cellular telephone service within a few years. Andrew Ramirez, 'A challenge to cellular's foothold', *NY Times*, 1 April 1993, at D1.

15. Open network architecture policies of the Federal Communications Commission encourage the ROBCs to deploy technologies that give outside communications companies the same access to their switching networks as the RBOCs themselves enjoy. Edmund Andrews, 'Business technology: opening nation's phone networks', *NY Times*, 16 Jan. 1991, at D5. A similar policy already governs long-distance phone service, where customers can select AT&T or any of its competitors to handle their long-distance calls without having to press a score of numbers on their phones. Bruce Keppel, 'FCC lets phone companies offer wide range of services', *LA Times*, 18 Nov. 1988, at 4.2. The FCC first proposed open network architecture in 1985. Edmund Andrews, 'FCC moves to expand service choices', *NY Times*, 22 Nov. 1991, at D2.

16. *United States* v. *Western Elec. Co.*, 714 F. Supp. 1 (D.D.C. 1988), *aff'd*, 900 F. 2d 283 (2d Cir. 1990).

17. Telephone Co.–Cable Television Cross Ownership Rules, 7 F.C.C.R. 5781 (1992) (second report and order, recommendation to Congress and second further notice of proposed rulemaking).

18. Aziz Lakhani, *Video Dialtone*, (1992) (unpublished manuscript, on file with author). Another observer notes that 'the U.S. already lags [behind] many countries in digitization, SS7 implementation, and fiber deployment'. W. Davidson et al., 'Telecommunications infrastructure policy and performance: a global perspective', 5–38 (6 Jan 1993) (on file with Center for Telecommunications Management, University of Southern California).

19. Larry J. Yokell, 'Cable TV moves into telecom markets', *Bus. Comm. Rev.*, Nov. 1994, at 43.

20. *Id.*

21. *Id.*

22. John Maynard Keynes, *The General Theory of Employment, Interest, and Money*, 384 (First Harvest/HBJ ed. 1964) (1936).

23. R. Schmalensee, *The Control of Natural Monopolies*, 143 (1979).

24. *Id.*

25. See, for example, F.M. Scherer, *Industrial Market Structure and Economic Performance* (1980).

26. See, for example, W.J. Baumol et al., *Contestable Markets and the Theory of Industrial Structure* (2nd ed. 1988).

27. *Id.*

28. Interexchange service is the carriage of voice or data traffic across LATA boundaries, the connection between 'exchanges'. Intraexchange service remains within a LATA. Kellogg et al., *supra* note 13, at 856.

29. T.R. Reid, '21st century promises marriage of telephone, computer', *Wash. Post*, 15 Sept. 1986, at F23.

30. A variety of authors have investigated the impact of alternative technology. For example, D. Reed, *Residential Fiber Optic Networks: An Engineering and Economic Analysis* (1992); G. Calhoun, *Wireless Access and the Local Telephone Network* (1992); P. Huber et al., *The Geodesic Network II: 1993 Report on Competition in the Telephone Industry* (1992); D. Reed, 'Putting it all together: the cost structure of personal comunnications services', FCC Office of Plans and Policy Working Paper No. 28 (Nov. 1992); E. DeSurvire, 'Lightwave communications: the fifth generation', *Scientific American*, Jan. 1992, at 114; B. Egan, *Information Superhighways: The Economics of Advanced Public Communication Networks* (1991).

31. Andrew Adonis, 'Survey of mobile communications', *Financial Times*, 5 Sept. 1994, at 1.

32. Sarah Curtis, 'Beyond cellular', *Maclean's*, 23 Jan. 1995, at 46.

33. 'Nextel installs all digital integrated wireless communications in Los Angeles', *RBOC Update*, Sept. 1994.

34. *Id.*

35. Mike Holderness, 'Computer: and thou beside me in the wilderness', *The Guardian*, 19 Aug. 1993, at 19.

36. Note that both technologies have been experiencing significant decreases in cost, but if transmission costs decrease more rapidly than switching costs, system designers will substitute transmission for switching at the margin. See Huber, *supra* note 30, at 3.37.

37. CPE is used on the customer's premises 'to originate, route, or terminate telecommunications'. *U.S.* v. *AT&T*, *supra* note 1, at 228. Examples of CPE are telephone sets and answering machines.

38. R. Hartman et al., 'Assessing market power in regimes of rapid technological change', in *Industrial and Corporate Change*, 318, 321 (1993) (discussion of the impacts of competition on a variety of features in addition to price).

39. A Private Branch Exchange (PBX) is a customer-provided switch that automatically transfers, or switches calls between the customer's private telephone station and other locations. Carolyn Whitman Malanga, Note, '*California* v. *Federal Communications Commission*: Continuing the

40. Centrex provides remote switching service with customer-tailored capabilities such as four digit dialling for business and institutional customers. See Kellogg et al., *supra* note 13, at 852.

41. An unbundled network, in theory, provides independent information service providers with more complete information about network features and allows them to choose the specific features they need. See, for example, *United States* v. *Western Electric Co, Inc.*, 767 F. Supp. 308, 319 (D.D.C. 1991).

42. Ameritech filed its Customer First Plan with the FCC in 1993 and also filed a request with the Department of Justice for a long-distance waiver in Illinois. Jim Dilorenzo, 'AT&T challenges Ameritech in opening local competition', *Telephony*, 18 Apr. 1994, at 6. Since the presentation of this article, the Department of Justice had filed a motion in support of Ameritech's CFP. See *infra* notes 104–107 and accompanying text.

43 Carriers offer switching service by allowing users to change the end point of a circuit in a similar fashion to how individuals do when dialling a voice phone number. 'A Wan communications glossary', *Network Computing*, 1 January 1993, at 76.

44. According to TCI's President and CEO, Dr. John Malone, in 1992 TCI became the largest single buyer of fibre in the world, based on mileage. Charles F. Mason, 'AT&T takes center stage at national cable T.V. convention', *Telephony*, 11 May 1992, at 6. Time Warner already offers local connections to long-distance carriers in Indianapolis and Kansas City. 'Time Warner, Baby Bell may compete in San Diego', *Wall St. J.*, 24 June 1993, at B7.

45. 'US West bets on cable with Time Warner', *Telephone Week*, 24 May 1993.

46. *Id.*

47. Randall M. Sukow and Rich Brown, 'Time Warner unveils "full service" TV', *Broadcasting*, 1 Feb. 1993, at 6. Time Warner is also seeking regulatory approval to offer telecommunications services in San Diego. The services, which are scheduled to begin in 1995, would compete directly with Pacific Bell for business customers. Time Warner plans to connect local businesses with long-distance carriers and link the offices of area companies by building a fibre-optic network. 'Time Warner, Baby Bell may compete in San Diego', *supra* note 44, at B7.

48. Don Clark, 'New visions of communications: "data highways" lure billions in investment', *S.F. Chron.*, 23 Nov. 1992, at B1.

49. *Id.*

50. Anthony Ramirez, 'Head start on data superhighway', *NY Times*, 8 Sept. 1993, at D13. Comcast is not only the third largest cable company but also the fifth largest independent cellular telephone provider, giving them a significant presence as a local service provider. *Id.*

51. *Id.*

52. *Id.*

53. *Id.*

54. Cable and Wireless, 1993 Report and Accounts 12 (1994).

55. Edmond L. Andrews, 'The AT&T deal's big losers', *NY Times,* 25 Aug. 1993, at C1.

56. See discussion of Telular Inc.'s 'magic box' in John J. Keller, 'Telecommunications: a "magic box" turns wired into wireless', *Wall St. J.*, 1 Oct. 1993, at B1.

57. 'Telecommunications expected to grow steadily in 1992, commerce says', *Common Carrier Week*, 6 Jan. 1992, at 1.

58. For example, Yokell, *supra* note 19.

59. See 'US West bets on cable with Time Warner', *supra* note 44.\

60. Daniel W. Edwards et al., 'Telecommunications services', *US Industrial Outlook*, Jan. 1994, at 29.

61 Sprint has formed an alliance with TCI, Cox, and Comcast to target local markets. Edmund Andrews, 'Ameritech forcefully stays home', *NY Times*, 22 Nov. 1994, at D1. AT&T, despite its protestations to the contrary, will also enter the local service business with its imminent acquisition of McCaw Cellular. Jerry A. Goldstone, 'Wireless market nears boiling point', *Bus. Comm. Rev.*, Nov. 1994, at 4.

62. Gregory F. Borton and Fred S. Knight 'Seeds of change in CTI', *Bus. Comm. Rev.*, Mar. 1994, at 35.

63. For example, Bob Stanzione, AT&T vice president of transmission systems, recently acknowledged that for AT&T to compete in the delivery of multimedia communications services, the company will 'have to have alliances of some sort with the companies that provide the last-mile access to the home'. John Eckhouse, 'Cable television's growing pains', *S.F. Chron.*, 7 June 1993, at E1. These statements diminish the credibility of AT&T's public pronouncements that its acquisition of McCaw does not make it a local phone company. Earlier this year, Arno Penzias, vice president of research at AT&T's Bell Laboratories, touted AT&T's vertical integraition as being 'a far greater asset than it's ever been in the past'. The article went on to say that the

'ability to merge all the elements – the fiber, the chips and the software to run them – is what makes [a] network valuable' in today's marketplace. Gary Slutsker, 'The tortoise and the hare', *Forbes*, 1 Feb. 1993, at 67.

64. 'States meander toward rules to foster CAP competition', *Telco Bus. Rep.*, 5 July 1994, at 1.

65. 'New visions of communications', *supra* note 48, at B 1.

66. 'Local competition by CAPS still embryonic in Western states', *St. Telephone Reg. Rep.*, 8 June 1992.

67. MCI has purchased a significant amount of right-of-way from Western Union. *Telecommunications Alert*, 1 May 1992, at 1. MCI has also recently filed for state certification as a CAP in Indiana. See 'States meander toward rules to foster CAP competition', *supra* note 64, at 1.

68. According to an MCI expert economist, Kenneth Baseman, 'the marginal activation costs and marginal operating costs for new circuits activated on facilities already in place are generally quite low and do not differ significantly depending on whether the IXC is co-located or the ICX's POP is several miles away'. *In the Matter of Expanded Interconnection with Local Telephone Company Facilities; Amendment of Part 69 Allocation of General Support Facility Costs*, 7 F.C.C.R. 7369, (19 Oct. 1992) (citing Affidavit of Kenneth Baseman at 23–24).

69. 'MFS Communications Co.: unit tries to win customers from New York telephone', *Wall St. J.*, 6 Oct. 1993, at A4.

70. 'Local service resellers target small businesses in 41 states', *St. Telephone Reg. Rep.*, 21 Oct. 1993, at 1.

71. See 'MFS Communications Co.', *supra* note 69.

72. *Id.*

73. *Id.* at B7.

74. 'Continental and Comcast each acquire 20% share of Teleport', *Fiber Optic News*, 28 Dec. 1992.

75. *Goldman Sachs, Communicopia: A Digital Communication Bounty* 20 (1992).

76. *Id.* at 21.

77. Although the New Zealand government completely deregulated the industry with far less apparent competition. See generally L. Evans et al., *supra* note 8; See also 'Intervention and openness and economic performance: New Zealand', *OECD Economic Surveys*, Oct. 1994.

78. R. Harris and D. Teece, 'Telecommunications in transition: innovation, unbundling, and reintegration' (forthcoming) (manuscript on file with author).

79. Vince Vittore, 'Rochester tel: blueprint for change', *America's Network*, 15 Jan. 1995, at 24.

80. Signaling System Seven is an out-of-band network overlaid on the public telephone network to provide network management. An SS7 signal is a request to any number of facilities that switches down the line to open up circuits, engage billing systems, and otherwise prepare to carry, process, bill, answer, block, screen, record or respond to a call. Kellogg et al., *supra* note 13, at 863.

81. NXX codes are any three-digit codes. In telephone convention, 'N' is any number from two to nine; 'X' is any number from zero to nine. *Id.* at 860.

82. Paolo Sylos-Labini, *Oligopolio e Progresso Technico* (1956).

83. Joseph A. Schumpeter, *Capitalism, Socialism and Democracy* (3rd edn., 1950).

84. W.J. Baumol et al., *supra* note 26.

85. W.J. Baumol, 'On the Ameritech proposal for entry into interLATA services 12' (February 1994) (unpublished manuscript, on file with author).

86. *Id.* at 10.

87. *Id.* at 11.

88. *Id.* at 3.

89. These tariffs are no higher than those which Professor Baumol advances under his Efficient Component Pricing rule. William J. Baumol and J. Gregory Sidak, *Toward Competition in Local Telephony* (1994).

90. Elizabeth E. Bailey and William J. Baumol, 'Deregulation and the theory of contestable markets', *1 Yale J. on Reg.*, 111, 123 (1984).

91. See *U.S. v. AT&T*, *supra* note 1, at 194–95.

92. InterLATA entry would involve integration by Ameritech of local and long-distance service.

93. Oliver. E. Williamson, *Markets and Hierarchies*, 115 (1975).

94. See *U.S. v. AT&T*, *supra* note 1, at 194–95.

95. *Id.* at 231.

96. See Bailey and Baumol, *supra* note 90, at 135.

97. *Id.*

98. *Id.* at 131.

99. The thrust of telecommunications innovation has been to erase the confines of geography.

satellite technologies are greatly reducing the significance of distance as a factor in cost, and new providers are modelling their networks and their equipment to serve a pattern based not on geography but on communities of interest: educational institutions, hospitals, financial markets, corporations, and so on.

100.   Integrated Services Digital Network (ISDN) is a standardized, all-digital network that integrates voice and data communications through existing copper wiring. See Kellogg et al., *supra* note 13, at 856.

101.   See *U.S.* v. *AT&T*, *supra* note 1, at 141.

102.   Ameritech eventually sold Ticon to Octel Corp. 'Long distance ban forces Ameritech to sell Tigon to Octel', *Enhanced Services Outlook*, Oct. 1992, at 1.

103.   *Id.*; see also Robert S. Vinton, 'Can the RHCs get a slice of the enhanced services pie?', *Telephony*, 16 Apr. 1990, at 104.

104.   'Long distance ban forces Ameritech to sell Tigon to Octel', *supra* note 102, at 1; Vinto, *supra* note 103, at 104.

105.   See, for example, Edmund L. Andrews, 'Bill to revamp communications dies in Congress', *NY Times*, 24 Sept. 1994, at 1.

106.   'Local phone wars just one call away', *Chi. Trib.*, 4 Apr. 1995, at 1.

107.   *Id.*

108.   'Opening the local market', *Chi. Trib.*, 10 Apr. 1995, at 12.

109.   'Communications, Justice Department approves plan to allow Bell Company into long-distance', *Daily Rep. for Executives*, 4 Apr. 1995, at A64.

110.   Edmund L. Andrews, 'MCI maps plan for local phone services', *NY Times*, 6 Mar. 1995, at D1. See also Frederick H. Lowe, 'Phone service on cable lines to be tested in Arlington Hts.', *Chi. Sun-Times*, 13 Oct. 1994, at 57.

111.   'Major players in Valley Fiber Optics Competition', *The Ariz. Republic*, 14 Nov. 1993, at H1.

112.   Jon Van, 'MCI's new front in phone wars: local service; Ameritech rival says it will offer discount rates', *Chi. Trib.*, 5 Jan. 1994, at 1.

113.   'Phone service on cable lines to be tested in Arlington Hts.', *supra* note 110, at 57.

114.   'Communications, Justice Department approves plan to allow Bell Company into long-distance', *supra* note 109, at 65.

[25]

Globalism and Localism in Telecommunications
E.M. Noam and A.J. Wolfson (Editors)
© 1997 Elsevier Science B.V. All rights reserved.

Competition and "Local" Communications: Innovation, Entry and Integration

Gregory L. Rosston
David J. Teece

1. Introduction

"Local" communications, but for regulation, is about to become an anachronism. Its utility as a meaningful economic concept has faded. Its viability rests solely on the continuation of state and federal regulatory distinctions and the enforcement of the provisions of the Modified Final Judgment (MFJ). The MFJ provisions -- which are now nearly 10 years old -- set up artificial LATA boundaries to separate inter- and intra-exchange calls. The size of LATAs reflected the minimum traffic requirements considered necessary a decade ago to ensure competition for interLATA services rather than any technical or economic requirements or "natural monopoly" characteristics present in the "local" exchange.

In this paper we suggest that if the local exchange was ever a natural monopoly by virtue of underlying cost conditions (rather than regulation), the imminent introduction of new local access competition using existing and new technologies will prove it is no longer. We question whether the fundamental economics of the local exchange really requires regulation of local telephone service rather than the narrow regulation of interconnection. Furthermore, we point out that technological development is sharpening competitive forces in practically all aspects of telecommunication, blurring competitive distinctions of all kinds, and requiring new organizational forms. Moreover, the willingness of some local exchange providers like Ameritech and Frontier Corp. to unbundle has laid the foundation for a further rollback of regulation in several parts of the country so that competitive forces, currently checked by regulation, can be unleashed.[1]

With the removal of regulation an avalanche of new services will be advanced which will greatly benefit consumers and U.S. competitiveness. We also contend that because of regulatory lags, regulation must take a forward looking perspective and attempt to deal with the industry as it will be, not as it was. This is particularly true when technology is advancing rapidly. While there is often considerable uncertainty with respect to the way technologies can unfold, there is often enough definition to the trajectory of technology to enable one to take the future into account without making egregious errors. Thus, in our view, it is appropriate to minimize constraints on an industry with only modest competition which is nevertheless being inexorably propelled towards greater competition.

2

2. Local telephone service as a "natural" monopoly?

Background

John Maynard Keynes remarked over half a century ago that "in the field of economic and political philosophy there are not many who are influenced by new theories -- so that the ideas which civil servants and politicians and even agitators apply are not likely to be the newest."[2] Civil servants, politicians, agitators and even some economists have been far to quick to see the local exchange as a natural monopoly. "The defining characteristic of natural monopoly is the necessity to have production done by a single enterprise if costs are to be minimized."[3] To the extent that the regulation of the local exchange has any grounding in economic theory, it is in the theory of natural monopoly. According to this theory, in industries characterized by cost conditions such that market demand is insufficient for all but one supplier (the "natural" monopolist) to install facilities of optimal scale, society is better off accepting the condition of monopoly -- since industry costs are thereby minimized -- but then regulating to prevent the charging of monopoly prices.

The traditional case for regulation assumed the existence of a "natural" monopoly -- a situation where economies of scale persist over all relevant ranges of demand so that a single firm can serve the market at lower cost than two or more firms. Textbook treatments (e.g., Scherer 1980) then typically use electric power and gas distribution, local telephone service, rail transport between small and medium city pairs and the long distance pipeline transport of petroleum and gasoline as examples of natural monopolies. It was often assumed, because detailed analysis was rarely performed or even reported, that regulation was necessary in such instances to protect consumers from the monopoly pricing behavior.

Recently, however, the scholarly literature has begun to recognize that natural monopolies are not only extremely rare, but that they do not necessarily have to be regulated. The theory of contestable markets demonstrates that it is not necessary for large numbers of actively producing firms to be present to produce efficient outcomes. Where costlessly reversible entry -- sometimes referred to as "hit and run" entry -- is possible, firms which are characterized by economies of scale will still price at efficient levels. Put differently, the threat of potential competition can, under certain conditions, produce efficient outcomes even in markets where there is only one supplier, or where a single supplier holds a substantial market share. The argument here, however, is not that markets characterized by natural monopolies do not need to be regulated. Although in some circumstances that is true. Rather, the proposition that the local exchange is not a natural monopoly any more, if it ever was.

In the telephone business, local telephone service has almost since the beginning been provided by a copper pair of wires strung to each house. Since the major cost of providing local phone service was the cost of the wire, and the wire was sufficient to carry the calls of each customer, it was significantly cheaper to have a single provider of local services. The cost savings from a single provider led to the widespread belief that a "natural monopoly" existed.

3. History

An historical perspective can help to explain the current status of telecommunications provision as well as to understand the nature of the need for a network of networks[4] and the organizational structure to enhance innovation. The development of the telecommunications infrastructure in the U.S. illustrates several points that are important for analyzing the current and likely future status of the telecommunications industry: 1) competition existed in the local exchange in the early days; 2) the industry may well have continued as competitive if AT&T had not invited regulation upon itself; 3) interconnection was, and remains, the primary requirement for supporting a competitive and efficient telecommunications industry.

The Era of Competition
The telephone initially competed with the telegraph. Moreover, Western Union, the dominant provider of telegraph services formed the American Speaking Telephone Company in 1877 to go after the telephone business. Western Union hired Thomas Edison to advance the technology and he quickly came up with the carbon transmitter which provided voice quality superior to Bell, thus giving Western Union a considerable competitive advantage. With Theodore Vail as CEO in the late 1870s, Bell competed head to head with Western Union in installation, racing to install exchanges in large cities and pushing on technological development. Bell's ability to install phone lines was hindered by Western Union's control of the telegraph lines because Western Union refused services to places that installed Bell telephones, thus effectively prohibiting Bell installation in hotels, railways and newspaper offices that needed Western Union telegraph services.[5]

In September, 1878, Bell filed a patent infringement suit against Western Union over its telephone patents. As part of a settlement to this litigation, in 1879 Western Union agreed to withdraw from telephone service for seventeen years and to sell its telephone business -- then 56,000 subscribers in 55 cities -- to Bell. In return, Bell agreed to stay out of the telegraph business. Bell kept its rights to compete against Western Union for long distance services. Thus Bell was free to compete with Western Union at all levels, so long as it stayed out of telegraph, but Western Union and the telegraph was basically killed as a competitor to Bell.[6] It is unlikely that such an agreement would be sanctioned under the antitrust laws in place today. (At the time, however, the telephone and telegraph were complementary as the telephone technically did not have the capacity for long distance services and the telegraph was not competitive for local service because it required skilled operators. The telegraph increased the value of telephone service by allowing long distance communication.)

From 1879 on, Bell had a virtual monopoly on telephone service until its patents expired in the mid-1890s. Following the 1879 Western Union agreement, the Bell Company was reorganized as the American Bell Company in 1880. The agreement eliminated Bell's strongest competition and according to one observer, "left Bell close to the position of a textbook pure monopolist until 1894."[7]

Bell's market position was not based on natural monopoly; rather it was based on Bell's patent position and its market division arrangement with Western Union. In 1893 and 1894, with the expiration of two key Bell patents -- though another 900 or so covering every aspect of the telephone and related equipment remained alive -- entry rapidly occurred, despite the network externalities and scale economies that Bell enjoyed.[8] In 1894, 80 commercial systems and seven mutual systems were established. By the end of the year, new entrants had 5% of the market, or 15,000 installed phones. "By 1900 telephone competition was widespread."[9] (By 1902, 3,000 non-Bell commercial systems had been established.) The non-Bells controlled 38% of the installed phones in the U.S., and "provided direct competition to almost all Bell operating

4

companies."[10] The large number of providers present and viable does not appear to be indicative of strong natural monopoly conditions.

Generally Bell prices fell after competitors entered.[11] Bell itself pushed to compete by expanding its long distance offerings, which it did through innovation and investment. Competition clearly worked; in fact it worked very well, despite the lack of interconnection. Moreover, " the price reduction, selling efforts and service improvements of the competitive era created a dramatic surge in telephone demand -- the total number of telephones doubled during the last 10 years of monopoly, but were multiplied by a factor of 12 during the first 10 years of competition."[12]

As Bell lost market share to the independents, it began a series of mergers and acquisitions. This policy reversed Bell's decline in market share. The political opposition to Bell began to mount, however, so in 1913 the company entered the Kingsbury commitment with the Department of Justice. The Kingsbury Commitment required AT&T to interconnect its long distance service with the remaining independent telephone companies and be subject to state and federal regulation. It did not have to divest any operating companies other than Western Union, which it had acquired five years earlier. In addition, it was able to continue to acquire local telephone operating companies. In fact, in 1921, Congress immunized telephone and telegraph company mergers from the antitrust laws.[13]

The Era of Regulation
While the market had clearly demonstrated that it could support competition, the political winds in the early decades of this century favored regulation. Vail's strategy was to embrace regulation rather than to fight it. In Bell's 1907 annual report, Vail stated:

> "It is contended that if there is to be no competition, there should be public control. It is not believed that there is any serious objection to such control, provided it is independent, intelligent, considerate, thorough and just, recognizing, as does the Interstate Commerce Commission in its report recently issued, that capital is entitled to its fair return, and good management or enterprise to its reward."

In a 1915 speech, Vail forthrightly stated that regulation "is as necessary for the protection of corporations from each other as for protection to, or from, the public." With the support of both Bell and the independents, the Interstate Commerce Act was amended in 1910 to bring interstate telephone companies under the jurisdiction of the ICC. Regulation simultaneously stabilized rates, increased the difficulty of new entry and calmed public criticism of Bell. Regulation in subsequent decades helped maintain AT&T's dominance against the threat of new technologies, such as microwave radio. With the assistance of regulation, social subsidies were strengthened at first to advance Vail's vision of universal service, then subsequently to redistribute income. The economic concept of natural monopoly was used to ratify the logic of regulation.

The divestiture of AT&T in 1984 supposedly marked the separation of the "natural monopoly" portion of the telecommunication infrastructure from the competitive portion. Divestiture was accomplished with such a broad brush, however, that "natural monopoly" boundaries, if they existed, could not possibly have been honored. In addition, changes in technology since divestiture, both in the "local" exchange and long distance transmission, have significantly altered the economics of transport such that any relation of the LATA boundaries to fundamental cost discontinuities must be purely coincidental.

Changes due to technological advance since divestiture are continuing, pushing at the boundaries of the local exchange from many different directions. The next section will explore the variety of technologies that are and will soon be available and how those technologies affect the economics and definition of local service.

4. New technologies and and the "natural monopoly"

For the past 20 years, technology has further challenged the notion of the natural monopoly. Technology is not only making the local exchange more susceptible to competition, it is further blurring the distinction between interexchange and intraexchange services. Regulatory distinctions between categories of service themselves affect technical choice and network design and therefore may themselves be an important factor in determining the direction of innovation and the nature of competition.

For example, the introduction of fiber optics into the telephone networks has significantly reduced the cost of transport so that the cost of calls is very insensitive to distance. As a result, depending on the amount of switching, the real resource cost of a 10 mile "local" call may not be very different than the cost of a 100 or 1,000 mile long distance call. However, because of regulation and imbedded subsidies, the prices for these calls may be very different. In response to these price-cost discrepancies, many companies have been able to arbitrage the difference, and route calls through the least cost jurisdiction even if it is not the least resource cost routing. This results both from the implicit subsidies as well as the decrease in cost of call transport.

The implementation of fiber optic technology is not the only change that is affecting the economics of local communications. There are a variety of technological advances that have lowered local exchange costs, changed the nature of local exchange costs to threaten the natural monopoly and reduced the difference between long distance and local telephone calls.[14]

New enabling technologies have and will lead to alternative provision and enhanced provision of telephone service. The advance of technology has come in many different arenas and from many different enterprises in response to several different regulatory regimes. Especially pertinent to the discussion of "local" telephony are the impact of radio based technology, the introduction of fiber optics and significant advances and decreases in prices of microelectronics and computing power.

Radio based technology

Radio based technologies are rapidly increasing quality, capacity and decreasing costs of wireless telephone service. The combination of these three factors makes radio based local loops much more of a competitive threat to the traditional wireline based local "natural" monopoly. Radio has gone through a series of advances since it was first introduced. These advances are currently most evident in the explosion of cellular phone usage that has occurred over the past ten years. Last year, there were more new cellular phone "lines" activated than local exchange lines. Despite its success, and the predictions that cellular might compete with landline service, it has yet to provide significant price competition for landline telephone service.[15] In some respects, this may be due to capacity limitations and the inability of providers to price discriminate for mobile versus fixed service. The first problem, capacity constraints, is in the process of being

6

rectified for the majority of the country with the conversion to digital signaling. Digital cellular transmission is expected to bring an immediate 3-fold increase in capacity. System capacity at that level will be sufficient to provide a competitive alternative to wireline service in all but the very largest areas of the country.[16]

Although cellular is currently providing only modest competition to landline service, several factors are likely to reduce cellular prices in the near future and make it more of a competitive alternative to landline service. Cellular is likely to face price competition from two sides in the near future. Nextel has begun implementing its digital, cellular specialized mobile radio (SMR) service in Los Angeles and other cities and is endeavoring to provide national coverage. The addition of a third high quality mobile service provider would expand capacity further and put downward pressure on prices. Other SMR operators also appear to have plans to introduce digital cellular technology to their networks.

In addition, future wireless competition will put pressure on both cellular and landline service. PCS is expected to provide mobile communications and to add significantly to wireless capacity. Because the higher PCS frequencies have limited effective ranges, the handsets will be smaller than comparable cellular phones. However, the systems will require significantly more cells, and thus may impose limitations on mobility, but will provide concomitant increases in capacity. This will cause them to charge lower prices than cellular systems and serve as competitors to portable and wireline phones in addition to many portable cellular phones.

The additional capacity offered by the introduction of digital signaling and the increase in spectrum available for mobile communications will eliminate the capacity constraint in most areas. At that time, service prices should be based on the cost of installing the infrastructure and maintaining the system. In many cases, these costs will be comparable to, or lower than, the costs faced by a traditional wireline company. Especially as one moves away from dense urban areas, wireline costs increase, spectrum scarcity decreases and cell siting becomes less expensive. As a result, the wireless technologies become much more competitive with wireline service.

In addition to terrestrial-based radio projects, there are a number of different satellite projects projected to begin service in the next few years. Motorola has proposed a Low Earth Orbit (LEO) satellite project called Iridium to provide world-wide satellite service interconnected to the landline network. There are a number of other "Big LEO" satellite system that have recently been assigned spectrum by the FCC and who propose to begin service in the near future. In addition, a number of other satellite systems, propose to provide ubiquitous high speed, high capacity service anywhere in the country. Although these services may be relatively expensive, they will provide alternatives, especially in high cost areas and may someday turn "local" communications into global communications.

Fiber optics
Fiber optics have dramatically changed the nature of competition in communications. Because fiber is so much more efficient than microwave technology, the cost of transmission of calls is much less sensitive to distance than it was at the time of divestiture. Because of the negligible cost differences, it is hard to determine why a 10 mile call should be "local" and a 100 mile call long distance. The decline in transmission costs will lead to the substitution of fiber for switching. It will become more cost effective to circuitously route calls over fiber networks if it allows the network to minimize its switching costs, if the cost of transmission decreases relative to the cost of switching.[17]

Fiber has not only affected the cost structure of the interLATA carriers, it has become an integral part of the local exchange. Local telephone and cable companies are racing to introduce fiber into their networks. Just as Bell and the other telephone companies competed to wire networks, current competitors are racing to be the first to have a high capacity two-way network and to reap the benefits of early adoption. There are many issues to be resolved about the introduction of fiber -- whether it will be fiber to the home, fiber to the curb or fiber to the neighborhood -- but it is clear that fiber and its carrying capacity have had a strong impact on the nature and cost structure of communications.

The development of fiber optic technology has led to the first competitive alternative to the LECs -- competitive access providers. CAPs have deployed fiber optic networks through dense downtown areas. In addition to the arguments that they are able to avoid the social subsidies embedded in LEC access rates, the CAPs claim that they are satisfying a need for high capacity, high quality, high speed data transmission links. Without the transmission quality of fiber, CAPs would not be able to fill this need and therefore might not be able to justify their existence, and the competitive pressure they bring to bear on LEC rates.

The preceding two sections show the complementary nature of the competitive effects of fiber and wireless technologies. Fiber is being introduced by CAPs and cable companies in dense urban areas to provide high capacity service. In these areas, the costs of wiring per telephone is relatively low since the density is high. In these areas, spectrum is also relatively scarce and expensive. Construction and operation of a high quality cellular-like system would be expensive because of the opportunity cost of the spectrum, the high price of the land rental for cell sites and the requirement of a large number of cell sites. On the other hand, in suburban and rural areas, it is more expensive to string wires, but spectrum is less intensely used and there is more choice for cell sites. As a result, technology is changing the nature of the natural monopoly in both high population and low population areas.

Equipment costs

The relentless advance in power and decrease in price of microelectronics and computing technology has had a large impact on the price and performance of customer premise equipment as well as central office switching equipment. For example, these cost decreases affect the total cost of cellular service since the handsets have become significantly cheaper, and operators pay lower prices for incremental switching capacity. Because switching and controller costs have decreased, the costs to provide alternative forms of local access have decreased. Cable, CAPs and radio based carriers will benefit from these lower costs as they begin to compete with local exchange carriers. The decline in microelectronics prices will make it easier for cable companies to compete with LECs. The customer premises equipment to link into a 500 channel interactive broadband network will be significantly cheaper and more sophisticated than it would have been only a few years ago. As a result, even if the cable and telco networks provide different levels of service, the overall competition from the variety of features ensures that the cost reductions to provide cable telephony will make them more competitive with LEC providers.[18]

The pace of electronics advance has blurred the distinction between transmission and switching as well as between central office equipment and customer premises equipment. For example, the increase in central office technology has allowed the offering of advanced voice messaging systems. While these may offer more features than standard home answering machines, they provide direct competition for each other. PBXs are an example of an advance

8

outside the central office that also increased the competition between central office services, Centrex, and customer premises equipment. PBXs not only provide competition for central office services, but because they provide switching services, they allow users to reduce their use of loops, and to pay for fewer lines.

The next section analyzes the effect of these technologies on the entry strategies of potential entrants into the local exchange.

5. Entry

Entry can be divided into two broad categories: entrants using existing local distribution technology and entrants using new technologies. This discussion will also consider entry in the context of an unbundled network like the one proposed by Ameritech in its Customers First Plan. This analysis seems to be applicable for other regions as well since the FCC has steadily been decreasing the scope of the "bottleneck" and increasingly allowing competition. The recent switched and special access orders and expanded interconnection have opened traffic on the local exchange network to competition beginning just outside the local switch.

Cable companies
Cable companies are positioning themselves to provide local exchange services. Cable companies have capacity to provide transport from LEC end offices to IXC POPs.[19] They are also interconnecting their headends with fiber to offer advertisers the ability to reach region-wide audiences.[20] One indirect, but non-trivial result is the creation of capacity for the transport of telephone calls. Cable companies are also putting fiber further into their networks, giving them the ability to provide end-to-end voice and video service.

Perhaps the most obvious example of cable company entry into telephony is the ownership of Teleport by TCI and other cable companies. In addition TCI's success with its CATV/telephony venture in the U.K. is another example of the cable company's interest in the provision of telephony. Finally, TCI has joined with other cable companies and Sprint to bid in the recent PCS auctions and to form Sprint Telecommunications Ventures which will compete for local service using both wireless and wireline technology.

In a cable and RBOC joint effort, Time Warner/US West recently made a presentation disclosing that they intend to upgrade their physical plant to begin the provision of telephone service.[21] Their proposed service seeks to target residences and small businesses in addition to large businesses. They expect to charge rates that will undercut LEC rates. The partners are both well-financed, experienced companies. Time Warner claimed in its presentation that it has been very successful competing against British Telecom in England.[22]

Time Warner's Orlando, Florida trial is another example of cable competition for local service.[23] The system as envisioned will be based on a fiber optic backbone/copper to the home architecture, digital compression technology and digital storage and switching systems. The network will give the cable company the ability to offer, among other things, voice and data transmission services and PCS. Jones InterCable recently announced a test of telephone service over its cable system. With the help of MCI and Scientific Atlanta, the test will allow users to bypass the LEC and receive faxes while using the phone and have access to interactive games.[24]

Comcast is also poised to begin telephone service.[25] The New York Times reported that Comcast had continuing talks with both AT&T and MCI, indicating their interest in telephone service. Comcast also is one of the owners of Nextel, a specialized mobile radio company that recently received FCC approval to provide cellular-like service in a number of major cities. Furthermore, Comcast offers cable and telephone service in Britain. In the U.S., Brian Roberts, President of Comcast says "Long term, the cable companies want to look like the phone companies with ubiquitous coverage. We've wired up nearly all the homes, but not the businesses. So that's why we're investing in Teleport."[26]

Once these ventures and others begin offering services to consumers, a significant marketing advantage will emerge. A cable company can package its programming and phone service, offering the customer the convenience of one stop shopping and possibly adjusting the prices of the individual services to convince the customer to subscribe. Such bundling has proven highly successful in the U.K. Cable and Wireless, a British telecommunications and cable company, is now signing-up close to 15,000 residential customers per month through the local cable companies.[27] There is no reason not to expect similar scenarios in the U.S., especially with an interconnected network of networks.

Wireless entry

Wireless carriers provide both immediate and future competitive entry alternatives for local exchange service. AT&T's $18 billion purchase of McCaw Cellular will position wireless technology as a direct competitor to the RBOCs' local telephone business.[28] Their purchases of licenses in the recent PCS auction also give them nearly nationwide presence as a competitive alternative. The company's brand name, marketing prowess and financial resources eliminate any doubt that an AT&T backed cellular venture could quickly become a nationwide player in the local telecommunications services area. Furthermore, the merger places AT&T in the enviable position of being able to offer its subscribers a complete package of local, cellular and long-distance calling.

"Nonwireline" cellular carriers provide nearly ubiquitous service throughout the country. While their "loops" may not currently provide a complete competitive alternative to LEC loops, they are positioned to do so easily. Cellular carriers have sophisticated switches and, in some cases, fully functional networks and office support in place that will allow them to use spectrum for "fixed" loops and to provide competitive local service. Cellular carriers also possess a select list of customers with a high demand for telecommunications services.

Cellular and other wireless carriers appear well situated to provide future competition for the local loop, especially in rural areas where the costs of wireline loops is relatively high. In these areas, spectrum is used less intensively than in major metropolitan areas, so providing competitive wireless loops would not divert spectrum from a relatively more valuable use.

In the future, the combination of leased wireline access and wireless access may give the cellular carriers a unique advantage in marketing to customers. With their new PCS licenses, wireless carriers would provide customers with new options for "loops."[29] In one scenario, the wireless provider can position a cell site directly adjacent to a wireless PBX serving a large corporate complex. The wireless carrier could handle local mobile traffic and serve as the local carrier for all interLATA traffic originating and terminating at the PBX. Though the coverage for the wireless portion of the traffic would be more limited than for wireline traffic, the volume of traffic, combined with the absence of interconnect charges for the wireless carrier, would offset at least some of the gap.[30]

10

With the imminent conversion to digital signaling for cellular, there are a number of cellular operators that will have significant excess capacity. In addition, there will be significant increases in capacity from the new digital PCS carriers. They can market this capacity for use as simple local service. In fact, products are being developed to allow cellular operators to sell wireless service to wireline customers that is transparent to the user.[31] Other implementations could include selling "loops" to serve as connections for alarms that need only infrequent access. As a result, the competition from wireless providers is likely to occur on a number of fronts -- mobility, standard service, and specialized services.

Amalgamations and alliances

Given the infrastructure of cable companies, CAPs and cellular carriers, and the emergence of alliances among them,[32] a possible future competitive alternative combination would be to use CAPs to provide downtown loops, cable companies to provide loops for suburban and residential customers, and cellular companies to provide loops in rural areas. Combinations of the various technologies also lead to greater geographic coverage. An entry strategy using a combination of the assets of these companies would be reflected in the pervasive entry at multiple nodes shown in Figure 2(pg. 15).

The combination of Sprint and its cable partners in Sprint Telecommunications Ventures is a vivid example of this strategy. They have the complementary assets of Sprint's local and long distance telephony expertise, the wireless expertise of both Sprint and Comcast and the cable operations of the four cable companies. The group has stated that they expect to provide local exchange competition through both their wireless licenses and their cable plant.

Another group of potentially formidable competitors, and moving closer to a position of actual entry with each passing month, are the LECs from other regions. The RBOCs and GTE are all large, financially sound carriers with the requisite technical engineering, marketing and billing capabilities to provide local exchange services.

As already noted, US West (with Time Warner) intends to enter other regions and begin providing local exchange service within 2 years. Entry by the other LECs is just as likely. Both Sprint and GTE have local exchange operations and it would be logical for them to expand their service areas through a combination of resale and facilities construction. Most RBOCs have cellular operations in areas outside their local exchange territories. The market presence of these companies provides a natural springboard for the extension of the scope of their services into the local exchange. Even though three of the RBOCs have teamed together for their wireless operations, they have wireless operation in non-affiliated regions and the other RBOCs and GTE have wireless operations in Bell Atlantic, Nynex and US West's regions. Such a strategy could be accomplished via their own facilities, or by a pooling of talents and resources with the other potential entrants.

Entry using existing technology

Competitors using existing technology, depending on their specific capabilities, are poised to compete for either the entire market or for distinct subsets of customers. Because each potential competitor has different competitive advantages, the range of customers benefiting from new entry and expanded competition nearly spans the gamut of local exchange customers. In addition, the ability to enter with minimal investment and to act as a reseller in an unbundled local network gives an entrant complete market presence with little risk.[33]

Interexchange carriers

The most likely source of immediate and influential entry into local service will be the IXCs, especially the large, nationwide carriers like AT&T, MCI and Sprint.[34]   AT&T has itself advanced the case for seamless end-to-end integration through its Megacom service and private networks.   The McCaw acquisition is the *sine qua non* of a company positioning itself for the end-to-end provision of service.   AT&T's purchase shows the obvious synergies between the two businesses and the expected future synergies.   Indeed, AT&T's public statements suggest that the company's strategy is to provide their customers with end-to-end service.[35]

MCI has formed a subsidiary, MCI Metro, for the express purpose of providing local telephone service.   In addition, through its subsidiary Access Transmission Services, MCI has filed for a permit to begin competitive access service provision in Indiana.   MCI also recently announced the planned test of cable telephony with Jones InterCable.   Sprint is already an active participant in local exchange telephony.   MCI and Sprint will now have incentives to use competitive trunks from high volume end offices to their POPs because of changes to the rules regarding switched and special access .   This will create excess capacity and position them to take advantage of the unbundling and switch integration plan.

All three companies have the ability to self-supply transport, and, once the necessary construction and right-of-way expenses are incurred, the incremental cost to add traffic is quite small.[36]   Specifically, once the IXCs have successfully developed the transport segment of their network, they will be able to sign up additional subscribers at little added cost in an unbundled environment since they can rent loops from the LEC and transport the traffic to their own switches.[37]   In addition, as a major manufacturer of switches, AT&T is in the position to obtain switching at a lower cost than any of its competitors and could easily position switches for local service.

IXCs enjoy their highest margins in the small and mid-size business segment.[38] Consequently, IXCs are likely to pursue these customers first for their provision of end-to-end service.[39]   AT&T, as well as other large IXCs, could compete by installing switches (or using excess capacity on its existing switches) to supply dial tone and usage services and routing the traffic to one of their many existing POPs.   This could be economical even in an area with a small amount of traffic because the large IXCs could either share capacity on a nearby existing long distance switch or economically use a somewhat distant switch to provide local dial tone until traffic justifies a truly local switch.   Adding switch capacity is relatively simple with modern modular switches such as the 5ESS.   Since the IXCs have fiber facilities in place with excess capacity, the cost of transport to take advantage of a distant "local" switch would be minimal.

An unbundled local network means that the IXCs, and everyone else for that matter, will always be able to access LEC facilities; entry can occur before proprietary facilities are built, or even planned.   New construction can be delayed until such time as the current or forecasted volume of traffic justifies the investment.   As a result, entrants avoid large, risky infrastructure investment.

Competitive access providers

Competitive access providers (CAPs) have entered many major cities by deploying fiber loops through dense downtown areas.   They are already providing competition for local exchange

12

carriers without the benefit of unbundled local networks. With the recent FCC orders discussed above, the competition for transport services will increase the traffic on CAP networks, decreasing their average unit costs and making them more effective competitors for a larger portion of business.

CAPs appear to have their eyes on expanded services. MFS has recently announced that it will offer local and long distance services in New York City.[40] To support this effort, it plans to install Ericsson switches in its network. The service will be "available immediately in Manhattan and will be extended to the rest of the New York metropolitan area over 'the next few months.'"[41] MFS does not intend to stop with New York. According to its half page advertisement for this new service, "Service is available in New York now. National expansion is underway."[42]

CAPs have invested in loops that give them access to a large number of customers with a relatively high demand for telephone service. CAPs may not be positioned to compete for customers throughout the local service areas, but they are well beyond the venture capital stage and now represent formidable competitors to the local exchange carriers. The largest CAP, Teleport, is owned by several large cable companies, including TCI, Comcast and Cox, and thus possesses the financial backing to ensure its ability to effectively compete. In addition, the cable investment in a telephone service provider indicates that synergies may be expected and that the CAPs are expected to provide some of the telephony expertise.

Investment houses and the CAPs themselves believe that CAPs will play a significant role in local telecommunications. In discussing the acquisition of Teleport by TCI and Cox Communications, Goldman Sachs says that the alternative access market is "substantial" and represents a significant opportunity for cable companies.[43] TCI's CEO, Dr. John Malone, believes that there is a potential market for alternative access carriers of as much as $40 billion annually; he expects that the business will be at least $1 billion in three years with a potential to represent 25% of the total access marketplace.[44] Such heady numbers, while obviously not precise, are indicative of the potential for CAPs to become significant access providers.

With LEC switch integration, CAPs with switches can easily become the local phone service provider to those businesses passed by their network. In addition, the ability to rent loops in areas their networks do not pass means that they can provide service, with little incremental investment, to any business or residence that is served by the end offices they pass with their loops. CAPs can also expand their geographic coverage sequentially and determine the optimal path for their new fiber loops by leasing capacity in the short term while determining where to install plant expansions. Finally, the CAPs will be able to compete to serve multi-location businesses even when they do not have a physical presence near each of the satellite offices.

CAPs will be able to increase their target customer base significantly with unbundling. CAPs already reach a significant number of high volume customers. With unbundling, CAPs may deploy fiber in other areas, giving them even more potential customers. CAPs can use unbundling to determine demand for their services and perform true market research by purchasing pieces of LECs' networks before determining where to construct their own facilities. They can greatly reduce the risk of new construction by acquiring an active customer base prior to completion of their facilities.

Unbundling and integration

Because of the network nature of telecommunications, stand-alone networks cannot always deliver head to head competitive threats to existing telephone systems. There are many instances where private networks, or arrangements which provide direct access to IXCs through CAPs, provide competition to LECs without interconnection to the LEC network. However, these networks do not always provide the entire communications needs of their customers, and they are generally not stand-alone networks. In short, mutual interconnection is very important for the success of alternate "local" networks.

Ameritech recently proposed its Customers First plan to the FCC. Under this plan, Ameritech proposes not only to provide mutual interconnection to other local carriers, but it will unbundle its local network. Frontier Corp. also proposed fundamental unbundling of its network elements, including unbundling the local loop from switching. In addition, they proposed full interconnection, including interconnection with SS7 network. In essence, the unbundling allows for immediate competitive local service entry by any of the parties discussed above. They can use portions of their own networks and combine them with portions of the unbundled LEC network to provide service. Unbundling means that entry requirements will be lowered dramatically.[45] Any portion of the network that involves significant investment will be leased to competitors by the most efficient provider (initially this is likely to be the incumbent) so that if there are economies of scale or scope, all competitors and consumers will benefit. When scale and scope economies are not present, or consumers desire specific services, other providers can tailor their network services to fill those needs.

Figure 1 shows the current status of the local exchange. The majority of traffic originating at the CPE uses the LEC network. However, for some large customers, CAPs provide an alternative. Note that the diagram ignores the presence of alternative local loops such as cellular. Figure 2 shows the change in the structure of the local exchange with unbundling in place. The variety of options for traffic carriage is significantly greater with unbundling. A large number of options are available to potential entrants to take advantage of the ability to purchase pieces of the LEC network and to self supply the remaining portions, whether they be transport or switching.

One possible concern is that the threat of entry may not be sufficient to discipline prices for each individual portion of the network. To make sure that it does not exploit any remaining power over a bottleneck portion of the local exchange, Ameritech has agreed to freeze prices for 3 years and then subject them to price cap regulation. The combination of this pricing proposal ensures that Ameritech will not take advantage of any remaining power to disadvantage its competitors while waiting for the implementation of alternative local loops. As noted earlier, advances in technology are accelerating local exchange competition. The coupling of unbundling and price caps makes sure that if there is temporary market power, it will not be extended to competitive services through cross subsidies or discrimination. With unbundling and integration, an efficient network of networks will develop and be priced at competitive levels.

Comparisons with other industries are instructive because they demonstrate the feasibility of unbundling and switch integration; and how entry in industries believed to have certain natural monopoly features can be assisted by such mechanisms. This section provides a brief overview of unbundling and entry in two regulated industries: natural gas and electricity.

14

Figure 1
Current Status of the Local Exchange

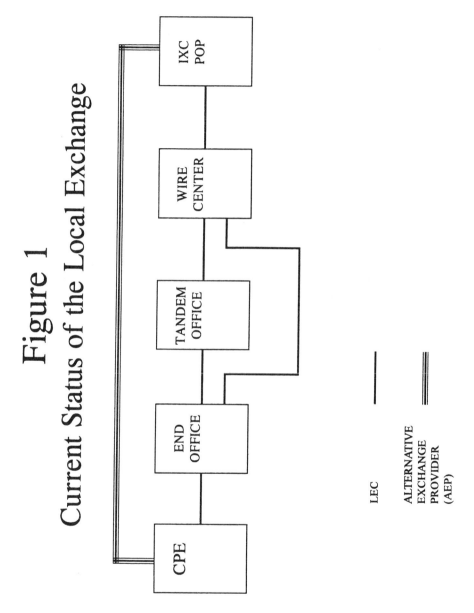

CPE — END OFFICE — TANDEM OFFICE — WIRE CENTER — IXC POP

LEC

ALTERNATIVE
EXCHANGE
PROVIDER
(AEP)

Figure 2

The Local Exchange with Unbundling

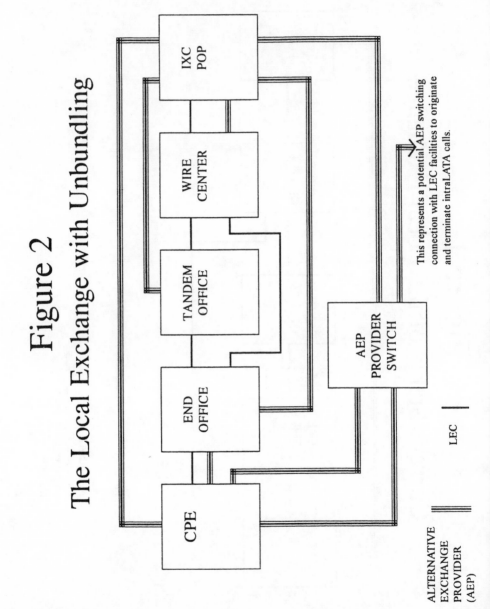

This represents a potential AEP switching connection with LEC facilities to originate and terminate intraLATA calls.

A. Natural Gas

The natural gas interstate pipeline business represents a clear instance where unbundling has led to substantial entry. Traditionally, interstate natural gas pipeline service involved the purchase of natural gas at the wellhead, followed by transportation and sale at the city gate all provided on a bundled basis by interstate pipelines. Pipelines were both merchants and shippers. As discrepancies widened between gas prices at the wellhead and the city gate, pressures arose to gain access to transportation on an unbundled basis.

In 1985, FERC (Federal Energy Regulatory Commission) responded with Order 436, which represented a limited form of unbundling; it did not *require* that pipelines carry natural gas for sale in their city gate market but established nondiscriminatory tariff provisions. Despite the limited form of unbundling represented by Order 436, the effects were dramatic. The share of natural gas sold in competition with the pipeline in its city gate markets rose from approximately 15 percent of total gas carried by interstate pipelines in 1985 to over 70 percent of total gas carried in 1989. Entry was also rapid. Initially most entry was by former pipeline customers buying natural gas for their own account. Increasingly however, new marketers entered, purchased natural gas at the wellhead and resold it in competition with the pipeline's own sales business downstream.

FERC Order 636 represents a further step in the unbundling process because pipeline control of facilities will be reduced. Potential shippers will now be able to acquire rights to pipeline capacity as well as rights to storage.[46] Pipeline customers will also be able to trade such rights, allowing them to realign allocated capacity and obtain the flexible services customers desire. The competitive forces set in motion by Order 636 are still working their way through the regulatory process and the market. Even so, new companies have emerged and offer new services using the pipeline's unbundled transportation and storage capacity.

B. Electricity

Various parts of the electrical system have likewise been unbundled. In most regions of the United States there are markets in which utilities can buy and sell bulk power. Interruptible power can be sold separately from reliable capacity that is provided under long term contracts. Furthermore, intermediate commodities can also be sold by one utility to another. Examples of these include commitments to have a certain plant available for an intermediate period of time to provide back up in case of unanticipated changes in demand at a second utility.

Unbundling has provided benefits, allowing electric utilities to sell power from plants that are underutilized on a seasonal basis, thereby reducing unit costs. It has also permitted the shut down of inefficient plants, since the owners can purchase power from more efficient utilities.

The evidence from gas and electricity indicates that opening up the local exchange is feasible, and that at least in the case of gas it indicates that new entry is facilitated. Moreover, because new entrants can access the embedded facilities of the incumbent at the incumbent's costs, it causes the incumbent to yield the basis of its own competitive advantage from scale to its competitors. Clearly, unbundling is great for new entrants, as it in essence enables them to rent the competitive advantage of the incumbent, at the incumbent's cost.

Assessment

Many different entry strategies are likely to arise. Some new entrants may be better suited for niche plays; others may choose more comprehensive strategies. Both can coexist in the marketplace. Entrants can target high profit customers by supplying a small dedicated system catered to the specific customer's needs. This would make them more difficult for an LEC to dislodge them. Such niche players are likely to be very successful since unbundling enables the niche player to take advantage of LECs' scale economies.

A critical characteristic of local/intraLATA service to note here is the concentration of revenue in a handful of business customers. On average, 30% of a LEC's revenues, and a still larger percentage of its profits, come from 1% of the customer base.[47] A new entrant need not win over many customers to have a noticeable impact in the marketplace. The top 1% of customers account for more than 30% of profits because they purchase large volumes of high margin services. Thus, while CAPs only have a small geographic presence, their actual market presence is significant. With unbundling, a new entrant can avoid large capital outlays and can focus its limited resources on several key business customers to quickly achieve a positive cash flow. These funds can then be used to secure additional customers leading to a self-sustaining cycle of profitability.

AT&T and MCI are unlikely to be content with niche plays. These companies have expressly stated their interest in providing end-to-end service for their customers.[48] Unbundling offers the opportunity to provide ubiquitous service and the IXCs will have the added advantage of being able to complement their existing assets with the use of unbundled portions of service from the LEC. They can also obtain all of a customer's traffic without the need to provide local switching or loops.

While many of these entry strategies appear likely, it is instructive to examine and contrast the status of AT&T's competitors at the time of divestiture with the status of local exchange competitors now to see how facilities-based entry occurred in that segment of the business. The meteoric rise of MCI and Sprint and the concurrent rapid dissipation of AT&T's market position in long distance are well known and need not be repeated here. However, it is informative to compare AT&T's competitors as they existed in 1983 to LEC competitors today. Specifically, this exercise convincingly demonstrates that actual and potential competitors, not least among them AT&T, MCI and Sprint, all possess financial and marketing wherewithal and installed facilities that far surpass anything facing AT&T back in 1983. Indeed, the FCC has already noted that competition for access will "develop much more rapidly than interexchange competition did."[49]

This point is made clearly by the comparisons in Table 1. Compared with the 1983 versions of Sprint and MCI, actual and potential LEC competitors have considerable financial muscle.[50] AT&T is the leading communications provider in the world. AT&T provides long-distance service to three-quarters of all U.S. households; owns one of the five most recognizable brand names in the country; annually spends $3 billion on R&D; and is vertically integrated across major business lines.[51] Furthermore, the McCaw deal immediately made AT&T the nation's largest cellular provider. AT&T's entry into local/intraLATA will be vigorous, as the company has all the relevant complementary assets needed to be a successful competitor.

Implications of entry for "natural" monopoly arguments
Although not all of these entry scenarios will take place immediately, the threat of entry and ability of entrants to target specific groups have significant implications for the natural monopoly arguments put forth to justify regulation of local telephone service. New entry is evidence that either the monopoly is not natural or it is not sustainable. Given the number of different entry strategies, it seems obvious that a large number of urban and suburban customers will be passed

18

Table 1

Selected Financial Statistics
(All Amounts in $Millions)

Selected AT&T Competitors in 1983

	Sales	Current Assets	Market Value	Net Plant	EBITD
Sprint (United Tel.)	1,966	656	937	4,285	1,073
MCI	1,073	713	1,335	1,324	420

Selected LEC Competitors in 1994

IXCs					
AT&T	75,094	37,611	78,843	22,035	12,305
MCI	13,338	4,888	10,878	9,059	2,609
Sprint	12,662	2,189	9,622	10,879	3,266
RBOCs					
BellSouth	16,845	4,728	26,859	25,162	7,328
NYNEX	13,307	3,798	15,391	20,623	4,411
Bell Atlantic	13,791	3,783	21,751	16,938	3,364
Ameritech	12,570	2,891	23,725	13,455	2,147
US West	10,953	2,766	16,720	13,997	4,777
Southwestern Bell	11,619	3,493	25,052	17,317	4,952
Pacific Telesis	9,235	2,898	12,083	16,114	4,059
Other					
Time-Warner	7,396	2,817	13,323	753	1,250
TCI	4,318	204	12,421	5,579	1,685

Notes:
a)Market Value is calculated as: (number of common shares outstanding)*(12/31 closing price)
   (except for MCI in 1983, market value is calculated using the 3/31 closing price)
b)EBITD = Earnings Before Interest, Tax and Depreciation
c)Market Value for TCI is calculated using Class A common stock only
d)TCI "Current Assets" is the sum of Cash and Accounts Receivable - it does not include investments in Liberty
Media and other affiliates of Turner Broadcasting

Source: Company Reports-respective years, Jan. 1995 S&P Stock Guide and electronic data retrieval for 1983 prices

by two wires capable of providing two-way voice grade service in the near future (either cable or CAP in addition to the LEC). In addition, advances in radio technology and the release of additional spectrum will provide an alternative for rural customers. Thus it appears that for two-way voice grade telephone service, the natural monopoly will not continue (if it exists now).

Unbundling adds force to the entry scenarios. With unbundling, uncommitted entry can occur quickly. The Department of Justice distinguishes between committed and uncommitted entry in it Merger Guidelines.[52] Uncommitted entrants are defined as firms whose "supply responses must be likely to occur within one year and without the expenditure of significant sunk costs of entry and exit, in response to a 'small but significant and nontransitory' price increase."[53] Such uncommitted entry does not have significant costs and is a continuing competitive threat, even when potential entrants are not actually participating actively.[54] With unbundling, the local exchange business will be contestable since up front expenditures by new entrants will be minimal. This is because potential competitors can rent/lease various components of the LEC's embedded investment while determining the demand for their services. In this way, entrants can reduce their risk by performing real market research in advance of making large capital investments. For potential entrants, unbundling creates a market for non-redeployable assets. In addition, entrants can benefit from any LEC scale and scope economies, augmented by their own competitive advantages. Unbundling essentially drives entry and exit costs to zero for the unbundled components. As a result, the market becomes contestable and, in a contestable market, market power cannot exist, regardless of market share.

However, the future appears to be somewhat different. Voice grade telephone service may soon become simply an ancillary service provided with interactive two-way video service. In this case, bandwidth needs of wireless providers may currently be too great to pose an alternative to a wire-based technology. In addition, the cost to upgrade a system to provide advanced services may justify only a single wire-based system. However, the recent spate of mergers and the investment projects by both cable and telephone companies projects a world where a large number of homes will be passed by two high capacity wires and the homes will also be addressable by a large variety of wireless service providers.

6. Organizational structure and innovation

All aspects of the telecommunications industry -- local and long distance -- have been exposed to rapid innovation since the birth of the industry. Indeed, overall telecommunications productivity growth has been about 3% per year since 1948.[55] In particular, the digital electronics revolution has brought about vast improvements in telecommunication equipment. Much of this innovation was autonomous, or made to be so. That is, it could be integrated into the network so long as it met compatibility standards. In short, one could upgrade one piece without having to abandon the existing investment in the network. Sometimes innovation isn't autonomous but is systemic thereby requiring investment throughout the network, as with Common Channel Interface Signaling (CCIS). In the pre-divestiture days, AT&T was able to bring forward such investment, even through not all of the local companies benefited equally. Complex negotiations could be avoided as the administrative apparatus -- an integrated AT&T -- was available to get it done.

Innovation has continued since divestiture, though it is of a different kind. Terminal equipment, switching and non-network technology have been beneficiaries of innovation in the

20

post divestiture period. There does not appear to be significant innovation that has required the cooperation of long distance carriers with the LEC's, with the exception of advanced intelligent network features that require out of band transport. Indeed, when innovative integrated service offering became compelling, the organizational response has been merger, as with AT&T and McCaw.

Now the opportunity for a new family of innovations is becoming apparent. We refer in particular to interactive TV, multimedia and the information superhighway. The amount of electronic material the superhighway can carry is dizzying compared to the relatively narrow range of broadcast TV and the limited number of cable channels. These new systems, when commercialized, will support a wide range of new services: home shopping, on-line information, classified ads, teleconferencing, movies on demand, video games, travel services, and distance learning. When in place, these new services will be available when needed, and users rather than providers will determine when they are used, thereby putting a greater degree of control back with the user.

At this point the technical barriers to building this platform and loading services upon it have largely been broken. The challenge, it would seem, is to overcome the organizational barriers. The key success factors which are relevant include equipment design, software, programming and network management. The current industrial structure is not as yet well aligned with respect to the compilation of these assets. Telephone companies have terrific capabilities in network management; cable companies have broadband transmission capabilities. More importantly cable companies often have ownership in programming, and understand how to match programming to markets. Software development skills, with the possible exception of Bell Labs and Bellcore, lie mainly outside the current boundaries of the industry: Microsoft, Apple Computer, and Lotus are among the repositories of such skills.

Colliding technological trajectories in telephony, computers and fiber optics suggest the need for a rich network of alliances as well as possible cross ownership arrangements to bring forward these technologies in a timely and cost effective fashion. The pioneers are likely to need common ownership of key elements of the system in order to speed concerted action. The Sprint Telecommunications Ventures alliance appears to be motivated by these considerations. Once scale economies and installed base economies have been achieved, and the commercial aspects of the technology proven, business routines will emerge which may obviate the need of following firms to integrate to the same degree. As we note elsewhere:

> "Integration facilitates systemic innovations by facilitating information flows, and the coordination of investment plans. It also removes institutional barriers to innovation where the innovation in question requires allocating costs and benefits, or placing specialized investments into several parts of an industry. In the absence of integration, there will be a reluctance on the part of both parties to make the necessary investments in specialized assets, even is this would yield mutual gains. One reason is that both parties know that the exercise of opportunism might yield even greater benefits to one of the parties. Hence, in the absence of common ownership of the parts, there will be reluctance on the part of one or more of the parties to adopt a systemic innovation."[56]

While integration may be necessary to create the information superhighway platform, alliances and partial equity arrangement may suffice to place new products and services on the platform. Indeed, whatever organizational arrangements come into place to build the platform, we expect to see a plethora of alliances and partial equity links formed in order to organize and deploy services onto these new platforms. As we state elsewhere:

> "With rapid learning, colliding technological trajectories and tight selection, on can expect to see incumbent firms becoming enveloped in a dense skein of inter-corporate relationships involving partial equity holdings and joint ventures. Such firms might be called "network" firms."[57]

Local telecommunications is thus about to become buried in this rich plethora of new arrangements designed to bring forward the bandwidth hungry technologies of tomorrow. Not only will fiber cause distance to shrink -- making everything "local" -- but telecommunications will itself become transformed. The LECs as we now know them will no longer dominate the local landscape. Cable-CAP amalgamations are already there, and out of town LECs will be in town as the MFJ's interLATA restrictions fold. Radio will bring in new players providing ESMR, PCS or Iridium like services which will compete with some aspects of what we consider local telecommunications. The identity of the players will thus change dramatically as will the nature of local service. Customers will have such a menu of new services available to them that POTS will no longer have a recognizable meaning.

7. Conclusions

Our brief survey of the history of the industry, and our analysis of technological challenges at work today make it quite clear that the so-called "local" portion of the telephone business is now, and likely has always been, capable of supporting competition. Regulation and limited interconnection are the main reasons why competition is not more powerful there today. Alternative technologies such as radio and cable remove any shadow of doubt about the fundamental ability of the local exchange to support competition. A forward looking view recognizes the impending actual competition; recognition of the multiple sources of new competition makes the disciplinary effect of potential competition a reality.

Unbundling plans put forward by some incumbent local exchange companies such as Ameritech and Frontier Corp. will sharpen local exchange competition by facilitating or indeed assisting new entry. These unbundling plans represent a bold step and involve some sacrifice of market position; but they make transparent to all -- especially regulators and judges -- that in at least in those parts of country where unbundling is to be implemented, the myth of monopoly has been buried. Just as Theodore Vail embraced regulation, the executives of Ameritech and Frontier Corp. are embracing competition. Unbundling will serve not only to promote entry, but to eliminate the excuse of the MFJ's restrictions on interLATA service, (i.e., the provision of interLATA service is inappropriate for an LEC because of the alleged ability of the LECs to use their monopoly power in the local exchange to deleteriously affect the terms of competition in interLATA services through cross subsidies and discrimination.) With unbundling, the fig leaf is removed. Eventually, the MFJ must collapse.

What lies ahead is a new industry -- the distinctions between local and long distance will disappear in their entirety, and the distinction between telephone, computer and television will also evaporate. The future is one where local exchange telephone companies as we know them

22

today will barely be recognizable, even a decade from now, and regulation -- except for antitrust enforcement -- will most probably be swept to the side. Technology is of course the key driver. It not only is rendering unworkable the organizational and regulatory structures of the past, but will also advance whole new streams of services of great benefit to society.

Endnotes

1. Professor Teece has testified in support of the Ameritech plan to the the U.S. Department of Justice and the Federal Communications Commission. Dr. Rosston assisted Dr. Teece in the preparation of his testimony as a Senior Economist at the Law & Economics Consulting Group.

2. Keynes, J. *The General Theory of Employment, Interest, and Money*, MacMillan: London, 1936, p.384.

3. Schmanlensee, R. *The Control of Natural Monopolies*, D.C. Heath & Co.: Lexington, NJ, 1979, p.143.

4. See Noam (1993) for the origins for these terms.

5. See Brock, G., *The Telecommunications Industry*, p. 94.

6. This "surely was one of the most one-sided deals ever struck." Noll, R.G. and Owen, B.M. "The Anticompetitive Uses of Regulation: *United States v. AT&T*" in Kwoka, J.E. and White, L.J. (eds.) *The Antitrust Revolution*, 1989, p. 291.

7. Brock, G., *The Telecommunications Industry*, p. 99.

8. As Brock notes on p.110, "While it would be practically impossible for a new entrant to establish a system equal to Bell's in a short period of time, the systems advantage to Bell was reduced by the fact that most telephone subscribers communicated with a relatively small number of people. Although the value of having a telephone would rise with the total number of people connected, the amount of increase would depend on the existing subscribers' desire to communicate with new subscribers. If a new entrant could connect to a small but homogeneous subgroup of the population, its service would be valuable despite the limited total number of phones in the system. If the Bell system and the new competitor generally served different social classes in the same city (as often happened during the period of competition), the advantage of having the two systems interconnected could be relatively small. The fact that telegraph service was far more pervasive than long-distance telephone service at the expiration of the patents also reduced the systems advantage by allowing subscribers to an isolated telephone exchange to conduct long-distance business via telegraph."

9. Brock, p. 114.

10. Brock, p. 124. See also Noll, R.G. and Owen, B.M. "The Anticompetitive Uses of Regulation: *United States v. AT&T*" in Kwoka, J.E. and White, L.J. (eds.) *The Antitrust Revolution*, 1989, p. 291.

11. Irwin, M. "The Telephone Industry," in Adams, W. (ed.) *The Structure of American Industry*, 6th ed. 1982, p-300.

12. Brock, p.122.

13. Irwin, M. "The Telephone Industry," in Adams, W. (ed.) *The Structure of American Industry*, 6th ed. 1982, p-301.

14. A variety of authors have investigated the impact of alternative technology. Rapid technological change has made it difficult for the references to remain up to date, but a few include Reed, D. *Residential Fiber Optic Networks: An Engineer and Economic Analysis*, Artec House, 1992, Calhoun, G. *Wireless Access and the Local Telephone*

Network, Artec House, 1992, Huber, P. Kellogg, M. and Thorne, J. *The Geodesic Network II: 1993 Report on Competition in the Telephone Industry*, The Geodesic Company: Washington D.C., 1992, Reed, D. "Putting it all Together: The Cost Structure of Personal Communications Services," FCC Office of Plans and Policy Working Paper No. 28, November 1992, DeSurvire, E. "Lightwave Communications: The Fifth Generation," *Scientific American*, January 1992, p. 114, and Egan, B. *Information Superhighways: The Economics of Advanced Public Communication Networks*, Artec House, 1991.

15. Calhoun, G., *Wireless Access and the Local Telephone Network*, Artec House: Boston, MA, 1992, Hatfield D.N., Ax, G.G. and Dunmore, K.R. "A Comparison of the Costs of Providing Ordinary Telephone Service Using Conventional Wireline and Cellular Radio Technology" October 1985, Hatfield Associates, Denver, CO.

16. Rosston, G. "An Economic Analysis of the Effects of FCC Regulation on Land Mobile Radio," Stanford University Ph.D. thesis, 1994, Harris, R., Rosston, G., and Teece, D.,"Competition and Unbundling in Local Telecommunications: Implications for Antitrust Policy," in *Toward a Competitive Telecommunication Industry: Selected Papers from the 1994 Telecommunications Policy Research Conference*, Brock, G. ed., 1995.

17. Note that both technologies have been experiencing significant decreases in cost, but if transmission costs decrease more rapidly than switching costs, system designers will substitute transmission for switching at the margin. See Huber, P. Kellogg, M. and Thorne, J. *The Geodesic Network II: 1993 Report on Competition in the Telephone Industry*, The Geodesic Company, 1992, p 3.37, and DeSurvire, E. "Lightwave Communications: The Fifth Generation," *Scientific American*, January 1992.

18. See Hartman, R., D. Teece, W. Mitchell and T. Jorde, "Assess Market Power in Regimes of Rapid Technological Change," *Industrial and Corporate Change*, 2, 317-350, 1993, for a discussion of the impacts of competition on a variety of features in addition to price.

19. TCI, in 1992, became the largest single buyer of fiber in the world, based on mileage. (Telephony, May 11, 1992, v.222(19), p. 6.) Time Warner already offers local connections to long-distance carriers in Indianapolis and Kansas City. Wall Street Journal, "Time Warner, Baby Bell May Compete in San Diego," June 24, 1993, p. B7.

20. The headend is the originating point of a signal in cable TV systems.

21. Time Warner/US West presentation to the Ameritech Region Regulatory Council Customers First Ad Hoc Committee (a group of state regulators from the Ameritech region who are jointly reviewing Ameritech's Customers First Plan)

22. Time Warner's success in England comes without the benefit of the unbundling and switch integration proposed in Ameritech's Plan. As a result, the exclusionary practices opponents suggest Ameritech might engage in are distinct possibilities in England and yet have not served to prevent competition.

23. Time Warner is also seeking regulatory approval to offer telecommunications services in San Diego. The services, which are scheduled to begin in 1995, would compete directly with Pacific Bell for business customers. The company has said it will build a fiber-optic network to connect the local businesses to long-distance carriers and to link offices of companies in the area. Time Warner will also offer video conferencing and data transport. (Wall Street Journal, "Time Warner, Baby Bell May Compete in San Diego," June 24, 1993, p. B7.).

24. San Francisco Chronicle, November 23, 1993, p. B1.

25. Comcast is not only the third largest cable company, they are also the fifth largest independent cellular telephone provider, giving them a significant presence as a local service provider.

26. New York Times, September 8, 1993, p. C13.

27. Cable and Wireless, Report and Accounts 1993, p. 12.

28. The New York Times, August 25, 1993, pp. C1, C2.

29. Goldman Sachs, analyzing the recent AT&T/McCaw deal, wrote that the "relationship opens up a major opportunity for McCaw to provide bypass services for AT&T,..." (Goldman Sachs Investment Research, The McCaw/AT&T Alliance, November 24, 1992, p. 1.).

30. See Goldman Sachs Investment Research, The McCaw/AT&T Alliance, November 24, 1992, p. 14, for an example of such a strategy.

31. See the discussion of Telular Inc.'s "magic box." Keller, John J., "A 'Magic Box' Turns Wired Into Wireless," Wall Street Journal, October 4, 1993, p. B1.

32. For example, one of the largest CAPs, Teleport, is owned by some of the largest cable companies including TCI.

33. See Porter, Michael E., "Competition in the Long Distance Telecommunications Market," p. 9, Appendix A to "Motion for Reclassification of American Telephone and Telegraph as a Nondominant Carrier." In the Matter of Policy and Rules Concerning Rates for Competitive Common Carrier Services and Facilities Authorization Therefor, CC Docket No. 79-252. He discusses the entry of WilTel and others into interLATA service by employing a niche strategy in combination with resale to expand service to the entire marketplace.

34. Indeed, Sprint already provides local wireline service. In 1991, the company had local service revenue of $2.3 billion for the nation, $478 million in the Ameritech region alone. (Table 29, FCC Preliminary Statistics of Communications Common Carriers, 1991.) AT&T, despite its protestations to the contrary, will also enter the local service business with its imminent acquisition of McCaw Cellular.

35. For example, Bob Stanzione, AT&T Vice President of transmission systems, recently acknowledged that for AT&T to compete in the delivery of multimedia communications services, the company will "have to have alliances of some sort with the companies that provide the last-mile access to the home." San Francisco Chronicle, June 7, 1993, p. E7. These actions diminish the credibility of AT&T's public pronouncements that its acquisition of McCaw does not make it a local phone company.
   In an interview with Forbes, AT&T's vertical integration was touted by Arno Penzias, vice-president of research at AT&T's Bell Laboratories, as being "a far greater asset than it's ever been in the past." The article went on to say that "the ability to merge all the elements" - wireless, voice, data and video - is "what makes [a] network valuable" in today's marketplace. Forbes, February 1, 1993, p. 67. See also AT&T 1993 Annual Report.

36. MCI has purchased a significant amount of right of way from Western Union. Telecommunications Alert, "MCI Could Use Western Union Right-of-Ways as Bypass," May 11, 1992, V.09, No.91.

37. According to an MCI expert economist, Kenneth Baseman, "the marginal activation costs and marginal operating costs for new circuits activated on facilities already in place are generally quite low and do not differ significantly depending on whether the IXC is collocated or the IXC's POP is several miles away." Affidavit of Kenneth Baseman in Federal Communications Commission, *Report and Order and Further Notice of Proposed Rulemaking in CC Docket 91-141, 92-222,* 2 FCC Rcd 7369, October 1992.

38. "Long Distance - A Healthy Industry Ready To Conquer New Territory", Bernstein Research: New York, May 1993, p. 10.

39. IntraLATA margins are also quite high for this customer class. The average revenue per line, at $60-80 (which can be computed from Ameritech's access revenues by customer class), is far above the overall per line average of $45-50.

40. Wall Street Journal, "Business Brief -- MFS Communications Co.: Unit Tries to Win Customers from New York Telephone," October 6, 1993, p. A4. MFS has also filed a petition in Illinois to provide dialtone service.

41. Id.

42. Wall Street Journal, "Business Brief -- MFS Communications Co.: Unit Tries to Win Customers from New York Telephone," October 6, 1993, p. A4.

43. Goldman Sachs, *Communicopia: A Digital Communication Bounty*, July, 1992, p. 20.

44. Id. at 21.

45. The provision of a bundle of services may create entry barriers when combined with network externalities. However, the implementation of interconnection and the unbundling plan means that the possible competitive problems from the provision of a bundle of services will not constitute arise since all competitors can realize the same network externalities.

46. Limitations on pipeline space and use of storage meant that sellers of natural gas could not offer service fully comparable to pipeline sales service; especially in winter months when demands typically peak. Potential competitors were therefore precluded from offering winter service. Limited delivery and withdrawal flexibility prevented sellers from reaching all the customers they would have liked and similarly limited customers from purchasing natural gas from as full a range of sellers as possible. For example, distribution customers typically have highly variable delivery needs even over limited geographical areas as weather and operational conditions on their systems vary.

47. Federal Communications Commission, Bypass of the Public Switched Network, 3d Report and Order, rel'd May 26, 1987, at 32. Note that any attempt to evaluate the state of local competition with references to shares based upon the customer base are entirely misleading and inapt. What is directly relevant is the share of revenues and, more importantly, profits that are exposed to competitive pressures.

48. Even MFS has set it sights on becoming a full service provider. In its recent prospectus, MFS states that "Through MFS Intelenet, the Company will offer a single source for telecommunications services to small and medium sized business." (Prospectus of MFS Communications Company, Inc., May 19, 1993, p. 18.)

49. Federal Communications Commission *Report and Order and Further Notice of Proposed Rulemaking in CC Docket 91-141, 92-222,* 2 FCC Rcd 7369, October 1992.

50. For example, Sprint, in 1987, began a $3 billion fiber deployment program.

51. "Long Distance - A Healthy Industry Ready To Conquer New Territory", Bernstein Research, p. 14.

52. See DOJ Merger Guidelines, sections 1.3 and 3.0, Department of Justice, *1992 Department of Justice -- Federal Trade Commission Horizontal Merger Guidelines,* 4 Trade Reg. Report (CCH), 1992.

53. DOJ Merger Guidelines, section 1.3. Department of Justice, *1992 Department of Justice -- Federal Trade Commission Horizontal Merger Guidelines,* 4 Trade Reg. Report (CCH), 1992.

54. See Baumol, Panzar and Willig (1982) Contestable Markets and the Theory of Industry Structure.

55. Note that the 3% per year productivity increase is a combination of both long distance and local telephone service.

56. Teece, "Technological Change and the Nature of the Firm," in G. Dosi, C. Freeman, R. Nelson, G. Silverberg, and L.Soete (eds.) *Technical Change and Economic Theory,* Pinter: London, 1988, p. 256-281.

57. Hartman et al, 1993.

[26]

Competition in Local Telecommunications: Implications of Unbundling for Antitrust Policy

Robert G. Harris
University of California, Berkeley

Gregory L. Rosston
Federal Communications Commission

David J. Teece
University of California, Berkeley

In the past two decades, competition has increased substantially in telecommunications equipment and interexchange services, through a combination of technological advances and changes in public policies. Innovations in microwave communications, for example, combined with the allocation of radio frequency spectrum (the "above 890" decision by the FCC), enabled Microwave Communications, Inc.—now MCI—to enter into interexchange services. More recently, technological innovations in fiber optics have stimulated additional entry into interexchange services. That process has been long and drawn out, in part because a sea change in public policy was required, from a belief that "the system is the solution" to the view that competition is the best method of providing quality services at lower prices. The waves of change—"gales of creative destruction," Schumpeter would say—are now hitting the beaches of local telecommunications, first through *targeted* competition from competitive access providers (CAPs), then through *ubiquitous* competition from cable systems and mobile communications.

Technological change is increasing the range of services that can be economically provided by each mode of communications, thereby increasing the potential for intermodal competition in communications. During this decade, intermodal competition will greatly intensify in communications, just as it has in transportation (e.g., railroads, motor carriers, waterways, pipelines, and air freight). Intermodal competition will emerge from

- Gas and electric utilities deploying optical fiber and wireless technologies to exploit their extensive rights of way, which reach virtually every home and office.
- Cable systems operators deploying new digital technologies to significantly increase the capacity of cable systems, and enable two-way communications over those systems.
- Cellular personal communications services (PCS) carriers deploying digital technologies that will dramatically increase capacity, reduce costs and prices so that cellular service competes directly with wireline.
- Satellite-based communications services, including VSAT, DBS (direct broadcast satellite) and LEOs (low earth-orbiting satellites), expanding rapidly with digital technology.

Combinations of communications modes through strategic alliances, cross-ownership, and intermodal mergers will further facilitate competitive entry and intermodal competition. In addition to the growing size and increasing resources of competitors, most competitors have undertaken a variety of acquisitions, mergers, joint ventures, and strategic alliances to further strengthen their competitive capabilities.

The revolution in telecommunications, though, is not just a story of escalating competition, it is also a story of complementarity and cooperation. Even as intramodal and intermodal competition increase, most communications will span networks, the interconnection and interoperability of which are absolutely essential. In this chapter, we address the emergence and acceleration of competition and complementarity in local access and exchange services, the unbundling and interconnection of competitive networks, and the implications of these developments for antitrust policy in telecommunications. As reviewed in the next section, the deployment of fiber optics in local telecommunications networks by CAPs has begun to break through the market dominance of LECs, by targeting areas with high concentrations of intense users of local telecommunications services. The CAPs are growing at markedly faster rates now than did MCI at a comparable stage in its development, owing in part to the radical character of the technological innovations in the use of fiber optics in the local loop, as well as regulatory changes that have lowered entry barriers.

Yet, the "gales of creative destruction" have just begun to blow in local telecommunications. In the next few years, through the widespread deployment of fiber optics and interactive communications capabilities by cable system operators, the potential for wireline competition in local telecommunications services will explode. As discussed later, this process is well underway, and is likely to accelerate markedly within the next few years. As it does, local exchange companies (LECs) will face ubiquitous competition for local access and exchange services. Conversely, LECs will be upgrading their networks to provide broadband services to end users, which means that customers will have at least two wireline options for both video and telephone services.

In a later section, we discuss the impacts of current and pending changes in wireless technologies for competition in local telecommunications services. With the advent of digital wireless systems and a multiple increase in the allocation of spectrum for mobile communications, true head-to-head competition between wireline and wireless services will develop over the next 5 to 10 years. Whereas the prices of cellular service remains well above local wireline service, radical innovations and heightened competition in wireless communications will surely drive prices way below current levels, with substantial increases in capacity and substantial improvements in service quality.

It is evident from these technological and competitive developments that communications will be provided over an increasingly complex array of networks offering competing and complementary services. In many cases, one network will both provide inputs to, and compete with, another network. Cable companies and LECs, for example, will both sell transport services to PCS providers, as well as compete with them in the provision of local telecommunications services to end users. In another section, we describe and discuss the Ameritech proposal for unbundling and interconnecting their network in exchange for relief from the Modification of Final Judgment (MFJ) interLATA (Local Access and Transport Area) restriction.[1] It is our view that the adoption of appropriate unbundling and interconnection rules will facilitate the advance of competition and promote economic efficiency in local telecommunications services. Finally, we consider the implications of these developments and the Ameritech plan for antitrust policy in telecommunications, specifically, the MFJ interLATA restriction.

TARGETED COMPETITION FROM COMPETITIVE ACCESS PROVIDERS

The demand for local telecommunications services is highly concentrated: A small percentage of customers, lines, and geographic areas account for a very large share of the revenues in most service categories because the intensity of access and usage varies dramatically across customers and space. In addition, the density of customers varies dramatically across space; that is, the most intensive customers tend to be highly concentrated geographically. Because demand has also become very highly concentrated, entrants with geographically limited networks can reach a very substantial share of access revenues. Business customers located in just 1% of the total land area served by LECs in 10 large states constitute 30% of total LEC revenues; 75% of total revenues are located in just 8% of the land area. It should also be noted that, because user demands are so highly con-

---

1. Professor Teece has testified in support of the Ameritech plan to the U.S. Department of Justice and the Federal Communications Commission. Dr. Rosston assisted Dr. Teece in the preparation of his testimony as a Senior Economist at the Law & Economics Consulting Group. Professor Harris has testified in support of the plan to the Illinois Commerce Commission.

centrated in telecommunications services, one of the most important forms of competition is "self-supply" or "contract carriage" by large, intensive users.[2]

A substantial portion of LEC revenue is derived from business customers.[3] LECs derived approximately 41% of their local revenues from commercial customers in 1993. Business customer growth is expected to be 80% greater than residential customer growth over the next 5 years.[4] Thus, business customers are an important part of the telephony market, and will become even more so in the future. Because basic residential service is not as profitable to LECs as other services, it is likely that business customers represent the principal source of profits to LECs.

Because revenues are highly concentrated in local telecommunications services, these markets are easily segmentable and targetable. A new entrant does not need to serve all geographic or customer segments to compete effectively in one or a few segments. Instead, the rational entrant will target its initial entry at the small share of the customers who account for a large share of revenues. Moreover, although LECs have been allowed to deaverage their prices to a small degree, there are still customers with very different costs of service who pay the same prices. Hence, profitability is even more highly concentrated than revenues, because the highest volume customers and those in the most densely populated areas are also, typically, the lowest cost customers. Whereas an LEC has an obligation to serve all customers, entrants and competitors can and do target their investments, facilities, operations, and marketing efforts at those segments with the highest expected returns.

By successfully targeting the most profitable geographic areas and customers, CAPs are growing at extraordinary rates. CAPs are currently operating networks in 222 cities and have announced plans to enter 41 more. CAPs have begun to install switches and thus can provide switched as well as special access services and have formed alliances with cable companies and interexchange carriers (IXCs) to help extend the reach of their networks. MFS has switching capabilities in New York City and has authorization to provide switched services in Chicago and Baltimore;[5] Teleport also provides switched services in New York City, Boston, Chicago, and San Francisco.[6]

---

2. Although there is nothing inherently wrong with the rapid growth in private networks, there is reason to believe that at least in some cases, they are stimulated by regulations that require uneconomic pricing and/or inhibit the offering of new services by the LEC. In those cases, self-supply through private networks is contrary to economic efficiency and other public policy objectives.

3. Network access revenues account for nearly 25% of LEC revenues and other services (e.g., directory advertising and equipment sales) account for an additional 22% of revenues. Long-distance service, such as intraLATA toll calling, comprises an additional 12% of revenues. Thus, nearly 59% of LEC revenues come from sources other than local service.

4. INSIGHT Research Corporation.

5. See "MFS Intelenet Launches Full Service Phone Company Providing Both Local and Long Distance Services," MFS Communications Company News Release, October 5, 1993.

6. "Teleport Communications Prepares for Local Service Offensive," *Local Competition Report*, October 4, 1993.

Once a CAP has built its core fiber ring in a metropolitan area, the incremental cost of serving additional customers is quite low, relative to the potential gain in revenue. Having established strong footholds in downtown urban areas, one should expect continuing rapid growth by CAPs, as they sign up more customers and expand their networks over larger geographic areas. Because CAPs target their entry selectively to high-volume, high-density business customers (or smaller customers located in the same or adjacent buildings), they can exploit LECs' price averaging requirements. Because CAPs choose not to serve high-cost areas, they have a distinct cost advantage over LECs. CAPs can exploit these advantages of asymmetric regulation as they expand into switched access and exchange services as well. CAPs have expanded beyond central business districts in major metropolitan areas: Linkatel from Los Angeles to Anaheim and Santa Monica; Intelcom Group from Denver to Boulder and Colorado Springs; Tampa Electric Company from Tampa to Sarasota. The ability to serve customers in a concentrated geographic area allows the CAPs to maintain relatively low start-up costs. CAPs can establish a fiber ring in a downtown area for a relatively small investment, as low as $1 million in certain cases.[7]

The targeting strategy has enabled CAPs to grow rapidly. CAP networks, as measured by route miles, multiplied by 24 times between 1987 and 1992. CAP investment in local loop networks is now well in excess of $1 billion.[8] CAP revenues increased by 43% between 1992 and 1993. The annual route growth rate for MFS and Teleport, two of the largest CAPs, equalled 65.9% and 94.3%, respectively, between 1987 and 1992. In the past 3 years, MFS has grown at the phenomenal rate of 919%, from $10 million to $140 million in revenues, indicating that the company is competitive and that the environment for competition is hospitable to the new entrant. For that reason, some sources expect CAP revenue to more than triple between 1993 and 1996.[9] Perhaps the strongest evidence of the rapid growth prospects of CAPs is their extraordinary market valuations. MFS ranked second in *BusinessWeek*'s market value ranking of firms with under $150 million in sales with a 1993 value of $1.9 billion on sales of $141 million.[10]

In a study commissioned by the Regional Bell Operating Companies (RBOCs), Quality Strategies analyzed LEC high-capacity service (special access and intra-LATA point-to-point services for DS0, DS1, DS3, etc.) in 10 metropolitan areas in which CAPs were operating. Based on 4,500 customers, they found that CAPs have captured approximately 30% of high-capacity transport services. A recent study conducted for Pacific Telesis found that CAPs have captured 36% and 32% of revenue for high-capacity transport services from point (customer or POP) to point in downtown Los Angeles and San Francisco, respectively. In response to

---

7. Peter Huber, *The Geodesic Network: Report on Competition in the Telephone Industry*, 1992, p. 2.69.

8. *A CAP Market Update*, The Yankee Group, July 1993, p. ii.

9. *Ibid.*

10. "The Business Week 1000," *Business Week*, March 28, 1994, p. 69.

these CAP inroads, LECs have substantially reduced their special access rates; since 1991, for example, Illinois Bell's price for DS1 service has fallen by 39%.

CAPs have been sufficiently successful to attract the IXCs into local telecommunications services. MCI, for example, has announced plans to spend $20 billion developing "network MCI," a national network providing local and long-distance telephony services. Included in these plans is "MCI Metro"—a $2 billion plan to build local networks in 20 major cities. Through its purchase of Western Union conduits, MCI already has rights of way to build networks in these cities.

We do not mean to suggest, by concentrating this discussion on CAPs and IXCs, that there are not other significant competitors in local telecommunications. Gas and electric utilities, for example, have rights of way to almost every residential and business customer within their service area, and have begun to install and utilize broadband networks to provide local telecommunications services to themselves and others. For example:

- Entergy Corp., whose subsidiaries serve 1.9 million customers in Arkansas, Mississippi, Texas, and Louisiana, is testing an energy management technology called "PowerView." In addition to its "intelligent utility" capability, the technology enables the utility to support cable TV service and telephone services.[11]

- The Electric Plant Board of Glasgow, Kentucky has installed a coax-based broadband network from which spare capacity is being used for cable television, wide-area public data networking, local telephony, and long-distance access.

- A subsidiary of Citizens Utilities Company, ELI, has filed with the Washington State Utilities and Transportation Commission to offer intrastate interexchange and exchange switched services. ELI currently owns and operates networks in Seattle and Portland and is constructing networks in Phoenix, Salt Lake, and Sacramento.

EMERGING COMPETITION FROM CABLE SYSTEMS

Cable companies have an existing wire-based network that passes 90% of all homes and businesses in the United States.[12] Increasingly, the backbone distribution network of cable companies is fiber-based and thus capable of handling two-way communications. In fact, cable operators' use of fiber optics has increased 600% since 1988.[13] Thus, cable companies either possess or are installing the

---

11. "Utilities Emerging Role in Local Telecom Markets," *Telco Competition Report Special Report*, February 17, 1994, p. 15.

12. Paul Kagan Associates, *Cable TV Financial Databook*, 1992. About 60% of all homes actually subscribe to cable TV.

13. Cable companies in 1993 planned to install approximately 465,000 miles of new optical fiber cabling in their networks, for a cumulative installed total to data of about 28 yards of fiber per subscriber. Equivalently, telephone companies planned to install about 1.8 million miles of additional fiber in 1993, for a cumulative total of roughly 111 yards per subscriber (*Lightwave*, August 1993).

physical plant required to provide telephony services. In addition, the fiber optic cable used in their backbone loops for the provision of video services generally has unused capacity, which greatly reduces the cost of offering telephony services. Cable networks are already used for the backhaul of voice and data transmissions for cellular providers and CAPs. For example, AirTouch-Detroit has replaced some RBOC-provided local loop circuits with leased cable TV fiber to connect to IXCs' facilities and uses fiber in combination with microwave for its network.[14] In Kansas City, FiberNet, a cable venture begun in 1988, provides data and voice services to interexchange carriers, several airline reservation subsidiaries, and financial brokerage houses and other large firms.[15]

Moreover, cable companies are beginning to provide telephony services to end users directly over their cable networks. Time Warner is upgrading its facilities to offer telephony services in Rochester. Cablevision (in conjunction with AT&T) won a competitive bid over NYNEX to provide local telephone and cable services to Long Island University's C. W. Post campuses. Cablevision continues to build a fiber optic based network on Long Island and in New York City with the capability of offering video on demand, interactive games, and an alternative phone service to subscribers.[16] In addition, Cablevision has constructed on Long Island the fiber backbone of a high-speed communications network linking Stony Brook University and Brookhaven National Laboratory, termed FISHNet, using an ATM technology that allows voice, video, and data images to be processed together.[17]

Cable companies have also formed alliances with other telecommunications companies. MCI recently announced a joint trial with Jones Intercable to test phone service over the Jones cable network in Alexandria, Virginia. In June 1993, Teleport Communications Group (TCG) announced that it had signed letters of intent to establish joint ventures with 11 major cable operators to build new fiber networks and expand existing TCG networks (using some cable capacity for both projects).[18] In February 1993, Southwestern Bell purchased Hauser Cable in Montgomery County, Maryland, and has announced plans to offer telephone service to compete directly with Bell Atlantic. In May 1993, US West bought a 25% stake in Time Warner for $2.5 billion and BellSouth acquired 22.5% of Prime Management, which operates Prime Cable.[19] Bell Canada has purchased Jones Intercable. These "intermodal" alliances provide cable companies with significant financial backing and the technological know-how concerning the provision of two-way telephony and will thereby accelerate entry by cable companies into telecommunications.

A recent study has estimated that the costs of upgrading existing cable plant to provide telephony services (assuming the cable company has already upgraded its

14. Peter W. Huber, *The Enduring Myth of the Local Bottleneck*, March 14, 1994, p. 39.

15. Fred Dawson, "In Teleport's Shadow," *Cablevision*, September 21, 1992, p. 31.

16. Joshua Quittner, "Cable's Vision," *Newsday*, February 25, 1993, pp. 3, 18.

17. See "Cablevision Seeks to Catch Big Fish in its High-Speed Long Island Net," *Communications Engineering and Design*, April 1994, p. 8, and "Information Superhighway Adds Lane," *Currents*, April 1994, p. 1.

18. 1993 Connecticut Research, VII-80.

19. Huber (1994), p. 26.

backbone transmission plant to fiber optics) would be about $207 per subscriber. If both telephone and distributed video services were provided, the cost per subscriber would only increase to $297 due to significant economies of scope in the provision of telephony and distributed video services. The analysis further demonstrates that upgrades to existing plant represent a large cost advantage to deployment of new networks and that there may be economies of scope between distributed video services and PCS. The author concludes "this outcome increases the value of the incumbent cable television network."[20] Similar conclusions have been reached by a leading investment analyst:

> The reason for the enormity of the financial implications of this technological change is that . . . *the cost of adding telephony to a cable system is far less than the cost of the existing telephone plant* (italics in original). The cost of upgrading a cable system by adding fiber trunks is less than $150 per subscriber. The cost is so low that the reduction in maintenance expenditures alone is adequate to more than pay for the upgrade, so effectively the cost is zero. The cost of adding telephony to an upgraded cable system is less than $400 per subscriber, and it is only incurred for the subscribers who purchase the new service.[21]

The cable industry is well aware of the enormous opportunities ahead. In July 1994, Cable Television Laboratories issued a "Request for Proposals for a Telecommunications Delivery System over a Hybrid Fiber/Coax (HFC) Architecture." The purpose of the RFP is to "expedite the design, test, production and phased implementation of practical, cost-effective approaches to telecommunications services over the evolving cable infrastructure."[22] It also announces that TCI, Comcast, Continental Cablevision, Cox Cable, Time Warner and Viacom—the majority owners of CableLabs, "intend to individually purchase equipment under this RFP."

The transformation of cable systems to interactive, broadband networks capable of offering a wide range of telecommunications and video services means that, within a decade or so, the millions of miles of LECs' existing copper-twisted pair cables will be thoroughly obsolete. As noted by Philip Sirlin:

> The telecommunications industry is about to undergo a technology-driven earthquake of enormous magnitude . . . The financial epicenter of this metamorphosis will be in the . . . local loop [because] copper twisted pair is a very high cost, low functionality, archaic technology . . . The new

---

20. See David P. Reed, *The Prospects for Competition in the Subscriber Loop: The Fiber-to-Neighborhood Approach,* presented at Twenty-First Annual Telecommunications Research Policy Conference, September 1993.

21. Philip J. Sirlin, *The Digital Battlefield: Bellopoly—The End of the Game,* Investment Report by Wertheim Schroder & Co., March 22, 1994, p. 13.

22. Cable Television Laboratories, "Request for Proposals for a Telecommunications Delivery System over a Hybrid Fiber/Coax (HFC) Architecture," Boulder, Colorado, p. 6.

technologies—high capacity fiber circuits to large businesses, wireless (new cellular, SMR, and PCS) systems and telephony and video on fiber/coaxial cable systems—have lower costs and higher functionality than the existing copper twisted pair local loop . . . New entrants who can deploy the new technologies and gain market share will be very successful.[23]

As suggested by Sirlin, there is a strong affinity between CAPs and cable companies, both in terms of ownership structure and network deployment. Several of the leading CAPs are owned by cable companies; others have formed alliances with them, including the following:

- Cox, TCI, Continental, Comcast, Time Warner Cable, and Teleport: Cox and TCI acquired TCG, the largest CAP, and sold minority stakes to the two other multiple system operators (MSOs) in 1993. Cox owns a 25.05% stake, followed by TCI with 24.95%, and Time Warner, Comcast, and Continental with 16.67% each.

- TCI, ATC, and TeleCable: The MSOs have participated in a joint venture known as FiberNet since 1989 in and around Kansas City, MO. TCI, American Television and Communications (ATC), and TeleCable jointly own the all-fiber network, covering close to 200 route miles on both sides of the Missouri River. The network now serves upwards of eight interexchange carriers, several airline reservation subsidiaries, financial brokerage houses, and other large firms requiring diverse paths to carry their traffic.[24]

- Monmouth Cablevision, Adelphia Cable, and Comcast Cable Communications: The three cable operators in Central New Jersey began setting up an inexpensive fiber interconnect in 1993 through a joint venture that will open new business opportunities for them such as alternative access to long-distance services. Each company expects its cost for the interconnect to be less than $50,000.[25]

- Continental Cable and Hyperion: The MSO and the telecommunications subsidiary of Adelphia agreed to set up a metropolitan area network through a joint venture in Jacksonville, FL. The network will utilize Continental's existing fiber backbone and will require some construction of a series of fiber rings and fiber hookups to the premises of potential users. Between 30 and 40 large business users have been identified as likely connection points for the operation.[26]

- Continental Cable and Teleport: The MSO and CAP began building loops around greater Boston and in the Wilshire corridor of Los Angeles through a joint venture since 1992. TCG has been able to extend its business beyond the city limits via fiber routes available over Continental's suburban sys-

23. Sirlin, op. cit., p. 5.
24. "In Teleportís Shadow," *Cablevision*, September 21, 1992.
25. "RBOCs? Who Needs RBOCs?" *Cablevision*, December 6, 1993.
26. "In Teleport's Shadow," *Cablevision*, September 21, 1992, p. 31.

tems, allowing the MSO to enter the business without devoting a tremendous amount of startup effort.[27]

- Comcast and Eastern Telelogic: Comcast agreed to acquire a 51% stake in the CAP in July 1992 and subsequently expanded the CAP's operations in Philadelphia.[28]

The rate at which these deals are being struck indicates both the strong complementarity between CAP and cable networks and the mutuality of their business interests in competing with LECs. Not surprisingly, CAPs are, in many cities, laying fiber to connect the head-ends of cable systems and, therefore, connecting cable customers to the CAPs switches. These extended networks will be able to provide wireline services to end users, and transport services to interconnect wireless cell-sites and switching centers, both in competition with LECs.

EMERGING COMPETITION FROM WIRELESS

Wireless telecommunications providers already have infrastructure in place that allows them to provide telephone service to more than 90% of the population. With the introduction of satellite service, coverage will be ubiquitous and coverage will be available from a number of different providers. The two major questions about whether wireless can provide a real competitive alternative to wireline telephone service focus on price and capacity: Will costs be low enough so that competitive prices will entice enough customers to demand wireless service in place of wired service and will there be sufficient capacity to meet demand at those prices to force competitive pricing for the wireline alternatives?

Although wireless communications has been used for a relatively long time, there are two significant changes that will impact the nature of wireless communications.[29] Capacity increases of more than an order of magnitude resulting from continuing improvements in technology and new allocations of spectrum will yield enough capacity so that wireless can be more of a threat to wireline telephone service. In addition, regulatory flexibility will allow wireless service providers to use this capacity to serve an increasing variety of different consumer needs. The confluence of these technical and regulatory changes will have significant impacts on competition within and between wireless and wireline communications. This section examines the technological changes that are transforming wireless communications into a rapidly growing, high-quality service; the regulatory changes that have accompanied and complemented the changing technology to prompt the growth and competitiveness of wireless services; and the effects of these two forces on competition for local telecommunications services.

Wireless communications already plays a significant role in telecommunications. The success of wireless is much greater than was anticipated 10 years ago

---

27. *Ibid.*

28. *Ibid.*

29. Historically, wireless communications preceded wireline: The original telegraph system in France was a wireless system. See Noam (1993).

when the first cellular systems were licensed. At that point in time, analysts projected that mobile telephony would only serve a limited market and that there would be about 100,000 cellular subscribers by the year 2000.[30] The number of cellular subscribers has grown almost eightfold over the past 5 years;[31] there are currently more than 19 million cellular subscribers. In the last 6 months, more than 100,000 net new subscribers were added each week.[32] Cellular revenue in 1993 was almost six times as great as its level 5 years ago, totaling over $6 billion. Cellular traffic is increasing significantly as a result of the new subscribers, even though the average minutes of use per subscriber is decreasing. To meet the demand, cellular service providers have significantly increased system capacity through the installation of additional cells and the implementation of digital signaling. Existing analog cellular systems have added or "split" cells to substantially increase capacity. System operators employ small radius cells where there is significant demand so they can reuse frequencies more in these areas. Because each cell has historically cost approximately $1 million for the capital investment, cell splitting is only undertaken in areas where the traffic justifies the added expense. In areas where demand is relatively low, cells cover wide areas. Adding cells to current systems can increase capacity until the minimum size cell is reached. Because of the propagation characteristics of spectrum, there appears to be a limit to decreasing cell size and the additional costs of increasing the number of cells is causing systems to switch to higher capacity digital systems. To determine the ability of a cellular system to provide a significant competitive alternative to landline service, it is possible to determine the fraction of minutes of use accounted for currently by cellular systems and then determine the increase in capacity available from additional spectrum and digital signaling to estimate a minimum capacity available over cellular. This estimate is likely to provide a significant lower bound because there are many areas of the county where cell splitting has not even begun to approach the limit using current technology. In fact, some cellular systems have such low demand that they have not even used the additional 5 MHz of spectrum they were allocated in 1986.

It is possible to determine the current share of minutes of use from cellular systems by using data available on the number of "lines" and the average minutes of use for both cellular and wireline service. The ratio of cellular service to the total population is over 7% compared to about 56% for landline service. The average minutes of use for a cellular phone is about 70 minutes per month compared to more than 1,600 for the average landline phone.[33] Using these figures, it is

---

30. Huber (1992), op. cit., p. 4.22.

31. Cellular telephony's astounding growth is expected to continue. Link Resources Corp. estimates that the annual growth rate for cellular voice services through the year 1998 will be 20.2% and that the corresponding rate for cellular data services will be approximately 33.0%. *Wall Street Journal*, February 11, 1994, p. R5.

32. Cellular Telecommunications Industry Association, July 1994.

33. FCC Statistics of Common Carriers, July 1994, and Cellular Telecommunications Industry Association data. Calculation assumes $35 per month average service charge and $0.35 per minute average usage charge.

straightforward to calculate that cellular minutes of use account for approximately 0.5% of total minutes of telephone use. The cumulative capital investment in the cellular industry is now almost $14 billion, implying that the cellular infrastructure is becoming increasingly well positioned to compete against wired telephony.

The "new" wireless services can be both complementary to and competitive with existing communications services. The ability to provide high-quality voice and data services with wireless technology derives directly from advances in electronics that provide the backbone for the networks. Early wireless communication usually emanated from a high-power tower to multiple mobile units. The quality and privacy were very low. Advances in signal processing and microelectronics led directly to the development of higher quality cellularlike systems by making it possible for a mobile switching office to track thousands of mobile units, manage the allocation of spectrum and hand-offs, and perform normal telephone end office switching functions. In addition, the advances in circuitry and miniaturization combined with economies of scale in manufacturing have led to the decline in mobile telephone prices from $2,500 in 1984 at the initiation of cellular service to around $200 now.[34] The advances have increased the quality of service, and the capacity of service and have reduced the cost of the consumer and network equipment needed for service.

A number of cellular systems are currently converting to digital technology because they need to further increase their capacity. There appear to be two different "camps" within the cellular community—those who support Time Division Multiple Access (TDMA) and those who support Code Division Multiple Access (CDMA). Some systems are already in the process of converting to digital signaling and using TDMA because it is commercially available. Those who support CDMA must wait for the technology to become commercially available, but they feel that ultimately it will offer higher capacity and quality.[35] Both of the technologies result from advances in signal processing that derive directly from microelectronic advances. Also, digital phones will be able to be smaller, lighter, and use less power than their analog counterparts.

Although the ultimate capacity increase from the digital conversions is unknown, the initial increase from TDMA is expected to triple current capacity. PCS systems are expected to employ digital technology from the outset and smaller cell sizes than cellular so they will also have significant capacity available. A number of Specialized Mobile Radio (SMR) companies are converting their high-powered analog systems to cellular configurations with digital technology, which they estimate will increase their capacity by a factor of 15. Finally, mobile satellite providers expect to be able to offer a variety of different services on a nationwide or even global basis. Over time, digital technology is expected to significantly more than triple the capacity of current analog systems. This magnitude of in-

---

34. "Cellular Market and Profit Opportunities through Year 2000." Herschel Schostek Associates, Ltd, February 1992, Silver Spring, MD.

35. Qualcomm presentation at Telecommunications Policy Research Conference, Solomons, MD, October 1994.

crease will allow cellularlike systems to significantly increase sales, some of which are likely to displace local wireline calls.

There is 50 MHz of spectrum allocated to cellular service. There is also 14 MHz of SMR spectrum in the 800 MHz band that is currently being aggregated by operators so they can form more efficient and higher quality cellular systems. In addition, the FCC has allocated 120 MHz of additional spectrum for broadband personal communications services. The earlier calculation showed that current analog cellular accounts for about 0.5% of minutes of use. The additional 134 MHz of spectrum available for wireless telephony adds to the current 50 MHz of cellular spectrum to more than triple capacity. The introduction of digital technology will triple that increase again so that the effective increase will be approximately a factor of 10. It should be noted that this simple calculation does not take into account the fact that current analog cellular is not near its theoretical capacity, nor does it take into account the ability to implement significantly smaller cells using the 1.8 GHz spectrum associated with PCS. As a result, this capacity increase should be viewed as a significant lower bound. In any event, it shows that wireless systems would easily have the capacity to provide for more than 5% of the minutes of use across the country.

The previous exercise did not account for the fact discussed earlier that traffic is not uniform across the country, but rather is concentrated in specific areas. In 1985, Hatfield undertook a study showing that analog cellular with 20 MHz of spectrum could provide a competitive alternative to landline local loops for a significant portion of the San Francisco Bay area.[36] His study vividly illustrated the point that local loop costs are directly related to loop length, whereas the costs of wireless "loops" are relatively insensitive to loop length and much more sensitive to traffic. As a result, in less densely populated areas where loop lengths tend to be longer, the competitive threat from wireless loops will be stronger. In addition, in these less densely populated areas, the traffic demands on spectrum tend to be lower so that the opportunity costs for spectrum devoted to wireline competition will also be lower.

The FCC recently reclassified a variety of wireless services into a category called Commercial Mobile Radio Services (CMRS). CMRS encompasses a variety of radio services that historically faced different regulatory frameworks and service restrictions. By including all of these and adopting a forward-looking framework for establishing that all of these services should be considered "substantially similar" the FCC has determined that it expects that all of these services will compete with each other either now or in the future. The major components of CMRS include PCS, cellular, SMR, paging, and possibly mobile satellite services.

---

36. "A Comparison of the Costs of Providing Ordinary Telephone Service Using Conventional Wireline and Cellular Radio Technology," Hatfield, D. Ax, G. and Dunmore, K. Boulder, CO, October 1985.

The FCC specifically adopted a flexible definition for PCS.[37] In addition, it has issued a Notice of Proposed Rulemaking to increase flexibility for cellular and SMR providers.[38] These rules and changes will allow service providers greater ability to use their wireless capacity to respond to marketplace demands—whether they be for high quality mobile voice, dispatch, paging, or service more similar to residential fixed service.

Because of the flexible definition of PCS, a large number of companies are pursuing different visions of what PCS will be. To date, 187 companies have obtained experimental PCS licenses. About 10% of those companies are cable companies and cable companies are among the most active in a broad range of cities. For instance, Comcast is conducting trials in five cities, Hauser Communications is testing in five cities, Prime II is testing in six cities, Time Warner is testing in five cities, United Artists Cable is testing in five cities, Viacom is testing in five cities, Cable USA is testing in four cities, and Cablevision is testing in four cities. In addition, CableLabs, a research and development consortium of North American cable companies, is investigating using preexisting broadband cable infrastructure for PCS. Continental Cablevision, Cablevision of Boston, and Time Warner Cable became the first cable TV companies to interconnect their systems to demonstrate how PCS could be offered over cable TV systems in Boston in late 1993. The demonstration allowed the MSOs to overcome their problems with interconnecting with differing systems and offering telecommunications subscribers extended and seamless service by using a combination of technology and cooperation. The companies had to do very little to their basic cable infrastructure to offer wireless services and to bypass the local telephone company.[39]

New wireless PCS competitors are likely to begin service within the next 1 to 2 years. The FCC scheduled broadband auctions to begin on December 5, 1994. The new PCS providers will have to submit high bids at the auctions, go through the FCC licensing process, acquire and construct cell-sites, and, in some cases, negotiate for and effectuate the relocation of incumbent microwave users. In addition, because of the propagation characteristics of the 1.8 GHz PCS spectrum compared with the 800 MHz cellular spectrum, PCS providers will be required to use more cells than their cellular and Enhanced Specialized Mobile Radio (ESMR) counterparts to cover the same area. In addition, early PCS operators may enter into roaming agreements with neighboring cellular providers because PCS systems are not likely to become operational across the country at the same time. Based on these events, it will be from 6 months to 2 years before there is significant service from PCS providers.

These providers will have to compete with existing cellular and ESMR providers who are continuing to build their customer bases. Current cellular providers

---

37. The Commission adopted the following definition for broadband PCS: "Radio communications that encompass mobile and ancillary fixed communication services that provide services to individuals and businesses and can be integrated with a variety of competing networks." FCC Second Report and Order, GEN Docket No. 90-314, para. 24.

38. Notice of Proposed Rulemaking, GN Docket No. 94-90.

39. "CATV networks join to offer PCS," *Telephony*, November 22, 1993, p. 8.

have constructed systems that provide coverage for more than 90% of the U.S. population so that mobile wireless service is available nearly universally. The current belief is that service providers compete on coverage area in addition to price. For example, McCaw heavily advertises its "City of Florida" where customers can travel anywhere in the state and pay home rates and also call anywhere in the state without paying toll charges. PCS systems will start with smaller coverage areas, even though two of the major systems will be licensed on a Major Trading Area (MTA) basis. In fact, as discussed already, the early PCS systems are likely to be forced to negotiate roaming agreements with incumbent cellular providers in order to give their customers equivalent geographic coverage. To take advantage of the expanded coverage area, their customers will be forced to buy dual-mode handsets so they can operate on the different systems. Customers on existing cellular systems will only require a single-mode handset. When PCS is fully deployed, its handsets are expected to be somewhat smaller and lighter and to have a longer battery life because they will transmit with lower power. However, to acquire customers in the interim, PCS providers will either offer a more limited coverage area with a "better" phone or offer equivalent service with a somewhat less desirable phone. As a result, to acquire customers, PCS providers may have to compete with lower prices to compensate for their initial disadvantages.

In addition to targeting customers who do not require roaming, the cost characteristics of PCS favor a less mobile customer base. PCS will be transmitting with lower power and less propagation, which will require a larger number of cells to cover an area than a current cellular system. As a result, the number of hand-offs required for each call will be higher. The less "mobile" the user, the lower the burden will be on the switch and the lower the costs will be. As a result, the target for PCS is likely to be somewhat less mobile than the current cellular customer.

Regulation has made two contributions to the radical change taking place in wireless communications—the allocation of a significant amount of additional spectrum and the flexibility to allow service providers to respond to market forces in determining their product offerings. The increase in spectrum allocation and spectral efficiency have changed the ability of mobile radio service providers to compete with each other and with local wireline service. The technical characteristics are now such that the demand for mobile service may not be sufficiently high to demand all of the wireless spectrum. In addition, the change in capacity may make the costs characteristic of wireless service more applicable to wireline service. To encourage the efficient use of spectrum, the FCC has allowed providers to configure their product offerings to target the highest value use. Such policies are important to the development of competition in areas where it is warranted. By allowing flexible use of spectrum, wireless service providers will be able to target those areas of wireline service where their cost advantages allow them to charge lower prices than current providers. Motorola, for example, has already announced a PCS product designed to compete directly with wireline: "Tele-Density" is a low-power, high-quality, low-mobility handset combined with small, low-power base stations.[40] Alternatively, mobile service providers may charge somewhat higher prices than conventional landline services, but entice consumers away from wireline through increased functionality and more enhanced services.

The combined effects of these changes, technical, regulatory and competitive, lead experts to predict a very substantial role for wireless communications. Mercer Management recently conducted a national survey, analyzed several market and cost possibilities, and interviewed telecommunications industry experts:

> Nearly half of the industry experts that Mercer interviewed projected wireless service would become a "viable substitute" for traditional wireline service within 10 years . . . Half of those experts interviewed predicted more than 15 percent of the public would be using a wireless handset in five years, compared with the current 7 percent. They expect that figure to rise to more than 30 percent in 10 years."[41]

In order to reach anywhere near these predicted market penetration levels, wireless services must compete with—and take share from—traditional wireline providers of local access and exchange services.

UNBUNDLING AND INTERCONNECTING LOCAL TELECOMMUNICATIONS NETWORKS

In the prior sections, we have shown that competiion is developing rapidly in local telecommunications services. In the next few years, there will be a proliferation of communications technologies and networks. To a substantial degree, these networks will compete directly with each other. They will also serve as complements, in the sense that the communications needs of any given customer will be served by a combination of networks and service providers. Note that interconnection and interoperability will be essential, even if every single end user is served by a completely integrated service provider, so that customers served by one integrated provider can interact with customers served by other providers. To accommodate this "network of networks," public policies must promote both competition and cooperation. In this section, we describe and assess one company's proposal for doing so.

The Ameritech plan, as presented to the U.S. Department of Justice, Federal Communications Commission in 1993 and to the Illinois Commerce Commission in 1994,[42] is an effort by one company to address both key policy concerns and business realities.[43] The plan is, in essence, a quid pro quo: Ameritech would take steps to unbundle its local telecommunications services, offer a standard set of in-

---

40. Motorola press release, September 23, 1994.

41. *The New York Times*, February 9, 1994.

42. To be implemented throughout the Ameritech region, state regulatory approval in Indiana, Michigan, Ohio, and Wisconsin would also be required.

43. Rochester Telephone has a somewhat different proposal for unbundling its local network.

Figure 1: Current Status of the Local Exchange

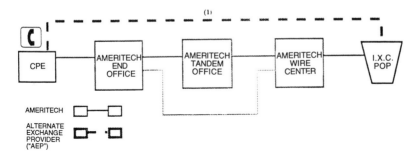

terconnection prices and arrangements, make the necessary network investments to promote further competition, and generally support removal of regulatory restrictions that may inhibit entry. In return, Ameritech seeks removal of the MFJ restriction so that it could offer interLATA services to customers in its region. Under the plan, Ameritech will open its network as follows:

- *Loops:* Offers local loops on an unbundled basis at tariff rates approved by state regulatory agencies; proposes rates above long-run incremental costs, not to exceed fully distributed costs; access to local loops at the main distribution frame or the digital cross-connect frame.

- *Switching:* Offers interconnection to its local switching with loops provided by others, enabling all providers to seamlessly connect to a "network of networks."

Figure 2: Local Exchange with Unbundling

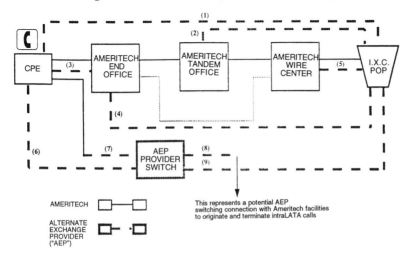

- *Signaling:* Unbundles SS7 call set-up capabilities and permits competitors to access the SS7 signaling network without subscribing to Ameritech's transport or switching service.
- *White Pages listings, 911 service, deaf-relay services:* Offers these network support services to competitors on an optional basis, at wholesale prices.
- *Cooperative engineering:* Offers cooperative engineering, operation, maintenance, and administrative practices.
- *Rights of way:* Will continue to make conduit and pole attachment space available on a non-discriminatory basis to authorized interconnectors where sufficient space permits.
- *Mutual compensation:* Offers mutual compensation arrangements for termination of traffic by state certified alternate exchange providers at reciprocal rates.
- *Numbering plans:* Makes available complete NXX codes to other qualified providers through a third-party administrator.
- *Local telephone number portability:* Provides portability to the fullest extent permitted by current technology and a commitment to support development of more robust options through industry forums.
- *Usage subscription:* Allows others to use Ameritech's loops and local dial tone provision while they carry all outbound traffic on their networks (in essence, intraLATA presubscription); a new entrant can offer alternative service without requiring the customer to change telephone numbers.

Unbundling and switch integration would facilitate entry and interconnection. A simplified graphical representation of the current status of the local exchange is shown in Fig. 4.1. Typically alternate exchange providers such as MFS connect directly to customers with their fiber loop and transport the traffic directly to the IXC point of presence (IXC POP). This is depicted by the bold dashed line labeled (1) that connects customer premise equipment (CPE) directly to the IXC POP. Figure 4.2 shows the potential effects of unbundling, with nine different places where alternative exchange providers can connect to and/or make use of portions of the local exchange network. The lines labeled (2), (4), and (5) show potential connections by competitive access providers to take advantage of traffic aggregation by the LEC and provide transport of the traffic from the end office (4) , tandem office (2), or wire center (5) to the IXC POP. Because of unbundling, the CAP can have its customers' traffic routed over the local exchange network until the point where it has facilities. Line (7) represents a provider who uses a portion of the local exchange provider's local loop and then transports the traffic to its own switch. Under the Ameritech plan, a provider might use the local loop, gather its traffic at the frame of the end office, and transfer the traffic to its own switch. Lines (3) and (6) represent alternative local loops. For example, a cable company may be able to provide a local loop, but wish to use some of the local exchange provider's switching capabilities, leading to a scenario represented by Line (3). A cellular company or cable company connecting to its own switch would be represented by Line (6), which directly connects the customer to the alternative exchange provider's own switch. Lines (8) and (9) represent connections from the

Figure 3: Possible IXC Entry with Unbundling

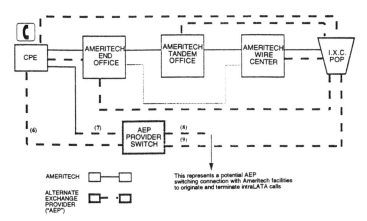

alternative exchange provider's switch to either Ameritech's network or to an interexchange provider.

Ameritech has stated in its filings that it will price its noncompetitive facilities
between incremental and fully distributed cost,[44] although the actual measurement of these costs is likely to be a source of contention.[45] For the implementation
of the Ameritech plan to support economic efficiency, prices for these noncompetitive services must be set so that efficient producers that use noncompetitive services as inputs are encouraged to provide their services and inefficient producers
are similarly discouraged from providing theirs. A "monopoly" provider of an input to a competitive product market can generally use the input itself to provide
downstream products, sell the input to other firms who provide the downstream
products, or both.[46] To ensure that the firm prices the input so that the most efficient firms provide the downstream product, price should be set equal to the average incremental cost plus the opportunity cost of that input.[47] In this way, prices
will not be set below cost, nor will they be set so as to discriminate against competitors. In the presence of scale and scope economies, prices need to be greater

---

44. Supplemental Materials to Ameritech's Petition for Declaratory Ruling and Related Waivers to
Establish a New Regulatory Model for the Ameritech Region, DA 93-481, Attachment 2 of 4, "Ameritech Customers First Expanded Network Interconnection Proposal," pp. 22–24. filed April 16, 1993;
Ameritech's Reply to Comments on its Petition for a Declaratory Ruling and Related Waivers to Establish a New Regulatory Model for the Ameritech Region, DA93-481, pp. 36–39, filed July 12, 1993.

45. Kelley, Daniel, & Mercer, Robert, "A General Approach to Local Exchange Carrier Pricing and
Interconnection Issues," Hatfield Associates, Inc., Working Paper, September 19, 1992, pp. 20–24.

46. Much of this discussion is based on Baumol, William J., & Sidak, J. Gregory, *Toward Competition in Local Telephony.* AEI Studies in Telecommunications Deregulation, Washington, 1994.

47. At this level, the sale will make the appropriate contribution to joint costs without distorting
downstream provision of alternative products.

Figure 4: Possible CAP Entry with Unbundling

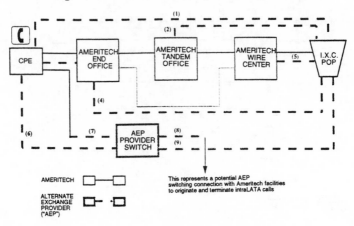

than incremental cost for at least some services in order to pay for the joint and common costs.

In conjunction with providing equal access, the plan has the feature of offering to competitors the scale and scope economies of the Ameritech network. Pricing is based on the long-run incremental costs of operating the Ameritech network. This is especially germane for smaller firms looking to enter specific niche services, as they will be able to compete with Ameritech and other large providers on a more equal footing. Perhaps most importantly, they will avoid the capital outlays and incumbent risks that typically accompany forays into new lines of business. As revenue streams are realized from initial ventures, the cash flow can be used to secure additional customers and offer new services.

Based on current market conditions, there are several classes of competitors positioned to take advantage of the unbundling, switch integration, and usage subscription offered under the plan. These competitors, depending on their specific capabilities, are poised to compete for either the entire market or for distinct subsets of customers. Because each potential competitor has different competitive advantages, the range of customers benefiting from new entry and expanded competition nearly spans the gamut of Ameritech's customer base. In addition, the ability to enter with minimal investment and to act as a reseller gives an entrant complete market presence with little risk.[48]

---

48. See Porter, Michael E., "Competition in the Long Distance Telecommunications Market," p. 9, Appendix A to "Motion for Reclassification of American Telephone and Telegraph as a Nondominant Carrier." In the Matter of Policy and Rules Concerning Rates for Competitive Common Carrier Services and Facilities Authorization Therefor, CC Docket No. 79-252. He discusses the entry of WilTel and others into interLATA service by employing a niche strategy in combination with resale to expand service to the entire marketplace.

Figure 5: Possible Cable Entry with Unbundling

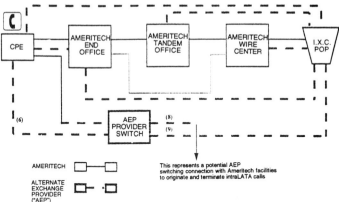

The most likely source of immediate and influential entry into local service will be the IXCs, especially the large, nationwide carriers like AT&T, MCI, and Sprint.[49] All three companies have the ability to self-supply transport, and, once the necessary construction and right-of-way expenses are incurred, the incremental cost to add traffic is quite small.[50] Specifically, once the IXCs have successfully developed the transport segment of their network, they will be able to sign up additional subscribers at little added cost because they can rent loops from Ameritech and transport the traffic to their own switches.[51] Figure 4.3 illustrates the network configuration of possible IXC entry under the plan.

IXCs enjoy their highest margins in the small and mid-size business segment.[52] Consequently, IXCs are likely to pursue these customers first for their provision of end-to-end service.[53] AT&T, as well as other large IXCs, could compete by in-

---

49. Indeed, Sprint already provides local wireline service. In 1991, the company had local service revenue of $2.3 billion for the nation, $478 million in the Ameritech region alone. Table 29, *FCC Preliminary Statistics of Communications Common Carriers*, 1991. AT&T, despite its protestations to the contrary, has also entered the local service business with its acquisition of McCaw Cellular.

50. MCI has purchased a significant amount of right of way from Western Union. *Telecommunications Alert*, May 11, 1992. MCI has also recently filed for state certification as a competitive access provider in Indiana.

51. According to an MCI expert economist, Kenneth Baseman, "the marginal activation costs and marginal operating costs for new circuits activated on facilities already in place are generally quite low and do not differ significantly depending on whether the IXC is collocated or the IXC's POP is several miles away." Affidavit of Baseman to FCC in CC Docket No. 91-141.

52. "Long Distance—A Healthy Industry Ready To Conquer New Territory," *Bernstein Research*, May 1993, p. 10.

53. IntraLATA margins are also quite high for this customer class. The average revenue per line, at $60 to $80 (which can be computed from Ameritech's access revenues by customer class), is far above the overall per line average of $45 to $50.

Figure 6: Possible Wireless Entry with Unbundling

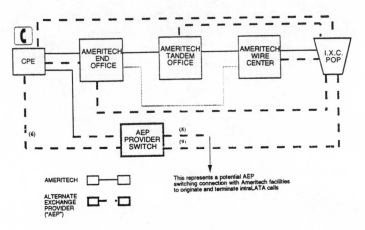

stalling switches (or using excess capacity on its existing switches) to supply dial tone and usage services and routing the traffic to one of their many existing POPs. This could be economical even in an area with a small amount of traffic because the large IXCs could either share capacity on a nearby existing long-distance switch or economically use a somewhat distant switch to provide a local dial tone until traffic justifies a truly local switch. Adding switch capacity is relatively simple with modern modular switches such as the 5ESS. Because the IXCs have fiber facilities in place with excess capacity, the cost of transport to take advantage of a distant "local" switch would be minimal. Moreover, the IXCs have customer-specific demand information that would enable them to target high-margin neighborhoods; they also have strong brandnames.[54] Existing IXC POPs are located within 242 of the 1,183 wire centers in the Ameritech region, thereby providing the IXCs with direct access to 44% of Ameritech's revenue base. The threat of such widespread competition would diminish Ameritech's ability to preserve and subsequently leverage market power. Much of Ameritech's customer base would be exposed to significantly greater competition.

CAPs have entered many major cities by deploying fiber loops through dense downtown areas. These loops give them access to a large number of customers with a relatively high demand for telephone service. With the switch integration portion of the Ameritech plan, CAPs with switches can easily become the local phone service provider to those businesses passed by their network. In addition, the ability to rent loops means that they can provide service, with little incremental investment, to any business or residence that is served by the end offices they pass with their loops. CAPs can also expand their geographic coverage sequentially

---

54. As a share of revenues, AT&T, MCI, and Sprint spend roughly three times as much on advertising as the average RBOC—15% versus 5%.

and determine the optimal path for their new fiber loops by leasing capacity in the short term while determining where to install plant expansions. Finally, the CAPs will be able to compete to serve multilocation businesses even when they do not have a physical presence near each of the satellite offices. Figure 4.4 depicts this possible CAP entry strategy.

CAPs will be able to increase their target customer base significantly upon implementation of the plan. CAPs currently have networks in 111 of Ameritech's 1,183 wire centers, giving them immediate access to 29% of Ameritech's revenue base. Under the plan, CAPs may deploy fiber in other areas, giving them even more potential customers. CAPs can use the plan to determine demand for their services and perform true market research by purchasing pieces of Ameritech's network before determining where to construct their own facilities. They can greatly reduce the risk of new construction by acquiring an active customer base prior to completion of their facilities. The unbundling and switch integration will make the CAPs' presence significant and immediate.

As shown in Fig. 4.5, a cable operator will be able to begin providing telecommunications services, even if it serves only a portion of a metropolitan area. It can employ its own cable to operate in currently served areas, providing competitive local loops attached to its own, Ameritech (or a third party) switch. It can purchase loops (and/or switching) from Ameritech to serve portions of the region where cable systems have not been upgraded to provide telephone service. If other cable systems are able to provide voice service, cable companies will then have a choice of purchasing facilities from Ameritech or from other cable companies. Under the plan, cable companies will be able to compete for local telephone service without having to ensure that other cable operators will also upgrade their facilities. This will allow cable companies to avoid the uncertainty of the payoff from investment in upgrading their systems. Cable companies are situated to immediately address a substantial portion of Ameritech's revenue base. The top four MSOs[55] have cable networks in 748 of Ameritech's 1,183 wire centers, giving them direct access to 77% of Ameritech's revenues. Their broad coverage of the Ameritech region reduces the incremental capital outlay associated with entering local telephone services and makes them a viable future competitive alternative.

Throughout the Ameritech region, "nonwireline" cellular carriers provide nearly ubiquitous service. Although their "loops" may not currently provide a complete competitive alternative to Ameritech's loops, they are positioned to take advantage of the plan, as shown in Fig. 4.6. They have sophisticated switches and, in some cases, fully functional networks and office support in place that will allow them to lease loops from Ameritech and provide local exchange services with little incremental investment. Their ubiquitous presence allows them to access almost all of Ameritech's revenue base immediately through leased loops, and use their wireless capacity to substitute for these loops in the future. Cellular carriers also possess a select list of customers with a high demand for telecommunications ser-

---

55. *Multiple System Operator.* The top four MSOs are Time Warner, TCI, Continental, and Comcast.

vices. Cellular carriers also possess a select list of customers with a high demand for telecommunications services.

In the future, the combination of leased wireline access and wireless access may give the cellular carriers a unique advantage in marketing to customers. If they succeed in their drive to receive PCS licenses, wireless carriers would provide customers with three options for "loops."[56] Under one example, the cellular provider can position a cell-site directly adjacent to a wireless private branch exchange (PBX) serving a large corporate complex. The cellular carrier could handle local mobile traffic and serve as the local carrier for all interLATA traffic originating and terminating at the PBX. Although the coverage for the cellular portion of the traffic would be lower than for wireline traffic, the volume of traffic, combined with the absence of interconnect charges for the cellular carrier, would make up some of the gap.[57] With the imminent conversion to digital signaling for cellular, there are a number of cellular operators that will have significant excess capacity. They can market this capacity for use as simple local service. In fact, products are being developed to allow cellular operators to sell service to wireline customers that is transparent to the user. Tellular's "magic box," for example, would enable a cellular customer to easily interconnect a cellular hand unit to its inside wiring (merely by inserting the unit into its charger-base station), thereby routing all long-distance calls from any phone in the house over the cellular carrier, rather than the customer's wireline carrier.[58]

As these examples suggest, the Ameritech plan facilitates many different entry possibilities. Some new entrants may be better suited for niche plays; others may choose more comprehensive strategies. Both can coexist in the marketplace. Although Ameritech ought to be able to competitively respond to new entrants, entrants can target high-profit customers by supplying a small dedicated system catered to the specific customer's needs. This would make them more difficult for Ameritech to dislodge. Such niche plays are likely to be very successful because the plan enables the niche player to take advantage of Ameritech's scale economies.

IMPLICATIONS FOR ANTITRUST POLICY AND INTERLATA RELIEF

Compared to other economically advanced nations, the telecommunications policymaking in the United States is highly fragmented, with substantial involvement by the various states and, especially since the AT&T divestiture, a division of federal policy responsibility between the FCC, the U.S. District Court, and the De-

56. Goldman Sachs, analyzing the recent AT&T/McCaw deal, wrote that the "relationship opens up a major opportunity for McCaw to provide bypass services for AT&T" Goldman Sachs Investment Research, *The McCaw/AT&T Alliance*, November 24, 1992, p. 1.

57. See Goldman Sachs Investment Research, *The McCaw/AT&T Alliance*, November 24, 1992, p. 14, for an example of such a strategy.

58. See the discussion of Tellular Inc.'s "magic box." *Wall Street Journal*, October 4, 1993, p. B1.

partment of Justice.[59] In that environment, Ameritech has proposed a multijurisdictional proposal intended to further the transition to competition in local telecommunications. One of the chief difficulties facing Ameritech is that no single decision maker has the authority to approve all, or even, most aspects of the plan, even though there is a high degree of interdependence among the main elements of the plan. The business, economic, and policy logic underlying the plan is dependent on each of the integral policy components being implemented by the appropriate jurisdictions, the District Court, the FCC, and the Illinois Commerce Commission, respectively. If any one of the integral components of the plan is not adopted by one jurisdiction, for whatever reasons, adoption of the other parts of the plan could have negative economic consequences for Ameritech.

From Ameritech's perspective, the plan is intended to break the "logjam" over the interLATA line of business restriction. As competition in local telecommunications grows and intraLATA service becomes increasingly competitive, Ameritech sees itself boxed into a corner—namely, the LATA boundaries.[60] Its competitors are taking steps to offer bundled or integrated packages of communications services designed to meet specific customer needs. In return, Ameritech is seeking authority to offer interLATA services. It does so in recognition of the increasing tendency for customers, especially business customers, to purchase network services to meet integrated voice, data, and video needs on a global basis. Through acquisitions and alliances, AT&T and MCI will be able to provide end-to-end services to consumers, whether it be information transmitted by PCS, cellular telephony, cable, or fiber optics. These cooperative relationships have special competitive significance when they involve, as they often do, complementary assets and resources. The AT&T-based alliance spans telecommunications equipment and wireline and wireless services. It has enormous financial, human, and technical resources and one of the best known name brands in the United States. The BT–MCI-based alliance includes global and domestic interexchange services, cable and wireless interests, and strong relationships with many competitive access providers. Most recently, France Telecom and Deutsche Telekom have announced their intent to buy substantial equity interests in Sprint.

Of course, Ameritech is also developing global corporate relationships spanning wireline and wireless services (e.g., equity interests in New Zealand Telecom; Ameritech Mobile, a cellular carrier). There is a fundamental difference, however, between Ameritech on the one hand, and the AT&T, MCI, and Sprint agglomerations on the other. The interLATA restriction geographically consigns Ameritech and other RBOCs to local transport areas. In the evolving world of corporate communications and personal mobility, that is an enormous competi-

---

59. For an extended discussion of jurisdictional conflicts in U.S. telecommunications and a comparison to the "synoptic" policy regimes of leading competitor nations, see Harris, Robert G., "Telecommunications Services as a Strategic Industry: Implications for United States Policy," in *Competition and the Regulation of Utilities*, Michael A. Crew, editor, Boston: Kluwer Academic Publishers, 1990; and Harris, Robert G., "Telecommunications Policy in Japan: Lessons for the U.S.," *California Management Review, 31* (3, Spring), 1989.

60. For idiosyncratic reasons, LATAs in Illinois are called MSAs.

tive liability. The management of Ameritech realized that to succeed in the global telecommunications marketplace, it must also offer integrated network services to its customers. Yet the MFJ and the interLATA restrictions, prevent it from doing so.

Because the premise of that restriction is that the RBOCs can and would use their monopoly power in local telecommunications to compete unfairly in interLATA services, the Ameritech plan is designed to reduce or eliminate its alleged "bottleneck monopoly" over local access and exchange services. Other RBOCs are taking the position that, even without unbundling, growing competition in local markets, regulatory and antitrust safeguards, and the ability of IXCs to detect discrimination are sufficient conditions for removing the interLATA restriction. Conversely, the IXCs argue that the restriction should be removed only after the RBOC can demonstrate that there is full and effective competition for access and exchange services in its region. Ameritech is taking a middle position, which is that the "market opening" elements of their plan—unbundling the network and numbering, plus usage presubscription with the LATAs—are sufficient to reduce or eliminate the threat that it could compete unfairly in interLATA by leveraging its position in intraLATA services. The main rationales for their position are that:

1. There are several different options for an IXC seeking to obtain local switching services under the plan. The carrier can provide the switching itself, or obtain it from another party. The carrier can access the customer directly by cross connecting to its (or a third party's) switch or the carrier can access the customer through Ameritech's usage subscription plan, whereby the customer loop is connected through the Ameritech switch and all traffic is directed to the carrier (or third party). The carrier can also resell Ameritech's exchange service.

2. Even after the implementation of the plan, Ameritech might appear to retain some transitory market power regarding the local loop until cable companies, CAPs, PCS, and other wireless providers complete their drives to create competitive local "loops." However, sources of new competition act as a restraint on current pricing because of the importance of customer goodwill and the desire on the part of the provider to enhance its long-run profitability. Furthermore, even without the new competition, loops will be subject to pricing constraints such as price caps to prevent anticompetitive abuses.

3. The entry-facilitating nature of unbundling will generate a larger pool of competitors upon its implementation. Thus, if a hypothetical monopolist had control of the local exchange, and were to attempt to raise prices for local exchange services under the plan, the price increase could be quickly defeated in a number of ways, including entry from outside the local exchange business. Hence, the relevant market must include the capacity of firms outside the local exchange that can readily enter.[61] In evaluating competition,

---

61. This supply-side component to market definition is recognized by the Department of Justice and the Federal Trade Commission in the *Merger Guidelines*, April 2, 1992, p. 47.

one must at a minimum include a portion of the capacity that would be added by those classes of competitors presently outside the local exchange that could easily enter in response to a significant and nontransitory price increase in local exchange services.

4. Ameritech entry into interLATA services would be procompetitive, given the evidence of rising prices and increasing price discrimination by IXCs. MacAvoy, for example, has found that the price–cost margins of AT&T, MCI, and Sprint all have increased in four long-distance service groups (MTS, inbound/outbound WATS, and VNS) and are high in absolute value relative to those in other industries.[62] These high margins would explain the political dynamics of interLATA relief: both why the RBOCs so badly want to enter interLATA services and why the IXCs want to keep them out. So too does the growth and profitability differentials between local and long-distance companies: Whereas RBOC revenues are growing just 2.3% a year, and profits only .9%, the long-distance revenues of AT&T, MCI, and Sprint are growing at an annual rate of 4.3%, and their profits are rising 10% per year.[63]

The Ameritech plan is currently under review by the Department of Justice (DOJ). It is expected to make its decision on the merits of the plan sometime soon. Typically, there are negotiations between DOJ and petitioners that could result in modifications to the plan. If the DOJ decides in the affirmative, it would then recommend the plan to Judge Green, who might accept or reject the recommendation. In either case, his decision would likely be appealed by the "losing" party. At the same time, consolidated proceedings on the Ameritech plan, an AT&T petition and proposed staff rules for interconnection and intraLATA presubscription are underway at the Illinois Commerce Commission. There, the IXCs have argued that the unbundling, dialing parity and number portability and other elements of the Ameritech plan should be adopted, whether or not the company is granted interLATA relief.

The long delay in considering—much less implementing—the Ameritech plan is quite unfortunate, considering that it offers an opportunity to conduct a great experiment in local telecommunications. There is much debate about what the effects of unbundling the local network will actually be, with disparate predictions of outcomes. Yet the best that can be offered are predictions based on economic theory and empirical inferences, because the plan proposed by Ameritech has never been done before—here or elsewhere. With no experience in unbundling, the best way to test the proposition is to try it and see what happens:

---

62. Price cost margins across 284 industries averaged 27%, or about one third of the 1993 margins for MTS, inbound WATS, and outbound WATS, and about 52% of the margin for VNS; MacAvoy, Paul W., affidavit to United States District Court for the District of Columbia Civil Action No. 82-0192, June 6, 1994, filed in support of motion to remove interLATA restriction submitted by four RBOCs.

63. Measured over the years 1990 through 1994 (estimated). Kupfer, Andrew, "The Future of the Phone Companies," *Fortune*, October 3, 1994, pp. 95–105.

- Does entry into local access and exchange actually occur? Does the unbundling of the local network facilitate entry or not?
- Do the proposed rules promote interconnection and interoperability? Is there progress in creating the network of networks?
- Do prices and service offerings in interLATA services indicate healthy competition? Are there benefits from Ameritech's entry?

In assessing the pros and cons of such an "experiment," one should remember that any relief granted from the MFJ could be temporary, conditional on Ameritech's performance under the waiver. One would expect the IXCs—to say nothing of Judge Green—to be vigilant in their monitoring of Ameritech's compliance with the regulatory safeguards included in the plan. The threat of removing the waiver would presumably be strong incentive for Ameritech to avoid conduct that would justify such a result. Conversely, evidence from the experiment could help resolve the issue of interLATA restrictions once and for all.

E

Technology Policy

[27]

TECHNOLOGICAL DEVELOPMENT AND THE ORGANISATION OF INDUSTRY

D. J. Teece
University of California, Berkeley

I. INTRODUCTION

Competition is essential to the innovation process and to capitalist economic development more generally. But so is co-operation. The challenge to policy analysts and to managers is to find the right balance of competition and co-operation, and the appropriate institutional structures within which competition and co-operation ought to take place.

Unfortunately, the economics textbooks tell us virtually nothing about these issues. Where there is usually some consideration given to the import of monopoly and competition on incentives to innovate, it is always implicitly assumed that the price mechanism can effectuate whatever co-ordination the economic system requires. Typically there is no discussion of how interfirm agreements, vertical and horizontal, can positively impact the process. If interfirm agreements are discussed, it is almost always in the context of cartel theory. It is not surprising, therefore, that the economics textbooks, at least those used in the West, do not convey a sense that interfirm co-operation is either desirable or a subject worthy of study.

Analysts and policy-makers have tended to stress the values of pluralism and rivalry as the best organisational arrangement to promote innovation. While these are important values, they are not the only ones. Moreover, with increased global competition, such values are now adequately represented in the global system. This paper does not question the value of rivalry and pluralism; rather, it asks whether at the margin such

I am grateful to Thomas Jorde for his commanding insights into interfirm contractual issues and their legal status in the United States, Europe, and Japan. I am also indebted to Michael Gerlach for help in understanding the differences in industrial organisation between the United States and Japan. Patrizia Zagnoli also provided useful comments into the theory and practice of strategic alliances.

values ought to be balanced by a recognition of the importance of co-ordination and co-operation to a well-functioning national system of innovation. In what follows, the relationship between technical innovation and aspects of industrial organisation, other than market structure and firm size, are examined. In particular, in section III, the role of co-operative arrangements (national and international) among firms are examined for their impact on innovation. Implications for corporate strategy and public policy are derived.

The basic conclusion of the paper is that co-operation is usually necessary to promote competition, particularly when industries are fragmented. Very few firms can successfully "go it alone" any more. Co-operation, in turn, requires interfirm agreements and alliances. In this regard, the Japanese form of industrial organisation, with complex interfirm relationships, may have distinct advantages. European and American firms are now only beginning to learn how to effectively co-operate in order to compete. Antitrust authorities in Europe and the United States appear increasingly willingly to let them try[1].

II.   INNOVATION AND COMPETITION

Schumpeter's claim that large firms were necessary to promote innovation has fostered exploration of the links between innovative performance and market structure. Schumpeter linked firm size and innovation for three distinct reasons. First, he contended that only large firms could afford the cost of R&D programmes. Second, large, diversified firms could absorb failures by innovating across broad technological fronts. Third, firms needed some element of market control to reap the rewards of innovation.   [409]

The Schumpeterian legacy has spurred discussion of the link between firm size and innovation, and between market structure and innovation. In this section, it is suggested that this discussion has been rather inconclusive, and that it is partly outmoded as it has not framed the firm size hypothesis in a particularly relevant way, given that the boundaries of the firm can no longer be assessed independently of the co-operative relationships that particular innovating firms may have forged. Indeed, this paper posits that the firms' ability to forge co-operative relationships can in may instances substitute for more comprehensive forms of integration. Put differently, in some circumstances co-operative agreements can enable smaller firms to emulate many of the functional aspects of large integrated enterprises, without suffering possible dysfunctions sometimes associated with large size. These points are now briefly explored.

Firm size, market concentration, and innovation

As a theoretical matter, economic models of the innovation process are decidedly non-robust, showing that competition can lead to too much or too little R&D investment[2]. In fragmented market structures, several kinds of market failures are commonly recognised. First, if firms are unable to exclude other firms from using technology they have developed, there is the classic "free rider" problem. Even if patents prevent direct mimicking, there is likely to be a technological "neighbourhood" illuminated by the innovation that is not foreclosed by the patent, so the externality problem remains, though in a different form. The second problem is what is sometimes referred to as "overbidding". This arises in the early development phase as competitors are stimulated to invest for the potential rewards that will go to the patent winner. Incentives to be the first to invent, or to be first to get to the patent office, may induce too many firms to try to invent early. In such a competitive race, too many resources may get applied too early. One consequence may be that firms drop out of the industry after the patent race is over but before the serious development work begins. A misallocation of resources is the unfortunate consequence.

A monopolised industry avoids both the free rider and the patent race problem. Moreover, the knowledge externalities that come from successful exploration of unchartered technological areas are internalised. Economies of scale and scope may also be available. But the cost is the output restriction that the monopolist will supposedly engineer. This in turn cuts R&D investment. The result, as Nelson and Winter (1982) explain, is that "it is hard to say whether there would be more or less R&D undertaken in the monopolised case than in the competitive case". However, Nelson and Winter surmise that the balance probably tips against the monopolist, because in a centralised R&D regime which monopoly would entail, the diversity of approaches characteristic of competition would probably fail, as managers adopt simplified decision-making styles. In short, the theoretical literature identifies a wide range of possible outcomes and, accordingly, provides little guide to policy.

Defining the firms' boundaries

As a practical matter, the economists' debate seems highly stylised and out of touch with global realities. Neither perfect competition nor complete monopoly is observable or realistically attainable in any industry today. Moreover, to abstract from industrial structure in such narrow terms is to miss key elements of industrial organisation.

First, the boundaries of the firm are extremely difficult to delineate, particularly when there are complex alliance structures in place. In Japan, for instance, Gerlach (1988) notes that alliances are "neither formal organisations with clearly defined, hierarchical structures, nor impersonal, decentralised markets. Business alliances operate instead in extended networks of relationships between companies, organised around identifiable groupings, and bound together in durable relationships which are based on long term reciprocity". Much of the complexity and subtlety of these arrangements is missed by economists who tend to focus on legal titles and the structure of property rights, narrowly defined. Even worse, since the most familiar model that economists have of co-operative behaviour is that of the cartel, many scholars have missed the efficiency-inducing characteristics of alliance structures in Japan and elsewhere. Indeed, Caves and Uekusa (1976, p. 158) appear to push alliances into the straightjacket of cartel theory when they contend that "Japanese industries are prone to collusive arrangements but are also rich in structural incentives for the conspirators to cheat. The net outcome for the gap between actual and ideal industrial output is, thus, hard to predict, but we do expect increased distortions from sporadic price discrimination, reciprocity, and the diversion of rivalry into uncontrolled nonprice forms".

Alliances are a form of contractual relationship, but they are much more than a legal contract. Alliance partners are not faceless entities operating at arms-length in Walrasian markets. Rather, exchange among alliance partners is characterised according to Gerlach by: *1.* an emphasis on relational, rather than transactional exchange, wherein the focus is toward the actors taking part rather than the objects of exchange; 2. a state of continuous indebtedness and mutual obligation between the parties; 3. the implicit negotiations of a socially significant order through symbolic activities and ceremonies. Alliances are defined by interests among specific subsets of firms that are familiar with each other through historical association, rather than immediate task requirements. [410]

The alliance structure in Japan appears to have enabled smaller Japanese firms to attain the degree of functional integration found within some large integrated American enterprises, but with less in the way of common ownership of the parts. Sub-contractors, trading companies, and distributors take on for the firm functions often done internally in the United States. While many American firms, particularly those in higher technology industries, rely on outside suppliers and distributors to a similar degree, the level of functional integration attained with these relationships in the United States is markedly lower. In Japan, the image is perhaps neither that of the "visible hand" nor the "invisible hand" but of the continuous handshake[3]. Japanese corporate strategy is, therefore, formulated to a considerable extent by maneuvering within alliance relationships, by industrial visions worked out among firms, and also by the broader industrial policies set by government.

Where the law permits, alliance and consortia structures are increasingly coming to characterise aspects of European and American business. Though more transactional and less relational than alliances in Japan, these structures nevertheless involve high levels of co-operation, particularly for new product development and commercialisation. So pervasive have these relationships become that one can no longer fruitfully explore industrial organisation questions in the neoclassical tradition. Discussions of firm size which do not take co-operative agreements into account seriously mischaracterise the nature of the business firm. Discussions of product market structure that do not take the market for know-how into account are also likely to mischaracterise the nature of competition faced by a firm in a fast-paced industry. In the remainder of this paper, co-operative agreements are explored more fully. The next section discusses both the importance of co-ordination for the innovation process, and the organisational mechanisms available to effectuate it.

III.   INNOVATION, CO-ORDINATION AND CO-OPERATION

The contention advanced in this paper is that the intensely competitive environment in which high-technology firms find themselves, coupled with the special needs for successful innovation and product commercialisation, requires some degree of national and international co-operation among competing firms. This paper stresses the need for both "operational" and "strategic" co-ordination to develop and profitably commercialise new technology.

The need for operational co-ordination

Innovation is a special kind of economic activity, with very special kinds of informational and co-ordination requirements. This sub-section examines these requirements, without addressing the question of whether they are organised more appropriately by markets, hierarchies, alliances or other organisational forms.

Accessing complementary assets

Innovative new products and processes will not yield value unless they are commercialised. It is during commercialisation that the greatest organisational challenges arise and where the bulk of the resource commitment occurs. The profitable commercialisation of technology requires timely access to complementary assets on competitive terms. Thus, an innovating firm or consortium that has developed a new product or process with good commercialisation prospects has taken only the first step. It must then secure access to complementary technologies and complementary assets on favourable terms in order to successfully commercialise the product or process[4].

Assets such as marketing, competitive manufacturing, reputation, and after-sales support are almost always needed. The range of complementary assets that are necessary is indicated in Figure 1. These assets need not bear a relationship to a firm that is either strictly vertical or horizontal. Moreover, services of these assets are often obtained from complementary assets which are specialised. For example, the commercialisation of a new drug is likely to require the dissemination of information over a specialised information channel. In some cases, the complementary

Figure 1

COMPLEMENTARY ASSETS NEEDED TO
COMMERCIALIZE AN INNOVATION

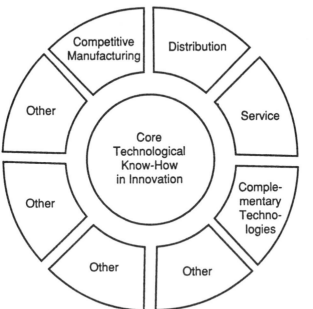

[411]

assets may be the other parts of a system. For instance, computer hardware typically requires the development of specialised software both for the operating system and for applications.

The interdependence between the innovation and the relevant complementary assets can very, of course, tremendously. At one extreme, the complementary assets may be virtually generic, have many potential suppliers, and be relatively unimportant when compared with the technological breakthrough represented by the innovation. At the other extreme, successful commercialisation of the innovation may depend critically on a bottleneck asset that has only one possible supplier. Between these two extremes there is the possibility of "co-specialisation" – where the innovation and the assets depend on each other. An example of this would be containerised shipping, which requires specialised trucks and terminals that can work only in conjunction with each other.

The main decision the innovator has to make with respect to commercialisation is what to do with respect to complementary assets. Although there are a myriad of possible arrangements, two pure types stand out. At one extreme, the innovator could attempt to integrate into (i.e. build or acquire) all of the necessary complementary assets. This is likely to be unnecessary as well as prohibitively expensive[5]. It is well to recognise that the variety of assets and competence which need to be accessed is likely to be quite large even for only modestly complex technologies. To produce a personal computer, for instance, expertise is needed in a range of technologies, including disk-drives, networking technology, keyboard technology, and power supplies. No company has kept pace on all of these areas by itself. At the other extreme, the innovator could attempt to access these assets through straightforward unilateral contractual relationships (e.g., component supply contracts, fabrication contracts, distribution contracts, etc.). In many instances, such contracts may suffice, although a contract does expose the innovator to various hazards and dependencies that it may well wish to avoid.

In short, the profitable commercialisation of new technology requires that various complementary assets be assembled and that technology transfer be effectuated out of the lab and into manufacturing, sales and service. This often takes place inside the corporation, [412] but it need not. Collaboration and strategic alliances with other firms elsewhere in the global economy are often desirable and sometimes necessary. These organisational issues are discussed in Section: "Governance structures to facilitate co-operation".

Coupling developer to user

A salient aspect of innovation is that it requires a close coupling of the developer of the new technology to the user. Commercially successful innovations require linking scientific, engineering, entrepreneurial and management skills with an intimate understanding of user needs. Indeed, in some fields, such as scientific instruments, it is often the user that stimulates innovation and comes up with a new product concept or product prototype which is passed back upstream for further development work. Hence, innovation requires considerable vertical interaction and communication flows. Moreover, these flows must occur expeditiously. With uncertainty, learning, and short-product life cycle, there must be organisational systems in place to facilitate timely feedback, mid-course correction, redesign, and rapid commercialisation. The necessary linkages and feedbacks are summarised in Figure 2.

Figure 2

MODEL SHOWING FLOW PATHS OF INFORMATION AND CO-OPERATION

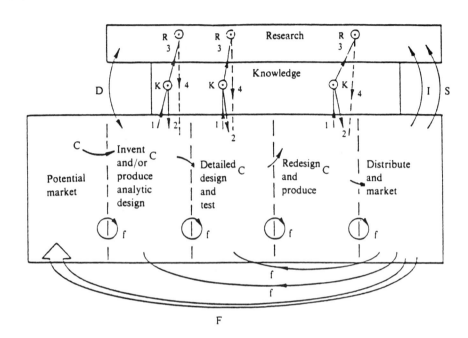

Symbols used on arrows:

C: Central chain of innovation
f: Feedback loops
F: Particularly important feedback

K–R: Links through knowledge to research and return paths. If problem solved at
    node K, link 3 to R not activated. Return from research (link 4) is
    problematic—therefore dashed line.
  D: Direct link to and from research from problems in invention and design.
  I: Support of scientific research by instruments, machines, tools and pro-
    cedures of technology.
  S: Support of research in sciences underlying product area to gain information
    directly and by monitoring outside work. The information obtained may
    apply anywhere along the chain.

This model recognises the existence and exercise of
tight linkages and feedback mechanisms that must
operate quickly and efficiently. These linkages must
exist within the firm, among firms, and between firms
and other organisations, such as universities. The positioning of the firm's boundaries – for example, its level
of vertical integration – determines in part whether the
required interactions are intrafirm or interfirm.

Corrections among technologies[6]

Another dimension of co-ordination is that which must take place among various technologies. Particular technological advances seldom stand alone. They are usually connected both to *a)* prior developments in the same technology; and *b)* to complementary or facilitating advances in related technologies. In addition, a generic technology may be capable of *c)* a wide variety of end-product applications. Each is discussed in turn, along with related reasons for co-operation[7].

Connections to prior technologies

Many technologies evolve in an evolutionary fashion, with today's round of R&D activities building on yesterday's, which in turn build on the day before's. Thus, with respect to memory devices, advance is cumulative along a particular technological trajectory, from 1K to 4K to 64K to 256K to 1 megabyte and so on, up to the theoretical limits of a particular technology. Similarly, in the aircraft industry the DC-3 improved upon the DC-2, and subsequent aircraft built on what was learned with the DC-3. Hence, whether an enterprise is able to participate in one technology often depends on whether it participated in the earlier generation. If it did not, and the technologies in question have path dependencies, then in order to enter at a subsequent stage the enterprise in question will have to link up, in some fashion, with the enterprises familiar with the prior art. Relatedly, experience and competence in a particular technological regime may count for little and may, in fact, be a handicap when a significant shift in technological regime occurs. A regime shift signals opportunities for new entrants, but to engage these opportunities, new entrants may need to link up with incumbent firms, who may not have the relevant new technology but do, in fact, have complementary capacities, such as market and distribution.

Connections to complementary technologies

Technological advances are often linked together because of systems interdependencies. Thus, the electric lighting system – dynamos, distribution system, and incandescent bulbs – was severely limited by the non-durable bulb filaments that existed until Edison and his associates invented a high resistance filament. Artificial intelligence technologies depend both on the availability of computer software and hardware. Containerisation of ocean shipping could not move forward until new facilities to handle containers had been put in place in ports, in distribution centres, and in railroads and trucking. The innovation, of course, also required the construction of ships with the requisite capacities. In a system technology, an advance in one part of the system may not only permit, but require, changes in other parts. The tightness of interdependence and the requirements for organisational connectedness are discussed later. Suffice to say here that tight interdependencies require interaction and information and materials flows among organisations. Whether the appropriate governance mechanism is a contract, a joint venture, equity cross-holdings, or merger is a matter we consider in Section IV.

Generic technologies

New technologies may simultaneously affect several different businesses, typically because they provide a common core technology to several businesses (e.g., microelectronics, composites biotechnology) or because they are systemic (e.g., instant photography). Both core technologies and systemic technologies create relatedness across the businesses they affect. In these instances, organisations must be designed in order to facilitate the complex co-operation that the development, and especially the commercialisation, of such technology requires. Thus entrusting an existing business unit with the responsibility of developing and commercialising a new technology with these characteristics, without providing mechanisms and incentives for the necessary co-operation, is likely to cause the technology to evolve slowly and to lead to missed opportunities. In sum, for core and system technologies, both differentiation from, and interdependence with, existing businesses are needed.   [413]

Cost reduction and risk spreading

Innovation and commercialisation of new products and processes are high-cost activities. The scale and scope of assets needed will often lie beyond the capabilities of a single firm. Thus, co-operation may be the only viable means for moving forward. In addition, co-operation will also reduce wasteful duplicate expenditures on research and development. Innovation also entails significant risk. While successful innovation and its financial rewards are often highly visible, behind the scenes there are usually many failed efforts and unproductive paths. "Dry holes" and "blind alleys" are commonplace. Risk can be diversified and spread through co-operation. Indeed, when risk is particularly high because the technology being pursued is both expensive and undeveloped, co-operation may be the only way that firms will undertake the needed effort.

Appropriability and diffusion

The ability to appropriate the rents of innovation is critically important. Intellectual property rights may not adequately protect innovation. A survey conducted at Yale has provided robust evidence that most US industries are characterised by weak appropriability regimes[8]. Leakage and free riding are commonplace, forcing firms to rely more on business strategy and conduct to secure adequate returns to innovation. Co-operation in innovation can be an important mechanism for appropriability because it brings together potential free riders in a cost-sharing relationship. Co-operation can also ensure diffusion of technology, at least among the co-operating firms.

The need for strategic co-ordination

In the preceding section, the technical-operational aspects of co-ordination were sketched without addressing the question of how various organisational arrangements, such as markets, hierarchies, alliances or other intermediate forms, would accomplish this. (That will be discussed in the next section.) It was indicated that to develop and commercialise new technology, it is necessary to link the developer to the user, the developers of complementary technologies to the owners of complementary assets and to prior art. Co-operation is also an important means of reducing costs and spreading risk and of simultaneously appropriating the returns to innovation while diffusing technology. These linkages are technical-operational in that they focus on the transactions among different organisation units or individuals necessary to get the job done. A related question is how to assemble the different organisational units among which these interactions take place. The latter question is what is meant by strategic co-ordination.

Clearly, the economic prospects for innovation depend upon the size of the prospective market, the costs of supplying it, and appropriability regime, and relatedly the number and strength of competitors, and so forth. It is the essence of private enterprise economy that, although its individual members are independent, their activities are nevertheless interrelated. Any single investment will only be profitable provided first that the volume of competitive investment does not exceed a limit set by demand and, second, that the volume of complementary investment reaches the correct level[9].

However, there is no special machinery in a private enterprise, market economy to ensure that investment programmes are made known to all concerned at the time of their inception. Price movements, by themselves, do not generally form an adequate system of signalling. Indeed, Tjalling Koopmans (1957) has been rather critical of what he calls the "overextended belief" of certain economists in the efficiency of competitive markets as a means of allocating resources in a world characterised by ubiquitous uncertainty. The main source of this uncertainty, according to Koopmans, is the ignorance that firms have with respect to their competitors' future actions, preferences, and states of technological information. In the absence of a complete set of forward markets in which anticipation and intentions could be tested and adjusted, there is no reason to believe that with uncertainty competitive markets of the kind described in the textbooks produce efficient outcomes[10]. The information-circulating function which economic theory attributes to competitive markets is not discharged by any existing arrangements with the detail and forward extension necessary to support efficient outcomes[11].

There is no arena in which uncertainty is higher and the need to co-ordinate greater than in the development and commercialisation of new technology. There are no theoretical grounds for believing that an economy that is all tooth and claw will outperform one that involves a judicious mix of tooth, claw, and intramarket and intermarket co-operation. Adam Smith's[12] warning – that "people of the same trade seldom meet together, even for merriment and diversion, but the conversation ends in a conspiracy against the public, or in some contrivance to raise prices" – needs to be tempered with the recognition that in global markets the difficulty of assembling all the relevant parties to effectuate an international conspiracy is an insurmountable challenge in industries experiencing rapid technological change. It also needs to be tempered with a recognition that industrial structure and competition policy effects the degree to which firms in an industry can effectuate the necessary strategic co-ordination.

But the informational requirements are usually greater than that which is embedded in price, especially if a complete set of future prices does not exist, which is in fact the case. As a practical matter, entrepreneurs need, and have, access to much more information than the Walrasian model presents. Thus, if there is a shortage of a key component, entrepreneurs [414] necessarily delve behind today's price in an attempt to examine the cause of the price run-up, and estimate its likely duration. They care about, and typically discover through investment in information acquisition, whether there is a capacity problem, a government policy intervention, a natural disaster, unexpected demand growth, etc.

Prices clearly are not sufficient signals in many cases. In the United States there is nevertheless great antitrust suspicion placed on firms if they exchange market data on price, capacity, and plans. However, if third parties obtain the information and publish it, there is much less concern[13]. The result is sometimes the same – competitors may get to know about each other's prices and capacity – yet the law treats the two exchanges as fundamentally different.

One can obtain complete antitrust exemption after one consummates a legal merger. There are no antitrust strictures in the United States, the European Community or Japan against information exchange and strategic co-ordination inside the firm. Indeed, if this activity does not occur smoothly and efficiently, the enterprise would be considered mismanaged. Yet such activities between unaffiliated enterprises create considerable antitrust concerns in some countries and, under certain poorly defined circumstances, are in fact likely to be illegal in the United States if they involve agreement among competitors.

This suggests that when firms are engaged in innovation, a much more relaxed antitrust standard should be applied with respect to discussion, exchanges, and agreements among competitors when they relate to innovative activities because there is the need to co-ordinate disparate activities and because there is so little possibility of establishing a cartel in an industry experiencing rapid technological change, especially if that industry is open to international trade. Accordingly, there is no reason why firms in fragmented industries experiencing rapid technological change should not be able to communicate, co-ordinate and agree on many things.

Importantly, communication could build the basis for socially beneficial co-operation. While co-operation is often possible without direct communication – antagonists in trench warfare learned to co-operate based upon reciprocity[14] – communication can speed it up and make it durable, particularly when complex technical and market matters are at issue. The need for communication and co-operation among firms is likely to be especially strong when an industry is highly fragmented[15]. The next section examines various organisational or governance models by which the necessary co-operation might take place.

Governance structures to facilitate co-operation

The preceding two sections have helped establish that innovation typically requires the co-ordination of a variety of activities and a multitude of actors. In many theoretical treatments, the necessary co-ordination takes place using the price system (the pure market solution). Alternatively, and at the other extreme, it could take place inside one giant enterprise (the pure hierarchy solution), perhaps formed by a merger. Intermediate solutions include bilateral contracts, interfirm agreements, and other forms of alliance. It is these intermediate forms that will not be analysed.

In the traditional textbook treatment of these issues, the price system magically allows all of the necessary co-ordination to occur smoothly and efficiently. In the Walrasian system, which is implicit in textbook thinking about equilibrium price determination, profits cause output expansion, losses contraction. In equilibrium, firms make neither profits nor losses. In this system, entrepreneurs, together with the auctioneer, act as co-ordinators to bring harmony to the competitive pursuit of self-interest[16]. In this simple view, the only information firms need to develop and commercialise innovation is provided by the auctioneer in terms of price.

At the other extreme, co-ordination is achieved inside integrated and usually hierarchically structured firms. But the full integration solution has liabilities, not least of which is that it can impair the autonomy so necessary for aspects of the innovation process to proceed. Still, it has obvious advantages for effectuating strategic co-ordination. For example, Michael Borrus (1988) recognises that new institutional forms are needed in US microelectronics if the industry is to compete effectively in the future and at the same time avoid antitrust problems[17]. However, his solution – the establishment of a number of holding companies for Silicon Valley firms – implicitly endorses a merger approach to the problem[18]. While it may be better than the current fragmented structure, there are many reasons why one should be sceptical of its viability. Many of these relate to the change in incentives and compensation structures that the arrangements would imply[19]. As explained below, when high technology activities are at issue, contractual agreements, alliances, and joint ventures are likely to be superior to merger. This is particularly true if they are bilateral.

Relationships are bilateral when A agrees to secure Y from B as a condition for making X available, and both parties understand that relationship, and associated transactions will be continued only if reciprocity is observed[20]. These relationships can be referred to as "strategic alliances". While the term is often used rather loosely, a strategic alliance is defined here as a bilateral relationship characterised by the commitment of two or more partner firms to reach a common goal, entailing the pooling of their resources and activities. Thus, a strategic alliance might include one or more of the following: *i)* an exclusive purchase agreement; *ii)* exclusive market or manufacturing rights; *iii)* technology swaps; *iv)* joint R&D or co-development. Thus, [415] a strategic alliance denotes some form of mutual control. By its nature, it is not a passive instrument.

Strategic alliances can be differentiated from exchange transactions, such as a simple licensing agreement with specified royalties, because with an exchange transaction the object of the transaction is supplied by the selling firm to the buying firm in exchange for cash because it would not be bilateral. A strategic alliance by definition can never have one side receiving only cash. They need not involve equity swaps or equity investments, though they often do. Strategic alliances without equity typically consist of contracts between, or among, partner firms that are non-affiliated. Equity alliances can take many forms, including minority equity holdings, consortia, and joint ventures.

Strategic alliances have increased in frequency in recent years, and are particularly characteristic of high technology industries. Joint R&D, know-how, manufacturing, and marketing agreements go well beyond exchange agreements because they can be used to access complementary technologies and complementary assets. The object of the transaction, such as the development and launch of a new product, usually does not exist at the time the contracts are inked. Whether equity or non-equity forms of alliances are the most desirable governance structures depends on a variety of circumstances[21]. Governance structures are summarised in Table 1.

Table 1. **Taxonomy of Interfirm Arrangements**

	Non-equity	Equity
Exchange	short-medium-term cash-based contracts	passive stock holdings for portfolio diversification
Alliance	mid- long-term bilateral contracts (non-cash based)	joint venture (operating or nonoperating), consortium, minority equity holdings, and cross holdings
Merger	0	wholly-owned affiliate or subsidiary

IV. CONCLUSION

Successful technological innovation requires complex forms of business organisation. Innovating organisations must form linkages to others, upstream and downstream, lateral and horizontal. Advanced technological systems do not, and cannot, get created in splendid isolation. The communication and co-ordination requirements are often quite stupendous, and in practice the price system alone does not suffice to achieve the necessary co-ordination.

A variety of organisational arrangements exist to bring about the necessary co-ordination. The price system provides only a useful backdrop in market-oriented economies. By itself, it is not up to task, because not all of what must be exchanged can be transacted in faceless markets. Fully integrated companies, on the other hand, must be careful not to suffocate creativity and to dampen incentives.

Increasingly, however, firms must co-operate, vertically, horizontally, and laterally, to effectuate innovation and to be competitive. Alliance structures of various kinds can facilitate innovation, and are increasingly necessary as the sources of innovation and the capacities necessary to effectuate commercialisation become increasingly dispersed.

A variety of implications follow for management and public policy. Managers must become adept at managing not just their own organisation, but also their relationships and alliances with other firms. Very often, different skills are required for each, which makes management tasks more complex and challenging. Strategic alliances must also be designed to be self-reinforcing. There is the danger that changing circumstances can upset delicate balances, thereby causing relationships and agreements to unravel. Equity can be judiciously used to anchor alliances, but it may not suffice as the safeguard if inadequate in amount and if not bolstered by other mechanisms. At present there is considerable organisational learning occurring with respect to such matters, both nationally and internationally, and new arrangements that are balanced and durable will undoubtedly be crafted.

The greatest challenge probably goes to public policy, particularly in the United States, where there has been a failure to recognise that co-operation is as important as competition. This has manifested itself in the absence of interagency co-ordination in the federal government, with science and technology policy appearing to be weak and unco-ordinated, and a reluctance to permit and encourage the private sector to forge the interfirm agreements, alliances and consortia necessary to develop and commercialise new technologies like high-density television or superconductors. A key reason for this is the shadow that neoclassical economic thinking casts over antitrust policy. It renders antitrust policy hostile to many forms of beneficial collaboration, because of fear that such arrangements are a subterfuge for cartelisation and other forms of anticompetitive behaviour. Until a greater understanding emerges as to the organisational requirements of the innovation process, antitrust policy and managerial attitudes in the United States are likely to remain barriers to innovation. Co-operation must become recognised as a tool to effectuate competition and competitiveness.   [416]

NOTES

1. For a discussion of the antitrust treatment of co-operative agreements in Japan, Europe and the United States, see T.M. Jorde and D.J. Teece (1988).
2. For a useful survey, see W. Baldwin and J.T. Scott (1987).
3. See Gerlach (1988), p. 2.
4. See Teece (1986), pp. 286-305.

5. Needless to say, incumbent firms may already have integrated into many of the necessary capabilities.

6. This treatment is based in part on R. Nelson (1984), pp. 8-10.

7. It is obvious that the treatment here breaks with the traditional "book of blueprints" approach to technology often embedded in economic models of the innovation process. We implicitly postulate market failure in the market for know-how. For a more extensive treatment, see D. Teece (1980).

8. See Levin, Klevorick, Nelson, and Winter (1987), p. 3.

9. See G. Richardson (1960), p. 31.

10. Koopmans (1957, p. 146) points out that because of this deficiency economic theorists are not able to speak with anything approaching scientific authority on matters relating to individual versus collective enterprise.

11. *Ibid.*, p. 163.

12. This did not appear to be an important part of Smith's (1976, Chapter 10, Part II, p. 144) overall thesis.

13. For a recent theoretical treatment of information sharing, see Kirby (1988), pp. 138-146.

14. See R. Axelrod (1984).

15. As mentioned earlier, such communication takes place routinely within firms.

16. The prices of goods and services are set by the auctioneer, who adjusts them according to the law of supply and demand. Given a system of prices, the excess of sales price of entrepreneurial output over the cost of production may be either positive, null, or negative. This excess is termed "benefice de l'entreprise" by Walras (1954, p. 423). A positive or negative "benefice" is a sign of disequilibrium, and entrepreneurs respond to this signal according to the law of cost price; that is, they increase their scale of production when the "benefice" is positive, and reduce it when the "benefice" is negative. The presumption that firms strive for higher incomes and lower losses through entry and exit is implicit. However, entrepreneurs in their purely functional roles are only catalytic agents who accelerate combinations of atomistic factors of production only when the "benefice" is positive. Thus, in a state of equilibrium, entrepreneurs make neither profit nor loss. "Profit in the sense of 'benefice de l'entreprise'... depends upon exceptional and not upon normal circumstances."

17. Borrus (1988, p. 231) comments: "Almost a decade ago it was clear that Japanese producers would emerge as enduring players in the semiconductor industry, and would, as a consequence, radically alter the industry's terms of competition. Yet it has taken almost that long for US firms to co-operate sufficiently to begin to devise appropriate responses. It is almost a truism that had the

industry been able to co-ordinate its actions strategically a decade ago, an adequate response would have been far less costly and far more likely to succeed. To accomplish such strategic co-ordination, the US chip industry needs an ongoing analytic capacity, embedded in an electronics industry-wide institution, with the ability to carry on competitive analysis of foreign market and technology strategies, and with sufficient prestige to offer strategic direction on which planning can occur. There is, of course, a substantial problem associated with industry-strategic planning. To assure its health, the industry needs strategic co-ordination short of market sharing. All US industries facing international competition ought to be permitted to develop industry-wide competitive assessment capability, at least whenever the industry can demonstrate substantial involvement of foreign governments in assisting foreign competitors."

18. Borrus (1988, p. 233): "It is possible to envision chip-firm holding companies built around common manufacturing facilities(...) R&D resources shared among the holding company's chip firms would eliminate the problem of duplication of R&D among smaller companies. The high capital costs of staying in the technology race could be share among firms in the form of shared flexible fabrication facilities(...). Shared facilities would permit high usage of capacity(...). In essence, the holding company structure would gain the advantages associated with consolidation without the disadvantages associated with integration."

19. See in particular O.E. Williamson (1985), Chapter 6.

20. *Ibid.*, p. 191.

21. For a fuller treatment, see G. Pisano and D. J. Teece (1988).   [417]

References

Axelrod, R. (1984), *The Evolution of Co-operation,* New York, Basic Books.

Baldwin, W. and J. T. Scott (1987), *Market Structure and Technological Change,* Chur, Switzerland: Harwood Publishers.

Borrus, M. (1988), *Competing for Control: America's Stake in Microelectronics,* Cambridge, MA: Ballinger.

Caves, R. and M. Uekusa (1976), *Industrial Organization in Japan,* Washington, DC: Brookings Institution.

Davis, D. (1985) 'R&D consortia pooling industries' resources', *High Technology,* V, October, 42–7.

Gerlach, M. (1988), *Alliances and the Social Organization of Japanese Business,* unpublished MS, University of California at Berkeley.

Jorde, T. M. and D. J. Teece (1988), 'Innovation, strategic alliances, and antitrust', unpublished paper, University of California at Berkeley, December.

Kirby, A. (1988), 'Trade associations as information exchange mechanisms', *Rand Journal of Economics,* 19(1), 138–46.

Kline, S. J. and N. Rosenberg (1986), 'An Overview of Innovation' in N. Rosenberg and R. Landau (eds), *The Positive Sum Strategy: Harnessing Technology for Economic Growth*, Washington, DC: National Academy Press.

Koopmans, T. (1957), *Three Essays on the State of Economic Science*, New York: McGraw-Hill.

Levin, R. and P. Reiss (1984), 'Tests of a Schumpeterian Model of R&D and Market Structure' in Z. Griliches (ed.), *R&D, Patents, and Productivity*, (NBER), Chicago and London: University of Chicago Press.

Levin, R., A. Klevorick, R. Nelson and S. Winter (1987), 'Appropriating the returns from industrial research and development', *Brookings Papers on Economic Activity*, 3, 783–831.

Nelson, R. (1984), *High Technology Policies*, Washington, DC: American Enterprise Institute.

Nelson, R. and S. Winter (1982), *An Evolutionary Theory of Economic Change*, Cambridge, MA: Harvard University Press.

Pisano, G. and D. J. Teece (1988), 'Collaborative arrangements and global technology strategy: some evidence from the telecommunication equipment industry', working Paper IB–10, Center for Research in Management, University of California, Berkeley.

Richardson, G. (1960), *Information and Investment: A Study in the Working of the Competitive Economy*, London and New York: Oxford University Press.

Rosenberg, N. (1972), *Technology and American Economic Growth*, New York: Harper and Row.

Rosenberg, N. (1982), *Inside the Black Box: Technology and Economics*, Cambridge and New York: Cambridge University Press.

Scherer, F. M. (1970), *Industrial Market Structure and Economic Performance*, Chicago: Rand-McNally.

Schumpeter, J. A. (1942), *Capitalism, Socialism, and Democracy*, New York: Harper.

Smith, A. (1976), *Wealth of Nations*, Book 1, Chicago: University of Chicago Press.

Stiglitz, J. (1987), 'Technical change, sunk costs, and competition', *Brookings Papers on Economic Activity*, 3.

Teece, D. J. (1980), 'Economies of scope and the scope of the enterprise', *Journal of Economic Behavior and Organization*, 3(1), 223–47.

Teece, D. J. (1986), 'Profiting from technological innovation', *Research Policy*, 15 (6), 285–305.

von Hippel, E. (1977), 'The dominant role of the user in semiconductor and electronic subassembly process innovation', *IEEE Transactions on Engineering Management*, EM-24(2), May, 60–71.

von Hippel, E. (1988), *The Sources of Innovation*, New York: Oxford University Press.

Walras, L. (1954), *Elements of Pure Economics*, (Republished in French in 1976), Paris: Librairie générale de droit et de jurisprudence.

Williamson, O. E. (1985), *The Economic Institution of Capitalism*, New York: Free Press.

[28]

Foreign Investment and Technological Development in Silicon Valley

David J. Teece

Few topics excite intellectual and political passions in the United States as much as inward foreign investment, particularly inward foreign investment in high-technology industries. This article takes a cursory look at inward foreign investment over the last decade in Silicon Valley. I use "Silicon Valley" partly as a geographical representation—loosely as the San Francisco Bay Area, and more particularly the Santa Clara Valley and places nearby—and partly as a metaphor to represent high-technology industry in California, and the United States more generally. My data are sketchy and my conclusions highly preliminary. Yet the issues are of considerable interest to both managers and policy makers in the United States and elsewhere.

Foreign Direct Investment in California

Investments in California by persons or companies from outside the state have played a major role throughout the state's history. Indeed, British financing of the railroads opened California to the rest of the Continent. However, foreign direct investment—which is defined here as the establishment or purchase by residents of another country of a significant ownership share and some management voice in a business enterprise or real

I wish to thank Nick Argyres, Janet Bercowitz, Marty Graham, Dan McFetridge, and L. G. Teece for helpful comments and assistance.

This is an adapted version of an article that originally appeared in *Foreign Investment, Technology and Economic Growth* (University of Calgary Press, 1991). Reproduced with the permission of the Minister of Supply and Services Canada, 1992.

property—is a relatively recent phenomena and became prominent in the 1970s. While statistics on the level and growth of Foreign Direct Investment (hereafter FDI) in California are outdated and of questionable reliability, the state's data show an increase from 31 transactions in 1976 to 244 in 1987 (Table 1). Often these were in the form of mergers and acquisitions, but joint ventures and strategic alliances were also prominent (Table 2).

In addition to the traditional modes of direct foreign investment, the 1980s have seen a marked increase in indirect investment via venture capital funds. Eventually, when the funds are dissolved—perhaps a decade or more after their domination—the limited partners obtain ownership shares in the portfolio companies in which the venture fund has invested. In the interim, the venture funds act as a kind of intermediary between the foreign investor and the ultimate investee.

Data from Venture Economics indicate that on average over $100 million a year was invested in California funds by foreign individuals or entities over the period 1980-1989 (see Table 3). This is not a large amount, but it does indicate that foreign firms see venture capital funds as one vehicle for investing in California high-technology firms. However, as discussed later, traditional forms of venture capital are unlikely to be attractive in the future to investors desiring something other than a financial relationship with the companies in the venture fund's portfolio.

Table 1. Number and Value of Foreign Investment Transactions in California by Year, 1976–1986

Year	Number	Number Where Value is Recorded	Value ($Mil)
1976	31	17	$ 194.3
1977	27	19	638.8
1978	103	49	544.9
1979	134	64	4,850.1
1980	184	76	2,395.5
1981	149	49	4,197.1
1982	120	50	2,116.8
1983	114	56	2,318.0
1984	155	73	3,769.2
1985	147	66	6,173.6
1986	179	80	3,296.2
1987	244	NA	NA

Source: California Department of Commerce, Office of Economic Research. Calculations from U.S. Department of Commerce, International Trade Administration (ITA), *Foreign Direct Investment in the United States: Completed Transactions, 1974-1983, Volume III: State Location,* June 1985; *1984 Transactions,* September 1985; *1985 Transactions,* September 1986, *1986 Transactions,* September 1987.

Table 2. Number and Value of Foreign Investment Transactions in California by Type of Investment, 1976–1986

Type	Number	Number Where Value Is Recorded	Value ($ Mil)	Average Value ($ Mil)
Total	1,343	599	$30,494.5	$50.9
Acquisition/Merger	382	208	16,286.4	78.3
Equity Increase	56	33	1,257.5	38.1
Joint Venture	54	13	712.2	39.6
New Plant	95	36	526.9	14.6
Plant Expansion	34	23	860.3	37.4
Real Estate	328	198	9,054.6	45.7
Other	326	58	950.8	16.4
Unknown	68	25	845.8	33.8

Source: California Department of Commerce, Office of Economic Research. Calculations from U.S. Department of Commerce, International Trade Administration (ITA), *Foreign Direct Investment in the Unitred States: Completed Transactions, 1974-1983, Volume III: State Location,* June 1985; *1984 Transactions,* September 1985; *1985 Transactions,* September 1986, *1986 Transactions,* September 1987.

Table 3. Foreign Investments in California Funds, 1980–1989 (in $ millions)

	Financial Corp.	Industrial Corp.	Family/ Individual	Unknown Type	Total
1980	2.8	1.75	1.0	18.5	24.05
1981	11.45	8.5	8.95	1.65	30.55
1982	8.9	4.65	10.9	2.5	26.95
1983	17.2	2.8	7.1	191.8	218.90
1984	47.6	17.15	5.55	4.8	75.10
1985	173.0	23.0	4.8	10.6	211.40
1986	18.4	13.6	1.5	19.2	52.70
1987	59.3	53.8	4.55	64.5	182.15
1988	28.8	21.0	1.35	6.75	57.90
1989	34.5	21.5	4.25	——	60.25

Country of origin statistics indicate that since 1986 Japan has been the leading foreign investor in California. In 1987, Japanese companies owned $8.1 billion gross book value of property, plant, and equipment in California.[1] Canada and the United Kingdom has the second and third rankings respectively. The largest share of foreign investment (measured by gross book value) was in real estate (27.5%), followed by manufacturing. High-technology investments constitute a significant and possibly growing proportion of total foreign direct investment in California.

It is by no means clear, however, that the economic moment of foreign direct investment can be adequately summarized by statistics on gross investment. A clearer picture of what is going on, and possibly what is at stake, can be gleaned from Table 4 which identifies certain investee and investor firms that have participated in foreign direct investment in California in the period 1981 to 1990 in three industries: semiconductors, biotechnology, and computers. To illustrate this phenomenon, I briefly discuss five recent instances.

Genentech—On February 2, 1990, Genentech announced an arrangement for Roche Holdings of Basil, Switzerland to purchase 60 percent of the South San Francisco biotech firm—the nation's largest, best capitalized, and most visible biotech firm. The agreement was effective on September 7, 1990. Genentech will stay organizationally separate from Roche for at least the next five years, with Roche not interfering in the management of operations and controlling only two of Genentech's 13 board seats. This transaction is of great interest because of its potential impact on technological development in the biotechnology industry.

Genentech's motivations appeared to be both financial and strategic. Genentech appeared concerned that further technological development and the worldwide commercialization of new biotechnology applications would require cash as well as access to assets and capabilities that it currently did not have. Roche's cash infusion ($492 million) will undoubtedly invigorate Genentech's R&D, enabling projects put on hold to move into active development.

As a result of this investment, Roche obtains a substantial augmentation of its technological position in biotechnology in the United States. While already operating laboratories in New Jersey, Roche does not appear to have been very successful in recombinant technology in the United States or elsewhere. In the short run technology transfer opportunities for Roche are limited as Genentech technology is not licensed to Roche under the agreement, and there is no technology "transparency" for five years. However, after five years, Roche has the right to buy the remainder of Genentech's stock at its fair market value at the time. It then will have complete access to Genentech's intellectual property and products in the pipeline and to future research results.

Table 4. Examples of Direct Foreign Investment in California, 1981–1990

Firm	Investor	Country	Amount of Investment (millions)	Holding (percent)	Year
Semiconductors and Equipment					
Exel Microelectronics	Rohm Corp.	Japan	5.7	60.7	1986
US Semiconductor	Osaka Titanium	Japan		100	1986
NBK Corp.	Kawasaki Steel	Japan	9.4	100	1985
T.A. Hand, Inc.	Showa Musen Kogyo	Japan	9.4	100	1981
Syncor Int'l	Gov't of France	France	24.2	100	1983
Telmos	Merlin Gerin SA	France	4.1	100	1985
Zymos	Daewoo Corp.	S. Korea	13.4	35	1986
Telmos' Production Facility	Rohm Co.	Japan	1.5	100	1987
Tera Micro Systems	ASCII Corp.	Japan		25	1990
Semi-Gas	Nippon Sanso	Japan		100	1990
Aegis Inc.	Asahi Glass/Olin	Japan		50	1987
Monsanto's Polysilicon Unit	Huels	Germany		100	1989
Siltec	Mitsubishi	Japan	32.0	33	1986
Panatech's Semicond. Div.	Ricoh Co.	Japan	1.1	100	1987
Siscan Systems	Mitsubishi	Japan		11.5	1985
GTI Corp.	individual	So. Africa	6.0	100	1987
Varian's Tube Division	Thorn EMI	UK		100	1983
Marumen Integ. Cir.	Toshiba	Japan		2.7	1980
Xicor	S.G. de l'Horlogerie	Switzerland		15	1983
(NEC)	NEC	Japan		100	1981
Diamon Images	Kanematsu-Gosho	Japan		10	
Waferscale Integ.	Sharp	Japan		3.5	
Benzing	Kanematsu	Japan		7	1984
Micro Linear	Kyocera	Japan		ND	ND
Vitelic	Sony	Japan		ND	ND
Exar	Rohm	Japan		61	1985
Focus Semicond.	MIP Equity	Netherlands	5.0	100	1987
Integrated CMOS	Toshiba	Japan	4.0	14	1989
Vitesse Semicond.	Thomson	France		ND	1990
(Toshiba Semicond.)	Toshiba	Japan		100	1986
Biotechnology					
Cytel	Sandoz	Switzerland	30.0	20	1989
Zoecon	Sandoz	Switzerland		100	1983
Intermedics Intraocular	Pharmacia AB	Sweden		100	1986
Immunetech	Tanabe Seiyaku	Japan			1988
Chiron	CIBA-Geigy	Switzerland		6.2	1989
Cetus	Roche Holdings	Switzerland		3.5	1989
Mycogen	Kubota	Japan		9.6	1987
Gen-Probe	Chugai Pharm.	Japan		100	1989
Genencor	Cultor Oy/Kodak	Finland/U.S.		100	1990
Codon	Shering AG	Germany		100	1990
Adv. Genetic Sci.	AB Cardo	Italy		100	1986
Intl. Immunology	Nitto Boski Co.	Japan		100	1986
Genentech	Roche Holdings	Switzerland		60	1990

Table 4. Examples of Direct Foreign Investment in California, 1981–1990

Firm	Investor	Country	Amount of Investment (millions)	Holding (percent)	Year
Computer Hardware/Peripherals					
Dataproducts	Hitachi Koki/N. Sanso	Japan		100	1990
Silicon Graphics	NKK Corp.	Japan	5.0	3590	
Akhasic Memories	Kubota	Japan	15.0	100	1987
Komag	Asahi Glass	Japan	20.0	17	1986
Komag	Kobe Steel	Japan	20.0	20	1990
C-Cube Microsystems	Kubota	Japan		ND	ND
Lam Research	Sumitomo Metal	Japan	5.0	5	
Maxoptix	Kubota	Japan	12.0	12	
MIPS Computer	Kubota	Japan	15.0	25	1987
NeXT	Canon	Japan	100	17	1989
Poquet Computer	Fujitsu	Japan		38	ND
Ardent Computer	Kubota	Japan	26.0	44	1989
Counterpoint Computer	Acer	Taiwan		100	1986
Wyse	investor group	Taiwan		100	1990
Atari GamesNamco		Japan			
Britton Lee	Mitsubishi	Japan		ND	ND
David Systems	Pirelli	Italy	2.0	100	1985
LaPine	Kyocera	Japan	2.1	ND	1987
SyQuest	JAFCC, Nippon Sys.	Japan		ND	ND
Tolerant (Eritas)	Digital Ltd.	Japan		1	1986
Dana Computer	Kubota	Japan	20.0	100	1986
Momenta	group	Singapore		1990	
System Integrators	Birmingham	UK		100	1985
National Controls	Stavely Inc.	UK		100	1985
Apple's plant	Alps Electric	Japan		100	1985
Forward Technologies	Digital Computer	Japan		100	1985
Victor Technologies	Datatronics AB	Sweden		100	1985
Datametrics	Oranje-Nassau	Netherlands	.8	100	1986
Fortune Systems	Govt. of France	France		100	1986
Micro Five Corp.	Samsung	S. Korea	.9	100	1986
Saber Labs	BMW	Germany			1986
Calay Sys.	Agiv	Germany		100	1987
Corporate Data Sciences	Telfos TLC	UK		100	1987
Calcomp's Systems Div.	ISI-CAD	Germany		100	1987

* = Southern California location   ND = not disclosed

Source: The data was compiled from the following sources: International Trade Administration (ITA), *Foreign Investment Transactions,* 1980–1988, various issues of *Japan Economic Institute Report, Business Week, Bio/Technology, San Francisco Chronicle,* and a coinversation with a representative of the Semiconductor Industry Association. One hundred percent ownership represents an acquisition or merger as identified in the ITA data.

Since the ITA data rely heavily on business and trade publications sources, as opposed to more systematic surveys, the data here may not be representative of actual FDI activity in California.

Roche's investment can be seen in part as a reaction to the high risks and costs associated with using U.S. public markets to finance technological development in the biotechnology industry.[2] For example, Genentech's stock fell from 47½ to 14⅜ in 1988 because of disappointing sales of its heart attack drug, TPA. Likewise in August 1990, Cetus stock fell from about 15 to 3 because of a temporary setback in its ability to obtain FDA approval for its anti-cancer drug, Interluken II, which had already been approved in Europe. In part, it is also a recognition that Genentech and other U.S. companies have the lead in this industry; by far the cheapest way for the European and Japanese to catch up is for them to acquire U.S. biotech firms.[3] It is also a reflection of the fact that stand-alone biotech companies like Genentech—without substantial downstream facilities in manufacturing and marketing—need to team with established firms to accomplish this end. Previously it had appeared that strategic alliances would suffice; the Genentech experience may portend that further integration is necessary. But it is also important to bear in mind that Genentech was already profitable and had considerable cash reserves.[4] Some have interpreted the sale as evidence that Genentech's owners did not have the tenacity or patience to stick it out.[5] However, it is difficult to avoid the conclusion that U.S. equity markets are not the place to finance long gestation industries and that the owners were worried about the long-run viability of Genentech in the absence of a significant of internal cash flow steam.

Wyse—Established in 1981, Wyse Technology, a San Jose-based manufacturer of computer terminals, was an independent company for nine years before being purchased, following a period of financial distress, by Channel Intercorporation Corporation. This Taiwanese consortium, which consists of China Trust Co., a Taiwan Government development fund (the Executive Yuan Development fund), two petrochemical companies, and Taiwan's second largest computer company (Mitac International Corporation)—purchased Wyse in late 1989. The sale marked the first time a Taiwanese concern had purchased all the stock of a U.S. company. Interestingly, two of the founders of Wyse, Grace and Bernie Tse, were themselves U.S.-educated Taiwanese citizens, residing in the United States.

In 1986, five-year old Wyse Technology was the world's largest independent terminal supplier, second only to IBM in terminal volume. The San Jose-based company manufactured its terminals at a high-volume, vertically integrated, and automated factory in Taiwan. However, in the last half of 1980 sales fell by more than 50 percent. The company faced a collapsing computer market, an associated industry-wide memory chip shortage, and competitive new product introductions. Wyse, being locked into a high-volume and vertically integrated strategy, seemed unable to adjust.[6] In the same period, Wyse lost a great deal of money due to an ill-timed diversification into PC clones. The company responded to its problems by taking on debt and by cutting personnel in the United States and Taiwan. But after losses of $7.6 million on (projected) sales of $231.4 million in 1990, Wyse was sold to the Taiwanese consortium for close to $270 million in cash.

For the buyers, the principle advantage in purchasing Wyse appeared to be access to the company's extensive distribution channel in the United States.[7] Mitac, which in the past had little success in selling its brand-name computers in the United States, will benefit directly by exploiting Wyse's relationship with Businessland Inc. The company may be better positioned to place products onto crowded retail shelves and capture margin and control by moving downstream into the distribution network.[8] Wyse's well-established brand name and "good will" presented additional benefits for the investors.

The Taiwanese consortium will not be passive investors. The group announced plans to install Morris Chang as Wyse's new chairman. Mr. Chang currently heads the government sponsored Industrial Technology Research Institute (ITRI).

Fairchild—In 1979, Schlumberger bought Fairchild Camera and Instrument, one of the world's first semiconductor producers, for $425 million.[9] Despite Fairchild's fading product line and the 1982-83 semiconductor slump, Schlumberger, a French oil services company, tried to implement a radically new business strategy almost overnight. Under Schlumberger's direction, Fairchild laid off half of its workforce, decentralized its corporate structure, and refocused on semiconductors. Schlumberger poured cash into R&D and into new plant and equipment.

But the strategy failed. By 1984, it had been eclipsed by its four major spinoffs—Signetics, Advanced Micro Devices, National, and Intel. In the face of mounting losses, Schlumberger shut down Fairchild's opto-electronics division in February 1983. In March, it disbanded Fairchild's MOS operation, and by mid-1983 Fairchild's presence in EPROMs, SRAMs, and DRAMs had virtually disappeared. Fairchild also ceased manufacturing its custom hybrid circuit modules, and began phasing out a test and assembly plant in Indonesia. The massive retreat was accompanied by an equally massive exodus of experienced managers. Thomas Roberts, a Schlumberger manager who was installed as Fairchild president and CEO, was heavily criticized, as was Schlumberger's imposition of top managers who had no semiconductor experience. In 1983, Schlumberger sought out semiconductor expertise, hiring Texas Instruments senior vice president Donald Brooks. But the losses continued, and in October 1986 Schlumberger agreed to sell 80 percent of its position in Fairchild to Fujitsu.

The proposed deal with Fujitsu had several purported short- and long-run benefits for Fairchild and Fujitsu. In the short run, Fujitsu would provide capital resources to shore up Fairchild finances. Fujitsu would gain the onshore production capabilities it was seeking. It also would get access to

Fairchild's first-tier distribution network. This was potentially important, since some distributors, including Wyse Labs, refused to "handle any product with a Japanese brand name on it."[10] Wilfred Corrigan, chairman of LSI Logic, called the proposed investment "a backdoor way to buy into U.S. manufacturing," as well as a "backdoor to distribution channels."

In the longer term, Fujitsu promised to be a source of patient capital with a commitment to R&D. It was also expected that it might share its advanced optoelectronics technology. There were other potential technological complementarities as well. Fujitsu's MOS capabilities would have replaced those lost to Fairchild back in 1983, and were seen as important in the development of a new generation of bipolar circuits. Fairchild perhaps had some technological advantage over competitors with respect to this class of circuits, but was by no means the only producer. But more generally, the development of custom chips had made the relationships between systems producers and chip manufacturers much closer. Many industry managers and analysts cited the high degree of vertical integration of Japanese firms as a reason for their relative success. It was Brooks' view that co-development of system hardware and software with semiconductor technology was the logical extension of the increased customer role in the innovation process.[11]

Specifically, one element of the plan appears to have been to merge Fairchild's capabilities in bipolar gate arrays with Fujitsu's capabilities in supercomputing in order to boost supercomputers' power, and even build new "minisupers." These would put supercomputer power in the hands of conventional mainframe customers and could catapult the two firms into the next era of computing. It was here, however, where the deal got into trouble.

The Pentagon voiced concern since one group of bipolar circuits manufactured by Fairchild, using emitter-coupler logic (ECL), were particularly crucial to the operation of computers embedded in certain advanced weapons. Defense Secretary Weinberger argued to the Administration that the merger would make the Defense department dependent on foreign sources for a key technology. On the surface, this would seem to be a questionable argument, since no similar concern was raised when the French company Schlumberger bought Fairchild. But concerns expressed by certain personnel at Cray Research, the major U.S. supercomputer producer and Pentagon supplier, gave support to Weinberger's position. Apparently, sources at Cray and at ETA Systems complained that they had trouble getting shipments of certain Japanese integrated circuits. Lloyd Thorndike, president of ETA Systems had said that "Japanese firms with supercomputer lines were withholding new high-speed IC's from U.S. firms."[12] Potential leakage of Cray supercomputer designs to Fujitsu was also a concern.

Commerce Secretary Malcolm Baldridge also urged the Administration to block the transaction. He criticized Japanese protection of their home supercomputer market and saw the merger as a threat to the competitiveness of the U.S. supercomputer industry. The mounting political furor caused Fujitsu to back away from the deal. But the saga was not yet over. Fairchild pursued ties with Fujitsu anyway, and eventually Fujitsu joined a management group in a buyout attempt. The group was outbid by National Semiconductor, which bought Fairchild for $122 million in stock and warrants, some 25 percent of the Schlumberger purchase price seven years earlier. National's acquisition created a $2 to $4 billion company; industry executives praised the deal, saying it would help National and U.S. industry compete worldwide. The acquisition also marked the end of an epoch, with an industry pioneer being acquired by one of its former spinouts.

It appears, however, that emotions, not national technological issues, carried the day. Fairchild was made out to be an industry technological leader and a unique U.S. supplier of a key technology. Neither of these appear to have been true. Rather than dealing with the fundamental problems, the government moved to block the transaction, amidst considerable confusion about the intentions of all parties to the transaction.[13] It is probably the case that Fujitsu would have enhanced Fairchild's technological position. Yet Fairchild, and its potential sale to Fujitsu, became a symbol of Silicon Valley's proud heritage and declining American competitiveness, and the deal came unstuck.

Akhasic Memories and MIPS—Both Akhasic and MIPS have taken in significant investment in recent years from Kubota. Kubota Ltd. is a 100-year-old Japanese heavy machinery maker, perhaps best known for its farm equipment business, with sales in the $5.5 billion range. It is one of the major foreign investors in U.S. high-tech companies. As of July 1990, it had invested approximately $200 million in the United States. In California, these investments include equity stakes in Stardent Computer, C-Cube Microsystems, MIPS Computer, Rasna Computer, and Maxoptix. Investees outside of California include ownership of Domain Technology (purchased for $66 million) and a $6 million, 9.2 percent stake in Exabyte of Boulder, Colorado.

Founded in 1982, Akhasic was in trouble by 1986. It had run out of cash and was two and a half years late to market with its thin-film memory disk. Meanwhile Komag, its closest competitor, had marketed its version of the disk a year earlier, gone public, and raised $135 million. In Japan, Kubota had just built a disk production plant in Osaka, but was having trouble exporting to the U.S. market, which represented 90 percent of the world memory disk market. Kubota believed its problems stemmed from a technology gap, which would take three years to close, along with the strong yen. Acquiring Akhasic Memories solved the first problem, while turning the second on its head. It would boost Kubota's access to technology and take advantage of the strong yen which made the acquisition look cheap.

The timing was good for Akhasic as well. Despite the $3.5 million revenues it had obtained by 1986, venture capital funds had become "very jaded toward the disk drive business and anything associated with it."[14] Akhasic needed at least $10 million to bring production up to profitable levels. The firms settled on a $20 million buyout price. Kubota immediately sent a team of 10 technicians to Akhasic, who spent two weeks studying the technology.

MIPS is primarily a designer of reduced instruction-set computing, or RISC microprocessors and systems and related software and components. Founded in 1985, it became one of the fastest growing hardware firms in Silicon Valley, reaching $40 million in revenues by its third year. The first years were spent promoting the RISC idea to potential buyers such as concept DEC, Stardent (then Ardent), and Tandem Computers. Buyers and venture capitalists were convinced and remained so. By mid-1987, the latter had invested $37 million, and DEC bought a 5 percent equity stake in 1988. In October 1987, Kubota offered $25 million, just when MIPS was at a breakeven point in its financing. Kubota agreed to a base valuation of $120 million for MIPS, which was unheard of for a company of MIPS' level of development. A pure financial motivation for the offer by Kubota appears unlikely. Paradoxically, pure financial motivation by MIPS seems likely, as MIPS needed cash to pursue its business objectives. The Kubota money solidified MIPS' position in the market. The investment by Kubota was not a rescue effort, as with Akhasic Memories. Kubota appears to have sought access to a technology with high potential, as well as a "listening post" to aid in further moves in the United States. Moreover, the RISC technology was a crucial technology for Kubota's long-term strategy to be a presence in the workstation and supercomputer markets.

Kubota's corporate strategy, with respect to these and other deals, is widely understood to be long term. It appears to have two facets. On the one hand, Kubota is interested in new computer technologies that will transform its traditional businesses in machinery and mechanical automation. On the other hand, Kubota appears inntent on diversification, and views the workstation and supercomputer markets as desirable because of their growth prospects.

Kubota's investments in Stardent (previously Ardent before its merger with Stellar Computer), Rasna, and MIPS all serve to illustrate these dual motivations. The association with Stardent, a graphics supercomputer firm, has enabled Kubota to manufacture Stardent's sophisticated titan mini-supercomputer in a new $200 million factory in Yamagashi, Japan, while maintaining access to Stardent's technology. These computers use components from MIPS, another Kubota investee. Rasna, a software firm, is known for its work on programs for computer-aided design with mechanical engineering and machinery-design applications. Computer tools for fluid modelling in refinery development are one set of applications of particular interest. To achieve their goals in a world where technologies are converging, Kubota appears to be investing in both microelectronics hardware and software. There can be little doubt that some significant U.S. technology is being transferred to Kubota, and that the net flow is outward, although the direction may change in the future.

The long-term nature of Kubota's investment plans appear to be real. Naohisa Matsuda, a vice president of Kubota, explains his company's actions with respect to technology transfer from Stardent by saying, "We are only manufacturing the machines. All the designs are done in the United States."[15] He went on to say that it would take 20 years for Kubota to develop the design skills of Stardent and other major computer makers.

Observations on Foreign Direct Investment in California

Silicon Valley is perhaps the world's most prosaic and creative incubator of new technology-based firms, particularly in semiconductors, biotechnology, and computers. The region has an unmatched capacity to spawn new enterprises and sustain them through early technological development. A principal reason for foreign direct investment in Silicon Valley manufacturing from the perspective of investors, is to access technology and the distribution channels for high-technology products.

As development expenses mount and as cash constraints become critical, the financial infrastructure on which so many Silicon Valley firms depend —venture capital and small amounts of bank debt collateralized by receivables or equipment—is either inadequate or too expensive to propel growth at levels necessary to maintain international competitiveness. Invariably, internal corporate financing, provided by companies with a keen interest in the technology and/or the distribution facilities of the investee, offers the most likely source of additional capital. The firms with the capital and the willingness to commit it are generally foreign, and frequently Japanese.

The willingness to invest in this fashion is far too commonly attributed to the higher cost of capital in the United States.[16] This difference was never great and has now evaporated. The different patterns of investment behavior is mainly due to differences in management approaches and to the difference in corporate governance between U.S. and foreign firms. Either the foreign firms are private, such as Roche Holdings and Schlumberger, or they are large Japanese enterprises that are beholden less to (short-term) stockholder interests than their American counterparts. This reflects differences in industrial structure between the United States and Japan, with Japanese firms commonly embedded in *keiretsu* structures with ready access to bank capital and with less propensity to allocate earnings to dividends or stock buybacks. Differences in ownership and industrial structure support a longer time horizon on the part of many foreign firms— particularly Japanese firms, as the Kubota example illustrates. This reflects not only the different financial structures between U.S. and Japanese firms but also the greater managerial concern with building technological competences rather than particular products.[17] With technological competence and capabilities put center stage, Japanese firms are free to focus on the long run and to imagine constellations of future products deriving from technological capabilities.

The growing importance of Japanese direct investment in California industry is of great interest in the United States, if not elsewhere. Such investment takes a number of forms. First, there are corporate investments, as when a Japanese company takes a direct equity stake in a U.S. venture. This form is illustrated by Kubota's investment in MIPS and Stardent.

Another major form of investment is through a venture capital vehicle, such as a partnership. In this structure, Japanese corporate investors, often with other investors, place monies in venture capital funds which in turn take equity positions in non publicly-traded ventures. Kubota has actively used this vehicle in Silicon Valley. So has Mitsubishi. In practically all such instances, Japanese investors have much more than a financial interest in their investee, whether they are direct investors or whether the investee is simply one of several companies in the venture capitalist's portfolio. As discussed earlier, in many instances immediate financial returns are decidedly secondary. This explains in part the willingness of the Japanese to pay high prices for equity positions.

What the Japanese usually want with their investments in Silicon Valley, but do not always receive, is a window on new technologies and markets. Because the Japanese system does not have the entrepreneurial capacity of Silicon Valley,[18] it is most important for Japanese firms to find ways to access new technology and to legitimize internal efforts at developing new technology. Silicon Valley firms often become the pilot fish of large Japanese enterprises, providing new early-stage technologies and windows on market evolution. This not only propels innovation in Japan, it also legitimatizes new initiatives. Because failure is "costly" in Japan—the individuals associated with leading a company down a blind alley often face levels of ostracism uncommon in California—the guiding light provided by Silicon Valley firms is often of considerable moment.

Moreover, so often venture-funded U.S. firms are unable to finish what they start. Japanese corporate investors often provide what the U.S. firms lack—patient capital, engineering talent, manufacturing excellence, and access to the Japanese market. Clearly there is a symbiotic relationship here which generally benefits both parties. But the United States must recognize that Japanese investment signifies a failure of U.S. organizational structures and capital markets to provide large-scale investments to support uncertain new technologies.

It is important to recognize, however, that it is not just existing Japanese competitors that take strategic investment in high-tech Silicon Valley companies. Often large low-tech firms, like the tobacco and steel companies, use such investments to underpin their diversification strategies. These firms are not only cash rich; they have strategic visions going ahead 99 years. An acquisition now is often seen as a way to preserve options into the future. U.S. firms often are delighted to have such firms as part of their investor group.

The "success" of an investment from the Japanese perspective —particularly if it occurs through venture funds—is likely to depend importantly on whether personal relationships develop between representatives from the Japanese investor and the Silicon Valley investee. Opportunities for technology transfer and market success depend on the continued flow of information and personnel. In this regard, the use of a traditional venture capitalist as an intermediary often serves to stifle information exchange and block all but occasional interaction among the principals. Perhaps the traditional forms of venture capital will wane in relative importance over time as mechanisms to place Japanese investment in Silicon Valley. A new breed of "relational" venture capitalists may well displace them.

Strategic Trade Policy, the Theory of the Multinational Enterprise, and Direct Foreign Investment

Mainstream academic research has contributed very little to our understanding of the motivation for and effects of direct foreign investment in high-technology industries. The most recent flurry—the literature on strategic trade and investment policy—is unfortunately no exception. As Harris notes, "the heart of the strategic trade policy argument revolves around the presence of oligopoly rents due to barriers to entry. Barriers to entry may stem from either large economies of scale in production or distribution, or the presence of substantial sunk costs in the form of R&D expenditures."[19] The new strategic trade theory has shown that under a rather restrictive set of assumptions, nation states can intervene in markets to shift rents from foreign firms to domestic firms.

At least with respect to trade and foreign investment involving Silicon Valley firms, oligopoly theory is almost useless in helping us understand what is going on. The technological rivalry which can be witnessed between U.S. firms and Japanese firms is not primarily about the division of monopoly profits in identifiable product markets; rather it is about the accumulation of firm-specific capabilities. Until the theory of trade and investment is able to build within itself a meaningful model of the business enterprise, academic and policy research in this area will continue to flounder. It has been suggested that the firm should be represented not by production functions or cost curves, but by the capabilities they possess, and their capacity to employ and augment them.[20] It must also be recognized that the firm's resources endowments are substantially "sticky": firms are often stuck with what they have and may have to live with what they lack, at least in the short term. Many assets are simply not readily tradeable. Certainly tacit know-how falls into this category. Thus, differences in capabilities cannot easily equilibrate through factor markets or through the market for know-how. The market for corporate control—as with direct foreign investment—may provide certain, though limited, opportunities for transferring know-how. If such investments are coupled with long-run efforts to build relationships and transfer technology, capabilities can be transferred.

If control over idiosyncratic capabilities can be the source of (Ricardian) rents, then it follows that such issues as skill accumulation and learning become fundamental to building firm-level competitive advantage. Direct foreign investment needs to be understood in this context. In short, it is not monopoly rents which are at issue in foreign direct investment, rather it is the Ricardian and Schumpeterian rents flowing from the gradual transfer of firm-specific capabilities in production and innovation. Hence, earlier work on foreign direct investment[21] which analyzed the relative efficiency of equity positions and licensing as the way to do business abroad may have missed an issue which is becoming increasingly important, at least in Silicon Valley—the role that direct foreign investment can play in technological accumulation and business development.

The emerging theory of corporate capabilities provides concepts which, if adopted, promise to yield a better theory of direct foreign investment.[22] Foreign direct investment cannot be well understood unless explicit attention is given to the organizational requirements of the innovation process, including the need of pioneers to access complementary assets[23] in order to be successful in bringing a new product or process to market. Such an approach to the business enterprise may help provide a framework for understanding how foreign investment fits into business strategy and technological development. As John Dunning suggested: "It is to be hoped that the next generation of scholars will give more attention to issues of innovation and entrepreneurship as they impinge upon the internationalization of business."[24]

Policy Issues

Should government be encouraging or discouraging foreign investment in Silicon Valley? What are the benefits, and what are the costs? The answers to these questions are not at all straightforward. Nevertheless, as a philosophical matter, I will begin with the presumption that there should be no restrictions on direct foreign investment. This is not quite U.S. government policy at present, as there are at least two avenues currently available for restricting direct foreign investment.

One is Exon-Florio. Following the Fairchild Fujitsu debacle discussed earlier, the Exon-Florio amendment[25] was passed which provided authority for the pre-existing Committee on Foreign Investment in the United States (CFIUS) of the executive branch to intervene in foreign acquisitions of U.S. companies when such acquisition might imperil "national security." The law does not explicitly define this term or give examples of adverse effects. CFIUS has not been at all activist and has been criticized for its liberal stance.[26] In the context of CFIUS's controversial approval of the sale of Semi-Gas to Nippon-Sanso, the President's Science Advisor, D. Allan Bromiley, on August 14, 1990 is reported to have written the Department of Defense warning of the cumulative effect of CFIUS approvals. CFIUS has apparently approved 28 foreign acquisitions of semiconductor equipment and materials firms. Bromiley is reported to have argued that "our technological base can be nibbled from under us through the coherent plan of [foreign] purchasing of entrepreneurial companies, many of whom have been assisted directly or indirectly by the federal government in developing their technological strengths."[27] The Deputy Assistant Treasury Secretary meanwhile argued that the Nippon-Sanso acquisition would benefit the U.S. industry because of capital investment and technology transfer that the Japanese company would make to Semi-Gas.[28]

The other avenue open to block the foreign acquisition of a U.S. company is the antitrust laws, again illustrated by the Semi-Gas debacle. The DOJ and the FTC have the capacity to block acquisitions by either domestic or foreign firms when the effect is to substantially lessen competition. In the Semi-Gas case, Congressman Bingamen and Bentsen lobbied the DOJ arguing that if the acquisition went through, Nippon-Sanso could dominate the world market in critical semiconductor gas distribution systems. The Department of Justice *Merger Guidelines* (revised 1984) clearly lay out the level of concentration that will cause it to challenge a merger. However, the market definition approach which the antitrust agencies employ of course does not exclude substitute products from the definition of the market, even if those products use different technologies. At the time of this writing (November 1990), the Semi-Gas acquisition was still pending.

There is not the opportunity here to resolve whether the existing regulatory mechanisms are adequate and whether the presumption in favor of a liberal approach to foreign direct investment can be adequately supported. However, in order to address these issues, I believe it is necessary, at least in the context of DFI in Silicon Valley, to adopt a forward-looking posture which examines the impact of DFI on the dynamic capabilities of U.S. firms. If this is resolved positively by looking at the evidence, it is probably the case the U.S. welfare is enhanced by DFI, and vice versa. Certainly the narrow consumer-oriented approach embedded in the antitrust laws is unlikely to capture all of what ought to be considered. Clearly this is an area that invites careful empirical scholarship that examines the impact of DFI on skills and capabilities.

A looming issue for the 1990s is the aggressive program by the Japanese to set up labs in Silicon Valley and elsewhere.[29] Leading Japanese computer and electronic companies are opening up labs in the United States and competing for top talent, particularly in computer software. NEC has opened a research lab in Princeton, Matsushita is reported to be opening a new lab in San Francisco in 1991, and Canon is opening one in Stanford, California. The Japanese appear to be targeting sites near universities with leading computer science departments—hence the two proposed labs in the San Francisco Bay Area. If the Japanese characteristically offer top dollar for this talent, U.S. universities and research facilities will need to stretch in order to keep their best talent.

If these new labs focus on basic research, the world scientific community will be the beneficiary, because the technology will simply leak out. But if the labs develop a strong proprietary focus, the effect may well be to deplete the United States of one of its few remaining competitive advantages in high-technology—the clear superiority of its early stage research. The ability of the Japanese to bring ideas to market will be further enhanced by such labs, but the distributional implications are by no means clear.

Conclusion

Foreign direct investment in Silicon Valley has important implications for U.S. economic welfare. It is the arena where global competition in the future is being shaped today. The shortcomings of the Silicon Valley industrial system—the absence of patient capital, the lack of manufacturing skills, and poor capacity to access to foreign markets—mean that high-technology companies that get launched here often land elsewhere. This is a natural consequence of global competition—natural in the sense that it reflects the competitive advantage of the firms and nations engaged in global competition.

Is there cause for alarm? Possibly so. Significant foreign investment signals the inability of U.S. high-tech firms to grow to maturity without infusion of capital and other resources from abroad. It signals tremendous dynamic capabilities in early-stage technological development, followed by subsequent failure. The solution is unlikely to require impeding the flow of foreign investment. Rather, it may lie in building the infrastructure —education, skills, savings, employee commitment, and the like—and new organizational systems which will support the development of later-stage firm level capacities in the innovation process. Failure to do so may enable firms outside the United States to disproportionately profit from the pioneering activity for which "the Valley" is so famous.

References

1. California Department of Commerce, Office of Economic Research, *Foreign Direct Investment in California*, February 1990.
2. G. Kirk Raab, Genentech's CEO, noted that "the quarterly pressures of the stock market, although real and understandable, were inevitably going to inhibit our taking advantage of the wonderful brain trust that works here on this 36 acres in South San Francisco." *San Jose Mercury News*, February 12, 1990.
3. The deal values Genentech at more than U.S. \$4 billion—100 times 1989 earnings.
4. 1989 revenues of \$400.5 million, and profits of \$43.9 million.
5. Genentech founder and former CEO Robert Swanson collected \$67 million on the transaction, while still keeping a large portion of his stock.
6. Wyse was particularly hurt in 1988 by Compaq's introduction of a 30386-based machine at 30286 prices and IBM's re-entry into the PC-AT market with a low-priced machine.
7. According to Daniel Wu, the consortium's president-designate of Wyse, the consortium was named Channel International Corporation to reflect investors' belief that Wyse's prime asset is its well-established U.S. marketing channel. *Far Eastern Economic Review*, December 28, 1989.
8. According to Colley Hwang of the Market Intelligence Centre (MIC), Mitac will obtain a share of the 30% average mark-up distributors place on PC products. *Asian Business* (May 1990).
9. Fairchild was founded by the late Robert Noyce. Much of the early research leading to the microelectronics age was done at Fairchild in the late 1950s and 1960s, including the Integrated Circuit.
10. Charley Clough, president of Wyse Labs, quoted in *Electronic News*, November 3, 1986, p. 10.
11. *Electronic News*, February 24, 1986, pp. 72-75.
12. Quoted in *Electronic News*, March 30, 1987, p. 10.
13. According to one member of the Committee for Foreign Investment in the United States, which spent weeks reviewing the Fujitsu proposal, "The reasons [for blocking the Fujitsu deal] varied from week to week." *San Jose Mercury News*, September 7, 1987).
14. William Hart, general partner at Technology Partners, is one of three venture capital firms that had put \$9 million into Akhasic.
15. Quoted in *Tokyo Business Today*, November 1989, p. 23.
16. In a recent paper, Frankel argues that while the cost of capital has generally been lower in Japan than in the United States, recent increases in interest rates or declines in stock values in Japan have left the cost of capital there approximately as high as in the United States. J. Frankel, "Japanese Finance in the 1980s: A Survey," in P. Krugman, ed., *Trade with Japan: Has the Door Opened Wider?* (Chicago, IL: Univ. of Chicago Press, 1991).
17. See David J. Teece, Gary Pisano, and Amy Shuen, "Firm Capabilities, Resources, and the Concept of Strategy," *Foreign Investment and Economic Growth* (University of Calgary Press, 1991), for a discussion of the dynamic capabilities approach to strategic management.
18. Many large American companies are similarly afflicted with a lack of entrepreneurial capacity. However, there are more mechanisms available in the United States to counter this deficiency, other than an equity play in Silicon Valley. For the Japanese, links to Silicon Valley firms often provide a unique capacity to identify new technologies.
19. R.G. Harris, "Strategic Trade Policy, Technological Spillovers and Foreign Investment," Simon Fraser University, August 1990.

20. Teece, Pisano, and Shuen, op. cit.
21. P.J. Buckley and M. C. Casson, *The Future of the Multinational Enterprise* (London: Macmillan, 1976); David J. Teece, "The Multinational Enterprise: Market Failure and Market Power Considerations," *Sloan Management Review*, 22/3 (Spring 1981): 3-17; David J. Teece, "Multinational Enterprise, Internal Governance, and Industrial Organization," *American Economic Review*, 75/2 (May 1985): 233-238; David J. Teece, "Transactions Cost Economics and the Multinational Enterprise: An Assessment," *Journal of Economic Behavior and Organization*, 7 (1986): 21-45; David J. Teece, "Profiting from Technological Innovation," *Research Policy*, 15/6 (December 1986): 285-305.
22. Teece et al., op. cit.
23. Teece (1986), op. cit.
24. John Dunning, "The Theory of International Production," *The International Trade Journal* (1989).
25. Exon-Florio was an amendment to the Omnibus Trade and Competitiveness Act of 1988.
26. As of February 1990, 270 cases had come before CFIUS. Seven of these cases were investigated, four recommendations were referred to the President, and one foreign investor, a Chinese national firm, was ordered to divest its share in a U.S. aerospace firm.
27. Quoted in *Electronic News*, October 15, 1990.
28. Ibid.
29. See "Japanese Computer Labs in the U.S. Are Luring America's Top Experts," *New York Times*, November 11, 1990, p. 15.

CALIFORNIA MANAGEMENT REVIEW Reprint Series
© 1993 by The Regents of the University of California
CMR, Volume 35, Number 2, Winter 1993

Japan's Growing Capabilities in Industrial Technology: Implications for U.S. Managers and Policymakers

David C. Mowery   David J. Teece

During the past 20 years, Japan's role within the global network of public and private institutions that influence the creation and adoption of new technologies has changed. **Along with dramatic structural change in the Japanese economy, this period has witnessed a transformation in Japanese tech-** nological capabilities. From its position in the 1960s as an economy that relied extensively on the transfer and modification of externally developed technologies, Japan has emerged as an economy with many firms that define the technological frontier in their industries.

This transformation in Japanese technological capabilities has created complex challenges for U.S. managers and public officials. The rapidly expanding network of "strategic alliances" among U.S. and Japanese firms has fueled concern that the pursuit by U.S. managers of corporate interests may not coincide with the advancement of U.S. national economic interests. The contrasting structure of the U.S. and Japanese "national innovation systems"[1] means that U.S. firms may have more difficulty accessing

Another version of this article was presented at a National Research Council conference and appeared under the title "The Changing Place of Japan in the Global Scientific and Technological Enterprise" in Thomas S. Arrison, C. Fred Bergsten, Edward M. Graham, and Martha Caldwell Harris, eds., *Japan's Growing Technological Capability: Implications for the U.S. Economy*, copyright 1992 by the National Academy of Sciences, National Academy Press, Washington, D.C.

Research for this article was aided by support from the Alfred P. Sloan Foundation and the Sasakawa Peace Foundation through the Consortium on Competitiveness and Cooperation at the University of California at Berkeley. We also wish to thank Tom Cottrell for research assistance and William Finan, Ulrike Schaede, John Cantwell, and an anonymous referee for valuable comments. Dr. Takebi Otsubo also assisted us in obtaining data on interfirm alliances. We are most grateful for all of this assistance.

Japanese scientific and technological research than Japanese firms face in gaining access to U.S. research activities and results. Added to these and other challenges for public policy is that of assessing the "lessons," if any, of postwar Japanese government industrial and technology policies for a U.S. economy that has produced minimal growth in median household incomes or hourly earnings and compensation during the past two decades.

Japan's Changing Technological Position, 1960-1990

A number of indicators suggest that Japanese firms have progressed during the postwar period from borrowing, modifying, and successfully commercializing foreign technologies to operating at the technological frontier. No individual indicator is definitive, but together they are suggestive. The average annual rate of growth in Japanese payments for imports of technology declined from 31 percent in the 1950s to 6 percent in the late 1970s, according to Uekusa.[2] Data from the surveys of Japanese technology imports and exports conducted by the Management and Coordination Agency show that the ratio of the value of Japan's technology exports to technology imports has increased from 39.4 percent in fiscal 1975 to 99.8 percent in fiscal 1989, i.e., virtual equality between imports and exports of technology (measured as the value of licensing fees and royalties) in fiscal 1989.[3] These data incorporate many older licenses, and they say little about the balance of trade in new technology licensing agreements. Data collected by the Management and Coordination Agency on new technology agreements indicate that the value of Japanese exports of new technology (i.e., new agreements and contracts undertaken during a given fiscal year) has exceeded that of imports for all but two years of the fiscal 1975-1989 period, and in fiscal 1989 amounted to 137 percent of the value of imports.[4]

Alone among the industrial nations, Japan registered an increase, rather than a decrease, in the number of patents received per scientist and engineer during 1967-84, as well as an increase in the number of patents received in foreign countries. Pavitt and Patel point out that on a per capita (adjusted by home-country population) basis, Japanese patenting in the U.S. increased by more than 650 percent during the period from 1963-68 to 1980-85, far more than any other industrial economy.[5] The U.S. National Science Foundation reported in 1988 that Japanese firms accounted for the largest single share of foreign-origin U.S. patents.[6] A comparison of U.S. patenting by U.S. and Japanese firms in 1975 and 1986 reveals dramatic improvements in Japanese patenting performance, relative to that of U.S. firms, in selected technologies (see Table 1). Moreover, according to the NSF report, Japanese-origin U.S. patents were cited more than proportionately in other patent applications, an indicator of the high quality of the Japanese patents.[7] Japan outstripped the combined totals of Germany, France, and England in patents granted in the United States in 1990 (see Table 2).

Table 1. U.S. and Japanese Shares of Total Patents Granted in the United States for Selected Technologies: 1975 and 1986 (percent)

Selected Technologies	United States		Japan	
	1975 %	1986 %	1975 %	1986 %
Lasers	63	50	14	35
Telecommunications	66	52	14	26
Steel and Iron	48	37	18	29
Internal Combustion Engines	54	28	17	44
Semiconductor Devices and Manufacture	68	57	13	29
Jet Engines	66	60	4	9
General Purpose Programmable Digital Computer Systems	77	69	5	19
Robots	63	50	20	29
Machine Tools—Metalworking	65	51	8	17
All technologies	65	54	9	19

Sources: National Science Foundation (1988).

Other indicators of technological performance suggest considerable Japanese strength. Technology adoption is a critical factor in national competitive performance, and in some technologies Japanese adoption performance appears to exceed that of the U.S. economy. The rate of adoption and intensity of utilization of advanced manufacturing technologies (including robotics, computer-integrated-manufacturing workcells, and flexible manufacturing systems) in Japanese manufacturing both considerably exceed their levels in U.S. manufacturing.[8] Clark et al.[9] and Clark and Fujimoto[10] have documented the ability of Japanese automotive firms to bring new models to market more rapidly than U.S. auto firms, and Mansfield[11] found that for technologies based on sources of knowledge outside of the firm, Japanese firms exhibit significantly shorter development and commercialization cycles. Mansfield's research also indicates that Japanese firms devote twice as large a share of their R&D budget to process research as U.S. firms. Interestingly, Mansfield's econometric analyses suggest that the returns to R&D investments in Japanese industry substantially exceed those in U.S. industry.[12]

This remarkable record of technological achievement has rested largely on R&D funding from private industry, rather than from government. The

Table 2. Patent Applications (Registrations) in Selected Countries, by Nationality, 1990

Nationality of Applic.	Country of Applic.						
	Japan	U.S.	FRG	France	U.K.	U.S.S.R.	Others
Japan	317.609 (54.743)	33.104 (20.168)	14.454 (6.888)	10.765 (4.294)	12.938 (5.440)	202. (102.)	43.598 (13.932)
U.S.	17.563 (3.779)	82.956 (50.185)	18.693 (7.135)	17.483 (6.118)	19.598 (6.859)	1.664 (167.)	161.087 (44.092)
FRG	7.436 (1.813)	13.245 (8.303)	43.265 (16.904)	13.471 (6.832)	13.075 (6.179)	830. (240.)	87.999 (32.720)
France	2.624 (654.)	4.960 (3.140)	5.115 (2.752)	15.468 (8.301)	4.920 (2.422)	291. (86.)	37.545 (15.139)
U.K.	2.861 (432.)	6.502 (3.100)	4.778 (1.637)	4.461 (1.471)	24.031 (4.234)	489. (50.)	43.242 (10.470)
U.S.S.R	357 (108.)	570. (161.)	459 (227.)	365. (126.)	403. (87.)	146.021 (83.348)	5.420 (1.552)
Other	9.014 (1.752)	20.323 (10.482)	15.663 (16.690)	12.929 (5.737)	15.269 (5.676)	2.311 (584.)	
Total	357.464 (63.301)	161.660 (95.539)	102.427 (42.233)	74.942 (32.879)	90.234 (30.897)	151.808 (84.577)	
% of Foreign Applics	11.1 (13.5)	48.7 (47.5)	57.8 (60.0)	79.4 (74.8)	73.4 (86.3)	3.8 (1.5)	

Numbers in thousands; figures in parentheses are registrations.

Source: Kagaku gijutsu-cho (Science and Technology Agency) (ed.), *Kagaku gijutsu hakusho heisei 3 nendo: Kagaku gijutsu katsudo no guroobarizeeshion no shinten to wagakuni no kadai* (1990 White Paper on R&D: Developments towards the Globalization of R&D and Japan's Tasks); 1990, Tokyo: Okurasho Insatsukyoku.

share of national R&D that is privately financed is higher in Japan than in the United States or other industrial countries.[13] The share of national R&D expenditures financed by the Japanese government was only 20 percent in 1987, and this included grants-in-aid to national and private universities. The comparable figure for the United States in 1987 was 49 percent.[14] The large military R&D budget in the United States accounts for much of this difference, but the Japanese share of R&D financed by the private sector is larger than that for the United States even if we consider only nondefense R&D.[15] When military R&D expenditures are removed from the figures for both countries, the share of GNP devoted to R&D in Japan has exceeded the American figure since the early 1960s.

The U.S.-Japan contrasts in the direct role of government R&D funding are linked to other important differences in the structure of the U.S. and Japanese "national research systems" (a term meant to include both public and private research organizations). Along with a relatively open market for imports and foreign investment, the U.S. maintains a relatively open research system. More than 50 percent of the basic research performed within the U.S. economy is carried out within universities (including federally funded R&D centers, FFRDCs). The structural characteristics of the U.S. R&D system—including high mobility of engineers, scientists, and entrepreneurs among firms, heavy reliance on university research for basic science and training and on small firms for technology commercialization—facilitate access by foreign firms to U.S. scientific and technological advances.[16]

The structure of both the Japanese and U.S. R&D systems is changing,[17] but in the near future, the U.S. system is likely to remain unparalleled as a performer of basic research, even as the Japanese R&D system strengthens its capabilities in the creation, modification, and adoption of technology. Among other things, the deeply rooted nature of differences in the structure of the Japanese and U.S. R&D systems means that changes in public policy will work slowly and incompletely to remove structural impediments to access.

U.S. Firms' Growing Links with the Japanese R&D System

The rise of Japan as a technological powerhouse has been parallelled by growth in the importance of the domestic Japanese market for consumer and industrial goods. Foreign firms have pursued a number of approaches to improving their access to Japanese technology and markets, including the establishment of R&D facilities in Japan and the development of complex "strategic alliances" with Japanese firms. Remarkably, in view of the urgency and importance of this issue for U.S. public policy and private managers, U.S. government agencies provide only the most rudimentary data on U.S. and foreign R&D investment in Japan or on the growth of U.S.-Japanese strategic alliances. In this section, we review the development of both of these channels for access to Japanese R&D and markets, relying on fragmentary data from the Japanese Ministry of International Trade and Industry and other sources.[18] One of the most important implications of the growth of Japanese technological capabilities is the need for better data on the private and public relationships between U.S. and Japanese entities in technology development, transfer, and exchange. All too often, U.S. policy toward Japanese industrial R&D is formulated in a factual vacuum.

Foreign Patenting and R&D Activity in Japan—Data on patenting by foreign firms in postwar Japan indicate that foreign firms have had a long-standing interest in utilizing their technology in Japan. Though the data we have found are extremely sketchy and relate only to patent applications, they indicate that foreign firms accounted for 23.2 percent of the total of all patent applications in Japan in 1970, though by 1978 this had fallen to 14.8 percent.[19] Chemicals was the most active of these sectors in foreign patenting within Japan during the 1970-78 period. The United States accounted for 42.7 percent of the total number of patents (30,089) in 1989. Germany was the second most significant applicant in 1989, with 19.4 percent of the total (see Figure 1). Table 2 also indicates that foreign firms have been far less active in patenting in Japan than in the United States, Germany, France, or England.[20]

Of greater interest are the R&D activities of foreign firms in Japan.[21] Table 3 contains data from a MITI survey of foreign R&D laboratories in Japan during 1975-90 in manufacturing, the sector that accounts for the vast majority of foreign R&D activity.[22] The number of foreign-owned Japanese R&D facilities in manufacturing grew from 51 in 1975 to 123 in 1990; by 1990, this study suggests that total foreign R&D expenditures within Japan amounted to more than 200 billion yen ($1.5 billion). Interestingly, despite widespread perceptions that Japanese technological strengths are concentrated in electronics and manufacturing process technologies, Table 3 indicates that the chemicals and pharmaceuticals industries account for the largest number of foreign-owned R&D facilities in both 1975 and 1990 and the largest share of foreign firms' R&D investment in 1990. A substantial portion of foreign pharmaceutical firms' R&D investment is linked to their efforts to obtain regulatory approval for the introduction of new drugs into the Japanese market. Although foreign clinical trial data are increasingly acceptable to Japanese regulatory authorities, the use of domestic medical personnel and researchers for such trials remains a more effective strategy for gaining regulatory approval. Much of foreign pharmaceuticals firms' R&D investment, therefore, is linked to growth in the Japanese consumer market. This market access motive seems to underpin much of the foreign R&D investment in Japan.

A separate tabulation compiled as part of the MITI study contains data on the number and expenditures of Japanese R&D facilities owned by U.S. and non-U.S. firms in 1990 (including nonmanufacturing industries). According to this analysis, U.S. firms operated 83 R&D laboratories at a cost of nearly 83.5 billion yen in 1990. European firms accounted for 58 laboratories, but invested a larger amount, more than 122 billion yen. The apparent differences in the average size of U.S. and European R&D laboratories in Japan are not explained in the study, but may reflect differences in the industrial composition of U.S.- and European-owned R&D laboratories within Japan. The European R&D presence within Japan may contain a

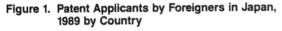

Figure 1. Patent Applicants by Foreigners in Japan, 1989 by Country

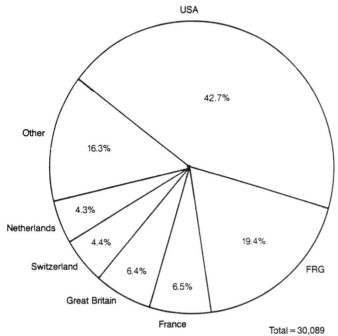

Source: Kagaku gijutsu-cho (Science and Technology Agency) (ed.), *Kagaku gijutsu hakusho heisei 3 nendo: Kagaku gijutsu katsudo no guroobarizeeshion no shinten to wagakuni no kadai* (1990 White Paper on R&D: Developments towards the Globalization of R&D and Japan's Tasks); 1989, Tokyo: Kurasho Insatsukyoku.

larger share of chemicals and pharmaceuticals firms, which typically operate large laboratories, than the U.S. industrial R&D investment, which contains a higher share of software and electronics firms. In the absence of additional data, however, any such conclusion is speculative.

These data on foreign firms' R&D investment in Japan differ somewhat from the portrait of foreign firms' innovative activities in Japan presented in Cantwell.[23] Cantwell's data are based on U.S. patents received by large U.S. and foreign firms' Japanese research facilities, and suggest that the contribution of foreign-owned R&D in Japan during 1978-86 was greatest in motor vehicles, scientific and measurement instruments, and electrical

Table 3. Foreign R&D Facilities in Japan, 1975 and 1990
Foreign Firms' R&D Expenditures in Japan, 1990

	No. of labs 1975	No. of labs 1990	R&D exp. 1990 (¥ billions)	R&D exp. 1990 ($ millions)
Chemicals	26	59	25.9	199.23
Pharmaceuticals	12	25	127.3	979.23
Electrical Machinery	3	11	15.5	119.23
Non-elec. Machinery	1	5	8.6	66.15
Instruments	1	5	0.6	4.61
Transportation Equip.	1	4	3.1	23.85
Petroleum	3	3	14.9	114.62
Food	1	2	1.1	8.46
Paper/Pulp	2	2	0.3	2.31
Ceramics	0	2	0.1	7.69
Non-ferrous Metals	1	2	2.2	16.92
Rubber Products	0	1	0.01	0.08
Total Manufacturing	**51**	**123**	**202.9**	**1,560.76**
Retail Services	4	15	2.9	22.31
Other Services	0	5	4.0	30.77
Petroleum Extraction	4	4	15.2	116.92
Total number of foreign R&D labs in Japan	**59**	**137**		
Total foreign firms' R&D expenditures in Japan			**211.4**	**1,626.15**

Source: Ministry of International Trade and Industry (1990). Exchange rate for 1990 from Bank of America, San Francisco. Yen converted to dollars at 1990 exchange rate of 130 yen per dollar.

equipment (including semiconductors). The modest contribution of foreign-owned pharmaceuticals research in Japan to these firms' U.S. patents is consistent with our characterization of this R&D investment in Japan as concerned with clinical testing and approval of new drugs for the Japanese domestic market.

The great contribution of foreign-owned R&D to motor vehicles patenting in Japan, however, does not appear to be matched by high levels of foreign R&D investment or large numbers of foreign-owned facilities in this industry within Japan. There are at least two possible explanations for this disparity. Cantwell's patent data are classified by the field of application of the patent, but the data presented above are classified by "primary indus-try" of the investing firm. Cantwell's data thus classify a patent received on a ceramic engine part by a foreign-owned chemicals R&D laboratory in Japan as a "motor vehicles" patent, but the data in Table 3 classify this laboratory and its associated costs as a chemicals industry R&D facility.

Alternatively, this disparity may reflect a failure by foreign motor vehicle firms to reward the significant technological contributions of their Japanese R&D facilities with higher levels of investment.

A recent contractor report to the National Science Foundation provides additional information (some of which appears to be inconsistent with the MITI data) on U.S. firms' R&D presence within Japan.[24] The NSF study found 71 U.S. firms with R&D operations in Japan; 36 of these firms responded to a detailed questionnaire. The authors of the study note that their count of U.S.-owned R&D laboratories yielded a smaller number than was tabulated in the MITI study discussed above.[25] As in the MITI survey, the NSF study found that more than half of the firms responding to the survey were from the pharmaceuticals, chemicals, or petroleum industries, rather than the electronics sector.[26] The NSF study also obtained information on staffing patterns and on U.S. firms' motives for establishing Japanese R&D facilities.

Despite the importance of Japan as a source of new industrial technology, the NSF study suggests that most U.S. firms continue to use Japanese R&D laboratories as instruments for improving or maintaining access to Japanese markets. This conclusion, which must be qualified by an acknowledgement of the low response rate to the NSF team's questionnaire, is based on respondents' characterization of their motives for establishing a Japanese R&D laboratory:

> Objectives [in establishing a Japanese R&D lab] considered "very important" or "important" were: developing products for the Japanese market; to improve the quality and consumer acceptance of their products (by utilizing Japanese manufacturing technology); and entry into the Japanese R&D scene. Objectives considered "least important" were to establish a research base in the Far East; to increase the effectiveness of absorbing technology generated in Japan; and to qualify for Japanese government grants and loans for industrial R&D.[27]

U.S. firms also staffed their Japanese R&D facilities largely with Japanese scientists and engineers, rather than rotating personnel from other research facilities through their Japanese research facilities. This policy may impede the transfer of Japanese-developed technologies to their U.S. or global operations.[28]

In other words, U.S. firms appear to be utilizing their Japanese R&D facilities to modify products for Japanese consumers and thereby improve their access to the growing Japanese market,[29] instead of using their Japanese R&D operations as part of a global technology development strategy. If the NSF study accurately characterizes U.S. firms' motives and R&D operations in Japan, it suggests that many U.S. managers have yet to modify their strategies in recognition of Japan's importance as a source of new technologies. This apparent lack of awareness may also be responsible for the relatively modest presence of U.S. electronics firms in Japan. Much more detailed research on the motives for and returns to U.S. firms' R&D investments in Japan is needed in order to illuminate the reasons for their modest efforts thus far to penetrate the Japanese R&D system.

Japanese R&D Activity in the United States—Do Japanese firms adopt a different approach to their U.S. R&D? A survey of 100 Japanese subsidiaries in the United States, 10 of which were established through acquisition of U.S. firms, showed that 45 percent conducted in-house R&D.[30] The managers surveyed frequently claimed that "the primary R&D objective of these subsidiary plants with in-house R&D was to expand present business and support present business, "apparently through new product development."[31] These results tell us little, however, about how these objectives are pursued. Respondents to the survey indicated that technology transferred from their Japanese parent company was overwhelmingly the most important source of technology. Little basic research is conducted in the United States by Japanese subsidiaries, although there are exceptions (e.g., NEC's Princeton laboratory). Many Japanese firms use their U.S. research facilities to adapt technology to the U.S. market, in much the same fashion as U.S. firms historically have used their Japanese R&D facilities. In addition, of course, Japanese firms utilize their U.S. R&D facilities to monitor and assimilate U.S. technological and scientific advances.[32]

Sectoral differences are considerable. Japanese firms have established at least 70 electronics R&D facilities in the United States, according to data collected by Genther and Dalton and reproduced here as Table 4.[33] Although many of these labs may be modifying Japanese technology for the U.S. market, there is little doubt that in the area of software development Japanese firms are shoring up their historic weaknesses by hiring U.S. talent.

"Strategic Alliances" between Japanese and Foreign Firms—Another important channel for foreign access to Japanese markets and technologies is through long-term agreements among firms that cover joint activities in R&D, product development, manufacturing, or marketing. Such "alliances" between U.S. and Japanese, U.S. and European, and Japanese and European firms have grown significantly in number during the past 20 years. Although international joint ventures have long been a mainstay of international business operations, the "alliances" of the past two decades focus more intensively on technology-intensive activities and industries, and frequently are concerned with product development or manufacture for a global, rather than a local, market. Most such alliances involving private firms are motivated by one or more of the following three factors: access to foreign markets; access to foreign technologies; and access to low-cost capital.

In industries like telecommunications equipment or commercial aircraft, the longstanding importance of governments as purchasers or sources of

Table 4. Major R&D Facilities of Japanese Electronics Companies in the United States

Company	Location of Facility	R&D Activities in Electronics
Computers:		
Canon	Lake Success, New York	Desktop publishing and workstations (1988)
Epson	Epson Technology Center, Silicon Valley, CA	Personal computers (1988)
Fujitsu	Fujitsu America, Longmont, CO	Disk storage devices (1989)
Hitachi	Boston, MA	Workstation and software development (1989)
Konica	Sunnyvale, CA	Data storage
Matsushita	N. Calif. Research Lab, Palo Alto, CA	Computer document processing systems
Mitsubishi	Cambridge, MA	Super-parallel computers (1991)
Nakamichi	Mountain View, CA	Disk drives (1988)
NEC	NEC Information Systems, Foxboro, MA	Workstations
NEC	NEC Home Electronics, San Jose, CA	Laptop personal computers
Oki Electric	Sunnyvale, CA	Computer hardware/software (1989)
Sony	Palo Alto, CA	Workstations (1988)
Computer Software:		
Ascii	San Francisco, CA	Software and media
Canon	Los Angeles, CA	Software, data processing (1990)
Fujitsu	Fujitsu Systems, San Diego, CA	Software engineering
Hitachi	Hitachi Microsystems, San Jose, CA	Software engineering, design and engineering support
Hitachi	Atlanta, GA	Software (1988)
JAIS	Gardena, CA	Software
JAIS	New York, NY	Software
Kobe Steel	Palo Alto, CA	Magnetic memories, artificial intelligence (1990)
Matsushita	Information Technology Laboratory Princeton, NJ	Computer graphics, document processing, software (1991)
Matsushita	Ind. Equip. Research Lab, Wooddale, IL	Software for PCS (1987)
NEC	NEC Research Institute, Princeton, NJ (1990)	AI, parallel computing, machine learning
Ricoh	American Software, San Jose, CA	Software
Seiko Instruments	San Jose, CA	Computer aided design
Semiconductors:		
Fujitsu	Fujitsu Microelectronics, Boston, MA	Custom gate array design
Fujitsu	Fujitsu Microelectronics, Dallas, TX	
Fujitsu	Fujitsu Microelectronics, Santa Clara, CA	
Hitachi	Detroit, MI	Electronic components for automotive use (1989)
Hitachi	San Francisco, CA	Semiconductors (1989)
Kobe Steel	Research Triangle Park, NC	GAAS and superconductive ceramics (1989)
Mitsubishi	Durham, NC	Semiconductors (1984)
NEC	NEC Home Electronics, Natick, MA	Semiconductors (ASICs) (1987)
NEC	Sunnyvale, CA	VLSI (1986)
Ricoh	San Jose, CA	ASICs, CMOS (1989)
Sharp	Vancouver, WA	Semiconductors (1988)
Toshiba	Beaverton, OR	ASIC design center (1990)

Table 4. Major R&D Facilities of Japanese Electronics Companies in the United States (continued)

Telecommunications Equipment:

Applied Telesis	Seattle, WA	Data communications equipment (1989)
Fujitsu	Fujitsu Network Systems, Raleigh, NC	Telecommunications equipment
Fujitsu	Anaheim, CA	Telecommunications equipment
Matsushita	Applied Research Lab., Burlington, NJ	Video broadcasting (1981)
Matsushita	Communications Systems Lab, Secaucus, NJ	Digital cable TV systems
NEC	NEC Telecommunications, Irving, TX	Central office switches (1989)
Oki Electric	Hackensack, NJ	Telecommunications (1989)
Ricoh	Santa Clara, CA	Facsimile equipment (1979)
Sony	Sony Telecommunications Technology	Telecommunications
TDK	Components Engineering, Torrance, CA	Microwave-related components

Optoelectronics:

Hoya Corp.	Northern California	Optoelectronics (1989)
NTT	Photonic Integration Research, Columbus, OH	Optoelectronics (1989)
Olympus	Torrance, CA	Optical and electronic products
Sumitomo	Raleigh, CA	Optoelectronics

Television:

Hitachi	Hitachi America, Princeton, NJ	HDTV (1991)
Matsushita	Advanced TV-Video Lab, Burlington, NJ	NDTV (1990)
Sony	Sony Technology Engineering Operations, San Jose, CA	HDTV (1989)
Sony	Sony America, San Diego, CA	TV components
Toshiba	Lebanon, TN	HDTV (1990)
Toshiba	Wayne, NJ	HDTV receivers (1990)

Semiconductor Materials and Equipment:

Kyocera	San Diego, CA	Ceramics
Nikon	San Bruno, CA	Wafer steppers applications lab (1990)
Shinetsu	California	Advanced silicon material (1987)
ULVAC	Fremont, CA	Semiconductor equipment applications lab (1990)

Other Industries:

Asahi Optical	Englewood, CO	Optical disks (1985)
Canon	Newport News, NJ	Copiers, CA (1990)
JAIS	Washington, DC	Information products; system design
Matsushita	Speech Technology Lab, Santa Barbara, CA	Speech recognition, information processing (1981)
Matsushita	Avionics Development Corp., Irvine, CA	In-flight audio, video systems for passengers (1990)
Matsushita	Franklin Park, IL	Factory Automation Technology Center (1991)
Ricoh	Advanced Technology, West Caldwell, NJ	Office automation
Sharp	Hycom, Inc., Irvine, CA	Flat panel displays (1989)
Sony	Portland, OR	Optical recording media (1984)
Tescon Corp.	Milpitas, CA	PCB test equipment (1989)

Sources: Dept. of Commerce ITA, Office of Computers. Japan Economic Institute. Company officials.

influence over purchasers have made international collaborative ventures an
important means for improving market access. In the semiconductor industry, bilateral trade disputes and the resulting "managed trade" agreements
calling for improved market access also appear to have contributed to an
increase in collaborative activity.[34] Political factors and market access
restrictions, however, are not the only factors behind the recent growth
in U.S.-Japan joint ventures. The sheer complexities of transferring and
accessing external technologies through licenses,[35] along with the growing
technological prowess of Japanese firms, also have played an important role
in the growth of U.S.-Japanese collaboration in industrial technology
development.

Tables 5-7 are drawn from a 1987 report by the Japanese Ministry of
International Trade and Industry on Japanese participation in international
research joint ventures. The report appears to have employed a fairly narrow, legalistic definition of a joint venture, in view of the differences between its tabulation and those drawn from other sources. Nevertheless, the
tables yield important information on the growing technological linkages
between foreign and Japanese firms. Table 5 displays trends in joint venture
formation during 1982-87, and together with Table 6 yields several interesting insights. Table 5 shows the acceleration in the number of newly
formed international research joint ventures, which increased from 7 in
1982 to 36 in 1987.[36] Table 5 also suggests a high concentration of international joint ventures in the chemicals industry, which accounts for almost
one-fifth of the total number of ventures formed during this period. Chemicals ranks second only to electronics in the number of joint ventures formed
during 1982-87. The importance of chemicals (which in this table includes
pharmaceuticals) as a focus of international collaboration between U.S.
and Japanese firms appears broadly consistent with the prominent role of
pharmaceuticals and chemicals in the Japanese R&D investments of foreign
firms discussed above.

Table 6 contains information on the nationality of the foreign participants
in the international joint ventures covered in the MITI study, and categorizes the joint ventures by technology field. U.S. firms dominate both
the "conventional" and "advanced" technology fields, accounting for 49
percent and 85 percent of the international joint ventures in the two categories respectively. U.S. dominance in computers and communications,
biotechnology, integrated circuits, and factory and office automation (all of
which are included in the "advanced" technology category) is even more
pronounced. Table 7 disaggregates the international joint ventures by
research activity. These data support the findings of other studies, that
international joint ventures among private firms rarely focus on basic or
fundamental research.[37] Instead, consistent with the blend of technology
access and market access motives that underpin many such undertakings,
they are focused on product development and/or modification for global

Table 5. Formation of New International Research Joint Ventures Involving Japanese Firms, by Year and Industry, 1982-87

Japanese IRDJVs	1982	1983	1984	1985	1986	1987	Cum Total
Total	7	7	23	37	25	36	135
%	100	100	100	100	100	100	100
Manufacturing:	6	7	19	29	18	30	109
%	85.7	100	82.6	78.4	72	83.3	80.7
Food	0	0	1	2	1	1	5
%	0	0	4.3	5.4	4	2.8	3.7
Textiles	0	0	0	2	0	3	5
%	0	0	0	5.4	0	8.3	3.7
Chemicals	1	1	7	7	4	4	24
%	14.3	14.3	30.4	18.9	16	11.1	17.8
Steel	1	1	4	0	0	2	8
%	14.3	14.3	17.4	0	0	5.6	5.9
General Machinery	1	0	1	2	2	5	11
%	14.3	0	4.3	5.4	8	13.9	8.1
Electrical Machinery	3	4	4	9	6	6	32
%	42.9	57.1	17.4	24.3	24	16.7	23.7
Heavy Electrical Machinery	3	1	0	4	3	0	11
%	42.9	14.3	0	10.8	12	0	8.1
Household Appliances	0	1	3	2	2	0	8
%	0	14.3	13	5.4	8	0	5.9
Communications/Computer	0	1	1	2	1	3	8
%	0	14.3	4.3	5.4	4	8.3	5.9
Other Electrical Machinery	0	1	0	1	0	3	5
%	0	14.3	0	2.7	0	8.3	3.7
Transportation Machinery	0	0	1	5	3	1	10
%	0	0	4.3	13.5	12	2.8	7.4
Instruments	0	1	1	1	0	3	6
%	0	14.3	4.3	2.7	0	8.3	4.4
Other Manufacturing	0	0	0	1	2	5	8
%	0	0	0	2.7	8	13.9	5.9
Non-Manufacturing:	1	0	4	8	7	6	26
%	14.3	0	17.4	21.6	26.9	17.1	19.3
Construction	0	0	1	1	0	1	3
%	0	0	4.3	2.7	0	2.8	2.2
Communications	0	0	1	2	1	0	4
%	0	0	4.3	5.4	4	0	3
Finance	0	0	2	3	1	2	9
%	0	0	8.7	8.1	4	8.3	6.7
Utilities	0	0	0	0	1	0	1
%	0	0	0	0	4	0	9
Other Services	1	0	0	2	4	2	9
%	14.3	0	0	5.4	16	5.6	6.7

Source: Ministry of International Trade and Industry, 1987.

Table 6. Technology Fields of International Research Joint Ventures Involving Japanese Firms, 1982-87, by Field of Technology and Nationality of Foreign Firm

IRJVs by nation, 1982-87	All Tech. Fields	Conv. Tech.	Advanced Tech.	Communications/Computers	Integrated Circuits	Factory & Office Automation	Medical	Biotech	New Materials	Nuclear Power
US	93	30	63	16	15	9	4	13	4	2
Canada	4	2	2	0	0	0	0	0	2	0
UK	13	8	5	2	0	1	0	2	0	0
Germany	9	7	2	0	1	0	0	1	0	0
France	7	6	1	0	0	1	0	0	0	0
Italy	5	5	0	0	0	0	0	0	0	0
Other	4	3	1	0	0	0	0	1	0	0
TOTAL	135	61	74	18	16	11	4	17	6	2

Advanced technologies includes the seven columns to the right of this category, respectively communications and computers; integrated circuits; factory and office automation; medical technologies; biotechnology; new materials; and nuclear power.

Source: Ministry of International Trade and Industry, 1987.

Table 7. Technology Fields of International Research Joint Ventures Involving Japanese Firms, 1982-87, by Type of Research and Technology Field

Japan IRJVs/ Type of Research 1982-87	Conv. Tech.	Advanced Tech.	Communications/Computers	Integrated Circuits	Factory & Office Automation	Medical	Biotech	Materials	Nuclear Power
Basic Research	2	1	0	0	0	0	1	0	0
Applied Research	7	18	3	0	0	0	11	3	1
Product Oriented	23	38	9	10	3	3	7	4	2
Market Specified	28	23	6	7	6	1	2	1	0
Other	1	0	0	0	0	0	0	0	0
Unspecified	4	3	0	0	2	0	1	0	0
TOTAL	65	83	18	17	11	4	22	8	3

Source: Ministry of International Trade and Industry, 1987.

markets ("market-specified" R&D in Table 7 refers to incremental product modifications for new markets).

A recent study by the U.S. Department of Commerce examined a much broader array of linkages—what might be thought of as strategic alliances—between U.S. and Japanese firms, focusing on a "snapshot" of U.S.-Japan corporate linkages in 6 high-technology industries during 1989-90 (Table 8). Joint ventures account for less than 40 percent of the number of interfirm collaborative relationships in all of these industries, and in most instances are less common than are marketing collaborations and agreements.[38] The importance of the market access motive for many current interfirm alliances may be inferred from the substantial portion of collaborations in all of these industries that focus on marketing and/or the development of new products. Consistent with the MITI data on the research content of international joint ventures, very few of the U.S.-Japan joint ventures in Table 8 are concerned with research, as opposed to production, marketing and/or the development of products (an exception to this statement is the biotechnology industry).

Although the full impact of U.S.-Japanese collaboration on the competitiveness of U.S. firms will not be apparent for some time, the visible consequences of these collaborations thus far do not support the critical view of these ventures presented by Reich and Mankin.[39] Technology transfer within these ventures is more modest in scope and less uniformly "outbound" than some assessments assume. Just as U.S. industries vary in their trade balances in goods, the net inflow or outflow of technology through U.S.-Japan collaborations varies across industries. Requiring balance in technology transfer on an industry-by-industry basis makes no more sense than a requirement for such balance in goods trade. In a number of industries, including steel, automobiles, and portions of microelectronics, international collaboration can improve the international competitiveness of the U.S. participants.[40] In other industries, such as robotics, the competitiveness of U.S. systems engineering and software firms and the ability of large U.S. firms to offer a "full line" of factory automation hardware and software depend on access to foreign hardware through joint ventures and licensing. As we note below, however, the ability of U.S. firms to reap benefits from international collaboration depends on the care with which these ventures are organized and managed. In particular, U.S. firms entering into international joint ventures may need to strengthen their abilities to learn and absorb new technologies from their partners.

Many U.S.-Japan collaborative ventures involve the purchase by large Japanese firms of significant equity positions in small start-up firms. Do these foreign investments result in the export of critical technological assets that will strengthen Japanese competitors? Little is known about the economic or technological importance of foreign acquisitions of U.S. high-technology startup firms. Despite the numerous uncertainties that surround

Table 8. U.S.-Japan "Corporate Linkages," 1989-90, in Selected High-Technology Industries

U.S.-Japan Links 1989-90	Aerospace	Computers	Software	Semiconductors	SC Equipment	Biotechnology	Total
Marketing	19	36	38	33	11	22	159
Marketing/Development	0	2	3	1	1	0	7
Joint Venture:	15	18	27	34	10	30	134
R&D/Product	7	10	12	18	8	10	
Production	6	5	13	14	2	4	
Research	2	3	2	2	0	14	
Licensing	6	3	11	11	3	10	44
Technology	0	2	0	10	0	2	14
M&A	2	8	3	7	5	4	29
Direct Investment	0	12	8	2	5	5	32
Consortia	1	1	0	0	0	1	3
Internal Venture	0	0	0	4	2	4	10
Production	4	4	1	1	1	1	12
Other	0	1		2		1	4
TOTAL	47	87	91	105	38	80	448

Source: U.S. Department of Commerce, Japan Technology Program, *The Role of Corporate Linkages in U.S.-Japan Technology Transfer: 1991* (Washington, D.C.: NTIS, 1991).

this issue, the "leakage" of U.S. technology through these acquisitions is likely to have a modest economic impact. In many instances, start-up firms pursue international collaborative ventures because of their need for capital. Policies to reduce this supposed outflow of U.S. technology must address the availability of capital and/or the willingness of managers in established U.S. firms to support small start-up enterprises (e.g., overcoming resistance to technologies "not invented here"), rather than attempting to restrict collaboration.[41]

Smaller firms' "export" of technology through international collaborative ventures rarely means that opportunities for exploitation of these technologies are lost to U.S. firms—in most cases, the U.S. partner in such a collaborative venture does not change its management or its location, and protection from other U.S. firms of its intellectual property is not airtight.

The critical agents for the diffusion of these technologies (managers and employees of the small firm) remain in the U.S., where they move to other firms, present the results of their research to domestic audiences, and otherwise act to disseminate much of the technology domestically. Indeed, the basis for such domestic high-technology concentrations as Silicon Valley in California, Route 128 in Massachusetts, and North Carolina's Research Triangle is the tendency for critical technological assets (mainly people and specialized suppliers of goods and services) to remain regionally concentrated. If the enormous interregional flows of capital of the past 30 years have not diluted and diminished these regional concentrations within the United States, it seems unlikely that international capital flows will do so.

Conclusion

U.S. policymakers have yet to address the implications of change in the technological relationship between the U.S. and Japan. These changes pose a fundamental challenge to much current thinking in the Executive branch and Congress, which now all too often proposes that Japanese access to U.S. science and technology be limited. Restrictions on commercial technology transfer from U.S. universities or firms to Japanese entities, however, could provoke reciprocal restrictions that would harm U.S. competitiveness.

Paradoxically, the end of the postwar U.S. technological hegemony means that this nation has much more to lose and much less to gain by restricting foreign access to U.S. research and technology than at any previous point in the postwar era. In the current environment, U.S. firms stand to gain from continued improvements in their access to foreign markets, investment opportunities, and technologies. Achieving these improvements will be hampered if U.S. public policy restricts access to the U.S. research system.

The actions of many U.S. firms suggest that managers are beginning to pursue strategies designed to improve their access to the Japanese technological research system. Nonetheless, the evidence discussed above indicates that too many U.S. firms still view their Japanese R&D operations as oriented largely toward the domestic Japanese market, and are not working to exploit and transfer technologies from Japan into their global R&D networks. Japan's importance as a source of industrial technology means that U.S. firms must do more to gain access and to exploit Japanese technological strengths. This will require the expansion and establishment of corporate R&D facilities within Japan, as well as efforts to more closely link these facilities to corporate technology development strategies.

Similarly, the view that joint ventures with Japanese firms in research or product development "give away our future" must be qualified by an awareness of the potential and actual benefits of well-managed joint ventures for

U.S. firms. U.S. managers nonetheless must proceed carefully in cooperating with an actual or potential competitor, and manage their technological and other assets strategically. In most cases, this requires that one maintain or strengthen independent technological and other capabilities, improving or sustaining the value of one's contributions to the joint venture. Successful participation in joint ventures requires that senior managers understand their firms' technological and other capabilities and incorporate them into strategic planning. Strategies designed to learn from the joint venture partner must be actively pursued, for ultimately the distribution of the benefits and costs from joint ventures in high technology will swing on how well each party is able to learn from the other.

The growing web of U.S.-Japanese technological linkages among private firms complicates efforts by one or the other government to restrict access to its domestic research system. The effectiveness of Sematech's restrictions on foreign participation, for example, are not aided by collaborative relationships between U.S. participants in the consortium and such Japanese semiconductor producers as Hitachi (which is working with Texas Instruments on advanced memory chips) and Toshiba (working with Motorola on memory and microprocessor chips). The development of international collaborative ventures among corporations is likely to frustrate attempts to restrict international transfer of some or all of the results of domestic R&D consortia, even as such government policies provide powerful incentives for private firms to collaborate in R&D, marketing, and manufacture in order to improve their access to foreign markets.[42]

The growth of Japan's technological strengths has raised to high levels of the U.S. and Japanese governments the issue of access by foreign firms to the Japanese research system. This issue figured prominently, for example, in the 1988 negotiations over the renewal of the U.S.-Japanese agreement on scientific cooperation. The Japanese R&D system is difficult for foreign firms to penetrate for reasons that reflect the historic legacy of government policies, as well as differences in industry structure and in the structure of capital markets; these difficulties are not solely a result of current government policies. The complex origins of these structural differences in the organization of national R&D systems and their influences on the ease with which foreigners can gain access to national R&D systems mean that government-to-government negotiations and agreements cannot address all of the causes and consequences of "asymmetrical access."

The structural differences between the U.S. and foreign research systems are such that a strict requirement of reciprocity in access to research facilities is either worthless or infeasible. Assurances by the Japanese government of complete access to Japanese universities, for example, may be of limited interest to U.S. firms, in view of the modest amount of world-class research performed by Japanese university researchers. A "results-oriented" reciprocity requirement that mandated that Japanese firms open their industrial research facilities to foreign researchers could impose a similar requirement on U.S. firms, and is scarcely likely to elicit the support of U.S. firms.

Some evidence suggests that the structure of the U.S., Japanese, and Western European research systems may be converging somewhat. As and if the quality and amount of world-class research performed in Japanese universities and quasi-public "hybrid" institutions improve, for example, access to these facilities may become more attractive and important for informed U.S. and European firms. Reduction in the structural dissimilarities between these research systems could reduce the problems of reciprocal access, but this process of institutional change and convergence is likely to move so slowly that the issue of reciprocal access will remain very difficult for the foreseeable future. The serious impediments to U.S. acquisition of firms in other industrial economies, particularly Japan, are not exaggerated. They will continue to create serious tensions, exacerbating the effects of other structural differences in access to research projects and results, until they are reduced or circumvented.

The interdependent relationship between a scientifically strong U.S. research system and a technologically strong Japanese research system also raises complex issues of balancing national contributions and benefits to the global scientific and technological enterprise. The results of scientific research are increasingly mobile internationally and difficult to "appropriate" by the discoverer, a characterization that applies less accurately to the results of technology-oriented research. As a result, the possibility exists that the U.S. research system produces global "public goods," which can be exploited by (among others) Japanese firms for private profit. This characterization of scientific and technological research is at best a caricature, and understates the difficulties and costs of transferring and absorbing either type of information, but it captures an important difference between two research systems such as those of Japan and the United States.

The Japanese government has proposed several international scientific research projects (e.g., the Human Frontiers Science Program), in order to expand its contribution to global scientific research. The HFSP project has progressed quite slowly, however, and Japan's nonfinancial contributions to its advance are likely to remain modest. Significant Japanese participation in international scientific research projects in any but a financial role is likely to be hampered in the near term by the weakness of Japan's basic research capabilities in many areas. Japan's proposed Intelligent Manufacturing Systems (IMS) project, however, focuses on an area (advanced manufacturing process technologies) in which Japanese firms are in a leadership position and to which they could make significant contributions.[43] The IMS appears to contain considerable potential benefits for U.S. corporate participants.

Partly because U.S. government officials felt they had not been adequately consulted by the IMS project's Japanese sponsors, the U.S.

government was initially reluctant to support the IMS proposal. In addition to their concerns over the perceived lack of consultation, some U.S. officials felt that U.S. firms would contribute more to the undertaking than they would receive, transferring their technology to Japanese firms. This concern appears to be misplaced, for several reasons. It is based on an outdated assessment of U.S. and Japanese technological strengths in manufacturing. This view also attempts to substitute the technological judgements of U.S. policymakers for those of corporate managers. Finally, opposition to U.S. participation in the IMS may reinforce the already distressing tendencies of U.S. managers to ignore external sources of industrial technology. The ambivalent response of the U.S. government to this Japanese proposal for international collaboration on technology-oriented research suggests the need for a recognition by U.S. policymakers of Japan's technological capabilities and a more realistic appraisal of the costs and benefits of U.S. participation in international technology development programs. In addition, a more coherent U.S. domestic policy structure for evaluating and responding to such programmatic initiatives is badly needed.[44]

Intellectual property rights is another area of U.S.-Japan tension and negotiations that may now assume a different role in this bilateral economic relationship. During the past decade, U.S. pressure has led the government of Japan to improve the protection offered to foreign firms' intellectual property, and U.S. firms such as Texas Instruments have begun to reap significant royalty payments for such key patents as that covering the integrated circuit. Simultaneously, the Executive branch and Congress have taken a number of steps to strengthen the domestic protection of intellectual property rights in the United States. As was noted above, however, Japan now is increasingly a technology exporter and is a major patentor in the United States. Stronger international and domestic intellectual property rights protection thus may raise the costs to some U.S. firms of access to the increasingly important flow of technology from Japanese sources.[45]

As the example of intellectual property suggests, the effectiveness and value of specific technology policy initiatives depend critically on the level of technological development within an economy, both absolutely and relative to other economies. The Japanese government policies that are asserted to have contributed to the technological transformation of that economy now have many admirers and advocates within the United States. Even as some U.S. observers recommend emulation of Japanese research policies and institutions, however, a search is underway within Japan for new institutions to support the indigenous basic research believed necessary to underpin commercial innovation. Japanese cooperative research policies, for example, historically supported the diffusion and utilization of technological and scientific knowledge that was derived from external sources, and supported Japanese firms' efforts to "catch up" with global technology leaders. Within Japan, however, cooperative research rarely has served to advance the scientific or technological frontier, a purpose for which it is often promoted in the U.S. Moreover, uncritical imitation of this and other technology policies associated with the period of "catch-up" in the Japanese economy overlooks considerable evidence suggesting that Japanese policymakers are now considering policies, such as public funding of basic research, that have long been central features of the U.S. national research system.

As we noted above, the enduring structural contrasts between the U.S. and Japanese national R&D systems will not be removed quickly or solely through government actions. Certainly, the evidence presented here suggests that U.S. firms must do more to strengthen their presence within the domestic Japanese R&D system. But many of these complexities in U.S.-Japanese economic and technological relationships are a legacy of successful domestic and international policies. Japan's postwar rise to technological leadership is attributable in part to U.S. policies that assisted Japanese national security and economic reconstruction. U.S. and Japanese citizens alike should be proud of this remarkable accomplishment. Adjustment by policymakers and managers in both the United States and Japan to new technological realities nevertheless require fresh thinking on both sides of the Pacific. Failure to adjust to the new environment will result in missed opportunities and unnecessary friction.

References

1. See C. Freeman, *Technology Policy and Economic Performance: Lessons from Japan* (London: Frances Pinter, 1987); R.R. Nelson, ed., *National Innovation Systems: A Comparative Study* (New York, NY: Oxford University Press, forthcoming).
2. M. Uekusa, "Industrial Organization," in K. Yamamura and Y. Yasuba, eds., *The Political Economy of Japan, Vol. 1, The Domestic Transformation* (Stanford, CA: Stanford University Press, 1987).
3. See Japan Economic Institute, "Research and Development in Japan: 1991 Update," *JEI Report*, 36A, 9/27/91. Okimoto and Saxonhouse report a similar trend. D.I. Okimoto and G. R. Saxonhouse, "Technology and the Future of the Economy," in K. Yamamura and Y. Yasuba, eds., *The Political Economy of Japan, Vol. 1, The Domestic Transformation* (Stanford, CA: Stanford University Press, 1987), pp. 384-95.
4. The data suggests negative balance of trade in new technology agreements for 1987 and 1988, which is sharply reversed in fiscal 1989. Japan Economic Institute, op. cit.
5. K. Pavitt and P. Patel, "The International Distribution and Determinants of Technological Activities," *Oxford Review of Economic Policy*, 4 (1988): 35-55.
6. National Science Foundation, *The Science and Technology Resources of Japan: A Comparison with the United States*, NSF report 88-318 (Washington, D.C.: National Science Foundation, 1988), p. 33.
7. "Given their total representation in the U.S. patent system, Japanese patents account for 45 percent more of the top 1 percent most highly cited U.S. patents than expected. The highest citation rates for Japanese patents are in the automotive, semiconductor electronics, photocopying and photography,and pharmaceuticals patent classes." Ibid., p. xii. The relatively high quality of Japanese firms' U.S. patents, however, may reflect some tendency for these firms to seek U.S. patents only for their most important

technological advances. Taylor and Yamamura argue that Japanese firms are far more likely to seek domestic patent protection for minor technical advances than are U.S. firms. S. Taylor and K. Yamamura, "Japan's Technological Capabilities and Its Future: Overview and Assessments," in G. Heiduk and K. Yamamura, eds., *Technological Competition and Interdependence: The Search for Policy in the United States, West Germany, and Japan* (Seattle, WA: University of Washington Press, 1990). It is also possible, although there is no direct evidence to support such a speculation, that a Japanese firm is more likely to cite other patents received by itself than are U.S. or European firms.

8. K. Flamm, "The Changing Pattern of Industrial Robot Use," in R. M. Cyert and D. C. Mowery, eds., *The Impact of Technological Change on Employment and Economic Growth* (Cambridge, MA: Ballinger, 1988); E. Mansfield, "The Diffusion of Industrial Robots in Japan and the United States," *Research Policy*, 18 (1989): 183-192; C. Edquist and S. Jacobsson, *Flexible Automation: The Global Diffusion of New Technology in the Engineering Industry* (New York, NY: Blackwell, 1988).

9. K.B. Clark, W. B. Chew, and T. Fujimoto, "Product Development in the World Automobile Industry," *Brookings Papers on Economic Activity* (1987), pp. 729-771.

10. K.B. Clark and T. Fujimoto, *Product Development Performance: Strategy, Organization, and Management in the World Auto Industry* (Boston, MA: Harvard Business School Press, 1991).

11. E. Mansfield, "Industrial Innovation in Japan and the United States," *Science* (1988).

12. E. Mansfield, "Industrial R and D in Japan and the United States: A Comparative Study," *American Economic Review Papers and Proceedings* (1988).

13. D. Okimoto, "The Japanese Challenge in High Technology," in R. Landau and N. Rosenberg, eds., *The Positive Sum Strategy* (Washington, D.C.: National Academy Press, 1986), p. 551; Taylor and Yamamura, op. cit. p. 32.

14. H. Odagiri and A. Goto, "The Japanese System of Innovation: Past, Present and Future," in R. Nelson, ed., *National Innovation Systems: A Comparative Study* (New York, NY: Oxford University Press, forthcoming).

15. R&D expenditures constituted roughly 1.70 percent of Japanese GNP in the years 1975-1978. This ratio rose to 1.80 percent in 1979 and to 2.77 percent in 1985, exceeding the U.S. GNP share of 2.4 percent in that year.

16. See Cohen, Teece, Tyson, and Zysman for an early statement on this issue. S. Cohen, D. Teece, L. Tyson, and J. Zysman, "Competitiveness," *Global Competition: The New Reality*, Vol. III (Washington, D.C.: President's Commission on Industrial Competitiveness, 1985).

17. Stenberg, for example, notes that Japanese university research has played an important role in the development of molecular beam epitaxy (MBE), a semiconductor component manufacturing process: "While universities played a minor role in MBE-research in the early 1980s in Japan, they are ten years later contributing very actively, especially in research related to quantum materials and quantum-effect devices. The pattern is similar in other countries and partly a consequence of changes in MBE technology and related research topics. The development of MBE technology has, for example, become increasingly dependent on an understanding of the basic mechanisms of the MBE growth process and as the sophistication of MBE technology has grown it has become possible to grow materials and structures which can be used to study scientifically increasingly more interesting physical effects, changes which both have served to attract academic scientists to MBE-research. Although Japanese universities have responded vigorously to the new challenges opening up, their response has been weaker, in quantitative terms, than that of the American universities but comparable to that of European universities." L. Stenberg, "Molecular Beam Epitaxy—A Mesoview of Japanese Research Organization," unpublished manuscript, Research Policy Institute, University of Lund, Sweden, 1990, p. 56.

18. We are indebted to Dr. Takebi Otsubo of the Nomura School of Advanced Management for his assistance in obtaining these data.

19. Kagaku gijutsu-cho [Science and Technology Agency], ed., *Kagaku gijutsu hakusho heisei 3 nendo: Kagaku gijutsu katsudo no guroobarizeeshion no shinten to wagakuni no kadai* [1989 White Paper on R&D: Developments towards the Globalization of R&D and Japan's Tasks] (Tokyo: Kkurasho Insatsukyoku, 1989).

20. The data in Table 2 suggest that only 13.5 percent of the patent applications in Japan were from foreign sources, far below the 86.3 percent of all patent applications in the United Kingdom filed by foreign entities. Interpreting these differences is difficult without much more information, but they reflect differences in domestic intellectual property systems (e.g., the Japanese system imposes a low novelty requirement for receipt of a patent, encouraging large numbers of applications for minor patents), as well as underlying differences in foreign corporations propensity to patent in these economies.

21. Patent applications in Japan primarily reflect technology developed outside of Japan.

22. For purposes of the survey, "foreign-owned R&D" establishments are defined as those operated by foreign firms or joint ventures in which non-Japanese firms control more than 51 percent of the equity.

23. J. Cantwell, "Global R&D and U.K. Competitiveness," in M. Casson, ed., *Global Research Strategy and International Competitiveness* (Oxford: Blackwell, 1991).

24. National Science Foundation, *Survey of Direct U.S. Private Capital Investment in Research and Development Facilities in Japan*, contractor report for Science and Engineering Indicators program prepared by Global Competitiveness Corporation and Technology International, Inc. (Washington, D.C.: National Science Foundation, 1991).

25. "A major recent trend is the divestiture of established R&D operations in Japan by U.S. firms as a result of merger and acquisition (M&A) activity. Within the past four years, at least eleven U.S. firms with R&D facilities in Japan were either acquired by foreign companies or they sold off their R&D facilities . . . The divestiture of Japanese R&D facilities has been offset by a new wave. The latest group establishing R&D facilities has consisted primarily of software firms (CADEM, Lotus, MicroSoft, Nova Graphics) and medium-sized firms involved in electronics. In addition, a number of semiconductor and pharmaceutical firms are currently building R&D facilities or have indicated they will establish such facilities within the next two years. . . . However, the number of U.S. companies with R&D facilities in Japan is substantially less than that believed at the onset of this study." Ibid., p. 3.

26. "17 of the 30 responses (57%) show primary R&D activity in the related fields of chemicals, plastics, petroleum refining, and drugs. We had anticipated that electronics and related fields would prove to represent the majority interest." Ibid. p. 8.

27. Ibid., p. 43.

28. "Despite the recent publicity surrounding the potential technology transfer benefits from stationing U.S. R&D employees in Japan, this practice is very limited. Several respondents indicated that double taxation and fringe benefits make employment of U.S. expatriates very expensive compared to hiring Japanese nationals . . . the major activity of the Japanese R&D staff was product development, followed in importance by applied research." Ibid. p. 6.

29. The "market access" motive for offshore R&D has long been prominent in U.S. firms' foreign R&D investments. Mansfield et al. found that "In our sample, practically all of the firms doing R and D overseas say that the principal reason is to respond to special design needs of overseas markets. In their view, there are great advantages in doing R and D of this sort in close contact with the relevant overseas markets and manufacturing units of the firms." E. Mansfield, D. Teece, and A. Romeo, "Overseas Research and Development by U.S.-Based Firms," *Economica*, 46 (1979): 188. Cantwell's analysis of

trends in multinational firms' R&D investment behavior, however, emphasizes the recent growth in these enterprises' use of global R&D networks to support the growth of firm-specific technological capabilities drawn from a number of international and domestic sources. J. Cantwell, *Technological Innovation and Multinational Corporations* (Oxford: Basil Blackwell, 1987).

30. L. Peters, "Technology Strategies of Japanese Subsidiaries and Joint Ventures in the U.S.," Center for Science and Technology Policy, School of Management, Rensselaer Polytechnic Institute, 1991.

31. Ibid.

32. Some evidence [Mansfield, op. cit., 1988a] suggests that Japanese firms are considerably more effective than U.S. firms in developing innovations based on sources of knowledge outside of the firms. If these differences are present as well in their management of foreign R&D, Japanese firms may be able to derive returns from their offshore R&D investments that exceed those of U.S. firms.

33. P.A. Genther and D. Dalton, "Japanese Affiliated Electronics Companies and U.S. Technological Development: 1990 Assessment," Office of Business Analysis, Economics and Statistics Administration, U.S. Department of Commerce, August 1991.

34. D.C. Mowery, "Public Policy Influences on the Formation of International Joint Ventures," *International Trade Journal*, 6 (1991): 29-62.

35. D.J. Teece, "Transactions Cost Economics and the Multinational Enterprise: An Assessment," *Journal of Economic Behavior and Organization*, 7 (1986): 21-45.

36. Like many tabulations of trends in international joint venture activity, the MITI data in Tables 5-7 contain no information on terminated joint ventures. Since these undertakings are renowned for their high "mortality" rate, the MITI data may overstate somewhat the rate of growth in sustained collaborative activity. Any overstatement, however, almost certainly is more than offset by the effects of the MITI study's narrow definition of joint ventures.

37. E.g., D.C. Mowery, "Collaborative Ventures Between U.S. and Foreign Manufacturing Firms," *Research Policy*, 18 (1989): 19-32.

38. Unfortunately, the lack of data on the size of the ventures in Table 8 means that the only basis for comparison of the "importance" of different types of collaborative activity is their number. Adjusting these data for the size of individual collaborative undertakings might yield different conclusions regarding the relative importance of various types of ventures.

39. R. Reich and E. Mankin, "Joint Ventures with Japan Give Away Our Future," *Harvard Business Review* (March/April 1986).

40. For a recent example, see *Business Week*, "The Partners," February 10, 1992, pp. 102-107.

41. D.J. Teece, "Foreign Investment and Technological Development in Silicon Valley," in D. McFetridge, ed., *Foreign Investment, Technology and Economic Growth* (Calgary: University of Calgary Press, 1991), pp. 215-235.

42. Mowery (1991), op. cit. Chesnais has noted the complementary relationship between relatively closed domestic research programs in the EC and the U.S., such as JESSI and Sematech, and international product development and technology exchange agreements in microelectronics: "one finds a combination between *domestic* alliances in *pre-competitive* R&D (with all of the provisos attached to this notion), and a wide range of technology exchange and cross-licensing agreements among oligopolist rivals at the international level." [p. 95; emphasis in original]. Such international collaboration brings important benefits to the United States and other corporate participants, but it may undermine domestic political support for public financing of domestic R&D consortia that prohibit or restrict foreign participation. F. Chesnais, "Technical Cooperation Agreements Between Firms," *STI Review*, 4 (1988): 51-119.

43. G.R. Heaton, *International R&D Cooperation: Lessons from the Intelligent Manufacturing Systems Proposal*, Manufacturing Forum Discussion Paper #2 (Washington, D.C.: National Academy of Engineering, 1991).

44. D.C. Mowery, "Balancing Benefits and Obligations within the Global R&D System: The Changing Position of Japan," presented at the Georgetown University–Japan Economic Institute conference on "Japan's Future Global Role," Washington, D.C., March 11-14, 1992.

45. As Yoder's 1989 article pointed out, some Japanese firms already are aggressively pursuing infringement actions against South Korean firms. S.K. Yoder, "Hitachi Reaches Patent Accord with Samsung," *Wall Street Journal*, April 5, 1989, p. B3.

[30]

Review of Industrial Organization **11**: 737–751, 1996.
© 1996 *Kluwer Academic Publishers. Printed in the Netherlands.*

Estimating the Benefits from Collaboration:
The Case of SEMATECH *

ALBERT N. LINK[1], DAVID J. TEECE[2] and WILLIAM F. FINAN[3]
[1]*Department of Economics, University of North Carolina at Greensboro, Greensboro, NC 27412, U.S.A.;*
[2]*Institute for Management, Innovation, and Organization University of California at Berkeley, Berkeley, CA 94720, U.S.A.;*
[3]*Technecon Analytic Research, 2445 M Street, NW, Washington, DC 20037, U.S.A.*

Abstract. SEMATECH (SEmiconductor MAnufacturing TECHnology) was established in 1987 as a not-for-profit research consortium with an original mission to provide a pilot manufacturing facility where member companies could improve their semiconductor manufacturing process technology. Since its inception, SEMATECH's mission has become more general. This paper presents the findings from a quantitative case-based analysis of the returns to member companies from their investments in SEMATECH. The findings suggest that SEMATECH has provided an organizational structure in which important processes and technologies have been advanced which could not have been justified on economic grounds outside of a collaborative research arrangement.

Key words: SEMATECH, collaborative research, internal rate of return.

I. Introduction

SEMATECH (SEmiconductor MAnufacturing TECHnology) was established in 1987 as a not-for-profit research consortium with an original mission to provide a pilot manufacturing facility where member companies could improve their semiconductor manufacturing process technology.[1] Since its inception, SEMATECH's stated mission has evolved and become more general. The consortium currently defines its mission around solving the technical challenges presented by sustaining a leadership position for the United States in the global semiconductor industry.[2]

---

 * This research was funded by the Alfred P. Sloan Foundation through a grant to the Center for Research in Management at the University of California at Berkeley. We gratefully acknowledge the full cooperation of management at SEMATECH by providing crucial access to key individuals and requisite data. Extremely useful comments on the material summarized came from David Mowery, and Brian Silverman, both of the University of California at Berkeley, and Laura Bauer Beecy. The conclusions presented in this paper, which draws directly from Beecy, Link, Finan, and Teece (1994) are those of the authors and not of SEMATECH or the University of California at Berkeley. In addition, John T. Scott of Dartmouth College provided excellent editorial suggestions.

[1] See Public Law 100–180, section 272, December 4, 1987.

[2] It is important to distinguish between SEMATECH and the U.S. semiconductor industry because not all members of the industry are members of SEMATECH.

SEMATECH had fourteen founding semiconductor company members; but at present it has eleven: AT&T, AMD, Digital Equipment Corporation, Hewlett-Packard, IBM, Intel, Motorola, NCR, National Semiconductor, Rockwell, and Texas Instruments.[3] These eleven member companies fund approximately one-half of SEMATECH's annual $200 million operating budget.[4] The Defense Advanced Research Projects Agency (DARPA, now ARPA) matches annual company contributions, but SEMATECH has requested FY 1997 as the last year to receive government funds.[5] SEMATECH's operating revenues not only support research at its headquarters in Austin, Texas; but also they support related research at member companies, supplier sites, and universities.[6]

SEMATECH's budget for projects has grown from $3 million in 1988 to $141 million in 1993 – the last full year before this study was begun. Cumulative research spending over this time period has been nearly $500 million. The purpose of this paper is to report the returns to member companies from their investments in SEMATECH.

In Section II, the qualifications and limitations of the study are discussed. In Sections III and IV, the methodology used in the study is described in detail. In Section V, member company returns are estimated in terms of an internal rate of return and a benefit-to-cost ratio. The implications of the findings are discussed in Section VI in terms of SEMATECH, in particular, and collaborative research relationships in general.

II. Qualifications and Limitations of the Study

It is important to understand the scope of SEMATECH benefits in order to put the benefit analysis presented in this paper in context. First, there are four organizational groups linked to SEMATECH, all of which receive benefits. These groups include: (i) member companies, (ii) ARPA as a funding source, (iii) U.S.-headquartered semiconductor equipment and materials vendors, and (iv) other outside groups engaged in silicon-related research (e.g., universities and national laboratories). Interface organizations, such as the Technical Advisory Board (TAB) (between SEMATECH and the member companies), SEMI/SEMATECH (between SEMATECH and the U.S. semiconductor equipment and materials industry), and the SRC (between SEMATECH and universities and national laboratories) help to define

---

[3] Harris, LSI Logic, and Micron Technologies has left the organization after their initial five-year commitment.

[4] Company contributions are determined by a revenue-based formula.

[5] Originally, it was the intent of SEMATECH to become self-supporting. The political realities are that continued government funding is doubtful even if SEMATECH desired such support. The government is viewed by SEMATECH as imposing undesirable regulations on the direction of SEMATECH's research.

[6] University research is supported through SEMATECH's ongoing funding of the Semiconductor Research Corporation (SRC) in Research Triangle Park, North Carolina. University research is also supported through numerous projects that draw upon specific university research outside of SRC's operation.

SEMATECH's activities and to distribute results from SEMATECH's activities. Because of the magnitude and diversity of these organizational linkages, this study focuses on only one group of stakeholders, namely member companies.

Member companies are, after all, the constituency group that is most directly targeted by SEMATECH. Moreover, because the member companies financially support SEMATECH, it is important to quantify their returns for obvious internal managerial reasons.

The scope of this study is also limited as to the types of benefits measured. Generally speaking, SEMATECH benefits to each stakeholder group can be dichotomized into tangible and intangible benefits. Tangible (meaning quantifiable) and intangible benefits can flow either directly (e.g., from SEMATECH to the member company via the TAB) or indirectly (e.g., from SEMATECH to the member company from spillovers from another stakeholder group) to the benefit recipient. Only tangible direct benefits accruing to member companies, transferred through the TAB channel, were considered in this study.

Potential tangible benefits can be grouped into three general categories: (i) research management, (ii) research integration, and (iii) research results. The benefits from research management are important in that SEMATECH provides value to members by lowering the transaction costs associated with acquiring research results, improving the match of research capabilities to requirements, prioritizing the research agenda, and accelerating the delivery of research. The benefits from research integration are important because SEMATECH defines for its members a long-term research strategy that can lower the risk of advanced research and rationalize additional research funding by member companies. Furthermore, the benefits from research results are important because they embody the technical knowledge accumulated from specific research projects undertaken by SEMA-TECH. The benefits associated with research results were selected for this study.

During interviews with SEMATECH officials, it was clear that the benefits to member companies from research management and research integration, as well as the indirect benefits from spillovers, were more important than the tangible direct benefits flowing directly from research results. Interviews with TAB members and other individuals inside member companies reinforced this view. In other words, the benefit area focused on in this study is the smallest of all of the benefits areas defined above. Still, it was recognized that this effort to quantify the direct returns from research results to member companies, albeit limited, is nonetheless important to member companies and was manageable from a research perspective. As a result, the estimates presented here clearly understate the total returns to members, and certainly to the semiconductor industry as a whole, from SEMATECH.

III. General Methodology

1. PROJECT-BASED APPROACH

SEMATECH's research agenda is implemented on the basis of specific projects, formulated within the SEMATECH Roadmap.[7] Each year, SEMATECH's Board decides which projects, from a large number of proposed projects, will be initiated in that year. By the end of 1993, SEMATECH had completed 84 projects and 94 were underway. In 1994, 72 new projects were started.

The approach taken to evaluate the direct returns to member companies was based on a sample of SEMATECH projects. By studying a representative sample of projects in detail, it was believed that inferences about the overall direct returns could be made. The sample selected contained eleven projects, as described later in the paper.

To capture the project-specific returns to member companies, those individuals within each company who were knowledgeable about each project that was selected for the study were interviewed. With the assistance of the relevant SEMATECH project leaders, project-specific survey instruments were designed.

The survey instruments were distributed to the member companies through SEMATECH's Director of Technology Transfer, who wrote to the appropriate individual within each company for each project studied and (i) introduced the study, (ii) explained the importance of the study from SEMATECH's perspective, and (iii) asked that each project survey be distributed to the most knowledgeable individual within the organization.[8]

2. COLLECTION OF INFORMATION

In order to gain the full cooperation of the member companies, each was assured that its individual responses would remain strictly confidential.[9] Survey responses were collected either directly from the identified project-specific individual(s) within each company or from each member company's representative on the SEMATECH Technology Transfer Council. Each member company was assured that project-specific survey responses would neither be distributed to SEMATECH nor published. The survey responses were aggregated across projects within each company, and then across companies, as discussed below. Only aggregate values are discussed herein.[10]

---

[7] The Roadmap is a resource for planning. It provides a consensus view of how semiconductor technology will develop over the next ten to fifteen years and of the technology challenges that must be met for this schedule to be realized. See also Teece (1994).

[8] To facilitate this last step, SEMATECH project leaders prepared a list of individuals within each company who had previously been involved with each of the projects studied.

[9] Confidentiality agreements were signed with the three companies that so requested.

[10] It should be noted that one of the leading-edge producers refused to attempt to quantify any benefits to their company from any project, although its SEMATECH assignees represent that the company did receive significant benefits from many, if not all, of the projects. This company was the

3. ANALYSIS OF THE DATA

On the cost side, there are three separate issues to consider. The first issue related to the scope of the cost data that were obtained from SEMATECH's budget data. Second, because SEMATECH is partially funded from federal funds, there is an issue related to allocating the government's share to individual projects. The third issue relates to costs not included in SEMATECH budgets, but that should be considered in the analysis because they support research.

SEMATECH's accounting system is the only source available to obtain information on project-specific costs for each of the eleven sample projects. To be consistent, project costs were defined to include: (i) payments to third-party suppliers that participated in development and improvements projects; (ii) costs for equipment purchased by SEMATECH for specific projects; and, (iii) payments for miscellaneous other project-related services.[11] In order to allocate other project-specific costs (such as SEMATECH labor; the use of SEMATECH's facilities, equipment and consumables; and non-project-specific indirect costs) to the projects in the sample, SEMATECH's total budget information was used to calculate, from historical experiences, a factor with which to burden direct project costs.

With respect to the government's share of the project costs, no distinction was made between the federal and member company funds spent on each project. Thus, since one-half of the research budget is funded by the government, reported costs are viewed as 50 percent government funded. Non-project-specific costs are also assumed to be 50 percent government funded, with minor exceptions.[12]

The final issue to be addressed is that of costs not captured in SEMATECH's accounting system. First, as may be the case with most if not all research consortia, traditional cost accounting procedures do not capture all relevant costs associated with a particular research project. Separate from costs incurred at SEMATECH, member companies incur costs above their annual SEMATECH dues. For example, each Technology Transfer Council representative devotes member company time and resources to SEMATECH-related activities.

Second, the costs captured by the SEMATECH's accounting system are conceptually "push" costs—the costs related to "pushing" SEMATECH research results to member companies. However, pushing the results out to member companies is not sufficient for effective technology transfer. Member companies must also invest in "pulling" the research results into their organization. That is, they must invest in the acquisition and absorption of the technology generated by SEMATECH in order to internalize and adapt the results for their individual purposes. These research-pull costs are likely to vary across member companies. Although the absolute magni-

---

only company that refused to participate at this level of reporting. Accordingly, the benefits realized by this company were estimated to equal the average benefits realized by the other companies reporting benefit values.

[11] These cost classifications came from GAO (1992), p. 29.

[12] For example, government funds cannot be used to support the operation of SEMATECH's Washington, D.C. office. This represents only a very minor share of the total budget, however.

tude of the pull costs associated with the projects studied are not known, an attempt was made to account for them by asking each company to net these costs against reported benefits.

On the benefit side, the eleven projects were used to estimate the annual project-specific benefits to member companies from their investments in SEMATECH. Unlike SEMATECH's project-specific cost data, benefit data from the member companies were not tracked or recorded by the companies in any formal manner.

Project-specific surveys were developed after having discussions about each project's characteristics with SEMATECH project leaders.[13] A different survey instrument was developed for each project. Project-specific survey questions were accordingly tailored to each member company through follow-up telephone interviews with at least one individual in every participating company. The purpose of these follow-up interviews was to encourage participants' elaboration or clarification of their survey responses. This process allows diverse company-specific benefits from a particular project to be captured in a consistent manner.[14]

An inspection of the survey responses reveals that a variety of benefits were considered by the company respondents. Many companies either reported a range of benefits or noted that there were significant benefits that could not be accurately estimated.[15] When a range of benefits was reported, the mean of the range was used for aggregate quantitative purposes. When a company noted that there were benefits, but that they could not be estimated, a $0 benefit value was assigned to that company for that project. Because of this, the reported benefits to member companies from SEMATECH research is understated.

---

[13] While the survey instruments are confidential, the general approach taken, through a series of focused questions, was to obtain expressed preference information (as opposed to revealed preference or market information) about the economic state of the company in the absence of the research project. Benefit data were derived by comparing these responses to the current economic state of the company.

[14] Through these interviews, the quality of the benefit data was improved in two ways. First, evaluative consistency was achieved by applying uniformity of interpretation across companies. For example, it was possible to discover if member companies were interpreting questions incorrectly or inconsistently; as a result, the needed information could be extracted through an iterative process of correcting inconsistencies and inaccuracies. Where companies deviated in their responses from individual to individual, the interview process facilitated an understanding of the reason for this and offered a mechanism for accounting for it. Second, the interview process also provided a forum to allow for an explanation of member company responses. On occasion, a question had to be restated to make it more applicable to the individual company. In doing this, the original basis of the question was left intact while making it more applicable to each member company. Through these follow-up interviews, the interviewee was able to narrow the bands on range responses and to quantify their qualitative responses.

[15] In fact, in some cases a company would report that a project had significantly high non-quantifiable benefits, but low quantifiable ones.

IV. Sample of Projects Selected

1. POPULATION OF SEMATECH PROJECTS

As of April 1993, when the quantitative analysis was conducted, there were 76 completed research projects (totalling $137.2 million in expenditures) and 82 open or active projects (totalling $356.1 million, including estimated 1993 expenditures) at SEMATECH. However, only a subset of this population of 158 projects was used to define the population for this analysis. Fifty-six of the 158 projects lacked completed background files.[16] The remaining 102 projects (totalling $381.8 million) are therefore referred to herein as the population of projects available to study.

There are five distinguishing characteristics of the population of projects that are relevant for defining a representative sample. First, there is an overarching characteristic to much of what SEMATECH funds. Their research is oriented toward supporting the technological infrastructure of the industry as opposed to supporting company-specific technological needs.[17]

Second, the population contained three types of projects: Joint Development Projects (JDPs), Equipment Improvement Projects (EIPs), and SEMATECH Improvement Projects (SIPs). A JDP is a program in which a SEMATECH team partners with an external supplier (usually a SEMI/SEMATECH supplier), university, or national laboratory to develop a new tool, material, or process that supports phase requirements of future generations of technology.[18] An EIP, as the name suggests, is a program in which either existing manufacturing equipment or systems are improved from a competitive manufacturing perspective. An SIP is a program that generally resides at SEMATECH, requires a least six months to complete, and has a budget that exceeds $100,000. As shown in Table I, the majority of SEMATECH projects in the population fall into the JDP category.

Third, JDPs dominate SEMATECH's research agenda not only in terms of number of projects, but also in terms of budget. JDPs are the larger scale projects. As shown in Table II, the mean budget of a JDP is $5.0 million, contrasted with $3.5 million for an EIP and $1.3 million for an SIP.[19] Just over 69 percent of the total cost of all 102 projects is budgeted to JDPs. EIPs, as suggested from Table II, are the next most costly – 21.9 percent. SIPs account for only 8.8 percent

---

[16] In SEMATECH's project management process, Master Deliverables List (MDL) files are created once a project has been approved by SEMATECH's Investment Council and the supporting contracts have been signed with the project suppliers. Of the 56 projects with no or incomplete MDL files, 26 were new projects that had not progressed to the point where contracts were signed or the MDL records created. Of the remaining 30 projects, sixteen were small (under $100,000), internal SEMATECH projects for while no MDL files were not created. The remaining fourteen were projects: (i) aborted, (ii) started in the early years before SEMATECH began creating MDL files, or (iii) merged with other projects that had begun before MDL files were created.

[17] By this we mean that SEMATECH supports generic research.

[18] A SEMATECH team is comprised of assignees from member companies and direct SEMATECH hires.

[19] These means were calculated using nominal values of the total annual budget of each project, summed through 1993.

744   ALBERT N. LINK ET AL.

Table I. Distribution of population projects, by type
($n = 102$)

Project type	% of total
Equipment improvement projects	23.5%
Joint development projects	52.0%
SEMATECH improvement projects	24.5%

Table II. Mean budget for population projects, by type
($n = 102$)

Project type	Mean budget
Equipment improvement projects	$3.5 million
Joint development projects	$5.0 million
SEMATECH improvement projects	$1.3 million

of SEMATECH's total budget. Further, seven of the eight most costly projects previously conducted or currently being conducted by SEMATECH are JDPs. The most costly JDP in the population is $45.5 million, the most costly EIP is $26.5 million, and the most costly SIP is $8.3 million.

Fourth, the majority of projects in the population are budgeted within the $1.0 million to $10.0 million range. Just over one-third of all SEMATECH projects cost less than $1.0 million. Nearly 60 percent are within the $1.0 million to $10.0 million range, and only eight percent are budgeted at over $10.0 million.

Fifth, just over one-half — 56 percent — of the projects in the population are active.

Based on these characteristics of the population of projects, four criteria for the selection of a representative sample of projects were imposed on the study: (i) the sample should contain EIP, JDP, and SIP projects; (ii) the budget distribution associated with the sample of projects should be weighted toward JDPs; (iii) the range of sample projects, defined by budgets, should be large and should be dominated by projects in the $1.0 million to $10.0 million range; and (iv) the sample should contain both closed and open projects.

2. SAMPLE OF SEMATECH PROJECTS

After reviewing these criteria with SEMATECH officers, a list of candidate projects was formulated. During this process, a fifth criterion became explicit: only projects for which there is a SEMATECH individual who is both familiar with the project and available to provide background information will be considered.

Eleven projects were selected.[20] The sample conforms well to the five criteria listed above. First, it contains at least one project from each project-type – six EIPs, four JDPs, and one SIP. Although this numerical distribution of sample projects, by type, does not directly parallel the distribution of population projects in Table I, the distribution of sample projects by budget does, as discussed below.

It should also be noted that there is now a decreasing emphasis on SIPs at SEMATECH. For example, of the 25 SIPs in the population, only eight are active at the time of this study. Of those eight, none was begun in 1992 and only two were begun in 1993 (at a total estimated budget of less than $1 million). For this reason, only one SIP was included in the sample.

Second, the distribution of sample project budgets, by type of project, is similar to that of the population, as discussed above: 69.3 percent to JDPs, 21.9 percent to EIPs, and 8.8 percent to SIPs. Specifically, 58.9 percent of the total sample budget is allocated to JDPs, 41.0 percent to EIPs, and less than 1.0 percent to SIPs. While JDPs account for the largest share of budgets in the sample, EIP and SIP cost shares are not as equal as in the population. This distributional difference is by design, owing partly to the decreased emphasis on SIPs within SEMATECH.

Third, the range of project budgets parallels that of the population. Three of the eleven sample projects (27 percent) have budgets of less than $1.0 million; five (46 percent) are within the $1.0 million to $10.0 million range; and three are budgeted at more than $10.0 million. In addition, the sample contains one project that ranks among the smallest four projects in the population, and two projects that would rank among the largest four in the population.

Fourth, six of the eleven projects, or 55 percent, are open compared with 56 percent for the population. All of these open projects were near completion, allowing SEMATECH member firms to provide a reasonable expected benefit stream.

And fifth, SEMATECH individuals familiar with the sample projects were available to assist with the collection of background information.

V. Estimated Returns to Member Companies

1. RETURN ON INVESTMENT (ROI) CALCULATIONS

One method for evaluating the returns to collective investments in research is to calculate an internal rate of return. The internal rate of return is defined as that rate of discount, r, that reduces the flow of net economic benefits over t years from a research project or collection of research projects to zero. Stated alternatively, r is that rate which equates the present value of net benefits to zero.

---

[20] For reasons of confidentiality, neither the names of these projects nor a description of their technological focus are reported herein.

Time series values on net benefits were calculated for the SEMATECH projects as follows.[21] First, the costs for each project were obtained directly from the business analyst at SEMATECH. The cost values were then summed across projects to establish a total cost for each year. Second, for each year, survey-measured benefits were summed first across companies, and then across projects. Thus, for each time period, there is a total cost value and an aggregated total benefit value for the entire sample of projects. Costs were then subtracted from the aggregated benefit values, by year, resulting in annual net benefit values to use in an internal rate of return formulation. As described below, sensitivity tests were performed for several different internal rate of return calculations under alternative cost and aggregation methods.

Regarding aggregation, the internal rate of return was calculated on a weighted and an unweighted basis. The weighted calculations are based on aggregating reported company benefits across companies and then across projects. Similarly, costs were then aggregated across projects and subtracted from benefits, resulting in annual net benefits to use to calculate an internal rate of return. This is a stream of weighted net benefits because the size of each project is explicitly taken into account in terms of the value of net benefits. Alternatively, unweighted calculations are done by calculating the internal rate of return for each project separately, and then calculating the average (median) of the individual return estimate. This is an unweighted analysis because all sized projects are treated equally.

Regarding costs, they were quantified in two ways. First, because the original intent of the study was to analyze the return to member companies resulting from their investment in SEMATECH, reported project costs were divided by two because the government funded one-half of the expenditures. For comparison, separate calculations were done using total costs; member plus government costs. Finally, SEMATECH's project cost accounting, especially in the early years, did not allow for the allocation of some internal expenses, such as facility costs, labor, equipment and consumables, and other non-project indirect costs. Thus, project costs, as reported by SEMATECH, are exclusive of these charges. Internal rate of return estimates based on project costs alone and project costs burdened with overhead are also calculated for comparison purposes.

The results from the internal rate of return calculations are presented in Table III.[22] The weighted returns to SEMATECH member companies when only member company, unburdened costs are considered are 59 percent. When burdened, which is a more realistic cost consideration, the returns are 25 percent.

Because the investment base at SEMATECH includes more than just member contributions, although the return estimates above are of most interest to the members, internal rate of return estimates that include federal funds, especially those

---

[21] Project costs were incurred as early as 1989. Costs for 1994 were negligible and excluded from the analysis. Benefits were realized as early as 1990 for the selected projects, and they extend to 1998 for some of the projects.

[22] No multiple solutions were found for these calculations.

Table III. Internal rate of return analysis

Benefit definitions	Member company $		Member company plus federal $	
	Project cost only	Project cost with burden	Project cost only	Project cost with burden
Weighted	59%	25%	24%	2%
Unweighted	209%	124%	122%	63%

Table IV. Benefit-to-cost analysis

Benefit definitions	Member company $	
	Project cost only	Project cost with burden
Weighted	2.8	1.4
Unweighted	6.4	3.3

corresponding to burdened costs, provide a more accurate picture of the returns that members are receiving from private plus social cost outlays. When burdened federal dollars are included in the cost calculations, the direct, tangible weighted returns to members are 2 percent.[23]

While the sample of projects is representative of SEMATECH's past projects, SEMATECH is restructuring a number of its programs and, as a result, the sample considered in this study may not represent the mix of future projects. However, the estimated returns for unweighted benefits in the lower portion of Table III may be more indicative of the magnitude of returns possible in the future because SEMATECH expects most of its projects to be of comparable size. Looking at burdened member plus federal costs, the return estimate is 63 percent. This is perhaps the best estimate of the private returns to private and public investments in SEMATECH.

2. BENEFIT-TO-COST CALCULATIONS

The benefit-to-cost ratios that correspond to the data described above are reported in Table 4. As before, the reported benefits from each company were aggregated across companies, and then across projects, and finally across years in real terms.[24] Costs were aggregated in the same fashion.

Based on the weighted methodology, the ratio of benefits received by member companies to their cost contributions to SEMATECH research that generated those benefits is 2.8 based only on project costs, and 1.4 based on burdened project costs. In other words, on the basis of project costs alone, SEMATECH members receive

---

[23] Recall that the purpose of this paper is to present estimates of the returns to member companies as opposed to total social returns.

[24] The Consumer Price Index was used for these adjustments.

$280.00 in project-specific returns for each $100.00 they allocate to SEMATECH. Or, on the basis of burdened project costs, they receive $140.00 for each $100.00 they allocated.

As noted in terms of the internal rate of return analysis, the weighted analyses produce legitimate estimates, but they are not necessarily the best indicator of SEMATECH's performance for the mix of projects that may exist in the future. The unweighted ratio for fully-burdened cost is 3.3.

Of course, when federal dollars are added to the cost basis, all of the ratios in Table 4 are reduced in half.

VI. Summary Observations

In recent years, R&D consortia have become common in the United States. SEMA-TECH is perhaps the most ambitious of these and certainly the one that has received the lion's share of attention and government support. It is not surprising, then, that there has been much debate about whether or not SEMATECH has been successful. This intense and continuing scrutiny of SEMATECH indicates the importance of carefully evaluating its effectiveness.

The intent of this paper is to add to the body of information available to all interested parties as they seek to gauge the usefulness not only of SEMATECH, but also of collaborative research arrangements in general. Further, most studies to date of SEMATECH have been qualitative in nature or, when quantitative, they have lacked methodological rigor.[25] The emphasis of the research conducted here was on measuring net benefits in a methodologically rigorous manner. Only an empirically-based study can provide the necessary insights into SEMATECH's effectiveness and would thus assist in informing the overall debate about the usefulness of collaborative research.

The decision to go forward with a study stressing quantitative measurement of tangible benefits dictated several outcomes with regard to the final design of the study. First, to some degree it limited the scope of potential SEMATECH benefits that were examined to only those that could be quantified. Thus, even though interviewees referenced intangible benefits that they felt were extremely important, no attempt was made to explore these systematically. Second, only benefits flowing from research results were considered – clearly the category of tangible benefits that members and SEMATECH officers believed generated the fewest member benefits.

It is important to emphasize that spillover benefits to other constituents were not considered. Examining these categories of benefits and benefit recipients was defined to be outside the scope of the study. As a result, caution should be exercised when comparing the return measure presented here to social rates of return presented by other researchers.

---

[25] A notable exception is Irwin and Klenow (1994).

The fact that each SEMATECH member company appeared to be able to internalize a significant return on their own contribution to SEMATECH raises an important issue about the appropriability of the research funded by SEMATECH. It is not unreasonable to speculate, based on these findings, that absent the government funding the projects studied would not have been undertaken. As we noted earlier, the eleven projects studied create technology infrastructure for the industry. Firms have a difficult time appropriating returns from this type of research if it is not funded collectively or publicly.[26]

In light of the findings presented here, it is interesting that three of the original fourteen members exited the consortium. Clearly, the fact that some firms have exited after the end of their initial five- year commitment indicated that there is a variance in the returns perceived by member companies. While it was beyond the scope of this study to determine the reasons for their exit, the study does nevertheless offer several potential insights about cooperative research arrangements in general. Because SEMATECH is a complex research organism – with activities spanning research integration, research results, and research communities – there is a fairly high threshold of commitment required by a member company to obtain a high return on its investment. In other words, companies need to establish a "pull mechanism" in order to extract full value from SEMATECH's menu of research endeavors. Companies that are not prepared or equipped to effectively extract and integrate SEMATECH research results are likely not to perceive sufficient returns on their investments.

In this regard, there are several lessons from SEMATECH. As conjecture, the more complex a research consortium agenda (i.e., the broader its menu of research activities), the higher the threshold of pull-related investments that are required in the member companies to obtain adequate perceived returns. Second, the more the research results relate to pre-commercial, generic know-how, the greater the threshold of commitment to make complementary investments for pulling relevant know-how from the consortium.

Several lessons learned from this study can perhaps be generalized to other research consortia. First, while economic theory would predict that the benefits to sponsoring companies are the "glue" that binds a collaborative research organization, more often than not, participating companies in SEMATECH had a difficult time quantifying the benefits that they received. In only a few cases did the company endeavor to quantify benefits on their own (i.e., independent of this study). Companies seem to rely mostly on "resonance" benefits to justify their continued participation.[27] This suggests, perhaps, that the intangible benefits may weigh more importantly in the sponsoring companies' decision to continue to participate.

Second, collaborative research does not seem to inhibit competition. While performing this research, it became apparent that SEMATECH collectively would

---

[26] See Leyden and Link (1992) and Tassey (1992) for support of this proposition.

[27] "Resonance" benefits can be thought of as those that result from an industry-wide focusing effect that would not have occurred in the absence of SEMATECH.

investigate some technology A, while a member company on its own would investigate competing technology B in the event that the results of SEMATECH's research were not directly applicable. This is not surprising because, while SEMATECH's research is at the generic end of the research spectrum, the member companies are still competing with each other in terms of new and improved market projects. Further, such behavior indicates that even though SEMATECH assists in developing a strategic approach to the technology development — pursing the development of a common technology roadmap — companies are still vigorously exploring various alternatives in order to enhance their competitive position.[28] Indeed, the U.S. semiconductor industry has advanced its overall competitive position vis-a-vis Japanese based rivals, and some consider SEMATECH to have been a factor.

Third, in evaluating the benefit-to-cost ratios, defining appropriate costs is easier than defining appropriate benefits. That said, traditional cost accounting procedures may not capture all relevant costs associated with a particular research project. Collaborative research organizations should seek to put in place a cost allocation system that provides accurate historical cost tracking. As to measuring member company costs, there are several steps that member organizations can take to develop a more complete awareness on their costs of participating, such as establishing a specific cost center for all direct costs of participation. As to measuring benefits, consortia can seek to obtain a consensus on their benefit categories and seek to devise simple tracking approaches to monitor benefits generated. Even if the approach is too fraught with practical problems, at the very least member companies should achieve an agreed upon taxonomy of perceived benefits that they can qualitatively refer to over time in assessing the benefits of continued participation.

In conclusion, SEMATECH has provided an organizational structure in which important processes and technologies have been advanced, which could not have been justified on economic grounds, based on the estimates presented herein, outside of a collaborative research arrangement. Government funding has been helpful. The results presented here suggest the members can justify their membership, given government funding, based on tangible research benefits alone. Certainly there are many other categories of perceived benefits not captured in the focused analysis of this study, and if analyzed would present a more optimistic picture for SEMATECH. Once government support terminates in 1997, SEMATECH management will be challenged to adapt to the loss of government support by selecting a mix of projects that continues to benefit the industry as a whole and at the same time provides companies a sufficient return to justify their continued membership.

References

Beecy, Laura L., Albert N. Link, William F. Finan, and David J. Teece (1994) 'Quantifying the Private Rates of Return to Collaborative Research: The Case of SEMATECH', mimeo.

---

[28] See Teece (1994).

Grindley, Peter, David C. Mowery, and Brian Silverman (1994) 'SEMATECH and Collaborative Research: Lessons in the Design of a High-Technology Consortia', *Journal of Policy Analysis and Management*, **13**, 723–785.

Irwin, Douglas A. and Peter J. Klenow (1994) 'High Tech R&D Subsidies: Estimating the Effects of SEMATECH', NBER Working Paper 4974.

Leyden, Dennis P. and Albert N. Link (1992) *Government's Role in Innovation*, Boston, Kluwer Academic Publishers.

Link, Albert N. (1996) *Evaluating Public Sector Research and Development*, Boston, Kluwer Academic Publishers.

Tassey, Gregory (1992) *Technology Infrastructure and Competitive Advantage*, Boston, Kluwer Academic Publishers.

Teece, David J. (1994) 'Information Sharing, Innovation, and Antitrust', *Antitrust Law Journal*, **62**, 465–481.

U.S. Government Accounting Office (GAO) (1992) 'SEMATECH's Technological Progress and Proposed R&D Program', Briefing Report to the Chairman, Subcommittee on Defense, Committee on Appropriations, U.S. Senate.

[31]

STRATEGIC ALLIANCES AND INDUSTRIAL RESEARCH

David C. Mowery and David J. Teece

FOR THE PAST FIFTEEN YEARS, U.S. industrial research has been in the throes of a restructuring that has changed the position of industrially funded in-house research within the corporate innovation process. A number of central corporate research laboratories have undergone significant cutbacks or, in a few instances, have been eliminated entirely. Since 1980, as Nelson and Rosenberg's chapter in this book and numerous other studies have noted, U.S. firms have expanded their funding for and relationships with university-based research. In addition, numerous domestic and international intercorporate alliances that span R&D, manufacturing, and marketing have sprung up. This chapter considers the motives for and some implications of these trends, which reflect efforts by many U.S. firms to "externalize" a larger share of the industrially financed R&D that formerly was performed within their boundaries.

Some analyses (for example, the National Science Foundation's 1992 study) have speculated that the recent expansion in external research relationships has reduced growth in spending on in-house research and is responsible, at least in part, for declines in the rate of growth in industry-funded R&D expenditures. Although the growth in alliances and research consortia certainly has affected the role of in-house research, we believe that those who think that alliances and consortia can fulfill all of the functions of in-house R&D are mistaken.

The growth in strategic alliances in R&D is part of a broad restructuring of the U.S. national R&D system that involves change in the funding and functions of industry, universities, and government agencies. United States firms were among the pioneers in the development of in-house industrial research laboratories in the late nineteenth and early twentieth centuries. For decades, industrial research laboratories stood at the "heart of the system" of public and private institutions that financed and managed the creation, commercialization, and adoption of new technologies within the U.S. economy (Nelson 1991). Industry accounted for roughly 50 percent of the national R&D investment during much of the postwar period, but it was responsible for performing more than 70 percent of the nation's·R&D (National Science Foundation 1992). Thus, today's growth in strategic alliances should be seen in its broader context of declining rates of growth in U.S. industry-financed R&D.[1]

Industrial research laboratories were first established within many large corporations as part of an effort to strengthen central, strategic functions within the firm; that is, to prevent long-range planning and investment decisions from being dominated by day-to-day operating concerns (Chandler 1962; 1977; 1990; see also Teece 1977; 1988). To be successful, however, R&D, like other operations of central corporate management, has to be integrated effectively with both day-to-day and long-range decision making. Many of the problems that have contributed to recent managerial skepticism of corporate research laboratories stem from the failure to integrate R&D strategies with corporate strategies in today's environment in which the demands for rapid response are far more compelling than they were in the beginning of the century.

By itself, outsourcing R&D does not address this failure. Instead, corporate strategists need to manage external and internal R&D activities as complementary activities within a coherent research program that links R&D and corporate strategy. In-house R&D can monitor, absorb, and exploit the results of research performed in research consortia and at other external sites, including universities. Corporate managers also must improve their management of technology transfer and absorption from joint development projects with erstwhile competitors or suppliers. Better management of these relationships can raise the returns to R&D investments.

In contrast to the arguments that portray knowledge transfer and exploitation as virtually costless (Teece 1988; Mowery 1983; Mowery and Rosenberg 1989; Cohen and Levinthal 1990), these arguments are built on a portrayal that emphasizes the costs and importance of managing the transfer and exploitation of scientific and technological information. Finally, as Teece, Pisano, and Shuen (1992) and Prahalad and Hamel (1990) have noted, there is a need for a dynamic view of the firm and the competencies or capabilities for the enduring competitiveness of firms. Although innovation is prominent among the sources of dynamic competitive advantage, the integration of R&D and firm strategy requires an understanding of the role of technology and a discriminating commitment to its support by senior corporate management.

EXTERNAL SOURCING OF R&D

In several respects, today's efforts by R&D managers to expand their links to external sources of new technology have revived an important function of corporate R&D laboratories during much of the period preceding 1940. Early research facilities of such firms as DuPont, Eastman Kodak, General Electric, and AT&T were expected to monitor technological advances occurring elsewhere within their industries and to advise senior management on the acquisition of technologies from other firms and independent inventors (Hounshell and Smith 1988; Reich 1985; Mueller 1962; and Jenkins 1975). In many cases, in-house R&D laboratories modified and commercialized patents or technologies acquired from external sources. In addition, as Nelson and Rosenberg's chapter has pointed out, a number of pre–World War II corporate research laboratories worked with researchers at U.S. universities.

After World War II, however, the outward orientation of many large corporate research laboratories changed. Several factors influenced this shift in R&D strategy, which has been discussed most thoroughly by Hounshell and Smith (1988) for the DuPont Corporation. The wartime demonstration of the power of organized engineering and innovation and the postwar surge in federal R&D contracts led many large firms to develop or expand central research facilities that had weak links with operating divisions. Having been encouraged or requested to do so by federal funders of classified R&D projects, some corporations created autonomous central research "campuses." University researchers also benefited from the expansion in federal research funding and in doing so shifted their attention and fund-raising efforts away from industry (Swann 1988). The tough antitrust policy that emerged in the late 1930s under Thurman Arnold and remained in place through much of the 1970s also made a number of large firms reluctant to seek external sources for new technologies, which had been a key element of their R&D strategies.

Thus, the "golden years" of corporate research described in the introduction to this book were associated with the inward orientation of industrial R&D. While the growth of central corporate research may be associated with improvements in the basic research capabilities of many corporations, all too often, as Hounshell and Smith (1988), Graham (1986), and anecdotal histories of such facilities as the Xerox Corporation's Palo Alto Research Center (Uttal 1983) suggest, this research was not linked effectively to a corporate strategy for its exploitation. In our view, any reorganization or "externalization" of corporate research that does not include restructuring the relationship between corporate strategy and the firm's internal and external R&D investments will not improve innovative performance.

During the 1970s and 1980s, a series of events contributed to the decision of many firms to seek alternatives to exclusive reliance on in-house sources of expertise in the innovation and technology commercialization processes. First, the U.S. antitrust climate changed significantly during the 1980s, as illustrated by the National Cooperative Research Act of 1984 and the 1993 relaxation of federal antitrust restrictions on joint production ventures. Second, the costs of R&D, especially those associated with the development of new products, grew dramatically (in commercial aircraft, for example, new product development costs grew at an average annual rate of more than 10 percent throughout the postwar period), and became increasingly difficult for individual firms to shoulder in an economic environment characterized by high capital costs and intense competition from other domestic and foreign firms. Third, the recovery from the global political and economic upheaval that occurred between 1914 and 1945 meant that the capability to develop and commercialize new technologies had diffused throughout the world by the 1970s (Nelson 1991). Many of the U.S. firms that had dominated R&D and innovation in their industries during the 1950s and 1960s now faced more technologically sophisticated competitors, which increased the financial penalties associated with slow commercialization. Widespread distribution of the technological and nontechnological (marketing and manufacturing) assets needed to bring a new product to market meant that low-cost access to these complementary assets could be achieved most effectively through collaboration with other firms. Finally, scientific and technological advances increased the demands on firms to develop expertise in a wide array of technologies. Firms in food processing and pharmaceuticals, for example, confronted the challenges of biotechnology; telecommunications and computer technologies virtually merged; and advanced materials increased their importance in a broad range of manufacturing industries. Even the largest U.S. corporations, many of which also faced demands for improved financial performance, could not shoulder the costs of in-house development of expertise in an expanding array of strategic technologies. Thus, other firms, consortia, or universities offered possibilities for sharing the costs of developing the required new capabilities.

These forces and others that are specific to each type of collaborative activity have influenced the development of three broad forms of R&D collaboration during the past 15 years. These forms can be characterized as international strategic alliances, precommercial research consortia, and university-industry research collaborations. Collaborative ventures between U.S. and foreign firms now focus on activities, such as joint product development, that did not figure prominently in many of the international joint ventures of the 1950s and 1960s. Domestic consortia of U.S. firms, such as the Microelectronics and Computer Technology Corporation (MCC) have been organized during the past decade to carry out "precommercial" research. University-industry research collaborations now involve larger flows of funds and more U.S. firms.

Each of these forms of collaboration differs somewhat in activities, strategy, and goals. Therefore, the effects of each on in-house corporate research usually differ. International strategic alliances focus mainly on development, production, and marketing rather than precommercial research.[2] Thus far, most domestic collaborations among U.S. firms have concerned research that is not closely linked to specific commercial products. Despite the aspirations of several of them at the time of their founding, these collaborations have rarely focused on basic research. University-industry research collaborations appear to incorporate scientific and engineering research that extends downstream from basic research but typically is not specific to a single commercial product. Thus, two of the three forms of research collaboration do not concern development, the D of R&D that accounts for more than two-thirds of all U.S. R&D spending. In other words, a considerable portion of the research collaboration occurring in U.S. firms involves a relatively small share of their R&D investment.

International Strategic Alliances

International joint ventures have long been common in extractive industries such as mining and petroleum production (Stuckey 1983) and have accounted for a significant share of the foreign investment by U.S. manufacturing firms since World War II.[3] Recently, however, the number of collaborations (between U.S. and foreign enterprises) has grown.

Furthermore, such collaborations now appear in a wide range of industries.[4] The activities that are central to many of these recent ventures, including research, product development, and production for world markets, were absent from most of the ventures of the pre-1975 era, which focused primarily on production and marketing for the domestic market of the non-U.S. firm.

While these ventures are primarily responses to the rising costs and risks of unassisted product development, the growth of technological strengths within foreign firms, the prominent role of nontariff trade barriers in world markets, and government support for the development of advanced technologies, there are other important reasons for their creation. Many recent domestic and international alliances have been formed in the effort to create "bandwagons" behind a particular technical standard. For example, Matsushita's victory over Sony in the Beta-VHS competition in videocassette recorders, for example, owed much to the firm's success in gaining the allegiance of other Japanese and foreign firms to its VCR architecture (Cusumano et al., 1992; Grindley 1990).[5] On the other hand, U.S. firms have created international strategic alliances to improve their access to foreign markets, especially high-technology markets in which governments are engaged in managing trade flows.[6] The search for foreign capital and technological resources also has motivated U.S. firms to enter international joint ventures in industries ranging from semiconductors to steel.[7]

Firms engaged in international strategic alliances need to maintain a strong intrafirm competence in technologies related to the joint venture, for several reasons. Although the central activities of many international joint ventures usually are focused on the development and/or manufacture of specific products or technologies, they provide many opportunities for all parties to learn from their collaborators. According to some scholars (Prahalad and Hamel 1990), some firms, such as NEC of Japan, have developed technology-based core competences relatively inexpensively through their use of joint ventures as learning opportunities. Thus, focusing solely on the completion of the development project may limit opportunities for learning from joint venture partners. Moreover, because many joint development projects produce intellectual property by-products, it is important for firms to negotiate carefully the provisions governing the valuation, exploitation, and sharing of any revenues associated with these by-products.[8]

Exploiting learning opportunities requires an intrafirm capacity to absorb and apply the fruits of the venture. Joint venture participants should create mechanisms for absorbing technology transferred from their partners. The creation of these mechanisms often requires complementary in-house investments. One such investment is the rotation of research and engineering personnel from the firm through a collaborative project. However, it is not enough for an employee simply to capture knowledge (both codified and tacit) or skills from other firms. The employee must be given opportunities to communicate that knowledge to others within the parent firm. This can be done through parallel development and engineering activities within the parent firm.

Because international joint ventures act as vehicles for technology transfer and skills acquisition, the value of the knowledge or capabilities contributed by any single partner depreciates, *ceteris paribus*. As technology is transferred through a collaborative venture, learning by the other participants reduces the value of the technological capabilities that were originally unique to one or another participant. Depreciation may be even more rapid in ventures in which one firm contributes its marketing knowledge and network or other "country-specific" expertise. Although an alliance may be an essential means to gain access to new knowledge, as the other participants improve their knowledge of the markets in which this partner has specialized, they are likely to choose to continue without it.[9] This fact has played a role in the breakup of a number of collaborative ventures between Japanese and U.S. producers of auto parts. As the Japanese partners in these ventures have gained knowledge about local markets and production conditions (particularly when selling to Japanese transplant operations in the United States), they have withdrawn from the joint venture to continue independently (Phillips 1989). Although technology-based assets are likely to depreciate more slowly, especially if technology transfer is closely managed, Hamel, Doz, and Prahalad (1989) suggest that process technologies are less easily exploited by other participants than product technologies, which are more transparent to venture partners.[10]

Depreciation in the value of assets within a joint venture is no less inevitable than depreciation of physical capital assets within a manufacturing plant. In both cases, participants must take steps to reduce erosion in the value of their contribution and, at the same time, seek ways to offset the consequences of such depreciation. Intrafirm investments in technology development are essential to the creation or maintenance of the quality of the technological assets contributed to the joint venture. Therefore, participant firms must sustain in-house technology development activities in product lines and technologies that are related to the joint venture and managers need to pursue ways to offset the depreciation that will occur, for example, by exploiting learning opportunities. If the collaborative venture aids in the establishment of a product design as a market standard or a venture with an established firm provides an endorsement of a technology, some of the detrimental effects of this depreciation also can be reduced. When a firm provides a static asset like market access, the collaborative venture may function most effectively as a means for exiting the industry or as a temporary channel for learning process and product technologies.

For many U.S. firms, joint ventures involve closer work with suppliers. In these user-supplier ventures, more responsibility for the development of components to meet specific performance parameters is delegated to the supplier and the risks and costs of development are shared. In the semiconductor industry, these ventures often team U.S. and Japanese firms and generate considerable product-specific and technology-specific know-how and intellectual property. Shuen's research (1993) suggests that the failure of some U.S. semiconductor firms to invest sufficient resources in monitoring and absorbing jointly developed intellectual property has reduced their returns from these relationships. It would appear that U.S. managers need to broaden the channels through which they obtain technologies from external sources. Know-how and technological capabilities do not come exclusively from formal "horizontal" joint ventures. They also flow from marketing, supplier, and numerous other relationships. Moreover, as firms come to rely more heavily on these relationships, they need better channels for transfer and absorption.

In addition to improving market access, reducing risk, and lowering the costs and time required for new product development, international joint ventures in product development can raise the efficiency of a firm's internal R&D. These ventures allow firms to exercise greater selectivity in their in-house technology investments. However, selectivity must be based on a careful analysis of the firm's strengths and weaknesses, and the long-run impact of reducing investment in specific technologies on corporate strategy must be clearly laid out. In other words, entry into an international joint venture should be based on an integrated analysis of technological and firm strategy. Such an assessment should include some evaluation of the competitive sensitivity of specific parts—the firm's "crown jewels"—of its technology portfolio. The uncertainties associated with technology-based competition mean that any such analysis is likely to rely more heavily on the construction and evaluation of scenarios than on the illusory precision of quantitative estimates. Moreover, the firm pursuing this selective approach still will require in-house expertise to evaluate the strengths and weaknesses in the technologies of its prospective collaborators.

Precommercial Research Consortia

Research consortia, funded entirely or in part by industry funds and focusing on precommercial research activities, are a recent innovation in U.S. firms. In most cases, these consortia have involved U.S. firms only (some consortia that are funded in part from public sources, for example, SEMATECH, have formal policies excluding foreign firms). More than 450 such ventures have been registered with the U.S. Justice Department through 1994 under the terms of the 1984 National Cooperative Research Act (Evan and Olk 1990; Werner 1992; Link 1995).

Several of the most widely publicized consortia founded during the first half of the 1980s, such as MCC, were established in response to Japanese cooperative research programs (Peck 1986), particularly the VLSI program of the 1970s and the Fifth Generation Computing project that was undertaken during the 1980s as a successor to the VLSI program. Computer industry executives in the United States concluded that Japanese cooperative programs supported the type of long-range research that no single firm would undertake; projects like MCC were created to fill this void in the U.S. computer industry.

The short history of MCC and the experiences of consortia in other industries (for example, the Electric Power Research Institute, which serves the U.S. electric utility industry) suggest that research consortia rarely sustain a long-range focus but rather shift their focus to research on generic technology issues of more immediate interest to member firms. Both SEMATECH and the National Center for Manufacturing Sciences are now pursuing technology-focused research that seeks to improve vertical relationships between users and suppliers of capital equipment (Grindley et al. 1994). Interestingly, the Japanese industry consortia that sparked U.S. concern have rarely undertaken basic research. Instead, they have focused on technology development and dissemination among their members. Japan's Fifth Generation Computing project, which pursued a longer-term research agenda, has been relatively unsuccessful.

Like international strategic alliances, most research consortia focus on technology development. In contrast to alliances, however, agendas of consortia usually are not highly product-specific. Indeed, the example of SEMATECH suggests that agreement among consortium members on an agenda that focuses on specific (and often proprietary) product or process technologies may be difficult if not impossible to achieve (Grindley et al. 1994). For this reason, the near-term competitive risks from participating in a consortium may be less significant than the risks associated with an international joint venture. The financial costs of consortium participation also are likely to be lower than the costs of a joint venture. Therefore, decisions on consortium participation, management, and so forth may raise fewer long-term corporate strategy issues and do not require the same degree of senior management participation as decisions on international joint ventures.

Although there are a number of important differences in their goals and structure, the requirements for maximizing technology-based benefits from consortia closely resemble the requirements associated with strategic alliances. Complementary investments in R&D within member firms, the creation of channels of communication and technology transfer with the consortium, and the development of an in-house receptor are necessary to increase the returns from participation. For example, MCC's reliance on its own research staff, in contrast to SEMATECH's use of assignees from member firms, made it difficult for member firms to absorb the results of MCC research. The complex structure of MCC, which established barriers to some firms' access to certain research areas, further impeded technology transfer.

University-Industry Research Collaboration

Much of the recent expansion in domestic research collaboration involves a renewal of the link among state governments, publicly supported universities, and industry that languished during the post-1945 period (Mowery and Rosenberg 1993). The huge size, decentralized structure, and research-intensive character of the American universities are unique and increase the potential payoff from collaboration between universities and industry. Nevertheless, clearly defined "deliverables" often are of secondary importance in successful university-industry collaborations (Mowery and Rosenberg 1989; Rosenberg and Nelson 1994).

Thus far, university-industry collaborations appear better suited to the support of long-term, precommercial research than interfirm consortia. This tentative conclusion is based on the tendency of consortia to shift their agenda toward near-term research. The personnel flows between firm and research laboratory that often figure prominently in university-industry collaborations also aid communication between university and corporate research establishments.

Because U.S. universities include education as well as research in their activities, they are important sources of scientific and engineering personnel for industry. Firms can use collaborative ventures as filters for hiring research personnel, since the ventures allow them to observe the performance of potential researchers before making employment commitments. Moreover, the hiring of graduates of these programs facilitates the transfer of knowledge and technology even more effectively than does the rotation of industry personnel through university research facilities. Given the interdisciplinary character of current industrial technological and research challenges, the training of research personnel is an especially important benefit to industry that may emerge from industry-university collaborations. Firms in the semiconductor, biotechnology, or robotics industries now need individuals with interdisciplinary research training. Industrial funding, like federal government research support during the 1960s and 1970s, can aid in the establishment of university interdisciplinary research and education programs, which are notoriously difficult to develop without external funds.[11]

Thus, through interdisciplinary research and education programs, collaboration with universities can provide firms with "windows" for monitoring novel research areas and filters for hiring research and technical personnel. While the results of university-industry research collaborations may rarely be applied directly to commercial innovation, by improving access to university research, they can improve the efficiency of in-house research activities. As Nelson and Levin (1986) and David, Mowery, and Steinmueller (1992) have argued, many of the economic benefits of university research and other basic research are realized through the ability of the research findings to improve the efficiency of applied research; that is, basic research results lead to a better informed, and therefore more efficient, "search" process in technology development. It is the general knowledge produced by this research, rather than any specific discoveries, that provides many of the economic benefits.[12]

What does this characterization of the economic payoffs from these collaborations imply for managers who wish to increase the competitive benefits arising from such relationships? As in the case of strategic alliances and research consortia, the creation and maintenance of good channels of communication and transfer are critical and require both the hiring of graduates and the rotation of firm personnel through university research facilities. Managers also must maintain "receptors" within the firm to absorb and apply university research findings to technology development. One of the few empirical studies of the role of external basic research in innovative performance found that pharmaceuticals firms with strong intrafirm "academic," or basic, research capabilities more successfully exploited such research than firms lacking these capabilities (Gambardella 1992). In other words, university-based research must complement in-house research activities. Without some capability to understand and exploit the results produced in collaborative research relationships, the returns to these external investments are likely to be low. University research collaborations may allow for greater selectivity in the in-house basic research agenda, but they cannot be effective without complementary in-house research activities.

CONCLUSION

This chapter has provided a taxonomy for understanding the external research relationships that have recently sprung up within U.S. industrial research and has suggested some ways in which the management of these relationships influences in-house research activities and innovative performance. Although some recent experiments in strategic alliances represent a revival of the earlier, outward-oriented R&D strategy followed by many of the pioneers in U.S. industrial research, the outcomes of these new undertakings remain uncertain. The restructuring of U.S. corporate research is likely to continue for some time because of severe competitive and financial pressures on U.S. firms.

In order to utilize research collaboration as an effective competitive solution, managers must define the problem they are addressing. Undertaking external R&D relationships primarily or solely as a means of reducing the corporate R&D budgets, for example, may do little to improve the long-term returns to corporate R&D investments. The disappointing returns to many R&D investments reflect a frequent failure to maintain links between R&D priorities and corporate strategy rather than excessive levels of R&D investment. This problem is not addressed by external R&D, and without a solution to it, external R&D

may well fail. Research collaboration provides opportunities for R&D cost reduction or improved market access, but entry into such ventures solely for these purposes is ill-advised. Collaborative research ventures should be undertaken and managed for their potential to strengthen the capabilities that underpin firms' competitive strength.

While external research ventures can support learning from other firms or research institutions and a more focused in-house R&D agenda and budget, to do so successfully corporate strategy and R&D priorities must be well integrated. The failure to integrate may then prove to be counterproductive causing R&D collaboration to erode, rather than strengthen, corporate competitive advantage. To improve the payoff from external research ventures, a firm must invest in activities that facilitate the inward transfer of knowledge and technology, but this is insufficient by itself. Complementary investments in intrafirm R&D are also necessary to provide opportunities for the exploitation and "absorption" of the fruits of external research. As noted earlier, managing these external research relationships as complements to an in-house research portfolio can facilitate a more efficient alloca- tion of intrafirm R&D investments among technologies or strategic opportunities.

Successful management of external research relationships also re- quires a good fit between the type of external research venture and corporate or business unit goals. Using a university-industry collabo- ration to accelerate the development of a product or using a precom- mercial research consortium to strengthen basic research capabilities is likely to prove disappointing. Furthermore, the failure to recognize that these activities may yield multiple types of benefits can reduce their payoffs. Joint product development ventures often yield significant learning by-products and may develop intellectual property in related areas or technologies. Capturing these benefits and managing their exploitation requires careful consideration of different approaches to organizing and negotiating the terms of a venture.

As noted earlier, the focus of many of these collaborations on the lower-cost phases of industrial innovation means that their effects on in-house R&D spending may have been overstated. Moreover, as noted repeatedly, the successful exploitation of external R&D requires com- plementary in-house R&D investments. In light of these conclusions, recent flat trends in industrially funded R&D spending may not reflect improvements in efficiency or productivity as a result of collaborations. Indeed, policies that seek to improve industrial competitiveness by encouraging externally based research networks (for example, tax incentives or direct subsidies) may not offset the effects of declining intrafirm R&D if the impact of these collaborations on innovative performance depends on intrafirm R&D investment. These policies also cannot address performance problems that reflect deficiencies in the integration of corporate strategy and R&D management and priorities.

Notes

1. Real annual growth rates in industry-financed R&D spending have declined since 1984. Rates reached zero in 1986–87 and in 1990–91 (National Science Foundation 1992). The share of GDP accounted for by industry funded R&D in the United States has lagged behind the share of GDP in both Germany and Japan by a widening margin during the past decade.

2. A number of regional programs in Western Europe, such as ESPRIT and EUREKA, focus on precommercial research. For purposes of this discussion, however, these consortia within an economically unified region are treated as similar to domestic research consortia.

3. Indeed, although their relative importance has declined, the absolute size and number of joint ventures in the extractive industries remain substantial and may have increased. Karen Hladik's analysis (1985) of data from the Harvard Multinational Enterprise Project concluded that 39 percent of the number of foreign subsidiaries established by U.S. manufacturing firms from 1951 to 1975 were joint ventures. Benjamin Gomes-Casseres (1988) analyzed these data and found a significant decline in the share of joint ventures within U.S. multinationals' international subsidiaries from 1961 to 1968, followed by a resumption of growth in the share of joint ventures from 1969 to 1975.

4. Kathryn Harrigan (1984) concluded that domestic joint ventures involving U.S. firms had grown during the previous decade. In the 1960s, joint ventures were concentrated in the chemicals, primary metals, paper, and stone, clay, and glass industries, but they now extend beyond these sectors. Karen Hladik (1985) found significant growth from 1975 to 1982 in the number of international joint ventures involving U.S. firms. This trend has almost certainly continued through the present.

5. These alliances are not always successful, however. The Advanced Computer Environment (ACE) failed to establish the RISC microprocessor architecture developed by MIPS Computer Systems as a standard. See Jonathan Khazam and David C. Mowery (1994).

6. U.S. firms are not the only ones to use joint ventures in this manner. Foreign firms have found that joint ventures can improve their access to U.S. markets.

7. Historically, in industries such as telecommunications, technical standards have been established through multilateral or plurilateral negotiations

among governments. These negotiations are heavily affected by governments' perceptions of the effects of a particular standard on the competitive fortunes of "national champions," many of which are government-owned or controlled. By establishing a network of international alliances, U.S. telecommunications firms have sought to gain advantage in negotiations over government-sponsored technical standards. See David C. Mowery (1989).

8. David J. Teece (1992) argues that the importance of such by-products and the development of provisions for their exploitation may favor the use of a shared-equity ownership structure for joint ventures.

9. Michael E. Porter and Mark B. Fuller (1986) have observed that collaborative ventures centered on marketing "may be particularly unstable, however, because they frequently are formed because of the access motive on one or both sides. For example, one partner needs market access while the other needs access to product. As the foreign partner's market knowledge increases, there is less and less need for a local partner" (p. 334).

10. "The type of skill a company contributes is an important factor in how easily its partner can internalize the skills. The potential for transfer is greatest when a partner's contribution is easily transported (in engineering drawings, on computer tapes, or in the heads of a few technical experts); easily interpreted (it can be reduced to commonly understood equations or symbols); and easily absorbed (the skill or competence is independent of any particular cultural context). . . . Western companies face an inherent disadvantage because their skills are generally more vulnerable to transfer. The magnet that attracts so many companies to alliances with Asian competitors is their manufacturing excellence—a competence that is less transferable than most" (Gary Hamel, Yves Doz, and C. K. Prahalad 1989, 136). The converse is also true. A central technological asset contributed by Boeing to its collaborative ventures with Japanese firms is its expertise in production technology and in the management of fluctuations in production volume for commercial airframes (Mowery 1987).

11. The departmental structure of U.S. universities appears to make this task easier than it is in many Western European universities: "Among the factors cited to explain West Germany's slow entry into commercial biotechnology is an educational system that prevents the kind of interdisciplinary cooperation that is viewed by most experts as essential to the development of this field. In particular, the traditional separation of technical faculties from their arts and sciences counterparts means that process technicians, usually located in the technical schools, rarely come into contact with colleagues holding university appointments in biochemistry or microbiology" (U.S. House of Representatives, Office of Technology Assessment 1985, 424).

12. D. M. Hercules and J. W. Enyart (1983, 7) report that the following four areas of collaboration had very high potential payoffs and currently lacked sufficient activity: (1) lectureships by academic scientists at industrial sites; (2) student interns at industrial sites; (3) continuing education programs at

industrial sites; and (4) corporate support for employees to obtain advanced degrees. Note that none of these areas involve significant transfers to industry of intellectual property or other deliverables.

References

Chandler, Alfred D., Jr. 1962. *Strategy and Structure.* Cambridge, Mass.: MIT Press.

Clark, Kim B. 1989. "What Technology Can Do for Strategy." *Harvard Business Review* (November–December): 94–8.

Cohen, Wesley M., and David A. Levinthal. 1990. "Absorptive Capacity: A New Perspective on Learning and Innovation." *Administrative Sciences Quarterly* 35: 128–52.

Cohen, Wesley, Richard Florida, and Richard Goe. 1994. *University-Industry Research Centers in the United States.* Pittsburgh: Carnegie Mellon University.

Cusumano, Michael, Yorgis Mylonadis, and Richard Rosenbloom. 1992. "Strategic Maneuvering and Mass-Market Dynamics: The Triumph of Beta over VHS." *Business History Review* 66: 51–94.

David, Paul A., David C. Mowery, and W. Edward Steinmueller, "Analyzing the Economic Payoffs to Basic Research." *Economics of Innovation and New Technology* 2: 73–90.

Evan, William M., and Paul Olk. 1990. "R&D Consortia: A New Organizational Form." *Sloan Management Review* 31 (Spring): 37–46.

Feller, I. 1990. "Universities as Engines of R&D-Based Economic Growth: They Think They Can." *Research Policy* 19: 335–48.

Gambardella, A. 1992. "Competitive Advantages from In-House Scientific Research: The U.S. Pharmaceutical Industry in the 1980s." *Research Policy* 21: 391–407.

Ghemawat, P., M. E. Porter, and R. A. Rawlinson. 1986. "Patterns of International Coalition Activity." In *Competition in Global Industries* edited by Michael E. Porter. Boston, Mass.: Harvard Business School Press.

Gomes-Casseres, Benjamin. 1988. "Joint Venture Cycles: The Evolution of Ownership Strategies of U.S. MNEs, 1945–75." In *Cooperative Strategies in International Business,* edited by F. J. Contractor and P. Lorange. Lexington, Mass.: Lexington Books.

Graham, Margaret B. W. 1986. *RCA and the Videodisc: The Business of Research.* New York: Cambridge University Press.

Graham, Margaret B. W., and Bettye H. Pruitt. 1990. *R&D for Industry: A Century of Technical Innovation at Alcoa.* New York: Cambridge University Press.

Grindley, P. 1990. "Winning Standards Contests: Using Product Standards in Business Strategy." *Business Strategy Review* 1 (Spring): 71–84.

Grindley, P., David C. Mowery, and B. Silverman. 1994. "Sematech and Collaborative Research: Lessons in the Design of High-Technology Consortia." *Journal of Policy Analysis and Management* 13: 723–58.

Hamel, Gary, Yves Doz, and C. K. Prahalad. 1989. "Collaborate with Your Competitors—and Win." *Harvard Business Review* (January–February): 133–39.

Harrigan, Kathryn R. 1984. "Joint Ventures and Competitive Strategy." Working paper, Graduate School of Business, Columbia University, New York.

Hercules, D. M., and J. W. Enyart. 1983. "Report on the Questionnaire on Current Exchange Programs Between Industries and Universities." Council on Chemical Research, University-Industry Interaction Committee.

Hladik, Karen. 1985. *International Joint Ventures*. Lexington, Mass.: D.C. Heath.

Hounshell, David A., and John Kenly Smith. 1988. *Science and Corporate Strategy: Du Pont R&D, 1902–1980*. New York: Cambridge University Press.

Jenkins, Reese V. 1975. *Images and Enterprise: Technology and the American Photographic Industry, 1839–1925*. Baltimore: The Johns Hopkins University Press.

Khazam, J., and D. C. Mowery. 1994. "The Commercialization of RISC: Strategies for the Creation of Dominant Designs." *Research Policy* 23: 89–102.

Link, A. N. 1995. "Research Joint Ventures: Patterns from *Federal Register* Filings." Economics working paper, Center for Applied Research, Bryan School of Business and Economics, University of North Carolina-Greensboro.

Mowery, David C. 1983. "Economic Theory and Government Technology Policy." *Policy Sciences* 16, no. 2: 27–43.

———. 1987. *Alliance Politics and Economics: Multinational Joint Ventures in Commercial Aircraft*. Cambridge, Mass.: Ballinger.

Mowery, David C., and N. Rosenberg. 1989. *Technology and the Pursuit of Economic Growth*. New York: Cambridge University Press.

———. 1993. "The U.S. National Innovation System." In *National Innovation Systems: A Comparative Analysis*, edited by Richard R. Nelson. New York: Oxford University Press.

Mueller, W. F. 1962. "The Origins of the Basic Inventions Underlying Du Pont's Major Product and Process Inventions, 1920 to 1950." In *The Rate and Direction of Inventive Activity*, edited by Richard R. Nelson. Princeton, N.J.: Princeton University Press.

National Science Foundation. National Science Board. 1992. Committee on Industrial Support for R&D. *The Competitive Strength of U.S. Industrial*

Science and Technology: Strategic Issues. Washington, D.C.: U.S. Government Printing Office.

Nelson, Richard R. 1990. "U.S. Technological Leadership: Where Did It Come From and Where Did It Go?" *Research Policy* 19: 117–132.

———. 1991. "Capitalism as an Engine of Progress." *Research Policy* 20: 193–214.

Nelson, Richard R., and Richard C. Levin. 1986. "The Influence of Science University Research and Technical Societies on Industrial R&D and Technical Advance," Research Program on Technological Change Policy discussion paper 3, Yale University, New Haven, Conn.

New York Times. 1992. "University of California Proposes Laboratory-to-Marketplace Link," 11 December, A14.

Pavitt, Keith. 1991. "What Makes Basic Research Economically Useful?" *Research Policy* 20: 109–19.

Peck, Merton J. 1986. "Joint R&D: The Case of the Microelectronics and Computer Technology Corporation." *Research Policy* 15: 219–32.

Phillips, S. 1989. "When U.S. Joint Ventures with Japan Go Sour." *Business Week* (24 July): 30–31.

Porter, Michael E., and Mark B. Fuller. 1986. "Coalitions and Global Strategy." In *Competition in Global Industries,* edited by M. E. Porter, Boston: Harvard Business School Press.

Prahalad, C. K., and Gary Hamel. 1990. "The Core Competence of the Corporation." "Harvard Business Review" (May–June): 79–91.

Reich, Leonard S. 1985. *The Making of Industrial Research: Science and Business at GE and Bell, 1876–1926.* New York: Cambridge University Press.

Rosenberg, Nathan. 1990. "Why Do Firms Do Basic Research (With Their Own Money)?" *Research Policy* 19: 165–74.

Rosenberg, Nathan, and Richard R. Nelson. 1994. "American Universities and Technical Advance in Industry." *Research Policy* 23: 323–48.

Servos, John W. 1994. "Changing Partners: The Mellon Institute, Private Industry, and the Federal Patron." *Technology and Culture* 35 (April): 221–57.

Shuen, Amy S. 1993. "Co-Developed Know-how Assets in Technology Partnerships." Haas School of Business, University of California, Berkeley.

Stuckey, J. S. 1983. *Vertical Integration and Joint Ventures in the Aluminum Industry.* Cambridge, Mass.: Harvard University Press.

Swann, John P. 1988. *Academic Scientists and the Pharmaceutical Industry: Cooperative Research in Twentieth-Century America.* Baltimore: The Johns Hopkins University Press.

Teece, David J. 1977. *The Multinational Corporation and the Costs of International Technology Transfer.* Cambridge, Mass.: Ballinger.

————. 1988. "Technological Change and the Nature of the Firm." In *Technical Change and Economic Theory,* edited by G. Dosi, C. Freeman, R. Nelson, G. Silverberg, and L. Soete. London: Frances Pinter.

————. 1992. "Competition, Cooperation, and Innovation: Organizational Arrangements for Regimes of Rapid Technological Progress," *Journal of Economic Behavior and Organization* 18, no. 1: 1–25.

Teece, David J., Gary Pisano, and Amy Shuen. 1992. "Dynamic Capabilities and Strategic Management." Working paper, Haas School of Business, University of California, Berkeley.

U.S. House of Representatives. 1985. Office of Technology Assessment. *Commercial Biotechnology: An International Analysis* (Washington, D.C.: U.S. Government Printing Office, 1985).

Uttal, Bro. 1983. "The Lab that Ran Away from Xerox." *Fortune* 108 (5 September): 97–102.

Wall Street Journal. 1991. "U.S.'s DNA Patent Moves Upset Industry," 22 October, B4.

Werner, Jerry. 1992. "Technology Transfer in Consortia." *Research-Technology Management* 35, no. 3: 38–43.

Index

Economists of the Twentieth Century